Marketing | An Introduction

7/e

Gary Armstrong
University of North Carolina

Philip Kotler
Northwestern University

PEARSON
Prentice Hall

Pearson Education International

Acquisitions Editor: Katie Stevens
VP/Editorial Director: Jeff Shelstad
Editorial Assistant: Rebecca Cummings
Assistant Editor: Melissa Pellerano
AVP/Executive Marketing Manager: Michelle O'Brien
Marketing Assistant: Amanda Fisher
Senior Managing Editor (Production): Judy Leale
Production Editor: Cindy Durand
Production Assistant: Joe DeProspero
Manufacturing Buyer: Diane Peirano
Design Manager: Maria Lange
Designer: Jill Little
Cover Illustration/Photo: N. Gleis/Raw Talent Photo
Image Manager: Keri Jean Miksza
Photo Researcher: Sheila Norman
Image Permission Coordinator: Charles Morris
Manager, Print Production: Christy Mahon
Composition/Full-Service Project Management: Lynn Steines, Carlisle Communications
Printer/Binder: Courier/Kendallville

Credits and acknowledgments borrowed from other sources and reproduced,with permission, in this textbook appear on the appropriate page within text; photo credits appear on page CR1.

If you purchased this book within the United States or Canada you should be aware that it has been wrongfully imported without the approval of the Publisher or the Author.

Pearson Education LTD.
Pearson Education Singapore, Pte., Ltd
Pearson Education, Canada, Ltd
Pearson Education-Japan
Pearson Education Australia PTY, Limited

Pearson Education North Asia Ltd
Pearson Educaión de Mexico, S.A. de C.V.
Pearson Education Malaysia, Pte. Ltd
Pearson Education, Upper Saddle River, New Jersey

10 9 8 7 6 5 4 3 2 1
ISBN 0-13-127312-4

To Kathy, Betty, Mandy, Matt, K.C., Keri, and Delaney;
Nancy, Amy, Melissa, and Jessica

About the Authors

As a team, Gary Armstrong and Philip Kotler provide a blend of skills uniquely suited to writing an introductory marketing text. Professor Armstrong is an award-winning teacher of undergraduate business students. Professor Kotler is one of the world's leading authorities on marketing. Together they make the complex world of marketing practical, approachable, and enjoyable.

Gary Armstrong is Crist W. Blackwell Distinguished Professor of Undergraduate Education in the Kenan-Flagler Business School at the University of North Carolina at Chapel Hill. He holds undergraduate and masters degrees in business from Wayne State University in Detroit, and he received his Ph.D. in marketing from Northwestern University. Dr. Armstrong has contributed numerous articles to leading business journals. As a consultant and researcher, he has worked with many companies on marketing research, sales management, and marketing strategy. But Professor Armstrong's first love is teaching. His Blackwell Distinguished Professorship is the only permanent endowed professorship for distinguished undergraduate teaching at the University of North Carolina at Chapel Hill. He has been very active in the teaching and administration of Kenan-Flagler's undergraduate program. His recent administrative posts include Chair of the Marketing Faculty, Associate Director of the Undergraduate Business Program, Director of the Business Honors Program, and others. He works closely with business student groups and has received several campus-wide and business school teaching awards. He is the only repeat recipient of the school's highly regarded Award for Excellence in Undergraduate Teaching, which he won three times. In 2004, Professor Armstrong received the UNC Board of Governors Award for Excellence in Teaching, the highest teaching honor bestowed at the University of North Carolina at Chapel Hill.

Philip Kotler is the S. C. Johnson & Son Distinguished Professor of International Marketing at the Kellogg Graduate School of Management, Northwestern University. He received his master's degree at the University of Chicago and his Ph.D. at M.I.T., both in economics. Dr. Kotler is author of *Marketing Management: Analysis, Planning, Implementation, and Control* (Prentice Hall), now in its eleventh edition and the most widely used marketing textbook in graduate schools of business. He has authored several successful books and has written over 100 articles for leading journals. He is the only three-time winner of the coveted Alpha Kappa Psi award for the best annual article in the *Journal of Marketing*. Dr. Kotler's numerous major honors include the Paul D. Converse Award given by the American Marketing Association to honor "outstanding contributions to science in marketing" and the Stuart Henderson Britt Award as Marketer of the Year. He was named the first recipient of two major awards: the Distinguished Marketing Educator of the Year Award given by the American Marketing Association and the Philip Kotler Award for Excellence in Health Care Marketing presented by the Academy for Health Care Services Marketing. He has also received the Charles Coolidge Parlin Award which each year honors an outstanding leader in the field of marketing. In 1995, he received the Marketing Educator of the Year Award from Sales and Marketing Executives International. Dr. Kotler has served as chairman of the College on Marketing of the Institute of Management Sciences (TIMS) and a director of the American Marketing Association. He has received honorary doctorate degrees from DePaul University, the University of Zurich, and the Athens University of Economics and Business. He has consulted with many major U.S. and foreign companies on marketing strategy.

v

Brief Contents

Contents

PART FOUR | Extending Marketing 478

Welcome to the Seventh Edition of
Marketing: An Introduction!

As we present this new edition, we want to take a moment to thank you and the millions of other marketing students and professors who have used our texts over the years. You've helped to make this text an international best seller and Prentice Hall Business Publishing's book of the year! Thank you.

Our goal with the seventh edition is to create an even more effective text from which to learn about and teach marketing. Most students learning marketing, whether majors or non-majors, want a complete picture of basic marketing principles and practices. However, they don't want to drown in a sea of details or to be overwhelmed by marketing's complexities. They want a text that's complete yet easy to manage and master.

The seventh edition of *Marketing: An Introduction* strikes a careful balance between depth of coverage and ease of learning. The seventh edition presents the latest marketing thinking. It builds upon a marketing framework which positions marketing simply as the art and science of creating value *for* customers in order to capture value *from* customers in return. It explains how marketing works with other company departments—such as accounting, information technology, finance, operations, and human resources—and with marketing partners outside the company to jointly bring value to customers.

Finally, the seventh edition takes a practical approach—concepts are applied through examples in which well-known and lesser-known companies assess and solve marketing challenges. An entirely new and comprehensive set of teaching resources, both print and digital, has been developed to support this edition. Our goal is this: offer innovative supplements that simplify—that are easier to find, access, manage, and use. You won't have to sift through boxes and books to find what you need.

In all, we think that this edition of *Marketing: An Introduction* is the best edition yet. We hope that you'll enjoy your journey down the road to learning marketing. So buckle up, and let's get rolling!

Gary Armstrong
University of North Carolina at Chapel Hill

Philip Kotler
Northwestern University

Preface

The seventh edition of *Marketing: An Introduction* presents an innovative framework for understanding and learning about marketing. Today's marketing is all about building profitable customer relationships. It starts with understanding consumer needs and wants, deciding which target markets the organization can serve best, and developing a compelling value proposition by which the organization can attract, keep, and grow targeted consumers. If the organization does these things well, it will reap the rewards in terms of market share, profits, and customer equity. Simply put, marketing is the art and science of creating value *for* customers in order to capture value *from* customers in return. From beginning to end, the seventh edition of *Marketing: An Introduction* presents and develops this customer-relationships/customer-equity framework.

What's New: Customer Value Is the Key

Marketing: An Introduction has been thoroughly revised to reflect the major trends and forces that are changing marketing in this new age of customer relationships. It offers important new thinking and expanded coverage on:

1. A "customer-relationships/customer-equity" framework:

■ *The customer relationship management/customer equity framework* is established from the start of the text, in the completely revised Chapter 1, *Marketing: Managing Profitable Customer Relationships*, and carried forward throughout the text.

■ The framework is presented in a five-step model of the marketing process, a model that details how marketing creates customer value and captures value in return. This model can be found in simplified form on page 7 and expanded form on page 33.

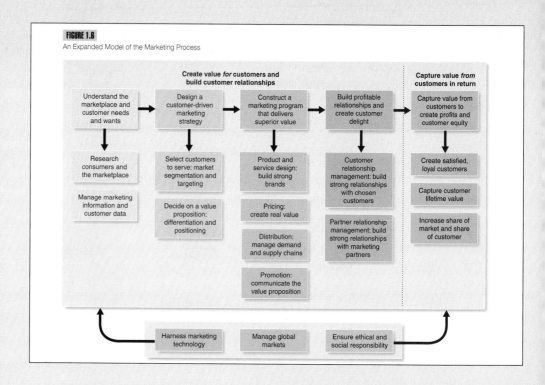

FIGURE 1.6
An Expanded Model of the Marketing Process

Many reviewers at other colleges and universities provided valuable comments and suggestions for this and previous editions. We are indebted to the following colleagues: Ron Lennon, Barry University; Alan Brokaw, Michigan Technological University; Mernoush Banton, University of Miami; Gordon Snider, California Poly-Technical School of San Luis Obispo; Karen Stone, Southern New Hampshire University; Martha Leham, Diablo Valley College; Thomas Drake, University of Miami; Rebecca Ratner, University of North Carolina—Chapel Hill; and Steve Hoeffler, University of North Carolina–Chapel Hill.

Seventh Edition Reviewers:

Rajshri Agarwal, Iowa State University

S. Allen Broyles, University of Tennessee

Mee-Shew Cheung, University of Tennessee

Renee Florsheim, Loyola Marymount University

Charles Goeldner, University of Colorado, Boulder

Carol Gwin, Baylor University

Richard Hansen, Ferris State University

Kathy Illing, Greenville Technical College

Jerry L. Thomas, San Jose State University

Merv Yeagle, University of Maryland

Robert Jones, California State University, Fullerton

Ann Kuzma, Minnesota State University, Mankato

Mark Mitchell, University of South Carolina, Spartanburg

William Rodgers, St. Cloud State University

Jeff Schmidt, U. Illinois, Champaign-Urbana

Roberta Schultz, Western Michigan University

Donald Self, Auburn University, Montgomery

Steve Taylor, Illinois State University

Ron Young, Kalamazoo Valley Community College

Former Reviewers:

Gemmy Allen, Mountain View College

Abi Almeer, Nova University

Arvid Anderson, University of North Carolina, Wilmington

Mernoush Banton, University of Miami

Arnold Bornfriend, Worcester State College

Alan Brokaw, Michigan Technological University

Donald Boyer, Jefferson College

Alejandro Camacho, University of Georgia

William Carner, University of Texas, Austin

Gerald Cavallo, Fairfield University

Lucette Comer, Florida International University

Ron Cooley, South Suburban College

Michael Conard, Teikyo Post University

June Cotte, University of Connecticut

Ronald Cutter, Southwest Missouri State University

John de Young, Cumberland County College

Lee Dickson, Florida International University

Mike Dotson, Appalachian State University

Peter Doukas, Westchester Community College

Thomas Drake, University of Miami

David Forlani, University of North Florida

Jack Forrest, Middle Tennessee State University

John Gauthier, Gateway Technical Institute

Eugene Gilbert, California State University, Sacramento

Diana Grewel, University of Miami

Esther Headley, Wichita State University

Sandra Heusinkveld, Normandale Community College

Steve Hoeffler, University of North Carolina, Chapel Hill

James Jeck, North Carolina State University

Eileen Keller, Kent State University

James Kennedy, Navarro College

Eric Kulp, Middlesex Community College

Ed Laube, Macomb Community College

Martha Leham, Diablo Valley College

Ron Lennon, Barry University

Gregory Lincoln, Westchester Community College

John Lloyd, Monroe Community College

Dorothy Maas, Delaware County Community College

Ajay Manrai, University of Delaware

Lalita Manrai, University of Delaware

James McAlexander, Oregon State University

Donald McBane, Clemson University

Debbora Meflin-Bullock, California State Polytechnic University

Randall Mertz, Mesa Community College

Herbert Miller, University of Texas, Austin

Veronica Miller, Mt. St. Mary's College

Joan Mizis, St. Louis Community College

Melissa Moore, University of Connecticut

Robert Moore, University of Connecticut

William Morgenroth, University of South Carolina, Columbia

Linda Moroble, Dallas County Community College

Sandra Moulton, Technical College of Alamance

Jim Muney, Valdosta State

Lee Neuman, Bucks County Community College

Dave Olsen, North Hennepin Community College

Thomas Paczkowski, Cayuga Community College

George Paltz, Erie Community College

Tammy Pappas, Eastern Michigan University

Alison Pittman, Brevard Community College

Lana Podolak, Community College of Beaver County

Joel Porrish, Springfield College

Robert L. Powell, Gloucester County College

Eric Pratt, New Mexico State University

Rebecca Ratner, University of North Carolina, Chapel Hill

Robert Ross, Wichita State University

Andre San Augustine, University of Arizona

Dwight Scherban, Central Connecticut College

Eberhard Scheuing, St. John's University

Pamela Schindler, Wittenburg University

Raymond Schwartz, Montclair State University

Raj Sethuraman, University of Iowa

Reshima H. Shah, University of Pittsburgh

Jack Sheeks, Broward Community College

Herbert Sherman, Long Island University, Southhampton

Dee Smith, Lansing Community College

Gordon Snider, California Poly-Technical School of San Luis Obispo

Jim Spiers, Arizona State University

Karen Stone, Southern New Hampshire University

Peter Stone, Spartanburg Technical College

Ira Teich, Long Island University

Donna Tillman, California State Polytechnic University

Andrea Weeks, Fashion Institute of Design and Merchandising

Summer White, Massachusetts Bay Community College

Bill Worley, Allan Hancock College

We also owe a great deal to the people at Prentice Hall who helped develop this book. Marketing Editors Katie Stevens and Bruce Kaplan provided caring and valuable advice and assistance through several phases of this revision. To Michelle O'Brien, we thank you for your energy and creative efforts in marketing our text. We also thank the members of our outstanding production team at Prentice Hall for their expertise in taking a rough manuscript and creating a beautiful, living text: Judy Leale, Senior Managing Editor; Cindy Durand and Virginia Somma, Production Editors; Jill Little, Designer; and Keri Miksza, Image Manager.

Finally, we owe many thanks to our families for all of their support and encouragement — Kathy, Betty, Mandy, Matt, KC, Keri, and Delaney from the Armstrong family and Nancy, Amy, Melissa, and Jessica from the Kotler family. To them, we dedicate this book.

Gary Armstrong

Philip Kotler

Marketing: An Introduction
7/e

amazon.com.

| VIEW CART | WISH LIST | YOUR ACCOUNT | HELP |

WELCOME | YOUR STORE | BOOKS | APPAREL & ACCESSORIES | ELECTRONICS | TOYS & GAMES | KITCHEN & HOUSEWARES | TRAVEL | ► SEE MORE STORES

► INTERNATIONAL | ► TOP SELLERS | ► ⊙ TARGET | ► TODAY'S DEALS | ► SELL YOUR STUFF

amazon.com.

Dear Customers,

The American Customer Satisfaction Index is, by far, the most authoritative and widely followed survey of customer satisfaction. Last year, Amazon.com received an ACSI score of 84, the highest ever recorded -- not just online, not just in retailing -- but the highest score ever recorded in any service industry. This year, Amazon.com scored an 88 -- again the highest score ever recorded in any service industry.

In ACSI's words:

"Amazon.com continues to show remarkably high levels of customer satisfaction. With a score of 88 (up 5%), it is generating satisfaction at a level unheard of in the service industry...Can customer satisfaction for Amazon climb more? The latest ACSI data suggest that it is indeed possible. Both service and the value proposition offered by Amazon have increased at a steep rate".

Thank you very much for being a customer, and we'll work even harder for you in the future. (We already have lots of customer experience improvements planned for 2003.)

On behalf of everyone at Amazon.com,

Sincerely,

Jeff Bezos
Founder & CEO

■ *After studying this chapter, you should be able to*

1. *Define* marketing and outline the steps in the marketing process **2.** *Explain* the importance of understanding customers and the marketplace, and identify the five core marketplace concepts **3.** *Identify* the key elements of a customer-driven marketing strategy, and discuss the marketing management orientations that guide marketing strategy **4.** *Discuss* customer relationship management, and identify strategies for creating value *for* customers and capturing value *from* customers in return **5.** *Describe* the major trends and forces that are changing the marketing landscape in this new age of relationships

Marketing: Managing Profitable Customer Relationships

ROAD MAP | Previewing the Concepts

Welcome to the exciting world of marketing! In this chapter, to start you off, we will introduce you to the basic concepts. We'll start with a simple question: What *is* marketing? Simply put, marketing is building profitable customer relationships. The aim of marketing is to create value for customers and to capture value in return. Chapter 1 is organized around five steps in the marketing process—from understanding customer needs, to designing customer-driven marketing strategies and constructing marketing programs, to building customer relationships and capturing value for the firm. Throughout the chapter, we focus on the most important concept of modern marketing—managing customer relationships. Understanding these basic concepts, and forming your own ideas about what they really mean to you, will give you a solid foundation for all that follows.

To set the stage, let's look first at Amazon.com. In only a few years, Amazon.com has blossomed from an obscure dot-com upstart into one of the best-known names on the Internet. In the process, it has forever changed the practice of marketing. It pioneered the use of Web technology to build strong, one-to-one customer relationships based on creating genuine customer value. The only problem: This seemingly successful company has yet to prove that it can turn long-term profits. As you read on, ask yourself: Will Amazon.com eventually become the Wal-Mart of the Internet? Or will it become just another interactive catalog company?

Chances are, when you think of shopping on the Web, you think of Amazon.com. Amazon.com first opened its virtual doors in mid-July 1995, selling books out of founder Jeff Bezos's garage in suburban Seattle. It still sells books—by the millions. But it now sells products in a dozen other categories as well: from music, videos, consumer electronics, and computers to tools and hardware, kitchen and housewares, apparel, and toys and baby products. "We have the Earth's Biggest Selection," declares the company's Web site.

In less than a decade, Amazon.com has become one of the best-known names on the Net. In perfecting the art of online selling, it has also rewritten the rules of marketing. Its most ardent fans view Amazon.com as *the* model for New Economy businesses of the twenty-first century. If any dot-com can make it big, they believe, Amazon.com can.

But not everything has clicked smoothly for Amazon.com. If you believe the skeptics, the company will never become a workable business. Attracting customers and sales hasn't been a problem. Over the past six years, Amazon.com's customer base has grown more than 23-fold, to 35 million customers in more than 220 countries. Sales have rocketed from a modest $15 million a year in 1996 to more than $4 billion today, and they are growing by more than 20 percent per year. Some analysts confidently predict that sales will reach $8 billion by 2007. So, what's the problem? Profits—or a lack thereof. Although its losses continue to shrink, and although it made first-quarter profits in 2002 and 2003, Amazon.com has yet to experience a profitable year. Doubters say that Amazon.com's Web-only model can never be truly profitable.

No matter what your view on its future, there's little doubt that Amazon.com is an outstanding marketing company. To its core, the company is relentlessly customer driven. "The thing that drives everything is creating genuine value for customers," says founder Jeff Bezos. "Nothing happens without that." A few years back, when asked when Amazon.com would start putting profits first rather than growth, Bezos replied, "Customers come first. If you focus on what customers want and build a relationship, they will allow you to make money."

The relationship with customers is the key to the company's future. Anyone at Amazon.com will tell you that the company wants to do much more than just sell books or DVDs or digital cameras. It wants to deliver a special *experience* to every customer. "The customer experience really matters," says Bezos. "We've focused on just having a better store, where it's easier to shop, where you can learn more about the products, where you have a bigger selection, and where you have the lowest prices. You combine all of that stuff together and people say, 'Hey, these guys really get it.' "

And they do get it. Most Amazon.com regulars feel a surprisingly strong and personal relationship with the company, especially given the almost complete lack of actual human interaction. For each of the last two years, the American Customer Satisfaction Index has rated Amazon the highest ever in customer satisfaction for a service company, regardless of industry. Analyst Geoffrey Colvin comments:

> I travel a lot and talk with all kinds of people and I'm struck by how many of them speak passionately about their retail experience with Amazon.com. . . . How can people get so cranked up about an experience in which they don't see, touch, or hear another soul? The answer is that Amazon.com creates a more human relationship than most people realize. . . . The experience has been crafted so carefully that most of us actually enjoy it.

Amazon.com obsesses over making each customer's experience uniquely personal. For example, the site's "Your Recommendations" feature prepares personalized product recommendations, and its "New for You" feature links customers through to their own personalized home pages. Amazon.com was the first to use "collaborative filtering" technology, which sifts through each customer's past purchases and the purchasing patterns of customers with similar profiles to come up with personalized site content. "We want Amazon.com to be the right store for you as an individual," says Bezos. "If we have 35 million customers, we should have 35 million stores."

Visitors to Amazon.com's Web site receive a unique blend of benefits: huge selection, good value, convenience, and what Amazon vice president Jason Kilar calls "discovery." In books alone, for example, Amazon.com offers an easily searchable virtual selection of more than 3 million titles, 15 times more than in any physical bookstore. Good value comes in the form of reasonable prices. And at Amazon.com, it's irresistibly convenient to buy. You can log on, find what you want, and order with a single mouse click, all in less time than it takes to find a parking space at the local mall.

But it's the "discovery" factor that makes the Amazon.com experience really special. Once on the Web site, you're compelled to stay for a while—looking, learning, and discovering. Amazon.com has become a kind of online community, in which customers can browse for products, research purchase alternatives, share opinions and reviews with other visitors, and chat online with authors and experts. In this way, Amazon.com does much more than just sell goods on the Web. It creates customer relationships and satisfying online experiences.

In fact, Amazon.com has become so good at managing online relationships that many traditional "brick-and-mortar" retailers are turning to Amazon for help in adding more "clicks" to their "bricks." For example, Amazon.com now partners with well-known retailers such as Target, Toys "R" Us, Circuit City, and Borders to help them run their Web interfaces. The brick-and-mortar partners handle purchasing and inventory; Amazon.com oversees the customer experience—maintaining the Web site, attracting customers, and managing customer service. Amazon.com has also formed alliances with dozens, even hundreds, of retailers who sell their wares through the Amazon site. For example, Amazon's "apparel store" is more of a mall, featuring the products of partners such as Gap, Old Navy, Eddie Bauer, Spiegel, Foot Locker, Nordstrom, and Sears-owned Lands' End.

So, what do you think? Will Amazon eventually become the Wal-Mart of the Web? Or will it end up as just another interactive catalog company? Despite its successes and improving financials, until Amazon proves that it can be profitable, the debate will continue. But here's one analyst's conclusion:

> I'm betting on Amazon.com. . . . In the old days, only small outfits could keep track of customers: your local tailor, the local barber, the butcher at the grocery store. [Lately,] we've bemoaned the loss of that personal touch. [Amazon.com can bring it back. It] understands that the real opportunity is in using the technology to build long-term relationships. . . . What Amazon.com has done is invent and implement a model for interacting with millions of customers, one at a time. Old-line companies can't do that. . . . Amazon.com's technology gives me exactly what I want, in an extraordinarily responsive way.

Whatever its fate, Amazon.com has forever changed the face of marketing. "No matter what becomes of Amazon," says the analyst, "it has taught us something new."[1]

Today's successful companies at all levels have one thing in common: Like Amazon.com, they are strongly customer focused and heavily committed to marketing. These companies share a passion for understanding and satisfying customer needs in well-defined target markets. They motivate everyone in the organization to help build lasting customer relationships through superior customer value and satisfaction. As cofounder Bernie Marcus of Home Depot asserted, "All of our people understand what the Holy Grail is. It's not the bottom line. It's an almost blind, passionate commitment to taking care of customers."

■▌ What Is Marketing?

Marketing, more than any other business function, deals with customers. Building customer relationships based on customer value and satisfaction is at the very heart of modern marketing. Although we will soon explore more-detailed definitions of marketing, perhaps the simplest definition is this one: Marketing is managing profitable customer relationships.

The twofold goal of marketing is to attract new customers by promising superior value and to keep and grow current customers by delivering satisfaction.

Wal-Mart has become the world's largest retailer, and the world's largest company, by delivering on its promise, "Always low prices. Always!" Ritz-Carlton promises—and delivers—truly "memorable experiences" for its hotel guests. At Disney theme parks, "imagineers" work wonders in their quest to "make a dream come true today." Dell Computer leads the personal computer industry by consistently making good on its promise to "be direct." Dell makes it easy for customers to custom-design their own computers and have them delivered quickly to their doorsteps or desktops. These and other highly successful companies know that if they take care of their customers, market share and profits will follow.

Sound marketing is critical to the success of every organization—large or small, for-profit or not-for-profit, domestic or global. Large for-profit firms such as Procter & Gamble, Microsoft, Sony, Wal-Mart, IBM, and Marriott use marketing. But so do not-for-profit organizations such as colleges, hospitals, museums, symphony orchestras, and even churches. Moreover, marketing is practiced not only in the United States but also in the rest of the world.

You already know a lot about marketing—it's all around you. You see the results of marketing in the abundance of products in your nearby shopping mall. You see marketing in the advertisements that fill your TV screen, spice up your magazines, stuff your mailbox, or enliven your Web pages. At home, at school, where you work, and where you play, you see marketing in almost everything you do. Yet, there is much more to marketing than meets the consumer's casual eye. Behind it all is a massive network of people and activities competing for your attention and purchases.

This book will give you a more complete and formal introduction to the basic concepts and practices of today's marketing. In this chapter, we begin by defining marketing and the marketing process.

Marketing Defined

What does the term *marketing* mean? Many people think of marketing only as selling and advertising. And no wonder—every day we are bombarded with television commercials, newspaper ads, direct-mail offers, sales calls, and Internet pitches. However, selling and advertising are only the tip of the marketing iceberg.

Today, marketing must be understood not in the old sense of making a sale—"telling and selling"—but in the new sense of *satisfying customer needs.* If the marketer does a good job of understanding consumer needs; develops products that provide superior value; and prices, distributes, and promotes them effectively, these products will sell very easily. Thus, selling and advertising are only part of a larger "marketing mix"—a set of marketing tools that work together to affect the marketplace.

Marketing
A social and managerial process by which individuals and groups obtain what they need and want through creating and exchanging value with others.

We define **marketing** as a social and managerial process by which individuals and groups obtain what they need and want through creating and exchanging value with others.[2] In a business setting, marketing involves building and managing profitable exchange relationships with customers.

The Marketing Process

Figure 1.1 presents a simple five-step model of the marketing process. In the first four steps, companies work to understand consumers, create customer value, and build strong customer relationships. In the final step, companies reap the rewards of creating superior customer value. By creating value *for* consumers, they in turn capture value *from* consumers in the form of sales, profits, and long-term customer equity.[3]

In this and the next chapter, we will examine the steps of this simple model of marketing. In this chapter, we'll review each step but focus more on the customer relationship steps—understanding consumers, building customer relationships, and capturing value from customers. In Chapter 2, we'll look more deeply into the second and third steps—designing marketing strategies and constructing marketing programs.

FIGURE 1.1
A Simple Model of the
Marketing Process

■ Understanding the Marketplace and Consumer Needs

The marketing process begins, continues, and ends with consumers. As a first step, marketers need to understand customer needs and wants and the marketplace within which they operate. We now examine five core marketplace concepts: needs, wants, and demands; marketing offers (products, services, and experiences); value and satisfaction; exchanges, transactions, and relationships; and markets.

Needs, Wants, and Demands

The most basic concept underlying marketing is that of human needs. Human **needs** are states of felt deprivation. They include basic *physical* needs for food, clothing, warmth, and safety; *social* needs for belonging and affection; and *individual* needs for knowledge and self-expression. These needs were not created by marketers; they are a basic part of the human makeup.

    Wants are the form human needs take as they are shaped by culture and individual personality. An American *needs* food but *wants* a Big Mac, french fries, and a soft drink. A person in Mauritius *needs* food but *wants* a mango, rice, lentils, and beans. Wants are shaped by one's society and are described in terms of objects that will satisfy needs. When backed by buying power, wants become **demands**. Given their wants and resources, people demand products with benefits that add up to the most value and satisfaction.

    Outstanding marketing companies go to great lengths to learn about and understand their customers' needs, wants, and demands. They conduct consumer research and analyze mountains of customer data. Their people at all levels—including top management—stay close to customers. For example, top executives from Wal-Mart spend two days each week visiting stores and mingling with customers. At Disney World, at least once in his or her career, each manager spends a day touring the park in a Mickey, Minnie, Goofy, or other character costume.

    At consumer products giant Procter & Gamble, top executives even visit with ordinary consumers in their homes and on shopping trips. "We read the data and look at the charts," says one P&G executive, "but to shop [with consumers] and see how the woman is changing retailers to save 10 cents on a loaf of bread [so she can] spend it on things that are more important—that's important to us to keep front and center."[4]

Marketing Offers—Products, Services, and Experiences

Consumers' needs and wants are fulfilled through a **marketing offer**—some combination of products, services, information, or experiences offered to a market to satisfy a need or want. Marketing offers are not limited to physical *products*. Marketing offers also include *services*, activities or benefits offered for sale that are essentially intangible and do not result in the ownership of anything. Examples include banking, airline, hotel, tax preparation, and home repair services. More broadly, marketing offers also include other entities, such as *persons*, *places*, *organizations*, *information,* and *ideas*.

    Many sellers make the mistake of paying more attention to the specific products they offer than to the benefits and experiences produced by these products. These sellers suffer

Needs
States of felt deprivation.

Wants
The form human needs take as shaped by culture and individual personality.

Demands
Human wants that are backed by buying power.

Marketing offer
Some combination of products, services, information, or experiences offered to a market to satisfy a need or want.

■ Products do not have to be physical objects. Here the "product" is an idea—protecting animals.

from "*marketing myopia.*" They are so taken with their products that they focus only on existing wants and lose sight of underlying customer needs.[5] They forget that a product is only a tool to solve a consumer problem. A manufacturer of quarter-inch drill bits may think that the customer needs a drill bit. But what the customer *really* needs is a quarter-inch hole. These sellers will have trouble if a new product comes along that serves the customer's need better or less expensively. The customer with the same *need* will *want* the new product.

Smart marketers look beyond the attributes of the products and services they sell. They create *brand meaning* and *brand experiences* for consumers. For example, Coca-Cola means much more to consumers than just something to drink—it has become an American icon with a rich tradition and meaning. And Nike is more than just shoes, it's what the shoes do for you and where they take you.

By orchestrating several services and products, companies can create, stage, and market brand experiences. Disney World is an experience; so is a ride on a Harley-Davidson motorcycle. You experience a visit to Barnes & Noble or surfing Sony's playstation.com Web site. And you don't just watch a NASCAR race, you immerse yourself in the NASCAR experience (see Marketing at Work 1.1). In fact, experiences have emerged for many firms as the next step in differentiating the company's offer. "What consumers really want [are offers] that dazzle their senses, touch their hearts, and stimulate their minds," declares one expert. "They want [offers] that deliver an experience."[6]

Value and Satisfaction

Consumers usually face a broad array of products and services that might satisfy a given need. How do they choose among these many marketing offers? Consumers make choices based on their perceptions of the value and satisfaction that various products and services deliver. Customers form expectations about the value of various marketing offers and buy accordingly. Satisfied customers buy again and tell others about their good experiences. Dissatisfied customers often switch to competitors and disparage the product to others.

Marketers must be careful to set the right level of expectations. If they set expectations too low, they may satisfy those who buy but fail to attract enough buyers. If they raise expectations too high, buyers will be disappointed. Customer value and customer satisfaction are key building blocks for developing and managing customer relationships. We will revisit these core concepts later in the chapter.

Exchange, Transactions, and Relationships

Exchange
The act of obtaining a desired object from someone by offering something in return.

Transaction
A trade of values between two parties.

Marketing occurs when people decide to satisfy needs and wants through exchange. **Exchange** is the act of obtaining a desired object from someone by offering something in return. Whereas exchange is the core concept of marketing, a transaction, in turn, is marketing's unit of measurement. A **transaction** consists of a trade of values between two parties: One party gives X to another party and gets Y in return. For example, you pay Sears $350 and receive a television set.

In the broadest sense, the marketer tries to bring about a response to some marketing offer. The response may be more than simply buying or trading products and services. A political candidate, for instance, wants votes, a church wants membership, and a social action group wants idea acceptance.

Marketing at Work | 1.1

NASCAR: Creating Customer Experiences

When you think of NASCAR, do you think of tobacco-spitting rednecks and run-down race tracks? Think again! These days, NASCAR (the National Association for Stock Car Auto Racing) is much, much more. In fact, it's one great marketing organization. And for fans, NASCAR is a lot more than a stock car race. It's a high-octane, totally involving experience.

As for the stereotypes, throw them away. NASCAR is now the second-highest-rated regular season sport on TV—only the NFL draws more viewers. NASCAR fans are young (58 percent are between the ages of 18 and 34). They are affluent (42 percent earn in excess of $50,000 a year). And they are decidedly family oriented (40 percent are women). What's more, they are 75 million strong—4 of every 10 people in the United States regularly watch or attend NASCAR events. Most important, they are passionate about NASCAR. An ardent NASCAR fan experiences almost 9 hours of NASCAR media coverage per week and spends nearly $700 a year on NASCAR-related clothing, collectibles, and other items.

What's NASCAR's secret? Its incredible success results from a single-minded focus: creating memorable experiences that translate into lasting customer relationships. The NASCAR experience consists of a careful blend of live racing events, abundant media coverage, and compelling Web sites.

Each year, fans experience the adrenaline-charged, heart-stopping excitement of NASCAR racing first-hand by attending national tours to some two dozen tracks around the country. NASCAR races attract the largest crowds of any U.S. sporting event. About 140,000 people attended the recent Daytona 500, twice as many as attended the Super Bowl. At these events, fans hold tailgate parties, camp and cook out, watch the cars roar around the track, meet the drivers, and swap stories with other NASCAR enthusiasts. To get fans even closer to the action, in addition to grandstands and skyboxes, track facilities include RV parks next to and right inside the racing oval.

NASCAR really cares about its customers and goes out of its way to show them a good time. For example, rather than fleecing fans with overpriced food and beer, NASCAR tracks encourage fans to bring their own. Marvels one sponsor, "[In] what other sport can you drive your beat-up RV or camper into the stadium and sit on it to watch the race? . . . How many NFL stadiums go so far as to print the allowable cooler dimensions on the back of the ticket?" Such actions mean that NASCAR might lose a sale today, but it will keep the customer tomorrow.

To further the experience, NASCAR makes the sport a wholesome family affair. Tracks feature professionally landscaped grounds, with manicured flower beds, no litter, and ample restrooms. The environment is safe for kids—uniformed security guards patrol the track to keep things in line. The family atmosphere extends to the drivers, too. Unlike the aloof and often distant athletes in other sports, NASCAR drivers seem like regular guys. They are approachable, friendly, and readily available to mingle with fans and sign autographs. Many drivers have children, brothers, sisters, or parents who work for NASCAR as drivers or pit crew. As a result, fans view drivers as good role models, and the long NASCAR tradition of family involvement creates the next generation of loyal fans.

Can't make it to the track? No problem. NASCAR TV coverage reaches 20 million viewers weekly. Well-orchestrated coverage and in-car cameras put fans in the middle of the action, giving them vicarious thrills that keep them glued to the

NASCAR's incredible success results from creating memorable experiences that translate into lasting customer relationships. The resulting fan loyalty attracts hundreds of marketers, who pay to sponsor cars and get their corporate logos emblazoned on team uniforms and on the hoods or side panels of cars.

(continued)

screen. "When the network gets it right, my surround-sound bothers my neighbors but makes my ears happy," says Angela Kotula, a 35-year-old human resources professional.

NASCAR also delivers the NASCAR experience through its engaging Web sites. NASCAR.com serves up a glut of news and entertainment to more than 2 million fans each month—in-depth news, driver bios, background information, online games, community discussions, and merchandise. True die-hard fans can subscribe to TrackPass for $4.95 a month (or $29.95 for the year) to get up-to-the-minute standings, race video, streaming audio from the cars, and access to a host of archived audio and video highlights. For another $3 per month, TrackPass with PitCommand delivers a real-time data feed, complete with the GPS locations of cars and data from drivers' dashboards.

Ready access to NASCAR races, drivers, and information makes fans feel more a part of the sport. But a big part of the NASCAR experience is the feeling that the sport itself is personally accessible. Anyone who knows how to drive feels that he or she, too, could be a champion NASCAR driver. As 48-year police officer Ed Sweat puts it: "Genetics did not bless me with the height of a basketball player, nor was I born to have the bulk of a lineman in the NFL. But . . . on any given Sunday, with a rich sponsor, the right car, and some practice, I could be draftin' and passin', zooming to the finish line, trad-

ing paint with Tony Stewart. . . . Yup, despite my advancing age and waistline, taking Zocor, and driving by a gym . . . I could be Dale Jarrett!" Some NASCAR tracks even have driving schools and let the public test their driving skills on the track.

Ultimately, all of this fan enthusiasm translates into financial success for NASCAR, and for its sponsors. Television networks pay some $2.4 billion per year for the rights to broadcast NASCAR events. And the sport is third in licensed merchandise sales, behind only the NFL and the NCAA. It rings up more than $1.3 billion in sales of NASCAR-branded retail merchandise every year.

Marketing studies show that NASCAR's fans are more loyal to the sport's sponsors than fans of any other sport. They are three times as likely to purchase a sponsor's product rather than a nonsponsor's product. Indeed, 71 percent always buy sponsors' products, and 42 percent will switch to support a sponsor. Just ask dental hygienist Jenny German, an ardent fan of NASCAR driver Jeff Gordon. According to one account: "She actively seeks out any product he endorses. She drinks Pepsi instead off Coke, eats Edy's ice cream for desert, and owns a pair of Ray-Ban sunglasses. 'If they sold underwear with the number 24 on it, I'd have it on,' German says."

Because of such loyal fan relationships, NASCAR has attracted more than 250 big-name sponsors, from Wal-Mart, Home Depot, and AT&T to Procter & Gamble, M&Ms, Wrangler, and the U.S.

Army. Sponsors eagerly pay up to $10 million per year to sponsor a top car and to get their corporate colors and logos emblazoned on team uniforms and on the hoods or side panels of team cars. Or they pay $3 million to $5 million a year to become the "official (fill-in-the-blank)" of NASCAR racing. They also invest in their own NASCAR promotions, which can produce amazing results. For example, in a recent Coca-Cola "Racing Family" promotion, 175 million NASCAR commemorative bottles flew off retailers' shelves in a matter of weeks.

So if you're still thinking of NASCAR as rednecks and moonshine, you'd better think again. NASCAR is a premier marketing organization that knows how to create customer experiences that translate into deep and lasting customer relationships. "Better than any other sport," says a leading sports marketing executive, "NASCAR listens to its fans and gives them what they want."

Sources: Quotes and other information from Mark Woods, "Readers Try to Explain Why Racin' Rocks," *The Florida Times Union*, February 16, 2003, p. C1; Tina Grady, "NASCAR Fan Base More Than Just Blue Collar," *Aftermarket Business*, May 2002, p. 11; George Pyne, "In His Own Words: NASCAR Sharpens Winning Strategy," *Advertising Age*, October 28, 2002, p. S6; Peter Spiegel, "Heir Gordon," *Forbes*, December 14, 1998, pp. 42–46; Tony Kontzer, "Backseat Drivers—NASCAR Puts You in the Race," *InformationWeek*, March 25, 2002, p. 83; Lisa Matte, "The Race Is On: Marketing Partnerships with Racing Teams Increase Awareness of, Loyalty to Hotel Brands," *Hotel & Motel Management*, August 2002, p. 127; Matthew Futterman, "What Fuels NASCAR," *The Star-Ledger*, February 16, 2003, p. 1; and www.NASCAR.com, July 2003.

Marketing consists of actions taken to build and maintain desirable *exchange relationships* with target audiences involving a product, service, idea, or other object. Beyond simply attracting new customers and creating transactions, the goal is to retain customers and grow their business with the company. Marketers want to build strong economic and social relationships by consistently delivering superior value. We will expand on the important concept of customer relationship management later in the chapter.

Markets

Market
The set of all actual and potential buyers of a product or service.

The concepts of exchange and relationships lead to the concept of a market. A **market** is the set of actual and potential buyers of a product. These buyers share a particular need or want that can be satisfied through exchange relationships. The size of a market depends on the number of people who exhibit the need, have resources to engage in exchange, and are willing to exchange these resources for what they want.

Marketers are keenly interested in markets. Marketing means managing markets to bring about profitable exchange relationships. However, creating exchange relationships

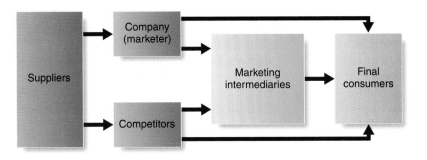

FIGURE 1.2
Elements of a Modern
Marketing System

takes work. Sellers must search for buyers, identify their needs, design good marketing offers, set prices for them, promote them, and store and deliver them. Activities such as product development, research, communication, distribution, pricing, and service are core marketing activities.

Although we normally think of marketing as being carried out by sellers, buyers also carry out marketing. Consumers do marketing when they search for the goods they need at prices they can afford. Company purchasing agents do marketing when they track down sellers and bargain for good terms.

Figure 1.2 shows the main elements in a modern marketing system. In the usual situation, marketing involves serving a market of final consumers in the face of competitors. The company and the competitors send their respective offers and messages to consumers, either directly or through marketing intermediaries. All of the actors in the system are affected by major environmental forces (demographic, economic, physical, technological, political/legal, social/cultural).

Each party in the system adds value for the next level. Thus, a company's success at building profitable relationships depends not only on its own actions but also on how well the entire system serves the needs of final consumers. Wal-Mart cannot fulfill its promise of low prices unless its suppliers provide merchandise at low costs. And Ford cannot deliver high quality to car buyers unless its dealers provide outstanding service.

■■ Designing a Customer-Driven Marketing Strategy

Once it fully understands consumers and the marketplace, marketing management can design a customer-driven marketing strategy. We define **marketing management** as the art and science of choosing target markets and building profitable relationships with them. The marketing manager's aim is to get, keep, and grow target customers by creating, delivering, and communicating superior customer value. To design a winning marketing strategy, the marketing manager must answer two important questions: What customers will we serve (what's our target market)? and How can we serve these customers best (what's our value proposition)? We will discuss these marketing strategy concepts briefly here, then look at them in more detail in the next chapter.

Marketing management
The art and science of choosing target markets and building profitable relationships with them.

Selecting Customers to Serve

The company must first decide *who* it will serve. It does this by dividing the market into segments of customers (*market segmentation*) and selecting which segments it will cultivate (*target marketing*). Some people think of marketing management as finding as many customers as possible and increasing demand. But marketing managers know that they cannot serve all customers in every way. Trying to serve all customers may result in not serving any customers well. Instead, the company wants to select customers that it can serve well and profitably. For example, Porsche profitably targets affluent professionals; Family Dollar stores profitably target families with more modest means.

Some marketers may seek *fewer* customers and reduced demand. For example, Yosemite National Park is badly overcrowded in the summer. And power companies sometimes have trouble meeting demand during peak usage periods. In these and other cases of excess demand, **demarketing** may be required to reduce the number of customers or to shift their demand temporarily or permanently. For instance, to reduce demand for space on congested expressways in Washington, D.C., the Metropolitan Washington Council of Governments has set up a Web site encouraging commuters to carpool and use mass transit.[7]

Demarketing
Marketing to reduce demand temporarily or permanently; the aim is not to destroy demand but only to reduce or shift it.

Thus, marketing managers must decide which customers they want to target, and on the level, timing, and nature of their demand. Simply put, marketing management is *customer management* and *demand management*.

**What a dog feels
when the leash breaks.**

Instant freedom, courtesy of the Boxster S. The 250 horsepower boxer engine launches you forward with its distinctive growl. Any memory of life on a leash evaporates in the wind rushing overhead. It's time to run free. Contact us at 1-800-PORSCHE or porsche.com.

PORSCHE

■ Value propositions: Porsche targets affluent buyers with promises of driving excitement: "What a dog feels like when the leash breaks."

Deciding on a Value Proposition

The company must also decide *how* it will serve targeted customers—how it will *differentiate and position* itself in the marketplace. A company's *value proposition* is the set of benefits or values it promises to deliver to consumers to satisfy their needs. Porsche promises driving performance and excitement: "What a dog feels when the leash breaks." Tide laundry detergent promises powerful, all-purpose cleaning, whereas Gain "cleans and freshens like sunshine." Altoids positions itself as "the curiously strong mint."

Such value propositions differentiate one brand from another. They answer the customer's question "Why should I buy your brand rather than a competitor's?" Companies must design strong value propositions that give them the greatest advantage in their target markets.

■ Marketing Management Orientations

Marketing management wants to design strategies that will build profitable relationships with target consumers. But what *philosophy* should guide these marketing strategies? What weight should be given to the interests of customers, the organization, and society? Very often these interests conflict.

There are five alternative concepts under which organizations design and carry out their marketing strategies: the production, product, selling, marketing, and societal marketing concepts.

Production concept
The idea that consumers will favor products that are available and highly affordable.

The Production Concept The **production concept** holds that consumers will favor products that are available and highly affordable. Therefore, management should focus on improving production and distribution efficiency. This concept is one of the oldest orientations that guides sellers.

The production concept is still a useful philosophy in two types of situations. The first occurs when the demand for a product exceeds the supply. Here, management should look for ways to increase production. The second situation occurs when the product's cost is too high and improved productivity is needed to bring it down. For example, Henry Ford's philosophy was to perfect the production of the Model T so that its cost could be reduced and more people could afford it. He joked about offering people a car of any color as long as it was black.

Although useful in some situations, the production concept can lead to marketing myopia. Companies adopting this orientation run a major risk of focusing too narrowly on their own operations and losing sight of the real objective—building customer relationships by satisfying customers' needs.

The Product Concept The **product concept** holds that consumers will favor products that offer the most in quality, performance, and innovative features. Under this concept, marketing strategy should focus on making continuous product improvements. Some manufacturers believe that if they can build a better mousetrap, the world will beat a path to their door.[8] But they are often rudely shocked. Buyers may well be looking for a better solution to a mouse problem but not necessarily for a better mousetrap. The solution might be a chemical spray, an exterminating service, or something that works better than a mousetrap. Furthermore, a better mousetrap will not sell unless the manufacturer designs, packages, and prices it attractively; places it in convenient distribution channels; brings it to the attention of people who need it; and convinces buyers that it is a better product.

Thus, the product concept also can lead to marketing myopia. For instance, railroad management once thought that users wanted *trains* rather than *transportation* and overlooked the growing challenge of airlines, buses, trucks, and automobiles. Kodak assumed that consumers wanted photographic film rather than a way to capture and share memories and at first overlooked the challenge of digital cameras. Although it now leads the digital camera market in sales, it has yet to make significant profits from this business.[9]

The Selling Concept Many companies follow the **selling concept**, which holds that consumers will not buy enough of the firm's products unless it undertakes a large-scale selling and promotion effort. The concept is typically practiced with unsought goods—those that buyers do not normally think of buying, such as insurance or blood donations. These industries must be good at tracking down prospects and selling them on product benefits.

Most firms practice the selling concept when they face overcapacity. Their aim is to sell what they make rather than make what the market wants. Such a marketing strategy carries high risks. It focuses on creating sales transactions rather than on building long-term, profitable customer relationships. It assumes that customers who are coaxed into buying the product will like it. Or, if they don't like it, they will possibly forget their disappointment and buy it again later. These are usually poor assumptions. Most studies show that dissatisfied customers do not buy again. Worse yet, whereas the average satisfied customer may tell four or five others about good experiences, the average dissatisfied customer tells twice as many others about his or her bad experiences.[10]

The Marketing Concept The **marketing concept** holds that achieving organizational goals depends on knowing the needs and wants of target markets and delivering the desired satisfactions better than competitors do. Under the marketing concept, customer focus and value are the *paths* to sales and profits.

Instead of a product-centered "make and sell" philosophy, the marketing concept is a customer-centered "sense and respond" philosophy. It views marketing not as "hunting," but as "gardening." The job is not to find the right customers for your product, but the right products for your customers. As stated by famed direct marketer Lester Wunderman, "The chant of the Industrial Revolution was that of the manufacturer who said, 'This is what I make, won't you please buy it.' The call of the Information Age is the consumer asking, 'This is what I want, won't you please make it.' "[11]

Figure 1.3 contrasts the selling concept and the marketing concept. The selling concept takes an *inside-out* perspective. It starts with the factory, focuses on the company's existing products, and calls for heavy selling and promotion to obtain profitable sales. It focuses primarily on customer conquest—getting short-term sales with little concern about who buys or why.

In contrast, the marketing concept takes an *outside-in* perspective. As Herb Kelleher, Southwest Airlines's colorful CEO, puts it, "We don't have a Marketing Department; we have a Customer Department." And in the words of one Ford executive, "If we're not customer driven, our cars won't be either." The marketing concept starts with a well-defined

Product concept
The idea that consumers will favor products that offer the most quality, performance, and features and that the organization should therefore devote its energy to making continuous product improvements.

Selling concept
The idea that that consumers will not buy enough of the firm's products unless it undertakes a large-scale selling and promotion effort.

Marketing concept
The marketing management philosophy that holds that achieving organizational goals depends on knowing the needs and wants of target markets and delivering the desired satisfactions better than competitors do.

FIGURE 1.3

The Selling and Marketing
Concepts Contrasted

Starting point	Focus	Means	Ends
Factory	Existing products	Selling and promoting	Profits through sales volume

The selling concept

Market	Customer needs	Integrated marketing	Profits through customer satisfaction

The marketing concept

market, focuses on customer needs, and integrates all the marketing activities that affect customers. In turn, it yields profits by creating long-term customer relationships with the right customers based on customer value and satisfaction. Many successful and well-known companies have adopted the marketing concept. Procter & Gamble, Disney, Wal-Mart, Marriott, Nordstrom, Dell Computer, and Southwest Airlines follow it faithfully.

Implementing the marketing concept often means more than simply responding to customers' stated desires and obvious needs. *Customer-driven* companies research current customers deeply to learn about their desires, gather new product and service ideas, and test proposed product improvements. Such customer-driven marketing usually works well when a clear need exists and when customers know what they want.

In many cases, however, customers *don't* know what they want or even what is possible. For example, 20 years ago, how many consumers would have thought to ask for cell phones, fax machines, home copiers, 24-hour Internet brokerage accounts, DVD players, handheld global satellite positioning systems, or wearable PCs? Such situations call for *customer-driving* marketing—understanding customer needs even better than customers themselves do and creating products and services that will meet existing and latent needs, now and in the future.

As Sony's visionary leader, Akio Morita, puts it: "Our plan is to lead the public with new products rather than ask them what kinds of products they want. The public does not know what is possible, but we do." And according to an executive at 3M, "Our goal is to lead customers where they want to go before *they* know where they want to go."[12]

Societal marketing concept

A principle of enlightened marketing that holds that a company should make good marketing decisions by considering consumers' wants, the company's requirements, consumers' long-run interests, and society's long-run interests.

■ Customer-driving marketing: How many of us would have thought to ask for a "wearable PC." Marketers must often understand customer needs even better than customers themselves do.

The Societal Marketing Concept   The **societal marketing concept** questions whether the pure marketing concept overlooks possible conflicts between consumer *short-run wants* and consumer *long-run welfare*. Is a firm that senses, serves, and satisfies immediate needs, wants, and interests of target markets always doing what's best for consumers and society in the long run? The societal marketing concept holds that marketing strategy should deliver value to customers in a way that maintains or improves both the consumer's *and the society's* well-being.

Consider the fast-food industry. You may see today's giant fast-food chains as offering tasty and convenient food at reasonable prices. Yet many consumer and environmental groups have voiced concerns. Critics point out that hamburgers, fried chicken, french fries, and most other foods sold by fast-food restaurants are high in fat and salt. Meals are now "super-sized," leading consumers to overeat and contributing to a national obesity epidemic. The products are wrapped in convenient packaging, but this leads to waste and pollution. Thus, in satisfying short-term consumer wants, the highly successful fast-food chains may be harming consumer health and causing environmental problems in the long run.[13]

As Figure 1.4 shows, the societal marketing concept calls on marketers to balance three considerations in setting their marketing strategies:

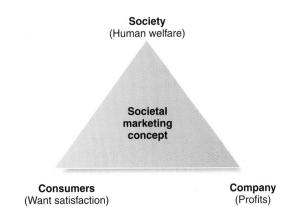

FIGURE 1.4

Three Considerations Underlying the Societal Marketing Concept

company profits, consumer wants, *and* society's interests. Originally, most companies based their marketing decisions largely on short-run company profit. Eventually, they recognized the long-run importance of satisfying consumer wants, and the marketing concept emerged. Now most companies consider society's interests when making their marketing decisions.

One such company is Johnson & Johnson, which has been rated each year in a *Fortune* magazine poll as one of America's most admired companies. Johnson & Johnson's concern for societal interests is summarized in a company document called "Our Credo," which stresses honesty, integrity, and putting people before profits. Under this credo, Johnson & Johnson would rather take a big loss than ship a bad batch of one of its products.

Consider the tragic tampering case in which eight people died from swallowing cyanide-laced capsules of Tylenol, a Johnson & Johnson brand. Although Johnson & Johnson believed that the pills had been altered in only a few stores, not in the factory, it quickly recalled all of its product. The recall cost the company $240 million in earnings. In the long run, however, the company's swift recall of Tylenol strengthened consumer confidence and loyalty, and Tylenol remains one of the nation's leading brands of pain reliever.

In this and other cases, Johnson & Johnson management has found that doing what's right benefits both consumers and the company. Says Johnson & Johnson's chief executive, "The Credo should not be viewed as some kind of social welfare program . . . it's just plain good business. If we keep trying to do what's right, at the end of the day we believe the marketplace will reward us." Thus, over the years, Johnson & Johnson's dedication to consumers and community service has made it one of America's most-admired companies *and* one of the most profitable.[14]

■ Preparing a Marketing Plan and Program

The company's marketing strategy outlines which customers the company will serve and how it will create value for these customers. Next, guided by the marketing strategy, the marketer constructs a marketing program that will actually deliver the intended value to its target customers. The marketing program builds customer relationships by transforming the strategy into action. It consists of the firm's *marketing mix*, the set of marketing tools the firm uses to implement its marketing strategy.

The major marketing tools are classified into four broad groups, called the *four Ps* of marketing: product, price, place, and promotion. To deliver on its value proposition, the firm must first create a need-satisfying marketing offer (product). It must decide

Our Credo

We believe our first responsibility is to the doctors, nurses and patients, to mothers and fathers and all others who use our products and services. In meeting their needs everything we do must be of high quality. We must constantly strive to reduce our costs in order to maintain reasonable prices. Customers' orders must be serviced promptly and accurately. Our suppliers and distributors must have an opportunity to make a fair profit.

We are responsible to our employees, the men and women who work with us throughout the world. Everyone must be considered as an individual. We must respect their dignity and recognize their merit. They must have a sense of security in their jobs. Compensation must be fair and adequate, and working conditions clean, orderly and safe. We must be mindful of ways to help our employees fulfill their family responsibilities. Employees must feel free to make suggestions and complaints. There must be equal opportunity for employment, development and advancement for those qualified. We must provide competent management, and their actions must be just and ethical.

We are responsible to the communities in which we live and work and to the world community as well. We must be good citizens — support good works and charities and bear our fair share of taxes. We must encourage civic improvements and better health and education. We must maintain in good order the property we are privileged to use, protecting the environment and natural resources.

Our final responsibility is to our stockholders. Business must make a sound profit. We must experiment with new ideas. Research must be carried on, innovative programs developed and mistakes paid for. New equipment must be purchased, new facilities provided and new products launched. Reserves must be created to provide for adverse times. When we operate according to these principles, the stockholders should realize a fair return.

Johnson & Johnson

■ Johnson & Johnson's concern for society is summarized in its credo and in the company's actions over the years.

how much it will charge for the offer (price) and how it will make the offer available to target consumers (place). Finally, it must communicate with target customers about the offer and persuade them of its merits (promotion).

We will explore marketing programs and the marketing mix in much more detail in Chapter 2. Then, in later chapters, we'll look more deeply into each element of the marketing mix.

Linking the Concepts

Stop here for a moment and stretch your legs. What have you learned so far about marketing? For the moment, set aside the more formal definitions we've examined and try to develop your own understanding of marketing.

- In *your own words*, what *is* marketing? Write down *your* definition. Does your definition include key concepts such as customer value and relationships?
- What does marketing *mean* to you? How does it affect your daily life?
- What marketing management philosophy appears to guide NASCAR? How does this compare with the marketing philosophy that guides Johnson & Johnson? Can you think of another company guided by a very different philosophy? Is there one marketing management philosophy that's best for all companies?

◼▌ Building Customer Relationships

The first three steps in the marketing process—understanding the marketplace and customer needs, designing a customer-driven marketing strategy, and constructing marketing programs—all lead up to the fourth and most important step: building profitable customer relationships.

Customer Relationship Management

Customer relationship management (CRM) is perhaps the most important concept of modern marketing. Until recently, CRM has been defined narrowly as a customer data management activity. By this definition, it involves managing detailed information about individual customers and carefully managing customer "touchpoints" in order to maximize customer loyalty. We will discuss this narrower CRM activity later in a chapter dealing with marketing information.

More recently, however, customer relationship management has taken on a broader meaning. In this broader sense, **customer relationship management** is the overall process of building and maintaining profitable customer relationships by delivering superior customer value and satisfaction. It deals with all aspects of acquiring, keeping, and growing customers.

Customer relationship management

The overall process of building and maintaining profitable customer relationships by delivering superior customer value and satisfaction.

Relationship Building Blocks: Customer Value and Satisfaction The key to building lasting customer relationships is to create superior customer value and satisfaction. Satisfied customers are more likely to be loyal customers and to give the company a larger share of their business.

Customer Value. Attracting and retaining customers can be a difficult task. Customers often face a bewildering array of products and services from which to choose. A customer buys from the firm that offers the highest **customer perceived value**—the customer's evaluation of the difference between all the benefits and all the costs of a marketing offer relative to those of competing offers.

Customer perceived value

The difference between total customer value and total customer cost.

For example, FedEx customers gain a number of benefits. The most obvious is fast and reliable package delivery. However, by using FedEx, customers also may receive some status and image values. Using FedEx usually makes both the package sender and the receiver feel more important. When deciding whether to send a package via FedEx, customers will weigh these and other perceived values against the money, effort, and psychological costs of using the service. Moreover, they will compare the value of using FedEx against the value of using other shippers—UPS, Airborne, the U.S. Postal Service. They will select the service that gives them the greatest perceived value.

Customers often do not judge product values and costs accurately or objectively. They act on *perceived* value. For example, does FedEx really provide faster, more reliable delivery? If so, is this better service worth the higher prices FedEx charges? The U.S. Postal Service argues that its express service is comparable, and its prices are much lower. However, judging by market share, most consumers perceive otherwise. Each day, they entrust FedEx with a 46 percent share of their next-day air shipping business, compared with the Postal Service's 6 percent share. The Postal Service's challenge is to change these customer value perceptions.[15]

■ Is FedEx's service worth the higher price? FedEx thinks so. It promises reliability, speed, and piece of mind. FedEx ads say "Need to get it there or else? Don't worry. There's a FedEx for that."

Customer Satisfaction. Customer satisfaction depends on the product's perceived performance relative to a buyer's expectations. If the product's performance falls short of expectations, the customer is dissatisfied. If performance matches expectations, the customer is satisfied. If performance exceeds expectations, the customer is highly satisfied or delighted.

Outstanding marketing companies go out of their way to keep important customers satisfied. Highly satisfied customers make repeat purchases and tell others about their good experiences with the product. The key is to match customer expectations with company performance. Smart companies aim to *delight* customers by promising only what they can deliver, then delivering *more* than they promise (see Marketing at Work 1.2).[16]

The American Customer Satisfaction Index, which tracks customer satisfaction in more than two dozen U.S. manufacturing and service industries, shows that overall customer satisfaction has been declining slightly in recent years.[17] It is unclear whether this has resulted from a decrease in product and service quality or from an increase in customer expectations. In either case, it presents an opportunity for companies that can consistently deliver superior customer value and satisfaction.

However, although the customer-centered firm seeks to deliver high customer satisfaction compared with its competitors, it does not attempt to *maximize* customer satisfaction. A company can always increase customer satisfaction by lowering its price or increasing its services. But this may result in lower profits. Thus, the purpose of marketing is to generate customer value profitably. This requires a very delicate balance: The marketer must continue to generate more customer value and satisfaction but not "give away the house."

Customer satisfaction

The extent to which a product's perceived performance matches a buyer's expectations.

Customer Relationship Levels and Tools

Companies can build customer relationships at many levels, depending on the nature of the target market. At one extreme, a company with many low-margin customers may seek to develop *basic relationships* with them. For example, Procter & Gamble does not phone or call on all of its Tide customers to get to know them personally. Instead, P&G creates relationships through brand-building advertising, sales promotions, a 1-800 customer response number, and its Tide Fabric Care Network Web site (www.Tide.com).

At the other extreme, in markets with few customers and high margins, sellers want to create *full partnerships* with key customers. For example, P&G customer teams work closely with Wal-Mart, Safeway, and other large retailers. And Boeing partners with American Airlines, Delta, and other airlines in designing airplanes that fully satisfy their requirements. In between these two extreme situations, other levels of customer relationships are appropriate.

Marketing at Work | *1.2*

Customer Relationships: Delighting Customers

Top-notch marketing companies know that delighting customers involves more than simply opening a complaint department, smiling a lot, and being nice. These companies set very high standards for customer satisfaction and often make seemingly outlandish efforts to achieve them. Consider the following examples:

■ A man bought his first new Lexus—a $45,000 piece of machinery. He could afford a Mercedes, a Jaguar, or a Cadillac, but he bought the Lexus. He took delivery of his new honey and started to drive it home, luxuriating in the smell of the leather interior and the glorious handling. On the interstate, he put the pedal to the metal and felt the Gs in the pit of his stomach. The lights, the windshield washer, the cup holder that popped out of the dashboard, the seat heater that warmed his bottom on a cold winter morning—he tried all of these with mounting pleasure. On a whim, he turned on the radio. His favorite classical music station came on in splendid quadraphonic sound that ricocheted around the interior. He pushed the second button; it was his favorite news station. The third button brought his favorite talk station that kept him awake on long trips. The fourth button was set to his daughter's favorite rock station. In fact, every button was set to his specific tastes. The customer knew the car was smart, but was it psychic? No. The mechanic at Lexus had noted the radio settings on his trade-in and duplicated them on the new Lexus. The customer was delighted. This was his car now—through and through! No one told the mechanic to do it. It's just

part of the Lexus philosophy: Delight a customer and continue to delight that customer, and you will have a customer for life. What the mechanic did cost Lexus nothing. Not one red cent. Yet it solidified the relationship that could be worth high six figures to Lexus in customer lifetime value.

■ Don and Betts Jackson are two of the most fun and outgoing people around. And Betts is one of the great chefs of the world. Their holiday party at their farmhouse in Delaware—usually filled to overflowing with friends, relatives, neighbors, and members of the local chamber of commerce—is a stunner, with an array of foods, drinks, and wines that would shame a Michelin four-star restaurant in Lyons. Several years ago, the Jacksons gave each other $1,500 worth of kitchen gear

from Williams-Sonoma as their main gifts to go under the Christmas tree. Don placed the order in plenty of time for Christmas delivery. The order never arrived. It was a bleak sight under the tree, made bleaker by the knowledge that Betts needed the new implements for the upcoming holiday party. The next day, Jackson got a Williams-Sonoma sales rep on the phone and told him the sad story. A combination of factors was involved: a FedEx slow-down, a computer glitch in Williams-Sonoma's eastern distribution center, and unexpected snow all conspired to delay the order. The rep took instant action. "Here's what I'm going to do for you," he said. "First, I'm going to reassemble the order and get it out to you by FedEx overnight, so you'll have it tomorrow morning. Second, I'm

The Lexus philosophy: Delight a customer and continue to delight that customer, and you will have a customer for life.

Today, most leading companies are developing customer loyalty and retention programs. Beyond offering consistently high value and satisfaction, marketers can use specific marketing tools to develop stronger bonds with consumers.[18] First, a company might build value and satisfaction by adding financial benefits to the customer relationship. For example, many companies now offer frequency marketing programs that reward customers who buy frequently or in large amounts. Airlines offer frequent-flier programs, hotels give room upgrades to their frequent guests, and supermarkets give patronage discounts to "very important customers."

going to enclose merchandise return labels, so when the old order arrives, you can slap the labels on the packages and call FedEx to take them away. Third, I'm going to forgive all shipping costs for the original order, for the returns, and for this new order that you'll get tomorrow morning. And fourth, I'm going to send you a present—a thank-you for your patience and for being a customer of Williams-Sonoma." Jackson hung up the phone feeling better. The next day, the merchandise arrived as promised, together with the return labels and a giant, top-of-the-line, blue-glass turkey baster as the free gift. Despite the original goof, the Jacksons were delighted.

■ When a customer arrived early one winter morning at an Enterprise Rent-A-Car office in Cambridge, Massachusetts, to pick up an SUV to drive on a ski vacation to the Sugarbush resort in Vermont (a three-hour-plus drive away), there was no vehicle and no record of his reservation. Cambridge's customer service representative apologized profusely and called nearby branches until he found the car the customer wanted, a Chevy Trailblazer at a location several miles away. So far, so good. But then the customer service rep drove the customer back to his house to pick up his ski gear, and to the other branch to retrieve the Trailblazer. He knocked 20 percent off the rental price, provided the customer the two-dollar toll he would have to pay to get on the highway (which he wouldn't have had to pay leaving from Cambridge) and gave him a half-tank of gas. Within a month, the delighted customer had rented twice more from Enterprise and "will probably rent more," he says.

Studies show that going to extremes to keep customers happy, although sometimes costly, goes hand in hand with good financial performance. Delighted customers come back again and again. Thus, in today's highly competitive marketplace, companies can well afford to lose money on one transaction if it helps to cement a profitable long-term customer relationship.

For companies interested in delighting customers, exceptional value and service are more than a set of policies or actions—they are a companywide attitude, an important part of the overall company culture. American Express loves to tell stories about how its people have rescued customers from disasters ranging from civil wars to earthquakes, no matter what the cost. The company gives cash rewards of up to $1,000 to "Great Performers," such as Barbara Weber, who moved mountains of U.S. State Department and Treasury Department bureaucracy to refund $980 in stolen traveler's checks to a customer stranded in Cuba.

Southwest Airlines is well known for its low fares and prompt arrivals. But its friendly and often funny flight staff goes to great lengths to delight customers. In one instance, after pushing away from the departure gate, a Southwest pilot spied an anguished passenger, sweat streaming from her face, racing down the jetway only to find that that she'd arrived too late. He returned to the gate to pick her up. Says Southwest's executive vice president for customers, "It broke every rule in the book, but we congratulated the pilot on a job well done."

Four Seasons Hotels, long known for its outstanding service, tells its employees the story of Ron Dyment, a doorman in Toronto, who forgot to load a depart-

ing guest's briefcase into his taxi. The doorman called the guest, a lawyer in Washington, D.C., and learned that he desperately needed the briefcase for a meeting the following morning. Without first asking for approval from management, Dyment hopped on a plane and returned the briefcase. The company named Dyment Employee of the Year.

Similarly, the Nordstrom department store chain thrives on stories about its service heroics, such as employees dropping off orders at customers' homes or warming up cars while customers spend a little more time shopping. In one case, a salesclerk reportedly gave a customer a refund on a tire—Nordstrom doesn't carry tires, but the store prides itself on a no-questions-asked return policy. There's even a story about a man whose wife, a loyal Nordstrom customer, died with her Nordstrom account $1,000 in arrears. Not only did Nordstrom settle the account, it also sent flowers to the funeral.

There's no simple formula for taking care of customers, but neither is it a mystery. According to the president of L.L. Bean, "A lot of people have fancy things to say about customer service . . . but it's just a day-in, day-out, ongoing, never-ending, unremitting, persevering, compassionate type of activity." For the companies that do it well, it's also very rewarding.

Sources: The Lexus and Williams-Sonoma examples are adapted from Denny Hatch and Ernie Schell, "Delight Your Customers," *Target Marketing,* April 2002, pp. 32–39. The Enterprise example is from Dana James, "Lighting the Way," *Marketing News,* April 1, 2002, pp. 1, 11. Also see Patricia Sellers, "Companies That Serve You Best," *Fortune,* May 31, 1993, pp. 74-88; Len Ellis, "Customer Loyalty," *Executive Excellence,* July 2001, pp. 13–14; "Toyota [Lexus] Tops Rankings," *The Washington Post,* May 7, 2003, p. E02; and "Lexus Awards and Accolades," accessed online at www.lexus.com, May 2003.

A second approach is to add *social benefits* as well as financial benefits. Many companies sponsor *club marketing programs* that offer members special discounts and create member communities. For example[19]:

Swiss watchmaker, Swatch, uses its club to cater to collectors, who on average buy nine of the company's quirky watches every year. "Swatch: The Club" members get additional chances to buy limited edition Swatch specials.

■ Building customer relationships: Harley-Davidson sponsors the Harley Owners Group (H.O.G.), which gives Harley owners "an organized way to share their passion and show their pride." The worldwide club now numbers more than 1,300 local chapters and 700,000 members.

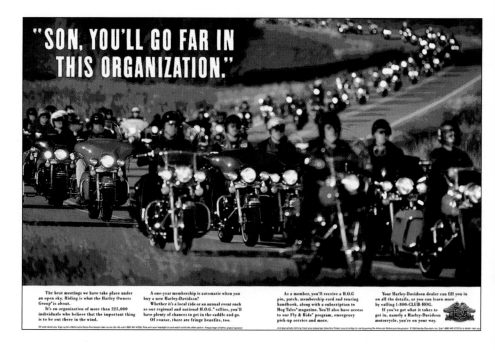

They also receive the *Swatch World Journal*, a magazine filled with Swatch-centric news from the four corners of the globe. And the club's Web site is the ultimate meeting place for Swatch enthusiasts. Swatch counts on enthusiastic word of mouth from club members as a boost to business. "Our members are like walking billboards," says the manager of Swatch's club, Trish O'Callaghan. "They love, live, and breathe our product. They are ambassadors for Swatch."

Harley-Davidson sponsors the Harley Owners Group (H.O.G.), which gives Harley riders "an organized way to share their passion and show their pride." H.O.G. membership benefits include two magazines (*Hog Tales* and *Enthusiast*), a *H.O.G. Touring Handbook,* a roadside assistance program, a specially designed insurance program, theft reward service, a travel center, and a "Fly & Ride" program that enables members to rent Harleys while on vacation. The company also maintains an extensive H.O.G. Web site, which offers information on H.O.G. chapters, rallies, events, and benefits. The worldwide club now numbers more than 1,300 local chapters and 700,000 members.

A third approach to building customer relationships is to add *structural ties* as well as financial and social benefits. For example, a business marketer might supply customers with special equipment or computer links that help them manage their orders, payroll, or inventory. McKesson Corporation, a leading pharmaceutical wholesaler, has invested millions of dollars in such linkages. It has set up direct computer links with drug manufacturers and an online system to help small pharmacies manage their inventories, their order entry, and their shelf space. FedEx offers Web links to its customers to keep them from defecting to competitors such as UPS. Customers can use the Web site to arrange shipments and track the status of their FedEx packages anywhere in the world.

The Changing Nature of Customer Relationships

Dramatic changes are occurring in the ways in which companies are relating to their customers. Yesterday's companies focused on mass marketing to all customers at arm's length. Today's companies are building more direct and lasting relationships with more carefully selected customers. Here are some important trends in the way companies are relating to their customers.

Relating with More Carefully Selected Customers Few firms today still practice true mass marketing—selling in a standardized way to any customer who comes along. Today, most marketers realize that they don't want relationships with every customer. Instead, companies are now targeting fewer, more profitable customers.

At the same time that companies are finding new ways to deliver more value *to* customers, they are also beginning to assess carefully the value *of* customers to the firm. Called *selective relationship management*, many companies now use customer profitability analysis to weed out losing customers and target winning ones for pampering. Once they identify profitable customers, firms can create attractive offers and special handling to capture these customers and earn their loyalty.

But what should the company do with unprofitable customers? If it can't turn them into profitable ones, it may even want to "fire" customers that are too unreasonable or that cost more to serve than they are worth. For example, the banking industry has led the way in assessing customer profitability. After decades of casting a wide net to lure as many customers as possible, many banks are now mining their vast databases to identify winning customers and cut out losing ones.

> Banks now routinely calculate customer value based on such factors as an account's average balances, account activity, services usage, branch visits, and other variables. A bank's customer service reps use such customer ratings when deciding how much—or how little—leeway to give a customer who wants, say, a lower credit-card interest rate or to escape the bank's bounced-check fee. Profitable customers often get what they want; for customers whose accounts lose money for the bank, the reps rarely budge.

This sorting-out process, of course, has many risks. For one, future profits are hard to predict. A high school student on his or her way to a Harvard MBA and a plum job on Wall Street might be unprofitable now but worth courting for the future. Or that shabby-looking guy might actually be or become an eccentric billionaire—so you may not want to give him the bum's rush.

Still, most banks believe that the benefits outweigh the risks. For example, after First Chicago imposed a three-dollar teller fee in 1995 on some of its money-losing customers, 30,000 of them—or close to 3 percent of the bank's customers—closed their accounts. However, many marginal customers became profitable by boosting their account balances high enough to avoid the fee or by visiting ATMs instead of tellers. On balance, imposing the fee improved the profitability of the bank's customer base.[20]

Relating for the Long Term Just as companies are being more selective about which customers they choose to serve, they are serving those they choose in a deeper, more lasting way. Today's companies are going beyond designing strategies to *attract* new customers and create *transactions* with them. They are using customer relationship management to *retain* current customers and build profitable, long-term *relationships* with them. The new view is that marketing is the science and art of finding, retaining, *and* growing profitable customers.

Why the new emphasis on retaining and growing customers? In the past, many companies took their customers for granted. Facing an expanding economy and rapidly growing markets, companies could practice a "leaky bucket" approach to marketing. Growing markets meant a plentiful supply of new customers. Companies could keep filling the marketing bucket with new customers without worrying about losing old customers through holes in the bottom of the bucket.

However, companies today face some new marketing realities. Changing demographics, more sophisticated competitors, and overcapacity in many industries mean that there are fewer customers to go around. Many companies are now fighting for shares of flat or fading markets. As a result, the costs of attracting new consumers are rising. In fact, on average, it costs 5 to 10 times as much to attract a new customer as it does to

■ Selective relationship management: BankOne in Louisiana lets its "Premier One" customers know that they are "special, exclusive, privileged, and valued." For example, after presenting a special gold card to the "concierge" near the front door, they are whisked away to a special teller window with no line or to the desk of a specially trained bank officer.

keep a current customer satisfied. Sears found that it costs 12 times more to attract a customer than to keep an existing one.[21] Given these new realities, companies now go all out to keep profitable customers.

Relating Directly Beyond connecting more deeply with their customers, many companies are also connecting more *directly*. In fact, direct marketing is booming. Consumers can now buy virtually any product without going to a store—by telephone, mail-order catalogs, kiosks, and online. Business purchasing agents routinely shop on the Web for items ranging from standard office supplies to high-priced, high-tech computer equipment.

Some companies sell *only* via direct channels—firms such as Dell Computer, Expedia, 1-800-Flowers, and Amazon.com, to name only a few. Other companies use direct connections to supplement their other communications and distribution channels. For example, Sony sells Playstation consoles and game cartridges through retailers, supported by millions of dollars of mass-media advertising. However, Sony uses its www.PlayStation.com Web site to build relationships with game players of all ages. The site offers information about the latest games, news about events and promotions, game guides and support, and even online forums in which game players can swap tips and stories.

Some marketers have hailed direct marketing as the "marketing model of the next century." They envision a day when all buying and selling will involve direct connections between companies and their customers. Others, although agreeing that direct marketing will play a growing and important role, see it as just one more way to approach the marketplace. We will take a closer look at world of direct marketing in Chapter 13.

Partner Relationship Marketing

When it comes to creating customer value and building strong customer relationships, today's marketers know that they can't go it alone. They must work closely with a variety of marketing partners. In addition to being good at *customer relationship management*, marketers must also be good at **partner relationship management**. Major changes are occurring in how marketers partner with others inside and outside the company to jointly bring more value to customers.

Partners Inside the Company Traditionally, marketers have been charged with understanding customers and representing customer needs to different company departments. The old thinking was that marketing is done only by marketing, sales, and customer support people. However, in today's more connected world, marketing no longer has sole ownership of customer interactions. Every functional area can interact with customers, especially electronically. The new thinking is that every employee must be customer focused. David Packard, co-founder of Hewlett-Packard, wisely said, "Marketing is far too important to be left only to the marketing department."[22]

Today, rather than letting each department go its own way, firms are linking all departments in the cause of creating customer value. Rather than assigning only sales and marketing people to customers, they are forming cross-functional customer teams. For example, Procter & Gamble assigns "customer development teams" to each of its major retailer accounts. These teams—consisting of sales and marketing people, operations specialists, market and financial analysts, and others—coordinate the efforts of many P&G departments toward helping the retailer be more successful.

Marketing Partners Outside the Firm Changes are also occurring in how marketers connect with their suppliers, channel partners, and even competitors. Most companies today are networked companies, relying heavily on partnerships with other firms.

Marketing channels consist of distributors, retailers, and others who connect the company to its buyers. The *supply chain* describes a longer channel, stretching from raw materials to components to final products that are carried to final buyers. For example, the supply chain for personal computers consists of suppliers of computer chips and other components, the computer manufacturer, and the distributors, retailers, and others who sell the computers.

Through *supply chain management*, many companies today are strengthening their connections with partners all along the supply chain. They know that their fortunes rest not just on how well they perform. Success at building customer relationships also rests on how well their entire supply chain performs compared with competitors' supply chains. These companies don't treat suppliers just as vendors and distributors just as customers. They treat both as partners in delivering customer value. On the one hand, for example, Lexus works closely with carefully selected suppliers to improve quality and operations efficiency. On the other hand, it works with its franchise dealers to provide top-grade sales and service support that will bring customers in the door and keep them coming back.

Beyond managing the supply chain, today's companies are also discovering that they need *strategic* partners if they hope to be effective. In the new, more competitive global environment, going it alone is going out of style. *Strategic alliances* are booming across almost all industries and services. For example, Dell Computer recently ran advertisements telling how it partners with Microsoft and Intel to provide customized e-business solutions. The ads ask: "Why do many corporations choose Windows running on Dell PowerEdge servers with Intel Pentium processors to power their e-business solutions?" The answer: "At Dell, Microsoft, and Intel, we specialize in solving the impossible." As Jim Kelly, former CEO at UPS, puts it, "The old adage 'If you can't beat 'em, join 'em,' is to being replaced by 'Join 'em and you can't be beat.' "[23]

▪▮ Capturing Value from Customers

The first four steps in the marketing process involve building customer relationships by creating and delivering superior customer value. The final step involves capturing value in return, in the form of current and future sales, market share, and profits. By creating superior customer value, the firm creates highly satisfied customers who stay loyal and buy more. This, in turn, means greater long-term returns for the firm. Here, we discuss the outcomes of creating customer value: customer loyalty and retention, share of market and share of customer, and customer equity.

Creating Customer Loyalty and Retention

Good customer relationship management creates customer delight. In turn, delighted customers remain loyal and talk favorably to others about the company and its products. Studies show big differences in the loyalty of customers who are less satisfied, somewhat satisfied, and completely satisfied. Even a slight drop from complete satisfaction can create an enormous drop in loyalty. Thus, the aim of customer relationship management is to create not just customer satisfaction, but customer delight.[24]

Companies are realizing that losing a customer means losing more than a single sale. It means losing the entire stream of purchases that the customer would make over a lifetime of patronage. For example, here is a dramatic illustration of **customer lifetime value**:

Customer lifetime value
The value of the entire stream of purchases that the customer would make over a lifetime of patronage.

> Stew Leonard, who operates a highly profitable three-store supermarket chain, says that he sees $50,000 flying out of his store every time he sees a sulking customer. Why? Because his average customer spends about $100 a week, shops 50 weeks a year, and remains in the area for about 10 years. If this customer has an unhappy experience and switches to another supermarket, Stew Leonard's has lost $50,000 in revenue. The loss can be much greater if the disappointed customer shares the bad experience with other customers and causes them to defect. To keep customers coming back, Stew Leonard's has created what the *New York Times* has dubbed the "Disneyland of Dairy Stores," complete with costumed characters, scheduled entertainment, a petting zoo, and animatronics throughout the store. From its humble beginnings as a small dairy store in 1969, Stew Leonard's has grown at an amazing pace. It has built 29 additions onto the original store, which now serves more that 250,000 customers each week. This legion of loyal shoppers is largely a result of the store's passionate approach to customer service. Rule #1 at Stew Leonard's—The customer is always right. Rule #2—If the customer is ever wrong, reread rule #1![25]

Stew Leonard is not alone in assessing customer lifetime value. Lexus estimates that a single satisfied and loyal customer is worth $600,000 in lifetime sales. The customer lifetime

■ Customer lifetime value: To keep customers coming back, Stew Leonard's has created the "Disneyland of dairy stores," Rule #1—the customer is always right. Rule #2—if the customer is ever wrong, reread rule #1!

Share of customer

The portion of the customer's purchasing in its product categories that a company gets.

Customer equity

The total combined customer lifetime values of all of the company's customers.

value of a Taco Bell customer exceeds $12,000.[26] Thus, working to retain and grow customers makes good economic sense. In fact, a company can lose money on a specific transaction but still benefit greatly from a long-term relationship.

This means that companies must aim high in building customer relationships. Customer delight creates an emotional relationship with a product or service, not just a rational preference. Hanging on to customers is "so basic, it's scary," claims one marketing executive. "We find out what our customers' needs and wants are, and then we overdeliver."[27]

Growing Share of Customer

Beyond simply retaining good customers to capture customer lifetime value, good customer relationship management can help marketers to increase their **share of customer**—the share they get of the customer's purchasing in their product categories. Many marketers are now spending less time figuring out how to increase share of market and more time trying to grow share of customer. Thus, banks want to increase "share of wallet." Supermarkets and restaurants want to get a greater "share of stomach." Car companies want to increase "share of garage" and airlines want greater "share of travel."

To increase share of customer, firms can leverage customer relationships by offering greater variety to current customers. Or they can train employees to cross-sell and up-sell in order to market more products and services to existing customers. For example, Amazon.com is highly skilled at leveraging relationships with its 35 million customers to increase its share of each customer's purchases. Originally an online bookseller, Amazon now offers customers music, videos, gifts, toys, consumer electronics, office products, home improvement items, lawn and garden products, apparel and accessories, and an online auction. In addition, based on each customer's purchase history, the company recommends related books, CDs, or videos that might be of interest. In this way, Amazon.com captures a greater share of each customer's leisure and entertainment budget.

Building Customer Equity

We can now see the importance of not just acquiring customers, but of keeping and growing them as well. Customer relationship management is oriented toward the long term. Today's smart companies not only want to create profitable customers, they want to "own" them for life, capture their customer lifetime value, and earn a greater share of their purchases.

What Is Customer Equity? The ultimate aim of customer relationship management is to produce high **customer equity**.[28] Customer equity is the total combined customer lifetime values of all of the company's customers. Clearly, the more loyal the firm's profitable customers, the higher the firm's customer equity. Customer equity may be a better measure of a firm's performance than current sales or market share. Whereas sales and market share reflect the past, customer equity suggests the future. Consider Cadillac:

In the 1970s and 1980s, Cadillac had some of the most loyal customers in the industry. To an entire generation of car buyers, the name "Cadillac" defined American luxury. Cadillac's share of the luxury car market reached a whopping 51 percent in 1976. Based on market share and sales, the brand's future looked rosy. However, measures of customer equity would have painted a bleaker picture. Cadillac customers were getting older (average age, 60), and average customer lifetime value was falling. Many Cadillac buyers were on their last car. Thus, although

Cadillac's market share was good, its customer equity was not. Compare this with BMW. Its more youthful and vigorous image didn't win BMW the early market share war. However, it did win BMW younger customers with higher customer lifetime values. The result: Cadillac now captures only about a 15 percent market share, lower than BMW's. And BMW's customer equity remains much higher—it has more customers with a higher average customer lifetime value. Thus, market share is not the answer. We should care not just about current sales but also about future sales. Customer lifetime value and customer equity are the name of the game.[29]

Building the Right Relationships with the Right Customers Companies should manage customer equity carefully. They should view customers as assets that need to be managed and maximized. But not all customers, not even all loyal ones, are good investments. Surprisingly, some loyal customers can be unprofitable, and some disloyal customers can be profitable. Which customers should the company acquire and retain? "Up to a point, the choice is obvious: Keep the consistent big spenders and lose the erratic small spenders," says one expert. "But what about the erratic big spenders and the consistent small spenders? It's often unclear whether they should be acquired or retained, and at what cost."[30]

The company can classify customers according to their potential profitability and manage its relationships with them accordingly. Figure 1.5 classifies customers into one of four relationship groups, according to their profitability and projected loyalty.[31] Each group requires a different relationship management strategy. "Strangers" show low profitability and little projected loyalty. There is little fit between the company's offerings and their needs. The relationship management strategy for these customers is simple: don't invest anything in them.

"Butterflies" are profitable but not loyal. There is a good fit between the company's offerings and their needs. However, like real butterflies, we can enjoy them for only a short while and then they're gone. An example is stock market investors who trade shares often and in large amounts, but who enjoy hunting out the best deals without building a regular relationship with any single brokerage company. Efforts to convert butterflies into loyal customers are rarely successful. Instead, the company should enjoy the butterflies for the moment. It should use promotional blitzes to attract them, create satisfying and profitable transactions with them, and then cease investing in them until the next time around.

"True friends" are both profitable and loyal. There is a strong fit between their needs and the company's offerings. The firm wants to make continuous relationship investments to delight these customers and nurture, retain, and grow them. It wants to turn true friends into "true believers," who come back regularly and tell others about their good experiences with the company.

"Barnacles" are highly loyal but not very profitable. There is a limited fit between their needs and the company's offerings. An example is smaller bank customers who bank regularly but do not generate enough returns to cover the costs of maintaining their accounts. Like barnacles on the hull of a ship, they create drag. Barnacles are perhaps the most problematic customers. The company might be able to improve their profitability by selling them more, raising their fees, or reducing service to them. However, if they cannot be made profitable, they should be "fired."

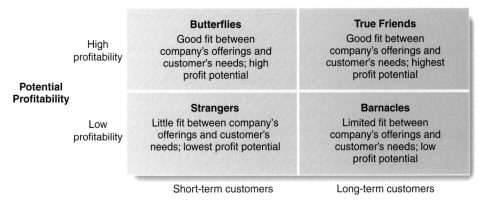

		Butterflies	**True Friends**
	High profitability	Good fit between company's offerings and customer's needs; high profit potential	Good fit between company's offerings and customer's needs; highest profit potential
Potential Profitability	Low profitability	**Strangers** Little fit between company's offerings and customer's needs; lowest profit potential	**Barnacles** Limited fit between company's offerings and customer's needs; low profit potential
		Short-term customers	Long-term customers
		Projected loyalty	

FIGURE 1.5

Customer Relationship Groups

Source: Reprinted by permission of *Harvard Business Review.* Adapted from "The Mismanagement of Customer Loyalty" by Werner Relnartz and V. Kumar, July 2002, p. 93. Copyright © by the president and fellows of Harvard College; all rights reserved.

The point here is an important one: different types of customer require different relationship management strategies. The goal is to build the *right relationships* with the *right customers*.

| Linking the | Concepts |

We've covered a lot of territory. Again, slow down for a moment and develop *your own* thoughts about marketing.

- In *your own words*, what *is* marketing and what does it seek to accomplish?
- How well does Lexus manage its relationships with customers? What customer relationship management strategy does it use? What relationship management strategy does Wal-Mart use?
- Think of a company for which you are a "true friend." What strategy does this company use to manage its relationship with you?

The New Marketing Landscape

As the world spins into the first decade of the twenty-first century, dramatic changes are occurring in the marketing arena. Richard Love of Hewlett-Packard observes, "The pace of change is so rapid that the ability to change has now become a competitive advantage." Yogi Berra, the legendary New York Yankees catcher, summed it up more simply when he said, "The future ain't what it used to be." Technological advances, rapid globalization, and continuing social and economic shifts—all are causing profound changes in the marketplace. As the marketplace changes, so must those who serve it.

In this section, we examine the major trends and forces that are changing the marketing landscape and challenging marketing strategy. We look at five major developments: the new digital age, rapid globalization, the call for more ethics and social responsibility, the growth in not-for-profit marketing, and the new world of marketing relationships.

The New Digital Age

The recent technology boom has created a new digital age. The explosive growth in computer, telecommunications, information, transportation, and other technologies has had a major impact on the ways companies bring value to their customers. Now, more than ever before, we are all connected to each other and to things near and far in the world around us. Moreover, we are relating in new and different ways. Where it once took weeks or months to travel across the United States, we can now travel around the globe in only hours or days. Where it once took days or weeks to receive news about important world events, we now see them as they are occurring through live satellite broadcasts. Where it once took weeks to correspond with others in distant places, they are now only moments away by phone or the Internet.

The technology boom has created exciting new ways to learn about and track customers, and to create products and services tailored to individual customer needs. Technology is helping companies to distribute products more efficiently and effectively. And it's helping them to communicate with customers in large groups or one-to-one. For example, through videoconferencing, marketing researchers at a company's headquarters in New York can look

■ The New Digital Age: The recent technology boom has had a major impact on the ways marketers connect with and bring value to their customers.

in on focus groups in Chicago or Paris without ever stepping onto a plane. With only a few clicks of a mouse button, a direct marketer can tap into online data services to learn anything from what car you drive to what you read to what flavor of ice cream you prefer.

Using today's vastly more powerful computers, marketers create detailed databases and use them to target individual customers with offers designed to meet their specific needs and buying patterns. Technology has also brought a new wave of communication and advertising tools—ranging from cell phones, fax machines, CD-ROMs, and interactive TVs to video kiosks at airports and shopping malls. Marketers can use these tools to zero in on selected customers with carefully targeted messages. Through e-commerce, customers can learn about, design, order, and pay for products and services—without ever leaving home. Then, through the marvels of express delivery, they can receive their purchases in less than 24 hours. From virtual reality displays that test new products to online virtual stores that sell them, the technology boom is affecting every aspect of marketing.

The Internet Perhaps the most dramatic new technology is the **Internet**. Today, the Internet links individuals and businesses of all types to each other and to information around the world. The Internet has been hailed as the technology behind a New Economy. It allows anytime, anywhere connections to information, entertainment, and communication. Companies are using the Internet to build closer relationships with customers and marketing partners. Beyond competing in traditional marketplaces, they now have access to exciting new market*spaces*.

> **Internet**
> A vast public web of computer networks, which connects users of all types all around the world to each other and to an amazingly large information repository.

Internet usage surged in the 1990s with the development of the user-friendly World Wide Web. Entering the twenty-first century, Internet penetration in the United States has reached 67 percent, with some 160 million people accessing the Web in any given month. The Internet is truly a global phenomenon—the number of Internet users worldwide reached 655 million last year and is expected to approach 1.5 billion by 2007.[32] This growing and diverse Internet population means that all kinds of people are now going to the Web for information and to buy products and services.

These days, it's hard to find a company that doesn't use the Web in a significant way. Most traditional "brick-and-mortar" companies have now become "click-and-mortar" companies. They have ventured online to attract new customers and build stronger relationships with existing ones. The Internet also spawned an entirely new breed of "click-only" companies—the so-called dot-coms. During the Web frenzy of the late 1990s, dot-coms popped up everywhere, selling anything from books, toys, and CDs to furniture, home mortgages, and 100-pound bags of dog food via the Internet. The frenzy cooled during the "dot-com meltdown" of 2000, when many poorly conceived e-tailers and other Web start-ups went out of business. Today, despite its turbulent start, online consumer buying is growing at a healthy rate, and many of the dot-com survivors face promising futures. More than half of the companies that survived the meltdown are now profitable.[33]

If consumer e-commerce looks promising, business-to-business e-commerce is just plain booming. Business-to-business transactions online amounted to $3.9 trillion last year and are expected to reach $4.3 trillion in 2005, compared with only $107 billion in consumer purchases. By 2005, more than 500,000 businesses will engage in e-commerce as buyers, sellers, or both. It seems that almost every major business has set up shop on the Web. Giants such as GE, IBM, Dell, Cisco Systems, Microsoft, and many others have moved quickly to exploit the power of the Internet.[34]

Thus, the technology boom is providing exciting new opportunities for marketers. We will explore the impact of the new digital age in more detail in Chapter 14.

Rapid Globalization

As they are redefining their relationships with customers and partners, marketers are also taking a fresh look at the ways in which they connect with the broader world around them. In an increasingly smaller world, many marketers are now connected *globally* with their customers and marketing partners.

The world economy has undergone radical change during the past two decades. Geographical and cultural distances have shrunk with the advent of jet planes, fax

■ Many U.S. companies have developed truly global operations. Coca-Cola offers more than 300 different brands in more than 200 countries including BPM Energy drink in Ireland, Mare Rosso Bitter in Spain, Sprite Ice Cube in Belgium, Fanta in Chile, and NaturAqua in Hungary.

machines, world satellite television broadcasts, global Internet hookups, and other technical advances. This has allowed companies to greatly expand their geographical market coverage, purchasing, and manufacturing. The result is a vastly more complex marketing environment for both companies and consumers.

Today, almost every company, large or small, is touched in some way by global competition. A neighborhood florist buys its flowers from Mexican nurseries, while a large U.S. electronics manufacturer competes in its home markets with giant Japanese rivals. A fledgling Internet retailer finds itself receiving orders from all over the world at the same time that an American consumer-goods producer introduces new products into emerging markets abroad.

American firms have been challenged at home by the skillful marketing of European and Asian multinationals. Companies such as Toyota, Siemens, Nestlé, Sony, and Samsung have often outperformed their U.S. competitors in American markets. Similarly, U.S. companies in a wide range of industries have found new opportunities abroad. General Motors, ExxonMobil, IBM, General Electric, DuPont, Motorola, and dozens of other American companies have developed truly global operations, making and selling their products worldwide. Coca-Cola offers a mind-boggling 300 different brands in more than 200 countries. Even MTV has joined the elite of global brands, delivering localized versions of its pulse-thumping fare to teens in 140 countries around the globe (see Marketing at Work 1.3).

Today, companies are not only trying to sell more of their locally produced goods in international markets, they also are buying more supplies and components abroad. For example, Bill Blass, one of America's top fashion designers, may choose cloth woven from Australian wool with designs printed in Italy. He will design a dress and e-mail the drawing to a Hong Kong agent, who will place the order with a Chinese factory. Finished dresses will be air-freighted to New York, where they will be redistributed to department and specialty stores around the country.

Thus, managers in countries around the world are increasingly taking a global, not just local, view of the company's industry, competitors, and opportunities. They are asking: What is global marketing? How does it differ from domestic marketing? How do global

Marketing at Work | 1.3

MTV Global: Music Is the Universal Language

Some say love is the universal language. But for MTV, the universal language is *music*. In 1981, MTV began offering its unique brand of programming for young music lovers across the United States. The channel's quirky but pulse-thumping lineup of shows soon attracted a large audience in its targeted 12-to-34 age group. MTV quickly established itself as the nation's youth-culture network, offering up "everything young people care about." With success in the United States secured, MTV went global in 1986, selling a few hours of programming to Japan's Asahi network. A short time later, in 1987, it launched MTV Europe, and the network has experienced phenomenal global growth ever since.

MTV now offers programming in 140 countries, including Brazil, Canada, France, Holland, India, Italy, Japan, Korea, Latin America, Poland, Russia, Southeast Asia, Spain, Taiwan, Hong Kong, the United Kingdom, and Germany. It recently became the first U.S. cable network to provide round-the-clock programming in China. The result of this global expansion? Today, MTV reaches twice as many people around the world as CNN, and 8 of 10 MTV viewers live outside the United States. Altogether, MTV reaches into an astounding 384 million households in 19 different languages on 31 different channels and 17 Web sites.

What is the secret to MTV's roaring international success? Of course, it offers viewers around the globe plenty of what made it so popular in the United States. Tune in to the network in Paris, or Beijing, or Moscow, or Tierra del Fuego, or anywhere else and you'll see all of the elements that make it uniquely MTV anywhere in the world—the global MTV brand symbols, fast-paced format, veejays, rockumentaries, and music, music, music. But rather than just offering a carbon copy of its U.S. programming to international viewers, MTV carefully localizes its fare. Each channel

serves up a mix that includes 70 percent local programming tailored to the specific tastes of viewers in local markets. A *Business Week* analyst notes:

[MTV is] shrewd enough to realize that while the world's teens want American music, they really want the local stuff, too. So, MTV's producers and veejays scour their local markets for the top talent. The result is an endless stream of overnight sensations that keep MTV's global offerings fresh. Just over a year ago, for example, Lena Katina and Yulia Volkova were no different than most Moscow schoolgirls. Today, Katina, 16, and Volkova, 15, make up Tatu, one of the hottest bands ever to come out of Russia.

Tatu is just one of a slew of emerging local music groups gaining international exposure through MTV and a wider audience in the United States, too. Colombian rock singer Shakira, unknown outside Latin America until 1999 when she recorded an MTV

Unplugged CD—the acoustic live concerts recorded by MTV—is now the winner of one U.S. Grammy and two Latin Grammy awards. Her CD has gone platinum, selling more than 2 million copies worldwide.

[MTV's] policy of 70 percent local content has resulted in some of the network's most creative shows, such as MTV Brazil's month-long *Rockgol*, a soccer championship that pits Brazilian musicians against record industry executives. In Russia, the locally produced *Twelve Angry Viewers* was voted one of Russia's top three talk programs. In a colorful studio amid bright blue steps and large green cushions, a dozen teens watch and discuss the latest videos. Periodically, they break into spontaneous dance or pop one another over the head with inflatable lollipops. Okay, it's not Chekhov. But Russian groups beg to be featured on it.

Ceding so much control to local channels does result in the occasional misstep. While watching MTV in Taiwan, [MTV executives were] aghast to see nude wrestling. That was one time

MTV has joined the ranks of the global brand elite. It reaches into an astounding 384 million households in 19 different languages on 33 different channels and 17 Web sites. From Germany to China, "MTV's version of globalization rocks."

(continued)

[they] had to intervene. And when MTV first entered the Indian market in 1996, Hindi film music—the romantic soundtracks of Bollywood movies—was wildly popular, but [MTV's] locally hired programmers disdained it as uncool. Viewers abandoned the channel, forcing it to [relent and] air Bollywood music. Since then its ratings have soared by some 700 percent.

At the center of MTV's global growth machine is Bill Roedy, president of MTV Networks International. He's a nonstop ambassador on a mission to make MTV available in every last global nook and cranny.

To give kids their dose of rock, [Roedy] has breakfasted with former Israeli Prime Minister Shimon Peres, dined with Singapore founder Lee Kuan Yew, and chewed the fat with Chinese leader Jiang Zemin. [He] even met with El Caudillo himself—

Cuban leader Fidel Castro—who wondered if MTV could teach Cuban kids English. Says Roedy: "We've had very little resistance once we explain that we're not in the business of exporting American culture."

MTV's unique blend of international and local programming is not only popular, it's also highly profitable. The network's hold on a young, increasingly wealthy population makes its programming especially popular with advertisers. Altogether, its mix of local and international content, combined with early entry in international markets, makes it tough to beat. "MTV Networks International makes buckets of money year after year from a potent combination of cable subscriber fees, advertising, and, increasingly, new media," concludes the analyst. "Revenues at MTV Networks International increased 19 percent [last year] . . . while operating

profits grew a hefty 50 percent. They are expected to more than double by 2004." Meanwhile, the competition struggles just to break even. VIVA, MTV's strongest competitor in Europe, has yet to turn a profit.

Thus, in only two decades, MTV has joined the ranks of the global brand elite, alongside such icons as Coke, Levi's, and Sony. Concludes the analyst: "MTV's version of globalization rocks."

Sources: Excerpts from Kerry Capell, "MTV's World: Mando-Pop. Mexican Hip Hop. Russian Rap. It's All Fueling the Biggest Global Channel," *Business Week,* February 18, 2002, pp. 81–84. Also see Lynn Elber, "U.S. TV Networks Expand Interests Overseas," *Marketing News,* November 7, 1994, p. 7; Alkman Granitsas, "MTV Is Launching a 24-Hour Network in Indonesian Cities," *Wall Street Journal,* March 13, 2002, p. B7; "MTV to Begin 24-Hour Service in Part of China," *New York Times,* March 27, 2003, p. C.13; the MTV Worldwide Web site, www.mtv.com/mtvinternational; and "MTV: Music Television: The Facts," accessed online at www.viacom.com/prodbyunit1.tin?ixBusUnit=19, May 2003.

competitors and forces affect our business? To what extent should we "go global"? Many companies are forming strategic alliances with foreign companies, even competitors, who serve as suppliers or marketing partners. Winning companies in the next century may well be those that have built the best global networks. We will discuss the global marketplace in more detail in Chapter 15.

The Call for More Ethics and Social Responsibility

Marketers are reexamining their relationships with social values and responsibilities and with the very Earth that sustains us. As the worldwide consumerism and environmentalism movements mature, today's marketers are being called upon to take greater responsibility for the social and environmental impacts of their actions. Corporate ethics and social responsibility have become hot topics for almost every business. And few companies can ignore the renewed and very demanding environmental movement.

The social-responsibility and environmental movements will place even stricter demands on companies in the future. Some companies resist these movements, budging only when forced to by legislation or organized consumer outcries. More forward-looking companies, however, readily accept their responsibilities to the world around them. They view socially responsible actions as an opportunity to do well by doing good. They seek ways to profit by serving the best long-run interests of their customers and communities.

Some companies—such as Ben & Jerry's, Saturn, Honest Tea, and others—are practicing "caring capitalism" and distinguishing themselves by being more civic-minded and caring. They are building social responsibility and action into their company value and mission statements. For example, consider Ben & Jerry's, a division of Unilever. Its mission statement challenges all employees, from top management to ice cream scoopers in each store, to include concern for individual and community welfare in their day-to-day decisions. We will revisit the relationship between marketing and social responsibility in greater detail in Chapter 16.[35]

The Growth of Not-for-Profit Marketing

In the past, marketing has been most widely applied in the for-profit business sector. In recent years, however, marketing also has become a major part of the strategies of many not-for-profit organizations, such as colleges, hospitals, museums, symphony orchestras, and even churches. Consider the following example:

> "Want to feed your soul?" implores a subway ad for Marble Collegiate Church in New York City. "We've got a great menu." Indeed, Marble Collegiate has something on its plate for almost every type of hungering spiritual consumer. It has ministries targeting senior citizens; young singles; older singles; gays and lesbians; entrepreneurs; artists, actors, and writers; men; women; children; and people who love singing gospel music, to name a few. The church is now at work on yet another program. Called the New Spirit Café, it's a hip kind of spiritual eatery designed to feed the souls—and stomachs—of those who may be disillusioned by organized religion. The New Spirit Café aims to establish Marble Collegiate's "brand" with spiritually minded people in their twenties and thirties who may be wary of conventional religious organizations. It is purposely located several blocks from the sanctuary and offers its fare of hot food, snacks, and seminars six days a week.

Marble Collegiate is not alone in turning to marketing. To maintain their shrinking flocks, religious institutions have increasingly borrowed marketing tools and tactics from companies selling more worldly goods. Many are tailoring their core product—religion itself—to the needs of specific demographic groups. To get its message out, Marble Collegiate anointed a Madison Avenue advertising agency as its missionary. The agency produced a slick marketing campaign with hip, youth-oriented messages. One ad urges potential parishioners to "Make a friend in a very high place." Exhorts another: "Our product really does perform miracles." All the marketing seems to be working. Marble Collegiate's Web site traffic has increased by 30 percent since its ad campaign launched, and the church has had its highest attendance in more than 30 years.[36]

Similarly, private colleges, facing declining enrollments and rising costs, are using marketing to compete for students and funds. Many performing arts groups—even the Lyric Opera Company of Chicago, which has seasonal sellouts—face huge operating deficits that they must cover by more aggressive donor marketing. Finally, many

■ Broadening connections: Marble Collegiate Church's advertising agency has produced ads with hip, youth-oriented messages.

long-standing not-for-profit organizations—the YMCA, the Salvation Army, the Girl Scouts—have lost members and are now modernizing their missions and "products" to attract more members and donors.[37]

Government agencies have also shown an increased interest in marketing. For example, the U.S. Army has a marketing plan to attract recruits, and various government agencies are now designing *social marketing campaigns* to encourage energy conservation and concern for the environment or to discourage smoking, excessive drinking, and drug use. Even the once-stodgy U.S. Postal Service has developed innovative marketing to sell commemorative stamps, promote its priority mail services against those of its competitors, and lift its image. It invests some $100 million annually in advertising.[38]

Every type of organization—for-profit, not-for-profit, governmental—can connect through marketing. The continued growth of not-for-profit and public-sector marketing presents new and exciting challenges for marketing managers.

The New World of Marketing Relationships

As our discussion of the marketing process suggests, the major new developments in marketing can be summed up in a single word: *relationships*. Today, smart marketers of all kinds are taking advantage of new opportunities for building relationships with their customers, their marketing partners, and the world around them. Table 1.1 compares the old marketing thinking with the new. The old marketing thinking saw marketing as little more than selling or advertising. It viewed marketing as customer acquisition rather than customer care. It emphasized trying to make a profit on each sale rather than trying to profit by managing long-term customer equity. And it concerned itself with trying to sell products rather than to understand, create, communicate, and deliver real value to customers.

Fortunately, this old marketing thinking is now giving way to newer ways of thinking. Modern marketing companies are improving their customer knowledge and customer relationships. They are targeting profitable customers, then finding innovative ways to capture

TABLE 1.1   Marketing Relationships in Transition

The Old Marketing Thinking	The New Marketing Thinking
Relationships with Customers	
Be sales and product centered	Be market and customer centered
Practice mass marketing	Target selected market segments or individuals
Focus on products and sales	Focus on customer satisfaction and value
Make sales to customers	Develop customer relationships
Get new customers	Keep old customers
Grow share of market	Grow share of customer
Serve any customer	Serve profitable customers, "fire" losing ones
Communicate through mass media	Connect with customers directly
Make standardized products	Develop customized products
Relationships with Marketing Partners	
Leave customer satisfaction and value to sales and marketing	Enlist all departments in the cause of customer satisfaction and value
Go it alone	Partner with other firms
Relationships with the World Around Us	
Market locally	Market locally *and* globally
Assume profit responsibility	Assume social and environmental responsibility
Market for profits	Market for nonprofits
Conduct commerce in market*places*	Conduct e-commerce in market*spaces*

and keep these customers. They are forming more-direct connections with customers and building lasting customer relationships. Using more-targeted media and integrating their marketing communications, they are delivering meaningful and consistent messages through every customer contact. They are employing more technologies such as videoconferencing, sales automation software, and the Internet, intranets, and extranets. They view their suppliers and distributors as partners, not adversaries. In sum, today's companies are connecting in new ways to deliver superior value to and build relationships with their customers.

■■ So, What Is Marketing? Pulling It All Together

At the start of this chapter, Figure 1.1 presented a simple model of the marketing process. Now that we've discussed all of the steps in the model, Figure 1.6 presents an expanded model that will help you pull it all together. What is marketing? Simply put, marketing is the process of building profitable customer relationships by creating value for customers and capturing value in return.

The first four steps of the marketing process focus on creating value for customers. The company starts by researching consumer needs and wants and managing marketing information to gain a full understanding of the marketplace. It then designs a customer-driven marketing strategy based on the answers to two simple questions. The first question is "What consumers will we serve?" (market segmentation and targeting). Good marketing companies know that they cannot serve all customers in every way. They need to focus their resources on the customers they can serve best and most profitably. The

FIGURE 1.6

An Expanded Model of the Marketing Process

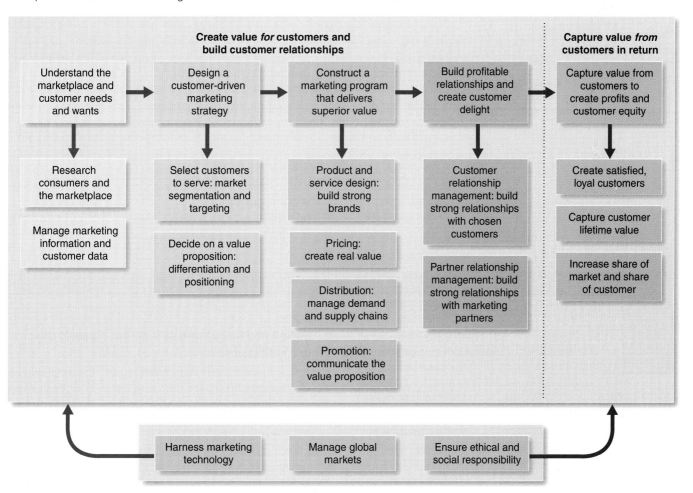

second marketing strategy question is "How can we best serve targeted customers?" (differentiation and positioning). Here, the marketer outlines a value proposition that spells out what benefits and values the company will deliver in order to win target customers.

With its marketing strategy decided, the company now constructs a marketing program—consisting of the four marketing mix elements, or the four Ps—that transforms the marketing strategy into real value for customers. The company develops product offers and creates strong brand identities for them. It prices these offers to create real customer value and distributes the offers to make them available to target consumers. Finally, the company develops promotion programs that communicate the value proposition to target consumers and persuade them to act on the marketing offer.

Perhaps the most important step in the marketing process involves building value-laden, profitable relationships with target customers. Throughout the process, marketers practice customer relationship management to create customer satisfaction and delight. In creating customer value and relationships, however, today's outstanding marketing companies know that they cannot go it alone. They must work closely with marketing partners inside the company and throughout the marketing system. Thus, in addition to practicing good customer relationship management, firms must also practice good partner relationship management.

The first four steps in the marketing process create value *for* customers. In the final step, the company reaps the rewards of the strong customer relationships by capturing value *from* customers. Delivering superior customer value creates highly satisfied customers who will buy more and will buy again. This helps the company to capture customer lifetime value and a greater share of customer. The result is increased long-term customer equity for the firm.

Finally, in the face of today's changing marketing landscape, companies must take into account three additional factors. In building customer and partner relationships, they must harness marketing technology, take advantage of global opportunities, and ensure that they act in an ethical and socially responsible way.

Figure 1.6 provides a good roadmap to future chapters of the text. Chapters 1 and 2 introduce the marketing process, with a focus on perhaps the most important steps—building customer relationships and capturing value from customers. These steps result from and provide a guiding framework for the earlier steps. Chapters 3, 4, and 5 address the first step of the marketing process—understanding the marketing environment, managing marketing information, and understanding consumer behavior. In Chapter 6, we look more deeply into the two major marketing strategy decisions: selecting which customers to serve (segmentation and targeting) and deciding on a value proposition (differentiation and positioning). Chapters 7 through 13 discuss the marketing mix variables, one by one. Then, the final three chapters examine special marketing considerations: marketing technology in this new digital age, global marketing, and marketing ethics and social responsibility.

So, here we go, down the road to learning marketing. We hope you'll enjoy the journey!

REST STOP:
Reviewing the Concepts

Today's successful companies—whether large or small, for-profit or not-for-profit, domestic or global—share a strong customer focus and a heavy commitment to marketing. The goal of marketing is to build and manage profitable customer relationships. Marketing seeks to attract new customers by promising superior value and to keep and grow current customers by delivering satisfaction. Marketing operates within a dynamic environment, which can quickly make yesterday's winning strategies obsolete. To be successful, companies will have to be strongly customer focused.

1. Define marketing and outline the steps in the marketing process.

Marketing is a social and managerial process whereby individuals and groups obtain what they need and want through creating and exchanging products and value with others. More simply, it's managing profitable customer relationships.

The marketing process involves five steps. The first four steps in the marketing process create value *for* customers. First, marketers need to understand the marketplace and customer needs and wants. Next, marketers design a customer-driven marketing strategy with the goal of getting, keeping, and growing target customers. In the third step, marketers construct a marketing program that actually delivers superior value. All of these steps form the basis for the fourth step, building profitable customer relationships and create customer delight. In the final step, the company reaps the rewards of the strong customer relationships by capturing value *from* customers.

2. Explain the importance of understanding customers and the marketplace, and identify the five core marketplace concepts.

Outstanding marketing companies go to great lengths to learn about and understand their customers' needs, wants, and demands. This understanding helps them to design want-satisfying marketing offers and build value-laden customer relationships by which they can capture customer lifetime value and greater share of customer. The result is increased long-term customer equity for the firm.

The core marketplace concepts are *needs, wants,* and *demands; marketing offers (products, services, and experiences); value* and *satisfaction; exchange, transactions,* and *relationships;* and *markets. Wants* are the form taken by human needs when shaped by culture and individual personality. When backed by buying power, wants become *demands.* Companies address needs by putting forth a *value proposition,* a set of benefits that they promise to consumers to satisfy their needs. The value proposition is fulfilled through a *marketing offer,* which delivers customer value and satisfaction, resulting in long-term exchange relationships with customers.

3. Identify the key elements of a customer-driven marketing strategy, and discuss marketing management orientations that guide marketing strategy.

To design a winning marketing strategy, the company must first decide *who* it will serve. It does this by dividing the market into segments of customers (*market segmentation*) and selecting which segments it will cultivate (*target marketing*). Next, the company must decide *how* it will serve targeted customers (how it will *differentiate and position* itself in the marketplace).

Marketing management can adopt one of five competing market orientations. The *production concept* holds that management's task is to improve production efficiency and bring down prices. The *product concept* holds that consumers favor products that offer the most in quality, performance, and innovative features; thus, little promotional effort is required. The *selling concept* holds that consumers will not buy enough of the organization's products unless it undertakes a large-scale selling and promotion effort. The *marketing concept* holds that achieving organizational goals depends on determining the needs and wants of target markets and delivering the desired satisfactions more effectively and efficiently than competitors do. The *societal marketing concept* holds that generating customer satisfaction *and* long-run societal well-being are the keys to both achieving the company's goals and fulfilling its responsibilities.

4. Discuss customer relationship management, and identify strategies for creating value *for* customers and capturing value *from* customers in return.

Broadly defined, *customer relationship management* is the overall process of building and maintaining profitable customer relationships by delivering superior customer value and satisfaction. The aim of customer relationship management is to produce high *customer equity,* the total combined customer lifetime values of all of the company's customers.

The key to building lasting relationships is the creation of superior *customer value* and *satisfaction,* and companies need to understand the determinants of these important elements. *Customer perceived value* is the difference between total customer value and total customer cost. Customers will usually choose the offer that maximizes their perceived value. *Customer satisfaction* results when a company's performance has fulfilled a buyer's expectations. Customers are dissatisfied if performance is below expectations, satisfied if performance equals expectations, and delighted if performance exceeds expectations. Highly satisfied customers buy more, are less price sensitive, talk favorably about the company, and remain loyal longer.

Companies want not only to acquire profitable customers, but to build relationships that will keep them and grow "share of customer." Companies must decide the level at which they want to build relationships with different market segments and individual customers, ranging from basic relationships to full partnerships. Today's marketers use a number of specific marketing tools to develop stronger bonds with customers by adding *financial* and *social benefits* or *structural ties.* Different types of customers require different customer relationship management strategies. The marketer's aim is to build the *right relationships* with the *right customers.* In return for creating value *for* targeted customers, the company captures value *from* customers in the form of profits and customer equity.

In building customer relationships, good marketers realize that they cannot go it alone. They must work closely with marketing partners inside and outside the company. In addition to being good at customer relationship management, they must also be good at *partner relationship management.*

5. Describe the major trends and forces that are changing the marketing landscape in this new age of relationships.

As the world spins into the twenty-first century, dramatic changes are occurring in the marketing arena. The explosive growth in computer, telecommunications, information, transportation, and other technologies has had a major impact on marketing. The technology boom has created exciting new ways to learn about and track customers, and to create products and services tailored to individual customer needs.

In an increasingly smaller world, many marketers are now connected *globally* with their customers and marketing partners. Today, almost every company, large or small, is touched in some way by global competition. Thus, managers in countries around the world are increasingly taking a global, not just local, view of the company's industry, competitors, and opportunities.

Today's marketers are also reexamining their social values and societal responsibilities. As the worldwide consumerism and environmentalism movements mature, marketers are being called upon to take greater responsibility for the social and environmental impacts of their actions. Corporate ethics and social responsibility have become hot topics for almost every business. And few companies can ignore the renewed and very demanding environmental movement.

In the past, marketing has been most widely applied in the for-profit business sector. In recent years, however, marketing also has become a major part of the strategies of many not-for-profit organizations, such as colleges, hospitals, museums, symphony orchestras, and even churches. Finally, as discussed throughout the chapter, the major new developments in marketing can be summed up in a single word: *relationships*. Today, smart marketers of all kinds are taking advantage of new opportunities for building relationships with their customers, their marketing partners, and the world around them.

Navigating the Key Terms

Customer equity
Customer lifetime value
Customer perceived value
Customer relationship
 management
Customer satisfaction
Demands
Demarketing
Exchange

Internet
Market
Marketing
Marketing concept
Marketing management
Marketing offer
Needs
Partner relationship
 management

Product concept
Production concept
Share of customer
Selling concept
Societal marketing concept
Transaction
Wants

Travel Log

Discussing the Issues

1. Why is understanding customer wants so critical for marketers? How are the concepts of value and satisfaction related to each other? Explain the difference between transactions and relationships.

2. Why is target-market selection important for a customer-driven marketing strategy? Discuss some of the negative consequences a company might incur from not paying enough attention to selecting its target market.

3. Discuss the differences between the production, product, selling, marketing, and societal marketing concepts. Identify circumstances where each one may be appropriate.

4. What are the advantages for a company in building relationships with its customers? What are some ways in which a company can build customer relationships?

5. Discuss the potential for technological advances and globalization to change the manner in which companies interact with their customers and business partners.

6. Think of a company in your town with which you have a relationship. What value do you get from that relationship and how does that company capture value from you in return?

Application Questions

1. Human *needs* are a basic desire for things one does not have (e.g., clothing). These needs are transformed into specific

wants by one's individual personality and the culture in which one lives. Consider the basic need of self-expression. This need can be transformed into a variety of "wants." For example, clothing, hairstyles, tattoos, and body piercing could satisfy this need. Discuss the degree to which a company offering clothing should consider other companies offering hairstyles, tattoos, and body piercing as competitors for consumers motivated by self-expression.

2. Specific marketing tools to develop stronger bonds with consumers include financial benefits, social benefits, and structural ties. Identify three companies you feel exemplify each of these tools. Explain how each company uses the tool to build customer relationships. Among the three companies you identified, consider if it would be advisable for those using the financial or social benefits approach to also include structural ties.

3. Companies using the concept of customer lifetime value consider the potential profit from customers over their entire life with the company, not just their profit from a single transaction. When banks began tracking the profitability of individual customers, some found that a large percentage of them actually cost them more to do business with than the revenue they produced. Considering the lifetime value of a customer concept, should companies "fire" their unprofitable customers? What are the consequences of such an action? What factors should a company consider before taking steps to eliminate their unprofitable customers?

Under the Hood: Focus on Technology

While the Internet has provided a medium for companies to develop relationships with customers, it has also created a means by which customers can share consumption experiences with other customers. Some companies, such as amazon.com, allow customers to post product reviews directly on the company's Web site. In addition, dedicated consumer opinion Web sites (e.g., epinions.com, consumerreview.com, and rateitall.com) provide consumers with the opportunity to read other consumers' consumption opinions and experiences, as well as to write their own on just about any product or service sold.

Visit the rating Web sites listed above and read some of the reviews for a product in one of the following categories: digital cameras, video game systems, or athletic shoes. Next respond to the following questions with this product in mind.

1. How much influence do you think consumer-to-consumer ratings have on the purchase decision for this product? What factors may make this influence stronger or weaker?

2. Discuss whether the ability of a consumer to receive product performance information directly from other consumers helps or harms this company's promotional efforts?

3. What might this company do to use consumer rating Web sites to its advantage?

Focus on Ethics

The marketing concept focuses on satisfying consumers' needs, but what if doing so places the consumer at risk? A variety of legal products are sold that may have harmful effects on consumers. The health impact of tobacco and alcohol are well known. More recently, many individuals and the Food and Drug Administration have become concerned about the level of trans-fatty acids present in some food products. Companies such as McDonald's, Kraft Foods, and Frito-lay have recently been reevaluating their offerings and have begun to initiate changes to make their food healthier. For example, McDonald's will soon test a Happy Meal that will allow the option of replacing french fries with a bag of sliced fruit.

1. What ethical responsibility do companies producing products that have potentially adverse health effects have to consumers?

2. Are the goals of increasing profits and of the societal marketing concept at odds with one another?

3. Break into groups of four to six students. Within each group, half of the students should consider reasons for why marketing potentially unhealthy products, like McDonald's french fries, is ethical. The other half of the group should consider reasons for why such actions are unethical. Debate the issue.

4. What ethical concerns exist behind a McDonald's order taker asking *all* customers if they want to supersize their meal? Is this giving consumers what they want, or is this inducing many overweight people to eat more than necessary? Debate the issue.

Videos

The Subaru video case that accompanies this chapter is located in Appendix 1 at the back of the book.

Student Materials

Need a tune-up? A study guide and OneKey access code are available to aid in your review of chapter material. Your instructor may choose to have these items shrink-wrapped with your text or you may purchase them separately at www.prenhall.com/marketing.

■ *After studying this chapter, you should be able to*

   1. Explain companywide strategic planning and its four steps   *2. Discuss* how to design business portfolios and develop growth strategies   *3. Explain* marketing's role in strategic planning and how marketing works with its partners to create and deliver customer value   *4. Describe* the elements of a customer-driven marketing strategy and mix, and the forces that influence it   *5. List* the marketing management functions, including the elements of a marketing plan

Company and Marketing Strategy:
Partnering to Build Customer Relationships

2

ROAD MAP | Previewing the Concepts

Ready to travel on? In the first chapter, we explored the marketing process by which companies create value for consumers in order to capture value in return. On this leg of our journey, we'll dig more deeply into steps two and three of the marketing process—designing customer-driven marketing strategies and constructing marketing programs. But first we'll examine marketing's role in the broader organization. We start with the companywide strategic planning process. Marketing contributes to and is guided by the company's overall strategic plan. First, marketing urges a whole-company philosophy that puts customers at the center. Then, under the overall strategic plan, marketers work with other company functions to design marketing strategies for delivering value to carefully targeted customers. Finally, marketers develop "marketing mixes"—consisting of product, price, distribution, and promotion tactics—to carry out these strategies profitably. These first two chapters will give you a full introduction to the basics of marketing, the decisions marketing managers make, and where marketing fits into an organization. After that, we'll take a look at the external environments in which marketing operates.

First stop: The Walt Disney Company. When you hear the name Disney, you probably think of wholesome family entertainment. Most people do. With its theme parks and family films, Disney long ago mastered the concepts of customer relationship building and customer delight that we examined in Chapter 1. For generations, it has woven its special "Disney magic" to create and fulfill fantasies for people around the world. But what you may not know is that The Walt Disney Company has now grown to include much, much more than just theme parks and family films. As you read on, think about all the strategic planning challenges facing Disney's modern-day Magic Kingdom.

When you think of The Walt Disney Company, you probably think first of theme parks and animated films. And no wonder. Since the release of its first Mickey Mouse cartoon 75 years ago, Disney has grown to become the undisputed master of family entertainment. It perfected the art of movie animation. From pioneering films such as *Snow White and the Seven Dwarfs, Fantasia, Pinocchio,* and *Song of the South* to more recent features such as *The Lion King, Toy Story,* and *Monsters, Inc.,* Disney has brought pure magic to the theaters, living rooms, and hearts and minds of audiences around the world.

But perhaps nowhere is the Disney magic more apparent than at the company's premier theme parks. Each year, nearly 40 million people flock to the Walt Disney World Resort alone—15 times more than visit Yellowstone National Park—making it the world's number one tourist attraction. What brings so many people to Walt Disney World Resort? Part of the answer lies in its many attractions. The resort's four major theme parks—Magic Kingdom, Epcot, Disney-MGM Studios, and Disney's Animal Kingdom—brim with attractions such as Cinderella's Castle, Space Mountain, The Twilight Zone Tower of Terror, Body Wars, the Kilimanjaro Safaris, Big Thunder Mountain Railroad, Typhoon Lagoon, Buzz Lightyear's Space Ranger Spin, and Honey I Shrunk the Audience.

But these attractions reveal only part of the Walt Disney World Resort value proposition. In fact, what visitors like even more, they say, is the park's sparkling cleanliness and the friendliness of Walt Disney World Resort employees. In an increasingly rude, dirty, and mismanaged world, Disney offers warmth, cleanliness, and order. As one observer notes, "In the Magic Kingdom, America still works the way it is supposed to. Everything is clean and safe, quality and service still matter, and the customer is always right."

Thus, the real "Disney Magic" lies in the company's obsessive dedication to its mission to "make people happy" and to "make a dream come true." The company orients all of its people—from the executive in the corner office, to the monorail driver, to the ticket seller at the gate—around the customer's experience. On their first day, all new Walt Disney World Resort employees report for a three-day motivational course at Disney University in Orlando, where they learn about the hard work of making fantasies come true. They learn that they are in the entertainment business—"cast members" in the Walt Disney World Resort "show." The job of each cast member is to enthusiastically serve Disney's "guests."

Before they receive their "theme costumes" and go "on stage," employees take courses titled Traditions I and Traditions II, in which they learn the Disney language, history, and culture. They are taught to be enthusiastic, helpful, and *always* friendly. They learn to do good deeds, such as volunteering to take pictures of guests, so that the whole family can be in the picture. Rumor has it that Disney is so confident that its cast members will charm guests that it forces contact. For example, many items in the park's gift shops bear no price tags, requiring shoppers to ask the price.

Cast members are taught never to say, "It's not my job." When a guest asks a question—whether it's "Where's the nearest restroom?" or "What are the names of Snow White's Seven Dwarfs?"—they need to know the answer. If they see a piece of trash on the ground, they pick it up. They go to extremes to fulfill guests' expectations and dreams. For example, to keep the Magic Kingdom feeling fresh and clean, five times a year the Main Street painters strip every painted rail in the park down to bare metal and apply a new coat of paint. Disney's customer-delight mission and marketing have become legendary. Its theme parks are so highly regarded for outstanding customer service that many of America's leading corporations send managers to Disney University to learn how Disney does it.

As it turns out, however, theme parks are only a small part of a much bigger Disney story. These units make up only a small part of today's Walt Disney Company empire. In recent years, Disney has become a real study in strategic planning. Throughout the 1990s, seeking growth, Disney diversified rapidly, transforming itself into a $25 billion international media and entertainment conglomerate. You might be surprised to learn that, beyond its theme parks, The Walt Disney Company now owns or has a major stake in all of the following:

- A major television and radio network—ABC—along with 10 company-owned television stations, 29 radio stations, and 13 international broadcast channels
- Sixteen cable networks (including the Disney Channel, Toon Disney, SoapNet, ESPN, A&E, the History Channel, Lifetime Television, E! Entertainment, and the ABC Family Channel)

- Four television production companies and eight movie production and distribution companies (including Walt Disney Pictures, Touchstone Pictures, Hollywood Pictures, Miramax Films, and Buena Vista Productions)
- Five book and magazine publishing groups (including Hyperion Books and Miramax Books)
- Five music labels (including Hollywood Records and Mammoth Records)
- Nineteen Internet groups (including Disney Online, Disney's Blast, ABC.com, ESPN.com, FamilyFun.com, NASCAR.com, NBA.com, and NFL.com)
- Disney Interactive (which develops and markets computer software, video games, and CD-ROMS)
- The Disney Store—660 retail store locations carrying Disney-related merchandise
- Disney Cruise Line

It's an impressive list. However, for Disney, managing this diverse portfolio of businesses has become a real *Monsters, Inc.* Although hurting recently because of the travel slump caused by a down economy and increased fears of terrorism, Disney's theme park and family movie operations have been wonderfully successful over the years. During the last half of the 1980s, the smaller, more focused Disney experienced soaring sales and profits. Revenues grew at an average rate of 23 percent annually; net income grew at 50 percent a year. In contrast, the new and more complex Disney has struggled for growth and profitability. During the most recent five years, the more diversified Disney's sales have grown at an average rate of only 3 percent annually; net income has *fallen* 23 percent a year.

Thus, for Disney, bigger isn't necessarily better. Many critics assert that Disney has grown too large, too diverse, and too distant from the core strengths that made it so successful over the years. Others, however, believe that such diversification is essential for profitable long-term growth. One thing seems certain—creating just the right blend of businesses to make up the new Magic Kingdom won't be easy. It will take masterful strategic planning—along with some big doses of the famed "Disney magic"—to give the modern Disney story a happy-ever-after ending.[1]

Marketing strategies and programs operate within the context of broader, companywide strategic plans. Thus, to understand the role of marketing within an organization, we must first understand the organization's overall strategic planning process. Like Disney, all companies must look ahead and develop long-term strategies to meet the changing conditions in their industries and ensure long-term survival.

In this chapter, we look first at the organization's overall strategic planning. Next, we discuss how marketers, guided by the strategic plan, work closely with others inside and outside the firm to serve customers. Finally, we examine marketing strategy and planning—how marketers choose target markets, position their marketing offers, and develop marketing mix programs.

■▌ Companywide Strategic Planning: Defining Marketing's Role

The hard task of selecting an overall company strategy for long-run survival and growth is called *strategic planning*. Each company must find the game plan that makes the most sense given its specific situation, opportunities, objectives, and resources. This is the focus of **strategic planning**—the process of developing and maintaining a strategic fit between the organization's goals and capabilities and its changing marketing opportunities.

Strategic planning sets the stage for the rest of the planning in the firm. Companies usually prepare annual plans, long-range plans, and strategic plans. The annual and long-

Strategic planning
The process of developing and maintaining a strategic fit between the organization's goals and capabilities and its changing marketing opportunities. It involves defining a clear company mission, setting supporting objectives, designing a sound business portfolio, and coordinating functional strategies.

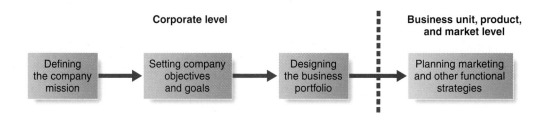

FIGURE 2.1

Steps in Strategic Planning

range plans deal with the company's current businesses and how to keep them going. In contrast, the strategic plan involves adapting the firm to take advantage of opportunities in its constantly changing environment.

At the corporate level, the company starts the strategic planning process by defining its overall purpose and mission (see Figure 2.1). This mission then is turned into detailed supporting objectives that guide the whole company. Next, headquarters decides what portfolio of businesses and products is best for the company and how much support to give each one. In turn, each business and product develops detailed marketing and other departmental plans that support the companywide plan. Thus, marketing planning occurs at the business-unit, product, and market levels. It supports company strategic planning with more detailed plans for specific marketing opportunities.[2]

Defining a Market-Oriented Mission

An organization exists to accomplish something. At first, it has a clear purpose or mission, but over time its mission may become unclear as the organization grows, adds new products and markets, or faces new conditions in the environment. When management senses that the organization is drifting, it must renew its search for purpose. It is time to ask: What is our business? Who is the customer? What do consumers value? What should our business be? These simple-sounding questions are among the most difficult the company will ever have to answer. Successful companies continuously raise these questions and answer them carefully and completely.

Many organizations develop formal mission statements that answer these questions. A **mission statement** is a statement of the organization's purpose—what it wants to accomplish in the larger environment. A clear mission statement acts as an "invisible hand" that guides people in the organization.

Some companies define their missions myopically in product or technology terms ("We make and sell furniture" or "We are a chemical-processing firm"). But mission statements should be *market oriented* and defined in terms of customer needs. Products and technologies eventually become outdated, but basic market needs may last forever.

A market-oriented mission statement defines the business in terms of satisfying basic customer needs. For example, Charles Schwab isn't just a brokerage firm—it sees itself as the "guardian of our customers' financial dreams." At Hill's Pet Nutrition, "Our mission is to enrich and lengthen the special relationship between people and their pets." Likewise, eBay's mission isn't simply to hold online auctions. Instead, it connects individual buyers and sellers in "the world's online marketplace." Its mission is to be a unique Web community in which people can shop around, have fun, and get to know each other, for example, by chatting at the eBay Cafe. Table 2.1 provides several other examples of product-oriented versus market-oriented business definitions.

Management should avoid making its mission too narrow or too broad. A pencil manufacturer that says it is in the communication equipment business is stating its mission too broadly. Missions should be *realistic*. Singapore Airlines would be deluding itself if it adopted the mission to become the world's largest airline. Missions should also be *specific*. Many mission statements are written for public relations purposes and lack specific, workable guidelines. Too often, companies develop mission statements that look much like this tongue-in-cheek version:

> We are committed to serving the quality of life of cultures and communities everywhere, regardless of sex, age, sexual preference, religion, or disability, whether

Mission statement
A statement of the organization's purpose—what it wants to accomplish in the larger environment.

TABLE 2.1 Market-Oriented Business Definitions

Company	Product-Oriented Definition	Market-Oriented Definition
Amazon.com	We sell books, videos, CDs, toys, consumer electronics, hardware, housewares, and other products.	We make the Internet buying experience fast, easy, and enjoyable—we're the place where you can find and discover anything you want to buy online.
America Online	We provide online services.	We create customer connectivity, anytime, anywhere.
Disney	We run theme parks.	We create fantasies—a place where America still works the way it's supposed to.
eBay	We hold online auctions.	We connect individual buyers and sellers in the world's online marketplace, a unique Web community in which they can shop around, have fun, and get to know each other.
Home Depot	We sell tools and home repair and improvement items.	We provide advice and solutions that transform ham-handed homeowners into Mr. and Mrs. Fixits.
Nike	We sell shoes.	We help people experience the emotion of competition, winning, and crushing competitors.
Revlon	We make cosmetics.	We sell lifestyle and self-expression; success and status; memories, hopes, and dreams.
Ritz-Carlton Hotels	We rent rooms.	We create the Ritz-Carlton experience—one that enlivens the senses, instills well-being, and fulfills even the unexpressed wishes and needs of our guests.
Wal-Mart	We run discount stores.	We deliver low prices, every day.

they be customers, suppliers, employees, or shareholders—we serve the planet—to the highest ethical standards of integrity, best practice, and sustainability, through policies of openness and transparency vetted by our participation in the International Quality Business Global Audit forum, to ensure measurable outcomes worldwide. . . .[3]

Such generic statements sound good but provide little real guidance or inspiration.

Missions should fit the *market environment*. The Girl Scouts of America would not recruit successfully in today's environment with its former mission: "to prepare young girls for motherhood and wifely duties." Today, its mission is to be the place "where girls grow strong." The organization should base its mission on its *distinctive competencies*. McDonald's could probably enter the solar energy business, but that would not take advantage of its core competence—providing low-cost food and fast service to large groups of customers.

Finally, mission statements should be *motivating*. A company's mission should not be stated as making more sales or profits—profits are only a reward for undertaking a useful activity. A company's employees need to feel that their work is significant and that it contributes to people's lives. For example, Walt Disney Company's aim is to "make people happy." Celestial Seasonings' pursues this mission: "To create and sell healthful, naturally oriented products that nurture people's bodies and uplift their souls."[4]

Setting Company Objectives and Goals

The company's mission needs to be turned into detailed supporting objectives for each level of management. Each manager should have objectives and be responsible for reaching them. For example, Monsanto operates in many businesses, including agriculture, pharmaceuticals, and food products. The company defines its mission as creating "abundant food and a healthy environment." It seeks to help feed the world's exploding population while at the same time sustaining the environment.

This mission leads to a hierarchy of objectives, including business objectives and marketing objectives. Monsanto's overall objective is to build profitable customer relationships by creating environmentally better products and getting them to market faster at lower costs. For

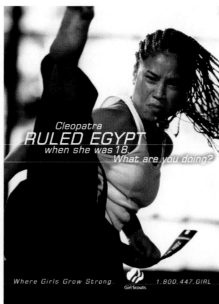
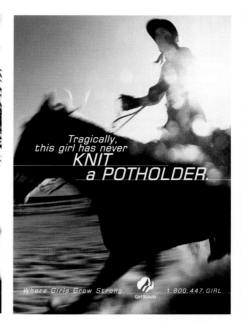

■ Mission statements: The Girl Scouts' mission is to be a place "Where Girls Grow Strong."

its part, the agricultural division's objective is to increase agricultural productivity and reduce chemical pollution. It does this by researching new pest- and disease-resistant crops that produce higher yields without chemical spraying. But research is expensive and requires improved profits to plow back into research programs. So improving profits becomes another major Monsanto objective. Profits can be improved by increasing sales or reducing costs. Sales can be increased by improving the company's share of the U.S. market, by entering new foreign markets, or both. These goals then become the company's current marketing objectives.

Marketing strategies and programs must be developed to support these marketing objectives. To increase its U.S. market share, Monsanto might increase its products' availability and promotion. To enter new foreign markets, the company may cut prices and target large farms abroad. These are its broad marketing strategies. Each broad marketing strategy must then be defined in greater detail. For example, increasing the product's promotion may require more salespeople and more advertising; if so, both requirements will have to be spelled out. In this way, the firm's mission is translated into a set of objectives for the current period.

Designing the Business Portfolio

Business portfolio

The collection of businesses and products that make up the company.

Guided by the company's mission statement and objectives, management now must plan its **business portfolio**—the collection of businesses and products that make up the company. The best business portfolio is the one that best fits the company's strengths and weaknesses to opportunities in the environment. Business portfolio planning involves two steps. First, the company must analyze its *current* business portfolio and decide which businesses should receive more, less, or no investment. Second, it must shape the *future* portfolio by developing strategies for growth and downsizing.

Portfolio analysis

A tool by which management identifies and evaluates the various businesses making up the company.

Analyzing the Current Business Portfolio The major activity in strategic planning is business **portfolio analysis**, whereby management evaluates the products and businesses making up the company. The company will want to put strong resources into its more profitable businesses and phase down or drop its weaker ones.

Management's first step is to identify the key businesses making up the company. These can be called the strategic business units. A *strategic business unit* (SBU) is a unit of the company that has a separate mission and objectives and that can be planned independently from other company businesses. An SBU can be a company division, a product line within a division, or sometimes a single product or brand.

The next step in business portfolio analysis calls for management to assess the attractiveness of its various SBUs and decide how much support each deserves. Most companies are well advised to "stick to their knitting" when designing their business portfolios. It's usually a good idea to focus on adding products and businesses that fit closely with the firm's core philosophy and competencies.

The purpose of strategic planning is to find ways in which the company can best use its strengths to take advantage of attractive opportunities in the environment. So most standard portfolio-analysis methods evaluate SBUs on two important dimensions—the attractiveness of the SBU's market or industry and the strength of the SBU's position in that market or industry. The best-known portfolio-planning method was developed by the Boston Consulting Group, a leading management consulting firm.

The Boston Consulting Group Approach. Using the Boston Consulting Group (BCG) approach, a company classifies all its SBUs according to the **growth-share matrix** shown in Figure 2.2. On the vertical axis, *market growth rate* provides a measure of market attractiveness. On the horizontal axis, *relative market share* serves as a measure of company strength in the market. The growth–share matrix defines four types of SBUs:

> **Stars.**   Stars are high-growth, high-share businesses or products. They often need heavy investment to finance their rapid growth. Eventually their growth will slow down, and they will turn into cash cows.
>
> **Cash cows.**   Cash cows are low-growth, high-share businesses or products. These established and successful SBUs need less investment to hold their market share. Thus, they produce a lot of cash that the company uses to pay its bills and to support other SBUs that need investment.
>
> **Question marks.**   Question marks are low-share business units in high-growth markets. They require a lot of cash to hold their share, let alone increase it. Management has to think hard about which question marks it should try to build into stars and which should be phased out.
>
> **Dogs.**   Dogs are low-growth, low-share businesses and products. They may generate enough cash to maintain themselves but do not promise to be large sources of cash.

The 10 circles in the growth-share matrix represent a company's 10 current SBUs. The company has two stars, two cash cows, three question marks, and three dogs. The areas of the circles are proportional to the SBU's dollar sales. This company is in fair shape, although not in good shape. It wants to invest in the more promising question marks to make them stars and to maintain the stars so that they will become cash cows as their markets mature. Fortunately, it has two good-sized cash cows. Income from these cash cows will help finance the company's question marks, stars, and dogs. The company should take some decisive action concerning its dogs and its question marks. The picture

Growth–share matrix

A portfolio-planning method that evaluates a company's strategic business units in terms of their market growth rate and relative market share. SBUs are classified as stars, cash cows, question marks, or dogs.

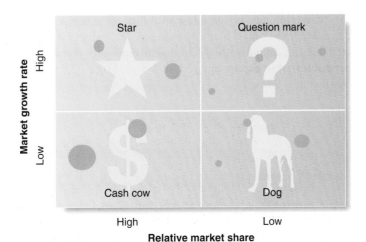

FIGURE 2.2

The BCG Growth-Share Matrix

would be worse if the company had no stars, if it had too many dogs, or if it had only one weak cash cow.

Once it has classified its SBUs, the company must determine what role each will play in the future. One of four strategies can be pursued for each SBU. The company can invest more in the business unit in order to *build* its share. Or it can invest just enough to *hold* the SBU's share at the current level. It can *harvest* the SBU, milking its short-term cash flow regardless of the long-term effect. Finally, the company can *divest* the SBU by selling it or phasing it out and using the resources elsewhere.

As time passes, SBUs change their positions in the growth-share matrix. Each SBU has a life cycle. Many SBUs start out as question marks and move into the star category if they succeed. They later become cash cows as market growth falls, then finally die off or turn into dogs toward the end of their life cycles. The company needs to add new products and units continuously so that some of them will become stars and, eventually, cash cows that will help finance other SBUs.

Problems with Matrix Approaches. The BCG and other formal methods revolutionized strategic planning. However, such approaches have limitations. They can be difficult, time-consuming, and costly to implement. Management may find it difficult to define SBUs and measure market share and growth. In addition, these approaches focus on classifying *current* businesses but provide little advice for *future* planning.

Formal planning approaches can also place too much emphasis on market-share growth or growth through entry into attractive new markets. Using these approaches, many companies plunged into unrelated and new high-growth businesses that they did not know how to manage—with very bad results. At the same time, these companies were often too quick to abandon, sell, or milk to death their healthy mature businesses. As a result, many companies that diversified too broadly in the past now are narrowing their focus and getting back to the basics of serving one or a few of the industries that they know best.

Because of such problems, many companies have dropped formal matrix methods in favor of more customized approaches that are better suited to their specific situations. Unlike former strategic-planning efforts, which rested mostly in the hands of senior managers at company headquarters, today's strategic planning has been decentralized. Increasingly, companies are placing responsibility for strategic planning in the hands of cross-functional teams of managers who are close to their markets. Some teams even include customers and suppliers in their strategic-planning processes.[5]

Developing Strategies for Growth and Downsizing

Beyond evaluating current businesses, designing the business portfolio involves finding businesses and products the company should consider in the future. Companies need growth if they are to compete more effectively, satisfy their stakeholders, and attract top talent. "Growth is pure oxygen," states one executive. "It creates a vital, enthusiastic corporation where people see genuine opportunity." At the same time, a firm must be careful not to make growth itself an objective. The company's objective must be "profitable growth."

Marketing has the main responsibility for achieving profitable growth for the company. Marketing must identify, evaluate, and select market opportunities and lay down strategies for capturing them. One useful device for identifying growth opportunities is the **product/market expansion grid**, shown in Figure 2.3.[6] We apply it here to Starbucks (see Marketing at Work 2.1).

Product/market expansion grid
A portfolio-planning tool for identifying company growth opportunities through market penetration, market development, product development, or diversification.

FIGURE 2.3
The Product/Market Expansion Grid

	Existing products	New products
Existing markets	Market penetration	Product development
New markets	Market development	Diversification

Marketing at Work | 2.1

Starbucks Coffee: Where Things Are Really Perking

Back in 1983, Howard Schultz hit on the idea of bringing a European-style coffeehouse to America. People needed to slow down, he believed—to "smell the coffee" and enjoy life a little more. The result was Starbucks, the coffeehouse chain that started the trend in America of enjoying coffee to its fullest. Starbucks doesn't sell just coffee, it sells *The Starbucks Experience*. As one Starbucks executive puts it, "We're not in the business of filling bellies, we're in the business of filling souls." Says another, "We changed the way people live their lives, what they do when they get up in the morning, how they reward themselves, and where they meet."

Starbucks is now a powerhouse premium brand in a category in which only cheaper commodity products once existed. As the brand has perked, Starbucks's sales and profits have risen like steam off a mug of hot java. Some 20 million customers visit the company's more than 5,900 stores worldwide each week. During just the past 5 years, Starbucks's sales and earnings have both more than tripled. Over the past decade, its stock has soared more than 2,200 percent, outperforming such superstars as Wal-Mart, General Electric, Coca-Cola, Microsoft, and IBM in total return.

Starbucks's success, however, has drawn a full litter of copycats, ranging from direct competitors such as Caribou Coffee to fast-food merchants. These days it seems that everyone is peddling its own brand of premium coffee. In the early 1990s, there were only 200 coffee houses in the United States. Today there are more than 14,000. To maintain its phenomenal growth in an increasingly overcaffeinated marketplace, Starbucks has brewed up an ambitious, multipronged growth strategy. Let's examine the key elements of this strategy:

More store growth: *Almost 85 percent of Starbucks's sales comes from*

its stores. So, not surprisingly, Starbucks is opening new stores at a breakneck pace. Seven years ago, Starbucks had just 1,015 stores, total—that's 200 fewer than it built last year alone. Starbucks's strategy is to put stores everywhere. In Seattle, there's a Starbucks for every 9,400 people; in Manhattan, there's one for every 12,000. One three-block stretch in Chicago contains six of the trendy coffee bars. In fact, cramming so many stores close together caused one satirical publication to run this headline: "A New Starbucks Opens in the Restroom of Existing Starbucks." Although it may seem that there aren't many places left without a Starbucks, there's still plenty of room to expand. Amazingly, there are still eight U.S. states with no Starbucks at all. Worldwide, Starbucks claims that it will grow to at least 10,000 stores worldwide by 2005, and to 25,000 stores ultimately.

Beyond opening new shops, Starbucks is adding in-store products

and features that get customers to stop in more often, stay longer, and buy more. Its beefed-up menu now includes hot breakfast sandwiches plus lunch and dinner items, increasing the average customer sales ticket. The chain has tested everything from Krispy Kreme doughnuts and Fresh Fields gourmet sandwiches to Greek pasta salads and assorted chips. To get customers to hang around longer, Starbucks now offers high-speed wireless Internet access in many of its stores. Out of cash? No problem— just swipe your prepaid Starbucks card on the way out ("a Starbucks store in your wallet," according to the company's Web site). And while you're at it, pick up the latest Starbucks compilation music CD, a board game, and a Starbucks coffee mug for home.

New retail channels: The vast majority of coffee in America is bought in retail stores and brewed at home. To capture this demand,

To maintain its phenomenal growth in an increasingly overcaffeinated marketplace, Starbucks has brewed up an ambitious, multipronged growth strategy.

(continued)

Starbucks is also pushing into America's supermarket aisles. However, rather than going head-to-head in this new channel, Starbucks struck a co-branding deal with Kraft. Under this deal, Starbucks will continue to roast and package its coffee while Kraft will market and distribute it. The deal gave Starbucks quick entry into 18,000 U.S. supermarkets, supported by the marketing muscle of 3,500 Kraft salespeople.

Beyond supermarkets, Starbucks has forged an impressive set of new ways to bring its brand to market. Some examples: Host Marriott operates Starbucks kiosks in America's airports and several airlines serve Starbucks coffee to their passengers. Westin and Sheraton hotels offer packets of Starbucks brew in their rooms. Starbucks recently signed deals to install coffee shops in all Borders Books and Target stores. Starbucks also sells gourmet coffee, tea, gifts, and related goods through business and consumer catalogs. And its Web site, Starbucks.com, has become a kind of "lifestyle portal" on which it sells coffee, tea, coffee-making equipment, compact discs, gifts, and collectibles.

New products and store concepts: Starbucks has partnered with several firms to extend its brand into new categories. For example, it joined with PepsiCo to stamp the Starbucks brand on bottled

Frappuccino drinks and its DoubleShot espresso drink. Starbucks ice cream, marketed in a joint venture with Dreyer's, is now the leading brand of coffee ice cream. Starbucks has also examined a number of new store concepts. In San Francisco, for example, it's testing Circadia—a kind of bohemian coffeehouse concept with tattered rugs, high-speed Internet access, and live music as well as coffee specialties.

International growth: Finally, Starbucks has taken its American-brewed concept global. In 1996, the company had only 11 coffeehouses outside North America. By 2003, the number had grow to more than 1,300 stores in 30 international markets, including more than 440 in Japan, 300 in the UK, 102 in Taiwan, and 90 in China. Last year, Starbucks opened close to 400 international stores, entering nine new international markets, from Austria, Spain, and Greece to Indonesia and Oman. And it's now moving rapidly into Latin and South America, where it plans to build 900 stores by 2005.

Although Starbucks's growth strategy so far has met with great success, some analysts express strong concerns. What's wrong with Starbucks's rapid expansion? Some critics worry that the company may be overextending the Starbucks brand name. "People

pay [up to $5.00] for a caffe latte because it's supposed to be a premium product," asserts one such critic. "When you see the Starbucks name on what an airline is pouring, you wonder." Others fear that, by pursuing such a broad-based growth strategy, Starbucks will stretch its resources too thin or lose its focus.

Still others, however, remain true believers. Some even see similarities between Starbucks and a young McDonald's, which rode the humble hamburger to such incredible success. "The similar focus on one product, the overseas opportunities, the rapid emergence as the dominant player in a new niche," says Goldman Sachs analyst Steve Kent, "this all applies to Starbucks, too." Only time will tell whether Starbucks turns out to be the next McDonald's—it all depends how well the company manages growth. For now, things are really perking. But Starbucks has to be careful that it doesn't boil over.

Sources: Quotes and other information from Cora Daniels, "Mr. Coffee," *Fortune,* April 14, 2003, pp. 139–140; Nelson D. Schwartz, "Still Perking after All These Years," *Fortune,* May 24, 1999, pp. 203–210; Stephane Fitch, "Latte Grande, Extra Froth," *Forbes,* March 19, 2001, p. 58; Jacqueline Doherty, "Make It Decaf," *Barrons,* May 20, 2002, pp. 20–21; Stanley Holmes, "Planet Starbucks: To Keep Up the Growth, It Must Go Global Quickly," *Business Week,* September 9, 2002, pp. 100–110; "Starbucks Corporation," *Hoover's Company Profiles,* Austin, May 1, 2003; and information accessed online at www.starbucks.com, July 2003.

Market penetration
A strategy for company growth by increasing sales of current products to current market segments without changing the product.

Market development
A strategy for company growth by identifying and developing new market segments for current company products.

First, Starbucks management might consider whether the company can achieve deeper **market penetration**—making more sales to current customers without changing its products. It might add new stores in current market areas to make it easier for more customers to visit. In fact, Starbucks is adding an average of 23 stores a week, 52 weeks a year. Improvements in advertising, prices, service, menu selection, or store design might encourage customers to stop by more often, stay longer, or to buy more during each visit. For example, Starbucks now features high-speed wireless Internet access in many of its stores. And it recently introduced a company debit card, which lets customers prepay for coffee and snacks or give the gift of Starbucks to family and friends. Customers using the card move through stores faster and return more often.[7] Basically, Starbucks would like to increase patronage by current customers and attract competitors' customers to Starbucks shops.

Second, Starbucks management might consider possibilities for **market development**—identifying and developing new markets for its current products. For instance, managers could review new *demographic markets*. Perhaps new groups—such as seniors or ethnic groups—could be encouraged to visit Starbucks coffee shops for the first time or to buy more from them. Managers also could review new *geographical markets*. Starbucks is now expanding swiftly into new U.S. markets, especially in the Southeast and Southwest. It is also developing its international markets, with stores popping up rapidly in Asia, Europe, Australia, and Latin and South America.

Third, management could consider **product development**—offering modified or new products to current markets. For example, Starbucks recently added hot breakfast sandwiches to its menu to steal some early-morning business from McDonald's and Burger King. It also increased its midday and evening food offerings to attract more business during the lunch and dinner hours. Finally, Starbucks has partnered with other firms to sell coffee in supermarkets and to extend its brand to new products, such as coffee ice cream (with Dreyers) and bottled coffee drinks (with PepsiCo).

Fourth, Starbucks might consider **diversification**. It could start up or buy businesses outside of its current products and markets. For example, in 1999, Starbucks purchased Hear Music and began making compilation music CDs to play and sell in its stores. And it has also tested new restaurant concepts—such as Circadia in San Francisco—in an effort to offer new formats to related but new markets. In a more extreme diversification, Starbucks might consider leveraging its strong brand name by making and marketing a line of branded casual clothing consistent with the "Starbucks Experience." However, this would probably be unwise. Companies that diversify too broadly into unfamiliar products or industries can lose their market focus, something that some critics are already concerned about with Starbucks.

Companies must not only develop strategies for *growing* their business portfolios but also strategies for **downsizing** them. There are many reasons that a firm might want to abandon products or markets. The market environment might change, making some of the company's products or markets less profitable. This might happen during an economic recession or when a strong competitor opens next door. The firm may have grown too fast or entered areas where it lacks experience. This can occur when a firm enters too many foreign markets without the proper research or when a company introduces new products that do not offer superior customer value. Finally, some products or business units just age and die.

When a firm finds products or businesses that no longer fit its overall strategy, it must carefully prune, harvest, or divest them. Weak businesses usually require a disproportionate amount of management attention. Managers should focus on promising growth opportunities, not fritter away energy trying to salvage fading ones.

Strategic Planning and Small Businesses

Many discussions of strategic planning focus on large corporations with many divisions and products. However, small businesses can also benefit from sound strategic planning. Whereas most small ventures start out with extensive business and marketing plans used to attract potential investors, strategic planning often falls by the wayside once the business gets going.

Entrepreneurs and presidents of small companies are more likely to spend their time "putting out fires" than planning. But what does a small firm do when it finds that it has taken on too much debt, or when its growth is exceeding production capacity. What does it do when it's losing market share to a competitor with lower prices? Strategic planning can help small business managers to anticipate such situations and determine how to prevent or handle them.

King's Medical Company of Hudson, Ohio, provides an example of how one small company has used very simple strategic-planning tools to chart its course every three years. King's Medical owns and manages magnetic-resonance-imaging (MRI) equipment—million-dollar-plus machines that produce X-ray-type pictures. Several years ago, William Patton, then a consultant and the company's "planning guru," pointed to strategic planning as the key to this small company's very rapid growth and high profit margins. Patton claimed, "A lot of literature

Product development
A strategy for company growth by offering modified or new products to current market segments.

Diversification
A strategy for company growth through starting up or acquiring businesses outside the company's current products and markets.

Downsizing
Reducing the business portfolio by eliminating products or business units that are not profitable or that no longer fit the company's overall strategy.

says there are three critical issues to a small company: cash flow, cash flow, cash flow. I agree those issues are critical, but so are three more: planning, planning, planning."

King's Medical's planning process, which hinges on an assessment of the company, its place in the market, and its goals, includes the following steps.[8]

1. Identify the major elements of the business environment in which the organization has operated over the past few years.
2. Describe the mission of the organization in terms of its nature and function for the next two years.
3. Explain the internal and external forces that will have an impact on the mission of the organization.
4. Identify the basic driving force that will direct the organization in the future.
5. Develop a set of long-term objectives that will identify what the organization will become in the future.
6. Outline a general plan of action that defines the logistical, financial, and personnel factors needed to integrate the long-term objectives into the total organization.

Clearly, strategic planning is crucial to a small company's future. Thom Wellington, president of Wellington Environmental Consulting and Construction, Inc., says that it's important to do strategic planning at a site away from the office. An off-site location offers neutral ground where employees can be "much more candid." And it takes entrepreneurs away from the scene of the fires they spend so much time stamping out.[9]

■▌ Planning Marketing: Partnering to Build Customer Relationships

The company's strategic plan establishes what kinds of businesses the company will be in and its objectives for each. Then, within each business unit, more detailed planning takes place. The major functional departments in each unit—marketing, finance, accounting, purchasing, operations, information systems, human resources, and others—must work together to accomplish strategic objectives.

Marketing plays a key role in the company's strategic planning in several ways. First, marketing provides a guiding *philosophy*—the marketing concept—that suggests that company strategy should revolve around building profitable relationships with important consumer groups. Second, marketing provides *inputs* to strategic planners by helping to identify attractive market opportunities and by assessing the firm's potential to take advantage of them. Finally, within individual business units, marketing designs *strategies* for reaching the unit's objectives. Once the unit's objectives are set, marketing's task is to help carry them out profitably.

Customer value and satisfaction are important ingredients in the marketer's formula for success. However, as we noted in Chapter 1, marketers alone cannot produce superior value for customers. Although it plays a leading role, marketing can be only a partner in attracting, keeping, and growing customers. In addition to *customer relationship management*, marketers must also practice *partner relationship management*. They must work closely with partners in other company departments to form an effective *value chain* that serves the customer. Moreover, they must partner effectively with other companies in the marketing system to form a competitively superior *value-delivery network*. We now take a closer look at the concepts of a company value chain and value-delivery network.

Partnering with Other Company Departments

Value chain

The series of departments that carry out value-creating activities to design, produce, market, deliver, and support a firm's products.

Each company department can be thought of as a link in the company's **value chain**.[10] That is, each department carries out value-creating activities to design, produce, market, deliver, and support the firm's products. The firm's success depends not only on how well each department performs its work but also on how well the activities of various departments are coordinated.

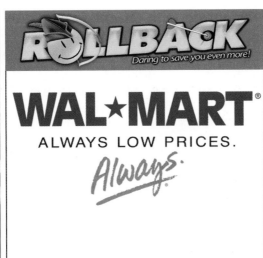

■ The value chain: Wal-Mart's ability to offer the right products at low prices depends on the contributions of people in all of the company's departments—marketing, purchasing, information systems, and operations.

For example, Wal-Mart's goal is to create customer value and satisfaction by providing shoppers with the products they want at the lowest possible prices. Marketers at Wal-Mart play an important role. They learn what customers need and want and stock the store's shelves with the desired products at unbeatable low prices. They prepare advertising and merchandising programs and assist shoppers with customer service. Through these and other activities, Wal-Mart's marketers help deliver value to customers. However, the marketing department needs help from the company's other departments. Wal-Mart's ability to offer the right products at low prices depends on the purchasing department's skill in tracking down the needed suppliers and buying from them at low cost. Similarly, Wal-Mart's information technology department must provide fast and accurate information about which products are selling in each store. And its operations people must provide effective, low-cost merchandise handling.

A company's value chain is only as strong as its weakest link. Success depends on how well each department performs its work of adding value for customers and on how well the activities of various departments are coordinated. At Wal-Mart, if purchasing can't wring the lowest prices from suppliers, or if operations can't distribute merchandise at the lowest costs, then marketing can't deliver on its promise of having the lowest prices.

Ideally, then, a company's different functions should work in harmony to produce value for consumers. But, in practice, departmental relations are full of conflicts and misunderstandings. The marketing department takes the consumer's point of view. But when marketing tries to develop customer satisfaction, it can cause other departments to do a poorer job *in their terms*. Marketing department actions can increase purchasing costs, disrupt production schedules, increase inventories, and create budget headaches. Thus, the other departments may resist the marketing department's efforts.

Yet marketers must find ways to get all departments to "think consumer" and to develop a smoothly functioning value chain. Marketing management can best gain support for its goal of customer satisfaction by working to understand the company's other departments. Marketing managers need to work closely with managers of other functions to develop a system of functional plans under which the different departments can work together to accomplish the company's overall strategic objectives.

Jack Welch, General Electric's highly regarded former CEO, told his employees: "Companies can't give job security. Only customers can!" He emphasized that all General Electric people, regardless of their department, have an impact on customer satisfaction and retention. His message: "If you are not thinking customer, you are not thinking."[11]

Value-delivery network
The network made up of the company, suppliers, distributors, and ultimately customers who "partner" with each other to improve the performance of the entire system.

Partnering with Others in the Marketing System

In its quest to create customer value, the firm needs to look beyond its own value chain and into the value chains of its suppliers, distributors, and, ultimately, customers. Consider McDonald's. McDonald's 30,000 restaurants worldwide serve more than 46 million customers daily, capturing a 43 percent share of the burger market.[12] People do not swarm to McDonald's only because they love the chain's hamburgers. In fact, consumers typically rank McDonald's behind Burger King and Wendy's in taste. Consumers flock to the McDonald's *system*, not just to its food products. Throughout the world, McDonald's finely tuned system delivers a high standard of what the company calls QSCV—quality, service, cleanliness, and value. McDonald's is effective only to the extent that it successfully partners with its franchisees, suppliers, and others to jointly deliver exceptionally high customer value.

More companies today are partnering with the other members of the supply chain to improve the performance of the customer **value-delivery network**. For example, Honda has designed a program for working closely with its suppliers to help them reduce their costs and improve quality. When Honda chose Donnelly Corporation to supply all of the mirrors for its U.S.-made cars, it sent engineers swarming over Donnelly's plants, looking for ways to improve its products and operations. This helped Donnelly reduce its costs by 2 percent in the first year. As a result of its improved performance, Donnelly's sales to Honda grew from $5 million annually to more than $60 million in less than 10 years. In turn, Honda gained an efficient, low-cost supplier of quality components. And Honda customers received greater value in the form of lower-cost, higher-quality cars.[13]

Increasingly in today's marketplace, competition no longer takes place between individual competitors. Rather, it takes place between the entire value-delivery networks created by these competitors. Thus, Honda's performance against Toyota depends on the quality of Honda's overall value-delivery network versus Toyota's. Even if Honda makes the best cars, it might lose in the marketplace if Toyota's dealer network provides more customer-satisfying sales and service.

■ The value-delivery network: Toyota and its dealers must work together to sell cars. Toyota makes good cars and builds the brand; dealerships like Modern Toyota bring value to customers and communities.

SPEED BUMP

Linking the Concepts

Here's a good place to pause for a moment to think about and apply what you've read in the first part of this chapter.

- Why are we talking about companywide strategic planning in a marketing textbook? What *does* strategic planning have to do with marketing?
- What are Starbucks's mission and strategy? What role does marketing play in helping Starbucks to accomplish this mission and strategy?
- What roles do other Starbucks functional departments play, and how can Starbucks's marketers partner with these others to maximize overall customer value?

■■▌ Marketing Strategy and the Marketing Mix

The strategic plan defines the company's overall mission and objectives. Marketing's role and activities are shown in Figure 2.4, which summarizes the major activities involved in managing marketing strategy and the marketing mix.

Consumers stand in the center. The goal is to build strong and profitable customer relationships. Next comes **marketing strategy**—the marketing logic by which the company hopes to achieve these profitable relationships. Through market segmentation, targeting, and positioning, the company decides which customers it will serve and how. It identifies the total market, then divides it into smaller segments, selects the most promising segments, and focuses on serving and satisfying these segments.

Guided by marketing strategy, the company designs a marketing mix made up of factors under its control—product, price, place, and promotion. To find the best marketing strategy and mix, the company engages in marketing analysis, planning, implementation, and control. Through these activities, the company watches and adapts to the actors and forces in the marketing environment. We will now look briefly at each activity. Then, in later chapters, we will discuss each one in more depth.

Customer-Centered Marketing Strategy

As we emphasized throughout Chapter 1, to succeed in today's competitive marketplace, companies need to be customer centered. They must win customers from competitors, then keep and grow them by delivering greater value. But before it can satisfy consumers, a company must first understand their needs and wants. Thus, sound marketing requires a careful customer analysis.

Companies know that they cannot profitably serve all consumers in a given market— at least not all consumers in the same way. There are too many different kinds of consumers with too many different kinds of needs. And most companies are in a position to serve some segments better than others. Thus, each company must divide up the total market, choose the best segments, and design strategies for profitably serving chosen segments. This process involves three steps: *market segmentation*, *target marketing*, and *market positioning*.

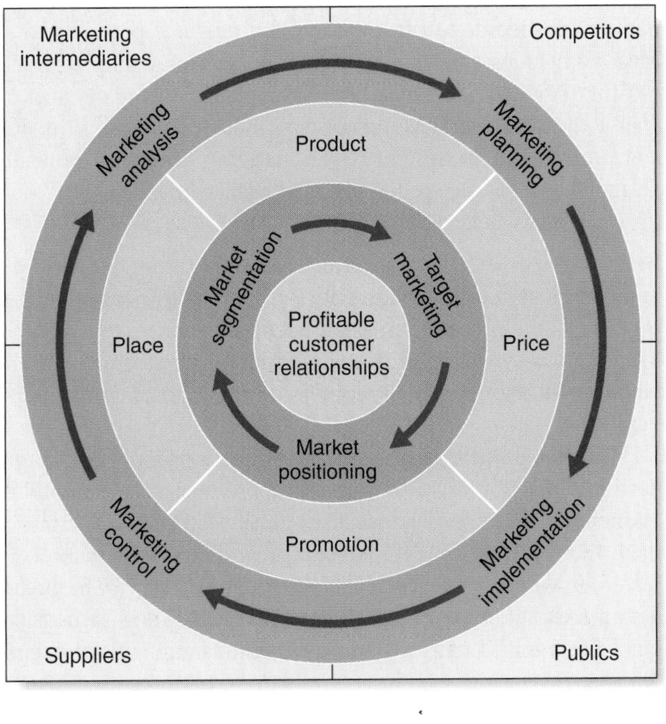

Marketing strategy
The marketing logic by which the company hopes to achieve strong and profitable customer relationships. It involves deciding which customers to serve (segmentation and targeting) and with what value proposition (differentiation and positioning).

FIGURE 2.4
Managing Marketing Strategy and the Marketing Mix

Market Segmentation The market consists of many types of customers, products, and needs. The marketer has to determine which segments offer the best opportunity for achieving company objectives. Consumers can be grouped and served in various ways based on geographic, demographic, psychographic, and behavioral factors. The process of dividing a market into distinct groups of buyers with different needs, characteristics, or behavior who might require separate products or marketing programs is called **market segmentation**.

Market segmentation

Dividing a market into distinct groups of buyers who have distinct needs, characteristics, or behavior and who might require separate products or marketing mixes.

Every market has segments, but not all ways of segmenting a market are equally useful. For example, Tylenol would gain little by distinguishing between male and female users of pain relievers if both respond the same way to marketing efforts. A **market segment** consists of consumers who respond in a similar way to a given set of marketing efforts. In the car market, for example, consumers who choose the biggest, most comfortable car regardless of price make up one market segment. Customers who care mainly about price and operating economy make up another segment. It would be difficult to make one car model that was the first choice of consumers in both segments. Companies are wise to focus their efforts on meeting the distinct needs of individual market segments.

Market segment

A group of consumers who respond in a similar way to a given set of marketing efforts.

Target Marketing After a company has defined market segments, it can enter one or many segments of a given market. **Target marketing** involves evaluating each market segment's attractiveness and selecting one or more segments to enter. A company should target segments in which it can profitably generate the greatest customer value and sustain it over time.

Target marketing

The process of evaluating each market segment's attractiveness and selecting one or more segments to enter.

A company with limited resources might decide to serve only one or a few special segments or "market niches." Such "nichers" specialize in serving market segments that major competitors overlook or ignore. For example, Arm & Hammer has a lock on the baking soda corner of most consumer goods categories, including toothpaste, deodorizers, and others. Oshkosh Truck has found its niche as the world's largest producer of airport rescue trucks and front-loading concrete mixers. And Veterinary Pet Insurance provides 82 percent of all health insurance policies for our furry—or feathery—friends (see Marketing at Work 2.2).

Alternatively, a company might choose to serve several related segments—perhaps those with different kinds of customers but with the same basic wants. Pottery Barn, for example, targets kids, teens, and adults with the same lifestyle-themed merchandise in different outlets: the original Pottery Barn, Pottery Barn Kids, and PB Teen. Or a large company might decide to offer a complete range of products to serve all market segments. Most companies enter a new market by serving a single segment, and if this proves successful, they add segments. Large companies eventually seek full market coverage. They want to be the General Motors of their industry. GM says that it makes a car for every "person, purse, and personality." The leading company normally has different products designed to meet the special needs of each segment.

Market Positioning After a company has decided which market segments to enter, it must decide what positions it wants to occupy in those segments. A product's *position* is the place the product occupies relative to competitors in consumers' minds. Marketers want to develop unique market positions for their products. If a product is perceived to be exactly like others on the market, consumers would have no reason to buy it.

Market positioning

Arranging for a product to occupy a clear, distinctive, and desirable place relative to competing products in the minds of target consumers.

Market positioning is arranging for a product to occupy a clear, distinctive, and desirable place relative to competing products in the minds of target consumers. Thus, marketers plan positions that distinguish their products from competing brands and give them the greatest strategic advantage in their target markets. For example, Saturn is "a different kind of company, different kind of car"; Chevy Blazer is "like a rock"; the Hummer is "like nothing else"; and Toyota's hybrid Prius is "a revelation brilliantly disguised as a car." Lexus avows "the passionate pursuit of excellence" and Mercedes says, "In a perfect world, everyone would drive a Mercedes." The luxurious Bentley promises

Marketing at Work | 2.2

Niching: Health Insurance for Our Furry—or Feathery—Friends

Health insurance for pets? MetLife, Prudential, Northwestern Mutual, and most other large insurance companies haven't paid much attention to it. But that leaves plenty of room for more-focused nichers, for whom pet health insurance has become a lucrative business. The largest of the small competitors is Veterinary Pet Insurance (VPI). VPI's mission is to "make the miracles of veterinary medicine affordable to all pet owners."

VPI was founded in 1980 by veterinarian Jack Stephens. He never intended to leave his practice, but his life took a dramatic turn when he visited a local grocery store and was identified by a client's daughter as "the man who killed Buffy." Stephens had euthanized the family dog 2 weeks earlier. He immediately began researching the possibility of creating medical pet insurance. "There is nothing more frustrating for a veterinarian than knowing that you can heal a sick patient, but the owner lacks the financial resources and instructs you to put the pet down," says Stephens. "I wanted to change that."

Pet insurance is a still-small but fast-growing segment of the insurance business. Insiders think the industry offers huge potential. Currently, there are more than 60 million dogs and 68 million cats in the United States—more than 60 percent of all U.S. households own one or the other or both. Another 4.6 million U.S. households own one or more of about 300 species of birds; 2 million more own pet rabbits. Many people treat their pets as family members—and they buy accordingly. In fact, Americans now spend a whopping $28.5 billion a year on their pets.

Unlike in Sweden and Britain, where more than half of all pets owners carry pet health insurance, only 1 percent of pet owners in the United States carry such coverage. However, a recent study of pet owners found that nearly 75 per-

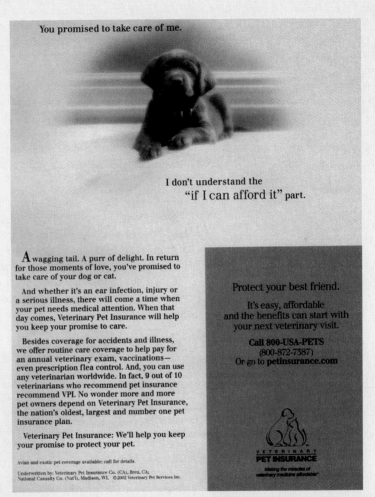

You promised to take care of me.

I don't understand the "if I can afford it" part.

A wagging tail. A purr of delight. In return for those moments of love, you've promised to take care of your dog or cat.

And whether it's an ear infection, injury or a serious illness, there will come a time when your pet needs medical attention. When that day comes, Veterinary Pet Insurance will help you keep your promise to care.

Besides coverage for accidents and illness, we offer routine care coverage to help pay for an annual veterinary exam, vaccinations—even prescription flea control. And, you can use any veterinarian worldwide. In fact, 9 out of 10 veterinarians who recommend pet insurance recommend VPI. No wonder more and more pet owners depend on Veterinary Pet Insurance, the nation's oldest, largest and number one pet insurance plan.

Veterinary Pet Insurance: We'll help you keep your promise to protect your pet.

Avian and exotic pet coverage available; call for details.

Underwritten by: Veterinary Pet Insurance Co. (CA), Brea, CA; National Casualty Co. (Nat'l), Madison, WI. ©2002 Veterinary Pet Services Inc.

Protect your best friend.

It's easy, affordable and the benefits can start with your next veterinary visit.

Call 800-USA-PETS
(800-872-7387)
Or go to **petinsurance.com**

VETERINARY
PET INSURANCE
Making the miracles of veterinary medicine affordable

Nichers: Market nicher VPI is growing faster than a new-born puppy. Its mission is to "make the miracles of veterinary medicine affordable to all pet owners."

cent are willing to go into debt to pay for veterinary care for their furry—or feathery—companions. And for many pet medical procedures, they'd have to! If not diagnosed quickly, even a mundane ear infection in a dog can result in $1,000 worth of medical treatment. A more complicated feline kidney transplant can run as much as $6,500. Cancer treatments, including radiation and chemotherapy, could cost a pet owner more than $10,000. All of this adds up to a lot of potential growth for pet health insurers.

VPI's plans cover more than 6,400 pet medical problems and conditions. The insurance helps pay for office calls, prescriptions, treatments, lab fees, x-rays, surgery, and hospitalization. Like its handful of competitors, VPI issues health insurance policies for dogs and cats. Unlike its competitors, VPI recently expanded its coverage to a menagerie of exotic pets as well. Among other critters, the new Avian and Exotic Pet Plan covers birds, rabbits, ferrets, rats, guinea pigs, snakes (except extra large

(continued)

ones) and other reptiles, iguanas, possums, turtles, hedgehogs, and pot belly pigs. "There's such a vast array of pets," says a VPI executive, "and people love them. We have to respect that."

How's VPI doing in its niche? It's growing like a newborn puppy. VPI is by far the largest of the handful of companies that offer pet insurance, providing more than 85 percent of all U.S. pet insurance policies. Since its inception, VPI has issued more than 1 million policies, and it now serves more than 350,000 policyholders. Sales have grown 40 percent in each of the past seven years, reaching nearly $72 million last year. That might not amount to much for the likes of Prudential or Northwestern Mutual, which rack up tens of billions of dollars in yearly revenues. But it's profitable business for nichers like VPI.

"Pet health insurance is no longer deemed so outlandish in a world where acupuncture for cats, hospice of dogs, and Prozac for ferrets are part of a veterinarian's routine," says one analyst. Such insurance is a real godsend for VPI's policyholders. Just ask Joe and Paula Sena, whose cocker spaniel, Elvis, is receiving radiation treatments for cancer. "He is not like our kids—he is our kid," says Ms. Pena. "He is a kid in a dog's body." VPI is making Elvis's treatments possible by picking up a lion's share of the costs. "Cost often becomes the deciding factor in the level of care owners can provide," says VPI founder Stephens. "We [always will] strive to make the miracles of modern medicine affordable."

Sources: **AD:** As advertised in *Time,* Inc. MAGAZINE; Michelle Desai, "VPI—Twenty Years and Still Going Strong," VPI press release, January 13, 2002; Michelle Leder, "How Much Is That $100 Deductible in the Window?" *New York Times*, Jul 22, 2001, p. 3.10; Jane Bennett Clark, "Cover Your Tail," *Kiplinger's Personal Finance,* Jan 2002, pp. 108–112; Yilu Zhao, "Break a Leg, Fluffy, If You Have Insurance," *New York Times,* June 30, 2002, p. 9.11; and information from the Veterinary Health Insurance Web site at www.petinsurance.com, June 2003.

"18 handcrafted feet of shameless luxury." Such deceptively simple statements form the backbone of a product's marketing strategy.

In positioning its product, the company first identifies possible competitive advantages upon which to build the position. To gain competitive advantage, the company must offer greater value to target consumers. It can do this either by charging lower prices than competitors do or by offering more benefits to justify higher prices. But if

■ Positioning: Toyota's hybrid Prius is "a revelation brilliantly disguised as a car." The Hummer is "like nothing else—Sport utility? Define Sport!"

the company positions the product as *offering* greater value, it must then *deliver* that greater value. Thus, effective positioning begins with actually *differentiating* the company's marketing offer so that it gives consumers more value. Once the company has chosen a desired position, it must take strong steps to deliver and communicate that position to target consumers. The company's entire marketing program should support the chosen positioning strategy.

Developing the Marketing Mix

Once the company has decided on its overall marketing strategy, it is ready to begin planning the details of the marketing mix, one of the major concepts in modern marketing. The **marketing mix** is the set of controllable, tactical marketing tools that the firm blends to produce the response it wants in the target market. The marketing mix consists of everything the firm can do to influence the demand for its product. The many possibilities can be collected into four groups of variables known as the "four *P*s": *product*, *price*, *place*, and *promotion*. Figure 2.5 shows the particular marketing tools under each *P*.

Product means the goods-and-services combination the company offers to the target market. Thus, a Ford Taurus product consists of nuts and bolts, spark plugs, pistons, headlights, and thousands of other parts. Ford offers several Taurus styles and dozens of optional features. The car comes fully serviced and with a comprehensive warranty that is as much a part of the product as the tailpipe.

Price is the amount of money customers have to pay to obtain the product. Ford calculates suggested retail prices that its dealers might charge for each Taurus. But Ford dealers rarely charge the full sticker price. Instead, they negotiate the price with each customer, offering discounts, trade-in allowances, and credit terms. These actions adjust prices for the current competitive situation and bring them into line with the buyer's perception of the car's value.

Place includes company activities that make the product available to target consumers. Ford partners with a large body of independently owned dealerships that sell the company's many different models. Ford selects its dealers carefully and supports them strongly. The dealers keep an inventory of Ford automobiles, demonstrate them to potential buyers, negotiate prices, close sales, and service the cars after the sale.

Promotion means activities that communicate the merits of the product and persuade target customers to buy it. Ford spends more than $2.4 billion each year on advertising to

Marketing mix
The set of controllable tactical marketing tools—product, price, place, and promotion—that the firm blends to produce the response it wants in the target market.

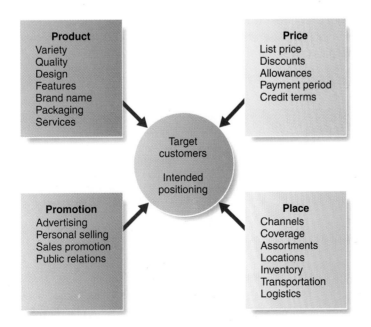

FIGURE 2.5

The Four *P*s of the Marketing Mix

tell consumers about the company and its many products.[14] Dealership salespeople assist potential buyers and persuade them that Ford is the best car for them. Ford and its dealers offer special promotions—sales, cash rebates, low financing rates—as added purchase incentives.

An effective marketing program blends all of the marketing mix elements into a coordinated program designed to achieve the company's marketing objectives by delivering value to consumers. The marketing mix constitutes the company's tactical tool kit for establishing strong positioning in target markets.

Some critics feel that the four Ps may omit or underemphasize certain important activities. For example, they ask, "Where are services?" Just because they don't start with a P doesn't justify omitting them. The answer is that services, such as banking, airline, and retailing services, are products too. We might call them *service products*. "Where is packaging?" the critics might ask. Marketers would answer that they include packaging as just one of many product decisions. All said, as Figure 2.5 suggests, many marketing activities that might appear to be left out of the marketing mix are subsumed under one of the four Ps. The issue is not whether there should be four, six, or ten Ps so much as what framework is most helpful in designing marketing programs.

There is another concern, however, that is valid. It holds that the four Ps concept takes the seller's view of the market, not the buyer's view. From the buyer's viewpoint, in this age of customer relationships, the four Ps might be better described as the four Cs[15]:

Four *Ps*	Four *Cs*
Product	Customer solution
Price	Customer cost
Place	Convenience
Promotion	Communication

Thus, while marketers see themselves as selling products, customers see themselves as buying value or solutions to their problems. And customers are interested in more than just the price; they are interested in the total costs of obtaining, using, and disposing of a product. Customers want the product and service to be as conveniently available as possible. Finally, they want two-way communication. Marketers would do well to think through the four Cs first and then build the four Ps on that platform.

■ Managing the Marketing Effort

In addition to being good at the *marketing* in marketing management, companies also need to pay attention to the *management* in marketing management. Managing the marketing process requires the four marketing management functions shown in Figure 2.6—*analysis*, *planning*, *implementation*, and *control*. The company first develops companywide strategic plans, then translates them into marketing and other plans for each division, product,

FIGURE 2.6

Marketing Analysis, Planning, Implementation, and Control

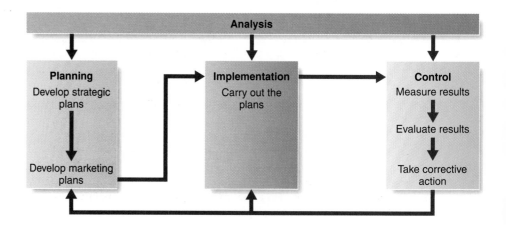

and brand. Through implementation, the company turns the plans into actions. Control consists of measuring and evaluating the results of marketing activities and taking corrective action where needed. Finally, marketing analysis provides information and evaluations needed for all of the other marketing activities.

Marketing Analysis

Managing the marketing function begins with a complete analysis of the company's situation. The company must analyze its markets and marketing environment to find attractive opportunities and avoid environmental threats. It must analyze company strengths and weaknesses as well as current and possible marketing actions to determine which opportunities it can best pursue. Marketing provides input to each of the other marketing management functions. We discuss marketing analysis more fully in Chapter 4.

■ Marketers must continually plan their analysis, implementation, and control activities.

Marketing Planning

Through strategic planning, the company decides what it wants to do with each business unit. Marketing planning involves deciding on marketing strategies that will help the company attain its overall strategic objectives. A detailed **marketing plan** is needed for each business, product, or brand. What does a marketing plan look like? Our discussion focuses on product or brand plans.

Table 2.2 outlines the major sections of a typical product or brand plan. The plan begins with an executive summary, which forms a quick overview of major assessments, goals, and recommendations. The main section of the plan presents a detailed analysis of the current marketing situation as well as potential threats and opportunities. It next states major objectives for the brand and outlines the specifics of a marketing strategy for achieving them.

A *marketing strategy* consists of specific strategies for target markets, positioning, the marketing mix, and marketing expenditure levels. In this section, the planner explains how each strategy responds to the threats, opportunities, and critical issues spelled out earlier in the plan. Additional sections of the marketing plan lay out an action program for implementing the marketing strategy along with the details of a supporting *marketing budget*. The last section outlines the controls that will be used to monitor progress and take corrective action.

Marketing plan
A detailed plan for a product or brand that assesses the current marketing situation and outlines marketing objectives, a marketing strategy, action programs, budgets, and controls.

Marketing Implementation

Planning good strategies is only a start toward successful marketing. A brilliant marketing strategy counts for little if the company fails to implement it properly. **Marketing implementation** is the process that turns marketing *plans* into marketing *actions* in order to accomplish strategic marketing objectives. Implementation involves day-to-day, month-to-month activities that effectively put the marketing plan to work. Whereas marketing planning addresses the *what* and *why* of marketing activities, implementation addresses the *who*, *where*, *when*, and *how*.

Many managers think that "doing things right" (implementation) is as important as, or even more important than, "doing the right things" (strategy). The fact is that both are critical to success, and companies can gain competitive advantages through effective implementation.[16] One firm can have essentially the same strategy as another, yet win in the marketplace through faster or better execution. Still, implementation is difficult—it is often easier to think up good marketing strategies than it is to carry them out.

Marketing implementation
The process that turns marketing strategies and plans into marketing actions in order to accomplish strategic marketing objectives.

TABLE 2.2   Contents of a Marketing Plan

Section	Purpose
Executive summary	Presents a brief summary of the main goals and recommendations of the plan for management review, helping top management to find the plan's major points quickly. A table of contents should follow the executive summary.
Current marketing situation	Describes the target market and company's position in it, including information about the market, product performance, competition, and distribution. This section includes: • A *market description* that defines the market and major segments, then reviews customer needs and factors in the marketing environment that may affect customer purchasing. • A *product review,* that shows sales, prices, and gross margins of the major products in the product line. • A review of *competition*, which identifies major competitors and assesses their market positions and strategies for product quality, pricing, distribution, and promotion. • A review of *distribution*, which evaluates recent sales trends and other developments in major distribution channels.
Threats and opportunity analysis	Assesses major threats and opportunities that the product might face, helping management to anticipate important positive or negative developments that might have an impact on the firm and its strategies.
Objectives and issues	States the marketing objectives that the company would like to attain during the plan's term and discusses key issues that will affect their attainment. For example, if the goal is to achieve a 15 percent market share, this section looks at how this goal might be achieved.
Marketing strategy	Outline the broad marketing logic by which the business unit hopes to achieve its marketing objectives and the specifics of target markets, positioning, and marketing expenditure levels. It outlines specific strategies for each marketing-mix element and explains how each responds to the threats, opportunities, and critical issues spelled out earlier in the plan.
Action programs	Spells out how marketing strategies will be turned into specific action programs that answer the following questions: *What* will be done? *When* will it be done? *Who* is responsible for doing it? *How* much will it cost?
Budgets	Details a supporting marketing budget that is essentially a projected profit-and-loss statement. It shows expected revenues (forecasted number of units sold and the average net price) and expected costs (of production, distribution, and marketing). The difference is the projected profit. Once approved by higher management, the budget becomes the basis for materials buying, production scheduling, personnel planning, and marketing operations.
Controls	Outlines the control that will be used to monitor progress and allow higher management to review implementation results and spot products that are not meeting their goals.

In an increasingly connected world, people at all levels of the marketing system must work together to implement marketing strategies and plans. At Black &Decker, for example, marketing implementation for the company's power tool products requires day-to-day decisions and actions by thousands of people both inside and outside the organization. Marketing managers make decisions about target segments, branding, packaging, pricing, promoting, and distributing. They connect with people elsewhere in the company to get support for their products and programs. They talk with engineering about product design, with manufacturing about production and inventory levels, and with finance about funding and cash flows. They also connect with outside people, such as advertising agencies to plan ad campaigns and the media to obtain publicity support. The sales force urges Home Depot, Wal-Mart, and other retailers to advertise Black & Decker products, provide ample shelf space, and use company displays.

Successful marketing implementation depends on how well the company blends its people, organizational structure, decision and reward systems, and company culture into a cohesive action program that supports its strategies. At all levels, the company must be staffed by people who have the needed skills, motivation, and personal characteristics. The company's formal organization structure plays an important role in implementing marketing strategy; so do its decision and reward systems. For example, if a company's compensation system rewards managers for short-term profit results, they will have little incentive to work toward long-term market-building objectives.

Finally, to be successfully implemented, the firm's marketing strategies must fit with its company culture, the system of values and beliefs shared by people in the organization. A study of America's most successful companies found that these companies have almost cultlike cultures built around strong, market-oriented missions. At companies such as Wal-Mart, Dell, Microsoft, Nordstrom, Citicorp, Procter &Gamble, and Walt Disney, "employees share such a strong vision that they know in their hearts what's right for their company."[17]

Marketing Department Organization

The company must design a marketing organization that can carry out marketing strategies and plans. If the company is very small, one person might do all of the research, selling, advertising, customer service, and other marketing work. As the company expands, a marketing department emerges to plan and carry out marketing activities. In large companies, this department contains many specialists. Thus, General Electric and Microsoft have product and market managers, sales managers and salespeople, market researchers, advertising experts, and other specialists.

Modern marketing departments can be arranged in several ways. The most common form of marketing organization is the *functional organization*. Under this organization, different marketing activities are headed by a functional specialist—a sales manager, advertising manager, marketing research manager, customer service manager, or new-product manager. A company that sells across the country or internationally often uses a *geographic organization*. Its sales and marketing people are assigned to specific countries, regions, and districts. Geographic organization allows salespeople to settle into a territory, get to know their customers, and work with a minimum of travel time and cost.

Companies with many very different products or brands often create a *product management organization*. Using this approach, a product manager develops and implements a complete strategy and marketing program for a specific product or brand. Product management first appeared at Procter & Gamble in 1929. A new company soap, Camay, was not doing well, and a young P&G executive was assigned to give his exclusive attention to developing and promoting this product. He was successful, and the company soon added other product managers.[18] Since then, many firms, especially consumer products companies, have set up product management organizations.

For companies that sell one product line to many different types of markets and customers that have different needs and preferences, a *market* or *customer management organization* might be best. A market management organization is similar to the product management organization. Market managers are responsible for developing marketing strategies and plans for their specific markets or customers. This system's main advantage is that the company is organized around the needs of specific customer segments.

Large companies that produce many different products flowing into many different geographic and customer markets usually employ some *combination* of the functional, geographic, product, and market organization forms. This ensures that each function, product, and market receives its share of management attention. However, it can also add costly layers of management and reduce organizational flexibility. Still, the benefits of organizational specialization usually outweigh the drawbacks.

Marketing organization has become an increasingly important issue in recent years. As we discussed in Chapter 1, many companies are finding that today's marketing environment calls for less focus on products, brands, and territories and more focus on customers and customer relationships. More and more companies are shifting their brand management focus toward *customer relationship management*—moving away from managing just product or brand profitability and toward managing customer profitability and customer equity.[19] And many companies now organize their marketing operations around major customers. For example, companies such as Procter & Gamble, Black & Decker,

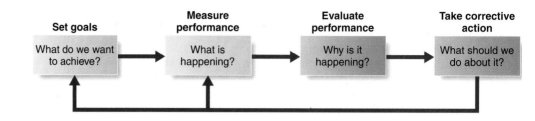

FIGURE 2.7

The Marketing Control Process

and Newell Rubbermaid have large teams, or even whole divisions, set up to serve large customers like Wal-Mart, Target, or Home Depot.

Marketing Control

Marketing control

The process of measuring and evaluating the results of marketing strategies and plans, and taking corrective action to ensure that objectives are achieved.

Because many surprises occur during the implementation of marketing plans, the marketing department must practice constant marketing control. **Marketing control** involves evaluating the results of marketing strategies and plans and taking corrective action to ensure that objectives are attained. Figure 2.7 shows that marketing control involves four steps. Management first sets specific marketing goals. It then measures its performance in the marketplace and evaluates the causes of any differences between expected and actual performance. Finally, management takes corrective action to close the gaps between its goals and its performance. This may require changing the action programs or even changing the goals.

Operating control involves checking ongoing performance against the annual plan and taking corrective action when necessary. Its purpose is to ensure that the company achieves the sales, profits, and other goals set out in its annual plan. It also involves determining the profitability of different products, territories, markets, and channels.

Strategic control involves looking at whether the company's basic strategies are well matched to its opportunities. Marketing strategies and programs can quickly become outdated, and each company should periodically reassess its overall approach to the marketplace. A major tool for such strategic control is a **marketing audit**. The marketing audit is a comprehensive, systematic, independent, and periodic examination of a company's environment, objectives, strategies, and activities to determine problem areas and opportunities. The audit provides good input for a plan of action to improve the company's marketing performance.[20]

Marketing audit

A comprehensive, systematic, independent, and periodic examination of a company's environment, objectives, strategies, and activities to determine problem areas and opportunities and to recommend a plan of action to improve the company's marketing performance.

The marketing audit covers *all* major marketing areas of a business, not just a few trouble spots. It assesses the marketing environment, marketing strategy, marketing organization, marketing systems, marketing mix, and marketing productivity and profitability. The audit is normally conducted by an objective and experienced outside party. The findings may come as a surprise—and sometimes as a shock—to management. Management then decides which actions make sense and how and when to implement them.

■■ The Marketing Environment

Managing the marketing function would be hard enough if the marketer had to deal with only the controllable marketing mix variables. But the company operates in a complex marketing environment, consisting of uncontrollable forces to which the company must adapt. The environment produces both threats and opportunities. The company must carefully analyze its environment so that it can avoid the threats and take advantage of the opportunities.

The company's marketing environment includes forces close to the company that affect its ability to serve consumers, such as other company departments, channel members, suppliers, competitors, and publics. It also includes broader demographic and economic forces, political and legal forces, technological and ecological forces, and social and cultural forces. Marketers need to consider all of these forces in the process of building and maintaining profitable relationships with customers and marketing partners. We will examine the marketing environment more fully in Chapter 3.

REST STOP:
Reviewing the Concepts

What have you learned so far on your journey through marketing? In Chapter 1, we defined marketing and outlined the steps in the marketing process. We learned that the aim of marketing is to create value for customers in order to capture value in return. In this chapter, we examined companywide strategic planning and marketing's role in the organization. Then, we looked more deeply into marketing strategy and the marketing mix, and reviewed the major marketing management functions. So you've had a pretty good overview of the fundamentals of modern marketing. In future chapters, we'll expand on these fundamentals.

1. Explain companywide strategic planning and its four steps.

Strategic planning sets the stage for the rest of the company's planning. Marketing contributes to strategic planning, and the overall plan defines marketing's role in the company. Although formal planning offers a variety of benefits to companies, not all companies use it or use it well. Although many discussions of strategic planning focus on large corporations, small business also can benefit greatly from sound strategic planning.

Strategic planning involves developing a strategy for long-term survival and growth. It consists of four steps: defining the company's mission, setting objectives and goals, designing a business portfolio, and developing functional plans. *Defining a clear company mission* begins with drafting a formal mission statement, which should be market oriented, realistic, specific, motivating, and consistent with the market environment. The mission is then transformed into detailed *supporting goals and objectives* to guide the entire company. Based on those goals and objectives, headquarters designs a *business portfolio*, deciding which businesses and products should receive more or fewer resources. In turn, each business and product unit must develop *detailed marketing plans* in line with the companywide plan. Comprehensive and sound marketing plans support company strategic planning by detailing specific opportunities.

2. Discuss how to design business portfolios and develop strategies for growth and downsizing.

Guided by the company's mission statement and objectives, management plans its *business portfolio*, or the collection of businesses and products that make up the company. The firm wants to produce a business portfolio that best fits its strengths and weaknesses to opportunities in the environment. To do this, it must analyze and adjust its *current* business portfolio and develop growth and downsizing strategies for adjusting the *future* portfolio. The company might use a formal portfolio-planning method. But many companies are now designing more-customized portfolio-planning approaches that better suit their unique situations. The *product/market expansion grid* suggests four possible growth paths: market penetration, market development, product development, and diversification.

3. Assess marketing's role in strategic planning and explain how marketers partner with others inside and outside the firm to build profitable customer relationships.

Under the strategic plan, the major functional departments— marketing, finance, accounting, purchasing, operations, information systems, human resources, and others—must work together to accomplish strategic objectives. Marketing plays a key role in the company's strategic planning by providing a *marketing-concept philosophy* and *inputs* regarding attractive market opportunities. Within individual business units, marketing designs *strategies* for reaching the unit's objectives and helps to carry them out profitably.

Marketers alone cannot produce superior value for customers. It can be only a partner in attracting, keeping, and growing customers. A company's success depends on how well each department performs its customer value-adding activities and how well the departments work together to serve the customer. Thus, marketers must practice *partner relationship management*. They must work closely with partners in other company departments to form an effective *value chain* that serves the customer. And they must partner effectively with other companies in the marketing system to form a competitively superior *value-delivery network*.

4. Describe the elements of a customer-driven marketing strategy and mix, and the forces that influence it.

Consumer relationships are at the center of marketing strategy and programs. Through market segmentation, target marketing, and market positioning, the company divides the total market into smaller segments, selects the segments it can best serve, and decides how it wants to bring value to target consumers. It then designs a *marketing mix* to produce the response it wants in the target market. The marketing mix consists of product, price, place, and promotion decisions.

5. List the marketing management functions, including the elements of a marketing plan.

To find the best strategy and mix and to put them into action, the company engages in marketing analysis, planning, implementation, and control. The main components of a *marketing plan* are the executive summary, current marketing situation, threats and opportunities, objectives and issues, marketing strategies, action programs, budgets, and controls. To plan good strategies is often easier than to carry them out. To be successful, companies must also be effective at *implementation—* turning marketing strategies into marketing actions.

Much of the responsibility for implementation goes to the company's marketing department. Modern marketing departments can be organized in one or a combination of ways: *functional marketing organization, geographic organization, product management organization*, or *market management organization*. In this age of customer relationships, more and more companies are now changing their organizational focus from product or territory management to customer relationship management. Marketing organizations carry out *marketing control*, both operating control and strategic control. They use *marketing audits* to determine marketing opportunities and problems and to recommend short-run and long-run actions to improve overall marketing performance. Through these activities, the company watches and adapts to the marketing environment.

Navigating the Key Terms

Business portfolio	Market segmentation	Portfolio analysis
Diversification	Marketing audit	Product development
Downsizing	Marketing control	Product/market expansion grid
Growth-share matrix	Marketing implementation	Strategic planning
Market development	Marketing mix	Target marketing
Market penetration	Marketing planning	Value chain
Market positioning	Marketing strategy	Value-delivery network
Market segment	Mission statement	

Travel Log

Discussing the Issues

1. Four steps are identified in the strategic planning process. Why are they arranged in this order? What consequences might a company experience if one of the steps was performed out of order? What should be the role of marketing in the strategic planning process?

2. How can the BCG growth-share matrix be used to assess the current product portfolio and to plan for the future? What limitations does portfolio analysis have? Discuss how a product/market expansion grid can aid companies in identifying profitable growth opportunities.

3. Discuss the concept of the value chain. Is it true that the value chain is only as strong as its weakest link? Explain why or why not. How can partnering with other organizations to form a value delivery network further strengthen a firm's performance?

4. Discuss the differences between the following terms: market segmentation, target marketing, and market positioning.

5. Discuss the various activities encompassed by each of the four Ps. What insight might a firm develop by considering the four Cs, instead of the four Ps?

6. What role do analysis, planning, implementation, and control play in managing the marketing process? How are these four marketing management functions related to one another?

Application Questions

1. The product/market expansion grid can be useful in identifying growth opportunities for companies through market penetration, product development, market development, and diversification. Consider a food retailer like Subway, which makes sandwiches and offers chips and drinks. Think creatively to describe four growth opportunities for Subway that fit into each of the four product/market expansion grid cells.

2. Propel is a new lightly flavored, vitamin-enhanced "fitness" water from the maker of Gatorade. It comes in flavors such as berry, black cherry, and kiwi-strawberry. Describe the likely target market for this beverage. How should this beverage be positioned relative to competitive products such as sports drinks, bottled water, orange juice, and milk?

3. Nike has recently entered the golf market with a line of clubs, balls, bags, footwear, and clothing. Most visibly, Nike has enlisted the services of Tiger Woods to promote its golf products. Discuss the four-step marketing control process as it would apply to Nike's evaluation of Tiger Woods as its celebrity endorser.

Under the Hood: Focus on Technology

In order to improve 911 emergency services, the FCC has put forth guidelines that require cell phone carriers to be able to establish subscribers' locations within 100 meters by the end of 2005. Two different approaches are being considered by wireless carriers. One uses phones with built-in GPS chips, while the other uses triangulation between three or more cell towers to pinpoint a caller's location. This technology, already in use in Hong

Kong, Tokyo, and Helsinki, has drawn the interest of marketers who envision other uses such as sending promotional offers to customers as they walk past their stores. In the beginning, the technology will likely be used to give subscribers directions to particular stores.

1. In a small group, brainstorm potential marketing uses for this technology other than those discussed above.

2. Assume you are a member of a cell phone carrier's marketing team selling this technology to retailers. Develop both a product-oriented and a market-oriented mission statement for the company.

3. What limitations does the product-oriented mission statement have that the market-oriented statement overcomes?

Focus on Ethics

High-profile scandals involving companies such as Enron and WorldCom have renewed interest in understanding how such debacles might be avoided. Corporate accountability is the new theme for concerned investors and politicians. Many agree that the culture of an organization influences the ethical and socially responsible behavior of its employees.

1. Discuss the role that a company's mission statement can play in encouraging ethical corporate behavior.

2. As more firms partner with suppliers, distributors, and even customers to improve their value delivery network, what challenges exist for monitoring and encouraging responsible decision making across the entire value delivery network? What can be done to address these challenges?

3. What function does a marketing audit play in avoiding scandals?

Videos

The Dunkin' Donuts video case that accompanies this chapter is located in Appendix 1 at the back of the book.

Student Materials

Need a tune-up? A study guide and OneKey access code are available to aid in your review of chapter material. Your instructor may choose to have these items shrink-wrapped with your text or you may purchase them separately at www.prenhall.com/marketing.

■ *After studying this chapter, you should be able to*

1. *Describe* the environmental forces that affect the company's ability to serve its customers **2.** *Explain* how changes in the demographic and economic environments affect marketing decisions **3.** *Identify* the major trends in the firm's natural and technological environments **4.** *Explain* the key changes in the political and cultural environments **5.** *Discuss* how companies can react to the marketing environment

The Marketing Environment

3

ROAD MAP | Previewing the Concepts

In Part 1 (Chapters 1 and 2), you learned about the basic concepts of marketing and the steps in the marketing process for building profitable relationships with targeted consumers. In Part 2, we'll look more deeply into the first step of the marketing process—understanding the marketplace and customer needs and wants. In this chapter, you'll discover that marketing does not operate in a vacuum, but rather in a complex and changing marketplace environment. Other *actors* in this environment—suppliers, intermediaries, customers, competitors, publics, and others—may work with or against the company. Major environmental *forces*—demographic, economic, natural, technological, political, and cultural—shape marketing opportunities, pose threats, and affect the company's ability to serve customers and develop profitable relationships with them. To understand marketing, and to develop effective marketing strategies, you must first understand the context in which marketing operates.

At our first stop, we'll check out a major development in the marketing environment, millennial fever, and the nostalgia boom that it has produced. Volkswagen responded with the introduction of a born-again New Beetle. As you read on, ask yourself: What has made this little car so right for the times?

As we hurtle into the new millennium, social experts are busier than ever assessing the impact of a host of environmental forces on consumers and the marketers who serve them. "An old year turns into a new one," reflects one such expert, "and the world itself, at least for a moment, seems to turn also. Images of death and rebirth, things ending and beginning, populate . . . and haunt the mind. Multiply this a thousand-fold, and you get 'millennial fever' . . . driving consumer behavior in all sorts of interesting ways."

Such millennial fever has hit the nation's baby boomers, the most commercially influential demographic group in history, especially hard. The oldest boomers, now in their mid- to late 50s, are resisting the aging process with the vigor they once reserved for antiwar protests. Other factors are also at work. Today, people of all ages seem to feel a bit overworked, overstimulated, overloaded, and technostressed. "Americans are overwhelmed . . . by the breathtaking onrush of the Information Age, with its high-speed modems, cell phones, and pagers," suggests the expert. "While we hail the benefits of these wired [times], at the same time we are buffeted by the rapid pace of change."

The result of this millennial fever is a yearning to turn back the clock, to return to simpler times. This yearning has in turn produced a massive nostalgia wave. Marketers of all kinds have responded to these nostalgia pangs by recreating products and images that help take consumers back to the good old days. "In these tough times," says another expert, "nostalgia for rosier days seems to be driving a consumer appetite for retro products and design."

Examples are plentiful: Kellogg has revived old Corn Flakes packaging and car makers have created retro roadsters such as the Porsche Boxter and Chrysler's PT Cruiser. A Pepsi commercial rocks to the Rolling Stones's "Brown Sugar," James Brown's "I Feel Good" helps sell Senokot laxatives, and Janis Joplin's raspy voice crows, "Oh Lord, won't you buy me a Mercedes-Benz?" Heinz reintroduced its classic glass ketchup bottle, supported by nostalgic "Heinz was there" ads showing two 1950s-era boys eating hot dogs at a ballpark. And the television networks launched what one analyst calls a "retro feeding frenzy" of reunion programs "that revisit the good (*M*A*S*H*, *L.A. Law*, *The Cosby Show*, *The Mary Tyler Moore Show*), the bad (*That's Incredible!*, *Laverne & Shirley*), and the truly ancient (*American Bandstand*, *The Honeymooners*).

Perhaps no company has been more successful in riding the nostalgia wave than Volkswagen. The original Volkswagen Beetle first sputtered into America in 1949. With its simple, buglike design, no-frills engineering, and economical operation, the Beetle was the antithesis of Detroit's chrome-laden gas guzzlers. Although most owners would readily admit that their Beetles were underpowered, noisy, cramped, and freezing in the winter, they saw these as endearing qualities. Overriding these minor inconveniences, the Beetle was cheap to buy and own, dependable, easy to fix, fun to drive, and anything but flashy.

During the 1960s, as young baby boomers by the thousands were buying their first cars, demand exploded and the Beetle blossomed into an unlikely icon. Bursting with personality, the understated Bug came to personify an era of rebellion against conventions. It became the most popular car in American history, with sales peaking at 423,000 in 1968. By the late 1970s, however, the boomers had moved on, Bug mania had faded, and Volkswagen had dropped Beetle production for the United States. Still, decades later, the mere mention of these chugging oddities evokes smiles and strong emotions. Almost everyone over the age of 30, it seems, has a "feel-good" Beetle story to tell.

In an attempt to surf the nostalgia wave, Volkswagen introduced a New Beetle in 1998. Outwardly, the reborn Beetle resembles the original, tapping the strong emotions and memories of times gone by. Beneath the skin, however, the New Beetle is packed with modern features. According to an industry analyst, "The Beetle comeback is . . . based on a combination of romance and reason. . . . Built into the dashboard is a bud vase perfect for a daisy plucked straight from the 1960s. But right next to it is a high-tech multi-speaker stereo—and options like power windows, cruise control, and a power sunroof make it a very different car than the rattly old Bug. The new version . . . comes with all the modern features car buyers demand, such as four air bags and power outlets for cell phones. But that's not why . . . folks buy it. With a familiar bubble shape that still makes people smile as it skitters by, the new Beetle offers a pull that is purely emotional."

Initial advertising for the New Beetle played strongly on the nostalgia theme, while at the same time refreshing the old Beetle heritage. "If you sold your soul in the '80s," tweaked one ad, "here's your chance to buy it back." Other ads read, "Less flower, more power," and "Comes with wonderful new features. Like heat." Still another ad declared "0 to 60? Yes."

Volkswagen invested $560 million to bring the New Beetle to market. The investment paid big dividends as demand quickly outstripped supply. Even before the first cars reached VW showrooms, dealers across the country had long waiting lists of people who'd paid for the car without ever seeing it, let alone driving it. The New Beetle turned out to be a cross-generational hit, appealing to more than just Woodstock-recovered baby boomers. Even kids too young to remember the original Bug loved this new one.

Volkswagen's first-year sales projections of 50,000 New Beetles in North America proved pessimistic. After only nine months, the company had sold more than 64,000 of the new Bugs in the United States and Canada. Sales are still sizzling—the New Beetle now accounts for more than a quarter of Volkswagen's U.S. sales and has helped win VW a fivefold increase in sales during the past decade.

To follow up, Volkswagen launched the spunky little New Beetle convertible in early 2003. By the time they were introduced, more than half of the convertibles arriving at dealerships had already been sold. "It's just a nice, happy ride," notes one delighted owner. Upbeat ads for the new model evoke images of simpler, gentler times. One ad shows a chain reaction of smiles, as one person walking on a city sidewalk stops to help someone else, who in turn helps another, and so on. At the end, the ad rewinds to show what sparked the first smile: a VW convertible.

For an encore, Volkswagen plans to introduce a reincarnation of its old cult-classic flower-power Microbus in 2005. Although most younger buyers won't remember much about the original Microbus unless they encountered one at a Grateful Dead concert, test models have received rave reviews at auto shows in Japan and Europe.

"Millennial fever" results from the convergence of a wide range of forces in the marketing environment—from technological, economic, and demographic forces to cultural, social, and political ones. Most trend analysts believe that the nostalgia craze will only grow as the population ages and as times get more complex. If so, the New Beetle, so full of the past, has a very bright future. "The Beetle is not just empty nostalgia," says Gerald Celente, publisher of *Trend Journal*. "It is a practical car that is also tied closely to the emotions of a generation." Says another trend analyst, the New Beetle "is our romantic past, reinvented for our hectic here-and-now. Different, yet deeply familiar—a car for the times."[1]

As noted in previous chapters, marketers need to be good at building relationships with customers, others in the company, and external partners. To do this effectively, marketers must understand the major environmental forces that surround all of these relationships. A company's **marketing environment** consists of the actors and forces outside marketing that affect marketing management's ability to build and maintain successful relationships with target customers. The marketing environment offers both opportunities and threats. Successful companies know the vital importance of constantly watching and adapting to the changing environment.

Marketing environment
The actors and forces outside marketing that affect marketing management's ability to build and maintain successful relationships with target customers.

As we move into the twenty-first century, both consumers and marketers wonder what the future will bring. The environment continues to change rapidly. More than any other group in the company, marketers must be the trend trackers and opportunity seekers. Although every manager in an organization needs to observe the outside environment, marketers have two special aptitudes. They have disciplined methods—marketing intelligence and marketing research—for collecting information about the marketing environment. They also spend more time in the customer and competitor environments. By carefully studying the environment, marketers can adapt their strategies to meet new marketplace challenges and opportunities.

The marketing environment is made up of a *microenvironment* and a *macroenvironment*. The **microenvironment** consists of the actors close to the company that affect its ability to serve its customers—the company, suppliers, marketing intermediaries, customer markets, competitors, and publics. The **macroenvironment** consists of the larger societal forces that affect the microenvironment—demographic, economic, natural, technological, political, and cultural forces. We look first at the company's microenvironment.

Microenvironment
The actors close to the company that affect its ability to serve its customers—the company, suppliers, marketing intermediaries, customer markets, competitors, and publics.

Macroenvironment
The larger societal forces that affect the microenvironment—demographic, economic, natural, technological, political, and cultural forces.

▪◼ The Company's Microenvironment

Marketing management's job is to build relationships with customers by creating customer value and satisfaction. However, marketing managers cannot do this alone. Figure 3.1 shows the major actors in the marketer's microenvironment. Marketing success will require building relationships with other company departments, suppliers, marketing intermediaries, customers, competitors, and various publics, which combine to make up the company's value delivery network.

The Company

In designing marketing plans, marketing management takes other company groups into account—groups such as top management, finance, research and development (R&D), purchasing, operations, and accounting. All these interrelated groups form the internal environment. Top management sets the company's mission, objectives, broad strategies, and policies. Marketing managers make decisions within the strategies and plans made by top management.

Marketing managers must also work closely with other company departments. Finance is concerned with finding and using funds to carry out the marketing plan. The R&D department focuses on designing safe and attractive products. Purchasing worries about getting supplies and materials, whereas operations is responsible for producing and distributing the desired quality and quantity of products. Accounting has to measure revenues and costs to help marketing know how well it is achieving its objectives. Together, all of these departments have an impact on the marketing department's plans and actions. Under the marketing concept, all of these functions must "think consumer." They should work in harmony to provide superior customer value and satisfaction.

Suppliers

Suppliers form an important link in the company's overall customer value delivery system. They provide the resources needed by the company to produce its goods and services. Supplier problems can seriously affect marketing. Marketing managers must watch supply availability—supply shortages or delays, labor strikes, and other events can cost sales in the short run and damage customer satisfaction in the long run. Marketing managers also monitor the price trends of their key inputs. Rising supply costs may force price increases that can harm the company's sales volume.

Most marketers today treat their suppliers as partners in creating and delivering customer value. Wal-Mart goes to great lengths to work with its suppliers. For example, it helps them to test new products in its stores. And its Supplier Development Department publishes a Supplier Proposal Guide and maintains a supplier Web site, both of which help suppliers to navigate the complex Wal-Mart buying process. It knows that good partnership relationship management results in success for Wal-Mart, suppliers, and, ultimately, its customers.

FIGURE 3.1

Actors in the Microenvironment

Marketing Intermediaries

Marketing intermediaries help the company to promote, sell, and distribute its goods to final buyers. They include *resellers, physical distribution firms, marketing services agencies*, and *financial intermediaries. Resellers* are distribution channel firms that help the company find customers or make sales to them. These include wholesalers and retailers, who buy and resell merchandise. Selecting and partnering with resellers is not easy. No longer do manufacturers have many small, independent resellers from which to choose. They now face large and growing reseller organizations such as Wal-Mart, Target, Home Depot, Costco, and Best Buy. These organizations frequently have enough power to dictate terms or even to shut the manufacturer out of large markets.

Physical distribution firms help the company to stock and move goods from their points of origin to their destinations. Working with warehouse and transportation firms, a company must determine the best ways to store and ship goods, balancing factors such as cost, delivery, speed, and safety. *Marketing services agencies* are the marketing research firms, advertising agencies, media firms, and marketing consulting firms that help the company target and promote its products to the right markets. When the company decides to use one of these agencies, it must choose carefully because these firms vary in creativity, quality, service, and price. *Financial intermediaries* include banks, credit companies, insurance companies, and other businesses that help finance transactions or insure against the risks associated with the buying and selling of goods. Most firms and customers depend on financial intermediaries to finance their transactions.

Like suppliers, marketing intermediaries form an important component of the company's overall value delivery system. In its quest to create satisfying customer relationships, the company must do more than just optimize its own performance. It must partner effectively with marketing intermediaries to optimize the performance of the entire system.

Thus, today's marketers recognize the importance of working with their intermediaries as partners rather than simply as channels through which they sell their products. For example, Coca-Cola has a 10-year deal with Wendy's that makes it the fast-food chain's exclusive soft drink provider. In the deal, Coca-Cola provides Wendy's much more than just soft drinks. It also pledges powerful marketing support.

Along with the soft drinks, Wendy's gets a cross-functional team of 50 Coke employees who are dedicated to understanding the finer points of Wendy's business. It also benefits from Coke dollars spent in joint marketing campaigns. Bigger still is the staggering amount of consumer research that Coca-Cola provides its partners. Coke . . . goes to great lengths to understand beverage drinkers—and to make sure its partners can use those insights. The company has also analyzed the demographics of every zip code in the country and used the information to create a software program called Solver. By answering questions about their target audience, Wendy's franchise owners can determine which Coke brands are preferred by the customers in their area. Coca-Cola also has even studied the design of drive-through menu boards to better understand which layouts, fonts, letter sizes, colors, and visuals induce consumers to order more food and drink. Such intense partnering efforts have earned Coca-Cola a 65 percent share of the U.S. fountain soft drink market, compared with a 24 percent share for Pepsi.[2]

Marketing intermediaries
Firms that help the company to promote, sell, and distribute its goods to final buyers; they include resellers, physical distribution firms, marketing service agencies, and financial intermediaries.

■ Partnering with marketing intermediaries: Coca-Cola provides Wendy's with much more than just soft drinks. It also pledges powerful marketing support.

Customers

The company needs to study five types of customer markets closely. *Consumer markets* consist of individuals and households that buy goods and services for personal consumption. *Business markets* buy goods and services for further processing or for use in their production process, whereas *reseller markets* buy goods and services to resell at a profit. *Government markets* are made up of government agencies that buy goods and services to produce public services or transfer the goods and services to others who need them. Finally, *international markets* consist of these buyers in other countries, including consumers, producers, resellers, and governments. Each market type has special characteristics that call for careful study by the seller.

Competitors

The marketing concept states that to be successful, a company must provide greater customer value and satisfaction than its competitors do. Thus, marketers must do more than simply adapt to the needs of target consumers. They also must gain strategic advantage by positioning their offerings strongly against competitors' offerings in the minds of consumers.

No single competitive marketing strategy is best for all companies. Each firm should consider its own size and industry position compared to those of its competitors. Large firms with dominant positions in an industry can use certain strategies that smaller firms cannot afford. But being large is not enough. There are winning strategies for large firms, but there are also losing ones. And small firms can develop strategies that give them better rates of return than large firms enjoy.

Public

Any group that has an actual or potential interest in or impact on an organization's ability to achieve its objectives.

Publics

The company's marketing environment also includes various publics. A **public** is any group that has an actual or potential interest in or impact on an organization's ability to achieve its objectives. We can identify seven types of publics.

- *Financial publics* influence the company's ability to obtain funds. Banks, investment houses, and stockholders are the major financial publics.

- *Media publics* carry news, features, and editorial opinion. They include newspapers, magazines, and radio and television stations.

- *Government publics.* Management must take government developments into account. Marketers must often consult the company's lawyers on issues of product safety, truth in advertising, and other matters.

- *Citizen-action publics.* A company's marketing decisions may be questioned by consumer organizations, environmental groups, minority groups, and others. Its public relations department can help it stay in touch with consumer and citizen groups.

- *Local publics* include neighborhood residents and community organizations. Large companies usually appoint a community relations officer to deal with the community, attend meetings, answer questions, and contribute to worthwhile causes.

- *General public.* A company needs to be concerned about the general public's attitude toward its products and activities. The public's image of the company affects its buying.

■ Publics: In this ad, Wal-Mart recognizes the importance of both its local and employee publics. Its Good Works scholarship program "is just one of the reasons Wal-Mart associates in Mississippi (such as Tiffany, at lower right), and all over the country, are proud to get involved in the communities they serve."

■ *Internal publics* include workers, managers, volunteers, and the board of directors. Large companies use newsletters and other means to inform and motivate their internal publics. When employees feel good about their company, this positive attitude spills over to external publics.

A company can prepare marketing plans for these major publics as well as for its customer markets. Suppose the company wants a specific response from a particular public, such as goodwill, favorable word of mouth, or donations of time or money. The company would have to design an offer to this public that is attractive enough to produce the desired response.

■■ The Company's Macroenvironment

The company and all of the other actors operate in a larger macroenvironment of forces that shape opportunities and pose threats to the company. Figure 3.2 shows the six major forces in the company's macroenvironment. In the remaining sections of this chapter, we examine these forces and show how they affect marketing plans.

Demographic Environment

Demography is the study of human populations in terms of size, density, location, age, gender, race, occupation, and other statistics. The demographic environment is of major interest to marketers because it involves people, and people make up markets.

The world population is growing at an explosive rate. It now totals more than 6.3 billion and will exceed 8.2 billion by the year 2030.[3] The world's large and highly diverse population poses both opportunities and challenges. Think for a few minutes about the world and your place in it. If we reduced the world to a village of 1,000 people representative of the world's population, this would be our reality[4]:

■ Our village would have 520 females and 480 males including 330 children and 60 people over age 65, 10 college graduates, and 335 illiterate adults.

■ We'd have 52 North Americans, 55 Russians, 84 Latin Americans, 95 Europeans, 124 Africans, and 584 Asians.

■ Communication would be difficult: 165 of us would speak Mandarin, 85 English, 83 Hindi, 64 Spanish, 58 Russian, and 37 Arabic. The other half of us would speak one of more than 5,000 other languages.

■ Among us we'd have 329 Christians, 178 Moslems, 32 Hindus, 60 Buddhists, 3 Jews, 167 nonreligious, 45 atheists, and 86 others.

■ About one-third of our people would have access to clean, safe drinking water. About half of our children would be immunized against infections.

Demography
The study of human populations in terms of size, density, location, age, gender, race, occupation, and other statistics.

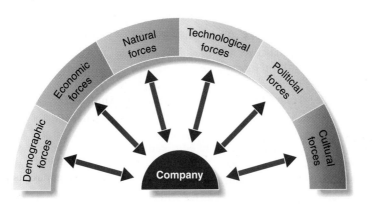

FIGURE 3.2

Major Forces in the Company's Macroenvironment

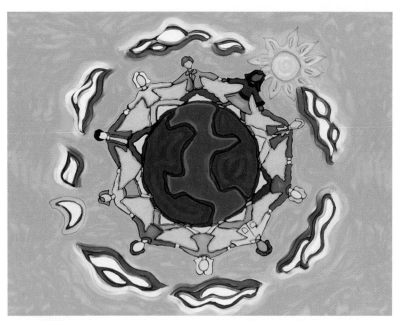

■ The world population is growing at an explosive rate, presenting both opportunities and challenges for marketers. Think for a few minutes about the world and your place in it.

■ The woodlands in our village would be decreasing rapidly and wasteland would be growing. Forty percent of the village's cropland, nourished by 83 percent of our fertilizer, would produce 72 percent of the food to feed its 270 well-fed owners. The remaining 60 percent of the land and 17 percent of the fertilizer would produce 28 percent of the food to feed the other 730 people. Five hundred people in the village would suffer from malnutrition.

■ Only 200 of the 1,000 people would control 75 percent of our village's wealth. Another 200 would receive only 2 percent of the wealth. Seventy people would own cars. One would have a computer, and that computer probably would not be connected to the Internet. Only 70 of us would own a car.

The explosive world population growth has major implications for business. A growing population means growing human needs to satisfy. Depending on purchasing power, it may also mean growing market opportunities. For example, to curb its skyrocketing population, the Chinese government has passed regulations limiting families to one child each. As a result, Chinese children are spoiled and fussed over as never before. Known in China as "little emperors and empresses," Chinese children are being showered with everything from candy to computers as a result of what's known as the "six-pocket syndrome." As many as six adults—including parents and two sets of doting grandparents—may be indulging the whims of each child. Parents in the average Beijing household now spend about 40 percent of their income on their cherished only child. This trend has encouraged toy companies such as Japan's Bandai Company (known for its Mighty Morphin Power Rangers), Denmark's Lego Group, and Mattel to enter the Chinese market. And McDonald's has triumphed in China in part because it has catered successfully to this pampered generation.[5]

Thus, marketers keep close track of demographic trends and developments in their markets, both at home and abroad. They track changing age and family structures, geographic population shifts, educational characteristics, and population diversity. Here, we discuss the most important demographic trends in the United States.

Changing Age Structure of the Population

The U.S. population stood at more than 291 million in 2003 and may reach 350 million by the year 2025.[6] The single most important demographic trend in the United States is the changing age structure of the population. As shown in Figure 3.3, the U.S. population contains seven generational groups. Here, we discuss the three largest age groups—the baby boomers, Generation X, and Generation Y—and their impact on today's marketing strategies.

Baby boomers

The 78 million people born during the baby boom following World War II and lasting until the early 1960s.

The Baby Boomers. The post–World War II baby boom produced 78 million **baby boomers**, born between 1946 and 1964. Since then, the baby boomers have become one of the most powerful forces shaping the marketing environment. The boomers have presented a moving target, creating new markets as they grew from infancy to their preadolescent, teenage, young adult, and now middle-age to mature years. Today's baby boomers account for about 28 percent of the population but earn more than half of all personal income.

Marketers typically have paid the most attention to the smaller upper crust of the boomer generation—its more educated, mobile, and wealthy segments. These segments have gone by many names. In the 1980s, they were called "yuppies" (young urban professionals), "bumpies" (black upwardly mobile professionals), "yummies" (young upwardly mobile mommies), and "DINKs" (dual-income, no-kids couples). In the 1990s, yuppies

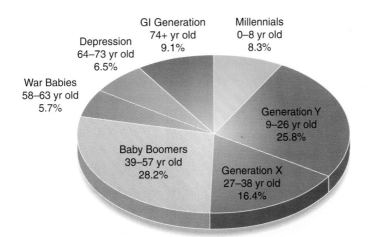

FIGURE 3.3

The Seven U.S. Generations

Source: Adapted from Alison Stein Wellner, "Generational Divide," *American Demographics*, October 2000, pp. 53-58.

and DINKs gave way to a new breed, with names such as "DEWKs" (dual-earners with kids) and "MOBYs" (mother older, baby younger). Now, to the chagrin of many in this generation, they are acquiring such titles as "WOOFs" (well-off older folks) or even "GRUMPIES" (just what the name suggests).

Although the more affluent boomers have grabbed most of the headlines, baby boomers cut across all walks of life, creating a diverse set of target segments for businesses. There are wealthy boomers but also boomers with more modest means. Boomers span a 20-year age range, and almost 25 percent of boomers belong to a racial or ethnic minority.[7]

The youngest boomers are now in their late 30s; the oldest are in their mid- to late 50s. In fact, somewhere in America, seven boomers will turn 50 every minute from now until 2014. By 2025, there will be 64 million baby boomers aged 61 to 79, a 90 percent increase in the size of this population from today. Thus, the boomers have evolved from the "youthquake generation" to the "backache generation." The maturing boomers are experiencing the pangs of midlife and rethinking the purpose and value of their work, responsibilities, and relationships. They are approaching life with a new stability and reasonableness in the way they live, think, eat, and spend. As they continue to age, they will create a large and important seniors market.

As they mature, the boomers are also reaching their peak earning and spending years. Thus, they constitute a lucrative market for new housing and home remodeling, financial services, travel and entertainment, eating out, health and fitness products, and high-priced cars and other luxuries. For example, more than half of all U.S. home remodeling expenditures last year were made by baby boomers.[8]

It would be a mistake to think of the boomers as aging and staid. In fact, the boomers are spending $30 billion a year on *anti*-aging products and services. Consider the following example[9]:

> Dave Conrath walked into the Grooming Lounge in downtown Washington D.C., with one thought in mind: turning back the clock. The 43-year-old commercial builder, who describes himself as "follically challenged," received a cut that puffed up the strands of his thinning blonde hair. He stretched out for a hot shave that seemed to take years off his sun-leathered skin. After a quick massage to loosen the knots in his neck, he headed to the display case for bottles of skin toner, moisturizer, and shaving oil. The trip cost him $100, but he left with a smile. "I feel like I'm 28 again," said Conrath, scrutinizing his reflection in the storefront window. "I work hard and feel that it's okay to drop 100 bucks to look young. . . . I deserve it."

Unlike previous generations, boomers are likely to postpone retirement. Many boomers are rediscovering the excitement of life and have the means to play it out. For

■ The baby boomers: It would be a mistake to think of the boomers as aging and staid. The personal watercraft industry has now virtually abandoned young adult consumers in favor of targeting middle-aged boomers.

example, according to the Travel Industry Association of America, one-half of all U.S. adults took adventure vacations within the past five years. Some 56 percent of these travelers were boomers. The median age of a Harley-Davidson buyer is 46 years old, squarely in the middle of the boomer age range. And the personal watercraft industry has now virtually abandoned young adult consumers in favor of targeting middle-aged boomers and their kids.[10]

> Those one-man, stand-up Jet Skis that used to terrorize beachgoers, with ab-ribbed guys in shell necklaces vaulting over waves on their water hogs, now represent only about 1 percent of the market. New models have wider seats and room for three or even four people, with storage space for coolers and spray shields to keep legs dry. They're practically minivans. . . . The boomers want youthful lifestyle forever.

Generation X

The 45 million people born between 1965 and 1976 in the "birth dearth" following the baby boom.

Generation X. The baby boom was followed by a "birth dearth," creating another generation of 45 million people born between 1965 and 1976. Author Douglas Coupland calls them **Generation X**, because they lie in the shadow of the boomers and lack obvious distinguishing characteristics. Others call them the "baby busters," the "shadow generation," or the "yiffies"—young, individualistic, freedom-minded few.

The Generation Xers are defined as much by their shared experiences as by their age. Increasing divorce rates and higher employment for their mothers made them the first generation of latchkey kids. Having grown up during times of recession and corporate downsizing, they have developed a more cautious economic outlook.

As a result, the GenXers are a more skeptical bunch, cynical of frivolous marketing pitches that promise easy success. They share new cultural concerns. They care about the environment and respond favorably to socially responsible companies. Although they seek success, they are less materialistic; they prize experience, not acquisition. They are cautious romantics who want a better quality of life and are more interested in job satisfaction than in sacrificing personal happiness and growth for promotion.

Once labeled as "the MTV generation" and as body-piercing slackers who whined about "McJobs," the GenXers have now grown up and are beginning to take over. They do surf the Internet more than other groups, but with serious intent. The GenXers are poised to displace the lifestyles, culture, and materialistic values of the baby boomers. They represent close to $736 billion in annual purchasing power. By the year 2010, they will have overtaken the baby boomers as a primary market for almost every product category.[11]

With so much potential, many companies are focusing on GenXers. Consider the following example:

> In a gritty Northside Chicago neighborhood, in a former grocery store here, under an L-train and next to a Trader Joe's, percolates CB2, the store where the definition of home for the next generation of consumers is being refined. Inside, the store pulses with techno-jazz and high-impact displays. The "CB" stands for Crate & Barrel, the "2" signals that the store is a spin-off, a cheekier cousin geared to price-and-design conscious customers in their twenties and thirties. Who are CB2's core consumers? GenXers. They're urban professionals, age 25 to 40, who

are more likely to live in a loft, apartment, or townhouse than a house in the suburbs. They are skeptical, impatient, and highly mobile. They like trends but not gimmicks, and they gravitate to the cool and casual. At CB2, it's taken three years to get the mix right. For example, while Crate & Barrel attracts cooks, CB2 discovered that its core customers spend more time at their computers than at the stove. So gourmet was scaled down and home office beefed up.[12]

Generation Y. Both the baby boomers and GenXers will one day be passing the reins to the latest demographic group, **Generation Y** (also called echo boomers). Born between 1977 and 1994, these children of the baby boomers now number 72 million, dwarfing the GenXers and almost equal in size to the baby boomer segment. Ranging from preteens to mid-20s, the echo boomer generation is still forming its buying preferences and behaviors.

The echo boom has created large kid and teen markets (see Marketing at Work 3.1). With an average disposable income of $100 a week, echo boomers already spend $150 billion a year and influence another $50 billion in family spending. After years of bust, markets for kids' and teen's toys and games, clothes, furniture, and food have enjoyed a boom. Designers and retailers have created new lines, new products, and even new stores devoted to children and teens—Tommy Hilfiger, DKNY, Gap, Toys "*R*" Us, Guess, Talbots, Pottery Barn, and Eddie Bauer, to name just a few. New media appeared that cater specifically to this market: *Time*, *Sports Illustrated*, and *People* have all started new editions for kids and teens. Banks have offered banking and investment services for young people, including investment camps.[13]

Generation Y oldsters are now graduating from college and beginning careers. Like the trailing edge

■ Targeting GenXers: Crate & Barrel's spin-off, CB2, sells edgy products aimed at price-and-design conscious customers aged 25 to 40.

of the Generation Xers ahead of them, one distinguishing characteristic of Generation Y is their utter fluency and comfort with computer, digital, and Internet technology. About 9 of 10 teens have a home computer, half have Internet access, and more than 50 percent of teens 12 to 17 own a mobile phone. In all, they are an impatient, now-oriented bunch. "Blame it on the relentless and dizzying pace of the Internet, 24-hour cable news cycles, cell phones, and TiVo for creating the on-demand, gotta-get-it-now universe in which we live," says one observer. "Perhaps nowhere is the trend more pronounced than among the Gen Y set."[14]

Generation Y represents a complex target for marketers. On average, Gen Ys have access to 62 TV channels, not to mention mobile phones, personal digital assistants (PDAs), and the Internet, offering broad media access. Studies have shown that Gen Y consumers are smart, aware, and fair-minded. They like to be entertained in ads directed at them but don't like ads that make fun of people. They love things that are "green" and they relate well to causes. Making connections now with Gen Ys will pay dividends to

Generation Y
The 72 million children of the baby boomers, born between 1977 and 1994.

Marketing at Work | 3.1

The Teen Market: Youth Will Be Served

Gone are the days when kids saved up their pennies for candy and ice cream at the corner soda fountain. Today's teens are big spenders. The average U.S. teen spends $101 each week; combined, the nation's 32 million 12-to-19-year-olds spend more than $170 billion a year. What's more, teens influence another $30 billion annually of their parents' spending. With so much cash to spend, teens represent a lucrative market for companies willing to cater to their often fickle, trend-driven tastes.

To tap into this vast market of potential new customers, all kinds of companies are targeting teens with new or modified products. Some of these products are naturals for the teen market, such as action movies, acne creams, teen magazines, cell phones, and N Sync. Others are less expected, such as Avon products, cars, and hotels. Here are just a few examples of companies attempting to cash in on the hot teen market:

■ *Wildseed:* Cell phone manufacturer Wildseed has spent years conducting research to develop cell phones for teens. For the past two years, the company has regularly summoned teenagers to focus groups, where it pays them $20 to lounge around, eat pizza, play Xbox video games, and give their thumbs up or thumbs down on various proposals. The research shows that for teenagers, a desirable cell phone is not about smaller, lighter, sleeker. What teens want from a cell phone ranges from the concrete (music, messaging, and games) to the abstract (style, personality, and individ-

uality). As a result, Wildseed phones have "smart skins"—replaceable faceplates with computer chips that allow teens to individualize the phone's functions and appearance to match their personalities. For example, skateboarders can choose graffiti-splattered

faceplates that come with edgy urban ringer tones and gritty icons.
■ *Teen Vogue:* After years of preliminary market testing, *Vogue* launched the first issue of the teen version of its popular women's magazine in early 2003. The publisher, Condé Nast,

Marketing to teens: Based on focus group research, Wildseed developed cell phones with "smart skins"—replaceable faceplates with computer chips that let teens individualize the phone's functions and appearance to match their personalities.

marketers beyond capturing their current spending. In future years, as they begin working and their buying power increases, this segment will more than rival the baby boomers in spending and market influence.[15]

Generational Marketing. Do marketers have to create separate products and marketing programs for each generation? Some experts caution that each generation spans decades

built an initial subscription base of more than 450,000 teens and expects the readership to expand to more than 750,000. In addition to including articles on fashion and stunning pictures, Condé Nast has decreased the size of the magazine, measuring only 6 3/4 inches by 9 1/8 inches, perfect for hiding in class.

■ *Hot Topic:* Clothing retailer Hot Topic targets the 17 percent of American high school students who consider themselves "alternative teens." Hot Topic's buyers go to rock concerts and raves to check out what performers and fashion-forward fans are wearing. The store carries an assortment of items you just won't find at Abercrombie & Fitch. Rather than khakis and tank tops, the store stocks pinstripe fishnet stockings, pink fur pants, feather boas, blue hair dye, black nail polish, and Morbid Makeup. Teens can buy T-shirts from TV shows such as "SpongeBob SquarePants," Kermit the Frog underwear, and licensed concert apparel from rockers such as Eminem, Marilyn Manson, Tool, and Linkin Park. Whereas Gap, American Eagle, and other teen retailers have recently reported flat or declining sales, Hot Topic's sales are, well, a hot topic. Sales have increased an average of 37 percent annually for the last three years.

■ *Avon:* Avon will soon roll out a Teen Business unit to target teenage buyers. The new department will employ teens as sales associates who sell to other teens through catalogs, the Internet, and slumber parties and other informal gatherings. Can a company known for its appeal to 25-to-55-year-old middle American-women sell successfully to teens and young women? Avon thinks so. The new brand is dis-

tinctly more upscale and trendier than Avon's traditional look. "This is very much not just another brand," says Avon's chief executive, Andrea Jung.

■ *Rockport:* When you think of Rockport, you probably think of casual shoes and clothing for the older set. However, in an attempt to build relationships with 12-to-19-year-olds, Rockport recently teamed up with Dubit, a youth-focused company in the United Kingdom, to produce a 3D online store targeting teens (www.dubit.co.uk). Teens roaming Dubit's virtual mall can enter the Rockport store and check out shoes with real youth appeal—such as the Copepoda Crustacean, a sleek "performance sandal with a rubber outsole," or the Tactonic Open Road, a "retro bowling style trainer with a contrast stitching." In the corner of the store, a deejay takes requests and spins digital tracks onto a personalized MP3 player.

■ *The Gorham Hotel:* Hotels and resorts are becoming more and more aware of the impact teens have on family vacation decisions. According to one study, 82 percent of parents said they choose vacations based on their kids' input. As a result, many hotels are catering to teens by offering family packages that include access to teen nightclubs, special teen-oriented outings, and computer rooms with unlimited Internet access. At the Gorham Hotel in New York, catering to teens means giving them a little space—in their parents' rooms. Special suites have denlike rooms with their own doors, pull-out sofas, televisions, phones, even Nintendo. Downstairs, in the lobby, the Gorham offers 24-hour access to the Internet.

■ *The National Cattlemen's Beef Association:* It's hard to imagine Robert Mitchum or Sam Elliott (the two men who have gruffly voiced the "Beef. It's what's for dinner" tagline) dominating discussion at a slumber party. . . . Yet the National Cattlemen's Beef Association is plenty interested in this young teen female cohort. It has been using Sasha Cohen, the 4-foot-11, 19-year-old figure skater, as a spokeswoman for the past several years. And now it has launched a girl-power-themed Web site, Cool-2B-Real.com, aimed at 8-to-12-year-olds (many of whom, the NCBA is well aware, are already vegetarians). Outfitted in pastel pinks, blues and yellows, the site looks a lot like Barbie.com, if you ignore the hamburger in the middle of the page. It offers games like "Burger Boggle" and "Grillin' & Chillin'," as well as polls, quizzes, chat rooms, message boards and, of course, recipes (almost all of which include beef).

Sources: Examples adapted from those found in Frand Washington, "Aim Young; No, Younger," *Advertising Age,* April 9, 2001; Nancy Keates, "Family Travel: Catering to Kids," *Wall Street Journal,* May 3, 2002, p. W-1; Jennifer Lee, "Youth Will Be Served, Wirelessly," *New York Times,* May 30, 2002, p. G1; Sally Beatty, "Avon Set to Sell to Teens," *Wall Street Journal,* October 17, 2002, p. B1; and Tim Nudd, "Beef. It's, Like, What's for Dinner," *Adweek,* March 17, 2003, p. 46. Also see "Hot Topic, Inc.," *Hoover Company Profiles,* Austin, May 15, 2003; Leslie Earnest, "California: Hot Topic Results Suit It to a Tee," *The Los Angeles Times,* March 5, 2003, p. C2; "Rockport Opens 3D Shop on Teen Web Site," *Marketing Week,* May 23, 2002, p. 39; Jon Fine, "Teen Vogue Takes Sophisticate Route," *Advertising Age,* January 13, 2003, p. 45; "Teens Spent $170 Billion in 2002," press release, Teenage Research Unlimited, February 17, 2003, accessed online at www.teenresearch.com/PRview.cfm?edit_id=152; and Arlene Weintraub, "Hotter Than a Pair of Vinyl Jeans," *Business Week,* June 9, 2003, pp. 84–85.

of time and many socioeconomic levels. For example, marketers often split the baby boomers into three smaller groups—leading boomers, core boomers, and trailing boomers—each with its own beliefs and behaviors. Similarly, they split Generation Y into Gen Y adults, Gen Y teens, and Gen Y kids. Thus, marketers need to form more precise age-specific segments within each group. More important, defining people by their birth date may be less effective than segmenting them by their lifestyle or life stage.

Others warn that marketers have to be careful about turning off one generation each time they craft a product or message that appeals effectively to another. "The idea is to try to be broadly inclusive and at the same time offer each generation something specifically designed for it," notes one expert. "Tommy Hilfiger has big brand logos on his clothes for teenagers and little pocket polo logos on his shirts for baby boomers. It's a brand that has a more inclusive than exclusive strategy."[16]

The Changing American Family The "traditional household" consists of a husband, wife, and children (and sometimes grandparents). Yet, the once American ideal of the two-child, two-car suburban family has lately been losing some of its luster. "Ward and June Cleaver used to represent the typical American household," says one demographer. "Today, marketers would be remiss in not incorporating the likes of Murphy Brown, Ally McBeal, and Will and Grace into their business plans."[17]

In the United States today, married couples with children now make up only about 34 percent of the nation's 105 million households, and this percentage is falling. Married couples and people living with other relatives make up 22 percent; single parents comprise another 12 percent. A full 32 percent are nonfamily households—single live-alones or adult live-togethers of one or both sexes.[18] More people are divorcing or separating, choosing not to marry, marrying later, or marrying without intending to have children. Marketers must increasingly consider the special needs of nontraditional households, because they are now growing more rapidly than traditional households. Each group has distinctive needs and buying habits.

■ The changing American family: Non-family households—single live-alones or adult live-togethers of one or both sexes—make up a full 32 percent of U.S. households. Today's marketers must incorporate "the likes of Murphy Brown, Ally McBeal, and Will and Grace into their business plans."

The number of working women has also increased greatly, growing from under 30 percent of the U.S. workforce in 1950 to just over 60 percent today.[19] However, that trend may be slowing. After increasing steadily for 25 years, the percentage of women with children under age 1 in the workforce has fallen during the past few years. Meanwhile, men are staying home with their children in record numbers. Last year, more than 1.7 million stay-at-home dads managed the household while their wives went to work.

The significant number of women in the workforce has spawned the child-day-care business and increased consumption of convenience foods and services, career-oriented women's clothing, financial services, and many other business opportunities. For example, new niche malls feature customized mixes of specialty shops with extended hours for working women who can find time to shop only before or after work. Stores in these malls feature targeted promotions and phone-in shopping. Busy shoppers can phone ahead with color choices and other preferences while store employees perform a "wardrobe consulting" service.[20]

Geographic Shifts in Population This is a period of great migratory movements between and within countries. Americans, for example, are a mobile people, with about 16 percent of all U.S. residents moving each year.[21] Over the past two decades, the U.S. population has shifted toward the Sunbelt states. The West and South have grown, while the Midwest and Northeast states have lost population. Such population shifts interest marketers because people in different regions buy differently. For example, research shows that people in Seattle buy more toothbrushes per capita than people in any other U.S. city; people in Salt Lake City eat more candy bars; people from New Orleans use more ketchup; and people in Miami drink more prune juice.

Also, for more than a century, Americans have been moving from rural to metropolitan areas. In the 1950s, they made a massive exit from the cities to the suburbs. Today, the migration to the suburbs continues. And more and more Americans are moving to "micropolitan areas," small cities located beyond congested metropolitan areas. These smaller micros offer many of the advantages of metro areas—jobs, restaurants, diversions, community organizations—but without the population crush, traffic jams, high crime rates, and high property taxes often associated with heavily urbanized areas.[22]

The shift in where people live has also caused a shift in where they work. For example, the migration toward micropolitan and suburban areas has resulted in a rapid increase in the number of people who "telecommute"—work at home or in a remote office and conduct their business by phone, fax, modem, or the Internet. This trend, in turn, has created a booming SOHO (small office/home office) market. One in every five Americans are now working out of their homes with the help of electronic conveniences such as personal computers, cell phones, fax machines, and handheld organizers. Many marketers are actively courting the home office segment of this lucrative SOHO market. One example is Kinko's:

> Founded in the 1970s as a campus photocopying business, Kinko's is now reinventing itself as a document solutions provider for businesses, ranging from small offices to Fortune 500 companies. For the SOHO segment, Kinko's has become a well-appointed office outside the home. Where once there were copy machines, Kinko's 1,100 stores in this country and abroad now feature a uniform mixture of fax machines, ultrafast color printers, and networks of computers equipped with popular software programs and high-speed Internet connections. People can come to a Kinko's store to do all their office jobs: They can copy, send and receive faxes, use various programs on the computer, go on the Internet, order stationery and other printed supplies, rent a conference room, and even teleconference. As more and more people join the work-at-home trend, Kinko's offers an escape from the isolation of the home office. Besides adding state-of-the-art equipment, the company is talking to Starbucks about opening up coffee shops adjacent to some Kinko's.[23]

A Better-Educated and More White-Collar Population The U.S. population is becoming better educated. For example, in 2002, 84 percent of the U.S. population over age 25 had completed high school and 27 percent had completed college, compared with 69 percent and 17 percent in 1980. Moreover, nearly two-thirds of high school graduates now enroll in college within 12 months of graduating.[24] The rising number of educated people will increase the demand for quality products, books, magazines, travel, personal computers, and Internet services.

The workforce also is becoming more white collar. Between 1950 and 1985, the proportion of white-collar workers rose from 41 percent to 54 percent, that of blue-collar workers declined from 47 percent to 33 percent, and that of service workers increased from 12 percent to 14 percent. Between 1983 and 1999, the proportion of managers and professionals in the work force increased from 23 percent to more than 30 percent. These trends have continued into the new century.[25]

Increasing Diversity Countries vary in their ethnic and racial makeup. At one extreme is Japan, where almost everyone is Japanese. At the other extreme is the United States, with people from virtually all nations. The United States has often been called a melting pot—diverse groups from many nations and cultures have melted into a single, more homogeneous whole. Instead, the United States seems to have become more of a "salad bowl," in which various groups have mixed together but have maintained their diversity by retaining and valuing important ethnic and cultural differences.

Marketers are facing increasingly diverse markets, both at home and abroad as their operations become more international in scope. The U.S. population is 71 percent white, with African Americans and Hispanics each making up another 12 percent. Asian Americans now totals about 4 percent of the U.S. population, with the remaining 1 percent made up of American Indian, Eskimo, and Aleut. These ethnic populations are expected to explode during the next 20 years. During that time, the number of African Americans will increase 25 percent, and the numbers of Hispanics and Asian Americans will double. Moreover, nearly 26 million people living in the United States—more than 9 percent of the population—were born in another country.[26]

Most large companies, from Sears, Wal-Mart, and Bank of America to Levi Strauss, Procter & Gamble, and General Mills, now target specially designed products and promotions to one or more of these groups. General Mills targets the African American market with separate campaigns for its Big G cereals—Cheerios, Trix, Honey Nut Cheerios, and Cinnamon Toast Crunch. The campaigns consist of advertising, sponsorships, sampling, and community-based promotions that feature a strong family emphasis. For example, for the past several years, Honey Nut Cheerios has been the title sponsor of the Universal Circus and for a "Soul Fest" music event that travels to 30 urban markets.

Similarly, Bank of America is quadrupling its multicultural budget this year, to $40 million. Based on customer research and careful study of cultural differences, it has developed different advertising messages for Hispanic, Asian, and African American markets.

For Asians, the brand platform is "tangibly committed to the success and growth of all Americans." One commercial shot in China, Korea, and Vietnam—

■ Based on careful study of cultural differences, Bank of America has developed targeted advertising messages for different cultural subgroups, here Asians and Hispanics.

the beginning of an immigrant's journey—flashes back to a boy teaching his younger brother to ride a bike in his homeland. It then draws parallels with the helping hand today of Bank of America with a mortgage. The bike used in the ad is the exact kind an Asian child would learn to ride, not an American kids' bicycle. In contrast, one of the Hispanic spots opens on an exaggerated stack of mortgage-related paperwork the size of a house, and details how Bank of America can reduce it by 80 percent. The ads will run in the appropriate language—Spanish, Chinese, Korean, or Vietnamese—to target consumers who prefer to communicate in their native tongue.[27]

Diversity goes beyond ethnic heritage. For example, many major companies have recently begun to target gay and lesbian consumers explicitly. A Simmons Research study of readers of the National Gay Newspaper Guild's 12 publications found that, compared to the average American, respondents are 12 times more likely to be in professional jobs, almost twice as likely to own a vacation home, 8 times more likely to own a notebook computer, and twice as likely to own individual stocks. They are twice as likely as the general population to have a household income between $60,000 and $250,000. More than two-thirds have graduated from college, and 20 percent hold a master's degree. In addition, gays and lesbians tend to be early adopters, with word-of-mouth clout in their communities, making them a very attractive market segment.

Although measuring the size and impact of the gay market can be difficult, some experts estimate that 5 to 6 percent of the U.S. population—some 14 to 15 million people—freely identify as gay. Others estimate that gays account for as much as 10 percent of the U.S. population, with buying power of $450 billion. As a result, many large companies now target their products and services directly to gay consumers. For example, ad spending to reach gay and lesbian consumers is booming. Gay.com, a Web site that attracts more than 2 million unique visitors each month, has attracted a diverse set of well-known advertisers, from IBM, eBay, Quicken Mortgage, Saturn, and AT&T to American Airlines and Neiman Marcus. Other companies that target gays directly include American Express, Ford, Miller Brewing Company, Absolut Vodka, Johnson & Johnson, and John Hancock Financial Services. Here are examples of gay and lesbian marketing efforts[28]:

> American Express Financial Advisors launched print ads that depict same-sex couples planning their financial futures. The ads ran in *Out* and *The Advocate*, the two highest-circulation national gay publications. The company's director of segment marketing, Margaret Vergeyle, said: "We're targeting gay audiences with targeted ads and promotions that are relevant to them and say that we understand their specific needs. Often, gay couples are very concerned about issues like Social Security benefits and estate planning, since same-sex marriages often are not recognized under the law."

> The sleek jaguar whizzes past a curve, with the advertising tag line: "Life is full of twists and turns. Care for a partner?" It's Ford's latest commercial pitch—one where the word "partner" has a double meaning. Gays and lesbians are the target market here. The Jaguar ads are noteworthy because they come from one of America's biggest corporations and are gay-specific, rather than simply a general-interest ad running in a gay publication. "We believe in messaging that connects with the consumer," says Jan Valentic, vice president of global marketing for Ford.

> Avis, the rental car company, dedicated about 5 percent of its advertising and marketing budget to the gay community in 2003. Its ad campaign highlights its policy for domestic partners to automatically be included as additional drivers. "It's a loyal group and an affluent group, and one that our research shows will respond to marketing that speaks directly to their consumer needs,

says an Avis spokesperson. Avis' strategy includes the sponsorship of gay pride festivals and the placement of coupons noting that for every rental, Avis will donate a dollar to the nonprofit Gay and Lesbian Alliance Against Defamation.

Miller Brewing Company recently ran an ad which featured two women trying to attract a man in a bar by buying him a Miller Lite. When a second man enters, the women grow even bubblier. Then the two men lock hands. The humor of the ad, via the disappointment of the women was "a real home run," say Howard Buford, of Prime Access, Inc., the multicultural ad agency that created the Miller and Jaguar ads. "Women enjoyed it and gay men really liked it. Straight men really enjoyed it."

Another attractive segment is the more than 54 million people with disabilities in the United States—a market larger than African Americans or Hispanics—representing almost $1 trillion in annual spending power. People with mobility challenges are an ideal target market for companies such as Peapod (www.peapod.com), which teams up with large supermarket chains in many heavily populated areas to offer online grocery shopping and home delivery. They also represent a growing market for travel, sports, and other leisure-oriented products and services. Consider the following examples[29]:

Julie Perez sees the difference when she goes to the Divi Hotels resort at Flamingo Beach on the Caribbean island of Bonaire. "It's famous for being totally accessible," she says. "The hotel brochures show the wheelchair access. The dive staff are trained and aware, and they really want to take disabled people diving. They're not afraid." Perez, 35, of Ventura, California, is an experienced scuba diver, a travel agent—and a quadriplegic. Before she had children, she made five trips a year to the Caribbean; these days, she gets there only once or twice a year.

Volkswagen targets people with disabilities who want to travel. For example, it recently launched a special marketing campaign for its EuroVan. The campaign touted the EuroVan's extra-wide doors, high ceilings, and overall roominess as features that accommodate most wheelchair lifts and make driving more fun for those traditionally ignored by mainstream automakers. To make the EuroVan even more accessible, Volkswagen offers its Mobility Access Program. Drivers with disabilities who purchase or lease any VW can take advantage of $1,500 in purchase assistance for modifications such as hand controls and wheelchair lifts. Volkswagen even modified its catchy tag line "Drivers Wanted" to appeal to motorists with disabilities, coining the new slogan "All Drivers Wanted." The VW Web site sums up, "We build cars for people who love to drive. Some just happen to use wheelchairs."

■ Volkswagon targets people with disabilities who want to travel. It offers a Mobility Access Program and has even modified its catchy "Drivers Wanted" tag line to appeal to motorists with disabilities: "All Drivers Wanted."

As the population in the United States grows more diverse, successful marketers will continue to diversify their marketing programs to take advantage of opportunities in fast-growing segments. Says one expert, "diversity will be more than a buzzword—diversity will be the key to economic survival."[30]

Linking the Concepts

SPEED BUMP

Pull over here for a moment and think about how deep an impact these demographic factors have on all of us and, as a result, on marketers' strategies.

- Apply these demographic developments to your own life. Think of some specific examples of how the changing demographic factors affect you and your buying behavior.
- Identify a specific company that has done a good job of reacting to the shifting demographic environment—generational segments (baby boomers, GenXers, or Generation Y), the changing American family, and increased diversity. Compare this company to one that's done a poor job.

Economic Environment

Markets require buying power as well as people. The **economic environment** consists of factors that affect consumer purchasing power and spending patterns. Nations vary greatly in their levels and distribution of income. Some countries have *subsistence economies*—they consume most of their own agricultural and industrial output. These countries offer few market opportunities. At the other extreme are *industrial economies*, which constitute rich markets for many different kinds of goods. Marketers must pay close attention to major trends and consumer spending patterns both across and within their world markets. Following are some of the major economic trends in the United States.

Economic environment
Factors that affect consumer buying power and spending patterns.

Changes in Income During the 1980s—tabbed the "roaring 80s" by some—American consumers fell into a consumption frenzy, fueled by income growth, federal tax reductions, rapid increases in housing values, and a boom in borrowing. They bought and bought, seemingly without caution, amassing record levels of debt. "It was fashionable to describe yourself as 'born to shop.' When the going gets tough, it was said, the tough go shopping."[31] Entering the 1990s, the baby boom generation moved into its prime wage-earning years, and the number of small families headed by dual-career couples continued to increase. Thus, many consumers continued to demand quality products and better service, and they were able to pay for them.

However, the free spending and high expectations of the 1980s were dashed by a recession in the early 1990s. In fact, the 1990s become the decade of the "squeezed consumer." Along with rising incomes in some segments came increased financial burdens. Consumers faced repaying debts acquired during earlier spending splurges, increased household and family expenses, and saving ahead for college tuition payments and retirement. These financially squeezed consumers sobered up, pulled back, and adjusted to their changing financial situations. They spent more carefully and sought greater value in the products and services they bought. *Value marketing* became the watchword for many marketers.

Now, in the 2000s, consumers continue to spend carefully.[32] Hence, the trend toward value marketing continues. Rather than offering high quality at a high price, or lesser quality at very low prices, marketers are looking for ways to offer today's more financially cautious buyers greater value—just the right combination of product quality and good service at a fair price.

Marketers should pay attention to *income distribution* as well as to average income. Income distribution in the United States is still very skewed. At the top are *upper-class* consumers, whose spending patterns are not affected by current economic events and who are a major market for luxury goods. There is a comfortable *middle class* that is somewhat careful about its spending but can still afford the good life some of the time. The *working class* must stick close to the basics of food, clothing, and shelter and must try hard to save. Finally, the *underclass* (persons on welfare and many retirees) must count their pennies when making even the most basic purchases.

Over the past three decades, the rich have grown richer, the middle class has shrunk, and the poor have remained poor. In 1998, the top 5 percent of income-earning households in the United States captured more than 21 percent of the aggregate income, up from 17.5 percent in 1967. Last year, 12 percent of American households had an annual income of $100,000 or more, compared to just 4 percent in the early 1990s. Meanwhile, the share of income captured by the bottom 20 percent of income-earning households decreased from 4 percent to 3.6 percent.[33] This distribution of income has created a two-tiered market. Many companies are aggressively targeting the affluent:

> Driven by [growing wealth in the affluent segment,] marketers have responded with a ceaseless array of pricey, upscale products aimed at satisfying wealthy Americans' appetite for "the very best": leather-lined SUVs as big as tanks, $1,300 sheets, restaurant-quality appliances, and vast cruise ships offering every form of luxurious coddling. . . . Huge increases in wealth among the very rich have fueled the sales of $17,500 Patek Philippe watches that are sold as family heirlooms (thus justifying the price tag), created the clamor for a $48,000 Lexus (options extra), and resulted in a two-year waiting list for $14,000 Hermes Kelly bags.[34]

Other companies are now tailoring their marketing offers to two different markets—the affluent and the less affluent. For example, Walt Disney Company markets two distinct Winnie-the-Pooh bears:

> The original line-drawn figure appears on fine china, pewter spoons, and pricey kids' stationery found in upscale specialty and department stores such as

■ Income distribution: Walt Disney markets two distinct Pooh bears to match its two-tiered market.

Upscale

Pewter cup **$56**

Classic Pooh dress **$85**

Stuffed bear by Gund **$25**

Royal Doulton dish set **$40**

Downscale

Kmart jumper **$14**

Plastic cup **$6**

Plush cartoon Pooh **$15**

Plastic dish set **$15**

Nordstrom and Bloomingdale's. The plump, cartoonlike Pooh, clad in a red shirt and a goofy smile, adorns plastic key chains, polyester bed sheets, and animated videos. It sells in Wal-Mart stores and five-and-dime shops. Except at Disney's own stores, the two Poohs do not share the same retail shelf. [Thus, Disney offers both] upstairs [upscale?] and downstairs [downscale?] Poohs, hoping to land customers on both sides of the [income] divide.[35]

Changing Consumer Spending Patterns Table 3.1 shows the proportion of total expenditures made by U.S. households at different income levels for major categories of goods and services. Food, housing, and transportation use up most household income. However, consumers at different income levels have different spending patterns. Some of these differences were noted over a century ago by Ernst Engel, who studied how people shifted their spending as their income rose (see Table 3.1). He found that as family income rises, the percentage spent on food declines, the percentage spent on housing remains about constant (except for utilities such as gas, electricity, and public services, which decrease), and both the percentage spent on most other categories and that devoted to savings increase. **Engel's laws** generally have been supported by later studies.

Changes in major economic variables such as income, cost of living, interest rates, and savings and borrowing patterns have a large impact on the marketplace. Companies watch these variables by using economic forecasting. Businesses do not have to be wiped out by an economic downturn or caught short in a boom. With adequate warning, they can take advantage of changes in the economic environment.

Engel's laws
Differences noted over a century ago by Ernst Engel in how people shift their spending across food, housing, transportation, health care, and other goods and services categories as family income rises.

Natural Environment

The **natural environment** involves the natural resources that are needed as inputs by marketers or that are affected by marketing activities. Environmental concerns have grown steadily during the past three decades. In many cities around the world, air and water pollution have reached dangerous levels. World concern continues to mount about the possibilities of global warming, and many environmentalists fear that we soon will be buried in our own trash.

Natural environment
Natural resources that are needed as inputs by marketers or that are affected by marketing activities.

TABLE 3.1   Consumer Spending at Different Income Levels

	Percent of Spending at Different Income Levels			
Expenditure	$10–15,000	$20–30,000	$30–40,000	$70,000 and Over
Food	16.5	15.7	14.3	11.9
Housing	26.5	24.7	23.6	26.0
Utilities	9.7	8.6	7.5	5.0
Clothing	4.2	3.7	4.6	4.6
Transportation	17.1	19.7	21.3	18.2
Health care	8.7	7.3	6.2	3.8
Entertainment	3.8	4.1	4.6	5.2
Contributions	2.9	3.1	3.0	3.6
Insurance	3.4	6.2	8.5	15.2

Source: Consumer Expenditure Survey, 2001, U.S. Department of Labor, Bureau of Labor Statistics, accessed online at www.bls.gov/cex/csxann01.pdf, April 2003.

Marketers should be aware of several trends in the natural environment. The first involves growing *shortages of raw materials*. Air and water may seem to be infinite resources, but some groups see long-run dangers. Air pollution chokes many of the world's large cities, and water shortages are already a big problem in some parts of the United States and the world. Renewable resources, such as forests and food, also have to be used wisely. Nonrenewable resources, such as oil, coal, and various minerals, pose a serious problem. Firms making products that require these scarce resources face large cost increases, even if the materials do remain available.

A second environmental trend is *increased pollution*. Industry will almost always damage the quality of the natural environment. Consider the disposal of chemical and nuclear wastes; the dangerous mercury levels in the ocean; the quantity of chemical pollutants in the soil and food supply; and the littering of the environment with nonbiodegradable bottles, plastics, and other packaging materials.

A third trend is *increased government intervention* in natural resource management. The governments of different countries vary in their concern and efforts to promote a clean environment. Some, like the German government, vigorously pursue environmental quality. Others, especially many poorer nations, do little about pollution, largely because they lack the needed funds or political will. Even the richer nations lack the vast funds and political accord needed to mount a worldwide environmental effort. The general hope is that companies around the world will accept more social responsibility, and that less expensive devices can be found to control and reduce pollution.

In the United States, the Environmental Protection Agency (EPA) was created in 1970 to set and enforce pollution standards and to conduct pollution research. In the future, companies doing business in the United States can expect continued strong controls from government and pressure groups. Instead of opposing regulation, marketers should help develop solutions to the material and energy problems facing the world.

Concern for the natural environment has spawned the so-called green movement. Today, enlightened companies go beyond what government regulations dictate. They are developing *environmentally sustainable* strategies and practices in an effort to create a world economy that the planet can support indefinitely. They are responding to consumer demands with ecologically safer products, recyclable or biodegradable packaging, recycled materials and components, better pollution controls, and more energy-efficient operations.

3M runs a Pollution Prevention Pays program that helps prevent pollution at the source—in products and manufacturing processes. Between 1975 and 2001, the program prevented 821,344 tons of pollutants and saved $857 million. AT&T uses a special software package to choose the least harmful materials, cut hazardous waste, reduce energy use, and improve product recycling in its operations. McDonald's eliminated polystyrene cartons years ago and now uses paper-based packaging and napkins that contain recycled content. Beyond this, the company has a long-standing rainforest policy and a commitment to purchasing recycled products and energy-efficient restaurant construction techniques. UPS's fleet now includes 1,800 energy-efficient, low-polluting alternative-fuel vehicles. And Starbucks is buying more organic and shade-grown coffee, a move that minimizes damage to rain forests. More and more, companies are recognizing the link between a healthy economy and a healthy ecology.[36]

■ Environmental responsibility: McDonald's has made a substantial commitment to the so-called "green movement."

Technological Environment

The **technological environment** is perhaps the most dramatic force now shaping our destiny. Technology has released such wonders as antibiotics, organ transplants, notebook computers, and the Internet. It also has released such horrors as nuclear missiles, chemical weapons, and assault rifles. It has released such mixed blessings as the automobile, television, and credit cards. Our attitude toward technology depends on whether we are more impressed with its wonders or its blunders. For example, what would you think about having tiny little transmitters implanted in all of the products you buy that would allow tracking products from their point of production though use and disposal? On the one hand, it would provide many advantages. On the other hand, it could be a bit scary. Either way, it probably won't be long before it happens (see Marketing at Work 3.2).

Technological environment
Forces that create new technologies, creating new product and market opportunities.

The technological environment changes rapidly. Think of all of today's common products that were not available 100 years ago or even 30 years ago. Abraham Lincoln did not know about automobiles, airplanes, radios, or the electric light. Woodrow Wilson did not know about television, aerosol cans, automatic dishwashers, air conditioners, antibiotics, or computers. Franklin Delano Roosevelt did not know about xerography, synthetic detergents, tape recorders, birth control pills, or earth satellites. John F. Kennedy did not know about personal computers, DVD players, or the World Wide Web.

New technologies create new markets and opportunities. However, every new technology replaces an older technology. Transistors hurt the vacuum-tube industry, xerography hurt the carbon-paper business, the auto hurt the railroads, and compact disks hurt phonograph records. When old industries fought or ignored new technologies, their businesses declined. Thus, marketers should watch the technological environment closely. Companies that do not keep up with technological change soon will find their products outdated. And they will miss new product and market opportunities.

■ Technological environment: Technology is perhaps the most dramatic force shaping the marketing environment. Here, a herder makes a call on his cell phone.

The United States leads the world in research and development spending. Total U.S. R&D spending reached an estimated $302 billion in 2003. The federal government was the largest R&D spender, at $108 billion.[37] Scientists today are researching a wide range of promising new products and services, ranging from practical solar energy, electric cars, and cancer cures to voice-controlled computers and genetically engineered food crops. Today's research usually is carried out by research teams rather than by lone inventors such as Thomas Edison, Samuel Morse, or Alexander Graham Bell. Many companies are adding marketing people to R&D teams to try to obtain a stronger marketing orientation. Scientists also speculate about fantasy products, such as flying cars, three-dimensional televisions, and space colonies. The challenge in each case is not only technical but also commercial—to make *practical, affordable* versions of these products.

As products and technology become more complex, the public needs to know that these are safe. Thus, government agencies investigate and ban potentially unsafe products. In the United States, the Food and Drug Administration (FDA) has set up complex regulations for testing new drugs. The Consumer Product Safety Commission sets safety standards for consumer products and penalizes companies that fail to meet them. Such regulations have resulted in much higher research costs and in longer times between new-product ideas and their introduction. Marketers should be aware of these regulations when applying new technologies and developing new products.

Marketing at Work | 3.2

Tiny Transmitters in Every Product: Is This Great Technology, or What?

Envision a world in which every product contains a tiny transmitter, loaded with information. Imagine a time when we could track every item electronically— anywhere in the world, at any time, automatically. Producers could track the precise flow of goods up and down the supply chain, ensuring timely deliveries and lowering inventory and distribution costs. Retailers could track real-time merchandise movements in their stores, helping them manage inventories, keep shelves full, and automatically reorder goods.

And think about the whole new world that such technology would create for consumers. Picture this futuristic scenario:

As you stroll through the aisles of your supermarket, you pluck a six-pack of your favorite beverage from the shelf. Shelf sensors detect your selection and beam an ad to the screen on your shopping cart. The ad offers special deals on salty snacks that might go great with your beverage. When you reach the shampoo section, electronic readers scan your cart and note that you haven't made the usual monthly purchase of your favorite brand. "Did you forget the shampoo?" asks the screen. As your shopping cart fills, scanners detect that you might be buying for a dinner party. The screen suggests a wine that complements the meal you've planned. After shopping, you bag your groceries and

head for home. Exit scanners automatically total up your purchases and charge them to your credit card. At home, readers track what goes into and out of your pantry, automatically updating your shopping list when stocks run low. To plan your Sunday dinner, you scan the Butterball turkey you just purchased. An embedded transmitter chip yields serving instructions and recipes for several side dishes. You pop the bird into your "smart oven," which follows instructions coded on the chip and cooks the Turkey to perfection. Is this great technology, or what?

Seem far-fetched? Not according to the Auto-ID Center. Founded in 1999,

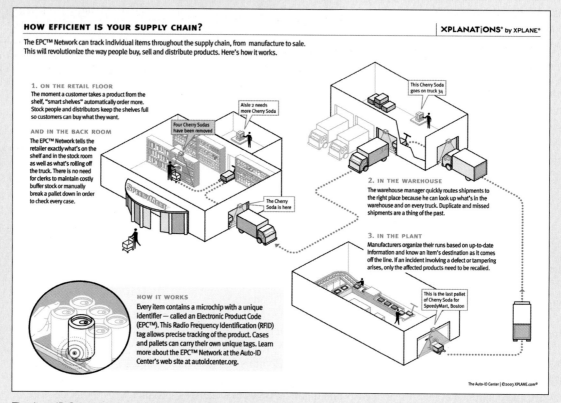

The Auto-ID Center aims "to change the world" by developing tiny transmitters that can be imbedded in products, benefiting both sellers and consumers.

the Center formed a unique partnership among almost 100 global companies and five of the world's leading research universities. The Auto-ID Center's aim was "to change the world . . . to give companies something that, until now, they have only dreamed of: near-perfect supply chain visibility." This seems like a lofty mission. But it might soon become a reality with the backing of such marketing heavyweights as Wal-Mart, Home Depot, Target, Best Buy, Procter & Gamble, Coca-Cola, IBM, Gillette, Michelin, and the U.S. Post Office.

The Auto-ID Center developed tiny, affordable radio-frequency identification (RFID) transmitters—or smart chips—that can be embedded in all of the products you buy. The transmitters are so small that several would fit on the head of a pin. Yet they can be packed with coded information and can be read and rewritten at any point in the supply chain. Auto-ID technology provides producers and retailers with amazing new ways to track inventories, trends, and sales. They can use embedded chips to follow products—everything from ice cream and cat food to tires, insulation, and jet engines—step by step from factories, to warehouses, to retail shelves, to recycling centers.

The smart chips make today's bar code systems seem badly outmoded. Whereas bar codes must be visible to be read, embedded RFID chips can be read in any location. Bar codes identify only a product's manufacturer. In contrast, the chips can identify each individual product item and can carry codes that, when paired with a database containing the details, reveal an almost endless supply of information. Thus, beyond identifying an item as a gallon of Borden 2% skim milk, an embedded smart chip can identify that *specific* gallon of milk—its manufacture date, expiration date, location in the supply chain, and a storehouse of other product-specific information.

Although it may seem futuristic, Auto-ID technology is already being tested at several sites across the United States and the United Kingdom. Recently, Gillette ordered a half-billion chips and launched two RFID pilot projects. The first project uses embedded transmitters to track products from the factory to grocery store shelves. Gillette hopes that the technology will improve service to its retail customers while at the same time reducing its inventories from 5 percent to 25 percent. In the second project, Gillette has installed readers on shelves in selected Wal-Mart and Tesco stores. It claims that retailers lose more than $30 billion a year in sales because shelves aren't fully stocked. The shelf readers track Gillette's razors as they come and go, and prompt store staff to restock when quantities dwindle. "We'll have a world where shelves are always full," says Gillette's vice president for global business management. The readers also alert staff when unusually large quantities of razors leave a shelf in a short time, helping to reduce theft.

Michelin is also testing the chips, in this case to help it comply with federal regulations that govern tracing products in the event of a recall. The tire maker plans to embed the chips in tires installed on passenger cars and light trucks for the 2005 model year. At the factory, it will include information such as time and date of manufacture, tire size and dimensions, plant location, and vehicle identification numbers.

In addition to mega-marketers like Gillette, Michelin, and Wal-Mart, smaller retailers are putting smart chips to work. Fashion retailer Prada recently installed the chips in its store in New York City. Based on scans of items in customers hands, video screens show personalized product demonstrations and designer sketches. In dressing rooms, readers identify each item of clothing a customer tries on and offers additional size, color, and design information through interactive touch screens.

With innovations like these, you'd think most consumers would welcome the tiny transmitters. But some consumers and many consumer advocates worry about invasion-of-privacy issues. If companies can link products to specific consumers and track consumer buying and usage, they fear, marketers would gain access to too much personal information. Says one analyst, "backers of the technology appear torn between the urge to hype its huge potential and fear that consumers will get spooked."

To counter these concerns, Auto-ID technology proponents point out that the transmitters have limited range, most under 20 feet. So reading chips inside consumers' homes or tracking them on the move would be nearly impossible. The Auto-ID industry is also working to address consumer privacy concerns. Among other things, it is drafting a privacy policy that includes giving customers the option of permanently disabling the chips at checkout. And according to an Auto-ID consultant, the basic mission is not to spy on consumers. It's to serve them better. "It's not Orwellian. That is absolutely, positively not the vision of Auto-ID," she says. "The vision is for . . . brand manufacturers and retailers to be able to have right-time, right-promotion, real-time eye-to-eye [contact] with the consumer."

Last year the Auto-ID Center transferred responsibility for the administration and development of its technology to EPC Global, ushering in a new phase of RFID research and application. In coming years, as smart chips appear on more and more products, Auto-ID technology will no doubt bring significant benefits to both marketers and the customers they serve. "The idea of someone using tiny radio transmitters to influence consumer purchase behavior was once only the stuff of paranoid delusions," says the analyst. "But in the not-so-distant future, it could become the basis of a new generation of marketing."

Sources: Jack Neff, "A Chip over Your Shoulder?" *Advertising Age,* April 22, 2002, p. 4; Kimberly Hill, "Prada Uses Smart Tags to Personalize Shopping," April 24, 2002, accessed online at www.crmdaily.com; "Business: The Best Thing Since the Bar-Code: The IT Revolution," *The Economist,* February 8, 2003, pp. 57–58; "Gillette, Michelin Begin RFID Pilots," *Frontline Solutions,* March 2003, p. 8; "RFID Benefits Apparent," *Chain Store Age,* March 2003, p. 63; Faith Keenan, "If Supermarket Shelves Could Talk," *Business Week,* March 31, 2003, pp. 66–67; and information accessed online at www.autoidcenter.org, July 2003, and information accessed online at www.autoidlabs.org, November 2003.

Political Environment

Marketing decisions are strongly affected by developments in the political environment. The **political environment** consists of laws, government agencies, and pressure groups that influence or limit various organizations and individuals in a given society.

Political environment

Laws, government agencies, and pressure groups that influence and limit various organizations and individuals in a given society.

Legislation Regulating Business Even the most liberal advocates of free-market economies agree that the system works best with at least some regulation. Well-conceived regulation can encourage competition and ensure fair markets for goods and services. Thus, governments develop *public policy* to guide commerce—sets of laws and regulations that limit business for the good of society as a whole. Almost every marketing activity is subject to a wide range of laws and regulations.

Increasing Legislation. Legislation affecting business around the world has increased steadily over the years. The United States has many laws covering issues such as competition, fair trade practices, environmental protection, product safety, truth in advertising, consumer privacy, packaging and labeling, pricing, and other important areas (see Table 3.2). The European Commission has been active in establishing a new framework of laws covering competitive behavior, product standards, product liability, and commercial transactions for the nations of the European Union.

Several countries have gone further than the United States in passing strong consumerism legislation. For example, Norway bans several forms of sales promotion—trading stamps, contests, premiums—as being inappropriate or unfair ways of promoting products. Thailand requires food processors selling national brands to market low-price brands also, so that low-income consumers can find economy brands on the shelves. In India, food companies must obtain special approval to launch brands that duplicate those already existing on the market, such as additional cola drinks or new brands of rice.

Understanding the public policy implications of a particular marketing activity is not a simple matter. For example, in the United States, there are many laws created at the national, state, and local levels, and these regulations often overlap. Aspirins sold in Dallas are governed both by federal labeling laws and by Texas state advertising laws. Moreover, regulations are constantly changing—what was allowed last year may now be prohibited, and what was prohibited may now be allowed. Marketers must work hard to keep up with changes in regulations and their interpretations.

Business legislation has been enacted for a number of reasons. The first is to *protect companies* from each other. Although business executives may praise competition, they sometimes try to neutralize it when it threatens them. So laws are passed to define and prevent unfair competition. In the United States, such laws are enforced by the Federal Trade Commission and the Antitrust Division of the Attorney General's office.

The second purpose of government regulation is to *protect consumers* from unfair business practices. Some firms, if left alone, would make shoddy products, tell lies in their advertising, and deceive consumers through their packaging and pricing. Unfair business practices have been defined and are enforced by various agencies.

The third purpose of government regulation is to *protect the interests of society* against unrestrained business behavior. Profitable business activity does not always create a better quality of life. Regulation arises to ensure that firms take responsibility for the societal costs of their production or products.

Changing Government Agency Enforcement. International marketers will encounter dozens, or even hundreds, of agencies set up to enforce trade policies and regulations. In the United States, Congress has established federal regulatory agencies such as the Federal Trade Commission, the Food and Drug Administration, the Federal Communications Commission, the Federal Energy Regulatory Commission, the Civil Aeronautics Board, the Consumer Product Safety Commission, and the Environmental Protection Agency. Because such government agencies have some discretion in enforcing the laws, they can have a major impact on a company's marketing performance. At times, the staffs of these

TABLE 3.2   Major U.S. Legislation Affecting Marketing

Legislation	Purpose
Sherman Antitrust Act (1890)	Prohibits monopolies and activities (price fixing, predatory pricing) that restrain trade or competition in interstate commerce.
Federal Food and Drug Act (1906)	Forbids the manufacture or sale of adulterated or fraudulently labeled foods and drugs. Created the Food and Drug Administration.
Clayton Act (1914)	Supplements the Sherman Act by prohibiting certain types of price discrimination, exclusive dealing, and tying clauses (which require a dealer to take additional products in a seller's line).
Federal Trade Commission Act (1914)	Establishes a commission to monitor and remedy unfair trade methods.
Robinson–Patman Act (1936)	Amends Clayton Act to define price discrimination as unlawful. Empowers FTC to establish limits on quantity discounts, forbid some brokerage allowances, and prohibit promotional allowances except when made available on proportionately equal terms.
Wheeler–Lea Act (1938)	Makes deceptive, misleading, and unfair practices illegal regardless of injury to competition. Places advertising of food and drugs under FTC jurisdiction.
Lanham Trademark Act (1946)	Protects and regulates distinctive brand names and trademarks.
National Traffic and Safety Act (1958)	Provides for the creation of compulsory safety standards for automobiles and tires.
Fair Packaging and Labeling Act (1966)	Provides for the regulation of packaging and labeling of consumer goods. Requires that manufacturers state what the package contains, who made it, and how much it contains.
Child Protection Act (1966)	Bans sale of hazardous toys and articles. Sets standards for child-resistant packaging.
Federal Cigarette Labeling and Advertising Act (1967)	Requires that cigarette packages contain the following statement: "Warning: The Surgeon General Has Determined That Cigarette Smoking Is Dangerous to Your Health."
National Environmental Policy Act (1969)	Establishes a national policy on the environment. The 1970 Reorganization Plan established the Environmental Protection Agency.
Consumer Product Safety Act (1972)	Establishes the Consumer Product Safety Commission and authorizes it to set safety standards for consumer products as well as exact penalties for failure to uphold those standards.
Magnuson–Moss Warranty Act (1975)	Authorizes the FTC to determine rules and regulations for consumer warranties and provides consumer access to redress, such as the class-action suit.
Children's Television Act (1990)	Limits number of commercials aired during children's programs.
Nutrition Labeling and Education Act (1990)	Requires that food product labels provide detailed nutritional information.
Telephone Consumer Protection Act (1991)	Establishes procedures to avoid unwanted telephone solicitations. Limits marketers' use of automatic telephone dialing systems and artificial or prerecorded voices.
Americans with Disabilities Act (1991)	Makes discrimination against people with disabilities illegal in public accommodations, transportation, and telecommunications.
Children's Online Privacy Protection Act (2000)	Prohibits Web sites or online services operators from collecting personal information from children without obtaining consent from a parent and allowing parents to review information collected from their children.

agencies have appeared to be overly eager and unpredictable. Some of the agencies sometimes have been dominated by lawyers and economists who lacked a practical sense of how business and marketing work. In recent years, the Federal Trade Commission has added staff marketing experts, who can better understand complex business issues.

New laws and their enforcement will continue to increase. Business executives must watch these developments when planning their products and marketing programs. Marketers need to know about the major laws protecting competition, consumers, and society. They need to understand these laws at the local, state, national, and international levels.

Increased Emphasis on Ethics and Socially Responsible Actions
Written regulations cannot possibly cover all potential marketing abuses, and existing laws

are often difficult to enforce. However, beyond written laws and regulations, business is also governed by social codes and rules of professional ethics.

Socially Responsible Behavior. Enlightened companies encourage their managers to look beyond what the regulatory system allows and simply "do the right thing." These socially responsible firms actively seek out ways to protect the long-run interests of their consumers and the environment.

The recent rash of business scandals and increased concerns about the environment have created fresh interest in the issues of ethics and social responsibility. Almost every aspect of marketing involves such issues. Unfortunately, because these issues usually involve conflicting interests, well-meaning people can honestly disagree about the right course of action in a given situation. Thus, many industrial and professional trade associations have suggested codes of ethics. And more companies are now developing policies, guidelines, and other responses to complex social responsibility issues. For example, 45 percent of Fortune 250 companies issued environmental, social, or sustainability reports in 2001, up from 35 percent in 1998.[38]

The boom in e-commerce and Internet marketing has created a new set of social and ethical issues. Online privacy issues are the primary concern. For example, Web site visitors often provide extensive personal information that might leave them open to abuse by unscrupulous marketers. Moreover, both Intel and Microsoft have been accused of covert, high-tech computer chip and software invasions of customers' personal computers to obtain information for marketing purposes.[39]

Throughout this book, we present Marketing at Work exhibits that summarize the main public policy and social responsibility issues surrounding major marketing decisions. These exhibits discuss the legal issues that marketers should understand and the common ethical and societal concerns that marketers face. In Chapter 16, we discuss a broad range of societal marketing issues in greater depth.

Cause-Related Marketing. To exercise their social responsibility and build more positive images, many companies are now linking themselves to worthwhile causes. These days, every product seems to be tied to some cause. Buy Purina cat food and help the American Association of Zoological Parks and Aquariums save endangered big cat species. Drink Tang and earn money for Mothers Against Drunk Driving. Drive a Dollar rental car and help support the Special Olympics. Buy from EddieBauer.com and have a percentage of your purchase go to support your local grade school. Buy a pink mixer from Kitchenaid and support breast cancer research. Or if you want to help the Leukemia Society of America, buy Helping Hand trash bags or toilet paper. Pay for these purchases with the right charge card and you can support a local cultural arts group or help fight cancer or heart disease.

Cause-related marketing has become a primary form of corporate giving. It lets companies "do well by doing good" by linking purchases of the company's products or services with fund-raising for worthwhile causes or charitable organizations. Companies now sponsor dozens of cause-related marketing campaigns each year. Many are backed by large budgets and a full complement of marketing activities. Consider these examples:

■ Cause-related marketing: KitchenAid donates $50 to breast cancer research for every pink mixer it sells and encourages consumers to host a "Cook for the Cure" dinner party.

In 1987, Johnson & Johnson teamed with the Children's National Medical Center and the National Safety Council to sponsor the National SAFE KIDS Campaign. Designed to reduce preventable children's injuries, the leading killer of children, the campaign offered consumers a free SAFE KIDS safety kit for children in exchange for proofs of purchase. Consumers could also buy a Child's Safety Video for $9.95. To promote the campaign, Johnson & Johnson distributed almost 50 million advertising inserts in daily newspapers. It also developed a special information kit for retailers containing posters, floor displays, and other in-store promotion materials. Started as a program of the Children's National Medical Center, the National SAFE KIDS Campaign has now grown into an independent organization, SAFE KIDS, made up of 300 state and local coalitions across America. Each May the organization teams with Johnson & Johnson to present National SAFE KIDS Week. J&J continues to support the organization with millions of dollars in annual grants, public awareness campaigns, corporate advertising, and retail promotions.

In 1996, General Mills launched its Box Tops for Education program. The program offers schools nationwide a chance to earn cash to pay for everything from field trips, to computers, to playground equipment. Box Tops for Education has really caught on. Today, more than 60 percent of the nation's elementary schools are enrolled. To participate, students and parents clip box tops and labels from any of more than 330 eligible products, including brands like Yoplait, Big G, Lloyd's, and Betty Crocker. General Mills then pays the school 10 cents for every box top redeemed. To date, the company has given nearly $70 million to local public, private, and parochial schools. Based on that success, General Mills has now teamed up with Visa to offer a Box Tops for Education credit card. Visa donates 1 percent of every purchase made to the cardholder's designated school. In addition, consumers who link to Web sites such as Amazon.com and EddieBauer.com from the Box Tops for Education Web site are guaranteed a donation to their schools amounting up to 10 percent of every purchase.

Cause-related marketing has stirred some controversy. Critics worry that cause-related marketing is more a strategy for selling than a strategy for giving—that "cause-related" marketing is really "cause-exploitative" marketing. Thus, companies using cause-related marketing might find themselves walking a fine line between increased sales and an improved image, and facing charges of exploitation.

However, if handled well, cause-related marketing can greatly benefit both the company and the cause. The company gains an effective marketing tool while building a more positive public image. The charitable organization or cause gains greater visibility and important new sources of funding. Cause-related marketing programs generate more than $700 million from U.S. corporations each year for various causes.[40] Thus, when cause marketing works, everyone wins.

Cultural Environment

The **cultural environment** is made up of institutions and other forces that affect a society's basic values, perceptions, preferences, and behaviors. People grow up in a particular society that shapes their basic beliefs and values. They absorb a world view that defines their relationships with others. The following cultural characteristics can affect marketing decision making.

Persistence of Cultural Values People in a given society hold many beliefs and values. Their core beliefs and values have a high degree of persistence. For example, most Americans believe in working, getting married, giving to charity, and being honest. These beliefs shape more specific attitudes and behaviors found in everyday life. *Core* beliefs and values are passed on from parents to children and are reinforced by schools, churches, businesses, and government.

Cultural environment

Institutions and other forces that affect society's basic values, perceptions, preferences, and behaviors.

Secondary beliefs and values are more open to change. Believing in marriage is a core belief; believing that people should get married early in life is a secondary belief. Marketers have some chance of changing secondary values but little chance of changing core values. For example, family-planning marketers could argue more effectively that people should get married later than that they should not get married at all.

Shifts in Secondary Cultural Values   Although core values are fairly persistent, cultural swings do take place. Consider the impact of popular music groups, movie personalities, and other celebrities on young people's hairstyling, clothing, and sexual norms. Marketers want to predict cultural shifts in order to spot new opportunities or threats. Several firms offer "futures" forecasts in this connection, such as the Yankelovich Monitor, Market Facts' BrainWaves Group, and the Trends Research Institute.

The Yankelovich Monitor has tracked consumer value trends for years. At the dawn of the twenty-first century, it looked back to capture lessons from the past decade that might offer insight into the 2000s. It identified the following eight major consumer themes[41]:

1. **Paradox:**   People agree that "life is getting better and worse at the same time."
2. **Trust not:**   Confidence in doctors, public schools, TV news, newspapers, federal government, and corporations drops sharply.
3. **Go it alone:**   More people agree with the statement "I rely more on my own instincts than on experts."
4. **Smarts really count:**   For example, fewer people agree with "It's risky to buy a brand you are not familiar with."
5. **No sacrifices:**   For example, many people claim that looks are important but not at any price, that keeping house for show instead of comfort is over, and that giving up taste for nutrition is no longer acceptable.
6. **Stress hard to beat:**   For example, more people claim that they are "concerned about getting enough rest."
7. **Reciprocity is the way to go:**   More people agree that "Everybody should feel free to do his or her own thing."
8. **Me 2:**   For example, people express the need to live in a world that is built by "me," not by you.

Yankelovich maintains that the decade drivers for the 2000s will primarily come from the baby boomers and Generation Xers. The baby boomers will be driven by four factors in the 2000s: "adventure" (fueled by a sense of youthfulness), "smarts" (fueled by a sense of empowerment and willingness to accept change), "intergenerational support" (caring for younger and older people, often in nontraditional arrangements), and "retreading" (embracing early retirement with second career or phase of their work life). GenXers will be driven by three factors: "redefining the good life" (being highly motivated to improve their economic well-being and remain in control), "new rituals" (returning to traditional values but with a tolerant mind-set and active lifestyle), and "cutting and pasting" (balancing work, play, sleep, family, and other aspects of their lives).

The major cultural values of a society are expressed in people's views of themselves and others, as well as in their views of organizations, society, nature, and the universe.

People's Views of Themselves.   People vary in their emphasis on serving themselves versus serving others. Some people seek personal pleasure, wanting fun, change, and escape. Others seek self-realization through religion, recreation, or the avid pursuit of careers or other life goals. People use products, brands, and services as a means of self-expression, and they buy products and services that match their views of themselves.

In the 1980s, personal ambition and materialism increased dramatically, with significant marketing implications. In a "me society," people buy their "dream cars" and take their "dream vacations." They tended to spend to the limit on self-indulgent goods and services. Today, in contrast, people are adopting more conservative behaviors and ambitions. As we move into the new millennium, materialism, flashy spending, and self-indulgence have been replaced by more sensible spending, saving, family concerns, and helping others. The maturing baby boomers are limiting their spending to products and services that improve their lives instead of boosting their images. This suggests a bright future for products and services that serve basic needs and provide real value rather than those relying on glitz and hype.

People's Views of Others. Recently, observers have noted a shift from a "me society" to a "we society," in which more people want to be with and serve others.[42]

> After years of serious "nesting"—staying close to the security and creature comforts of home and hearth—Americans are finally starting to tiptoe out of their homes to hang out in the real world. The nesting instinct has gone in and out of fashion before. When the first big wave hit in the early '80s, trend watchers coined the term "cocooning" to describe the surge of boomers buying their first homes and filling them up with oversized furniture and fancy gadgets. The dot-com boom set off another round, partly fueled by cool home gizmos like plasma TVs and PlayStations. Though many expected 9/11 to send people even deeper into nesting mode, sociologists say it actually got people out looking for companionship. After being hunkered down through terror alerts and the war in Iraq, many people were naturally itching to get out. "You can only cocoon with your family for so long," says one sociologist. "Even if they don't drive you nuts, they bore you."

Marketers are beginning to notice the shift. In Las Vegas, the Saks Fifth Avenue store is trying to ease folks back out of the house with a simulated living room, complete with sofas where shoppers can sit and mingle, or munch from bowls of candy and watch a giant TV. The Applebee's restaurant chain has dropped ads that focus on food in favor of feel-good spots with a community theme. The latest: a "Neighborhood Hero" contest in which diners nominate a local figure to be honored. And as people move away from the confines of their snug dens and out into the fresh air and sunshine, nesting icon Home Depot is expanding its gardening business, testing out landscape-supply stores.

More and more, people are wanting to get out of the house and be with others. This trend suggests a greater demand for "social support" products and services that improve direct communication between people, such as health clubs and family vacations.

People's Views of Organizations. People vary in their attitudes toward corporations, government agencies, trade unions, universities, and other organizations. By and large, people are willing to work for major organizations and expect them, in turn, to carry out society's work. The late 1980s saw a sharp decrease in confidence in and loyalty toward America's business and political organizations and institutions. In the workplace, there has been an overall decline in organizational loyalty. During the 1990s, waves of company downsizings bred cynicism and distrust. Recent corporate scandals at Enron, WorldCom, Tyco International, and other large companies resulted in a further loss of confidence in big business. Many people today see work not as a source of satisfaction but as a required chore to earn money to enjoy their nonwork hours. This trend suggests that organizations need to find new ways to win consumer and employee confidence.

People's Views of Society. People vary in their attitudes toward their society; patriots defend it, reformers want to change it, malcontents want to leave it. People's orientation to their society influences their consumption patterns and attitudes toward the marketplace. American patriotism has been increasing gradually for the past two decades. It surged, however, following the September 11 terrorist attacks and the Iraq war. For example, before the 9/11 attacks, Americans spent some $200 million a year on flags of all sizes and shapes. But in 2001, American flag sales quadrupled. Within the two weeks following the September 11 attacks, K-Mart alone sold more than 662,000 handheld flags nationwide. The summer following the Iraq war saw a surge of pumped-up

■ American patriotism has been increasing gradually for the past two decades but surged following the September 11 terrorist attacks. Marketers such as Mars, Inc. (the maker of M&Ms) responded with patriotic products and promotions.

Americans visiting U.S. historic sites, ranging from the Washington, D.C., monuments, Mount Rushmore, the Gettysburg battlefield, and the USS Constitution ("Old Ironsides") to Pearl Harbor and the Alamo.[43]

Marketers have responded with patriotic products and promotions, offering everything from floral bouquets to clothing with patriotic themes. For example, following the September 11 attacks, Mars introduced a new limited-edition patriotic package for its M&M brand, featuring red, white, and blue candy pieces. It donated 100 percent of the profits from the sale of those special packages to the American Red Cross. For Christmas, Hallmark offered a card showing a snowman bearing the American flag and reading "God Bless America!" Wal-Mart sold "Little Patriots Diapers" with tiny blue stars. The Heartland Brewery in Times Square even came out with a new beer, DetermiNation Ale. And a heart-rending Budweiser Super Bowl ad featured the venerable Budweiser Clydesdales bowing to honor the forever changed Manhattan skyline.[44]

Although most of these marketing efforts were tasteful and well received, waving the red, white, and blue proved tricky for some marketers. Following September 11, consumers quickly became wary of patriotic products and ads. Except in cases in which companies tied product sales to charitable contributions, "patriotism as a marketing program was largely unwelcome," says one analyst. They were often "seen by consumers as attempts to cash in on the tragedy." Another expert advises that marketers must take care when responding to such national emotions. Whatever their intentions, they must "be careful not to come across as saying 'Wasn't it awful, now go spend money on our product.'"[45]

People's Views of Nature. People vary in their attitudes toward the natural world. Some feel ruled by it, others feel in harmony with it, and still others seek to master it. A long-term trend has been people's growing mastery over nature through technology and the belief that nature is bountiful. More recently, however, people have recognized that nature is finite and fragile, that it can be destroyed or spoiled by human activities.

Love of nature is leading to more camping, hiking, fishing, bird-watching, and other outdoor activities. Business has responded by offering more products and services catering to these interests. Tour operators are offering more wilderness adventures, and retailers are offering more fitness gear and apparel. Marketing communicators are using appealing natural backgrounds in advertising their products. And food producers have found growing markets for natural and organic foods. Natural and organic products are now a $25 billion industry, growing at a rate of 20 percent annually. Niche marketers, such as Whole Foods Markets, have sprung up to serve this market, and traditional food chains such as Kroger and Safeway have added separate natural and organic food sections. Sales of White Wave's Silk soymilk, for example, have jumped from $10 mil-

It's not just for health nuts.
Regular nuts like it, too.

All natural, lactose free, high in protein, with a surprisingly good taste. Don't be so stubbo

■ Marketers are responding to changes in people's view of the natural environment by offering more natural and organic products. White Wave's Silk soymilk has found success in the $25 billion industry.

lion to $200 million in just two years. Even McDonald's has joined the movement, recently replacing its milk offering with cartons of organic milk.[46]

People's Views of the Universe. Finally, people vary in their beliefs about the origin of the universe and their place in it. Although most Americans practice religion, religious conviction and practice have been dropping off gradually through the years. Some futurists, however, have noted a renewed interest in spirituality, perhaps as a part of a broader search for a new inner purpose. People have been moving away from materialism and dog-eat-dog ambition to seek more permanent values—family, community, earth, faith— and a more certain grasp of right and wrong.

"Americans are on a spiritual journey," observes one expert, "increasingly concerned with the meaning of life and issues of the soul and spirit. The journey can encompass religion, but it is much more likely to take the form of . . . 'spiritual individualism'." This new spiritualism affects consumers in everything from the television shows they watch and the books they read to the products and services they buy. "Since consumers don't park their beliefs and values on the bench outside the marketplace," adds the expert, "they are bringing this awareness to the brands they buy. Tapping into this heightened sensitivity presents a unique marketing opportunity for brands."[47]

Linking the Concepts

SPEED BUMP

Slow down and cool your engine. You've now read about a large number of environmental forces. How are all of these environments *linked* with each other? With company marketing strategy?

- How are major demographic forces linked with economic changes? With major cultural trends? How are the natural and technological environments linked? Think of an example of a company that has recognized one of these links and turned it into a marketing opportunity.
- Is the marketing environment uncontrollable—something that the company can only prepare for and react to? Or can companies be proactive in changing environmental factors? Think of a good example that makes your point, then read on.

■ Responding to the Marketing Environment

Someone once observed, "There are three kinds of companies: those who make things happen, those who watch things happen, and those who wonder what's happened."[48] Many companies view the marketing environment as an uncontrollable element to which they must adapt. They passively accept the marketing environment and do not try to change it. They analyze the environmental forces and design strategies that will help the company avoid the threats and take advantage of the opportunities the environment provides.

Other companies take an **environmental management perspective**.[49] Rather than simply watching and reacting, these firms take aggressive actions to affect the publics and forces in their marketing environment. Such companies hire lobbyists to influence legislation affecting their industries and stage media events to gain favorable press coverage. They run advertorials (ads expressing editorial points of view) to shape public opinion. They press lawsuits and file complaints with regulators to keep competitors in line, and they form contractual agreements to better control their distribution channels.

Environmental management perspective
A management perspective in which the firm takes aggressive actions to affect the publics and forces in its marketing environment rather than simply watching and reacting to them.

Marketing at Work | 3.3

YourCompanySucks.com

Richard Hatch is one of the few people in this world with a passion for both Harley-Davidson motorcycles and collecting dolls and cute little toys. One day a few years ago, the tattooed, 210-pound Hatch got into a shouting match with an employee in his local Wal-Mart and was banned from the store. Hatch claims that his actions didn't warrant his ousting. He says he'd complained to store managers for months that employees were snapping up the best Hot Wheels and NASCAR collectible toy cars before they hit the shelves.

Wal-Mart didn't budge and the angry Hatch retaliated. He hired a Web designer and created the Wal-Mart Sucks Web site (www.walmartsucks.com). In only a few years, according to one account, the Web site "sprouted beyond Hatch's wildest dreams of revenge. [Thousands] of customers have written in to attack rude store managers, complain about alleged insects in the aisles, offer shoplifting tips, and, from time to time, write romantic odes to cashiers." Hatch, who had amassed some 5,000 Beanie Babies, also had a dispute with employees at his local Toys 'R' Us store about similar complaints. He was banished from there as well. His response? You guessed it: another sucks.com Web site (www.toysrussucks.com).

An extreme event? Not anymore. As more and more well-intentioned grassroots organizations, consumer watchdog groups, or just plain angry consumers take their gripes to the Web, such "sucks.com" sites are becoming almost commonplace. According to one source, more than half of the Fortune 1000 companies have encountered some type of Web site critical of their businesses. The sites target some highly respected companies with some highly *dis*respectful labels: Microsucks; Gapsucks.org; NonAmazon; Starbucked; BestBuy-sucks; The I Hate McDonald's Page; Just Do Not Do It (Nike); America Offline; NorthWorst Air; Untied Airlines: The Most Unfriendly Skies; The Unofficial BMW Lemon Site; AllStateInsurancesucks ("Their hands in your pockets"); and Dunkindonuts.org (featuring "unhappy tales about coffee, crullers, and cinnamon buns") to name only a few. Some of these attack sites are little more than a nuisance. Others, however, can draw serious attention and create real headaches. "The same people who used to stand on [the] corner and rail against things to 20 people now can put up a Web site and rail in front of 2 million people," says William Comcowich, whose firm helps companies monitor what's said about them on the Internet.

How should companies react to these attack sites? The real quandary

Environmental management: The best strategy for dealing with consumer hate sites is to address complaints directly. "If a company solves my problem, why would I keep up the Web site?"

Often, companies can find positive ways to overcome seemingly uncontrollable environmental constraints. For example:

> Cathay Pacific Airlines . . . determined that many travelers were avoiding Hong Kong because of lengthy delays at immigration. Rather than assuming that this was a problem they could not solve, Cathay's senior staff asked the Hong Kong government how to avoid these immigration delays. After lengthy discussions, the airline agreed to make an annual grant-in-aid to the government to hire more immigration inspectors—but these reinforcements would service primarily

for targeted companies is figuring out how far they can go to protect their image without fueling the fire already raging at the sites. One point upon which all experts seem to agree: Don't try to retaliate in kind. "Avoid 'testosterosis'—or the urge to hit someone in the face because they are doing something you don't like," advises one consultant. "It's a free country, and the Web is completely unregulated. Don't get angry and think about doing foolish things."

Some companies have tried to silence the critics through lawsuits, but few have succeeded. For example, McDonald's sued one such site for libel; it spent $16 million on the case and won the suit but received only $94,000 in damages. Wal-Mart's attorneys threatened Hatch with legal action unless he shut down his Wal-Mart sucks Web site. However, Hatch stood up to the $250 billion retailer, and Wal-Mart eventually backed down. As it turns out, a company has legal recourse only when the unauthorized use of its trademarks, brand names, or other intellectual property is apt to be confusing to the public. And no reasonable person is likely to be confused that Wal-Mart maintains and supports a site tagged Walmartsucks.com.

Beyond the finer legal points, Wal-Mart also feared that a lawsuit would draw only more attention to the consumer hate site. An industry analyst comments: "Those who operate hate sites adore posting cease-and-desist letters they receive from corporate attorneys. Such letters also validate their fight for the cause, whatever they perceive that to be, and they can use them to cast yet

another negative spotlight on the company. They revel in the attention."

Given the difficulties of trying to sue consumer hate sites out of existence, some companies have tried other strategies. For example, most big companies now routinely buy up Web addresses for their firm names preceded by the words "Ihate" or followed by "sucks.com." In general, however, attempts to block, counterattack, or shut down consumer hate sites may be shortsighted. Such sites are often based on real consumer concerns. Hence, the best strategy might be to proactively monitor these sites and respond positively to the concerns they express.

Some targeted companies actively listen to concerns posted on hate sites and develop Web presentations to tell their own side of the story. For example, Nike is the target of at least eight different attack sites, mostly criticizing it for alleged unfair labor practices in Southeast Asia. In response, Nike commissioned an independent investigation of labor practices in its Indonesian factories and presented the results on its own Web site (www.Nikebiz.com/social/labor).

Monitoring consumer hate sites can yield additional benefits. For example, some sites can actually provide the targeted company with useful information. "Most sites are full of genuine, free market research . . . on what is going wrong in customer service and product terms," advises an expert. "Rather than closing down such sites, companies should encourage them as a healthy outlet for unresolved anger."

According to James Alexander, president of EWatch, an Internet monitoring service, the best strategy for dealing

with consumer hate sites is to address their complaints directly. "If a company solves my problem," he says, "why would I keep up the Web site?" Take Dunkin' Donuts, for example:

After a disgruntled customer established dunkindonuts.org, *an attack site that appeared on many Internet search engines ahead of the company's own Web page, the company contacted about 25 people who had written in with complaints and offered them coupons for free donuts. "If this was where customers were going to post their comments, we thought it was important for us to go ahead and address them," says spokesperson Jennifer Rosenberg. Now, the company is in negotiations to buy the site from its founder, 25-year-old David Felton, who says he'll sell because "they have been taking complaints and responding."*

By proactively responding to a seemingly uncontrollable event in its environment, Dunkin' Donuts has been able to turn a negative into a positive. Dunkinsucks.com is now all smiles.com.

Sources: Quotes and excerpts from Leslie Goff, "<YourCompanyNameHere>sucks.com," *Computerworld*, July 20, 1998, pp. 57–58; Mike France, "A Site for Soreheads," *Business Week*, April 12, 1999, pp. 86–90; and Wanda Goldwag, "Complaint Sites Can Focus Firms on Issues to Fix," *Marketing*, September 5, 2002, p. 16. Also see Oscar S. Cisneros, "Legal Tips for Your 'Sucks' Site," accessed online at www.wired.com, August 14, 2000; Hilary Appelman, "I Scream, You Scream: Consumers Vent over the Net," *New York Times*, March 4, 2001, p. 3.13; Eric J. Sinrod, " 'Suck' Sites Live in the Eyes of the Courts," November 29, 2002, accessed online at www.USAToday.com; and Ronald F. Lopez, "Corporate Strategies for Addressing Internet "Complaint" Sites," accessed online at www.constructionweblinks.com, June 2003.

the Cathay Pacific gates. The reduced waiting period increased customer value and thus strengthened [Cathay's competitive advantage].[50]

Marketing management cannot always control environmental forces. In many cases, it must settle for simply watching and reacting to the environment. For example, a company would have little success trying to influence geographic population shifts, the economic environment, or major cultural values. But whenever possible, smart marketing managers will take a *proactive* rather than *reactive* approach to the marketing environment (see Marketing at Work 3.3).

REST STOP:
Reviewing the Concepts

In this chapter and the next two chapters, you'll examine the environments of marketing and how companies analyze these environments to discover marketplace opportunities and create effective marketing strategies. Companies must constantly watch and adapt to the *marketing environment* in order to seek opportunities and ward off threats. The marketing environment comprises all the actors and forces influencing the company's ability to transact business effectively with its target market.

1. Describe the environmental forces that affect the company's ability to serve its customers.

The company's *microenvironment* consists of other actors close to the company that combine to form the company's value delivery network or that affect its ability to serve its customers. It includes the company's *internal environment*—its several departments and management levels—as it influences marketing decision making. *Marketing-channel firms*—suppliers and marketing intermediaries, including resellers, physical distribution firms, marketing services agencies, and financial intermediaries—cooperate to create customer value. Five types of customer *markets* include consumer, business, reseller, government, and international markets. *Competitors* vie with the company in an effort to serve customers better. Finally, various *publics* have an actual or potential interest in or impact on the company's ability to meet its objectives.

The *macroenvironment* consists of larger societal forces that affect the entire microenvironment. The six forces making up the company's macroenvironment include demographic, economic, natural, technological, political, and cultural forces. These forces shape opportunities and pose threats to the company.

2. Explain how changes in the demographic and economic environments affect marketing decisions.

Demography is the study of the characteristics of human populations. Today's *demographic environment* shows a changing age structure, shifting family profiles, geographic population shifts, a better-educated and more white-collar population, and increasing diversity. The *economic environment* consists of factors that affect buying power and patterns. The economic environment is characterized by more consumer concern for value and shifting consumer spending patterns. Today's squeezed consumers are seeking greater value—just the right combination of good quality and service at a fair price. The distribution of income also is shifting. The rich have grown richer, the middle class has shrunk, and the poor have remained poor, leading to a two-tiered market. Many companies now tailor their marketing offers to two different markets—the affluent and the less affluent.

3. Identify the major trends in the firm's natural and technological environments.

The *natural environment* shows three major trends: shortages of certain raw materials, higher pollution levels, and more government intervention in natural resource management. Environmental concerns create marketing opportunities for alert companies. The marketer should watch for four major trends in the *technological environment*: the rapid pace of technological change, high R&D budgets, the concentration by companies on minor product improvements, and increased government regulation. Companies that fail to keep up with technological change will miss out on new product and marketing opportunities.

4. Explain the key changes in the political and cultural environments.

The *political environment* consists of laws, agencies, and groups that influence or limit marketing actions. The political environment has undergone three changes that affect marketing worldwide: increasing legislation regulating business, strong government agency enforcement, and greater emphasis on ethics and socially responsible actions. The *cultural environment* is made up of institutions and forces that affect a society's values, perceptions, preferences, and behaviors. The environment shows long-term trends toward a "we society," a lessening trust of institutions, increasing patriotism, greater appreciation for nature, a new spiritualism, and the search for more meaningful and enduring values.

5. Discuss how companies can react to the marketing environment.

Companies can passively accept the marketing environment as an uncontrollable element to which they must adapt, avoiding threats and taking advantage of opportunities as they arise. Or they can take an *environmental management perspective*, proactively working to change the environment rather than simply reacting to it. Whenever possible, companies should try to be proactive rather than reactive.

Navigating the Key Terms

Baby boomers
Cultural environment
Demography
Economic environment
Engel's laws
Environmental management
   perspective

Generation X
Generation Y
Macroenvironment
Marketing environment
Marketing intermediaries

Microenvironment
Natural environment
Political environment
Public
Technological environment

Travel Log

Discussing the Issues

1. The microenvironment includes a variety of publics that have an interest in the company or can have an impact on its operations. Discuss how the goals of some of these publics may be opposed to one another. How would opposing goals among a company's relevant publics have an impact on its strategy?

2. The changing structure of the American family was identified as an important demographic force shaping the opportunities and threats to the company. Explain how a grocery store could change its positioning to appeal to each of the following segments: married couples with children, single parents, and adults living alone.

3. Value marketing—the right combination of product quality and good service at a fair price—has increased in popularity. Pick an industry and identify two competing companies, one that is good at value marketing and one that is poor at value marketing. For the company that is poor at value marketing, discuss why consumers purchase from that company. What need is it fulfilling better than the firm that is good at value marketing?

4. The 2002 Sarbanes–Oxley Act, among other things, has made high-level corporate executives personally accountable for the accuracy of their company's earnings statements, requires public companies to improve their financial control systems, and calls for some board members to be from outside the company. What impact might this legislation have on business operations?

5. An environmental management perspective advocates taking a proactive, rather than reactive, approach to dealing with the marketing environment. Identify a company you feel characterizes this approach. What specific actions do they take to proactively influence their environment?

Application Questions

1. For an educational institution, the number, quality, and characteristics of its student body are heavily impacted by changes in the size and structure of the general population. Discuss how your school is likely to be impacted by the following trends: an aging population, a growing population, a changing definition of the family, geographic shifts in population, a more white-collar workforce, and increasing ethnic and cultural diversity. For the trends that have a negative impact, what strategy would you recommend for reducing the negative influence?

2. The text argues that major cultural values in society are defined by individuals' views of themselves and others, as well as their views of organizations, society, nature, and the universe. Break into groups of four to five students, with each group focusing on one of these six views. Noting the shift discussed in the text for your group's assigned area, identify a company that has benefited from the shift and one whose position has worsened. For those organizations that have not fared as well under the shift, what must they do to better adjust to this trend?

3. The Federal Trade Commission estimates that its national do-not-call registry will contain more than 60 million phone numbers by July 2004. In response, a telemarketing trade association has challenged the legality of this consumer telemarketing call-blocking service in federal court. Describe what activities might have been engaged in if the telemarketing industry had taken a more proactive environmental management perspective toward this issue. What is your opinion on balancing the privacy of consumers with the rights of legitimate telemarketing firms to conduct business?

Under the Hood: Focus on Technology

Customer loyalty for online travel companies is low, with the average consumer checking three travel websites for the best prices on airlines, hotels, and rental cars. Today, approximately 15 percent of all travel is purchased online, with airline ticket sales accounting for about half of that amount. Three online travel companies, Expedia (36 percent of the market), Travelocity (24 percent), and Orbitz (13 percent) account for the majority of online travel sales. While consumers have been focused on where to get the best deals, many online travel companies have been investing in new technology that will allow them to differentiate themselves with regard to the services they provide rather than the prices they offer.

1. What macroenvironmental forces do you feel will have the largest positive and largest negative impact on online travel companies? Why?

2. Discuss how online travel companies should address these negative impacts.

3. What do you think is the long-run future of the online travel industry?

4. What do you feel are the most significant environmental issues facing the online travel industry in the next 5 years?

Focus on Ethics

How many times have you or your parents purchased a new computer in the past 5 years? As computers become more and more powerful, regular updating of computer equipment has become common. Have you ever wondered where all of the old computers and monitors go? Are they sitting in your house somewhere, in the garage maybe?

Concerns over decreasing raw materials, increasing pollution levels, and global warming have gained momentum over the past several years. While many companies have been accused of polluting the environment, some have used society's concern over the natural environment to differentiate themselves from competitors. One such company is Dell Computer, which recently initiated a recycling program for businesses and consumers that includes computers, monitors, keyboards, and mice—all those items that may be hanging around in your house.

How does this work? You pay a fee of $15.00 per 50 pounds of weight, and Dell has someone pick up your computers and monitors. The average computer and monitor weigh more than 50 pounds but less than 100 pounds, so the cost is likely to be $30.00 to the customer. Dell then will either recycle or resell the old computer equipment, thus sparing landfills from the hazardous materials contained in much of today's existing computer equipment.

1. Assume that the price paid by the owners of the old computer equipment does not cover Dell's cost of recycling. What benefits might Dell gain that would be worth this expense?

2. What actions might the government take if it became concerned about the disposal of unwanted computer equipment? How can Dell's recycling efforts be considered similar to an environmental management perspective?

3. Might Dell's computer recycling program help to differentiate it from other computer manufacturers? How much influence would a recycling program like the one described above for Dell computer have on your decision to buy a computer from a particular company?

Videos

The Nike video case that accompanies this chapter is located in Appendix 1 at the back of the book.

Student Materials

Need a tune-up? A study guide and OneKey access code are available to aid in your review of chapter material. Your instructor may choose to have these items shrink-wrapped with your text or you may purchase them separately at www.prenhall.com/marketing.

■ *After reading this chapter, you should be able to*

1. Explain the importance of information to the company and its understanding of the marketplace **2.** *Define* the marketing information system and discuss its parts **3.** *Outline* the steps in the marketing research process **4.** *Explain* how companies analyze and distribute marketing information **5.** *Discuss* the special issues some marketing researchers face, including public policy and ethics issues

Managing Marketing Information

4

ROAD MAP | Previewing the Concepts

In the last chapter, you learned about the complex and changing marketing environment. In this chapter, we'll continue our exploration of how marketers go about understanding the marketplace and consumers. We'll look at how companies develop and manage information about important marketplace elements—information about customers, competitors, products, and marketing programs. We'll examine marketing information systems designed to give managers the right information, in the right form, at the right time to help them make better marketing decisions. We'll also take a close look at the marketing research process and at some special marketing research considerations. To succeed in today's marketplace, companies must know how to manage mountains of marketing information effectively.

We'll start the chapter with a look at a classic marketing blunder—Coca-Cola's ill-considered decision some years ago to introduce New Coke. The company based its decision on substantial marketing research, yet the new product fizzled badly. As you read on, ask yourself how a large and resourceful marketing company such as Coca-Cola could make such a huge research mistake. The moral: If it can happen to Coca-Cola, it can happen to any company.

I n 1985, in what has now become an all-time classic marketing tale, the Coca-Cola Company made a major marketing blunder. After 99 successful years, it set aside its long-standing rule—"Don't mess with Mother Coke"—and dropped its original-formula Coke! In its place came *New* Coke with a sweeter, smoother taste.

At first, amid the introductory flurry of advertising and publicity, New Coke sold well. But sales soon went flat, as a stunned public reacted. Coke began receiving sacks of mail and more than 1,500 phone calls each day from angry consumers. One angry consumer addressed his concerns in a letter sent to "Chief Dodo, The Coca-Cola Company." (Coke's CEO claimed that he was less concerned about the letter than about the fact that it was actually delivered to him!) Other consumers panicked, filling their basements with cases of the old tried-and-true. One man in Texas drove to a local bottler and bought $1,000 worth of the old Coca-Cola. A group called "Old Cola Drinkers" staged protests, handed out T-shirts, and threatened a class-action suit

unless Coca-Cola brought back the old formula. Meanwhile, Pepsi was so delighted that it declared April 23, 1985, New Coke's debut day, a corporate holiday.

After only three months, the Coca-Cola Company brought old Coke back. That July day, virtually every major newspaper featured the return of the "old Coke" on the front page. Now called "Coke Classic," the old formula sold side-by-side with New Coke on supermarket shelves. The company said that New Coke would remain its flagship brand, but consumers had a different idea. By the end of that year, Classic was outselling New Coke in supermarkets by two to one.

Quick reaction saved Coca-Cola from potential disaster. The company stepped up efforts for Coke Classic and slotted New Coke into a supporting role. Coke Classic again became the company's main brand and the country's leading soft drink. New Coke became the company's "attack brand"—its Pepsi stopper—and ads boldly compared New Coke's taste with Pepsi's. Still, New Coke managed only a 2 percent market share. In the spring of 1990, the company repackaged New Coke and relaunched it as a brand extension with a new name, Coke II. Today, Coke Classic captures more than 19 percent of the U.S. soft drink market; Coke II sells in only a few selected markets.

Why was New Coke introduced in the first place? What went wrong? Many analysts blame the blunder on poor marketing research.

In the early 1980s, although Coke was still the leading soft drink, it was slowly losing market share to Pepsi. For almost 15 years, Pepsi had successfully mounted the "Pepsi Challenge," a series of televised taste tests showing that consumers preferred the sweeter taste of Pepsi. By early 1985, although Coke led in the overall market, Pepsi led in share of supermarket sales by 2 percent. (That doesn't sound like much, but 2 percent of today's huge U.S. soft drink market amounts to almost $1.2 billion in retail sales!) Coca-Cola had to do something to stop the loss of its market share, and the solution appeared to be a change in Coke's taste.

Coca-Cola began the largest new-product research project in the company's history. It spent more than two years and $4 million on research before settling on a new formula. It conducted some 200,000 taste tests—30,000 on the final formula alone. In blind tests, 60 percent of consumers chose the new Coke over the old, and 52 percent chose it over Pepsi. Research showed that New Coke would be a winner, and the company introduced it with confidence. So what happened?

Looking back, we can see that Coke defined its marketing research problem too narrowly. The research looked only at taste; it did not explore consumers' feelings about dropping the old Coke and replacing it with a new version. It took no account of the *intangibles*—Coke's name, history, packaging, cultural heritage, and image. However, to many people, Coke stands alongside baseball, hot dogs, and apple pie as an American institution; it represents the very fabric of America. Coke's symbolic meaning turned out to be more important to many consumers than its taste. Research addressing a broader set of issues would have detected these strong emotions.

Coke's managers may also have used poor judgment in interpreting the research and planning strategies around it. For example, they took the finding that 60 percent of consumers preferred New Coke's taste to mean that the new product would win in the marketplace, as when a political candidate wins with 60 percent of the vote. But it also meant that 40 percent still liked the original formula. By dropping the old Coke, the company trampled the taste buds of the large core of loyal Coke drinkers who didn't want a change. The company might have been wiser to leave the old Coke alone and introduce New Coke as a brand extension, as it later did successfully with Cherry Coke.

The Coca-Cola Company has one of the largest, best-managed, and most advanced marketing research operations in America. Good marketing research has kept the company atop the rough-and-tumble soft drink market for decades. But marketing research is far from an exact science. Consumers are full of surprises, and figuring them out can be awfully tough. If Coca-Cola can make a large marketing research mistake, any company can.[1]

In order to produce superior value and satisfaction for customers, companies need information at almost every turn. As the New Coke story highlights, good products and marketing programs begin with a thorough understanding of consumer needs and wants. Companies also need an abundance of information on competitors, resellers, and other actors and forces in the marketplace.

Increasingly, marketers are viewing information not only as an input for making better decisions but also as an important strategic asset and marketing tool. A company's information may prove to be its chief competitive advantage. Competitors can copy each other's equipment, products, and procedures, but they cannot duplicate the company's information and intellectual capital. Several companies have recently recognized this by appointing vice presidents of knowledge, learning, or intellectual capital.

In today's more rapidly changing environments, managers need up-to-date information to make timely, high-quality decisions. In turn, with the recent explosion of information technologies, companies can now generate information in great quantities. In fact, today's managers often receive too much information.

One study found that with all the companies offering data, and with all the information now available through supermarket scanners, a packaged-goods brand manager is bombarded with 1 million to 1 *billion* new numbers each week. Another study found that large retailers typically now have the equivalent of 320 miles of bookshelves of information on their products. Wal-Mart, the largest retailer of all, has more than three and a half times that much information in it's data warehouse. Thus, running out of information is not a problem, but seeing through the "data smog" is. "In this oh-so-overwhelming Information age," comments one observer, "it's all too easy to be buried, burdened, and burned out by data overload.[2]

Despite this data glut, marketers frequently complain that they lack enough information of the *right* kind. One recent study found that managers lose as much as three hours a day looking for the right information, costing U.S. companies more than $2.5 billion annually. Another study found that although half of the managers surveyed said they couldn't cope with the volume of information coming at them, two-thirds wanted even more. The researcher concluded that, "despite the volume, they're still not getting what they want."[3] Thus, most marketing managers don't need *more* information, they need *better* information.

A former CEO at Unilever once said that if Unilever only knew what it knows, it would double its profits. The meaning is clear: Many companies sit on rich information but fail to manage and use it well.[4] Companies must design effective marketing information systems that give managers the right information, in the right form, at the right time to help them make better marketing decisions.

■ Information overload: "In this oh so overwhelming Information age, it's all too easy to be buried, burdened, and burned out by data overload."

A **marketing information system (MIS)** consists of people, equipment, and procedures to gather, sort, analyze, evaluate, and distribute needed, timely, and accurate information to marketing decision makers. Figure 4.1 shows that the MIS begins and ends with information users—marketing managers, internal and external partners, and others who need marketing information. First, it interacts with these information users to *assess information needs*. Next, it *develops needed information* from internal company databases, marketing intelligence activities, and marketing research. Then it helps users to analyze information to put it in the right form for making marketing decisions and managing customer relationships. Finally, the MIS *distributes* the marketing information and helps managers *use* it in their decision making.

Marketing information system (MIS)

People, equipment, and procedures to gather, sort, analyze, evaluate, and distribute needed, timely, and accurate information to marketing decision makers.

FIGURE 4.1

The Marketing Information System

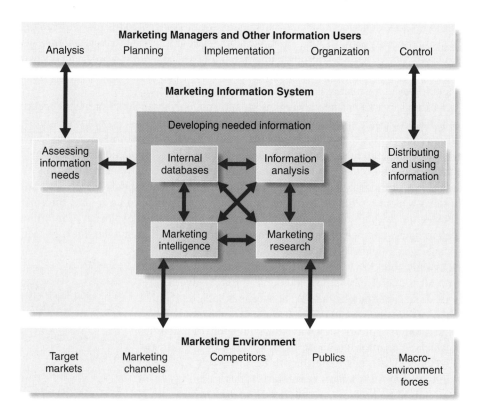

▪▪▪ Assessing Marketing Information Needs

The marketing information system primarily serves the company's marketing and other managers. However, it may also provide information to external partners, such as suppliers, resellers, or marketing services agencies. For example, Wal-Mart might give Procter & Gamble and other key suppliers access to information on customer buying patterns and inventory levels. In addition, important customers may be given limited access to the information system. Dell Computer creates tailored Premium Pages for large customers, giving them access to product design, order status, and product support and service information. FedEx lets customers into its information system to schedule and track shipments. In designing an information system, the company must consider the needs of all of these users.

A good marketing information system balances the information users would *like* to have against what they really *need* and what is *feasible* to offer. The company begins by interviewing managers to find out what information they would like. Some managers will ask for whatever information they can get without thinking carefully about what they really need. Too much information can be as harmful as too little. Other managers may omit things they ought to know, or they may not know to ask for some types of information they should have. For example, managers might need to know that a competitor plans to introduce a new product during the coming year. Because they do not know about the new product, they do not think to ask about it. The MIS must monitor the marketing environment in order to provide decision makers with information they should have to make key marketing decisions.

Sometimes the company cannot provide the needed information, either because it is not available or because of MIS limitations. For example, a brand manager might want to know how competitors will change their advertising budgets next year and how these changes will affect industry market shares. The information on planned budgets probably is not available. Even if it is, the company's MIS may not be advanced enough to forecast resulting changes in market shares.

Finally, the costs of obtaining, processing, storing, and delivering information can mount quickly. The company must decide whether the benefits of having additional information are worth the costs of providing it, and both value and cost are often hard to assess.

By itself, information has no worth; its value comes from its *use*. In many cases, additional information will do little to change or improve a manager's decision, or the costs of the information may exceed the returns from the improved decision. Marketers should not assume that additional information will always be worth obtaining. Rather, they should weigh carefully the costs of getting more information against the benefits resulting from it.

■ Developing Marketing Information

Marketers can obtain the needed information from *internal data, marketing intelligence,* and *marketing research*.

Internal Data

Many companies build extensive **internal databases**, electronic collections of information obtained from data sources within the company. Marketing managers can readily access and work with information in the database to identify marketing opportunities and problems, plan programs, and evaluate performance.

Information in the database can come from many sources. The accounting department prepares financial statements and keeps detailed records of sales, costs, and cash flows. Operations reports on production schedules, shipments, and inventories. The sales force reports on reseller reactions and competitor activities. The marketing department furnishes information on customer demographics, psychographics, and buying behavior. And the customer service department keeps records of customer satisfaction or service problems. Research studies done for one department may provide useful information for several others.

Here is an example of how one company uses its internal database to make better marketing decisions:

Internal databases
Electronic collections of information obtained from data sources within the company.

> USAA, which provides financial services to U.S. military personnel and their families, maintains a customer database built from customer purchasing histories and from information collected directly from customers. To keep the database fresh, the organization regularly surveys its 5 million customers worldwide to learn things such as whether they have children (and if so, how old they are), if they have moved recently, and when they plan to retire. USAA uses the database to tailor marketing offers to the specific needs of individual customers. For example, if the family has college-age children, the USAA sends those children information on how to manage their credit cards. If the family has younger children, it sends booklets on things like financing a child's education. Or, for customers looking toward retirement, it sends information on estate planning. Through skillful use of its database, USAA serves each customer uniquely, resulting in high levels of customer loyalty—the roughly $8.6 billion company retains 97 percent of its customers.[5]

Internal databases usually can be accessed more quickly and cheaply than other information sources, but they also present some problems. Because internal information was collected for other purposes, it may be incomplete or in the wrong form for making marketing decisions. For example, sales and cost data used by the accounting department for preparing financial statements must be adapted for use in evaluating the value of specific

■ Financial services provider USAA uses its extensive database to tailor marketing offers to the specific needs of individual customers, resulting in greater than 96 percent customer retention.

customers or segments or product, sales force, or channel performance. Data ages quickly; keeping the database current requires a major effort. In addition, a large company produces mountains of information, and keeping track of it all is difficult. The database information must be well integrated and readily accessible so that managers can find it easily and use it effectively.

Marketing Intelligence

Marketing intelligence

The systematic collection and analysis of publicly available information about competitors and developments in the marketing environment.

Marketing intelligence is the systematic collection and analysis of publicly available information about competitors and developments in the marketplace. The goal of marketing intelligence is to improve strategic decision making, assess and track competitors' actions, and provide early warning of opportunities and threats.

Competitive intelligence gathering has grown dramatically as more and more companies are now busily snooping on their competitors. Techniques range from quizzing the company's own employees and benchmarking competitors' products to researching the Internet, lurking around industry trade shows, and rooting through rivals' trash bins.

Much intelligence can be collected from people inside the rival companies—executives, engineers and scientists, purchasing agents, and the sales force. Consider the following example:

> Spies don't always enter a rival's lair through the back door. Sometimes they stride in, and are even welcomed by their hosts. Bob Ayling, ex-chief executive of British Airways, accomplished such a mission when he visited the offices of the recently launched EasyJet. . . . Ayling approached the company's founder, Stelios Haji-Ioannou, to ask whether he could visit, claiming to be fascinated as to how the Greek entrepreneur had made the budget airline formula work. Haji-Ioannou not only agreed, but allegedly showed Ayling his business plan. [A year later, British Air] announced the launch of Go. "It was a carbon copy of EasyJet," says . . . EasyGroup's director of corporate affairs. "Same planes, same direct ticket sales, same use of a secondary airport, and same idea to sell on-board refreshments. They succeeded in stealing our business model—it was a highly effective spying job."[6]

■ Marketing intelligence: Procter & Gamble admitted to "dumpster diving" at rival Unilever's Helene Curtis headquarters. When P&G's top management learned of the questionable practice, it stopped the project, voluntarily informed Unilever, and set up talks to right whatever competitive wrongs had been done.

The company can also obtain important intelligence information from suppliers, resellers, and key customers. Or it can get good information by observing competitors. It can buy and analyze competitors' products, monitor their sales, check for new patents, and examine various types of physical evidence. For example, one company regularly checks out competitors' parking lots—full lots might indicate plenty of work and prosperity; half-full lots might suggest hard times.

Some companies have even rifled their competitors' garbage, which is legally considered abandoned property once it leaves the premises. In one garbage-snatching incident, Oracle was caught rifling through rival Microsoft's dumpsters. Microsoft objected loudly. But a later investigation of the incident was closed because, technically, no crime had been committed. In another case, Procter & Gamble admitted to "dumpster diving" at rival Unilever's headquarters. The target was Unilever's hair-care products—including Salon Selectives, Finesse, Thermasilk, and Helen Curtis—which competed with P&G's own Pantene, Head & Shoulders, and Pert brands. "Apparently, the operation was a big success," notes an analyst. "P&G got its mitts on just about every iota of info there was to be had about Unilever's brands." However, when news of the questionable tactics reached top P&G managers, they were shocked. They immediately stopped the project, voluntarily informed Unilever, and set up negotiations to right whatever competitive wrongs had been done. Although P&G claims it broke no laws, the company reported that the dumpster raids "violated our strict guidelines regarding our business policies."[7]

Competitors may reveal intelligence information through their annual reports, business publications, trade show exhibits, press releases, advertisements, and Web pages. The Internet is proving to be a vast new source of competitor-supplied information. Most companies now place volumes of information on their Web sites, providing details to attract customers, partners, suppliers, or franchisees. Using Internet search engines, marketers can search specific competitor names, events, or trends and see what turns up.[8]

Even companies with the most basic technology can use it to gather intelligence, advises a competitive intelligence consultant. Keep tabs on your rivals' Web sites, and check to see if they have updated or altered their copy on any product lines. Have they redesigned the site or shifted its focus? What do search engines turn up on rivals? How is the press covering them? Your industry? Often, publicly accessible bulletin boards offer additional clues: Investors may log on to discuss rumors and tidbits of information. And keep watch for off-duty employees. They post, too. "Clients are often surprised that there's so much out there to know," says the consultant. "They're busy with their day-to-day operations and they don't realize how much information can be obtained with a few strategic keystrokes."

Intelligence seekers can also pore through any of thousands of online databases. Some are free. For example, the U.S. Security and Exchange Commission's database provides a huge stockpile of financial information on public competitors, and the U.S. Patent Office database reveals patents competitors have filed. And for a fee, companies can subscribe to any of more than 3,000 online databases and information search services such as Dialog, DataStar, LEXIS-NEXIS, Dow Jones News Retrieval, UMI ProQuest, and Dun & Bradstreet's Online Access.

Facing determined marketing intelligence efforts by competitors, most companies are now taking countermeasures. For example, Unilever has begun widespread competitive intelligence training. According to a former Unilever staffer, "We were told how to protect information, as well as how to get it from competitors. We were warned to always keep our mouths shut when traveling. . . . We were even warned that spies from competitors could be posing as drivers at the mini-cab company we used." Unilever even performs random checks on internal security. Says the former staffer, "At one [internal marketing] conference, we were set up when an actor was employed to infiltrate the group. The idea was to see who spoke to him, how much they told him, and how long it took to realize that no one knew him. He ended up being there for a long time."[9]

The growing use of marketing intelligence raises a number of ethical issues. Although most of the preceding techniques are legal, and some are considered to be shrewdly competitive, some may involve questionable ethics. Clearly, companies should take advantage of publicly available information. However, they should not stoop to snoop. With all the legitimate intelligence sources now available, a company does not have to break the law or accepted codes of ethics to get good intelligence.

Marketing Research

In addition to information about competitor and marketplace happenings, marketers often need formal studies of specific situations. For example, Sears wants to know what appeals will be most effective in its corporate advertising campaign. Or Toshiba wants to know how many and what kinds of people or companies will buy its new superfast notebook computer. In such situations, marketing intelligence will not provide the detailed information needed. Managers will need marketing research.

Marketing research is the systematic design, collection, analysis, and reporting of data relevant to a specific marketing situation facing an organization. Companies use marketing research in a wide variety of situations. For example, marketing research can help marketers understand customer satisfaction and purchase behavior. It can help them assess

Marketing research
The systematic design, collection, analysis, and reporting of data relevant to a specific marketing situation facing an organization.

market potential and market share or to measure the effectiveness of pricing, product, distribution, and promotion activities.

Some large companies have their own research departments that work with marketing managers on marketing research projects. This is how Kraft, Citigroup, and many other corporate giants handle marketing research. In addition, these companies—like their smaller counterparts—frequently hire outside research specialists to consult with management on specific marketing problems and conduct marketing research studies. Sometimes firms simply purchase data collected by outside firms to aid in their decision making.

The marketing research process has four steps (see Figure 4.2): *defining the problem and research objectives*, *developing the research plan*, *implementing the research plan*, and *interpreting and reporting the findings*.

Defining the Problem and Research Objectives

Marketing managers and researchers must work closely together to define the problem and agree on research objectives. The manager best understands the decision for which information is needed; the researcher best understands marketing research and how to obtain the information.

Defining the problem and research objectives is often the hardest step in the research process. The manager may know that something is wrong, without knowing the specific causes. For example, in the New Coke case, Coca-Cola defined its research problem too narrowly, with disastrous results. In another example, managers of a large discount retail store chain hastily decided that falling sales were caused by poor advertising. As a result, they ordered research to test the company's advertising. When this research showed that current advertising was reaching the right people with the right message, the managers were puzzled. It turned out that the real problem was that the chain was not delivering the prices, products, and service promised in the advertising. Careful problem definition would have avoided the cost and delay of doing advertising research.

After the problem has been defined carefully, the manager and researcher must set the research objectives. A marketing research project might have one of three types of objectives. The objective of **exploratory research** is to gather preliminary information that will help define the problem and suggest hypotheses. The objective of **descriptive research** is to describe things, such as the market potential for a product or the demographics and attitudes of consumers who buy the product. The objective of **causal research** is to test hypotheses about cause-and-effect relationships. For example, would a 10 percent decrease in tuition at a private college result in an enrollment increase sufficient to offset the reduced tuition? Managers often start with exploratory research and later follow with descriptive or causal research.

The statement of the problem and research objectives guides the entire research process. The manager and researcher should put the statement in writing to be certain that they agree on the purpose and expected results of the research.

Developing the Research Plan

Once the research problems and objectives have been defined, researchers must determine the exact information needed, develop a plan for gathering it efficiently, and present the plan to management. The research plan outlines sources of existing data and spells out the specific research approaches, contact methods, sampling plans, and instruments that researchers will use to gather new data.

Research objectives must be translated into specific information needs. For example, suppose Campbell decides to conduct research on how soup consumers would react to the introduction of new bowl-shaped plastic containers that it has used successfully for a number of its other products. The containers would cost more but would allow consumers to

Exploratory research
Marketing research to gather preliminary information that will help define problems and suggest hypotheses.

Descriptive research
Marketing research to better describe marketing problems, situations, or markets, such as the market potential for a product or the demographics and attitudes of consumers.

Causal research
Marketing research to test hypotheses about cause-and-effect relationships.

FIGURE 4.2
The Marketing Research Process

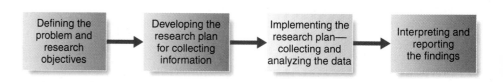

heat the soup in a microwave oven without adding water or milk and to eat it without using dishes. This research might call for the following specific information:

- The demographic, economic, and lifestyle characteristics of current soup users. (Busy working couples might find the convenience of the new packaging worth the price; families with children might want to pay less and wash the bowls.)

- Consumer-usage patterns for soup: how much soup they eat, where, and when. (The new packaging might be ideal for adults eating lunch on the go, but less convenient for parents feeding lunch to several children.)

- Retailer reactions to the new packaging. (Failure to get retailer support could hurt sales of the new package.)

- Consumer attitudes toward the new packaging. (The red-and-white Campbell can has become an American institution—will consumers accept the new packaging?)

- Forecasts of sales of both new and current packages. (Will the new packaging increase Campbell's profits?)

Campbell managers will need these and many other types of information to decide whether to introduce the new packaging.

The research plan should be presented in a *written proposal*. A written proposal is especially important when the research project is large and complex or when an outside firm carries it out. The proposal should cover the management problems addressed and the research objectives, the information to be obtained, and the way the results will help management decision making. The proposal also should include research costs.

To meet the manager's information needs, the research plan can call for gathering secondary data, primary data, or both. **Secondary data** consist of information that already exists somewhere, having been collected for another purpose. **Primary data** consist of information collected for the specific purpose at hand.

Gathering Secondary Data   Researchers usually start by gathering secondary data. The company's internal database provides a good starting point. However, the company can also tap a wide assortment of external information sources, including commercial data services and government sources (see Table 4.1).

Companies can buy secondary data reports from outside suppliers.[10] For example, Information Resources, Inc., sells supermarket scanner purchase data from a panel of 55,000 households nationally, with measures of trial and repeat purchasing, brand loyalty, and buyer demographics. The *Monitor* service by Yankelovich and Partners sells information on important social and lifestyle trends. These and other firms supply high-quality data to suit a wide variety of marketing information needs.

Using commercial **online databases**, marketing researchers can conduct their own searches of secondary data sources. General database services such as CompuServe, Dialog, and LEXIS-NEXIS put an incredible wealth of information at the keyboards of marketing decision makers. Beyond commercial Web sites offering information for a fee, almost every industry association, government agency, business publication, and news medium offers free information to those tenacious enough to find their Web sites. There are so many Web sites offering data that finding the right ones can become an almost overwhelming task.

Secondary data can usually be obtained more quickly and at a lower cost than primary data. For example, an Internet or online

Secondary data
Information that already exists somewhere, having been collected for another purpose.

Primary data
Information collected for the specific purpose at hand.

Online databases
Computerized collections of information available from online commercial sources or via the Internet.

■ Online database services such as Dialog put an incredible wealth of information at the keyboards of marketing decision makers. Dialog puts "information to change the world, or your corner of it," at your fingertips.

TABLE 4.1   Selected External Information Sources

For business data:

AC Nielsen Corporation (www.acnielsen.com) provides supermarket scanner data on sales, market share, and retail prices; data on household purchasing; and data on television audiences.

Information Resources, Inc. (www.infores.com) provides supermarket scanner data for tracking grocery product movement and new product purchasing data.

Arbitron (www.arbitron.com) provides local-market and Internet radio audience and advertising expenditure information, among other media and ad spending data.

NDC Health Information Services (www.ndchealth.com) reports on the movement of drugs, laboratory supplies, animal health products, and personal care products.

Simmons Market Research Bureau (www.smrb.com) provides detailed analysis of consumer patterns in 400 product categories in selected markets.

Dun & Bradstreet (www.dnb.com) maintains a database containing information on more than 50 million individual companies around the globe.

Media Metrix (www.mediametrix.com) provides audience measurement and geodemographic analysis of Internet and digital media users around the world.

Dialog (http://library.dialog.com) offers access to ABI/INFORM, a database of articles from 800+ publications and to reports, newsletters, and directories covering dozens of industries.

LEXIS-NEXIS (www.lexis-nexis.com) features articles from business, consumer, and marketing publications plus tracking of firms, industries, trends, and promotion techniques.

CompuServe (www.compuserve.com) provides access to databases of business and consumer demographics, government reports, and patent records, plus articles from newspapers, and research reports.

Dow Jones Interactive (www.djinteractive.com) specializes in in-depth financial, historical, and operational information on public and private companies.

Hoover's Online (www.hoovers.com) provides business descriptions, financial overviews, and news about major companies around the world.

CNN (www.cnn.com) reports U.S. and global news and covers the markets and news-making companies in detail.

American Demographics (www.americandemographics.com) reports on demographic trends and their significance for businesses.

For government data:

Securities and Exchange Commission Edgar database (www.sec.gov) provides financial data on U.S. public corporations.

Small Business Administration (www.sba.gov) features information and links for small business owners.

Federal Trade Commission (www.ftc.gov) shows regulations and decisions related to consumer protection and antitrust laws.

Stat-USA (www.stat-usa.gov) a Department of Commerce site, highlights statistics on U.S. business and international trade.

U.S. Census (www.census.gov) provides detailed statistics and trends about the U.S. population.

U.S. Patent and Trademark Office (www.uspto.gov) allows searches to determine who has filed for trademarks and patents.

For Internet data:

Cyber Atlas (http://cyberatlas.internet.com) brings together a wealth of information about the Internet and its users, from consumers to e-commerce.

Interactive Advertising Bureau (www.iab.net) covers statistics about advertising on the Internet.

Jupiter Research (www.jupiterresearch.com) monitors Web traffic and ranks the most popular sites.

database search might provide all the information Campbell needs on soup usage, quickly and at low cost. A study to collect primary information might take weeks or months and cost thousands of dollars. Also, secondary sources sometimes can provide data an individual company cannot collect on its own—information that either is not directly available or would be too expensive to collect. For example, it would be too expensive for Campbell to conduct a continuing retail store audit to find out about the market shares, prices, and displays of competitors' brands. But it can buy the InfoScan service from Information

TABLE 4.2   Planning Primary Data Collection

Research Approaches	Contact Methods	Sampling Plan	Research Instruments
Observation	Mail	Sampling unit	Questionnaire
Survey	Telephone	Sample size	Mechanical instruments
Experiment	Personal	Sampling procedure	
	Online		

Resources, Inc., which provides this information from thousands of scanner-equipped supermarkets in dozens of U.S. markets.

Secondary data can also present problems. The needed information may not exist—researchers can rarely obtain all the data they need from secondary sources. For example, Campbell will not find existing information about consumer reactions to new packaging that it has not yet placed on the market. Even when data can be found, they might not be very usable. The researcher must evaluate secondary information carefully to make certain it is *relevant* (fits research project needs), *accurate* (reliably collected and reported), *current* (up-to-date enough for current decisions), and *impartial* (objectively collected and reported).

Primary Data Collection   Secondary data provide a good starting point for research and often help to define problems and research objectives. In most cases, however, the company must also collect primary data. Just as researchers must carefully evaluate the quality of secondary information, they also must take great care when collecting primary data. They need to make sure that it will be relevant, accurate, current, and unbiased. Table 4.2 shows that designing a plan for primary data collection calls for a number of decisions on *research approaches*, *contact methods*, *sampling plan*, and *research instruments*.

Research Approaches.   Research approaches for gathering primary data include observation, surveys, and experiments. **Observational research** involves gathering primary data by observing relevant people, actions, and situations. For example, a consumer packaged-goods marketer might visit supermarkets and observe shoppers as they browse the store, pick up products and examine packages, and make actual buying decisions. Or a bank might evaluate possible new branch locations by checking traffic patterns, neighborhood conditions, and the location of competing branches. Fisher-Price even set up an observation lab in which it could observe the reactions of little tots to new toys:

The Fisher-Price Play Lab is a sunny, toy-strewn space where, since 1961, lucky kids have tested Fisher-Price prototypes. Today three boys and three girls,

Observational research

The gathering of primary data by observing relevant people, actions, and situations.

■ Observational research: Fisher-Price set up an observation lab in which it could observe the reactions of little tots to new toys.

all four-year-olds, speed through the front door. Two boys tug quietly, but firmly, for the wheel of a new radio-controlled race set—a brand-new offering. The girls skid to a stop near a small subdevelopment of dollhouses. And from behind the one-way glass, toy designers study the action intently, occasionally stepping out to join the play. At the Play Lab, creation and (attempted) destruction happily coexist. Over an eight week session with these kids, designers will test dozens of toy concepts, sending out crude models, then increasingly sophisticated revisions, to figure out what gets kids worked up into a new-toy frenzy.[11]

A wide range of companies now use *ethnographic research.* Ethnographic research involves sending trained observers to watch consumers in their "natural environments." Researchers observe consumers up close to learn how they use and feel about products and services. Consider the following example:

Four years ago, Sunbeam wanted to extend its Coleman brand—known for its distinctive forest green encased lanterns and its red coolers—into gas barbecue grills. But company execs couldn't decide how to design and position the new line. Even after hours of focus groups and reams of quantitative data, the outdoor cooking team felt like it had a whole lot of information but little insight. "We were hearing a lot of passion about grilling, particularly among men," says a Sunbeam marketer, "but they couldn't really describe *why* they had the passion." Sunbeam execs turned to ethnography for help. Researchers hoisted video cameras onto shoulders and headed to their consumers' native habitat: the backyard. By hanging out with the guys around the grill and listening in on the gab, the team eventually gathered a key insight: A gas grill isn't really a tool that cooks hamburgers and hot dogs. Rather, it's the centerpiece of warm family moments worthy of a summer highlights reel. So, rather than create and promote the new Coleman Grill in terms of BTUs, rotisserie options, and cooking square inches, Sunbeam designed the grill to evoke nostalgia for the camping experience with friends and family. The company positioned the product and grilling experience as "a relaxing ritual where the grilling area is the stage," an event that takes place in a "backyard oasis." The result: The Coleman Grill did a scorching $50 million in sales in its first year, making the product line one of the most successful launches in Sunbeam history.[12]

Ethnographic research often yields the kinds of intimate details that just don't emerge from traditional focus groups. For example, by videotaping consumers in the shower, plumbing fixture maker Moen uncovered safety risks that consumers didn't recognize—such as the habit some women have of shaving their legs while holding on to one unit's temperature control. Moen would find it almost impossible to discover such design flaws simply by asking questions.[13] To glean greater insights into buying behavior, one company even went so far as to set up an actual retail store that serves as an ethnographic lab (see Marketing at Work 4.1).

Many companies collect data through *mechanical* observation via machine or computer. For example, Nielsen Media Research attaches *people meters* to television sets in selected homes to record who watches which programs. Other companies use *checkout scanners* to record shoppers' purchases so that manufacturers and retailers can assess product sales and store performance. MediaMetrix places special software on consumers' PCs to monitor Web surfing patterns and produce ratings for top Web sites.

Observational research can obtain information that people are unwilling or unable to provide. In some cases, observation may be the only way to obtain the needed information. In contrast, some things simply cannot be observed, such as feelings, attitudes and motives, or private behavior. Long-term or infrequent behavior is also difficult to observe. Because of these limitations, researchers often use observation along with other data collection methods.

Survey research, the most widely used method for primary data collection, is the approach best suited for gathering *descriptive* information. A company that wants to know about people's knowledge, attitudes, preferences, or buying behavior can often find out by asking them directly.

Survey research

The gathering of primary data by asking people questions about their knowledge, attitudes, preferences, and buying behavior.

Some firms provide marketers with a more comprehensive look at buying patterns through **single-source data systems**. These systems start with surveys of huge consumer panels—carefully selected groups of consumers who agree to participate in ongoing research. Then, they electronically monitor survey respondents' purchases and exposure to various marketing activities. Combining the survey and monitoring information gives a better understanding of the link between consumer characteristics, attitudes, and purchase behavior.

The major advantage of survey research is its flexibility—it can be used to obtain many different kinds of information in many different situations. However, survey research also presents some problems. Sometimes people are unable to answer survey questions because they cannot remember or have never thought about what they do and why. People may be unwilling to respond to unknown interviewers or about things they consider private. Respondents may answer survey questions even when they do not know the answer in order to appear smarter or more informed. Or they may try to help the interviewer by giving pleasing answers. Finally, busy people may not take the time, or they might resent the intrusion into their privacy.

Whereas observation is best suited for exploratory research and surveys for descriptive research, **experimental research** is best suited for gathering *causal* information. Experiments involve selecting matched groups of subjects, giving them different treatments, controlling unrelated factors, and checking for differences in group responses. Thus, experimental research tries to explain cause-and-effect relationships.

For example, before adding a new sandwich to its menu, McDonald's might use experiments to test the effects on sales of two different prices it might charge. It could introduce the new sandwich at one price in one city and at another price in another city. If the cities are similar, and if all other marketing efforts for the sandwich are the same, then differences in sales in the two cities could be related to the price charged.

Contact Methods. Information can be collected by mail, telephone, personal interview, or online. Table 4.3 shows the strengths and weaknesses of each of these contact methods.

Mail questionnaires can be used to collect large amounts of information at a low cost per respondent. Respondents may give more honest answers to more personal questions on a mail questionnaire than to an unknown interviewer in person or over the phone. Also, no interviewer is involved to bias the respondent's answers. However, mail questionnaires are not very flexible—all respondents answer the same questions in a fixed order. Mail surveys usually take longer to complete, and the response rate—the number of people returning completed questionnaires—is often very low. Finally, the researcher often has little control over the mail questionnaire sample. Even with a good mailing list, it is hard to control *who* at the mailing address fills out the questionnaire.

Telephone interviewing is the one of the best methods for gathering information quickly, and it provides greater flexibility than mail questionnaires. Interviewers can explain difficult questions and, depending on the answers they receive, skip some questions or probe

Single-source data systems
Electronic monitoring systems that link consumers' exposure to television advertising and promotion (measured using television meters) with what they buy in stores (measured using store checkout scanners).

Experimental research
The gathering of primary data by selecting matched groups of subjects, giving them different treatments, controlling related factors, and checking for differences in group responses.

TABLE 4.3   Strengths and Weaknesses of Contact Methods

	Mail	Telephone	Personal	Online
Flexibility	Poor	Good	Excellent	Good
Quantity of data that can be collected	Good	Fair	Excellent	Good
Control of interviewer effects	Excellent	Fair	Poor	Fair
Control of sample	Fair	Excellent	Fair	Poor
Speed of data collection	Poor	Excellent	Good	Excellent
Response rate	Fair	Good	Good	Good
Cost	Good	Fair	Poor	Excellent

Source: Adapted with permission from *Marketing Research: Measurement and Method,* 7th ed., by Donald S. Tull and Dell Hawkins. Copyright 1993 by Macmillan Publishing Company.

Marketing at Work | 4.1

OnceFamous: Watching Consumers in Their Natural Settings

Microphones capture every word while cameras record the action. Observers, posted everywhere, document each move. The runway at the Academy Awards? Or the paparazzi shadowing the royal family in London? No, it's all happening at a retail store called OnceFamous, and the observers and microphones aren't focused on celebrities, they're scrutinizing consumers.

OnceFamous is a unique ethnographic laboratory for studying consumer behavior in a natural setting. Although designed to look and feel like an ordinary retail store, this boutique is anything but ordinary. For starters, surveillance is everywhere at OnceFamous. Ethnographers watch from behind mirrored glass, while salespeople interview would-be buyers. Store employees—both on the floor and hidden behind glass—study the meanderings, whims,

and buying behaviors of those who wander in. Five cameras track consumers as they prowl the store—documenting both the smiles and scowls of browsers. Sensitive hidden microphones catch every utterance, from shoppers' questions to salespeople to snide comments between friends. Later, researchers pore over the tapes and analyze each shopper's behavior, looking for clues.

Although it all sounds like a massive invasion of consumer privacy, there's no need to fear Big Brother here. The store posts a prominent sign, complete with flashing lights, to alert shoppers that the store is in "Testing Mode." Additional signs invite shoppers who don't wish to be observed to "kindly visit us when this sign has been removed."

This 2300-sq-ft retail store is the work of FAME, a retail brand advertising agency located in Minneapolis. In late

2001, FAME opened the unique observational research lab in a heavily trafficked downtown skyway. Stocked with fancy pillows, knickknacks, and hand-made arts and crafts, the store attracts a variety of shoppers. Mingled with the store's regular inventory is an ever-changing assortment of clients' test products, including everything from ornaments to a new line of funny infant T-shirts.

When it comes to consumer research, OnceFamous beats the sterile, artificial cubicles used in many opinion survey research situations. Rather than interrogate test subjects in an artificial environment, researchers at OnceFamous watch shoppers in their natural surroundings. In fact, much of the time OnceFamous is just a store like any other store—it doesn't stay in "test mode" all of the time and it even turns a profit on sales. Such ethnographic

Watching consumers in their natural settings: OnceFamous is an actual retail store that serves as an ethnographic lab to yield greater insights into buying behavior.

on others. Response rates tend to be higher than with mail questionnaires, and interviewers can ask to speak to respondents with the desired characteristics or even by name.

However, with telephone interviewing, the cost per respondent is higher than with mail questionnaires. Also, people may not want to discuss personal questions with an interviewer. The method also introduces interviewer bias—the way interviewers talk, how they

research often yields insights that just don't emerge from traditional survey or focus group studies.

For FAME and its clients, the store helps fill a big gap in everyone's understanding of that elusive species, the shopper. Retailers know from inventory records what is on the shelf, and they know from point-of-sale data what ends up in shopper's baskets. But they lack a true understanding of the mysterious, often fickle buying process that connects the shelf to the checkout counter. What causes a consumer to skip past one aisle but spend a half hour strolling down another? Why does a shopper peer at one shelf but not even glance at the next one? What leads a person to pick up a product, examine it, put it back, walk away, come back later, pick it up again, and then finally buy it? How do the off-hand or pointed comments of friends, spouses, or sales staff have an impact on the buying decision?

The video and audio data FAME collects at OnceFamous help marketers understand a bit more about consumers and how they interact with the wealth of sensory and social cues in a retail store. "Ninety percent of all purchases are made on impulse," says Jeri Quest, FAME's executive vice president for strategic development. "We can get really close to customers at the point of decision making."

To gain these valuable insights into consumer preferences, manufacturers and retailers pay anywhere from $40,000 to $200,000 to have their products stocked at OnceFamous. In addition to product tests, FAME uses the lab as a testing ground for a variety of retailing decisions, such as product placement and traffic flow. Although OnceFamous is usually outfitted as an eclectic home furnishings and gift bou-

tique, FAME can strip it to the walls and reconfigure it for other product categories in a matter of days.

OnceFamous experiments have yielded interesting details on how people shop, including differences in the shopping approaches of men and women. "Women find an object they like and visit it," Quest says. "Men look at how it's made, what's the construction." Men stand back and study things, but women can't wait to get their hands on merchandise. Such differences may go as far back as childhood shopping experiences. Mothers are more likely to tell their sons to keep their hands to themselves while shopping. As a result, as adults, men are much less likely to pick up a product to get a closer look unless explicitly invited to. In contrast, daughters who shop with mom are more likely to learn her approach to evaluating a product by experiencing it. As adults, women evaluate products based on the stories the products tell and what the products may say about their owners.

Based on results like these, many stores tailor their displays to appeal differently to men and women. Stores like Brookstone and Sharper Image, which target mostly men, provide details about design and construction. They post signs urging shoppers to push buttons, test out massage chairs, and ask questions. In contrast, Pottery Barn, with its largely female audience, displays products in quaint groupings, allowing shoppers to visualize merchandise in their own homes, experience the products more intimately, and discover what those products might say about them.

Other in-store research has revealed that consumers react strongly to colors. Researchers at OnceFamous conducted an experiment by launching three separate sales, all on the same merchandise and with the same signs and promo-

tions. The researchers varied only the colors of the signs. The sales promoted with signs colored blue and green failed, whereas the event with red signs enticed shoppers to buy. The conclusion? Consumers associate cool colors, including blue and green, with higher prices. They associate warm colors, such as red and yellow, with low prices. Consumers are so drawn to the warm colors that red and yellow signs posted toward the rear of a store will draw shoppers in and through the aisles.

In another case, a retailer was desperate to get customers to turn left instead of right when entering its store. But research shows that 9 of 10 customers turn right. OnceFamous tested a video fireplace placed to the left of its entrance and found that this made 8 in 10 customers turn left instead.

OnceFamous may be the first research lab of its kind, but it won't be the last. Analysts predict a rise in the number of such detailed, "retail ethnography" labs as the retail world grows more and more competitive. To keep up with demand for consumer behavior insights, FAME plans to open a second retail shop at the ultimate retailing venue, the Mall of America. We'll be watching.

Sources: Keyla Kokmen, "The Company Store," *City Pages Media*, June 5, 2002, accessed at www.citypages.com/databank/23/1122/article10444.asp; Erik Baard, "Going Retail with Market Research," *Wired News*, August 8, 2002, p.1; Bruce Horovitz, "Shop, You're on Candid Camera," *USA Today*, November 5, 2002, p. 1B; Timothy Henderson, "Shopping Guinea Pigs," *Stores*, December 2002, accessed at www.stores.org/archives/archives02.html; "Little Shop of Habits," *NACS (National Association of Convenience Stores) Online*, November 8, 2002; Stephanie Simon, "Shopping with Big Brother," *Los Angeles Times*, May 2, 2002, accessed at www.chicagotribune.com/technology/chi-020502shopping.story; information gathered from www.fameretail.com, August 2003; and interviews with Tina Wilcox, President and Chief Creative Officer, FAME, June 2003.

ask questions, and other differences may affect respondents' answers. Finally, different interviewers may interpret and record responses differently, and under time pressures some interviewers might even cheat by recording answers without asking questions.

Personal interviewing takes two forms—individual and group interviewing. *Individual interviewing* involves talking with people in their homes or offices, on the street, or in shopping malls. Such interviewing is flexible. Trained interviewers can guide interviews, explain difficult questions, and explore issues as the situation requires. They can show subjects actual products, advertisements, or packages and observe reactions and behavior. However, individual personal interviews may cost three to four times as much as telephone interviews.

Group interviewing consists of inviting 6 to 10 people to talk with a trained moderator about a product, service, or organization. Participants normally are paid a small sum for attending. The moderator encourages free and easy discussion, hoping that group interactions will bring out actual feelings and thoughts. At the same time, the moderator "focuses" the discussion—hence the name **focus group interviewing**. Researchers and marketers watch the focus group discussions from behind one-way glass, and comments are recorded in writing or on videotape for later study.

Focus group interviewing has become one of the major marketing research tools for gaining insight into consumer thoughts and feelings. However, focus group studies usually employ small sample sizes to keep time and costs down, and it may be hard to generalize from the results. Because interviewers have more freedom in personal interviews, the problem of interviewer bias is greater.

Today, many researchers are changing the way they conduct focus groups. Some are employing videoconferencing technology to connect marketers in distant locations with live focus group action. Using cameras and two-way sound systems, marketing executives in a far-off boardroom can look in and listen, even using remote controls to zoom in on faces and pan the focus group at will. Other researchers are changing the environments in which they conduct focus groups. To help consumers relax and to elicit more authentic responses, they are using settings that are more comfortable and more relevant to the products being researched. For example, they might conduct focus groups for cooking products in a kitchen setting, or focus groups for home furnishings in a living room setting. One research firm offers facilities that look just like anything from a living room or play room to a bar or even a courtroom.

Some firms are now going on-site to conduct focus group sessions. Target did this before designing a new line of products for students entering college:

> To hear firsthand from college-bound students about their concerns when shopping for their dorm rooms, and to get a sense from college students of what life in a dorm is like, Target hired research firm Jump Associates to conduct focus groups. But rather than inviting respondents to a research facility, Jump put a different spin on the traditional focus group. It sponsored a series of "game nights" at high school grads' homes, inviting incoming college freshman as well as students with a year of dorm living under their belts. To get teens talking about dorm life, Jump devised a board game that involved issues associated with going to college. The game naturally led to informal conversations—and questions—about college life. Jump researchers were on the sidelines to observe, while a video camera recorded the proceedings. The research paid off. Last year, Target launched the Todd Oldham Dorm Room product line designed for college freshman. Among the new offerings: Kitchen in a Box, which provides basic accessories for a budding college cook; Bath in a Box, which includes an extra-large bath towel to preserve modesty on the trek to and from the shower; and a laundry bag with instructions printed on the bag about how to actually do the laundry.[14]

Focus group interviewing
Personal interviewing that involves inviting 6 to 10 people to gather for a few hours with a trained interviewer to talk about a product, service, or organization. The interviewer "focuses" the group discussion on important issues.

■ A new spin on focus groups: Before designing a new line of products for students entering college, Target sponsored "game nights" at high school grads' homes, inviting incoming college freshmen as well as students with a year of dorm living under their belts. To get teens talking, Target devised a board game that involved issues associated with going to college.

Advances in communication technologies have resulted in a number of new high-tech contact methods. One is *computer-assisted telephone interviewing (CATI),* in which interviewers sit at computers, read questions on the screen, and type in respondents' answers. Another is *completely automated telephone surveys (CATS),* in which respondents are dialed by computer and asked prerecorded questions. They enter responses by voice or through the phone's touchpad. Other high-tech contact methods include disks-by-mail, e-mail surveys, and computer-based fax surveys.[15]

The latest technology to hit marketing research is the Internet. Increasingly, marketing researchers are collecting primary data through **online (Internet) marketing research**—*Internet surveys, experiments,* and *online focus groups*. Online focus groups offer advantages over traditional methods in terms of low cost, access to respondents, and speed. However, although online research offers much promise, and some analysts predict that the Internet will soon be the primary marketing research tool, others are much more cautious. Marketing at Work 4.2 summarizes the advantages, drawbacks, and prospects for conducting marketing research on the Internet.

Online (Internet) marketing research
Collecting primary data through Internet surveys and online focus groups.

Sampling Plan. Marketing researchers usually draw conclusions about large groups of consumers by studying a small sample of the total consumer population. A **sample** is a segment of the population selected to represent the population as a whole. Ideally, the sample should be representative so that the researcher can make accurate estimates of the thoughts and behaviors of the larger population.

Designing the sample requires three decisions. First, *who* is to be surveyed (what *sampling unit*)? The answer to this question is not always obvious. For example, to study the decision-making process for a family automobile purchase, should the researcher interview the husband, wife, other family members, dealership salespeople, or all of these? The researcher must determine what information is needed and who is most likely to have it.

Second, *how many* people should be surveyed (what *sample size*)? Large samples give more reliable results than small samples. It is not necessary to sample the entire target market or even a large portion to get reliable results, however. If well chosen, samples of less than 1 percent of a population can often give good reliability.

Third, *how* should the people in the sample be *chosen* (what *sampling procedure*)? Table 4.4 describes different kinds of samples. Using *probability samples,* each population member has a known chance of being included in the sample, and researchers can calculate confidence limits for sampling error. But when probability sampling costs too much or takes too much time, marketing researchers often take *nonprobability samples,* even though their sampling error cannot be measured. These varied ways of drawing samples have different costs and time limitations as well as different accuracy and statistical properties. Which method is best depends on the needs of the research project.

Sample
A segment of the population selected for marketing research to represent the population as a whole.

Research Instruments. In collecting primary data, marketing researchers have a choice of two main research instruments—the *questionnaire* and *mechanical devices*. The *questionnaire* is by far the most common instrument, whether administered in person, by phone, or online.

TABLE 4.4 Types of Samples

Probability Sample	
Simple random sample	Every member of the population has a known and equal chance of selection.
Stratified random sample	The population is divided into mutually exclusive groups (such as age groups), and random samples are drawn from each group.
Cluster (area) sample	The population is divided into mutually exclusive groups (such as blocks), and the researcher draws a sample of the groups to interview.

Nonprobability Sample	
Convenience sample	The researcher selects the easiest population members from which to obtain information.
Judgment sample	The researcher uses his or her judgment to select population members who are good prospects for accurate information.
Quota sample	The researcher finds and interviews a prescribed number of people in each of several categories.

Marketing at Work | 4.2

Online Marketing Research

As more and more consumers have connected with the Internet, an increasing number of marketers have begun conducting marketing research on the Web. Online research now accounts for 8 percent of all spending on quantitative marketing research, and most industry insiders predict healthy growth.

Web research offers some real advantages over traditional surveys and focus groups. The most obvious advantages are speed and low costs. Online focus groups require some advance scheduling, but results are practically instantaneous. Survey researchers routinely complete their online studies in a matter of only days or weeks. For example, consider a recent online survey by a soft drink company to test teenagers' opinions of new packaging ideas. The 10- to 15-minute Internet survey included dozens of questions, along with 765 different images of labels, bottle shapes, and such. Some 600 teenagers participated over a three- to four-day period. Detailed analysis from the survey was available just five days after all the responses had come in—lightning quick compared with offline efforts. Similarly, Hershey Foods now does all of its new product testing research online. Whereas the old system of mail testing took six weeks or more to complete, online results can be garnered in two weeks or less.

Internet research is also relatively low in cost. Participants can dial in for a focus group from anywhere in the world, eliminating travel, lodging, and facility costs. For surveys, the Internet eliminates most of the postage, phone, labor, and printing costs associated with other approaches. "The cost [of Web research] can be anywhere from 10 percent to 80 percent less," says

Tod Johnson, head of NPD Group, a firm that conducts online research. Moreover, sample size has little influence on costs. "There's not a huge difference between 10 and 10,000 on the Web," says Johnson.

Online surveys and focus groups are also excellent for reaching the hard-to-reach—the often-elusive teen, single, affluent, and well-educated audiences. "It's very solid for reaching . . . doctors, lawyers, professionals—people you might have difficulty reaching because they are not interested in taking part in surveys," says Paul Jacobson, an executive of Greenfield Online. "It's also a

good medium for reaching working mothers and others who lead busy lives. They can do it in their own space and at their own convenience." The Internet also works well for bringing together people from different parts of the country, especially those in higher-income groups who can't spare the time to travel to a central site.

However, using the Internet to conduct marketing research does have some drawbacks. For one, many consumers still don't have access to the Internet. That makes it difficult to construct research samples that represent a broad cross section of Americans.

Brand manager eliminates pilot costs, becomes hero

Testing new package designs online with rotating 3-D images not only saved the client expensive tooling costs but also saved time. Now manufacturers can design today and test tomorrow. Eliminating pilot costs and shortening "time to market" are just some of the many ways that Greenfield Online quantitative research beats the old-fashioned kind.
Put our expert consultants and advanced technology to work for you.
www.greenfield.com
888.291.9997

Greenfield Online
Leading the Research Revolution™

• Quantitative Studies
• Qualitative Studies
• Media Research
• Self-Directed Research
• Syndicated Studies
• Website Evaluations

HERO

More and more companies are moving their research onto the Web. According to this Greenfield Online ad, in many ways, it "beats the old-fashioned kind."

Still, as Internet usage broadens, many mainstream marketers are now using Web research. General Mills, for example, conducts 60 percent of its consumer research online, reducing costs by 50 percent. And UPS uses online research extensively. "Between 40 percent and 50 percent of our customers are online, so it makes sense," says John Gilbert, UPS marketing research manager. He finds little difference in the results of traditional and online studies, and the online studies are much cheaper and faster.

Another major problem of online research is controlling who's in the sample. Tom Greenbaum, president of Groups Plus, recalls a cartoon in *The New Yorker* in which two dogs are seated at a computer: "On the Internet, nobody knows you are a dog," one says to the other. "If you can't see a person with whom you are communicating, how do know who they really are?" he says. To overcome such sample and response problems, many online research firms use opt-in communities and respondent panels. For example, Greenfield Online maintains a 1.3-million-member Internet-based respondent panel, recruited through cooperative marketing arrangements with other sites. Because such respondents opt in and can answer questions whenever they are ready, they yield high response rates. Whereas response rates for telephone surveys have plummeted to less than 14 percent in recent years, online response rates typically reach 40 percent or higher.

Even when you reach the right respondents, online surveys and focus groups can lack the dynamics of more personal approaches. "You're missing all of the key things that make a focus group a viable method," says Greenbaum. "You may get people online to talk to each other and play off each other, but it's very different to

watch people get excited about a concept." The online world is devoid of the eye contact, body language, and direct personal interactions found in traditional focus group research. And the Internet format—running, typed commentary and online "emoticons" (punctuation marks that express emotion, such as :-) to signify happiness)—greatly restricts respondent expressiveness.

Increasingly, however, advances in technology—such as the integration of animation, streaming audio and video, and virtual environments—will help to overcome these limitations. "In the online survey of the not-so-distant-future," notes an online researcher, "respondents will be able to rotate, zoom in on, and manipulate (like change the color or size of) three-dimensional products. They'll be able to peruse virtual stores, take items off shelves, and see how they function."

Just as the impersonal nature of the Web hinders two-way interactions, it can also provide anonymity. This often yields less guarded, more honest responses, especially when discussing topics such as income, medical conditions, lifestyle, or other sensitive issues. "People hiding behind a keyboard get pretty brave," says one researcher. Adds another:

From those questions that may simply make you squirm a little ("How much money did you lose in the stock market last month?"), to those you most probably don't want to answer to another human being, even if you don't know the person on the other end of the line ("How often do you have sex each week?"), Internet-based surveys tend to draw more honest responses. I once conducted the same survey in a mall and via the Internet. The question was, "How often do you bathe or shower each week?" The average answer, via the

mall interview, was 6.2 times per week. The average via the Internet interview was 4.8 times per week, probably a more logical—and honest—response.

Perhaps the most explosive issue facing online researchers concerns consumer privacy. Critics worry that online researchers will spam our e-mail boxes with unsolicited e-mails to recruit respondents. They fear that unethical researchers will use the e-mail addresses and confidential responses gathered through surveys to sell products after the research is completed. They are concerned about the use of electronic agents (called Spambots or Spiders) that collect personal information without the respondents' consent. Failure to address such privacy issues could result in angry, less cooperative consumers and increased government intervention.

Although most researchers agree that online research will never completely replace traditional research, some are wildly optimistic about its prospects. Others, however, are more cautious. "Ten years from now, national telephone surveys will be the subject of research methodology folklore," proclaims one expert. "That's a little too soon," cautions another. "But in 20 years, yes."

Sources: "Market Trends: Online Research Growing," accessed at www.greenfieldcentral.com/research_solutions/rsrch_solns_main.htm, June 2003; Ian P. Murphy, "Interactive Research," *Marketing News,* January 20, 1997, pp. 1, 17; "NFO Executive Sees Most Research Going to Internet," *Advertising Age,* May 19, 1997, p. 50; Noah Shachtman, "Web Enhanced Market Research," *Advertising Age,* June 18, 2001, p. T18; Thomas W. Miller, "Make the Call: Online Results Are a Mixed Bag," *Marketing News,* September 24, 2001, pp. 30–35; Catherine Arnold, "Hershey Research Sees Net Gain," *Marketing News,* November 25, 2003, p. 17; Beth Mack, "Online Privacy Critical to Research Success," *Marketing News,* November 25, 2002, p. 21; and Nina M. Ray and Sharon W. Tabor, "Cybersurveys Come of Age," *Marketing Research,* Spring 2003, pp. 32–37.

TABLE 4.5 A Questionable Questionnaire

Suppose that a summer camp director had prepared the following questionnaire to use in interviewing the parents of prospective campers. How would you assess each question?

1. What is your income to the nearest hundred dollars? *People don't usually know their income to the nearest hundred dollars, nor do they want to reveal their income that closely. Moreover, a researcher should never open a questionnaire with such a personal question.*

2. Are you a strong or weak supporter of overnight summer camping for your children? *What do "strong" and "weak" mean?*

3. Do your children behave themselves well at a summer camp? Yes ( ) No ( ) *"Behave" is a relative term. Furthermore, are yes and no the best response options for this question? Besides, will people answer this honestly and objectively? Why ask the question in the first place?*

4. How many camps mailed literature to you last year? This year? *Who can remember this?*

5. What are the most salient and determinant attributes in your evaluation of summer camps? *What are salient and determinant attributes? Don't use big words on me!*

6. Do you think it is right to deprive your child of the opportunity to grow into a mature person through the experience of summer camping? *A loaded question. Given the bias, how can any parent answer yes?*

Questionnaires are very flexible—there are many ways to ask questions. *Closed-end questions* include all the possible answers, and subjects make choices among them. Examples include multiple-choice questions and scale questions. *Open-end questions* allow respondents to answer in their own words. In a survey of airline users, Southwest might ask simply, "What is your opinion of Southwest Airlines?" Or it might ask people to complete a sentence: "When I choose an airline, the most important consideration is. . . ." These and other kinds of open-end questions often reveal more than closed-end questions because respondents are not limited in their answers. Open-end questions are especially useful in exploratory research, when the researcher is trying to find out *what* people think but not measuring *how many* people think in a certain way. Closed-end questions, on the other hand, provide answers that are easier to interpret and tabulate.

Researchers should also use care in the *wording* and *ordering* of questions. They should use simple, direct, unbiased wording. Questions should be arranged in a logical order. The first question should create interest if possible, and difficult or personal questions should be asked last so that respondents do not become defensive. A carelessly prepared questionnaire usually contains many errors (see Table 4.5).

Although questionnaires are the most common research instrument, researchers also use *mechanical instruments* to monitor consumer behavior, such as supermarket scanners and people meters. Other mechanical devices measure subjects' physical responses. For example, a galvanometer detects the minute degree of sweating that accompanies emotional arousal. It can be used to measure the strength of interest or emotions aroused by a subject's exposure to marketing stimuli such as an ad or product. Eye cameras are used to study respondents' eye movements to determine at what points their eyes focus first and how long they linger on a given item. Here are examples of new technologies that capture information on consumers' emotional and physical responses[16]:

> Machine response to facial expressions that indicate emotions will soon be a commercial reality. The technology discovers underlying emotions by capturing an image of a user's facial features and movements—especially around the eyes and mouth—and comparing the image against facial feature templates in a database. Hence, an elderly man squints at an ATM screen and the font size doubles almost instantly. A woman at a shopping center kiosk smiles at a travel ad, prompting the device to print out a travel discount coupon. Several users at another kiosk frown at a racy ad, leading a store to pull it.

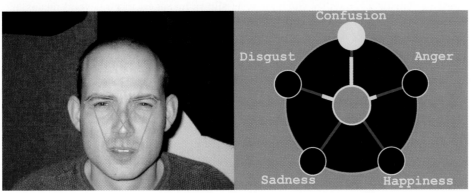

■ Mechanical measures of consumer response: devices are in the works that will allow marketers to measure facial expressions and adjust their offers or communications accordingly.

IBM is perfecting an "emotion mouse" that will figure out users' emotional states by measuring pulse, temperature, movement, and galvanic skin response. The company has mapped those measurements for anger, fear, sadness, disgust, happiness, and surprise. The idea is to create a style that fits a user's personality. An Internet marketer, for example, might offer to present a different kind of display if it senses that the user is frustrated.

Implementing the Research Plan The researcher next puts the marketing research plan into action. This involves collecting, processing, and analyzing the information. Data collection can be carried out by the company's marketing research staff or by outside firms. The data collection phase of the marketing research process is generally the most expensive and the most subject to error. Researchers should watch closely to make sure that the plan is implemented correctly. They must guard against problems with contacting respondents, with respondents who refuse to cooperate or who give biased answers, and with interviewers who make mistakes or take shortcuts.

Researchers must process and analyze the collected data to isolate important information and findings. They need to check data for accuracy and completeness and code it for analysis. The researchers then tabulate the results and compute averages and other statistical measures.

Interpreting and Reporting the Findings The market researcher must now interpret the findings, draw conclusions, and report them to management. The researcher should not try to overwhelm managers with numbers and fancy statistical techniques. Rather, the researcher should present important findings that are useful in the major decisions faced by management.

However, interpretation should not be left only to the researchers. They are often experts in research design and statistics, but the marketing manager knows more about the problem and the decisions that must be made. The best research is meaningless if the manager blindly accepts faulty interpretations from the researcher. Similarly, managers may be biased—they might tend to accept research results that show what they expected and to reject those that they did not expect or hope for. In many cases, findings can be interpreted in different ways, and discussions between researchers and managers will help point to the best interpretations. Thus, managers and researchers must work together closely when interpreting research results, and both must share responsibility for the research process and resulting decisions.

Analyzing Marketing Information

Information gathered in internal databases and through marketing intelligence and marketing research usually requires more analysis. And managers may need help in applying the information to their marketing problems and decisions. This help may include advanced statistical analysis to learn more about both the relationships within a set of data and their statistical reliability. Such analysis allows managers to go beyond means and standard deviations in the data and to answer questions about markets, marketing activities, and outcomes.

Information analysis might also involve a collection of analytical models that will help marketers make better decisions. Each model represents some real system, process, or outcome. These models can help answer the questions of *What if?* and *Which is best?* Marketing scientists have developed numerous models to help marketing managers make better marketing mix decisions, design sales territories and sales call plans, select sites for retail outlets, develop optimal advertising mixes, and forecast new-product sales.

Customer Relationship Management (CRM)

The question of how best to analyze and use individual customer data presents special problems. Most companies are awash in information about their customers. In fact, smart companies capture information at every possible customer *touch point*. These touch points include customer purchases, sales force contacts, service and support calls, Web site visits, satisfaction surveys, credit and payment interactions, market research studies—every contact between the customer and the company.

The trouble is that this information is usually scattered widely across the organization. It is buried deep in the separate databases, plans, and records of different company functions and departments. To overcome such problems, many companies are now turning to **customer relationship management (CRM)** to manage detailed information about individual customers and carefully manage customer "touchpoints" in order to maximize customer loyalty. In recent years, there has been an explosion in the number of companies using CRM. In fact, one research firm found that 97 percent of all U.S. businesses plan to boost spending on CRM technology within the next two years.[17]

CRM consists of sophisticated software and analytical tools that integrate customer information from all sources, analyze it in depth, and apply the results to build stronger customer relationships. CRM integrates everything that a company's sales, service, and marketing teams know about individual customers to provide a 360-degree view of the customer relationship. It pulls together, analyzes, and provides easy access to customer information from all of the various touch points. Companies use CRM analysis to assess the value of individual customers, identify the best ones to target, and customize the company's products and interactions to each customer.

CRM analysts develop *data warehouses* and use sophisticated *data mining* techniques to unearth the riches hidden in customer data. A data warehouse is a company-wide electronic storehouse of customer information—a centralized database of finely detailed customer data that needs to be sifted through for gems. The purpose of a data warehouse is not to gather information—many companies have already amassed endless stores of information about their customers. Rather, the purpose is to allow managers to integrate the information the company already has. Then, once the data warehouse brings the data together for analysis, the company uses high-powered data mining techniques to sift through the mounds of data and dig out interesting relationships and findings about customers.

Customer relationship management (CRM)

Managing detailed information about individual customers and carefully managing customer "touch points" in order to maximize customer loyalty.

Companies can gain many benefits from customer relationship management. By understanding customers better, they can provide higher levels of customer service and develop deeper customer relationships. They can use CRM to pinpoint high-value customers, target them more effectively, cross-sell the company's products, and create offers tailored to specific customer requirements. Consider the following examples[18]:

- FedEx recently launched a multimillion-dollar CRM system in an effort to cut costs, improve its customer support, and use its existing customer data to cross-sell and up-sell services to potential or existing customers. The new system gives every member of FedEx's 3,300-person sales force a comprehensive view of every customer, detailing each one's needs and suggesting services that might meet those needs. For instance, if a customer who does a lot of international shipping calls to arrange a delivery, a sales rep will see a detailed customer history on his or her computer screen, assess the customer's needs, and determine the most appropriate offering on the spot. Beleaguered sales reps can use such high-tech help. FedEx offers 220 different services—from logistics to transportation to customs brokerage—often making it difficult for salespeople to identify the best fit for customers. The new CRM system will also help FedEx conduct promotions and qualify potential sales leads. The CRM software analyzes market segments, points out market "sweet spots," and calculates how profitable those segments will be to the company and to individual salespeople.

- At Marks & Spencer—Britain's "most trusted retailer"—CRM plays an important role in helping achieve the company's mission "to focus on our customers and be driven by their needs." M&S has one of the richest customer databases of any retailer in the world. The database contains demographic and purchasing information on more than 3 million M&S charge account customers, point-of-sale information from 10 million store transactions per week, and a wealth of data from external sources such as the census. "We have at least 80 explanatory variables for every household in the UK, rising to more than 300 for any customer holding a charge card," says Steven Bond, head of the retailer's Customer Insight Unit (CIU). The CRM system organizes this wealth of data and analyzes it to tell Marks & Spencer a great deal about its customers. The result is better decisions on everything from corporate branding to targeted communications and sales promotions. "We have a much better idea of what kinds of offers to put in front of different customers and when, and what tone of voice to use, based on their individual tastes, preferences, and behavior," says Bond. For example, by identifying who shops and when—older customers tend to shop early to avoid the crowds, while younger male shoppers leave things until the last minute, for instance—M&S can align its product availability and marketing activity accordingly. Or a regular customer checking out of the store's food section might be enticed into the menswear department with a promotion personalized according to whether he or she is an "Egyptian cotton and silk tie" purchaser or has a lifestyle that demands non-iron shirts. CRM has put Marks & Spencer at the leading edge of customer analysis. The improved customer insights help Marks & Spenser make better marketing decisions. This, in turn, creates more satisfied customers and more profitable customer relationships.

Most experts believe that good customer data, by itself, can give companies a substantial competitive advantage. Just ask American Express. At a secret location in Phoenix, security guards watch over American Express's 500 billion bytes of data on how customers have used its 35 million green, gold, and platinum charge cards. Amex uses the database to design carefully targeted offers in its monthly mailing of millions of customer bills.

CRM benefits don't come without cost or risk, not only in collecting the original customer data but also in maintaining and mining it. U.S. companies will spend an estimated $10 billion to $20 billion this year on CRM software alone from companies such as Siebel Systems, Oracle, SAS, and SPSS. Yet more than half of all CRM efforts fail to meet their objectives. The most common cause of CRM failures is that companies mistakenly view CRM only as a technology and software solution.[19] But technology alone cannot build profitable customer relationships. "CRM is not a technology solution—you can't achieve . . . improved customer relationships by simply slapping in some software," says a CRM expert. Instead, CRM is just one part of an effective overall *customer relationship management strategy*. "Focus on the *R*," advises the expert. "Remember, a relationship is what CRM is all about."[20]

■ CRM: SAS offers CRM software that provides "a complete view of your customers." So you'll understand their needs, enhance their lifetime value, and achieve greater competitive advantage.

When it works, the benefits of CRM can far outweigh the costs and risks. Based on regular polls of its customers, Siebel Systems claims that customers using its CRM software report an average 16 percent increase in revenues and 21 percent increase in customer loyalty and staff efficiency. "No question that companies are getting tremendous value out of this," says a CRM consultant. "Companies [are] looking for ways to bring disparate sources of customer information together, then get it to all the customer touch points." The powerful new CRM techniques can unearth "a wealth of information to target that customer, to hit their hot button."[21]

■ Distributing and Using Marketing Information

Marketing information has no value until it is used to make better marketing decisions. Thus, the marketing information system must make the information available to the managers and others who make marketing decisions or deal with customers on a day-to-day basis. In some cases, this means providing managers with regular performance reports, intelligence updates, and reports on the results of research studies.

But marketing managers may also need nonroutine information for special situations and on-the-spot decisions. For example, a sales manager having trouble with a large customer may want a summary of the account's sales and profitability over the past year. Or a retail store manager who has run out of a best-selling product may want to know the current inventory levels in the chain's other stores. Increasingly, therefore, information distribution involves entering information into databases and making these available in a user-friendly and timely way.

Many firms use a company *intranet* to facilitate this process. The intranet provides ready access to research information, stored reports, shared work documents, contact information for employees and other stakeholders, and more. For example, iGo, a catalog and Web retailer, integrates incoming customer service calls with up-to-date database information about customers' Web purchases and e-mail inquiries. By accessing this information on the intranet while speaking with the customer, iGo's service representatives can get a well-rounded picture of each customer's purchasing history and previous contacts with the company.

In addition, companies are increasingly allowing key customers and value-network members to access account and product information and other data on demand on *extranets*. Suppliers, customers, and select other network members may access a company's extranet to update their accounts, arrange purchases, and check orders against inventories to improve customer service. For example, one insurance firm allows its 200 independent agents access to a Web-based database of claim information covering 1 million customers. This allows the agents to avoid high-risk customers and to compare claim data with their own customer databases. And Wal-Mart's Retail Link system provides suppliers with up to two years worth of data on how their products have sold in Wal-Mart stores.[22]

Thanks to modern technology, today's marketing managers can gain direct access to the information system at any time and from virtually any location. They can tap into the system while working at a home office, in a hotel room, at an airport—anyplace where they can turn on a laptop computer and link up. Such systems allow managers to get the information they need directly and quickly and to tailor it to their own needs. From just about anywhere, they can obtain information from company or outside data bases, analyze it using statistical software, prepare reports and presentations, and communicate directly with others in the network.

■▌ Other Marketing Information Considerations

This section discusses marketing information in two special contexts: marketing research in small businesses and nonprofit organizations, and international marketing research. Finally, we look at public policy and ethics issues in marketing research.

Marketing Research in Small Businesses and Nonprofit Organizations

Just like larger firms, small organizations need market information. Start-up businesses need information about their industries, competitors, potential customers, and reactions to new market offers. Existing small businesses must track changes in customer needs and wants, reactions to new products, and changes in the competitive environment.

Managers of small businesses and nonprofit organizations often think that marketing research can be done only by experts in large companies with big research budgets. True, large-scale research studies are beyond the budgets of most small businesses. However, many of the marketing research techniques discussed in this chapter also can be used by smaller organizations in a less formal manner and at little or no expense.

Managers of small businesses and nonprofit organizations can obtain good marketing information simply by *observing* things around them. For example, retailers can evaluate new locations by observing vehicle and pedestrian traffic. They can monitor competitor advertising by collecting ads from local media. They can evaluate their customer mix by recording how many and what kinds of customers shop in the store at different times. In addition, many small business managers routinely visit their rivals and socialize with competitors to gain insights. Tom Coohill, a chef who owns two Atlanta restaurants, gives managers a food allowance to dine out and bring back ideas. Atlanta jeweler Frank Maier Jr., who often visits out-of-town rivals, spotted and copied a dramatic way of lighting displays.[23]

Managers can conduct informal *surveys* using small convenience samples. The director of an art museum can learn what patrons think about new exhibits by conducting informal focus groups—inviting small groups to lunch and having discussions on topics of interest. Retail salespeople can talk with customers visiting the store; hospital officials can interview patients. Restaurant managers might make random phone calls during slack hours to interview consumers about where they eat out and what they think of various restaurants in the area. Bissell, a nicher in the carpet-cleaning industry, used a small convenience sample to quickly and cheaply test the market for its Steam Gun—a newly developed home-cleaning device that resembled a hand-held vacuum cleaner.

Bissell had only four weeks and a tight budget to get a feel for how consumers would respond to the new product. Aware that women with children often purchase such products, Bissell made a $1,500 donation to a local Parent Teacher Association (PTA) for the opportunity to make a presentation. After the presentation, it gave 20 interested women the Steam Gun to take home, along with journals to record their experiences. Following a two-week trial period, Bissell's marketing research director visited the mothers in their homes to watch them use the product. This "research on a shoestring" yielded several interesting discoveries. First, Bissell learned that the women weren't sold on the cleaning ability of hot water used without chemicals. Second, it would have to change the name of the product. When roped into chores, children would arm themselves with the Steam Gun and take aim at their siblings. One child was quoted as saying, "Freeze, or I'll melt your face off!" Finally, Bissell found that the product had special appeal to those who were serious about cleaning. They used it to get into hard to reach places and blast off tough grime. Based on these findings, Bissell changed the name of the product to the Steam 'n Clean and focused on the cleaning power of super hot steam when promoting the product. The Steam 'n Clean was successfully launched through infomercials and in nationwide retail chains.[24]

Managers also can conduct their own simple *experiments*. For example, by changing the themes in regular fund-raising mailings and watching the results, a nonprofit manager can learn much about which marketing strategies work best. By varying newspaper advertisements, a store manager can learn the effects of things such as ad size and position, price coupons, and media used.

Small organizations can obtain most of the secondary data available to large businesses. In addition, many associations, local media, chambers of commerce, and government agencies provide special help to small organizations. The U.S. Small Business Administration offers dozens of free publications and a Web site (www.sbaonline.sba.gov) that give advice on topics ranging from starting, financing, and expanding a small business to ordering business cards. Other excellent Web resources for small businesses include the U.S. Census Bureau (www.census.gov) and the Bureau of Economic Analysis (www.bea.doc.gov).

The business sections at local libraries can also be a good source of information. Local newspapers often provide information on local shoppers and their buying patterns. Finally, small businesses can collect a considerable amount of information at very little cost on the Internet. They can scour competitor and customer Web sites and use Internet search engines to research specific companies and issues.

In summary, secondary data collection, observation, surveys, and experiments can all be used effectively by small organizations with small budgets. Although these informal research methods are less complex and less costly, they still must be conducted carefully. Managers must think carefully about the objectives of the research, formulate questions in advance, recognize the biases introduced by smaller samples and less skilled researchers, and conduct the research systematically.[25]

International Marketing Research

International marketing researchers follow the same steps as domestic researchers, from defining the research problem and developing a research plan to interpreting and reporting the results. However, these researchers often face more and different problems. Whereas domestic researchers deal with fairly homogeneous markets within a single country, international researchers deal with differing markets in many different countries. These markets often vary greatly in their levels of economic development, cultures and customs, and buying patterns.

■ Many associations, media, and government agencies provide special help to small organizations. Here the U.S. Small Business Administration offers a Web site that gives advice on topics ranging from starting, financing, and expanding a small business to ordering business cards.

In many foreign markets, the international researcher sometimes has a difficult time finding good secondary data. Whereas U.S. marketing researchers can obtain reliable secondary data from dozens of domestic research services, many countries have almost no research services at all. Some of the largest international research services do operate in many countries. For example, AC Nielsen Corporation, the world's largest marketing research company, has offices in more than 100 countries. And 63 percent of the revenues of the world's 25 largest marketing research firms comes from outside their home countries.[26] However, most research firms operate in only a relative handful of countries. Thus, even when secondary information is available, it usually must be obtained from many different sources on a country-by-country basis, making the information difficult to combine or compare.

Because of the scarcity of good secondary data, international researchers often must collect their own primary data. Here again, researchers face problems not found domestically. For example, they may find it difficult simply to develop good samples. U.S. researchers can use current telephone directories, census tract data, and any of several sources of socioeconomic data to construct samples. However, such information is largely lacking in many countries.

Once the sample is drawn, the U.S. researcher usually can reach most respondents easily by telephone, by mail, on the Internet, or in person. Reaching respondents is often not so easy in other parts of the world. Researchers in Mexico cannot rely on telephone and mail data collection—most data collection is door to door and concentrated in three or four of the largest cities. In some countries, few people have phones; for example, there are only 32 phones per thousand people in Argentina. In other countries, the postal system is notoriously unreliable. In Brazil, for instance, an estimated 30 percent of the mail is never delivered. In many developing countries, poor roads and transportation systems make certain areas hard to reach, making personal interviews difficult and expensive. Finally, few people in developing countries are connected to the Internet.[27]

■ Some of the largest research services operate in many countries: Roper ASW, Inc. provides companies with information resources "from Brazil to Eastern Europe; from Cape Town to Beijing—if you are there, Roper is there."

Cultural differences from country to country cause additional problems for international researchers. Language is the most obvious obstacle. For example, questionnaires must be prepared in one language and then translated into the languages of each country researched. Responses then must be translated back into the original language for analysis and interpretation. This adds to research costs and increases the risk of errors.

Translating a questionnaire from one language to another is anything but easy. Many idioms, phrases, and statements mean different things in different cultures. For example, a Danish executive noted, "Check this out by having a different translator put back into English what you've translated from English. You'll get the shock of your life. I remember [an example in which] 'out of sight, out of mind' had become 'invisible things are insane'."[28]

Consumers in different countries also vary in their attitudes toward marketing research. People in one country may be very willing to respond; in other countries, nonresponse can be a major problem. Customs in some countries may prohibit people from talking with strangers. In certain cultures, research questions often are considered too personal. For example, in many Latin American countries, people may feel embarrassed to talk with researchers about their choices of shampoo, deodorant, or other personal care products. Similarly, in most Muslim countries, mixed-gender focus groups are taboo, as is videotaping female-only focus groups.[29]

Even when respondents are *willing* to respond, they may not be *able* to because of high functional illiteracy rates. And middle-class people in developing countries often make false claims in order to appear well off. For example, in a study of tea consumption in India, over 70 percent of middle-income respondents claimed that they used one of several national brands. However, the researchers had good reason to doubt these results—more than 60 percent of the tea sold in India is unbranded generic tea.

Despite these problems, the recent growth of international marketing has resulted in a rapid increase in the use of international marketing research. Global companies have little choice but to conduct such research. Although the costs and problems associated with international research may be high, the costs of not doing it—in terms of missed opportunities and mistakes—might be even higher. Once recognized, many of the problems associated with international marketing research can be overcome or avoided.

Public Policy and Ethics in Marketing Research

Most marketing research benefits both the sponsoring company and its consumers. Through marketing research, companies learn more about consumers' needs, resulting in more satisfying products and services and stronger customer relationships. However, the misuse of marketing research can also harm or annoy consumers. Two major public policy and ethics issues in marketing research are intrusions on consumer privacy and the misuse of research findings.

Intrusions on Consumer Privacy Many consumers feel positively about marketing research and believe that it serves a useful purpose. Some actually enjoy being interviewed and giving their opinions. However, others strongly resent or even mistrust marketing research. A few consumers fear that researchers might use sophisticated techniques to probe our deepest feelings and then use this knowledge to manipulate our buying. Or they worry that marketers are building huge databases full of personal information about customers.

For example, DoubleClick has profiles on 100 million Web users. Privacy groups have worried that such huge profiling databases could be merged with offline databases and threaten individual privacy. In fact, DoubleClick did integrate its online data with that collected by a consumer panel firm to construct frighteningly accurate consumer profiles. It stirred up much controversy when it announced that it would sell about 100,000 of these Web-user profiles to businesses, complete with names and contact information. However, in response to a Federal Trade Commission investigation and to settle federal and state class-action suits, DoubleClick recently adopted sweeping privacy standards.[30]

Others consumers may have been taken in by previous "research surveys" that actually turned out to be attempts to sell them something. Still other consumers confuse legitimate marketing research studies with telemarketing efforts and say "no" before the interviewer can even begin. Most, however, simply resent the intrusion. They dislike mail or telephone surveys that are too long or too personal or that interrupt them at inconvenient times.

Increasing consumer resentment has become a major problem for the research industry. One recent poll found that 82 percent of Americans worry that they lack control over how businesses use their personal information, and 41 percent said that businesses had invaded their privacy. These concerns have led to lower survey response rates in recent years. One study found that 45 percent of Americans had refused to participate in a survey over the past year, up from 24 percent 15 years ago. Another study found that 59 percent of consumers had refused to give information to a company because they thought it was not really needed or too personal, up from 42 percent five years earlier.[31]

The research industry is considering several options for responding to this problem. One example is the Council for Marketing and Opinion Research's "Your Opinion Counts" program to educate consumers about the benefits of marketing research and to distinguish it from telephone selling and database building. Another is the industry's effort to provide a toll-free number that people can call to verify that a survey is legitimate. The industry also has considered adopting broad standards, perhaps based on The International Chamber of Commerce's International Code of Marketing and Social Research Practice. This code outlines researchers' responsibilities to respondents and to the general public.

For example, it says that researchers should make their names and addresses available to participants, and it bans companies from representing activities such as database compilation or sales and promotional pitches as research.[32]

Many companies—including IBM, AT&T, American Express, DoubleClick, and Microsoft—are now appointing a "chief privacy officer (CPO)," whose job is to safeguard the privacy of consumers who do business with the company. The chief privacy officer for Microsoft says that his job is to come up with data policies for the company to follow, make certain that every program the company creates enhances customer privacy, and inform and educate company employees about privacy issues and concerns. At least 100 U.S. companies now employ such privacy chiefs and the number is expected to grow rapidly. In fact, one expert estimates that laws requiring companies to protect consumer privacy will create 30,000 CPO jobs by 2006.[33]

According to Sally Cowan, who runs the privacy operations of American Express, any business that deals with consumers' information has to take privacy issues seriously. "Privacy is not the new hot issue at American Express," she says. The company developed a set of formal privacy principles in 1991, and in 1998 it became one of the first companies to post privacy policies on its Web site. This penchant for customer privacy led American Express to introduce new services that protect consumers' privacy when they use an American Express card to buy items online. American Express views privacy as way to gain competitive advantage—as something that leads consumers to choose one company over another.[34]

In the end, if researchers provide value in exchange for information, customers will gladly provide it. For example, Amazon.com's customers do not mind if the firm builds a database of products they buy in order to provide future product recommendations. This saves time and provides value. Similarly, Bizrate users gladly complete surveys rating e-tail sites because they can view the overall ratings of others when making purchase decisions. The best approach is for researchers to ask only for the information they need, to use it responsibly to provide value, and to avoid sharing information without the customer's permission.

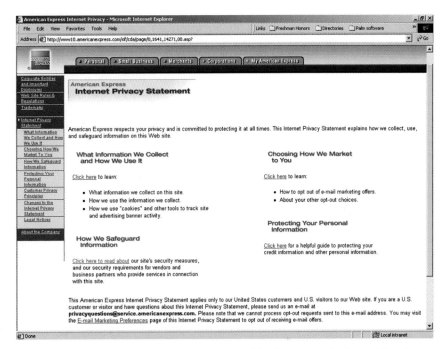

■ Consumer privacy: American Express was one of the first companies to post its privacy policies on the Web. "American Express respects your privacy and is committed to protecting it at all times."

Misuse of Research Findings Research studies can be powerful persuasion tools; companies often use study results as claims in their advertising and promotion. Today, however, many research studies appear to be little more than vehicles for pitching the sponsor's products. In fact, in some cases, the research surveys appear to have been designed just to produce the intended effect. Few advertisers openly rig their research designs or blatantly misrepresent the findings; most abuses tend to be subtle "stretches." Consider the following examples:[35]

> A study by Chrysler contends that Americans overwhelmingly prefer Chrysler to Toyota after test-driving both. However, the study included just 100 people in each of two tests. More importantly, none of the people surveyed owned a foreign car, so they appear to be favorably predisposed to U.S. cars.

> A Black Flag survey asked: "A roach disk . . . poisons a roach slowly. The dying roach returns to the nest and after it dies is eaten by other roaches. In turn

these roaches become poisoned and die. How effective do you think this type of product would be in killing roaches?" Not surprisingly, 79 percent said effective.

A poll sponsored by the disposable diaper industry asked: "It is estimated that disposable diapers account for less than 2 percent of the trash in today's landfills. In contrast, beverage containers, third-class mail, and yard waste are estimated to account for about 21 percent of the trash in landfills. Given this, in your opinion, would it be fair to ban disposable diapers?" Again, not surprisingly, 84 percent said no.

Thus, subtle manipulations of the study's sample or the choice or wording of questions can greatly affect the conclusions reached.

In others cases, so-called independent research studies are actually paid for by companies with an interest in the outcome. Small changes in study assumptions or in how results are interpreted can subtly affect the direction of the results. For example, at least four widely quoted studies compare the environmental effects of using disposable diapers to those of using cloth diapers. The two studies sponsored by the cloth diaper industry conclude that cloth diapers are more environmentally friendly. Not surprisingly, the other two studies, sponsored by the paper diaper industry, conclude just the opposite. Yet both appear to be correct *given* the underlying assumptions used.

Recognizing that surveys can be abused, several associations—including the American Marketing Association, the Council of American Survey Research Organizations, and the Marketing Research Association—have developed codes of research ethics and standards of conduct. In the end, however, unethical or inappropriate actions cannot simply be regulated away. Each company must accept responsibility for policing the conduct and reporting of its own marketing research to protect consumers' best interests and its own.

REST STOP:
Reviewing the Concepts

In the previous chapter, we discussed the marketing environment. In this chapter, we've continued our exploration of how marketers go about understanding the marketplace and consumers. We've studied tools used to gather and manage information that marketing managers and others can use to assess opportunities in the marketplace and the impact of a firm's marketing efforts. After this brief pause for rest and reflection, we'll head out again in the next chapter to take a closer look at the object of all of this activity—consumers and their buying behavior.

In today's complex and rapidly changing marketplace, marketing managers need more and better information to make effective and timely decisions. This greater need for information has been matched by the explosion of information technologies for supplying information. Using today's new technologies, companies can now handle great quantities of information, sometimes even too much. Yet marketers often complain that they lack enough of the *right* kind of information or have an excess of the *wrong* kind. In response, many companies are now studying their managers' information needs and

designing information systems to help managers develop and manage market and customer information.

1. Explain the importance of information to the company and its understanding of the marketplace.

The marketing process starts with a complete understanding of the marketplace and consumer needs and wants. Thus, the company needs sound information in order to produce superior value and satisfaction for customers. The company also requires information on competitors, resellers, and other actors and forces in the marketplace. Increasingly, marketers are viewing information not only as an input for making better decisions but also as an important strategic asset and marketing tool.

2. Define the marketing information system and discuss its parts.

The *marketing information system (MIS)* consists of people, equipment, and procedures to gather, sort, analyze, evaluate, and distribute needed, timely, and accurate information to marketing decision makers. A well-designed information system begins and ends with users. The MIS first *assesses information needs*. The marketing information system primarily serves the company's marketing and other managers. However, it may also provide information to external partners, such as suppliers or marketing services agencies. Then, the MIS *develops information* from internal databases, marketing intelligence activities, and marketing research. *Internal databases* provide information on the company's own sales, costs, inventories, cash flows, and accounts receivable and payable. Such data can be obtained quickly and cheaply but often needs to be adapted for marketing decisions. *Marketing intelligence* activities supply everyday information about developments in the external marketing environment. *Market research* consists of collecting information relevant to a specific marketing problem faced by the company. Lastly, the MIS *distributes information* gathered from these sources to the right managers in the right form and at the right time to help them make better marketing decisions.

3. Outline the steps in the marketing research process.

The first step in the marketing research process involves *defining the problem and setting the research objectives,* which may be exploratory, descriptive, or causal research. The second step consists of *developing a research plan* for collecting data from primary and secondary sources. The third step calls for *implementing the marketing research plan* by gathering, processing, and analyzing the information. The fourth step consists of *interpreting and reporting the findings*. Additional information analysis helps marketing managers apply the information and provides them with sophisticated statistical procedures and models from which to develop more rigorous findings.

Both *internal* and *external* secondary data sources often provide information more quickly and at a lower cost than primary data sources, and they can sometimes yield information that a company cannot collect by itself. However, needed information might not exist in secondary sources, and even if data can be found, they might be largely unusable. Researchers must also evaluate secondary information to ensure that it is *relevant, accurate, current,* and *impartial*. Primary research must also be evaluated for these features. Each primary data collection method—*observational, survey,* and *experimental*—has its own advantages and disadvantages.

Each of the various primary research contact methods—mail, telephone, personal interview, and online—also has its own advantages and drawbacks. Similarly, each contact method has its pluses and minuses.

4. Explain how companies analyze and distribute marketing information.

Information gathered in internal databases and through marketing intelligence and marketing research usually requires more analysis. This may include advanced statistical analysis or the application of analytical models that will help marketers make better decisions. In recent years, marketers have paid special attention to the analysis of individual customer data. Many companies have now acquired or developed special software and analysis techniques—called *customer relationship management (CRM)*—that integrate, analyze, and apply the mountains of individual customer data contained in their databases.

Marketing information has no value until it is used to make better marketing decisions. Thus, the marketing information system must make the information available to the managers and others who make marketing decisions or deal with customers. In some cases, this means providing regular reports and updates; in other cases it means making nonroutine information available for special situations and on-the-spot decisions. Many firms use company intranets and extranets to facilitate this process. Thanks to modern technology, today's marketing managers can gain direct access to the information system at any time and from virtually any location.

5. Discuss the special issues some marketing researchers face, including public policy and ethics issues.

Some marketers face special marketing research situations, such as those conducting research in small business, nonprofit, or international situations. Marketing research can be conducted effectively by small businesses and nonprofit organizations with limited budgets. International marketing researchers follow the same steps as domestic researchers but often face more and different problems. All organizations need to respond responsibly to major public policy and ethical issues surrounding marketing research, including issues of intrusions on consumer privacy and misuse of research findings.

Navigating the Key Terms

Causal research
Customer relationship
  management (CRM)
Descriptive research
Experimental research
Exploratory research
Focus group interviewing

Internal databases
Marketing information system
  (MIS)
Marketing intelligence
Marketing research
Observational research
Online databases

Online (Internet) marketing
  research
Primary data
Sample
Secondary data
Single-source data systems
Survey research

Travel Log

Discussing the Issues

1. Distinguish between internal databases, marketing intelligence, and marketing research as methods for developing marketing information. How does each of these three sources assist an organization differently in meeting its information needs?

2. Taking the role of a brand manager for Hawaiian Tropic suntan lotion, create an exploratory research objective, a descriptive research objective, and a causal research objective. How does the nature of each research objective guide data collection?

3. Small businesses face budget constraints that can limit the type and scope of research conducted. In a small group, brainstorm what a small furniture retailer might be able to do to gain competitor and consumer information on a limited budget.

4. Discuss some of the unique challenges U.S. researchers may encounter in conducting research in other countries. How might these obstacles be overcome?

5. What advantages do secondary data have over primary data? What advantages do primary data have over secondary data? Why is secondary data typically the starting point for marketing researchers?

6. How might observational research be used to understand a consumer's decision process in selecting greeting cards? What other information that is not observable might you want to know about the consumer's greeting card choices and how would you get it?

Application Questions

1. It has been reported that more than 7 million people have discontinued their regular home phone lines in favor of using cell phones at home to place and receive calls. Assume you work for one of the land-based telephone companies that is losing customers to cell phones. Describe both an experiment and a survey that would aid your company in understanding how to reverse this trend. Which approach makes the most sense for this research question?

2. You and three other students work for United Airlines and serve on a committee making decisions about an upcoming customer satisfaction questionnaire. Each team member is to be an advocate for one of the following contact methods: mail, telephone, personal, and online. Debate the pros and cons of the different contact methods and then have the group vote for using one of the four methods.

3. Browse through the list of external information sources provided in Table 4.1. Pick one Web site to visit from the business data section, government data section, and Internet data section of Table 4.1. What types of data can be found that would be useful to a Toyota car dealer interested in finding a location for a new dealership?

Under the Hood: Focus on Technology

SAP is the leading enterprise software company, claiming the majority of Fortune 500 companies among its clients. Its products are used to manage sales and distribution, production, inventory, and accounting, among other things. One of its products is a customer relationship management module that is designed to help companies manage the vast amounts of data associated with individual customers. Visit the SAP Web site (www.sap.com) and read about the customer relationship management tools under the "solutions" link.

1. Based on information available at the SAP Web site, describe some of the capabilities of CRM.

2. If you were creating a customer database to use individual customer data for CRM in a hotel chain, what types of information would you capture about the customer?

3. How would you collect information about the hotel customer and how could a marketing manager use it to improve the relationship with that customer?

Focus on Ethics

Survey research, either by phone or on the Internet, has become more difficult because even legitimate survey efforts are often viewed by suspicious consumers, who have been burned once too often, as thinly veiled sales calls. Furthermore, consumers are concerned with privacy and do not want their personal information misused. In addition, given the volume of unsolicited e-mail (SPAM) received (some estimates suggest that SPAM will account for over half of all e-mail in the near future), many people don't have time to try to separate legitimate research requests from unsolicited product advertisements, and end up deleting them all.

1. What ways might legitimate survey researchers overcome growing public resistance to online surveys and telephone surveys?

2. How have you responded in the past when asked to participate in a survey on the phone or Internet? Did you participate? Why or why not?

3. What methods might a company conducting an online survey use to distinguish its e-mail from SPAM?

Videos

The Burke, Inc. video case that accompanies this chapter is located in Appendix 1 at the back of the book.

Student Materials

Need a tune-up? A study guide and OneKey access code are available to aid in your review of chapter material. Your instructor may choose to have these items shrink-wrapped with your text or you may purchase them separately at www.prenhall.com/marketing.

■ *After studying this chapter, you should be able to*

1. Understand the consumer market and the major factors that influence consumer buyer behavior   *2. Identify* and discuss the stages in the buyer decision process   *3. Describe* the adoption and diffusion process for new products   *4. Define* the business market and identify the major factors that influence business buyer behavior   *5. List* and define the steps in the business buying decision process

Consumer and Business Buyer Behavior

5

ROAD MAP | Previewing the Concepts

In the previous chapter, you studied how marketers obtain, analyze, and use information to understand the marketplace and to assess marketing programs. In this chapter, you'll continue your marketing journey with a closer look at the most important element of the marketplace—customers. The aim of marketing is to affect how customers think about and behave toward the organization and its marketing offers. To affect the whats, whens, and hows of buying behavior, marketers must first understand the *whys*. We look first at *final consumer* buying influences and processes and then at the buying behavior of *business customers*. You'll see that understanding buying behavior is an essential but very difficult task.

Our first point of interest: Harley-Davidson, maker of the nation's top-selling heavy-weight motorcycles. Who rides these big Harley "Hogs"? What moves them to tattoo their bodies with the Harley emblem, abandon home and hearth for the open road, and flock to Harley rallies by the hundreds of thousands? *You* might be surprised, but Harley-Davidson knows *very* well.

F ew brands engender such intense loyalty as that found in the hearts of Harley-Davidson owners. Harley buyers are granitelike in their devotion to the brand. Observes the publisher of *American Iron*, an industry publication, "You don't see people tattooing Yamaha on their bodies." And according to the president of a motorcycle research company, "For a lot of people, it's not that they want a motorcycle; it's that they want a Harley—the brand is that strong."

Each year, in early March, more than 400,000 Harley bikers rumble through the streets of Daytona Beach, Florida, to attend Harley-Davidson's Bike Week celebration. Bikers from across the nation lounge on their low-slung Harleys, swap biker tales, and sport T-shirts proclaiming "I'd rather push a Harley than drive a Honda."

Riding such intense emotions, Harley-Davidson has rumbled its way to the top of the fast-growing heavyweight motorcycle market. Harley's "Hogs" capture more than one-fifth of all U.S. bike sales and more than half of the heavyweight segment. Both the segment and Harley's sales are growing rapidly. In fact, for several years running, sales have far outstripped supply, with customer waiting lists of up to two years for popular models and street prices running well above suggested list prices. "We've seen people buy a new Harley and then sell it in the parking

lot for $4,000 to $5,000 more," says one dealer. During just the past 5 years, Harley sales have quadrupled, and earnings have increased sixfold. By 2003, the company had experienced 17 straight years of record sales and income.

Harley-Davidson's marketers spend a great deal of time thinking about customers and their buying behavior. They want to know who their customers are, what they think and how they feel, and why they buy a Harley rather than a Yamaha or a Kawasaki or a big Honda American Classic. What is it that makes Harley buyers so fiercely loyal? These are difficult questions; even Harley owners themselves don't know exactly what motivates their buying. But Harley management puts top priority on understanding customers and what makes them tick.

Who rides a Harley? You might be surprised. It's no longer the Hell's Angels crowd—the burly, black-leather-jacketed rebels and biker chicks who once made up Harley's core clientele. Motorcycles are attracting a new breed of riders—older, more affluent, and better educated. Harley now appeals more to "rubbies" (rich urban bikers) than to rebels. The average Harley customer is a 46-year-old husband with a median household income of $78,300. "In case you haven't noticed," notes one observer, "the young motorcycle tough of American mythology has matured a bit. Less Easy Rider and more easy-fit Dockers."

Harley-Davidson makes good bikes, and to keep up with its shifting market, the company has upgraded its showrooms and sales approaches. But Harley customers are buying a lot more than just a quality bike and a smooth sales pitch. To gain a better understanding of customers' deeper motivations, Harley-Davidson conducted focus groups in which it invited bikers to make cut-and-paste collages of pictures that expressed their feelings about Harley-Davidsons. (Can't you just see a bunch of hard-core bikers doing this?) It then mailed out 16,000 surveys containing a typical battery of psychological, sociological, and demographic questions as well as subjective questions such as "Is Harley more typified by a brown bear or a lion?"

The research revealed seven core customer types: adventure-loving traditionalists, sensitive pragmatists, stylish status seekers, laid-back campers, classy capitalists, cool-headed loners, and cocky misfits. However, all owners appreciated their Harleys for the same basic reasons. "It didn't matter if you were the guy who swept the floors of the factory or if you were the CEO at that factory, the attraction to Harley was very similar," says a Harley executive. "Independence, freedom, and power were the universal Harley appeals."

These studies confirm that Harley customers are doing more than just buying motorcycles. "It's much more than a machine," says one analyst. "It is part of their own self expression and lifestyle." Another analyst suggests that owning a Harley makes you "the toughest, baddest guy on the block. Never mind that [you're] a dentist or an accountant. You [feel] wicked astride all that power." Your Harley renews your spirits and announces your independence. As the Harley Web site's home page announces, "Thumbing the starter of a Harley-Davidson does a lot more than fire the engine. It fires the imagination." Adds a Harley dealer: "We sell a dream here."

The classic look, the throaty sound, the very idea of a Harley—all contribute to its mystique. Owning this "American legend" makes you a part of something bigger, a member of the Harley family. The fact that you have to wait to get a Harley makes it all that much more satisfying to have one. In fact, the company deliberately restricts its output. "Our goal is to eventually run production at a level that's always one motorcycle short of demand," says Harley-Davidson's chief executive.

Such strong emotions and motivations are captured in a classic Harley-Davidson advertisement. The ad shows a close-up of an arm, the bicep adorned with a Harley-Davidson tattoo. The headline asks, "When was the last time you felt this strongly about anything?" The ad copy outlines the problem and suggests a solution: "Wake up in the morning and life picks up where it left off. You do what has to be done. Use what it takes to get there. And what once seemed exciting has now become part of the numbing routine. It all begins to feel the same. Except when you've got a Harley-Davidson. Something strikes a nerve. The heartfelt thunder rises up, refusing to become part of the background. Suddenly things are different. Clearer. More real. As they should have been all along. The feeling is personal. For some, owning a Harley is a statement of individuality. For others, owning a Harley means being a part of a homegrown legacy that was born in a tiny Milwaukee shed in 1903. . . . To the uninitiated, a Harley-Davidson motorcycle is associated with a certain look, a certain sound. Anyone who owns one will tell you it's much more than that. Riding a Harley changes you from within. The effect is permanent. Maybe it's time you started feeling this strongly. Things are different on a Harley."[1]

The Harley-Davidson example shows that many different factors affect consumer buying behavior. Buying behavior is never simple, yet understanding it is the essential task of marketing management. First we explore the dynamics of the consumer market and final-consumer buyer behavior. We then examine business markets and the business buying process.

◼ Consumer Markets and Consumer Buyer Behavior

Consumer buyer behavior refers to the buying behavior of final consumers—individuals and households who buy goods and services for personal consumption. All of these final consumers combine to make up the **consumer market**. The American consumer market consists of more than 290 million people who consume many trillions of dollars' worth of goods and services each year, making it one of the most attractive consumer markets in the world. The world consumer market consists of almost 6.3 *billion* people.[2]

Consumers around the world vary tremendously in age, income, education level, and tastes. They also buy an incredible variety of goods and services. How these diverse consumers connect with each other and with other elements of the world around them impacts their choices among various products, services, and companies. Here we examine the fascinating array of factors that affect consumer behavior.

Consumer buyer behavior
The buying behavior of final consumers—individuals and households who buy goods and services for personal consumption.

Consumer market
All the individuals and households who buy or acquire goods and services for personal consumption.

Model of Consumer Behavior

Consumers make many buying decisions every day. Most large companies research consumer buying decisions in great detail to answer questions about what consumers buy, where they buy, and how much they buy, when they buy, and why they buy. Marketers can study actual consumer purchases to find out what they buy, where, and how much. But learning about the *whys* of consumer buying behavior is not so easy—the answers are often locked deep within the consumer's head.

Penetrating the dark recesses of the consumer's mind is no easy task. Often, consumers themselves don't know exactly what influences their purchases. "Ninety-five percent of the thought, emotion, and learning [that drive our purchases] occur in the unconscious mind—that is, without our awareness," notes one consumer behavior expert.[3]

The central question for marketers is: How do consumers respond to various marketing efforts the company might use? The starting point is the stimulus–response model of buyer behavior shown in Figure 5.1. This figure shows that marketing and other stimuli enter the consumer's "black box" and produce certain responses. Marketers must figure out what is in the buyer's black box.

Marketing stimuli consist of the four *P*s: product, price, place, and promotion. Other stimuli include major forces and events in the buyer's environment: economic, technological, political, and cultural. All these inputs enter the buyer's black box, where they are turned into a set of observable buyer responses: product choice, brand choice, dealer choice, purchase timing, and purchase amount.

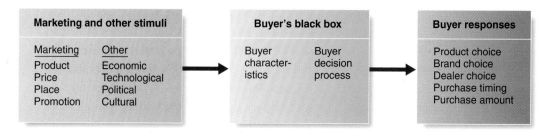

FIGURE 5.1

Model of Buyer Behavior

The marketer wants to understand how the stimuli are changed into responses inside the consumer's black box, which has two parts. First, the buyer's characteristics influence how he or she perceives and reacts to the stimuli. Second, the buyer's decision process itself affects the buyer's behavior. We look first at buyer characteristics as they affect buying behavior and then discuss the buyer decision process.

Characteristics Affecting Consumer Behavior

Consumer purchases are influenced strongly by cultural, social, personal, and psychological characteristics, as shown in Figure 5.2. For the most part, marketers cannot control such factors, but they must take them into account. We illustrate these characteristics for the case of a hypothetical consumer named Anna Flores. Anna is a married college graduate who works as a brand manager in a leading consumer packaged-goods company. She wants to find a new leisure-time activity that will provide some contrast to her working day. This need has led her to consider buying a camera and taking up photography. Many characteristics in her background will affect the way she evaluates cameras and chooses a brand.

Cultural Factors   Cultural factors exert a broad and deep influence on consumer behavior. The marketer needs to understand the role played by the buyer's *culture*, *subculture*, and *social class*.

Culture

The set of basic values, perceptions, wants, and behaviors learned by a member of society from family and other important institutions.

Culture.   **Culture** is the most basic cause of a person's wants and behavior. Human behavior is largely learned. Growing up in a society, a child learns basic values, perceptions, wants, and behaviors from the family and other important institutions. A child in the United States normally learns or is exposed to the following values: achievement and success, activity and involvement, efficiency and practicality, progress, material comfort, individualism, freedom, humanitarianism, youthfulness, and fitness and health. Every group or society has a culture, and cultural influences on buying behavior may vary greatly from country to country. Failure to adjust to these differences can result in ineffective marketing or embarrassing mistakes.

FIGURE 5.2

Factors Influencing Consumer Behavior

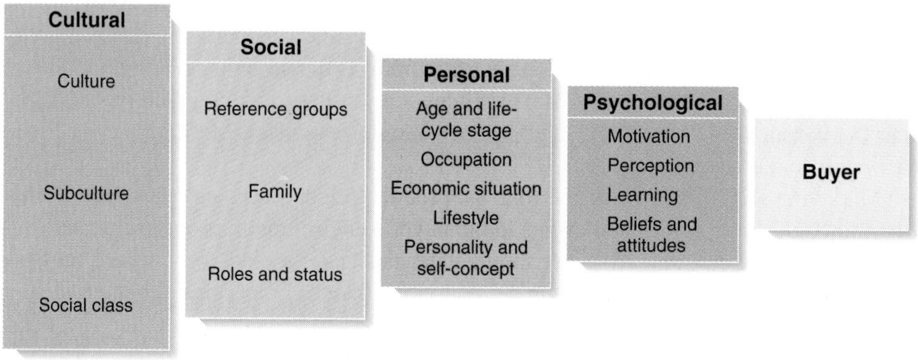

Cultural	**Social**	**Personal**	**Psychological**	**Buyer**
Culture	Reference groups	Age and life-cycle stage	Motivation	
		Occupation	Perception	
Subculture	Family	Economic situation	Learning	
		Lifestyle	Beliefs and attitudes	
	Roles and status	Personality and self-concept		
Social class				

Anna Flores's cultural background will affect her camera buying decision. Anna's desire to own a camera may result from her being raised in a modern society that has developed camera technology and a whole set of consumer learnings and values.

Marketers are always trying to spot *cultural shifts* in order to discover new products that might be wanted. For example, the cultural shift toward greater concern about health and fitness has created a huge industry for health and fitness services, exercise equipment and clothing, and lower-fat and more-natural foods. The shift toward informality has resulted in more demand for casual clothing and simpler home furnishings.

Subculture. Each culture contains smaller **subcultures**, or groups of people with shared value systems based on common life experiences and situations. Subcultures include nationalities, religions, racial groups, and geographic regions. Many subcultures make up important market segments, and marketers often design products and marketing programs tailored to their needs. Examples of four such important subculture groups include Hispanic, African American, Asian, and mature consumers.

Subculture
A group of people with shared value systems based on common life experiences and situations.

The U.S. *Hispanic market*—Americans of Cuban, Mexican, Central American, South American, and Puerto Rican descent—consists of almost 35 million consumers. Last year, Hispanic consumers bought more than $425 billion worth of goods and services, up 25 percent from just two years earlier. Expected to almost double in the next 20 years, this group will make up more than 19 percent of the total U.S. population by 2025.[4]

Hispanic consumers tend to buy more branded, higher-quality products—generics don't sell well to this group. And they tend to make shopping a family affair, and children have a big say in what brands they buy. Perhaps more important, Hispanics are brand loyal, and they favor companies who show special interest in them.[5]

Most marketers now produce products tailored to the Hispanic market and promote them using Spanish-language ads and media. For example, General Mills offers a line of Para su Familia (for your family) cereals for Hispanics, and Mattel has opened a Spanish-language site for its Barbie dolls—BarbieLatina.com—targeting U.S. Hispanic girls. Blockbuster recently set aside space in nearly 1,000 of its stores for videos dubbed in Spanish. Kmart launched an apparel line named after Mexican pop star Thalia.

Sears makes a special effort to market to Hispanic American consumers, especially for the 20 percent of its stores that are located in heavily Hispanic neighborhoods:

Sears is widely considered one of the most successful marketers to the U.S. Hispanic population. Last year, it spent some $25 million on advertising to Hispanics—more than any other retailer. Sears neighborhoods receive regular visits from a Fiesta Mobile, a colorful Winnebago that plays music, gives out prizes, and promotes the Sears credit card. Sears also sponsors major Hispanic cultural festivals and concerts. The retailer's Spanish-language Web site—Sears En Espanol (Sears in Spanish)—features content and events carefully tailored to Hispanic consumers. One of Sears's most successful marketing efforts is its magazine *Nuestra Gente*—which means Our People—the nation's largest Spanish-language magazine. The magazine features articles about Hispanic celebrities alongside glossy spreads of Sears fashions. As a result of this careful cultivation of Hispanic consumers, although Sears has lost sales in recent years to discount retailers, the Hispanic segment has remained steadfastly loyal.[6]

■ Sears is widely considered one of the most successful marketers to the U.S. Hispanic population. Its Spanish-language Web site features content and events carefully tailored to Hispanic consumers.

If the U.S. population of 35 million *African Americans* were a separate nation, its buying power of $646 billion annually would rank among the top 15 in the world. The black population in the United States is growing in affluence and sophistication. Although more price conscious than other segments, blacks are also strongly motivated by quality and selection. Brands are important. So is shopping—black consumers seem to enjoy shopping more than other groups, even for something as mundane as groceries. Black consumers are also the most fashion-conscious of the ethnic groups.[7]

In recent years, many companies have developed special products and services, packaging, and appeals to meet the needs of African Americans. For example, Hallmark launched its Afrocentric brand, Mahogany, with only 16 cards in 1987. Today the brand features more than 900 cards designed to celebrate African American culture, heritage, and traditions.

A wide variety of magazines, television channels, and other media now target African American consumers. Marketers are also reaching out to the African American virtual community. Per capita, black consumers spend twice as much as white consumers for online services. African Americans are increasingly turning to Web sites such as BlackPlanet.com, an African American community site with 5.8 million registered users. BlackPlanet.com's mission is to enable members to "cultivate meaningful personal and professional relationships, stay informed about the world, and gain access to goods and services that allow members to do more in life." Other popular sites include Afronet and Black Voices.[8]

Asian Americans, the fastest-growing and most affluent U.S. demographic segment, now number more than 12 million, with disposable income of $296 billion annually. Chinese Americans constitute the largest group, followed by Filipinos, Japanese Americans, Asian Indians, and Korean Americans. The U.S. Asian American population is estimated to reach 24 million by 2025. Asian consumers may be the most tech-savvy segment—more than a third made an Internet purchase last year. As a group, Asian consumers shop frequently and are the most brand-conscious of all the ethnic groups. Interestingly, they are also the least brand loyal—they change brands more often compared with the other groups.[9]

Because of the segment's rapidly growing buying power, many firms now target the Asian American market. For example, consider Wal-Mart. Today, in one Seattle store, where the Asian American population represents over 13 percent of the population, Wal-Mart stocks a large selection of CDs and videos from Asian artists, Asian-favored health and beauty products, and children's learning videos that feature multiple language tracks. Financial services provider Charles Schwab goes all out to court the large and particularly lucrative Chinese American market:

> Schwab estimates that there are over 3 million in the U.S. Asian community, half of whom are foreign-born and learned English as a second language. To cater to this audience, Schwab's Asia Pacific Services (APS) division has opened 14 Chinese American offices in hub locations such as New York's Chinatown and LA's Koreatown (many of which are open on Saturdays, when Asians tend to handle money matters). In addition, APS employs more than 200 people who speak Chinese, Korean, or Vietnamese at call centers serving Asian customers who prefer to speak their own languages. Schwab's Chinese-language Web site racks up millions of hits per month, including visits to an online Chinese-language news service, where customers can check real-time market activity, news headlines, and earnings estimates on their U.S. investments. Schwab's marketing to this segment focuses on educating clients on how to invest sensibly, whether they are short-term investors who trade frequently or long-term investors who are seeking investment or portfolio management advice. As a result, Schwab's APS' clients tend to be very loyal.[10]

As the U.S. population ages, *mature consumers* are becoming a very attractive market. Now 75 million strong, the population of U.S. seniors will more than double during in the next 25 years. The 65-and-over crowd alone numbers 35 million, more than 12 percent of the population. Mature consumers are better off financially than are younger consumer groups.[11] Because mature consumers have more time and money, they are an ideal market for exotic travel, restaurants, high-tech home entertainment products, leisure goods and services, designer furniture and fashions, financial services, and health care services.

Their desire to look as young as they feel also makes more-mature consumers good candidates for cosmetics and personal care products, health foods, fitness products, and

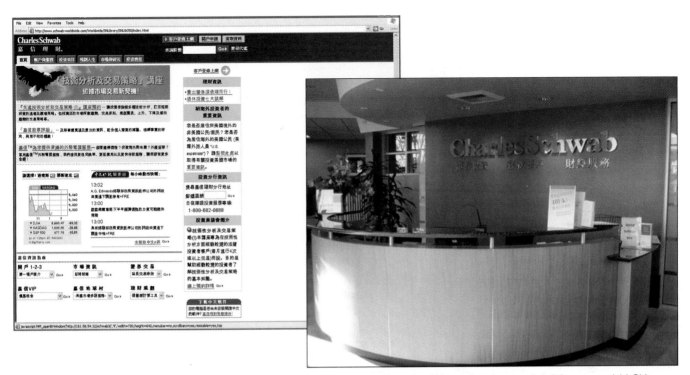

■ Financial services provider Charles Schwab goes all out to court the large and lucrative Chinese American market. It has opened 14 Chinese-language offices and its Chinese-language Web site racks up more than 5 million hits per month.

other items that combat the effects of aging. The best strategy is to appeal to their active, multidimensional lives. For example, Kellogg aired a TV spot for All-Bran cereal in which individuals ranging in age from 53 to 81 are featured playing ice hockey, water skiing, running hurdles, and playing baseball, all to the tune of "Wild Thing." A recent Pepsi ad features a young man in the middle of a mosh pit at a rock concert who turns around to see his father rocking out nearby. And an Aetna commercial portrays a senior who, after retiring from a career as a lawyer, fulfills a lifelong dream of becoming an archeologist.[12]

Anna Flores's buying behavior will be influenced by her subculture identification. These factors will affect her food preferences, clothing choices, recreation activities, and career goals. Subcultures attach different meanings to picture taking, and this could affect both Anna's interest in cameras and the brand she buys.

Social Class. Almost every society has some form of social class structure. **Social classes** are society's relatively permanent and ordered divisions whose members share similar values, interests, and behaviors. Social scientists have identified the seven American social classes shown in Figure 5.3.

Social class is not determined by a single factor, such as income, but is measured as a combination of occupation, income, education, wealth, and other variables. In some social systems, members of different classes are reared for certain roles and cannot change their social positions. In the United States, however, the lines between social classes are not fixed and rigid; people can move to a higher social class or drop into a lower one. Marketers are interested in social class because people within a given social class tend to exhibit similar buying behavior.[13]

Social classes show distinct product and brand preferences in areas such as clothing, home furnishings, leisure activity, and automobiles. Anna Flores's social class may affect her camera decision. If she comes from a higher social class background, her family probably owned an expensive camera and she may have dabbled in photography.

Social Factors A consumer's behavior also is influenced by social factors, such as the consumer's *small groups, family,* and *social roles* and *status.*

Social class
Relatively permanent and ordered divisions in a society whose members share similar values, interests, and behaviors.

FIGURE 5.3

The Major American Social Classes

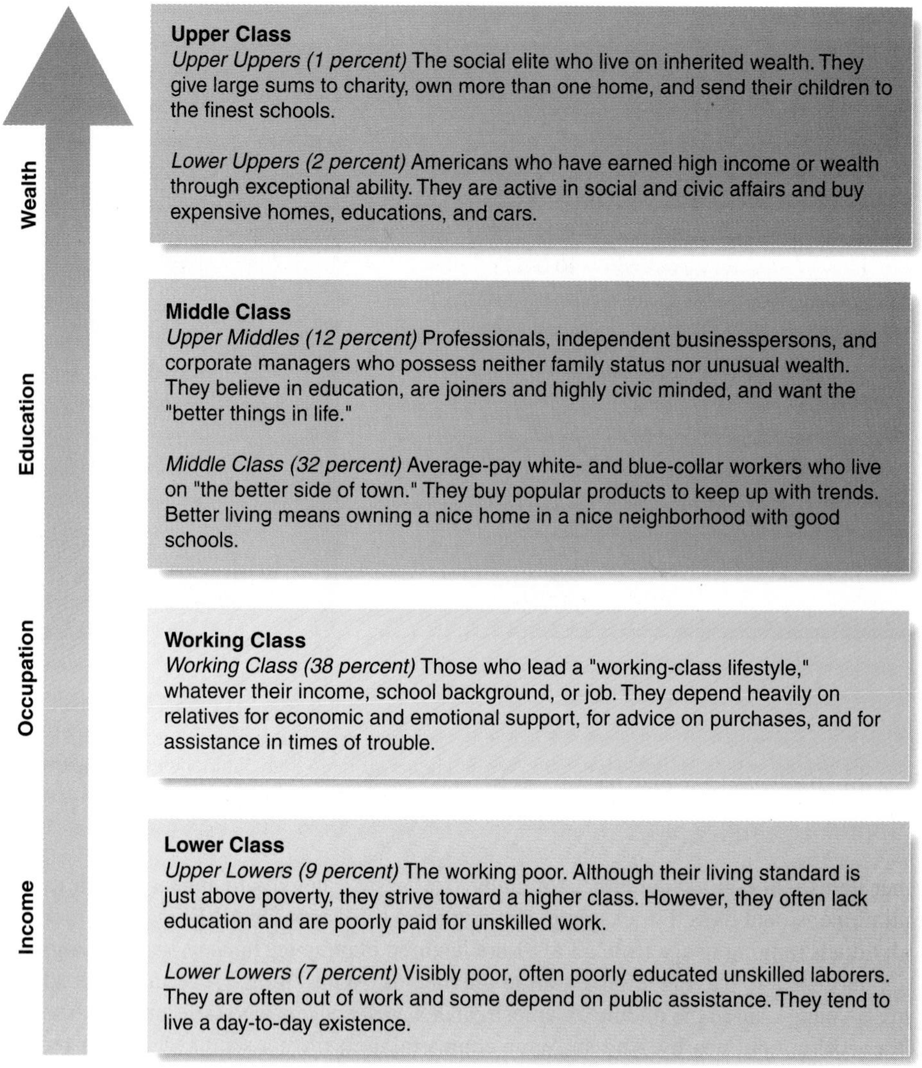

Wealth · Education · Occupation · Income (axis, bottom to top)

Upper Class
Upper Uppers (1 percent) The social elite who live on inherited wealth. They give large sums to charity, own more than one home, and send their children to the finest schools.

Lower Uppers (2 percent) Americans who have earned high income or wealth through exceptional ability. They are active in social and civic affairs and buy expensive homes, educations, and cars.

Middle Class
Upper Middles (12 percent) Professionals, independent businesspersons, and corporate managers who possess neither family status nor unusual wealth. They believe in education, are joiners and highly civic minded, and want the "better things in life."

Middle Class (32 percent) Average-pay white- and blue-collar workers who live on "the better side of town." They buy popular products to keep up with trends. Better living means owning a nice home in a nice neighborhood with good schools.

Working Class
Working Class (38 percent) Those who lead a "working-class lifestyle," whatever their income, school background, or job. They depend heavily on relatives for economic and emotional support, for advice on purchases, and for assistance in times of trouble.

Lower Class
Upper Lowers (9 percent) The working poor. Although their living standard is just above poverty, they strive toward a higher class. However, they often lack education and are poorly paid for unskilled work.

Lower Lowers (7 percent) Visibly poor, often poorly educated unskilled laborers. They are often out of work and some depend on public assistance. They tend to live a day-to-day existence.

Group

Two or more people who interact to accomplish individual or mutual goals.

Groups. A person's behavior is influenced by many small **groups**. Groups that have a direct influence and to which a person belongs are called *membership groups*. In contrast, *reference groups* serve as direct (face-to-face) or indirect points of comparison or reference in forming a person's attitudes or behavior. People often are influenced by reference groups to which they do not belong. For example, an *aspirational group* is one to which the individual wishes to belong, as when a teenage basketball player hopes to play someday for the Los Angeles Lakers. Marketers try to identify the reference groups of their target markets. Reference groups expose a person to new behaviors and lifestyles, influence the person's attitudes and self-concept, and create pressures to conform that may affect the person's product and brand choices.

The importance of group influence varies across products and brands. It tends to be strongest when the product is visible to others whom the buyer respects. Manufacturers of products and brands subjected to strong group influence must figure out how to reach **opinion leaders**—people within a reference group who, because of special skills, knowledge, personality, or other characteristics, exert influence on others. According to one recent study:

Opinion leader

Person within a reference group who, because of special skills, knowledge, personality, or other characteristics, exerts influence on others.

> One American in ten tells the other nine how to vote, where to eat, and what to buy. They are the influentials. They drive trends, influence mass opinion and, most importantly, sell a great many products. These are the early adopters who had a digital camera before everyone else and who were the first to fly again after September 11. They are the 10 percent of Americans who determine how the rest consume and live by chatting about their likes and dislikes.[14]

Many marketers try to identify opinion leaders for their products and direct marketing efforts toward them. They use *buzz marketing* by enlisting or even creating opinion leaders to spread the word about their brands. For example, one New York marketing firm, Big Fat Promotions, hires bar "leaners" to talk casually with tavern patrons about merits of certain liquors, doormen to stack packages from a particular online catalog company in their building lobbies, mothers to chat up new laundry products at their kids' little-league games, and commuters to play with new PDAs during the ride home.[15] Here's another buzz marketing example:

■ Opinion leaders: Marketers use *buzz marketing* by enlisting or even creating opinion leaders to spread the word about their brands. For example, scooter riding models on the Vespa payroll generate favorable word of mouth for the company's products.

> Frequent the right cafes . . . in and around Los Angeles this summer, and you're likely to encounter a gang of sleek, impossibly attractive motorbike riders who seem genuinely interested in getting to know you over an iced latte. Compliment them on their Vespa scooters glinting in the brilliant curbside sunlight, and they'll happily pull out a pad and scribble down an address and phone number—not theirs, but that of the local "boutique" where you can buy your own Vespa, just as (they'll confide) the rap artist Sisqo and the movie queen Sandra Bullock recently did. And that's when the truth hits you: This isn't any spontaneous encounter. Those scooter-riding models are on the Vespa payroll, and they've been hired to generate some favorable word of mouth for the recently reissued European bikes. Welcome to the new world of buzz marketing. Buzz marketers are now taking to the streets, as well as cafes, nightclubs, and the Internet, in record numbers. Vespa . . . has its biker gang. Hebrew National is dispatching "mom squads" to grill up its hot dogs in backyard barbecues, while Hasbro Games has deputized hundreds of fourth- and fifth-graders as "secret agents" to tantalize their peers with Hasbro's POX electronic game. Their goal: to seek out the trendsetters in each community and subtly push them into talking up their brand to their friends and admirers.[16]

Family. Family members can strongly influence buyer behavior. The family is the most important consumer buying organization in society, and it has been researched extensively. Marketers are interested in the roles and influence of the husband, wife, and children on the purchase of different products and services.

Husband–wife involvement varies widely by product category and by stage in the buying process. Buying roles change with evolving consumer lifestyles. In the United States, the wife traditionally has been the main purchasing agent for the family in the areas of food, household products, and clothing. But with 70 percent of women holding jobs outside the home and the willingness of husbands to do more of the family's purchasing, all this is changing. Whereas women make up just 40 percent of drivers, they now influence more than 80 percent of car-buying decisions. Men now account for about 40 percent of all food-shopping dollars. In all, women now make almost 85 percent of all purchases, spending $6 trillion each year.[17]

Such changes suggest that marketers who've typically sold their products to only men or only women are now courting the opposite sex. For example, consider home improvement retailer Lowe's:

> War has broken out over your home-improvement dollar, and Lowe's has superpower Home Depot on the defensive. Its not-so-secret ploy: Lure women, because they'll drag their Tim Allen tool-guy husbands behind them. According to Lowe's research, women initiate 80 percent of all home-improvement purchase decisions, especially the big-ticket orders like kitchen cabinets, flooring,

■ Family buying influences: To attract women shoppers, Lowe's focuses on aesthetics—bright and airy stores with wide, uncluttered aisles and supermarket-like signs. "Lure women, and they'll drag their Tim Allen tool-guy husbands behind them."

and bathrooms. And women appreciate Lowe's obsession with store aesthetics. Lowe's stores are bright and airy with wide, uncluttered aisles and supermarket-like signs that list what is in each aisle. Managers patrol every new store with light meters to make sure aisles are lit to the company standard of 90 foot-candles. Stack-outs, those pallets of merchandise set out on the floor in front of the main shelves, are banned. They add to revenue per square foot, but they also obstruct the aisles, triggering the dreaded "butt-brush" phenomenon: Female shoppers don't like to be touched by passersby. Pam and Shawn Panuline, a young North Carolina couple who just bought a three-bedroom home, have shopped the nearby Home Depot and Lowe's stores. For Pam, Lowe's felt friendlier and had far more choices in home decor, and she liked that it wasn't as contractor-oriented. "But it's not too froofy," says her husband. Lowe's focus on women has paid off handsomely. Over the past 10 years, Lowe's has earned a 30 percent annual return, compared with 10 percent for Home Depot.[18]

Children may also have a strong influence on family buying decisions. For example, children as young as age six may influence the family car purchase decision. Recognizing this fact, Toyota recently launched a new kid-focused ad campaign for its Sienna minivan. Whereas most other minivan ads have focused on soccer moms, the new Sienna ads show kids expressing what they want out of a minivan. In one spot, for example, engineers in Sienna's design center anxiously await what looks to be a shakedown by company big shots. Instead, in rush three little girls on bicycles who begin demanding certain features and offering other advice, "I want a hundred cup holders," says one. "Is 14 all right?" asks the engineer. In another ad, a sales-kid in a Toyota dealership makes a sales pitch to a kid-customer as the two bounce on a mini trampoline. "It's got a 230hpV6," says the sales-kid. "What's that?" asks the customer. "I'm not sure," he responds. The ad concludes: "Everything kids want. Everything you need."[19]

Roles and Status. A person belongs to many groups—family, clubs, organizations. The person's position in each group can be defined in terms of both role and status. With her parents, Anna Flores plays the role of daughter; in her family, she plays the role of wife; in her company, she plays the role of brand manager. A *role* consists of the activities people are expected to perform according to the people around them. Each of Anna's roles will influence some of her buying behavior. Each role carries a *status* reflecting the general esteem given to it by society. People often choose products that show their status in society. For example, the role of brand manager has more status in our society than does the role of daughter. As a brand manager, Anna will buy the kind of clothing that reflects her role and status.

Personal Factors A buyer's decisions also are influenced by personal characteristics such as the buyer's *age* and *life-cycle stage, occupation, economic situation, lifestyle,* and *personality* and *self-concept.*

Age and Life-Cycle Stage. People change the goods and services they buy over their lifetimes. Tastes in food, clothes, furniture, and recreation are often age related. Buying is also shaped by the stage of the *family life cycle*—the stages through which families might pass as they mature over time. Marketers often define their target markets in terms of life-cycle stage and develop appropriate products and marketing plans for each stage.

Traditional family life-cycle stages include young singles and married couples with children. Today, however, marketers are increasingly catering to a growing number of alternative, nontraditional stages such as unmarried couples, singles marrying later in life, childless couples, same-sex couples, single parents, extended parents (those with young adult children returning home), and others. For example, more and more companies are now reaching out to serve the fast-growing corps of the recently divorced (see Marketing at Work 5.1).

Sony recently overhauled its marketing approach in order to target products and services to consumers based on their life stages. It created a new unit called the Consumer Segment Marketing Division, which has identified seven life-stage segments. They include, among others, Gen Y (under 25), Young Professionals/DINKs (double income, no kids, 25 to 34), Families (35 to 54), and Zoomers (55 and over). A recent Sony ad aimed at Zoomers, people who have just retired or are close to doing so, shows a man living his dream by going into outer space. The ad deals not just with going into retirement, but with the psychological life-stage changes that go with it. "The goal is to get closer to consumers," says a Sony segment marketing executive.[20]

Occupation. A person's occupation affects the goods and services bought. Blue-collar workers tend to buy more rugged work clothes, whereas executives buy more business suits. Marketers try to identify the occupational groups that have an above-average interest in their products and services. A company can even specialize in making products needed by a given occupational group. Thus, computer software companies will design different products for brand managers, accountants, engineers, lawyers, and doctors.

Economic Situation. A person's economic situation will affect product choice. Anna Flores can consider buying an expensive Nikon if she has enough spendable income, savings, or borrowing power. Marketers of income-sensitive goods watch trends in personal income, savings, and interest rates. If economic indicators point to a recession, marketers can take steps to redesign, reposition, and reprice their products closely.

Lifestyle. People coming from the same subculture, social class, and occupation may have quite different lifestyles. **Lifestyle** is a person's pattern of living as expressed in his or her *psychographics*. It involves measuring consumers' major *AIO dimensions*—activities (work, hobbies, shopping, sports, social events), *interests* (food, fashion, family, recreation), and *opinions* (about themselves, social issues, business, products). Lifestyle captures something more than the person's social class or personality. It profiles a person's whole pattern of acting and interacting in the world.

Several research firms have developed lifestyle classifications. The most widely used is SRI Consulting's *Values and Lifestyles (VALS)* typology. VALS classifies people according to how they spend their time and money. It divides consumers into eight groups based on two major dimensions: primary motivation and resources. *Primary motivations* include ideals, achievement, and self-expression. According to SRI Consulting, consumers who are primarily motivated by ideals are guided by knowledge and principles. Consumers who are primarily motivated by *achievement* look for products and services that demonstrate success to their peers. Consumers who are primarily motivated by *self-expression* desire social or physical activity, variety, and risk.

Consumers within each orientation are further classified into those with *high resources* and those with *low resources*, depending on whether they have high or low levels of income, education, health, self-confidence, energy, and other factors. Consumers with either very high or very low levels of resources are classified without regard to their primary motivations (Innovators, Survivors). Innovators are people with so many resources that they exhibit all three primary motivations in varying degrees. In contrast,

Lifestyle

A person's pattern of living as expressed in his or her activities, interests, and opinions.

■ Lifestyles: To promote a new image, Iron City beer ads mingled images of the old Pittsburgh with those of the new, dynamic city and scenes of young Experiencers and Strivers having fun and working hard.

Survivors are people with so few resources that they do not show a strong primary motivation. They must focus on meeting needs rather than fulfilling desires.

Iron City beer, a well-known brand in Pittsburgh, used VALS to update its image and improve sales. Iron City was losing sales—its aging core users were drinking less beer, and younger men weren't buying the brand. VALS research showed that one VALS segment, Experiencers, drink the most beer, followed by Strivers. To assess Iron City's image problems, the company interviewed men in these categories. It gave the men stacks of pictures of different kinds of people and asked them to identify first Iron City brand users and then people most like themselves. The men pictured Iron City drinkers as blue-collar steelworkers stopping off at the local bar. However, they saw themselves as more modern, hardworking, and fun loving. They strongly rejected the outmoded, heavy-industry image of Pittsburgh. Based on this research, Iron City created ads linking its beer to the new self-image of target consumers. The ads mingled images of the old Pittsburgh with those of the new, dynamic city and scenes of young Experiencers and Strivers having fun and working hard. Within just one month of the start of the campaign, Iron City sales shot up by 26 percent.[21]

Lifestyle segmentation can also be used to understand how consumers use the Internet, computers, and other technology. Forrester developed its "Technographics" scheme, which segments consumers according to motivation, desire, and ability to invest in technology. The framework splits people into 10 categories, such as[22]:

■ *Fast Forwards:* the biggest spenders on computer technology. Fast Forwards are career focused, time-strapped, driven, and top users of technology.

■ *New Age Nurturers:* also big spenders. However, they are focused on technology for home uses, such as a family education and entertainment.

■ *Mouse Potatoes:* consumers who are dedicated to interactive entertainment and willing to spend for the latest in "technotainment."

■ *Techno-Strivers:* consumers who are up-and-coming believers in technology for career advancement.

■ *Traditionalists:* small-town folks, suspicious of technology beyond the basics.

Delta Airlines used Technographics to better target online ticket sales. It created marketing campaigns for time-strapped Fast Forwards and New Age Nurturers, and eliminated Technology Pessimists from its list of targets.

When used carefully, the lifestyle concept can help marketers understand changing consumer values and how they affect buying behavior. Anna Flores, for example, can choose to live the role of a capable homemaker, a career professional, or a free spirit— or all three. She plays several roles, and the way she blends them expresses her lifestyle. If she becomes a professional photographer, this would change her lifestyle, in turn changing what and how she buys.

Marketing at Work | 5.1

Targeting Nontraditional Life Stages: Just Divorced, Gone Shopping

When Los Angeles psychologist Leila Mesghali walked out of her marriage of three years, she didn't look back. She took only her clothes and some heirloom dishes. A few months later, however, the decorating urge kicked in. Even on a limited budget, she spent $6,000 on a dark teak armoire, sofa, and bedroom set. "I had a lot of motivation to fill my apartment up quickly," she said. "It was an opportunity to do my own thing."

Kim Lombard, a television producer in Toronto, also refurnished from scratch after splitting two years ago—although not of his own will. "When my wife left me, she took everything," he says. He quickly spent about $25,000 on a sofa, a good mattress, and a 50-inch television. Consider, too, the suddenly single Wall Street banker who spent $3,000 in an afternoon to outfit a bedroom for his 17-month-old twins just like the one they already knew. Or the newly separated publisher who visited an Arts and Crafts furniture store to buy a Gustav Stickley headboard and walked out with a recliner, a table, and an armoire as well.

The number of divorced people in the United States has quintupled over the past 30 years, from 4 million in 1970 to almost 20 million in 2000. With about half of all first marriages ending in divorce, marketers are beginning to recognize that divorcees represent a distinct consumer segment in a not so nontraditional life-cycle stage. When two people untie the knot, there's rarely an equitable split of their possessions. One person usually keeps the belongings; the other goes shopping.

"The divorce rate is keeping the furniture business alive," says a consultant who advises furniture retailers and manufacturers. "There's no doubt that life stages are driving consumers. They buy when they get married; they buy when

they get divorced." Like newlyweds, the newly separated need to stock their homes with everything from dish towels to four-poster beds (for her), from recliners to flat-screen televisions (for him). "Next year, at least half of the 2.4 million people who will get divorced in the United States and Canada are going to buy new beds," says Dan Couvrette, publisher of *Divorce Magazine*. "That's over a million people. You can't find a bigger niche."

Divorcees don't just buy out of necessity; the shopping cure can ease the pain. People going through a divorce, Couvrette says, "represent a tremendous market potential because they'll spend money to get stuff that makes them feel better." He adds that even those who suffer financial setbacks—often the case with women leaving long-term marriages—try to

treat themselves to the best they can afford. A survey of the magazine's readers found that 78 percent of the men bought new entertainment systems, while 69 percent of the women opted for new bedroom furniture.

Retail stores, such as Crate & Barrel, Sears, and Ikea, are learning to recognize and take care of the shopper who may be dazed and alone, trailing a long list of household needs. "Our salespeople say they sometimes feel like therapists," says a Crate & Barrel spokesperson. "They know they can't be all bubbly around someone who might be upset. It's clearly a situation that demands their most sensitive approach." One North Carolina furniture maker has trained its salespeople to keep an eye out for customers with such special needs. "We teach our sales associates to look out for that

Life-stage marketing: Marketers are discovering that when couples split, someone goes shopping. Divorcees, much like newly-weds, restock their homes with everything from pots and pans to televisions.

(continued)

man wandering around. He may have just been kicked out of the house," says a company's owner.

One Ikea spokeswoman estimates that as many as one-third of the customers she worked with over five years as a design consultant at the Ikea store in Elizabeth, New Jersey, were ex-husbands. Sometimes saleswomen find themselves playing surrogate wife. As a home furnishings consultant at Ikea in Chicago, Sharon Klein provides design advice to customers as they shop. She said she is frequently approached by "gentlemen who want help from someone with a woman's touch in buying just about everything. They come right up to you and say, 'Help!'" She adds that when it came to outfitting rooms for children, those same shoppers have bottomless wallets. "They always want a lot of extras to make their kid's new bedroom more exciting than the one at the other parent's house," she says.

In response to the growing market, advertisers are tentatively reaching out. Sears tested the waters with a coy tele-vision ad about divorce. A once-loving couple, having split their washer and dryer, are each shown while shopping at Sears for replacement appliances. They smile awkwardly at each other. "It was a humorous look at a real-life situation," says a Sears marketer.

Some years ago, Ikea ran a televi-sion ad that put a positive spin on shopping one's way to a fresh start. It showed a woman driving at night with her daughter asleep in the back seat. She muses aloud about her divorce and starting a new life. Flashbacks show her shopping up a storm in the aisles of Ikea. The campaign was well received by the press and the public.

Many marketers have shunned the divorcee segment as too downbeat. "Divorce is still a niche market with neg-ative connotations," says one analyst. "Historically, advertisers go with more positive images. But that's going to change in keeping with the whole trend to go after more targeted groups."

Montauk Sofas was among the first to run an upbeat breakup ad. A smiling woman cozies up in the embrace of a $1,900 extra-plush armchair. The text begins in bold type: "He left me. Good Riddance," and ends: "Who cares . . . I kept the sofa." The ad has generated such good feelings for Montauk, a Montreal-based furniture manufacturer with seven stores in the United States and Canada, that it has kept running it for five years. "We've gotten an excel-lent reaction from all walks of life and ages," said Tim Zyto, the owner of Montauk. "Women especially like it. They find it empowering."

It may be only a matter of time before the once taboo D-word comes to stand for "divorce registry." Mr. Couvrette at *Divorce Magazine* is confi-dent that that day is not far off. "It's not going to be called a divorce registry," he predicted, "but everyone's going to know what it's for."

Source: Adapted from Julie V. Iovine, "Just Divorced, Gone Shopping," *New York Times*, July 12, 2001, p. F1. Also see Pamela Sebastian Ridge, "Tool Sellers Tap Their Feminine Side," *Wall Street Journal*, March 29, 2002, p. B1; and David Anderson and Rosemary Clandos, "Dating after Divorce," *Psychology Today*, January/February 2003, pp. 46–56.

Personality

The unique psychological characteristics that lead to relatively consistent and lasting responses to one's own environment.

Personality and Self-Concept. Each person's distinct personality influences his or her buying behavior. **Personality** refers to the unique psychological characteristics that lead to relatively consistent and lasting responses to one's own environment. Personality is usu-ally described in terms of traits such as self-confidence, dominance, sociability, autonomy, defensiveness, adaptability, and aggressiveness. Personality can be useful in analyzing consumer behavior for certain product or brand choices. For example, coffee marketers have discovered that heavy coffee drinkers tend to be high on sociability. Thus, to attract customers, Starbucks and other coffeehouses create environments in which people can relax and socialize over a cup of steaming coffee.

The idea is that brands also have personalities, and that consumers are likely to choose brands whose personalities match their own. A *brand personality* is the specific mix of human traits that may be attributed to a particular brand. One researcher identified five brand personality traits[23]:

1. Sincerity (down-to-earth, honest, wholesome, and cheerful)
2. Excitement (daring, spirited, imaginative, and up-to-date)
3. Competence (reliable, intelligent, and successful)
4. Sophistication (upper class and charming)
5. Ruggedness (outdoorsy and tough)

The researcher found that a number of well-known brands tended to be strongly associated with one particular trait: Levi's with "ruggedness," MTV with "excitement," CNN with "competence," and Campbell's with "sincerity." Hence, these brands will attract persons who are high on the same personality traits.

Many marketers use a concept related to personality—a person's *self-concept* (also called *self-image*). The basic self-concept premise is that people's possessions contribute to and reflect their identities; that is, "we are what we have." Thus, in order to understand consumer behavior, the marketer must first understand the relationship between consumer self-concept and possessions.

Psychological Factors   A person's buying choices are further influenced by four major psychological factors: *motivation, perception, learning,* and *beliefs* and *attitudes.*

Motivation.   We know that Anna Flores became interested in buying a camera. Why? What is she *really* seeking? What *needs* is she trying to satisfy? A person has many needs at any given time. Some are *biological,* arising from states of tension such as hunger, thirst, or discomfort. Others are *psychological,* arising from the need for recognition, esteem, or belonging. A need becomes a *motive* when it is aroused to a sufficient level of intensity. A **motive** (or *drive*) is a need that is sufficiently pressing to direct the person to seek satisfaction. Psychologists have developed theories of human motivation. Two of the most popular—the theories of Sigmund Freud and Abraham Maslow—have quite different meanings for consumer analysis and marketing.

■ Heavy coffee drinkers tend to be high on sociability, so to attract customers Starbucks and other coffee houses create environments in which people can relax and socialize over a cup of steaming coffee.

Motive (drive)
A need that is sufficiently pressing to direct the person to seek satisfaction of the need.

Sigmund Freud assumed that people are largely unconscious about the real psychological forces shaping their behavior. He saw the person as growing up and repressing many urges. These urges are never eliminated or under perfect control; they emerge in dreams, in slips of the tongue, in neurotic and obsessive behavior, or ultimately in psychoses. Thus, Freud suggested that a person does not fully understand his or her motivation. If Anna Flores wants to purchase an expensive camera, she may describe her motive as wanting a hobby or career. At a deeper level, she may be purchasing the camera to impress others with her creative talent. At a still deeper level, she may be buying the camera to feel young and independent again.

The term *motivation research* refers to qualitative research designed to probe consumers' hidden, subconscious motivations. Motivation researchers collect in-depth information from small samples of consumers to uncover the deeper motives for their product choices. The techniques range from sentence completion, word association, and inkblot or cartoon interpretation tests, to having consumers describe typical brand users or form daydreams and fantasies about brands or buying situations (see Marketing at Work 5.2).

Abraham Maslow sought to explain why people are driven by particular needs at particular times. Why does one person spend much time and energy on personal safety and another on gaining the esteem of others? Maslow's answer is that human needs are arranged in a hierarchy, as shown in Figure 5.4 on page 158, from the most pressing at the bottom to the least pressing at the top. They include *physiological* needs, *safety* needs, *social* needs, *esteem* needs, and *self-actualization* needs.

A person tries to satisfy the most important need first. When that need is satisfied, it will stop being a motivator and the person will then try to satisfy the next most important need. For example, starving people (physiological need) will not take an interest in the latest happenings in the art world (self-actualization needs), nor in how they are seen or esteemed by others (social or esteem needs), nor even in whether they are breathing clean air (safety needs). But as each important need is satisfied, the next most important need will come into play.

What light does Maslow's theory throw on Anna Flores's interest in buying a camera? We can guess that Anna has satisfied her physiological, safety, and social needs; they do not motivate her interest in cameras. Her camera interest might come from a strong need for more esteem. Or it might come from a need for self-actualization—she might want to be a creative person and express herself through photography.

Marketing at Work | 5.2

"Touchy-Feely" Research: Psyching Out Consumers

Consumers often don't know or can't describe just why they act as they do. Thus, motivation researchers use a variety of probing techniques to uncover underlying emotions and attitudes toward brands and buying situations. These sometimes bizarre techniques range from free association and inkblot interpretation tests to having consumers form daydreams and fantasies about brands or buying situations. One writer offers the following tongue-in-cheek summary of a motivation research session:

Good morning, ladies and gentlemen. We've called you here today for a little consumer research. Now, lie down on the couch, toss your inhibitions out the window, and let's try a little free association. First, think about brands as if they were your friends. Imagine you could talk to your TV dinner. What would he say? And what would you say to him? . . . Now, think of your shampoo as an animal. Go on, don't be shy. Would it be a panda or a lion? A snake or a wooly worm? For our final exercise, let's all sit up and pull out our magic markers. Draw a picture of a typical cake-mix user. Would she wear an apron or a negligee? A business suit or a can-can dress?

Such projective techniques seem pretty goofy. But more and more, marketers are using such touchy-feely approaches to dig deeply into consumer psyches and develop better marketing strategies. For example, Shell Oil used motivation research in an attempt to uncover the real reasons behind a decade-long sales slump:

The manager of corporate advertising for Shell Oil, Sixtus Oeschle, was at his wits' end. For months, he and his team of researchers had pumped the consumer psyche. For months, they'd come up empty. "We tried psychographic memory triggers," he recalls. "We tried dream therapy." All to no avail. At one point, respondents were even given mounds of wet clay and urged to mold figures that expressed their inner feelings about Shell.

It was time, Oeschle decided, to try something radical. To craft a more potent appeal for its brand of gasoline, Shell would have to go deeper—much deeper. Oeschle called in a consumer researcher who specializes in focus groups conducted under hypnosis. The results, Oeschle says, wowed even the skeptics. "I've got to tell you, it was fascinating, fascinating stuff," he says. After dimming the lights, the researcher took respondents back, back—back all the way to their infancy. "He just kept taking them back and back," Oeschle says, "until . . . he's saying, 'Tell me about your first experience in a gas station.' And people were actually having memory flash-

The PT Cruiser: The phenomenally successful retro style car that's "part 1920s gangster car, part 1950s hot rod, and part London taxicab"—an actual chrome-and-sheet-metal incarnation of the popular will.

backs. I mean, they were going there. They were saying, 'I was three-and-a half years old. I was in the back of my dad's brand new Chevy.' It was like it was yesterday to them. I was stunned."

The real breakthrough, however, came after the respondents awoke out of their trance. "When he brought them all back out, he asked them who'd they prefer as a gasoline purveyor," Oeschle says. "What staggered me was that, to a person, it was always linked to that experience in their youth." One woman volunteered that she always made a point of filling up at Texaco. "We asked her why," Oeschle recalls. "And she said, 'I don't know, I guess I just feel good about Texaco.' Well, this was the little three-and-a-half-year-old in the back of her daddy's car speaking."

Shell is now designing new marketing approaches based on the insights gleaned from the groups of mesmerized motorists. Where Shell had gone wrong, it seems, was in reasoning that, since people don't start buying gas until at least age 16, there was no need to target the tiniest consumers. "They weren't even on Shell's radar," Oeschle laments. "It dawned on us . . . that we'd better figure out how to favorably impact people from an early age."

Similarly, DaimlerChrysler used a dose of deep motivation research to create a successful new concept car.

A few years back, DaimlerChrysler set out to find the next "wow car," the "segment buster" that would reach across age and income lines, into the subconscious. That meant doing more than the usual focus group research. So DaimlerChrysler hired psychologist Clothaire Rapaille to probe consumers' innermost feelings. The underlying premise: the products we buy mean something; they form

part of a greater whole. "The more we learn about American culture, the more we see how our vehicles fit into our psyche—the more we see how it is that we fit into the overall scheme of living," says David Bostwick, director of market research at DaimlerChrysler.

Rather than convening traditional focus groups, Rapaille used a method known as "archetype research." He had participants lie on soft mats, listen to mood music, and free-associate in the dark. According to Bostwick, this recreates the same brain activity you have when you first wake up from a dream. "It's a very special brain activity," he says. "It allows us to actually access some of those unconscious thoughts."

When the lights came back up, Rapaille had learned that Americans are entrepreneurial, individualistic, freedom loving, and inventive—but also juvenile and self-indulgent. More important, he discovered that many suffered nostalgia pangs. In these complex and often unsettling times, car buyers yearned for the good old days—for a time when things seemed simpler and more secure, and when people felt good about themselves. "What that said to us is that people are looking for something that offers protection on the outside, and comfort on the inside," says Bostwick. "We communicated that to our design team."

The result: the PT Cruiser, DaimlerChrysler's phenomenally successful retro style car. Described by the Wall Street Journal as "part 1920s gangster car, part 1950s hot rod, and part London taxicab," the PT Cruiser is what one analyst calls "a focus group on wheels—an actual chrome-and-sheet-metal incarnation of the popular will." Its nostalgic look and

protective exterior, combined with a well-appointed and highly functional interior, inspires an emotional reaction from almost everyone. In just two years following its introduction, U.S. consumers snapped up more than 225,000 PT Cruisers. "We didn't set out to create a market," Bostwick says earnestly. "We just tapped into what people had in their heads in the first place. . . . The vehicle takes you back, but not to a particular time in the century. It just takes you back to a time you felt cool." Says a PT Cruiser designer, "it's a celebration of automotive heritage . . . with a twist of rebellion."

Some marketers dismiss such motivation research as mumbo jumbo. However, like Shell and DaimlerChrysler, many companies are now delving into the murky depths of the consumer unconscious. "Such tactics have been worshipfully embraced by even the no-nonsense, jut-jawed captains of industry," claims an analyst. "At companies like Kraft, Coca-Cola, Proctor & Gamble, and DaimlerChrysler, the most sought-after consultants hail not from [traditional consulting firms like McKinsey. They come] from brand consultancies with names like Archetype Discoveries, PsychoLogics and Semiotic Solutions."

Sources: Examples adapted from Ruth Shalit, "The Return of the Hidden Persuaders," Salon Media, September 27, 1999, accessed online at www.salon.com. Also see Annetta Miller and Dody Tsiantar, "Psyching Out Consumers," *Newsweek*, February 27, 1989, pp. 46–47; Alison Stein Wellner, "Research on a Shoestring," *American Demographics*, April 2001, pp. 38–39; Phil Patton, "Car Shrinks," *Fortune*, March 18, 2002, pp. 187–190; "PT Cruiser," *Journal of Business and Design*, accessed online at the Corporate Design Foundation Web site, www.cdf.org, June 2003; "Taste—Review & Outlook: Sweet 16," *Wall Street Journal*, January 24, 2003, p. W13; and information found at www.ptcruiserclub.com, August 2003.

FIGURE 5.4

Maslow's Hierarchy of Needs

Sources: From *Motivation and Personality* by Abraham H. Maslow. Copyright © 1970 by Abraham H. Maslow. Copyright 1954, 1987 by Harper & Row Publishers, Inc. Reprinted by permission of Addison Wesley Educational Publishers, Inc. Also see Barbara Marx Hubbard, "Seeking Our Future Potentials," *The Futurist,* May 1998, pp. 29–32.

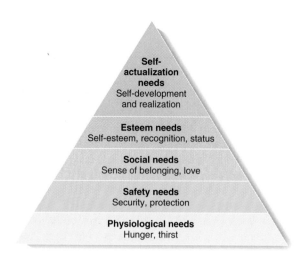

Perception

The process by which people select, organize, and interpret information to form a meaningful picture of the world.

Perception. A motivated person is ready to act. How the person acts is influenced by his or her own perception of the situation. All of us learn by the flow of information through our five senses: sight, hearing, smell, touch, and taste. However, each of us receives, organizes, and interprets this sensory information in an individual way. **Perception** is the process by which people select, organize, and interpret information to form a meaningful picture of the world.

People can form different perceptions of the same stimulus because of three perceptual processes: selective attention, selective distortion, and selective retention. People are exposed to a great amount of stimuli every day. For example, one analyst estimates that people are exposed to about 5,000 ads every day.[24] It is impossible for a person to pay attention to all these stimuli. *Selective attention*—the tendency for people to screen out most of the information to which they are exposed—means that marketers have to work especially hard to attract the consumer's attention.

Even noted stimuli do not always come across in the intended way. Each person fits incoming information into an existing mind-set. *Selective distortion* describes the tendency of people to interpret information in a way that will support what they already believe. Anna Flores may hear a salesperson mention some good and bad points about a competing camera brand. Because she already has a strong leaning toward Nikon, she is likely to distort those points in order to conclude that Nikon is the better camera. Selective distortion means that marketers must try to understand the mind-sets of consumers and how these will affect interpretations of advertising and sales information.

People also will forget much that they learn. They tend to retain information that supports their attitudes and beliefs. Because of *selective retention,* Anna is likely to remember good points made about the Nikon and to forget good points made about competing cameras. Because of selective exposure, distortion, and retention, marketers have to work hard to get their messages through. This fact explains why marketers use so much drama and repetition in sending messages to their market.

Interestingly, although most marketers worry about whether their offers will be perceived at all, some consumers worry that they will be affected by marketing messages without even knowing it—through *subliminal advertising.* In 1957, a researcher announced that he had flashed the phrases "Eat popcorn" and "Drink Coca-Cola" on a screen in a New Jersey movie theater every five seconds for 1/300 of a second. He reported that although viewers did not consciously recognize these messages, they absorbed them subconsciously and bought 58 percent more popcorn and 18 percent more Coke. Suddenly, advertisers and consumer-protection groups became intensely interested in subliminal perception. People voiced fears of being brainwashed, and California and Canada declared the practice illegal. Although the researcher later admitted to making up the data, the issue has not died. Some consumers still fear that they are being manipulated by subliminal messages.

Numerous studies by psychologists and consumer researchers have found no link between subliminal messages and consumer behavior. It appears that subliminal advertising simply doesn't have the power attributed to it by its critics. Most advertisers scoff at the notion of an industry conspiracy to manipulate consumers through "invisible" messages. Says one industry insider: "[Some consumers believe we are] wizards who can manipulate them at will. Ha! Snort! Oh my sides! As we know, just between us, most of [us] have difficulty getting a 2 percent increase in sales with the help of $50 million in media and extremely liminal images of sex, money, power, and other [motivators] of human emotion. The very idea of [us] as puppeteers, cruelly pulling the strings of consumer marionettes, is almost too much to bear."[25]

Learning.   When people act, they learn. **Learning** describes changes in an individual's behavior arising from experience. Learning theorists say that most human behavior is learned. Learning occurs through the interplay of *drives, stimuli, cues, responses,* and *reinforcement.*

We have seen that Anna Flores has a drive for self-actualization. A *drive* is a strong internal stimulus that calls for action. Her drive becomes a motive when it is directed toward a particular *stimulus object,* in this case a camera. Anna's response to the idea of buying a camera is conditioned by the surrounding cues. *Cues* are minor stimuli that determine when, where, and how the person responds. Seeing cameras in a shop window, hearing of a special sale price, and receiving her husband's support are all cues that can influence Anna's *response* to her interest in buying a camera.

Suppose Anna buys the Nikon. If the experience is rewarding, she will probably use the camera more and more. Her response to cameras will be *reinforced.* Then the next time she shops for a camera, binoculars, or some similar product, the probability is greater that she will buy a Nikon product. The practical significance of learning theory for marketers is that they can build up demand for a product by associating it with strong drives, using motivating cues, and providing positive reinforcement.

Beliefs and Attitudes.   Through doing and learning, people acquire beliefs and attitudes. These, in turn, influence their buying behavior. A **belief** is a descriptive thought that a person has about something. Anna Flores may believe that a Nikon camera takes great pictures, stands up well under hard use, and costs $450. These beliefs may be based on real knowledge, opinion, or faith, and may or may not carry an emotional charge. For example, Anna Flores's belief that a Nikon camera is heavy may or may not matter to her decision.

Marketers are interested in the beliefs that people formulate about specific products and services, because these beliefs make up product and brand images that affect buying behavior. If some of the beliefs are wrong and prevent purchase, the marketer will want to launch a campaign to correct them.

People have attitudes regarding religion, politics, clothes, music, food, and almost everything else. **Attitude** describes a person's relatively consistent evaluations, feelings, and tendencies toward an object or idea. Attitudes put people into a frame of mind of liking or disliking things, of moving toward or away from them. Thus, Anna Flores may hold attitudes such as "Buy the best," "The Japanese make the best products in the world," and "Creativity and self-expression are among the most important things in life." If so, the Nikon camera would fit well into Anna's existing attitudes.

Attitudes are difficult to change. A person's attitudes fit into a pattern, and to change one attitude may require difficult adjustments in many others. Thus, a company should usually try to fit its products into existing attitudes rather than attempt to change attitudes. Of course, there are exceptions in which the great cost of trying to change attitudes may pay off handsomely:

By 1994, milk consumption had been in decline for 20 years. The general perception was that milk was unhealthy, outdated, just for kids, or good only with cookies and cake. To counter these notions, the National Fluid Milk Processors Education Program (MilkPEP) began an ad campaign featuring milk be-

Learning
Changes in an individual's behavior arising from experience.

Belief
A descriptive thought that a person holds about something.

Attitude
A person's consistently favorable or unfavorable evaluations, feelings, and tendencies toward an object or idea.

got milk?

Try this at home.*

*We mean the drinking milk part.
Lowfat milk helps prevent osteoporosis
and keeps your bones supple.

■ Attitudes are difficult to change, but the National Fluid Milk Processors' wildly popular milk mustache campaign succeeded in changing attitudes toward milk.

mustached celebrities and the tag line "Got Milk?" The campaign has not only been wildly popular, it has been successful as well—not only did it stop the decline, milk consumption actually increased. The campaign is still running. Although initially the target market was women in their twenties, the campaign has been expanded to other target markets and has gained cult status with teens, much to their parents' delight. Teens collect the print ads featuring celebrities ranging from music stars Hanson and LeAnn Rimes, supermodel Tyra Banks, Kermit the Frog, and Garfield to sports idols such as Jeff Gordon, Mia Hamm, and Venus and Serena Williams. Building on this popularity with teens, the industry set up a Web site (www.whymilk.com) where young folks can make their own mustache, check out the latest Got Milk? ads, or get facts about "everything you every need to know about milk." The industry also promotes milk to them through grass-roots marketing efforts. It recently sponsored a traveling promotion event featuring a 28-foot truck that turns into a backdrop that looks like Manhattan's Times Square. Once recruited, teens can listen to music and do a 15-second "audition" on an artificial set of MTV's "Total Request Live." They can also enter a contest to make an appearance in *Rolling Stone* magazine with a milk mustache of their own. While there, teens are encouraged to drink milk rather than soda. Each is invited to sign a pledge to reduce the national "calcium debt."[26]

We can now appreciate the many forces acting on consumer behavior. The consumer's choice results from the complex interplay of cultural, social, personal, and psychological factors.

The Buyer Decision Process

Now that we have looked at the influences that affect buyers, we are ready to look at how consumers make buying decisions. Figure 5.5 shows that the buyer decision process consists of five stages: *need recognition, information search, evaluation of alternatives, purchase decision,* and *postpurchase behavior.* Clearly, the buying process starts long before actual purchase and continues long after. Marketers need to focus on the entire buying process rather than on just the purchase decision.

The figure implies that consumers pass through all five stages with every purchase. But in more routine purchases, consumers often skip or reverse some of these stages. A woman buying her regular brand of toothpaste would recognize the need and go right to the purchase decision, skipping information search and evaluation. However, we use the model in Figure 5.5 because it shows all the considerations that arise when a consumer faces a new and complex purchase situation.

Need Recognition The buying process starts with need recognition—the buyer recognizes a problem or need. The need can be triggered by *internal stimuli* when one of the

FIGURE 5.5
Buyer Decision Process

Need recognition → Information search → Evaluation of alternatives → Purchase decision → Postpurchase behavior

person's normal needs—hunger, thirst, sex—rises to a level high enough to become a drive. A need can also be triggered by *external stimuli*. Anna Flores might have felt the need for a new hobby when her busy season at work slowed down, and she thought of cameras after talking to a friend about photography or seeing a camera ad. At this stage, the marketer should research consumers to find out what kinds of needs or problems arise, what brought them about, and how they led the consumer to this particular product.

Information Search An interested consumer may or may not search for more information. If the consumer's drive is strong and a satisfying product is near at hand, the consumer is likely to buy it then. If not, the consumer may store the need in memory or undertake an information search related to the need. At the least, Anna Flores will probably pay more attention to camera ads, cameras used by friends, and camera conversations. Or Anna may actively look for reading material, phone friends, and gather information in other ways. The amount of searching she does will depend on the strength of her drive, the amount of information she starts with, the ease of obtaining more information, the value she places on additional information, and the satisfaction she gets from searching.

The consumer can obtain information from any of several sources. These include *personal sources* (family, friends, neighbors, acquaintances), *commercial sources* (advertising, salespeople, dealers, packaging, displays), *public sources* (mass media, consumer-rating organizations), and *experiential sources* (handling, examining, using the product). The relative influence of these information sources varies with the product and the buyer. Generally, the consumer receives the most information about a product from commercial sources—those controlled by the marketer. The most effective sources, however, tend to be personal. Commercial sources normally *inform* the buyer, but personal sources *legitimize* or *evaluate* products for the buyer.

As more information is obtained, the consumer's awareness and knowledge of the available brands and features increases. In her information search, Anna Flores learned about the many camera brands available. The information also helped her drop certain brands from consideration. A company must design its marketing mix to make prospects aware of and knowledgeable about its brand. It should carefully identify consumers' sources of information and the importance of each source.

Evaluation of Alternatives We have seen how the consumer uses information to arrive at a set of final brand choices. How does the consumer choose among the alternative brands? The marketer needs to know about alternative evaluation—that is, how the consumer processes information to arrive at brand choices. Unfortunately, consumers do not use a simple and single evaluation process in all buying situations. Instead, several evaluation processes are at work.

The consumer arrives at attitudes toward different brands through some evaluation procedure. How consumers go about evaluating purchase alternatives depends on the individual consumer and the specific buying situation. In some cases, consumers use careful calculations and logical thinking. At other times, the same consumers do little or no evaluating; instead they buy on impulse and rely on intuition. Sometimes consumers make buying decisions on their own; sometimes they turn to friends, consumer guides, or salespeople for buying advice.

Suppose Anna Flores has narrowed her choices to four cameras. And suppose that she is primarily interested in four attributes—picture quality, ease of use, camera size, and

■ Need recognition can be triggered by advertising. This ad from America's Dairy Farmers alerts consumers of their need for more dairy products to build strong bones.

price. Anna has formed beliefs about how each brand rates on each attribute. Clearly, if one camera rated best on all the attributes, we could predict that Anna would choose it. However, the brands vary in appeal. Anna might base her buying decision on only one attribute, and her choice would be easy to predict. If she wants picture quality above everything, she will buy the camera that she thinks has the best picture quality. But most buyers consider several attributes, each with different importance. If we knew the importance weights that Anna assigns to each of the four attributes, we could predict her camera choice more reliably.

Marketers should study buyers to find out how they actually evaluate brand alternatives. If they know what evaluative processes go on, marketers can take steps to influence the buyer's decision.

Purchase Decision   In the evaluation stage, the consumer ranks brands and forms purchase intentions. Generally, the consumer's purchase decision will be to buy the most preferred brand, but two factors can come between the purchase *intention* and the purchase *decision*. The first factor is the *attitudes of others*. If Anna Flores's husband feels strongly that Anna should buy the lowest-priced camera, then the chances of Anna's buying a more expensive camera will be reduced.

The second factor is *unexpected situational factors*. The consumer may form a purchase intention based on factors such as expected income, expected price, and expected product benefits. However, unexpected events may change the purchase intention. Anna Flores may lose her job, some other purchase may become more urgent, or a friend may report being disappointed in her preferred camera. Or a close competitor may drop its price. Thus, preferences and even purchase intentions do not always result in actual purchase choice.

Postpurchase Behavior   The marketer's job does not end when the product is bought. After purchasing the product, the consumer will be satisfied or dissatisfied and will engage in postpurchase behavior of interest to the marketer. What determines whether the buyer is satisfied or dissatisfied with a purchase? The answer lies in the relationship between the *consumer's expectations* and the product's *perceived performance*. If the product falls short of expectations, the consumer is disappointed; if it meets expectations, the consumer is satisfied; if it exceeds expectations, the consumer is delighted.

The larger the gap between expectations and performance, the greater the consumer's dissatisfaction. This suggests that sellers should make product claims that faithfully represent the product's performance so that buyers are satisfied. Some sellers might even understate performance levels to boost consumer satisfaction with the product. For example, Boeing's salespeople tend to be conservative when they estimate the potential benefits of their aircraft. They almost always underestimate fuel efficiency—they promise a 5 percent savings that turns out to be 8 percent. Customers are delighted with better-than-expected performance; they buy again and tell other potential customers that Boeing lives up to its promises.

Cognitive dissonance
Buyer discomfort caused by post-purchase conflict.

Almost all major purchases result in **cognitive dissonance**, or discomfort caused by postpurchase conflict. After the purchase, consumers are satisfied with the benefits of the chosen brand and are glad to avoid the drawbacks of the brands not bought. However, every purchase involves compromise. Consumers feel uneasy about acquiring the drawbacks of the chosen brand and about losing the benefits of the brands not purchased. Thus, consumers feel at least some postpurchase dissonance for every purchase.[27]

Why is it so important to satisfy the customer? Such satisfaction is important because a company's sales come from two basic groups—*new customers* and *retained customers*. It usually costs more to attract new customers than to retain current ones. And the best way to retain current customers is to keep them satisfied. Customer satisfaction is a key to building profitable relationships with consumers—to keeping and growing consumers and reaping their customer lifetime value. Satisfied customers buy a product again, talk favorably to others about the product, pay less attention to competing brands and advertising, and buy other products from the company. Many marketers go beyond merely *meeting* the expectations of customers—they aim to *delight* the customer.

A dissatisfied consumer responds differently. Bad word of mouth often travels farther and faster than good word of mouth. It can quickly damage consumer attitudes about a company and its products. But companies cannot simply rely on dissatisfied customers to volunteer their complaints when they are dissatisfied. Most unhappy customers never tell the company about their problem. Therefore, a company would be wise to measure customer satisfaction regularly. It should set up systems that *encourage* customers to complain. In this way, the company can learn how well it is doing and how it can improve.

But what should companies do about dissatisfied customers? At a minimum, most companies offer toll-free numbers and Web sites to handle complaints and inquiries. For example, over the past two decades, the Gerber help line (1-800-4-GERBER) has received more than 5 million calls. Help-line staffers, most of them mothers or grandmothers themselves, handle customer concerns and provide baby care advice 24 hours a day, 365 days a year to more than 2,400 callers a day. General Electric offers an online GE Answer Center. At this Web site, customers can find a wealth of information on GE's thousands of appliance products—from answers to frequently asked postpurchase questions to do-it-yourself installation and repair tips. Customers who can't find answers at the Web site can call GE's telephone Answer Center and talk directly with a GE customer service representative.

By studying the overall buyer decision, marketers may be able to find ways to help consumers move through it. For example, if consumers are not buying a new product because they do not perceive a need for it, marketing might launch advertising messages that trigger the need and show how the product solves customers' problems. If customers know about the product but are not buying because they hold unfavorable attitudes toward it, the marketer must find ways either to change the product or change consumer perceptions.

■ The adoption process: This ad encourages trial by offering a coupon.

The Buyer Decision Process for New Products

We have looked at the stages buyers go through in trying to satisfy a need. Buyers may pass quickly or slowly through these stages, and some of the stages may even be reversed. Much depends on the nature of the buyer, the product, and the buying situation.

We now look at how buyers approach the purchase of new products. A **new product** is a good, service, or idea that is perceived by some potential customers as new. It may have been around for a while, but our interest is in how consumers learn about products for the first time and make decisions about whether to adopt them. We define the **adoption process** as "the mental process through which an individual passes from first learning about an innovation to final adoption," and *adoption* as the decision by an individual to become a regular user of the product.[28]

New product

A good, service, or idea that is perceived by some potential customers as new.

Adoption process

The mental process through which an individual passes from first hearing about an innovation to final adoption.

Stages in the Adoption Process Consumers go through five stages in the process of adopting a new product:

■ *Awareness:* The consumer becomes aware of the new product, but lacks information about it.

■ *Interest:* The consumer seeks information about the new product.

■ *Evaluation:* The consumer considers whether trying the new product makes sense.

■ *Trial:* The consumer tries the new product on a small scale to improve his or her estimate of its value.

■ *Adoption:* The consumer decides to make full and regular use of the new product.

FIGURE 5.6

Adopter Categorization on the Basis of Relative Time of Adoption of Innovations

Source: Reprinted with the permission of The Free Press, a Division of Simon & Schuster, from *Diffusion of Innovations*, Fifth Edition, by Everett M. Rogers. Copyright © 2003 by The Free Press.

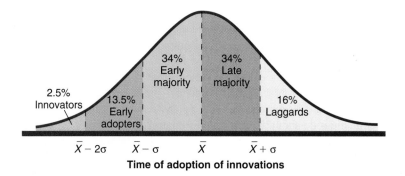

This model suggests that the new-product marketer should think about how to help consumers move through these stages. A manufacturer of large-screen televisions may discover that many consumers in the interest stage do not move to the trial stage because of uncertainty and the large investment. If these same consumers were willing to use a large-screen television on a trial basis for a small fee, the manufacturer should consider offering a trial-use plan with an option to buy.

Individual Differences in Innovativeness People differ greatly in their readiness to try new products. In each product area, there are "consumption pioneers" and early adopters. Other individuals adopt new products much later. People can be classified into the adopter categories shown in Figure 5.6. After a slow start, an increasing number of people adopt the new product. The number of adopters reaches a peak and then drops off as fewer nonadopters remain. Innovators are defined as the first 2.5 percent of the buyers to adopt a new idea (those beyond two standard deviations from mean adoption time); the early adopters are the next 13.5 percent (between one and two standard deviations); and so forth.

The five adopter groups have differing values. *Innovators* are venturesome—they try new ideas at some risk. *Early adopters* are guided by respect—they are opinion leaders in their communities and adopt new ideas early but carefully. The *early majority* are deliberate—although they rarely are leaders, they adopt new ideas before the average person. The *late majority* are skeptical—they adopt an innovation only after a majority of people have tried it. Finally, *laggards* are tradition bound—they are suspicious of changes and adopt the innovation only when it has become something of a tradition itself.

This adopter classification suggests that an innovating firm should research the characteristics of innovators and early adopters and should direct marketing efforts toward them. In general, innovators tend to be relatively younger, better educated, and have a higher income than later adopters and nonadopters. They are more receptive to unfamiliar things, rely more on their own values and judgment, and are more willing to take risks. They are less brand-loyal and more likely to take advantage of special promotions such as discounts, coupons, and samples.

Influence of Product Characteristics on Rate of Adoption The characteristics of the new product affect its rate of adoption. Some products catch on almost overnight (Beanie Babies), whereas others take a long time to gain acceptance (high-density television, or HDTV). Five characteristics are especially important in influencing an innovation's rate of adoption. For example, consider the characteristics of HDTV in relation to the rate of adoption:

- *Relative advantage:* the degree to which the innovation appears superior to existing products. The greater the perceived relative advantage of using HDTV—say, in picture quality and ease of viewing—the sooner HDTVs will be adopted.

- *Compatibility:* the degree to which the innovation fits the values and experiences of potential consumers. HDTV, for example, is highly compatible with the lifestyles found in upper-middle-class homes. However, it is not very compatible with the programming and broadcasting systems currently available to consumers.

- *Complexity:* the degree to which the innovation is difficult to understand or use. HDTVs are not very complex and, therefore, once programming is available and prices come down, it will take less time to penetrate U.S. homes than more complex innovations.

- *Divisibility:* the degree to which the innovation may be tried on a limited basis. HDTVs are still very expensive. To the extent that people can lease them with an option to buy, their rate of adoption will increase.

- *Communicability:* the degree to which the results of using the innovation can be observed or described to others. Because HDTV lends itself to demonstration and description, its use will spread faster among consumers.

Other characteristics influence the rate of adoption, such as initial and ongoing costs, risk and uncertainty, and social approval. The new-product marketer has to research all these factors when developing the new product and its marketing program.

Consumer Behavior Across International Borders

Understanding consumer behavior is difficult enough for companies marketing within the borders of a single country. For companies operating in many countries, however, understanding and serving the needs of consumers can be daunting. Although consumers in different countries may have some things in common, their values, attitudes, and behaviors often vary greatly. International marketers must understand such differences and adjust their products and marketing programs accordingly.

■ New-product adoption rate: Some products catch on almost overnight. Others, such as HDTV, take a long time to gain acceptance.

Sometimes the differences are obvious. For example, in the United States, where most people eat cereal regularly for breakfast, Kellogg focuses its marketing on persuading consumers to select a Kellogg brand rather than a competitor's brand. In France, however, where most people prefer croissants and coffee or no breakfast at all, Kellogg advertising simply attempts to convince people that they should eat cereal for breakfast. Its packaging includes step-by-step instructions on how to prepare cereal. In India, where many consumers eat heavy, fried breakfasts and many consumers skip the meal altogether, Kellogg's advertising attempts to convince buyers to switch to a lighter, more nutritious breakfast diet.

Often, differences across international markets are more subtle. They may result from physical differences in consumers and their environments. For example, Remington makes smaller electric shavers to fit the smaller hands of Japanese consumers and battery-powered shavers for the British market, where few bathrooms have electrical outlets. Other differences result from varying customs. In Japan, for example, where humility and deference are considered great virtues, pushy, hard-hitting sales approaches are considered offensive. Failing to understand such differences in customs and behaviors from one country to another can spell disaster for a marketer's international products and programs.

Marketers must decide on the degree to which they will adapt their products and marketing programs to meet the unique cultures and needs of consumers in various markets. On the one hand, they want to standardize their offerings in order to simplify operations and take advantage of cost economies. On the other hand, adapting marketing efforts within each country results in products and programs that better satisfy the needs of local consumers. The question of whether to adapt or standardize the marketing mix across international markets has created a lively debate in recent years.

Linking the Concepts

Here's a good place to pull over and apply the concepts you've examined in the first part of this chapter.

- Think about a specific major purchase you've made recently. What buying process did you follow? What major factors influenced your decision?
- Pick a company that we've discussed in a previous chapter—Coca-Cola, Starbucks, NASCAR, Disney, Wal-Mart, MTV, Volkswagen, Amazon.com, or another. How does the company you chose use its understanding of customers and their buying behavior to build better customer relationships?
- Think about a company like Intel, which sells its products to computer makers and other businesses rather than to final consumers. How would Intel's marketing to business customers differ from Starbucks's marketing to final consumers? The second part of the chapter deals with this issue.

Business Markets and Business Buyer Behavior

In one way or another, most large companies sell to other organizations. Many companies, such as DuPont, Boeing, Cisco Systems, Caterpillar, and countless other firms, sell *most* of their products to other businesses. Even large consumer-products companies, which make products used by final consumers, must first sell their products to other businesses. For example, General Mills makes many familiar consumer products—Cheerios, Betty Crocker cake mixes, Gold Medal flour, and others. But to sell these products to consumers, General Mills must first sell them to the wholesalers and retailers that serve the consumer market.

Business buyer behavior

The buying behavior of the organizations that buy goods and services for use in the production of other products and services or for the purpose of reselling or renting them to others at a profit.

Business buyer behavior refers to the buying behavior of the organizations that buy goods and services for use in the production of other products and services that are sold, rented, or supplied to others. It also includes the behavior of retailing and wholesaling firms that acquire goods for the purpose of reselling or renting them to others at a profit. In the *business buying process*, business buyers determine which products and services their organizations need to purchase, and then find, evaluate, and choose among alternative suppliers and brands. Companies that sell to other business organizations must do their best to understand business markets and business buyer behavior.

Business Markets

The business market is *huge*. In fact, business markets involve far more dollars and items than do consumer markets. For example, think about the large number of business transactions involved in the production and sale of a single set of Goodyear tires. Various suppliers sell Goodyear the rubber, steel, equipment, and other goods that it needs to produce the tires. Goodyear then sells the finished tires to retailers, who in turn sell them to consumers. Thus, many sets of *business* purchases were made for only one set of *consumer* purchases. In addition, Goodyear sells tires as original equipment to manufacturers, who install them on new vehicles, and as replacement tires to companies that maintain their own fleets of company cars, trucks, buses, or other vehicles.

Characteristics of Business Markets In some ways, business markets are similar to consumer markets. Both involve people who assume buying roles and make purchase decisions to satisfy needs. However, business markets differ in many ways from consumer markets. The main differences are in *market structure and demand*, the *nature of the buying unit*, and the *types of decisions and the decision process* involved.

Market Structure and Demand The business marketer normally deals with *far fewer but far larger buyers* than the consumer marketer does. For example, when Goodyear sells replacement tires to final consumers, its potential market includes the owners of the millions of cars currently in use in the United States and around the world. But Goodyear's fate in the business market depends on getting orders from one of only a handful of large auto makers. Even in large business markets, a few buyers often account for most of the purchasing. Similarly, Black & Decker sells its power tools and outdoor equipment to tens of millions of consumers worldwide. However, it must sell these products through three huge retail customers—Home Depot, Lowe's, and Wal-Mart—which combined account for more than half its sales.

Business markets are also *more geographically concentrated.* More than half the nation's business buyers are concentrated in eight states: California, New York, Ohio, Illinois, Michigan, Texas, Pennsylvania, and New Jersey. Furthermore, business demand is **derived demand**—it ultimately derives from the demand for consumer goods. General Motors buys steel because consumers buy cars. If consumer demand for cars drops, so will the demand for steel and all the other products used to make cars. Therefore, business marketers sometimes promote their products directly to final consumers to increase business demand.

For example, Intel's long-running "Intel Inside" advertising campaign sells personal computer buyers on the virtues of Intel microprocessors. The increased demand for Intel chips boosts demand for the PCs containing them, and both Intel and its business partners win. Similarly, DuPont promotes Teflon directly to final consumers as a key ingredient in many products—from nonstick cookware to stain-repellent, wrinkle-free clothing. You see Teflon Fabric Protector hangtags on clothing lines such as Levi's Dockers, Donna Karan's menswear, and Ralph Lauren denim.[29] By making Teflon familiar and attractive to final buyers, DuPont also makes the products containing it more attractive.

Nature of the Buying Unit Compared with consumer purchases, a business purchase usually involves *more decision participants* and a *more professional purchasing effort.* Often, business buying is done by trained purchasing agents, who spend their working lives learning how to buy better. The more complex the purchase, the more likely that several people will participate in the decision-making process. Buying committees made up of technical experts and top management are common in the buying of major goods. Beyond this, many companies are now upgrading their purchasing functions to "supply management" or "supplier development" functions. As one observer notes, "It's a scary thought:

Derived demand
Business demand that ultimately comes from (derives from) the demand for consumer goods.

■ Business markets: B2B marketers often role up their sleeves and partner with customers to jointly create solutions. Here, Fujitsu promises, "Our technology helps keep you moving upward. And our people won't let you down."

Today, business uses technology to gain a strategic advantage. And the higher the technology, the greater the advantage. So long as the technology does what it's supposed to do, that is. At Fujitsu, ours does. ◇ We create, from the components up, computer, communications and microelectronic products of not only the highest technology, but the highest quality and reliability as well. ◇ And we support them in ways that few other companies do. With extended warranties. Liberal replacement policies. And superior technical support. ◇ Moreover, as part of a company at the forefront of today's emerging and converging computer and communications technologies, our systems support teams offer unique expertise. ◇ Fujitsu. Our technology helps keep you moving upward. And our people won't let you down. To learn more about Fujitsu, our products and support programs, see us at www.fujitsu.com.

THE HIGHER THE TECHNOLOGY, THE MORE IMPORTANT THE SUPPORT.

FUJITSU

COMPUTERS, COMMUNICATIONS, MICROELECTRONICS

Your customers may know more about your company and products than you do. . . . Companies are putting their best and brightest people on procurement patrol."[30] Therefore, business marketers must have well-trained salespeople to deal with well-trained buyers.

Types of Decisions and the Decision Process Business buyers usually face *more complex* buying decisions than do consumer buyers. Purchases often involve large sums of money, complex technical and economic considerations, and interactions among many people at many levels of the buyer's organization. Because the purchases are more complex, business buyers may take longer to make their decisions. The business buying process also tends to be *more formalized* than the consumer buying process. Large business purchases usually call for detailed product specifications, written purchase orders, careful supplier searches, and formal approval.

Finally, in the business buying process, buyer and seller are often much *more dependent* on each other. Consumer marketers are often at a distance from their customers. In contrast, B2B marketers may roll up their sleeves and work closely with their customers during all stages of the buying process—partnering to jointly create solutions to the customer's problems and to support customer operations.

Business Buyer Behavior

At the most basic level, marketers want to know how business buyers will respond to various marketing stimuli. Figure 5.7 shows a model of business buyer behavior. In this model, marketing and other stimuli affect the buying organization and produce certain buyer responses. As with consumer buying, the marketing stimuli for business buying consist of the four *P*s: product, price, place, and promotion. Other stimuli include major forces in the environment: economic, technological, political, cultural, and competitive. These stimuli enter the organization and are turned into buyer responses: product or service choice; supplier choice; order quantities; and delivery, service, and payment terms. In order to design good marketing mix strategies, the marketer must understand what happens within the organization to turn stimuli into purchase responses.

Within the organization, buying activity consists of two major parts: the buying center, made up of all the people involved in the buying decision, and the buying-decision process. The model shows that the buying center and the buying decision process are influenced by internal organizational, interpersonal, and individual factors as well as by external environmental factors.

The model in Figure 5.7 suggests four questions about business buyer behavior: What buying decisions do business buyers make? Who participates in the buying process? What are the major influences on buyers? How do business buyers make their buying decisions?

FIGURE 5.7

A Model of Business Buyer Behavior

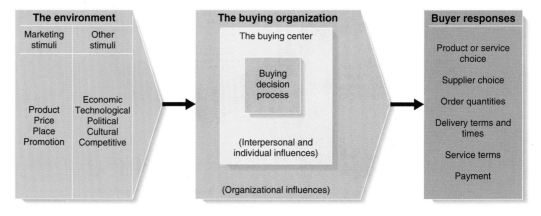

Major Types of Buying Situations There are three major types of buying situations.[31] At one extreme is the *straight rebuy*, which is a fairly routine decision. At the other extreme is the *new task*, which may call for thorough research. In the middle is the *modified rebuy*, which requires some research.

In a **straight rebuy**, the buyer reorders something without any modifications. It is usually handled on a routine basis by the purchasing department. Based on past buying satisfaction, the buyer simply chooses from the various suppliers on its list. "In" suppliers try to maintain product and service quality. They often propose automatic reordering systems so that the purchasing agent will save reordering time. "Out" suppliers try to offer something new or exploit dissatisfaction with other suppliers so that the buyer will consider them.

In a **modified rebuy**, the buyer wants to modify product specifications, prices, terms, or suppliers. The modified rebuy usually involves more decision participants than does the straight rebuy. The in suppliers may become nervous and feel pressured to put their best foot forward to protect an account. Out suppliers may see the modified rebuy situation as an opportunity to make a better offer and gain new business.

A company buying a product or service for the first time faces a **new-task** situation. In such cases, the greater the cost or risk, the larger the number of decision participants and the greater their efforts to collect information will be. The new-task situation is the marketer's greatest opportunity and challenge. The marketer not only tries to reach as many key buying influences as possible but also provides help and information.

The buyer makes the fewest decisions in the straight rebuy and the most in the new-task decision. In the new-task situation, the buyer must decide on product specifications, suppliers, price limits, payment terms, order quantities, delivery times, and service terms. The order of these decisions varies with each situation, and different decision participants influence each choice.

Many business buyers prefer to buy a packaged solution to a problem from a single seller. Instead of buying and putting all the components together, the buyer may ask sellers to supply the components *and* assemble the package or system. The sale often goes to the firm that provides the most complete system meeting the customer's needs. Thus, **systems selling** is often a key business marketing strategy for winning and holding accounts. For example, ChemStation provides a complete solution for its customers' industrial cleaning problems:

> ChemStation sells industrial cleaning chemicals to a wide range of business customers, ranging from car washes to the U.S. Air Force. Whether a customer is washing down a fleet or a factory, a store or a restaurant, a distillery or an Army base, ChemStation comes up with the right cleaning solution every time. It supplies thousands of products in hundreds of industries. But ChemStation does more than just sell chemicals. First, ChemStation works closely with each individual customer to concoct a soap formula specially designed for that customer. It has brewed special formulas for cleaning hands, feathers, mufflers, flutes, perfume vats, cosmetic eye makeup containers, yacht-making molds, concrete trucks, ocean-going trawlers, and about anything else you can imagine. Next, ChemStation delivers the custom-made mixture to a tank installed at the customer's site. Finally, it maintains the tank by monitoring usage and automatically refilling the tank when supplies run low. Thus, ChemStation sells an entire system for dealing with the customer's special cleaning problems. The company's motto: "Our

Straight rebuy
A business buying situation in which the buyer routinely reorders something without any modifications.

Modified rebuy
A business buying situation in which the buyer wants to modify product specifications, prices, terms, or suppliers.

New task
A business buying situation in which the buyer purchases a product or service for the first time.

Systems selling
Buying a packaged solution to a problem from a single seller, thus avoiding all the separate decisions involved in a complex buying situation.

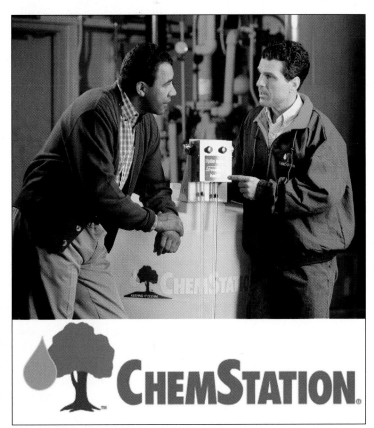

■ ChemStation does more than simply supply its customers with cleaning chemicals. "Our customers . . . think of us as more of a partner than a supplier."

system is your solution!" Partnering with an individual customer to find a full solution creates a lasting relationship that helps ChemStation to lock out the competition. As noted in the a recent issue of *Insights*, ChemStation's customer newsletter, "Our customers . . . oftentimes think of us as more of a partner than a supplier."[32]

Participants in the Business Buying Process   Who does the buying of the trillions of dollars' worth of goods and services needed by business organizations? The decision-making unit of a buying organization is called its **buying center**: all the individuals and units that participate in the business decision-making process. The buying center includes all members of the organization who play a role in the purchase decision process. This group includes the actual users of the product or service, those who make the buying decision, those who influence the buying decision, those who do the actual buying, and those who control buying information.

Buying center

All the individuals and units that participate in the business buying-decision process.

The buying center is not a fixed and formally identified unit within the buying organization. It is a set of buying roles assumed by different people for different purchases. Within the organization, the size and makeup of the buying center will vary for different products and for different buying situations. For some routine purchases, one person—say a purchasing agent—may assume all the buying center roles and serve as the only person involved in the buying decision. For more complex purchases, the buying center may include 20 or 30 people from different levels and departments in the organization.

The buying center concept presents a major marketing challenge. The business marketer must learn who participates in the decision, each participant's relative influence, and what evaluation criteria each decision participant uses. For example, the medical products and services group of Cardinal Health sells disposable surgical gowns to hospitals. It identifies the hospital personnel involved in this buying decision as the vice president of purchasing, the operating room administrator, and the surgeons. Each participant plays a different role. The vice president of purchasing analyzes whether the hospital should buy disposable gowns or reusable gowns. If analysis favors disposable gowns, then the operating room administrator compares competing products and prices and makes a choice. This administrator considers the gown's absorbency, antiseptic quality, design, and cost, and normally buys the brand that meets requirements at the lowest cost. Finally, surgeons affect the decision later by reporting their satisfaction or dissatisfaction with the brand.

■ Buying center: Cardinal Health deals with a wide range of buying influences, from purchasing executives and hospital administrators to the surgeons who actually use its products.

The buying center usually includes some obvious participants who are involved formally in the buying decision. For example, the decision to buy a corporate jet will probably involve the company's CEO, chief pilot, a purchasing agent, some legal staff, a member of top management, and others formally charged with the buying decision. It may also involve less obvious, informal participants, some of whom may actually make or strongly affect the buying decision. Sometimes, even the people in the buying center are not aware of all the buying participants. For example, the decision about which corporate jet to buy may actually be made by a corporate board member who has an interest in flying and who knows a lot about airplanes. This board member may work behind the scenes to sway the decision. Many business buying decisions result from the complex interactions of ever-changing buying center participants.

Major Influences on Business Buyers   Business buyers are subject to many influences when they make their buying decisions. Some marketers assume that the major

■ Emotions play an important role in business buying: This Volvo truck ad mentions objective factors, such as efficiency and ease of maintenance. But it stresses more emotional factors such as the raw beauty of the truck and its comfort and roominess, features that make "drivers a lot more possessive."

influences are economic. They think buyers will favor the supplier who offers the lowest price or the best product or the most service. They concentrate on offering strong economic benefits to buyers. However, business buyers actually respond to both economic and personal factors. Far from being cold, calculating, and impersonal, business buyers are human and social as well. They react to both reason and emotion.

Today, most business-to-business marketers recognize that emotion plays an important role in business buying decisions. For example, you might expect that an advertisement promoting large trucks to corporate fleet buyers would stress objective technical, performance, and economic factors. However, a recent ad for Volvo heavy-duty trucks shows two drivers arm-wrestling and claims, "It solves all your fleet problems. Except who gets to drive." It turns out that, in the face of an industrywide driver shortage, the type of truck a fleet provides can help it to attract qualified drivers. The Volvo ad stresses the raw beauty of the truck and its comfort and roominess, features that make it more appealing to drivers. The ad concludes that Volvo trucks are "built to make fleets more profitable and drivers a lot more possessive."

Figure 5.8 lists various groups of influences on business buyers—environmental, organizational, interpersonal, and individual. *Environmental factors* play a major role. For example, buyer behavior can be heavily influenced by factors in the current and expected economic environment, such as the level of primary demand, the economic outlook, and the cost of money. Another environmental factor is shortages in key materials. Many companies now are more willing to buy and hold larger inventories of scarce materials to

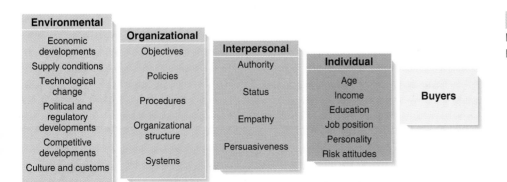

FIGURE 5.8

Major Influences on
Business Buyer Behavior

ensure an adequate supply. Business buyers also are affected by technological, political, and competitive developments in the environment. Finally, culture and customs can strongly influence business buyer reactions to the marketer's behavior and strategies, especially in the international marketing environment (see Marketing at Work 5.3).

Business buyer behavior is also influenced strongly by *organizational factors*. Each buying organization has its own objectives, policies, procedures, structure, and systems, and the business marketer must understand these factors well. Questions such as these arise: How many people are involved in the buying decision? Who are they? What are their evaluative criteria? What are the company's policies and limits on its buyers?

The buying center usually includes many participants who influence each other, so *interpersonal factors* also influence the business buying process. However, it is often difficult to assess such interpersonal factors and group dynamics. As one writer notes, "Managers do not wear tags that say 'decision maker' or 'unimportant person.' The powerful are often invisible, at least to vendor representatives."[33] Nor does the buying center participant with the highest rank always have the most influence. Participants may influence the buying decision because they control rewards and punishments, are well liked, have special expertise, or have a special relationship with other important participants. Interpersonal factors are often very subtle. Whenever possible, business marketers must try to understand these factors and design strategies that take them into account.

Finally, business buyers are influenced by *individual factors*. Each participant in the business buying decision process brings in personal motives, perceptions, and preferences. These individual factors are affected by personal characteristics such as age, income, education, professional identification, personality, and attitudes toward risk. Also, buyers have different buying styles. Some may be technical types who make in-depth analyses of competitive proposals before choosing a supplier. Other buyers may be intuitive negotiators who are adept at pitting the sellers against one another for the best deal.

The Business Buying Process Figure 5.9 lists the eight stages of the business buying process.[34] Buyers who face a new-task buying situation usually go through all stages of the buying process. Buyers making modified or straight rebuys may skip some of the stages. We will examine these steps for the typical new-task buying situation.

Problem Recognition. The buying process begins when someone in the company recognizes a problem or need that can be met by acquiring a specific product or service. Problem recognition can result from internal or external stimuli. Internally, the company may decide to launch a new product that requires new production equipment and materials. Or a machine may break down and need new parts. Perhaps a purchasing manager is unhappy with a current supplier's product quality, service, or prices. Externally, the buyer may get some new ideas at a trade show, see an ad, or receive a call from a salesperson who offers a better product or a lower price. In fact, in their advertising, business marketers often alert customers to potential problems and then show how their products provide solutions.

FIGURE 5.9

Stages of the Business Buying Process

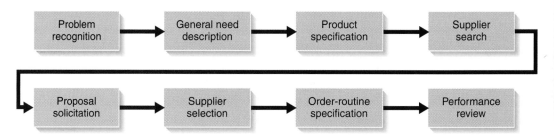

Marketing at Work | *5.3*

International Marketing Manners: When in Rome, Do As the Romans Do

Picture this: Consolidated Amalgamation, Inc., thinks it's time that the rest of the world enjoyed the same fine products it has offered American consumers for two generations. It dispatches Vice President Harry E. Slicksmile to Europe, Africa, and Asia to explore the territory. Mr. Slicksmile stops first in London, where he makes short work of some bankers—he rings them up on the phone. He handles Parisians with similar ease: After securing a table at La Tour d'Argent, he greets his luncheon guest, the director of an industrial engineering firm, with the words, "Just call me Harry, Jacques."

In Germany, Mr. Slicksmile is a powerhouse. Whisking through a lavish, state-of-the-art marketing presentation, complete with flip charts and audiovisuals, he shows 'em that this Georgia boy *knows* how to make a buck. Heading on to Milan, Harry strikes up a conversation with the Japanese businessman sitting next to him on the plane. He flips his card onto the guy's tray and, when the two say good-bye, shakes hands warmly and clasps the man's right arm. Later, for his appointment with the owner of an Italian packaging design firm, our hero wears his comfy corduroy sport coat, khaki pants, and Topsiders. Everybody knows Italians are zany and laid back.

Mr. Slicksmile next swings through Saudi Arabia, where he coolly presents a potential client with a multimillion-dollar proposal in a classy pigskin binder. His final stop is Beijing, China, where he talks business over lunch with a group of Chinese executives. After completing the meal, he drops his chopsticks into his bowl of rice and presents each guest with an elegant Tiffany's clock as a reminder of his visit.

A great tour, sure to generate a pile of orders, right? Wrong. Six months

later, Consolidated Amalgamation has nothing to show for the trip but a stack of bills. Abroad, they weren't wild about Harry.

This hypothetical case has been exaggerated for emphasis. Americans are seldom such dolts. But experts say success in international business has a lot to do with knowing the territory and its people. By learning English and extending themselves in other ways, the world's business leaders have met Americans more than halfway. In contrast, Americans too often do little except assume that others will march to their music. "We want things to be 'American' when we travel. Fast. Convenient. Easy. So we become 'ugly

Americans' by demanding that others change," says one American world trade expert. "I think more business would be done if we tried harder."

Poor Harry tried, all right, but in all the wrong ways. The British do not, as a rule, make deals over the phone as much as Americans do. It's not so much a "cultural" difference as a difference in approach. A proper Frenchman neither likes instant familiarity—questions about family, church, or alma mater— nor refers to strangers by their first names. "That poor fellow, Jacques, probably wouldn't show anything, but he'd recoil. He'd *not* be pleased," explains an expert on French business practices. "It's considered poor taste,"

This HSBC ad recognizes the difficulties of doing business globally and understanding international customers needs and customs.

(continued)

he continues. "Even after months of business dealings, I'd wait for him or her to make the invitation [to use first names]. . . . You are always right, in Europe, to say 'Mister.'"

Harry's flashy presentation would likely have been a flop with the Germans, who dislike overstatement and ostentatiousness. According to one German expert, however, German businessmen have become accustomed to dealing with Americans. Although differences in body language and customs remain, the past 20 years have softened them. "I hugged an American woman at a business meeting last night," he said. "That would be normal in France, but [older] Germans still have difficulty [with the custom]." He says that calling secretaries by their first names would still be considered rude: "They have a right to be called by the surname. You'd certainly ask—and get—permission first." In Germany, people address each other formally and correctly—someone with two doctorates (which is fairly common) must be referred to as "Herr Doktor Doktor."

When Harry Slicksmile grabbed his new Japanese acquaintance by the arm, the executive probably considered him disrespectful and presumptuous. Japan, like many Asian countries, is a "no-contact culture" in which even shaking hands is a strange experience.

Harry made matters worse by tossing his business card. Japanese people revere the business card as an extension of self and as an indicator of rank. They do not *hand* it to people, they *present* it—with both hands. In addition, the Japanese are sticklers about rank. Unlike Americans, they don't heap praise on subordinates in a room; they will praise only the highest-ranking official present.

Hapless Harry also goofed when he assumed that Italians are like Hollywood's stereotypes of them. The flair for design and style that has characterized Italian culture for centuries is embodied in the businesspeople of Milan and Rome. They dress beautifully and admire flair, but they blanch at garishness or impropriety in others' attire.

To the Saudi Arabians, the pigskin binder would have been considered vile. An American salesman who really did present such a binder was unceremoniously tossed out, and his company was blacklisted from working with Saudi businesses. In China, Harry's casually dropping his chopsticks could have been misinterpreted as an act of aggression. Stabbing chopsticks into a bowl of rice and leaving them signifies death to the Chinese. The clocks Harry offered as gifts might have confirmed such dark

intentions. To "give a clock" in Chinese sounds the same as "seeing someone off to his end."

Thus, to compete successfully in global markets, or even to deal effectively with international firms in their home markets, companies must help their managers to understand the needs, customs, and cultures of international business buyers. "When doing business in a foreign country and a foreign culture—particularly a non-Western culture—assume nothing," advises an international business specialist. "Take nothing for granted. Turn every stone. Ask every question. Dig into every detail. Because cultures really are different, and those differences can have a major impact." So the old advice is still good advice: When in Rome, do as the Romans do.

Sources: Portions adapted from Susan Harte, "When in Rome, You Should Learn to Do What the Romans Do," *The Atlanta Journal-Constitution,* January 22, 1990, pp. D1, D6. Additional examples from Terri Morrison, Wayne A. Conway, and Joseph J. Douress, *Dun & Bradstreet's Guide to Doing Business Around the World* (Upper Saddle River, NJ: Prentice Hall, 2000); Craig S. Smith, "Beware of Green Hats in China and Other Cross-Cultural Faux Pas," *New York Times,* April 30, 2002, p. C11; James K. Sebenius, "The Hidden Challenge of Cross-Border Negotiations," *Harvard Business Review,* March 2002, pp. 76–85; and Daniel Joseph, "Dangerous Assumptions," *Ceramic Industry,* January 2003, p. 120.

General Need Description. Having recognized a need, the buyer next prepares a general need description that describes the characteristics and quantity of the needed item. For standard items, this process presents few problems. For complex items, however, the buyer may have to work with others—engineers, users, consultants—to define the item. The team may want to rank the importance of reliability, durability, price, and other attributes desired in the item. In this phase, the alert business marketer can help the buyers define their needs and provide information about the value of different product characteristics.

Value analysis

An approach to cost reduction in which components are studied carefully to determine if they can be redesigned, standardized, or made by less costly methods of production.

Product Specification. The buying organization next develops the item's technical product specifications, often with the help of a value analysis engineering team. **Value analysis** is an approach to cost reduction in which components are studied carefully to determine if they can be redesigned, standardized, or made by less costly methods of production. The team decides on the best product characteristics and specifies them accordingly. Sellers, too, can use value analysis as a tool to help secure a new account. By showing buyers a better way to make an object, outside sellers can turn straight rebuy situations into new-task situations that give them a chance to obtain new business.

Supplier Search. The buyer now conducts a supplier search to find the best vendors. The buyer can compile a small list of qualified suppliers by reviewing trade directories, doing a

■ Supplier development: Wal-Mart's Supplier Development Department offers a Supplier Proposal Guide and maintains a Web site offering advice to suppliers wishing to do business with Wal-Mart.

computer search, or phoning other companies for recommendations. Today, more and more companies are turning to the Internet to find suppliers. For marketers, this has leveled the playing field—the Internet gives smaller suppliers many of the same advantages as larger competitors.

These days, many companies are viewing supplier search more as *supplier development*. These companies want to develop a system of supplier-partners that can help it bring more value to its customers. For example, Wal-Mart's Supplier Development Department seeks out qualified suppliers and helps them through the complex Wal-Mart buying process.

The newer the buying task, and the more complex and costly the item, the greater the amount of time the buyer will spend searching for suppliers. The supplier's task is to get listed in major directories and to build a good reputation in the marketplace. Salespeople should watch for companies in the process of searching for suppliers and make certain that their firm is considered.

Proposal Solicitation. In the proposal-solicitation stage of the business buying process, the buyer invites qualified suppliers to submit proposals. In response, some suppliers will send only a catalog or a salesperson. However, when the item is complex or expensive, the buyer will usually require detailed written proposals or formal presentations from each potential supplier.

Business marketers must be skilled in researching, writing, and presenting proposals in response to buyer proposal solicitations. Proposals should be marketing documents, not just technical documents. Presentations should inspire confidence and should make the marketer's company stand out from the competition.

Supplier Selection. The members of the buying center now review the proposals and select a supplier or suppliers. During supplier selection, the buying center often will draw up a list of the desired supplier attributes and their relative importance. In one survey, purchasing executives listed the following attributes as most important in influencing the relationship between supplier and customer: quality products and services, on-time delivery, ethical corporate behavior, honest communication, and competitive prices. Other important factors include repair and servicing capabilities, technical aid and advice, geographic location, performance history, and reputation. The members of the buying center will rate suppliers against these attributes and identify the best suppliers.

Buyers may attempt to negotiate with preferred suppliers for better prices and terms before making the final selections. In the end, they may select a single supplier or a few suppliers. Many buyers prefer multiple sources of suppliers to avoid being totally dependent on one supplier and to allow comparisons of prices and performance of several suppliers over time.

Order-Routine Specification. The buyer now prepares an order-routine specification. It includes the final order with the chosen supplier or suppliers and lists items such as technical specifications, quantity needed, expected time of delivery, return policies, and warranties. In the case of maintenance, repair, and operating items, buyers may use *blanket contracts* rather than periodic purchase orders. A blanket contract creates a long-term relationship in which the supplier promises to resupply the buyer as needed at agreed prices for a set period. A blanket order eliminates the expensive process of renegotiating a purchase each time that stock is required. It also allows buyers to write more, but smaller, purchase orders, resulting in lower inventory levels and carrying costs.

Blanket contracting leads to more single-source buying and to buying more items from that source. This practice locks the supplier in more tightly with the buyer and makes it difficult for other suppliers to break in unless the buyer becomes dissatisfied with prices or service.

Performance Review. In this stage, the buyer reviews supplier performance. The buyer may contact users and ask them to rate their satisfaction. The performance review may lead the buyer to continue, modify, or drop the arrangement. The seller's job is to monitor the same factors used by the buyer to make sure that the seller is giving the expected satisfaction.

We have described the stages that typically would occur in a new-task buying situation. The eight-stage model provides a simple view of the business buying decision process. The actual process is usually much more complex. In the modified-rebuy or straight-rebuy situation, some of these stages would be compressed or bypassed. Each organization buys in its own way, and each buying situation has unique requirements. Different buying center participants may be involved at different stages of the process. Although certain buying-process steps usually do occur, buyers do not always follow them in the same order, and they may add other steps. Often, buyers will repeat certain stages of the process. Finally, a customer relationship might involve many different types of purchases ongoing at a given time, all in different stages of the buying process. The seller must manage the total customer relationship, not just individual purchases.

Business Buying on the Internet

During the past few years, advances in information technology have changed the face of the business-to-business marketing process. Online purchasing, often called **e-procurement**, is growing rapidly. In a recent survey, almost 75 percent of business buyers indicated that they use the Internet to make at least some of their purchases. Another study found that e-procurement accounts for 14 percent of the average company's spending. One research firm estimates that the dollar value of materials purchased online swelled from $75 billion in 2000 to more than $3 trillion in 2003.[35] In addition to

e-procurement
Online purchasing.

their own Web pages on the Internet, companies are establishing extranets that link a company's communications and data with its regular suppliers and distributors.

Much online purchasing also takes place on public and private online trading exchanges, or through *reverse auctions,* in which sellers put their purchasing requests online and invite suppliers to bid for the business. For example, public trading exchanges like the auto industry's Covisint exchange offer a faster, more efficient way to communicate, collaborate, buy, sell, trade, and exchange information business to business. The exchange handled more that $50 billion in auto-parts orders last year.

E-procurement gives buyers access to new suppliers, lowers purchasing costs, and hastens order processing and delivery. In turn, business marketers can connect with customers online to share marketing information, sell products and services, provide customer support services, and maintain ongoing customer relationships.

So far, most of the products bought online are MRO materials—maintenance, repair, and operations. For instance, Los Angeles County purchases everything from chickens to light bulbs over the Internet. National Semiconductor has automated almost all of the company's 3,500 monthly requisitions to buy materials ranging from the sterile booties worn in its fabrication plants to state-of-the-art software. The actual dollar amount spent on these types of MRO materials pales in comparison with the amount spent for items such as airplane parts, computer systems, and steel tubing. Yet, MRO materials make up 80 percent of all business orders and the transaction costs for order processing are high. Thus, companies have much to gain by streamlining the MRO buying process on the Web.

General Electric, one of the world's biggest purchasers, plans to be buying *all* of its general operating and industrial supplies online within the next few years. Five years ago, GE set up its Global eXchange Services network—a central Web site through which all GE business units could make their purchases. The site was so successful that GE has now opened it up to other companies, creating a vast electronic e-purchasing clearinghouse.

Business-to-business e-procurement yields many benefits. First, it shaves transaction costs and results in more efficient purchasing for both buyers and suppliers. A Web-powered purchasing program eliminates the paperwork associated with traditional requisition and ordering procedures. On average, companies can trim the costs of purchased goods alone by 15 to 20 percent. For example, Owens Corning estimates that e-procurement has shaved 10 percent off its annual purchasing bill of $3.4 billion. And Microsoft recently reduced its purchasing costs by $700 million after implementing its MS Market e-procurement system.[36] E-procurement reduces the time between order and delivery. Time savings are particularly dramatic for companies with many overseas suppliers. Adaptec, a leading supplier of computer storage, used an extranet to tie all of its Taiwanese chip suppliers together in a kind of virtual family. Now messages from Adaptec flow in seconds from its headquarters to its Asian partners, and Adaptec has reduced the time between the order and delivery of its chips from as long as 16 weeks to just 55 days—the same turnaround time for companies that build their own chips.

Finally, beyond the cost and time savings, e-procurement frees purchasing people to focus on more-strategic issues. For many purchasing professionals, going online means reducing drudgery and paperwork and spending more time managing inventory and working creatively with suppliers.

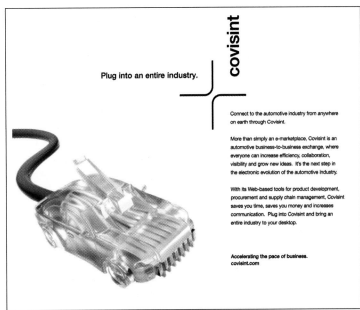

■ Online purchasing—or e-procurement: Public trading exchanges like the auto industry's Covisint exchange offer "a faster, more efficient way to communicate, collaborate, buy, sell, trade, and exchange information—business to business. The exchange handled more than $50 billion in auto-parts orders last year.

The rapidly expanding use of e-purchasing, however, also presents some problems. For example, at the same time that the Web makes it possible for suppliers and customers to share business data and even collaborate on product design, it can also erode decades-old customer–supplier relationships. Many firms are using the Web to search for better suppliers.

E-purchasing can also create potential security disasters. More than 80 percent of companies say security is the leading barrier to expanding electronic links with customers and partners. Although e-mail and home banking transactions can be protected through basic encryption, the secure environment that businesses need to carry out confidential interactions is still lacking. Companies are spending millions for research on defensive strategies to keep hackers at bay. Cisco Systems, for example, specifies the types of routers, firewalls, and security procedures that its partners must use to safeguard extranet connections. In fact, the company goes even further—it sends its own security engineers to examine a partner's defenses and holds the partner liable for any security breach that originates from its computer.

REST STOP:
Reviewing the Concepts

This chapter is the last of three chapters that address understanding the marketplace and consumers. Here, we've looked closely at consumers and their buying behavior. The American consumer market consists of more than 290 million people who consume many trillions of dollars' worth of goods and services each year. The business market involves far more dollars and items than the consumer market. Final consumers and business buyers vary greatly in their characteristics and circumstances. Understanding *consumer* and *business buyer behavior* is one of the biggest challenges marketers face.

1. Describe the consumer market and the major factors that influence consumer buyer behavior.

The *consumer market* consists of all the individuals and households who buy or acquire goods and services for personal consumption. A simple stimulus–response model of consumer behavior suggests that marketing stimuli and other major forces enter the consumer's "black box." This black box has two parts: buyer characteristics and the buyer's decision process. Once in the black box, the inputs result in observable buyer responses, such as product choice, brand choice, dealer choice, purchase timing, and purchase amount.

Consumer buyer behavior is influenced by four key sets of buyer characteristics: cultural, social, personal, and psychological. Understanding these factors can help marketers to identify interested buyers and to shape products and appeals to serve consumer needs better. *Culture* is the most basic determinant of a person's wants and behavior. People in different cultural, subcultural, and social class groups have different product and brand preferences. *Social factors*—such as small group and family influences—strongly affect product and brand choices, as do *personal characteristics,* such as age, life-cycle stage, occupation, economic circumstances, lifestyle, and personality. Finally, consumer buying behavior is influenced by four major sets of *psychological factors*—motivation, perception, learning, and beliefs and attitudes. Each of these factors provides a different perspective for understanding the workings of the buyer's black box.

2. Identify and discuss the stages in the buyer decision process.

When making a purchase, the buyer goes through a decision process consisting of need recognition, information search, evaluation of alternatives, purchase decision, and postpurchase behavior. During *need recognition*, the consumer recognizes a problem or need that could be satisfied by a product or service. Once the need is recognized, the consumer moves into the *information search* stage. With information in hand, the consumer proceeds to *alternative evaluation* and assesses brands in the choice set. From there, the consumer makes a *purchase decision* and actually buys the product. In the final stage of the buyer decision process, *postpurchase behavior,* the consumer takes action based on satisfaction or dissatisfaction. The marketer's job is to understand the buyer's behavior at each stage and the influences that are operating.

3. Describe the adoption and diffusion process for new products.

The product *adoption process* is comprised of five stages: awareness, interest, evaluation, trial, and adoption. New-product marketers must think about how to help consumers move through these stages. With regard to the *diffusion process* for new products, consumers respond at different rates, depending on consumer and product characteristics. Consumers may be innovators, early adopters, early majority, late majority, or laggards. Each group may require different marketing approaches. Marketers often try to bring their new products to the attention of potential early adopters, especially those who are opinion leaders.

4. Define the business market and identify the major factors that influence business buyer behavior.

The *business market* comprises all organizations that buy goods and services for use in the production of other products and services or for the purpose of reselling or renting them to others at a profit. As compared with consumer markets, business markets usually have fewer, larger buyers who are more geographically concentrated. Business demand is derived demand, and the business buying decision usually involves more, and more professional, buyers.

Business buyers make decisions that vary with the three types of *buying situations:* straight rebuys, modified rebuys, and new tasks. The decision-making unit of a buying organization—the *buying center*—can consist of many different persons playing many different roles. The business marketer needs to know the following: Who are the major buying center participants? In what decisions do they exercise influence, and to what degree? What evaluation criteria does each decision participant use? The business marketer also needs to understand the major environmental, organizational, interpersonal, and individual influences on the buying process.

5. List and define the steps in the business buying decision process.

The *business buying decision process* itself can be quite involved, with eight basic stages: problem recognition, general need description, product specification, supplier search, proposal solicitation, supplier selection, order-routine specification, and performance review. Buyers who face a new-task buying situation usually go through all stages of the buying process. Buyers making modified or straight rebuys may skip some of the stages. Companies must manage the overall customer relationship, which often includes many different buying decisions in various stages of the buying decision process.

Recent advances in information technology have given birth to "e-purchasing," by which business buyers are purchasing all kinds of products and services electronically, either through electronic data interchange links (EDI) or on the Internet. Such cyber-buying gives buyers access to new suppliers, lowers purchasing costs, and hastens order processing and delivery. However, it can also erode customer–supplier relationships and create potential security problems. Still, business marketers are increasingly connecting with customers online to share marketing information, sell products and services, provide customer support services, and maintain ongoing customer relationships.

Navigating the Key Terms

Adoption process	Derived demand	Opinion leader
Attitude	e-procurement	Perception
Belief	Groups	Personality
Business buyer behavior	Learning	Social class
Buying center	Lifestyle	Straight rebuy
Cognitive dissonance	Modified rebuy	Subculture
Consumer buyer behavior	Motive (drive)	Systems selling
Consumer market	New product	Value analysis
Culture	New task	

Travel Log

Discussing the Issues

1. Describe how the subcultures individuals belong to and their social classes can influence their choices of an automobile. Which of these two influences is likely to have the largest influence?

2. Reference groups with which an individual desires to become associated are called aspirational groups. What is one of your aspirational groups? What types of products could marketers effectively sell using the aspirational group you selected?

3. Learning is described as changes in an individual's behavior arising from experience. In what ways do marketers attempt to get consumers to experience their products in order to influence their buying behavior?

4. Sometimes a consumer conducts an information search and other times a very minimal search. What factors might influence how much information searching a consumer does?

5. Think about a new type of product you have recently purchased. Discuss how you proceeded through the five stages of the product adoption process. Did you skip any stages?

Were any of the stages in a different order from that presented in the text?

6. Discuss how business buyer behavior is different from consumer buyer behavior. What does this mean for a company attempting to sell goods to other organizations?

Application Questions

1. Go to SRI Consulting's Web site (www.sric-bi.com/VALS/presurvey.html) and complete the VALS survey online. How accurately are you described by your primary and secondary VALS types? Do you think you will be in a different VALS category in 5 to 10 years? Discuss how Kraft food marketers might use this information to sell Velveeta cheese.

2. Examine the five adopter categories and how they differ from one another. Pick a recent technology-oriented product such as a PDA or a DVD player and discuss how such a product should be positioned differently to appeal to each of the five adopter categories. To which group do you feel would be easiest to sell? Which group might be the most profitable?

3. Relationships between the seller and buyer are often mentioned as being more critical in business-to-business transactions than in business-to-consumer transactions. Do you agree or disagree with this? What types of activities might a firm use to develop closer relations with another organization?

Under the Hood: Focus on Technology

 This chapter discusses how consumer and business markets differ from one another. How do you think the company Web sites of a company selling directly to consumers will compare with one selling directly to other businesses? Visit and investigate the corporate Web sites for Dow Chemical (www.dow.com) and for Kellogg's (www.kelloggs.com).

1. How are the Web sites different?

2. Who is each Web site designed for?

3. What types of information are present on both Web sites?

4. How well does each Web site communicate with its intended audience?

Focus on Ethics

 As pointed out in the chapter, mature consumers are an attractive market because of their growing ranks, financial stability, and increasing free time. Health-related products are often pitched toward these markets in an effort to help them look as young as they feel and to combat the effects of aging.

Traditionally, prescription drug advertising has been aimed directly at physicians. Recently, there has been a rise in prescription drug advertising aimed directly at the consumer, particularly the mature consumer. The goal is clear: if a patient is aware of new drugs that supposedly help combat aging, the patient will ask the physician to prescribe them. The expected result?—an increase in sales for the advertised drug.

Drug manufacturers have increased the amount of direct-to-consumer advertising, from $800 million in 1996 to $2.7 billion in 2001. While a better-educated consumer is a laudable goal, critics suggest that direct-to-consumer advertising partly fuels the escalating cost of prescription drugs, which are rising at an average of 17 percent per year. The advertising appears to be working. From 1990 to 2000, the volume prescribed of the 50 most advertised drugs increased by 24.6 percent, compared with only 4.3 percent for all other prescription drugs. Perhaps most disturbing, a study in the *Journal of Family Practice* reported that 71 percent of family physicians felt direct-to-consumer advertising pressured them to prescribe medication they wouldn't otherwise prescribe.

1. How do you feel about the rise in direct-to-consumer advertising for prescription drugs? What are some of the pros and cons of such advertising?

2. What actions, if any, should drug manufacturers take to be socially responsible in the creation of consumer advertising?

3. Does direct-to-consumer advertising in the drug industry have any negative consequences for pharmaceutical companies?

Videos

The Subaru video case that accompanies this chapter is located in Appendix 1 at the back of the book.

Student Materials

Need a tune-up? A study guide and OneKey access code are available to aid in your review of chapter material. Your instructor may choose to have these items shrink-wrapped with your text or you may purchase them separately at www.prenhall.com/marketing.

■ *After studying this chapter, you should be able to*

1. *Define* the three steps of target marketing: market segmentation, market targeting, and market positioning
2. *List* and discuss the major bases for segmenting consumer and business markets   **3.** *Explain* how companies
identify attractive market segments and choose a target marketing strategy   **4.** *Discuss* how companies position
their products for maximum competitive advantage in the marketplace

Segmentation, Targeting, and Positioning: Building the Right Relationships with the Right Customers

6

ROAD MAP | Previewing the Concepts

So far in your marketing journey, you've learned what marketing is and about the complex environments in which it operates. Marketing works with partners inside and outside the company to build profitable customer relationships in a complex and changing marketplace. With that as background, in Part 3 of the book, we'll travel more deeply into marketing strategy and tactics. The key to smart marketing is to build the *right relationships* with the *right customers*. This chapter looks further into key marketing strategy decisions—how to divide up markets into meaningful customer groups (market segmentation), choose which customer groups to serve (target marketing), and create a value proposition that best serves targeted customers (positioning). The chapters that follow explore in depth the tactical marketing tools—the *4Ps*—through which marketers bring these strategies to life.

Next stop: Procter & Gamble, one of the world's premier consumer goods companies. Some 99 percent of all U.S. households use at least one P&G brand, and the typical household regularly buys and uses from one to two *dozen* P&G brands. How many P&G products can you name? Why does this superb marketer compete with itself on supermarket shelves by marketing eight different brands of laundry detergent? The P&G story provides a great example of how smart marketers use segmentation, targeting, and positioning.

Procter & Gamble (P&G) sells eight brands of laundry detergent in the United States (Tide, Cheer, Bold, Gain, Era, Dreft, Febreze, and Ivory Snow). It also sells six brands of hand soap (Ivory, Safeguard, Camay, Olay, Zest, and Old Spice); five brands of shampoo (Pantene, Head & Shoulders, Pert, Physique, and Vidal Sassoon); four brands of dishwashing detergent (Dawn, Ivory, Joy, and Cascade); three brands each of tissues and towels (Charmin, Bounty, Puffs), and deodorant (Secret, Sure, and Old Spice) ; and two brands each of fabric softener (Downy and Bounce), cosmetics (Cover Girl and Max Factor), skin care potions (Olay and Noxzema), and disposable diapers (Pampers and Luvs). Moreover, P&G has many additional brands in each category for different international markets. For example, it sells 16 different laundry product brands in Latin America and 19 in Europe, the Middle East, and Africa. (See Procter & Gamble's Web site at www.pg.com for a full look at the company's impressive lineup of familiar brands.)

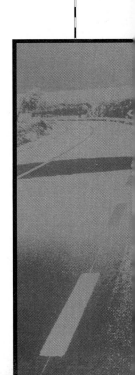

These P&G brands compete with one another on the same supermarket shelves. But why would P&G introduce several brands in one category instead of concentrating its resources on a single leading brand? The answer lies in the fact that different people want different *mixes of benefits* from the products they buy. Take laundry detergents, for example. People use laundry detergents to get their clothes clean. But they also want other things from their detergents—such as economy, bleaching power, fabric softening, fresh smell, strength or mildness, and lots of suds or only a little. We all want *some* of every one of these benefits from our detergent, but we may have different *priorities* for each benefit. To some people, cleaning and bleaching power are most important; to others, fabric softening matters most; still others want a mild, fresh-scented detergent. Thus, there are groups—or segments—of laundry detergent buyers, and each segment seeks a special combination of benefits.

Procter & Gamble has identified at least seven important laundry detergent segments, along with numerous subsegments, and has developed a different brand designed to meet the special needs of each. The seven brands are positioned for different segments as follows:

- *Tide* provides "fabric cleaning and care at its best." It's the all-purpose family detergent that is "tough on greasy stains."
- *Cheer* is the "color expert." It helps protect against fading, color transfer, and fabric wear, with or without bleach. *Cheer Free* is "dermatologist tested . . . contains no irritating perfume or dye."
- *Bold* is the detergent with built-in fabric softener and pill/fuzz removal.
- *Gain*, originally P&G's "enzyme" detergent, was repositioned as the detergent that gives you clean, fresh-smelling clothes. It "cleans and freshens like sunshine. Great cleaning power and a smell that stays clean."
- *Era* is "the power tool for stain removal and pretreating." It contains advanced enzymes to fight a family's tough stains and help get the whole wash clean. *Era Max* has three types of active enzymes to help fight many stains that active families encounter.
- *Ivory Snow* is "Ninety-nine and forty-four one hundredths percent pure." It provides "mild cleansing benefits for a pure and simple clean."
- *Dreft* "helps remove tough baby stains . . . for a clean you can trust." It's "pediatrician recommended and the first choice of mothers." It "doesn't remove the flame resistance of children's sleepwear."

Within each segment, Procter & Gamble has identified even *narrower* niches. For example, you can buy regular Tide (in powder or liquid form) or any of several formulations:

- *Tide with Bleach* helps to "keep your whites white and your colors bright." Available in regular or "mountain spring" scents.
- *Tide Liquid with Bleach Alternative* uses active enzymes in pretreating and washing to break down and remove the toughest stains while whitening whites.
- *Tide High Efficiency* "unlocks the cleaning power of high-efficiency top-loading machines"— it prevents oversudsing.
- *Tide Clean Breeze* gives the fresh scent of laundry line-dried in a clean breeze.
- *Tide Mountain Spring* lets you "bring the fresh clean scent of the great outdoors inside—the scent of crisp mountain air and fresh wildflowers."
- *Tide Free* "provides all the stain removal benefits without any dyes or perfumes."
- *Tide Rapid Action Tablets* are portable and powerful. It's Tide "all concentrated into a little blue and white tablet that fits into your pocket."

By segmenting the market and having several detergent brands, Procter & Gamble has an attractive offering for consumers in all important preference groups. As a result, P&G is really cleaning up in the $4 billion U.S. laundry detergent market. Tide, by itself, captures a whopping 38 percent market share. All P&G brands combined take a 60 percent share of the U.S. market—more than three times that of nearest rival Unilever and much more than any single brand could obtain by itself.[1]

Companies today recognize that they cannot appeal to all buyers in the marketplace, or at least not to all buyers in the same way. Buyers are too numerous, too widely scattered, and too varied in their needs and buying practices. Moreover, the companies themselves vary widely in their abilities to serve different segments of the market. Instead, they must design strategies to build the *right* relationships with the *right* customers. Rather than trying to compete in an entire market, sometimes against superior competitors, each company must identify the parts of the market that it can serve best and most profitably.

Thus, most companies are being more choosy about the customers with whom they wish to build relationships. Most have moved away from mass marketing and toward *market segmentation and targeting*—identifying market segments, selecting one or more of them, and developing products and marketing programs tailored to each. Instead of scattering their marketing efforts (the "shotgun" approach), firms are focusing on the buyers who have greater interest in the values they create best (the "rifle" approach).

Figure 6.1 shows the three major steps in target marketing. The first is **market segmentation**—dividing a market into smaller groups of buyers with distinct needs, characteristics, or behaviors who might require separate products or marketing mixes. The company identifies different ways to segment the market and develops profiles of the resulting market segments. The second step is **target marketing**—evaluating each market segment's attractiveness and selecting one or more of the market segments to enter. The third step is **market positioning**—setting the competitive positioning for the product and creating a detailed marketing mix. We discuss each of these steps in turn.

◼◼ Market Segmentation

Markets consist of buyers, and buyers differ in one or more ways. They may differ in their wants, resources, locations, buying attitudes, and buying practices. Through market segmentation, companies divide large, heterogeneous markets into smaller segments that can be reached more efficiently and effectively with products and services that match their unique needs. In this section, we discuss four important segmentation topics: segmenting consumer markets, segmenting business markets, segmenting international markets, and requirements for effective segmentation.

Segmenting Consumer Markets

There is no single way to segment a market. A marketer has to try different segmentation variables, alone and in combination, to find the best way to view the market structure. Table 6.1 outlines the major variables that might be used in segmenting consumer markets. Here we look at the major *geographic, demographic, psychographic,* and *behavioral variables.*

Geographic Segmentation   **Geographic segmentation** calls for dividing the market into different geographical units such as nations, regions, states, counties, cities, or

Market segmentation
Dividing a market into distinct groups with distinct needs, characteristics, or behaviors who might require separate products or marketing mixes.

Target marketing
The process of evaluating each market segment's attractiveness and selecting one or more segments to enter.

Market positioning
Arranging for a product to occupy a clear, distinctive, and desirable place relative to competing products in the minds of target consumers.

Geographic segmentation
Dividing a market into different geographical units such as nations, states, regions, counties, cities, or neighborhoods.

Market segmentation	Target marketing	Market positioning
Identify bases for segmenting the market	Develop measure of segment attractiveness	Develop positioning for target segments
Develop segment profiles	Select target segments	Develop a marketing mix for each segment

FIGURE 6.1
Steps in Market Segmentation, Targeting, and Positioning

TABLE 6.1 Major Segmentation Variables for Consumer Markets

Geographic

World region or country	North America, Western Europe, Middle East, Pacific Rim, China, India, Canada, Mexico
Country region	Pacific, Mountain, West North Central, West South Central, East North Central, East South Central, South Atlantic, Middle Atlantic, New England
City or metro size	Under 5,000; 5,000–20,000; 20,000–50,000; 50,000–100,000; 100,000–250,000; 250,000–500,000; 500,000–1,000,000; 1,000,000–4,000,000; 4,000,000 or over
Density	Urban, suburban, rural
Climate	Northern, southern

Demographic

Age	Under 6, 6–11, 12–19, 20–34, 35–49, 50–64, 65+
Gender	Male, female
Family size	1–2, 3–4, 5+
Family life-cycle	Young, single; young, married, no children; young, married with children; older, married with children; older, married, no children under 18; older, single; other
Income	Under $10,000; $10,000–$20,000; $20,000–$30,000; $30,000–$50,000; $50,000–$100,000; $100,000 and over
Occupation	Professional and technical; managers, officials, and proprietors; clerical; sales; craftspeople; supervisors; operatives; farmers; retired; students; homemakers; unemployed
Education	Grade school or less; some high school; high school graduate; some college; college graduate
Religion	Catholic, Protestant, Jewish, Muslim, Hindu, other
Race	Asian, Hispanic, black, white
Generation	Baby boomer, Generation X, Generation Y
Nationality	North American, South American, British, French, German, Italian, Japanese

Psychographic

Social class	Lower lowers, upper lowers, working class, middle class, upper middles, lower uppers, upper uppers
Lifestyle	Achievers, strivers, strugglers
Personality	Compulsive, gregarious, authoritarian, ambitious

Behavioral

Occasions	Regular occasion; special occasion
Benefits	Quality, service, economy, convenience, speed
User status	Nonuser, ex-user, potential user, first-time user, regular user
User rates	Light user, medium user, heavy user
Loyalty status	None, medium, strong, absolute
Readiness stage	Unaware, aware, informed, interested, desirous, intending to buy
Attitude toward product	Enthusiastic, positive, indifferent, negative, hostile

even neighborhoods. A company may decide to operate in one or a few geographical areas, or to operate in all areas but pay attention to geographical differences in needs and wants.

Many companies today are localizing their products, advertising, promotion, and sales efforts to fit the needs of individual regions, cities, and even neighborhoods. For example, Campbell sells Cajun gumbo soup in Louisiana and Mississippi and makes its nacho cheese soup spicier in Texas and California. Starbucks offers more desserts and larger, more comfortable coffee shops in the South, where customers tend to arrive later in the day and to stay longer. And Parker Brothers offers localized versions of its popular Monopoly game for several major cities, including Chicago, New York, San Francisco, St. Louis, and Las Vegas. The Las Vegas version features a black board with The Strip rather than Boardwalk, hotel casinos, red Vegas dice, and custom pewter tokens including blackjack cards, a wedding chapel, and a roulette wheel.[2]

Other companies are seeking to cultivate as-yet untapped geographic territory. For example, many large companies are fleeing the fiercely competitive major cities and suburbs to set up shop in small-town America. Hampton Inns has opened a chain of smaller-format motels in towns too small for its standard-size units. For example, Townsend, Tennessee, with a population of only 329, is small even by small-town standards. But looks can be deceiving. Situated on a heavily traveled and picturesque route between Knoxville and the Smoky Mountains, the village serves both business and vacation travelers. Hampton Inns opened a unit in Townsend and plans to open 100 more in small towns. It costs less to operate in these towns, and the company builds smaller units to match lower volume. The Townsend Hampton Inn, for example, has 54 rooms instead of the usual 135.

In contrast, other retailers are developing new store concepts that will give them access to higher-density urban areas. For example, Home Depot is introducing neighborhood stores that look a lot like its traditional stores but at about two-thirds the size. It is placing these stores in high-density markets where full-size stores are impractical. Similarly, Wal-Mart is testing Neighborhood Market grocery stores to complement its supercenters.[3]

Demographic Segmentation **Demographic segmentation** divides the market into groups based on variables such as age, gender, family size, family life cycle, income, occupation, education, religion, race, generation, and nationality. Demographic factors are the most popular bases for segmenting customer groups. One reason is that consumer needs, wants, and usage rates often vary closely with demographic variables. Another is that demographic variables are easier to measure than most other types of variables. Even when market segments are first defined using other bases, such as benefits sought or behavior, their demographic characteristics must be known in order to assess the size of the target market and to reach it efficiently.

Age and Life-Cycle Stage. Consumer needs and wants change with age. Some companies use **age and life-cycle segmentation**, offering different products or using different marketing approaches for different age and life-cycle groups. For example, for kids,

Demographic segmentation
Dividing the market into groups based on demographic variables such as age, gender, family size, family life cycle, income, occupation, education, religion, race, generation, and nationality.

Age and life-cycle segmentation
Dividing a market into different age and life-cycle groups.

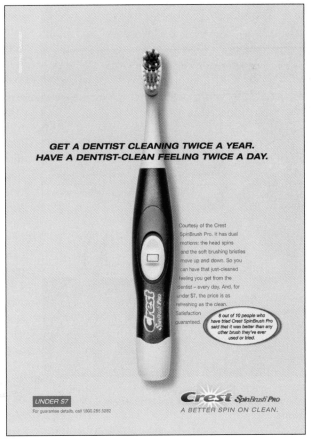

■ Age and life-cycle segmentation: For kids, Procter & Gamble sells Crest Spinbrushes featuring favorite children's characters. For adults, it sells more serious models, promising "a dentist-clean feeling twice a day."

Procter & Gamble sells Crest Spinbrushes featuring children's favorite characters and lots of fun. For adults, it sells more serious models, promising "a dentist-clean feeling twice a day."[4] Gap has branched out to target people at different life stages. In addition to its standard line of clothing, the retailer now offers baby Gap, Gap kids, and Gap Maternity. Here's another example[5]:

> In several of its stores around the country, clothing retailer Eddie Bauer places large, high-definition video screens in its storefront windows to draw in customers who might otherwise walk on by. The screens allow stores to customize in-store advertising to target different generational segments, depending on the time of day. For example, a store might post images featuring older models during the morning hours when retirees frequently shop, then change the posters to reflect the younger shopping crowd of the evening. In one initial nine-month test, sales at one location rose 56 percent from the previous nine months.

Marketers must be careful to guard against stereotypes when using age and life-cycle segmentation. For example, although some 70-year-olds require wheelchairs, others play tennis. Similarly, whereas some 40-year-old couples are sending their children off to college, others are just beginning new families. Thus, age is often a poor predictor of a person's life cycle; health, work, or family status; needs; and buying power. Companies marketing to mature consumers usually employ positive images and appeals. For example, ads for Olay ProVital—designed to improve the elasticity and appearance of the "maturing skin" of women over 50—feature attractive older spokeswomen and uplifting messages.

Gender segmentation
Dividing a market into different groups based on gender.

Gender. **Gender segmentation** has long been used in clothing, cosmetics, toiletries, and magazines. For example, Procter & Gamble was among the first with Secret, a brand specially formulated for a woman's chemistry, packaged and advertised to reinforce the female image. More recently, other marketers have noticed opportunities for targeting women. Citibank launched Women & Co. to sell financial services "designed to help women with all their personal finance and investing needs." Leatherman, which has traditionally targeted its multipurpose combination tool to men, now makes Leatherman Juice for women, hip and stylish tools offered in five vibrant colors. And after its research showed that women make 90 percent of all home improvement decisions, home improvement retailer Lowe's recently launched a family-oriented advertising campaign that reaches out to women buyers. Similarly, Owens-Corning aimed a major advertising campaign for home insulation at women after a study showed that two-thirds of all women were involved in materials installation, with 13 percent doing it themselves. Half the women surveyed compared themselves to Bob Vila, whereas less than half compared themselves to Martha Stewart.[6]

Even the National Football League and advertisers on the Super Bowl, long the holy day of testosterone, are now targeting women. The 30 million or more women who watch the average Super Bowl make up more than 36 percent of the game's audience. And advertisers know that these women influence 80 percent of all household consumer purchases. Moreover, women now account for almost half of all NFL-licensed merchandise purchases. Anheuser-Busch, the biggest advertiser in the game, actively targets its Super Bowl

■ Gender Segmentation: Leatherman targets women with its "juice" tool in five vibrant colors, with ads like this one in *Cooking Light* magazine.

advertising to both genders. Whereas its competitors are still courting men with big doses of babes and sophomoric humor, A-B is showing a more sensitive side. "Women are a huge part of this audience," says A-B's vice president of brand management. "We've been working hard for five years not to do the typical guy jokes."[7]

A growing number of Web sites also target women. For example, Oxygen Media runs a Web site "designed for women by women" (www.oxygen.com). It appeals to 18- to 34-year-old women with fresh and hip information, features, and exchanges on a wide variety of topics—from health and fitness, money and work, and style and home to relationships and self-discovery. The leading women's online community, iVillage (www.iVillage.com), offers "real solutions for real women" and entreats visitors to "join our community of smart, compassionate, real women." Various iVillage channels cover topics ranging from babies, food, fitness, pets, and relationships to careers, finance, and travel.[8]

Income. **Income segmentation** has long been used by the marketers of products and services such as automobiles, boats, clothing, cosmetics, financial services, and travel. Many companies target affluent consumers with luxury goods and convenience services. Stores such as Neiman Marcus pitch everything from expensive jewelry and fine fashions to glazed Australian apricots priced at $20 a pound. To cater to its best customers, Neiman Marcus created its InCircle Rewards program:

Income segmentation
Dividing a market into different income groups.

> InCircle members, who must spend $3,000 a year using their Neiman Marcus credit cards to be eligible, earn points with each purchase—one point for each dollar charged. They then cash in points for anything from drinks and appetizers with

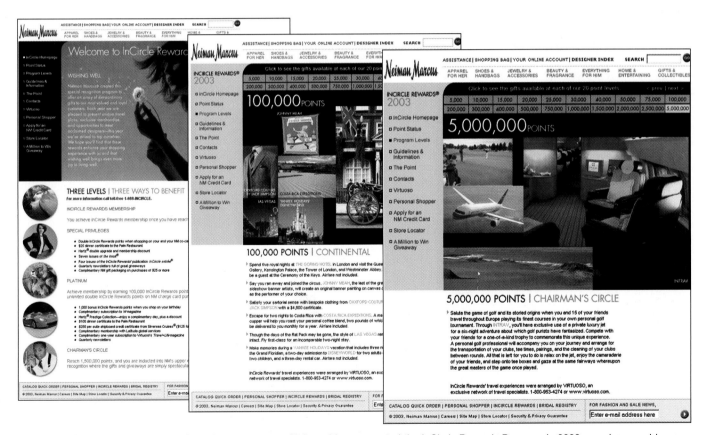

■ Income segmentation: To thank its very best customers, Neiman Marcus created the InCircle Rewards Program. In 2003, members could redeem 5 million points for a tour of Europe's finest golf courses in a private luxury jet with fifteen close friends.

friends at the St. Regis in New York (5000 points) or a one-year membership in the American Airlines Admirals club (15,000 points) to two nights at a deluxe hotel in Montréal complete with free museum admissions, a guided walking tour of the city, VIP admission to Montréal Casino, and a night as an assistant chef for the acclaimed Le Gutenberg restaurant (50,000 points). For 500,000 points, InCircle members can get an all expense paid, 10-day trip to Morocco, and for 1.5 million points, a commemorative Steinway grand piano. The top prize (for 5 million points!) is a tour of Europe's finest golf courses in a private luxury jet with 15 close friends. The trip includes a personal golf professional to arrange tee times, create the pairings for a personal tournament, and clean the member's clubs between rounds.[9]

However, not all companies that use income segmentation target the affluent. Despite their lower spending power, the nearly one-third of the nation's households that earn less than $25,000 per year offer an attractive market. For example, Greyhound Lines, with its inexpensive nationwide bus network, targets lower-income consumers. Almost half of 25 million yearly passengers have annual incomes under $15,000. Many retailers also target this lower-income group, including chains such as Dollar General and Family Dollar stores. When Family Dollar real-estate experts scout locations for new stores, they look for lower-middle-class neighborhoods where people wear less expensive shoes and drive old cars that drip a lot of oil. The typical Family Dollar customer household earns about $25,000 a year, and the average customer spends only about $8 per trip to the store. Similarly, half of Dollar General's customers earn less than $20,000 a year, and about half of its target shoppers do not work. Yet both stores' low-income strategy has put them among the fastest-growing and most-profitable discount chains in the country.[10]

Levi Strauss sells jeans to consumers spanning several income levels. It sells Levi Strauss Signature jeans in Wal-Mart at $23 a pair, Type 1 jeans at Macy's for as much as $65, and Levi Red jeans at luxury stores like Barneys for $150 or more.[11]

Psychographic segmentation

Dividing a market into different groups based on social class, lifestyle, or personality characteristics.

Psychographic Segmentation **Psychographic segmentation** divides buyers into different groups based on social class, lifestyle, or personality characteristics. People in the same demographic group can have very different psychographic makeups.

In Chapter 5, we discussed how the products people buy reflect their *lifestyles*. As a result, marketers often segment their markets by consumer lifestyles. For example, Duck Head apparel targets a casual student lifestyle claiming "You can't get them old until you get them new." And Pottery Barn sells more than just home furnishings; it sells an entire lifestyle—all that its customers aspire to be (see Marketing at Work 6.1). One forward-looking grocery store found that segmenting its self-service meat products by lifestyle had a big payoff:

> Walk by the refrigerated self-service meat cases of most grocery stores and you'll usually find the offering grouped by type of meat. Pork is in one case, lamb is another, and chicken is in a third. However, a Nashville, Tennessee, Kroger supermarket decided to experiment and offer groupings of different meats by lifestyle. For instance, the store had a section called "Meals in Minutes," one called "Cookin' Lite," another, filled with prepared products like hot dogs and ready-made hamburger patties, called "Kids Love This Stuff," and one called "I Like to Cook." By focusing on lifestyle needs and not on protein categories, Kroger's test store encouraged habitual beef and pork buyers to consider lamb and veal as well. As a result, the 16-foot service case has seen a substantial improvement in both sales and profits.[12]

Marketers also have used *personality* variables to segment markets. For example, the marketing campaign for Honda's Reflex and Elite motor scooters *appears* to target hip and trendy 22-year-olds. But it is *actually* aimed at a much broader personality group. One ad, for example, shows a delighted child bouncing up and down on his bed while the announcer says, "You've been trying to get there all your life." The ad reminds viewers of the euphoric feelings they got when they broke away from authority and did things their parents told them not to do. It suggests that they can feel that way again by riding a Honda scooter. Thus, Honda is appealing to the rebellious, independent kid in all of us. As Honda notes on its Web page, "Fresh air, freedom, and flair—on a Honda scooter, every day is independence day! When it comes to cool, this scooter is off the charts!" In fact, more than half of Honda's scooter sales are to young professionals and older buyers—15 percent are purchased by the over-50 group. Aging baby boomers, now thrill-seeking middle-agers, caused a 26 percent jump in scooter sales last year.[13]

■ Psychographic Segmentation: When Honda markets its Reflex and Elite scooters, it appeals to the rebellious, independent kid in all of us.

Behavioral Segmentation
Behavioral segmentation divides buyers into groups based on their knowledge, attitudes, uses, or responses to a product. Many marketers believe that behavior variables are the best starting point for building market segments.

Occasions. Buyers can be grouped according to occasions on which they get the idea to buy, actually make their purchase, or use the purchased item. **Occasion segmentation** can help firms build up product usage. For example, orange juice is most often consumed at breakfast, but orange growers have promoted drinking orange juice as a cool and refreshing drink at other times of the day. In contrast, Coca-Cola's "Coke in the Morning" advertising campaign attempts to increase Coke consumption by promoting the beverage as an early morning pick-me-up.

Some holidays, such as Mother's Day and Father's Day, were originally promoted partly to increase the sale of candy, flowers, cards, and other gifts. And many marketers prepare special offers and ads for holiday occasions. For example, Altoids offers a special "Love Tin," the "curiously strong valentine." Beatrice Foods runs special Thanksgiving and Christmas ads for Reddi-wip during November and December, months that account for 30 percent of all whipped cream sales. Hershey wraps its Hershey's Kisses in special

Behavioral segmentation
Dividing a market into groups based on consumer knowledge, attitude, use, or response to a product.

Occasion segmentation
Dividing the market into groups according to occasions when buyers get the idea to buy, actually make their purchase, or use the purchased item.

■ Occasion segmentation: For Valentine's Day, Altoids created a special "Love Tin"—a "curiously strong valentine."

Marketing at Work | 6.1

Pottery Barn: Oh, What a Lifestyle!

Shortly after Hadley MacLean got married, she and her husband, Doug, agreed that their old bed had to go. It was a mattress and box spring on a cheap metal frame, a relic of Doug's Harvard days. But Hadley never anticipated how tough it would be to find a new bed. "We couldn't find anything we liked, even though we were willing to spend the money," says Hadley, a 31-year-old marketing director. It turned out to be much more than just finding a piece of furniture at the right price. It was a matter of emotion: They needed a bed that meshed with their lifestyle—with who they are and where they are going.

The couple finally ended up at the Pottery Barn on Boston's upscale Newbury Street, where Doug fell in love with a mahogany sleigh bed that Hadley had spotted in the store's catalog. The couple was so pleased with how great it looked in their Dutch Colonial home that they hurried back to the store for a set of end tables. And then they bought a quilt. And a mirror for the living room. And some stools for the dining room. "We got kind of addicted," Hadley confesses.

The MacLeans aren't alone. Pottery Barn's smart yet accessible product mix, seductive merchandising, and first-rate customer service have made it the front-runner in the fragmented home furnishings and housewares industry—not just because of the products that it sells, but also because of the connections that it makes with customers. Pottery Barn does more than just sell home furnishings. It sells an entire lifestyle.

Three thousand miles away from Hadley MacLean's home in Massachusetts, Laura Alber is obsessed with a towel. A tall, slim blond with pale-blue eyes and no makeup, Alber could be the poster child for the Pottery Barn lifestyle. The 34-year-old California mother of two says that she enjoys entertaining, describes herself as living "holistically," and has just bought the company's Westport sectional sofa, with its kid-resistant twill slipcovers. She also happens to be Pottery Barn's president.

"Feel how great this is," says Alber, pulling a large white bath towel from a stack. "It's thick, it's got a beautiful dobby [the woven band a few inches from the towel's edge], it's highly absorbent, and it's $24. I can say with great confidence that you can't top this." To some merchants, a towel is just a towel. But to Alber, the towel is a fluffy icon of the lifestyle to which Pottery Barn customers aspire: upscale but casual, active but laid back, family-

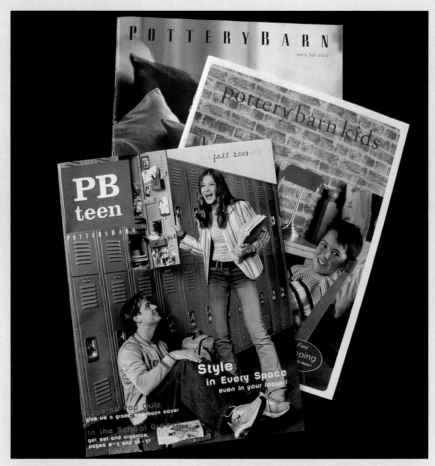

Pottery Barn sells more than just home furnishings; it sells all that its customers aspire to be. It offers idyllic scenes of the perfect childhood at Pottery Barn Kids; trendy, fashion-forward self-expression at PB Teen; and an upscale yet casual, family- and friend-focused life style at its flagship Pottery Barn stores.

and friend-focused, affluent but sensibly so.

Everyone at Pottery Barn works obsessively to understand the store's customers—who they are, how they live, and what they want out of life. They study customers first-hand and scour the marketplace for ideas. Like Alber, most staffers actually live the lifestyle themselves. They use their deep insights to develop products and store concepts that deliver the Pottery Barn lifestyle to customers.

To pass muster, a potential new Pottery Barn product needs to pass a strict five-point test. First, it has to look good, but not be too cutting edge. Second, the product has to feel good, and third, it must be of high quality. Fourth, it has to be durable—the question "Can the kids jump on it?" is a veritable mantra among Pottery Barn staffers, many of whom have children of their own to road-test the merchandise. Finally, it must pass the ultimate hurdle: "I ask my designers, 'Will you take it home or give it as a present to your best friends,'" says Celia Tejada, head of Pottery Barn's design and product development. "If they hesitate, I say, 'Throw it in the garbage.' Emotionally, it has to feel right."

It's a process that relies more on gut instinct than on rational science. At Pottery Barn, there are no panels of focus groups and no teams of market researchers. To create a powerful lifestyle brand, Tejada says, you must first have a life. So staffers are encouraged to go to restaurants and notice how the tables are set. To scavenge flea markets for interesting artifacts. To cruise real-estate open houses and model homes, looking for new architectural and design trends. To entertain friends and note what products they wish that they had: a bigger platter, a nicer serving utensil, a better bowl for salsa—anything that may be a good addition to the lifestyle line.

Individual products or lines of merchandise aren't the only things inspired by the personal lives of Pottery Barn staffers. It's no coincidence that the first Pottery Barn Kids catalog debuted simultaneously with the birth of Laura Alber's first child. The company's president was frustrated at trying to put together a good-looking nursery. She and her team developed a business plan for extending the Pottery Barn lifestyle to the bedrooms of newborns and young children. There are now 64 Pottery Barn Kids stores, with 16 more scheduled to open this year. As you might expect, Pottery Barn Kids delivers the ultimate kid lifestyle. Stores and catalogs create idyllic scenes of the perfect childhood, featuring themed bedrooms packed with accessories: fluttering curtains, cozy quilts, and stuffed animals. "My husband would tell you the furniture was for me and not the baby," says one mom. It's "a reflection of what I want her to be."

The latest Pottery Barn sibling is PBteen, which targets the lifestyles of tweens and teens. The first PBteen catalog featured furry beanbag chairs, animal-print sheets, and desks that look like lockers. The core products consist of basic things a teenager's room needs: from shag rugs and CD stands to furniture, pillows, and frames. There are some fashion-forward offerings—a skateboard headboard, for instance—but the majority have timeless designs, in keeping with Pottery Barn's other lifestyle offerings. "We've got the stuff that fits your world," says the PBteen Web site. "Go to my room?" it concludes. "Gladly."

The PBteen concept seems like a natural extension for Pottery Barn, but it was one that required significant sleuthing to divine just the right product mix. Pottery Barn staffers spent months trying to get inside the heads of their teenage customers and better understand their lifestyles. "Our designers [were] going to concerts, hanging out at schools, and watching MTV," says one VP. A contest asking kids to mail in snapshots of their rooms generated photographs that gave PBteen staffers a view into the real life-spaces of teenagers. Staffers pored over them like CIA analysts. "The kids are all little pack rats," says one, "with every stuffed animal they've gotten since they were born. That's a huge opportunity for us. We hope to get parents to buy stuff that will impose some order."

Regardless of which family member it targets, Pottery Barn gives customers an attainable and inspirational vision of what a really great lifestyle might look like. That may be the reason why, when Conde Nast magazine recently asked readers to name their favorite home-decorating magazine, an overwhelming number cited the Pottery Barn catalog.

The Pottery Barn lifestyle suits the company as well as its customers. Pottery Barn sales were up almost 12 percent last year; sales at Pottery Barn Kids increased by almost half. The chain's success has helped Pottery Barn's parent company, Williams-Sonoma, to achieve a 6-fold increase in revenues during the past decade, and a 10-fold increase in earnings. Pottery Barn's allure is no mystery to Tejada. "Our brand [embraces a lifestyle]. It's a state of mind. And customers can make it their own."

Sources: Adapted from Linda Tischler, "How Pottery Barn Wins with Style," *Fast Company*, June 2003, pp. 106–113. Additional information from Amy Merrick, "Child's Play for Furniture Retailers?—Amid Signs of a Baby Boom, the Big Chains Rush to Expand Offerings to Newborns, Kids," *Wall Street Journal*, September 25, 2002, p. B1; Charlyne Varkonyi Schaub, "Pottery Barn Tailoring Itself for Teens," *Sun-Sentinel*, May 9, 2003, accessed online at www.sun-sentinel.com; "William's Sonoma, Inc.," *Hoover's Company Profiles*, Austin, May 15, 2003; and information accessed at www.pbteen.com, July 2003.

holiday colors—75 percent of the demand for Kisses is focused around Valentine's Day, Easter, and other holiday time periods. Butterball, on the other hand, advertises "Happy Thanksgrilling" during the summer to increase the demand for turkeys on non-Thanksgiving occasions.

Kodak, Konica, Fuji, and other camera makers use occasion segmentation in designing and marketing their one-time-use cameras. By mixing lenses, film speeds, and accessories, they have developed special disposable cameras for about any picture-taking occasion, from underwater photography to taking baby pictures. The Kodak Water & Sport one-time-use camera is water resistant to 50 feet deep and features a shock-proof frame, a sunscreen and scratch-resistant lens, and 800 speed film. "It survives where your regular camera won't!" claims Kodak.[14]

Benefit segmentation

Dividing the market into groups according to the different benefits that consumers seek from the product.

Benefits Sought. A powerful form of segmentation is to group buyers according to the different *benefits* that they seek from the product. **Benefit segmentation** requires finding the major benefits people look for in the product class, the kinds of people who look for each benefit, and the major brands that deliver each benefit. For example, our chapter-opening example pointed out that Procter & Gamble has identified several different laundry detergent segments. Each segment seeks a unique combination of benefits, from cleaning and bleaching to economy, fabric softening, fresh smell, strength or mildness, and lots of suds or only a little.

The Champion athletic wear division of Sara Lee Corporation segments its markets according to benefits that different consumers seek from their activewear. For example, "fit and polish" consumers seek a balance between function and style—they exercise for results but want to look good doing it. "Serious sports competitors" exercise heavily and live in and love their activewear—they seek performance and function. By contrast, "value-seeking moms" have low sports interest and low activewear involvement—they buy for the family and seek durability and value. Thus, each segment seeks a different mix of benefits. Champion must target the benefit segment or segments that it can serve best and most profitably using appeals that match each segment's benefit preferences.

User Status. Markets can be segmented into groups of nonusers, ex-users, potential users, first-time users, and regular users of a product. For example, one study found that blood donors are low in self-esteem, low risk takers, and more highly concerned about their health; nondonors tend to be the opposite on all three dimensions. This suggests that social agencies should use different marketing approaches for keeping current donors and attracting new ones.

A company's market position also influences its focus. Market share leaders focus on attracting potential users, whereas smaller firms focus on attracting current users away from the market leader.

Usage Rate. Markets can also be segmented into light, medium, and heavy product users. Heavy users are often a small percentage of the market but account for a high percentage of total consumption. Marketers usually prefer to attract one heavy user to their product or service rather than several light users.

For example, in the fast-food industry, heavy users make up only 20 percent of patrons but eat up about 60 percent of all the food served. A single heavy user, typically a single male who doesn't know how to cook, might spend as much as $40 in a day at fast-food restaurants and visit them more than 20 times a month. Heavy users "come more often, they spend more money, and that's what makes the cash registers ring," says a Burger King marketing executive. Interestingly, although fast-food companies such as Burger King, McDonald's, and KFC depend a lot on heavy users and do all they can to keep them satisfied with every visit, these companies often target light users with their ads and promotions. The heavy users "are in our restaurants already," says the Burger King marketer. The company's marketing dollars are more often spent trying to convince light users that they want a burger in the first place.[15]

Loyalty Status. A market can also be segmented by consumer loyalty. Consumers can be loyal to brands (Tide), stores (Wal-Mart), and companies (Ford). Buyers can be divided into groups according to their degree of loyalty. Some consumers are completely loyal—they buy one brand all the time. Others are somewhat loyal—they are loyal to two or three brands of a given product or favor one brand while sometimes buying others. Still other buyers show no loyalty to any brand. They either want something different each time they buy or they buy whatever's on sale.

A company can learn a lot by analyzing loyalty patterns in its market. It should start by studying its own loyal customers. For example, to better understand the needs and behavior of its core soft drink consumers, Pepsi observed them in places where its products are consumed—in homes, in stores, in movie theaters, at sporting events, and at the beach. "We learned that there's a surprising amount of loyalty and passion for Pepsi's products," says Pepsi's director of consumer insights. "One fellow had four or five cases of Pepsi in his basement and he felt he was low on Pepsi and had to go replenish." The company used these and other study findings to pinpoint the Pepsi target market and develop marketing appeals.[16]

By studying its less loyal buyers, the company can detect which brands are most competitive with its own. If many Pepsi buyers also buy Coke, Pepsi can attempt to improve its positioning against Coke, possibly by using direct-comparison advertising. By looking at customers who are shifting away from its brand, the company can learn about its marketing weaknesses. As for nonloyals, the company may attract them by putting its brand on sale.

Using Multiple Segmentation Bases Marketers rarely limit their segmentation analysis to only one or a few variables. Rather, they are increasingly using multiple segmentation bases in an effort to identify smaller, better-defined target groups. Thus, a bank may not only identify a group of wealthy retired adults but also, within that group, distinguish several segments based on their current income, assets, savings and risk preferences, and lifestyles. Companies often begin by segmenting their markets using a single base, then expand using other bases.

One good example of multivariable segmentation is "geodemographic" segmentation. Several business information services have arisen to help marketing planners link U.S. Census data with lifestyle patterns to better segment their markets down to ZIP codes, neighborhoods, and even city blocks. One of the leading lifestyle segmentation systems is PRIZM "You Are Where You Live" system by Claritas. By marrying a host of demographic factors—such as age, education, income, occupation, family life cycle, housing, ethnicity, and urbanization—with lifestyle information taken from consumer surveys, the PRIZM system classifies every one of the more than 260,000 U.S. neighborhoods into one of 62 clusters. Clusters carry such exotic names as "Kids & Cul-de-Sacs," "Blue Blood Estates," "Money & Brains," "Young Literati," "Shotguns & Pickups," "American Dreams," "New Eco-topias," "Mobility Blues," and "Gray Power."

Each cluster exhibits unique characteristics and buying behavior. For example, "Blue Blood Estates" neighborhoods are suburban areas populated by elite, super-rich families. People in this cluster are more likely to belong to health clubs, take expensive trips, buy classical music, and read *Architectural Digest*. In contrast, the "Shotguns & Pickups" cluster is populated by rural, blue-collar workers and families. People in this group are more likely to go fishing, use chain saws, own a dog, drink RC Cola, watch ESPN2, and read *Motor Trend*. People in the "Hispanic Mix" cluster are highly brand conscious, quality conscious, and brand loyal. They have a strong family and home orientation.

Such segmentation provides a powerful tool for segmenting markets, refining demand estimates, selecting target markets, and shaping promotion messages. For example, in marketing its Suave shampoo, Unilever's Helene Curtis division uses PRIZM to identify neighborhoods with high concentrations of working women. Such women respond best to advertising messages that with Suave, "looking great doesn't have to cost a fortune." Bookseller Barnes & Noble locates its stores where there are concentrations of

■ In marketing its Suave shampoo, Helene Curtis uses PRIZM to identify neighborhoods with high concentrations of working women. Such women respond best to advertising messages that with Suave, "looking great doesn't have to cost a fortune."

"Money & Brains" consumers, because they buy lots of books.[17]

Segmenting Business Markets

Consumer and business marketers use many of the same variables to segment their markets. Business buyers can be segmented geographically, demographically (industry, company size), or by benefits sought, user status, usage rate, and loyalty status. Yet, business marketers also use some additional variables, such as customer *operating characteristics*, *purchasing approaches*, *situational factors*, and *personal characteristics*.

By going after segments instead of the whole market, companies have a much better chance to deliver value to consumers and to receive maximum rewards for close attention to consumer needs. Hewlett-Packard's Computer Systems Division targets specific industries that promise the best growth prospects, such as telecommunications and financial services. Its "red team" sales force specializes in developing and serving major customers in these targeted industries.[18] Within the chosen industry, a company can further segment by *customer size* or *geographic location*. For example, Hewlett-Packard's "blue team" telemarkets to smaller accounts and to those that don't fit neatly into the strategically targeted industries on which HP focuses.

A company might also set up separate systems for dealing with larger or multiple-location customers. For example, Steelcase, a major producer of office furniture, first segments customers into 10 industries, including banking, insurance, and electronics. Next, company salespeople work with independent Steelcase dealers to handle smaller, local, or regional Steelcase customers in each segment. But many national, multiple-location customers, such as Exxon/Mobil or IBM, have special needs that may reach beyond the scope of individual dealers. So Steelcase uses national accounts managers to help its dealer networks handle its national accounts.

Within a given target industry and customer size, the company can segment by purchase approaches and criteria. As in consumer segmentation, many marketers believe that *buying behavior* and *benefits* provide the best basis for segmenting business markets.[19]

Segmenting International Markets

Few companies have either the resources or the will to operate in all, or even most, of the countries that dot the globe. Although some large companies, such as Coca-Cola or Sony, sell products in more than 200 countries, most international firms focus on a smaller set. Operating in many countries presents new challenges. Different countries, even those that are close together, can vary greatly in their economic, cultural, and political makeup. Thus, just as they do within their domestic markets, international firms need to group their world markets into segments with distinct buying needs and behaviors.

Companies can segment international markets using one or a combination of several variables. They can segment by *geographic location*, grouping countries by regions such as Western Europe, the Pacific Rim, the Middle East, or Africa. Geographic segmentation assumes that nations close to one another will have many common traits and behaviors. Although this is often the case, there are many exceptions. For example, although the United States and Canada have much in common, both differ culturally and economically from neighboring Mexico. Even within a region, consumers can differ widely. For example, many U.S. marketers think that all Central and South American countries are the same, including their 400 million inhabitants. However, the Dominican Republic is no more like Brazil than Italy is like Sweden. Many Latin Americans don't speak Spanish, including 140 million Portuguese-speaking Brazilians and the millions in other countries who speak a variety of Indian dialects.

World markets can also be segmented on the basis of *economic factors*. For example, countries might be grouped by population income levels or by their overall level of economic development. Some countries, such as the United States, Britain, France, Germany, Japan, Canada, Italy, and Russia, have established, highly industrialized economies. Other countries have newly industrialized or developing economies (Singapore, Taiwan, Korea, Brazil, Mexico). Still others are less developed (China, India). A company's economic structure shapes its population's product and service needs and, therefore, the marketing opportunities it offers.

Countries can be segmented by *political and legal factors* such as the type and stability of government, receptivity to foreign firms, monetary regulations, and the amount of bureaucracy. Such factors can play a crucial role in a company's choice of which countries to enter and how. *Cultural factors* can also be used, grouping markets according to common languages, religions, values and attitudes, customs, and behavioral patterns.

Segmenting international markets on the basis of geographic, economic, political, cultural, and other factors assumes that segments should consist of clusters of countries. However, many companies use a different approach called **intermarket segmentation**. Using this approach, they form segments of consumers who have similar needs and buying behavior even though they are located in different countries. For example, Mercedes-Benz targets the world's well-to-do, regardless of their country.

Intermarket segmentation
Forming segments of consumers who have similar needs and buying behavior even though they are located in different countries.

MTV targets the world's teenagers. The world's teens have a lot in common: They study, shop, and sleep. They are exposed to many of the same major issues: love, crime, homelessness, ecology, and working parents. In many ways, they have more in common with each other than with their parents. "Last year I was in seventeen different countries," says one expert, "and it's pretty difficult to find anything that is different, other then language, among a teenager in Japan, a teenager in the UK, and a teenager in China." Says another, "Global teens in Buenos Aires, Beijing, and Bangalore swing to the beat of MTV while sipping Coke." MTV bridges the gap between cultures, appealing to what teens around the world have in common. Sony, Reebok, Nike, Swatch, and many other firms also actively target global teens.[20]

■ Intermarket segmentation: Teens show surprising similarity no matter where in the world they live. For instance, these two teens could live almost anywhere. Thus, many companies target teenagers with worldwide marketing campaigns.

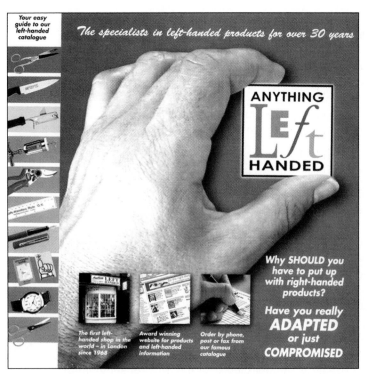

■ The "Leftie" segment can be hard to identify and measure. As a result, few companies tailor their offers to left-handers. However, some nichers such as Anything Left-Handed in the UK target this segment.

Requirements for Effective Segmentation

Clearly, there are many ways to segment a market, but not all segmentations are effective. For example, buyers of table salt could be divided into blond and brunette customers. But hair color obviously does not affect the purchase of salt. Furthermore, if all salt buyers bought the same amount of salt each month, believed that all salt is the same, and wanted to pay the same price, the company would not benefit from segmenting this market.

To be useful, market segments must be

■ *Measurable:* The size, purchasing power, and profiles of the segments can be measured. Certain segmentation variables are difficult to measure. For example, there are 32.5 million left-handed people in the United States—almost equaling the entire population of Canada. Yet few products are targeted toward this left-handed segment. The major problem may be that the segment is hard to identify and measure. There are no data on the demographics of lefties, and the U.S. Census Bureau does not keep track of left-handedness in its surveys. Private data companies keep reams of statistics on other demographic segments but not on left-handers. As a result, only market nichers like Anything Left-Handed in the UK target this segment.

■ *Accessible:* The market segments can be effectively reached and served. Suppose a fragrance company finds that heavy users of its brand are single men and women who stay out late and socialize a lot. Unless this group lives or shops at certain places and is exposed to certain media, its members will be difficult to reach.

■ *Substantial:* The market segments are large or profitable enough to serve. A segment should be the largest possible homogeneous group worth pursuing with a tailored marketing program. It would not pay, for example, for an automobile manufacturer to develop cars especially for people whose height is greater than seven feet.

■ *Differentiable:* The segments are conceptually distinguishable and respond differently to different marketing mix elements and programs. If married and unmarried women respond similarly to a sale on perfume, they do not constitute separate segments.

■ *Actionable:* Effective programs can be designed for attracting and serving the segments. For example, although one small airline identified seven market segments, its staff was too small to develop separate marketing programs for each segment.

SPEED BUMP

Linking the Concepts

Slow down a bit and smell the roses. How do the companies you do business with employ the segmentation concepts you're reading about here?

■ Can you identify specific companies, other than the examples already discussed, which practice the different types of segmentation just discussed?

■ Using the segmentation bases you've just read about, segment the U.S. footwear market. Describe each of the major segments and subsegments. Keep these segments in mind as you read the next section on target marketing.

Target Marketing

Market segmentation reveals the firm's market segment opportunities. The firm now has to evaluate the various segments and decide how many and which segments it can serve best. We now look at how companies evaluate and select target segments.

Evaluating Market Segments

In evaluating different market segments, a firm must look at three factors: segment size and growth, segment structural attractiveness, and company objectives and resources.

Segment Size and Growth   The company must first collect and analyze data on current segment sales, growth rates, and expected profitability for various segments. It will be interested in segments that have the right size and growth characteristics. But "right size and growth" is a relative matter. The largest, fastest-growing segments are not always the most attractive ones for every company. Smaller companies may lack the skills and resources needed to serve the larger segments. Or they may find these segments too competitive. Such companies may select segments that are smaller and less attractive, in an absolute sense, but that are potentially more profitable for them.

Segment Structural Attractiveness   The company also needs to examine major structural factors that affect long-run segment attractiveness.[21] For example, a segment is less attractive if it already contains many strong and aggressive *competitors*. The existence of many actual or potential *substitute products* may limit prices and the profits that can be earned in a segment. The relative *power of buyers* also affects segment attractiveness. Buyers with strong bargaining power relative to sellers will try to force prices down, demand more services, and set competitors against one another—all at the expense of seller profitability. Finally, a segment may be less attractive if it contains *powerful suppliers* who can control prices or reduce the quality or quantity of ordered goods and services.

Company Objectives and Resources   Even if a segment has the right size and growth and is structurally attractive, the company must consider its own objectives and resources in relation to that segment. Some attractive segments could be dismissed quickly because they do not mesh with the company's long-run objectives. The company must consider whether it possesses the skills and resources needed to succeed in that segment. If the company lacks the needed strengths and cannot readily obtain them, it should not enter the segment. Even if the company possesses the *required* strengths, it needs to employ skills and resources *superior* to those of the competition in order to really win in a market segment. The company should enter only segments in which it can offer superior value and gain advantages over competitors.

Selecting Target Segments

After evaluating different segments, the company must now decide which and how many segments it will target. A **target market** consists of a set of buyers who share common needs or characteristics that the company decides to serve.

Because buyers have unique needs and wants, a seller could potentially view each buyer as a separate target market. Ideally, then, a seller might design a separate marketing program for each buyer. However, although some companies do attempt to serve buyers individually, most face larger numbers of smaller buyers and do not find individual targeting worthwhile. Instead, they look for broader segments of buyers. More generally, target marketing can be carried out at several different levels. Figure 6.2 shows that companies can target very broadly (undifferentiated marketing), very narrowly (micromarketing), or somewhere in between (differentiated or concentrated marketing).

Target market

A set of buyers sharing common needs or characteristics that the company decides to serve.

FIGURE 6.2
Target Marketing Strategies

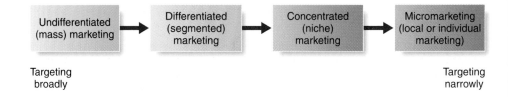

Targeting
broadly

Targeting
narrowly

Undifferentiated (mass) marketing

A market-coverage strategy in which a firm decides to ignore market segment differences and go after the whole market with one offer.

Undifferentiated Marketing Using an **undifferentiated marketing** (or **mass marketing**) strategy, a firm might decide to ignore market segment differences and target the whole market with one offer. This mass-marketing strategy focuses on what is *common* in the needs of consumers rather than on what is *different*. The company designs a product and a marketing program that will appeal to the largest number of buyers. It relies on mass distribution and mass advertising, and it aims to give the product a superior image in people's minds.

As noted earlier in the chapter, most modern marketers have strong doubts about this strategy. Difficulties arise in developing a product or brand that will satisfy all consumers. Moreover, mass marketers often have trouble competing with more focused firms that do a better job of satisfying the needs of specific segments and niches.

Differentiated (segmented) marketing

A market-coverage strategy in which a firm decides to target several market segments and designs separate offers for each.

Differentiated Marketing Using a **differentiated marketing** (or **segmented marketing**) strategy, a firm decides to target several market segments and designs separate offers for each. General Motors tries to produce a car for every "purse, purpose, and personality." Nike offers athletic shoes for a dozen or more different sports, from running, fencing, golf, and aerobics to baseball and bicycling. Marriott markets to a variety of segments—business travelers, families, and others—with hotel formats and packages adapted to their varying needs. And American Express offers not only its traditional green cards but also gold cards, platinum cards, corporate cards, and even a black card, called the Centurian, with a $1,000 annual fee aimed at a segment of "superpremium customers."

Estée Lauder offers dozens of different products aimed at carefully defined segments:

> The four best-selling prestige perfumes in the United States belong to Estée Lauder. So do 7 of the top 10 prestige makeup products and 8 of the 10 best-selling prestige skin care products. Estée Lauder is an expert in creating differentiated brands that serve the tastes of different market segments. There's the original Estée Lauder brand, which appeals to older, Junior League types. Then there's Clinique, perfect for the middle-aged mom with a GMC Suburban and no time to waste. For the youthful hipster, there's the hip M.A.C. line. And, for the New Age type, there's upscale Aveda, with its aromatherapy line, and earthy Origins, which the company expects will become a $1 billion brand. The company even offers downscale brands, such as Jane by Sassaby, for teens at Wal-Mart and Rite Aid.[22]

By offering product and marketing variations to segments, companies hope for higher sales and a stronger position within each market segment. Developing a stronger position within several segments creates more total sales than undifferentiated marketing across all segments. Procter & Gamble gets more total market share with seven brands of laundry detergent than it could with only one. And Estée Lauder's combined brands give it a much greater market share than any single brand could. The Estée Lauder and Clinique brands alone reap a combined 40 percent share of the prestige cosmetics market.

But differentiated marketing also increases the costs of doing business. A firm usually finds it more expensive to develop and produce, say, 10 units of 10 different products than 100 units of 1 product. Developing separate marketing plans for the separate segments requires extra marketing research, forecasting, sales analysis, promotion planning, and channel management. And trying to reach different market segments with different advertising increases promotion costs. Thus, the company must weigh increased sales against increased costs when deciding on a differentiated marketing strategy.

Concentrated Marketing   A third market-coverage strategy, **concentrated marketing** (or **niche marketing**), is especially appealing when company resources are limited. Instead of going after a small share of a large market, the firm goes after a large share of one or a few segments or niches. For example, Oshkosh Truck is the world's largest producer of airport rescue trucks and front-loading concrete mixers. Tetra sells 80 percent of the world's tropical fish food, and Steiner Optical captures 80 percent of the world's military binoculars market.

Concentrated (niche) marketing
A market-coverage strategy in which a firm goes after a large share of one or a few segments, or niches.

Whereas segments are fairly large and normally attract several competitors, niches are smaller and may attract only one or a few competitors. Through concentrated marketing, the firm achieves a strong market position because of its greater knowledge of consumer needs in the niches it serves and the special reputation it acquires. It can market more *effectively* by fine-tuning its products, prices, and programs to the needs of carefully defined segments. It can also market more *efficiently*, targeting its products or services, channels, and communications programs toward only the consumers that it can serve best and most profitably.

Niching offers smaller companies an opportunity to compete by focusing their limited resources on serving niches that may be unimportant to or overlooked by larger competitors. Consider Apple Computer. Although it once enjoyed a better than 13 percent market share, Apples now a market nicher, capturing only about 3.5 percent of its market. Rather than competing head-on with other PC makers as they slash prices and focus on volume, Apple invests in research and development, making it the industry trendsetter. Such innovation has created a loyal base of consumers who are willing to pay more for Apple's cutting edge products.[23]

■ Niching: Rather than competing head-on with other PC makers, Apple has invested in research and development, creating a loyal base of consumers who are willing to pay more for Apple's cutting edge products.

Many companies start as nichers to get a foothold against larger, more resourceful competitors, then grow into broader competitors. For example, Southwest Airlines began by serving intrastate, no-frills commuters in Texas but is now one of the nation's eight largest airlines. Wal-Mart, which got its start by bringing everyday low prices to small towns and rural areas, is now the world's largest company. In contrast, as markets change, some mega-marketers are developing niche markets to create sales growth. For example, Pepsi has recently introduced several products that appeal to specific niche markets, such as Sierra Mist, Pepsi Blue, and Mountain Dew Code Red. Together, these brands account for barely 5 percent of Pepsi's overall soft-drink sales. That may not seem much, but that's the idea. Says Pepsi-Cola North America's chief marketing officer, "The era of the mass brand has been over for a long time."[24]

Today, the low cost of setting up shop on the Internet makes it even more profitable to serve seemingly minuscule niches. Small businesses, in particular, are realizing riches from serving small niches on the Web. Here is a "Webpreneur" who achieved astonishing results:

Whereas Internet giants like Amazon.com have yet to even realize a consistent profit, Steve Warrington is earning a six-figure income selling ostriches— and every product derived from them—online (www.ostrichesonline.com). Launched for next to nothing on the Web in 1996, Ostrichesonline.com now boasts that it sends newsletters to 33,000 subscribers and sells 17,500 ostrich products to more than 18,000 satisfied clients in more than 125 countries. The site tells visitors everything they ever wanted to know about ostriches and much,

much more—it supplies ostrich facts, ostrich pictures, an ostrich farm index, and a huge ostrich database and reference index. Visitors to the site can buy ostrich meat, feathers, leather jackets, videos, eggshells, and skin care products derived from ostrich body oil.[25]

Concentrated marketing can be highly profitable. At the same time, it involves higher-than-normal risks. Companies that rely on one or a few segments for all of their business will suffer greatly if the segment turns sour. Or larger competitors may decide to enter the same segment. California Cooler's early success in the wine cooler segment attracted many large competitors, causing the original owners to sell to a larger company that had more marketing resources. For these reasons, many companies prefer to diversify in several market segments.

Micromarketing Differentiated and concentrated marketers tailor their offers and marketing programs to meet the needs of various market segments and niches. At the same time, however, they do not customize their offers to each individual customer. **Micromarketing** is the practice of tailoring products and marketing programs to suit the tastes of specific individuals and locations. Rather than seeing a customer in every individual, micromarketers see the individual in every customer. Micromarketing includes *local marketing* and *individual marketing*.

Local Marketing. **Local marketing** involves tailoring brands and promotions to the needs and wants of local customer groups—cities, neighborhoods, and even specific stores. Retailers such as Sears and Wal-Mart routinely customize each store's merchandise and promotions to match its specific clientele. Citibank provides different mixes of banking services in its branches, depending on neighborhood demographics. Kraft helps supermarket chains identify the specific cheese assortments and shelf positioning that will optimize cheese sales in low-income, middle-income, and high-income stores and in different ethnic communities.

Micromarketing
The practice of tailoring products and marketing programs to the needs and wants of specific individuals and local customer groups—includes *local marketing* and *individual marketing*.

Local marketing
Tailoring brands and promotions to the needs and wants of local customer groups—cities, neighborhoods, and even specific stores.

Local marketing has some drawbacks. It can drive up manufacturing and marketing costs by reducing economies of scale. It can also create logistics problems, as companies try to meet the varied requirements of different regional and local markets. Furthermore, a brand's overall image might be diluted if the product and message vary too much in different localities.

Still, as companies face increasingly fragmented markets, and as new supporting technologies develop, the advantages of local marketing often outweigh the drawbacks. Local marketing helps a company to market more effectively in the face of pronounced regional and local differences in demographics and lifestyles. It also meets the needs of the company's first-line customers—retailers—who prefer more fine-tuned product assortments for their neighborhoods.

■ Local marketing: Some marketers tailor their offers to the needs and wants of local customers. Video screens in some Eddie Bauer storefront windows allow each store to customize in-store advertising to its specific customer mix.

Individual marketing
Tailoring products and marketing programs to the needs and preferences of individual customers—also labeled "markets-of-one marketing," "customized marketing," and "one-to-one marketing."

Individual Marketing. In the extreme, micromarketing becomes **individual marketing**—tailoring products and marketing programs to the needs and preferences of individual customers. Individual marketing has also been labeled *one-to-one marketing, customized marketing,* and *markets-of-one marketing*.

The widespread use of mass marketing has obscured the fact that for centuries consumers were served as individuals: The tailor custom-made the suit, the cobbler designed shoes for the individual, the cabinetmaker made furniture to order. Today, however, new technologies are permitting many companies to return to customized marketing. More powerful computers, detailed databases, robotic production and flexible manufacturing, and interactive communication media such as e-mail, fax, and the Internet—all have combined to foster "mass customization." *Mass customization* is the process through which firms interact one-to-one with masses of customers to design products and services tailor-made to individual needs (see Marketing at Work 6.2).

Dell Computer delivers computers to individual customers loaded with customer-specified hardware and software. Hockey stick maker Branches Hockey lets customers choose from more than two-dozen options—including stick length, blade patterns, and blade curve—and turns out a customized stick in five days. And Ritz-Carlton Hotels creates custom-designed experiences for its delighted guests:

> Check into any Ritz-Carlton hotel around the world, and you'll be amazed at how well the hotel's employees anticipate your slightest need. Without ever asking, they seem to know that you want a nonsmoking room with a king-size bed, a nonallergenic pillow, and breakfast with decaffeinated coffee in your room. How does Ritz-Carlton work this magic? The hotel employs a system that combines information technology and flexible operations to customize the hotel experience. At the heart of the system is a huge customer database, which contains information gathered through the observations of hotel employees. Each day, hotel staffers—from those at the front desk to those in maintenance and housekeeping—discreetly record the unique habits, likes, and dislikes of each guest on small "guest preference pads." These observations are then transferred to a corporatewide "guest preference database." Every morning, a "guest historian" at each hotel reviews the files of all new arrivals who have previously stayed at a Ritz-Carlton and prepares a list of suggested extra touches that might delight each guest. Guests have responded strongly to such markets-of-one service. Since inaugurating the guest-history system, Ritz-Carlton has boosted guest retention by 23 percent. An amazing 95 percent of departing guests report that their stay has been a truly memorable experience. Business-to-business marketers are also finding new ways to customize their offerings.

For example, Becton-Dickinson, a major medical supplier, offers to customize almost anything for its hospital customers. It offers custom-designed labeling, individual packaging, customized quality control, customized computer software, and customized billing. And John Deere manufactures seeding equipment that can be configured in more than 2 million versions to individual customer specifications. The seeders are produced one at a time, in any sequence, on a single production line.[26]

The move toward individual marketing mirrors the trend in consumer *self-marketing*. Increasingly, individual customers are taking more responsibility for determining which products and brands to buy. Consider two business buyers with two different purchasing styles. The first sees several salespeople, each trying to persuade him to buy his or her product. The second sees no salespeople but rather logs on to the Internet. She searches for information on available products; interacts electronically with various suppliers, users, and product analysts; and then makes up her own mind about the best offer. The second purchasing agent has taken more responsibility for the buying process, and the marketer has had less influence over her buying decision.

As the trend toward more interactive dialogue and less advertising monologue continues, self-marketing will grow in importance. As more buyers look up consumer reports, join Internet product discussion forums, and place orders via phone or online, marketers will have to influence the buying process in new ways. Many companies now practice *customerization*.[27] They combine operationally driven mass customization with customized marketing to empower consumers to design products and services to their own preferences. They involve customers more in all phases of the product development and buying processes, increasing opportunities for buyers to practice self-marketing.

Choosing a Target Marketing Strategy Companies need to consider many factors when choosing a target-marketing strategy. Which strategy is best depends on *company resources*. When the firm's resources are limited, concentrated marketing makes

Marketing at Work   6.2

Markets of One: Treating Customers As Individuals

Imagine walking into a booth that bathes your body in patterns of white light and, in a matter of seconds, captures your exact three-dimensional form. The digitized data are then imprinted on a credit card, which you use to order customized clothing. No, this isn't a scene from the next Star Wars sequel; it's a peek ahead at how you will be able to buy clothing in the not-so-distant future. A consortium of over 100 apparel companies, including Levi-Strauss, has banded together to develop body-scanning technology in the hope of making mass customization commonplace.

Although body-scanning technology and smart cards carrying customer measurements are still in development, many companies are now using existing technologies to tailor products to individual customers. Dell creates custom-configured computers, Reflect.com formulates customized beauty products,

Ford lets buyers "build a vehicle" from a palette of options, and Golf to Fit crafts custom clubs based on consumer measurements and preferences. Companies selling all kinds of products—from candy, clothing, and hockey sticks to fire trucks—are customizing their offerings to the needs of individual buyers.

Here are some other examples of companies in the forefront of the mass-customization economy:

Levi-Strauss. *In 1994, Levi began making measure-to-fit women's jeans under its in-store Personal Pair program. Consumer response was so positive that Levi developed an expanded in-store customization concept called Original Spin, which works a lot like the futuristic sizing scenario described above. Original Spin lets buyers create their own jeans from scratch or modify an*

existing pair. Customers—both men and women—enter a booth in which a 3-D Body Scanner creates personalized measurements against a backdrop of strobe lights and space-age music. Using the Original Spin terminals, customers can then choose from a range of cuts and styles that represent hundreds of different pairs of jeans available for purchase. Whereas a fully stocked Levi's store carries 130 pairs of ready-to-wear jeans for a given waist and inseam, with Original Spin the number jumps to 750.

Mattel. *Girls can log on to the "My Design" page of the Barbie Web site (www.barbie.com) and create their very own "friend of Barbie" doll. They choose the doll's skin tone, eye color, hairstyle and hair color, clothes, accessories, personality, and name. They even fill out a questionnaire detailing their doll's likes*

Mass customization: M&M's Colorworks site lets customers special order the tasty little candies in whatever combination of 21 colors suits their fancy.

and dislikes. When Barbie's special friend arrives in the mail, the girls find the doll's name on the packaging along with a computer-generated paragraph about her personality.

Mars M&Ms. Looking to sweeten up a party or special celebration? Try the M&M's Colorworks site, where you can special order the tasty little candies in whatever combination of colors suits your fancy. Mix up a patriotic combo of red, white, and blue M&Ms for the chocolate lovers at your Fourth of July celebration. Or special order a blend of your school colors for the next tailgate party. Send promotional packs featuring your company colors to special customers. Don't know what colors to choose? No problem. The site is packed with suggestions for just about any occasion. Colorworks lets you pick from a palette of 21 colors and order in 8-ounce or 5-pound customized bags. It's a bit spendy—nearly three times the cost of regular M&Ms. But business is booming, with sales doubling every year. Next up? Along with the famous "m" on its candies, the company is trying out personalized messages. How about "boo" your Halloween M&Ms, or "HO HO HO" at Christmas? "Want to see your name on a batch of aqua-green M&Ms?" asks one analyst. "It could happen."

Consumer goods marketers aren't the only ones going one-to-one. B2B marketers also provide customers with tailor-made goods, often more cheaply and quickly than it used to take to make standardized ones. Particularly for small companies, mass customization provides a way to stand out against larger competitors:

Oshkosh Truck. Oshkosh Truck specializes in making fire, garbage,

cement, and military trucks. Oshkosh is small—one-tenth the size of larger rivals such as Paccar and Navistar International—and the truck industry is slumping. Yet Oshkosh has more than doubled its sales and increased its earnings sixfold over the past five years. What's the secret to Oshkosh's success? Mass customization—the ability to personalize its products and services to the needs of individual customers. For example, when firefighters order a truck from Oshkosh, it's an event. They travel to the plant to watch the vehicle, which may cost as much as $800,000, take shape. The firefighters can choose from 19,000 options. A stripped-down fire truck costs $130,000, but 75 percent of Oshkosh's customers order lots of extras, like hideaway stairs, ladders, special doors, compartments, and firefighting foam systems for those difficult-to-extinguish fires. Some bring along paint chips so they can customize the color of their fleet. Others are content just to admire the vehicles, down to the water tanks and hideaway ladders. "Some chiefs even bring their wives; we encourage it," says the president of Oshkosh's firefighting unit, Pierce Manufacturing. "Buying a fire truck is a very personal thing." Indeed, Pierce customers are in town so often the Holiday Inn renamed its lounge the Hook and Ladder. Through such customization and personalization, smaller Oshkosh has gained a big edge over its languishing larger rivals.

Two trends underlie the growth in one-to-one marketing. First, today's consumers have very high expectations—they expect products and services that meet their individual needs. Yet, it would be too expensive or downright impossible to meet these individual demands if it weren't for another

trend: rapid advances in technology. Data warehouses now allow companies to store trillions of bytes of customer information. Computer-controlled factory equipment and industrial robots can now quickly readjust assembly lines. Bar code scanners make it possible to track parts and products. Most important, the Internet ties it all together and makes it easy for a company to interact with customers, learn about their preferences, and respond. Indeed, the Internet appears to be the ultimate one-to-one medium.

Unlike mass production, which eliminates the need for human interaction, mass customization has made relationships with customers more important than ever. For instance, when Levi's sells made-to-order jeans, the company not only captures consumer data in digitized form but also becomes the customer's "jeans adviser." And Mattel is building a database of information on all the customers of My Design dolls so it can start long-term, one-to-one relationships with each customer.

Just as mass production was the marketing principle of the past century, mass customization is becoming a marketing principle for the twenty-first century. The world appears to be coming full circle—from the good old days when customers were treated as individuals, to mass marketing when nobody knew your name, and back again.

Sources: See James H. Gilmore and B. Joseph Pine, Markets of One: Creating Customer-Unique Value Through Mass Customization (Boston: Harvard Business School Press, 2001); Don Peppers and Martha Rogers, One to One B2B: Customer Development Strategies for the Business-to-Business World (New York, NY: Doubleday, 2001); Faith Keenan, "A Mass Market of One," Business Week, December 2, 2002, pp. 68–72; "Oshkosh Truck Corporation," Hoover's Company Profiles, Austin, May 15, 2003; and information accessed at www.us.levi.com, www.colorworks.com, www.Barbie.com/Activities/Fashion_Fun/MyDesign/look.asp, and www.oshkoshtruck.com, October 2003.

the most sense. The best strategy also depends on the degree of *product variability*. Undifferentiated marketing is more suited for uniform products such as grapefruit or steel. Products that can vary in design, such as cameras and automobiles, are more suited to differentiation or concentration.

The *product's life-cycle stage* also must be considered. When a firm introduces a new product, it may be practical to launch only one version, and undifferentiated marketing or concentrated marketing may make the most sense. In the mature stage of the product life cycle, however, differentiated marketing begins to make more sense. Another factor is *market variability*. If most buyers have the same tastes, buy the same amounts, and react the same way to marketing efforts, undifferentiated marketing is appropriate. Finally, *competitors' marketing strategies* are important. When competitors use differentiated or concentrated marketing, undifferentiated marketing can be suicidal. Conversely, when competitors use undifferentiated marketing, a firm can gain an advantage by using differentiated or concentrated marketing.

Socially Responsible Target Marketing

Smart targeting helps companies to be more efficient and effective by focusing on the segments that they can satisfy best and most profitably. Targeting also benefits consumers—companies reach specific groups of consumers with offers carefully tailored to satisfy their needs. However, target marketing sometimes generates controversy and concern. Issues usually involve the targeting of vulnerable or disadvantaged consumers with controversial or potentially harmful products.

For example, over the years, the cereal industry has been heavily criticized for its marketing efforts directed toward children. Critics worry that premium offers and high-powered advertising appeals presented through the mouths of lovable animated characters will overwhelm children's defenses. The marketers of toys and other children's products have been similarly battered, often with good justification.

Other problems arise when the marketing of adult products spills over into the kid segment—intentionally or unintentionally. For example, the Federal Trade Commission and citizen action groups have accused tobacco companies of targeting underage smokers. And a recent FTC study found that 80 percent of R-rated movies and 70 percent of video games with a mature rating were targeted to children under 17.[28] Some critics have even called for a complete ban on advertising to children. To encourage responsible advertising to children, the Children's Advertising Review Unit, the advertising industry's self-regulatory agency, has published extensive children's advertising guidelines that recognize the special needs of child audiences.

Cigarette, beer, and fast-food marketers have also generated much controversy in recent years by their attempts to target inner-city minority consumers. For example, McDonald's and other chains have drawn criticism for pitching their high-fat, salt-laden fare to low-income, inner-city residents, who are much more likely than are suburbanites to be heavy consumers. Last year, McDonald's faced lawsuits alleging that its marketing practices are responsible for teenage obesity. Similarly, R.J. Reynolds took heavy flak in the early 1990s when it announced plans to market Uptown, a menthol cigarette targeted toward low-income blacks. It quickly dropped the brand in the face of a loud public outcry and heavy pressure from black leaders.

G. Heileman Brewing made a similar mistake with PowerMaster, a potent malt liquor. Because malt liquor had become the drink of choice among many in the inner city, Heileman focused its marketing efforts for PowerMaster on inner-city consumers. However, this group suffers disproportionately from liver diseases brought on by alcohol, and the inner city is already plagued by alcohol-related problems such as crime and violence. Thus, Heileman's targeting decision drew substantial criticism.[29]

The meteoric growth of the Internet and other carefully targeted direct media has raised fresh concerns about potential targeting abuses. The Internet allows increasing refinement of audiences and, in turn, more precise targeting. This might help makers of questionable products or deceptive advertisers to more readily victimize the most vulnerable audiences.

As one expert observes, "In theory, an audience member could have tailor-made deceptive messages sent directly to his or her computer screen."[30]

Not all attempts to target children, minorities, or other special segments draw such criticism. In fact, most provide benefits to targeted consumers. For example, Colgate makes a large selection of toothbrushes and toothpaste flavors and packages for children—from Colgate Barbie Sparkling Bubble Fruit, Colgate Barney Mild Bubble Fruit, and Colgate Looney Tunes Tazmanian Devil Wild Mint toothpastes to Colgate Pokemon and Disney Monsters, Inc. character toothbrushes. Such products help make tooth brushing more fun and get children to brush longer and more often.

Golden Ribbon Playthings developed a highly acclaimed and very successful black character doll named "Huggy Bean" targeted toward minority consumers. Huggy comes with books and toys that connect her with her African heritage. Nacara Cosmetiques markets cosmetics for "ethnic women

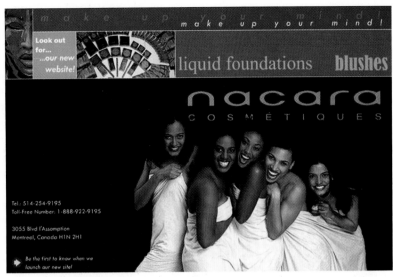

■ Most target marketing benefits both the marketer and the consumer. Nacara Cosmetiques markets cosmetics for "ethnic women who have a thirst for the exotic."

who have a thirst for the exotic." The line is specially formulated to complement the darker skin tones of African American women and dark-skinned women of Latin American, Indian, and Caribbean origins. Black-owned ICE theaters noticed that although moviegoing by blacks has surged, there are few inner-city theaters. The chain has opened a theater in Chicago's South Side as well as two other Chicago theaters, and it plans to open in four more cities this year. ICE partners with the black communities in which it operates theaters, using local radio stations to promote films and featuring favorite food items at concession stands.

Thus, in target marketing, the issue is not really *who* is targeted but rather *how* and for *what*. Controversies arise when marketers attempt to profit at the expense of targeted segments—when they unfairly target vulnerable segments or target them with questionable products or tactics. Socially responsible marketing calls for segmentation and targeting that serve not just the interests of the company but also the interests of those targeted.

Linking the Concepts

SPEED BUMP

Time to coast for a bit and take stock.

■ At the last speed bump, you segmented the U.S. footwear market. Refer to Figure 6.2 and select two companies that serve this market. Describe their segmentation and targeting strategies. Can you come up with one that targets many different segments versus another that focuses on only one or a few segments?

■ How does each company you chose differentiate its marketing offer and image? Has each done a good job of establishing this differentiation in the minds of targeted consumers? The final section in this chapter deals with such positioning issues.

■ Positioning for Competitive Advantage

Product position
The way the product is defined by consumers on important attributes—the place the product occupies in consumers' minds relative to competing products.

Beyond deciding which segments of the market it will target, the company must decide what positions it wants to occupy in those segments. A **product's position** is the way the product is *defined by consumers* on important attributes—the place the product occupies

CAPPUCCINO & TIRAMISU

WE LOVE WHEN YOU HATE TO LEAVE.

*When you're here,
you're Family.*

■ Positioning: At Olive Garden restaurants, "When You're Here, You're Family."

in consumers' minds relative to competing products. Positioning involves implanting the brand's unique benefits and differentiation in customers' minds.

Tide is positioned as a powerful, all-purpose family detergent; Ivory Snow is positioned as the gentle detergent for fine washables and baby clothes. At Subway restaurants, you "Eat Fresh"; at Olive Garden restaurants, "When You're Here, You're Family." In the automobile market, the Toyota Echo and Ford Focus are positioned on economy, Mercedes and Cadillac on luxury, and Porsche and BMW on performance. Volvo positions itself powerfully on safety. And Toyota positions its fuel-efficient, hybrid Prius as a high-tech solution to the energy shortage. "How far will you go to save the planet?" it asks.

Consumers are overloaded with information about products and services. They cannot reevaluate products every time they make a buying decision. To simplify the buying process, consumers organize products, services, and companies into categories and "position" them in their minds. A product's position is the complex set of perceptions, impressions, and feelings that consumers have for the product compared with competing products.

Consumers position products with or without the help of marketers. But marketers do not want to leave their products' positions to chance. They must *plan* positions that will give their products the greatest advantage in selected target markets, and they must design marketing mixes to create these planned positions.

Positioning Maps

In planning their positioning strategies, marketers often prepare *perceptual positioning maps,* which show consumer perceptions of their brands versus competing products on important buying dimensions. Figure 6.3 shows a positioning map for the U.S. large luxury sport utility vehicle market.[31] The position of each circle on the map indicates the brand's perceived positioning on two dimensions—price and orientation (luxury versus performance). The size of each circle indicates the brand's relative market share. Thus, customers view the market-leading Cadillac Escalade as a moderately-priced large luxury SUV with a balance of luxury and performance.

The original Hummer H1 was positioned as a very high performance SUV with a price tag to match. Hummer targets the H1 toward a small segment of well-off rugged individualists. According to the H1 Web site, "The H1 was built around one central philosophy: function. Every aspect of the H1 was created to allow it to go where cars and trucks just aren't supposed to go. [It] gives you an incredible sense of freedom and allows you to experience the world and your place in it." By contrast, although also oriented toward performance, the Hummer H2 is positioned as a more luxury-oriented and more reasonably priced luxury SUV. The H2 is targeted toward a larger segment of urban and suburban professionals. "In a world where SUVs have begun to look like their owners, complete with love handles and mushy seats, the H2 proves that there is still one out there that can drop and give you twenty," says the H2 Web site. The H2 "strikes a perfect balance between interior comfort, on-the-road capability, and off-road capability."

Choosing a Positioning Strategy

Some firms find it easy to choose their positioning strategy. For example, a firm well known for quality in certain segments will go for this position in a new segment if there are enough buyers seeking quality. But in many cases, two or more firms will go after the same position. Then, each will have to find other ways to set itself apart. Each firm must differentiate its offer by building a unique bundle of benefits that appeals to a substantial group within the segment.

The positioning task consists of three steps: identifying a set of possible competitive advantages on which to build a position, choosing the right competitive advantages, and

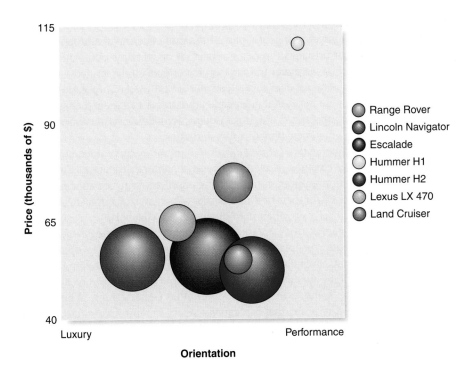

FIGURE 6.3
Positioning Map: Large Luxury SUVs

selecting an overall positioning strategy. The company must then effectively communicate and deliver the chosen position to the market.

Identifying Possible Competitive Advantages   The key to winning target customers and building profitable relationships with them is to understand their needs better than competitors do and to deliver more value. To the extent that a company can position itself as providing superior value, it gains **competitive advantage**. But solid positions cannot be built on empty promises. If a company positions its product as *offering* the best quality and service, it must then *deliver* the promised quality and service. Thus, positioning begins with actually *differentiating* the company's marketing offer so that it will give consumers more value than competitors' offers do.

To find points of differentiation, marketers must think through the customer's entire experience with the company's product or service. An alert company can find ways to differentiate itself at every point where it comes in contact with customers. In what specific ways can a company differentiate its offer from those of competitors? A company or market offer can be differentiated along the lines of *product, services, channels, people,* or *image.*

Product differentiation takes place along a continuum. At one extreme we find physical products that allow little variation: chicken, steel, aspirin. Yet even here some meaningful differentiation is possible. For example, Perdue claims that its branded chickens are better—fresher and more tender—and gets a 10 percent price premium based on this differentiation. At the other extreme are products that can be highly differentiated, such as automobiles, clothing, and furniture. Such products can be differentiated on features, performance, or style and design. Thus, Volvo provides new and better safety features; Whirlpool designs its dishwasher to run more quietly; Bose positions its speakers on their striking design characteristics. Similarly, companies can differentiate their products on attributes such as consistency, durability, reliability, or repairability.

Beyond differentiating its physical product, a firm can also differentiate the services that accompany the product. Some companies gain *services differentiation* through speedy, convenient, or careful delivery. For example, BankOne has opened full-service branches in supermarkets to provide location convenience along with Saturday, Sunday, and weekday-evening hours.

Competitive advantage
An advantage over competitors gained by offering consumers greater value, either through lower prices or by providing more benefits that justify higher prices.

Installation can also differentiate one company from another, as can repair services. Many an automobile buyer will gladly pay a little more and travel a little farther to buy a car from a dealer that provides top-notch repair services. Some companies differentiate their offers by providing customer training service or consulting services—data, information systems, and advising services that buyers need. McKesson Corporation, a major drug wholesaler, consults with its 12,000 independent pharmacists to help them set up accounting, inventory, and computerized ordering systems. By helping its customers compete better, McKesson gains greater customer loyalty and sales.

Firms that practice *channel differentiation* gain competitive advantage through the way they design their channel's coverage, expertise, and performance. Caterpillar's success in the construction-equipment industry is based on superior channels. Its dealers worldwide are renowned for their first-rate service. And Amazon.com, Dell Computer, and Avon distinguish themselves by their high-quality direct channels.

Companies can gain a strong competitive advantage through *people differentiation*—hiring and training better people than their competitors do. Disney people are known to be friendly and upbeat. Singapore Airlines enjoys an excellent reputation largely because of the grace of its flight attendants. IBM offers people who make sure that the solution customers want is the solution they get: "People Who Get It. People Who Get It Done." People differentiation requires that a company select its customer-contact people carefully and train them well. For example, Disney trains its theme park people thoroughly to ensure that they are competent, courteous, and friendly—from the hotel check-in agents, to the monorail drivers, to the ride attendants, to the people who sweep Main Street USA. Each employee is carefully trained to understand customers and to "make people happy."

Even when competing offers look the same, buyers may perceive a difference based on company or brand *image differentiation*. A company or brand image should convey the product's distinctive benefits and positioning. Developing a strong and distinctive image calls for creativity and hard work. A company cannot develop an image in the public's mind overnight using only a few advertisements. If Ritz-Carlton means quality, this image must be supported by everything the company says and does. Symbols—such as the McDonald's golden arches, the Prudential rock, the Nike swoosh, the Intel Inside logo, or the Pillsbury doughboy—can provide strong company or brand recognition and image differentiation. The company might build a brand around a famous person, as Nike did with its Air Jordan basketball shoes and Tiger Woods golfing products. Some companies even become associated with colors, such as IBM (blue), Campbell (red and white), or UPS (brown). The chosen symbols, characters, and other image elements must be communicated through advertising that conveys the company's or brand's personality.

Choosing the Right Competitive Advantages

Suppose a company is fortunate enough to discover several potential competitive advantages. It now must choose the ones on which it will build its positioning strategy. It must decide *how many* differences to promote and *which ones*.

How Many Differences to Promote? Many marketers think that companies should aggressively promote only one benefit to the target market. Ad man Rosser Reeves, for example, said a company should develop a *unique selling proposition* (USP) for each brand and stick to it. Each brand should pick an attribute and tout itself as "number one" on that attribute. Buyers tend to remember number one better, especially in an overcommunicated society. Thus, Crest toothpaste consistently promotes its anticavity protection and Volvo promotes safety. A company that hammers away at one of these positions and consistently delivers on it probably will become best known and remembered for it.

Other marketers think that companies should position themselves on more than one differentiator. This may be necessary if two or more firms are claiming to be best on the same attribute. Today, in a time when the mass market is fragmenting into many small segments, companies are trying to broaden their positioning strategies to appeal to more segments. For example, Unilever introduced the first three-in-one bar soap—Lever 2000—offering cleansing, deodorizing, *and* moisturizing benefits. Clearly, many buyers want all three benefits. The challenge was to convince them that one brand can deliver all three. Judging from Lever 2000's outstanding success, Unilever easily met the challenge. However, as companies increase the number of claims for their brands, they risk disbelief and a loss of clear positioning.

In general, a company needs to avoid three major positioning errors. The first is *underpositioning*—failing ever to really position the company at all. Some companies discover that buyers have only a vague idea of the company or that they do not really know anything special about it. The second error is *overpositioning*—giving buyers too narrow a picture of the company. Thus, a consumer might think that the Steuben glass company makes only fine glass costing $1,000 and up, when in fact it makes affordable fine glass starting at around $50.

Finally, companies must avoid *confused positioning*—leaving buyers with a confused image of a company. For example, Kmart has not fared well against more strongly positioned competitors. Wal-Mart positions itself forcefully as offering "Always low prices. Always!" Target has positioned itself as the trendier "upscale discounter." But most consumers have difficulty positioning Kmart favorably on any specific differentiating attributes.

Which Differences to Promote? Not all brand differences are meaningful or worthwhile; not every difference makes a good differentiator. Each difference has the potential to create company costs as well as customer benefits. Therefore, the company must carefully select the ways in which it will distinguish itself from competitors. A difference is worth establishing to the extent that it satisfies the following criteria:

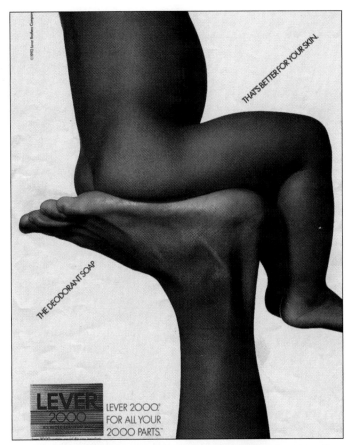

■ Unilever positioned its bestselling Lever 2000 soap on three benefits in one: cleansing, deodorizing, and moisturizing benefits. It's good "for all your 2000 parts."

- *Important:* The difference delivers a highly valued benefit to target buyers.

- *Distinctive:* Competitors do not offer the difference, or the company can offer it in a more distinctive way.

- *Superior:* The difference is superior to other ways that customers might obtain the same benefit.

- *Communicable:* The difference is communicable and visible to buyers.

- *Preemptive:* Competitors cannot easily copy the difference.

- *Affordable:* Buyers can afford to pay for the difference.

- *Profitable:* The company can introduce the difference profitably.

Many companies have introduced differentiations that failed one or more of these tests. The Westin Stamford hotel in Singapore advertises that it is the world's tallest hotel, a distinction that is not important to most tourists—in fact, it turns many off. Polaroid's Polarvision, which produced instantly developed home movies, bombed too. Although Polarvision was distinctive and even preemptive, it was inferior to another way of capturing motion, namely, camcorders. When Pepsi introduced clear Crystal Pepsi some years ago, customers were unimpressed. Although the new drink was distinctive, consumers didn't see "clarity" as an important benefit in a cola drink. Thus, choosing competitive advantages on which to position a product or service can be difficult, yet such choices may be crucial to success.

Selecting an Overall Positioning Strategy Consumers typically choose products and services that give them the greatest value. Thus, marketers want to position their brands on the key benefits that they offer relative to competing brands. The full positioning

FIGURE 6.4

Possible Value Propositions

Price

	More	The same	Less
More	More for more	More for the same	More for less
The same			The same for less
Less			Less for much less

(Benefits on vertical axis)

Value proposition

The full positioning of a brand—the full mix of benefits on which it is positioned.

of a brand is called the brand's **value proposition**—the full mix of benefits on which the brand is positioned. It is the answer to the customer's question "Why should I buy your brand?" Volvo's value proposition hinges on safety but also includes reliability, roominess, and styling, all for a price that is higher than average but seems fair for this mix of benefits.

Figure 6.4 shows possible value propositions on which a company might position its products. In the figure, the five blue cells represent winning value propositions—positioning that gives the company competitive advantage. The red cells represent losing value propositions. The center yellow cell represents at best a marginal proposition. In the following sections, we discuss the five winning value propositions on which companies can position their products: more for more, more for the same, the same for less, less for much less, and more for less.[32]

More for More. "More for more" positioning involves providing the most upscale product or service and charging a higher price to cover the higher costs. Ritz-Carlton Hotels, Mont Blanc writing instruments, Mercedes-Benz automobiles—each claims superior quality, craftsmanship, durability, performance, or style and charges a price to match. Not only is the marketing offer high in quality, it also gives prestige to the buyer. It symbolizes status and a loftier lifestyle. Often, the price difference exceeds the actual increment in quality.

Sellers offering "only the best" can be found in every product and service category, from hotels, restaurants, food, and fashion to cars and kitchen appliances. Consumers are sometimes surprised, even delighted, when a new competitor enters a category with an unusually high-priced brand. Starbucks coffee entered as a very expensive brand in a largely commodity category; Häagen-Dazs came in as a premium ice cream brand at a price never before charged.

In general, companies should be on the lookout for opportunities to introduce a "much-more-for-much-more" brand in any underdeveloped product or service category. Yet "more-for-more" brands can be vulnerable. They often invite imitators who claim the same quality but at a lower price. Luxury goods that sell well during good times may be at risk during economic downturns when buyers become more cautious in their spending.

More for the Same. Companies can attack a competitor's more-for-more positioning by introducing a brand offering comparable quality but at a lower price. For example, Toyota introduced its

Before we knew it we were having Häagen~Dazs.

Fall deeply in Häagen-Dazs.

■ "Much more for much more" value proposition: Häagen-Dazs offers its superpremium ice cream at a price never before charged.

Lexus line with a "more-for-the-same" value proposition. Its headline read: "Perhaps the first time in history that trading a $72,000 car for a $36,000 car could be considered trading up." It communicated the high quality of its new Lexus through rave reviews in car magazines and through a widely distributed videotape showing side-by-side comparisons of Lexus and Mercedes automobiles. It published surveys showing that Lexus dealers were providing customers with better sales and service experiences than were Mercedes dealerships. Many Mercedes owners switched to Lexus, and the Lexus repurchase rate has been 60 percent, twice the industry average.

The Same for Less. Offering "the same for less" can be a powerful value proposition—everyone likes a good deal. For example, Dell Computer offers equivalent-quality computers at a lower "price for performance." Discounts stores such as Wal-Mart and "category killers" such as Best Buy, Circuit City, and Sportmart also use this positioning. They don't claim to offer different or better products. Instead, they offer many of the same brands as department stores and specialty stores but at deep discounts based on superior purchasing power and lower-cost operations. Other companies develop imitative but lower-priced brands in an effort to lure customers away from the market leader. For example, AMD makes less expensive versions of Intel's market-leading microprocessor chips.

Less for Much Less. A market almost always exists for products that offer less and therefore cost less. Few people need, want, or can afford "the very best" in everything they buy. In many cases, consumers will gladly settle for less than optimal performance or give up some of the bells and whistles in exchange for a lower price. For example, many travelers seeking lodgings prefer not to pay for what they consider unnecessary extras, such as a pool, attached restaurant, or mints on the pillow. Motel chains such as Motel 6 suspend some of these amenities and charge less accordingly.

"Less for much less" positioning involves meeting consumers' lower performance or quality requirements at a much lower price. For example, Family Dollar and Dollar General stores offer more affordable goods at very low prices. Sam's Club and Costco warehouse stores offer less merchandise selection and consistency, and much lower levels of service; as a result, they charge rock-bottom prices. Southwest Airlines, the nation's most profitable air carrier, also practices less for much less positioning. It charges incredibly low prices by not serving food, not assigning seats, and not using travel agents (see Marketing at Work 6.3).

More for Less. Of course, the winning value proposition would be to offer "more for less." Many companies claim to do this. For example, Dell Computer claims to have better products *and* lower prices for a given level of performance. Procter & Gamble claims that its laundry detergents provide the best cleaning *and* everyday low prices. In the short run, some companies can actually achieve such lofty positions. For example, when it first opened for business, Home Depot had arguably the best product selection, the best service, *and* the lowest prices compared to local hardware stores and other home improvement chains.

Yet in the long run, companies will find it very difficult to sustain such best-of-both positioning. Offering more usually costs more, making it difficult to deliver on the "for less" promise. Companies that try to deliver both may lose out to more focused competitors. For example, facing determined competition from Lowe's stores, Home Depot must now decide whether it wants to compete primarily on superior service or on lower prices.

All said, each brand must adopt a positioning strategy designed to serve the needs and wants of its target markets. "More for more" will draw one target market, "less for much less" will draw another, and so on. Thus, in any market, there is usually room for many different companies, each successfully occupying different positions.

The important thing is that each company must develop its own winning positioning strategy, one that makes it special to its target consumers. Offering only "the same for the same" provides no competitive advantage, leaving the firm in the middle of the pack. Companies offering one of the three losing value propositions—"the same for more," "less

Marketing at Work | 6.3

Southwest's Value Proposition: "Less for Much Less"

In an industry beset by hard times, Southwest Airlines flies well above its competition. In the wake of a global economic slump and the effects of September 11 and increased terrorism, most airlines are suffering huge losses, or even declaring bankruptcy. Industry leader American Airlines lost more than $3.5 billion last year. Yet even in these bleak times, Southwest has yet to suffer a loss in a single quarter. Amazingly, Southwest has experienced 30 straight years of profits. What's the secret? Southwest is the most strongly and clearly positioned airline in the world. It offers a classic "less-for-much-less" value proposition.

From the start, Southwest has positioned itself firmly as *the* no-frills, low-price airline. Its average flight time is just one hour; its average one-way fare just $86. Southwest's passengers have learned to fly without the amenities. For example, the airline provides no meals—just packaged snacks. It also offers no first-class section, only three-across seating in all of its planes. There's no such thing as a reserved seat on a Southwest flight. Passengers are assigned to one of three boarding groups when checking in and then herded onto the plane by group. "Southwest will get you and your luggage where you're going," comments an industry analyst, "but we don't call their planes cattle cars for nothing. It's a mercy that Southwest is a short-haul airline, because you can get pretzelated on their planes p.d.q."

Why, then, do so many passengers love Southwest? Perhaps most importantly, Southwest excels at the basics of getting passengers where they want to go and on time. In 1992, Southwest received the U.S. Department of

Southwest offers a classic "less for much less" value proposition, with lots of zany fun. It all starts at the top with company founder and chairman Herb Kelleher.

Transportation's first-ever Triple Crown Award for best on-time service, best baggage handling, *and* best customer service, a feat it repeated for the next five straight years. For more than a decade, Southwest has been among

---

Positioning statement

A statement that summarizes company or brand positioning—it takes this form: *To (target segment and need) our (brand) is (concept) that (point-of-difference).*

for more," and "less for the same"—will inevitably fail. Customers soon realize that they've been underserved, tell others, and abandon the brand.

Developing a Positioning Statement Company and brand positioning should be summed up in a **positioning statement.** The statement should follow the form: *To (target segment and need) our (brand) is (concept) that (point-of-difference).*[33] For example: "To busy professionals who need to stay organized, Palm Pilot is an electronic organizer that*

the industry leaders in on-time performance. All this makes Southwest passengers a satisfied bunch. For the past 12 consecutive years, Southwest has ranked number one in fewest customer complaints in the Department of Transportation's Air Travel Consumer Report. And last year it rated number one in its industry in customer satisfaction on the American Customer Satisfaction Index.

Beyond the basics, however, there are two key elements to Southwest's strong positioning. The analyst sums up Southwest's positioning this way: "It is not luxurious, . . . but it's cheap and it's fun." Southwest is a model of efficiency and low-cost operations. As a result, its prices are shockingly low. When it enters a new market, Southwest proclaims: "Southwest is coming to town, and airline prices are coming down." In fact, prices are so low that when Southwest enters a market, it actually increases total air traffic by attracting customers who might otherwise travel by car or bus. For example, when Southwest began its Louisville-to-Chicago flight at a one-way rate of $49 versus competitors' $250, total weekly air passenger traffic between the two cities increased from 8,000 to 26,000.

No frills and low prices, however, don't mean drudgery. To lighten things up, Southwest adds another key positioning ingredient—lots of good, clean fun. With its happy-go-lucky Chairman and co-founder, Herb Kelleher, leading the charge, Southwest refuses to take itself seriously. Cheerful employees go out of their way to amuse, surprise, or

somehow entertain passengers. According to one account:

Southwest employees are apt to dress as leprechauns on St. Patrick's Day, rabbits on Easter, and almost anything on Halloween. I have heard flight attendants sing the safety lecture as country music, blues, and rap; I have heard them compare the pilot to Rocky Raccoon and insist that passengers introduce themselves to one another, then hug, then kiss, then propose marriage.

Kelleher himself has been known to dress up as Klinger from "MASH" at company parties and hands out snacks to passengers when flying on his airline.

During delays at the gate, ticket agents will award prizes to the passenger with the largest hole in his or her sock. Flight attendants have been known to hide in overhead luggage bins and then pop out when passengers start filing on board. Veteran Southwest fliers have learned to listen up to announcements over the intercom. On a recent flight, the pilot suggested, "Flight attendants will please prepare their hair for departure." Later in the flight, he announced, "Good morning, ladies and gentlemen. Those of you who wish to smoke will please file out to our lounge on the wing, where you can enjoy our feature film, *Gone with the Wind*." Safety instructions from the flight attendant included the advice. "In the unlikely event of a water landing, please remember to paddle, kick, kick, paddle, kick, kick, all the way back." One passenger recalls a flight on which the pilot told everyone

on the plane's left side, toward the terminal, to put their faces in the window and smile "so our competitors can see what a full flight looks like."

As a result of its strong positioning, Southwest has grown to become the nation's fourth-largest domestic carrier. The company has successfully beaten off determined challenges from several major competitors who have tried to copy its winning formula, including Continental Lite, Delta Express, and Shuttle by United. Southwest now makes 2,800 flights a day, serving 58 cities in 30 states. Its revenues have grown 250 percent during the past decade. And in the recent industry downdraft, Southwest has been the *only* major airline to turn a profit.

Simple, clear positioning has made Southwest *Fortune* magazine's most admired airline for the past seven years running. And last year, Southwest was *Fortune's* number two most admired company overall. Southwest not only promises an appealing value proposition, it delivers on the promise. It's not ritzy, but it gets you where you want to go, when you want to get there. You get low, low prices and lots of good fun. Just the ticket when you need a good lift!

Sources: Quotes from Molly Ivins, "From Texas, with Love and Peanuts," *New York Times*, March 14, 1999, p. 11; Wendy Zellner, "Southwest: After Kelleher, More Blue Skies," *Business Week*, April 2, 2001, p. 45; and Ron Suskind, "Humor Has Returned After 9/11 Hiatus," *Wall Street Journal*, January 13, 2003, p. A1. Also see Wendy Zellner, "Holding Steady," *Business Week*, February 3, 2003, pp. 66–68; "Airline of the Year: Southwest Airlines," *Air Transport World*, February 2003, pp. 26–27; and *Southwest Airlines Fact Sheet*, June 6, 2003, accessed at www.southwest.com.

allows you to backup files on your PC more easily and reliably than competitive products." Sometimes a positioning statement is more detailed:

To young, active soft-drink consumers who have little time for sleep, Mountain Dew is the soft drink that gives you more energy than any other brand because it has the highest level of caffeine. With Mountain Dew, you can stay alert and keep going even when you haven't been able to get a good night's sleep.[34]

Note that the positioning first states the product's membership in a category (Mountain Dew is a soft drink) and then shows its point-of-difference from other members of the category (has more caffeine). Placing a brand in a specific category suggests similarities that it might share with other products in the category. But the case for the brand's superiority is made on its points of difference. Sometimes marketers put a brand in a surprisingly different category before indicating the points of difference:

> DiGiorno's is a frozen pizza whose crust rises when the pizza is heated. Instead of putting it in the frozen pizza category, the marketers positioned it in the delivered pizza category. Their ad shows party guests asking which pizza delivery service the host used. But, says the host, "It's not delivery, its DiGiorno!" This helped highlight DiGiorno's fresh quality and superior taste over the normal frozen pizza.

Communicating and Delivering the Chosen Position

Once it has chosen a position, the company must take strong steps to deliver and communicate the desired position to target consumers. All the company's marketing mix efforts must support the positioning strategy. Positioning the company calls for concrete action, not just talk. If the company decides to build a position on better quality and service, it must first *deliver* that position. Designing the marketing mix—product, price, place, and promotion—involves working out the tactical details of the positioning strategy. Thus, a firm that seizes on a more-for-more position knows that it must produce high-quality products, charge a high price, distribute through high-quality dealers, and advertise in high-quality media. It must hire and train more service people, find retailers who have a good reputation for service, and develop sales and advertising messages that broadcast its superior service. This is the only way to build a consistent and believable more-for-more position.

Companies often find it easier to come up with a good positioning strategy than to implement it. Establishing a position or changing one usually takes a long time. In contrast, positions that have taken years to build can quickly be lost. Once a company has built the desired position, it must take care to maintain the position through consistent performance and communication. It must closely monitor and adapt the position over time to match changes in consumer needs and competitors' strategies. However, the company should avoid abrupt changes that might confuse consumers. Instead, a product's position should evolve gradually as it adapts to the ever-changing marketing environment.

REST STOP:
Reviewing the Concepts

Time to stop and stretch your legs. In this chapter, you've learned about the major elements of marketing strategy: segmentation, targeting, and positioning. Marketers know that they cannot appeal to all buyers in their markets, or at least not to all buyers in the same way. Buyers are too numerous, too widely scattered, and too varied in their needs and buying practices. Therefore, most companies today are moving away from mass marketing. Instead, they practice *target marketing*—identifying market segments, selecting one or more of them, and developing products and marketing mixes tailored to each. In this way, sellers can develop the right product for each target market and adjust their prices, distribution channels, and advertising to reach the target market efficiently.

1. Define the three steps of target marketing: market segmentation, target marketing, and market positioning.

Target marketing involves designing strategies to build the *right relationships* with the *right customers. Market segmentation* is the act of dividing a market into distinct groups of buyers with different needs, characteristics, or behaviors who might require separate products or marketing mixes. Once the groups have been identified, *target marketing* evaluates each market segment's attractiveness and selects one or more segments to serve. *Market positioning* consists of deciding how to best serve target customer—setting the competitive positioning for the product and creating a detailed marketing plan.

2.   List and discuss the major bases for segmenting consumer and business markets.

There is no single way to segment a market. Therefore, the marketer tries different variables to see which give the best segmentation opportunities. For consumer marketing, the major segmentation variables are geographic, demographic, psychographic, and behavioral. In *geographic segmentation,* the market is divided into different geographical units such as nations, regions, states, counties, cities, or neighborhoods. In *demographic segmentation,* the market is divided into groups based on demographic variables, including age, gender, family size, family life cycle, income, occupation, education, religion, race, generation, and nationality. In *psychographic segmentation,* the market is divided into different groups based on social class, lifestyle, or personality characteristics. In *behavioral segmentation,* the market is divided into groups based on consumers' knowledge, attitudes, uses, or responses to a product.

Business marketers use many of the same variables to segment their markets. But business markets also can be segmented by business consumer *demographics* (industry, company size), *operating characteristics, purchasing approaches, situational factors,* and *personal characteristics.* The effectiveness of segmentation analysis depends on finding segments that are *measurable, accessible, substantial, differentiable,* and *actionable.*

3.   Explain how companies identify attractive market segments and choose a target marketing strategy.

To target the best market segments, the company first evaluates each segment's size and growth characteristics, structural attractiveness, and compatibility with company objectives and resources. It then chooses one of four target marketing strategies—ranging from very broad to very narrow targeting. The seller can ignore segment differences and target broadly using *undifferentiated (or mass) marketing.* This involves mass producing, mass distributing, and mass promoting about the same product in about the same way to all consumers. Or the seller can adopt *differentiated marketing*—developing different market offers for several segments. *Concentrated marketing* (or *niche marketing*) involves focusing on only one or a few market segments. Finally, *micromarketing* is the practice of tailoring products and marketing programs to suit the tastes of specific individuals and locations. Micromarketing includes *local marketing* and *individual marketing.* Which targeting strategy is best depends on company resources, product variability, product life-cycle stage, market variability, and competitive marketing strategies.

4.   Discuss how companies position their products for maximum competitive advantage in the marketplace.

Once a company has decided which segments to enter, it must decide on its *market positioning* strategy—on which positions to occupy in its chosen segments. The positioning task consists of three steps: identifying a set of possible competitive advantages on which to build a position, choosing the right competitive advantages, and selecting an overall positioning strategy. The brand's full positioning is called its *value proposition*—the full mix of benefits on which the brand is positioned. In general, companies can choose from one of five winning value propositions on which to position their products: more for more, more for the same, the same for less, less for much less, or more for less. Company and brand positioning are summarized in positioning statements that state the target segment and need, positioning concept, and specific points of difference. The company must then effectively communicate and deliver the chosen position to the market.

Navigating the Key Terms

Age and life-cycle
   segmentation
Behavioral segmentation
Benefit segmentation
Competitive advantage
Concentrated (niche) marketing
Demographic segmentation
Differentiated (segmented)
   marketing

Gender segmentation
Geographic segmentation
Income segmentation
Individual marketing
Intermarket segmentation
Local marketing
Market positioning
Market segmentation
Micromarketing

Occasion segmentation
Positioning statement
Product position
Psychographic segmentation
Target market
Target marketing
Undifferentiated (or mass)
   marketing
Value proposition

Travel Log

Discussing the Issues

1. What are the differences between mass marketing, segment marketing, niche marketing, and micro marketing? Discuss actual products that use each of these market segmentation levels.

2. For each of these three products—DVD Player, shoes, and salsa—consider each of the segmentation variables listed in Table 6.1 and assess the degree to which it is useful to segment the market for the product based on that variable.

3. Describe the student market segments for your university. To what extent are these segments measurable, accessible, substantial, differentiable, and actionable?

4. The George Foreman Grilling Machine is a compact cooking appliance with a double-sided cooking surface that is angled to allow fat to drip off the food and out of the grill. Describe a likely target market for this product. How does this target market rate with respect to size, growth, and structural attractiveness.

5. Discuss how Mountain Dew has differentiated itself from other soft drink brands on the basis of product, services, channels, people, and image differentiation.

6. Study Figure 6.4. Give examples of a hotel chain that falls into each of the five value propositions. What does each hotel you selected do on the benefits dimension to offer more, the same, or less than competitors?

Application Questions

1. One direction Levi's has gone in personalizing the shopping experience is to allow the use of a virtual model to try on clothing at the company's Web site (www.levi.com). Visitors can even customize the model to look more like themselves (or what they wish they looked like) and save this representation for future visits. Visit the company Web site and virtually try on some of the clothing in the "fitting room." What do you think of this experience? How does this feature fit with the notion of individual marketing? Do you feel that the virtual fitting room differentiates the Levi brand from other clothing companies?

2. Pick five different brands of deodorant. Based on your own perception, rate each one on the attributes of scent, price, and odor protection (use a 1 to 10 scale, with 1 being low and 10 being high). Pick two of the attributes and plot your ratings of each brand. How are the brands different and similar to each other? Are there any areas on the graph that are void of competitors? Do these represent an opportunity for a deodorant manufacturer?

3. Cable television news organizations have become more popular in recent years as consumers have started to expect and demand news coverage 24 hours a day, 7 days a week. Spend some time watching CNN, MSNBC, and Fox news. List the ways each news program tries to differentiate itself from the others. Evaluate the worthiness of their differentiation strategies using the following criteria: important, distinctive, communicable, preemptive, affordable, and profitable.

Under the Hood: Focus on Technology

Birds of a feather flock together. This is the philosophy behind Claritas's PRIZM lifestyle segmentation system. Operating under the presumption that people with similar lifestyles tend to live near each other, Claritas has classified neighborhoods into 1 of 62 categories based on census data, consumer surveys, and other public and private sources of demographic and consumer information. Companies use this geodemographic information to understand and target customers better, to develop the content for advertisements, to decide the specific media in which to place ads, to help decide where to put new stores, and to decide what kind of merchandise should go in those stores.

Claritas offers a limited version of the PRIZM segmentation online at www.yawyl.claritas.com. Visit this Web site and respond to the following questions.

1. Enter the ZIP code where you live into the PRIZM Web site and read about the descriptions of the different customer segments. Do you think it accurately describes your area?

2. What are some products that might be successfully targeted at the most popular market segment in your area?

3. How might a business selling Caribbean cruises be able to use the Claritas PRIZM segmentation tool?

Focus on Ethics

Many companies consider children an attractive market segment because of their spending power. A strategy in some middle schools and high schools is to develop exclusive "pouring rights" contracts with soft drink companies, which allow the company to be the exclusive soft drink sold on campus in exchange for payments equaling hundreds of thousands of dollars. Pepsi and Coca-Cola have led this charge in recent years, encouraged by school districts in desperate need of additional funding. However, some parents feel that soft drinks are an unhealthy beverage alternative and have lobbied to have soft drinks removed from campuses. Indeed, the nation's two largest school districts—New York and Los Angeles—have banned soft-drink sales.

1. Why would soft drink companies pay such large sums for exclusive access to middle and high school campuses? How might the controversy damage the image of the soft drink manufacturers?

2. In your mind, are there any ethical issues associated with this practice?

3. What sort of compromise might be worked out between supporters and opponents of this practice?

Videos

The Marriott video case that accompanies this chapter is located in Appendix 1 at the back of the book.

Student Materials

Need a tune-up? A study guide and OneKey access code are available to aid in your review of chapter material. Your instructor may choose to have these items shrink-wrapped with your text or you may purchase them separately at www.prenhall.com/marketing.

■ *After studying this chapter, you should be able to:*

1. *Define product* and the major classifications of products and services **2.** *Describe* the decisions companies make regarding their individual products and services, product lines, and product mixes **3.** *Discuss* branding strategy—the decisions companies make in building and managing their brands **4.** *Identify* the four characteristics that affect the marketing of a service **5.** *Discuss* two additional product issues

Product, Services, and Branding Strategy

7

ROAD MAP | Previewing the Concepts

Now that you've had a good look at marketing strategy, we'll journey on into the marketing mix—the tactical tools that marketers use to implement their strategies. In this and the next chapter, we'll study how companies develop and manage products. Then, in the chapters that follow, we'll look at pricing, distribution, and marketing communication tools. The product is usually the first and most basic marketing consideration. How well firms manage their individual brands and their overall product and service offerings has a major impact on their success in the marketplace. We'll start with a seemingly simple question: What *is* a product? As it turns out, however, the answer is not so simple.

First stop on this leg of the journey: cosmetics marketing. Remember that seemingly simple question—what is a product? The cosmetics industry example shows why there is no easy answer. What, really, *are* cosmetics? Cosmetics makers like Aveda know that when a woman buys cosmetics, she buys much, much more than scented ingredients in fancy bottles.

Each year, cosmetics companies sell billions of dollars' worth of potions, lotions, and fragrances to consumers around the world, part of a $160 billion global beauty industry. In one sense, these products are no more than careful mixtures of oils and chemicals that have nice scents and soothing properties. But the cosmetics companies know that they sell much more than just mixtures of ingredients—they sell the promise of what these concoctions will do for the people who use them.

Of course, in the cosmetics business, like anywhere else, quality and performance contribute to success or failure. For example, perfume marketers agree, "No smell; no sell." However, $180-an-ounce perfume may cost no more than $10 to produce. Thus, to perfume consumers, many things beyond the scent and a few dollars' worth of ingredients add to a perfume's allure. Fragrance names such as Obsession, Passion, Gossip, Wildheart, Opium, Joy, White Linen, Youth Dew, Eternity, and Love suggest that the perfumes will do something more than just make you smell better.

What *is* the promise of cosmetics? The following account by a *New York Times* reporter suggests the extent to which cosmetics take on meaning far beyond their physical makeup.

Last week I bathed in purple water (*I Trust* bubble bath, made by Philosophy) and powdered up with pink powder (*Rebirth*, by 5S, "to renew the spirit and recharge the soul"). My moisturizer was *Bliss* (Chakra VII by Aveda, for "the joyful enlightenment and soaring of the spirit"); my nail polish was *Spiritual* (by Tony and Tina, "to aid connection with the higher self"). My teeth were clean, my heart was open—however, my bathroom was so crowded with bottles and brochures, the latest tools and totems from the human potential movement, that I could hardly find my third eye. Still, my "Hope in a Jar" package (from Philosophy) pretty well summed it up: "Where there is hope there can be faith. Where there is faith miracles can occur."

If you are looking for enlightenment in all the wrong places, cosmetics companies are eager to help. Because today, feeling good is the new religion. And cosmetics companies are the newest of the new prophets, turning the old notion of hope in a jar on its head.

"Cosmetics are our satellite to the divine!" This is what you'll hear from Tony and Tina, for example. Tony and Tina (Anthony Gillis and Cristina Bornstein) are nice young artists. He's from London, she grew up in New York. Chakra nail polish, which they invented for an installation at the Gershwin Gallery in Manhattan two years ago, was intended as an ironic commentary on the beauty business. But then a friend suggested they get into the beauty business, and now Tony and Tiny have a $2 million cosmetics company with a mission statement: "To aid in the evolution of human consciousness." Their products include nail polishes (Vibrational Remedies) in colors meant to do nice things to your chakras, as well as body glitter and hair mascara, lipstick and eyeshadow. You can buy them at Fred Segal, Nordstrom, and Bloomingdale's, where last month they outsold Hard Candy and Urban Decay. "We think color therapy is going to be the new medicine," said Tony.

Rainbows are proliferating as rapidly in the New Age as angels once did. Philosophy, a 3-year-old Arizona company, makes a sort of head/heart kit—"a self-help program," the company insists—called the *Rainbow Connection*. You pay $45 for seven bottles of colored bubble bath in a metal box. "Choose your colored bath according to the area of your emotional life that needs attention, i.e. self-love, self-worth," the brochure reads. "My role as I see it," said Christina Carlino, Philosophy's founder, "is to help you stay on your destiny path. It's not about what you look like. Beauty is defined by your deeds."

5S, a sprout of the Japanese cosmetics company Shiseido, offers a regimen that plays, the company says, on the "fundamental and mythical significance of 5" (Five Pillars of Islam, Five Classics of Confucianism, and so on), and which is organized into emotional rather than physical categories. At the 5S store in SoHo, you don't buy things for dry skin, you buy things that are "energizing" or "nurturing" or "adoring." The company also believes in color therapy. Hence, *Rebirth*, products tinted "nouveau pink" (the color of bubble gum). A customer can achieve rebirth with 5S pink soap, pink powder, and pink toner.

Here are products that are not intended to make you look better, but to make you act better, feel better, and be a better person. You don't need a month's visit to India to find your higher self; you need only buy this bubble bath, that lipstick, this night cream. The beauty business' old come-on (trap your man!) has been swept away in favor of a new pitch. I don't have wrinkles anymore. I've got a chakra blockage.

Of course, who knew about chakras before Aveda? In 1989, the plant-based, eco-friendly cosmetics company Aveda trademarked Chakras I through VII to use as titles for moisturizers and scents. Chakra products were perhaps a little ahead of their time back then. However, the purchase of Aveda [a while] ago by the Estée Lauder Companies, the General Motors of the cosmetics world, suggests that the pendulum of history has finally caught up. "Aveda isn't a marketing idea," says Jeanette Wagner, the vice chairman of Estée Lauder. "It is a passionately held belief. From my point of view, the appeal is first the spirituality, and then the products."

All this might sound like only so much flimflam, but the underlying point is legitimate. The success of such brands affirms that products really are more than just the physical entities. When a woman buys cosmetics, she really does buy much, much more than just oils, chemicals, and fragrances. The cosmetic's image, its promises and positioning, its ingredients, its name and package, the company that makes it, the stores that sell it—all become a part of the total cosmetic product. When Aveda, Philosophy, and 5S sell cosmetics, they sell more than just tangible goods. They sell lifestyle, self-expression, exclusivity, and spirituality; achievement, success, and status; romance, passion, and fantasy; memories, hopes, and dreams.[1]

Clearly, cosmetics are more than just cosmetics when Aveda sells them. This chapter begins with a deceptively simple question: *What is a product*? After answering this question, we look at ways to classify products in consumer and business markets. Then we discuss the important decisions that marketers make regarding individual products, product lines, and product mixes. Next, we look into the critically important issue of how marketers build and manage brands. Finally, we examine the characteristics and marketing requirements of a special form of product—services.

■▌ What Is a Product?

A Sony DVD player, a Ford Taurus, a Costa Rican vacation, a Caffé Mocha at Starbucks, Fidelity online investment services, and advice from your family doctor—all are products. We define a **product** as anything that can be offered to a market for attention, acquisition, use, or consumption and that might satisfy a want or need. Products include more than just tangible goods. Broadly defined, products include physical objects, services, events, persons, places, organizations, ideas, or mixes of these entities. Thus, throughout this book, we use the term *product* broadly to include any or all of these entities.

Because of their importance in the world economy, we give special attention to services. **Services** are a form of product that consists of activities, benefits, or satisfactions offered for sale that are essentially intangible and do not result in the ownership of anything. Examples are banking, hotel, airline, retail, tax preparation, and home repair services. We will look at services more closely later in this chapter.

Product
Anything that can be offered to a market for attention, acquisition, use, or consumption that might satisfy a want or need.

Service
Any activity or benefit that one party can offer to another that is essentially intangible and does not result in the ownership of anything.

Products, Services, and Experiences

Product is a key element in the *market offering.* Marketing-mix planning begins with formulating an offering that brings value to target customers and satisfies their needs. This offering becomes the basis on which the company builds profitable relationships with customers.

A company's market offering often includes both tangible goods and services. Each component can be a minor or a major part of the total offer. At one extreme, the offer may consist of a *pure tangible good,* such as soap, toothpaste, or salt—no services accompany the product. At the other extreme are *pure services,* for which the offer consists primarily of a service. Examples include a doctor's exam or financial services. Between these two extremes, however, many goods-and-services combinations are possible.

Today, as products and services become more and more commoditized, many companies are moving to a new level in creating value for their customers. To differentiate their offers, beyond simply making products and delivering services, companies are staging, marketing, and delivering memorable customer *experiences.* Whereas products are tangible and services are intangible, experiences are memorable. Whereas products and services are external, experiences are personal and take place in the minds of individual consumers.

Experiences have always been important in the entertainment industry—Disney has long manufactured memories through its movies and theme parks. Today, however, all kinds of firms are recasting their traditional goods and services to create experiences. For example, restaurants create value well beyond the food they serve. Starbucks patrons are paying for more than just coffee. The company treats customers to poetry on its wallpaper,

Marketing at Work | *7.1*

Krispy Kreme: A Truly Sweet Experience

Want a doughnut? What's the first name that comes to mind? Five years ago, you probably would have said Dunkin' Donuts, still the world's largest coffee and doughnut chain. But today, thanks to the hot popularity of Krispy Kreme, the southern phenomenon, your answer might be different. The Krispy Kreme name and famous bowtie logo have cropped up throughout the country and around the world, bringing the company's delicious yeast-raised doughnuts to more and more satisfied customers.

Krispy Kreme is changing the way the world eats doughnuts. The company and its franchisees now make 7.5 million doughnuts each day—2.7 *billion* doughnuts each year. Larger outlets make more than 12,000 of the sweet-tasting delicacies an hour. In about 22 seconds, Krispy Kreme stores worldwide can produce enough doughnuts to make a stack as high as the empire state building. That's enough doughnuts each week to stretch from New York City to Los Angeles. In the process, they use 1.3 million pounds of sprinkles and enough chocolate to fill nearly five Olympic size swimming pools.

But to a true believer, a Krispy Kreme isn't just a doughnut. It's an *experience*. A magical moment. With every doughnut the company sells, it creates a happy customer. And each happy customer can't wait to tell others about the experience. If you haven't had a gooey, hot glazed Krispy Kreme, they'd say, you simply haven't lived.

Krispy Kreme's magical moments date all the way back to 1933, when Vernon Rudolph bought a doughnut shop in Paducah, Kentucky. The deal came with the secret recipe for the unique, yeast-raised Krispy Kreme doughnut that has become so popular today. In 1937 the Rudolph family

moved the business to Winston-Salem, North Carolina. It was there that Vernon responded to customer requests by installing a retail window through which he could sell fresh, hot doughnuts directly to customers.

As the company expanded through franchises, Rudolph saw the need to

To a true believer, a Krispy Kreme isn't just a doughnut. It's a truly sweet experience. *A magical moment.*

apron-clad performers behind espresso machines, and a warm but modern interior ambience that leaves them feeling more affluent and fulfilled. And Krispy Kreme doesn't just sell doughnuts, it creates carefully staged "magical moments" for just about anyone within "aroma range" of a Krispy Kreme store (see Marketing at Work 7.1).

Many retailers also stage experiences. Niketown stores create "shoppertainment" by offering interactive displays, engaging activities, and promotional events in a stimulating shopping environment. At stores such as Sharper Image and Brookstone, people play with the latest gadgets, sit in massage chairs, and enjoy the experience more than the merchan-

provide a consistent Krispy Kreme experience at every outlet. So he built a mix plant and developed a distribution system that delivered the same dry mix to each store. He also began manufacturing equipment that would automate each store's doughnut-making process.

This focus on consistency continues today. The company painstakingly plans every Krispy Kreme store decision—from product placement and store design to the color of the employees' uniforms. Every poster and every sign, every piece of equipment, every light fixture, and every bag of flour, sugar, sprinkles, and icing must be purchased from Krispy Kreme. Thus, every Krispy Kreme customer experiences the same magical moment with every visit, at any Krispy Kreme store, anywhere.

The Krispy Kreme magical moment seems to appeal to everyone, regardless of age, sex, ethnicity, or socioeconomic background. And, it has built a host of fervent followers that most competitors could only dream about. Says Krispy Kreme's Senior Vice President of Store Development, "people wait in line for hours to get into a new store opening and they have fun . . . they talk to each other, share their Krispy Kreme stories . . . amazing. How many businesses could you be in where people are willing to stand in line for hours? I've never seen anything that even comes close to the passion people feel for this brand."

Krispy Kreme is so focused on the experience it creates that it actually defines its brand through the store experience. Its "Retail Environments" book, which details new store design,

states "Our brand and how our customers experience Krispy Kreme is the platform that supports us all. Nothing can be more important than the preservation and nurturing of these valuable possessions." This undying demand for perfection, unwavering consistency, and a passion for the consumer–brand relationship forms the foundation of Krispy Kreme's success.

Krispy Kreme's powerful brand experience makes it easy to attract customers in new markets. The company has an almost cult-like following. So, for many neighborhoods the arrival of a Krispy Kreme is an event to celebrate. Consumers in Clackamas, Oregon, greeted the groundbreaking for a new Krispy Kreme store with the local marching band and hordes of supporters. When a new store opened just outside of Seattle, eager customers camped out on the sidewalk overnight to be the first inside at 5:30 A.M. the next morning. When Krispy Kreme debuted in Denver, morning traffic was snarled for hours.

For those who have never heard of Krispy Kreme, word travels quickly about the chain's tasty doughnuts. But to ensure that the message gets out, local franchisees often deliver several dozen glazed doughnuts to a local radio station, or to—you guessed it—the town's fire and police stations. When a new store opened in Phoenix, Sheriff Joe Arpaio, the infamous "toughest sheriff in America"—the lawman known for making prisoners wear pink underwear—was one of the first people to try a fresh Krispy Kreme doughnut. In front of a sea of television cameras, he

uttered the perfect phrase: "These doughnuts are so good, they should be illegal." Such free promotion is the norm for Krispy Kreme. The delicious doughnuts have also played cameo roles in the movie Primary Colors and on such TV shows as Ally McBeal, NYPD Blue, and The Tonight Show with Jay Leno.

Thus, Krispy Kreme does more than sell doughnuts. It creates carefully crafted magical moments for its customers, moments that are gaining popularity with just about anyone within "aroma range" of a Krispy Kreme store. Notes marketing manager Jennifer Gardner, "I've seen a blue-collar worker, an expectant mother, a biker, a businessman, and a woman who was driven up in a Rolls Royce all standing in line inside a Krispy Kreme store, and they were talking to each other like long-lost friends." Says Krispy Kreme fan Jamie Karn, "You have to experience one. You have to eat it to understand it!" More than a doughnut, Krispy Kreme is a truly sweet customer experience. Creating magical moments for customers has also been a pretty sweet experience for Krispy Kreme. The company's sales have increased more than 73 percent in just the past two years.

Sources: Portions adapted from a case written by Peter Attwater, student at the University of North Carolina at Chapel Hill, April 2003. Other information from "It's Official: Krispy Kreme Coming to Clackamas," April 8, 2003, accessed online at www.katu.com; Sarah MacDonald, "It's a Drive-Thru or No Go," April 17, 2003, *Daily News Transcript*, accessed online at www.neponset valleydailynews.com; Christina Dyrness, "Hot Technology Now," *News & Observer*, April 23, 2003, p. 1F, 3F; and information accessed online at www.krispykreme.com/mediarelations.html, July 2003.

dise. And you don't just shop at the Toys "*R*" Us store on Times Square store in New York City, you *experience* it.

Step into Toys "*R*" Us Times Square to enjoy three levels of incredible fun right on Broadway! Take a ride on a 60-foot-high Ferris Wheel with cool character-themed cabs. Feel like a celebrity in our amazing two-story Barbie Dollhouse. Take a stroll through our life-size Candy Land. Gaze up in wonder at our LEGO Empire State Building. And for a classic Jurassic experience, say

■ Marketing experiences: You don't just shop at the Toys "R" Us store on Times Square in New York City, you *experience* it.

hello to a larger than life, 20-foot-tall, T-Rex with realistic moves and a mighty roar. You really have to see it to believe it![2]

Companies that market experiences realize that customers are really buying much more than just products and services. They are buying what those offers will *do* for them.[3]

Levels of Product and Services   Product planners need to think about products and services on three levels (see Figure 7.1). Each level adds more customer value. The most basic level is the *core benefit*, which addresses the question *What is the buyer really buying?* When designing products, marketers must first define the core, problem-solving benefits or services that consumers seek. A woman buying lipstick buys more than lip color. Charles Revson of Revlon saw this early: "In the factory, we make cosmetics; in the store, we sell hope." Charles Schwab does more than sell financial services—it promises to fulfill customers' "financial dreams."

At the second level, product planners must turn the core benefit into an *actual product*. They need to develop product and service features, design, a quality level, a brand name, and packaging. For example, a Sony camcorder is an actual product. Its name, parts, styling, features, packaging, and other attributes have all been combined carefully to

FIGURE 7.1

Three Levels of Product

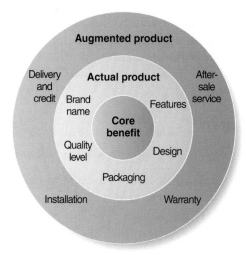

deliver the core benefit—a convenient, high-quality way to capture important moments.

Finally, product planners must build an *augmented product* around the core benefit and actual product by offering additional consumer services and benefits. Sony must offer more than just a camcorder. It must provide consumers with a complete solution to their picture-taking problems. Thus, when consumers buy a Sony camcorder, Sony and its dealers also might give buyers a warranty on parts and workmanship, instructions on how to use the camcorder, quick repair services when needed, and a toll-free telephone number to call if they have problems or questions.

Consumers see products as complex bundles of benefits that satisfy their needs. When developing products, marketers first must identify the *core* consumer needs the product will satisfy. They must then design the *actual* product and find ways to *augment* it in order to create the bundle of benefits that will provide the most satisfying customer experience.

Product and Service Classifications

Products and services fall into two broad classes based on the types of consumers that use them—*consumer products* and *industrial products*. Broadly defined, products also include other marketable entities such as experiences, organizations, persona, places, and ideas.

Consumer Products   **Consumer products** are products and services bought by final consumers for personal consumption. Marketers usually classify these products and services further based on how consumers go about buying them. Consumer products include *convenience products*, *shopping products*, *specialty products*, and *unsought products*. These products differ in the ways consumers buy them and therefore in how they are marketed (see Table 7.1).

■ Core, actual, and augmented product: Consumers perceive this Sony Handycam as a complex bundle of intangible features and services that deliver a core benefit—a convenient, high-quality way to capture important moments.

TABLE 7.1   Marketing Considerations for Consumer Products

Marketing Considerations	Type of Consumer Product			
	Convenience	Shopping	Specialty	Unsought
Customer buying behavior	Frequent purchase, little planning, little comparison or shopping effort, low customer involvement	Less frequent purchase, much planning and shopping effort, comparison of brands on price, quality, style	Strong brand preference and loyalty, special purchase effort, little comparison of brands, low price sensitivity	Little product awareness, knowledge (or, if aware, little or even negative interest)
Price	Low price	Higher price	High price	Varies
Distribution	Widespread distribution, convenient locations	Selective distribution in fewer outlets	Exclusive distribution in only one or a few outlets per market area	Varies
Promotion	Mass promotion by the producer	Advertising and personal selling by both producer and resellers	More carefully targeted promotion by both producer and resellers	Aggressive advertising and personal selling by producer and resellers
Examples	Toothpaste, magazines, laundry detergent	Major appliances, televisions, furniture, clothing	Luxury goods, such as Rolex watches or fine crystal	Life insurance, Red Cross blood donations

Consumer product
Product bought by final consumer for personal consumption.

Convenience product
Consumer product that the customer usually buys frequently, immediately, and with a minimum of comparison and buying effort.

Shopping product
Consumer good that the customer, in the process of selection and purchase, characteristically compares on bases such as suitability, quality, price, and style.

Specialty product
Consumer product with unique characteristics or brand identification for which a significant group of buyers is willing to make a special purchase effort.

Unsought product
Consumer product that the consumer either does not know about or knows about but does not normally think of buying.

Convenience products are consumer products and services that the customer usually buys frequently, immediately, and with a minimum of comparison and buying effort. Examples include soap, candy, newspapers, and fast food. Convenience products are usually low priced, and marketers place them in many locations to make them readily available when customers need them.

Shopping products are less frequently purchased consumer products and services that customers compare carefully on suitability, quality, price, and style. When buying shopping products and services, consumers spend much time and effort in gathering information and making comparisons. Examples include furniture, clothing, used cars, major appliances, and hotel and airline services. Shopping products marketers usually distribute their products through fewer outlets but provide deeper sales support to help customers in their comparison efforts.

Specialty products are consumer products and services with unique characteristics or brand identification for which a significant group of buyers is willing to make a special purchase effort. Examples include specific brands and types of cars, high-priced photographic equipment, designer clothes, and the services of medical or legal specialists. A Lamborghini automobile, for example, is a specialty product because buyers are usually willing to travel great distances to buy one. Buyers normally do not compare specialty products. They invest only the time needed to reach dealers carrying the wanted products.

Unsought products are consumer products that the consumer either does not know about or knows about but does not normally think of buying. Most major new innovations are unsought until the consumer becomes aware of them through advertising. Classic examples of known but unsought products and services are life insurance, cemetery plots, and blood donations to the Red Cross. By their very nature, unsought products require a lot of advertising, personal selling, and other marketing efforts.

Industrial product
Product bought by individuals and organizations for further processing or for use in conducting a business.

Industrial Products **Industrial products** are those purchased for further processing or for use in conducting a business. Thus, the distinction between a consumer product and an industrial product is based on the *purpose* for which the product is bought. If a consumer buys a lawn mower for use around home, the lawn mower is a consumer product. If the same consumer buys the same lawn mower for use in a landscaping business, the lawn mower is an industrial product.

The three groups of industrial products and services include materials and parts, capital items, and supplies and services. *Materials and parts* include raw materials and manufactured materials and parts. Raw materials consist of farm products (wheat, cotton, livestock, fruits, vegetables) and natural products (fish, lumber, crude petroleum, iron ore). Manufactured materials and parts consist of component materials (iron, yarn, cement, wires) and component parts (small motors, tires, castings). Most manufactured materials and parts are sold directly to industrial users. Price and service are the major marketing factors; branding and advertising tend to be less important.

Capital items are industrial products that aid in the buyer's production or operations, including installations and accessory equipment. Installations consist of major purchases such as buildings (factories, offices) and fixed equipment (generators, drill presses, large computer systems, elevators). Accessory equipment includes portable factory equipment and tools (hand tools, lift trucks) and office equipment (computers, fax machines, desks). They have a shorter life than installations and simply aid in the production process.

■ Business Services: Aramark offers everything from food, housekeeping, laundry, and office services, to equipment maintenance, to facilities and supply chain management.

The final group of business products is *supplies and services*. Supplies include operating supplies (lubricants, coal, paper, pencils) and repair and maintenance items (paint, nails, brooms). Supplies are the convenience products of the industrial field because they are usually purchased with a minimum of effort or comparison. Business services include maintenance and repair services (window cleaning, computer repair) and business advisory services (legal, management consulting, advertising). Such services are usually supplied under contract. For example, Aramark offers everything from food, housekeeping, laundry, and office services, to equipment maintenance, to facilities and supply chain management.

Organizations, Persons, Places, and Ideas In addition to tangible products and services, in recent years marketers have broadened the concept of a product to include other market offerings—organizations, persons, places, and ideas.

Organizations often carry out activities to "sell" the organization itself. *Organization marketing* consists of activities undertaken to create, maintain, or change the attitudes and behavior of target consumers toward an organization. Both profit and not-for-profit organizations practice organization marketing. Business firms sponsor public relations or corporate advertising campaigns to polish their images. *Corporate image advertising* is a major tool companies use to market themselves to various publics. For example, Lucent puts out ads with the tag line "We make the things that make communications work." IBM wants to establish itself as the company to turn to for "e-Business Solutions." And General Electric stands for "imagination at work." Similarly, nonprofit organizations, such as churches, colleges, charities, museums, and performing arts groups, market their organizations in order to raise funds and attract members or patrons.

People can also be thought of as products. *Person marketing* consists of activities undertaken to create, maintain, or change attitudes or behavior toward particular people. All kinds of people and organizations practice person marketing. Today's presidents market themselves, their parties, and their platforms to get needed votes and program support. Entertainers and sports figures use marketing to promote their careers and improve their impact and incomes. Professionals such as doctors, lawyers, accountants, and architects market themselves in order to build their reputations and increase business. Businesses, charities, sports teams, fine arts groups, religious groups, and other organizations also use person marketing. Creating or associating with well-known personalities often helps these organizations achieve their goals better. That's why more than a dozen different companies combined—including Nike, Target, Buick, American Express, Disney, and Titleist—pay more than $100 million a year to link themselves with golf superstar Tiger Woods.[4]

Place marketing involves activities undertaken to create, maintain, or change attitudes or behavior toward particular places. Cities, states, regions, and even entire nations compete to attract tourists, new residents, conventions, and company offices and factories. Texas advertises "It's Like a Whole Other Country" and New York State shouts, "I Love New York!"[5] Michigan says "Great Lakes, Great Times" to attract tourists, "Great Lakes, Great Jobs" to attract residents, and "Great Lakes, Great Location" to attract businesses. The Irish Development Agency has attracted more than 1,200 companies to locate their plants in Ireland. At the same time, the Irish

■ Organization marketing: Companies use corporate image advertising to market themselves to various publics. General Electric stands for "imagination at work."

Tourist Board has built a flourishing tourism business by advertising "Live a different life: friendly, beautiful, relaxing." And the Irish Export Board has created attractive markets for Irish exports.[6]

Ideas can also be marketed. In one sense, all marketing is the marketing of an idea, whether it be the general idea of brushing your teeth or the specific idea that Crest toothpastes "create smiles every day." Here, however, we narrow our focus to the marketing of *social ideas*. This area has been called **social marketing**, defined by the Social Marketing Institute as the use of commercial marketing concepts and tools in programs designed to influence individuals' behavior to improve their well-being and that of society.[7]

Social marketing

The design, implementation, and control of programs seeking to increase the acceptability of a social idea, cause, or practice among a target group.

Social marketing programs include public health campaigns to reduce smoking, alcoholism, drug abuse, and overeating. Other social marketing efforts include environmental campaigns to promote wilderness protection, clean air, and conservation. Still others address issues such as family planning, human rights, and racial equality. The Ad Council of America has developed dozens of social advertising campaigns, involving issues ranging from preventive health, education, and personal safety to environmental preservation (see Marketing at Work 7.2).

But social marketing involves much more than just advertising—the Social Marketing Institute encourages the use of a broad range of marketing tools. "Social marketing goes well beyond the promotional '*P*' of the marketing mix to include every other element to achieve its social change objectives," says the SMI's executive director.[8]

■■ Product and Service Decisions

Marketers make product and services decisions at three levels: individual product decisions, product line decisions, and product mix decisions. We discuss each in turn.

Individual Product and Service Decisions

Figure 7.2 shows the important decisions in the development and marketing of individual products and services. We will focus on decisions about *product attributes*, *branding*, *packaging*, *labeling*, and *product support services*.

Product and Service Attributes Developing a product or service involves defining the benefits that it will offer. These benefits are communicated and delivered by product attributes such as *quality*, *features*, and *style and design*.

Product Quality. **Product quality** is one of the marketer's major positioning tools. Quality has a direct impact on product or service performance; thus, it is closely linked to customer value and satisfaction. In the narrowest sense, quality can be defined as "freedom from defects." But most customer-centered companies go beyond this narrow definition. Instead, they define quality in terms of customer satisfaction. The American Society for Quality defines quality as the characteristics of a product or service that bear on its ability to satisfy stated or implied customer needs. Similarly, Siemens defines quality this way: "Quality is when our customers come back and our products don't."[9] These customer-focused definitions suggest that quality begins with customer needs and ends with customer satisfaction.

Total quality management (TQM) is an approach in which all the company's people are involved in constantly improving the quality of products, services, and business

Product quality

The ability of a product to perform its functions; it includes the product's overall durability, reliability, precision, ease of operation and repair, and other valued attributes.

FIGURE 7.2

Individual Product Decisions

Product attributes → Branding → Packaging → Labeling → Product support services

Marketing at Work | 7.2

The Ad Council: Advertising for the Common Good

How are these for familiar phrases? "Friends don't let friends drive drunk." "Only you can prevent forest fires." "Take a bite out of crime." "A mind is a terrible thing to waste." "Loose lips sink ships." "I am an American." Or how about these familiar characters: Smokey Bear, Rosie the Riveter, the Crash Test Dummies, and McGruff the Crime Dog? What do all of these phrases and icons have in common? They were all created by the Ad Council, a private, nonprofit organization with a long history of using advertising to create positive change.

The Ad Council was formed in 1942, at a time when people were especially cynical about advertising and all the money spent on it, to show the good that advertising can do. Its mission is "to identify a select number of significant public issues and stimulate action on those issues through communications programs that make a measurable difference in our society." To that end, the Ad Council works to connect ad agencies (who donate their time), sponsors (who donate money), and media (who donate advertising time and space) with worthy nonprofit organizations and governmental agencies that need a promotional voice.

Through this joint volunteer effort, the Ad Council has created thousands of public service campaigns on issues such as improving the quality of life for children, preventive health, education, community well-being, environmental preservation, personal safety, and strengthening families. These campaigns have produced more than just catchy slogans—they've produced positive and lasting social change as well. Ad Council campaigns have achieved significant results on a wide breadth of issues:

■ *Environment:*   Launched in 1944, Smokey Bear has been urging children

and adults not to play with matches, not to leave a campfire unattended, and to keep a bucket of water and a shovel nearby. Since the campaign began, the number of forest acres lost

to fires annually has decreased from 22 million to 4 million.

■ *Education:*   The Ad Council teamed with Young & Rubicam advertising agency to create a campaign

The Ad Council has created thousands of public service campaigns that have produced positive and lasting social change.

(continued)

message, "A mind is a terrible thing to waste." Now in its 30th year, the campaign has helped raise more than $1.9 billion for the United Negro College Fund and helped more than 300,000 minority students graduate college.

■ *Health:* In the 1940s, Ad Council campaigns urged Americans to get vaccinated against polio—not an easy sell at the time because the vaccination involved three sets of unpleasant shots. Today, polio is virtually unheard-of in this country.

■ *Crime awareness and prevention:* In 1978, working with the National Crime Prevention Council and the ad firm Saatchi & Saatchi, the Ad Council helped give birth to McGruff the Crime Dog. Since then, McGruff has taught both children and adults valuable crime awareness and crime prevention lessons, encouraging all of us to "Take A Bite Out Of Crime," The familiar blood-hound in a trench coat has become a popular icon. A 2000 study showed that 92 percent of American children recognize the character and believes he offers advice that helps them stay safe. In 1989 and 1990, McGruff the Crime Dog's popularity was surpassed only by that of Mickey Mouse.

■ *Seat-Belt Use:* When Vince & Larry, the crash-test dummies, first flew through a windshield on network TV in 1985, seat-belt usage was at 21 percent and most states did not mandate seat belt usage by law. Since then, most states have adopted seat-belt laws and safety-belt usage has

increased from 21 percent to 73 percent, saving an estimated 85,000 lives.

■ *Drunk Driving:* Since the Ad Council began its drunk-driving prevention campaign, the old saying "One more for the road" has been replaced with "Friends Don't Let Friends Drive Drunk." Some 68 percent of Americans say they have personally stopped someone from driving drunk.

■ *Social Issues:* More than 6,000 children were paired with a mentor in just the first 18 months of the Ad Council's mentoring campaign. And public awareness about child abuse has increased from just 10 percent in the mid-1970s to more than 90 percent today. According to the CEO of Prevent Child Abuse America, "When we first started our child abuse prevention campaign, the public's understanding of the issue was very low. But our partnership with the Ad Council has brought child abuse and neglect out into the open."

The Ad Council has drawn widespread support for its social marketing mission. Some 28,000 media outlets have contributed free ad space and time, and hundreds of socially conscious corporations, foundations, and individuals have provided crucial operating funds. Big ad agencies like J. Walter Thompson, Young & Rubicam, BBDO, Doyle Dane Bernbach, and Foote, Cone & Belding, and Marstellar willingly donate their creative energies to create Ad Council campaigns. And

the campaigns often turn out to be some of their very best work. For example, Marstellar's "People start pollution, people can stop it" campaign on behalf of Keep America Beautiful rates as one of the most memorable campaigns in history. The campaign ranked 50th on Advertising Age's list of top 100 ad campaigns of the century. And Foote, Cone & Belding's Smokey Bear and "Only you can prevent forest fires" campaign ranked 26th on the Ad Age top 100 list.

The Ad Council has established social marketing campaigns as an effective, admirable side of the advertising industry. It has proven that advertising can be used to do good, and its success has spawned other social marketing efforts. Nonprofit groups such as Partnership for a Drug-Free America have followed suit with additional public service announcements. And TV networks now routinely use their stars to promote worthy causes (such as NBC's "The More You Know . . . " series). "The Ad Council was a model that proved it could work," says former Ad Council president Ruth Wooden. Advertising no longer just pushes products—it improves, and even saves, human lives.

Sources: See Bob Garfield, "Inspiration and Urge-to-Serve Mark the Best of the Ad Council," *Advertising Age,* April 29, 2002, pp. c2–c20; and MEDIAWEEK Special Advertising Section, June 10, 2002. Portions adapted from "The Advertising Council," accessed at www.adcouncil.org/about/, July 2003.

processes. During the past two decades, companies large and small have credited TQM with greatly improving their market shares and profits. Recently, however, the total quality management movement has drawn criticism. Too many companies viewed TQM as a magic cure-all and created token total quality programs that applied quality principles only superficially. Still others became obsessed with narrowly defined TQM principles and lost sight of broader concerns for customer value and satisfaction. As a result, many such programs failed, causing a backlash against TQM.

When applied in the context of creating customer satisfaction, however, *total quality* principles remain a requirement for success. Although many firms don't use the TQM label anymore, for most top companies customer-driven quality has become a way of doing business. Today, companies are taking a "return on quality" approach, viewing quality as an investment and holding quality efforts accountable for bottom-line results.[10]

Product quality has two dimensions—level and consistency. In developing a product, the marketer must first choose a *quality level* that will support the product's position in the target market. Here, product quality means *performance quality*—the ability of a product to perform its functions. For example, a Rolls-Royce provides higher performance quality than a Chevrolet: It has a smoother ride, handles better, and lasts longer. Companies rarely try to offer the highest possible performance quality level—few customers want or can afford the high levels of quality offered in products such as a Rolls-Royce automobile, a Sub-Zero refrigerator, or a Rolex watch. Instead, companies choose a quality level that matches target market needs and the quality levels of competing products.

Beyond quality level, high quality also can mean high levels of quality *consistency*. Here, product quality means *conformance quality*—freedom from defects and *consistency* in delivering a targeted level of performance. All companies should strive for high levels of conformance quality. In this sense, a Chevrolet can have just as much quality as a Rolls-Royce. Although a Chevy doesn't perform as well as a Rolls, it can as consistently deliver the quality that customers pay for and expect.

Many companies today have turned customer-driven quality into a potent strategic weapon. They create customer satisfaction and value by consistently and profitably meeting customers' needs and preferences for quality.

Product Features. A product can be offered with varying features. A stripped-down model, one without any extras, is the starting point. The company can create higher-level models by adding more features. Features are a competitive tool for differentiating the company's product from competitors' products. Being the first producer to introduce a needed and valued new feature is one of the most effective ways to compete.

How can a company identify new features and decide which ones to add to its product? The company should periodically survey buyers who have used the product and ask these questions: How do you like the product? Which specific features of the product do you like most? Which features could we add to improve the product? The answers provide the company with a rich list of feature ideas. The company can then assess each feature's *value* to customers versus its *cost* to the company. Features that customers value little in relation to costs should be dropped; those that customers value highly in relation to costs should be added.

Product Style and Design. Another way to add customer value is through distinctive *product style and design*. Design is a larger concept than style. *Style* simply describes the appearance of a product. Styles can be eye-catching or yawn producing. A sensational style may grab attention and produce pleasing aesthetics, but it does not necessarily make the product *perform* better. Unlike style, *design* is more than skin deep—it goes to the very heart of a product. Good design contributes to a product's usefulness as well as to its looks.

Good style and design can attract attention, improve product performance, cut production costs, and give the product a strong competitive advantage in the target market. Here are two examples:

> Apple's original iMac—which featured a sleek, egg-shaped monitor and hard drive, all in one unit, in a futuristic translucent turquoise casing—redefined the look and feel of the personal computer. There was no clunky tower or desktop hard drive to clutter up your office area. Featuring one-button Internet access, this machine was designed specifically for cruising the Internet (that's what the "i" in "iMac" stands for). The dramatic iMac won raves for design and lured buyers in droves. Within a year, it had sold more than a million units, marking Apple's reemergence in the personal computer industry. Before it was over, Apple had sold more than 10 million of the original iMacs. "If they had not done that," says an industry insider, "they probably would have gone under. It captured the world's attention and put Apple back on the map." Four years later, Apple did it again with a stunning new iMac design—a clean, futuristic machine featuring a flat-panel display that seems to float in the air. Within only three months, Apple-lovers had snapped up nearly one-quarter million of these eye-pleasing yet functional machines.[11]

■ Product design: The design of the dramatic iMac helped reestablish Apple as a legitimate contender in the PC industry. The innovative Discover 2GO card is a gotta-have-it accessory for people who want to dash off to the gym, the mall, or a restaurant with nothing more than their keys and a credit card.

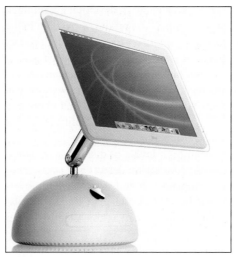
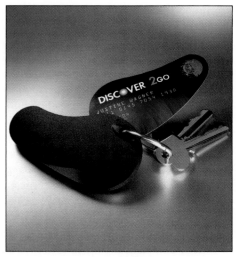

You turn the flat, kidney-shaped plastic gadget over in your hands, puzzling over what it does. Then you realize that a sliver of red plastic pivots out of the black case like a pocketknife blade. You recognize a familiar strand of embossed numbers, a magnetic stripe, and a signature bar. It's a credit card! To be precise, it's a Discover 2GO card, complete with a key chain, belt clip, and protective case. In consumer terms, the Discover 2GO card is a gotta-have-it accessory for people who want to dash off to the gym, the mall, or a restaurant with nothing more than their keys and a credit card. In industry terms, it's a big design innovation in a business that has rarely thought much outside the 2-by-3-inch box. The Discover 2GO card's design won it recognition as one of the best products of the year last year by *USA Today* and *Business Week*. It has also drawn praise from card marketing experts. "This is slick. It's different, which is good. And it's functional," says one consultant. "It's the card you'll use when you have your keys in your hand."[12]

Branding Perhaps the most distinctive skill of professional marketers is their ability to create, maintain, protect, and enhance brands of their products and services. A **brand** is a name, term, sign, symbol, or design, or a combination of these, that identifies the maker or seller of a product or service. Consumers view a brand as an important part of a product, and branding can add value to a product. For example, most consumers would perceive a bottle of White Linen perfume as a high-quality, expensive product. But the same perfume in an unmarked bottle would likely be viewed as lower in quality, even if the fragrance were identical.

Brand
A name, term, sign, symbol, or design, or a combination of these intended to identify the goods or services of one seller or group of sellers and to differentiate them from those of competitors.

Branding has become so strong that today hardly anything goes unbranded. Salt is packaged in branded containers, common nuts and bolts are packaged with a distributor's label, and automobile parts—spark plugs, tires, filters—bear brand names that differ from those of the auto makers. Even fruits, vegetables, and poultry are branded—Sunkist oranges, Dole pineapples, Chiquita bananas, Fresh Express salad greens, and Perdue chickens.

Branding helps buyers in many ways. Brand names help consumers identify products that might benefit them. Brands also tell the buyer something about product quality. Buyers who always buy the same brand know that they will get the same features, benefits, and quality each time they buy. Branding also gives the seller several advantages. The brand name becomes the basis on which a whole story can be built about a product's special qualities. The seller's brand name and trademark provide legal protection for unique product features that otherwise might be copied by competitors. And branding helps the seller to segment markets. For example, General Mills can offer Cheerios, Wheaties, Total, Kix, Lucky Charms, Trix, and many other cereal brands, not just one general product for all consumers.

Building and managing brands is perhaps the marketer's most important task. We will discuss branding strategy in more detail later in the chapter.

Packaging **Packaging** involves designing and producing the container or wrapper for a product. The package includes a product's primary container (the tube holding Colgate Total toothpaste). It may also include a secondary package that is thrown away when the product is about to be used (the cardboard box containing the tube of Colgate). Finally, it can include a shipping package necessary to store, identify, and ship the product (a corrugated box carrying six dozen tubes of Colgate). Labeling, printed information appearing on or with the package, is also part of packaging.

Traditionally, the primary function of the package was to contain and protect the product. In recent times, however, numerous factors have made packaging an important marketing tool. Increased competition and clutter on retail store shelves means that packages must now perform many sales tasks—from attracting attention, to describing the product, to making the sale.

Companies are realizing the power of good packaging to create instant consumer recognition of the company or brand. For example, in an average supermarket, which stocks 15,000 to 17,000 items, the typical shopper passes by some 300 items per minute, and more than 60 percent of all purchases are made on impulse. In this highly competitive environment, the package may be the seller's last chance to influence buyers. "Not long ago, the package was merely the product's receptacle, and the brand message was elsewhere—usually on TV," says a packaging expert. But changes in the marketplace environment are now "making the package itself an increasingly important selling medium."[13]

Innovative packaging can give a company an advantage over competitors. Consumer packaged goods firms have recently upped their investments in packaging research to develop package designs that grab more shelf attention or make life easier for customers. Notable examples include Skippy Squeez'It peanut butter, dispensed from tubes for on-the-go families, and Coca-Cola beverage packs designed to fit neatly onto refrigerator shelves. Dutch Boy recently came up with a long overdue innovation—paint in plastic containers with twist-off caps:

> How did Dutch Boy Paint stir up the paint business? It's so simple, it's scary. Imagine a paint can that's easy to carry, doesn't take a screwdriver to pry open, doesn't dribble when pouring, and doesn't take a hammer to bang closed again. It's here—in the form of Dutch Boy's new Twist and Pour paint container. The new container is an all-plastic gallon container with a twist-off lid, side handle, and pour spout. It's lighter weight than a can and rust-proof, too. "It's so much easier to use," says Dutch Boy's marketing director. "You can hold it like a cup of coffee." It kind of makes you wonder: Why did it take so long to come up with an idea like this? The new containers cost a dollar or two more than traditional cans, but consumers don't seem to mind. More than 50 percent of Dutch Boy's customers are now buying the plastic containers, and new stores, like Wal-Mart, are now carrying it. "It's an amazing innovation. Worth noticing," says one observer. "Not only did the new packaging increase sales, but it also got them more distribution at a higher retail price!"[14]

In contrast, poorly designed packages can cause headaches for consumers and lost sales for the company (see Marketing at Work 7.3). For example, a few years ago, Planters Lifesavers Company attempted to use innovative packaging to create an association between fresh-roasted peanuts and fresh-roasted coffee. It packaged its Fresh Roast Salted Peanuts in vacuum-packed "Brik-Pacs," similar to those used for ground coffee. Unfortunately, the coffeelike

Packaging
The activities of designing and producing the container or wrapper for a product.

INTRODUCING THE NEW TWIST AND POUR™ PAINT CONTAINER, ONLY FROM DUTCH BOY®

THE NEAT NEW PAINT 'CAN' WITH A TWIST

Easy to hold
Easy to open
Easy to pour

Dutch Boy®

For a Twist and Pour retailer near you, call 1-800-828-5669 or visit www.dutchboy.com
* U.S. and foreign patents pending

■ Innovative packaging: Dutch Boy recently came up with a long overdue innovation—paint in plastic containers with twist-off caps. Imagine a paint can that's easy to carry, doesn't take a screwdriver to pry open, doesn't dribble when pouring, and doesn't take a hammer to bang closed again.

Marketing at Work 7.3

Those Frustrating, Not-So-Easy-To-Open Packages

Some things, it seems, will never change. This classic letter from an angry consumer to Robert D. Stuart, then chairman of Quaker Oats, beautifully expresses the utter frustration all of us have experienced in dealing with so-called easy-opening packages.

Dear Mr. Stuart:

I am an 86-year-old widow in fairly good health. (You may think of this as advanced age, but for me that description pertains to the years ahead. Nevertheless, if you decide to reply to this letter I wouldn't dawdle, actuarial tables being what they are.)

As I said, my health is fairly good. Feeble and elderly, as one understands these terms, I am not. My two Doberman Pinschers and I take a brisk 3-mile walk every day. They are two strong and energetic animals and it takes a bit of doing to keep "brisk" closer to a stroll than a mad dash. But I manage because as yet I don't lack the strength. You will shortly see why this fact is relevant.

I am writing to call your attention to the cruel, deceptive, and utterly [false] copy on your Aunt Jemima buttermilk complete pancake and waffle mix. The words on your package read, "to open—press here and pull back."

Mr. Stuart, though I push and press and groan and strive and writhe and curse and sweat and jab and push, poke and ram . . . whew!—I have never once been able to do what the package instructs—to "press here and pull back" the [blankety-blank]. It can't be done! Talk about failing strength! Have you ever tried and succeeded?

My late husband was a gun collector who among other lethal weapons kept a Thompson machine gun in a locked cabinet. It was a good thing that the cabinet was locked. Oh, the number of times I was tempted to give your package a few short bursts.

That lock and a sense of ladylike delicacy kept me from pursuing that vengeful fantasy. Instead, I keep a small cleaver in my pantry for those occasions when I need to open a package of your delicious Aunt Jemima pancakes.

For many years that whacking away with my cleaver served a dual purpose. Not only to open the [blankety-blank] package but also to vent my fury at your sadists who willfully and maliciously did design that torture apparatus that passes for a package.

Sometimes just for the [blank] of it I let myself get carried away. I don't stop after I've lopped off the top. I whack away until the package is utterly destroyed in an outburst of rage, frustration, and vindictiveness. I wind up with a floorful of your delicious Aunt Jemima pancake mix. But that's a small price to pay for blessed release. (Anyway, the Pinschers lap up the mess.)

So many ingenious, considerate (even compassionate) innovations in package closures have been designed since Aunt Jemima first donned her red bandana. Wouldn't you consider the introduction of a more humane package to replace the example of marketing malevolence to which you resolutely cling? Don't you care, Mr. Stuart?

I'm really writing this to be helpful and in that spirit I am sending a copy to Mr. Tucker, president of Container Corp. I'm sure their clever young designers could be of immeasurable help to you in this matter. At least I feel it's worth a try.

Really, Mr. Stuart, I hope you will not regard me as just another cranky old biddy. I am The Public, the source of your fortunes.

Ms. Roberta Pavloff
Malvern, Pa.

Source: This letter was reprinted in "Some Designs Should Just Be Torn Asunder," *Advertising Age*, January 17, 1983, p. M54.

An easy to open package?

packaging worked too well: Consumers mistook the peanuts for a new brand of flavored coffee and ran them through supermarket coffee-grinding machines, creating a gooey mess, disappointed customers, and lots of irate store managers.[15]

Developing a good package for a new product requires making many decisions. First, the company must establish the *packaging concept,* which states what the package should *be* or *do* for the product. Should it mainly offer product protection, introduce a new dispensing method, suggest certain qualities about the product, or do something else? Decisions then must be made on specific elements of the package, such as size, shape, materials, color, text, and brand mark. These elements must work together to support the product's position and marketing strategy.

In recent years, product safety has also become a major packaging concern. We have all learned to deal with hard-to-open "childproof " packages. And after the rash of product tampering scares during the 1980s, most drug producers and food makers now put their products in tamper-resistant packages. In making packaging decisions, the company also must heed growing environmental concerns. Fortunately, many companies have gone "green" by reducing their packaging and using environmentally responsible packaging materials. For example, SC Johnson repackaged Agree Plus shampoo in a stand-up pouch using 80 percent less plastic. P&G eliminated outer cartons from its Secret and Sure deodorants, saving 3.4 million pounds of paperboard per year.

Labeling Labels may range from simple tags attached to products to complex graphics that are part of the package. They perform several functions. At the very least, the label *identifies* the product or brand, such as the name Sunkist stamped on oranges. The label might also *describe* several things about the product—who made it, where it was made, when it was made, its contents, how it is to be used, and how to use it safely. Finally, the label might *promote* the product through attractive graphics.

There has been a long history of legal concerns about packaging and labels. The Federal Trade Commission Act of 1914 held that false, misleading, or deceptive labels or packages constitute unfair competition. Labels can mislead customers, fail to describe important ingredients, or fail to include needed safety warnings. As a result, several federal and state laws regulate labeling. The most prominent is the Fair Packaging and Labeling Act of 1966, which set mandatory labeling requirements, encouraged voluntary industry packaging standards, and allowed federal agencies to set packaging regulations in specific industries.

Labeling has been affected in recent times by *unit pricing* (stating the price per unit of a standard measure), *open dating* (stating the expected shelf life of the product), and *nutritional labeling* (stating the nutritional values in the product). The Nutritional Labeling and Educational Act of 1990 requires sellers to provide detailed nutritional information on food products, and recent sweeping actions by the Food and Drug Administration regulate the use of health-related terms such as *low-fat, light,* and *high-fiber.* Sellers must ensure that their labels contain all the required information.

Product Support Services Customer service is another element of product strategy. A company's offer to the marketplace usually includes some support services, which can be a minor or a major part of the total offering. Later in the chapter, we will discuss services as products in themselves. Here, we discuss services that augment actual products.

The first step is to survey customers periodically to assess the value of current services and to

■ Innovative labeling can help to promote a product.

obtain ideas for new ones. For example, Cadillac holds regular focus group interviews with owners and carefully watches complaints that come into its dealerships. From this careful monitoring, Cadillac has learned that buyers are very upset by repairs that are not done correctly the first time.

Once the company has assessed the value of various support services to customers, it must next assess the costs of providing these services. It can then develop a package of services that will both delight customers and yield profits to the company. Based on its consumer interviews, Cadillac has set up a system directly linking each dealership with a group of 10 engineers who can help walk mechanics through difficult repairs. Such actions helped Cadillac jump, in one year, from 14th to 7th in independent rankings of service. For the past several years, Cadillac has rated at or near the top of its industry on the American Customer Satisfaction Index.[16]

Many companies are now using a sophisticated mix of phone, e-mail, fax, Internet, and interactive voice and data technologies to provide support services that were not possible before. Consider the following example:

> It's February 14, and you've just remembered that it's Valentine's Day. There's no time for florist shops, so you jump online to www.1800FLOWERS.com. Then you pause. Red roses? Boxed or in a vase? One dozen or two? Just as your head starts to pound, you notice a button on the Web site. Click on it, and you're connected to a customer service rep at the call center who can help sniff out your options. A chat page opens on your screen, allowing a real-time dialog with the agent. The service rep even "pushes" pages to your browser so you can see different floral arrangements and how much they cost. In minutes, you have placed your order online, with a little hand-holding. Like 1-800-Flowers, many e-marketers now offer live interaction with service reps. Some feature real-time chat sessions, others voice-over-Web capabilities. In the future, a "call cam" will even let consumers see an agent on their computer screen.[17]

Product Line Decisions

Product line

A group of products that are closely related because they function in a similar manner, are sold to the same customer groups, are marketed through the same types of outlets, or fall within given price ranges.

Beyond decisions about individual products and services, product strategy also calls for building a product line. A **product line** is a group of products that are closely related because they function in a similar manner, are sold to the same customer groups, are marketed through the same types of outlets, or fall within given price ranges. For example, Nike produces several lines of athletic shoes and apparel, Nokia produces several lines of telecommunications products, and Charles Schwab produces several lines of financial services.

The major product line decision involves *product line length*—the number of items in the product line. The line is too short if the manager can increase profits by adding items; the line is too long if the manager can increase profits by dropping items. The company should manage its product lines carefully. Product lines tend to lengthen over time, and most companies eventually need to prune unnecessary or unprofitable items from their lines to increase overall profitability.

Product line length is influenced by company objectives and resources. For example, one objective might be to allow for up-selling. Thus, BMW wants to move customers up from its 3-series models to 5- and 7-series models. Another objective might be to allow cross-selling: Hewlett-Packard sells printers as well as cartridges. Still another objective might be to protect against economic swings: Gap runs several clothing-store chains (Gap, Old Navy, Banana Republic) covering different price points.

A company can lengthen its product line in two ways: by *line stretching* or by *line filling*. *Product line stretching* occurs when a company lengthens its product line beyond its current range. The company can stretch its line downward, upward, or both ways.

Companies located at the upper end of the market can stretch their lines *downward*. A company may stretch downward to plug a market hole that otherwise would attract a new competitor or to respond to a competitor's attack on the upper end. Or it may add low-end products because it finds faster growth taking place in the low-end segments. DaimlerChrysler stretched its Mercedes line downward for all these reasons. Facing a slow-growth luxury car market and attacks by Japanese auto makers on its high-end positioning, it successfully introduced its Mercedes C-Class cars. These models sell at less than $30,000 without harming the firm's ability to sell other Mercedes for $100,000 or more. Similarly, Rolex launched its Rolex Tudor watch retailing for about $1,350, compared with a Rolex Submariner, usually priced at $3,875.

Companies at the lower end of a market can stretch their product lines *upward*. Sometimes, companies stretch upward in order to add prestige to their current products. Or they may be attracted by a faster growth rate or higher margins at the higher end. For example, each of the leading Japanese auto companies introduced an upmarket automobile: Toyota launched Lexus; Nissan launched Infinity; and Honda launched Acura. They used entirely new names rather than their own.

Companies in the middle range of the market may decide to stretch their lines in *both directions*. Marriott did this with its hotel product line. Along with regular Marriott hotels, it added the Renaissance Hotel line to serve the upper end of the market and the TownePlace Suites line to serve the moderate and lower ends. Each branded hotel line is aimed at a different target market. Renaissance aims to attract and please top executives; Marriotts, upper and middle managers; Courtyards, salespeople and other "road warriors"; and Fairfield Inns, vacationers and business travelers on a tight travel budget. ExecuStay by Marriott provides temporary housing for those relocating or away on long-term assignments of 30 days or longer. Marriott's Residence Inn provides a relaxed, residential atmosphere—a home away from home for people who travel for a living. Marriott TownePlace Suites provide a comfortable atmosphere at a moderate price for extended-stay travelers.[18] The major risk with this strategy is that some travelers will trade down after finding that the lower-price hotels in the Marriott chain give them pretty much everything they want. However, Marriott would rather capture its customers who move downward than lose them to competitors.

An alternative to product line stretching is *product line filling*—adding more items within the present range of the line. There are several reasons for product line filling: reaching for extra profits, satisfying dealers, using excess capacity, being the leading full-line company, and plugging holes to keep out competitors. Sony filled its Walkman line by adding solar-powered and waterproof Walkmans, an ultralight model that attaches to a sweatband for exercisers, the MiniDisc Walkman, the CD Walkman, and the Memory Stick Walkman, which enables users to download tracks straight from the Net. However, line

■ Product line stretching: Marriott offers a full line of hotel brands, each aimed at a different target market.

filling is overdone if it results in cannibalization and customer confusion. The company should ensure that new items are noticeably different from existing ones.

Product Mix Decisions

Product mix (or product assortment)

The set of all product lines and items that a particular seller offers for sale.

An organization with several product lines has a product mix. A **product mix** (or **product assortment**) consists of all the product lines and items that a particular seller offers for sale. Avon's product mix consists of five major product lines: beauty products, wellness products, jewelry and accessories, gifts, and "inspirational" products (inspiring gifts, books, music, and home accents). Each product line consists of several sublines. For example, the beauty line breaks down into makeup, skin care, bath and beauty, fragrance, and outdoor protection products. Each line and subline has many individual items. Altogether, Avon's product mix includes 1,300 items. In contrast, a typical Kmart stocks 15,000 items, 3M markets more than 60,000 products, and General Electric manufactures as many as 250,000 items.

A company's product mix has four important dimensions: width, length, depth, and consistency. Product mix *width* refers to the number of different product lines the company carries. Procter & Gamble markets a fairly wide product mix consisting of 250 brands organized into many product lines. These lines include fabric and home care; baby, feminine, and family care; beauty care; health care; and food and beverage products. Product mix *length* refers to the total number of items the company carries within its product lines. P&G typically carries many brands within each line. For example, it sells seven laundry detergents, six hand soaps, five shampoos, and four dishwashing detergents.

Product line *depth* refers to the number of versions offered of each product in the line. P&G's Crest toothpaste comes in 13 varieties, ranging from Crest Multicare, Crest Cavity Protection, and Crest Tartar Protection to Crest Sensitivity Protection, Crest Dual Action Whitening, Crest Whitening Plus Scope, Kid's Cavity Protection, and Crest Baking Soda & Peroxide Whitening formulations.[19] (Talk about niche marketing! Remember our Chapter 6 discussion?)

Finally, the *consistency* of the product mix refers to how closely related the various product lines are in end use, production requirements, distribution channels, or some other way. P&G's product lines are consistent insofar as they are consumer products that go through the same distribution channels. The lines are less consistent insofar as they perform different functions for buyers.

These product mix dimensions provide the handles for defining the company's product strategy. The company can increase its business in four ways. It can add new product lines, widening its product mix. In this way, its new lines build on the company's reputation in its other lines. The company can lengthen its existing product lines to become a more full-line company. Or it can add more versions of each product and thus deepen its product mix. Finally, the company can pursue more product line consistency—or less—depending on whether it wants to have a strong reputation in a single field or in several fields.

SPEED BUMP

Linking the Concepts

Slow down for a minute. To get a better sense of how large and complex a company's product offering can become, investigate Procter & Gamble's product mix.

■ Using P&G's Web site (www.pg.com), its annual report, or other sources, develop a list of all the company's product lines and individual products. What surprises you about this list of products?

■ Is P&G's product mix consistent? What overall strategy or logic appears to have guided the development of this product mix?

■ Branding Strategy: Building Strong Brands

Some analysts see brands as *the* major enduring asset of a company, outlasting the company's specific products and facilities. John Stewart, co-founder of Quaker Oats, once said, "If this business were split up, I would give you the land and bricks and mortar, and I would keep the brands and trademarks, and I would fare better than you." The CEO of McDonald's agrees[20]:

> A McDonald's board member who worked at Coca-Cola once talked to us about the value of our brand. He said if every asset we own, every building, and every piece of equipment were destroyed in a terrible natural disaster, we would be able to borrow all the money to replace it very quickly because of the value of our brand. And he's right. The brand is more valuable than the totality of all these assets.

Thus, brands are powerful assets that must be carefully developed and managed. In this section, we examine the key strategies for building and managing brands.

Brand Equity

Brands are more than just names and symbols. Brands represent consumers' perceptions and feelings about a product and its performance—everything that the product or service *means* to consumers. In the final analysis, brands exist in the minds of consumers. Thus, the real value of a strong brand is its power to capture consumer preference and loyalty.

Brands vary in the amount of power and value they have in the marketplace. Some brands—such as Coca-Cola, Tide, Nike, Harley-Davidson, Volkswagen, and others—become larger-than-life icons that maintain their power in the market for years, even generations. "These brands win competitive battles not [just] because they deliver distinctive benefits, trustworthy service, or innovative technologies," notes a branding expert. "Rather, they succeed because they forge a deep connection with the culture."[21]

A powerful brand has high *brand equity.* **Brand equity** is the positive differential effect that knowing the brand name has on customer response to the product or service. A measure of a brand's equity is the extent to which customers are willing to pay more for the brand. One study found that 72 percent of customers would pay a 20 percent premium for their brand of choice relative to the closest competing brand; 40 percent said they would pay a 50 percent premium.[22] Tide and Heinz lovers are willing to pay a 100 percent premium. Loyal Coke drinkers will pay a 50 percent premium and Volvo users a 40 percent premium.

A brand with strong brand equity is a very valuable asset. *Brand valuation* is the process of estimating the total financial value of a brand. Measuring such value is difficult. However, according to one estimate, the brand value of Coca-Cola is almost $70 billion, Microsoft is $65 billion, and IBM is $52 billion. Other brands rating among the world's most valuable include General Electric, Intel, Nokia, Disney, McDonald's, Marlboro, and Mercedes.[23]

High brand equity provides a company with many competitive advantages. A powerful brand enjoys a high level of consumer brand awareness and loyalty. Because consumers expect stores to

Brand equity
The positive differential effect that knowing the brand name has on customer response to the product or service.

■ A strong brand is a valuable asset. How many familiar brands and brand symbols can you find in this picture?

carry the brand, the company has more leverage in bargaining with resellers. Because the brand name carries high credibility, the company can more easily launch line and brand extensions, as when Coca-Cola used its well-known brand to introduce Diet Coke and Vanilla Coke, and when Procter & Gamble introduced Ivory dishwashing detergent. A powerful brand offers the company some defense against fierce price competition.

Above all, a powerful brand forms the basis for building strong and profitable customer relationships. Therefore, the fundamental asset underlying brand equity is *customer equity*—the value of the customer relationships that the brand creates. A powerful brand is important, but what it really represents is a set of loyal customers. The proper focus of marketing is building customer equity, with brand management serving as a major marketing tool.[24]

Building Strong Brands

Branding poses challenging decisions to the marketer. Figure 7.3 shows that the major brand strategy decisions involve brand positioning, brand name selection, brand sponsorship, and brand development.

Brand Positioning Marketers need to position their brands clearly in target customers' minds. They can position brands at any of three levels.[25] At the lowest level, they can position the brand on *product attributes.* Thus, marketers of Dove soap can talk about the product's attribute of one-quarter cleansing cream. However, attributes are the least desirable level for brand positioning. Competitors can easily copy attributes. More important, customers are not interested in attributes as such; they are interested in what the attributes will do for them.

A brand can be better positioned by associating its name with a desirable *benefit.* Thus, Dove marketers can go beyond the brand's cleansing cream attribute and talk about the resulting benefit of softer skin. Some successful brands positioned on benefits are Volvo (safety), Hallmark (caring), Harley-Davidson (adventure), FedEx (guaranteed overnight delivery), Nike (performance), and Lexus (quality).

The strongest brands go beyond attribute or benefit positioning. They are positioned on strong *beliefs and values.* These brands pack an emotional wallop. Thus, Dove's marketers can talk not just about cleansing cream attributes and softer skin benefits, but about how these will make you more attractive. Brand expert Marc Gobe argues that successful brands must engage customers on a deeper level, touching a universal emotion.[26] His brand design agency, which has worked on brands such as Starbucks, Victoria's Secret, Godiva, Versace, and Lancôme, relies less on a product's tangible attributes and more on creating surprise, passion, and excitement surrounding a brand.

When positioning a brand, the marketer should establish a mission for the brand and a vision of what the brand must be and do. A brand is the company's promise to deliver a specific set of features, benefits, services, and experiences consistently to the buyers. It can be thought of as a contract to the customer regarding how the product or service will deliver value and satisfaction. The brand contract must be simple and honest. Motel 6, for example, offers clean rooms, low prices, and good service but does not promise expensive furniture or large bathrooms. In contrast, Ritz-Carlton offers luxurious rooms and a truly memorable experience but does not promise low prices.

Brand Name Selection A good name can add greatly to a product's success. However, finding the best brand name is a difficult task. It begins with a careful review of the product and its benefits, the target market, and proposed marketing strategies.

■ Brand positioning: The strongest brands go beyond attribute or benefit positioning. They are positioned on what the brand will *do* for those who use it. Godiva says, "let your imagination out of its shell."

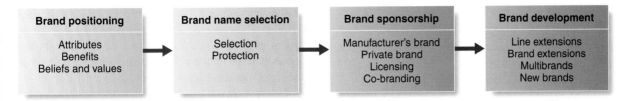

FIGURE 7.3

Major Brand Strategy Decisions

Desirable qualities for a brand name include the following: (1) It should suggest something about the product's benefits and qualities. Examples: Beautyrest, Craftsman, Snuggles, Merrie Maids, OFF! bug spray. (2) It should be easy to pronounce, recognize, and remember. Short names help. Examples: Tide, Crest, Puffs. But longer ones are sometimes effective. Examples: "Love My Carpet" carpet cleaner, "I Can't Believe It's Not Butter" margarine. (3) The brand name should be distinctive. Examples: Taurus, Kodak, Oracle. (4) It should be extendable: Amazon.com began as an online bookseller but chose a name that would allow expansion into other categories. (5) The name should translate easily into foreign languages. Before spending $100 million to change its name to Exxon, Standard Oil of New Jersey tested several names in 54 languages in more than 150 foreign markets. It found that the name Enco referred to a stalled engine when pronounced in Japanese. (6) It should be capable of registration and legal protection. A brand name cannot be registered if it infringes on existing brand names.

Once chosen, the brand name must be protected. Many firms try to build a brand name that will eventually become identified with the product category. Brand names such as Kleenex, Levi's, Jell-O, Scotch Tape, Formica, Ziploc, and Fiberglass have succeeded in this way. However, their very success may threaten the company's rights to the name. Many originally protected brand names—such as cellophane, aspirin, nylon, kerosene, linoleum, yo-yo, trampoline, escalator, thermos, and shredded wheat—are now generic names that any seller can use.

Brand Sponsorship   A manufacturer has four sponsorship options. The product may be launched as a *manufacturer's brand* (or national brand), as when Kellogg and IBM sell their output under their own manufacturer's brand names. Or the manufacturer may sell to resellers who give it a *private brand* (also called a *store brand* or *distributor brand*). Although most manufacturers create their own brand names, others market *licensed brands*. Finally, two companies can join forces and *co-brand* a product.

Manufacturer's Brands Versus Private Brands.   Manufacturers' brands have long dominated the retail scene. In recent times, however, an increasing number of retailers and wholesalers have created their own **private brands** (or *store brands*). For example, Sears has created several names—DieHard batteries, Craftsman tools, Kenmore appliances, and Weatherbeater paints. Wal-Mart offers Sam's Choice beverages and food products, Spring Valley nutritional products, Ol' Roy dog food (named for Sam Walton's Irish setter), and White Cloud brand toilet tissue, diapers, detergent, and fabric softener to compete against major national brands. Best Buy introduced its own brand of personal computers, VPR, which competes head to head with Dell. JCPenney has six core private label brands, including Stafford, St. John's Bay, and Arizona. In some cases, private brands even go head to head against designer brands. For example, Saks Fifth Avenue carries its own Platinum clothing line, which features $1,000 jackets and $500 cotton dress shirts. Private brands can be hard to establish and costly to stock and promote. However, they also yield higher profit margins for the reseller. And they give resellers exclusive products that cannot be bought from competitors, resulting in greater store traffic and loyalty.

In the so-called *battle of the brands* between manufacturers' and private brands, retailers have many advantages. They control what products they stock, where they go on the shelf, what prices they charge, and which ones they will feature in local circulars. Retailers

Private (or store) brand
A brand created and owned by a reseller of a product or service.

■ Store brands: Loblaw's President's Choice brand has become so popular that the company licenses it to retailers across the United States and in fifteen other countries where Loblaws has no stores of its own.

price their store brands lower than comparable manufacturers' brands, thereby appealing to budget-conscious shoppers, especially in difficult economic times. And most shoppers believe that store brands are often made by one of the larger manufacturers anyway.

Most retailers also charge manufacturers *slotting fees*—payments demanded by retailers before they will accept new products and find "slots" for them on the shelves. Slotting fees have recently received much scrutiny from the Federal Trade Commission, which worries that they might dampen competition by restricting retail shelf access for smaller manufacturers who can't afford the fees.[27]

As store brands improve in quality and as consumers gain confidence in their store chains, store brands are posing a strong challenge to manufacturers' brands. Consider the case of Loblaws, the Canadian supermarket chain.

Loblaws' President's Choice Decadent Chocolate Chip Cookies brand is now the leading cookie brand in Canada. Its private label President's Choice cola racks up 50 percent of Loblaws' canned cola sales. Based on this success, the private label powerhouse has expanded into a wide range of food and even nonfood categories. For example, it now offers more than 3,500 items under the President's Choice label, ranging from frozen desserts, paper, prepared foods, and boxed meats to pet foods, beauty care, and lawn and garden items. And the company has launched PC Financial, a Web-based bank that offers no-fee bank accounts and mortgages. The brand has become so popular that Loblaws now licenses it to retailers across the United States and fifteen other countries where Loblaws has no stores of its own. The company also offers a Web site where consumers can purchase its branded products directly.[28]

In U.S. supermarkets, taken as a single brand, private-label products are the number one, two, or three brand in over 40 percent of all grocery product categories. In all, they capture more than a 20 percent share of sales in U.S. supermarkets, drug chains, and mass merchandise stores. Private-label apparel captures a 36 percent share of all U.S. apparel sales.[29] To fend off private brands, leading brand marketers will have to invest in R&D to bring out new brands, new features, and continuous quality improvements. They must design strong advertising programs to maintain high awareness and preference. They must find ways to "partner" with major distributors in a search for distribution economies and improved joint performance.

Licensing. Most manufacturers take years and spend millions to create their own brand names. However, some companies license names or symbols previously created by other manufacturers, names of well-known celebrities, or characters from popular movies and books. For a fee, any of these can provide an instant and proven brand name.

Apparel and accessories sellers pay large royalties to adorn their products—from blouses to ties, and linens to luggage—with the names or initials of well-known fashion innovators such as Calvin Klein, Tommy Hilfiger, Gucci, or Armani. Sellers of children's products attach an almost endless list of character names to clothing, toys, school supplies, linens, dolls, lunch boxes, cereals, and other items. Licensed character names range from classics such as *Sesame Street*, Disney, Peanuts, Winnie the Pooh, the Muppets, Scooby Doo, and Dr. Seuss characters to the more recent Teletubbies, Pokemon, Powerpuff Girls, Rugrats, Blue's Clues, and Harry Potter characters. Almost half of all retail toy sales come from products based on television shows and movies such as *Scooby Doo, SpongeBob SquarePants, The Rugrats Movie, The Lion King, Batman, Star Trek, Star Wars, Spider-Man, Men in Black,* or *Harry Potter.*[30]

Name and character licensing has grown rapidly in recent years. Annual retail sales of licensed products in the United States and Canada has grown from only $4 billion in 1977 to $55 billion in 1987 and more than $71 billion today. Licensing can be a highly profitable business for many companies. For example, Warner Brothers has turned *Looney Tunes* characters into one of the world's most sought-after licenses. More than 225 licensees generate $6 billion in annual retail sales of products sporting Bugs Bunny, Daffy Duck, Foghorn Leghorn, or one of more than 100 other *Looney Tunes* characters. Warner Brothers has yet to tap the full potential of many of its secondary characters. The Tazmanian Devil, for example, initially appeared in only five cartoons. But through cross-licensing agreements with organizations such as Harley-Davidson and the NFL, Taz has become something of a pop icon. Warner Brothers sees similar potential for Michigan Frog or Speedy Gonzales for the Hispanic market.[31]

The fastest-growing licensing category is corporate brand licensing, as more and more for-profit and not-for-profit organizations are licensing their names to generate additional revenues and brand recognition. Coca-Cola, for example, has some 320 licensees in 57 countries producing more than 10,000 products, ranging from baby clothes and boxer shorts to earrings, a Coca-Cola Barbie doll, and even a fishing lure shaped like a tiny Coke can. Last year, licensees sold more than $1 billion worth of licensed Coca-Cola products.[32]

■ Character licensing: Warner Brothers has turned Looney Tunes characters into one of the world's most sought-after licenses. More than 225 licensees generate $6 billion in annual retail sales of products sporting one of more than 100 Looney Tunes characters.

Co-Branding. Although companies have been **co-branding** products for many years, there has been a recent resurgence in co-branded products. Co-branding occurs when two established brand names of different companies are used on the same product. For example, Nabisco joined forces with Pillsbury to create Pillsbury Oreo Bars baking mix, and Kellogg joined with ConAgra to co-brand Healthy Choice from Kellogg's cereals. Ford and Eddie Bauer co-branded a sport utility vehicle—the Ford Explorer, Eddie Bauer edition. General Electric worked with Culligan to develop its Water by Culligan Profile Performance refrigerator with a built-in Culligan water-filtration system. Mattel teamed with Coca-Cola to market Soda Fountain Sweetheart Barbie. In most co-branding situations, one company licenses another company's well-known brand to use in combination with its own.

Co-branding offers many advantages. Because each brand dominates in a different category, the combined brands create broader consumer appeal and greater brand equity. Co-branding also allows a company to expand its existing brand into a category it might otherwise have difficulty entering alone. For example, by licensing its Healthy Choice brand to Kellogg, ConAgra entered the breakfast segment with a solid product. In return, Kellogg could leverage the broad awareness of the Healthy Choice name in the cereal category.

Co-branding also has limitations. Such relationships usually involve complex legal contracts and licenses. Co-branding partners must carefully coordinate their advertising, sales promotion, and other marketing efforts. Finally, when co-branding, each partner must trust that the other will take good care of its brand. For example, consider the marriage between Kmart and the Martha Stewart housewares brand. When Kmart declared bankruptcy, it cast a shadow on the Martha Steward brand. In turn, when Martha Steward was accused of unethical or illegal financial dealings, it created negative associations for Kmart. As one Nabisco manager puts it, "Giving away your brand is a lot like giving away your child—you want to make sure everything is perfect."[33]

Co-branding
The practice of using the established brand names of two different companies on the same product.

FIGURE 7.4

Brand Development Strategies

		PRODUCT CATEGORY	
		Existing	**New**
BRAND NAME	**Existing**	Line extension	Brand extension
	New	Multibrands	New brands

Brand Development A company has four choices when it comes to developing brands (see Figure 7.4). It can introduce *line extensions* (existing brand names extended to new forms, sizes, and flavors of an existing product category), *brand extensions* (existing brand names extended to new product categories), *multibrands* (new brand names introduced in the same product category), or *new brands* (new brand names in new product categories).

Line extension

Using a successful brand name to introduce additional items in a given product category under the same brand name, such as new flavors, forms, colors, added ingredients, or package sizes.

Line Extensions. Line extensions occur when a company introduces additional items in a given product category under the same brand name, such as new flavors, forms, colors, ingredients, or package sizes. Thus, Dannon introduced several line extensions, including seven new yogurt flavors, a fat-free yogurt, and a large, economy-size yogurt. And Morton Salt has expanded its line to include regular iodized salt plus Morton Coarse Kosher Salt, Morton Lite Salt (low in sodium), Morton Popcorn Salt, and Morton Nature's Season seasoning blend. The vast majority of all new-product activity consists of line extensions.

A company might introduce line extensions as a low-cost, low-risk way to introduce new products. Or it might want to meet consumer desires for variety, to use excess capacity, or simply to command more shelf space from resellers. However, line extensions involve some risks. An overextended brand name might lose its specific meaning, or heavily extended brands can cause consumer confusion or frustration. For example, a consumer buying cereal at the local supermarket will be confronted by more than 150 brands, up to 30 different brands, flavors, and sizes of oatmeal alone. By itself, Quaker offers its original Quaker Oats, several flavors of Quaker instant oatmeal, and several dry cereals such as Oatmeal Squares, Toasted Oatmeal, and Toasted Oatmeal-Honey Nut.

■ Line extensions: Morton sells an entire line of salts and seasonings for every occasion.

Another risk is that sales of an extension may come at the expense of other items in the line. For example, the original Nabisco Fig Newtons cookies have now morphed into a full line of Newtons Fruit Chewy Cookies, including Cranberry Newtons, Blueberry Newtons, and Apple Newtons. Although all doing well, the original Fig Newton brand now seems like just another flavor. A line extension works best when it takes sales away from competing brands, not when it "cannibalizes" the company's other items.

Brand Extensions. A **brand extension** involves the use of a successful brand name to launch new or modified products in a new category. Mattel has extended its enduring Barbie Doll brand into new categories ranging from Barbie home furnishings, Barbie cosmetics, and Barbie electronics to Barbie books, Barbie sporting goods, and even a Barbie band—Beyond Pink. Honda uses its company name to cover different products such as its automobiles, motorcycles, snowblowers, lawn mowers, marine engines, and snowmobiles. This allows Honda to advertise that it can fit "six Hondas in a two-car garage." Swiss Army brand sunglasses, Disney Cruise Lines, Cosmopolitan low-fat dairy products, Century 21 Home Improvements, and Brinks home security systems—all are brand extensions.

A brand extension gives a new product instant recognition and faster acceptance. It also saves the high advertising costs usually required to build a new brand name. At the same time, a brand extension strategy involves some risk. Brand extensions such as Bic pantyhose, Heinz pet food, LifeSavers gum, and Clorox laundry detergent met early deaths. The extension may confuse the image of the main brand. And if a brand extension fails, it may harm consumer attitudes toward the other products carrying the same brand name. Furthermore, a brand name may not be appropriate to a particular new product, even if it is well made and satisfying—would you consider buying Texaco milk or Alpo chili? A brand name may lose its special positioning in the consumer's mind through overuse. Companies that are tempted to transfer a brand name must research how well the brand's associations fit the new product.[34]

Multibrands. Companies often introduce additional brands in the same category. Thus, P&G markets many different brands in each of its product categories. *Multibranding* offers a way to establish different features and appeal to different buying motives. It also allows a company to lock up more reseller shelf space. Or the company may want to protect its major brand by setting up *flanker* or *fighter brands*. Seiko uses different brand names for its higher-priced watches (Seiko Lasalle) and lower-priced watches (Pulsar) to protect the flanks of its mainstream Seiko brand.

A major drawback of multibranding is that each brand might obtain only a small market share, and none may be very profitable. The company may end up spreading its resources over many brands instead of building a few brands to a highly profitable level. These companies should reduce the number of brands they sell in a given category and set up tighter screening procedures for new brands.

New Brands. A company might believe that the power of its existing brand name is waning and a new brand name is needed. Or a company may create a new brand name when it enters a new product category for which none of the company's current brand names is appropriate. For example, Honda created the Acura brand to differentiate its luxury car from the established Honda line. Toyota created the separate Scion automobile, now available in California, targeted toward GenY consumers. Japan's Matsushita uses separate names for its different families of products: Technics, Panasonic, National, and Quasar.

As with multibranding, offering too many new brands can result in a company spreading its resources too thin. And in some industries, such as consumer packaged goods, consumers and retailers have become concerned that there are already too many brands, with too few differences between them. Thus, Procter & Gamble, Frito-Lay, and other large consumer-product marketers are now pursuing *megabrand* strategies—weeding out weaker brands and focusing their marketing dollars only on brands that can achieve the number one or number two market share positions in their categories.

Brand extension
Using a successful brand name to launch a new or modified product in a new category.

Managing Brands

Companies must carefully manage their brands. First, the brand's positioning must be continuously communicated to consumers. Major brand marketers often spend huge amounts on advertising to create brand awareness and to build preference and loyalty. For example, AT&T spends almost a billion dollars annually to promote its brands. McDonald's spends more than $600 million.[35]

Such advertising campaigns can help to create name recognition, brand knowledge, and maybe even some brand preference. However, the fact is that brands are not maintained by advertising but by the *brand experience*. Today, customers come to know a brand through a wide range of contacts and touch points. These include advertising, but also personal experience with the brand, word of mouth, personal interactions with company people, telephone interactions, company Web pages, and many others. Any of these experiences can have a positive or negative impact on brand perceptions and feelings. The company must put as much care into managing these touch points as it does into producing its ads.

The brand's positioning will not take hold fully unless everyone in the company lives the brand. Therefore the company needs to train its people to be customer-centered. Even better, the company should build pride in its employees regarding their products and services so that their enthusiasm will spill over to customers. Companies such as Nordstrom, Lexus, Dell, and Harley-Davidson have succeeded in turning all of their employees into enthusiastic brand builders. Companies can carry on internal brand building to help employees to understand, desire, and deliver on the brand promise. Many companies go even further by training and encouraging their distributors and dealers to serve their customers well.

All of this suggests that managing a company's brand assets can no longer be left only to brand managers. Brand managers do not have enough power or scope to do all the things necessary to build and enhance their brands. Moreover, brand managers often pursue short-term results, whereas managing brands as assets calls for longer-term strategy. Thus, some companies are now setting up brand asset management teams to manage their major brands. Canada Dry and Colgate-Palmolive have appointed *brand equity managers* to maintain and protect their brands' images, associations, and quality, and to prevent short-term actions by overeager brand managers from hurting the brand. Similarly, Hewlett-Packard has appointed a senior executive in charge of the customer experience in each of its two divisions, consumer and B2B. Their job is to track, measure, and improve the customer relationship with H-P products. They report directly to the presidents of their respective divisions.

Finally, companies need to periodically audit their brands' strengths and weaknesses.[36] They should ask: Does our brand excel at delivering benefits that consumers truly value? Is the brand properly positioned? Do all of our consumer touch points support the brand's positioning? Do the brand's managers understand what the brand means to consumers? Does the brand receive proper, sustained support?

The brand audit may turn up brands that need to be repositioned because of changing customer preferences or new competitors. Some cases may call for completely *rebranding* a product, service, or company. The recent wave of corporate mergers and acquisitions has set off a flurry of corporate rebranding campaigns. A prime example is Verizon Communication, created by the merger of Bell Atlantic and GTE. The company decided that neither of the old names properly positioned the new company. "We needed a master brand to leave all our old names behind," says Verizon's senior vice president of brand management and marketing services. The old names created too much confusion, conjured up an image of old-fashioned phone companies, and "held us back from marketing in new areas of innovation—high speed Internet and wireless services." The new branding effort appears to have worked. Verizon Wireless is now the leading provider of wireless phone services, with better than a 21 percent market share. Number two is Cingular Wireless, another new brand created through a joint venture between Bell South and SBC Communications.[37]

However, building a new image and re-educating customers can be a huge undertaking. The cost of Verizon's brand overhaul included tens of millions of dollars just for a special four-week advertising campaign to announce the new name, followed by considerable ongoing advertising expenses. And that was only the beginning. The company had to repaint its fleet of 70,000 trucks, along with its garages and service centers. The campaign also required relabeling 250,000 pay phones, redesigning 91 million customer billing statements, and producing videos and other in-house employee educational materials.

■▊ Services Marketing

Services have grown dramatically in recent years. Services now account for 74 percent of U.S. gross domestic product and nearly 60 percent of personal consumption expenditures. Whereas service jobs accounted for 55 percent of all U.S. jobs in 1970, today they account for 82 percent of total employment. Services are growing even faster in the world economy, making up a quarter of the value of all international trade.[38]

Service industries vary greatly. *Governments* offer services through courts, employment services, hospitals, military services, police and fire departments, postal services, and schools. *Private not-for-profit organizations* offer services through museums, charities, churches, colleges, foundations, and hospitals. A large number of *business organizations* offer services—airlines, banks, hotels, insurance companies, consulting firms, medical and law practices, entertainment companies, real estate firms, advertising and research agencies, and retailers.

Nature and Characteristics of a Service

A company must consider four special service characteristics when designing marketing programs: *intangibility*, *inseparability*, *variability*, and *perishability* (see Figure 7.5).

Service intangibility means that services cannot be seen, tasted, felt, heard, or smelled before they are bought. For example, people undergoing cosmetic surgery cannot see the result before the purchase. Airline passengers have nothing but a ticket and the promise that they and their luggage will arrive safely at the intended destination, hopefully at the same time. To reduce uncertainty, buyers look for "signals" of service quality. They draw conclusions about quality from the place, people, price, equipment, and communications that they can see.

Therefore, the service provider's task is to make the service tangible in one or more ways and to send the right signals about quality. One analyst calls this *evidence management,* in which the service organization presents its customers with organized, honest evidence of its capabilities. The Mayo Clinic practices good evidence management[39]:

> Nobody likes going to the hospital. The experience is at best unnerving and often frightening. What's more, it's very hard for the average patient to judge the quality of the "product." You can't try it on, you can't return it if you don't like it, and you need an advanced degree to understand it. And so, when we're considering a medical facility, most of us unconsciously turn detective, looking for evidence of competence, caring, and integrity. The Mayo Clinic doesn't leave that evidence to chance. By carefully managing a set of visual and experiential clues, Mayo offers patients and their families concrete evidence of its strengths and values. For example, staff people at the clinic are trained to act in a way that clearly signals its patient-first focus. "My doctor calls me at home to check on how I am

Service intangibility
A major characteristic of services—they cannot be seen, tasted, felt, heard, or smelled before they are bought.

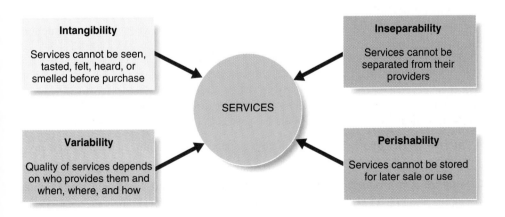

FIGURE 7.5
Four Service Characteristics

doing," marvels one patient. "She wants to work with what is best for my schedule." Mayo's physical facilities also send the right signals. They've been carefully designed to relieve stress, offer a place of refuge, create positive distractions, convey caring and respect, signal competence, accommodate families, and make it easy to find your way around. The result? Exceptionally positive word-of-mouth and abiding customer loyalty, which have allowed Mayo Clinic to build what is arguably the most powerful brand in health care—with very little advertising.

Service inseparability

A major characteristic of services—they are produced and consumed at the same time and cannot be separated from their providers, whether the providers are people or machines.

Physical goods are produced, then stored, later sold, and still later consumed. In contrast, services are first sold, then produced and consumed at the same time. **Service inseparability** means that services cannot be separated from their providers, whether the providers are people or machines. If a service employee provides the service, then the employee is a part of the service. Because the customer is also present as the service is produced, *provider–customer interaction* is a special feature of services marketing. Both the provider and the customer affect the service outcome.

Service variability

A major characteristic of services—their quality may vary greatly, depending on who provides them and when, where, and how.

Service variability means that the quality of services depends on who provides them as well as when, where, and how they are provided. For example, some hotels—say, Marriott—have reputations for providing better service than others. Still, within a given Marriott hotel, one registration-desk employee may be cheerful and efficient, whereas another standing just a few feet away may be unpleasant and slow. Even the quality of a single Marriott employee's service varies according to his or her energy and frame of mind at the time of each customer encounter.

Service perishability

A major characteristic of services—they cannot be stored for later sale or use.

Service perishability means that services cannot be stored for later sale or use. Some doctors charge patients for missed appointments because the service value existed only at that point and disappeared when the patient did not show up. The perishability of services is not a problem when demand is steady. However, when demand fluctuates, service firms often have difficult problems. For example, because of rush-hour demand, public transportation companies have to own much more equipment than they would if demand were even throughout the day. Thus, service firms often design strategies for producing a better match between demand and supply. Hotels and resorts charge lower prices in the off-season to attract more guests. And restaurants hire part-time employees to serve during peak periods.

Marketing Strategies for Service Firms

Just like manufacturing businesses, good service firms use marketing to position themselves strongly in chosen target markets. Southwest Airlines positions itself as a no-frills, short-haul airline charging very low fares. Wal-Mart promises "Always Low Prices, Always." Ritz-Carlton Hotels positions itself as offering a memorable experience that "enlivens the senses, instills well-being, and fulfills even the unexpressed wishes and needs of our guests." At the Mayo Clinic, "the needs of the patient come first." These and other service firms establish their positions through traditional marketing mix activities.

However, because services differ from tangible products, they often require additional marketing approaches. In a product business, products are fairly standardized and can sit on shelves waiting for customers. But in a service business, the customer and front-line service employee *interact* to create the service. Thus, service providers must interact effectively with customers to create superior value during service encounters. Effective interaction, in turn, depends on the skills of front-line service employees and on the support processes backing these employees.

Service-profit chain

The chain that links service firm profits with employee and customer satisfaction.

The Service-Profit Chain Successful service companies focus their attention on *both* their customers and their employees. They understand the **service-profit chain**, which links service firm profits with employee and customer satisfaction. This chain consists of five links[40]:

- *Internal service quality:* superior employee selection and training, a quality work environment, and strong support for those dealing with customers, which results in . . .

- *Satisfied and productive service employees:* more satisfied, loyal, and hardworking employees, which results in . . .

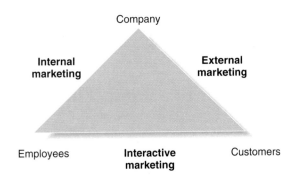

FIGURE 7.6
Three Types of Service Marketing

- *Greater service value:* more effective and efficient customer value creation and service delivery, which results in . . .

- *Satisfied and loyal customers:* satisfied customers who remain loyal, repeat purchase, and refer other customers, which results in . . .

- *Healthy service profits and growth:* superior service firm performance.

Therefore, reaching service profits and growth goals begins with taking care of those who take care of customers (see Marketing at Work 7.4).

Thus, service marketing requires more than just traditional external marketing using the four Ps. Figure 7.6 shows that service marketing also requires *internal marketing* and *interactive marketing*. **Internal marketing** means that the service firm must effectively train and motivate its customer-contact employees and supporting service people to work as a *team* to provide customer satisfaction. Marketers must get everyone in the organization to be customer-centered. In fact, internal marketing must *precede* external marketing. Ritz-Carlton orients its employees carefully, instills in them a sense of pride, and motivates them by recognizing and rewarding outstanding service deeds.

Interactive marketing means that service quality depends heavily on the quality of the buyer–seller interaction during the service encounter. In product marketing, product quality often depends little on how the product is obtained. But in services marketing, service quality depends on both the service deliverer and the quality of the delivery. Service marketers, therefore, have to master interactive marketing skills. Thus, Ritz-Carlton selects only "people who care about people" and instructs them carefully in the fine art of interacting with customers to satisfy their every need.

In today's marketplace, companies must know how to deliver interactions that are not only "high-touch" but also "high-tech." For example, customers can log on to the Charles Schwab Web site and access account information, investment research, real-time quotes, after-hours trading, and the Schwab learning center. They can also participate in live online events and chat online with customer service representatives. Customers seeking more-personal interactions can contact service reps by phone or visit a local Schwab branch office. Thus, Schwab has mastered interactive marketing at all three levels—calls, clicks, *and* visits.[41]

Today, as competition and costs increase, and as productivity and quality decrease, more service marketing sophistication is needed. Service companies face three major marketing tasks: They want to increase their *competitive differentiation*, *service quality*, and *productivity*.

Managing Service Differentiation   In these days of intense price competition, service marketers often complain about the difficulty of differentiating their services from those of competitors. To the extent that customers view the services of different providers as similar, they care less about the provider than the price.

The solution to price competition is to develop a differentiated offer, delivery, and image. The *offer* can include innovative features that set one company's offer apart from competitors' offers. Some hotels offer car rental, banking, and business center services in their lobbies. Airlines introduced innovations such as in-flight movies, advance seating,

Internal marketing
Marketing by a service firm to train and effectively motivate its customer-contact employees and all the supporting service people to work as a team to provide customer satisfaction.

Interactive marketing
Marketing by a service firm that recognizes that perceived service quality depends heavily on the quality of buyer–seller interaction.

Marketing at Work | 7.4

Ritz-Carlton: Taking Care of Those Who Take Care of Customers

Ritz-Carlton, a chain of luxury hotels renowned for outstanding service, caters to the top 5 percent of corporate and leisure travelers. The company's Credo sets lofty customer service goals: "The Ritz-Carlton Hotel is a place where the genuine care and comfort of our guests is our highest mission. We pledge to provide the finest personal service and facilities for our guests, who will always enjoy a warm, relaxed yet refined ambience. The Ritz-Carlton experience enlivens the senses, instills well-being, and fulfills even the unexpressed wishes and needs of our guests." The company's Web page concludes: "Here a calm settles over you. The world, so recently at your door, is now at your feet."

The Credo is more than just words on paper—Ritz-Carlton delivers on its promises. In surveys of departing guests, some 95 percent report that they've had a truly memorable experience. In fact, at Ritz-Carlton, exceptional service encounters have become almost commonplace. Take the experiences of Nancy and Harvey Heffner of Manhattan, who stayed at the Ritz-Carlton Naples, in Naples, Florida (recently rated the best hotel in the United States, fourth best in the world, by *Travel & Leisure* magazine). As reported in the *New York Times*:

"The hotel is elegant and beautiful," Mrs. Heffner said, "but more important is the beauty expressed by the staff. They can't do enough to please you." When the couple's son became sick last year in Naples, the hotel staff brought him hot tea with honey at all hours of the night, she said. When Mr. Heffner had to fly home on business for a day and his return flight was delayed, a driver for the hotel waited in the lobby most of the night.

Such personal, high-quality service has also made the Ritz-Carlton a favorite among conventioneers. "They not only treat us like kings when we hold our top-level meetings in their hotels, but we just never get any complaints," comments one convention planner. "Perhaps the biggest challenge a planner faces when recommending The Ritz-Carlton at Half Moon Bay to the boss, board, and attendees is convincing them that meeting there truly is work," says another. "The . . . first-rate catering and service-oriented convention services staff [and] the Ritz-Carlton's ambience and beauty—the elegant, Grand Dame-style lodge, nestled on a bluff between two championship golf courses

THE RITZ-CARLTON®

CREDO

The Ritz-Carlton Hotel is a place where the genuine care and comfort of our guests is our highest mission.

We pledge to provide the finest personal service and facilities for our guests who will always enjoy a warm, relaxed yet refined ambience.

The Ritz-Carlton experience enlivens the senses, instills well-being, and fulfills even the unexpressed wishes and needs of our guests.

THREE STEPS OF SERVICE

1
A warm and sincere greeting. Use the guest name, if and when possible.

2
Anticipation and compliance with guest needs.

3
Fond farewell. Give them a warm good-bye and use their name, if and when possible.

THE EMPLOYEE PROMISE

At The Ritz-Carlton, our Ladies and Gentlemen are the most important resource in our service commitment to our guests.

By applying the principles of trust, honesty, respect, integrity and commitment, we nurture and maximize talent to the benefit of each individual and the company.

The Ritz-Carlton fosters a work environment where diversity is valued, quality of life is enhanced, individual aspirations are fulfilled, and The Ritz-Carlton mystique is strengthened.

"We Are Ladies and Gentlemen Serving Ladies and Gentlemen"

The Credo and Employee Promise: Ritz-Carlton knows that to take care of customers, you must first take care of those who take care of customers.

air-to-ground telephone service, and frequent flyer award programs to differentiate their offers. British Airways even offers international travelers beds and private "demi-cabins," hot showers, and cooked-to-order breakfasts.

Service companies can differentiate their service *delivery* by having more able and reliable customer-contact people, by developing a superior physical environment in which the service product is delivered, or by designing a superior delivery process. For example,

overlooking the Pacific Ocean—makes a day's work there seem anything but."

In 1992, Ritz-Carlton became the first hotel company to win the Malcolm Baldrige National Quality Award. Since its incorporation in 1983, the company has received virtually every major award that the hospitality industry bestows. More importantly, service quality has resulted in high customer retention. More than 90 percent of Ritz-Carlton customers return. And despite its hefty room rates, the chain enjoys a 70 per-cent occupancy rate, almost nine points above the industry average.

Most of the responsibility for keeping guests satisfied falls to Ritz-Carlton's customer-contact employees. Thus, the hotel chain takes great care in finding just the right personnel. "We don't hire or recruit, we select," says Ritz-Carlton's director of human resources. "We want only people who care about people," notes the company's vice president of quality. Once selected, employees are given intensive training in the art of cod-dling customers. New employees attend a two-day orientation, in which top man-agement drums into them the "20 Ritz-Carlton Basics." Basic number one: "The Credo will be known, owned, and energized by all employees."

Employees are taught to do every-thing they can never to lose a guest. "There's no negotiating at Ritz-Carlton when it comes to solving customer problems," says the quality executive. Staff learn that *anyone* who receives a customer complaint *owns* that com-plaint until it's resolved (Ritz-Carlton Basic number eight). They are trained to drop whatever they're doing to help a customer—no matter what they're doing or what their department. Ritz-Carlton employees are empowered to handle problems on the spot, without

consulting higher-ups. Each employee can spend up to $2,000 to redress a guest grievance. And each is allowed to break from his or her routine for as long as needed to make a guest happy. "We master customer satisfaction at the individual level," adds the executive. "This is our most sensitive listening post . . . our early warning system." Thus, while competitors are still reading guest comment cards to learn about customer problems, Ritz-Carlton has already resolved them.

Ritz-Carlton instills a sense of pride in its employees. "You serve," they are told, "but you are not servants." The company motto states, "We are ladies and gentlemen serving ladies and gen-tlemen." Employees understand their role in Ritz-Carlton's success. "We might not be able to afford a hotel like this," says employee Tammy Patton, "but we can make it so people who can afford it will want to keep coming here."

And so they do. When it comes to customer satisfaction, no detail is too small. Customer-contact people are taught to greet guests warmly and sin-cerely, using guest names when possi-ble. They learn to use the proper lan-guage with guests—phrases such as *Good morning, Certainly, I'll be happy to, Welcome back,* and *My pleasure,* never *Hi* or *How's it going*? The Ritz-Carlton Basics urge employees to escort guests to another area of the hotel rather than pointing out directions, to answer the phone within three rings and with a "smile," and to take pride and care in their personal appearance. As the general manager of the Ritz-Carlton Naples puts it, "When you invite guests to your house, you want every-thing to be perfect."

Ritz-Carlton recognizes and rewards employees who perform feats

of outstanding service. Under its 5-Star Awards program, outstanding performers are nominated by peers and managers, and winners receive plaques at dinners celebrating their achievements. For on-the-spot recog-nition, managers award Gold Standard Coupons, redeemable for items in the gift shop and free weekend stays at the hotel. Ritz-Carlton further moti-vates its employees with events such as Super Sports Day, an employee tal-ent show, luncheons celebrating employee anniversaries, a family pic-nic, and special themes in employee dining rooms. As a result, Ritz-Carlton's employees appear to be just as satisfied as its customers. Employee turnover is less than 30 per-cent a year, compared with 45 percent at other luxury hotels.

Ritz-Carlton's success is based on a simple philosophy: To take care of customers, you must first take care of those who take care of customers. Satisfied employees deliver high ser-vice value, which then creates satisfied customers. Satisfied customers, in turn, create sales and profits for the company.

Sources: Quotes and other information from Edwin McDowell, "Ritz-Carlton's Keys to Good Service," *New York Times,* March 31, 1993, p. D1; Howard Schlossberg, "Measuring Customer Satisfaction Is Easy to Do—Until You Try," *Marketing News,* April 26, 1993, pp. 5, 8; Ginger Conlon, "True Romance," *Sales & Marketing Management,* May 1996, pp. 85–90; "The Ritz-Carlton, Half Moon Bay," *Successful Meetings,* November 2001, p. 40; and the Ritz-Carlton Web site at www.ritzcarlton.com, August 2003. Also see Patricia Sheehan, "Back to Bed: Selling the Perfect Night's Sleep," *Lodging Hospitality,* March 15, 2001, pp. 22–24; Nicole Harris, "Can't Sleep? Try the Eye Gel in the Minibar—Hotels Roll Out Products to Help Tired Travelers Snooze," *Wall Street Journal,* June 20, 2002, p. D1; and Scott Neuman, "Relax, Put Your Feet Up," *Far Eastern Economic Review,* April 17, 2003, p. 36.

many banks offer their customers Internet banking as a better way to access banking ser-vices than having to drive, park, and wait in line.

Finally, service companies also can work on differentiating their *images* through sym-bols and branding. The Harris Bank of Chicago adopted the lion as its symbol on its sta-tionery, in its advertising, and even as stuffed animals offered to new depositors. The well-known Harris lion confers an image of strength. Other well-known service symbols

■ Service differentiation: British Airways differentiates its offer by providing first-class world travelers private "demi-cabins" and other amenities.

include The Merrill Lynch's bull, MGM's lion, and Allstate's "good hands."

Managing Service Quality One of the major ways a service firm can differentiate itself is by delivering consistently higher quality than its competitors do. Like manufacturers before them, most service industries have now joined the customer-driven quality movement. And like product marketers, service providers need to identify what target customers expect concerning service quality. Unfortunately, service quality is harder to define and judge than is product quality. For instance, it is harder to agree on the quality of a haircut than on the quality of a hair dryer. Customer retention is perhaps the best measure of quality—a service firm's ability to hang onto its customers depends on how consistently it delivers value to them.[42]

Top service companies are customer obsessed and set high service quality standards. They watch service performance closely, both their own and that of competitors. They do not settle for merely good service; they aim for 100 percent defect-free service. A 98 percent performance standard may sound good, but using this standard, 64,000 FedEx packages would be lost each day, 10 words would be misspelled on each printed page, 400,000 prescriptions would be misfilled daily, and drinking water would be unsafe 8 days a year.[43]

Unlike product manufacturers, who can adjust their machinery and inputs until everything is perfect, service quality will always vary, depending on the interactions between employees and customers. As hard as they try, even the best companies will have an occasional late delivery, burned steak, or grumpy employee. However, good *service recovery* can turn angry customers into loyal ones. In fact, good recovery can win more customer purchasing and loyalty than if things had gone well in the first place. Therefore, companies should take steps not only to provide good service every time but also to recover from service mistakes when they do occur.

The first step is to *empower* front-line service employees—to give them the authority, responsibility, and incentives they need to recognize, care about, and tend to customer needs. At Marriott, for example, well-trained employees are given the authority to do whatever it takes, on the spot, to keep guests happy. They are also expected to help management ferret out the cause of guests' problems and to inform managers of ways to improve overall hotel service and guests' comfort.

Managing Service Productivity With their costs rising rapidly, service firms are under great pressure to increase service productivity. They can do so in several ways. They can train current employees better or hire new ones who will work harder or more skillfully. Or they can increase the quantity of their service by giving up some quality. The provider can "industrialize the service" by adding equipment and standardizing production, as in McDonald's assembly-line approach to fast-food retailing. Finally, the service provider can harness the power of technology. Although we often think of technology's power to save time and costs in manufacturing companies, it also has great—and often untapped—potential to make service workers more productive.

However, companies must avoid pushing productivity so hard that doing so reduces quality. Attempts to industrialize a service or to cut costs can make a service company more efficient in the short run. But they can also reduce its longer-run ability to innovate, maintain service quality, or respond to consumer needs and desires. In short, they can take the "service" out of service.

▪▪ Additional Product Considerations

Here, we discuss two additional product policy considerations: social responsibility in product decisions and issues of international product and services marketing.

Product Decisions and Social Responsibility

Product decisions have attracted much public attention. Marketers should carefully consider public policy issues and regulations involving acquiring or dropping products, patent protection, product quality and safety, and product warranties.

Regarding new products, the government may prevent companies from adding products through acquisitions if the effect threatens to lessen competition. Companies dropping products must be aware that they have legal obligations, written or implied, to their suppliers, dealers, and customers who have a stake in the dropped product. Companies must also obey U.S. patent laws when developing new products. A company cannot make its product illegally similar to another company's established product.

Manufacturers must comply with specific laws regarding product quality and safety. The Federal Food, Drug, and Cosmetic Act protects consumers from unsafe and adulterated food, drugs, and cosmetics. Various acts provide for the inspection of sanitary conditions in the meat- and poultry-processing industries. Safety legislation has been passed to regulate fabrics, chemical substances, automobiles, toys, and drugs and poisons. The Consumer Product Safety Act of 1972 established a Consumer Product Safety Commission, which has the authority to ban or seize potentially harmful products and set severe penalties for violation of the law.

If consumers have been injured by a product that has been designed defectively, they can sue manufacturers or dealers. Product liability suits are now occurring in federal and state courts at the rate of almost 110,000 per year, with a median jury award of $1.8 million and individual awards often running into the tens of millions of dollars.[44] This phenomenon has resulted in huge increases in product liability insurance premiums, causing big problems in some industries. Some companies pass these higher rates along to consumers by raising prices. Others are forced to discontinue high-risk product lines. Some companies are now appointing "product stewards," whose job is to protect consumers from harm and the company from liability by proactively ferreting out potential product problems.[45]

Many manufacturers offer written product warranties to convince customers of their products' quality. To protect consumers, Congress passed the Magnuson–Moss Warranty Act in 1975. The act requires that full warranties meet certain minimum standards, including repair "within a reasonable time and without charge" or a replacement or full refund if the product does not work "after a reasonable number of attempts" at repair. Otherwise, the company must make it clear that it is offering only a limited warranty. The law has led several manufacturers to switch from full to limited warranties and others to drop warranties altogether.

International Product and Services Marketing

International product and service marketers face special challenges. First, they must figure out what products and services to introduce and in which countries. Then, they must decide how much to standardize or adapt their products and services for world markets.

On the one hand, companies would like to standardize their offerings. Standardization helps a company to develop a consistent worldwide image. It also lowers manufacturing costs and eliminates duplication of research and development, advertising, and product design efforts. On the other hand, consumers around the world differ in their cultures, attitudes, and buying behaviors. And markets vary in their economic conditions, competition, legal requirements, and physical environments. Companies must usually respond to these differences by adapting their product offerings. Something as simple as an electrical outlet can create big product problems:

> Those who have traveled across Europe know the frustration of electrical plugs, different voltages, and other annoyances of international travel. . . . Philips, the

electrical appliance manufacturer, has to produce 12 kinds of irons to serve just its European market. The problem is that Europe does not have a universal [electrical] standard. The ends of irons bristle with different plugs for different countries. Some have three prongs, others two; prongs protrude straight or angled, round or rectangular, fat, thin, and sometimes sheathed. There are circular plug faces, squares, pentagons, and hexagons. Some are perforated and some are notched. One French plug has a niche like a keyhole. Looking for a fix? One online travel service sells an elaborate 10-piece adapter plug set for international travelers for $65.00.[46]

Packaging also presents new challenges for international marketers. Packaging issues can be subtle. For example, names, labels, and colors may not translate easily from one country to another. A firm using yellow flowers in its logo might fare well in the United States but meet with disaster in Mexico, where a yellow flower symbolizes death or disrespect. Similarly, although Nature's Gift might be an appealing name for gourmet mushrooms in America, it would be deadly in Germany, where *gift* means poison. Packaging may also have to be tailored to meet the physical characteristics of consumers in various parts of the world. For instance, soft drinks are sold in smaller cans in Japan to fit the smaller Japanese hand better. Thus, although product and package standardization can produce benefits, companies must usually adapt their offerings to the unique needs of specific international markets.

Service marketers also face special challenges when going global. Some service industries have a long history of international operations. For example, the commercial banking industry was one of the first to grow internationally. Banks had to provide global services in order to meet the foreign exchange and credit needs of their home country clients wanting to sell overseas. In recent years, many banks have become truly global. Germany's Deutsche Bank, for example, serves more than 12 million customers in 75 countries. For its clients around the world who wish to grow globally, Deutsche Bank can raise money not only in Frankfurt but also in Zurich, London, Paris, and Tokyo.[47]

Professional and business services industries such as accounting, management consulting, and advertising have only recently globalized. The international growth of these firms followed the globalization of the client companies they serve. For example, as their clients began to employ worldwide marketing and advertising strategies, advertising agencies responded by globalizing their own operations. McCann-Erickson Worldwide, the largest U.S. advertising agency, operates in more than 130 countries. It serves international clients such as Coca-Cola, General Motors, ExxonMobil, Microsoft, Johnson & Johnson, and Unilever in markets ranging from the United States and Canada to Korea to Kazakhstan. Moreover, McCann-Erikson is one company in the Interpublic Group of Companies, an immense, worldwide network of advertising and marketing services companies.[48]

Retailers are among the latest service businesses to go global. As their home markets become saturated, American retailers such as Wal-Mart, Kmart, Toys 'R' Us, Office Depot, Saks Fifth Avenue, and Disney are expanding into faster-growing markets abroad. For example, every year since 1995, Wal-Mart has entered a new country; its international division's sales grew more than 10 percent last year, skyrocketing to more than $35 billion. Foreign retailers are making similar moves. The Japanese retailer Yaohan now operates the largest shopping center in Asia, the 21-story Nextage Shanghai Tower in China, and Carrefour of France is the leading retailer in Brazil and Argentina. Asian shoppers now buy American products in Dutch-owned Makro stores, now Southeast Asia's biggest store group, with sales in the region of more than $2 billion.[49]

■ Retailers are among the latest service businesses to go global. Here Asian shoppers buy American products in a Dutch-owned Makro store in Kuala Lumpur.

Service companies wanting to operate in other countries are not always welcomed with open arms. Whereas manufacturers usually face straightforward tariff, quota, or currency restrictions when attempting to sell their products in another country, service providers are likely to face more subtle barriers. In some cases, rules and regulations affecting international service firms reflect the host country's traditions. In others, they appear to protect the country's own fledgling service industries from large global competitors with greater resources. In still other cases, however, the restrictions seem to have little purpose other than to make entry difficult for foreign service firms.

Despite such difficulties, the trend toward growth of global service companies will continue, especially in banking, airlines, telecommunications, and professional services. Today service firms are no longer simply following their manufacturing customers. Instead, they are taking the lead in international expansion.

REST STOP:
Reviewing the Concepts

Time to kick back and reflect on the key concepts in this first marketing mix chapter on products and services. A product is more than a simple set of tangible features. In fact, many marketing offers consist of combinations of both tangible goods and services, ranging from *pure tangible goods* at one extreme to *pure services* at the other. Each product or service offered to customers can be viewed on three levels. The *core product* consists of the core problem-solving benefits that consumers seek when they buy a product. The *actual product* exists around the core and includes the quality level, features, design, brand name, and packaging. The *augmented product* is the actual product plus the various services and benefits offered with it, such as warranty, free delivery, installation, and maintenance.

1. Define *product* and the major classifications of products and services.

Broadly defined, a *product* is anything that can be offered to a market for attention, acquisition, use, or consumption that might satisfy a want or need. Products include physical objects but also services, events, persons, places, organizations, ideas, or mixes of these entities. *Services* are products that consist of activities, benefits, or satisfactions offered for sale that are essentially intangible, such as banking, hotel, tax preparation, and home repair services.

Products and services fall into two broad classes based on the types of consumers that use them. *Consumer products*—those bought by final consumers—are usually classified according to consumer shopping habits (convenience products, shopping products, specialty products, and unsought products). *Industrial products*—purchased for further processing or for use in conducting a business—include materials and parts, capital items, and supplies and services. Other marketable entities—such as organizations, persons, places, and ideas—can also be thought of as products.

2. Describe the decisions companies make regarding their individual products and services, product lines, and product mixes.

Individual product decisions involve product attributes, branding, packaging, labeling, and product support services. *Product attribute* decisions involve product quality, features, and style and design. *Branding* decisions include selecting a brand name and developing a brand strategy. *Packaging* provides many key benefits, such as protection, economy, convenience, and promotion. Package decisions often include designing *labels*, which identify, describe, and possibly promote the product. Companies also develop *product support services* that enhance customer service and satisfaction and safeguard against competitors.

Most companies produce a product line rather than a single product. A *product line* is a group of products that are related in function, customer-purchase needs, or distribution channels. *Line stretching* involves extending a line downward, upward, or in both directions to occupy a gap that might otherwise be filled by a competitor. In contrast, *line filling* involves adding items within the present range of the line. The set of product lines and items offered to customers by a particular seller make up the *product mix*. The mix can be described by four dimensions: width, length, depth, and consistency. These dimensions are the tools for developing the company's product strategy.

3. Discuss branding strategy—the decisions companies make in building and managing their brands.

Some analysts see brands as *the* major enduring asset of a company. Brands are more than just names and symbols—they embody everything that the product or service *means* to consumers. *Brand equity* is the positive differential effect that knowing the brand name has on customer response to the product or service. A brand with strong brand equity is a very valuable asset.

In building brands, companies need to make decisions about brand positioning, brand name selection, brand sponsorship, and brand development. The most powerful *brand positioning* builds around strong consumer beliefs and values. *Brand name selection* involves finding the best brand name based on a careful review of product benefits, the target market, and proposed marketing strategies. A manufacturer has four *brand sponsorship* options: it can launch a *manufacturer's brand* (or national brand), sell to resellers who use a *private brand*, market *licensed brands*, or join forces with another company to *co-brand* a product. A company also has four choices when it comes to developing brands. It can introduce *line extensions, brand extensions, multibrands,* or *new brands* (new brand names in new product categories).

Companies must build and manage their brands carefully. The brand's positioning must be continuously communicated to consumers. Advertising can help, but brands are not maintained by advertising but by the *brand experience.* Customers come to know a brand through a wide range of contacts and interactions. The company must put as much care into managing these touch points as it does into producing its ads. Thus, managing a company's brand assets can no longer be left only to brand managers. Some companies are now setting up brand asset management teams to manage their major brands. Finally, companies must periodically audit their brands' strengths and weaknesses. In some cases, brands may need to be repositioned because of changing customer preferences or new competitors. Other cases may call for completely *rebranding* a product, service, or company.

4. Identify the four characteristics that affect the marketing of a service and the additional marketing considerations that services require.

Services are characterized by four key characteristics; they are *intangible, inseparable, variable,* and *perishable.* Each characteristic poses problems and marketing requirements. Marketers work to find ways to make the service more tangible, to increase the productivity of providers who are inseparable from their products, to standardize quality in the face of variability, and to improve demand movements and supply capacities in the face of service perishability.

Good service companies focus attention on *both* customers and employees. They understand the *service-profit chain,* which links service firm profits with employee and customer satisfaction. Services marketing strategy calls not only for external marketing but also for *internal marketing* to motivate employees and *interactive marketing* to create service delivery skills among service providers. To succeed, service marketers must create *competitive differentiation,* offer high *service quality,* and find ways to increase *service productivity.*

5. Discuss two additional product issues: socially responsible product decisions and international product and services marketing.

Marketers must consider two additional product issues. The first is *social responsibility.* These include public policy issues and regulations involving acquiring or dropping products, patent protection, product quality and safety, and product warranties. The second involves the special challenges facing international product and service marketers. International marketers must decide how much to standardize or adapt their offerings for world markets.

Navigating the Key Terms

Brand	Line extension	Service inseparability
Brand equity	Packaging	Service intangibility
Brand extension	Private (or store) brand	Service perishability
Co-branding	Product	Service-profit chain
Consumer product	Product line	Service variability
Convenience product	Product mix (or product	Shopping product
Industrial product	assortment)	Social marketing
Interactive marketing	Product quality	Specialty product
Internal marketing	Service	Unsought product

Travel Log

Discussing the Issues

1. Brand equity is the positive differential effect that knowing the brand name has on customer response to the product or service. Name three firms that you feel have high brand equity. How does having high brand equity help them compete against rival companies?

2. Visit a grocery store and look at the packages for competing products in two or three different product categories. Which packages are the best? Why? What functions do the packages perform?

3. Visit the Kraft Foods company Web site (www.kraft.com/index.html) and examine its list of different brands. Evaluate the company's product mix on the dimensions of width, length, depth, and consistency.

4. Consider how Cheerios cereal has been positioned in terms of product attributes, desired benefits, and strong beliefs and values.

5. What issues should a manufacturer of canned green beans consider when deciding between selling the product as a manufacturer's brand, store brand, licensed brand, or co-branded product?

6. Discuss how the services offered by a dry cleaning company are different from the products offered by an auto parts store in terms of intangibility, inseparability, variability, and perishability.

Application Questions

1. Consider the following brand extensions and evaluate how well the brand's associations fit the new product: Kodak extending from film into batteries, Winnebago motor homes extending into tents, Fisher-Price toys extending into children's eyeglass frames, Harley-Davidson motorcycles extending into cigarettes, and Dunkin' Donuts extending into cereal. What about the proposed brand extensions works or does not work for you?

2. Develop a list of five characteristics that a good brand name should possess. Based on the characteristics in your list, come up with three good brand names and three poor brand names of actual products currently sold. Imagine you are opening up a pizza restaurant. What would be a good name for the restaurant based on the characteristics in your list?

3. Describe a product you feel must be customized or adapted to sell in different markets around the world and one you feel can sell in a standardized format. Discuss what it is about the two products that requires customization in one case, but not the other. Can you articulate your reasons into general principles a company might use when considering the need to customize?

Under the Hood: Focus on Technology

The Hilton hotel's product mix is represented by nine different hotel brands located around the world. Visit the Web pages of three of Hilton's hotel brands (www.hilton.com, www.hamptoninn.com, and www.conradhotels.com) and respond to the questions below.

1. How are these three hotel brands positioned relative to each other?

2. Discuss Hilton's various hotel brands with respect to the concepts of product line stretching and product-line filling.

3. Why does Hilton use different brand names for each hotel? Do you agree or disagree with this approach?

Focus on Ethics

Companies have an interest in protecting their brand names, whether they be in the physical world or the cyberworld. The term "cybersquatting" has been used to refer to an individual registering a domain name that is identical or confusingly similar to a distinctive, famous trademark. For example, consider the Web site amazo**m**.com compared with amazo**n**.com. Cybersquaters typically did this with the goals of either using the similar Web address to bring traffic to their own Web site or with the hope of selling the domain name back to the company for a substantial profit. Cybersquatting was made illegal in the United States by the 2000 Anti-Cybersquatting Consumer Protection Act.

Under this law, individuals that are found to have registered a domain name in "bad faith" are subject to fines up to $100,000 per domain name.

1. Why should companies care about cybersquatters?

2. Some people feel that domain names should be on a "first come, first served" basis with no company or individual having a claim on unregistered domain names. How do you feel about that perspective?

3. How does protecting one's brand name in cyberspace compare with trademark protection?

Videos

The Accenture video case that accompanies this chapter is located in Appendix 1 at the back of the book.

Student Materials

Need a tune-up? A study guide and OneKey access code are available to aid in your review of chapter material. Your instructor may choose to have these items shrink-wrapped with your text or you may purchase them separately at www.prenhall.com/marketing.

■ *After studying this chapter, you should be able to*

1. *Explain* how companies find and develop new-product ideas   **2.** *List* and define the steps in the new-product development process   **3.** *Describe* the stages of the product life cycle   **4.** *Describe* how marketing strategies change during the product's life cycle

New-Product Development and Product Life-Cycle Strategies

8

In the previous chapter, you learned about decisions that marketers make in managing individual brands and entire product mixes. In this chapter, we'll cruise on into two additional product topics: developing new products and managing products through their life cycles. New products are the lifeblood of an organization. However, new-product development is risky, and many new products fail. So, the first part of this chapter lays out a process for finding and growing successful new products. Once introduced, marketers want their products to enjoy a long and happy life. In the second part of the chapter, you'll see that every product passes through several life-cycle stages and that each stage poses new challenges requiring different marketing strategies and tactics.

First point of interest: Microsoft. The chances are good that you use several Microsoft products and services. Microsoft's Windows software owns a mind-boggling 97 percent share of the PC operating system market and its Office software captures a 90 percent share! However, this $25 billion company doesn't rest on past performance. As you'll see, it owes much of this success to a passion for innovation, abundant new-product development, and its quest for "the Next Big Thing."

N o matter what brand of computer you're using or what you're doing on it, you're almost certain to be using some type of Microsoft product or service. In the world of computer and Internet software and technology, Microsoft dominates.

Microsoft's Windows operating system captures an astonishing 97 percent share of the PC market and a better than 40 percent share in the business server market. Microsoft Office, the company's largest moneymaker, grabs 90 percent of all office applications suite sales. The company's MSN Internet portal (www.msn.com) attracts more than 300 million unique surfers per month, second only to Yahoo!. Its MSN Internet-access service, with 9 million subscribers, trails only America Online as the most popular way for consumers to get onto the Web. Microsoft's Hotmail is the world's most used free e-mail service, hosting more than 100 million accounts, and its instant messaging service has more than 34 million users.

These and other successful products and services have made Microsoft incredibly profitable. During its first 27 years, the software giant racked up more than $50 billion in profits. An investment of $2,800 in 100 shares of Microsoft stock made back when the company went public

would by now have mushroomed into 14,400 shares worth a cool $1 million. All this has made Microsoft co-founder Bill Gates the world's richest man, worth over $43 billion.

A happy ending to a rags-to-riches fairy tale? Not quite. In Microsoft's fast-changing high-tech world, nothing lasts forever—or even for long. Beyond maintaining its core products and businesses, Microsoft knows that its future depends on its ability to conquer new markets with innovative new products.

Microsoft hasn't always been viewed as an innovator. In fact, it has long been regarded as "a big fat copycat." Gates bought the original MS/DOS operating system software upon which he built the company's initial success from a rival programmer for $50,000. Later, Microsoft was accused of copying the user-friendly Macintosh "look and feel." More recently, the company was accused of copying Netscape's Internet browser. It wasn't innovation that made Microsoft, critics claim, but rather its brute-force use of its PC operating system monopoly to crush competitors and muscle into markets. But no more. The technology giant is now innovating at a breakneck pace.

Thanks to its Windows and Office monopolies, and to Microsoft's legendary cash horde of more than $36 billion, the company has plenty of resources to pump into new products and technologies. This year alone, it will spend $5.2 billion on R&D, more than competitors America Online, Sun Microsystems, and Oracle combined. Along with the cash, Microsoft has a strong, visionary leader in its efforts to innovate—no less than Bill Gates himself. Three years ago, Gates turned the CEO-ship of the company over to longtime number two, Steve Ballmer, and named himself "Chief Software Architect." He now spends most of his time and considerable talents happily attending to the details of Microsoft's new-product and technology development.

At the heart of Gates's innovation strategy is the Internet. "Gates sees a day when Microsoft software will . . . be at nearly every point a consumer or corporation touches the Web, . . . easily connecting people to the Internet wherever they happen to be," says *Business Week* analyst Jay Greene. In this new world, any software application on your computer—or on your cell phone, handheld device, or home electronics device—will tap directly into Internet services that help you manage your work and your life. To prepare for such "anytime, anywhere" computing, Microsoft will transform itself from a software company into an Internet services company. As a part of its Web services, Microsoft will one day rent out the latest versions of its software programs via the Net. "Once that happens," says Greene, "Microsoft hopes to deliver software like a steady flow of electricity, collecting monthly or annual usage fees that will give it a lush, predictable revenue stream."

This vision drives a major new Microsoft initiative—dubbed *.NET Services*. It's all part of a strategy to connect people, information, and systems through Web services. Its initial service, called *.NET Passport*, lets registered users enter a single set of sign-in credentials—such as an e-mail address and a password—and then use this single "digital passport" to enter other Web sites without having to remember numerous passwords and user names. The idea is to make signing in to Web sites fast and easy, for anything from purchasing merchandise to scheduling airline tickets to performing transactions on eBay. Passport members can subscribe to other *.NET* services, such as notifying them of specific events or automatically updating their calendars when they make an appointment online.

Within this broad strategic framework, Microsoft is now unleashing its biggest-ever new-products assault. "We've never had a year with this many new products," crows Gates. Here are just a few of the new products and technologies that Microsoft has launched recently or will soon introduce (as described in recent *Business Week* and *Fortune* accounts):

- *.NET Services:* technology that lets unrelated Web sites talk with one another and with PC programs. One click can trigger a cascade of actions without the user having to open new programs or visit new Web sites.

- *Smartphone:* Microsoft's latest software for cell phones. It allows mobile phone users to e-mail, instant message, surf the Web, listen to music, play games, and much more.

- *Natural-language processing:* software that will let computers respond to questions or commands in everyday language, not just computerese or a long series of mouse clicks. Combine that with speech recognition—another area in which Microsoft researchers are plugging away—and one day you'll be able to talk to your computer the same way you do to another person.

- *Face mapping:* using a digital camera to scan a PC user's head into a 3D image. Software then adds a full range of emotions. The point? Microsoft thinks that gamers will want to use their own images in role-playing games.

- *Information agents:* software agents that help you sort the deluge of electronic information. One day, an agent will study what types of messages you read first and know your schedule. Then it will sort e-mail and voice mail, interrupting you with only key messages.

- *The digital home:* next-generation technologies aimed at making the PC the electronic hub of the twenty-first-century digital home. The new technologies will route music, movies, TV programming, e-mail, and news between the Web and PCs, TV set-top boxes, gadgets, and wall-size viewing screens, and sound systems that would make the neighbors call the cops. "Everything in the home will be connected," predicts Gates. And if he gets his way, most of the gizmos will use Microsoft software. The first major Microsoft connected-home product will be a gizmo code-named Mira. It's a flat-panel monitor that detaches from its stand and continues to connect wirelessly to the PC from anywhere in the house. With a stylus tapping icons or scrawling letters on a touch screen, Mom can check e-mail from the kitchen, the kids can chat with online buddies from the couch while watching MTV, and Dad can shop at Amazon.com from the back porch.

- *Smart Personal Objects Technology (SPOT):* Using chips developed in partnership with National Semiconductor, refrigerator magnets, watches, and key chains will receive FM radio waves delivering everything from traffic reports and stock quotes to movie times and sports scores. Eventually, the technology may enable alarm clocks to ring extra early when an accident is likely to lengthen your commute.

So, far from resting on its remarkable past successes, Microsoft is on a quest to discover tomorrow's exciting new technologies. "Even while its latest products are waiting on the launchpad, it continues to pour money into R&D in search of the Next Big Thing," comments Greene. Gates is jazzed about the future. "He gets wound up like a kid over stuff like creating a computer that watches your actions with a small video camera and determines if you're too busy to be interrupted with a phone call or e-mail," says Greene. An excited Gates shares the simple but enduring principle that guides innovation at Microsoft: "The whole idea of valuing the user's time, that's the Holy Grail," he says.[1]

A company has to be good at developing and managing new products. Every product seems to go through a life cycle—it is born, goes through several phases, and eventually dies as newer products come along that better serve consumer needs. This product life cycle presents two major challenges: First, because all products eventually decline, a firm must be good at developing new products to replace aging ones (the challenge of *new-product development*). Second, the firm must be good at adapting its marketing strategies in the face of changing tastes, technologies, and competition as products pass through life-cycle stages (the challenge of *product life-cycle strategies*). We first look at the problem of finding and developing new products and then at the problem of managing them successfully over their life cycles.

■ New-Product Development Strategy

New-product development
The development of original products, product improvements, product modifications, and new brands through the firm's own R&D efforts.

Given the rapid changes in consumer tastes, technology, and competition, companies must develop a steady stream of new products and services. A firm can obtain new products in two ways. One is through *acquisition*—by buying a whole company, a patent, or a license to produce someone else's product. The other is through **new-product development** in the company's own research-and-development department. By *new products* we mean original products, product improvements, product modifications, and new brands that the firm develops through its own research-and-development efforts. In this chapter, we concentrate on new-product development.

Innovation can be very risky. Ford lost $350 million on its Edsel automobile; RCA lost $580 million on its SelectaVision videodisk player; and Texas Instruments lost a staggering $660 million before withdrawing from the home computer business. Even these amounts pale in comparison to the failure of the $5 billion Iridium global satellite-based wireless telephone system. Other costly product failures from sophisticated companies include New Coke (Coca-Cola Company), Eagle Snacks (Anheuser-Busch), Zap Mail electronic mail (FedEx), Polarvision instant movies (Polaroid), Premier "smokeless" cigarettes (R.J. Reynolds), Clorox detergent (Clorox Company), and Arch Deluxe sandwiches (McDonald's).[2]

New products continue to fail at a disturbing rate. One source estimates that no more than 10 percent of new products are still on the market and profitable after three years. Another study suggested that of the staggering 25,000 new consumer food, beverage, beauty, and health care products to hit the market each year, only 40 percent will be around five years later. Moreover, failure rates for new industrial products may be as high as 30 percent. Still another estimates new-product failures to be as high as 95 percent.[3]

Why do so many new products fail? There are several reasons. Although an idea may be good, the market size may have been overestimated. Perhaps the actual product was not designed as well as it should have been. Or maybe it was incorrectly positioned in the market, priced too high, or advertised poorly. A high-level executive might push a favorite idea despite poor marketing research findings. Sometimes the costs of product development are higher than expected, and sometimes competitors fight back harder than expected. The reasons behind some new-product failure seem pretty obvious. Try the following on for size[4]:

Strolling the aisles at Robert McMath's New Product Showcase and Learning Center is like finding yourself in some nightmare version of a supermarket. There's Gerber food for adults (pureed sweet-and-sour pork and chicken Madeira), Hot Scoop microwaveable ice cream sundaes, Ben-Gay aspirin, Premier smokeless cigarettes, and Miller Clear Beer. How about Avert Virucidal Tissues, Dr. Care Aerosol Toothpaste, Richard Simmons Dijon Vinaigrette Salad Spray, and Look of Buttermilk shampoo? Most of the 80,000 products on display were abject flops. Behind each of them are squandered dollars and hopes.

McMath, the genial curator of this Smithsonian of consumerism, gets lots of laughs when he asks his favorite question, "What were they thinking?" For example, R.J. Reynolds's Premier smokeless cigarettes seemed like a good idea at the time—who could argue against a healthier, nonpolluting cigarette? But what is a cigarette without smoke? McMath notes, "The only people who loved the product were

■ Visiting the New Product Showcase and Learning Center is like finding yourself in some nightmare version of a supermarket. Each product failure represents squandered dollars and hopes.

nonsmokers, and they somehow aren't the market RJR was trying to reach." Looking back, what was RJR thinking?

Other companies failed because the attached trusted brand names to something totally out of character. For example, when you hear the name Ben-Gay, you immediately think of the way Ben-Gay cream sears and stimulates your skin. Can you imagine swallowing Ben-Gay aspirin? Or how would you feel about quaffing a can of Exxon fruit punch or Kodak quencher? Other misbegotten attempts to stretch a good name include Cracker Jack cereal, Smucker's premium ketchup, and Fruit of the Loom laundry detergent. "What *were* they thinking?" asks McGrath. You can tell that some innovative products were doomed as soon as you hear their names: Toaster Eggs. Cucumber antiperspirant spray. Health-Sea sea sausage. Look of Buttermilk shampoo. Dr. Care Aerosol Toothpaste (many parents questioned the wisdom of arming their kids with something like this!). Really, what were they thinking?

Because so many new products fail, companies are anxious to learn how to improve their odds of new-product success. One way is to identify successful new products and find out what they have in common. Another is to study new-product failures to see what lessons can be learned. In all, to create successful new products, a company must understand its consumers, markets, and competitors and develop products that deliver superior value to customers.

So companies face a problem—they must develop new products, but the odds weigh heavily against success. The solution lies in strong new-product planning and in setting up a systematic *new-product development process* for finding and growing new products. Figure 8.1 shows the eight major steps in this process.

Idea Generation

New-product development starts with **idea generation**—the systematic search for new-product ideas. A company typically has to generate many ideas in order to find a few good ones. According to one well-known management consultant, "For every 1,000 ideas, only 100 will have enough commercial promise to merit a small-scale experiment, only 10 of those will warrant substantial financial commitment, and of those, only a couple will turn out to be unqualified successes."[5] His conclusion? "If you want to find a few ideas with the power to enthrall customers, foil competitors, and thrill investors, you must first generate hundreds and potentially thousands of unconventional strategic ideas."

Major sources of new-product ideas include internal sources and external sources such as customers, competitors, distributors and suppliers, and others.

Idea generation
The systematic search for new-product ideas.

FIGURE 8.1

Major Stages in New-Product Development

Internal Idea Sources Using *internal sources*, the company can find new ideas through formal research and development. It can pick the brains of its executives, scientists, engineers, manufacturing staff, and salespeople. Some companies have developed successful "intrapreneurial" programs that encourage employees to think up and develop new-product ideas. For example, 3M's well-known "15 percent rule" allows employees to spend 15 percent of their time "bootlegging"—working on projects of personal interest, whether or not those projects directly benefit the company. "For more than a century," notes one source, "3M's culture has fostered creativity and given employees the freedom to take risks and try new ideas." The spectacularly successful Post-it notes evolved out of this program. Similarly, Texas Instruments's IDEA program provides funds for employees who pursue their own ideas. Among the successful new products to come out of the IDEA program was TI's Speak 'n' Spell, the first children's toy to contain a microchip. Many other speaking toys followed, ultimately generating several hundred million dollars for TI.[6]

Companies sometimes look for creative approaches to innovation that overcome barriers to the free flow of new product ideas. For example, firms like Eureka! Ranch—a well-known "new-product hatchery"—employ both "method" and "madness" in helping companies to jumpstart their new-product idea generation process (see Marketing at Work 8.1).

External Idea Sources Good new-product ideas also come from watching and listening to *customers*. The company can analyze customer questions and complaints to find new products that better solve consumer problems. Company engineers or salespeople can meet with and work alongside customers to get suggestions and ideas. The company can conduct surveys or focus groups to learn about consumer needs and wants.

Heinz did just that when its researchers approached children, who consume more than half of the ketchup sold, to find out what would make ketchup more appealing to them. "When we asked them what would make the product more fun," says a Heinz spokesperson, "changing the color was among the top responses." So, Heinz developed and launched EZ Squirt, green ketchup that comes in a soft, squeezable bottle targeted at kids. The new product was a smash hit, so Heinz followed up with an entire rainbow of EZ Squirt colors, including Funky Purple, Passion Pink, Awesome Orange, Totally Teal, and Stellar Blue. The EZ Squirt bottle's special nozzle also emits a thin ketchup stream, "so tykes can

■ When Heinz asked kids what would make the product more fun, they said "Change the color!" So, Heinz developed and launched EZ Squirt, now in a variety of colors targeted at kids. The EZ Squirt bottle's special nozzle also emits a thin ketchup stream, so tykes can autograph their burgers.

autograph their burgers (or squirt someone across the table, though Heinz neglects to mention that)." In all, the new line earned the company a 5 percent increase in sales in the first year after hitting the grocery shelf.[7]

Consumers often create new products and uses on their own, and companies can benefit by finding these products and putting them on the market. For example, Avon capitalized on new uses discovered by consumers for its Skin-So-Soft bath oil and moisturizer. For years, customers have been spreading the word that Skin-So-Soft bath oil is also a terrific bug repellent. Whereas some consumers were content simply to bathe in water scented with the fragrant oil, others carried it in their backpacks to mosquito-infested campsites or kept a bottle on the deck of their beach houses. Now, Avon offers a complete line of Skin-So-Soft Bug Guard products, including Bug Guard Mosquito Repellant Moisturizing Towelettes and Bug Guard Plus, a combination moisturizer, insect repellent, and sunscreen.[8]

Finally, some companies even give customers the tools and resources to design their own products.

> Many companies have abandoned their efforts to figure out exactly what products their customers want. Instead, they have equipped customers with tools that let them design their own products. The user-friendly tools employ new technologies like computer simulation and rapid prototyping to make product development faster and less expensive. For example, Bush Boake Allen (BBA), a global supplier of specialty flavors to companies like Nestle, provides a tool kit that lets its customers develop their own flavors, which BBA then manufactures. Similarly, GE Plastics gives customers access to company data sheets, engineering expertise, simulation software, and other Web-based tools for designing better plastics products. Companies like LSI Logic and VLSI Technology provide customers with do-it-yourself tools that let them design their own specialized chips and customized integrated circuits. Using customers as innovators has become a hot new way to create value.[9]

Companies must be careful not to rely too heavily on customer input when developing new products. For some products, especially highly technical ones, customers may not know what they need. In such cases, "customers should not be trusted to come up with solutions; they aren't expert or informed enough for that part of the innovation process," says the head of an innovation management consultancy. "That's what your R&D team is for. Rather, customers should be asked only for outcomes—that is, what they want a product or service to *do* for them."[10]

Competitors are another good source of new-product ideas. Companies watch competitors' ads and other communications to get clues about their new products. They buy competing new products, take them apart to see how they work, analyze their sales, and decide whether they should bring out a new product of their own. *Distributors and suppliers* can also contribute many good new-product ideas. Resellers are close to the market and can pass along information about consumer problems and new-product possibilities. Suppliers can tell the company about new concepts, techniques, and materials that can be used to develop new products. Other idea sources include trade magazines, shows, and seminars; government agencies; new-product consultants; advertising agencies; marketing research firms; university and commercial laboratories; and inventors.

The search for new-product ideas should be systematic rather than haphazard. Otherwise, few new ideas will surface and many good ideas will sputter and die. Top management can avoid these problems by installing an *idea management system* that directs the flow of new ideas to a central point where they can be collected, reviewed, and evaluated. In setting up such a system, the company can do any or all of the following[11]:

- Appoint a respected senior person to be the company's idea manager.

- Create a cross-functional idea management committee consisting of people from R&D, engineering, purchasing, operations, finance, and sales and marketing to meet regularly and evaluate proposed new product and service ideas.

Marketing at Work | *8.1*

Eureka! Ranch: Method and Madness in Finding New-Product Ideas

Having trouble thinking up the next hot new-product idea? Try a visit to Eureka! Ranch. For $75,000 to $150,000, you can send a dozen key marketing managers to loosen up, have some fun, and get the creative juices flowing. Located on 80 acres, with a sand volleyball court, a water sports lake, and a three-hole golf course, Eureka! Ranch seems more like an executive resort than a new-product hatchery. But Eureka! Ranch isn't just about relaxing and having fun. Instead, it's all about the very serious business of creating new product ideas.

Founded by Doug Hall, a former Procter & Gamble "Master Marketing Inventor," the Ranch seems at first to be sheer madness. Consider this account:

Executives from Gardetto's, a Milwaukee-based snack foods company, stream through the doors of Eureka! Ranch. A two-man zydeco band cranks out early morning Cajun tunes. Amid the high-energy music, Doug Hall and his staff greet their visitors with laughs, handshakes, and platters of muffins, bagels, and other breakfast goodies. Hall, the opposite of Wall Street chic, in a blue Hawaiian shirt and faded jeans, soon gathers his clients in the center of the living room and welcomes everyone. A large blanket-covered mound lurks near his bare feet. After a brief introduction, in which he notes, "Today, reality isn't relevant," Hall rips the blanket off, revealing a pile of Nerf guns. With a commando yell, he grabs a foam assault rifle and starts firing away at the momentarily shocked participants. In an instant, however, they too join the battle, blasting away at one another in a frenzy of multicolored projectiles and screams. Let the games begin.

But there's method to the madness in Eureka! Ranch's intensive multi-day ses-

sions. Doug Hall, once described as "a combination of Bill Gates, Ben Franklin, and Bozo the Clown," is dedicated to helping participants throw off the self-imposed constraints that keep them from innovating. Eureka! Ranch creates a unique combination of sensory overload and a supportive environment that breaks down defensiveness and self-censorship that too often stifle creativity in a corporate conference room. The

result: breakthrough ideas and strategies for new products and services.

Gardetto's—whose main product is called Snak-ens, a mixture of seasoned pretzels, rye crisps, and breadsticks—took 15 of its people to Eureka! Ranch's standard two-and-a-half-day program. The agenda for Eureka's program was serious and simple in concept. "I'm not looking for a line extension or just a good idea," said executive vice president Nan

"When Doug meets Disney, creativity ne'er wanes; Our team explodes when he jump starts our brains!"
**Ellen Guidera, Vice President
The Walt Disney Company**

"A rigorous, quantifiable process for inventing breakthrough ideas for clients. Unlike many creative gurus hustling ideation wares in the corporate marketplace, Eureka! Inventing processes are quantified every step of the way."
CIO Magazine

"Eureka! has developed more new products than any other organization in America."
New York Magazine

**Need Growth?
We Can Help!**

"Former Procter & Gamble marketing whiz Doug Hall goes to any length to encourage a fresh perspective ...clients say it works."
The Wall Street Journal

"Eureka! Ranch's unconventional approach has won raves from some of the biggest corporations in the country."
CNN

"Doug Hall is THE idea man. The former P&G marketer has guided big corporation marketing team after big corporation marketing team to stunning new product breakthroughs."
Tom Peters

**JUMP START
YOUR BUSINESS
BRAIN**

**WIN MORE • LOSE LESS
and MAKE MORE MONEY**
with your New Products, Services, Sales & Advertising

EUREKA! RANCH®

The Eureka! Ranch delivers OUTSTANDING client satisfaction. More than 80% of Eureka! Ranch business is REPEAT from such world class companies as The Ford Motor Company, Fidelity, Tenneco, Johnson & Johnson, Walt Disney, Frito-Lay, Compaq Computer, Procter & Gamble and American Express.

Generating new product ideas: Eureka! Ranch now combines creative passion with a more systematic process and real-world data. But along with the scientific method, there's still a healthy portion of madness thrown into the brew.

Gardetto. "I'm looking for something really breakthrough." But from day one, in execution, the program was free-wheeling and action-packed. Heart-pumping Nerf bullet battles replaced mind-numbing PowerPoint bullet lectures. The majority of the first day was devoted to generating as many wild ideas as possible. Reality? Not relevant!

At Eureka! Ranch, fast-paced play and idea-generating zaniness open the flood gates for new ideas. It starts with brainstorming exercises that expand people's minds and generate new ideas around the client's problem. No idea is too far-fetched or impractical on the first day, and everything gets written down. By the time they sit down to a gourmet dinner at the ranch, clients have typically spawned some 1,500 to 2,000 ideas. Only after dinner do the participants start judging the fruits of their fun. For the Gardetto's team, ideas like Gar-Chia—a Chia-pet-like snack that expands in water—get tossed. But other ideas receive numerous votes of support. At 11 P.M., after the clients have retired for the night, Eureka! Ranch's tireless staff—its "Trained Brains"—debrief and refine the day's results.

Day 2 begins with a hearty breakfast and a stiff mug of Brain Brew coffee. Then the Gardetto's team gathers around a large board, to which Eureka! Ranch staffers have tacked the 12 most popular new product ideas and the 19 most popular new positioning ideas from the previous day. The team reviews the concepts, adds depth and refinement to the better ones, and votes again. They spend the rest of the day assessing each surviving idea in more detail. "After the previous day's anything-that-pops-up-in-your-head brainstorming," says one observer, "today is more focused; people sense that they're discussing ideas that may evolve into a completely new line of snacks."

Yet even as the group tackles the serious issues, the atmosphere remains lighthearted. "Just the fact that a Nerf ball comes whistling at your head [during an exercise] makes you think of something different. [It's] harnessed chaos," says one participant. "You'd like to have it at the office, but that's not the real world." When the day's session ends, the Gardetto's team heads out for a relaxing dinner at a local restaurant. Meanwhile, Doug Hall and his staff prepare for the final day. They whittle down the list of ideas and write concept statements for what they think are the most viable new-product options.

The final day: "Another foggy morning, another hearty breakfast, another mug of Brain Brew," notes the observer. Hall, dressed in a long purple robe and still barefoot, presents the results of the Gardetto's team's efforts—the best of the best. The team talks through each product idea. Some are sent packing—such as Saturday night Snack 'Ems (featuring Charlie's skillet corn bread) and Bistro Baguettes (sweet bread with raspberry-champagne and cream cheese). But other ideas garner enthusiastic support. Gardetto's leaves satisfied, with 16 new packaging ideas, 9 new logos, and several new snack food concepts for the R&D kitchens.

Gardetto's satisfying experience is typical. *Human Resource Executive* recently named Eureka! Ranch as one of the top 10 training programs in the country. Eighty-five percent of participants rate the program as the best training they've ever attended. And more than 80 percent of Eureka! Ranch sessions are repeat business from such world-class companies as Ford, Fidelity, Tenneco, Johnson & Johnson, Walt Disney, Nike, Frito-Lay, Procter & Gamble, and American Express. "When Doug meets Disney, creativity never wanes," says a Disney executive after a visit to Eureka! Ranch. "Our team explodes when he jumps starts our brains."

In working with more than 4,000 new products and 6,000 front-line development groups, Eureka! Ranch has learned a good many lessons on creativity itself. Interestingly, one lesson is that zany fun is only part of the process for generating creative ideas. In fact, in recent years, Eureka! Ranch sessions are becoming more serious and less chaotic. The Ranch now tackles the tough job of being creative by balancing the "madness" with a stronger mix of "method."

There's still plenty of fast-paced action and creative brainstorming (video games still line the walls), and the Ranch promises sessions that will "wake up and shake up" your thinking. But sessions are now supported by the heaps of qualitative and quantitative data gleaned from Eureka! Ranch's years of new-product development experience. Along with the brainstorming, clients now learn "the three laws of marketing physics" and the "laws of capitalist creativity." Refined product-development tools and more methodical processes now supplement the open-ended fun of previous days. For example, Eureka! Ranch has developed its Merwyn software, a scoring system for new ideas. The Merwyn software contains over one million data points that help it predict the likely market success of new products.

What has emerged is a more effective version of Eureka! Ranch. Under Hall's notions of "capitalist creativity," new-product success "is not random. . . . There are reproducible scientific lessons and laws that . . . can help you win more, lose less, and make more money." Eureka! Ranch now combines creative passion with a more systematic process and real-world data. But along with the scientific method, there's still a healthy portion of madness thrown into the brew.

Sources: Quotes and other information from Todd Datz, "Romper Ranch," *CIO,* May 15, 1999; Lori Dahm, "Pursue Passion," *Stagnito's New Products Magazine,* October 2002, p. 58; Eva Kaplan-Leiserson, "Eureka!: This little-Ranch-that-Could Teaches You to 'Win More, Lose Less, and Make More Money,'" *T&D,* December 2001, p. 50(14); Geoff Williams, "I've Got an Idea!" *Entrepreneur,* December 2001, p. 36; Monique Reece, "Expert Shares His Ideas to Jumpstart Businesses," *Denver Business Journal,* September 28, 2001, p. 33A; Doug Hall, *Jump Start Your Business Brain* (Whitehall, VA: Betterway Publications, 2002); John Eckberg, "New Radio Host takes on Small Biz," *The Cincinnati Enquirer,* January 13, 2003, p. 7B; and www.eurekaranch.com, August 2003.

- Set up a toll-free number or Web site for anyone who wants to send a new idea to the idea manager.

- Encourage all company stakeholders—employees, suppliers, distributors, dealers—to send their ideas to the idea manager.

- Set up formal recognition programs to reward those who contribute the best new ideas.

The idea manager approach yields two favorable outcomes. First, it helps create an innovation-oriented company culture. It shows that top management supports, encourages, and rewards innovation. Second, it will yield a larger number of ideas, among which will be found some especially good ones. As the system matures, ideas will flow more freely. No longer will good ideas wither for the lack of a sounding board or a senior product advocate.

Idea Screening

Idea screening
Screening new-product ideas in order to spot good ideas and drop poor ones as soon as possible.

The purpose of idea generation is to create a large number of ideas. The purpose of the succeeding stages is to *reduce* that number. The first idea-reducing stage is **idea screening**, which helps spot good ideas and drop poor ones as soon as possible. Product development costs rise greatly in later stages, so the company wants to go ahead only with the product ideas that will turn into profitable products. As one marketing executive suggests, "Three executives sitting in a room can get 40 good ideas ricocheting off the wall in minutes. The challenge is getting a steady stream of good ideas out of the labs and creativity campfires, through marketing and manufacturing, and all the way to consumers."[12]

Many companies require their executives to write up new-product ideas on a standard form that can be reviewed by a new-product committee. The write-up describes the product, the target market, and the competition. It makes some rough estimates of market size, product price, development time and costs, manufacturing costs, and rate of return. The committee then evaluates the idea against a set of general criteria. For example, at Kao Company, the large Japanese consumer-products company, the committee asks questions such as these: Is the product truly useful to consumers and society? Is it good for our particular company? Does it mesh well with the company's objectives and strategies? Do we have the people, skills, and resources to make it succeed? Does it deliver more value to customers than do competing products? Is it easy to advertise and distribute? Many companies have well-designed systems for rating and screening new-product ideas.

Concept Development and Testing

Product concept
A detailed version of the new-product idea stated in meaningful consumer terms.

An attractive idea must be developed into a **product concept**. It is important to distinguish between a product idea, a product concept, and a product image. A *product idea* is an idea for a possible product that the company can see itself offering to the market. A *product concept* is a detailed version of the idea stated in meaningful consumer terms. A *product image* is the way consumers perceive an actual or potential product.

Concept Development DaimlerChrysler is getting ready to commercialize its experimental fuel-cell-powered electric car. This car's nonpolluting fuel-cell system runs directly on methanol, which delivers hydrogen to the fuel cell with only water as a by-product. It is highly fuel efficient (75 percent more efficient than gasoline engines) and gives the new car an environmental advantage over standard internal combustion engine cars or even today's superefficient gasoline–electric hybrid cars.

■ DaimlerChrysler's task is to develop its fuel-cell-powered-electric car into alternative product concepts, find out how attractive each is to customers, and choose the best one.

DaimlerChrysler is currently road-testing its NECAR 5 (New Electric Car) subcompact prototype and plans to deliver the first fuel-cell cars to customers in 2004. Based on the tiny Mercedes A-Class, the car accelerates quickly, reaches speeds of 90 miles per hour, and has a 280-mile driving range, giving it a huge edge over battery-powered electric cars that travel only about 80 miles before needing 3 to 12 hours of recharging.[13]

DaimlerChrysler's task is to develop this new product into alternative product concepts, find out how attractive each concept is to customers, and choose the best one. It might create the following product concepts for the fuel-cell electric car:

Concept 1   A moderately priced subcompact designed as a second family car to be used around town. The car is ideal for running errands and visiting friends.

Concept 2   A medium-cost sporty compact appealing to young people.

Concept 3   An inexpensive subcompact "green" car appealing to environmentally conscious people who want practical transportation and low pollution.

Concept 4   A high-end SUV appealing to those who love the space SUVs provide but lament the poor gas mileage.

Concept Testing   **Concept testing** calls for testing new-product concepts with groups of target consumers. The concepts may be presented to consumers symbolically or physically. Here, in words, is concept 3:

> An efficient, fun-to-drive, fuel-cell-powered electric subcompact car that seats four. This methanol-powered high-tech wonder provides practical and reliable transportation with virtually no pollution. It goes up to 90 miles per hour and, unlike battery-powered electric cars, it never needs recharging. It's priced, fully equipped, at $20,000.

For some concept tests, a word or picture description might be sufficient. However, a more concrete and physical presentation of the concept will increase the reliability of the concept test. Today, some marketers are finding innovative ways to make product concepts more real to consumer subjects. For example, some are using virtual reality to test product concepts. Virtual reality programs use computers and sensory devices (such as gloves or goggles) to simulate reality. A designer of kitchen cabinets can use a virtual reality program to help a customer "see" how his or her kitchen would look and work if remodeled with the company's products. Hairdressers have used virtual reality for years to show consumers how they might look with a new style. Although virtual reality is still in its infancy, its applications are increasing daily.[14]

After being exposed to the concept, consumers then may be asked to react to it by answering questions such as those in Table 8.1. The answers will help the company decide which concept has the strongest appeal. For example, the last question asks about the consumer's intention to buy. Suppose 10 percent of the consumers said they

Concept testing
Testing new-product concepts with a group of target consumers to find out if the concepts have strong consumer appeal.

TABLE 8.1   Questions for Fuel-Cell Electric Car Concept Test

1. Do you understand the concept of a fuel-cell-powered electric car?

2. Do you believe the claims about the car's performance?

3. What are the major benefits of the fuel-cell-powered electric car compared with a conventional car?

4. What are its advantages compared with a battery-powered electric car?

5. What improvements in the car's features would you suggest?

6. For what uses would you prefer a fuel-cell-powered electric car to a conventional car?

7. What would be a reasonable price to charge for the car?

8. Who would be involved in your decision to buy such a car? Who would drive it?

9. Would you buy such a car? (definitely, probably, probably not, definitely not)

"definitely" would buy and another 5 percent said "probably." The company could project these figures to the full population in this target group to estimate sales volume. Even then, the estimate is uncertain because people do not always carry out their stated intentions.

Many firms routinely test new-product concepts with consumers before attempting to turn them into actual new products. For example, each month AcuPOLL tests 40 new-product concepts in person on 100 nationally representative grocery store shoppers, rating them as "Pure Gold" or "Fool's Gold" concepts. In past polls, Nabisco's Oreo Chocolate Cones concept received a rare A+ rating, meaning that consumers think it is an outstanding concept that they would try and buy. Glad Ovenware, Reach Whitening Tape dental floss, and Lender's Bake at Home Bagels were also big hits. Other product concepts didn't fare so well. Nubrush Anti-Bacterial Toothbrush Spray disinfectant, from Applied Microdontics, received an F. Consumers found Nubrush to be overpriced, and most don't think they have a problem with "infected" toothbrushes. Nor did consumers think much of Excedrin Tension Headache Cooling Pads. Another concept that fared poorly was Chef Williams 5 Minute Marinade, which comes with a syringe customers use to inject the marinade into meats. "I can't see that on grocery shelves," comments an AcuPOLL executive. Some consumers might find the thought of injecting something into meat a bit repulsive, and "it's just so politically incorrect to have this syringe on there."[15]

Hershey does its product concept testing on the Web. It uses online test subjects to gain insight to all aspects of its product concepts. Consumers might be shown pictures of proposed candy bars or baking mixes, quizzed about flavors, and asked about potential product names. Says one Hershey researcher, "You need to test maybe 100 concepts to get one good product that might make it to market." Putting concept testing online has cut the time Hershey spends on new-product development by two-thirds.[16]

Marketing Strategy Development

Suppose DaimlerChrysler finds that concept 3 for the fuel-cell-powered electric car tests best. The next step is **marketing strategy development**, designing an initial marketing strategy for introducing this car to the market.

The *marketing strategy statement* consists of three parts. The first part describes the target market; the planned product positioning; and the sales, market share, and profit goals for the first few years. Thus:

> The target market is younger, well-educated, moderate-to-high-income individuals, couples, or small families seeking practical, environmentally responsible transportation. The car will be positioned as more economical to operate, more fun to drive, and less polluting than today's internal combustion engine or hybrid cars. It is also less restricting than battery-powered electric cars, which must be recharged regularly. The company will aim to sell 100,000 cars in the first year, at a loss of not more than $15 million. In the second year, the company will aim for sales of 120,000 cars and a profit of $25 million.

The second part of the marketing strategy statement outlines the product's planned price, distribution, and marketing budget for the first year:

> The fuel-cell-powered electric car will be offered in three colors—red, white, and blue—and will have optional air-conditioning and power-drive features. It will sell at a retail price of $20,000—with 15 percent off the list price to dealers. Dealers who sell more than 10 cars per month will get an additional discount of 5 percent on each car sold that month. An advertising budget of $50 million will be split 50-50 between a national media campaign and local advertising. Advertising will emphasize the car's fun spirit and low emissions. During the first year, $100,000 will be spent on marketing research to find out who is buying the car and their satisfaction levels.

Marketing strategy development
Designing an initial marketing strategy for a new product based on the product concept.

The third part of the marketing strategy statement describes the planned long-run sales, profit goals, and marketing mix strategy:

> DaimlerChrysler intends to capture a 3 percent long-run share of the total auto market and realize an after-tax return on investment of 15 percent. To achieve this, product quality will start high and be improved over time. Price will be raised in the second and third years if competition permits. The total advertising budget will be raised each year by about 10 percent. Marketing research will be reduced to $60,000 per year after the first year.

Business Analysis

Once management has decided on its product concept and marketing strategy, it can evaluate the business attractiveness of the proposal. **Business analysis** involves a review of the sales, costs, and profit projections for a new product to find out whether they satisfy the company's objectives. If they do, the product can move to the product development stage.

To estimate sales, the company might look at the sales history of similar products and conduct surveys of market opinion. It can then estimate minimum and maximum sales to assess the range of risk. After preparing the sales forecast, management can estimate the expected costs and profits for the product, including marketing, R&D, operations, accounting, and finance costs. The company then uses the sales and costs figures to analyze the new product's financial attractiveness.

Business analysis
A review of the sales, costs, and profit projections for a new product to find out whether these factors satisfy the company's objectives.

Product Development

So far, for many new-product concepts, the product may have existed only as a word description, a drawing, or perhaps a crude mock-up. If the product concept passes the business test, it moves into **product development**. Here, R&D or engineering develops the product concept into a physical product. The product development step, however, now calls for a large jump in investment. It will show whether the product idea can be turned into a workable product.

The R&D department will develop and test one or more physical versions of the product concept. R&D hopes to design a prototype that will satisfy and excite consumers and that can be produced quickly and at budgeted costs. Developing a successful prototype can take days, weeks, months, or even years.

Often, products undergo rigorous tests to make sure that they perform safely and effectively, or that consumers will find value in them. Here are some examples of such product tests[17]:

Product development
Developing the product concept into a physical product in order to ensure that the product idea can be turned into a workable product.

> A scuba-diving Barbie doll must swim and kick for 15 straight hours to satisfy Mattel that she will last at least one year. But because Barbie may find her feet in small owners' mouths rather than in the bathtub, Mattel has devised another, more torturous test: Barbie's feet are clamped by two steel jaws to make sure that her skin doesn't crack, and choke potential owners.

> P&G spends $150 million on 4,000 to 5,000 studies a year, testing everything from the ergonomics of picking up a shampoo bottle to how long women can keep their hands in sudsy water. On any given day, subjects meet in focus groups, sell their dirty laundry to researchers, put prototype diapers on their babies' bottoms, and rub mysterious creams on their faces. Last year, one elementary school raised $17,000 by having students and parents take part in P&G product tests. Students tested toothpaste and shampoo and ate brownies, while their mothers watched advertising for Tempo tissue, P&G's paper wipes packaged to fit in a car. This year, P&G is paying the school to have 48 students and parents wear new sneakers that they hand in every month for six months. Half the shoes return cleaned. No one knows what P&G is testing, and the company won't say.

> Taco Time International, a Canadian Mexican restaurant chain, wanted to taste test its new line of green and red hot sauces. So it decided to get input from

some real experts on hot stuff: the residents of Villa Hermosa in Mexico. Now Villa Hermosa isn't just any Mexican city, it's the capital of the state of Tabasco, which is, of course, known as the source of one of the world's most famous hot sauces. When the people of hot-sauce city reacted favorably to the firm's concoctions, Taco Time videotaped the tastings and produced the video for its franchisees. It also put shots of the tastings on its Web site and on restaurant tray liners. Straight to the source—now that's authentic!

At Gillette, almost everyone gets involved in new-product testing. Every working day at Gillette, 200 volunteers from various departments come to work unshaven, troop to the second floor of the company's gritty South Boston plant, and enter small booths with a sink and mirror. There they take instructions from technicians on the other side of a small window as to which razor, shaving cream, or aftershave to use. The volunteers evaluate razors for sharpness of blade, smoothness of glide, and ease of handling. In a nearby shower room, women perform the same ritual on their legs, underarms, and what the company delicately refers to as the "bikini area." "We bleed so you'll get a good shave at home," says one Gillette employee.

A new-product must have the required functional features and also convey the intended psychological characteristics. The fuel-cell electric car, for example, should strike consumers as being well built, comfortable, and safe. Management must learn what makes consumers decide that a car is well built. To some consumers, this means that the car has "solid-sounding" doors. To others, it means that the car is able to withstand heavy impacts in crash tests. Consumer tests are conducted, in which consumers test-drive the car and rate its attributes.

■ Product testing: Gillette uses employee-volunteers to test new shaving products—"We bleed so you'll get a good shave at home," says one Gillette employee.

Test Marketing

Test marketing
The stage of new-product development in which the product and marketing program are tested in more realistic market settings.

If the product passes functional and consumer tests, the next step is **test marketing**, the stage at which the product and marketing program are introduced into more realistic market settings. Test marketing gives the marketer experience with marketing the product before going to the great expense of full introduction. It lets the company test the product and its entire marketing program—positioning strategy, advertising, distribution, pricing, branding and packaging, and budget levels.

The amount of test marketing needed varies with each new product. Test marketing costs can be high, and it takes time that may allow competitors to gain advantages. When the costs of developing and introducing the product are low, or when management is already confident about the new product, the company may do little or no test marketing. In fact, test marketing by consumer packaged-goods firms has been declining in recent years. Companies often do not test-market simple line extensions or copies of successful competitor products. For example, Procter & Gamble introduced its Folger's decaffeinated coffee crystals without test marketing, and Pillsbury rolled out Chewy granola bars and chocolate-covered Granola Dipps with no standard test market.

However, when introducing a new product requires a big investment, or when management is not sure of the product or marketing program, a company may do a lot of test marketing. For instance, Lever USA spent two years testing its highly successful Lever 2000 bar soap in Atlanta before introducing it internationally. Frito-Lay did 18 months of testing in three markets on at least five formulations before introducing its Baked Lays line of low-fat snacks. Both Procter & Gamble and Unilever spent many months testing their new Juvian and MyHome valet laundry and home fabric care services. And Nokia test-marketed its new N-Gage cell phone/mobile game player extensively in London before introducing it worldwide.[18]

Although test-marketing costs can be high, they are often small when compared with the costs of making a major mistake. For example, McDonald's made a costly mistake when it introduced its low-fat burger, the McLean Deluxe, nationally without the chain's normal and lengthy testing process. The new product failed after a big investment but lean results. And Nabisco's launch of one new product without testing had disastrous—and soggy—results[19]:

■ Test marketing: Nokia test-marketed its new N-Gage cell phone/mobile game player extensively before introducing it worldwide.

> Nabisco hit a marketing home run with its Teddy Grahams, teddy-bear-shaped graham crackers in several different flavors. So, the company decided to extend Teddy Grahams into a new area. In 1989, it introduced chocolate, cinnamon, and honey versions of Breakfast Bears Graham Cereal. When the product came out, however, consumers didn't like the taste enough, so the product developers went back to the kitchen and modified the formula. But they didn't test it. The result was a disaster. Although the cereal may have tasted better, it no longer stayed crunchy in milk, as the advertising on the box promised. Instead, it left a gooey mess of graham mush on the bottom of cereal bowls. Supermarket managers soon refused to restock the cereal, and Nabisco executives decided it was too late to reformulate the product again. So a promising new product was killed through haste to get it to market.

Still, test marketing doesn't guarantee success. For example, Procter & Gamble tested its new Fit produce rinse heavily for five years and Olay cosmetics for three years. Although market tests suggested the products would be successful, P&G had to pull the plug on both shortly after their introductions.[20]

Commercialization

Test marketing gives management the information needed to make a final decision about whether to launch the new product. If the company goes ahead with **commercialization**—introducing the new product into the market—it will face high costs. The company will have to build or rent a manufacturing facility. And it may have to spend, in the case of a new consumer packaged good, between $10 million and $200 million for advertising, sales promotion, and other marketing efforts in the first year.

The company launching a new product must first decide on introduction *timing*. If DaimlerChrysler's new fuel-cell electric car will eat into the sales of the company's other cars, its introduction may be delayed. If the car can be improved further, or if the economy is down, the company may wait until the following year to launch it.

Next, the company must decide *where* to launch the new product—in a single location, a region, the national market, or the international market. Few companies have the confidence, capital, and capacity to launch new products into full national or international distribution. They will develop a planned *market rollout* over time. In particular, small companies may enter attractive cities or regions one at a time. Larger companies, however, may quickly introduce new models into several regions or into the full national market.

Commercialization
Introducing a new product into the market.

Companies with international distribution systems may introduce new products through global rollouts. Colgate-Palmolive used to follow a "lead-country" strategy. For example, it launched its Palmolive Optima shampoo and conditioner first in Australia, the Philippines, Hong Kong, and Mexico, then rapidly rolled it out into Europe, Asia, Latin America, and Africa. However, most international companies now introduce their new products in swift global assaults. More recently, in its fastest new-product rollout ever, Colgate introduced its Actibrush battery-powered toothbrush into 50 countries in a year, generating $115 million in sales. Such rapid worldwide expansion solidified the brand's market position before foreign competitors could react.[21]

Organizing for New-Product Development

Many companies organize their new-product development process into the orderly sequence of steps shown in Figure 8.1, starting with idea generation and ending with commercialization. Under this **sequential product development** approach, one company department works individually to complete its stage of the process before passing the new product along to the next department and stage. This orderly, step-by-step process can help bring control to complex and risky projects. But it also can be dangerously slow. In fast-changing, highly competitive markets, such slow-but-sure product development can result in product failures, lost sales and profits, and crumbling market positions. "Speed to market" and reducing new-product development cycle time have become pressing concerns to companies in all industries.

In order to get their new products to market more quickly, many companies are adopting a faster, team-oriented approach called **simultaneous product development** (or team-based or collaborative product development). Under this approach, company departments work closely together through cross-functional teams, overlapping the steps in the product development process to save time and increase effectiveness. Instead of passing the new product from department to department, the company assembles a team of people from various departments that stays with the new product from start to finish. Such teams usually include people from the marketing, finance, design, manufacturing, and legal departments, and even supplier and customer companies.

Top management gives the product development team general strategic direction but no clear-cut product idea or work plan. It challenges the team with stiff and seemingly contradictory goals—"turn out carefully planned and superior new products, but do it quickly"—and then gives the team whatever freedom and resources it needs to meet the challenge. In the sequential process, a bottleneck at one phase can seriously slow the entire project. In the simultaneous approach, if one functional area hits snags, it works to resolve them while the team moves on.

The Allen-Bradley Company, a maker of industrial controls, realized tremendous benefits by using simultaneous development. Under its old sequential approach, the company's marketing department handed off a new-product idea to designers, who worked in isolation to prepare concepts that they then passed along to product engineers. The engineers, also working by themselves, developed expensive prototypes and handed them off to manufacturing, which tried to find a way to build the new product. Finally, after many years and dozens of costly design compromises and delays, marketing was asked to sell the new product, which it often found to be too high priced or sadly out of date. Now, all of Allen-Bradley's departments work together to develop new products. The results have been astonishing. For example, the company recently developed a new electrical control in just two years; under the old system, it would have taken six years.

The simultaneous team-based approach does have some limitations. Superfast product development can be riskier and more costly than the slower, more orderly sequential approach. Moreover, it often creates increased organizational tension and confusion. And the company must take care that rushing a product to market doesn't adversely affect its quality—the objective is not only to create products faster, but to create them *better* and faster.

Sequential product development
A new-product development approach in which one company department works to complete its stage of the process before passing the new product along to the next department and stage.

Simultaneous (or team-based) product development
An approach to developing new products in which various company departments work closely together, overlapping the steps in the product-development process to save time and increase effectiveness.

Despite these drawbacks, in rapidly changing industries facing increasingly shorter product life cycles, the rewards of fast and flexible product development far exceed the risks. Companies that get new and improved products to the market faster than competitors often gain a dramatic competitive edge. They can respond more quickly to emerging consumer tastes and charge higher prices for more advanced designs. As one auto industry executive states, "What we want to do is get the new car approved, built, and in the consumer's hands in the shortest time possible. . . . Whoever gets there first gets all the marbles."[22]

Thus, new-product success requires more than simply thinking up a few good ideas, turning them into products, and finding customers for them. It requires a systematic approach for finding new ways to create value for target consumers, from generating and screening new-product ideas to creating and rolling out want-satisfying products to customers. More than this, successful new-product development requires a total-company commitment. At companies known for their new-product prowess—such as 3M, Gillette, Nokia, and Intel— the entire culture encourages, supports, and rewards innovation (see Marketing at Work 8.2).

Linking the Concepts

SPEED BUMP

Take a break. Think about new products and how companies find and develop them.

- Suppose that you're on a panel to nominate the "best new products of the year." What products would you nominate and why? See what you can learn about the new-product development process for one of these products.
- Applying the new-product development process you've just studied, develop an idea for an innovative new snack food product and sketch out a brief plan for bringing it to market. Loosen up and have some fun with this.

Product Life-Cycle Strategies

After launching the new product, management wants the product to enjoy a long and happy life. Although it does not expect the product to sell forever, the company wants to earn a decent profit to cover all the effort and risk that went into launching it. Management is aware that each product will have a life cycle, although its exact shape and length is not known in advance.

Figure 8.2 shows a typical **product life cycle (PLC)**, the course that a product's sales and profits take over its lifetime. The product life cycle has five distinct stages:

1. **Product development** begins when the company finds and develops a new-product idea. During product development, sales are zero and the company's investment costs mount.

Product life cycle (PLC)
The course of a product's sales and profits over its lifetime. It involves five distinct stages: product development, introduction, growth, maturity, and decline.

FIGURE 8.2
Sales and Profits Over the Product's Life from Inception to Decline

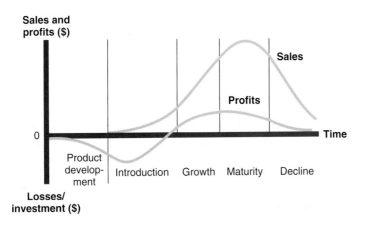

Marketing at Work 8.2

3M: A Culture for Innovation

You see the headline in every 3M ad: "Innovation Working for You." But at 3M, innovation isn't just an advertising pitch. 3M views *innovation* as its path to growth and new products as its lifeblood. It markets more than 50,000 products. These products range from sandpaper, adhesives, and sponges to power cable splices, to optical lenses, pharmaceuticals, and futuristic synthetic ligaments; from coatings that sleeken boat hulls to hundreds of sticky tapes—Scotch Tape, masking tape, superbonding tape, acid-free photo and document tape, and even refastening-disposable-diaper tape.

3M's goal is to derive an astonishing 30 percent of each year's sales from products introduced within the previous four years. More astonishing, it usually succeeds! Each year 3M launches more than 200 new products. And last year, a full third of its $16 billion in sales came from products introduced within the past four years. This legendary emphasis on innovation has consistently made 3M one of America's most admired companies. In 2003, 3M once again placed among the leaders in *Fortune's* list of companies most admired for innovation. At 3M, new products don't just happen. The company works hard to create an environment that supports innovation. Last year, it invested more than $1 billion, or 6 percent of annual sales, in research and development—almost twice as much as the average company.

3M encourages everyone to look for new products. The company's renowned "15 percent rule" allows technical employees to spend up to 15 percent of their time "bootlegging"—working on projects of personal inter-

1 The world wants thinner electronics.

2 We're getting it all on tape.

3M has

pioneered a whole

new technology: Microflex

Circuits – the world's leading

mass-produced electronic circuits on tape.

They're thinner, smaller, highly reliable, and allow for

more connections than rigid circuit boards. They'll go anywhere a

designer can dream up: phones, pagers, laptops and printers. We expand

the possibilities because we make the leap *from need to...*

3M *Innovation*

For more information, call 1-800-3M-HELPS, or Internet: http://www.mmm.com

3M views innovation as its path to growth and new products as its lifeblood. Its entire culture encourages, supports, and rewards innovation.

2. **Introduction** is a period of slow sales growth as the product is introduced in the market. Profits are nonexistent in this stage because of the heavy expenses of product introduction.
3. **Growth** is a period of rapid market acceptance and increasing profits.
4. **Maturity** is a period of slowdown in sales growth because the product has achieved acceptance by most potential buyers. Profits level off or decline because of increased marketing outlays to defend the product against competition.
5. **Decline** is the period when sales fall off and profits drop.

Not all products follow this product life cycle. Some products are introduced and die quickly; others stay in the mature stage for a long, long time. Some enter the decline stage and are then cycled back into the growth stage through strong promotion or repositioning.

est. "The 15% rule is absolutely essential to 3M for generating those unique ideas and breakthrough products," says 3M's Vice President of R&D. When a promising idea comes along, 3M forms a team made up of the researcher who developed the idea and volunteers from manufacturing, sales, marketing, and legal. Team members stay with the product until it succeeds or fails. Some teams have tried three or four times before finally making a success of an idea. Each year, 3M hands out Golden Step Awards to venture teams whose new products earned more than $2 million in U.S. sales, or $4 million in worldwide sales, within three years of introduction.

3M knows that it must try thousands of new-product ideas to hit one big jackpot. One well-worn slogan at 3M is, "You have to kiss a lot of frogs to find a prince." "Kissing frogs" often means making mistakes, but 3M accepts blunders and dead ends as a normal part of creativity and innovation. In fact, its philosophy seems to be "If you aren't making mistakes, you probably aren't doing anything."

As it turns out, "blunders" have turned into some of 3M's most successful products. Old-timers at 3M love to tell the story about the early 3M scientist who had a deathly fear of shaving with a straight razor. Instead, he invented a very fine, waterproof sandpaper which he used to sand the stubble from his face each morning. Although this invention never caught on as a shaving solution, it became one of 3M's best-selling products—wet-dry sandpaper, now used for a wide variety of commercial and industrial applications.

And then there's the one about 3M scientist Spencer Silver. Silver started out to develop a superstrong adhesive; instead he came up with one that didn't stick very well at all. He sent the apparently useless substance on to other 3M researchers to see whether they could find something to do with it. Nothing happened for several years. Then Arthur Fry, another 3M scientist, had a problem—and an idea. As a choir member in a local church, Mr. Fry was having trouble marking places in his hymnal—the little scraps of paper he used kept falling out. He tried dabbing some of Mr. Silver's weak glue on one of the scraps. It stuck nicely and later peeled off without damaging the hymnal. Thus were born 3M's Post-It Notes, a product that is now one of the top-selling office supply products in the world!

Thus, 3M could easily amend its long-running "Innovation Working for You" ad line to include "and for *3M*." Still, there are limits. Some analysts question whether such a free-wheeling, no-questions-asked creative culture is appropriate given the cost-reduction pressures of today's tougher economic times. In fact, 3M's new CEO, Jim McNerney, recently launched a "take-no-prisoners" campaign against inefficiencies. He's cutting costs and slimming down the company's workforce.

He is also overhauling the 3M R&D organization and culture, one in which even 3M old-timers agree that money hasn't always been spent wisely. According to one analyst, McNerney "vows to take an organization of myriad product and research fiefdoms—which happens to be one of the most respected manufacturing concerns in the world—and hammer it into one shared corporate culture." He is carefully examining where R&D dollars are spent and setting uniform performance standards and accountability across the company.

The risk is that the changing culture and organizational restructuring might stifle 3M's hallmark creativity. "The most important thing about 3M—the single most important thing—is you get to do things your own way," says a senior 3M executive and 33-year veteran. McNerney understands the balancing act: efficiency versus hands-off R&D spending; accountability versus individual creative freedom. "My job is to add scale in a fast-moving, entrepreneurial environment," he says. "If I end up killing that entrepreneurial spirit, I will have failed."

Sources: Quotes from Rick Mullin, "Analysts Rate 3M's New Culture," *Chemical Week,* September 26, 2001, pp. 39–40; and Michael Arndt, "3M: A Lab for Growth," *Business Week,* January 21, 2002, pp. 50-51. Also see William H. Miller, "New Leader, New Era," November 2001, accessed online at www.industryweek.com; Nicholas Stein, "America's Most Admired Companies," *Fortune,* March 3, 2003, pp. 81–87; Tim Studt, "3M—Where Innovation Rules," *R & D,* April 2003, pp. 20-24; and information accessed online at www.3m.com, July 2003.

The PLC concept can describe a *product class* (gasoline-powered automobiles), a *product form* (SUVs), or a *brand* (the Ford Explorer). The PLC concept applies differently in each case. Product classes have the longest life cycles—the sales of many product classes stay in the mature stage for a long time. Product forms, in contrast, tend to have the standard PLC shape. Product forms such as "dial telephones" and "cassette tapes" passed through a regular history of introduction, rapid growth, maturity, and decline.

A specific brand's life cycle can change quickly because of changing competitive attacks and responses. For example, although laundry soaps (product class) and powdered detergents (product form) have enjoyed fairly long life cycles, the life cycles of specific brands have tended to be much shorter. Today's leading brands of powdered laundry soap are Tide and Cheer; the leading brands 75 years ago were Fels Naptha, Octagon, and Kirkman.[23]

FIGURE 8.3

Styles, Fashions, and Fads

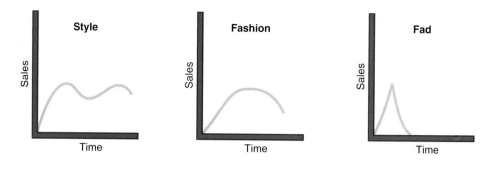

Style

A basic and distinctive mode of expression.

Fashion

A currently accepted or popular style in a given field.

Fad

A fashion that enters quickly, is adopted with great zeal, peaks early, and declines very quickly.

The PLC concept also can be applied to what are known as styles, fashions, and fads. Their special life cycles are shown in Figure 8.3. A **style** is a basic and distinctive mode of expression. For example, styles appear in homes (colonial, ranch, transitional), clothing (formal, casual), and art (realist, surrealist, abstract). Once a style is invented, it may last for generations, passing in and out of vogue. A style has a cycle showing several periods of renewed interest. A **fashion** is a currently accepted or popular style in a given field. For example, the more formal "business attire" look of corporate dress of the 1980s and early 1990s gave way to the "business casual" look of today. Fashions tend to grow slowly, remain popular for a while, and then decline slowly.

Fads are fashions that enter quickly, are adopted with great zeal, peak early, and decline very quickly. They last only a short time and tend to attract only a limited following. "Pet rocks" are a classic example of a fad. Upon hearing his friends complain about how expensive it was to care for their dogs, advertising copywriter Gary Dahl joked about his pet rock and was soon writing a spoof of a dog-training manual for it. Soon Dahl was selling some 1.5 million ordinary beach pebbles at four dollars a pop. Yet the fad, which broke in October 1975, had sunk like a stone by the next February. Dahl's advice to those who want to succeed with a fad: "Enjoy it while it lasts." Other examples of fads include Rubik's Cubes, lava lamps, CB radios, Pokemon cards, and scooters. Most fads do not survive for long because they normally do not satisfy a strong need or satisfy it well.[24]

The PLC concept can be applied by marketers as a useful framework for describing how products and markets work. But using the PLC concept for forecasting product performance or for developing marketing strategies presents some practical problems. For example, managers may have trouble identifying which stage of the PLC the product is in or pinpointing when the product moves into the next stage. They may also find it hard to determine the factors that affect the product's movement through the stages. In practice, it is difficult to forecast the sales level at each PLC stage, the length of each stage, and the shape of the PLC curve.

Using the PLC concept to develop marketing strategy also can be difficult because strategy is both a cause and a result of the product's life cycle. The product's current PLC position suggests the best marketing strategies, and the resulting marketing strategies affect product performance in later life-cycle stages. Yet, when used carefully, the PLC concept can help in developing good marketing strategies for different stages of the product life cycle.

We looked at the product development stage of the product life cycle in the first part of the chapter. We now look at strategies for each of the other life-cycle stages.

Introduction Stage

Introduction stage

The product life-cycle stage in which the new product is first distributed and made available for purchase.

The **introduction stage** starts when the new product is first launched. Introduction takes time, and sales growth is apt to be slow. Well-known products such as instant coffee, frozen orange juice, and powdered coffee creamers lingered for many years before they entered a stage of rapid growth.

In this stage, as compared to other stages, profits are negative or low because of the low sales and high distribution and promotion expenses. Much money is needed to attract distributors and build their inventories. Promotion spending is relatively high to inform consumers of the new product and get them to try it. Because the market is not generally ready for product refinements at this stage, the company and its few competitors produce basic versions of the product. These firms focus their selling on those buyers who are the most ready to buy.

A company, especially the *market pioneer*, must choose a launch strategy that is consistent with the intended product positioning. It should realize that the initial strategy is just the first step in a grander marketing plan for the product's entire life cycle. If the pioneer chooses its launch strategy to make a "killing," it will be sacrificing long-run revenue for the sake of short-run gain. As the pioneer moves through later stages of the life cycle, it will have to continuously formulate new pricing, promotion, and other marketing strategies. It has the best chance of building and retaining market leadership if it plays its cards correctly from the start.[25]

Growth Stage

If the new product satisfies the market, it will enter a **growth stage**, in which sales will start climbing quickly. The early adopters will continue to buy, and later buyers will start following their lead, especially if they hear favorable word of mouth. Attracted by the opportunities for profit, new competitors will enter the market. They will introduce new product features, and the market will expand. The increase in competitors leads to an increase in the number of distribution outlets, and sales jump just to build reseller inventories. Prices remain where they are or fall only slightly. Companies keep their promotion spending at the same or a slightly higher level. Educating the market remains a goal, but now the company must also meet the competition.

Profits increase during the growth stage, as promotion costs are spread over a large volume and as unit manufacturing costs fall. The firm uses several strategies to sustain rapid market growth as long as possible. It improves product quality and adds new product features and models. It enters new market segments and new distribution channels. It shifts some advertising from building product awareness to building product conviction and purchase, and it lowers prices at the right time to attract more buyers.

In the growth stage, the firm faces a trade-off between high market share and high current profit. By spending a lot of money on product improvement, promotion, and distribution, the company can capture a dominant position. In doing so, however, it gives up maximum current profit, which it hopes to make up in the next stage.

Maturity Stage

At some point, a product's sales growth will slow down, and the product will enter a **maturity stage**. This maturity stage normally lasts longer than the previous stages, and it poses strong challenges to marketing management. Most products are in the maturity stage of the life cycle, and therefore most of marketing management deals with the mature product.

The slowdown in sales growth results in many producers with many products to sell. In turn, this overcapacity leads to greater competition. Competitors begin marking down prices, increasing their advertising and sales promotions, and upping their R&D budgets to find better versions of the product. These steps lead to a drop in profit. Some of the weaker competitors start dropping out, and the industry eventually contains only well-established competitors.

Although many products in the mature stage appear to remain unchanged for long periods, most successful ones are actually evolving to meet changing consumer needs (see Marketing at Work 8.3). Product managers should do more than simply ride along with or defend their mature products—a good offense is the best defense. They should consider modifying the market, product, and marketing mix.

In *modifying the market*, the company tries to increase the consumption of the current product. It looks for new users and market segments, as when Johnson & Johnson targeted the adult market with its baby powder and shampoo. Or the company may want to reposition the brand to appeal to a larger or faster-growing segment, as Verizon did when it expanded into high speed Internet and wireless services. The company may also look for

Growth stage
The product life-cycle stage in which a product's sales start climbing quickly.

Maturity stage
The stage in the product life cycle in which sales growth slows or levels off.

ways to increase usage among present customers. Campbell does this by offering recipes and convincing consumers that "soup is good food." Amazon.com sends permission-based e-mails to regular customers letting them know when their favorite authors or performers publish new books or CDs. The WD-40 Company has shown a real knack for expanding the market by finding new uses for its popular substance.

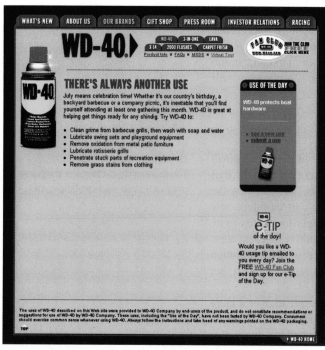

■ The WD-40 Company's knack for finding new uses has made this popular substance one of the truly essential survival items in most American homes.

In 2000, the company launched a search to uncover 2,000 unique uses for WD-40. After receiving 300,000 individual submissions, it narrowed the list to the best 2,000 and posted it on the company's Web site. Some consumers suggest simple and practical uses. One teacher uses WD-40 to clean old chalkboards in her classroom. "Amazingly, the boards started coming to life again," she reports. "Not only were they restored, but years of masking and Scotch tape residue came off as well." Others, however, report some pretty unusual applications. One man uses WD-40 to polish his glass eye; another uses it to remove a prosthetic leg. And did you hear about the nude burglary suspect who had wedged himself in a vent at a cafe in Denver? The fire department extracted him with a large dose of WD-40. Or how about the Mississippi naval officer who used WD-40 to repel an angry bear? Then there's the college student who wrote to say that a friend's nightly amorous activities in the next room were causing everyone in his dorm to lose sleep—he solved the problem by treating the squeaky bedsprings with WD-40.

The company might also try *modifying the product*—changing characteristics such as quality, features, or style to attract new users and to inspire more usage. It might improve the product's quality and performance—its durability, reliability, speed, or taste. It can improve the product's styling and attractiveness. Thus, car manufacturers restyle their cars to attract buyers who want a new look. The makers of consumer food and household products introduce new flavors, colors, ingredients, or packages to revitalize consumer buying. Heinz did this when it introduced ketchup in EZ Squirt packaging and new colors such as Blastin' Green and Awesome Orange.

Or the company might add new features that expand the product's usefulness, safety, or convenience. For example, Sony keeps adding new styles and features to its Walkman and Discman lines, and Volvo adds new safety features to its cars. Kimberly-Clark added a new twist to try to revitalize the product life cycle of an old standby, toilet tissue:

Almost without exception, every American family knows what the paper roll next to the toilet is for, knows how to use it, and purchases it faithfully. Selling an omnipresent household item requires a vital brand that stands out at the supermarket, but how do you make toilet tissue new and exciting? Kimberly-Clark, the maker of Cottonelle and Kleenex, has the answer with an unprecedented innovation: a premoistened toilet paper called Cottonelle Rollwipes, "the breakthrough product that is changing the toilet paper category." Like baby wipes on a roll, the product is designed to complement traditional toilet tissue. "In this category, your growth has to come from significant product Innovations," says a marketing director for Cottonelle. Another marketing executive agrees: "Without new products, old brands become older brands. In categories where there's basic satisfaction with the products, you still have to provide new benefits . . . to build brand share."[26]

Marketing at Work   8.3

Age-Defying Products or Just Skillful PLC Management?

Some products are born and die quickly. Others, however, seem to defy the product life cycle, enduring for decades, or even generations, with little or no apparent change in their makeup or marketing. Look deeper, however, and you'll find that such products are far from unchanging. Rather, skillful product life-cycle management keeps them fresh, relevant, and appealing to customers. Here are examples of two products that might have been only fads but instead were turned into long-term market winners with plenty of staying power.

Barbie

Talk about age-defying products. Although Mattel's Barbie has now reached 45, Mattel has kept her both timeless and trendy. Since her creation in 1959, Barbie has mirrored girls' dreams of what they'd like to be when they grow up. As such, Barbie has changed as girls' dreams have changed. Her aspirations have evolved from jobs such as stewardess, fashion model, and nurse to astronaut, rock singer, surgeon, and presidential candidate. These days, Barbie hardly notices her age—she's too busy being a WNBA basketball player, astronaut, Olympic skater, and NASCAR race car driver.

Pursuing its mission to "engage, enchant, and empower girls," Mattel introduces new Barbie dolls every year in order to keep up with the latest definitions of achievement, glamour, romance, adventure, and nurturing. Barbie also reflects America's diverse and changing population. Mattel has produced African American Barbie dolls since 1968 and has since introduced Hispanic and Asian dolls as well. In recent years, Mattel has introduced Crystal Barbie (a gorgeous glamour doll), Puerto Rican Barbie (part of its "dolls of the world" collection), Great Shape Barbie (to tie into the fitness craze), Flight Time Barbie (a pilot), Soccer Barbie (to tie in with the recent boom in girls' soccer), and Children's Doctor Barbie (the first in the "I Can Be" Career Series Barbies). Barbie herself has received several makeovers. The most recent one gave her a wider face, her first belly button, slightly less prominent breasts, and a more athletic body.

As a result of Mattel's adept product life-cycle handling, Barbie has kept her market allure as well as her youth. Available in 150 countries, Barbie now sells at a rate of two each second worldwide and racks up sales of more than $1.5 billion a year. If you placed head to foot every doll ever sold, Barbie and her friends would circle the globe 72 times.

Crayola Crayons

Over the past 100 years or so, Binney & Smith's Crayola crayons have become a household staple in more than 80 countries around the world. Few people can forget their first pack of "64s"—64 beauties neatly arranged in the familiar green and yellow flip-top box with a sharpener on the back. The aroma of a freshly opened Crayola box still drives kids into a frenzy and takes members of the older generation back to some of their fondest childhood memories.

In some ways, Crayola crayons haven't changed much since 1903, when they were sold in an eight-pack for a nickel. But a closer look reveals that Binney & Smith has made many adjustments to keep the brand out of decline. The company has added a steady stream of new colors, shapes, sizes, and packages. It has gradually increased the number of colors from the original eight in 1903 (red, yellow, blue, green, orange, black, brown, and white) to 120 in 2003. Binney & Smith has also extended the Crayola brand to new markets such as Crayola Markers, scissors, watercolor paints, gel pens, themed stamps and stickers, and activity kits. The company has licensed the Crayola brand for use on everything from

Some products seem to defy the product life cycle: Over the years, Crayola has lived a colorful life cycle, adding a steady steam of new colors, forms, and packages.

(continued)

camera outfits, backpacks, and book-ends to cartoon cups and mousepads. Finally, the company has added several programs and services to help strengthen its relationships with Crayola customers. Its *Crayola Kids* magazine and Crayola Web site offer features for children along with interactive art and craft suggestions for parents and edu-cators on helping develop reading skills and creativity.

Not all of Binney & Smith's life-cycle adjustments have been greeted favor-ably by consumers. For example, in 1990, to make room for more modern colors, it retired eight colors from the time-honored box of 64—raw umber, lemon yellow, maize, blue grey, orange yellow, orange red, green blue, and vio-let blue—into the Crayola Hall of Fame. The move unleashed a groundswell of protest from loyal Crayola users, who formed such organizations as the RUMPS—the Raw Umber and Maize Preservation Society—and the National Committee to Save Lemon Yellow. Company executives were flabber-gasted—"We were aware of the loyalty and nostalgia surrounding Crayola crayons," a spokesperson says, "but we didn't know we [would] hit such a nerve." The company reissued the old standards in a special collector's tin—it sold all of the 2.5 million tins made.

Thus, Crayola continues its long and colorful life cycle. Through smart product life-cycle management, Binney & Smith, now a subsidiary of Hallmark, has domi-nated the crayon market for almost a century. The company now makes nearly 3 billion crayons a year, enough to circle the globe six times. By the age of 10, the average American child has worn down 730 crayons. Sixty-five percent of all American children between the ages of two and seven pick up a crayon at least once a day and color for an average of 28 minutes. Nearly 80 percent of the time, they pick up a Crayola crayon.

Sources: See "Hue and Cry over Crayola May Revive Old Colors," *Wall Street Journal*, June 14, 1991, p. B1; Margaret O. Kirk, "Coloring Our Children's World Since '03," *Chicago Tribune*, October 29, 1986, sec. 5, p. 1; "Crayola Trivia," accessed online at www.crayola.com, July 2003; Alice Cuneo and Laura Petrecca, "Barbie Has to Work Harder to Help Out Sagging Mattel," *Advertising Age*, March 6, 2000, p. 4; Christopher Palmeri, "Mattel: Up the Hill Minus Jill," *Business Week*, April 9, 2001, pp. 53–54; Alexandria Peers, "Art Journal: Goodbye Dolly!" *Wall Street Journal*, January 4, 2002, p. W1 Kate MacArthur, "Plastic Surgery: Barbie Gets a Real Makeover," *Advertising Age*, November 4, 2002, pp. 4, 53; and www.barbie.com, August 2003.

Finally, the company can try *modifying the marketing mix*—improving sales by changing one or more marketing mix elements. It can cut prices to attract new users and competitors' customers. It can launch a better advertising campaign or use aggressive sales promotions—trade deals, cents-off, premiums, and contests. Hormel Foods Corporation, maker of SPAM, recently launched a new advertising campaign and other promotions to reposition and revitalize its mature product, which has been around since the late 1930s.[27]

■ Revitalizing a mature brand: Hormel, maker of Spam, recently launched a new "crazy tasty" advertising and promotion campaign, complete with the SPAM-MOBILE, to reposition and revitalize its mature product, which has been around since the late 1930s.

Joe is the everyman that impresses crowds at barbecues, beach get-togethers, and breakfasts by offering basic-assembly SPAM recipes. . . . The pitch is that the taste of SPAM makes eggs, pizza—almost any-thing—better. And it's done with all the over-the-top fervor of "Monty Python's Flying Circus" famed SPAM routine. In the spots, people literally eat up the stuff, and when there's none left, Joe is able to clap his hands, yell out "More SPAM!" and call up a SPAMMOBILE that crashes the party out of the clear blue to deliver up more of the "crazy tasty" stuff. The crowd, of course, barely notices the unusual delivery, as they only have eyes for the little tins of love. The campaign tries to capture the American boldness of the brand.

In addition to pricing and promotion, the com-pany can also move into larger market channels, using mass merchandisers, if these channels are growing. Finally, the company can offer new or improved services to buyers.

Linking the	Concepts

Pause for a moment and think about some products that, like Crayola Crayons, have been around for a long time.

- Ask a grandparent or someone else who shaved back then to compare a 1940s or 1950s Gillette razor to the most current model. Is Gillette's latest razor really a new product or just a "retread" of the previous version? What do you conclude about product life cycles?
- The Monopoly board game has been around for decades. How has Parker Bothers protected Monopoly from old age and decline (check out www.monopoly.com)?

Decline Stage

The sales of most product forms and brands eventually dip. The decline may be slow, as in the case of oatmeal cereal, or rapid, as in the case of phonograph records. Sales may plunge to zero, or they may drop to a low level at which they continue for many years. This is the **decline stage**.

Sales decline for many reasons, including technological advances, shifts in consumer tastes, and increased competition. As sales and profits decline, some firms withdraw from the market. Those remaining may prune their product offerings. They may drop smaller market segments and marginal trade channels, or they may cut the promotion budget and reduce their prices further.

Carrying a weak product can be very costly to a firm, and not just in profit terms. There are many hidden costs. A weak product may take up too much of management's time. It often requires frequent price and inventory adjustments. It requires advertising and sales force attention that might be better used to make "healthy" products more profitable. A product's failing reputation can cause customer concerns about the company and its other products. The biggest cost may well lie in the future. Keeping weak products delays the search for replacements, creates a lopsided product mix, hurts current profits, and weakens the company's foothold on the future.

For these reasons, companies need to pay more attention to their aging products. The firm's first task is to identify those products in the decline stage by regularly reviewing sales, market shares, costs, and profit trends. Then, management must decide whether to maintain, harvest, or drop each of these declining products.

Management may decide to *maintain* its brand without change in the hope that competitors will leave the industry. For example, Procter & Gamble made good profits by remaining in the declining liquid soap business as others withdrew. Or management may decide to reposition or reformulate the brand in hopes of moving it back into the growth stage of the product life cycle. Frito-Lay did this with the classic Cracker Jack brand:

> When Cracker Jack passed the 100-year-old mark, it seemed that the timeless brand was running out of time. By the time Frito-Lay acquired the classic snack-food brand from Borden Foods in 1997, sales and profits had been declining for five straight years. Frito-Lay set out to reconnect the box of candy-coated popcorn, peanuts, and a prize with a new generation of kids. "We made the popcorn bigger and fluffier with more peanuts and bigger prizes, and we put it in bags, as well as boxes," says Chris Neugent, VP-marketing for wholesome snacks for Frito-Lay. New promotional programs shared a connection with baseball and fun

Decline stage
The product life-cycle stage in which a product's sales decline.

■ Back into the growth stage: When this timeless brand was running out of time, Frito-Lay reconnected it with a new generation of kids. Sales more than doubled during the two years following the acquisition.

for kids, featuring baseball star Mark McGwire, Rawlings Sporting Goods trading cards, F.A.O. Schwartz, and Pokemon and Scooby Doo characters. The revitalized marketing pulled Cracker Jack out of decline. Sales more than doubled during the two years following the acquisition, and the brand has posted double-digit increases each year since.[28]

Management may decide to *harvest* the product, which means reducing various costs (plant and equipment, maintenance, R&D, advertising, sales force) and hoping that sales hold up. If successful, harvesting will increase the company's profits in the short run. Or management may decide to *drop* the product from the line. It can sell it to another firm or simply liquidate it at salvage value. In recent years, Procter & Gamble has sold off a number of lesser or declining brands such as Oxydol detergent and Jif peanut butter. If the company plans to find a buyer, it will not want to run down the product through harvesting.

Table 8.2 summarizes the key characteristics of each stage of the product life cycle. The table also lists the marketing objectives and strategies for each stage.[29]

TABLE 8.2   Summary of Product Life-Cycle Characteristics, Objectives, and Strategies

	Introduction	Growth	Maturity	Decline
Characteristics				
Sales	Low sales	Rapidly rising sales	Peak sales	Declining sales
Costs	High cost per customer	Average cost per customer	Low cost per customer	Low cost per customer
Profits	Negative	Rising profits	High profits	Declining profits
Customers	Innovators	Early adopters	Middle majority	Laggards
Competitors	Few	Growing number	Stable number beginning to decline	Declining number
Marketing objectives	Create product and trial	Maximize market share	Maximize profit while defending market share	Reduce expenditure and milk the brand
Strategies				
Product	Offer a basic product	Offer product extensions, service, warranty	Diversify brand and models	Phase out weak items
Price	Use cost-plus formula	Price to penetrate market	Price to match or best competitors	Cut price
Distribution	Build selective distribution	Build intensive distribution	Build more intensive distribution	Go selective: Phase out unprofitable outlets
Advertising	Build product awareness among early adopters and dealers	Build awareness and interest in the mass market	Stress brand differences and benefits	Reduce to level needed to retain hard-core loyals
Sales promotion	Use heavy sales promotion to entice trial	Reduce to take advantage of heavy consumer demand	Increase to encourage brand switching	Reduce to minimal level

Source: Philip Kotler, *Marketing Management: Analysis, Planning, Implementation, and Control,* 11th ed. (Upper Saddle River, NJ: Prentice Hall, 2003), Chapter 10.

REST STOP:
Reviewing the Concepts

Well, there's one more travel sticker on your marketing bumper. Before we move on to the next marketing mix destination, let's review the important new product and product life-cycle concepts. A company's current products face limited life spans and must be replaced by newer products. But new products can fail—the risks of innovation are as great as the rewards. The key to successful innovation lies in a total-company effort, strong planning, and a systematic *new-product development* process.

1. Explain how companies find and develop new-product ideas.

Companies find and develop new-product ideas from a variety of sources. Many new-product ideas stem from *internal sources.* Companies conduct formal research and development, pick the brains of their employees, and brainstorm at executive meetings. By conducting surveys and focus groups and analyzing *customer* questions and complaints, companies can generate new-product ideas that will meet specific consumer needs. Companies track *competitors'* offerings and inspect new products, dismantling them, analyzing their performance, and deciding whether to introduce a similar or improved product. *Distributors and suppliers* are close to the market and can pass along information about consumer problems and new-product possibilities.

2. List and define the steps in the new-product development process.

The new-product development process consists of eight sequential stages. The process starts with *idea generation.* Next comes *idea screening,* which reduces the number of ideas based on the company's own criteria. Ideas that pass the screening stage continue through *product concept development,* in which a detailed version of the new-product idea is stated in meaningful consumer terms. In the next stage, *concept testing,* new-product concepts are tested with a group of target consumers to determine whether the concepts have strong consumer appeal. Strong concepts proceed to *marketing strategy development,* in which an initial marketing strategy for the new product is developed from the product concept. In the *business analysis* stage, a review of the sales, costs, and profit projections for a new product is conducted to determine whether the new product is likely to satisfy the company's objectives. With positive results here, the ideas become more concrete through *product development* and *test marketing* and finally are launched during *commercialization.*

3. Describe the stages of the product life cycle.

Each product has a *life cycle* marked by a changing set of problems and opportunities. The sales of the typical product follow an S-shaped curve made up of five stages. The cycle begins with the *product development stage* when the company finds and develops a new-product idea. The *introduction stage* is marked by slow growth and low profits as the product is distributed to the market. If successful, the product enters a *growth stage,* which offers rapid sales growth and increasing profits. Next comes a *maturity stage,* when sales growth slows down and profits stabilize. Finally, the product enters a *decline stage,* in which sales and profits dwindle. The company's task during this stage is to recognize the decline and to decide whether it should maintain, harvest, or drop the product.

4. Describe how marketing strategies change during the product's life cycle.

In the *introduction stage*, the company must choose a launch strategy consistent with its intended product positioning. Much money is needed to attract distributors and build their inventories and to inform consumers of the new product and achieve trial. In the *growth stage*, companies continue to educate potential consumers and distributors. In addition, the company works to stay ahead of the competition and sustain rapid market growth by improving product quality, adding new product features and models, entering new market segments and distribution channels, shifting advertising from building product awareness to building product conviction and purchase, and lowering prices at the right time to attract new buyers. In the *maturity stage,* companies continue to invest in maturing products and consider modifying the market, the product, and the marketing mix. When *modifying the market,* the company attempts to increase the consumption of the current product. When *modifying the product,* the company changes some of the product's characteristics—such as quality, features, or style—to attract new users or inspire more usage. When *modifying the marketing mix,* the company works to improve sales by changing one or more of the marketing mix elements. Once the company recognizes that a product has entered the *decline stage,* management must decide whether to *maintain* the brand without change, hoping that competitors will drop out of the market; *harvest* the product, reducing costs and trying to maintain sales; or *drop* the product, selling it to another firm or liquidating it at salvage value.

Navigating the Key Terms

Business analysis
Commercialization
Concept testing
Decline stage
Fad
Fashion
Growth stage
Idea generation

Idea screening
Introduction stage
Marketing strategy
   development
Maturity stage
New-product development
Product concept
Product development

Product life cycle (PLC)
Sequential product
   development
Simultaneous (or team-based)
   product development
Style
Test marketing

Travel Log

Discussing the Issues

1. Describe some general reasons that so many new products fail. How can marketing managers use this information in the new-product development process?

2. Describe the major internal and external sources of new-product ideas. Which source do you think develops the best ideas? Which source delivers the most ideas? Explain your answer.

3. Discuss the difference between the following terms: product idea, product concept, and product image. How are they related to each other?

4. Compare sequential product development to simultaneous product development. What are the advantages and disadvantages of each approach?

5. Describe product classes that you feel represent each stage of the product life cycle. For each product class you came up with, do you think it will progress through all five stages of the product life cycle?

6. Explain the difference between maintaining, harvesting, and dropping a brand. Why would a company select one of these strategies over the other in a declining market?

Application Questions

1. Develop this new-product idea into three different product concepts: a sensor about the size of a quarter that measures ultraviolet rays from the sun and can sound an alarm when it is exposed to dangerous levels for a sustained time. Which product concept do you think is most viable? Explain your answer.

2. Take one of the product concepts you developed in the previous question and conduct a limited concept test by asking 10 people the questions in Table 8.1. The questions will have to be modified for your particular product concept. Summarize and report the results at the next class meeting.

3. Discuss a product that you feel has been modified to meet changing consumer needs and thus has been able to stay in the maturity stage of the PLC. What was modified: the market, the product, or the marketing mix? Explain your answer.

Under the Hood: Focus on Technology

Instead of trying to figure out exactly what consumers want, some firms let consumers design their own products. Nike has done just that by allowing consumers to completely design the look and performance of its Air Pegasus 2000 running shoe over the Internet. Consumers can select the outer-sole to best suit the type of surface they run on, the density of the midsole for their foot shape, the shoe width, the color for eight different areas of the shoe, and even a personalized name on the heel of the shoe.

Go to www.nikerunning.com and click on "create your own shoe" under the "gear" link (note that this feature requires the Macromedia Flash plug-in be installed on your computer—you will be prompted to download this if it is not currently installed). Go through the steps of creating an Air Pegasus 2000 running shoe and then respond to the following questions.

1. What do you think of the ability to create your own running shoe online? Do you think this capability provides a competitive advantage for Nike over rival running shoe manufacturers?

2. Why doesn't Nike just select several variations and sell those rather than allow consumers to customize the shoe? Describe the target market most likely to make its own shoes with this process.

3. What disadvantages might there be for Nike in allowing consumers to create their own running shoes? How can those disadvantages be minimized?

In 2004, Honda will become the first auto manufacturer to sell natural-gas-powered cars to the general public. Typically these vehicles have been sold in small fleets to entities, often governmental organizations, which use them for short trips and have the capacity to own their own natural gas refilling locations. That will change as Honda introduces a device that will allow owners to refill their vehicles in their own garages. Honda envisions eventually selling tens of thousands of these natural-gas-powered vehicles, mainly as a family's second vehicle or as a commuter car. Natural gas vehicles cost about 80 percent of what it costs to run gasoline vehicles.

1. Describe how you would construct a test market for this new product.

2. What major activities will Honda need to accomplish to make the commercialization phase of this new product launch successful?

3. How should Honda position the new natural gas powered vehicles relative to its traditional line of cars?

Focus on Ethics

Beating competitors to the marketplace with a product can result in substantial first-mover advantages for the initial market entrant. At times, this places tremendous pressure on a company's employees to speed through the product development process as fast as possible. In such cases, skipping or reducing the level of effort placed on stages in the development process (e.g., comprehensive safety testing) may become attractive alternatives for meeting tight timelines. Even the false reporting of outcomes associated with product testing may be encountered when employees are pressured to get a product to market as soon as possible.

1. What can a company do to ensure that all the necessary product development steps are adequately followed under the pressure of being first to market? What controls might be put in place?

2. Discuss the potential negative consequences of rushing a new product to market.

Videos

The eGo Bikes video case that accompanies this chapter is located in Appendix 1 at the back of the book.

Student Materials

Need a tune-up? A study guide and OneKey access code are available to aid in your review of chapter material. Your instructor may choose to have these items shrink-wrapped with your text or you may purchase them separately at www.prenhall.com/marketing.

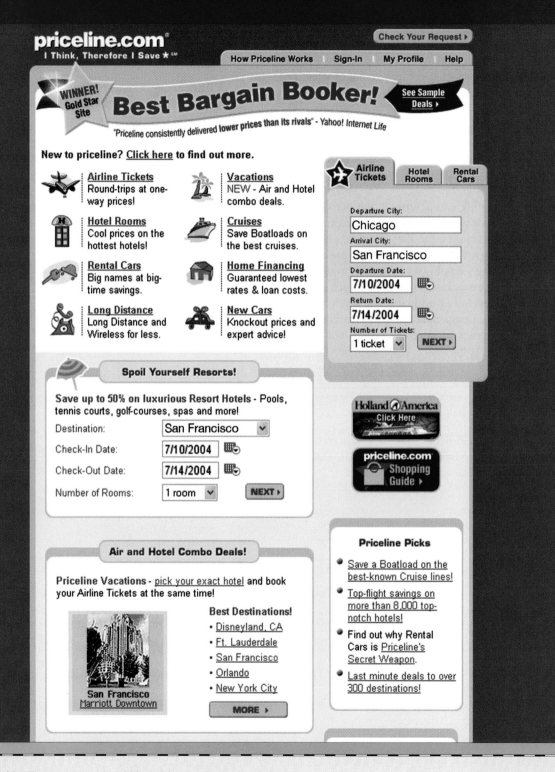

■ *After studying this chapter, you should be able to*

1. Identify and explain the external and internal factors affecting a firm's pricing decisions *2. Contrast* the three general approaches to setting prices *3. Describe* the major strategies for pricing imitative and new products *4. Explain* how companies find a set of prices that maximizes the profits from the total product mix *5. Discuss* how companies adjust their prices to take into account different types of customers and situations *6. Discuss* the key issues related to initiating and responding to price changes

Pricing Considerations and Strategies

9

We continue your marketing journey with a look at a second major marketing mix tool—pricing. According to one pricing expert, "If effective product development, promotion, and distribution sow the seeds of business success, effective pricing is the harvest."[1] Good pricing, he continues, "involves finding a balance between the customer's desire to obtain good value and the firm's need to cover costs and earn profits." Yet, despite its importance, many firms do not handle pricing well. In this chapter, we'll examine factors that affect pricing decisions, general pricing approaches, and specific pricing strategies.

To start, let's look at one of the most dramatic new developments in the fast-changing world of pricing—the impact of the Internet. Five years ago, Priceline.com burst onto the Web with a simple but compelling new pricing concept—let consumers name their own prices! This radical new idea caught on, making Priceline one of today's few profitable dot-coms. Sound too good to be true? It could only happen on the Internet.

T he headlines scream: *Name your own price deals! Top-flight savings on more than 8,000 top-notch hotels! Last-minute deals to more than 300 destinations! Save a boatload on best-known cruise lines! Low rates right now on home financing or refinancing!* Just the usual come-ons from fly-by-night operators? Too good to be true? Not at Priceline.com, at least not according to *Yahoo! Internet Life Magazine,* which recently proclaimed Priceline as the "Best Bargain Booker" on the Web. Priceline's byline: "I Think. Therefore I Save."

In 1998, founder Jay Walker launched Priceline as a radical new Internet service. It was based on an ingeniously simple concept—let consumers name their own prices, then dangle their offers in front of sellers and see who bites. Such transactions, he reasoned, benefited both buyers and sellers—buyers got lower prices; sellers turned excess inventory into profits. Although simple in concept, however, such "buyer-driven commerce" represented a dramatic departure from long-held pricing practices in which sellers—not buyers—set prices. Still, the idea caught on. Priceline has now grown to become the leading name-your-own-price Internet service.

Priceline deals primarily in travel-related products—plane tickets, hotel rooms, rental cars, cruises, and vacation packages. Here's how it works—say, for a hotel room. First, you select your destination and desired dates. If it's a big city, you can scan Priceline's maps to narrow down the area in which you'd like to stay. You can also select the types of hotels you're willing

to stay in—from one-star ("economy hotels that provide comfort with no frills") to five-star ("the best that money can buy"). Give Priceline the usual billing information and a credit card number and decide how much you'd like to bid. Click on "Buy My Hotel Room," then sit back and wait for Priceline to broker the deal. Within 15 minutes, Priceline e-mails you with the news. If no suitable hotel is willing to accept your price, you can bid again later. If Priceline finds a taker, it immediately charges your credit card no refunds, changes, or cancellations allowed and lets you know where you'll be staying.

The concept of setting your own prices over the Internet has real appeal to consumers. It starts with a good value proposition—getting really low prices. Beyond that, "name-your-price is a great hook," say a Priceline marketing executive. "If you get it, it's like 'I won!'" As a result, Priceline is attracting more and more customers. Its customer base has grown to almost 17 million users, and as many as 9 million people visit the Priceline site monthly. Through its recent acquisition of Lowestfare.com and by forging strategic partnerships with companies such as eBay and AOL, over the past year Priceline has extended its online audience by 810 percent, now reaching more than 85 million unique Web users. Since it opened for business in 1998, Priceline has sold more than 15 million airline tickets, 7 million hotel room nights, and 6.5 million rental car days.

Despite accepting fire-sale prices, sellers also benefit from Priceline's services. It's especially attractive to those who sell products that have "time sensitivity." "If airlines or hotels don't sell seats on particular flights or rooms for certain nights, those assets become worthless," comments an analyst. "Such businesses are a natural fit for Priceline." Moreover, notes the analyst, "by requiring customers to commit to payment up front with their credit card, retailers face little risk in dumping excess inventory. It's particularly attractive in markets that have huge fixed costs from creating capacity and relatively small marginal costs, like air travel, cruise ships, and automobiles."

Priceline makes its money by buying up unsold rooms, seats, or vacation packages at heavily discounted rates, marking them up, and selling them to consumers for as much as a 12 percent return. So, on a $215 plane ticket, Priceline makes about $35, compared to the $10 gross profit made by a traditional travel agent.

Along with the successes and recent profitability, however, Priceline has encountered some formidable obstacles. For example, not all products lend themselves to Priceline's quirky business model, and the company has met with uneven success in attempts to grow beyond travel services. Although it currently takes bids in other categories, such as home financing products (home mortgages, refinancing, and home equity loans), selling products and services that aren't time sensitive has proven difficult. Priceline has tried its hand unsuccessfully at selling a variety of things, including new cars and long distance services. Last year's efforts to expand into gasoline also blew up. Priceline had no trouble lining up customers interested in buying gas over the Internet. Unfortunately, however, gas and oil companies had no incentive to dump excess inventories because gas is not a perishable good. As a result, after only eight months but millions of dollars in losses, Priceline closed its virtual gas pumps.

Moreover, not all customers are thrilled with their Priceline experiences. Forcing customers to commit to purchases before they know the details such as which hotel or airline, flight times, and hotel locations can leave some customers feeling cheated. One frustrated user recently summed up his Priceline experience this way: "You don't get what you think you're gonna get."

But for every disappointed customer, Priceline has hundreds or thousands of happy ones. Some 64 percent of those who now visit Priceline to name their own prices are repeat customers. You don't have to go far to get positive testimonials such as these:

Using Priceline.com has worked out great! I remember the first time I used it. I'm not very technically savvy, but after navigating around the site, I set what I thought was a low-ball price. It turns out that my offer was accepted and I saved more than 50 percent off the normal room rate. The hotel was great. In fact, I usually stay there when traveling, so I also knew I was getting it for a great price.

I discovered Priceline.com and decided to try it out to visit my college roommate. She's in Albuquerque, New Mexico, and I'm in Hanover, Germany. The best price from the airlines was too high. After reading about priceline.com, I decided I had nothing to lose by trying it to get a better deal. I offered a low price but was sure I wouldn't stand the slightest chance of an acceptance. To my amazement, within 20 minutes of logging in, I received a happy "congratulations" e-mail from Priceline. The visit was wonderful, my friend was amazed, and I've been telling everyone (lots of seasoned travelers who didn't believe my story at first) from Germany to the United States about this spectacular new way to travel.

More than just changing how people pay for travel services, Priceline is perhaps the best example of how the Internet is changing today's pricing practices. "Only through the Web could you match millions of bids with millions of products, all without a fixed price," says one analyst. "In the offline world, this would be a strange market indeed," says another. Try to imagine a real-world situation in which "buyers attach money to a board, along with a note stating what they want to buy for the sum. Later, sellers come along and have a look. If they like an offer, they take the money and deliver the goods." It couldn't happen anywhere but on the Web.[2]

Companies today face a fierce and fast-changing pricing environment. The recent economic downturn has put many companies in a "pricing vise." One analyst sums it up this way: "They have virtually no pricing power. It's impossible to raise prices, and often, the pressure to slash them continues unabated." It seems that almost every company is slashing prices, and that is hurting their profits.[3]

Yet, cutting prices is often not the best answer. Reducing prices unnecessarily can lead to lost profits and damaging price wars. It can signal to customers that price is more important than brand. Instead, companies should "sell value, not price."[4] They should persuade customers that paying a higher price for the company's brand is justified by the greater value it delivers. The challenge is to find the price that will let the company make a fair profit by harvesting the customer value it creates.

◼▮ What Is a Price?

In the narrowest sense, **price** is the amount of money charged for a product or service. More broadly, price is the sum of all the values that consumers exchange for the benefits of having or using the product or service. Historically, price has been the major factor affecting buyer choice. However, in recent decades, nonprice factors have become more important in buyer-choice behavior.

Throughout most of history, prices were set by negotiation between buyers and sellers. *Fixed price* policies—setting one price for all buyers—is a relatively modern idea that arose with the development of large-scale retailing at the end of the nineteenth century. Now, some one hundred years later, many companies are reversing the fixed pricing trend. They are taking us back to an era of **dynamic pricing** charging different prices depending on individual customers and situations (see Marketing at Work 9.1). The Internet, corporate networks, and wireless communications are connecting sellers and buyers as never before. Web sites such as Compare.Net and PriceScan.com allow buyers to compare products and prices quickly and easily. Online auction sites such as eBay.com and Amazon.com Auctions make it easy for buyers and sellers to negotiate prices on thousands of items—from refurbished computers to antique tin trains. Sites like Priceline let customers set their own prices. At the same time, new technologies allow sellers to collect

Price

The amount of money charged for a product or service, or the sum of the values that consumers exchange for the benefits of having or using the product or service.

Dynamic pricing

Charging different prices depending on individual customers and situations.

Marketing at Work | 9.1

Back to the Future: Dynamic Pricing on the Web

The Internet is more than simply a new "marketspace"—it's actually changing the rules of commerce. Take pricing, for example. From the mostly fixed pricing practices of the past century, the Web seems now to be taking us back—into a new age of fluid pricing. "Potentially, [the Internet] could push aside sticker prices and usher in an era of dynamic pricing," says *Business Week* writer Robert Hof, "in which a wide range of goods would be priced according to what the market will bear—instantly, constantly." Here's how the Internet is changing the rules of pricing for both sellers and buyers.

Sellers Can . . .

charge lower prices, reap higher margins. Web buying and selling can result in much lower costs, allowing online sellers to charge lower prices and still make higher margins. "Thanks to their Internet connections, buyers and sellers around the world can connect at almost no cost—making instant bargaining [economically feasible]," observes Hof. Reduced inventory and distribution costs add to the savings. For example, by selling made-to-order computers online, Dell Computer greatly reduces inventory costs and eliminates retail markups. It shares the savings with buyers in the form of the "lowest price per performance."

monitor customer behavior and tailor offers to individuals. With the help of new technologies, Web merchants can now target special prices to specific customers. For example, Internet sellers such as Amazon.com can mine their databases to gauge a specific shopper's desires, measure his or her means, instantaneously tailor products

to fit that shopper's behavior, and price products accordingly. However, companies must be careful in how they apply dynamic pricing. When it recently came to light that Amazon.com had been charging different prices to different customers for the same DVDs, many customers were angry. Amazon.com claims that the pricing variations were a "pure and simple price test" and stopped the practice as soon as complaints began coming in, just five days after the "test" began. Despite these difficulties, Amazon still employs dynamic pricing by offering individualized suggestions to customers each time they log in. By doing so, it gives customers better value while also depleting unwanted inventory.

change prices on the fly according to changes in demand or costs. Just ask online catalog retailers such as L.L. Bean, Spiegel, or Fingerhut. With printed catalogs, a price is a price, at least until the next catalog is printed. Online sellers, however, can change prices for specific items on a day-by-day or even hour-by-hour basis, adjusting quickly to changing costs and merchandise movement. Many B2B marketers monitor inventories, costs, and demand at any given moment and adjust prices instantly. For example, IBM automatically adjusts prices on its servers based on customer demand and product life-cycle factors. As a result, customers will find that prices change dynamically when they visit the IBM Web site on any given day. Dell also uses dynamic online pricing. "If the price of memory or processors decreases, we pass those savings along to the customer almost in real time," says a Dell spokesperson.

Both Sellers and Buyers Can . . .

negotiate prices in online auctions and exchanges. Suddenly the centuries-old art of haggling is back in vogue. Want to sell that antique pickle jar that's been collecting dust for generations? Post it on eBay, the world's biggest online flea market. Want to purchase vintage baseball cards at a bargain price? Go to Boekhout's Collectibles Mall at www.azww.com/mall/. Want to set your own price for a hotel room or rental car? Visit Priceline.com or another reverse-auction site. Want to dump that excess inventory? Try adding an auction feature to your own Web site. Sharper Image claims it's getting 40 percent of retail for excess goods sold via its online auction site, compared with only 20 percent from liquidators.

Of the dozens of Internet auction sites, eBay is the largest. eBay began when its owner used the Web to find a market for his girlfriend's vintage Pez dispenser collection. Now, on any given day, it now lists more than 12 million items across 18,000 categories, generating almost $15 billion in trades annually. Buyers like auctions because, quite simply, they like the bargains they find. Sellers like auctions because, over the Internet, the cost per transaction drops dramatically. Thus, it becomes practical—even profitable—to auction an item for mere dollars rather than thousands of dollars. For example, the seller can program its computers to accept the 3,000 best bids higher than $2.10 for 3,000 pieces of costume jewelry. Business marketers, whose transactions account for 68 percent of online auction sales, also use auctions to offer time-sensitive

detailed data about customers' buying habits, preferences—even spending limits—so they can tailor their products and prices.[5]

In the current environment, pricing is the number one problem facing many marketing executives. Yet, many companies do not handle pricing well. One frequent problem is that

deals and gauge interest on possible price points for new products.

Buyers Can . . .

get instant price comparisons from thousands of vendors.   The Internet gives consumers access to reams of data about products and prices. Online comparison guides such as CompareNet and PriceSCAN give product and price comparisons at the click of a mouse. Other sites offer intelligent shopping agents—such as mySimon that seek out products, prices, and reviews. mySimon (www.mySimon.com), for instance, takes a buyer's criteria for a PC, camcorder, or collectible Barbie, then roots through top sellers' sites to find the best match at the best price.

find and negotiate lower prices. With market information and access come buyer power. In addition to simply finding the vendor with the best price, customers armed with price information can often negotiate lower prices. Here are examples of both consumers and industrial buyers exercising this newfound power:

In search of the best possible deal on a Palm organizer, Stephen Manes first checked PriceSCAN.com, where he learned that buysoware.com had the high-tech gadget for only $358. Buysoware, however, was "out of stock," as was the second-lowest-priced vendor, mcglen.com. Undaunted, Stephen skipped to the other end of the list where he found that PC Zone was offering the device for $449, and it was in stock. "Time to haggle," said Stephen. "I picked up the phone. In seconds, an eager

salesperson quoted me the official price. 'I saw it at buy.com for $358,' I said, omitting mention of the word[s 'out of stock']. 'I don't know if I can match buy.com,' came the response. 'But we can do it for $375.'" Stephen snapped up the offer, saving himself a bundle off the store price.

Business buyers have also learned the price advantages of shopping the Web. For example, hoping to save some money, United Technologies Corporation tried something new last year. Instead of the usual haggling with dozens of individual vendors to secure printed circuit boards for various subsidiaries worldwide, UTC put the contract out on FreeMarkets, an online marketplace for industrial goods. To the company's delight, bids poured in from 39 suppliers, saving UTC a cool $10 million off its initial $24 million estimate. Says a UTC executive, "The technology drives the lowest price in a hurry."

Will dynamic pricing sweep the marketing world? "Not entirely," says Hof. "It takes a lot of work to haggle—which is why fixed prices happened in the first place." However, he continues, "Pandora's E-box is now open, and pricing will never be the same. For many . . . products, millions of buyers figure a little haggling is a small price to pay for a sweet deal."

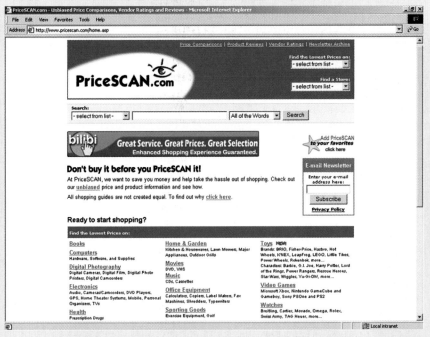

The Internet is ushering in a new era of fluid pricing. Online comparison guides—such as PriceSCAN—give product and price comparisons at the click of a mouse. In addition to simply finding the vendor with the best price, customers armed with price information can often negotiate lower prices.

Sources: Quotes, extracts, and other information from Robert D. Hof, "Going, Going, Gone," *Business Week,* April 12, 1999, pp. 30–32; Hof, "The Buyer Always Wins," *Business Week,* March 22, 1999, pp. EB26–EB28; Mui Kung, Kent B. Monroe, and Jennifer L. Cox, "Pricing on the Internet," *The Journal of Product and Brand Management,* 2002, pp. 274–287; Stephen Manes, "Off-Web Dickering," *Forbes,* April 5, 1999, p. 134; Walter Baker, Mike Marn, and Craig Zawada, "Price Smarter on the Net," *Harvard Business Review,* February 2001, pp. 122–127; Charles Fishman, "Which Price Is Right?" *Fast Company,* March 2003, pp. 92–102; Faith Keenan, "The Price Is Really Right," *Business Week,* March 31, 2003, pp. 60–67; and information accessed at www.ebay.com, July 2003.

companies are too quick to reduce prices in order to get a sale rather than convincing buyers that their products are worth a higher price. Other common mistakes include pricing that is too cost oriented rather than customer-value oriented and pricing that does not take the rest of the marketing mix into account.

FIGURE 9.1

Factors Affecting Pricing Decisions

In this chapter, we focus on the process of setting prices. We look first at the factors marketers must consider when setting prices and at general pricing approaches. Then, we examine pricing strategies for new-product pricing, product mix pricing, price adjustments for buyer and situational factors, and price changes.

Factors to Consider When Setting Prices

A company's pricing decisions are affected by both internal company factors and external environmental factors (see Figure 9.1).[6]

Internal Factors Affecting Pricing Decisions

Internal factors affecting pricing include the company's marketing objectives, marketing mix strategy, costs, and organizational considerations.

Marketing Objectives Before setting price, the company must decide on its strategy for the product. If the company has selected its target market and positioning carefully, then its marketing mix strategy, including price, will be fairly straightforward. For example, when Honda and Toyota decided to develop their Acura and Lexus brands to compete with European luxury-performance cars in the higher-income segment, this required charging a high price. In contrast, Motel 6, EconoLodge, and Red Roof Inn have positioned themselves as motels that provide economical rooms for budget-minded travelers; this position requires charging a low price. Thus, pricing strategy is largely determined by decisions on market positioning.

At the same time, the company may seek additional general or specific objectives. General objectives include survival, current profit maximization, market share leadership, and product quality leadership. At a more specific level, a company can set prices low to prevent competition from entering the market or set prices at competitors' levels to stabilize the market. Prices can be set to keep the loyalty and support of resellers or to avoid government intervention. Prices can be reduced temporarily to create excitement for a product or to draw more customers into a retail store. One product may be priced to help the sales of other products in the company's line. Thus, pricing may play an important role in helping to accomplish the company's objectives at many levels.

Marketing Mix Strategy Price is only one of the marketing mix tools that a company uses to achieve its marketing objectives. Price decisions must be coordinated with product design, distribution, and promotion decisions to form a consistent and effective marketing program. Decisions made for other marketing mix variables may affect pricing decisions. For example, producers using many resellers who are expected to support and promote their products may have to build larger reseller margins into their prices. The

■ Product quality leadership: Four Seasons starts with very-high-quality service—"we await you with the perfect sanctuary." It then charges a price to match.

decision to position the product on high-performance quality will mean that the seller must charge a higher price to cover higher costs.

Companies often position their products on price and then tailor other marketing mix decisions to the prices they want to charge. Here, price is a crucial product-positioning factor that defines the product's market, competition, and design. Many firms support such price-positioning strategies with a technique called **target costing**, a potent strategic weapon. Target costing reverses the usual process of first designing a new product, determining its cost, and then asking, "Can we sell it for that?" Instead, it starts with an ideal selling price based on customer considerations, then targets costs that will ensure that the price is met.

P&G used target costing to price and develop its highly successful Crest SpinBrush electric toothbrush:

> P&G usually prices its goods at a premium. But with Crest SpinBrush, P&G reversed its usual thinking. It started with an attractive low market price, and then found a way to make a profit at that price. SpinBrush's inventors first came up with the idea of a low-priced electric toothbrush while walking through their local Wal-Mart, where they saw Sonicare, Interplak, and other electric toothbrushes priced at more than $50. These pricy brushes held only a fraction of the overall toothbrush market. A less expensive electric toothbrush, the designers reasoned, would have huge potential. They decided on a target price of just $5, batteries included—only $1 more than the most expensive manual brushes—and set out design a brush they could sell at that price. Every design element was carefully considered with the targeted price in mind. To meet the low price, P&G passed on the usual lavish new-product launch campaign. Instead, to give SpinBrush more point-of-sale impact, it relied on "Try Me" packaging that allowed consumers to turn the brush on in stores. Target cost pricing has made Crest SpinBrush one of P&G's most successful new products ever. It has now become the nation's best-selling toothbrush, manual or electric, with a more than 40 percent share of the electric toothbrush market. Says brand manager Darin Yates, "It's hard for P&G's business models to conceive of a business growing as quickly as SpinBrush."[7]

Other companies deemphasize price and use other marketing mix tools to create *nonprice* positions. Often, the best strategy is not to charge the lowest price, but rather to differentiate the marketing offer to make it worth a higher price. For example, Sony builds more value into its consumer electronics products and charges a higher price than many competitors. Customers recognize Sony's higher quality and are willing to pay more to get it.

Thus, marketers must consider the total marketing mix when setting prices. If the product is positioned on nonprice factors, then decisions about quality, promotion, and distribution will strongly affect price. If price is a crucial positioning factor, then price will strongly affect decisions made about the other marketing mix elements. But even when featuring price, marketers need to remember that customers rarely buy on price alone. Instead, they seek products that give them the best value in terms of benefits received for the price paid.

Costs Costs set the floor for the price that the company can charge. The company wants to charge a price that both covers all its costs for producing, distributing, and selling the product and delivers a fair rate of return for its effort and risk. A company's costs may be an important element in its pricing strategy. Many companies, such as Southwest Airlines, Wal-Mart, and Union Carbide, work to become the "low-cost producers" in their industries. Companies with lower costs can set lower prices that result in greater sales and profits.

A company's costs take two forms, fixed and variable. **Fixed costs** (also known as overhead) are costs that do not vary with production or sales level. For example, a company must pay each month's bills for rent, heat, interest, and executive salaries, whatever the company's output. **Variable costs** vary directly with the level of production. Each personal computer produced by Compaq involves a cost of computer chips, wires, plastic, packaging, and other inputs. These costs tend to be the same for each unit produced. They

Target costing
Pricing that starts with an ideal selling price, then targets costs that will ensure that the price is met.

Fixed costs
Costs that do not vary with production or sales level.

Variable costs
Costs that vary directly with the level of production.

Total costs

The sum of the fixed and variable costs for any given level of production.

are called variable because their total varies with the number of units produced. **Total costs** are the sum of the fixed and variable costs for any given level of production. Management wants to charge a price that will at least cover the total production costs at a given level of production.

The company must watch its costs carefully. If it costs the company more than it costs competitors to produce and sell its product, the company will have to charge a higher price or make less profit, putting it at a competitive disadvantage.

Organizational Considerations Management must decide who within the organization should set prices. Companies handle pricing in a variety of ways. In small companies, prices are often set by top management rather than by the marketing or sales departments. In large companies, pricing is typically handled by divisional or product-line managers. In industrial markets, salespeople may be allowed to negotiate with customers within certain price ranges. Even so, top management sets the pricing objectives and policies, and it often approves the prices proposed by lower-level management or salespeople.

In industries in which pricing is a key factor (aerospace, steel, railroads, oil companies), companies often have a pricing department to set the best prices or help others in setting them. This department reports to the marketing department or top management. Others who have an influence on pricing include sales managers, production managers, finance managers, and accountants.

External Factors Affecting Pricing Decisions

External factors that affect pricing decisions include the nature of the market and demand, competition, and other environmental elements.

The Market and Demand Whereas costs set the lower limit of prices, the market and demand set the upper limit. Both consumer and industrial buyers balance the price of a product or service against the benefits of owning it. Thus, before setting prices, the marketer must understand the relationship between price and demand for its product. In this section, we explain how the price–demand relationship varies for different types of markets and how buyer perceptions of price affect the pricing decision. We then discuss methods for measuring the price–demand relationship.

Pricing in Different Types of Markets. The seller's pricing freedom varies with different types of markets. Economists recognize four types of markets, each presenting a different pricing challenge.

Under *pure competition*, the market consists of many buyers and sellers trading in a uniform commodity such as wheat, copper, or financial securities. No single buyer or seller has much effect on the going market price. A seller cannot charge more than the going price, because buyers can obtain as much as they need at the going price. Nor would sellers charge less than the market price, because they can sell all they want at this price. If price and profits rise, new sellers can easily enter the market. In a purely competitive market, marketing research, product development, pricing, advertising, and sales promotion play little or no role. Thus, sellers in these markets do not spend much time on marketing strategy.

Under *monopolistic competition*, the market consists of many buyers and sellers who trade over a range of prices rather than a single market price. A range of prices occurs because sellers can differentiate their offers to buyers. Either the physical product can be varied in quality, features, or style, or the accompanying services can be varied. Buyers see differences in sellers' products and will pay different prices for them. Sellers try to develop differentiated offers for different customer segments and, in addition to price, freely use branding, advertising, and personal selling to set their offers apart. Thus, Kinko's differentiates its offer through strong branding and advertising, reducing the impact of price. Because there are many competitors in such markets, each firm is less affected by competitors' pricing strategies than in oligopolistic markets.

Under *oligopolistic competition*, the market consists of a few sellers who are highly sensitive to each other's pricing and marketing strategies. The product can be uniform (steel, aluminum) or nonuniform (cars, computers). There are few sellers because it is difficult for new sellers to enter the market. Each seller is alert to competitors' strategies and moves. If a steel company slashes its price by 10 percent, buyers will quickly switch to this supplier. The other steelmakers must respond by lowering their prices or increasing their services.

In a *pure monopoly*, the market consists of one seller. The seller may be a government monopoly (the U.S. Postal Service), a private regulated monopoly (a power company), or a private nonregulated monopoly (DuPont when it introduced nylon). Pricing is handled differently in each case. In a regulated monopoly, the government permits the company to set rates that will yield a "fair return," one that will let the company maintain and expand its operations as needed. Nonregulated monopolies are free to price at what the market will bear. However, they do not always charge the full price for a number of reasons: a desire not to attract competition, a desire to penetrate the market faster with a low price, or a fear of government regulation.

Consumer Perceptions of Price and Value. In the end, the consumer will decide whether a product's price is right. Pricing decisions, like other marketing mix decisions, must be buyer oriented. When consumers buy a product, they exchange something of value (the price) to get something of value (the benefits of having or using the product). Effective, buyer-oriented pricing involves understanding how much value consumers place on the benefits they receive from the product and setting a price that fits this value.

■ Monopolistic competition: Canadian pickle marketer Bick's sets its pickles apart from other brands by using both price and nonprice factors.

A company often finds it hard to measure the values customers will attach to its product. For example, calculating the cost of ingredients in a meal at a fancy restaurant is relatively easy. But assigning a value to other satisfactions such as taste, environment, relaxation, conversation, and status is very hard. And these values will vary both for different consumers and different situations. Still, consumers will use these values to evaluate a product's price. If customers perceive that the price is greater than the product's value, they will not buy the product. If consumers perceive that the price is below the product's value, they will buy it, but the seller loses profit opportunities.

Analyzing the Price–Demand Relationship. Each price the company might charge will lead to a different level of demand. The relationship between the price charged and the resulting demand level is shown in the **demand curve** in Figure 9.2. The demand curve shows the number of units the market will buy in a given time period at different prices that might be charged. In the normal case, demand and price are inversely related; that is, the higher the price, the lower the demand. Thus, the company would sell less if it raised its price from P_1 to P_2. In short, consumers with limited budgets probably will buy less of something if its price is too high.

In the case of prestige goods, the demand curve sometimes slopes upward. Consumers think that higher prices mean more quality. For example, Gibson Guitar Corporation

Demand curve

A curve that shows the number of units the market will buy in a given time period at different prices that might be charged.

FIGURE 9.2

Demand Curve

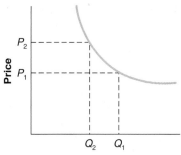

Quantity demanded per period

recently toyed with the idea of lowering its prices to compete more effectively with Japanese rivals such as Yamaha and Ibanez. To its surprise, Gibson found that its instruments didn't sell as well at lower prices. "We had an inverse [price–demand relationship]," noted Gibson's chief executive officer. "The more we charged, the more product we sold." At a time when other guitar manufacturers have chosen to build their instruments more quickly, cheaply, and in greater numbers, Gibson still promises guitars that "are made one-at-a-time, by hand. No shortcuts. No substitutions." It turns out that low prices simply aren't consistent with "Gibson's century old tradition of creating investment-quality instruments that represent the highest standards of imaginative design and masterful craftsmanship."[8] Still, if the company charges too high a price, the level of demand will be lower.

Most companies try to measure their demand curves by estimating demand at different prices. The type of market makes a difference. In a monopoly, the demand curve shows the total market demand resulting from different prices. If the company faces competition, its demand at different prices will depend on whether competitors' prices stay constant or change with the company's own prices.

Price Elasticity of Demand. Marketers also need to know **price elasticity**—how responsive demand will be to a change in price. If demand hardly changes with a small change in price, we say demand is *inelastic*. If demand changes greatly, we say the demand is *elastic*.

What determines the price elasticity of demand? Buyers are less price sensitive when the product they are buying is unique or when it is high in quality, prestige, or exclusiveness. They are also less price sensitive when substi-

■ The demand curve sometimes slopes upward: Gibson was surprised to learn that its high-quality instruments didn't sell as well at lower prices.

Price elasticity

A measure of the sensitivity of demand to changes in price.

tute products are hard to find or when they cannot easily compare the quality of substitutes. Finally, buyers are less price sensitive when the total expenditure for a product is low relative to their income or when the cost is shared by another party.[9]

If demand is elastic rather than inelastic, sellers will consider lowering their price. A lower price will produce more total revenue. This practice makes sense as long as the extra costs of producing and selling more do not exceed the extra revenue. At the same time, most firms want to avoid pricing that turns their products into commodities. In recent years, forces such as deregulation and the instant price comparisons afforded by the Internet and other technologies have increased consumer price sensitivity, turning products ranging from telephones and computers to new automobiles into commodities in consumers' eyes. Marketers need to work harder than ever to differentiate their offerings when a dozen competitors are selling virtually the same product at a comparable or lower price. More than ever, companies need to understand the price sensitivity of their customers and prospects and the trade-offs people are willing to make between price and product characteristics. In the words of marketing consultant Kevin Clancy, those who target only the price sensitive are "leaving money on the table."

Competitors' Costs, Prices, and Offers   Another external factor affecting the company's pricing decisions is competitors' costs and prices and possible competitor reactions to the company's own pricing moves. A consumer who is considering the purchase of a Sony digital camera will evaluate Sony's price and value against the prices and values of comparable products made by Nikon, Kodak, and others. In addition, the company's pricing strategy may affect the nature of the competition it faces. If Sony follows a high-price, high-margin strategy, it may attract competition. A low-price, low-margin strategy, however, may stop competitors or drive them out of the market. Sony needs to benchmark its costs and value against competitors' costs and value. It can then use these benchmarks as a starting point for its own pricing.

Other External Factors   When setting prices, the company also must consider other factors in its external environment. *Economic conditions* can have a strong impact on the firm's pricing strategies. Economic factors such as boom or recession, inflation, and interest rates affect pricing decisions because they affect both the costs of producing a product and consumer perceptions of the product's price and value. The company must also consider what impact its prices will have on other parties in its environment. How will *resellers* react to various prices? The company should set prices that give resellers a fair profit, encourage their support, and help them to sell the product effectively. The *government* is another important external influence on pricing decisions. Finally, *social concerns* may have to be taken into account. In setting prices, a company's short-term sales, market share, and profit goals may have to be tempered by broader societal considerations.

General Pricing Approaches

The price the company charges will be somewhere between one that is too low to produce a profit and one that is too high to produce any demand. Figure 9.3 summarizes the major considerations in setting price. Product costs set a floor to the price; consumer perceptions of the product's value set the ceiling. The company must consider competitors' prices and other external and internal factors to find the best price between these two extremes.

Companies set prices by selecting a general pricing approach that includes one or more of these three sets of factors. We will examine the following approaches: the *cost-based approach* (cost-plus pricing, break-even analysis, and target profit pricing), the *buyer-based approach* (value-based pricing), and the *competition-based approach* (going-rate and sealed-bid pricing).

Cost-Based Pricing

The simplest pricing method is **cost-plus pricing**—adding a standard markup to the cost of the product. For example, an appliance retailer might pay a manufacturer $20 for a toaster and mark it up to sell at $30, a 50 percent markup on cost. The retailer's gross margin is $10. If the store's operating costs amount to $8 per toaster sold, the retailer's profit margin will be $2.

Cost-plus pricing
Adding a standard markup to the cost of the product.

Product costs	Competitors' prices and other internal and external factors	Consumer perceptions of value
Price floor No profits below this price		**Price ceiling** No demand above this price

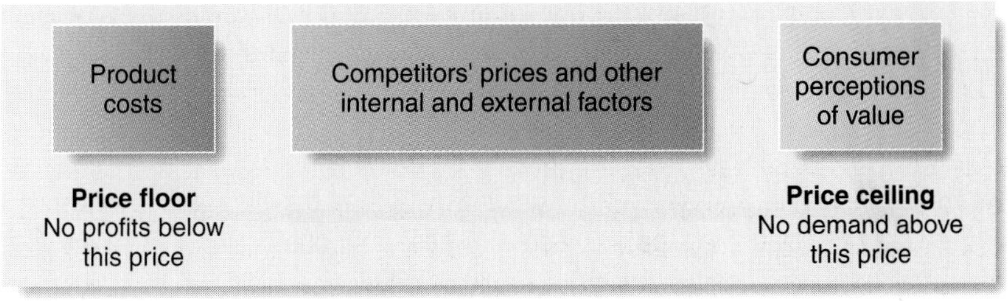

FIGURE 9.3

Major Considerations in Setting Price

The manufacturer that made the toaster probably used cost-plus pricing. If the manufacturer's standard cost of producing the toaster was $16, it might have added a 25 percent markup, setting the price to the retailers at $20. Similarly, construction companies submit job bids by estimating the total project cost and adding a standard markup for profit. Lawyers, accountants, and other professionals typically price by adding a standard markup to their costs. Some sellers tell their customers they will charge cost plus a specified markup; for example, aerospace companies price this way to the government.

Does using standard markups to set prices make sense? Generally, no. Any pricing method that ignores demand and competitor prices is not likely to lead to the best price. Still, markup pricing remains popular for many reasons. First, sellers are more certain about costs than about demand. By tying the price to cost, sellers simplify pricing—they do not have to make frequent adjustments as demand changes. Second, when all firms in the industry use this pricing method, prices tend to be similar, and price competition is thus minimized. Third, many people feel that cost-plus pricing is fairer to both buyers and sellers. Sellers earn a fair return on their investment but do not take advantage of buyers when buyers' demand becomes great.

Break-even pricing (target profit pricing)

Setting price to break even on the costs of making and marketing a product; or setting price to make a target profit.

Another cost-oriented pricing approach is **break-even pricing**, or a variation called **target profit pricing**. The firm tries to determine the price at which it will break even or make the target profit it is seeking. Target pricing uses the concept of a *break-even chart*, which shows the total cost and total revenue expected at different sales volume levels. Figure 9.4 shows a break-even chart for the toaster manufacturer discussed here. Here, fixed costs are $6 million regardless of sales volume, and variable costs are $5 per unit. Variable costs are added to fixed costs to form total costs, which rise with each unit sold. The slope of the total revenue curve reflects the price. Here, the price is $15 (for example, the company's revenue is $12 million on 800,000 units, or $15 per unit).

At the $15 price, the company must sell at least 600,000 units to *break even*—that is, at this level, total revenues will equal total costs of $9 million. If the company wants a target profit of $2 million, it must sell at least 800,000 units to obtain the $12 million of total revenue needed to cover the costs of $10 million plus the $2 million of target profits. In contrast, if the company charges a higher price, say $20 million, it will not need to sell as many units to break even or to achieve its target profit. In fact, the higher the price, the lower the company's break-even point will be.

However, as the *price* increases, *demand* decreases, and the market may not buy even the lower volume needed to break even at the higher price. Much depends on the relationship between price and demand. For example, suppose the company calculates that given its current fixed and variable costs, it must charge a price of $30 for the product in order to earn its desired target profit. But marketing research shows that few consumers will pay more than $25. In this case, the company will have to trim its costs in order to lower the break-even point so that it can charge the lower price consumers expect.

FIGURE 9.4

Break-Even Chart for Determining Target Price

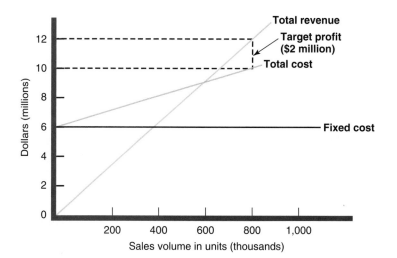

Thus, although break-even analysis and target profit pricing can help the company to determine minimum prices needed to cover expected costs and profits, they do not take the price–demand relationship into account. When using this method, the company must also consider the impact of price on sales volume needed to realize target profits and the likelihood that the needed volume will be achieved at each possible price.

Value-Based Pricing

An increasing number of companies are basing their prices on the product's perceived value. **Value-based pricing** uses buyers' perceptions of value, not the seller's cost, as the key to pricing. Value-based pricing means that the marketer cannot design a product and marketing program and then set the price. Price is considered along with the other marketing mix variables *before* the marketing program is set.

Figure 9.5 compares cost-based pricing with value-based pricing. Cost-based pricing is product driven. The company designs what it considers to be a good product, totals the costs of making the product, and sets a price that covers costs plus a target profit. Marketing must then convince buyers that the product's value at that price justifies its purchase. If the price turns out to be too high, the company must settle for lower markups or lower sales, both resulting in disappointing profits.

Value-based pricing reverses this process. The company sets its target price based on customer perceptions of the product value. The targeted value and price then drive decisions about product design and what costs can be incurred. As a result, pricing begins with analyzing consumer needs and value perceptions, and the price is set to match consumers' perceived value. It's important to remember that "good value" is not the same as "low price." For example, a Steinway piano sells at a higher price than many competing brands. But to those who buy one, it's a great value. For them, as a recent ad proclaims, "a Steinway takes you places you've never been."

A company using value-based pricing must find out what value buyers assign to different competitive offers. However, measuring perceived value can be difficult. Sometimes, companies ask consumers how much they would pay for a basic product and for each benefit added to the offer. Or a company might conduct experiments to test the perceived value of different product offers. According to an old Russian proverb, there are

■ Perceived value: A less expensive piano might play well, but would it take you places you've never been?

Value-based pricing
Setting price based on buyers' perceptions of value rather than on the seller's cost.

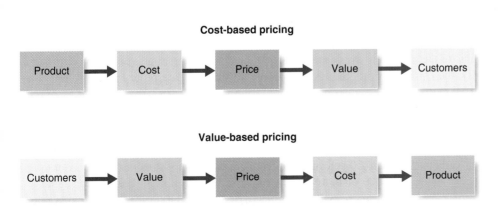

FIGURE 9.5
Cost-Based Versus Value-Based Pricing

Source: Thomas T. Nagle and Reed K. Holden, *The strategy and Tactics of Pricing*, 3rd ed. (Upper Saddle River, NJ: Prentice Hall, 2002), p. 4.

two fools in every market—one who asks too much and one who asks too little. If the seller charges more than the buyers' perceived value, the company's sales will suffer. If the seller charges less, it products sell very well, but they produce less revenue than they would if they were priced at the level of perceived value.

Value pricing

Offering just the right combination of quality and good service at a fair price.

Value Pricing   During the past decade, marketers have noted a fundamental shift in consumer attitudes toward price and quality. Many companies have changed their pricing approaches to bring them into line with changing economic conditions and consumer price perceptions. More and more, marketers have adopted **value pricing** strategies—offering just the right combination of quality and good service at a fair price. In many cases, this has involved introducing less expensive versions of established, brand name products. Campbell introduced its Great Starts Budget frozen-food line, Holiday Inn opened several Holiday Express budget hotels, Revlon's Charles of the Ritz offered the Express Bar collection of affordable cosmetics, and fast-food restaurants such as Taco Bell and McDonald's offered "value menus." In other cases, value pricing has involved redesigning existing brands to offer more quality for a given price or the same quality for less.

An important type of value pricing at the retail level is *everyday low pricing (EDLP)*. EDLP involves charging a constant, everyday low price with few or no temporary price discounts. In contrast, *high-low pricing* involves charging higher prices on an everyday basis but running frequent promotions to lower prices temporarily on selected items. In recent years, high-low pricing has given way to EDLP in retail settings ranging from Saturn car dealerships to upscale department stores such as Nordstrom.

The king of EDLP is Wal-Mart, which practically defined the concept. Except for a few sale items every month, Wal-Mart promises everyday low prices on everything it sells. In contrast, Kmart's recent attempts to match Wal-Mart's EDLP strategy failed. To offer everyday low prices, a company must first have everyday low costs. However, because Kmart's costs are much higher than Wal-Mart's, it could not make money at the lower prices and quickly abandoned the attempt.[10]

Value-Added Marketing   In many business-to-business marketing situations, the challenge is to build the company's *pricing power* its power to escape price competition and to justify higher prices and margins without losing market share. To do this, many companies adopt *value-added* strategies. Rather than cutting prices to match competitors, they attach value-added services to differentiate their offers and thus support higher margins.

When a company finds its major competitors offering a similar product at a lower price, the natural tendency is to try to match or beat that price. Although the idea of undercutting competitor's prices and watching customers flock in is tempting, there are dangers. Price-cutting can lead to price wars that erode the profit margins of all competitors in an industry. Or worse, discounting a product can cheapen it in the minds of customers. This greatly reduces the seller's power to maintain profitable prices in the long term. "It ends up being a losing battle," notes one marketing executive. "You focus away from quality, service, prestige—the things brands are all about."[11]

So, how can a company keep its pricing power when a competitor undercuts its price? Often, the best strategy is not to price below the competitor, but rather to price above and convince customers that the product is worth it. The company should ask, "What is the value of the product to the customer?" then stand up for what the product is worth. In this way, the company shifts the focus from price to value. Caterpillar is a master at value-added marketing[12]:

> Caterpillar charges premium prices for its heavy construction and mining equipment by convincing customers that its products and service justify every additional cent—or, rather, the extra tens of thousands of dollars. Caterpillar typically reaps a 20 to 30 percent price premium over competitors that can amount to an extra $200,000 or more on one of those huge yellow million-dollar dump trucks. When a large potential customer says, "I can get it for less from a competi-

tor," rather than discounting the price, the Caterpillar dealer explains that, even at the higher price, Cat offers the best value. Caterpillar equipment is designed with modular components that can be removed and repaired quickly, minimizing machine downtime. Caterpillar dealers carry an extensive parts inventory and guarantee delivery within 48 hours anywhere in the world, again minimizing downtime. Cat's products are designed to be rebuilt, providing a "second life" that competitors cannot match. As a result, Caterpillar used-equipment prices are often 20 to 30 percent higher. In all, the dealer explains, even at the higher initial price, Caterpillar equipment delivers the lowest total cost per cubic yard of earth moved, ton of coal uncovered, or mile of road graded over the life of the product—guaranteed! Most customers seem to agree with Caterpillar's value proposition—the company dominates its markets with a more than 40 percent worldwide market share.

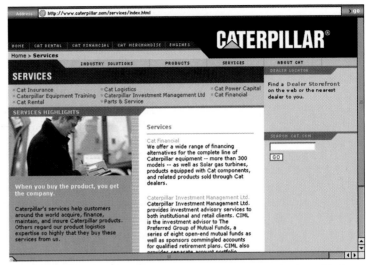

■ Value added: Caterpillar offers its dealers a wide range of value-added services—from guaranteed parts delivery to investment management advice and equipment training. Such added value supports a higher price.

Linking the Concepts

The concept of value is critical to good pricing and to successful marketing in general. Slow down for a minute and be certain that you appreciate what value really means.

■ A few years ago, Buick pitched its top-of-the-line Park Avenue model as "America's best car value." Does this fit with your idea of value?
■ Pick two competing brands from a familiar product category (watches, perfume, consumer electronics, restaurants)—one low priced and the other high priced. Which, if either, offers the greatest value?
■ Does "value" mean the same thing as "low price"? How do these concepts differ?

Competition-Based Pricing

Consumers will base their judgments of a product's value on the prices that competitors charge for similar products. One form of **competition-based pricing** is *going-rate pricing*, in which a firm bases its price largely on competitors' prices, with less attention paid to its own costs or to demand. The firm might charge the same as, more than, or less than its major competitors. In oligopolistic industries that sell a commodity such as steel, paper, or fertilizer, firms normally charge the same price. The smaller firms follow the leader: They change their prices when the market leader's prices change, rather than when their own demand or costs change. Some firms may charge a bit more or less, but they hold the amount of difference constant. Thus, minor gasoline retailers usually charge a few cents less than the major oil companies, without letting the difference increase or decrease.

Going-rate pricing is quite popular. When demand elasticity is hard to measure, firms feel that the going price represents the collective wisdom of the industry concerning the price that will yield a fair return. They also feel that holding to the going price will prevent harmful price wars.

Competition-based pricing is also used when firms *bid* for jobs. Using *sealed-bid pricing*, a firm bases its price on how it thinks competitors will price rather than on its own costs or on the demand. The firm wants to win a contract, and winning the contract

Competition-based pricing
Setting prices based on the prices that competitors charge for similar products.

requires pricing less than other firms. Yet the firm cannot set its price below a certain level. It cannot price below cost without harming its position. In contrast, the higher the company sets its price above its costs, the lower its chance of getting the contract.

No matter what general pricing approach the company uses, pricing decisions are subject to an incredibly complex array of environmental and competitive forces. A company sets not a single price, but rather a *pricing structure* that covers different items in its line. This pricing structure changes over time as products move through their life cycles. The company adjusts product prices to reflect changes in costs and demand and to account for variations in buyers and situations. As the competitive environment changes, the company considers when to initiate price changes and when to respond to them.

We now examine the major dynamic pricing strategies available to management. In turn, we look at *new-product pricing strategies* for products in the introductory stage of the product life cycle, *product mix pricing strategies* for related products in the product mix, *price-adjustment strategies* that account for customer differences and changing situations, and strategies for initiating and responding to *price changes*.[13]

◾▌ New-Product Pricing Strategies

Pricing strategies usually change as the product passes through its life cycle. The introductory stage is especially challenging. Companies bringing out a new product face the challenge of setting prices for the first time. They can choose between two broad strategies: *market-skimming pricing* and *market-penetration pricing*.

Market-Skimming Pricing

Market-skimming pricing

Setting a high price for a new product to skim maximum revenues layer by layer from the segments willing to pay the high price; the company makes fewer but more profitable sales.

Many companies that invent new products initially set high prices to "skim" revenues layer by layer from the market. Sony frequently uses this strategy, called **market-skimming pricing**. When Sony introduced the world's first high-definition television (HDTV) to the Japanese market in 1990, the high-tech sets cost $43,000. These televisions were purchased only by customers who could afford to pay a high price for the new technology. Sony rapidly reduced the price over the next several years to attract new buyers. By 1993, a 28-inch HDTV cost a Japanese buyer just over $6,000. In 2001, a Japanese consumer could buy a 40-inch HDTV for about $2,000, a price that many more customers could afford. An entry-level HDTV set now sells for just $1,000 in the United States. In this way, Sony skimmed the maximum amount of revenue from the various segments of the market.[14]

Market skimming makes sense only under certain conditions. First, the product's quality and image must support its higher price, and enough buyers must want the product at that price. Second, the costs of producing a smaller volume cannot be so high that they cancel the advantage of charging more. Finally, competitors should not be able to enter the market easily and undercut the high price.

Market-Penetration Pricing

Market-penetration pricing

Setting a low price for a new product in order to attract a large number of buyers and a large market share.

Rather than setting a high initial price to skim off small but profitable market segments, some companies use **market-penetration pricing**. They set a low initial price in order to *penetrate* the market quickly and deeply—to attract a large number of buyers quickly and win a large market share. The high sales volume results in falling costs, allowing the company to cut its price even further. For example, Wal-Mart and other discount retailers use penetration pricing. And Dell used penetration pricing to enter the personal computer market, selling high-quality computer products through lower-cost direct channels. Its sales soared when IBM, Apple, and other competitors selling through retail stores could not match its prices.

Several conditions must be met for this low-price strategy to work. First, the market must be highly price sensitive so that a low price produces more market growth. Second, production and distribution costs must fall as sales volume increases. Finally, the low price must help keep out the competition, and the penetration pricer must maintain its low-price position—otherwise, the price advantage may be only temporary. For example, Dell faced difficult times when IBM and other competitors established their own direct distribution channels. However, through its dedication to low production and distribution costs, Dell has retained its price advantage and established itself as the industry's number one personal computer maker.

Product Mix Pricing Strategies

The strategy for setting a product's price often has to be changed when the product is part of a product mix. In this case, the firm looks for a set of prices that maximizes the profits on the total product mix. Pricing is difficult because the various products have related demand and costs and face different degrees of competition. We now take a closer look at five product mix pricing situations: *product line pricing, optional-product pricing, captive-product pricing, by-product pricing,* and *product bundle pricing.*

Product Line Pricing

Companies usually develop product lines rather than single products. For example, Snapper makes many different lawn mowers, ranging from simple walk-behind versions priced at $259.95, $299.95, and $399.95, to elaborate "Yard Cruisers" and lawn tractors priced at $1,000 or more. Each successive lawn mower in the line offers more features. Sony offers not just one type of television, but several lines of televisions, each containing many models. It offers everything from Watchman portable color TVs starting at $99.99, to flat-screen Trinitrons ranging from $200 to $1,500, to its top-of-the-line plasma WEGA flat-panel sets running from $6,000 to $8,000. And Gramophone makes a complete line of high quality sound systems, ranging in price from $5,000 to $120,000. Notes the company, "Mozart sacrificed his life to create beautiful music. Surely you can afford $10,000." In **product line pricing**, management must decide on the price steps to set between the various products in a line.

There are two things you'll find only at Gramophone: The finest sound systems from $5,000 to $120,000. And a dedication to music that matches the passion of the people who created it.

GRAMOPHONE
VERY, VERY, VERY HI-FI
Lutherville 821-5800 • Ellicott City 465-5500

■ Product line pricing: Gramophone makes a complete line of high quality sound systems, ranging in price from $5,000 to $120,000.

The price steps should take into account cost differences between the products in the line, customer evaluations of their different features, and competitors' prices. In many industries, sellers use well-established *price points* for the products in their line. Thus, men's clothing stores might carry men's suits at three price levels: $185, $325, and $495. The customer will probably associate low-, average-, and high-quality suits with the three price points. Even if the three prices are raised a little, men normally will buy suits at their own preferred price points. The seller's task is to establish perceived quality differences that support the price differences.

Product line pricing

Setting the price steps between various products in a product line based on cost differences between the products, customer evaluations of different features, and competitors' prices.

Optional-Product Pricing

Many companies use **optional-product pricing**—offering to sell optional or accessory products along with their main product. For example, a car buyer may choose to order power windows, cruise control, and a CD changer. Refrigerators come with optional ice makers.

Pricing these options is a sticky problem. Automobile companies have to decide which items to include in the base price and which to offer as options. Until recent years, General Motors' normal pricing strategy was to advertise a stripped-down model at a base price to pull people into showrooms and then to devote most of the showroom space to showing option-loaded cars at higher prices. The economy model was stripped of so many comforts and conveniences that most buyers rejected it. Then, GM and other U.S. car makers followed the example of the Japanese and German automakers and included in the sticker price many useful items previously sold only as options. Most advertised prices

Optional-product pricing

The pricing of optional or accessory products along with a main product.

today represent a well-equipped car. However, during the recent economic downturn, the auto companies began to move some features back into the "options" category in order to reduce the prices of standard models.

Captive-Product Pricing

Captive-product pricing
Setting a price for products that must be used along with a main product, such as blades for a razor and film for a camera.

Companies that make products that must be used along with a main product are using **captive-product pricing**. Examples of captive products are razor blades, camera film, video games, and printer cartridges. Producers of the main products (razors, cameras, video game consoles, and printers) often price them low and set high markups on the supplies. Thus, Gillette sells low-priced razors but makes money on the replacement cartridges. U-Haul rents out trucks at low rates but commands high margins on accessories such as boxes, pads, insurance, and storage space rental. HP makes very low margins on its printers but very high margins on printer cartridges and other supplies.

Nintendo sells its game consoles at low prices and makes money on video games. In fact, whereas Nintendo's margins on its consoles run a mere 1 to 5 percent, margins on its game cartridges run close to 45 percent. Video game sales contribute more than half of the company's profits. Similarly, Sony loses money on sales of its PlayStation 2 game console. But the games themselves, while accounting for only 17 percent of sales, generate more than a third of Sony's profits.[15]

In the case of services, this strategy is called *two-part pricing*. The price of the service is broken into a *fixed fee* plus a *variable usage rate*. Thus, amusement parks charge admission plus fees for food, midway attractions, and rides over a minimum. Theaters charge admission, then generate additional revenues from concessions. And cell phone companies charge a flat rate for a basic calling plan, then charge for minutes over what the plan allows. The service firm must decide how much to charge for the basic service and how much for the variable usage. The fixed amount should be low enough to induce use of the service; profit can be made on the variable fees.

By-Product Pricing

By-product pricing
Setting a price for by-products in order to make the main product's price more competitive.

In producing processed meats, petroleum products, chemicals, and other products, there are often by-products. If the by-products have no value and if getting rid of them is costly, this will affect the pricing of the main product. Using **by-product pricing**, the manufacturer will seek a market for these by-products and should accept any price that covers more than the cost of storing and delivering them.

By-products can even turn out to be profitable. For example, many lumber mills sell bark chips and sawdust profitably as decorative mulch for home and commercial landscaping. EcoStrat, a consulting firm in Canada, takes the idea further. The firm partnered with WoodworkingSite.com to give wood product companies a place to sell their chips, shavings, dust, and other by-products. To find buyers, a manufacturer can log on to WoodworkingSite.com, answer a few questions, and hit "send." EcoStrat does the rest.[16]

Sometimes, companies don't realize how valuable their by-products are. For example, most zoos don't realize that one of their by-products—their occupants' manure—can be an excellent source of additional revenue. But the Zoo Doo Compost Company has helped many zoos understand the costs and opportunities involved with these by-products. Zoo Doo licenses its name to zoos and receives royalties on manure sales. "Many zoos don't even know how much manure they are producing or the cost of disposing of it," explains president and founder Pierce Ledbetter. They are often so pleased with any savings they can find on disposal that they don't think to move into active by-product sales.

However, sales of the fragrant by-product can be substantial. So far, novelty sales have been the largest, with tiny containers of Zoo Doo (and even "Love, Love Me Doo" valentines) available in 160 zoo stores and 700 additional retail outlets. You can also buy Zoo Doo products online ("the easiest way to buy our crap," says Zoo Doo) or even send a friend (or perhaps a foe) a free Poopy Greeting via e-mail. For the long-term market, Zoo Doo looks to organic gardeners who buy 15 to 70 pounds of manure at a time. Zoo Doo is already planning a "Dung-of-the-Month" club to reach this lucrative by-products market. Other zoos sell their by-products on their own. For example, the Woodland Park Zoo in Seattle sponsors annual Fecal Fests, selling processed manure by the trash can and truck load to lucky lottery winners.[17]

Product Bundle Pricing

Using **product bundle pricing**, sellers often combine several of their products and offer the bundle at a reduced price. For example, theaters and sports teams sell season tickets at less than the cost of single tickets; hotels sell specially priced week-end packages that include room, meals, and entertainment; computer makers include attractive software packages with their personal computers; and Internet service providers sell packages that include Web access, Web hosting, e-mail, and an Internet search program. Some marketers price bundle the offerings of other organizations. For example, cityPASS bundles tickets to many attractions in any of several selected cities at combined low prices. Price bundling can promote the sales of products consumers might not otherwise buy, but the combined price must be low enough to get them to buy the bundle.[18]

■ Product bundle pricing: cityPASS bundles tickets to many attractions at a low combined price.

Product bundle pricing
Combining several products and offering the bundle at a reduced price.

■ Price-Adjustment Strategies

Companies usually adjust their basic prices to account for various customer differences and changing situations. Here we examine the six price adjustment strategies: *discount and allowance pricing, segmented pricing, psychological pricing, promotional pricing, geographical pricing,* and *international pricing.*

Discount and Allowance Pricing

Most companies adjust their basic price to reward customers for certain responses, such as early payment of bills, volume purchases, and off-season buying. These price adjustments—called *discounts* and *allowances*—can take many forms.

The many forms of **discounts** include a *cash discount*, a price reduction to buyers who pay their bills promptly. A typical example is "2/10, net 30," which means that although payment is due within 30 days, the buyer can deduct 2 percent if the bill is paid within 10 days. A *quantity discount* is a price reduction to buyers who buy large volumes. A typical example might be "$10 per unit for less than 100 units, $9 per unit for 100 or more units." Such discounts provide an incentive to the customer to buy more from one given seller, rather than from many different sources.

A *functional discount* (also called a *trade discount*) is offered by the seller to trade-channel members who perform certain functions, such as selling, storing, and record keeping. A *seasonal discount* is a price reduction to buyers who buy merchandise or services out of season. For example, lawn and garden equipment manufacturers offer seasonal discounts to retailers during the fall and winter months to encourage early ordering in anticipation of the heavy spring and summer selling seasons. Seasonal discounts allow the seller to keep production steady during an entire year.

Allowances are another type of reduction from the list price. For example, *trade-in allowances* are price reductions given for turning in an old item when buying a new one. Trade-in allowances are most common in the automobile industry but are also given for

Discount
A straight reduction in price on purchases during a stated period of time.

Allowance
Promotional money paid by manufacturers to retailers in return for an agreement to feature the manufacturer's products in some way.

other durable goods. *Promotional allowances* are payments or price reductions to reward dealers for participating in advertising and sales support programs.

Segmented Pricing

Segmented pricing
Selling a product or service at two or more prices, where the difference in prices is not based on differences in costs.

Companies will often adjust their basic prices to allow for differences in customers, products, and locations. In **segmented pricing**, the company sells a product or service at two or more prices, even though the difference in prices is not based on differences in costs.

Segmented pricing takes several forms. Under *customer-segment* pricing, different customers pay different prices for the same product or service. Museums, for example, may charge a lower admission for students and senior citizens. Under *product-form pricing,* different versions of the product are priced differently but not according to differences in their costs. For instance, the most expensive Black & Decker iron is priced at $54.98, which is $12 more than the price of the next most expensive Black & Decker iron. The top model has a self-cleaning feature, yet this extra feature costs only a few more dollars to make.

Using *location pricing*, a company charges different prices for different locations, even though the cost of offering each location is the same. For instance, theaters vary their seat prices because of audience preferences for certain locations, and state universities charge higher tuition for out-of-state students. Finally, using *time pricing*, a firm varies its price by the season, the month, the day, and even the hour. Some public utilities vary their prices to commercial users by time of day and weekend versus weekday. Resorts give weekend and seasonal discounts.

Segmented pricing goes by many names. Robert Cross, a longtime consultant to the airlines, calls it *revenue management.* According to Cross, the practice ensures that "companies will sell the right product to the right consumer at the right time for the right price." Airlines, hotels, and restaurants call it *yield management* and practice it religiously. The airlines, for example, routinely set prices on an hour-by-hour—even minute-by-minute—basis, depending on seat availability, demand, and competitor price changes.

Continental Airlines launches about 2,000 flights every day. Each flight has between 10 and 20 prices. Continental starts booking flights 330 days in advance, and every flying day is different from every other flying day. As a result, at any given moment, Continental may have nearly 7 million prices in the market. It's a daunting marketing task—all of those prices need to be managed, all of the time. For Continental, setting prices is a complex process of balancing demand and customer satisfaction against company profitability.[19]

> The airlines know full well that we are puzzled by the frantic pricing and repricing that they do—puzzled, that is, when we aren't infuriated. "I do not set the prices," says Jim Compton, senior vice president of pricing and revenue management at Continental Airlines. "The market sets prices." That's point one. Point two: "I have a really perishable product. It's gone when the door of the plane closes. An empty seat is lost revenue." The most valuable airline seat is the one that somebody must have an hour before takeoff and is willing to pay almost any price for. An airline seat gets more profitable with time—right up to the moment it goes from being worth $1,000 one-way to being worth $0.
>
> Here's how Compton and his colleagues think about this: You want to sell every seat on the plane, except that you also want to have a handful left at the very end, for your most profitable (not to mention most grateful) customers. The airlines could easily sell out every seat, every flight, every day. They'd price 'em pretty low, book 'em up, and wait for takeoff. But that would mean there'd never be any seats available two or three weeks before a flight took off. How exasperated would customers be to call and find no seats three days out? When you understand that dilemma, all of a sudden, airline prices don't seem so exploitive. Although all of the seats on that New York–Miami flight are going to the same place, they aren't the same product. You pay less when you commit to a ticket four weeks in advance; Continental assumes a risk for holding a seat until the end—and wants to be paid a lot to balance the times when saving that last seat for you means that the seat flies empty.

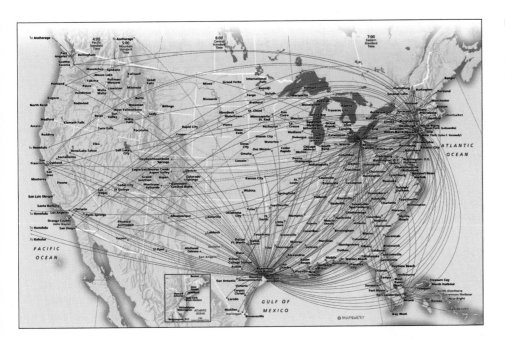

■ Segmented pricing: At any given moment, Continental may have nearly 7 million prices in the market. All of those prices need to be managed, all of the time.

Segmented pricing and yield management aren't really new ideas. For instance, Marriott Corporation used seat-of-the-pants yield-management approaches long before it installed its current sophisticated system.

> Back when Bill Marriott was a young man working at the family's first hotel, the Twin Bridges in Washington, D.C., he sold rooms from a drive-up window. As Bill tells it, the hotel charged a flat rate for a single occupant, with an extra charge for each additional person staying in the room. When room availability got tight on some nights, Bill would lean out the drive-up window and assess the cars waiting in line. If some of the cars were filled with passengers, Bill would turn away vehicles with just a single passenger to sell his last rooms to those farther back in line who would be paying for multiple occupants. He might have accomplished the same result by charging a higher rate at peak times, regardless of the number of room occupants.[20]

For segmented pricing to be an effective strategy, certain conditions must exist. The market must be segmentable, and the segments must show different degrees of demand. The costs of segmenting and watching the market cannot exceed the extra revenue obtained from the price difference. Of course, the segmented pricing must also be legal. Most importantly, segmented prices should reflect real differences in customers' perceived value. Otherwise, in the long run, the practice will lead to customer resentment and ill will.

Psychological Pricing

Price says something about the product. For example, many consumers use price to judge quality. A $100 bottle of perfume may contain only $3 worth of scent, but some people are willing to pay the $100 because this price indicates something special.

In using **psychological pricing**, sellers consider the psychology of prices and not simply the economics. For example, consumers usually perceive higher-priced products as having higher quality. When they can judge the quality of a product by examining it or by calling on past experience with it, they use price less to judge quality. But when they cannot judge quality because they lack the information or skill, price becomes an important quality signal:

> Heublein produces Smirnoff, America's leading vodka brand. Some years ago, Smirnoff was attacked by another brand. Wolfschmidt, priced at one dollar

Psychological pricing

A pricing approach that considers the psychology of prices and not simply the economics; the price is used to say something about the product.

■ Psychological pricing: What do the prices marked on this tag suggest about the product and buying situation?

Reference prices
Prices that buyers carry in their minds and refer to when they look at a given product.

less per bottle, claimed to have the same quality as Smirnoff. To hold on to market share, Heublein considered either lowering Smirnoff's price by one dollar or holding Smirnoff's price but increasing advertising and promotion expenditures. Either strategy would lead to lower profits, and it seemed that Heublein faced a no-win situation. At this point, however, Heublein's marketers thought of a third strategy. They *raised* the price of Smirnoff by one dollar! Heublein then introduced a new brand, Relska, to compete with Wolfschmidt. Moreover, it introduced yet another brand, Popov, priced even *lower* than Wolfschmidt. This clever strategy positioned Smirnoff as the elite brand and Wolfschmidt as an ordinary brand, producing a large increase in Heublein's overall profits. The irony is that Heublein's three brands are pretty much the same in taste and manufacturing costs. Heublein knew that a product's price signals its quality. Using price as a signal, Heublein sells roughly the same product at three different quality positions.

Another aspect of psychological pricing is **reference prices**—prices that buyers carry in their minds and refer to when looking at a given product. The reference price might be formed by noting current prices, remembering past prices, or assessing the buying situation. Sellers can influence or use these consumers' reference prices when setting price. For example, a company could display its product next to more expensive ones in order to imply that it belongs in the same class. Department stores often sell women's clothing in separate departments differentiated by price: Clothing found in the more expensive department is assumed to be of better quality. Companies can also influence consumers' reference prices by stating high manufacturer's suggested prices, by indicating that the product was originally priced much higher, or by pointing to a competitor's higher price.

Even small differences in price can suggest product differences. Consider a stereo priced at $300 compared to one priced at $299.95. The actual price difference is only 5 cents, but the psychological difference can be much greater. For example, some consumers will see the $299.95 as a price in the $200 range rather than the $300 range. The $299.95 will more likely be seen as a bargain price, whereas the $300 price suggests more quality. Some psychologists argue that each digit has symbolic and visual qualities that should be considered in pricing. Thus, 8 is round and even and creates a soothing effect, whereas 7 is angular and creates a jarring effect.[21]

Promotional Pricing

Promotional pricing
Temporarily pricing products below the list price, and sometimes even below cost, to increase short-run sales.

With **promotional pricing**, companies will temporarily price their products below list price and sometimes even below cost to create buying excitement and urgency. Promotional pricing takes several forms. Supermarkets and department stores will price a few products as *loss leaders* to attract customers to the store in the hope that they will buy other items at normal markups. For example, supermarkets often sell disposable diapers at less than cost in order to attract family buyers who make larger average purchases per trip. Sellers will also use *special-event pricing* in certain seasons to draw more customers. Thus, linens are promotionally priced every January to attract weary Christmas shoppers back into stores.

Manufacturers sometimes offer *cash rebates* to consumers who buy the product from dealers within a specified time; the manufacturer sends the rebate directly to the

■ Promotional pricing: Companies offer promotional prices to create buying excitement and urgency.

customer. Rebates have been popular with auto makers and producers of durable goods and small appliances, but they are also used with consumer packaged goods. Some manufacturers offer *low-interest financing*, *longer warranties*, or *free maintenance* to reduce the consumer's "price." This practice has become a favorite of the auto industry. Or, the seller may simply offer *discounts* from normal prices to increase sales and reduce inventories.

Promotional pricing, however, can have adverse effects. Used too frequently and copied by competitors, price promotions can create "deal-prone" customers, who wait until brands go on sale before buying them. Or, constantly reduced prices can erode a brand's value in the eyes of customers. Marketers sometimes use price promotions as a quick fix instead of sweating through the difficult process of developing effective longer-term strategies for building their brands. In fact, one observer notes that price promotions can be downright addicting to both the company and the customer: "Price promotions are the brand equivalent of heroin: easy to get into but hard to get out of. Once the brand and its customers are addicted to the short-term high of a price cut it is hard to wean them away to real brand building. . . . But continue and the brand dies by 1,000 cuts."[22]

The frequent use of promotional pricing can also lead to industry price wars. Such price wars usually play into the hands of only one or a few competitors—those with the most efficient operations. For example, until recently, the computer industry avoided price wars.

Computer companies, including IBM, Hewlett-Packard, and Gateway, showed strong profits as their new technologies were snapped up by eager consumers. When the market cooled, however, many competitors began to unload PCs at discounted prices. In response, Dell, the industry's undisputed low-cost leader, started a price war that only it could win.

In mid-2000, Dell declared a brutal price war just as the industry slipped into its worst slump ever. The result was nothing short of a rout. While Dell chalked up $361 million in profits the following year, the rest of the industry logged $1.1 billion in losses. Dell's edge starts with its direct-selling approach. By taking orders straight from customers and building machines to order, Dell avoids paying retailer markups, getting stuck with unsold PCs, and keeping costly inventories. For example, at any given moment, Dell's warehouses hold just four days of stock, compared with 24 days for competitors. That gives it a gigantic edge in a market where the price of chips, drives, and other parts typically falls 1 percent a week. Moreover, Dell has mastered supply chain management. Last year, it required suppliers to use sophisticated software that wires them straight into Dell's factory floor, allowing Dell's plants to replenish supplies only as needed throughout the day. That software alone saved Dell $50 million in the first six months of use. Since launching the price war, the price of a Dell computer has dropped more than 18 percent, leaving competitors with few effective weapons. IBM has responded by outsourcing its PC production and sales. And HP and Compaq merged in hopes of finding strength in numbers. Last year, Dell extended its low-price attack into the printer market, threatening lucrative HP's hold. "They're going after HP's golden egg," says one analyst. "If they are even moderately successful, you're going to see major trouble for HP." Says Michael Dell, "When we sell these products, we make money. When our competitors sell them, they lose money."[23]

By contrast, Kmart's mishandling of promotional pricing started a price war that the struggling discount retailer could never win, plunging the firm into bankruptcy (see Marketing at Work 9.2). The point is that promotional pricing can be an effective means of generating sales in certain circumstances but can be damaging if taken as a steady diet.

SPEED BUMP

Linking the Concepts

Here's a good place to take a brief break. Think about some of the companies and industries you deal with that are "addicted" to promotional pricing.

- Many industries have created "deal-prone" consumers through the heavy use of promotional pricing—fast food, automobiles, airlines, tires, furniture, and others. Pick a company in one of these industries and suggest ways that it might deal with this problem.
- How does the concept of value relate to promotional pricing? Does promotional pricing add to or detract from customer value?

Geographical Pricing

A company also must decide how to price its products for customers located in different parts of the country or world. Should the company risk losing the business of more-distant customers by charging them higher prices to cover the higher shipping costs? Or should the company charge all customers the same prices regardless of location? We will look at five geographical pricing strategies for the following hypothetical situation:

The Peerless Paper Company is located in Atlanta, Georgia, and sells paper products to customers all over the United States. The cost of freight is high

Marketing at Work | *9.2*

BlueLight Specials Mean "Lights Out" for Kmart

Kmart was once the top discount retailer in the United States, with more stores and sales than any other chain in the country. Then came Wal-Mart. With its low-cost operations, efficient distribution, and "Always Low Prices, Always" positioning, Wal-Mart quickly left Kmart in its wake. Consumers soon learned that, day in and day out, without a doubt, Wal-Mart is the low-price leader—always. Throughout the 1980s and 1990s, Kmart struggled as Wal-Mart grew.

Then, in the 1990s, shoppers seeking a slightly classier store environment but unwilling to pay for it found Target, which offers an alternative to the bare-bones Wal-Mart atmosphere. Target positions itself strongly as the "upscale discounter." With its promise of "Expect More, Pay Less," Target delivers value with an upscale feel for those who are price conscious but not price obsessed.

The emergence of Wal-Mart and Target left Kmart in a positioning no-man's-land. With its prices higher than Wal-Mart's, and its stores less chic than Target's, Kmart could find no meaningful way to differentiate itself. So in early 2001, a desperate Kmart launched a repositioning campaign. It targeted family buyers and set out to establish itself as the place for moms to find great values every day on items ranging from clothing to cereal. However, rather than building the Kmart brand on value, the repositioning effort quickly degenerated into a focus on price. It hinged on a seemingly contradictory combination of everyday low prices—to make Kmart more price-competitive with Wal-Mart—and promotional pricing—to lend new excitement and pull in shoppers.

For starters, Kmart slashed its every-day prices on more than 50,000 items in stores around the country to bring them within 2 percent of Wal-Mart's prices, as compared to 9 percent before the campaign. On top of this, Kmart resurrected

an old promotional pricing ploy. As the centerpiece of its new positioning, Kmart rekindled its age-old BlueLight Specials, first offered years ago by an industrious store manager. For many consumers, the BlueLight Specials still symbolize Kmart's early success.

In December 1965, Earl Bartell, a 24-year-old Kmart store manager in Fort Wayne, Indiana, was having a problem getting rid of some holiday wrapping paper he had put on sale. Frankly, people were having trouble finding it. After thinking it over, he went to the sporting goods section and picked up a flashing lantern. He taped the lantern to the end of a two-by-four, which in turn he taped to a little stock cart. He rolled the cart to the sale aisle, turned on the flashing light, and made another announcement. This time, everyone went to the right place. Bartell continued to use this

gimmick to feature other discounted items, and after watching sales steadily improve, he sent a short report back to the home office. Within six months, the flashing lights were part of the landscape of every Kmart store in the country. The presence of BlueLight Specials in Kmart stores continued for more than 20 years. But the retail scene was changing dramatically, and by 1984 Wal-Mart had overtaken Kmart as the number one discount department store chain. By the late 1980s, Kmart was close to bankruptcy, and a typical BlueLight Special had devolved into mismatched socks or two left shoes. In 1991, after 26 years, Kmart officially killed the BlueLight Special in an effort to turn the chain around by cleaning house and getting rid of every reminder of the past. To this day, however, when many consumers think back to the good old days at

Blue lights out for Kmart: BlueLight Specials and Dare to Compare campaigns kicked off a price war that Kmart had no chance of winning.

(continued)

Kmart, they remember those BlueLight Specials.

To kick off the repositioning campaign, Kmart launched a series of television ads featuring hip, animated blue spotlights dancing to Motown tunes and lowering everyday prices across the store. And, with hopes running high, Kmart introduced a new and improved version of its BlueLight Specials. The new program involved daylong discounts on certain items brought out in a cart every hour, flagged by sirens and a flashing blue light.

Despite the high hopes, the flashing blue lights signaled little more than "lights out" for Kmart. On the everyday-low-price front, Kmart simply could not outprice Wal-Mart. Its purchasing, distribution, and operating costs averaged 15 to 20 percent higher than Wal-Mart's. So in order to match Wal-Mart's prices, or even to come close, Kmart had to drop prices below cost.

To make matters worse, Kmart also failed to deliver consistently on the featured BlueLight Specials promotional pricing program. As a result of disorganization and poor management, some stores carried the signage but didn't offer the specials. Accounts like the following were all too common:

At one Chicago Kmart recently, a banner proclaims, "You are now entering the BlueLight Zone. Remain calm." Everyone does, because there is no BlueLight Special to be seen. A manager said one would be broadcast that day; pressed further, he promised it would happen within the hour. It didn't.

In addition, in too many cases, shoppers never had a chance to take advantage of BlueLight Always items, those supposedly offered at everyday low prices. Customers drawn to Kmart stores for advertised items often encountered only empty shelves.

At the height of the madness, Kmart launched a "Dare to Compare" campaign, in which it directly compared Kmart prices on specific products with those of other discounters, including Target and Wal-Mart. The campaign turned out to be a disaster. Kmart often got the comparisons wrong. In some cases, it quoted outdated or incorrect prices; in others, it compared products that other stores didn't even carry.

In the end, the BlueLight Specials and Dare to Compare campaigns kicked off a price war that Kmart had no chance of winning. Wal-Mart, the undisputed king of the discounters, responded in its usual ruthless way—by buckling down and cutting prices further. For Kmart, the results were disastrous—its losses mounted to more than $2.4 billion for the year. In early 2002, the once-dominant discount chain was forced into bankruptcy, closing nearly a third of its stores and letting go more than 60,000 employees. Kmart's stock dropped by 68 percent in just three weeks. During that same time, sales at Target and Wal-Mart rose 8 percent.

Kmart emerged from bankruptcy in May of 2003 still searching for a tenable position. Wherever it goes from here, Kmart's not likely to start another price war with Wal-Mart. "To go head-to-head with a 10,000-pound gorilla is non-sense," asserts one retail consultant. "It's like Switzerland declaring war on the United States. That, of course, doesn't work. Wal-Mart ate Kmart's lunch."

Sources: Excerpts adapted from Ann Zimmerman and Amy Merrick, "Kmart Rivals Appear to Benefit from BlueLight," *Wall Street Journal*, September 7, 2001, p. B1; and Mark Danzig, "By Design: The BlueLight Brand Story," *Design Management Journal*, Winter 2002, pp. 26–32. Also see Amy Merrick, "Target Sues Kmart Claiming Ads Misstate Prices in Comparisons," *Wall Street Journal*, August 22, 2001, p. B8; Debbie Howell, "Kmart's New Ad Campaign Puts Spotlight on EDLP," *DSN Retailing Today*, September 17, 2001, pp. 1, 67; Alice Z. Cuneo, "Ailing Kmart Surrenders in Price War," *Advertising Age*, January 21, 2002, pp. 1, 43; Keith Naughton, "Crisis at Kmart: Not a Good Thing," *Newsweek*, January 28, 2002, p. 38; Constance L. Hays, "Kmart Reports $2.42 Billion Annual Loss," *New York Times*, May 16, 2002, p. C1; Constance L. Hays, "A New Start, a New Name. But Have Things Really Changed as Kmart Comes Out of Bankruptcy?" *New York Times*, May 7, 2003, p. C9; and "Kmart Corporation," *Hoover's Company Profiles*, Austin, June 15, 2003.

and affects the companies from whom customers buy their paper. Peerless wants to establish a geographical pricing policy. It is trying to determine how to price a $100 order to three specific customers: Customer A (Atlanta), Customer B (Bloomington, Indiana), and Customer C (Compton, California).

One option is for Peerless to ask each customer to pay the shipping cost from the Atlanta factory to the customer's location. All three customers would pay the same factory price of $100, with Customer A paying, say, $10 for shipping; Customer B, $15; and Customer C, $25. Called *FOB-origin pricing,* this practice means that the goods are placed *free on board* (hence, *FOB*) a carrier. At that point the title and responsibility pass to the customer, who pays the freight from the factory to the destination. Because each customer picks up its own cost, supporters of FOB pricing feel that this is the fairest way to assess freight charges. The disadvantage, however, is that Peerless will be a high-cost firm for distant customers.

Uniform-delivered pricing is the opposite of FOB pricing. Here, the company charges the same price plus freight to all customers, regardless of their location. The freight charge is set at the average freight cost. Suppose this is $15. Uniform-delivered pricing therefore results in a higher charge to the Atlanta customer (who pays $15 freight instead of $10) and a lower charge to the Compton customer (who pays $15 instead of $25). Although the Atlanta customer would prefer to buy paper from another local paper company that uses

FOB-origin pricing, Peerless has a better chance of winning over the California customer. Other advantages of uniform-delivered pricing are that it is fairly easy to administer and it lets the firm advertise its price nationally.

Zone pricing falls between FOB-origin pricing and uniform-delivered pricing. The company sets up two or more zones. All customers within a given zone pay a single total price; the more distant the zone, the higher the price. For example, Peerless might set up an East Zone and charge $10 freight to all customers in this zone, a Midwest Zone in which it charges $15, and a West Zone in which it charges $25. In this way, the customers within a given price zone receive no price advantage from the company. For example, customers in Atlanta and Boston pay the same total price to Peerless. The complaint, however, is that the Atlanta customer is paying part of the Boston customer's freight cost.

Using *basing-point pricing,* the seller selects a given city as a "basing point" and charges all customers the freight cost from that city to the customer location, regardless of the city from which the goods are actually shipped. For example, Peerless might set Chicago as the basing point and charge all customers $100 plus the freight from Chicago to their locations. This means that an Atlanta customer pays the freight cost from Chicago to Atlanta, even though the goods may be shipped from Atlanta. If all sellers used the same basing-point city, delivered prices would be the same for all customers and price competition would be eliminated. Industries such as sugar, cement, steel, and automobiles used basing-point pricing for years, but this method has become less popular today. Some companies set up multiple basing points to create more flexibility: They quote freight charges from the basing-point city nearest to the customer.

Finally, the seller who is anxious to do business with a certain customer or geographical area might use *freight-absorption pricing.* Using this strategy, the seller absorbs all or part of the actual freight charges in order to get the desired business. The seller might reason that if it can get more business, its average costs will fall and more than compensate for its extra freight cost. Freight-absorption pricing is used for market penetration and to hold on to increasingly competitive markets.

International Pricing

Companies that market their products internationally must decide what prices to charge in the different countries in which they operate. In some cases, a company can set a uniform worldwide price. For example, Boeing sells its jetliners at about the same price everywhere, whether in the United States, Europe, or a third-world country. However, most companies adjust their prices to reflect local market conditions and cost considerations.

The price that a company should charge in a specific country depends on many factors, including economic conditions, competitive situations, laws and regulations, and development of the wholesaling and retailing system. Consumer perceptions and preferences also may vary from country to country, calling for different prices. Or the company may have different marketing objectives in various world markets, which require changes in pricing strategy. For example, Panasonic might introduce a new product into mature markets in highly developed countries with the goal of quickly gaining mass-market share—this would call for a penetration-pricing strategy. In contrast, it might enter a less developed market by targeting smaller, less price-sensitive segments; in this case, market-skimming pricing makes sense.

Costs play an important role in setting international prices. Travelers abroad are often surprised to find that goods that are relatively inexpensive at home may carry outrageously higher price tags in other countries. A pair of Levi's selling for $30 in the United States goes for about $63 in Tokyo and $88 in Paris. A McDonald's Big Mac selling for a modest $2.25 here costs $5.75 in Moscow, and an Oral-B toothbrush selling for $2.49 at home costs $10 in China. Conversely, a Gucci handbag going for only $60 in Milan, Italy, fetches $240 in the United States. In some cases, such *price escalation* may result from differences in selling strategies or market conditions. In most instances, however, it is simply a result of the higher costs of selling in another country—the additional costs of product modifications, shipping and insurance, import tariffs and taxes, exchange-rate fluctuations, and physical distribution.

■ Companies that market products internationally must decide what prices to charge in the different countries.

For example, Campbell found that distribution in the United Kingdom cost 30 percent more than in the United States. U.S. retailers typically purchase soup in large quantities—48-can cases of a single soup by the dozens, hundreds, or carloads. In contrast, English grocers purchase soup in small quantities—typically in 24-can cases of *assorted* soups. Each case must be hand-packed for shipment. To handle these small orders, Campbell had to add a costly extra wholesale level to its European channel. The smaller orders also mean that English retailers order two or three times as often as their U.S. counterparts, bumping up billing and order costs. These and other factors caused Campbell to charge much higher prices for its soups in the United Kingdom.[24]

Thus, international pricing presents some special problems and complexities. We discuss international pricing issues in more detail in Chapter 15.

■ Price Changes

After developing their pricing structures and strategies, companies often face situations in which they must initiate price changes or respond to price changes by competitors.

Initiating Price Changes

In some cases, the company may find it desirable to initiate either a price cut or a price increase. In both cases, it must anticipate possible buyer and competitor reactions.

Initiating Price Cuts Several situations may lead a firm to consider cutting its price. One such circumstance is excess capacity. In this case, the firm needs more business and cannot get it through increased sales effort, product improvement, or other measures. It may drop its "follow-the-leader pricing"—charging about the same price as its leading competitor—and aggressively cut prices to boost sales. But as the airline, construction equipment, fast-food, and other industries have learned in recent years, cutting prices in an industry loaded with excess capacity may lead to price wars, as competitors try to hold on to market share.

Another situation leading to price changes is falling market share in the face of strong price competition. Several American industries—automobiles, consumer electronics, cameras, watches, and steel, for example—lost market share to Japanese competitors whose high-quality products carried lower prices than did their American counterparts. In response, American companies resorted to more-aggressive pricing action.

A company may also cut prices in a drive to dominate the market through lower costs. Either the company starts with lower costs than its competitors, or it cuts prices in the hope of gaining market share that will further cut costs through larger volume. Bausch & Lomb used an aggressive low-cost, low-price strategy to become an early leader in the competitive soft contact lens market.

Initiating Price Increases A successful price increase can greatly increase profits. For example, if the company's profit margin is 3 percent of sales, a 1 percent price increase will increase profits by 33 percent if sales volume is unaffected. A major factor in price increases is cost inflation. Rising costs squeeze profit margins and lead companies to pass cost increases along to customers. Another factor leading to price increases is overdemand: When a company cannot supply all that its customers need, it can raise its prices, ration products to customers, or both.

Companies can increase their prices in a number of ways to keep up with rising costs. Prices can be raised almost invisibly by dropping discounts and adding higher-priced units to the line. Or prices can be pushed up openly. In passing price increases on to customers, the company must avoid being perceived as a price gouger. Companies also need to think of who will bear the brunt of increased prices. Customers have long memories, and they will eventually turn away from companies or even whole industries that they perceive as charging excessive prices.

This happened to the cereal industry in the 1990s. Industry leader Kellogg covered rising costs and preserved profits by steadily raising prices without also increasing customer value. Eventually, frustrated consumers retaliated with a quiet fury by shifting away from branded cereals toward cheaper private-label brands. Worse, many consumers switched to less expensive, more portable handheld breakfast foods, such as bagels, muffins, and breakfast bars. As a result, total American cereal sales began falling off by 3 to 4 percent a year. Moreover, private brands now capture almost 20 percent of the U.S. cereal market, and Kellogg's market share has slumped to about 33 percent, down from more than 42 percent less than a decade ago. Thus, customers paid the price in the short run but Kellogg paid the price in the long run.[25]

There are some techniques for avoiding this problem. One is to maintain a sense of fairness surrounding any price increase. Price increases should be supported by company communications telling customers why prices are being increased. Making low-visibility price moves first is also a good technique: some examples include eliminating discounts, increasing minimum order sizes, and curtailing production of low-margin products. The company sales force should help business customers find ways to economize.

Wherever possible, the company should consider ways to meet higher costs or demand without raising prices. For example, it can consider more cost-effective ways to produce or distribute its products. It can shrink the product instead of raising the price, as candy bar manufacturers often do. It can substitute less expensive ingredients or remove certain product features, packaging, or services. Or it can "unbundle" its products and services, removing and separately pricing elements that were formerly part of the offer. IBM, for example, now offers training and consulting as separately priced services.

Buyer Reactions to Price Changes Whether the price is raised or lowered, the action will affect buyers, competitors, distributors, and suppliers and may interest government as well. Customers do not always interpret prices in a straightforward way. They may view a price *cut* in several ways. For example, what would you think if Joy perfume, "the costliest fragrance in the world," were to cut its price in half? Or what if IBM suddenly cut its personal computer prices drastically? You might think that the computers are about to be replaced by newer models or that they have some fault and are not selling well. You might think that IBM is abandoning the computer business and may not stay in this business long enough to supply future parts. You might believe that quality has been reduced. Or you might think that the price will come down even further and that it will pay to wait and see.

Similarly, a price *increase*, which would normally lower sales, may have some positive meanings for buyers. What would you think if IBM *raised* the price of its latest personal computer model? On the one hand, you might think that the item is very "hot" and may be unobtainable unless you buy it soon. Or you might think that the computer is an unusually good value. On the other hand, you might think that IBM is greedy and charging what the traffic will bear.

Competitor Reactions to Price Changes A firm considering a price change has to worry about the reactions of its

TEN PERFECTLY RATIONAL REASONS FOR WEARING THE COSTLIEST FRAGRANCE IN THE WORLD.

1. "JOY ADDS LENGTH TO MY LEGS, WIT TO MY CONVERSATION AND A BETTER ACCENT TO MY FRENCH."

2. "A SINGLE WHIFF OF JOY TURNS A RICH MAN INTO A GENEROUS MAN."

3. "JOY IS THAT RARE BOUQUET OF 10,400 JASMINE FLOWERS AND 28 DOZEN ROSES THAT NEVER NEEDS WATERING AND NEVER DIES."

4. "A DAB OF JOY ON MY CHECK WRITING WRIST HELPS THE ZEROS FLOW WITH EASE."

5. "MY 76 YEAR OLD GRANDMOTHER WEARS JOY, AND SHE'S LIVING WITH HER 28 YEAR OLD FENCING INSTRUCTOR."

6. "MY ANTIDOTE FOR BAD DAYS IS A SPLASH OF JOY AND A GLASS OF CHAMPAGNE. ON WORSE DAYS, I DOUBLE THE RECIPE."

7. "MONEY CAN'T BUY HAPPINESS, BUT IT CAN FILL THE CUPBOARDS WITH JOY."

8. "JOY BODY CREAM MAKES ME FEEL LIKE A MILLION WITHOUT SPENDING A MINT."

9. "A SPLASH OF JOY BEFORE COFFEE AND CORNFLAKES PUTS THE GLAMOUR BACK INTO BREAKFAST."

10. "I WEAR DIAMONDS BEFORE FIVE, BLACK BEFORE DARK AND JOY EAU DE TOILETTE BEFORE EVERYTHING."

The most precious flowers on earth are just a few of the things that make JOY the costliest fragrance in the world.

■ Buyer reactions to price changes: What would you think if the price of Joy was suddenly cut in half?

competitors as well as those of its customers. Competitors are most likely to react when the number of firms involved is small, when the product is uniform, and when the buyers are well informed.

How can the firm anticipate the likely reactions of its competitors? The problem is complex because, like the customer, the competitor can interpret a company price cut in many ways. It might think the company is trying to grab a larger market share, or that it's doing poorly and trying to boost its sales. Or it might think that the company wants the whole industry to cut prices to increase total demand.

The company must guess each competitor's likely reaction. If all competitors behave alike, this amounts to analyzing only a typical competitor. In contrast, if the competitors do not behave alike—perhaps because of differences in size, market shares, or policies—then separate analyses are necessary. However, if some competitors will match the price change, there is good reason to expect that the rest will also match it.

Responding to Price Changes

Here we reverse the question and ask how a firm should respond to a price change by a competitor. The firm needs to consider several issues: Why did the competitor change the price? Was it to take more market share, to use excess capacity, to meet changing cost conditions, or to lead an industrywide price change? Is the price change temporary or permanent? What will happen to the company's market share and profits if it does not respond? Are other companies going to respond? And what are the competitor's and other firms' responses to each possible reaction likely to be?

Besides these issues, the company must make a broader analysis. It has to consider its own product's stage in the life cycle, the product's importance in the company's product mix, the intentions and resources of the competitor, and the possible consumer reactions to price changes. The company cannot always make an extended analysis of its alternatives at the time of a price change, however. The competitor may have spent much time preparing this decision, but the company may have to react within hours or days. About the only way to cut down reaction time is to plan ahead for both possible competitor's price changes and possible responses.

Figure 9.6 shows the ways a company might assess and respond to a competitor's price cut. Suppose the company learns that a competitor has cut its price and decides that this price cut is likely to harm company sales and profits. It might simply decide to hold its current price and profit margin. The company might believe that it will not lose too much market share, or that it would lose too much profit if it reduced its own price. Or it might

FIGURE 9.6

Assessing and Responding to Competitor Price Changes

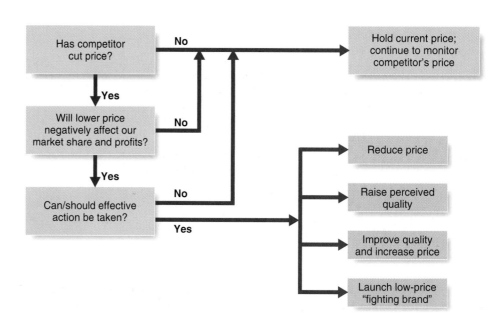

decide that it should wait and respond when it has more information on the effects of the competitor's price change. The argument against this holding strategy, however, is that the competitor may get stronger and more confident as its sales increase and that your company might wait too long to act.

If the company decides that effective action can and should be taken, it might make any of four responses. First, it could *reduce its price* to match the competitor's price. It may decide that the market is price sensitive and that it would lose too much market share to the lower-priced competitor. Or it might worry that recapturing lost market share later would be too hard. Cutting the price will reduce the company's profits in the short run. Some companies might also reduce their product quality, services, and marketing communications to retain profit margins, but this will ultimately hurt long-run market share. The company should try to maintain its quality as it cuts prices.

Alternatively, the company might maintain its price but *raise the perceived value* of its offer. It could improve its communications, stressing the relative quality of its product over that of the lower-price competitor. The firm may find it cheaper to maintain price and spend money to improve its perceived value than to cut price and operate at a lower margin.

Or, the company might *improve quality and increase price*, moving its brand into a higher-price position. The higher quality justifies the higher price, which in turn preserves the company's higher margins. Or the company can hold price on the current product and introduce a new brand at a higher-price position.

Finally, the company might *launch a low-price "fighting brand"*—adding a lower-price item to the line or creating a separate lower-price brand. This is necessary if the particular market segment being lost is price sensitive and will not respond to arguments of higher quality. Thus, when challenged on price by store brands and other low-price entrants, Procter & Gamble turned a number of its brands into fighting brands, including Luvs disposable diapers, Joy dishwashing detergent, and Camay beauty soap. In turn, P&G competitor Kimberly-Clark positions its value-priced Scott Towels brand as "the Bounty killer." It advertises Scott Towels as "Common Sense on a Roll." The brand scores well on customer satisfaction measures but sells for a lower price than P&G's Bounty brand.[26]

■ Fighting brands: Kimberly-Clark offers its value-priced Scott Towels brand as "the Bounty killer." It scores well on customer satisfaction but sells for a lower price than P&G's Bounty.

■ Public Policy and Pricing

Price competition is a core element of our free-market economy. In setting prices, companies are not usually free to charge whatever prices they wish. Many federal, state, and even local laws govern the rules of fair play in pricing. In addition, companies must consider broader societal pricing concerns (see Marketing at Work 9.3). The most important pieces of legislation affecting pricing are the Sherman, Clayton, and Robinson–Patman acts, initially adopted to curb the formation of monopolies and to regulate business practices that might unfairly restrain trade. Because these federal statutes can be applied only to interstate commerce, some states have adopted similar provisions for companies that operate locally.

Figure 9.7 on page 324 shows the major public policy issues in pricing. These include potentially damaging pricing practices within a given level of the channel (price-fixing and predatory pricing) and across levels of the channel (retail price maintenance, discriminatory pricing, and deceptive pricing).[27]

Pricing within Channel Levels

Federal legislation on *price fixing* states that sellers must set prices without talking to competitors. Otherwise, price collusion is suspected. Price fixing is illegal per se—that

Marketing at Work | *9.3*

Pricing Pharmaceutical Products: More Than Sales and Profits

The U.S. pharmaceutical industry has historically been one of the nation's most profitable industries. However, critics claim that this success has come at the expense of consumers. The U.S. population spent more than $161 billion on prescription medications last year, and this amount will more than double to $360 billion by 2010. Prescription prices have risen rapidly over the years. One study suggests that the price of brand-name drugs will rise, on average, more than 5.5 percent this year, much higher than the overall inflation rate.

After intense political pressure a decade ago, many drug makers pledged to keep their prices at or below inflation. However, as threats of price controls fade, the drug makers are again pushing up the prices. For example, last year, Pfizer raised the price of its cholesterol-fighting Lipitor, the world's largest selling drug, by 11 percent. Similarly, Wyeth boosted the price of its flagship drug, Premarin, by 17 percent, and Merck raised the price of its asthma remedy Singulair by 11 percent. High drug prices have sent many consumers, especially seniors with limited budgets and fixed-income, to Mexico and Canada in search of cheaper alternatives, including copycat versions of popular drugs like Zocor and Celebrex. Says one senior after a visit to Mexico, "If we couldn't get cheap meds, I wouldn't live."

The critics claim that competitive forces do not operate well in the pharmaceutical market, allowing companies to charge excessive prices. Unlike purchases of other consumer products, drug purchases cannot be postponed. Consumers don't usually shop for the best deal on medicines—they simply take what the doctor orders. Because physicians who write the prescriptions don't pay for the medicines they recommend, they have little incentive to be price conscious. Moreover, because of

patents and FDA approvals, few competing brands exist to force lower prices, and existing brands don't go on sale. Finally, expensive advertising and promotional efforts dictate higher prices at the same time that they build demand for more expensive remedies. These market factors leave pharmaceutical companies free to practice monopoly pricing, the critics claim, resulting in seemingly outlandish cases of price gouging.

One classic case involved the drug levamisole. Forty years ago, Johnson & Johnson introduced levamisole as a drug used to deworm sheep. When

farmers using the drug noticed that dewormed sheep also suffered fewer cases of shipping fever, researchers began investigating the drug for human use. They found that levamisole, in combination with another drug, proved effective for patients with advanced colon cancer, reducing recurrence of the disease by 40 percent and cutting deaths by a third.

The FDA quickly approved levamisole for human use, and the Janssen division of Johnson & Johnson introduced the drug under the brand name Ergamisol. All went well until an Illinois farm woman noticed that her

The critics claim that the lack of competitive forces in the pharmaceutical market lets companies charge excessive prices. Here, the AARP advises, "Avoid paying too much for your prescriptions" and "don't let advertising sell you on drugs you don't need."

cancer pills contained the same active ingredient as the medicine she used to deworm her sheep. It wasn't the fact that both humans and sheep were using the drug that disturbed her. What really rankled her was that the sheep medicine sold for pennies a pill, whereas the human medicine sold for $5 to $6 per tablet. In a year's time, humans had to spend $1,250 to $3,000 for Ergamisol; the cost for treating sheep was only about $14.95.

The price discrepancy caused quite a stir. One consumer even filed suit against Janssen, claiming that he was forced to pay "an outrageous, unconscionable, and extortionate price for a lifesaving drug" that is sold at a fraction of the cost for treating sheep. Janssen replied that the price reflected decades of costly research and testing conducted to determine if levamisole could be used to treat humans. The company said it had conducted over 1,400 studies with 40,000 subjects. Critics disagreed, claiming that the National Cancer Institute, funded by the American taxpayer, had sponsored the levamisole studies. Furthermore, they asserted, Janssen had had 25 years to recoup its investment before it ever sold the drug to humans.

The levamisole case may be extreme, but at one time or another we've all gulped at the prices we've had to pay for prescription drugs. Even when doctors or pharmacists recommend less expensive generic drugs, consumers may pay substantial markups. Pharmacies may look like good guys when they encourage the use of generics to save consumers money, but they also pocket a handsome profit. One recent study found that drugstores and pharmacies are marking up the price of some generics by more than 1,000 percent. For their part, pharmacies argue that the high gross margins for generics don't tell the whole story. Just as a patient who visits a doctor and gets handed a Band-Aid is not billed for just the Band-Aid, a pharmacy customer has to pay for the phar-

macist's time and other expenses of maintaining a pharmacy department.

These examples highlight many important drug-pricing issues. Most consumers appreciate the steady stream of beneficial drugs produced by the U.S. pharmaceutical industry. And there is no question that developing new drugs is a risky endeavor, involving legions of scientists, expensive technology, and often years of effort with no certainty of success. However, there is much concern that the industry may be taking advantage of its monopoly-pricing power. Perhaps the most serious concern is that high drug prices may have life-and-death consequences. Without levamisole, for example, many of the 22,000 patients diagnosed with advanced colon cancer each year would die. Thus, some critics claim that drug company profits may come at the expense of human life.

As a result of recent soaring prices, the industry is again facing pressure from the federal government, insurance companies, managed-care providers, and consumer advocates to exercise restraint in setting prices. Rather than waiting for tougher legislation on prices—or simply because it's the right thing to do—some forward-thinking drug companies have taken action on their own. Some voluntarily provide discounts to agencies such as the U.S. Public Health Service and to federally funded drug- and alcohol-treatment centers. Still other companies make drugs available free or at low prices to people who cannot afford them. Consider the following example:

Abbott Laboratories CEO Miles White returned from a recent eye-opening visit to Tanzania—where the HIV/AIDS epidemic rages almost unabated—with a new mission for his company. Among other things, he learned firsthand that when local doctors decide whether or not to use a drug, the biggest consideration is its price, not whether it is the right drug.

"I found out how much the price of drugs matters," says White. As a result, within days, he decided to reduce the price of Abbott's AIDS drugs to below cost for poor African nations. White also learned that the cost of the company's "rapid" AIDS detection test was the main reason it wasn't being used as a crucial tool in helping prevent the spread of the virus from infected pregnant women to their unborn children. Once detected, virus transmission can be blocked with the one-time use of a drug being given away by a competitor. But without an easy-to-use detection test, many expectant mothers are unaware they are infected. White now plans to give away 20 million test kits during the next five years. Asked how he can explain taking money out of the company coffers to fund such price cuts and give-aways, he says he'll tell shareholders that Abbott is doing "our part because we can." But, in a refreshing bit of honesty, he adds, "There is a practical business reason. If we don't lower prices and provide other help, we'll find governments altering patent laws."

Thus, Abbott and other companies recognize that in setting prices, their short-term sales, market share, and profit goals must be tempered by broader societal considerations. They know that in the long run, socially responsible pricing will benefit both the consumer and the company.

Sources: Abbott example adapted from Michael Waldholz, "Abbott Labs Improves Its Effort to Combat AIDS in Africa," *Wall Street Journal*, June 27, 2002, p. D4. Also see Marilyn Chase, "Doctor Assails J&J Price Tag on Cancer Drug," *Wall Street Journal*, May 20, 1992, p. B1; "Cancer Patient Sues Johnson & Johnson over Drug Pricing," *Wall Street Journal*, August 13, 1992, p. B6; Mike King, "Colon Cancer Drug: 5 Cents for an Animal, $5 for Humans," *Atlanta Constitution*, March 11, 1991, p. E1; Joel Millman, "Not Your Generic Smugglers—American Seniors Flock to Border Town for Cheap Prescriptions," *Wall Street Journal*, March 20, 2003, p. D.3; John Fetto, "Off the Map," *American Demographics*, March 2003, p. 48; and Scott Hensley, "Follow the Money: Drug Prices Rise at a Faster Clip, Placing Burden on Consumers," *Wall Street Journal*, April 15, 2003, p. D4.

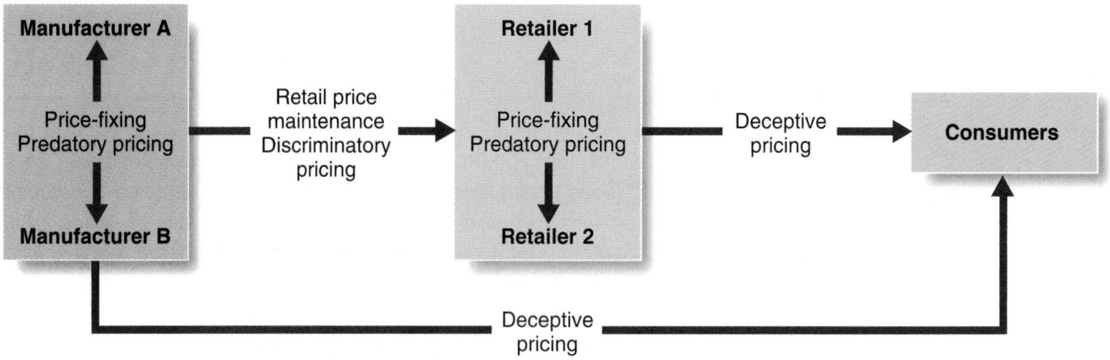

FIGURE 9.7

Public Policy Issues in Pricing

is, the government does not accept any excuses for price fixing. Companies found guilty of such practices can receive heavy fines. For example, when the U.S. Justice Department found that Archer Daniels Midland Company and three of its competitors had met regularly in the early 1990s to illegally fix prices, the four companies paid more than $100 million to settle the charges. Similarly, Sotheby's and Christie's, two auction houses that for years have dominated the market for high-end sales, were recently convicted of collusion and price-fixing. The collusion reportedly saved the companies in excess of $33 million a year, but they ended paying more than $512 million in fines and settlements.[28] Recently, governments at the state and national levels have been aggressively enforcing price-fixing regulations in industries ranging from tobacco, gasoline, and newsprint to vitamins and compact disks.[29]

Sellers are also prohibited from using *predatory pricing*—selling below cost with the intention of punishing a competitor or gaining higher long-run profits by putting competitors out of business. This protects small sellers from larger ones who might sell items below cost temporarily or in a specific locale to drive them out of business. The biggest problem is determining just what constitutes predatory pricing behavior. Selling below cost to sell off excess inventory is not considered predatory; selling below cost to drive out competitors is. Thus, the same action may or may not be predatory depending on intent, and intent can be very difficult to determine or prove.

In recent years, several large and powerful companies have been accused of this practice. For example, Wal-Mart has been sued by dozens of small competitors charging that it lowered prices in their specific areas to drive them out of business. In another case, the Justice Department sued American Airlines for allegedly using predatory pricing to muscle three small competitors—Vanguard Airlines, Sun Jet, and Western Pacific—out of its huge Dallas–Fort Worth hub.

> Every time a fledgling airline tried to get a toehold in the Dallas market, for example, American met its fares and added flights. As soon as the rival retreated, American jacked fares back up. Between Dallas and Kansas City, for instance, American's average one-way ticket was $108 before low-cost startup Vanguard Airlines entered the market. That prompted American to cut fares to $80 and almost double the number of daily flights, to 14. When Vanguard gave up [less than a year later], American jacked up prices to $147 and scaled back the number of flights. Justice lawyers even had memos from American execs plotting the upstarts' demise.

Despite such evidence, the case against American was dismissed. American had consistently priced flights higher than variable costs, thus avoiding predatory pricing. American won by arguing that it was just being a tough competitor.[30]

Pricing Across Channel Levels

The Robinson–Patman Act seeks to prevent unfair *price discrimination* by ensuring that sellers offer the same price terms to customers at a given level of trade. For example, every retailer is entitled to the same price terms from a given manufacturer, whether the retailer is Sears or the local bicycle shop. However, price discrimination is allowed if the seller can prove that its costs are different when selling to different retailers—for example, that it costs less per unit to sell a large volume of bicycles to Sears than to sell a few bicycles to a local dealer. Or the seller can discriminate in its pricing if the seller manufactures different qualities of the same product for different retailers. The seller has to prove that these differences are proportional. Price differentials may also be used to "match competition" in "good faith," provided the price discrimination is temporary, localized, and defensive rather than offensive.

Retail price maintenance is also prohibited—a manufacturer cannot require dealers to charge a specified retail price for its product. Although the seller can propose a manufacturer's *suggested* retail price to dealers, it cannot refuse to sell to a dealer who takes independent pricing action, nor can it punish the dealer by shipping late or denying advertising allowances. For example, the Florida attorney general's office recently investigated Nike for allegedly fixing the retail price of its shoes and clothing. It was concerned that Nike might be withholding items from retailers who were not selling its most expensive shoes—like the Air Jordan and Shox lines—at prices the company considered suitable.[31]

Deceptive pricing occurs when a seller states prices or price savings that mislead consumers or are not actually available to consumers. This might involve bogus reference or comparison prices, as when a retailer sets artificially high "regular" prices then announces "sale" prices close to its previous everyday prices. Such comparison pricing is widespread:

> Open any Sunday newspaper and find hundreds of such promotions being offered by a variety of retailers, such as supermarkets, office supply stores, furniture stores, computer stores, appliance stores, pharmacies and drugstores, car dealers, department stores, and others. Surf the Internet and see similar price promotions. Watch the shopping channels on television and find more of the same. It seems that, today, selling prices rarely stand alone. Instead retailers are using an advertised reference price (e.g., regular price, original price, manufacturer's suggested price) to suggest that buyers will save money if they take advantage of the "deal" being offered.[32]

■ Deceptive pricing concerns: The widespread use of checkout scanners has led to increasing complaints of retailers overcharging their customers.

Such claims are legal if they are truthful. However, the FTC's *Guides Against Deceptive Pricing* warns sellers not to advertise a price reduction unless it is a saving from the usual retail price, not to advertise "factory" or "wholesale" prices unless such prices are what they are claimed to be, and not to advertise comparable value prices on imperfect goods.[33]

Other deceptive pricing issues include *scanner fraud* and price confusion. The widespread use of scanner-based computer checkouts has led to increasing complaints of retailers overcharging their customers. Most of these overcharges result from poor management—from a failure to enter current or sale prices into the system. Other cases, however, involve intentional overcharges. *Price confusion* results when firms employ pricing methods that make it difficult for consumers to understand just what price they are really paying. For example, consumers are sometimes misled regarding the real price of a home mortgage or car leasing agreement. In other cases, important pricing details may be buried in the "fine print."

Many federal and state statutes regulate against deceptive pricing practices. For example, the Automobile Information Disclosure Act requires automakers to attach a statement to new-car windows stating the manufacturer's suggested retail price, the prices of optional equipment, and the dealer's transportation charges. However, reputable sellers go beyond what is required by law. Treating customers fairly and making certain that they fully understand prices and pricing terms is an important part of building strong and lasting customer relationships.[34]

REST STOP:
Reviewing the Concepts

Before you put pricing in the rearview mirror, let's review the important concepts. *Price* can be defined as the sum of the values that consumers exchange for the benefits of having and using the product or service. It is the only marketing mix element that produces revenue; all other elements represent costs. Even so, many companies are not good at handling pricing. Pricing decisions are subject to an incredibly complex array of environmental and competitive forces.

1. Identify and define the external and internal factors affecting a firm's pricing decisions.

External factors that influence pricing decisions include the nature of the *market* and *demand*; *competitors' costs, prices, and offers;* and factors such as *the economy, reseller needs,* and *government actions.* The seller's pricing freedom varies with different types of markets. Ultimately, the consumer decides whether the company has set the right price. The consumer weighs the price against the perceived values of using the product—if the price exceeds the sum of the values, consumers will not buy. Therefore, *demand* and *consumer value perceptions* set the ceiling for prices. Consumers also compare a product's price to the prices of *competitors'* products. As a result, a company must learn the price and quality of competitors' offers.

Many *internal factors* influence the company's pricing decisions, including the firm's *marketing objectives, marketing mix strategy, costs*, and *organization for pricing.* Common pricing objectives include survival, current profit maximization, market share leadership, and product quality leadership. The pricing strategy is largely determined by the company's *target market* and *positioning objectives.* Pricing decisions affect and are affected by product design, distribution, and promotion decisions and must be carefully coordinated with these other marketing mix variables. *Costs* set the floor for the company's price—the price must cover all the costs of making and selling the product, plus a fair rate of return. Finally, in order to coordinate pricing goals and decisions, management must decide who within the organization is responsible for setting price.

2. Contrast the three general approaches to setting prices.

A company can select one or a combination of three general pricing approaches: the *cost-based approach* (cost-plus pricing, break-even analysis, and target profit pricing); the *value-based approach*; and the *competition-based approach.* Cost-based pricing sets prices based on the seller's cost structure, whereas value-based pricing relies on consumer perceptions of value to drive pricing decisions. Competition-based pricing involves setting prices based on what competitors are charging or are expected to charge.

3. Describe the major strategies for pricing imitative and new products.

Pricing is a dynamic process. Companies design a *pricing structure* that covers all their products. They change this structure over time and adjust it to account for different customers and situations. Pricing strategies usually change as a product passes through its life cycle. The company can decide on one of several price quality strategies for introducing an imitative product, including premium pricing, economy pricing, good-value pricing, or overcharging. In pricing innovative new products, it can follow a *skimming policy* by initially setting high prices to "skim" the maximum amount of revenue from various segments of the market. Or it can use *penetration pricing* by setting a low initial price to penetrate the market deeply and win a large market share.

4. Explain how companies find a set of prices that maximizes the profits from the total product mix.

When the product is part of a product mix, the firm searches for a set of prices that will maximize the profits from the total mix. In *product line pricing,* the company decides on price steps for the entire set of products it offers. In addition, the company must set prices for *optional products* (optional or accessory products included with the main product), *captive products* (products that are required for use of the main product), *by-products* (waste or residual products produced when making the main product), and *product bundles* (combinations of products at a reduced price).

5. Discuss how companies adjust their prices to take into account different types of customers and situations.

Companies apply a variety of *price-adjustment strategies* to account for differences in consumer segments and situations. One is *discount and allowance pricing*, whereby the company establishes cash, quantity, functional, or seasonal discounts, or varying types of allowances. A second strategy is *segmented pricing*, whereby the company sells a product at two or more prices to accommodate different customers, product forms, locations, or times. Sometimes companies consider more than economics in their pricing decisions, using *psychological pricing* to better communicate a product's intended position. In *promotional pricing*, a company offers discounts or temporarily sells a product below list price as a special event, sometimes even selling below cost as a loss leader. Another approach is *geographical pricing*, whereby the company decides how to price to near and distant customers. Finally, *international pricing* means that the company adjusts its price to meet conditions and expectations in different world markets.

6. Discuss the key issues related to initiating and responding to price changes.

When a firm considers initiating a *price change*, it must consider customers' and competitors' reactions. There are different implications to *initiating price cuts* and *initiating price increases*. Buyer reactions to price changes are influenced by the meaning customers see in the price change. Competitors' reactions flow from a set reaction policy or a fresh analysis of each situation. There are also many factors to consider in responding to a competitor's price changes. The company that faces a price change initiated by a competitor must try to understand the competitor's intent as well as the likely duration and impact of the change. If a swift reaction is desirable, the firm should preplan its reactions to different possible price actions by competitors. When facing a competitor's price change, the company might sit tight, reduce its own price, raise perceived quality, improve quality and raise price, or launch a fighting brand.

Companies are not usually free to charge whatever prices they wish. Many federal, state, and even local laws govern the rules of fair play in pricing. The major public policy issues in pricing include potentially damaging pricing practices within a given level of the channel (price-fixing and predatory pricing) and across levels of the channel (retail price maintenance, discriminatory pricing, and deceptive pricing).

Navigating the Key Terms

Allowance
Break-even pricing
 (target profit pricing)
By-product pricing
Captive-product pricing
Competition-based pricing
Cost-plus pricing
Demand curve
Discount

Dynamic pricing
Fixed costs
Market-penetration pricing
Market-skimming pricing
Optional-product pricing
Price
Price elasticity
Product bundle pricing
Product line pricing

Promotional pricing
Psychological pricing
Reference prices
Segmented pricing
Target costing
Total costs
Value pricing
Value-based pricing
Variable costs

Travel Log

Discussing the Issues

1. Imagine that you are setting flight prices for Southwest Airlines. How would the internal and external factors identified in Figure 9.1 have an impact on your pricing decision?

2. Explain the differences between cost-based pricing, value-based pricing, and competition-based pricing. Under what conditions might a company favor one approach over the others?

3. Given that higher-priced products are often perceived as being higher in quality, what implications does a low price have for marketers using promotional pricing strategies?

4. Your major competitor has just cut its prices by 20 percent on all products. How should you react? What information do you want to have before you craft a response?

5. Review the geographical pricing strategies of FOB-origin pricing, uniform-delivered pricing, zone pricing, basing-point pricing, and freight-absorption pricing. What factors influence the choice of a geographical pricing strategy?

Application Questions

1. Your company is about to launch a new brand of paper towels that are more absorbent and durable than paper towels currently being sold. Your boss wants you to consider both market-skimming and market-penetration pricing strategies. What factors should you consider in making your decision?

2. Select an athletic team, theater series, or other event at your school for which tickets can be purchased individually or in a bundle (i.e., season tickets). Get pricing information for both single event/game and bundled tickets. Is the cost on a per-ticket basis less expensive for the bundled price? Does the price difference entice you to buy the bundle instead of individual tickets? Aside from maximizing revenue, what else might an event marketer be concerned with in deciding how to set ticket prices?

3. Visit a department store and find brands in three different product categories (e.g., televisions, refrigerators, tennis racquets) that engage in product-line pricing. Do you feel that the price-to-attribute/feature trade-off in the product line is appropriate? Pick the product in each line that offers the most value to you. Describe a market segment that would have selected a different product as having the most value. What market segment is each product trying to reach with its offerings?

Under the Hood: Focus on Technology

 The ability to quickly compare prices over the Internet has been a boon to consumers, and either a blessing or a curse to retailers (depending on which side of the "pricing fence" you're on). Web sites such as Streetprices.com, Nextag.com, and PriceScan.com allow consumers to quickly comparison shop for specific products at dozens of retailers. Imagine how long that would take if you were trying to drive all over town to accomplish the same thing! Some will even e-mail you when the product you are interested in reaches or falls below your target price.

Go to one of the Web sites listed above and do a comparison for a television and a vacuum cleaner. Then respond to the questions below.

1. What do you think of this service? Do you trust the retailers offering the lowest prices? What concerns might a consumer have using one of these Web sites to select a seller?

2. How can a local "brick-and-mortar" store in your town compete with the companies offering products through these Web sites?

3. What other features of these Web sites make them attractive for buyers?

Focus on Ethics

 In order to promote competition, federal laws prohibit price fixing—competitors agreeing on what price levels to set. Some companies find themselves in the media spotlight after being accused of price fixing. In recent years, rival auction houses Christie's and Sotheby's have been found guilty of fixing the commission rates they earned from auctions. More recently, some of the top modeling agencies have come under investigation for conspiring to fix the commissions they charge models to book their assignments. Being found guilty of price fixing in the United States can bring jail time and large fines.

1. Why is price fixing dealt with so harshly in the United States? Why shouldn't companies be able to discuss price levels and set whatever price they agree on?

2. What might a company do to discourage employees from engaging in price fixing? What factors might encourage companies to collude on prices?

3. Does the rapid availability of competitive price information on the Internet help to facilitate price fixing?

Videos

The NEXTEL video case that accompanies this chapter is located in Appendix 1 at the back of the book.

Student Materials

Need a tune-up? A study guide and OneKey access code are available to aid in your review of chapter material. Your instructor may choose to have these items shrink-wrapped with your text or you may purchase them separately at www.prenhall.com/marketing.

■ *After studying this chapter, you should be able to*

1. *Explain* why companies use distribution channels and discuss the functions these channels perform **2.** *Discuss* how channel members interact and how they organize to perform the work of the channel **3.** *Identify* the major channel alternatives open to a company **4.** *Explain* how companies select, motivate, and evaluate channel members **5.** *Discuss* the nature and importance of marketing logistics and integrated supply chain management

Marketing Channels and Supply Chain Management

10

ROAD MAP | Previewing the Concepts

We now arrive at the third marketing mix tool—distribution. Firms rarely work alone in bringing value to customers and building profitable customer relationships. Instead, most are only a single link in a larger supply chain and distribution channel. As such, an individual firm's success depends not only on how well *it* performs but also on how well its *entire distribution channel* competes with competitors' channels. For example, Ford can make the world's best cars but still not do well if its dealers perform poorly in sales and service against the dealers of Toyota, GM, Chrysler, or Honda. Ford must choose its channel partners carefully and work with them effectively. To be good at customer relationship management, a company must also be good at partner relationship management. The first part of this chapter explores the nature of distribution channels and the marketer's channel design and management decisions. We then examine physical distribution—or logistics—an area that is growing dramatically in importance and sophistication. In the next chapter, we'll look more closely at two major channel intermediaries—retailers and wholesalers.

While your engine's warming up, we'll take a look at Caterpillar. You might think that Caterpillar's success, and its ability to charge premium prices, rests on the quality of the heavy construction and mining equipment that it produces. But Caterpillar sees things differently. The company's dominance, it claims, results from its unparalleled distribution and customer support system—from the strong and caring partnerships that it has built with independent Caterpillar dealers. Read on and see why.

For more than seven decades, Caterpillar has dominated the world's markets for heavy construction and mining equipment. Its familiar yellow tractors, crawlers, loaders, bulldozers, and trucks are a common sight at any construction area. Caterpillar sells more than 300 products in nearly 200 companies, generating sales of more than $20 billion annually. It captures 27 percent of the worldwide construction-equipment business, more than double that of number two Komatsu. Its share of the North American market is more than twice that of competitors Komatsu and Deere combined.

Many factors contribute to Caterpillar's enduring success—high-quality products, flexible and efficient manufacturing, a steady stream of innovative new products, and a lean organization that is responsive to customer needs. Although Caterpillar charges premium prices for its equipment,

its high quality and trouble-free operation provide greater long-term value. Yet these are not the most important reasons for Caterpillar's dominance. Instead, Caterpillar credits its focus on customers and its corps of 220 outstanding independent dealers worldwide, who do a superb job of taking care of every customer need. According to former Caterpillar CEO Donald Fites:

> After the product leaves our door, the dealers take over. They are the ones on the front line. They're the ones who live with the product for its lifetime. They're the ones customers see. Although we offer financing and insurance, they arrange those deals for customers. They're out there making sure that when a machine is delivered, it's in the condition it's supposed to be in. They're out there training a customer's operators. They service a product frequently throughout its life, carefully monitoring a machine's health and scheduling repairs to prevent costly downtime. The customer . . . knows that there is a $20-billion-plus company called Caterpillar. But the dealers create the image of a company that doesn't just stand *behind* its products but *with* its products, anywhere in the world. Our dealers are the reason that our motto—Buy the Iron, Get the Company—is not an empty slogan.

Caterpillar's dealers build strong customer relationships in their communities. "Our independent dealer in Novi, Michigan, or in Bangkok, Thailand, knows so much more about the requirements of customers in those locations than a huge corporation like Caterpillar could," says Fites. Competitors often bypass their dealers and sell directly to big customers to cut costs or make more profits for themselves. However, Caterpillar wouldn't think of going around its dealers. "The knowledge of the local market and the close relations with customers that our dealers provide are worth every penny," he asserts with passion. "We'd rather cut off our right arm than sell directly to customers and bypass our dealers."

"Buy the Iron, Get the Company"—that's a powerful value proposition. It means that when you buy Cat equipment, you become a member of the Caterpillar family. Caterpillar and its dealers work in close harmony to find better ways to bring value to customers. The entire system is linked by a single worldwide computer network. For example, working at their desktop computers, Caterpillar managers can check to see how many Cat machines in the world are waiting for parts. Closely linked dealers play a vital role in almost every aspect of Caterpillar's operations, from product design and delivery, to product service and support, to market intelligence and customer feedback.

In the heavy-equipment industry, in which equipment downtime can mean big losses, Caterpillar's exceptional service gives it a huge advantage in winning and keeping customers. Consider Freeport-McMoRan, a Cat customer that operates one of the world's largest copper and gold mines, 24 hours a day, 365 days a year. High in the mountains of Indonesia, the mine is accessible only by aerial cableway or helicopter. Freeport-McMoRan relies on more than 500 pieces of Caterpillar mining and construction equipment—worth several hundred million dollars—including loaders, tractors, and mammoth 240-ton, 2,000-plus-horsepower trucks. Many of these machines cost well over $1 million apiece. When equipment breaks down, Freeport-McMoRan loses money fast. Freeport-McMoRan gladly pays a premium price for machines and service it can count on. It knows that it can count on Caterpillar and its outstanding distribution network for superb support.

The close working relationship between Caterpillar and its dealers comes down to more than just formal contracts and business agreements. The powerful partnership rests on a handful of basic principles and practices:

■ *Dealer profitability:* Caterpillar's rule: "Share the gain as well as the pain." When times are good, Caterpillar shares the bounty with its dealers rather than trying to grab all the riches for itself. When times are bad, Caterpillar protects its dealers. In the mid-1980s, facing a depressed global construction-equipment market and cutthroat competition, Caterpillar sheltered its dealers by absorbing much of the economic damage. It lost almost $1 billion dollars in just three years but didn't lose a single dealer. In contrast, competitors' dealers struggled and many failed. As a result, Caterpillar emerged with its distribution system intact and its competitive position stronger than ever.

- *Extraordinary dealer support:* Nowhere is this support more apparent than in the company's parts-delivery system, the fastest and most reliable in the industry. Caterpillar maintains 36 distribution centers and 1,500 service facilities around the world, which stock 320,000 different parts and ship 84,000 items per day, every day of the year. In turn, dealers have made huge investments in inventory, warehouses, fleets of trucks, service bays, diagnostic and service equipment, and information technology. Together, Caterpillar and its dealers guarantee parts delivery within 48 hours anywhere in the world. The company ships 80 percent of parts orders immediately and 99 percent on the same day the order is received. In contrast, it's not unusual for competitors' customers to wait four or five days for a part.

- *Communications:* Caterpillar communicates with its dealers—fully, frequently, and honestly. According to Fites, "There are no secrets between us and our dealers. We have the financial statements and key operating data of every dealer in the world. . . . In addition, virtually all Caterpillar and dealer employees have real-time access to continually updated databases of service information, sales trends and forecasts, customer satisfaction surveys, and other critical data. . . . [Moreover,] virtually everyone from the youngest design engineer to the CEO now has direct contact with somebody in our dealer organizations."

- *Dealer performance:* Caterpillar does all it can to ensure that its dealerships are run well. It closely monitors each dealership's sales, market position, service capability, financial situation, and other performance measures. It genuinely wants each dealer to succeed, and when it sees a problem, it jumps in to help. As a result, Caterpillar dealerships, many of which are family businesses, tend to be stable and profitable. The average Caterpillar dealership has remained in the hands of the same family for more than 50 years. Some actually predate the 1925 merger that created Caterpillar.

- *Personal relationships:* In addition to more formal business ties, Cat forms close personal ties with its dealers in a kind of family relationship. One Caterpillar executive relates the following example: "When I see Chappy Chapman, a retired executive vice-president . . . out on the golf course, he always asks about particular dealers or about their children, who may be running the business now. And every time I see those dealers, they inquire, 'How's Chappy?' That's the sort of relationship we have. . . . I consider the majority of dealers personal friends."

Thus, Caterpillar's superb distribution system serves as a major source of competitive advantage. The system is built on a firm base of mutual trust and shared dreams. Caterpillar and its dealers feel a deep pride in what they are accomplishing together. As Fites puts it, "There's a camaraderie among our dealers around the world that really makes it more than just a financial arrangement. They feel that what they're doing is good for the world because they are part of an organization that makes, sells, and tends to the machines that make the world work."[1]

Most firms cannot bring value to customers by themselves. Instead, they must work closely with other firms in a larger value delivery network.

■ Supply Chains and the Value Delivery Network

Producing a product or service and making it available to buyers requires building relationships not just with customers, but also with key suppliers and resellers in the company's *supply chain.* This supply chain consists of "upstream" and "downstream" partners, including suppliers, intermediaries, and even intermediaries' customers.

Upstream from the manufacturer or service provider is the set of firms that supply the raw materials, components, parts, information, finances, and expertise needed to create a product or service. Marketers, however, have traditionally focused on the "downstream" side of the supply chain—on the *marketing channels* or *distribution channels* that look forward toward the customer. Marketing channel partners such as wholesalers and retailers form a vital connection between the firm and its target consumers.

Both upstream and downstream partners may also be part of other firms' supply chains. But it is the unique design of each company's supply chain that enables it to deliver superior value to customers. An individual firm's success depends not only on how well *it* performs but also on how well its entire supply chain and marketing channel competes with competitors' channels.

The term *supply chain* may be too limited—it takes a *make-and-sell* view of the business. It suggests that raw materials, productive inputs, and factory capacity should serve as the starting point for market planning. A better term would be *demand chain* because it suggests a *sense-and-respond* view of the market. Under this view, planning starts with the needs of target customers, to which the company responds by organizing resources with the goal of building profitable customer relationships.

Even a demand-chain view of a business may be too limited, because it takes a step-by-step linear view of purchase–production–consumption activities. With the advent of the Internet and other technologies, however, companies are forming more numerous and complex relationships with other firms. For example, Ford manages numerous supply chains. It also sponsors or transacts on many B2B Web sites and online purchasing exchanges as needs arise. Like Ford, most large companies today are engaged in building and managing a continuously evolving *value delivery network.*

Companies today are increasingly taking a full-value-delivery-network view of their businesses. As defined in Chapter 2, a **value delivery network** is made up of the company, suppliers, distributors, and ultimately customers who "partner" with each other to improve the performance of the entire system. For example, Palm, the leading manufacturer of handheld devices, manages a whole community of suppliers and assemblers of semiconductor components, plastic cases, LCD displays, and accessories. Its network also includes offline and online resellers, and 45,000 complementors who have created over 5,000 applications for the Palm operating systems. All of these diverse partners must work effectively together to bring superior value to Palm's customers.

This chapter focuses on marketing channels—on the downstream side of the value delivery network. However, it is important to remember that this is only part of the full value network. To bring value to customers, companies need upstream supplier partners just as they need downstream channel partners. To provide banking services, for example, Citibank buys equipment and supplies such as automated teller machines (ATMs), printed deposit slips, and computers. To make its services available to customers and obtain information about customer transactions, the bank maintains a distribution channel consisting of company-owned bank branches and Web sites as well as thousands of ATMs owned by other banks. Increasingly, marketers are participating in and influencing their company's upstream activities as well as its downstream activities. More than marketing channel managers, they are becoming full network managers.

Value delivery network
A network made up of the company, suppliers, distributors, and ultimately customers who "partner" with each other to improve the performance of the entire system.

mp3 player
camera
appointment reminder

The Palm™ Zire™ 71 handheld. Perfect in so many ways. Only $299.** Visit palmOne.com.

Zire 71

■ Value delivery network: Palm manages a whole community of suppliers, assemblers, resellers, and complementors who must work effectively together to make life easier for Palm's customers.

This chapter examines four major questions concerning marketing channels: What is the nature of marketing channels and why are they important? How do channel firms interact and organize to do the work of the channel? What problems do companies face in designing and managing their channels? What role do physical distribution and supply chain management play in attracting and satisfying customers? In Chapter 11, we will look at marketing channel issues from the viewpoint of retailers and wholesalers.

The Nature and Importance of Marketing Channels

Few producers sell their goods directly to the final users. Instead, most use intermediaries to bring their products to market. They try to forge a **marketing channel** (or **distribution channel**)—a set of interdependent organizations involved in the process of making a product or service available for use or consumption by the consumer or business user.[2]

A company's channel decisions directly affect every other marketing decision. The company's pricing depends on whether it works with national discount chains, uses high-quality specialty stores, or sells directly to consumers via the Web. The firm's sales force and communications decisions depend on how much persuasion, training, motivation, and support its channel partners need. Whether a company develops or acquires certain new products may depend on how well those products fit the capabilities of its channel members.

Companies often pay too little attention to their distribution channels, sometimes with damaging results. In contrast, many companies have used imaginative distribution systems to *gain* a competitive advantage. FedEx's creative and imposing distribution system made it a leader in the small-package delivery industry. Dell Computer revolutionized its industry by selling personal computers directly to consumers rather than through retail stores. And Charles Schwab & Company pioneered the delivery of financial services via the Internet.

Distribution channel decisions often involve long-term commitments to other firms. For example, companies such as Ford, IBM, and McDonald's can easily change their advertising, pricing, or promotion programs. They can scrap old products and introduce new ones as market tastes demand. But when they set up distribution channels through contracts with franchisees, independent dealers, or large retailers, they cannot readily replace these channels with company-owned stores or Web sites if conditions change. Therefore, management must design its channels carefully, with an eye on tomorrow's likely selling environment as well as today's.

How Channel Members Add Value

Why do producers give some of the selling job to channel partners? After all, doing so means giving up some control over how and to whom the products are sold. The use of intermediaries results from their greater efficiency in making goods available to target markets. Through their contacts, experience, specialization, and scale of operation, intermediaries usually offer the firm more than it can achieve on its own.

Figure 10.1 shows how using intermediaries can provide economies. Figure 10.1A shows three manufacturers, each using direct marketing to reach three customers. This system requires nine different contacts. Figure 10.1B shows the three manufacturers working through one distributor, which contacts the three customers. This system requires only six contacts. In this way, intermediaries reduce the amount of work that must be done by both producers and consumers.

Marketing channel (distribution channel)
A set of interdependent organizations involved in the process of making a product or service available for use or consumption by the consumer or business user.

■ FedEx's creative and imposing distribution system made it a market leader in express delivery.

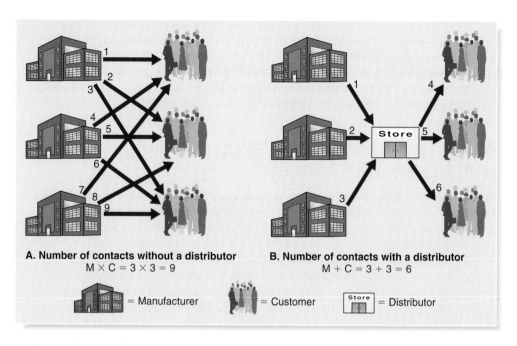

A. Number of contacts without a distributor
$M \times C = 3 \times 3 = 9$

B. Number of contacts with a distributor
$M + C = 3 + 3 = 6$

= Manufacturer   = Customer   = Distributor

FIGURE 10.1

How a Distributor Reduces the Number of Channel Transactions

From the economic system's point of view, the role of marketing intermediaries is to transform the assortments of products made by producers into the assortments wanted by consumers. Producers make narrow assortments of products in large quantities, but consumers want broad assortments of products in small quantities. In the marketing channels, intermediaries buy large quantities from many producers and break them down into the smaller quantities and broader assortments wanted by consumers. Thus, intermediaries play an important role in matching supply and demand.

In making products and services available to consumers, channel members add value by bridging the major time, place, and possession gaps that separate goods and services from those who would use them. Members of the marketing channel perform many key functions. Some help to complete transactions:

- *Information:* Gathering and distributing marketing research and intelligence information about actors and forces in the marketing environment needed for planning and aiding exchange.

- *Promotion:* Developing and spreading persuasive communications about an offer.

- *Contact:* Finding and communicating with prospective buyers.

- *Matching:* Shaping and fitting the offer to the buyer's needs, including activities such as manufacturing, grading, assembling, and packaging.

- *Negotiation:* Reaching an agreement on price and other terms of the offer so that ownership or possession can be transferred.

Others help to fulfill the completed transactions:

- *Physical distribution:* Transporting and storing goods.

- *Financing:* Acquiring and using funds to cover the costs of the channel work.

- *Risk taking:* Assuming the risks of carrying out the channel work.

The question is not *whether* these functions need to be performed—they must be—but rather *who* will perform them. To the extent that the manufacturer performs these functions, its costs go up and its prices have to be higher. When some of these functions are shifted to intermediaries, the producer's costs and prices may be lower, but the intermediaries must charge more to cover the costs of their work. In dividing the work of the channel, the various functions should be assigned to the channel members who can add the most value for the cost.

Number of Channel Levels

Companies can design their distribution channels to make products and services available to customers in different ways. Each layer of marketing intermediaries that performs some work in bringing the product and its ownership closer to the final buyer is a **channel level**. Because the producer and the final consumer both perform some work, they are part of every channel.

The *number of intermediary levels* indicates the *length* of a channel. Figure 10.2A shows several consumer distribution channels of different lengths. Channel 1, called a **direct marketing channel**, has no intermediary levels; the company sells directly to consumers. For example, Avon and Amway sell their products door-to-door, through home and office sales parties, and on the Web; L.L. Bean sells clothing direct through mail catalogs, by telephone, and online; and a university sells education on its campus or through distance learning. The remaining channels in Figure 10.2A are **indirect marketing channels**, containing one or more intermediaries.

Figure 10.2B shows some common business distribution channels. The business marketer can use its own sales force to sell directly to business customers. Or it can sell to various types of intermediaries, who in turn sell to these customers. Consumer and business marketing channels with even more levels are sometimes found, but not often. From the producer's point of view, a greater number of levels means less control and greater channel complexity. Moreover, all of the institutions in the channel are connected by several types

Channel level
A layer of intermediaries that performs some work in bringing the product and its ownership closer to the final buyer.

Direct marketing channel
A marketing channel that has no intermediary levels.

Indirect marketing channel
A channel containing one or more intermediary levels.

FIGURE 10.2

Consumer and Business Marketing Channels

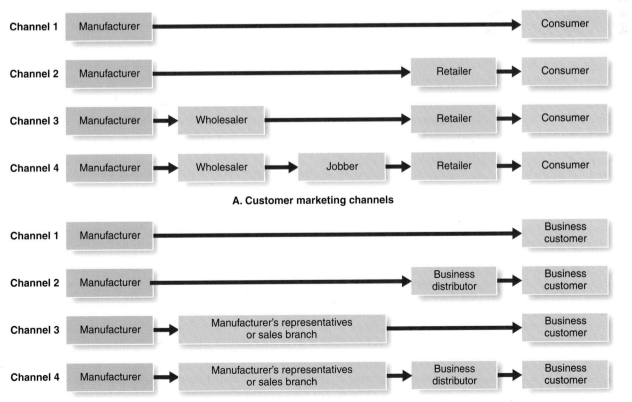

A. Customer marketing channels

B. Business marketing channels

of *flows*. These include the *physical flow* of products, the *flow of ownership*, the *payment flow*, the *information flow*, and the *promotion flow*. These flows can make even channels with only one or a few levels very complex.

■ Channel Behavior and Organization

Distribution channels are more than simple collections of firms tied together by various flows. They are complex behavioral systems in which people and companies interact to accomplish individual, company, and channel goals. Some channel systems consist only of informal interactions among loosely organized firms. Others consist of formal interactions guided by strong organizational structures. Moreover, channel systems do not stand still—new types of intermediaries emerge and whole new channel systems evolve. Here we look at channel behavior and at how members organize to do the work of the channel.

Channel Behavior

A marketing channel consists of firms that have partnered for their common good. Each channel member depends on the others. For example, a Ford dealer depends on Ford to design cars that meet consumer needs. In turn, Ford depends on the dealer to attract consumers, persuade them to buy Ford cars, and service cars after the sale. The Ford dealer also depends on other dealers to provide good sales and service that will uphold the brand's reputation. In fact, the success of individual Ford dealers depends on how well the entire Ford marketing channel competes with the channels of other auto manufacturers.

Each channel member plays a specialized role in the channel. For example, Sony's role is to produce personal consumer electronics products that consumers will like and to create demand through national advertising. Circuit City's role is to display these Sony products in convenient locations, to answer buyers' questions, and to complete sales. The channel will be most effective when each member is assigned the tasks it can do best.

Ideally, because the success of individual channel members depends on overall channel success, all channel firms should work together smoothly. They should understand and accept their roles, coordinate their activities, and cooperate to attain overall channel goals. However, individual channel members rarely take such a broad view. Cooperating to achieve overall channel goals sometimes means giving up individual company goals. Although channel members depend on one another, they often act alone in their own short-run best interests. They often disagree on who should do what and for what rewards. Such disagreements over goals, roles, and rewards generate **channel conflict**.

Channel conflict
Disagreement among marketing channel members on goals and roles—who should do what and for what rewards.

Horizontal conflict occurs among firms at the same level of the channel. For instance, some Ford dealers in Chicago might complain that the other dealers in the city steal sales from them by pricing too low or by selling outside their assigned territories. Or Holiday Inn franchisees might complain about other Holiday Inn operators overcharging guests or giving poor service, hurting the overall Holiday Inn image.

Vertical conflict, conflicts between different levels of the same channel, is even more common. For example, H&R Block franchisees complained when the parent company began using the Internet to deal directly with customers. Similarly, McDonald's created conflict with some of its California dealers when it placed new stores in areas that took business from existing locations. And office furniture maker Herman Miller created conflict with its dealers when it opened an online store—www.hmstore.com—and began selling its products directly to customers. Although Herman Miller believed that the Web site was reaching only smaller customers who weren't being served by current channels, dealers complained loudly. As a result, the company closed down its online sales operations. Tupperware faced similar conflicts with its army of in-home sales consultants—who bring in more than 90 percent of its sales—when it decided to sell its familiar containers at retail through Target stores. However, Tupperware avoided conflict by inviting the in-home consultants into the stores to demonstrate products.[3]

Some conflict in the channel takes the form of healthy competition. Such competition can be good for the channel—without it, the channel could become passive and noninnovative. But severe or prolonged conflict can disrupt channel effectiveness and cause lasting harm to channel relationships. Companies should manage channel conflict to keep it from getting out of hand. Here's an example:

P&G recently moved to manage channel conflict stemming from its change to multichannel distribution for Iams pet products. Traditionally, Iams had been distributed through specialized pet stores and veterinary offices. After studies showed that 70 percent of pet-food buyers never visit pet stores, P&G decided to add 25,000 grocery stores and mass retailers to its channel. To head off conflict with traditional channels, P&G's president wrote to the specialty stores and veterinarians, explaining that the new arrangements would increase brand awareness and not hurt brand equity. Although some pet stores stopped carrying Iams, most continued on, helping Iams boost sales and market share for all of its dealers.[4]

■ Channel conflict: When it decided to sell its familiar containers at retail through Target stores, Tupperware avoided conflicts with its army of in-home sales consultants—who bring in more than 90 percent of its sales—by inviting the in-home consultants into the stores to demonstrate products.

Vertical Marketing Systems

For the channel as a whole to perform well, each channel member's role must be specified and channel conflict must be managed. The channel will perform better if it includes a firm, agency, or mechanism that provides leadership and has the power to assign roles and manage conflict.

Historically, *conventional distribution channels* have lacked such leadership and power, often resulting in damaging conflict and poor performance. One of the biggest channel developments over the years has been the emergence of *vertical marketing systems* that provide channel leadership. Figure 10.3 contrasts the two types of channel arrangements.

A **conventional distribution channel** consists of one or more independent producers, wholesalers, and retailers. Each is a separate business seeking to maximize its own profits, even at the expense of the system as a whole. No channel member has much control over the other members, and no formal means exists for assigning roles and resolving channel conflict. In contrast, a **vertical marketing system (VMS)** consists of producers, wholesalers, and retailers acting as a unified system. One channel member owns the others, has contracts with them, or wields so much power that they must all cooperate. The VMS can be dominated by the producer, wholesaler, or retailer.

We look now at three major types of VMSs: *corporate, contractual,* and *administered.* Each uses a different means for setting up leadership and power in the channel.

Corporate VMS   A **corporate VMS** integrates successive stages of production and distribution under single ownership. Coordination and conflict management are attained through regular organizational channels. For example, Sears obtains more than 50 percent of its goods from companies that it partly or wholly owns. Giant Food Stores operates an ice-making facility, a soft drink bottling operation, an ice cream plant, and a bakery that supplies Giant stores with everything from bagels to birthday cakes. And little-known Italian eyewear maker Luxottica produces many famous eyewear brands—including Ray-Ban, Vogue, Anne Klein, Ferragamo, and Armani. It sells these brands through two of the world's largest optical chains, LensCrafters and Sunglass Hut, which it also owns.[5]

Controlling the entire distribution chain has turned Spanish clothing chain Zara into the world's fastest-growing fashion retailer.

Conventional distribution channel
A channel consisting of one or more independent producers, wholesalers, and retailers, each a separate business seeking to maximize its own profits even at the expense of profits for the system as a whole.

Vertical marketing system (VMS)
A distribution channel structure in which producers, wholesalers, and retailers act as a unified system. One channel member owns the others, has contracts with them, or has so much power that they all cooperate.

Corporate VMS
A vertical marketing system that combines successive stages of production and distribution under single ownership—channel leadership is established through common ownership.

FIGURE 10.3
Comparison of Conventional Distribution Channel with Vertical Marketing System

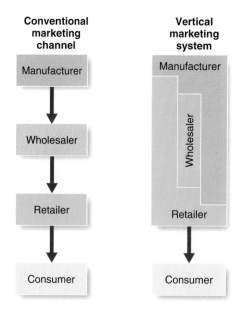

The secret to Zara's success is its control over almost every aspect of the supply chain, from design and production to its own worldwide distribution network. Zara makes 40 percent of its own fabrics and produces more than half of its own clothes, rather than relying on a hodgepodge of slow-moving suppliers. New styles take shape in Zara's own design centers, supported by real-time sales data. New designs feed into Zara manufacturing centers, which ship finished products directly to 600 Zara stores in 30 countries, saving time, eliminating the need for warehouses, and keeping inventories low. Effective vertical integration makes Zara faster, more flexible, and more efficient than international competitors such as Gap, Benetton, and Sweden's H&M. Its finely tuned distribution systems makes Zara seem more like Dell or Wal-Mart than Gucci or Louis Vuitton. Zara can make a new line from start to finish in just three weeks, so a look seen on MTV can be in Zara stores within a month, versus an industry average of nine months. And Zara's low costs let it offer midmarket chic at downmarket prices. The company's stylish but affordable offerings have attracted a cult following, and the company's sales have more than doubled to $2.3 billion in the past five years.[6]

Contractual VMS
A vertical marketing system in which independent firms at different levels of production and distribution join together through contracts to obtain more economies or sales impact than they could achieve alone.

Contractual VMS A **contractual VMS** consists of independent firms at different levels of production and distribution who join together through contracts to obtain more

■ Contractual VMS: An estimated 2,000 franchised U.S. companies with over 320,000 outlets account for some $1 trillion in annual sales.

economies or sales impact than each could achieve alone. Coordination and conflict management are attained through contractual agreements among channel members.

The **franchise organization** is the most common type of contractual relationship—a channel member called a *franchisor* links several stages in the production–distribution process. An estimated 1,600 U.S. franchisors with over 320,000 outlets account for some $1 trillion in annual sales. Industry analysts estimate that a new franchise outlet opens somewhere in the United States every eight minutes and that about 1 of every 12 retail business outlets is a franchised business.[7] Almost every kind of business has been franchised—from motels and fast-food restaurants to dental centers and dating services, from wedding consultants and maid services to fitness centers and funeral homes.

There are three types of franchises. The first type is the *manufacturer-sponsored retailer franchise system*—for example, Ford and its network of independent franchised dealers. The second type is the *manufacturer-sponsored wholesaler franchise system*—Coca-Cola licenses bottlers (wholesalers) in various markets who buy Coca-Cola syrup concentrate and then bottle and sell the finished product to retailers in local markets. The third type is the *service-firm-sponsored retailer franchise system*—examples are found in the auto-rental business (Hertz, Avis), the fast-food service business (McDonald's, Burger King), and the motel business (Holiday Inn, Ramada Inn).

The fact that most consumers cannot tell the difference between contractual and corporate VMSs shows how successfully the contractual organizations compete with corporate chains. Chapter 11 presents a fuller discussion of the various contractual VMSs.

Administered VMS In an **administered VMS**, leadership is assumed not through common ownership or contractual ties but through the size and power of one or a few dominant channel members. Manufacturers of a top brand can obtain strong trade cooperation and support from resellers. For example, General Electric, Procter & Gamble, and Kraft can command unusual cooperation from resellers regarding displays, shelf space, promotions, and price policies. Large retailers such as Wal-Mart, Home Depot, and Barnes & Noble can exert strong influence on the manufacturers that supply the products they sell.

Horizontal Marketing Systems

Another channel development is the **horizontal marketing system**, in which two or more companies at one level join together to follow a new marketing opportunity. By working together, companies can combine their financial, production, or marketing resources to accomplish more than any one company could alone.

Companies might join forces with competitors or noncompetitors. They might work with each other on a temporary or permanent basis, or they may create a separate company. For example, the Lamar Savings Bank of Texas arranged to locate its savings offices and automated teller machines in Safeway stores. Lamar gained quicker market entry at a low cost, and Safeway was able to offer in-store banking convenience to its customers. Similarly, McDonald's now places "express" versions of its restaurants in Wal-Mart stores. McDonald's benefits from Wal-Mart's heavy store traffic, while Wal-Mart keeps hungry shoppers from having to go elsewhere to eat.

Such channel arrangements also work well globally. For example, because of its excellent coverage of international markets, Nestlé jointly sells General Mills's cereal brands in 80 countries outside North America. Coca-Cola and Nestlé formed a joint venture to market ready-to-drink coffee and tea worldwide. Coke provides worldwide experience in marketing and distributing beverages, and Nestlé contributes two established brand names—

Franchise organization
A contractual vertical marketing system in which a channel member, called a franchiser, links several stages in the production–distribution process.

Administered VMS
A vertical marketing system that coordinates successive stages of production and distribution, not through common ownership or contractual ties, but through the size and power of one of the parties.

Horizontal marketing system
A channel arrangement in which two or more companies at one level join together to follow a new marketing opportunity.

The perfect handful for your little handful.

Made from four healthy whole grains-corn, oats, rice and wheat-Cheerios are the perfect choice for growing families. Small and round, they make ideal finger food for toddlers too. **There's a whole lot of good in those little 'o's.**

■ Horizontal marketing systems: Nestlé jointly sells General Mills cereal brands in markets outside North America.

Nescafé and Nestea. Seiko Watch's distribution partner in Japan, K. Hattori, markets Schick's razors there, giving Schick the leading market share in Japan, despite Gillette's overall strength in many other markets.[8]

Multichannel Distribution Systems

Multichannel distribution system
A distribution system in which a single firm sets up two or more marketing channels to reach one or more customer segments.

In the past, many companies used a single channel to sell to a single market or market segment. Today, with the proliferation of customer segments and channel possibilities, more and more companies have adopted **multichannel distribution systems**—often called *hybrid marketing channels*. Such multichannel marketing occurs when a single firm sets up two or more marketing channels to reach one or more customer segments. The use of multichannel systems has increased greatly in recent years.

Figure 10.4 shows a hybrid channel. In the figure, the producer sells directly to consumer segment 1 using direct-mail catalogs, telemarketing, and the Internet and reaches consumer segment 2 through retailers. It sells indirectly to business segment 1 through distributors and dealers and to business segment 2 through its own sales force.

These days, almost every large company and many small ones distribute through multiple channels. Charles Schwab reaches customers by telephone, over the Internet, and through its branch offices. It invites its customer to "call, click, or visit" Schwab. Staples markets through its traditional retail outlets, a direct-response Internet site, virtual malls, and 30,000 links on affiliated sites.

IBM uses multiple channels to serve dozens of segments and niches, ranging from large corporate buyers to small businesses to home office buyers. In addition to selling through its vaunted sales force, IBM also sells through a full network of distributors and value-added resellers, which sell IBM computers, systems, and services to a variety of special business segments. Final consumers can buy IBM personal computers from specialty computer stores or any of several large retailers. IBM uses telemarketing to service the needs of small and medium-size businesses. And both business and final consumers can buy online from the company's Web site (www.ibm.com).

Multichannel distribution systems offer many advantages to companies facing large and complex markets. With each new channel, the company expands its sales and market coverage and gains opportunities to tailor its products and services to the specific needs of diverse customer segments. But such multichannel distribution systems are harder to control, and they generate conflict as more channels compete for customers and sales. For example, when IBM began selling directly to customers through telemarketing and its own Web site, many of its retail dealers cried "unfair competition" and threatened to drop the IBM line or to give it less emphasis. Many outside salespeople felt that they were being undercut by the new "inside channels."

FIGURE 10.4

Hybrid Marketing Channel

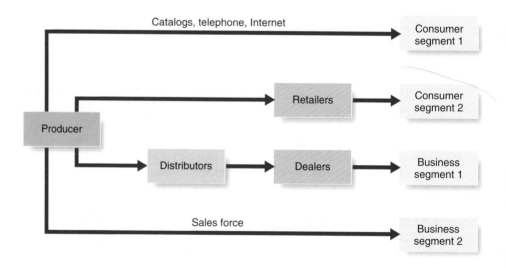

Changing Channel Organization

Changes in technology and the explosive growth of direct and online marketing are having a profound impact on the nature and design of marketing channels. One major trend is toward **disintermediation**—a big term with a clear message and important consequences. Disintermediation means that more and more, product and service producers are bypassing intermediaries and going directly to final buyers, or that radically new types of channel intermediaries are emerging to displace traditional ones.

Thus, in many industries, traditional intermediaries are dropping by the wayside. For example, companies such as Dell Computer and American Airlines are selling directly to final buyers, eliminating retailers from their marketing channels. E-commerce is growing rapidly, taking business from traditional brick-and-mortar retailers. Consumers can buy Flowers from 1-800-Flowers.com; books, videos, CDs, toys, consumer electronics, and other goods from Amazon.com; and clothes from llbean.com or gap.com, all without ever visiting a store.

Disintermediation presents problems and opportunities for both producers and intermediaries (see Marketing at Work 10.1). To avoid being swept aside, traditional intermediaries must find new ways to add value in the supply chain. To remain competitive, product and service producers must develop new channel opportunities, such as Internet and other direct channels. However, developing these new channels often brings them into direct competition with their established channels, resulting in conflict.

To ease this problem, companies often look for ways to make going direct a plus for both the company and its channel partners. For example, to trim costs and add business, Hewlett-Packard opened three direct-sales Web sites—Shopping Village (for consumers), H-P Commerce Center (for businesses buying from authorized resellers), and Electronic Solutions Now (for existing contract customers). However, to avoid conflicts with its established reseller channels, HP forwards all its Web orders to resellers, who complete the orders, ship the products, and get the commissions. In this way, HP gains the advantages of direct selling but also boosts business for resellers.

Disintermediation

The displacement of traditional resellers from a marketing channel by radical new types of intermediaries.

Stop here for a moment and apply the distribution channel concepts we've discussed so far.

- Compare the Caterpillar and IBM channels. Draw a diagram that shows the types of intermediaries in each channel. What kind of channel system does each company use?
- What are the roles and responsibilities of the members in each channel? How well do these channel members work together toward overall channel success?

▪▪ Channel Design Decisions

We now look at several channel decisions manufacturers face. In designing marketing channels, manufacturers struggle between what is ideal and what is practical. A new firm with limited capital usually starts by selling in a limited market area. Deciding on the best channels might not be a problem: The problem might simply be how to convince one or a few good intermediaries to handle the line.

If successful, the new firm might branch out to new markets through the existing intermediaries. In smaller markets, the firm might sell directly to retailers; in larger markets, it might sell through distributors. In one part of the country, it might grant exclusive franchises; in another, it might sell through all available outlets. Then, it might add a Web store that sells directly to hard-to-reach customers. In this way, channel systems often evolve to meet market opportunities and conditions.

Disintermediation: A Fancy Word but a Clear Message

Sunflower Travel of Wichita, Kansas, typifies the kind of business most threatened by the advent of new marketing channels, particularly the surge in Internet selling. Like other traditional travel agencies, Sunflower faces some scary new-age competitors. In recent years, it has seen a flurry of online competitors—ranging from giant travel supersites such as Expedia, Travelocity, Priceline, Hotels.com, and Orbitz to newcomers like Trip.com and Hotwire.com—that let consumers surf the Web for rock-bottom travel deals. To make matters worse, the airlines themselves now sell more than half of their own tickets online and no longer pay travel agencies commissions on ticket sales.

These new channels give consumers more choices, but they threaten the very existence of Sunflower Travel and other traditional travel agents. Since the mid-1990s, the number of U.S. travel agents has dropped by 25 percent, and some studies suggest that another 25 percent will go out of business during the next few years.

Resellers in dozens of industries face similar situations as new channel forms threaten to make them obsolete. There's even a fancy 17-letter word to describe this phenomenon: *disintermediation*. Strictly speaking, disintermediation means the elimination of a layer of intermediaries from a marketing channel. For example, for years personal computer makers assumed that customers needed hands-on buying experience, with lots of point-of-sale inventory and hand-holding sales assistance from retailers. Then, along came Dell Computer with its direct model. By eliminating retailers, Dell eliminated many costs and inefficiencies from the traditional computer supply chain.

More broadly, disintermediation includes not only the elimination of channel levels through direct marketing but also the displacement of traditional resellers by radically new types of intermediaries. For example, the publishing industry had for decades assumed that book buyers wanted to purchase their books from small, intimate, neighborhood

bookshops. Then, along came the book superstores—Barnes & Noble and Borders—with their huge inventories and low prices. Disintermediation occurred as the new intermediaries rapidly displaced traditional independent booksellers. Then online bookseller Amazon.com emerged to threaten the category killers. Amazon.com doesn't eliminate the retail channel—it's actually a new type of retailer that increases consumers' channel choices rather than reducing them. Still, disintermediation has occurred as Amazon.com and the superstores' own

Web sites are displacing traditional brick-and-mortar retailers.

Disintermediation is often associated with the surge in online selling. And, in fact, the Internet is a major disintermediating force. By facilitating direct contact between buyers and sellers, the Internet is displacing channels in industries ranging from books, apparel, and consumer electronics to travel, stock brokerage, and real estate services. However, disintermediation can involve almost any new form of channel competition. For example, Dell bypassed retailers through tele-

Disintermediation: Travel supersites such as Expedia, Travelocity, Priceline, Hotels.com, and Orbitz have threatened the very existence of traditional travel agents.

phone and mail-order selling long before it took to the Internet.

Disintermediation works only when a new channel form succeeds in bringing greater value to consumers. Thus, if Amazon.com weren't giving buyers greater convenience, selection, and value, it wouldn't be able to lure customers away from traditional retailers. If Dell's direct channel weren't more efficient and effective in serving the needs of computer buyers, traditional retail channels would have little to fear. However, the success of these new channels suggests that they *are* bringing greater value to significant segments of consumers.

From a producer's viewpoint, although eliminating unneeded intermediaries makes sense, disintermediation can be very difficult. One analyst summarizes it this way:

You thought e-commerce would bring nothing but good news. Here at last, you reasoned, is a way to add customers, boost market share, and cut sales costs. All manufacturers have to do is set up an electronic conduit between themselves and their customers and voilá, instant sales channel. There's just one little hitch. Those same thoughts terrify the retailers, distributors, and resellers that account for up to 90 percent of manufacturers' revenues. They fear that their role between company and customer will be rendered obsolete by the virtual marketplace. And that puts manufacturers in a bind. Either they surrender to the seductions of e-commerce and risk a mutiny from those valuable partners, or they do nothing and risk the wrath of [successful e-commerce competitors].

Thus, although bypassing channel intermediaries can help a company compete, it also may create conflict with the established channel partners that most companies count on for the bulk of their sales.

Still, most producers know that when more-effective channels come along, they have no choice but to change. Despite the risks, most companies are more afraid of being late to the party than of angering their channel partners. The major question often is

not whether to move to a new, high-growth channel but how quickly to do it and what to do with the established channel. One answer is to join forces with channel partners so that both benefit from new channel opportunities. For example, consider Maytag:

Appliance giant Maytag wanted to leverage its powerful brand name and great quality reputation by selling appliances on the Web. Maytag's goal was to sell to customers without forcing them to travel to a dealer, where they might be seduced by other brands. However, Maytag didn't want to damage its relationships with the thousands of dealers around the country that sell the bulk of its appliances. The solution was to help dealers close sales online. The company created My Maytag, a feature on its main Web site, by which customers could learn about and purchase Maytag products. But rather than filling the orders directly, the company handed them off to dealers. With My Maytag, everyone wins: Online consumers get a convenient and seamless shopping experience, dealers get the sales, and Maytag avoids channel conflict and boosts its business.

What about traditional resellers? How can they avoid being "Delled" or "Amazoned"? The answer lies in continually looking for new ways to create real customer value. For example, Sunflower Travel now works at adding value in ways that online competitors can't—by getting to know consumers and specializing in market niches. It has even turned the Web from foe to friend by using it as a tool for ferreting out new customers and serving them better.

To meet the Internet threat, Sunflower began focusing on packaged tours in the South Pacific, an area that owner Barbara Hansen loves and has traveled to extensively. She established a strong business relationship with a wholesaler who works in Australia and New Zealand, and began promoting packaged tours. In addition to her Sunflower Web site, she launched a new one: ANZtours.com. She made certain that the New Zealand Tourist Office in

New York had a link to her site. To put together tour groups, Hansen began scouring Web sites for wine stores, sending them information about food and wine tours through Australia. She's been in touch with garden clubs and florists, and is selling a package tour to Canberra, Australia's "Floriade," a horticultural show. She knows the music director for a local chamber group who hails from New Zealand, and is making him part of a tour of musical performances Down Under. "The Internet is so neat," she says, "You can go and search for these groups, and let them know what you are doing." The lesson: New technologies can put entire industries out of business. But the same technologies open doors, too, for entrepreneurs with the courage to walk through them.

Discount brokerage Charles Schwab also proves the value point. Facing a horde of price-cutting e-commerce competitors who got there first—including E*Trade and Ameritrade—Schwab jumped into the Internet with both feet. However, instead of becoming just another no-frills Internet trading operation, Schwab did competitors one better. It plied customers with a wealth of tools and information for managing their accounts, assuming the role of an investment adviser. Rather than dragging its feet or fighting the change, Schwab embraced the new channel as a competitive opportunity.

Thus, disintermediation is a big word but the meaning is clear. Those who continually seek new ways to add real value for customers have little to fear. However, those who fall behind in adding value risk being swept aside by their customers and channel partners.

Sources: Extracts adapted from Rochelle Garner, "Mad as Hell," *Sales & Marketing Management*, June 1999, pp. 55–61; Maricris G. Briones, "What Technology Wrought: Distribution Channel in Flux," *Marketing News*, February 1, 1999, pp. 3, 15; Barb Gomolski, "No Channel Conflict," *InfoWorld*, July 9, 2001, p. 10; and Paulette Thomas, "Case Study: Travel Agency Meets Technology's Threats," *Wall Street Journal*, May 21, 2002, p. B4. Additional information from Ted Kemp, "Beware the Pitfalls of Bypassing the Channel," *B to B*, February 11, 2002, pp. 1, 28; Barry Estabrook, "Agents' Survival Strategy," *The New York Times*, November 24, 2003, p. 5.6; and www.anztours.com, July 2003.

For maximum effectiveness, however, channel analysis and decision making should be more purposeful. Designing a channel system calls for analyzing consumer needs, setting channel objectives, identifying major channel alternatives, and evaluating them.

Analyzing Consumer Needs

As noted previously, marketing channels are part of the overall *customer value delivery network*. Each channel member adds value for the customer. Thus, designing the marketing channel starts with finding out what target consumers want from the channel. Do consumers want to buy from nearby locations or are they willing to travel to more distant centralized locations? Would they rather buy in person, over the phone, through the mail, or via the Internet? Do they value breadth of assortment or do they prefer specialization? Do consumers want many add-on services (delivery, credit, repairs, installation), or will they obtain these elsewhere? The faster the delivery, the greater the assortment provided, and the more add-on services supplied, the greater the channel's service level.

Providing the fastest delivery, greatest assortment, and most services may not be possible or practical. The company and its channel members may not have the resources or skills needed to provide all the desired services. Also, providing higher levels of service results in higher costs for the channel and higher prices for consumers. The company must balance consumer needs not only against the feasibility and costs of meeting these needs but also against customer price preferences. The success of discount retailing—on and off the Web—shows that consumers will often accept lower service levels in exchange for lower prices.

Setting Channel Objectives

Companies should state their marketing channel objectives in terms of targeted levels of customer service. Usually, a company can identify several segments wanting different levels of service. The company should decide which segments to serve and the best channels to use in each case. In each segment, the company wants to minimize the total channel cost of meeting customer service requirements.

The company's channel objectives are also influenced by the nature of the company, its products, its marketing intermediaries, its competitors, and the environment. For example, the company's size and financial situation determine which marketing functions it can handle itself and which it must give to intermediaries. Companies selling perishable products may require more direct marketing to avoid delays and too much handling.

In some cases, a company may want to compete in or near the same outlets that carry competitors' products. In other cases, producers may avoid the channels used by competitors. Avon and Mary Kay Cosmetics, for example, use door-to-door selling rather than going head-to-head with other cosmetics makers for scarce positions in retail stores. And GEICO markets auto insurance directly to consumers via the telephone and Web rather than through agents. Finally, environmental factors such as economic conditions and legal constraints may affect channel objectives and design. For example, in a depressed economy, producers want to distribute their goods in the most economical way, using shorter channels and dropping unneeded services that add to the final price of the goods.

Identifying Major Alternatives

When the company has defined its channel objectives, it should next identify its major channel alternatives in terms of *types* of intermediaries, the *number* of intermediaries, and the *responsibilities* of each channel member.

Types of Intermediaries A firm should identify the types of channel members available to carry out its channel work. For example, suppose a manufacturer of test equipment has developed an audio device that detects poor mechanical connections in machines with

moving parts. Company executives think this product would have a market in all industries in which electric, combustion, or steam engines are made or used. The company's current sales force is small, and the problem is how best to reach these different industries. The following channel alternatives might emerge from management discussion:

Company sales force: Expand the company's direct sales force. Assign outside salespeople to territories and have them contact all prospects in the area or develop separate company sales forces for different industries. Or, add an inside telesales operation in which telephone salespeople handle small or midsize companies.

Manufacturer's agency: Hire manufacturer's agents—independent firms whose sales forces handle related products from many companies—in different regions or industries to sell the new test equipment.

Industrial distributors: Find distributors in the different regions or industries who will buy and carry the new line. Give them exclusive distribution, good margins, product training, and promotional support.

Number of Marketing Intermediaries   Companies must also determine the number of channel members to use at each level. Three strategies are available: intensive distribution, exclusive distribution, and selective distribution. Producers of convenience products and common raw materials typically seek **intensive distribution**—a strategy in which they stock their products in as many outlets as possible. These goods must be available where and when consumers want them. For example, toothpaste, candy, and other similar items are sold in millions of outlets to provide maximum brand exposure and consumer convenience. Kraft, Coca-Cola, Kimberly-Clark, and other consumer goods companies distribute their products in this way.

By contrast, some producers purposely limit the number of intermediaries handling their products. The extreme form of this practice is **exclusive distribution**, in which the producer gives only a limited number of dealers the exclusive right to distribute its products in their territories. Exclusive distribution is often found in the distribution of new automobiles and prestige women's clothing. For example, Bentley retailers are few and far between—even large cities may have only one retailer. By granting exclusive distribution, Bentley gains stronger distributor selling support and more control over retailer prices, promotion, credit, and services. Exclusive distribution also enhances the car's image and allows for higher markups.

Intensive distribution
Stocking the product in as many outlets as possible.

Exclusive distribution
Giving a limited number of dealers the exclusive right to distribute the company's products in their territories.

■ Exclusive distribution: Luxury car makers sell exclusively through a limited number of dealerships. Such limited distribution enhances the car's image and generates stronger dealer support.

Selective distribution

The use of more than one, but fewer than all, of the intermediaries who are willing to carry the company's products.

Between intensive and exclusive distribution lies **selective distribution**—the use of more than one, but fewer than all, of the intermediaries who are willing to carry a company's products. Most television, furniture, and small-appliance brands are distributed in this manner. For example, KitchenAid, Maytag, Whirlpool, and General Electric sell their major appliances through dealer networks and selected large retailers. By using selective distribution, they do not have to spread their efforts over many outlets, including many marginal ones. They can develop good working relationships with selected channel members and expect a better-than-average selling effort. Selective distribution gives producers good market coverage with more control and less cost than does intensive distribution.

Responsibilities of Channel Members
The producer and intermediaries need to agree on the terms and responsibilities of each channel member. They should agree on price policies, conditions of sale, territorial rights, and specific services to be performed by each party. The producer should establish a list price and a fair set of discounts for intermediaries. It must define each channel member's territory, and it should be careful about where it places new resellers.

Mutual services and duties need to be spelled out carefully, especially in franchise and exclusive distribution channels. For example, McDonald's provides franchisees with promotional support, a record-keeping system, training at Hamburger University, and general management assistance. In turn, franchisees must meet company standards for physical facilities, cooperate with new promotion programs, provide requested information, and buy specified food products.

Evaluating the Major Alternatives

Suppose a company has identified several channel alternatives and wants to select the one that will best satisfy its long-run objectives. Each alternative should be evaluated against economic, control, and adaptive criteria.

Using *economic criteria*, a company compares the likely sales, costs, and profitability of different channel alternatives. What will be the investment required by each channel alternative, and what returns will result? The company must also consider *control issues*. Using intermediaries usually means giving them some control over the marketing of the product, and some intermediaries take more control than others. Other things being equal, the company prefers to keep as much control as possible. Finally, the company must apply *adaptive criteria*. Channels often involve long-term commitments, yet the company wants to keep the channel flexible so that it can adapt to environmental changes. Thus, to be considered, a channel involving long-term commitments should be greatly superior on economic and control grounds.

Designing International Distribution Channels

International marketers face many additional complexities in designing their channels. Each country has its own unique distribution system that has evolved over time and changes very slowly. These channel systems can vary widely from country to country. Thus, global marketers must usually adapt their channel strategies to the existing structures within each country.

In some markets, the distribution system is complex and hard to penetrate, consisting of many layers and large numbers of intermediaries. Consider Japan:

The Japanese distribution system stems from the early seventeenth century when cottage industries and a [quickly growing] urban population spawned a merchant class. . . . Despite Japan's economic achievements, the distribution system has remained remarkably faithful to its antique pattern. . . . [It] encompasses a wide range of wholesalers and other agents, brokers, and retailers, differing more in number than in function from their American counterparts. There are myriad tiny retail shops. An even greater number of wholesalers supplies goods to them, layered tier upon tier, many more than most U.S. executives would think necessary. For example, soap may move through three wholesalers plus a sales company after it leaves

■ The Japanese distribution system has remained remarkably traditional. A profusion of tiny retail shops are supplied by an even greater number of small wholesalers.

the manufacturer before it ever reaches the retail outlet. A steak goes from rancher to consumers in a process that often involves a dozen middle agents. . . . The distribution network . . . reflects the traditionally close ties among many Japanese companies . . . [and places] much greater emphasis on personal relationships with users. . . . Although [these channels appear] inefficient and cumbersome, they seem to serve the Japanese customer well. . . . Lacking much storage space in their small homes, most Japanese homemakers shop several times a week and prefer convenient [and more personal] neighborhood shops.[9]

Many Western firms have had great difficulty breaking into the closely knit, tradition-bound Japanese distribution network.

At the other extreme, distribution systems in developing countries may be scattered and inefficient, or altogether lacking. For example, China and India would appear to be huge markets, each with populations over 1 billion. In reality, however, these markets are much smaller than the population numbers suggest. Because of inadequate distribution systems in both countries, most companies can profitably access only a small portion of the population located in each country's most affluent cities. China's distribution system is so fragmented that logistics costs amount to 15 percent of the nation's GDP, far higher than in most other countries.[10]

Thus, international marketers face a wide range of channel alternatives. Designing efficient and effective channel systems between and within various country markets poses a difficult challenge. We discuss international distribution decisions further in Chapter 15.

■ Channel Management Decisions

Once the company has reviewed its channel alternatives and decided on the best channel design, it must implement and manage the chosen channel. Channel management calls for selecting, managing, and motivating individual channel members and evaluating their performance over time.

Selecting Channel Members

Producers vary in their ability to attract qualified marketing intermediaries. Some producers have no trouble signing up channel members. For example, when Toyota first introduced its Lexus line in the United States, it had no trouble attracting new dealers. In fact, it had to turn down many would-be resellers. In some cases, the promise of exclusive or selective distribution for a desirable product will draw plenty of applicants.

At the other extreme are producers who have to work hard to line up enough qualified intermediaries. When Polaroid started, for example, it could not get photography stores to carry its new cameras, and it had to go to mass-merchandising outlets. Similarly, when the U.S. Time Company first tried to sell its inexpensive Timex watches through regular jewelry stores, most jewelry stores refused to carry them. The company then managed to get its watches into mass-merchandise outlets. This turned out to be a wise decision because of the rapid growth of mass merchandising.

When selecting intermediaries, the company should determine what characteristics distinguish the better ones. It will want to evaluate each channel member's years in business, other lines carried, growth and profit record, cooperativeness, and reputation. If the intermediaries are sales agents, the company will want to evaluate the number and character of other lines carried and the size and quality of the sales force. If the intermediary is a retail store that wants exclusive or selective distribution, the company will want to evaluate the store's customers, location, and future growth potential.

Managing and Motivating Channel Members

Once selected, channel members must be continuously managed and motivated to do their best. The company must sell not only *through* the intermediaries but *to* and *with* them. Most companies see their intermediaries as first-line customers and partners. They practice strong *partner relationship management (PRM)* to forge long-term partnerships with channel members. This creates a marketing system that meets the needs of both the company *and* the partners. (See Marketing at Work 10.2.)

In managing its channels, a company must convince distributors that they can succeed better by working together as a part of a cohesive value delivery system.[11] Thus, Procter & Gamble and Wal-Mart work together to create superior value for final consumers. They jointly plan merchandising goals and strategies, inventory levels, and advertising and promotion plans. Similarly, GE Appliances has created an alternative distribution system called *CustomerNet* to coordinate, support, and motivate its dealers.

GE CustomerNet gives dealers instant online access to GE Appliances' distribution and order-processing system, 24 hours a day, 7 days a week. By logging on to the GE CustomerNet Web site, dealers can obtain product specifications, photos, feature lists, and side-by-side model comparisons for hundreds of GE appliance models. They can check on product availability and prices, place orders, and review order status. They can even create custom brochures, order point-of-purchase materials, or download "advertising slicks"—professionally prepared GE appliance ads ready for insertion in local media. GE promises next-day delivery on most appliance models, so dealers need carry only display models in their stores. This greatly reduces inventory costs, making even small dealers more price competitive. GE CustomerNet also helps dealers to sell GE appliances more easily and effectively. A dealer can put a computer terminal on the showroom floor, where salespeople and customers together can use the system to dig through detailed product specifications and check availability for GE's entire line of appliances. Perhaps the biggest benefit to GE Appliances, however, is that the system builds strong bonds between the com-

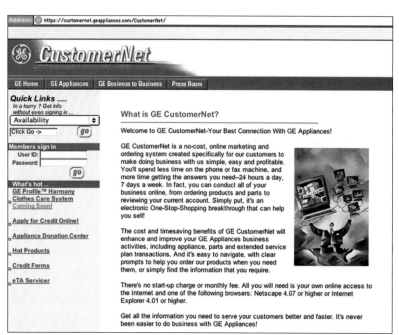

■ Creating dealer satisfaction and profitability: Using GE's CustomerNet system, dealers have instant online access to GE Appliances' distribution system, 24 hours a day, 7 days a week to check on product availability and prices, place orders, and review order status. "Simply put, it's an electronic one-stop shopping breakthrough that can help you sell."

Marketing at Work | *10.2*

Partner Relationship Management: Hewlett-Packard's No-Fly Zone

Hewlett-Packard has a long history of working *with* its channel partners, rather than *through* them or *against* them. It understands the great value that these partners add, both for HP and for customers. "Partners are core to HP's business go-to-market strategy," says Webb McKinney, president of HP's Business Customer Organization. "[Only by working closely] with our channel partners [can we] meet the diverse needs of our customers." Channel partners extend HP's reach far beyond its own capacity. They have a clear understanding of customers' needs and have the resources needed to build customer relationships and provide hands-on support. Managing channel relationships is one of the most important things HP does. "Put sim-

ply, it's a partnering world," adds Kevin Gilroy, general manager for HP's channel program.

A few years back, however, HP faced a difficult decision. Given competitor Dell's incredible success at selling direct to customers, HP had to decide whether it would do the same. Not only could direct selling reduce costs and increase profits, but some customers actually prefer to deal directly with HP. Says HP CEO Carly Fiorina, "The reality is there are some customers who prefer to order through a direct distribution capability *a la* Dell, and we have to satisfy those customers." So HP really had no choice: It had to go direct. The problem? By selling direct, HP would be competing directly with its traditional distribution channel partners. This, in turn, threatened HP's prized, and profitable, rela-

tionships with its distributors. "Two-thirds of our business comes as a direct result of our collaboration with our partners and our channel," says Fiorina.

Thus, HP had to find a way to both sell direct to customers *and* build support and trust among its traditional partners. To solve the problem, the company has developed a direct sales program that avoids infringing on its partners' turf. Whereas HP's competitors take business from their distributors through direct sales to even the smallest customers, HP has "drawn a line in the sand," Gilroy says. Its direct sales program, sometimes referred to as the "hard deck" program, clearly limits which accounts the company will target with direct selling.

"Hard deck" refers to an aviation term that defines a boundary under

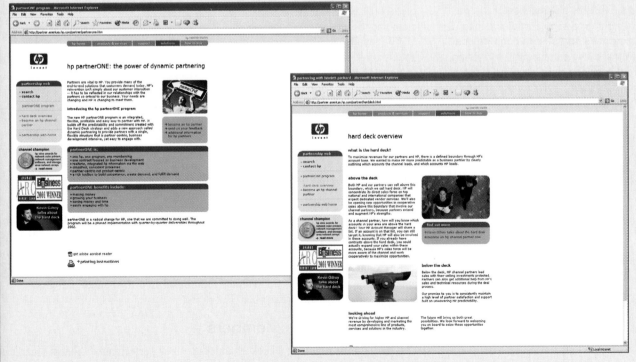

Partner relationship management: To support its channel partners and avoid conflict, HP's "hard deck" guideline clearly outlines "which accounts the channel leads and which accounts HP leads."

(continued)

which there is a "no-fly zone." For HP, it means that the company will sell direct only to potential customers that exceed a set of established specifications. To date, that includes about 1,000 large accounts. Customers falling below the specifications—those in the "no-fly zone"—are off limits to HP for direct sales. Such an arrangement allows HP to concentrate its direct sales force on the largest national and international companies, those that expect dedicated supplier service. At the same time, it creates a market for channel partners, below the hard deck, that is free from direct selling competition.

In addition to setting up the "no fly zone," HP goes out of the way to help its partners to sell the company's products and services. When HP sales reps get leads on accounts in the no-fly zone, they pass the information along to HP distributors, who make the sale and provide service and support. In addition, HP dedicates sales and technical resources to help channel members find the best customer solutions.

The day-to-day management of relationships with more than 20,000 channel partners, who sell everything from computer networks to pocket calculators, presents an immense challenge. Something as simple as distributing sales leads collected through various HP marketing campaigns—everything from business cards dropped in fish bowls at trade shows to requests for

product information from HP's Internet site—can be a daunting task. To manage these tasks, HP set up an integrating partner relationship management (PRM) system, which links HP directly with its channel partners and helps coordinate channelwide marketing efforts. Using a secure Web site, channel partners can log on at any time to obtain leads that have been generated for them. While at the Web site, they can also order literature and sales support materials, check product specifications, and obtain pricing information. In addition, HP communicates with channel members regularly, offering training seminars and promotional materials to support sales. In fact, many partners receive one or two e-mails a day offering information, resources, and support.

The PRM system not only provides strong support for channel partners, it improves their effectiveness and provides feedback to HP. Under the old system, says an HP manager, "we would generate a mass-mailing campaign, send it off to who knows where, out it would go, and we'd hope it would work. Now we can generate a targeted campaign, see when the opportunities start coming back, and . . . the channel partner tells us what happened. . . . It's changing the way we do campaigns."

The results of HP's partner relationship marketing efforts speak for themselves. HP has won multiple awards for its support of and relationships

with channel members. HP swept almost every category it was eligible for in last year's Channel Champions awards sponsored by Crn, a technology-focused trade journal. In surveys administered to determine the winners, one channel member offered that "you won't find a support network out there that's better. Overall, HP is a step above the rest." Referring to the support HP reps provide to channel partners, another distributor commented, "We treat our HP reps more like our sales managers. HP has high integrity. In a gray area, HP will always default to its partners." Adds CEO Fiorina, "Our success is measured on what we can achieve together with our partners."

Sources: Pat Curry, "Channel Changes," Industry Week, April 2, 2001, pp. 45–48; "Reinventing Partnership: Kevin Gilroy Answers Questions from the Channel," accessed online at http://partner. americas.HP.com/partner/harddeck.pdf, July 2003; Craig Zarley, "Making the Call," Crn, February 11, 2002, p. 14–17; Joseph F. Kovar, "Channel Champions 2002: HP Software Decisive," Crn, March 18, 2002, p. 52; Jennifer Hagendorf Follett, "Channel Champions 2002: HP's Hard Deck Is Aces," Crn, March 18, 2002, p. 66; Mike Cruz, "Channel Champions 2002: HP Takes All in Printers," Crn, March 18, 2002, p. 84; Jeff O'Heir, "HP's Fiorina: Know the Value You Add," CRN, April 14, 2003, pp. 6, 16; John Longwell, "Solution Provider Poll Looks at All the Variables in the Partner Satisfaction Equation," accessed at www.crn.com, July 2003; and information gathered from the Hewlett-Packard Web site at http://partner.americas.HP.com/partner/harddeck. pdf, July 2003.

pany and its dealers and motivates dealers to put more push behind the company's products.[12]

Many companies are now installing integrated high-tech partner relationship management systems to coordinate their whole-channel marketing efforts. Just as they use customer relationship management (CRM) software systems to help manage relationships with important customers, companies can now use PRM software to help recruit, train, organize, manage, motivate, and evaluate relationships with channel partners.[13]

Evaluating Channel Members

The producer must regularly check channel member performance against standards such as sales quotas, average inventory levels, customer delivery time, treatment of damaged and lost goods, cooperation in company promotion and training programs, and services to the customer. The company should recognize and reward intermediaries who are performing well and adding good value for consumers. Those who are performing poorly should be assisted or, as a last resort, replaced. A company may periodically "requalify" its intermediaries and prune the weaker ones.

Finally, manufacturers need to be sensitive to their dealers. Those who treat their dealers poorly risk not only losing dealer support but also causing some legal problems. The next section describes various rights and duties pertaining to manufacturers and their channel members.

Linking the Concepts

SPEED BUMP

Time for another break. This time, compare the Caterpillar and GE Appliances channel systems.

- Diagram the Caterpillar and GE Appliances systems. How do they compare in terms of channel levels, types of intermediaries, channel member roles and responsibilities, and other characteristics. How well is each system designed?
- Assess how well Caterpillar and GE Appliances have managed and supported their channels. With what results?

Public Policy and Distribution Decisions

For the most part, companies are legally free to develop whatever channel arrangements suit them. In fact, the laws affecting channels seek to prevent the exclusionary tactics of some companies that might keep another company from using a desired channel. Most channel law deals with the mutual rights and duties of the channel members once they have formed a relationship.

Exclusive Dealing

Many producers and wholesalers like to develop exclusive channels for their products. When the seller allows only certain outlets to carry its products, this strategy is called *exclusive distribution*. When the seller requires that these dealers not handle competitors' products, its strategy is called *exclusive dealing*. Both parties can benefit from exclusive arrangements: The seller obtains more loyal and dependable outlets, and the dealers obtain a steady source of supply and stronger seller support. But exclusive arrangements also exclude other producers from selling to these dealers. This situation brings exclusive dealing contracts under the scope of the Clayton Act of 1914. They are legal as long as they do not substantially lessen competition or tend to create a monopoly and as long as both parties enter into the agreement voluntarily.

Exclusive dealing often includes *exclusive territorial agreements*. The producer may agree not to sell to other dealers in a given area, or the buyer may agree to sell only in its own territory. The first practice is normal under franchise systems as a way to increase dealer enthusiasm and commitment. It is also perfectly legal—a seller has no legal obligation to sell through more outlets than it wishes. The second practice, whereby the producer tries to keep a dealer from selling outside its territory, has become a major legal issue.

Producers of a strong brand sometimes sell it to dealers only if the dealers will take some or all of the rest of the line. This is called full-line forcing. Such *tying agreements* are not necessarily illegal, but they do violate the Clayton Act if they tend to lessen competition substantially. The practice may prevent consumers from freely choosing among competing suppliers of these other brands.

Finally, producers are free to select their dealers, but their right to terminate dealers is somewhat restricted. In general, sellers can drop dealers "for cause." However, they cannot drop dealers if, for example, the dealers refuse to cooperate in a doubtful legal arrangement, such as exclusive dealing or tying agreements.[14]

■▊ Marketing Logistics and Supply Chain Management

In today's global marketplace, selling a product is sometimes easier than getting it to customers. Companies must decide on the best way to store, handle, and move their products and services so that they are available to customers in the right assortments, at the right time, and in the right place. Physical distribution and logistics effectiveness has a major impact on both customer satisfaction and company costs. Here we consider the nature and importance of logistics management in the supply chain, goals of the logistics system, major logistics functions, and the need for integrated supply chain management.

Nature and Importance of Marketing Logistics

Marketing logistics (physical distribution)

The tasks involved in planning, implementing, and controlling the physical flow of materials, final goods, and related information from points of origin to points of consumption to meet customer requirements at a profit.

Supply chain management

Managing upstream and downstream value-added flows of materials, final goods, and related information among suppliers, the company, resellers, and final consumers.

To some managers, marketing logistics means only trucks and warehouses. But modern logistics is much more than this. **Marketing logistics**—also called **physical distribution**—involves planning, implementing, and controlling the physical flow of goods, services, and related information from points of origin to points of consumption to meet customer requirements at a profit. In short, it involves getting the right product to the right customer in the right place at the right time.

In the past, physical distribution typically started with products at the plant and then tried to find low-cost solutions to get them to customers. However, today's marketers prefer customer-centered logistics thinking, which starts with the marketplace and works backward to the factory, or even to sources of supply. Marketing logistics addresses not only *outbound distribution* (moving products from the factory to resellers and ultimately to customers) but also *inbound distribution* (moving products and materials from suppliers to the factory) and *reverse distribution* (moving broken, unwanted, or excess products returned by consumers or resellers). That is, it involves entire **supply chain management**—managing upstream and downstream value-added flows of materials, final goods, and related information among suppliers, the company, resellers, and final consumers, as shown in Figure 10.5.

Thus, the logistics manager's task is to coordinate activities of suppliers, purchasing agents, marketers, channel members, and customers. These activities include forecasting, information systems, purchasing, production planning, order processing, inventory, warehousing, and transportation planning.

Companies today are placing greater emphasis on logistics for several reasons. First, companies can gain a powerful competitive advantage by using improved logistics to give customers better service or lower prices. Second, improved logistics can yield tremendous cost savings to both the company and its customers. As much as 20 percent of an average product's price is accounted for by shipping and transportation alone. Last year, American companies spent more than $900 billion—close to 10 percent of gross domestic product—to wrap, bundle, load, unload, sort, reload, and transport goods. By itself, Ford has more than 500 million tons of finished vehicles, production parts, and aftermarket parts in transit at any given time, running up an annual logistics bill of around $4 billion.[15] Shaving off even a small fraction of these costs can mean substantial savings.

Third, the explosion in product variety has created a need for improved logistics management. For example, in 1911 the typical A&P grocery store carried only 270 items. The store manager could keep track of this inventory on about 10 pages of notebook paper

FIGURE 10.5

Supply Chain Management

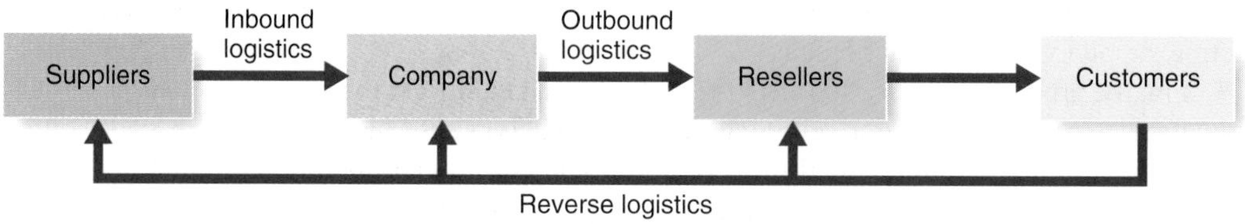

stuffed in a shirt pocket. Today, the average A&P carries a bewildering stock of more than 16,700 items. A Wal-Mart Supercenter stores carry more than 100,000 products, 30,000 of which are grocery products.[16] Ordering, shipping, stocking, and controlling such a variety of products presents a sizable logistics challenge.

Finally, improvements in information technology have created opportunities for major gains in distribution efficiency. Today's companies are using sophisticated supply chain management software, Web-based logistics systems, point-of-sale scanners, uniform product codes, satellite tracking, and electronic transfer of order and payment data. Such technology lets them quickly and efficiently manage the flow of goods, information, and finances through the supply chain.

Goals of the Logistics System

Some companies state their logistics objective as providing maximum customer service at the least cost. Unfortunately, no logistics system can *both* maximize customer service *and* minimize distribution costs. Maximum customer service implies rapid delivery, large inventories, flexible assortments, liberal returns policies, and other services—all of which raise distribution costs. In contrast, minimum distribution costs imply slower delivery, smaller inventories, and larger shipping lots—which represent a lower level of overall customer service.

The goal of marketing logistics should be to provide a *targeted* level of customer service at the least cost. A company must first research the importance of various distribution services to customers and then set desired service levels for each segment. The objective is to maximize *profits*, not sales. Therefore, the company must weigh the benefits of providing higher levels of service against the costs. Some companies offer less service than their competitors and charge a lower price. Other companies offer more service and charge higher prices to cover higher costs.

Major Logistics Functions

Given a set of logistics objectives, the company is ready to design a logistics system that will minimize the cost of attaining these objectives. The major logistics functions include *warehousing, inventory management, transportation,* and *logistics information management.*

Warehousing   Production and consumption cycles rarely match. So most companies must store their tangible goods while they wait to be sold. For example, Snapper, Toro, and other lawn mower manufacturers run their factories all year long and store up products for the heavy spring and summer buying seasons. The storage function overcomes differences in needed quantities and timing, ensuring that products are available when customers are ready to buy them.

A company must decide on *how many* and *what types* of warehouses it needs and *where* they will be located. The company might use either *storage warehouses* or *distribution centers*. Storage warehouses store goods for moderate to long periods. **Distribution centers** are designed to move goods rather than just store them. They are large and highly automated warehouses designed to receive goods from various plants and suppliers, take orders, fill them efficiently, and deliver goods to customers as quickly as possible.

Distribution center
A large, highly automated warehouse designed to receive goods from various plants and suppliers, take orders, fill them efficiently, and deliver goods to customers as quickly as possible.

For example, Wal-Mart operates a network of 78 huge U.S. distribution centers and another 37 around the globe. Almost 84 percent of the merchandise shipped to Wal-Mart stores is routed through one of its own distribution centers, giving Wal-Mart tremendous control over inventory management. One center, which might serve the daily needs of 165 Wal-Mart stores, typically contains more than a million square feet of space (about 24 football fields) under a single roof. Laser scanners route as many as 190,000 cases of goods per day along 11 miles of conveyer belts, and the center's 1,000 workers load or unload some 500 trucks daily. Wal-Mart's Monroe, Georgia, distribution center contains a 127,000-square-foot freezer that can hold 10,000 pallets—room enough for 58 million Popsicles.[17]

Like almost everything else these days, warehousing has seen dramatic changes in technology in recent years. Older, multistoried warehouses with outdated materials-handling methods are steadily being replaced by newer, single-storied *automated warehouses* with advanced, computer-controlled materials-handling systems requiring few employees. Computers and scanners read orders and direct lift trucks, electric hoists, or robots to gather goods, move them to loading docks, and issue invoices.

Inventory Management Inventory management also affects customer satisfaction. Here, managers must maintain the delicate balance between carrying too little inventory and carrying too much. With too little stock, the firm risks not having products when customers want to buy. To remedy this, the firm may need costly emergency shipments or production. Carrying too much inventory results in higher-than-necessary inventory-carrying costs and stock obsolescence. Thus, in managing inventory, firms must balance the costs of carrying larger inventories against resulting sales and profits.

Many companies have greatly reduced their inventories and related costs through *just-in-time* logistics systems. With such systems, producers and retailers carry only small inventories of parts or merchandise, often only enough for a few days of operations. For example, Dell Computer, a master just-in-time producer, carries just 3 days of inventory, whereas competitors might carry 40 days or even 60.[18] New stock arrives exactly when needed, rather than being stored in inventory until being used. Just-in-time systems require accurate forecasting along with fast, frequent, and flexible delivery so that new supplies will be available when needed. However, these systems result in substantial savings in inventory-carrying and handling costs.

■ Logistics technology: In the not-too-distant future, AutoID or "smart tag" technology could make the entire supply chain—which accounts for nearly 75 percent of a product's cost—intelligent and automated.

Marketers are always looking for new ways to make inventory management more efficient. In the not-too-distant future, handling inventory might even become fully automated. For example, in Chapter 3, we discussed AutoID or "smart tag" technology, by which small transmitter chips are embedded in products and packaging. "Smart" products could make the entire supply chain—which accounts for nearly 75 percent of a product's cost—intelligent and automated. Companies would know, at any time, exactly where a product—no matter how large or small—is located physically within the supply chain. "Smart shelves" would not only tell them when it's time to reorder, but would also place the order automatically with their suppliers. Such exciting new information technology applications will revolutionize distribution as we know it.[19]

Transportation The choice of transportation carriers affects the pricing of products, delivery performance, and condition of the goods when they arrive—all of which will affect customer satisfaction. In shipping goods to its warehouses, dealers, and customers, the company can choose among five main transportation modes: truck, rail, water, pipeline, and air, along with an alternative mode for digital products: the Internet.

Trucks have increased their share of transportation steadily and now account for 39 percent of total cargo ton-miles (more than 69 percent of actual tonnage).[20] They account for the largest portion of transportation *within* cities as opposed to *between* cities. Each year in the United States, trucks travel more than 600 billion miles—equal to nearly 1.3 million round trips to the moon—carrying 7.7 billion tons of freight. Trucks are highly flexible in their routing and time schedules, and they can usually offer faster service than railroads. They are efficient for short hauls of high-value merchandise. Trucking firms have added many services in recent years. For example, Roadway Express and most other major carriers now offers satellite tracking of shipments and sleeper tractors that move freight around the clock.

Railroads account for 38 percent of total cargo ton-miles moved. They are one of the most cost-effective modes for shipping large amounts of bulk products—coal, sand, minerals, and farm and forest products—over long distances. In recent years, railroads have increased their customer services by designing new equipment to handle special categories of goods, providing flatcars for carrying truck trailers by rail (piggyback), and providing in-transit services such as the diversion of shipped goods to other destinations en route and the processing of goods en route.

Water carriers, which account for about 10 percent of cargo ton-miles, transport large amounts of goods by ships and barges on U.S. coastal and inland waterways. Although the cost of water transportation is very low for shipping bulky, low-value, nonperishable products such as sand, coal, grain, oil, and metallic ores, water transportation is the slowest mode and may be affected by the weather.

Pipelines are a specialized means of shipping petroleum, natural gas, and chemicals from sources to markets. Most pipelines are used by their owners to ship their own products.

Although *air* carriers transport less than 1 percent of the nation's goods, they are an important transportation mode. Airfreight rates are much higher than rail or truck rates, but airfreight is ideal when speed is needed or distant markets have to be reached. Among the most frequently airfreighted products are perishables (fresh fish, cut flowers) and high-value, low-bulk items (technical instruments, jewelry). Companies find that airfreight also reduces inventory levels, packaging costs, and the number of warehouses needed.

The *Internet* carries digital products from producer to customer via satellite, cable modem, or telephone wire. Software firms, the media, music companies, and education all make use of the Internet to transport digital products. While these firms primarily use traditional transportation to distribute CDs, newspapers, and more, the Internet holds the potential for lower product distribution costs. Whereas planes, trucks, and trains move freight and packages, digital technology moves information bits.

Shippers also use **intermodal transportation**—combining two or more modes of transportation. *Piggyback* describes the use of rail and trucks; *fishyback*, water and trucks; *trainship*, water and rail; and *airtruck*, air and trucks. Combining modes provides advantages that no single mode can deliver. Each combination offers advantages to the shipper. For example, not only is piggyback cheaper than trucking alone but it also provides flexibility and convenience.

In choosing a transportation mode for a product, shippers must balance many considerations: speed, dependability, availability, cost, and others. Thus, if a shipper needs speed, air and truck are the prime choices. If the goal is low cost, then water or pipeline might be best.

■ Roadway and other trucking firms have added many services in recent years, such as satellite tracking of shipments and sleeper tractors that keep freight moving around the clock.

Intermodal transportation
Combining two or more modes of transportation.

Integrated Logistics Management

Today, more and more companies are adopting the concept of **integrated logistics management**. This concept recognizes that providing better customer service and trimming distribution costs require *teamwork*, both inside the company and among all the marketing channel organizations. Inside, the company's various departments must work closely together to maximize the company's own logistics performance. Outside, the company must integrate its logistics system with those of its suppliers and customers to maximize the performance of the entire distribution system.

Integrated logistics management
The logistics concept that emphasizes teamwork, both inside the company and among all the marketing channel organizations, to maximize the performance of the entire distribution system.

Cross-Functional Teamwork Inside the Company In most companies, responsibility for various logistics activities is assigned to many different functional units—marketing, sales, finance, operations, and purchasing. Too often, each function tries to optimize its own logistics performance without regard for the activities of the other functions. However, transportation, inventory, warehousing, and order-processing activities interact, often in an inverse way. Lower inventory levels reduce inventory-carrying costs. But they may also reduce customer service and increase costs from stock outs, back orders, special production runs, and costly fast-freight shipments. Because distribution activities involve

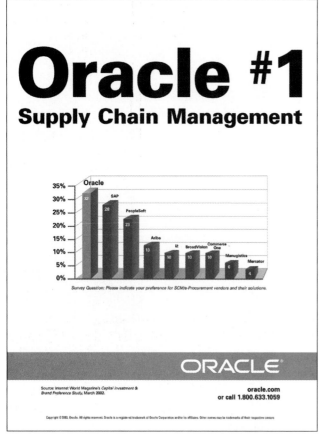

■ Supply chain management: Many companies use sophisticated, systemwide supply chain management software, such as that available from Oracle and other software providers.

Third-party logistics (3PL) provider

An independent logistics provider that performs any or all of the functions required to get its client's product to market.

strong trade-offs, decisions by different functions must be coordinated to achieve superior overall logistics performance.

The goal of integrated supply chain management is to harmonize all of the company's logistics decisions. Close working relationships among functions can be achieved in several ways. Some companies have created permanent logistics committees, made up of managers responsible for different physical distribution activities. Companies can also create management positions that link the logistics activities of functional areas. For example, Procter & Gamble has created supply managers, who manage all of the supply chain activities for each of its product categories. Many companies have a vice president of logistics with cross-functional authority. Finally, companies can employ sophisticated, systemwide supply chain management software, now available from Oracle and other software providers.[21] The important thing is that the company must coordinate its logistics and marketing activities to create high market satisfaction at a reasonable cost.

Building Logistics Partnerships Companies must do more than improve their own logistics. They must also work with other channel partners to improve whole-channel distribution. The members of a distribution channel are linked closely in delivering customer satisfaction and value and building customer relationships. One company's distribution system is another company's supply system. The success of each channel member depends on the performance of the entire supply chain. For example, Wal-Mart can charge the lowest prices at retail only if its entire supply chain—consisting of thousands of merchandise suppliers, transport companies, warehouses, and service providers—operates at maximum efficiency.

Smart companies coordinate their logistics strategies and forge strong partnerships with suppliers and customers to improve customer service and reduce channel costs. Many companies have created *cross-functional, cross-company teams*. For example, Procter & Gamble has a team of almost 100 people working in Bentonville, Arkansas, home of Wal-Mart. The P&Gers work jointly with their counterparts at Wal-Mart to find ways to squeeze costs out of their distribution system. Working together benefits not only P&G and Wal-Mart but also their final consumers.

Other companies partner through *shared projects*. For example, many larger retailers are working closely with suppliers on in-store programs. Home Depot allows key suppliers to use its stores as a testing ground for new merchandising programs. The suppliers spend time at Home Depot stores watching how their product sells and how customers relate to it. They then create programs specially tailored to Home Depot and its customers. Clearly, both the supplier and the customer benefit from such partnerships.

The point is that all supply chain members must work together in the cause of serving final consumers. "The functions that customers value deserve close, creative attention from all supply chain participants," says one expert. "Together, component suppliers, manufacturers, wholesalers, and retailers must . . . differentiate the way they provide and package these [values] to the ultimate customer."[22]

Third-Party Logistics Most businesses perform their own logistics functions. However, a growing number of firms now outsource some or all of their logistics to **third-party logistics (3PL) providers** such as Ryder Systems, UPS Worldwide Logistics, FedEx Logistics, Roadway Logistics Services, or Emory Global Logistics (see Marketing at Work 10.3). Such integrated logistics companies perform any or all of the functions required to get their clients' product to market.

For example, Emory's Global Logistics unit provides clients with coordinated, single-source logistics services, including supply chain management, customized information

Marketing at Work | *10.3*

Go Ryder, and Leave the Delivering to Us

Most big companies love to make and sell their products. But many loathe the associated logistics "grunt work." They detest bundling, loading, unloading, sorting, storing, reloading, transporting, and tracking required to supply their factories and to get products out to customers. They hate it so much that nearly two-thirds of the nation's largest manufacturing companies now outsource some or all of these functions, up from only 38 percent a decade ago.

Increasingly, companies are handing over their logistics to third-party logistics suppliers. These "3PLs" help companies to tighten up sluggish, overstuffed supply chains, slash inventories, and get products to customers more quickly and reliably. Below are some examples:

Ford: Ford uses an international logistics partner to move Ford products between continents. In North America, it uses third-party logistics partner UPS Autogistics to coordinate shipments from its 21 assembly plants, four rail centers, and 55 destination ramps to its 6,000-plus North American dealer network. That arrangement, in its first year alone, reduced Ford inventories by $1 billion, trimmed inventory carrying costs by $125 million, and decreased delivery time to dealers by four days, or 26 percent. The result: lower costs *and* better customer service.

Cisco Systems: This vendor of computer networking equipment and network management software ships tons of routers to Europe daily. It needs to know where each box is at any given time and may have to reroute orders on short notice to fill urgent customer requests. Moreover, Cisco's customers need to know exactly when orders will arrive. When Cisco handled its own logistics, deliveries took up to three weeks. Now, the company contracts its complex distribution process to UPS

Worldwide Logistics. Leveraging its knowledge of international plane, train, and trucking schedules, UPS Worldwide can speed routers to European customers in less than four days. Such superfast delivery saves Cisco Systems a bundle on inventories.

Cisco reaps some additional advantages from the logistics partnership. For example, UPS Worldwide has extensive knowledge of local customs laws and import duties. It recently arranged with Dutch customs to aggregate Cisco's import duties into a monthly bill, paid once customers

receive shipments instead of each time the routers land at the airport. The result: even more savings in time and paperwork.

National Semiconductor: In the early 1990s, National Semiconductor— whose chips end up inside everything from cars and computers to telecommunications gear— faced a logistics nightmare. National produced and assembled chips at 13 plants located in the United States, Britain, Israel, and Southeast Asia. Finished products were then shipped to an array of large customers—IBM, Toshiba, Ford,

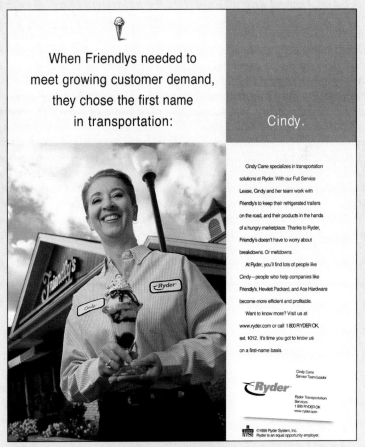

When Friendlys needed to meet growing customer demand, they chose the first name in transportation: Cindy.

Cindy Care specializes in transportation solutions at Ryder. With our Full Service Lease, Cindy and her team work with Friendly's to keep their refrigerated trailers on the road, and their products in the hands of a hungry marketplace. Thanks to Ryder, Friendly's doesn't have to worry about breakdowns. Or meltdowns.

At Ryder, you'll find lots of people like Cindy—people who help companies like Friendly's, Hewlett Packard, and Ace Hardware become more efficient and profitable.

Want to know more? Visit us at www.ryder.com or call 1 800 RYDER OK, ext. 1012. It's time you got to know us on a first-name basis.

Cindy Care
Service Team Leader

Ryder
Ryder Transportation
Services
1 800 RYDER OK
www.ryder.com

©1999 Ryder System, Inc.
Ryder is an equal opportunity employer.

Third-party logistics: Many companies are now outsourcing logistics tasks to companies like Ryder Integrated Logistics. Here, Ryder describes a system it designed to keep Friendly's refrigerated trucks on the road. "Thanks to Ryder, Friendly's doesn't have to worry about breakdowns. Or meltdowns."

(continued)

Siemens—each with factories scattered around the globe. On their way to customers, chips traveled any of 20,000 direct routes, mostly in the cargo holds of planes flown by 12 airlines, stopping along the way at 10 different warehouses. National's logistics performance left much to be desired: 95 percent of its products were delivered within 45 days of the order. The other 5 percent took as long as 90 days. Because customers never knew which 5 percent would be late, they demanded 90 days' worth of inventory in everything. "We had buffer stocks all along the line," comments a National executive. "The whole system was awash in inventory."

National's management set out to overhaul its global logistics network. However, whereas National knew a lot about making chips, it knew little about how to fix its logistics. Rather than hiring specialists, National hired UPS to handle its global distribution. UPS now runs National's distribution center in Singapore, conducting all storage, sorting, and shipping activities. The results have been startling. By outsourcing, National saves as much as 20 percent on distribution costs. At the same time, customer service and delivery performance have improved dramatically. National can now move products from the factory to global customers in an average of 48 hours.

Sony: Sony knows logistics. In fact, the company considers logistics to be one of its competitive advantages. So you might wonder why an industry leader would outsource half of its distri-

bution requirements in Mexico to Redwood Systems, a third-party logistics (3PL) provider with headquarters in Atlanta. It turns out that even a logistics leader needs help some of the time. The reasons are growth and speed to market. "In Mexico, logistics is challenging because of a lack of infrastructure," says Carlos Rojas, logistics division manager for Sony Electronicas, Mexico. "Given those limitations, we couldn't take advantage of a growing market without a 3PL partner who could quickly expand our operations. By relying on Redwood to manage the day-to-day details of our Mexico-based distribution, we can concentrate on marketing and sales instead of logistics, and do it without adding to our head count." Today, Redwood manages more than 500 different products and another 15,000 different parts for Sony. Product is received into the facility from all over the world, and in quantities ranging from parcel shipments to full containers. The 3PL supplier ships an estimated 200 orders per day, with an average of 10 line items per order.

Saturn: Saturn's just-in-time production system allows for almost no parts inventory at the plant. Instead, it relies on a world-class logistics system to keep parts flowing into the factory at precisely the times they're needed. Saturn is so good at managing its supply chain that in four years it has had to halt production just once—for only 18 minutes—because the right part failed to arrive at the right time. Most of the credit, however, goes to Ryder Integrated Logistics. Ryder, best known

for renting trucks, manages Saturn's far-ranging supply chain, moving the automaker's materials, parts, and products efficiently and reliably from supplier to factory to dealer showroom.

To keep Saturn's assembly lines humming, Ryder transports thousands of preinspected and presorted parts—more than 2,200 receiving-dock transactions every day—hitting delivery windows as narrow as five minutes. Ryder keeps its parts, people, and trucks in a nearly constant blur of high-tech motion. For example, according to one account, when delivering service parts to Saturn dealerships, Ryder's long-haul drivers "plug a plastic key, loaded with electronic data, into an onboard computer. The screen tells them exactly where to go, which route to take, and how much time to spend getting there." Ryder's effective supply chain management results in lower costs, improved operations, more productive dealers, and—in the end—more satisfied customers.

Sources: Quotes and other information from "Chipmaker Expands Its Relationship with 3PL into New Markets," *Purchasing,* March 20, 2003, pp. S11–S12; Ronald Henkoff, "Delivering the Goods," *Fortune,* November 28, 1994, pp. 64–77; Lisa H. Harrington, "Special Report on Contract Logistics," *Transportation & Distribution,* September 1996, pp. A–N; Scott Woolley, "Replacing Inventory with Information," *Forbes,* March 24, 1997, pp. 54–58; Martha Celestino, "Choosing a Third-Party Logistics Provider," *World Trade,* July 1999, pp. 54–56; "3PLs on the Rise," *Modern Materials Handling,* December 2001, p. 15; Mike Verespej, "Logistics' New Look? Now It's Service," *Frontline Solutions,* June 2002, pp. 24–33; and Robert E. Lieb, "3PLs Eye Further Supply Chain Integration," *Purchasing,* March 20, 2003, pp. S4–S8.

technology, inventory control, warehousing, transportation management, customer service and fulfillment, and freight auditing and control. "From sourcing raw materials to delivering finished products to stores," proclaims the Emery Web site, "our experts work with you to streamline and manage your entire supply chain and to keep you in control." Last year, U.S. manufacturers and distributors spent more than $61 billion on third-party logistics (also called *3PL, outsourced logistics,* or *contract logistics*) services. According to a recent survey, 3PL services are an integral part of the logistics strategies of nearly two-thirds of Fortune 500 manufacturers.[23]

Companies use third-party logistics providers for several reasons. First, because getting the product to market is their main focus, these providers can often do it more efficiently and at lower cost. According to one study, outsourcing typically results in 15 to 30 percent cost savings.[24] Second, outsourcing logistics frees a company to focus more intensely on its core business. Finally, integrated logistics companies understand increasingly complex logistics environments. This can be especially helpful to companies attempting to expand their global market coverage. For example, companies distributing their products across Europe face a bewildering array of environmental restrictions that affect logistics, including packaging standards, truck size and weight limits, and noise and emissions pollution controls. By outsourcing its logistics, a company can gain a complete pan-European distribution system without incurring the costs, delays, and risks associated with setting up its own system.

REST STOP:
Reviewing the Concepts

So, what have you learned about distribution channels and integrated supply chain management? Marketing channel decisions are among the most important decisions that management faces. A company's channel decisions directly affect every other marketing decision. Each channel system creates a different level of revenues and costs and reaches a different segment of target consumers. Management must make channel decisions carefully, incorporating today's needs with tomorrow's likely selling environment. Some companies pay too little attention to their distribution channels, but others have used imaginative distribution systems to gain competitive advantage.

1. Explain why companies use distribution channels and discuss the functions these channels perform.

Most producers use intermediaries to bring their products to market. They try to forge a *distribution channel*—a set of interdependent organizations involved in the process of making a product or service available for use or consumption by the consumer or business user. Through their contacts, experience, specialization, and scale of operation, intermediaries usually offer the firm more than it can achieve on its own. Distribution channels perform many key functions. Some help *complete* transactions by gathering and distributing *information* needed for planning and aiding exchange; by developing and spreading persuasive *communications* about an offer; by performing *contact* work—finding and communicating with prospective buyers; by *matching*—shaping and fitting the offer to the buyer's needs; and by entering into *negotiation* to reach an agreement on price and other terms of the offer so that ownership can be transferred. Other functions help to *fulfill* the completed transactions by offering *physical distribution*—transporting and storing goods; *financing*—acquiring and using funds to cover the costs of the channel work; and *risk taking*—assuming the risks of carrying out the channel work.

2. Discuss how channel members interact and how they organize to perform the work of the channel.

The channel will be most effective when each member is assigned the tasks it can do best. Ideally, because the success of individual channel members depends on overall channel success, all channel firms should work together smoothly. They should understand and accept their roles, coordinate their goals and activities, and cooperate to attain overall channel goals. By cooperating, they can more

effectively sense, serve, and satisfy the target market. In a large company, the formal organization structure assigns roles and provides needed leadership. But in a distribution channel made up of independent firms, leadership and power are not formally set. Traditionally, distribution channels have lacked the leadership needed to assign roles and manage conflict. In recent years, however, new types of channel organizations have appeared that provide stronger leadership and improved performance.

3. Identify the major channel alternatives open to a company.

Each firm identifies alternative ways to reach its market. Available means vary from direct selling to using one, two, three, or more intermediary *channel levels*. Marketing channels face continuous and sometimes dramatic change. Three of the most important trends are the growth of *vertical, horizontal,* and *hybrid marketing systems*. These trends affect channel cooperation, conflict, and competition. *Channel design* begins with assessing customer channel service needs and company channel objectives and constraints. The company then identifies the major channel alternatives in terms of the *types* of intermediaries, the *number* of intermediaries, and the *channel responsibilities* of each. Each channel alternative must be evaluated according to economic, control, and adaptive criteria. Channel management calls for selecting qualified intermediaries and motivating them. Individual channel members must be evaluated regularly.

4. Explain how companies select, motivate, and evaluate channel members.

Producers vary in their ability to attract qualified marketing intermediaries. Some producers have no trouble signing up channel members. Others have to work hard to line up enough qualified intermediaries. When selecting intermediaries, the company should evaluate each channel member's qualifications and select those who best fit its channel objectives. Once selected, channel members must be continuously motivated to do their best. The company must sell not only *through* the intermediaries but *to* them. It should work to forge long-term partnerships with their channel partners to create a marketing system that meets the needs of both the manufacturer *and* the partners. The company must also regularly check channel member performance against established performance standards, rewarding intermediaries who are performing well and assisting or replacing weaker ones.

5. Discuss the nature and importance of marketing logistics and integrated supply chain management.

Just as firms are giving the marketing concept increased recognition, more business firms are paying attention to *marketing logistics* (or *physical distribution*). Logistics is an area of potentially high cost savings and improved customer satisfaction. Marketing logistics addresses not only *outbound distribution* but also *inbound distribution* and *reverse distribution*. That is, it involves entire *supply chain management*—managing value-added flows between suppliers, the company, resellers, and final users. No logistics system can both maximize customer service and minimize distribution costs. Instead, the goal of logistics management is to provide a *targeted* level of service at the least cost. The major logistics functions include *order processing*, *warehousing*, *inventory management*, and *transportation*.

The *integrated supply chain management concept* recognizes that improved logistics requires teamwork in the form of close working relationships across functional areas inside the company and across various organizations in the supply chain. Companies can achieve logistics harmony among functions by creating cross-functional logistics teams, integrative supply manager positions, and senior-level logistics executives with cross-functional authority. Channel partnerships can take the form of cross-company teams, shared projects, and information-sharing systems. Today, some companies are outsourcing their logistics functions to third-party logistics providers to save costs, increase efficiency, and gain faster and more effective access to global markets.

Navigating the Key Terms

Administered VMS
Channel conflict
Channel level
Contractual VMS
Conventional distribution channel
Corporate VMS
Direct marketing channel
Disintermediation
Distribution center

Exclusive distribution
Franchise organization
Horizontal marketing system
Indirect marketing channel
Integrated logistics management
Intensive distribution
Intermodal transportation
Marketing channel (distribution channel)

Marketing logistics (physical distribution)
Multichannel distribution system
Selective distribution
Supply chain management
Third-party logistics (3PL) provider
Value delivery network
Vertical marketing system (VMS)

Travel Log

Discussing the Issues

1. Discuss the differences between a conventional distribution channel, a corporate VMS, a contractual VMS, and an administered VMS. Give an example of each.

2. Discuss the conditions under which a manufacturer would want its distribution intensity to be exclusive, selective, and intensive. Which distribution level makes sense for the following products: Mountain-Dew soft-drinks, Rolex watches, and Ford automobiles? Explain your answer.

3. While some channel members are removed through disintermediation, the functions performed by the channel must still take place. Using the travel industry as an example, explain how airlines and hotels will perform key distribution functions (e.g., information, promotion, contact, matching, and negotiation) that travel agents historically have performed.

4. With which major functions would someone managing the logistics area of a company be concerned? Give an example of decisions this manager would make for each major function.

5. Discuss the rationale behind the text's argument that "demand chain" may be a better term than "supply chain." Do you agree or disagree? How does the concept of a value delivery network fit with these two concepts?

Application Questions

1. Your company has just developed a new line of organic foods. Discuss the factors you should consider in selecting channel members. What methods will you use to motivate the channel members to work their best for you? Finally, how will you evaluate channel member performance?

2. Advances in technology and the increasingly widespread use of the Internet have led many firms to create Internet-based channels of distribution that bypass intermediaries and go right to the consumer. Provide an example of a specific company that has used this approach. What does the company gain from using a direct-to-consumer Internet strategy? What disadvantages are there for the manufacturer and consumers under this strategy?

3. One of the challenges for companies opting for an Internet distribution channel is providing timely customer service. One solution to this is to have "live" customer service representatives available to answer questions. Look at the "live chat" online customer service available at Landsend.com (www. landsend.com/)—click on the "Customer Service" tab at the top of the page, and then the "Lands' End Live" icon. What is your reaction to this type of customer service? Do you think it differentiates Lands' End from online retailers without this feature? Where do you think online customer service will be in 5 years?

Under the Hood: Focus on Technology

In the late 1990s, e-grocers promised to change the way we shop for milk, chicken, and paper towels. Imagine no more trips to the grocery store. With a few clicks of your mouse your shopping list would be sent to the grocery store and a few days later the groceries would appear at your door. Unfortunately, most e-grocers went bankrupt. But now Internet-based grocery stores are back and growing. Indeed, more groceries are sold online today than ever before, with annual sales in the online grocery industry expected to reach $1.6 billion in 2003. According to the Food Marketing Institute, a quarter of all grocery retailers now offer some form of Web-based shopping. This market segment is certainly attractive because online customers spend an average of $125 per customer, compared with only $25 per customer in traditional supermarkets.

Visit netgrocer.com (www.netgrocer.com/) and look around its Web site. Then respond to the following questions.

1. Would you use this service? Why or why not? Describe the market segment you feel is most likely to use an e-grocer to shop for groceries.

2. How big a threat is this channel to traditional grocery stores? Explain your response. Why would a traditional grocery store consider adding a Web-based component to their "bricks-and-mortar" offering?

3. What are likely to be the biggest challenges to success that online grocers will have to overcome? What can they do to minimize these obstacles?

Focus on Ethics

The music industry is one of the many industries that have started taking advantage of the speed and convenience of the Internet to add another distribution channel to their repertoire (e.g., www.apple.com/music/store). Unfortunately for the industry, this same channel lets consumers share music with each other for free. Music CD sales have dropped almost 15 percent in the past 2 years, according to the Recording Industry Association of America. What some consumers call "sharing," industry executives call online piracy or bootlegging, and they blame the illegal downloads for the decline in CD sales. It is reported that music-sharing Web sites have accounted for 2.6 billion files a month in illegal downloads, with much of the activity emanating from college campuses. The music industry estimates that it loses $300

million per year to illegal song copying and distribution. In the extreme, Senator Orrin Hatch of Utah has said that he is in favor of exploring technology that would remotely destroy computers used for illegal music downloads.

1. What is your position on this issue? Should users be able to share music freely over the Internet that they have legally purchased from retailers?

2. If you worked for a music recording company, what would you suggest that the recording industry do to address this issue?

3. Divide into two groups and have a debate in class over this issue. One group should take the side of the music industry, while the other group should take the side of consumers digitally sharing music.

Videos

The Snapple video case that accompanies this chapter is located in Appendix 1 at the back of the book.

Student Materials

Need a tune-up? A study guide and OneKey access code are available to aid in your review of chapter material. Your instructor may choose to have these items shrink-wrapped with your text or you may purchase them separately at www.prenhall.com/marketing.

■ *After studying this chapter, you should be able to*

1. *Explain* the roles of retailers and wholesalers in the distribution channel **2.** *Describe* the major types of retailers and give examples of each **3.** *Identify* the major types of wholesalers and give examples of each **4.** *Explain* the marketing decisions facing retailers and wholesalers

Retailing and Wholesaling

11

ROAD MAP | Previewing the Concepts

In the previous chapter, you learned the basics of distribution channel design and management. Now, we'll look more deeply into the two major intermediary channel functions, retailing and wholesaling. You already know something about retailing—you're served every day by retailers of all shapes and sizes. However, you probably know much less about the hoard of wholesalers that work behind the scenes. In this chapter, we'll navigate through the characteristics of different kinds of retailers and wholesalers, the marketing decisions they make, and trends for the future. You'll see that the retailing and wholesaling landscapes are changing rapidly to match explosive changes in markets and technology.

To start the tour, we'll look in on Wal-Mart, the ultimate retailer. This mega-retailer's phenomenal success has resulted from an unrelenting focus bringing value to its customers. Day in and day out, Wal-Mart lives up to its promise: Always low prices—*Always*. That focus on customer value has made Wal-Mart not just the world's largest retailer, but also the world's largest company.

I n 1962, Sam Walton and his brother opened the first Wal-Mart discount store in small-town Rogers, Arkansas. It was a big, flat, warehouselike store that sold everything from apparel to automotive supplies to small appliances at very low prices. Experts gave the fledgling retailer little chance—conventional wisdom suggested that discount stores could succeed only in large cities.

Yet, from these modest beginnings, the chain exploded onto the national retailing scene. Incredibly, Wal-Mart's annual sales now approach $275 billion—more than one and one-half times the sales of Target, Sears, Kmart, and JCPenney combined—making it the world's largest company. Wal-Mart's sales *grew* last year by the equivalent of the annual sales of one Microsoft, two Coca-Colas, or three Nikes. Wal-Mart's sales of $1.42 billion on one day last fall were larger than the GDPs of 36 countries. Each year in the United States, Wal-Mart sells one out of every four quarts of motor oil, one out of every five deodorants, and one out of every four replacement toilet seats. It sells a Timex watch every 7.4 seconds and a Barbie doll every 2 seconds. One out of every 220 men, women, and children in the United States is a Wal-Mart associate.

Wal-Mart's phenomenal growth shows few signs of slowing. The company is now well established in larger cities and is expanding rapidly into international markets. Within only a few years of entering the grocery business with its supercenters—and more recently with its smaller Neighborhood Market stores—Wal-Mart is now the nation's largest grocery retailer, with more than one and one-half times the food sales of number two Kroger. And many industry experts believe that Wal-Mart will one day dominate Internet marketspaces in the same way that it now dominates the physical marketplace. "At the end of the next four years," predicts one retailing industry consultant, "Wal-Mart will be number one on land and online."

What are the secrets behind this spectacular success? First and foremost, Wal-Mart is passionately dedicated to its value proposition of "Always Low Prices, *Always!*" Its mission is to "lower the world's cost of living." To deliver on this promise, it listens to and takes care of its customers, treats employees as partners, and keeps a tight rein on costs.

Wal-Mart knows its customers well and takes good care of them. As one analyst puts it, "The company gospel . . . is relatively simple: Be an agent for customers, find out what they want, and sell it to them for the lowest possible price." The company stays close to customers—for example, each top Wal-Mart executive spends at least two days a week visiting stores, talking directly with customers and getting a firsthand look at operations. Then, Wal-Mart delivers what customers want: a broad selection of carefully selected goods at unbeatable prices. Concludes Wal-Mart's current president and chief executive, "We're obsessed with delivering value to customers."

But the right merchandise at the right price isn't the only key to Wal-Mart's success. Compared with other discounters, Wal-Mart also provides the kind of service that keeps customers satisfied. A sign reading "Satisfaction Guaranteed" hangs prominently at each store's entrance. Another sign inside the store reads, "At Wal-Mart, our goal is: You're always next in line!" Customers are often welcomed by "people greeters" eager to lend a helping hand or just to be friendly. And, sure enough, the store opens extra checkout counters to keep waiting lines short.

Beyond listening to and taking care of customers, Wal-Mart also takes good care of employees. It believes that, in the final accounting, the company's people are what really make it better. Thus, it works hard to show employees that it cares about them. Wal-Mart was first to call employees "associates," a practice now widely copied by competitors. The associates work as partners, become deeply involved in operations, and share rewards for good performance.

> Everyone at Wal-Mart [is] an associate—from [the CEO] . . . to a cashier named Janet at the Wal-Mart on Highway 50 in Ocoee, Florida. "We," "us," and "our" are the operative words. Wal-Mart department heads, hourly associates who look after one of more than 30-some departments ranging from sporting goods to electronics, see figures that many companies never show general managers: costs, freight charges, profit margins. The company sets a profit margin for each store, and if the store exceeds it, then the hourly associates share part of the additional profit.

The partnership concept is deeply rooted in the Wal-Mart corporate culture. Wal-Mart's concern for its employees translates into high employee satisfaction, which in turn translates into greater customer satisfaction.

Finally, Wal-Mart delivers real value by keeping a sharp eye on costs. Wal-Mart is a lean, mean, distribution machine—it has the lowest cost structure in the industry. This lets the giant retailer charge lower prices but still reap higher profits. Wal-Mart's lower prices attract more shoppers, producing more sales, making the company more efficient, and enabling it to lower prices even more.

Wal-Mart's low costs result in part from superior management and more sophisticated technology. Its Bentonville, Arkansas, headquarters contains a computer communications system that the Defense Department would envy, giving managers around the country instant access to sales and operating information. And its huge, fully automated distribution centers employ the latest technology to supply stores efficiently. Wal-Mart also spends less than competitors on advertising as a percentage of sales. Because Wal-Mart has what customers want at the prices they'll pay, its reputation has spread rapidly by word of mouth. It has not needed more advertising.

Finally, Wal-Mart keeps costs down through good old "tough buying." Whereas the company is known for the warm way it treats customers, it is equally well known for the cold, calculated way it wrings low prices from suppliers. The following passage describes a visit to Wal-Mart's buying offices:

> Don't expect a greeter and don't expect friendly. . . . Once you are ushered into one of the spartan little buyers' rooms, expect a steely eye across the table and be prepared to cut your price. "They are very, very focused people, and they use their buying power more forcefully than anyone else in America," says the marketing vice president of a major vendor. "All the normal mating rituals are [forbidden]. Their highest priority is making sure everyone at all times in all cases knows who's in charge, and it's Wal-Mart. They talk softly, but they have piranha hearts, and if you aren't totally prepared when you go in there, you'll have your [head] handed to you."

Says one former Wal-Mart buyer of her $1 billion budget, "I had the biggest pencil in the United States of America and if someone didn't do what fit with our program, I could break my pencil, throw it on the table, and never come back." In response, many suppliers have set up entire teams and offices in Bentonville dedicated to Wal-Mart. Newell Rubbermaid's Bentonville office is just 60 seconds from Wal-Mart's headquarters and features an exact replica of the store on its first floor.

Some observers wonder whether Wal-Mart can be so big and still retain its focus and positioning. They wonder if an ever-larger Wal-Mart can stay close to its customers and employees. The company's managers are betting on it. No matter where it operates, Wal-Mart's announced policy is to take care of customers "one store at a time." Says one top executive: "We'll be fine as long as we never lose our responsiveness to the consumer."[1]

The Wal-Mart story provides many insights into the workings of one of today's most successful retailers. This chapter looks at *retailing* and *wholesaling*. In the first section, we look at the nature and importance of retailing, major types of store and nonstore retailers, the decisions retailers make, and the future of retailing. In the second section, we discuss these same topics as they relate to wholesalers.

■▮ Retailing

What is retailing? We all know that Wal-Mart, Home Depot, and Target are retailers, but so are Avon representatives, Amazon.com, the local Holiday Inn, and a doctor seeing patients. **Retailing** includes all the activities involved in selling products or services directly to final consumers for their personal, nonbusiness use. Many institutions—manufacturers, wholesalers, and retailers—do retailing. But most retailing is done by **retailers**: businesses whose sales come *primarily* from retailing.

Although most retailing is done in retail stores, in recent years *nonstore retailing* has been growing much faster than has store retailing. Nonstore retailing includes selling to final consumers through direct mail, catalogs, telephone, the Internet, TV home shopping shows, home and office parties, door-to-door contact, vending machines, and other direct

Retailing
All activities involved in selling goods or services directly to final consumers for their personal, nonbusiness use.

Retailer
Business whose sales come *primarily* from retailing.

selling approaches. We discuss such direct-marketing approaches in detail in Chapter 13. In this chapter, we focus on store retailing.

Types of Retailers

Retail stores come in all shapes and sizes, and new retail types keep emerging. The most important types of retail stores are described in Table 11.1 and are discussed in the following sections. They can be classified in terms of several characteristics, including the *amount of service* they offer, the breadth and depth of their *product lines*, the *relative prices* they charge, and how they are *organized*.

Amount of Service Different products require different amounts of service, and customer service preferences vary. Retailers may offer one of three levels of service—self-service, limited service, and full service.

Self-service retailers serve customers who are willing to perform their own "locate–compare–select" process to save money. Self-service is the basis of all discount operations and is typically used by sellers of convenience goods (such as supermarkets) and nationally branded, fast-moving shopping goods (such as Best Buy).

Limited-service retailers, such as Sears or JCPenney, provide more sales assistance because they carry more shopping goods about which customers need information. Their increased operating costs result in higher prices. In *full-service retailers*, such as specialty stores and first-class department stores, salespeople assist customers in every phase of the shopping process. Full-service stores usually carry more specialty goods for which customers like to be "waited on." They provide more services resulting in much higher operating costs, which are passed along to customers as higher prices.

Specialty store
A retail store that carries a narrow product line with a deep assortment within that line.

Product Line Retailers also can be classified by the length and breadth of their product assortments. Some retailers, such as **specialty stores**, carry narrow product lines with deep assortments within those lines. Today, specialty stores are flourishing. The increasing

---

TABLE 11.1 Major Store Retailer Types

Specialty Stores: Carry a narrow product line with a deep assortment, such as apparel stores, sporting-goods stores, furniture stores, florists, and bookstores. A clothing store would be a *single-line* store, a men's clothing store would be a *limited-line* store, and a men's custom-shirt store would be a *superspecialty* store. Examples: The Body Shop, Gap, The Athlete's Foot.

Department Stores: Carry several product lines—typically clothing, home furnishings, and household goods—with each line operated as a separate department managed by specialist buyers or merchandisers. Examples: Sears, Macy's, Marshall Field's.

Supermarkets: A relatively large, low-cost, low-margin, high-volume, self-service operation designed to serve the consumer's total needs for food and household products. Examples: Kroger, Vons, A&P, Food Lion.

Convenience Stores: Relatively small stores located near residential areas, open long hours seven days a week, and carrying a limited line of high-turnover convenience products at slightly higher prices. Examples: 7-Eleven, Stop-N-Go, Circle K.

Discount Stores: Carry standard merchandise sold at lower prices with lower margins and higher volumes. Examples: General—Wal-Mart, Target, Kmart; Specialty—Best Buy.

Off-Price Retailers: Sell merchandise bought at less-than-regular wholesale prices and sold at less than retail: often leftover goods, over-runs, and irregulars obtained at reduced prices from manufacturers or other retailers. These include *factory outlets* owned and operated by manufacturers (example: Mikasa); *independent off-price retailers* owned and run by entrepreneurs or by divisions of larger retail corporations (example: TJ Maxx); and *warehouse (or wholesale) clubs* selling a limited selection of brand-name groceries, appliances, clothing, other goods at deep discounts to consumers who pay membership fees (examples: Costco, Sam's, BJ's Wholesale Club).

Superstores: Very large stores traditionally aimed at meeting consumers' total needs for routinely purchased food and nonfood items. Includes *category killers,* which carry a deep assortment in a particular category and have a knowledgeable staff (examples: Best Buy, Petsmart, Staples); *supercenters,* combined supermarket and discount stores (examples: Wal-Mart Supercenters, SuperTarget, Super Kmart Center); and *hypermarkets* with up to 220,000 square feet of space combining supermarket, discount, and warehouse retailing (examples: Carrefour [France], Pyrca [Spain]).

use of market segmentation, market targeting, and product specialization has resulted in a greater need for stores that focus on specific products and segments.

In contrast, **department stores** carry a wide variety of product lines. In recent years, department stores have been squeezed between more focused and flexible specialty stores on the one hand, and more efficient, lower-priced discounters on the other. In response, many have added promotional pricing to meet the discount threat. Others have stepped up the use of store brands and single-brand "designer shops" to compete with specialty stores. Still others are trying mail-order, telephone, and Web selling. Service remains the key differentiating factor. Department stores such as Nordstrom, Saks, Neiman Marcus, and other high-end department stores are doing well by emphasizing high-quality service.

Supermarkets are the most frequently shopped type of retail store. Today, however, they are facing slow sales growth because of slower population growth and an increase in competition from convenience stores, discount food stores, and superstores. Supermarkets also have been hit hard by the rapid growth of out-of-home eating.

Thus, most supermarkets are making improvements to attract more customers. In the battle for "share of stomachs," many large supermarkets have moved upscale, providing from-scratch bakeries, gourmet deli counters, and fresh seafood departments. Others are cutting costs, establishing more efficient operations, and lowering prices in order to compete more effectively with food discounters. Finally, a few have added Web-based sales. Today, one quarter of all grocery stores sell their goods online. Forrester Research estimates that 18 percent of the nation's households will be good prospects for online grocery buying and that the number buying online will increase from 4.5 million households last year to more that 14 million by 2006.[2]

Department store

A retail organization that carries a wide variety of product lines—typically clothing, home furnishings, and household goods; each line is operated as a separate department managed by specialist buyers or merchandisers.

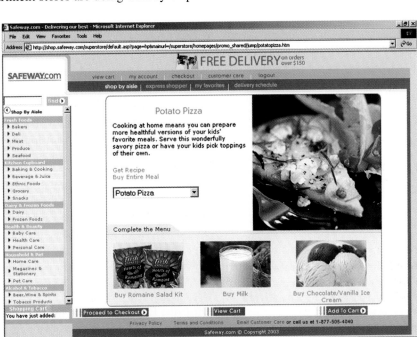

■ In the battle for "share of stomachs," Safeway and many large supermarkets have added Web-based sales. Today, one quarter of all grocery stores sell their goods online.

Convenience stores are small stores that carry a limited line of high-turnover convenience goods. Some 132,000 U.S. convenience stores posted sales last year of $290 billion. More than 60 percent of convenience store revenues come from sales of gasoline; more the 50 percent of in-store revenues are from cigarette and beverage sales.[3]

In recent years, the convenience store industry has suffered from overcapacity as its primary market of young, blue-collar men has shrunk. As a result, many chains are redesigning their stores to attract female shoppers. They are shedding the image of a "truck stop," where men go to buy beer, cigarettes, and magazines, and instead offer freshly prepared foods and cleaner, safer environments. Many are also applying micromarketing—tailoring each store's merchandise to the specific needs of its surrounding neighborhood. For example, a Stop-N-Go in an affluent neighborhood carries fresh produce, gourmet pasta sauces, chilled Evian water, and expensive wines. Stop-N-Go stores in Hispanic neighborhoods carry Spanish-language magazines and other goods catering to the specific needs of Hispanic consumers.

Superstores are much larger than regular supermarkets and offer a large assortment of routinely purchased food products, nonfood items, and services. Wal-Mart, Kmart, Target, and other discount retailers offer *supercenters*, combination food and discount stores that emphasize cross-merchandising. Toasters are above the fresh-baked bread, kitchen gadgets are across from produce, and infant centers carry everything from baby food to clothing. Supercenters are growing in the United States at an annual rate of

Supermarket

Large, low-cost, low-margin, high-volume, self-service store that carries a wide variety of food, laundry, and household products.

Convenience store

A small store, located near a residential area, that is open long hours 7 days a week and carries a limited line of high-turnover convenience goods.

Superstore

A store much larger than a regular supermarket that carries a large assortment of routinely purchased food and nonfood items and offers services such as dry cleaning, post offices, photo finishing, check cashing, bill paying, lunch counters, car care, and pet care.

25 percent, compared with a supermarket industry growth rate of only 1 percent. Wal-Mart, which opened its first supercenter in 1988, now has more than 1,250, capturing more than 70 percent of all supercenter volume.[4]

Recent years have also seen the explosive growth of superstores that are actually giant specialty stores, the so-called **category killers**. They feature stores the size of airplane hangars that carry a very deep assortment of a particular line with a knowledgeable staff. Category killers are prevalent in a wide range of categories, including books, baby gear, toys, electronics, home improvement products, linens and towels, party goods, sporting goods, even pet supplies. Another superstore variation, *hypermarkets*, are huge superstores, perhaps as large as *six* football fields. Although hypermarkets have been very successful in Europe and other world markets, they have met with little success in the United States.

Finally, for some retailers, the product line is actually a service. Service retailers include hotels and motels, banks, airlines, colleges, hospitals, movie theaters, tennis clubs, bowling alleys, restaurants, repair services, hair care shops, and dry cleaners. Service retailers in the United States are growing faster than product retailers.

Relative Prices Retailers can also be classified according to the prices they charge (see Table 11.1). Most retailers charge regular prices and offer normal-quality goods and customer service. Others offer higher-quality goods and service at higher prices. The retailers that feature low prices are discount stores and "off-price" retailers.

Discount Stores. A **discount store** sells standard merchandise at lower prices by accepting lower margins and selling higher volume. The early discount stores cut expenses by offering few services and operating in warehouselike facilities in low-rent, heavily traveled districts. In recent years, facing intense competition from other discounters and department stores, many discount retailers have "traded up." They have improved décor, added new lines and services, and expanding regionally and nationally, leading to higher costs and prices.

Off-Price Retailers. When the major discount stores traded up, a new wave of **off-price retailers** moved in to fill the low-price, high-volume gap. Ordinary discounters buy at regular wholesale prices and accept lower margins to keep prices down. In contrast, off-price retailers buy at less-than-regular wholesale prices and charge consumers less than retail. Off-price retailers can be found in all areas, from food, clothing, and electronics to no-frills banking and discount brokerages.

The three main types of off-price retailers are *independents, factory outlets,* and *warehouse clubs.* **Independent off-price retailers** either are owned and run by entrepreneurs or are divisions of larger retail corporations. Although many off-price operations are run by smaller independents, most large off-price retailer operations are owned by bigger retail chains. Examples include store retailers such as T.J.Maxx and Marshall's, owned by TJX Companies, and Web sellers such as Retail Exchange.com, Redtag.com, and CloseOut Now.com.

Factory outlets—such as the Manhattan's Brand Name Fashion Outlet and the factory outlets of Liz Claiborne, Carters, Levi Strauss, and other manufacturers—sometimes group together in *factory outlet malls* and *value-retail centers,* where dozens of outlet stores offer prices as low as 50 percent below retail on a wide range of items. Whereas outlet malls con-

Category killer

Giant specialty store that carries a very deep assortment of a particular line and is staffed by knowledgeable employees.

Discount store

A retail institution that sells standard merchandise at lower prices by accepting lower margins and selling at higher volume.

Off-price retailer

Retailer that buys at less-than-regular wholesale prices and sells at less than retail. Examples are factory outlets, independents, and warehouse clubs.

Independent off-price retailer

Off-price retailer that is either owned and run by entrepreneurs or is a division of a larger retail corporation.

Factory outlet

Off-price retailing operation that is owned and operated by a manufacturer and that normally carries the manufacturer's surplus, discontinued, or irregular goods.

■ Off-price retailing: Factory outlet malls and value-retail centers have blossomed in recent years, making them one of retailing's hottest growth areas.

sist primarily of manufacturers' outlets, value-retail centers combine manufacturers' outlets with off-price retail stores and department store clearance outlets. Factory outlet malls have become one of the hottest growth areas in retailing.

The malls now are moving upscale—and even dropping "factory" from their descriptions—narrowing the gap between factory outlet and more traditional forms of retailers. As the gap narrows, the discounts offered by outlets are getting smaller. However, a growing number of outlet malls now feature brands such as Coach, Polo Ralph Lauren, Dolce & Gabbana, Giorgio Armani, Gucci, and Versace, causing department stores to protest to the manufacturers of these brands. Given their higher costs, the department stores have to charge more than the off-price outlets. Manufacturers counter that they send last year's merchandise and seconds to the factory outlet malls, not the new merchandise that they supply to the department stores. The malls are also located far from urban areas, making travel to them more difficult. Still, the department stores are concerned about the growing number of shoppers willing to make weekend trips to stock up on branded merchandise at substantial savings.[5]

Warehouse clubs (or *wholesale clubs* or *membership warehouses*), such as Sam's Club, Costco, and BJ's, operate in huge, drafty, warehouselike facilities and offer few frills. Customers themselves must wrestle furniture, heavy appliances, and other large items to the checkout line. Such clubs make no home deliveries and often accept no credit cards. However, they do offer ultralow prices and surprise deals on selected branded merchandise. Whereas a weakening economy has slowed the growth of many traditional retailers, warehouse club sales have soared recently. These days, "consumers are laser-beam-focused on finding the best value," says an industry analyst, "and the absolute best value is at a club."[6]

Warehouse club
Off-price retailer that sells a limited selection of brand-name grocery items, appliances, clothing, and a hodgepodge of other goods at deep discounts to members who pay annual membership fees.

Organizational Approach Although many retail stores are independently owned, an increasing number are banding together under some form of corporate or contractual organization. The major types of retail organizations—*corporate chains*, *voluntary chains* and *retailer cooperatives*, *franchise organizations*, and *merchandising conglomerates*—are described in Table 11.2.

TABLE 11.2   Major Types of Retail Organizations

Type	Description	Examples
Corporate chain stores	Two or more outlets that are commonly owned and controlled, employ central buying and merchandising, and sell similar lines of merchandise. Corporate chains appear in all types of retailing, but they are strongest in department stores, variety stores, food stores, drugstores, shoe stores, and women's clothing stores.	Tower Records, Fayva (shoes), Pottery Barn (dinnerware and home furnishings)
Voluntary chains	Wholesaler-sponsored groups of independent retailers engaged in bulk buying and common merchandising.	Independent Grocers Alliance (IGA), Sentry Hardwares, Western Auto, True Value
Retailer cooperatives	Groups of independent retailers who set up a central buying organization and conduct joint promotion efforts.	Associated Grocers (groceries), Ace (hardware)
Franchise organizations	Contractual association between a *franchiser* (a manufacturer, wholesales, or service organization) and *franchisees* (independent businesspeople who buy the right to own and operate one or more units in the franchise system). Franchise organizations are normally based on some unique product, service, or method of doing business, or on a trade name or patent, or on goodwill that the franchiser had developed.	McDonald's, Subway, Pizza Hut, Jiffy Lube, Meineke Mufflers, 7-Eleven
Merchandising conglomerates	A free-form corporation that combines several diversified retailing lines and forms under central ownership, along with some integration of their distribution and management functions.	Target Corporation

Chain stores

Two or more outlets that are owned and controlled in common, have central buying and merchandising, and sell similar lines of merchandise.

Chain stores are two or more outlets that are commonly owned and controlled. They have many advantages over independents. Their size allows them to buy in large quantities at lower prices and to gain promotional economies. They can hire specialists to deal with areas such as pricing, promotion, merchandising, inventory control, and sales forecasting.

The great success of corporate chains caused many independents to band together in one of two forms of contractual associations. One is the *voluntary chain*—a wholesaler-sponsored group of independent retailers that engages in group buying and common merchandising—which we discussed in Chapter 10. Examples include Western Auto and Do it Best hardware stores. The other form of contractual association is the *retailer cooperative*—a group of independent retailers that bands together to set up a jointly owned, central wholesale operation and conducts joint merchandising and promotion efforts. Examples are Associated Grocers and Ace Hardware. These organizations give independents the buying and promotion economies they need to meet the prices of corporate chains.

Franchise

A contractual association between a manufacturer, wholesaler, or service organization (a franchiser) and independent businesspeople (franchisees) who buy the right to own and operate one or more units in the franchise system.

Another form of contractual retail organization is a **franchise**. The main difference between franchise organizations and other contractual systems (voluntary chains and retail cooperatives) is that franchise systems are normally based on some unique product or service; on a method of doing business; or on the trade name, goodwill, or patent that the franchiser has developed. Franchising has been prominent in fast foods, video stores, health and fitness centers, haircutting, auto rentals, motels, travel agencies, real estate, and dozens of other product and service areas.

Once considered upstarts among independent businesses, franchises now command 35 percent of all retail sales in the United States. These days, it's nearly impossible to stroll down a city block or drive on a suburban street without seeing a McDonald's, Subway, Jiffy Lube, or Holiday Inn. One of the best-known and most successful franchisers, McDonald's, now has more than 30,000 stores in 118 countries. It serves more than 46 million customers a day and racks up more than $41 billion in annual systemwide sales. More than 70 percent of McDonald's restaurants worldwide are owned and operated by franchisees. Gaining fast is Subway Sandwiches and Salads, one of the fastest-growing franchises, with nearly 20,000 shops in 74 countries, including some 16,000 in the United States. Franchising is even moving into new areas such as education. For example, LearnRight Corporation franchises its methods for teaching students thinking skills.[7]

Finally, *merchandising conglomerates* are corporations that combine several different retailing forms under central ownership. An example is Target Corporation, which operates Marshall Fields (upscale department stores), Target (upscale discount stores), Mervyn's (middle-market apparel and home soft goods), and Target.direct (online retailing and direct marketing). Diversified retailing, similar to a multi-branding strategy, provides superior management systems and economies that benefit all the separate retail operations, and is likely to increase.

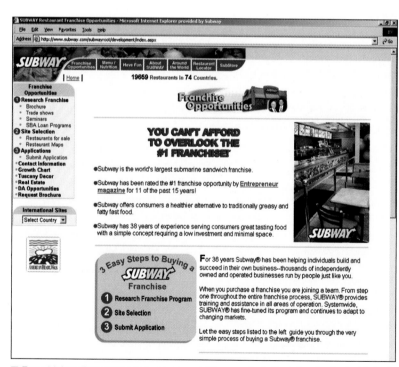

■ Franchising: Franchises now command 35 percent of all retail sales in the United States. Subway is one of the fastest-growing franchises, with nearly 20,000 shops in 74 countries.

Retailer Marketing Decisions

Retailers are always searching for new marketing strategies to attract and hold customers. In the past, retailers attracted customers with unique products, more or better services than their competitors offered, or credit cards. Today, national-brand manufacturers, in their drive for volume, have placed their branded goods everywhere. National brands are found not

■ Retailer communities: Sony Computer Entertainment America's Playstation.com Web site builds community among its customers. The site's message boards are incredibly active, discussing techie topics but also lifestyle issues, such as music and personal taste.

Brick-and-mortar retailers are not the only ones creating community. Others have also built virtual communities on the Internet:

> Sony actively builds community among its Playstation customers. Its recent Playstation.com campaign created message boards where its game players could post messages to one another. The boards are incredibly active, discussing techie topics but also providing the opportunity for members, fiercely competitive and opinionated, to vote on lifestyle issues, such as music and personal taste, no matter how trivial. Although Sony is laissez-faire about the boards and does not feed them messages, the company sees the value in having its customers' adamant conversations occur directly on its site. "Our customers are our evangelists. They are a very vocal and loyal fan base," says a Sony spokesperson. "There are things we can learn from them."[24]

Linking the Concepts

SPEED BUMP

Time out! So-called experts have long predicted that nonstore retailing eventually will replace store retailing as our primary way to shop. What do you think?

■ Shop for a good book at the Barnes & Noble Web site (www.bn.com), taking time to browse the site and see what it has to offer. Next, shop at a nearby Barnes & Noble, Borders Books, or other bookstore. Compare the two shopping experiences. Where would you rather shop? On what occasions? Why?

■ A Barnes & Noble store creates an ideal "community" where people can "hang out." How does its Web site compare on this dimension?

Wholesaling

All activities involved in selling goods and services to those buying for resale or business use.

Wholesaler

A firm engaged *primarily* in wholesaling activity.

◼◼ Wholesaling

Wholesaling includes all activities involved in selling goods and services to those buying for resale or business use. We call **wholesalers** those firms engaged *primarily* in wholesaling activity.

Wholesalers buy mostly from producers and sell mostly to retailers, industrial consumers, and other wholesalers. As a result, many of the nation's largest and most important wholesalers are largely unknown to final consumers. For example, you may never have heard of SuperValu, even though it's a $23 billion company and the nation's largest food wholesaler. Or how about Grainger, the leading wholesaler of maintenance, repair, and operating (MRO) supplies? (See Marketing at Work 11.3.)

But why are wholesalers used at all? For example, why would a producer use wholesalers rather than selling directly to retailers or consumers? Quite simply, wholesalers add value by performing one or more of the following channel functions:

- *Selling and promoting:* Wholesalers' sales forces help manufacturers reach many small customers at a low cost. The wholesaler has more contacts and is often more trusted by the buyer than the distant manufacturer.

- *Buying and assortment building:* Wholesalers can select items and build assortments needed by their customers, thereby saving the consumers much work.

- *Bulk breaking:* Wholesalers save their customers money by buying in carload lots and breaking bulk (breaking large lots into small quantities).

- *Warehousing:* Wholesalers hold inventories, thereby reducing the inventory costs and risks of suppliers and customers.

- *Transportation:* Wholesalers can provide quicker delivery to buyers because they are closer than the producers.

- *Financing:* Wholesalers finance their customers by giving credit, and they finance their suppliers by ordering early and paying bills on time.

- *Risk bearing:* Wholesalers absorb risk by taking title and bearing the cost of theft, damage, spoilage, and obsolescence.

- *Market information:* Wholesalers give information to suppliers and customers about competitors, new products, and price developments.

- *Management services and advice:* Wholesalers often help retailers train their salesclerks, improve store layouts and displays, and set up accounting and inventory-control systems.

Types of Wholesalers

Merchant wholesaler

An independently owned business that takes title to the merchandise it handles.

Broker

A wholesaler who does not take title to goods and whose function is to bring buyers and sellers together and assist in negotiation.

Agent

A wholesaler who represents buyers or sellers on a relatively permanent basis, performs only a few functions, and does not take title to goods.

Wholesalers fall into three major groups (see Table 11.3): *merchant wholesalers; agents and brokers,* and *manufacturers' sales branches and offices.* **Merchant wholesalers** are the largest single group of wholesalers, accounting for roughly 50 percent of all wholesaling. Merchant wholesalers include two broad types: full-service wholesalers and limited-service wholesalers. *Full-service wholesalers* provide a full set of services, whereas the various *limited-service wholesalers* offer fewer services to their suppliers and customers. The several different types of limited-service wholesalers perform varied specialized functions in the distribution channel.

Brokers and *agents* differ from merchant wholesalers in two ways: They do not take title to goods, and they perform only a few functions. Like merchant wholesalers, they generally specialize by product line or customer type. A **broker** brings buyers and sellers together and assists in negotiation. **Agents** represent buyers or sellers on a more permanent basis. *Manufacturers' agents* (also called manufacturers' representatives) are the most common type of agent wholesaler. The third major type of wholesaling is that done in

Marketing at Work | 11.3

Grainger: The Biggest Market Leader You've Never Heard Of?

Grainger may be the biggest market leader you've never heard of. It's a $4.6 billion business that offers more than 500,000 products and parts to more than 1.5 million customers. Its 600 North American branches, more than 15,000 employees, and innovative Web site handle more than 100,000 transactions a day. Grainger's customers include organizations ranging from factories, garages, and grocers to military bases and schools. Most American businesses are located within 20 minutes of a Grainger branch. Customers include notables such as Abbott Laboratories, General Motors, Campbell Soup, American Airlines, Mercedes-Benz, and the U.S. Postal Service. Grainger also operates one of the highest-volume B2B sites on the Web.

So, how come you've never heard of Grainger? Most likely it's because Grainger is a wholesaler. And like most wholesalers, it operates behind the scenes, selling only to other businesses. Moreover, Grainger operates in the not-so-glamorous world of maintenance, repair, and operating (MRO) supplies.

But whereas you might know little about Grainger, to its customers the company is very well known and much valued. Through its branch network, service centers, sales reps, catalog, and Web site, Grainger links customers with the supplies they need to keep their facilities running smoothly, everything from light bulbs, cleaners, and display cases to nuts and bolts, motors, valves, power tools, and test equipment. Grainger is by far the nation's largest MRO wholesaler. Notes one industry reporter, "If industrial America is an engine, Grainger is its lubricant."

Grainger serves as an important link between thousands of MRO supplies manufacturers on one side and millions of industrial and commercial customers on the other. It operates on a simple value proposition: to make it easier and less costly for customers to find and buy MRO supplies. It starts by acting as a one-stop shop for products to maintain facilities. Most customers will tell you that Grainger sells everything—everything—from the ordinary to the out-of-the-ordinary. For example, it stocks thousands of light bulbs—about every light bulb known to mankind. If you don't believe it, go to www.grainger.com and search "light bulbs"! As for the not-so-ordinary:

> Grainger sells 19 different models of floor-cleaning machines, has 49 catalog pages of socket wrenches, and offers nine different sizes of hydraulic service jacks, an assortment of NFL-licensed hard hats bearing

team logos, and item No. 6AV22, a $36.90 dispenser rack for two 1 gallon containers of Gatorade. According to corporate legend, [Grainger] is the only place that workers on the Alaskan Pipeline have been able to find repellent to cope with arctic bears during their mating season.

Beyond making it easier for customers to find the products they need, Grainger also helps them streamline their acquisition processes. For most companies, acquiring MRO supplies is a very costly process. In fact, 40 percent of the cost of MRO supplies stems from the purchase process, including finding a supplier, negotiating the best deal, placing the order, receiving the order, and paying the invoice. Grainger

Although you may never have heard it, Grainger is by far the world's leading wholesaler of maintenance, repair, and operating supplies.

(continued)

constantly seeks ways to reduce the costs associated with MRO supplies acquisition, both internally and externally. Says one analyst, "Grainger will reduce your search and your process costs for items, instead of your having to order 10 things from 10 different companies, and you'll get one invoice. That's pretty powerful."

One company found that working with Grainger cut MRO requisition time by more than 60 percent; lead times went from days to hours. Its supply chain dropped from 12,000 suppliers to 560—significantly reducing expenses. Similarly, a large timber and paper-products company has come to appreciate the value of Grainger's selection and streamlined ordering process. It orders two-thirds of its supplies from Grainger's Web site at an annual acquisition cost of only $300,000. By comparison, for the remainder of its needs, this company deals with more than 1,300 small distributors at an acquisition cost of $2.4 million each year, eight times the cost of dealing with Grainger for half of the volume. As a result, the company is now looking for ways to buy all of its MRO supplies from Grainger.

You might think that helping customers find what they need easily and efficiently would be enough to keep Grainger atop the MRO mountain. But Grainger goes even further. On a broader level, it builds lasting relationships with customers by helping them find *solutions* to their overall MRO problems. Acting as consultants, Grainger sales reps help buyers with everything from improving their supply chain management to reducing inventories and streamlining warehousing operations.

Branches . . . serve as the base for Grainger territory managers who provide on-site help to big facilities. . . . [Reps can] tour a factory or an office complex or even a hotel and suggest to its managers exactly what supplies they really need to keep the place up to snuff, right down to how many gallons of carpet cleaner they'll require each week. That's how Grainger knows, for example, that one Biltmore Hotel has 7,000 light bulbs. . . . "Our reps can pretty much stand outside a building and get a general feel for what kinds of products the customer needs" [says James Ryan, Grainger's executive vice president of marketing, sales, and service].

Grainger has launched a series of programs designed to add value to its commodity business. For example, through its "Click & Sell" program, Grainger uses information collected about customers, such as industry data and purchase histories, to help sales reps find solutions for customer needs. If, for example, a customer places an order for a pump to use with caustic chemicals, the Grainger rep might also suggest gloves and safety glasses. If an item is unavailable, the database identifies alternative products to get the job done.

Grainger also offers value to customers through its links to and clout with suppliers:

Jason Eastin is facilities operations director for JRV Management, a . . . company that runs community and private sports facilities in metropolitan Detroit. He relies on Grainger in part because of its clout with factory reps. When his company was opening up its newest complex, he asked Chris Clemons, a Grainger territory manager, for help figuring out the number and kinds of fixtures that would be required. Clemons summoned a rep from Rubbermaid, the household-products maker, who showed up with a laptop and a software program that churned out a reasonable supply chain within 20 minutes. Similarly, Clemens worked with a General Electric salesperson, who figured out how Eastin could stretch out "relamping" his facilities to every 2 years, instead of annually, and cut costs significantly as well by switching to a different kind of metal-halide bulb as the primary kind of illumination for his ice arenas. "To have General Electric provide that service to me at no charge would never happen," Eastin says. "But Grainger has that buying-power structure. They open up those kinds of opportunities to me."

So now you've heard of Grainger, a wholesaler that succeeds by making life easier and more efficient for commercial and industrial buyers and sellers. Although a market leader, Grainger still captures only 4 percent of the highly fragmented U.S. market for MRO goods. That leaves a lot of room for growth. But to take advantage of the opportunities, Grainger must continue to find innovative ways to add value. "Our system makes our business partners and suppliers more efficient," says Fred Loepp, vice president of product management at Grainger, "and that benefits the entire supply chain." Says Theresa Dubiel, branch manager at Grainger's Romulus, Michigan, branch, "If we don't save [customers] time and money every time they come [to us], they won't come back."

Sources: Excerpts from Dale Buss, "The New Deal," *Sales & Marketing Management*, June 2002, pp. 25–30; and Colleen Gourley, "Redefining Distribution," *Warehousing Management*, October 2000, pp. 28–30. Also see Leslie Langnau, "B2B E-commerce: A Look at What Works," *Material Handling Management*, February 2002, p. 42; Steve Konicki and Eileen Colkin, "Attitude Adjustment," *Informationweek*, March 25, 2002, pp. 20–22; "W.W. Grainger, Inc.," *Hoover's Company Profiles*, Austin, June 15, 2003; and information accessed at www.grainger.com, December 2003.

Manufacturers' sales branches and offices
Wholesaling by sellers or buyers themselves rather than through independent wholesalers.

manufacturers' sales branches and offices by sellers or buyers themselves rather than through independent wholesalers.

Wholesaler Marketing Decisions

Wholesalers now face growing competitive pressures, more demanding customers, new technologies, and more direct-buying programs on the part of large industrial, institutional,

TABLE 11.3   Major Types of Wholesalers

Type	Description
Merchant wholesalers	Independently owned businesses that take title to the merchandise they handle. In different trades they are called *jobbers,* distributors or *mill supply houses.* Include full-service wholesalers and limited-service wholesalers:
Full-service wholesalers	Provide a full line of services: carrying stock, maintaining a sales force, offering credit, making deliveries and providing management assistance. There are two types:
Wholesale merchants	Sell primarily to retailers and provide a full range of services. *General merchandise wholesalers* carry several merchandise lines, whereas *general line wholesalers* carry one or two lines in great depth. *Specialty wholesalers* specialize in carrying only part of a line. Examples: health food wholesalers, seafood wholesalers.
Industrial distributors	Sell to manufacturers rather than to retailers. Provide several services, such as carrying stock, offering credit, and providing delivery. May carry a broad range of merchandise, a general line, or a specialty line.
Limited-service wholesalers	Offer fewer services than full-service wholesalers. Limited-service wholesalers are of several types:
Cash-and-carry wholesalers	Carry a limited line of fast-moving goods and sell to small retailers for cash. Normally do not deliver. Example: A small fish store retailer may drive to a cash-and-carry fish wholesaler, buy fish for cash, and bring the merchandise back to the store.
Truck wholesalers (or truck jobbers)	Perform primarily a selling and delivery function. Carry limited line of semiperishable merchandise (such as milk, bread, snack foods), which they sell for cash as they make their rounds to supermarkets, small groceries, hospitals, restaurants, factory cafeterias, and hotels.
Drop shippers	Do not carry inventory or handle the product. On receiving an order, they select a manufacturer, who ships the merchandise directly to the customer. The drop shipper assumes title and risk from the time the order is accepted to its delivery to the customer. They operate in bulk industries, such as coal, lumber, and heavy equipment.
Rack jobbers	Serve grocery and drug retailers, mostly in nonfood items. They send delivery trucks to stores, where the delivery people set up toys, paperbacks, hardware items, health and beauty aids, or other items. They price the goods, keep them fresh, set up point-of-purchase displays, and keep inventory records. Rack jobbers retain title to the goods and bill the retailers only for the goods sold to consumers.
Producers' cooperatives	Owned by farmer members and assemble farm produce to sell in local markets. The co-op's profits are distributed to members at the end of the year. They often attempt to improve product quality and promote a co-op brand name, such as Sun Maid raisins, Sunkist oranges, or Diamond walnuts.
Mail-order wholesalers	Send catalogs to retail, industrial, and institutional customers featuring jewelry, cosmetics, specialty foods, and other small items. Maintain no outside sales force. Main customers are businesses in small outlying areas. Orders are filled and sent by mail, truck, or other transportation.
Brokers and agents	Do not take title to goods. Main function is to facilitate buying and selling, for which they earn a commission on the selling price. Generally specialize by product line or customer types.
Brokers	Chief function is bringing buyers and sellers together and assisting in negotiation. They are paid by the party who hired them and do not carry inventory, get involved in financing, or assume risk. Examples: food brokers, real estate brokers, insurance brokers, and security brokers.
Agents	Represent either buyers or sellers on a more permanent basis than brokers do. There are several types:
Manufacturers' agents	Represent two or more manufacturers of complementary lines. A formal written agreement with each manufacturer covers pricing, territories, order-handling, delivery service and warranties, and commission rates. Often used in such lines as apparel, furniture and electrical goods. Most manufacturers' agents are small businesses, with only a few skilled salespeople as employees. They are hired by small manufacturers who cannot afford their own field sales forces and by large manufacturers who use agents to open new territories or to cover territories that cannot support full-time salespeople.
Selling agents	Have contractual authority to sell a manufacturer's entire output. The manufacturer either is not interested in the selling function or feels unqualified. The selling agent serves as a sales department and has significant influence over prices, terms, and conditions of sale. Found in product areas such as textiles, industrial machinery and equipment, coal and coke, chemicals, and metals.

Continued

TABLE 11.3 (continued)

Type	Description
Purchasing agents	Generally have a long-term relationship with buyers and make purchases for them, often receiving, inspecting, warehousing, and shipping the merchandise to the buyers. They provide helpful market information to clients and help them obtain the best goods and prices available.
Commission merchants	Take physical possession of products and negotiate sales. Normally, they are not employed on a long-term basis. Used most often in agricultural marketing by farmers who do not want to sell their own output and do not belong to producers' cooperatives. The commission merchant takes a truckload of commodities to a central market, sells it for the best price, deducts a commission and expenses, and remits the balance to the producers.
Manufacturers' and retailers' branches and offices	Wholesaling operations conducted by sellers or buyers themselves rather than through independent wholesalers. Separate branches and offices can be dedicated to either sales or purchasing.
Sales branches and offices	Set up by manufacturers to improve inventory control, selling, and promotion. *Sales branches* carry inventory and are found in industries such as lumber and automotive equipment and parts. *Sales offices* do not carry inventory and are most prominent in dry-goods and notions industries.
Purchasing offices	Perform a role similar to that of brokers or agents but are part of the buyer's organization. Many retailers set up purchasing offices in major market centers such as New York and Chicago.

and retail buyers. As a result, they have had to take a fresh look at the marketing strategies. As with retailers, their marketing decisions include choices of target markets, positioning, and the marketing mix—product assortments and services, price, promotion, and place (see Figure 11.2).

Target Market and Positioning Decision Like retailers, wholesalers must define their target markets and position themselves effectively—they cannot serve everyone. They can choose a target group by size of customer (only large retailers), type of customer (convenience stores only), need for service (customers who need credit), or other factors. Within the target group, they can identify the more profitable customers, design stronger offers, and build better relationships with them. They can propose automatic reordering systems, set up management-training and advising systems, or even sponsor a voluntary chain. They can discourage less profitable customers by requiring larger orders or adding service charges to smaller ones.

Marketing Mix Decisions Like retailers, wholesalers must decide on product assortment and services, prices, promotion, and place. The wholesaler's "product" is the assortment of *products and services* that it offers. Wholesalers are under great pressure to carry a full line and to stock enough for immediate delivery. But this practice can damage profits. Wholesalers today are cutting down on the number of lines they carry, choosing to carry only the more profitable ones. Wholesalers are also rethinking which services count

FIGURE 11.2

Wholesaler Marketing Decisions

most in building strong customer relationships and which should be dropped or charged for. The key is to find the mix of services most valued by their target customers.

Price is also an important wholesaler decision. Wholesalers usually mark up the cost of goods by a standard percentage—say, 20 percent. Expenses may run 17 percent of the gross margin, leaving a profit margin of 3 percent. In grocery wholesaling, the average profit margin is often less than 2 percent. Wholesalers are trying new pricing approaches. They may cut their margin on some lines in order to win important new customers. They may ask suppliers for special price breaks when they can turn them into an increase in the supplier's sales.

Although *promotion* can be critical to wholesaler success, most wholesalers are not promotion minded. Their use of trade advertising, sales promotion, personal selling, and public relations is largely scattered and unplanned. Many are behind the times in personal selling—they still see selling as a single salesperson talking to a single customer instead of as a team effort to sell, build, and service major accounts. Wholesalers also need to adopt some of the nonpersonal promotion techniques used by retailers. They need to develop an overall promotion strategy and to make greater use of supplier promotion materials and programs.

Finally, *place* is important—wholesalers must choose their locations, facilities, and Web locations carefully. Wholesalers typically locate in low-rent, low-tax areas and tend to invest little money in their buildings, equipment, and systems. As a result, their materials-handling and order-processing systems are often outdated. In recent years, however, large and progressive wholesalers are reacting to rising costs by investing in automated warehouses and online ordering systems. Orders are fed from the retailer's system directly into the wholesaler's computer, and the items are picked up by mechanical devices and automatically taken to a shipping platform where they are assembled. Most large wholesalers are using technology to carry out accounting, billing, inventory control, and forecasting. Modern wholesalers are adapting their services to the needs of target customers and finding cost-reducing methods of doing business.

Trends in Wholesaling

As the wholesaling industry moves into the twenty-first century, it faces considerable challenges. The industry remains vulnerable to one of the most enduring trends of the last decade—fierce resistance to price increases and the winnowing out of suppliers who are not adding value based on cost and quality. Progressive wholesalers constantly watch for better ways to meet the changing needs of their suppliers and target customers. They recognize that, in the long run, their only reason for existence comes from adding value by increasing the efficiency and effectiveness of the entire marketing channel. To achieve this goal, they must constantly improve their services and reduce their costs.

McKesson HBOC, the nation's leading wholesaler of pharmaceuticals, health and beauty care, and home health care products, provides an example of progressive wholesaling. To survive, McKesson HBOC has to remain more cost effective than manufacturers' sales branches. Thus, the company has built efficient automated warehouses, established direct computer links with drug manufacturers, and set up extensive online supply management and accounts-receivable systems for customers. It offers retail pharmacists a wide range of online resources, including supply management assistance, catalog searches, real-time order tracking, and account management systems. Retailers can even use the McKesson system to maintain medical profiles on their customers. McKesson's medical–surgical supply and equipment customers receive a rich assortment of online solutions and supply management tools, including an online order-management system and real-time information on products

■ To improve efficiency and service, McKesson set up an extensive online supply management system by which customers can order, track, and manage their pharmaceutical and medical-surgical supplies. Retailers can even use the McKesson system to maintain medical profiles on their customers.

and pricing, inventory availability, and order status. According to McKesson, it adds value in the channel by providing "supply, information, and health care management products and services designed to reduce costs and improve quality across healthcare."[25]

The distinction between large retailers and large wholesalers continues to blur. Many retailers now operate formats such as wholesale clubs and hypermarkets that perform many wholesale functions. In return, many large wholesalers are setting up their own retailing operations. SuperValu and Fleming, both leading food wholesalers, now operate their own retailing operations. For example, SuperValu, the nation's largest food wholesaling company, is also the country's 11th largest food retailer. Almost 45 percent of the company's $23 billion in sales comes from its Bigg's, Cub Foods, Save-A-Lot, Farm Fresh, Hornbacher's, Laneco, Metro, Scott's Foods, Shop 'n Save, and Shoppers Food Warehouse stores.[26]

Wholesalers will continue to increase the services they provide to retailers—retail pricing, cooperative advertising, marketing and management information reports, accounting services, online transactions, and others. Rising costs on the one hand, and the demand for increased services on the other, will put the squeeze on wholesaler profits. Wholesalers who do not find efficient ways to deliver value to their customers will soon drop by the wayside. However, the increased use of computerized, automated, and Web-based systems will help wholesalers to contain the costs of ordering, shipping, and inventory holding, boosting their productivity.

Finally, facing slow growth in their domestic markets and developments such as the North American Free Trade Agreement, many large wholesalers are now going global. For example, in 1991, McKesson bought out its Canadian partner, Provigo. The company now receives about 3 percent of its total revenues from Canada.

REST STOP:
Reviewing the Concepts

Pull in here and reflect back on this retailing and wholesaling chapter, the last of two chapters on distribution channels. In this chapter, we first looked at the nature and importance of retailing, major types of retailers, the decisions retailers make, and the future of retailing. We then examined these same topics for wholesalers. Although most retailing is conducted in retail stores, in recent years, nonstore retailing has increased rapidly. In addition, although many retail stores are independently owned, an increasing number are now banding together under some form of corporate or contractual organization. Wholesalers, too, have experienced recent environmental changes, most notably mounting competitive pressures. They have faced new sources of competition, more demanding customers, new technologies, and more direct-buying programs on the part of large industrial, institutional, and retail buyers.

1. Explain the roles of retailers and wholesalers in the distribution channel.

Retailing and wholesaling consist of many organizations bringing goods and services from the point of production to the point of use. *Retailing* includes all activities involved in selling goods or services directly to final consumers for their personal, nonbusiness use. *Wholesaling* includes all the activities involved in selling goods or services to those who are buying for the purpose of resale or for business use. Wholesalers perform many functions, including selling and promoting, buying and assortment building, bulk breaking, warehousing, transporting, financing, risk bearing, supplying market information, and providing management services and advice.

2. Describe the major types of retailers and give examples of each.

Retailers can be classified as *store retailers* and *nonstore retailers*. Although most goods and services are sold through stores, nonstore retailing has been growing much faster than has store retailing. Store retailers can be further classified by the *amount of service* they provide (self-service, limited-service, or full-service), *product line sold* (specialty stores, department stores, supermarkets, convenience stores, superstores, and service businesses), and *relative prices* (discount stores and off-price retailers). Today, many retailers are banding together in corporate and contractual *retail organizations* (corporate chains, voluntary chains and retailer cooperatives, franchise organizations, and merchandising conglomerates).

3. Identify the major types of wholesalers and give examples of each.

Wholesalers fall into three groups. First, *merchant wholesalers* take possession of the goods. They include *full-service wholesalers* (wholesale merchants, industrial distributors) and *limited-service wholesalers* (cash-and-carry wholesalers, truck wholesalers, drop shippers, rack jobbers, producers' cooperatives, and mail-order wholesalers). Second, *brokers* and *agents* do not take possession of the goods but are paid a commission for aiding buying and selling. Finally, *manufacturers' sales branches and offices* are wholesaling operations conducted by nonwholesalers to bypass the wholesalers.

4. Explain the marketing decisions facing retailers and wholesalers.

Each retailer must make decisions about its target markets and positioning, product assortment and services, price, promotion, and place. Retailers need to choose target markets carefully and position themselves strongly. Today, wholesaling is holding its own in the economy. Progressive wholesalers are adapting their services to the needs of target customers and are seeking cost-reducing methods of doing business. Faced with slow growth in their domestic markets and developments such as the North American Free Trade Association, many large wholesalers are also now going global.

Navigating the Key Terms

Agent	Franchise	Shopping center
Broker	Independent off-price retailer	Specialty store
Category killer	Manufacturers' sales branches	Supermarket
Chain stores	and offices	Superstore
Convenience store	Merchant wholesaler	Warehouse club
Department store	Off-price retailer	Wheel-of-retailing concept
Discount store	Retailer	Wholesaler
Factory outlet	Retailing	Wholesaling

Travel Log

Discussing the Issues

1. Distinguish between the following types of retail forms: specialty stores, department stores, supermarkets, convenience stores, superstores, and category killers.

2. Identify a retailer in your town that has gone out of business in the past few years. What factors do you think led to this store's downfall?

3. As the chapter indicates, the popularity of nonstore retailing continues to grow. From a consumer's perspective, what are some of the advantages and disadvantages of shopping through mail-order catalogs, television shopping networks, and online?

4. Discuss the concept of retail convergence as it applies to wrist watches. How can smaller retailers compete in such an environment?

5. Describe the functions that wholesalers have traditionally performed. Which ones appear to be the most likely candidates for either large producers or large retailers to take over? Explain your response.

Application Questions

1. Develop a table with the retail characteristics of amount of service, product line length and breadth, relative prices, and organizational structure as the rows of the table. Place the following retailers at the top of each column in the table: Best Buy, Sears, Sam's Club, The Gap, Wal-Mart, and a local convenience store. Complete the cells in the table by describing each of the retailers for each of the characteristics. What implications can you draw from this table?

2. Pick one of these national retail chains (The Gap, Barnes and Noble, Foot Locker, or Walgreens) and a local retail firm that sell the same type and quality of merchandise. Compare and contrast the two retailers on their target market, product and service assortment, store atmosphere, prices, promotion tools, and location. Why would a shopper pick one of these retailers over the other when shopping for products they both carry?

3. Visit a store in your community that also has an e-commerce web site (e.g., Kmart, Kroger, Target, or Sears). After visiting both the store and the Web site, consider the following questions. Do the two retail shopping alternatives attract the same type of customer? Describe the customer who would shop at the bricks-and-mortar store location and the customer who would shop on the store's Web site. How are the store and Web site positioned differently? If they are not positioned differently, should they be? And how could this be accomplished? Are there any potential disadvantages for the store in having these two distribution channels?

Under the Hood: Focus on Technology

New technology may be coming to a grocery store near you. Shopping Buddy, currently in a test market in Massachusetts, is a small cart-mounted computer monitor and barcode reader. To begin using the cart, customers scan their customer card on the cart and their shopping history with the store is automatically downloaded to the cart. Customers can then scan items as they pull them off the shelf and place them directly into bags on the cart. When it is time to check out, they simply scan their card again and pay. No more waiting in lines as the cashier scans all your items.

But Shopping Buddy does more than just speed the checkout process. Because it knows your shopping history, it can remind you when you have not purchased an item in a while, it can tell you where in the store to find particular items you are looking for and how far away from it you are, it will alert you to any sale items that day, and you can even place your order at the Deli counter from the cart and it will alert you when it is ready to be picked up.

1. What is your initial reaction to this type of technology? Would you want to shop this way?

2. What advantages and disadvantages are there for stores implementing this technology?

3. What privacy concerns might shoppers have and how could a store minimize those concerns?

Focus on Ethics

Some individuals complain that big retailers like Wal-Mart, Home Depot, and Best Buy are hurting communities by driving smaller "mom and pop" operations out of business. These critics complain that the loss of these smaller retailers means that profits leave the community, service levels are reduced, and retail locations sit empty. On the other hand, proponents of large retailers suggest that these "big box" retailers offer consumers convenience, lower prices, and many employment opportunities.

1. What, if anything, should city governments do to protect local retailers from the threat of large retailers?

2. What are some alternative strategies smaller retailers can use to compete against large retailers, rather than going head-to-head with them on the basis of large selection and low prices?

3. Divide into teams of three to five students and take one side of this issue: Do large retailers like Wal-Mart, Home Depot, and Best Buy ultimately help or harm the communities they enter?

Videos

The Federated video case that accompanies this chapter is located in Appendix 1 at the back of the book.

Student Materials

Need a tune-up? A study guide and OneKey access code are available to aid in your review of chapter material. Your instructor may choose to have these items shrink-wrapped with your text or you may purchase them separately at www.prenhall.com/marketing.

The Duck Shops Here!

www.aflac.

About Us • Products • Policyholder Services • Employer Services • Investor Relations • Corporate Careers • Sales Opportu

QUICK ACTION

Get a Claim Form →
Find a State Sales Office →
Contact Us →
Request Information →

AFLAC Cancer Center News

Children's Healthcare of Atlanta and AFLAC Establish First Endowed Chair

see more ->

Shop for Duck Gear here !

Proceeds from the sale of the plush AFLAC Duck on this site go to the AFLAC Cancer Center.

60,770 AFLAC Ducks sold   Buy Now →

Internet Billing →   Policyholder Service Center
Press Center →   Formularios de Reclamacione
Ask About It At Work →   How to Use This Site →
Agent Login →   アフラック　日本社 →

■ *After reading this chapter, you should be able to*

   1. Discuss the process and advantages of integrated marketing communications   *2. Define* the five promotion tools and discuss the factors that must be considered in shaping the overall promotion mix   *3. Describe* and discuss the major decisions involved in developing an advertising program   *4. Explain* how sales promotion campaigns are developed and implemented   *5. Explain* how companies use public relations to communicate with their publics

Integrated Marketing Communication: Advertising, Sales Promotion, and Public Relations

12

ROAD MAP | Previewing the Concepts

We'll forge ahead now into the last of the marketing mix tools—promotion. You'll find that promotion is not a single tool but rather a mix of several tools. Ideally, under the concept of *integrated marketing communications,* the company will carefully coordinate these promotion elements to deliver a clear, consistent, and compelling message about the organization and its products. We'll begin by introducing you to the various promotion mix tools and to the importance of integrated marketing communications. Then, we'll look more carefully at three of the tools—advertising, sales promotion, and public relations. In the next chapter, we'll visit personal selling and direct marketing.

For starters, let's look closely at a highly successful advertising campaign that features an improbable spokesperson—er, spokes*duck*? As you read along, ask yourself just what is it that makes this such an effective advertising campaign?

Quick, name a supplemental insurance company! The chances are good that you thought of AFLAC, even if you're not entirely certain what supplemental insurance is. The highly successful $9.7 billion insurer is now by far the best-known firm in the supplemental insurance industry, which offers policies that kick in to pay expenses not covered by the standard health, life, and disability policies provided by most employers.

But AFLAC hasn't always enjoyed such high levels of recognition. Until recently, about the only people who'd ever heard of AFLAC lived either in Columbus, Georgia (where the company was founded), or in Japan (where it does more than 70 percent of its business, commands 85 percent of the supplemental insurance market, and serves 95 percent of the companies listed on the Tokyo Stock Exchange). Just a few years ago, only 13 percent of Americans even recognized the company's name. But now, thanks to an unorthodox advertising campaign—featuring an improbable squawking white duck—practically every American knows about AFLAC.

AFLAC's ads used to look just like every other insurance company's ads. They were what one analyst describes as "warm and fuzzy, with happy family members looking at one another lovingly." And while they were no better or worse than the competitors' efforts, these run-of-the-mill

ads were seriously overshadowed by the smart and funny ads of companies in other industries. "We realized we are competing for the attention of viewers who are not only watching [other] insurance ads, but [are also seeing] entertaining commercials for other products," says Kathleen Spencer, AFLAC's director of corporate communications.

So, in 1999, AFLAC began looking for a better way to build brand awareness and deliver its message to consumers. The company needed something radically different—ads that would break through today's unending advertising clutter. "We were at a point to try something new, and we were willing to take a risk," says Spencer.

The new brand-building effort presented challenges. According to the analyst, "Research showed that people didn't recognize the name, and coming up with a memory device was difficult, because the company's name is an acronym, not a word." (AFLAC stands for American Family Life Assurance Company.) However, someone on the creative team at AFLAC's advertising agency pointed out that "AFLAC" sounds like a duck squawk, and the rest is history. The idea gave birth to an American icon—an adenoidal white duck with a bright yellow beak and a blue bib that has made its "Aaaaaa-flaaack!" squawk a part of the American popular culture. The web-footer jolted AFLAC out of obscurity, raising the company's profile to soaring heights.

The campaign was risky. Some critics wondered whether the oddball spokesduck was suitable for the serious business of earning customer trust and selling insurance. But these fears proved unfounded—consumers love the duck. "He's the underduck," Spencer says. "We can rant and rave against policies and institutions, but as one person, we never feel as if we're heard. That's the role of the duck. He'll go on a roller coaster to tell the world about supplemental insurance."

Despite its humorous approach, the campaign delivers a serious message:

> AFLAC's campaign still hammers home the importance of making sure that family members are protected by having its duck pop up . . . to quack "Aaaaaa-flaaack!" in situations and at times when people seem likely to need supplemental insurance. For instance, in a spot set in an airport, a passenger trips over his luggage, prompting a couple of flight attendants to talk about a friend who was hurt on the job and lacked supplemental insurance. The duck, passing by on a people-mover, squawks "AFLAC!" . . . Another spot features a couple in the front car of a roller coaster, and the duck is in the car behind them to reassure them of their insurance coverage should the coaster jump the tracks.

The duck campaign has been incredibly successful in lifting both AFLAC's image and its sales. The company's name recognition jumped from 13 percent to 91 percent in the two years following the start of the campaign. More impressive, 4 out of 10 people in the United States not only recognize the name, they can identify AFLAC as a supplemental insurer. AFLAC experienced more sales leads in just the first two weeks following the start of the duck campaign than it had in the previous two years combined. As a result, despite flat industry performance, AFLAC's sales have grown almost 30 percent each year since the ads began running.

"We never dreamed it would be this successful," says Daniel Amos, CEO of AFLAC. "When you call on a person selling insurance, a wall goes up. . . . But people ask us about the AFLAC duck constantly, and when they do, that wall falls down. . . . It's hard to think what things would be like without the duck." The quirky duck has become so popular that AFLAC now sells a stuffed toy duck and other "duck gear"—ranging from T-shirts and baseball caps to golf club covers—on its Web site. So far, consumers have snapped up more than 56,000 stuffed ducks, generating $500,000 in proceeds that support the AFLAC Cancer Center and Blood Disorder Center at Children's Healthcare of Atlanta.

What is it that makes the AFLAC campaign so successful? First, it presents an important message about a worthwhile product. But as important, the duck ads break through the clutter and present the brand message in a very memorable way. "They stick in the mind," says one advertising critic. "You can remember [the duck] and the name of the company." And, says an AFLAC spokeswoman, "People enjoy the humor; they like the duck's attitude. The AFLAC duck also has helped consumers understand our business."

"You have to zig when everybody's zagging," concludes an executive from AFLAC's ad agency. "Emotion is the lightning rod, the trigger, to make a purchase," she adds. "A baby evokes a very warm response. A little duck waddling around with an attitude is funny." And a walking, talking duck sells.[1]

Modern marketing calls for more than just developing a good product, pricing it attractively, and making it available to target customers. Companies must also *communicate* with current and prospective customers, and what they communicate should not be left to chance. All of their communications efforts must be blended into a consistent and coordinated communications program. Just as good communication is important in building and maintaining any kind of relationship, it is a crucial element in a company's efforts to build customer relationships.

■ The Marketing Communications Mix

A company's total **marketing communications mix**—also called its **promotion mix**—consists of the specific blend of advertising, sales promotion, public relations, personal selling, and direct-marketing tools that the company uses to pursue its advertising and marketing objectives. Definitions of the five major promotion tools follow[2]:

> **Advertising:** Any paid form of nonpersonal presentation and promotion of ideas, goods, or services by an identified sponsor.
> **Sales promotion:** Short-term incentives to encourage the purchase or sale of a product or service.
> **Public relations:** Building good relations with the company's various publics by obtaining favorable publicity, building up a good corporate image, and handling or heading off unfavorable rumors, stories, and events.
> **Personal selling:** Personal presentation by the firm's sales force for the purpose of making sales and building customer relationships.
> **Direct marketing:** Direct connections with carefully targeted individual consumers to both obtain an immediate response and cultivate lasting customer relationships—the use of telephone, mail, fax, e-mail, the Internet, and other tools to communicate directly with specific consumers.

Each category involves specific tools. For example, advertising includes print, broadcast, Internet, outdoor, and other forms. Sales promotion includes point-of-purchase displays, premiums, discounts, coupons, specialty advertising, and demonstrations. Public relations includes press releases and special events. Personal selling includes sales presentations, trade shows, and incentive programs. Direct marketing includes catalogs, telephone marketing, kiosks, the Internet, and more. Thanks to technological breakthroughs, people can now communicate through traditional media (newspapers, radio, telephone, television) as well as through newer media forms (fax, cell phones, and computers).

At the same time, communication goes beyond these specific promotion tools. The product's design, its price, the shape and color of its package, and the stores that sell it—*all* communicate something to buyers. Thus, although the promotion mix is the company's primary communication activity, the entire marketing mix—promotion *and* product, price, and place—must be coordinated for greatest communication impact.

In this chapter, we begin by examining the rapidly changing marketing communications environment, the concept of integrated marketing communications, and the marketing communication process. Next, we discuss the factors that marketing communicators

Marketing communications mix (promotion mix)
The specific mix of advertising, personal selling, sales promotion, and public relations a company uses to pursue its advertising and marketing objectives.

Advertising
Any paid form of nonpersonal presentation and promotion of ideas, goods, or services by an identified sponsor.

Sales promotion
Short-term incentives to encourage the purchase or sale of a product or service.

Public relations
Building good relations with the company's various publics by obtaining favorable publicity, building up a good "corporate image," and handling or heading off unfavorable rumors, stories, and events.

Personal selling
Personal presentation by the firm's sales force for the purpose of making sales and building customer relationships.

Direct marketing
Direct connections with carefully targeted individual consumers to both obtain an immediate response and cultivate lasting customer relationships—the use of telephone, mail, fax, e-mail, the Internet, and other tools to communicate directly with specific consumers.

must consider in shaping an overall communication mix. We then summarize the legal, ethical, and social responsibility issues in marketing communications. Finally, we look at *mass-communication tools*—advertising, sales promotion, and public relations. Chapter 13 examines the *sales force* and *direct marketing* as communication and promotion tools.

Integrated Marketing Communications

During the past several decades, companies around the world have perfected the art of mass marketing—selling highly standardized products to masses of customers. In the process, they have developed effective mass-media advertising techniques to support their mass-marketing strategies. These companies routinely invest millions of dollars in the mass media, reaching tens of millions of customers with a single ad. However, as we move into the twenty-first century, marketing managers face some new marketing communications realities.

The Changing Communications Environment

Two major factors are changing the face of today's marketing communications. First, as mass markets have fragmented, marketers are shifting away from mass marketing. More and more, they are developing focused marketing programs designed to build closer relationships with customers in more narrowly defined micromarkets. Second, vast improvements in information technology are speeding the movement toward segmented marketing. Today's information technology helps marketers to keep closer track of customer needs—more information about consumers at the individual and household levels is available than ever before. New technologies also provide new communications avenues for reaching smaller customer segments with more-tailored messages.

The shift from mass marketing to segmented marketing has had a dramatic impact on marketing communications. Just as mass marketing gave rise to a new generation of mass-media communications, the shift toward one-to-one marketing is spawning a new generation of more specialized and highly targeted communications efforts.

Given this new communications environment, marketers must rethink the roles of various media and promotion mix tools. Mass-media advertising has long dominated the promotion mixes of consumer product companies. However, although television, magazines, and other mass media remain very important, their dominance is now declining. *Market* fragmentation has resulted in *media* fragmentation—in an explosion of more focused media that better match today's targeting strategies. Beyond the traditional mass-media channels, advertisers are making increased use of new, highly targeted media, ranging from highly focused specialty magazines and cable television channels to CD catalogs and Web coupon promotions, to airport kiosks and floor decals in supermarket aisles. In all, companies are doing less *broadcasting* and more *narrowcasting*.

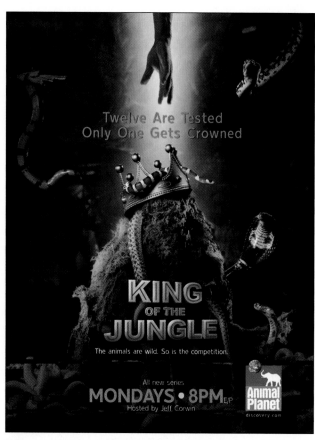

■ The new media environment: The relatively few major television networks have been replaced today by a host of highly focused cable channels. Animal Planet offers a variety of programs focused on animals, including *King of the Jungle*.

The Need for Integrated Marketing Communications

The shift from mass marketing to targeted marketing, and the corresponding use of a larger, richer mix of communication channels and promotion tools, poses a problem for marketers. Customers don't distinguish between message sources the way marketers do. In the consumer's mind, advertising messages from different media and different promotional approaches all become part of a single message about the company. Conflicting messages from these different sources can result in confused company images and brand positions.

All too often, companies fail to integrate their various communications channels. The result is a hodgepodge of communications to consumers. Mass-media advertisements say one thing, a price promotion sends a different signal, a product label creates still another message, company sales literature says something altogether different, and the company's Web site seems out of sync with everything else.

The problem is that these communications often come from different company sources. Advertising messages are planned and implemented by the advertising department or advertising agency. Personal selling communications are developed by sales management. Other functional specialists are responsible for public relations, sales promotion, direct marketing, Web sites, and other forms of marketing communications.

Recently, such functional separation has been a major problem for companies and their Internet communications. Many companies first organized their new Web and other digital communications operations into separate groups or divisions, isolating them from mainstream marketing activities. However, whereas some companies have compartmentalized the new communications tools, customers won't. According to one integrated marketing communications expert[3]:

> The truth is, most [consumers] won't compartmentalize their use of the new systems. They won't say, "Hey, I'm going off to do a bit of Web surfing. Burn my TV, throw out all my radios, cancel all my magazine subscriptions and, by the way, take out my telephone and don't deliver any mail anymore." It's not that kind of world for consumers, and it shouldn't be that kind of world for marketers either.

Thus, if treated as a special case, the Internet—or any other marketing communication tool—can be a *dis*integrating force in marketing communications. Instead, all the communication tools must be carefully integrated into the broader marketing communications

■ Today, all the marketing communication tools must be carefully integrated. For example, Saturn's television and print ads help build brand appeal while the company's Web site helps serious car buyers select a model, calculate payments, and find a dealer online.

FIGURE 12.1

Integrated Marketing Communications

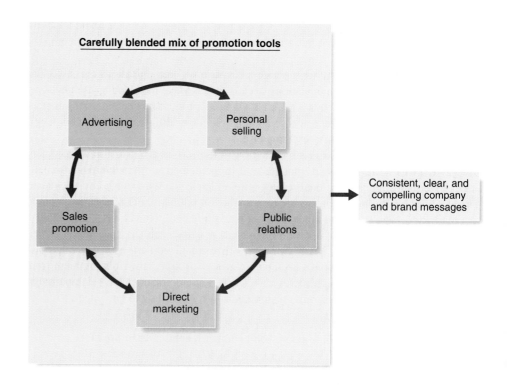

FIGURE 12.1

Integrated Marketing Communications

mix. Today, the best bet is to wed the emotional pitch and impact of traditional brand marketing with the interactivity and real service offered online. For example, print and television ads for Saturn build consumer preference for the brand. But the ads now point viewers to the company's Web site, which offers lots of help and very little hype. The site helps serious car buyers select a model, calculate payments, and find a dealer online.

In the past, no one person or department was responsible for thinking through the communication roles of the various promotion tools and coordinating the promotion mix. Today, however, more companies are adopting the concept of **integrated marketing communications (IMC)**. Under this concept, as illustrated in Figure 12.1, the company carefully integrates and coordinates its many communications channels to deliver a clear, consistent, and compelling message about the organization and its brands.[4]

Integrated marketing communications (IMC)

The concept under which a company carefully integrates and coordinates its many communications channels to deliver a clear, consistent, and compelling message about the organization and its products.

As one marketing executive puts it, "IMC builds a strong brand identity in the marketplace by tying together and reinforcing all your images and messages. IMC means that all your corporate messages, positioning and images, and identity are coordinated across all [marketing communications] venues. It means that your PR materials say the same thing as your direct mail campaign, and your advertising has the same 'look and feel' as your Web site."[5]

IMC calls for recognizing all contact points where the customer may encounter the company, its products, and its brands. Each *brand contact* will deliver a message, whether good, bad, or indifferent. The company must strive to deliver a consistent and positive message with each contact.

To help implement integrated marketing communications, some companies appoint a marketing communications director—or *marcom manager*—who has overall responsibility for the company's communications efforts. Integrated marketing communications produces better communications consistency and greater sales impact. It places the responsibility in someone's hands—where none existed before—to unify the company's image as it is shaped by thousands of company activities. It leads to a total marketing communication strategy aimed at showing how the company and its products can help customers solve their problems.

◼️ A View of the Communication Process

Integrated marketing communications involves identifying the target audience and shaping a well-coordinated promotional program to elicit the desired audience response. Too often, marketing communications focus on overcoming immediate awareness, image, or preference problems in the target market. But this approach to communication is too shortsighted. Today, marketers are moving toward viewing communications as *managing the customer relationship over time*. Because customers differ, communications programs need to be developed for specific segments, niches, and even individuals. And, given the new interactive communications technologies, companies must ask not only, "How can we reach our customers?" but also, "How can we find ways to let our customers reach us?"

Thus, the communications process should start with an audit of all the potential contacts target customers may have with the company and its brands. For example, someone purchasing a new computer may talk to others, see television ads, read articles and ads in newspapers and magazines, visit various Web sites, and try out computers in one or more stores. The marketer needs to assess what influence each of these communications experiences will have at different stages of the buying process. This understanding will help marketers allocate their communication dollars more efficiently and effectively.

◼️ Setting the Overall Communication Mix

The concept of integrated marketing communications suggests that the company must blend the promotion tools carefully into a coordinated *promotion mix*. But how does the company determine what mix of promotion tools it will use? Companies and brands within the same industry differ greatly in the design of their promotion mixes. For example, Avon spends most of its promotion funds on personal selling and direct marketing, whereas Covergirl spends heavily on consumer advertising. Hewlett Packard relies on advertising and promotion to retailers, whereas Dell Computer uses only direct marketing. We now look at factors that influence the marketer's choice of promotion tools.

The Nature of Each Promotion Tool Each promotion tool has unique characteristics and costs. Marketers must understand these characteristics in selecting their mix of tools.

◼️ Promotion mix: Companies within the same industry may use different mixes. Avon relies heavily on personal selling and direct marketing; Covergirl devotes significant resources to advertising.

Advertising. Advertising can reach masses of geographically dispersed buyers at a low cost per exposure, and it enables the seller to repeat a message many times. For example, television advertising can reach huge audiences. An estimated 137 million Americans tuned in to at least part of the most recent Super Bowl, more than 62 million people watched at least part of the last Academy Awards broadcast, and nearly 52 million watched the final episode of the first *Survivor* series. "If you want to get to the mass audience," says a media services executive, "broadcast TV is where you have to be." He adds, "For anybody introducing anything who has to lasso audience in a hurry—a new product, a new campaign, a new movie—the networks are still the biggest show in town."[6]

In addition to its reach, large-scale advertising says something positive about the seller's size, popularity, and success. Because of advertising's public nature, consumers tend to view advertised products as more legitimate. Advertising is also very expressive—it allows the company to dramatize its products through the artful use of visuals, print, sound, and color. On the one hand, advertising can be used to build up a long-term image for a product (such as Coca-Cola ads). On the other hand, advertising can trigger quick sales (as when Sears advertises a weekend sale).

Advertising also has some shortcomings. Although it reaches many people quickly, advertising is impersonal and cannot be as directly persuasive as can company salespeople. For the most part, advertising can carry on only a one-way communication with the audience, and the audience does not feel that it has to pay attention or respond. In addition, advertising can be very costly. Although some advertising forms, such as newspaper and radio advertising, can be done on smaller budgets, other forms, such as network TV advertising, require very large budgets.

Personal Selling. Personal selling is the most effective tool at certain stages of the buying process, particularly in building up buyers' preferences, convictions, and actions. It involves personal interaction between two or more people, so each person can observe the other's needs and characteristics and make quick adjustments. Personal selling also allows all kinds of relationships to spring up, ranging from matter-of-fact selling relationships to personal friendships. The effective salesperson keeps the customer's interests at heart in order to build a long-term relationship. Finally, with personal selling, the buyer usually feels a greater need to listen and respond, even if the response is a polite "No thank you."

These unique qualities come at a cost, however. A sales force requires a longer-term commitment than does advertising—advertising can be turned on and off, but sales force size is harder to change. Personal selling is also the company's most expensive promotion tool, on average costing companies $170 per sales call.[7] U.S. firms spend up to three times as much on personal selling as they do on advertising.

Sales Promotion. Sales promotion includes a wide assortment of tools—coupons, contests, cents-off deals, premiums, and others—all of which have many unique qualities. They attract consumer attention, offer strong incentives to purchase, and can be used to dramatize product offers and to boost sagging sales. Sales promotions invite and reward quick response—whereas advertising says, "Buy our product," sales promotion says, "Buy it now." Sales promotion effects are often short-lived, however, and often are not as effective as advertising or personal selling in building long-run brand preference.

Public Relations. Public relations is very believable—news stories, features, sponsorships, and events seem more real and believable to readers than ads do. Public relations can also reach many prospects who avoid salespeople and advertisements—the message gets to the buyers as "news" rather than as a sales-directed communication. And, as with advertising, public relations can dramatize a company or product. Marketers tend to under use public relations or to use it as an afterthought. Yet a well-thought-out public relations campaign used with other promotion mix elements can be very effective and economical.

Direct Marketing. Although there are many forms of direct marketing—telephone marketing, direct mail, online marketing, and others—they all share four distinctive charac-

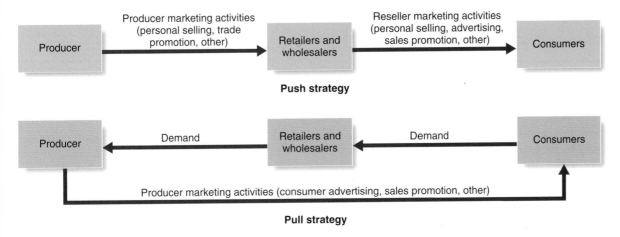

FIGURE 12.2
Push Versus Pull Promotion Strategy

teristics. Direct marketing is *nonpublic:* The message is normally directed to a specific person. Direct marketing is *immediate* and *customized*: Messages can be prepared very quickly and can be tailored to appeal to specific consumers. Finally, direct marketing is *interactive*: It allows a dialogue between the marketing team and the consumer, and messages can be altered depending on the consumer's response. Thus, direct marketing is well suited to highly targeted marketing efforts and to building one-to-one customer relationships.

Promotion Mix Strategies Marketers can choose from two basic promotion mix strategies—*push* promotion or *pull* promotion. Figure 12.2 contrasts the two strategies. The relative emphasis on the specific promotion tools differs for push and pull strategies. A **push strategy** involves "pushing" the product through distribution channels to final consumers. The producer directs its marketing activities (primarily personal selling and trade promotion) toward channel members to induce them to carry the product and to promote it to final consumers. Using a **pull strategy**, the producer directs its marketing activities (primarily advertising and consumer promotion) toward final consumers to induce them to buy the product. If the pull strategy is effective, consumers will then demand the product from channel members, who will in turn demand it from producers. Thus, under a pull strategy, consumer demand "pulls" the product through the channels.

Some industrial goods companies use only push strategies; some direct-marketing companies use only pull. However, most large companies use some combination of the two. For example, Kraft uses mass-media advertising and consumer promotions to pull its products and a large sales force and trade promotions to push its products through the channels. In recent years, consumer goods companies have been decreasing the pull portions of their mixes in favor of more push. This has caused concern that they may be driving short-run sales at the expense of long-term brand equity (see Marketing at Work 12.1).

Companies consider many factors when designing their promotion mix strategies, including *type of product/market* and the *product life-cycle stage*. For example, the importance of different promotion tools varies between consumer and business markets. B2C companies usually "pull" more, putting more of their funds into advertising, followed by sales promotion, personal selling, and then public relations. In contrast, B2B marketers tend to "push" more, putting more of their funds into personal selling, followed by sales promotion, advertising, and public relations. In general, personal selling is used more heavily with expensive and risky goods and in markets with fewer and larger sellers.

Now that we've examined the concept of integrated marketing communications and the factors that firms consider when shaping their promotion mixes, let's look more closely at the specific marketing communications tools.

Push strategy
A promotion strategy that calls for using the sales force and trade promotion to push the product through channels. The producer promotes the product to wholesalers, the wholesalers promote to retailers, and the retailers promote to consumers.

Pull strategy
A promotion strategy that calls for spending a lot on advertising and consumer promotion to build up consumer demand. If the strategy is successful, consumers will ask their retailers for the product, the retailers will ask the wholesalers, and the wholesalers will ask the producers.

Marketing at Work | 12.1

Are Consumer Goods Companies Getting Too Pushy?

Consumer packaged-goods companies such as Kraft, Procter & Gamble, Kellogg, General Mills, and Gillette grew into giants by using mostly pull promotion strategies. They used massive doses of national advertising to differentiate their products, gain market share, and build brand equity and customer loyalty. But during the past few decades, these companies have gotten more "pushy," deemphasizing national advertising and putting more of their marketing budgets into trade and consumer sales promotions.

General trade promotions (trade allowances, displays, cooperative advertising, slotting fees) now account for 49 percent of total marketing spending by consumer product companies. Another 10 percent of the marketing budget goes to the trade in the form of "account-specific" marketing expenditures—promotional spending personalized to the local needs of a specific retail chain that backs both the brand and the retailer. The total of 59 percent represents a 7-percentage-point increase in trade spending in just the past 5 years. Consumer promotions (coupons, cents-off deals, premiums) account for another 17 percent of the typical marketing budget. That leaves less than 24 percent of total marketing spending for mass-media advertising, down from 42 percent 20 years ago.

Why have these companies shifted so heavily toward push strategies? One reason is that mass-media campaigns have become more expensive and less effective in recent years. Network television costs have risen sharply while audiences have fallen off, making national advertising less cost effective. Companies have also increased their market segmentation efforts and are now tailoring their marketing programs more narrowly, making national advertising less suitable than localized retailer promotions. And in these days of brand extensions and me-too products, companies sometimes have trouble finding meaningful product differences to feature in advertising. So they have differentiated their products through price reductions, premium offers, coupons, and other push techniques.

Today's food marketers are using more and more push promotion, including consumer price promotions. But they must be careful that they don't win the battle for short-run sales at the expense of long-run brand equity.

■▪ Advertising

Advertising can be traced back to the very beginnings of recorded history. Archaeologists working in the countries around the Mediterranean Sea have dug up signs announcing various events and offers. The Romans painted walls to announce gladiator fights, and the Phoenicians painted pictures promoting their wares on large rocks along parade routes. Modern advertising, however, is a far cry from these early efforts. U.S. advertisers now run up an estimated annual advertising bill of more than $237 billion; worldwide ad spending

Another factor speeding the shift from pull to push has been the growing strength of retailers. Today's retailers are larger and have more access to product sales and profit information. Retail giants such as Wal-Mart, Kroger, Safeway, and A&P, now have the power to demand and get what they want—and what they want is more push. Whereas national advertising bypasses them on its way to the masses, push promotion benefits them directly. Consumer promotions give retailers an immediate sales boost, and cash from trade allowances and other trade promotions pads retailer profits. Thus, producers must often use push just to obtain good shelf space and advertising support from important retailers.

However, many marketers are concerned that the reckless use of push will lead to fierce price competition and a never-ending spiral of price slashing and deal making. This situation would mean lower margins, and companies would have less money to invest in the research and development, packaging, and advertising needed to improve products and maintain long-run consumer preference and loyalty.

If used improperly, push promotion can mortgage a brand's future for short-term gains. Sales promotion buys short-run reseller support and consumer sales, but advertising builds long-run brand equity and consumer preference. By robbing the media advertising budget to pay for more sales promotion, companies might win the battle for short-run earnings but lose the war for long-run brand equity, consumer loyalty, and market share. In fact, some analysts blame the shift away from advertising dollars for a recent two-decade long drop in the percentage of consumers who buy only well-known brands.

Of special concern is the overuse of price promotions. The regular use of price as a selling tool can destroy brand equity by encouraging consumers to seek value though price rather than through the benefits of the brand. Many marketers are too quick to drive short-term sales by reducing prices rather than building long-term brand equity through advertising. In fact, studies show that almost 60 percent of consumers now go to the store to make a purchase without a specific brand in mind. Once they get to the store, shoppers are often more swayed by special prices, sales, and coupons than by brand.

In cases where price is a key part of the brand's positioning, featuring price makes sense. But for brands where price does not underlie value, "price promotions are really desperate acts by brands that have their backs against the wall," says one marketing executive. "Generally speaking, it is better to stick to your guns with price and invest in advertising to drive sales."

Jack Trout, a well-known marketing consultant, cautions that some categories tend to self-destruct by always being on sale. Discount pricing has become routine for a surprising number of companies. Furniture, automobile tires, and many other categories of goods are rarely sold at anything near list price, and when auto makers get rebate happy, the market just sits back and waits for a deal. Even Coca-Cola and Pepsi, two of the world's popular brands, engage in regular price wars that ultimately tarnish their brand equity. Trout offers several "Commandments of Discounting," such as "Thou shalt not offer discounts because everyone else does," "Thou shalt be creative with your discounting," "Thou shalt put time limits on the deal," and "Thou shalt stop discounting as soon as you can."

Many consumer companies now are rethinking their promotion strategies and reversing the trend by shifting their promotion budgets back toward advertising. They have realized that it's not a question of sales promotion versus advertising, or of push versus pull. Success lies in finding the best mix of the two: consistent advertising to build long-run brand value and consumer preference, and sales promotion to create short-run trade support and consumer excitement. The company needs to blend both push and pull elements into an integrated promotion program that meets immediate consumer and retailer needs as well as long-run strategic needs.

Sources: Promotion spending statistics from *2002 Trade Promotion Spending & Merchandising Industry Study* (Cannondale Associates, Wilton, CT, May 2002), p. 13; and *Trade Promotion Spending & Merchandising 2003 Industry Study* (Wilton, CT: Cannondale Associates, 2003), p. 7. Other information from Jack Trout, "Prices: Simple Guidelines to Get Them Right," *Journal of Business Strategy*, November–December 1998, pp. 13–16; Tim Ambler, "Kicking Price Promotion Habit Is Like Getting Off Heroin—Hard," *Marketing*, May 27, 1999, p. 24; Robert Gray, "Driving Sales at Any Price," *Marketing*, April 11, 2002, pp. 24–25; Alan Mitchell, "When Push Comes to Shove, It's All about Pull," *Marketing Week*, January 9, 2003, pp. 26–27; and Kate Fitzgerald, "Packaging Is the Capper," *Advertising Age*, May 5, 2003, p. 22.

approaches an estimated $470 billion. General Motors, the nation's largest advertiser, last year spent more than $3.6 billion on U.S. advertising.[8]

Although advertising is used mostly by business firms, it also is used by a wide range of not-for-profit organizations, professionals, and social agencies that advertise their causes to various target publics. In fact, the 24th largest advertising spender is a not-for-profit organization—the U.S. government. Advertising is a good way to inform and persuade, whether the purpose is to sell Coca-Cola worldwide or to get consumers in a developing nation to use birth control.

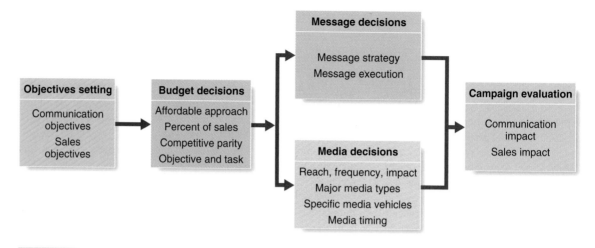

FIGURE 12.3

Major Decisions in Advertising

Marketing management must make four important decisions when developing an advertising program (see Figure 12.3): *setting advertising objectives, setting the advertising budget, developing advertising strategy* (*message decisions* and *media decisions*), and *evaluating advertising campaigns.*

Setting Advertising Objectives

The first step is to set *advertising objectives*. These objectives should be based on past decisions about the target market, positioning, and marketing mix, which define the job that advertising must do in the total marketing program.

Advertising objective

A specific communication *task* to be accomplished with a specific *target* audience during a specific period of *time*.

An **advertising objective** is a specific communication *task* to be accomplished with a specific *target* audience during a specific period of *time*. Advertising objectives can be classified by primary purpose—whether the aim is to *inform*, *persuade*, or *remind*. Table 12.1 lists examples of each of these objectives.

Informative advertising is used heavily when introducing a new product category. In this case, the objective is to build primary demand. Thus, producers of DVD players must first

TABLE 12.1 Possible Advertising Objectives

Informative advertising

Telling the market about a new product	Describing available services
Suggesting new uses for a product	Correcting false impressions
Informing the market of a price change	Reducing consumers' fears
Explaining how the product works	Building a company image

Persuasive advertising

Building brand preference	Persuading customer to purchase now
Encouraging switching to your brand	Persuading customer to receive a sales call
Changing customer's perception of product attributes	

Reminder advertising

Reminding consumer that the product may be needed in the near future	Keeping it in customer's mind during off seasons
Reminding consumer where to buy it	Maintaining its top-of-mind awareness

inform consumers of the image quality and convenience benefits of the new product. *Persuasive advertising* becomes more important as competition increases. Here, the company's objective is to build selective demand. For example, once DVD players are established, Sony begins trying to persuade consumers that *its* brand offers the best quality for their money.

Some persuasive advertising has become *comparative advertising*, in which a company directly or indirectly compares its brand with one or more other brands. Comparative advertising has been used for products ranging from soft drinks and computers to batteries, pain relievers, car rentals, and credit cards. For example, in its classic comparative campaign, Avis positioned itself against market-leading Hertz by claiming, "We're number two, so we try harder."

More recently, Progresso ran ads showing side-by-side comparisons of its soups versus Campbell's condensed soups, inviting consumers to "Enjoy a better soup . . . with a more adult taste." In its long-running comparative campaign, Visa has advertised, "American Express is offering you a new credit card, but you don't have to accept it. Heck, 7 million merchants don't." And Procter & Gamble recently ran an ad comparing its Tide with Bleach to Oxy10. In the ad, consumers spread iodine, tomato sauce, mud, and grass on a white t-shirt that was then cut in half and treated with the two detergents. All the while, "Anything You Can Do I Can Do Better" played in the background. Of course, Tide did a better job of removing stains. Advertisers should use comparative advertising with caution. All too often, such ads invite competitor responses, resulting in an advertising war that neither competitor can win.

Reminder advertising is important for mature products—it keeps consumers thinking about the product. Expensive Coca-Cola television ads primarily remind people about Coca-Cola rather than informing or persuading them.

■ Comparative advertising: Progresso makes side-by-side comparisons of its soup versus Campbell's, inviting consumers to "Enjoy a better soup . . . with a more adult taste."

Setting the Advertising Budget

After determining its advertising objectives, the company next sets its *advertising budget* for each product. No matter what method is used, setting the advertising budget is no easy task. How does a company know if it is spending the right amount?

Companies such as Coca-Cola and Kraft have built sophisticated statistical models to determine the relationship between promotional spending and brand sales, and to help determine the "optimal investment" across various media. Still, because so many factors affect advertising effectiveness, some controllable and others not, measuring the results of advertising spending remains an inexact science. In most cases, managers must rely on large doses of judgment along with more quantitative analysis when setting advertising budgets.

We look at four common methods used to set the total budget for advertising: the *affordable method*, the *percentage-of-sales method*, the *competitive-parity method*, and the *objective-and-task method*.[9]

Affordable Method   Some companies use the **affordable method**: They set the promotion budget at the level they think the company can afford. Small businesses often use this method, reasoning that the company cannot spend more on advertising than it has. They start with total revenues, deduct operating expenses and capital outlays, and then devote some portion of the remaining funds to advertising.

Unfortunately, this method of setting budgets completely ignores the effects of promotion on sales. It tends to place advertising last among spending priorities, even in situations

Affordable method
Setting the promotion budget at the level management thinks the company can afford.

in which advertising is critical to the firm's success. It leads to an uncertain annual promotion budget, which makes long-range market planning difficult. Although the affordable method can result in overspending on advertising, it more often results in underspending.

Percentage-of-sales method

Setting the promotion budget at a certain percentage of current or forecasted sales or as a percentage of the unit sales price.

Percentage-of-Sales Method Other companies use the **percentage-of-sales method**, setting their promotion budget at a certain percentage of current or forecasted sales. Or they budget a percentage of the unit sales price. The percentage-of-sales method has advantages. It is simple to use and helps management think about the relationships between promotion spending, selling price, and profit per unit.

Despite these claimed advantages, however, the percentage-of-sales method has little to justify it. It wrongly views sales as the *cause* of promotion rather than as the *result*. "A study in this area found good correlation between investments in advertising and the strength of the brands concerned—but it turned out to be effect and cause, not cause and effect. . . . The strongest brands had the highest sales and could afford the biggest investments in advertising!"[10] Thus, the percentage-of-sales budget is based on availability of funds rather than on opportunities. It may prevent the increased spending sometimes needed to turn around falling sales. Because the budget varies with year-to-year sales, long-range planning is difficult. Finally, the method does not provide any basis for choosing a *specific* percentage, except what has been done in the past or what competitors are doing.

Competitive-parity method

Setting the promotion budget to match competitors' outlays.

Competitive-Parity Method Still other companies use the **competitive-parity method**, setting their promotion budgets to match competitors' outlays. They monitor competitors' advertising or get industry promotion spending estimates from publications or trade associations, and then set their budgets based on the industry average.

Two arguments support this method. First, competitors' budgets represent the collective wisdom of the industry. Second, spending what competitors spend helps prevent promotion wars. Unfortunately, neither argument is valid. There are no grounds for believing that the competition has a better idea of what a company should be spending on promotion than does the company itself. Companies differ greatly, and each has its own special promotion needs. Finally, there is no evidence that budgets based on competitive parity prevent promotion wars.

Objective-and-task method

Developing the promotion budget by (1) defining specific objectives; (2) determining the tasks that must be performed to achieve these objectives; and (3) estimating the costs of performing these tasks. The sum of these costs is the proposed promotion budget.

Objective-and-Task Method The most logical budget-setting method is the **objective-and-task method**, whereby the company sets its promotion budget based on what it wants to accomplish with promotion. This budgeting method entails (1) defining specific promotion objectives, (2) determining the tasks needed to achieve these objectives, and (3) estimating the costs of performing these tasks. The sum of these costs is the proposed promotion budget.

The objective-and-task method forces management to spell out its assumptions about the relationship between dollars spent and promotion results. But it is also the most difficult method to use. Often, it is hard to figure out which specific tasks will achieve specific objectives. For example, suppose Sony wants 95 percent awareness for its latest camcorder model during the 6-month introductory period. What specific advertising messages and media schedules should Sony use to attain this objective? How much would these messages and media schedules cost? Sony management must consider such questions, even though they are hard to answer.

No matter what method is used, deciding how much to spend on advertising is one of the hardest marketing decisions a company faces. Measuring the results of advertising spending and "advertising return on investment" remains an inexact science. John Wanamaker, the department store magnate, once said, "I know that half of my advertising is wasted, but I don't know which half. I spent $2 million for advertising, and I don't know if that is half enough or twice too much." Thus, it is not surprising that companies vary widely in how much they spend on promotion. Even within a given industry, both low and high spenders can be found.

Developing Advertising Strategy

Advertising strategy consists of two major elements: creating advertising *messages* and selecting advertising *media*. In the past, companies often viewed media planning as secondary to the message-creation process. The creative department first created good advertisements, and then the media department selected the best media for carrying these advertisements to desired target audiences. This often caused friction between the creative types and the media planners.

Today, however, media fragmentation, soaring media costs, and more-focused target marketing strategies have promoted the importance of the media-planning function. More and more, advertisers are orchestrating a closer harmony between their messages and the media that deliver them. In some cases, an advertising campaign might start with a great message idea, followed by the choice of appropriate media. In other cases, however, a campaign might begin with a good media opportunity, followed by advertisements designed to take advantage of that opportunity. Among the more noteworthy ad campaigns based on tight media-creative partnerships is the pioneering campaign for Absolut vodka, marketed by Seagram.

The Absolut team and its ad agency meet once each year with a slew of magazines to set Absolut's media schedule. The schedule consists of up to 100 magazines, ranging from consumer and business magazines to theater playbills. The agency's creative department then creates media-specific ads. The result is a wonderful assortment of very creative ads for Absolut, tightly targeted to audiences of the media in which they appear. For example, an "Absolut Bravo" ad in playbills has roses adorning a clear bottle, while business magazines contain an "Absolut Merger" foldout. In New York–area magazines, "Absolut Manhattan" ads feature a satellite photo of Manhattan, with Central Park

■ Media planners for Absolut vodka work with creatives to design ads targeted to specific media audiences. "Absolut Bravo" appears in theater playbills. "Absolut Chicago" targets the Windy City.

assuming the distinctive outline of an Absolut bottle. In Chicago, the windy city, ads show an Absolut bottle with the letters on the label blown askew. An "Absolut Primary" ad run during the political season featured the well-known bottle spattered with mud. In some cases, the creatives even developed ads for magazines not yet on the schedule, such as a clever "Absolut Centerfold" ad for *Playboy* magazine. The ad portrayed a clear, unadorned playmate bottle ("11-inch bust, 11-inch waist, 11-inch hips"). In all, Absolut has developed more than 500 ads for the almost two-decades-old campaign. At a time of soaring media costs and cluttered communication channels, a closer cooperation between creative and media people has paid off handsomely for Absolut. Largely as a result of its breakthrough advertising; in the United States, Absolut is the number-three liquor brand. It's the nation's number-one imported vodka and captures a 63 percent share of the imported vodka market.[11]

Creating the Advertising Message No matter how big the budget, advertising can succeed only if advertisements gain attention and communicate well. Good advertising messages are especially important in today's costly and cluttered advertising environment. The average number of television channels beamed into U.S. homes has skyrocketed from 3 in 1950 to more than 50 today, and consumers have more than 17,300 magazines from which to choose.[12] Add the countless radio stations and a continuous barrage of catalogs, direct-mail and e-mail ads, and out-of-home media, and consumers are being bombarded with ads at home, at work, and at all points in between. One expert estimates that the average person is exposed to some 1,600 ad messages a day. Another puts the number at an eye-popping 5,000 ads a day.[13]

Breaking Through the Clutter. If all this advertising clutter bothers some consumers, it also causes big problems for advertisers. Take the situation facing network television advertisers. They regularly pay $200,000 or more for 30 seconds of advertising time during a popular prime-time program, even more if it's an especially popular program such as *Friends* ($456,000 per 30-second spot), *ER* ($438,000), *Will & Grace* ($377,000 per spot), or a mega-event such as the Super Bowl (as much as $2.4 million!). Then, their ads are sandwiched in with a clutter of other commercials, announcements, and network promotions, totaling more than 15 minutes of non–program material per hour.[14]

Until recently, television viewers were pretty much a captive audience for advertisers. Viewers had only a few channels from which to choose. But with the growth in cable and satellite TV, VCRs, and remote-control units, today's viewers have many more options. They can avoid ads by watching commercial-free cable channels. They can "zap" commercials by pushing the fast-forward button during taped programs. With remote controls, they can instantly turn off the sound during a commercial or "zip" around the channels to see what else is on. A recent study found that nearly half of all television viewers now switch channels when the commercial break starts.

Just to gain and hold attention, today's advertising messages must be better planned, more imaginative, more entertaining, and more rewarding to consumers. Many advertisers now see themselves as creating "advertainment"—ads that are both persuasive and entertaining. "Today we have to entertain and not just sell, because if you try to sell directly and come off as boring or obnoxious, people are going to press the remote on you," points out one advertising executive. "When most TV viewers are armed with remote channel switchers, a commercial has to cut through the clutter and seize the viewers in 1 to 3 seconds, or they're gone," comments another.[15] Some advertisers even create intentionally controversial ads to break through the clutter and gain attention for their products (see Marketing at Work 12.2).

Adding to the problem is the new wave of personal video recorders (PVRs) and personal television services—such as TiVo and ReplayTV—that have armed viewers with an arsenal of new-age zipping and zapping weapons. A recent study of TiVo and other PVR system users found that these users skip commercials 77 percent of the time, a

Marketing at Work | 12.2

Advertising on the Edge: You Either Hate 'Em or Love 'Em

You either love 'em or you hate 'em. Today's cluttered advertising environment has spawned a new genre of "gross-out" ads that go to extremes to get attention. These irreverent, cutting-edge ads intentionally create controversy, even if it means turning off some potential customers. "It's the age-old question of breaking through the clutter," says an ad agency creative director. You turn to "anything you can to get noticed," he says.

You see these controversial ads almost everywhere. While flipping through your favorite magazine, you might encounter a Toyota ad targeting Gen Ys with the headline "Attention nose pickers." Next comes an Altoids ad in which a man peers down the front of his boxer shorts: "Shrinkage may occur," proclaims the ad's headline. "The curiously strong mints." Other Altoids ads feature a women in a seductively devilish outfit, complete with horns, and headlines such as "Hot and bothered?" "Frigid?" and "Taste like hell!"

On television, a Fox Sports television ad shows an able-bodied young guy, engrossed in his Fox Sports Web site, casually ignoring an old man just a few feet away struggling to get a jar down from a shelf. An Orange Slice "twisted taste" commercial opens with the camera panning across a row of squeamish students in a science class, frog legs dangling from their dissection trays. As the teacher drones on about ruptured spleens and green discharges, one kid lunches on his lab project. During the Super Bowl, a Dodge Truck ad features a man choking on a piece of beef jerky lodged in his throat. The solution: the driver puts the truck through its testosterone-charged paces, then stops abruptly. The choking passenger hawks up the offending piece of meat, which splats against the windshield in a gooey mess. "Repulsive," says ad critic Bob Garfield.

Then, there's the "Blind Date" spot from SmartBeep, the retail paging-services provider. The spot, which generated enormous response, was part of a wacky five-part campaign that contrasted smart versus not-so-smart behavior to promote SmartBeep's free pagers and low rates on paging services. In it, a woman climbs into the front seat of her blind date's car. While he's crossing around to the other side, thinking she is alone, she leans to one side and lets rip a frat-house blast of gas. When her date hops in the car, she hesitates then turns red with embarrassment as he introduces her to another couple in the back seat. "You guys meet? Gregg, Janice?" he asks, to which Janice in the backseat responds, "We sure did." The announcer concludes, "That was stupid. . . . This is smart. A beeper service for just $1.99 a month." The ad closes: "We've got chemistry here. You feel it?" says the blind-date guy. "I felt it!" says Janice from the backseat. The ad became an immediate Internet cult item.

For pure gross-out value, few ads top the recent ad from FreshDirect, the online food retailer that delivers groceries directly to your home. In the ad, a woman with a cold and sniffles blows her nose and sneezes as she picks through a supermarket display of cheese and olives. As she sniffs an open bin of olives, one gets stuck in her right nostril. After checking to see that no one is watching, she closes off her left nostril with her index finger, exhales through her nose, and fires the olive back into the bin with a sploosh. "Where's *your* food been?" asks the ad.

To be truly cutting-edge, advertising must do more than just capture attention. Altoids' irreverent ads fit the brand's "curious, strong, original" positioning and appeal to its cutting-edge target customers.

(continued)

Such outrageous ads can grab attention, create word-of-mouth, and even win awards. However, such techniques often attract more attention to the ad itself than to the brand's selling proposition. If used improperly, controversial ads can boost viewer attention but actually *distract* from the selling message. For example, the Dodge Truck Super Bowl ad drew much attention, but most of it was bad. According to one expert, "it was the only commercial to be unanimously, roundly, and thoroughly bashed." To be effective, advertising must do more than just capture attention. It must support and enhance the brand and its positioning.

If used properly, cutting edge humor can help do that, as proved by Altoids and its "Curiously Strong" campaign. The campaign's irreverent, sometimes controversial ads fit the brand's "curious, strong, original" positioning. They also appeal to the tastes as well as the taste buds of Altoids' cutting-edge target consumers. As a result, in only 2 years, the small-budget but high-impact ad campaign propelled Altoids past long-time strong-mint market leader Tic Tac. "Altoids is now—improbably—the boss of the mint world," says an analyst. What's the power behind this cheeky campaign? The analyst confirms that "Everything links back to [the brand's] 'curiously strong' and 'original' [positioning]."

Sources: Tim Nudd and Jack Feuer, "Everyone's an Ad Critic," *Adweek,* February 3, 2003, p. 44; Tom Kurtz, "Unsettling TV Commercials: And Now, a Gross-Out from Our Sponsor," *New York Times,* July 25, 1999, p. 7; Stefano Hatfield, "Opinion: Olive Nose," accessed at www.adcritic.com/news/op/detail/?q=36945; and information accessed online at About Altoids at www.altoids.com, September 2003.

much higher rate than for those watching live television or using VCRs. One ad agency executive calls TiVo and Replay "electronic weed whackers." "These machines will rock the foundation of network advertising," he declares. "In time, the number of people using them to obliterate commercials will totally erode faith in the 30-second commercial.[16]

In response, some advertisers are trying to turn the TiVo trend into an opportunity. Companies like Porsche, Best Buy, and Universal Music have all tested "advertainment showcases" on TiVo. For example, when Porsche launched its Cayenne SUV, it targeted TiVo's half million customers with an opt-in ad that allowed them to pause the program and visit a branded showcase. Once there, consumers were offered additional product information, encouraged to visit the Web site, and given the opportunity to receive additional information. Best Buy ran a branded showcase on TiVo in which it offered subscribers the chance to access two exclusive videos, win a CD, and opt in to six entertaining product vignettes. Sixty-three percent of TiVo subscribers opted-in to the Best Buy showcase, staying an average of 3.36 minutes.[17]

Message Strategy. The first step in creating effective advertising messages is to plan a *message strategy*—to decide what general message will be communicated to consumers. The purpose of advertising is to get consumers to think about or react to the product or company in a certain way. People will react only if they believe that they will benefit from doing so. Thus, developing an effective message strategy begins with identifying customer *benefits* that can be used as advertising appeals. Ideally, advertising message strategy will follow directly from the company's broader positioning strategy.

Message strategy statements tend to be plain, straightforward outlines of benefits and positioning points that the advertiser wants to stress. The advertiser must next develop a compelling *creative concept*—or *"big idea"*—that will bring the message strategy to life in a distinctive and memorable way. At this stage, simple message ideas become great ad campaigns. Usually, a copywriter and art director

■ A new advertising challenge: The new wave of personal video recorders, such as TiVo, have armed viewers with an arsenal of new-age zipping and zapping weapons. One ad agency executive calls TiVo an "electronic weedwhacker."

will team up to generate many creative concepts, hoping that one of these concepts will turn out to be the big idea. The creative concept may emerge as a visualization, a phrase, or a combination of the two.

The creative concept will guide the choice of specific appeals to be used in an advertising campaign. *Advertising appeals* should have three characteristics: First, they should be *meaningful*, pointing out benefits that make the product more desirable or interesting to consumers. Second, appeals must be *believable*—consumers must believe that the product or service will deliver the promised benefits. However, the most meaningful and believable benefits may not be the best ones to feature. Appeals should also be *distinctive*—they should tell how the product is better than the competing brands. For example, the most meaningful benefit of owning a wristwatch is that it keeps accurate time, yet few watch ads feature this benefit. Instead, based on the distinctive benefits they offer, watch advertisers might select any of a number of advertising themes. For years, Timex has been the affordable watch that "Takes a lickin' and keeps on tickin'." In contrast, Swatch has featured style and fashion, whereas Rolex stresses luxury and status.

Message Execution.   The advertiser now has to turn the big idea into an actual ad execution that will capture the target market's attention and interest. The creative people must find the best style, tone, words, and format for executing the message. Any message can be presented in different *execution styles*, such as the following:

- *Slice of life:* This style shows one or more "typical" people using the product in a normal setting. For example, two mothers at a picnic discuss the nutritional benefits of Jif peanut butter.

- *Lifestyle:* This style shows how a product fits in with a particular lifestyle. For example, an ad for Mongoose mountain bikes shows a serious biker traversing remote and rugged but beautiful terrain and states, "There are places that are so awesome and so killer that you'd like to tell the whole world about them. But please, *don't.*"

- *Fantasy:* This style creates a fantasy around the product or its use. For instance, many ads are built around dream themes. Gap even introduced a perfume named Dream. Ads show a woman sleeping blissfully and suggests that the scent is "the stuff that clouds are made of."

- *Mood or image:* This style builds a mood or image around the product, such as beauty, love, or serenity. No claim is made about the product except through suggestion. Bermuda tourism ads create such moods.

- *Musical:* This style shows one or more people or cartoon characters singing about the product. For example, one of the most famous ads in history was a Coca-Cola ad built around the song "I'd Like to Teach the World to Sing."

- *Personality symbol:* This style creates a character that represents the product. The character might be *animated* (the Jolly Green Giant, Cap'n Crunch, Garfield the Cat) or *real* (the Marlboro man, Ol' Lonely the Maytag repairman, Morris the 9-Lives Cat, or the AFLAC duck).

- *Technical expertise:* This style shows the company's expertise in making the product. Thus, Maxwell House shows one of its buyers carefully selecting coffee beans, and Gallo tells about its many years of wine-making experience.

- *Scientific evidence:* This style presents survey or scientific evidence that the brand is better or better liked than one or more other brands. For years, Crest toothpaste has used scientific evidence to convince buyers that Crest is better than other brands at fighting cavities.

- *Testimonial evidence or endorsement:* This style features a highly believable or likable source endorsing the product. It could be ordinary people saying how much they like a given product or a celebrity presenting the product. For example, Apple recently ran ads featuring real people who'd recently switched from Microsoft Windows-based PCs to Macs. And many companies use actors or sports celebrities as product endorsers.

■ Humor in advertising: These days, it seems as though almost every company is using humor in its advertising, even the scholarly American Heritage Dictionary.

The advertiser also must choose a *tone* for the ad. Procter & Gamble always uses a positive tone: Its ads say something very positive about its products. P&G usually avoids humor that might take attention away from the message. In contrast, many advertisers now use edgy humor to break through the commercial clutter. These days, it seems as though almost every company is using humor in its advertising, from consumer product firms such as Anheuser-Busch and Levi Strauss, to high-tech product and service marketers such as Dell and Computer Associates, to the scholarly American Heritage Dictionary.

The advertiser must use memorable and attention-getting *words* in the ad. For example, rather than claiming simply that "a BMW is a well-engineered automobile," BMW uses more creative and higher-impact phrasing: "The ultimate driving machine." Instead of stating plainly that Hanes socks last longer than less expensive ones, Hanes suggests, "Buy cheap socks and you'll pay through the toes." It's not Häagen-Dazs is "a good-tasting luxury ice cream," it's "Our passport to indulgence: passion in a touch, perfection in a cup, summer in a spoon, one perfect moment."

Finally, *format* elements make a difference in an ad's impact as well as in its cost. A small change in ad design can make a big difference in its effect. The *illustration* is the first thing the reader notices—it must be strong enough to draw attention. Next, the *headline* must effectively entice the right people to read the copy. Finally, the *copy*—the main block of text in the ad—must be simple but strong and convincing. Moreover, these three elements must work *together* effectively.

Selecting Advertising Media   The major steps in media selection are (1) deciding on *reach*, *frequency*, and *impact*; (2) choosing among major *media types*; (3) selecting specific *media vehicles*; and (4) deciding on *media timing*.

Deciding on Reach, Frequency, and Impact.   To select media, the advertiser must decide on the reach and frequency needed to achieve advertising objectives. *Reach* is a measure of the *percentage* of people in the target market who are exposed to the ad campaign during a given period of time. For example, the advertiser might try to reach 70 percent of the target market during the first 3 months of the campaign. *Frequency* is a measure of how many *times* the average person in the target market is exposed to the message. For example, the advertiser might want an average exposure frequency of three.

The advertiser also must decide on the desired *media impact*—the *qualitative value* of a message exposure through a given medium. For example, for products that need to be demonstrated, messages on television may have more impact than messages on radio because television uses sight *and* sound. The same message in one magazine (say,

TABLE 12.2 Profiles of Major Media Types

Medium	Advantages	Limitations
Newspapers	Flexibility; timeliness; good local market coverage; broad accept- ability; high believability	Short life; poor reproduction quality; small pass-along audience
Television	Good mass-market coverage; low cost per exposure; combines sight, sound, and motion; appealing to the senses	High absolute costs; high clutter; fleeting exposure; less audience selectivity
Direct mail	High audience selectivity; flexibil- ity; no ad competition within the same medium; allows personalization	Relatively high cost per exposure; "junk mail" image
Radio	Good local acceptance; high geographic and demographic selectivity; low cost	Audio only; fleeting exposure; low attention ("the half-heard" medium) fragmented audiences
Magazines	High geographic and demo- graphic selectivity; credibility and prestige; high-quality repro- duction; long life and good pass-along readership	Long ad-purchase lead time; high cost; no guarantee of position
Outdoor	Flexibility; high repeat exposure; low cost; low message competi- tion; good positional selectivity	Little audience selectivity; creative limitations
Internet	High selectivity; low cost; immedi- acy; interactive capabilities	Small audience; relatively low impact; audience controls exposure

Newsweek) may be more believable than in another (say, *The National Enquirer*). In gen- eral, the more reach, frequency, and impact the advertiser seeks, the higher the advertising budget will have to be.

Choosing among Major Media Types. The media planner has to know the reach, fre- quency, and impact of each of the major media types. As summarized in Table 12.2, the major media types are newspapers, television, direct mail, radio, magazines, outdoor, and the Internet. Each medium has advantages and limitations.

Media planners consider many factors when making their media choices. The *media habits of target consumers* will affect media choice—advertisers look for media that reach target consumers effectively. So will the *nature of the product*—for example, fashions are best advertised in color magazines, and automobile performance is best demonstrated on television. Different *types of messages* may require different media. A message announc- ing a major sale tomorrow will require radio or newspapers; a message with a lot of tech- nical data might require magazines, direct mailings, or an online ad and Web site. *Cost* is another major factor in media choice. For example, network television is very expensive, whereas newspaper or radio advertising costs much less but also reaches fewer consumers. The media planner looks both at the total cost of using a medium and at the cost per expo- sure of reaching specific target customers.

Media impact and cost must be reexamined regularly. For a long time, television and magazines have dominated in the media mixes of national advertisers, with other media often neglected. Recently, however, as network television costs soar and audiences shrink, many advertisers are looking for new ways to reach consumers. The move toward micromarketing strategies, focused more narrowly on specific consumer groups, has also fueled the search for new media to replace or supplement network television. As a result, advertisers are increasingly shifting larger portions of their budgets to media that cost less and target more effectively.

Three media benefiting greatly from the shift are outdoor advertising, cable television, and digital satellite television systems. Billboards have undergone a resurgence in recent years. Gone are the ugly eyesores of the past; in their place we now see cleverly designed, colorful attention grabbers. Outdoor advertising provides an excellent way to reach important local consumer segments at a fraction of the cost per exposure of other major media. Cable television and digital satellite systems are also booming. Such systems allow narrow programming formats such as all sports, all news, nutrition, arts, gardening, cooking, travel, history, and others that target select groups. Advertisers can take advantage of such "narrowcasting" to "rifle in" on special market segments rather than use the "shotgun" approach offered by network broadcasting.

Outdoor, cable, and satellite media seem to make good sense. But, increasingly, ads are popping up in far less likely places. In their efforts to find less costly and more highly targeted ways to reach consumers, advertisers have discovered a dazzling collection of "alternative media" (see Marketing at Work 12.3).

Selecting Specific Media Vehicles. The media planner now must choose the best *media vehicles*—specific media within each general media type. For example, television vehicles include *Scrubs* and *ABC World News Tonight*. Magazine vehicles include *Newsweek*, *People*, *In Style*, and *Sports Illustrated*.

Media planners must compute the cost per thousand persons reached by a vehicle. For example, if a full-page, four-color advertisement in *Newsweek* costs $191,000 and *Newsweek*'s readership is 3.1 million people, the cost of reaching each group of 1,000 persons is about $62. The same advertisement in *Business Week* may cost only $99,000 but reach only 970,000 persons—at a cost per thousand of about $102. The media planner ranks each magazine by cost per thousand and favors those magazines with the lower cost per thousand for reaching target consumers.[18]

The media planner must also consider the costs of producing ads for different media. Whereas newspaper ads may cost very little to produce, flashy television ads may cost millions. On average, U.S. advertisers pay $332,000 to produce a single 30-second television commercial. A few years ago, Nike paid a cool $2 million to make a single ad called "The Wall."[19]

In selecting media vehicles, the media planner must balance media cost measures against several media impact factors. First, the planner should balance costs against the media vehicle's *audience quality*. For a baby lotion advertisement, for example, *New Parents* magazine would have a high exposure value; *Gentlemen's Quarterly* would have a low exposure value. Second, the media planner should consider *audience attention*. Readers of *Vogue*, for example, typically pay more attention to ads than do *Newsweek* readers. Third, the planner should assess the vehicle's *editorial quality*—*Time* and the *Wall Street Journal* are more believable and prestigious than *The National Enquirer*.

Deciding on Media Timing. The advertiser must also decide how to schedule the advertising over the course of a year. Suppose sales of a product peak in December and drop in March. The firm can vary its advertising to follow the seasonal pattern, to oppose the seasonal pattern, or to be the same all year. Most firms do some seasonal advertising. Some do *only* seasonal advertising: For example, Hallmark advertises its greeting cards only before major holidays. And ConAgra runs special Thanksgiving and Christmas ads for Reddi-Wip during November and December, months that account for 30 percent of all whipped cream sales.

Finally, the advertiser has to choose the pattern of the ads. *Continuity* means scheduling ads evenly within a given period. *Pulsing* means scheduling ads unevenly over a given time period. Thus, 52 ads could either be scheduled at one per week during the year or pulsed in several bursts. The idea is to advertise heavily for a short period to build awareness

Marketing at Work | 12.3

Advertisers Seek Alternative Media

As consumers, we're used to ads on television, in magazines and newspapers, on the radio, and along the roadways. But these days, no matter where you go or what you do, you probably will run into some new form of advertising.

Tiny billboards attached to shopping carts, ads on shopping bags, and even advertising decals on supermarket floors urge you to buy Jell-O Pudding Pops or Pampers. Signs atop parking meters hawk everything from Jeeps to Minolta cameras to Recipe dog food. A city bus rolls by, fully wrapped for Trix cereal. You escape to the ballpark, only to find billboard-size video screens running Budweiser ads while a blimp with an electronic message board circles lazily overhead. How about a quiet trip in the country? Sorry—you find an enterprising farmer using his milk cows as four-legged billboards mounted with ads for Ben & Jerry's ice cream.

You pay to see a movie at your local theater, only to learn that the movie is full of not-so-subtle promotional plugs for Pepsi, Domino's Pizza, MasterCard, Fritos, Mercedes, Ray Ban sunglasses, Rockport shoes, or any of a dozen other products. You head home for a little TV to find your favorite sitcom full of "virtual placements" of Coca-Cola, Sony, or M&M/Mars products digitally inserted into the program. You pop in the latest video game and find your action character jumping into a Jeep on the way to the skateboarding park.

At the local rail station, it's the Commuter Channel; at the airport, you're treated to the CNN Airport Network. Shortly after your plane lifts off the runway, you look out the window and spot a 500-foot-diameter crop circle carved into a farmer's field depicting Monster.com's mascot and corporate logo. As you wait to pick up your luggage, ads for Kenneth Cole baggage roll by on the luggage carousel conveyor belt.

These days, you're likely to find ads—well, anywhere. Boats cruise along public beaches flashing advertising messages for Sundown Sunscreen as sunbathers spread their towels over ads for Snapple pressed into the sand. Ad space is being sold on video cases, parking-lot tickets, golf scorecards, delivery trucks, gas pumps, ATMs, municipal garbage cans, police cars, and church bulletins. Reebok even rented space on the foreheads of college students for temporary advertising tattoos.

The following accounts takes a humorous look ahead at what might be in store for the future:

Tomorrow your alarm clock will buzz at 6 A.M., as usual. Then the digital readout will morph into an ad for Burger King's breakfast special. Hungry for a Croissan'wich, you settle for a bagel that you plop into the toaster. The coils burn a Toastmaster brand onto the sides. Biting into your embossed bread, you pour a cup of

Marketers have discovered a dazzling array of "alternative media."

(continued)

coffee as the familiar green-and-white Starbucks logo forms on the side. Sipping the brew, you slide on your Nikes to go grab the newspaper. The pressure-sensitive shoes leave a temporary trail of swooshes behind them wherever you step. Walking outside, you pick up the Times *and gaze at your lawn, where the fertilizer you put down last month time-releases ads for Scotts Turf Builder, Toro lawn mowers, Weber grills. . . .*

Even some of the current alternative media seem a bit far-fetched, and they sometimes irritate consumers who resent it all as "ad nauseam." But for

many marketers, these media can save money and provide a way to hit selected consumers where they live, shop, work, and play. "We like to call it the captive pause," says an executive of an alternative-media firm, where consumers "really have nothing else to do but either look at the person in front of them or look at some engaging content as well as 15-second commercials"—the average person waits in line about 30 minutes a day.

Of course, this may leave you wondering if there are any commercial-free havens remaining for ad-weary consumers. The back seat of a taxi, perhaps, or public elevators, or stalls in a

public restroom? Forget it! Each has already been invaded by innovative marketers.

Sources: See Cara Beardi, "From Elevators to Gas Stations, Ads Multiplying," *Advertising Age*, November 13, 2000, pp. 40–42; Charles Pappas, "Ad Nauseam," *Advertising Age*, July 10, 2000, pp. 16–18; Beardi, "Airport Powerhouses Make Connection," *Advertising Age*, October 2, 2000, p. 8; Wayne Friedman, "Eagle-Eye Marketers Find Right Spot," *Advertising Age*, January 22, 2001, pp. S2–S3; Jean Halliday, "Mercedes Ties Car to 'Men in Black II,'" *Advertising Age*, May 27, 2002, p. 4; and Cara Griffin, "Rockport, Ray-Ban Back in Black," *Sporting Goods Business*, April 2002, p. 14; Rich Thomaselli, "Reebok's Terry Tate Set to Play Dirty Ball," *Advertising Age*, April 21, 2003, p. 4; and Stephanie Mehta, "Ads Invade Video Games," *Fortune*, May 26, 2003, p. 46.

that carries over to the next advertising period. Those who favor pulsing feel that it can be used to achieve the same impact as a steady schedule but at a much lower cost. However, some media planners believe that although pulsing achieves minimal awareness, it sacrifices depth of advertising communications.

Recent advances in technology have had a substantial impact on the media planning and buying functions. Today, for example, computer software applications called *media optimizers* allow media planners to evaluate vast combinations of television programs and prices. Such programs help advertisers to make better decisions about which mix of networks, programs, and day parts will yield the highest reach per ad dollar.

Evaluating Advertising

The advertising program should regularly evaluate both the communication effects and the sales effects of advertising. Measuring the *communication effects* of an ad—*copy testing*—tells whether the ad is communicating well. Copy testing can be done before or after an ad is printed or broadcast. Before the ad is placed, the advertiser can show it to consumers, ask how they like it, and measure recall or attitude changes resulting from it. After the ad is run, the advertiser can measure how the ad affected consumer recall or product awareness, knowledge, and preference.

But what *sales* are caused by an ad that increases brand awareness by 20 percent and brand preference by 10 percent? The *sales effects* of advertising are often harder to measure than the communication effects. Sales are affected by many factors besides advertising—such as product features, price, and availability.

One way to measure the sales effect of advertising is to compare past sales with past advertising expenditures. Another way is through experiments. For example, to test the effects of different advertising spending levels, Coca-Cola could vary the amount it spends on advertising in different market areas and measure the differences in the resulting sales levels. It could spend the normal amount in one market area, half the normal amount in another area, and twice the normal amount in a third area. If the three market areas are similar, and if all other marketing efforts in the area are the same, then differences in sales in the three areas could be related to advertising level. More complex experiments could be designed to include other variables, such as differences in the ads or media used.

Other Advertising Considerations

In developing advertising strategies and programs, the company must address two additional questions. First, how will the company organize its advertising function—who will perform which advertising tasks? Second, how will the company adapt its advertising strategies and programs to the complexities of international markets?

Organizing for Advertising Different companies organize in different ways to handle advertising. In small companies, advertising might be handled by someone in the sales department. Large companies set up advertising departments whose job it is to set the advertising budget, work with the ad agency, and handle advertising not done by the agency. Most large companies use outside advertising agencies because they offer several advantages.

How does an **advertising agency** work? Advertising agencies were started in the mid-to-late 1800s by salespeople and brokers who worked for the media and received a commission for selling advertising space to companies. As time passed, the salespeople began to help customers prepare their ads. Eventually, they formed agencies and grew closer to the advertisers than to the media. Today's agencies employ specialists who can often perform advertising tasks better than can the company's own staff. Agencies also bring an outside point of view to solving the company's problems, along with lots of experience from working with different clients and situations. So, today, even companies with strong advertising departments of their own use advertising agencies.

Some ad agencies are huge—the largest U.S. agency, McCann-Erickson Worldwide, has worldwide annual gross revenue of more than $1.2 billion. In recent years, many agencies have grown by gobbling up other agencies, thus creating huge agency holding companies. The largest of these agency "megagroups," Omnicom Group, includes several large advertising, public relations, and promotion agencies with combined worldwide revenues of $7.5 billion.[20] Most large advertising agencies have the staff and resources to handle all phases of an advertising campaign for their clients, from creating a marketing plan to developing ad campaigns and preparing, placing, and evaluating ads.

International Advertising Decisions International advertisers face many complexities not encountered by domestic advertisers. The most basic issue concerns the degree to which global advertising should be adapted to the unique characteristics of markets in various countries. Some large advertisers have attempted to support their global brands with highly standardized worldwide advertising, with campaigns that work as well in Bangkok as they do in Baltimore. For example, DaimlerChrysler has created a worldwide image of ruggedness and reliability for its Jeep brand; Coca-Cola's Sprite brand uses standardized appeals to target the world's youth. Gillette's ads for its Venus razors for women are almost identical worldwide, with only minor adjustments to suit the local culture. Ericsson, the Swedish telecommunications giant, spent $100 million on a standardized global television campaign with the tag line "Make yourself heard," which features Agent 007, James Bond.

Standardization produces many benefits—lower advertising costs, greater global advertising coordination, and a more consistent worldwide image. But it also has drawbacks. Most importantly, it ignores the fact that country markets differ greatly in their cultures, demographics, and economic conditions. Thus, most international advertisers "think globally but act locally." They develop global advertising *strategies* that make their worldwide advertising efforts more efficient and consistent. Then they adapt their advertising

Advertising agency
A marketing services firm that assists companies in planning, preparing, implementing, and evaluating all or portions of their advertising programs.

■ Standardized worldwide advertising: Gillette's ads for its Gillette for Women Venus razors are almost identical world-wide, with only minor adjustments to suit the local culture.

programs to make them more responsive to consumer needs and expectations within local markets. For example, Coca-Cola has a pool of different commercials that can be used in or adapted to several different international markets. Some can be used with only minor changes—such as language—in several different countries. Local and regional managers decide which commercials work best for which markets.

Global advertisers face several special problems. For instance, advertising media costs and availability differ vastly from country to country. Countries also differ in the extent to which they regulate advertising practices. Many countries have extensive systems of laws restricting how much a company can spend on advertising, the media used, the nature of advertising claims, and other aspects of the advertising program. Such restrictions often require advertisers to adapt their campaigns from country to country.

For example, alcoholic products cannot be advertised or sold in Muslim countries. In many countries, Sweden, for example, no TV ads may be directed at children under 12. Moreover, Sweden is lobbying to extend that ban to all European Union member countries. To play it safe, McDonald's advertises itself as a family restaurant in Sweden. Comparative ads, while acceptable and even common in the United States and Canada, are less commonly used in the United Kingdom, are unacceptable in Japan, and are illegal in India and Brazil. China has restrictive censorship rules for TV and radio advertising; for example, the words *the best* are banned, as are ads that "violate social customs" or present women in "improper ways." Coca-Cola's Indian subsidiary was forced to end a promotion that offered prizes, such as a trip to Hollywood, because it violated India's established trade practices by encouraging customers to buy in order to "gamble."[21]

Thus, although advertisers may develop global strategies to guide their overall advertising efforts, specific advertising programs must usually be adapted to meet local cultures and customs, media characteristics, and advertising regulations.

Linking the Concepts

Think about what goes on behind the scenes for the ads we all tend to take for granted.

- Pick a favorite print or television ad. Why do you like it? Do you think that it's effective? Can you think of an ad that people like that may not be effective?
- Dig a little deeper and learn about the campaign *behind* your ad. What are the campaign's objectives? What is its budget? Assess the campaign's message and media strategies. Looking beyond your own feelings about the ad, is the campaign likely to be effective?

■ Sales Promotion

Advertising and personal selling often work closely with another promotion tool, sales promotion. *Sales promotion* consists of short-term incentives to encourage the purchase or sales of a product or service. Whereas advertising and personal selling offer reasons to buy a product or service, sales promotion offers reasons to buy *now*.

Examples of sales promotions are found everywhere. A freestanding insert in the Sunday newspaper contains a coupon offering $1 off Folgers coffee. An e-mail from Amazon.com offers free shipping on your next purchase over $35. The end-of-the-aisle display in the local supermarket tempts impulse buyers with a wall of Coke cartons. An executive who buys a new Sony laptop gets a free carrying case, or a family buys a new Taurus and receives a rebate check for $500. A hardware store chain receives a 10 percent discount on selected Black & Decker portable power tools if it agrees to advertise them in local newspapers. Sales promotion includes a wide variety of promotion tools designed to stimulate earlier or stronger market response.

Rapid Growth of Sales Promotion

Sales promotion tools are used by most organizations, including manufacturers, distributors, retailers, trade associations, and not-for-profit institutions. They are targeted toward final buyers (*consumer promotions*), retailers and wholesalers (*trade promotions*), business customers (*business promotions*), and members of the sales force (*sales force promotions*).

Today, in the average consumer packaged-goods company, sales promotion accounts for 76 percent of all marketing expenditures.[22]

Several factors have contributed to the rapid growth of sales promotion, particularly in consumer markets. First, inside the company, product managers face greater pressures to increase their current sales, and promotion is viewed as an effective short-run sales tool. Second, externally, the company faces more competition and competing brands are less differentiated. Increasingly, competitors are using sales promotion to help differentiate their offers. Third, advertising efficiency has declined because of rising costs, media clutter, and legal restraints. Finally, consumers have become more deal oriented, and ever-larger retailers are demanding more deals from manufacturers.

The growing use of sales promotion has resulted in *promotion clutter,* similar to advertising clutter. Consumers are increasingly tuning out promotions, weakening their ability to trigger immediate purchase. Manufacturers are now searching for ways to rise above the clutter, such as offering larger coupon values or creating more dramatic point-of-purchase displays.

In developing a sales promotion program, a company must first set sales promotion objectives and then select the best tools for accomplishing these objectives.

Sales Promotion Objectives

Sales promotion objectives vary widely. Sellers may use *consumer promotions* to increase short-term sales or to help build long-term market share. Objectives for *trade promotions* include getting retailers to carry new items and more inventory, getting them to advertise the product and give it more shelf space, and getting them to buy ahead. For the *sales force,* objectives include getting more sales force support for current or new products or getting salespeople to sign up new accounts. Sales promotions are usually used together with advertising, personal selling, or other promotion mix tools. Consumer promotions must usually be advertised and can add excitement and pulling power to ads. Trade and sales force promotions support the firm's personal selling process.

In general, rather than creating only short-term sales or temporary brand switching, sales promotions should help to reinforce the product's position and build long-term *customer relationships.* Increasingly, marketers are avoiding "quick fix," price-only promotions in favor of promotions designed to build brand equity.

Even price promotions can be designed to help build customer relationships. Examples include all of the "frequency marketing programs" and clubs that have mushroomed in recent years. For example, Waldenbooks sponsors a Preferred Reader Program, which has attracted more than 4 million members, each paying $5 to receive mailings about new books, a 10 percent discount on book purchases, toll-free ordering, and many other services. American Express's Custom Extras program automatically awards customers deals and discounts based on frequency of purchases at participating retailers. Lladró, maker of fine porcelain figurines, sponsors the Lladró Privilege Society. Members receive a subscription to the *Lladró Privilege Magazine,* access to exclusive Lladró sculptures, invitations to attend a variety of prestigious social gatherings and cultural events, as well as other relationship benefits. Norwegian Cruise Lines sponsors a loyalty program called Latitudes. Latitudes members receive exclusive deals and promotions, up to $200 of on-board credit, the services of a special person assigned to answer their questions at sea, savings on future sailings, and invitations to an exclusive captain's reception and escorted tours of the ship's bridge and galley, and *Latitudes* magazine, which contains special articles on NCL's

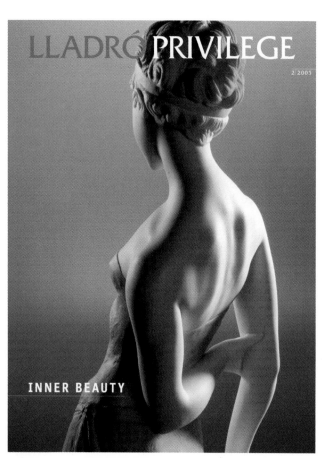

■ Consumer relationship building promotions: Benefits of the Lladró Privilege Society include a subscription to the *Lladró Privilege Magazine,* access to exclusive Lladró sculptures, invitations to attend a variety of prestigious social gatherings and cultural events, and other relationship benefits.

fleet and ports. If properly designed, every sales promotion tool has the potential to build consumer relationships.

Major Sales Promotion Tools

Many tools can be used to accomplish sales promotion objectives. Descriptions of the main consumer, trade, and business promotion tools follow.

Consumer Promotion Tools   The main *consumer promotion tools* include samples, coupons, cash refunds, price packs, premiums, advertising specialties, patronage rewards, point-of-purchase displays and demonstrations, and contests, sweepstakes, and games.

Samples are offers of a trial amount of a product. Sampling is the most effective—but most expensive—way to introduce a new product. For example, to launch Vanilla Coke, Coca-Cola distributed more than 1.3 million samples of the beverage. But the soft drink marketer didn't just hand out the samples. Instead, Coke staffers stopped targeted teen consumers at hangouts like malls, skate parks, concerts, and fairs, then delivered live commercials with messages like "Satisfy your curiosity, try a free Vanilla Coke." Says the president of Coca-Cola's promotion agency, "We wanted to get Vanilla Coke's target audience with a memorable live experience for the brand."[23]

Some samples are free; for others, the company charges a small amount to offset its cost. The sample might be delivered door-to-door, sent by mail, handed out in a store, attached to another product, or featured in an ad. Sometimes, samples are combined into sample packs, which can then be used to promote other products and services. Procter & Gamble has even distributed samples via the Internet[24]:

> When Procter & Gamble decided to relaunch Pert Plus shampoo, it extended its $20 million ad campaign by constructing a new Web site (www.pertplus.com). P&G had three objectives for the Web site: to create awareness for reformulated Pert Plus, get consumers to try the product, and gather data about Web users. The site's first page invited visitors to place their heads against the computer screen in a mock attempt to measure the cleanliness of their hair. After "tabulating the results," the site told visitors that they "need immediate help." The solution: "How about a free sample of new Pert Plus?" Visitors obtained the sample by filling out a short demographic form. The site offered other interesting features as well. For example, clicking "get a friend in a lather" produced a template that sent an e-mail to a friend with an invitation to visit the site and receive a free sample. How did the sampling promotion work out? Even P&G was shocked by the turnout. Within just 2 months of launching the site, 170,000 people visited and 83,000 requested samples. More surprising, given that the site was only 10 pages deep, the average person visited the site 1.9 times and spent a total of 7.5 minutes each visit.

Coupons are certificates that give buyers a saving when they purchase specified products. Most consumers love coupons. Manufacturers distribute 248 billion coupons year. Consumers clip some 3.7 billion of them, with an average face value of 81 cents, for a total savings of $3 billion.[25] Coupons can stimulate sales of a mature brand or promote early trial of a new brand. However, as a result of coupon clutter, redemption rates have been declining in recent years. Thus, most major consumer goods companies are issuing fewer coupons and targeting them more carefully.

Marketers are also cultivating new outlets for distributing coupons, such as supermarket shelf dispensers, electronic point-of-sale coupon printers, or "paperless coupon systems." An example is Catalina Marketing Network's Checkout Direct system, which dispenses personalized discounts to targeted buyers at the checkout counter in stores. Some companies also offer coupons on their Web sites or through online coupon services such as coolsavings.com, valupage.com, hotcoupons.com, and directcoupons.com. Last year, as a result of sites like these, the number of coupons distributed online more than doubled.[26]

Point-of-sale couponing: Using Checkout Direct technology, marketers can dispense personalized coupons to carefully targeted buyers at the checkout counter. This avoids the waste of poorly targeted coupons delivered through FSIs (coupon pages inserted into newspapers).

Cash refund offers (or *rebates*) are like coupons except that the price reduction occurs after the purchase rather than at the retail outlet. The consumer sends a "proof of purchase" to the manufacturer, who then refunds part of the purchase price by mail. For example, Toro ran a clever preseason promotion on some of its snowblower models, offering a rebate if the snowfall in the buyer's market area turned out to be below average. Competitors were not able to match this offer on such short notice, and the promotion was very successful.

Price packs (also called *cents-off deals*) offer consumers savings off the regular price of a product. The reduced prices are marked by the producer directly on the label or package. Price packs can be single packages sold at a reduced price (such as two for the price of one), or two related products banded together (such as a toothbrush and toothpaste). Price packs are very effective—even more so than coupons—in stimulating short-term sales.

Premiums are goods offered either free or at low cost as an incentive to buy a product, ranging from toys included with kids' products to phone cards and CDs. A premium may come inside the package (in-pack), outside the package (on-pack), or through the mail. In its "Treasure Hunt" promotion, for example, Quaker Oats inserted $5 million worth of gold and silver coins in Ken-L Ration dog food packages. Cutty Sark offered a brass tray with the purchase of one bottle of its scotch and a desk lamp with the purchase of two. United Airlines rewarded Chicago-area 75,000 Mileage Plus frequent-flier club members with a custom CD. The 10-song, Chicago-themed compilation disk, entitled "Chicago—Our Kind of Town," was widely played on local radio stations. It became so popular that United ended up selling it at record stores. The airline plans similar custom-designed premiums for four other major cities it serves.[27]

Advertising specialties, also called *promotional products*, are useful articles imprinted with an advertiser's name that are given as gifts to consumers. Typical items include pens, calendars, key rings, mouse pads, matches, tote bags, coolers, golf balls, T-shirts, caps, and coffee mugs. Such items can be very effective. In a recent study, 63 percent of all consumers surveyed were either carrying or wearing an ad specialty item. More than three-quarters of those who had an item could recall the advertiser's name or message before showing the item to the interviewer.[28]

Patronage rewards are cash or other awards offered for the regular use of a certain company's products or services. For example, airlines offer frequent flier plans, awarding points for miles traveled that can be turned in for free airline trips. Hotels have adopted honored-guest plans that award points to users of their hotels. And supermarkets issue frequent shopper cards that dole out a wealth of discounts at the checkout. Baskin-Robbins offers frequent-purchase awards—for every 10 purchases, customers receive a free quart of ice cream.

Point-of-purchase (POP) promotions include displays and demonstrations that take place at the point of purchase or sale. An example is a 5-foot-high cardboard display of Cap'n Crunch next to Cap'n Crunch cereal boxes. Unfortunately, many retailers do not like to handle the hundreds of displays, signs, and posters they receive from manufacturers each year. Manufacturers have responded by offering better POP materials, tying them in with television or print messages, and offering to set them up.

Contests, sweepstakes, and *games* give consumers the chance to win something, such as cash, trips, or goods, by luck or through extra effort. A *contest* calls for consumers to submit an entry—a jingle, guess, suggestion—to be judged by a panel that will select the best entries. A *sweepstakes* calls for consumers to submit their names for a drawing. A *game* presents consumers with something—bingo numbers, missing letters—every time they buy, which may or may not help them win a prize. A sales contest urges dealers or the sales force to increase their efforts, with prizes going to the top performers.

Trade Promotion Tools Manufacturers direct more sales promotion dollars toward retailers and wholesalers (78 percent) than to consumers (22 percent). Trade promotion can persuade resellers to carry a brand, give it shelf space, promote it in advertising, and push it to consumers. Shelf space is so scarce these days that manufacturers often have to offer price-offs, allowances, buy-back guarantees, or free goods to retailers and wholesalers to get products on the shelf and, once there, to stay on it.

Manufacturers use several trade promotion tools. Many of the tools used for consumer promotions—contests, premiums, displays—can also be used as trade promotions. Or the manufacturer may offer a straight *discount* off the list price on each case purchased during a stated period of time (also called a *price-off*, *off-invoice*, or *off-list*). Manufacturers also may offer an *allowance* (usually so much off per case) in return for the retailer's agreement to feature the manufacturer's products in some way. An *advertising allowance* compensates retailers for advertising the product. A *display allowance* compensates them for using special displays.

Manufacturers may offer *free goods*, which are extra cases of merchandise, to resellers who buy a certain quantity or who feature a certain flavor or size. They may offer *push money*—cash or gifts to dealers or their sales forces to "push" the manufacturer's goods. Manufacturers may give retailers free *specialty advertising items* that carry the company's name, such as pens, pencils, calendars, paperweights, matchbooks, memo pads, and yardsticks.

Business Promotion Tools Companies spend billions of dollars each year on promotion to industrial customers. These *business promotion tools* are used to generate business leads, stimulate purchases, reward customers, and motivate salespeople. Business promotion includes many of the same tools used for consumer or trade promotions. Here, we focus on two additional major business promotion tools—conventions and trade shows, and sales contests.

Many companies and trade associations organize *conventions and trade shows* to promote their products. Firms selling to the industry show their products at the trade show. More than 4,300 trade shows take place every year, drawing as many as 85 million people. Vendors receive many benefits, such as opportunities to find new sales leads, contact customers, introduce new products, meet new customers, sell more to present customers, and educate customers with publications and audiovisual materials. Trade shows also help companies reach many prospects not reached through their sales forces. About 90 percent of a trade show's visitors see a company's salespeople for the first time at the show. Business marketers may spend as much as 35 percent of their annual promotion budgets on trade shows.[29]

A *sales contest* is a contest for salespeople or dealers to motivate them to increase their sales performance over a given period. Sales contests motivate and recognize good company performers, who may receive trips, cash prizes, or other gifts. Some companies award points for performance, which the receiver can turn in for any of a variety of prizes. Sales contests work best when they are tied to measurable and achievable sales objectives (such as finding new accounts, reviving old accounts, or increasing account profitability).

■ More than 4,300 trade shows take place every year, drawing as many as 85 million people, giving sellers chances to introduce new products and meet new customers. At this consumer electronics trade show, 2,000 exhibitors attracted more than 91,000 professional visitors.

Developing the Sales Promotion Program

The marketer must make several other decisions in order to define the full sales promotion program. First, the marketer must decide on the *size of the incentive*. A certain minimum incentive is necessary if the promotion is to succeed; a larger incentive will produce more sales response. The marketer also must set *conditions for participation*. Incentives might be offered to everyone or only to select groups.

The marketer must then decide how to *promote and distribute the promotion* program itself. A 50-cents-off coupon could be given out in a package, at the store, by mail, or in an advertisement. Each distribution method involves a different level of reach and cost. Increasingly, marketers are blending several media into a total campaign concept. The *length of the promotion* is also important. If the sales promotion period is too short, many prospects (who may not be buying during that time) will miss it. If the promotion runs for too long, the deal will lose some of its "act now" force.

Evaluation is also very important. Yet many companies fail to evaluate their sales promotion programs, and others evaluate them only superficially. The most common evaluation method is to compare sales before, during, and after a promotion. Suppose a company has a 6 percent market share before the promotion, which jumps to 10 percent during the promotion, falls to 5 percent right after, and rises to 7 percent later on. The promotion seems to have attracted new triers and stimulated more buying by current customers. After the promotion, sales fell as consumers used up their inventories. The long-run rise to 7 percent means that the company gained some new users. If the brand's share had returned to the old level, then the promotion would have changed only the *timing* of demand rather than the *total* demand.

Consumer research would also show the kinds of people who responded to the promotion and what they did after it ended. *Surveys* can provide information on how many consumers recall the promotion, what they thought of it, how many took advantage of it, and how it affected their buying. Sales promotions also can be evaluated through *experiments* that vary factors such as incentive value, length, and distribution method.

Clearly, sales promotion plays an important role in the total promotion mix. To use it well, the marketer must define the sales promotion objectives, select the best tools, design the sales promotion program, implement the program, and evaluate the results. Moreover, sales promotion must be coordinated carefully with other promotion mix elements within the integrated marketing communications program.

■ Public relations is used to promote products, people, places, ideas, activities, organizations, and even nations. The state of New York turned its image around when its "I ❤ New York!" campaign took root, bringing in millions more tourists.

■ Public Relations

Another major mass-promotion tool is *public relations*—building good relations with the company's various publics by obtaining favorable publicity, building up a good corporate image, and handling or heading off unfavorable rumors, stories, and events. Public relations departments may perform any or all of the following functions[30]:

- *Press relations or press agency:* Creating and placing newsworthy information in the news media to attract attention to a person, product, or service.

- *Product publicity:* Publicizing specific products.

- *Public affairs:* Building and maintaining national or local community relations.

- *Lobbying:* Building and maintaining relations with legislators and government officials to influence legislation and regulation.

- *Investor relations:* Maintaining relationships with shareholders and others in the financial community.

- *Development:* Public relations with donors or members of nonprofit organizations to gain financial or volunteer support.

Public relations is used to promote products, people, places, ideas, activities, organizations, and even nations. Trade associations have used public relations to rebuild interest in declining commodities such as eggs, apples, milk, and potatoes. The state of New York turned its image around when its "I ❤ New York!" publicity and advertising campaign took root, bringing in millions more tourists. Johnson & Johnson's masterly use of public relations played a major role in saving Tylenol from extinction after its product-tampering scare. Nations have used public relations to attract more tourists, foreign investment, and international support.

The Role and Impact of Public Relations

Public relations can have a strong impact on public awareness at a much lower cost than advertising can. The company does not pay for the space or time in the media. Rather, it pays for a staff to develop and circulate information and to manage events. If the company develops an interesting story, it could be picked up by several different media, having the same effect as advertising that would cost millions of dollars. And it would have more credibility than advertising.

Public relations results can sometimes be spectacular. Here's how publisher Scholastic, Inc., used public relations to turn a simple new book introduction into a major international event, all on a very small budget:

Secret codes. A fiercely guarded text. Huddled masses lined up in funny hats at the witching hour. Welcome to one of the biggest and oddest literary events in history. As the clock crept past midnight, kids worldwide rushed to buy the next installment of the Harry Potter series. It was the fastest-shrinking book pile in history—with nearly 3 million copies selling in 48 hours in the United States alone. The spellbinding plots, written by Scottish welfare-mom-turned-millionaire J.K. Rowling, captivated kids everywhere, but the hidden hand of [public relations] played a role, too. With contests, theme parties, and giveaways, conditions were hot for Harry. How do you whip up a consumer frenzy with a mere $1.8 million promotion budget? Scholastic mixed in-store promotions with a few carefully

■ Public relations results can sometimes be spectacular. Scholastic sponsored low-cost sleepovers, games, and costume contests to whip up consumer frenzy for the fifth installment of its Harry Potter series.

placed ads [and a heap of public relations hype] to create a sense of celebration. It heightened the tension by keeping the title and book jacket under wraps almost until the last minute, even forcing booksellers to sign secrecy agreements.[31]

Despite its potential strengths, public relations is often described as a marketing stepchild because of its limited and scattered use. The public relations department is usually located at corporate headquarters. Its staff is so busy dealing with various publics—stockholders, employees, legislators, city officials—that public relations programs to support product marketing objectives may be ignored. Marketing managers and public relations practitioners do not always talk the same language. Many public relations practitioners see their job as simply communicating. In contrast, marketing managers tend to be much more interested in how advertising and public relations affect brand building, sales, and profits.

■ Public relations can be a powerful brand-building tool. Procter & Gamble used it to build prelaunch demand for Crest Whitestrips. On launch-day, Joan Rivers assured consumers that it is "Okay to Wear White after Labor Day."

This situation is changing, however. Although public relations still captures only a small portion of the overall marketing budgets of most firms, PR is playing an increasingly important brand-building role.

Public relations can be a powerful brand-building tool. Consider how Procter & Gamble used PR to launch Crest Whitestrips:

> Just before the product launch, to spread the word about Whitestrips, Procter & Gamble first identified key "influencer groups" to target: bridal consultants, salon and spa owners, and national and local sorority leaders. These influencers were considered image "experts." P&G held special conferences for these image experts to introduce them to Whitestrips. It also hired Joan and Melissa Rivers for Whitestrips launch-day celebrations. These celebrities, along with the permission slips they distributed and a giant billboard in Times Square, assured consumers that it is "Okay to Wear White after Labor Day." P&G also created an "Uppers Challenge" encouraging skeptics to use Whitestrips on only their upper teeth to reveal the real difference. Spokespeople who'd taken this challenge worked the crowds, showing the "uppers" difference. In all, the PR campaign brought 240 million media impressions, including broadcast coverage on the "Today" show and print coverage in *Good Housekeeping, Family Circle, Glamour, InStyle,* and *Elle.* And when Procter & Gamble launched its highly successful Whitestrips, prelaunch efforts generated $23 million in sales prior to retail availability. Of those sales, one-third were directly linked to public relations. Thus, PR played a highly significant role in building the Whitestrips brand.[32]

Two well-known marketing consultants even went so far as to conclude that advertising doesn't build brands, PR does. In their book *The Fall of Advertising and the Rise of PR,* the consultants proclaim that the era of advertising is over, and that public relations is quietly becoming the most powerful marketing communications tools[33]:

> The birth of a brand is usually accomplished with [public relations], not advertising. Our general rule is [PR] first, advertising second. [Public relations] is the nail, advertising the hammer. [PR] creates the credentials that provide the credibility for advertising. . . . Anita Roddick built the Body Shop into a major brand with no advertising at all. Instead, she traveled the world on a relentless quest for publicity. . . . Until recently Starbucks Coffee Co. didn't spend a hill of beans on advertising, either. In 10 years, the company spent less than $10 million on advertising, a trivial amount for a brand that delivers annual sales of $1.3 billion. Wal-Mart Stores became the world's largest retailer . . . with very little advertising. . . . On the Internet, Amazon.com became a powerhouse brand with virtually no advertising.[34]

Although the book created much controversy, and most advertisers wouldn't agree about the "fall of advertising" part of the title, the point is a good one. Advertising and public relations should work hand in hand to build and maintain brands.

Major Public Relations Tools

Public relations professionals use several tools. One of the major tools is *news*. PR professionals find or create favorable news about the company and its products or people. Sometimes news stories occur naturally, and sometimes the PR person can suggest events or activities that would create news. *Speeches* can also create product and company publicity. Increasingly, company executives must field questions from the media or give talks at trade associations or sales meetings, and these events can either build or hurt the company's image.

Another common PR tool is *special events*, ranging from news conferences, press tours, grand openings, and fireworks displays to laser shows, hot air balloon releases, multimedia presentations and star-studded spectaculars, or educational programs designed to reach and interest target publics. Many marketers are now designing *buzz marketing* campaigns that create excitement and generate favorable word-of-mouth communication for their brands. Buzz marketing creates publicity by getting consumers themselves to spread the brand message (see Marketing at Work 12.4).

Recently, *mobile marketing*—traveling promotional tours that bring the brand to consumers—has emerged as an effective way to build one-to-one relationships with targeted consumers[35]:

> These days, it seems that almost every company is putting its show on the road, with a record number of marketers launching nationwide tours. Not only are such tours relatively cheap, they offer an irresistible opportunity to build brands while attracting additional sponsorship dollars and promotional relationships with retailers and trade marketing partners. Home Depot recently brought do-it-yourself home project workshops and demonstrations to 26 NASCAR racetracks. Court TV launched a tour that visited malls in 20 cities, challenging consumers to solve a crime by visiting six "forensics labs" and interviewing a computerized virtual witness. Mattel's Matchbox Toys launched its first-ever tour last year, hitting store parking lots in 25 cities over 6 months to celebrate Matchbox's 50th anniversary. Events included interactive games, historic displays, free gifts, and an obstacle course for kids riding battery-powered vehicles. And Krispy Kreme recently unveiled a 53-foot-long, fully functioning store on wheels at an event in Winston-Salem, North Carolina, the chain's headquarters. It takes a day to set up the shop—which sells doughnuts, coffee, and logoed merchandise—so the company is targeting planned festivals, fairs, and events around the country. The mobile store is scheduled to be on the road approximately 250 days during the next year, visiting cities that are new to the company along with more established markets. It recently made an appearance for the homecoming of a U.S. Navy battleship group. Says one Krispy Kreme marketing executive, "the mobile store is a way to extend the Krispy Kreme experience."

Public relations people also prepare *written materials* to reach and influence their target markets. These materials include annual reports, brochures, articles, and company newsletters and magazines. *Audiovisual materials*, such as films, slide-and-sound programs, and video and audio cassettes, are being used increasingly as communication tools. *Corporate identity materials* can also help create a corporate identity that the public immediately recognizes. Logos, stationery, brochures, signs, business forms, business cards, buildings, uniforms, and company cars and trucks—all become marketing tools when they are attractive, distinctive, and memorable. Finally, companies can improve public goodwill by contributing money and time to *public service activities*.

A company's Web site can be a good public relations vehicle. Consumers and members of other publics can visit the site for information and entertainment. Such sites can be extremely popular. For example, Butterball's site (www.butterball.com), which features cooking and carving tips, received 550,000 visitors in 1 day during Thanksgiving week last year. Web sites can also be ideal for handling crisis situations. For example, when several bottles of Odwalla apple juice sold on the West Coast were found to contain *E. coli* bacteria, Odwalla initiated a massive product recall. Within only 3 hours, it set up a Web site laden with information about the crisis and Odwalla's response. Company staffers also combed the Internet looking for newsgroups discussing Odwalla and posted links to the site. In another example, American Home Products quickly set up a Web site to distribute accurate information and advice after a model died reportedly after inhaling its Primatene Mist. The Primatene site, up less than 12 hours after the crisis broke, remains in place today (www.primatene.com). In all, notes one analyst, "Today, public relations is reshaping the Internet and the Internet, in turn, is redefining the practice of public relations." Says another, "People look to the Net for information, not salesmanship, and that's the real opportunity for public relations."[36]

Marketing at Work | 12.4

Buzz Marketing: A Powerful New Way to Spread the Word

These days, buzz marketing is all the rage. Buzz marketing involves getting consumers themselves to spread information about a product or service to others in their communities. "In a successful buzz-marketing campaign, each carefully cultivated recipient of the brand message becomes a powerful carrier, spreading the word to yet more carriers, much as a virus rampages through a given population," says one expert. "Firms don't 'do' [buzz] marketing: It's done to you," says another. Companies of all kinds—from Procter & Gamble, Hebrew National, and Hasbro Games to Ford, Vespa, and IBM—are now using buzz marketing as a new way to connect with hard-to-reach consumers.

Why the new trend? For starters, buzz marketing is cheap. It's a great way to extend brand exposure without blowing out the marketing budget. Buzz marketing's increasing popularity can also be attributed to burgeoning Internet usage. Marketers can now use the Web to reach large numbers of consumers, particularly trend leaders, quickly and easily. Finally, buzz marketing provides a nonadvertising alternative for reaching the growing ranks of skeptical consumers—such as twenty-somethings—who are notoriously disdainful of mass-media advertising. Instead of the usual ad pitches, buzz marketing spreads the word through grassroots opinion leaders who are far removed from corporate America.

Perhaps the single most important reason that marketers are employing buzz marketing is that it really works. Consider the following examples.

Lee Dungarees: In recent years, VF had managed to reenergize the image of its stodgy Lee jeans brand among younger target consumers—mostly young males 17 to 22. But it needed to do more to convert that cooler image into sales at teen-toxic retailers like JCPenney and Sears Roebuck, its biggest outlets. So VF came up with one of the most free-

wheeling and influential buzz-marketing campaigns to date. The campaign played on target consumers' weakness for video games and computers. First, VF developed a list of 200,000 "influential" guys from a list of Web surfers. It then zapped them a trio of grainy video clips that were hilarious in their apparent stupidity. The videos appeared to be ultra-low-budget flicks

meant to draw visitors to the Web game sites of amateur film-makers, such as open-shirted Curry, a 23-year-old race car driver. To the young Web surfers who received them, the clips seemed like delicious examples of the oddball digital debris that litters the Web. So not many of the recipients who eagerly forwarded the flicks to their friends would have guessed that

Buzz marketing: The MINI USA unit of BMW of North America bucked car-advertising tradition by unleashing a torrent of unconventional tactics to create a buzz for its retro-looking MINI Cooper.

they actually were abetting in a marketing campaign orchestrated by Lee.

According to VF research, the "stupid little films" were so intriguing that, on average, recipients forwarded them to six friends apiece. Despite virtually no advertising, some 100,000 visitors stormed the fictional film makers' Web sites the week they went live, crashing the server. The marketing connection only became clear a few months later, after a TV and radio ad blitz finally revealed the three characters to be fictional antagonists developed as part of an online computer game. And that was a key to the program: To play the game at an advanced level, participants had to snag the product identification numbers—the "secret code"—off Lee items, which of course required a visit to a store. Ultimately, the effort drove thousands of kids age 17 to 22 into the stores and helped propel Lee sales upward by 20 percent last year.

Belly Washers: Shelby Coffey, a shy, blond 10-year-old in suburban Atlanta, loves BellyWashers. Really. There are 45 of the cartoon-character juice bottles in a place of honor on a shelf above her desk. There's a scarce Sylvester, a rare Blossom, and the much sought-after green Power Ranger. But Shelby is more than just a collector. With 15 young friends, she has organized a BellyWashers club to do community-service projects. They visit children's hospitals to pass out BellyWashers at Christmas, clean city parks under a BellyWashers banner, and donate proceeds of their yard sales to disadvantaged children. Over the past year, Shelby has amassed a 5-inch-thick binder of pictures and newspaper clippings documenting her work on behalf of the brand. Local TV stations have filmed her good deeds. The kicker: She does it all for free.

In Zone Brands, the company behind BellyWashers, has nurtured such buzz from the beginning, mostly because it's had to. A startup taking on giants in a fiercely competitive trade, it has never had the budget to sustain tra-

ditional mass marketing. But it knew that for kids, there is no advertising more effective than the peer influence of another kid. So, a year ago, the company launched its Kids Board, a national panel that acts as a mini-business unit within the company. Every year, In Zone selects some 15 kids to the board and sponsors their community-service projects. The kids help In Zone come up with new product ideas and, more important, build grassroots fervor. The Kids Board costs about $60,000 a year to manage and the exact impact is hard to calculate. But in the past year, board members have organized 40 community-service projects involving 60,000 kids, and generated an estimated 4 million media impressions. Not least, the buzz has fed a vibrant aftermarket: eBay recently listed 32 BellyWashers for sale; in May, a first-edition Powerpuff Girl bottle went for $35. Meanwhile, BellyWashers have rocketed off of the shelves at Kroger, Target, Toys "R" Us, and Wal-Mart. Last year, A.C. Nielsen clocked BellyWashers as the 37th most popular fruit-drink brand out of the 700 that it tracks—and that survey did not include convenience stores, BellyWashers' strongest channel. Thanks to effective buzz marketing, the company has logged 100 percent annual compounded growth over the past 3 years, and it expects sales to top $75 million this year.

MINI : The MINI USA division of BMW of North America bucked car-advertising tradition by using unconventional tactics to create a buzz for its MINI Cooper. To launch the return of the diminutive British-made sedan, "we wanted to be as different as we could because the car is so different from anything out there," says a MINI marketer. As a result, there was no national television advertising. Instead, MINI USA generated buzz for the MINI Cooper in less conventional ways. For example, the "MINI Ride" display touring the United States, which included an actual MINI, looked like a children's ride. "Rides $16,850. Quarters only, please" the sign

read. Displays in airports and other public places featured oversized newspaper vending machines, waste baskets, and pay phones next to posters showing the diminutive Mini and proclaiming, "Makes everything else seem a little too big." The car was also promoted on the Internet, in ads painted on city buildings, and on baseball-type cards handed out at auto shows. To intrigue passersby, MINI USA put MINIs on top of sport utilities and drove them around 24 cities. In addition, MINI USA sold unusual MINI-brand items including remote-control cars, speedometer watches, and cuckoo clocks on its Web site. The nation's 78 dealers, who agreed to build separate branded MINI showrooms, were deluged with orders. Within a year of the start of the campaign, MINI USA was selling MINIs faster than it could make them. The offbeat marketing campaign scooped up numerous advertising industry awards. And that interest was built from the ground up through buzz marketing. Just three years ago, only 2 percent of Americans had ever even heard of MINI. Today, MINI enjoys a 67 percent brand awareness.

Thus, buzz marketing can generate amazing results. For products that meet real needs with innovative or stylish designs, the positive word travels fast. Notes one global marketing executive, "Finding a revolutionary new way to market [a brand really works when] it's grounded in the product truth. . . . Great marketing is simply a megaphone for the truth, and when the 'buzz' is [right] it delivers unconventional messages very effectively to unconventional audiences."

Sources: Excerpts adapted from Gerry Khermouch and Jeff Green, "Buzz Marketing," Business Week, July 30, 2001, pp. 50–56; Jean Halliday, "Creating Max Buzz for New BMW Mini," Advertising Age, June 17, 2002, p. 12; and Linda Tischler, "Buzz without Bucks," Fast Company, August 2003, pp. 78–83. Also see James C. Schroer, "The Ultimate Buzz," Marketing Management, September–October 2001, p. 56; Laura Mazur, "Firms Can't 'Do' Viral Marketing: It Is Done to You," Marketing, June 27, 2002, p. 16; Mike Bierne, "Strip-Mining Slows, Low-Carb Pitches Grow," Brandweek, May 19, 2003, p. 14; and Joan Voight, "Mini's Wild Ride," Adweek, June 2, 2003, pp. 24–26.

As with the other promotion tools, in considering when and how to use product public relations, management should set PR objectives, choose the PR messages and vehicles, implement the PR plan, and evaluate the results. The firm's public relations should be blended smoothly with other promotion activities within the company's overall integrated marketing communications effort.

REST STOP:
Reviewing the Concepts

In this chapter, you've learned about the concept of integrated marketing communications (IMC), defined the major marketing communications tools, and overviewed the general promotion mix strategies. We've also explored three of the specific communications mix elements—advertising, sales promotion, and public relations—more deeply. Before moving on to other promotion tools, let's briefly review the important concepts.

Modern marketing calls for more than just developing a good product, pricing it attractively, and making it available to target customers. Companies also must *communicate* with current and prospective customers to inform them about product benefits and carefully position products in consumers' minds. To do this, they must blend five communication-mix tools, guided by a well-designed and well-implemented integrated marketing communications strategy.

1. Discuss the process and advantages of integrated marketing communications.

Recent shifts toward targeted or one-to-one marketing, coupled with advances in information technology, have had a dramatic impact on marketing communications. As marketing communicators adopt richer but more fragmented media and promotion mixes to reach their diverse markets, they risk creating a communications hodgepodge for consumers. To prevent this, more companies are adopting the concept of *integrated marketing communications (IMC)*. Guided by an overall IMC strategy, the company works out the roles that the various promotional tools will play and the extent to which each will be used. It carefully coordinates the promotional activities and the timing of when major campaigns take place. Finally, to help implement its integrated marketing strategy, the company appoints a marketing communications director who has overall responsibility for the company's communications efforts.

2. Define the five promotion tools and discuss factors that must be considered in shaping the overall promotion mix.

A company's total *marketing communications mix*—also called its *promotion mix*—consists of the specific blend of *advertising, personal selling, sales promotion, public relations,* and *direct-marketing* tools that the company uses to pursue its advertising and marketing objectives. Advertising includes any

paid form of nonpersonal presentation and promotion of ideas, goods, or services by an identified sponsor. In contrast, public relations focuses on building good relations with the company's various publics by obtaining favorable unpaid publicity. Personal selling is any form of personal presentation by the firm's sales force for the purpose of making sales and building customer relationships. Firms use sales promotion to provide short-term incentives to encourage the purchase or sale of a product or service. Finally, firms seeking immediate response from targeted individual customers use nonpersonal direct-marketing tools to communicate with customers.

The company wants to create an integrated *promotion mix*. It can pursue a *push* or a *pull* promotional strategy, or a combination of the two. The best specific blend of promotion tools depends on the type of product/market and the product life-cycle stage. People at all levels of the organization must be aware of the many legal and ethical issues surrounding marketing communications.

3. Describe and discuss the major decisions involved in developing an advertising program.

Advertising—the use of paid media by a seller to inform, persuade, and remind about its products or organization—is a strong promotion tool that takes many forms and has many uses. *Advertising decision making* involves decisions about the objectives, the budget, the message, the media, and, finally, the evaluation of results. Advertisers should set clear *objectives* as to whether the advertising is supposed to inform, persuade, or remind buyers. The advertising *budget* can be based on what is affordable, on sales, on competitors' spending, or on the objectives and tasks. The *message decision* calls for planning a message strategy and executing it effectively. The *media decision* involves defining reach, frequency, and impact goals; choosing major media types; selecting media vehicles; and deciding on media timing. Message and media decisions must be closely coordinated for maximum campaign effectiveness. Finally, *evaluation* calls for evaluating the communication and sales effects of advertising before, during, and after the advertising is placed.

4. Explain how sales promotion campaigns are developed and implemented.

Sales promotion covers a wide variety of short-term incentive tools—coupons, premiums, contests, buying allowances—designed to stimulate final and business consumers, the trade, and the company's own sales force. Sales promotion spending has been growing faster than advertising spending in recent years. A sales promotion campaign first calls for setting sales promotion objectives (in general, sales promotions should be *consumer relationship building*). It then calls for developing and implementing the sales promotion program by using consumer promotion tools (*samples, coupons, cash refunds* or *rebates, price packs, premiums, advertising specialties, patronage rewards*, and others); trade promotion tools (*discounts, allowances, free goods, push money*); and business promotion tools (*conventions, trade shows, sales contests*). The sales promotion effort should be coordinated carefully with the firm's other promotion efforts.

5. Explain how companies use public relations to communicate with their publics.

Public relations involves building good relations with the company's various publics. Its functions include *press agency,* *product publicity, public affairs, lobbying, investor relations,* and *development*. Public relations can have a strong impact on public awareness at a much lower cost than advertising can, and public relations results can sometimes be spectacular. Despite its potential strengths, however, public relations sometimes sees only limited and scattered use.

Public relations tools include *news, speeches, special events, buzz marketing, written materials, audiovisual materials, corporate identity materials*, and *public service activities*. A company's Web site can be a good public relations vehicle. In considering when and how to use product public relations, management should set PR objectives, choose the PR messages and vehicles, implement the PR plan, and evaluate the results. Public relations should be blended smoothly with other promotion activities within the company's overall integrated marketing communications effort.

Navigating the Key Terms

Advertising
Advertising agency
Advertising objective
Affordable method
Competitive-parity method

Direct marketing
Integrated marketing communications (IMC)
Marketing communications mix (promotion mix)
Objective-and-task method

Percentage-of-sales method
Personal selling
Public relations
Pull strategy
Push strategy
Sales promotion

Travel Log

Discussing the Issues

1. What are the five major promotional tools? Broadly speaking, what type of objective is each promotional tool best suited to accomplish?

2. Describe the four methods for setting the advertising budget discussed in the text. For each of the four methods, explain why a company might use that method over the other three.

3. Explain how the advertising factors of reach, frequency, and impact will influence consumer awareness of a brand. Is one more important than the others for increasing consumer awareness?

4. Consumer promotion tools include samples, coupons, cash refunds, price packs, premiums, advertising specialties, patronage rewards, point-of-purchase displays and demonstrations, and contests, sweepstakes, and games. Describe two of these promotional tools you have received or participated in. How did it have an impact on your purchase decision?

5. Compare and contrast the public relations functions of press relations, product publicity, public affairs, lobbying, investor relations, and development.

6. What are some of the likely challenges companies will face when trying to implement an integrated marketing communications program? How might these obstacles be overcome?

Application Questions

1. Find examples of advertisements in magazines that illustrate each of the execution styles presented in this chapter. Present your findings to the class, including a discussion explaining which execution styles you think are most effective for this type of product.

2. Assume that you have recently taken a position in the marketing area for a company manufacturing cellular phones that are capable of taking and transmitting pictures. Your boss has asked you to create a promotional plan that will include both push and pull strategies. Describe the plan and what objectives you hope to accomplish with each component.

3. Identify three advertisements for consumer goods or services (e.g., toothpaste, athletic shoes, insurance, beverages, restaurants, etc.), one from the radio, one from television, and one from a magazine. For each of the three, evaluate the advertising appeal. Specifically, rate each advertisement in terms of the appeals being meaningful, believable, and distinctive from those made for other brands. For the aspects you rated low, how could the advertisement be changed to improve that aspect of the advertising appeal?

Under the Hood: Focus on Technology

Although not yet as widespread as VCRs or DVDs, personal video recorders (PVRs) have been gaining popularity. However, the biggest names in the PVR industry, TiVo and RelayTV, have come under fire from the television industry for some of the features these new devices are capable of delivering. Perhaps of biggest concern to television executives is the ability of these machines to automatically skip over commercials, which the television industry claims is a violation of copyright laws. This takes consumers one big step beyond simply fast-forwarding through commercials using their VCRs. Because advertising is the primary source of income for television networks, they are justifiably concerned that this automatic channel-skipping technology will damage their ability to sell commercial time, or will at least decrease its value. Indeed, there are competing lawsuits working their way through the legal system with television and movie studios suing to stop this commercial-skipping feature and many users suing to give them the right to do exactly that.

1. Do you think that PVRs will ultimately change the nature of advertising on broadcast television?

2. Whose side are you on in the debate over the automatic commercial-skipping technology? Choose sides and debate the issue.

3. Beyond the current strategies discussed in the text, what alternatives might a company pursue to overcome the impact this new technology has on advertising?

Focus on Ethics

Straddling the line between advertising and publicity is cause-related marketing, which can be described as linking a company to a social cause or issue for their mutual benefit. Advocates of this approach suggest that it is an effective way of communicating the values of the company while at the same time supporting important social issues. For example, The Kellogg Company sponsors the Hannah Neil World of Children Awards, which provides $100,000 "to honor and recognize those people who make a world of difference in the lives of children across the globe."

1. When choosing between two products that are equal in all areas, what impact would knowing that one of the firms supports a cause that is meaningful to you have on your purchase decision?

2. Do companies have a moral responsibility to spend some of their profits assisting causes and issues that are of social value (e.g., funding cancer research, searching for missing children, preventing drug abuse, promoting environmental issues, etc.)?

3. Visit the Kellogg web site (www.kelloggs.com/kelloggco/) and click on the "corporate citizenship" link to learn more about the cause-related activities this company sponsors. Should a company that engages in these types of activities do more to make others aware of their activities? Should the support of activities such as these be considered a form of product promotion?

Videos

The AFLAC video case that accompanies this chapter is located in Appendix 1 at the back of the book.

Student Materials

Need a tune-up? A study guide and OneKey access code are available to aid in your review of chapter material. Your instructor may choose to have these items shrink-wrapped with your text or you may purchase them separately at www.prenhall.com/marketing.

LEAR
CORPORATI

■ *After studying this chapter, you should be able to*

1. *Discuss* the role of a company's salespeople in creating value for customers and building customer relationships
2. *Identify* and explain the six major sales force management steps **3.** *Discuss* the personal selling process, distinguishing between transaction-oriented marketing and relationship marketing **4.** *Define* direct marketing and discuss its benefits to customers and companies **5.** *Identify* and discuss the major forms of direct marketing

Integrated Marketing Communication: Personal Selling and Direct Marketing

13

In the previous chapter, you learned about integrated marketing communications (IMC) and three elements of the marketing communications mix—advertising, sales promotion, and publicity. In this chapter, we'll move on down the road to learn about the final two IMC elements—personal selling and direct marketing. Personal selling is the interpersonal arm of marketing communications in which the sales force interacts with customers and prospects to make sales and build relationships. Direct marketing consists of direct connections with carefully targeted consumers to both obtain an immediate response and cultivate lasting customer relationships. Actually, direct marketing can be viewed as more than just a communications tool. In many ways, it constitutes an overall marketing *approach*—a blend of communications and distribution channels all rolled into one. As you read on, remember that although this chapter examines personal selling and direct marketing as separate tools, they must be carefully coordinated with other elements of the marketing communication mix.

We'll begin this leg of the journey with a look at Lear Corporation's sales force. Although you may never have heard of Lear, the chances are good that you've spent lots of time in one or more of the car interiors that it supplies to the world's major automotive manufacturers. Before you read on, close your eyes for a moment and envision a typical salesperson. If what you see is a stereotypical glad-hander out to lighten your wallet or purse by selling you something that you don't really need, you might be in for a surprise.

W hen someone says "salesperson," what image comes to mind? Perhaps it's the stereotypical "traveling salesman"—the fast-talking, ever-smiling peddler who travels his territory foisting his wares on reluctant customers. Such stereotypes, however, are sadly out of date. Today, most professional salespeople are well-educated, well-trained men and women who work to build long-term, value-producing relationships with their customers. They succeed not by taking customers in but by helping them out—by assessing customer needs and solving customer problems.

Consider Lear Corporation, one of the largest, fastest-growing, and most successful automotive suppliers in the world. Each year, Lear produces more than $14 billion worth of automotive interiors—seat systems, instrument panels, door panels, floor and acoustic systems, overhead

systems, and electronic and electrical distribution systems. Its customers include all of the world's leading automotive companies, from Ford, DaimlerChrysler, General Motors, Fiat, Toyota, and Volvo to BMW, Ferrari, Rolls-Royce, and more than a dozen others. Lear now operates more than 280 facilities in 33 countries around the globe.

During the past few years, Lear has achieved record-breaking sales and earnings growth. Lear's sales during the past 5 years have more than doubled, and its "average content per car" in North America has increased more than fourfold since 1990. It owns about a 30 percent share of the North American interior components market. In addition, Lear was recently named by *Fortune* magazine as *America's Most Admired Company* in the motor vehicle parts industry.

Lear Corporation owes its success to many factors, including a strong customer orientation and a commitment to continuous improvement, teamwork, and customer value. But perhaps more than any other part of the organization, it's Lear's outstanding 145-person sales force that makes the company's credo, "Consumer driven. Customer focused," ring true. Lear's sales force was recently rated by *Sales & Marketing Management* magazine as one of "America's Best Sales Forces." What makes this an outstanding sales force? Lear knows that good selling these days takes much more than just a sales rep covering a territory and convincing customers to buy the product. It takes teamwork, relationship building, and doing what's best for the customer. Lear's sales force excels at these tasks.

Lear's sales depend completely on the success of its customers. If the auto makers don't sell cars, Lear doesn't sell interiors. So the Lear sales force strives to create not just sales, but customer success. In fact, Lear salespeople aren't "sales reps," they're "account managers," who function more as consultants than as order getters. "Our salespeople don't really close deals," notes a senior marketing executive. "They consult and work with customers to learn exactly what's needed and when."

To more fully match up with customers' needs, Lear has diversified its product line to become a kind of "one-stop shopping" source. Until a few years ago, Lear supplied only seats; now it sells almost everything for a car's interior. Providing complete interior solutions for customers also benefits Lear. "It used to be that we'd build a partnership and then get only a limited amount of revenue from it," the executive says. "Now we can get as much as possible out of our customer relationships."

Lear is heavily customer focused, so much so that it's broken up into separate divisions dedicated to specific customers. For example, there's a Ford, a General Motors, and a Fiat division—each operates as its own profit center. Within each division, high-level "platform teams"—made up of salespeople, engineers, and program managers—work closely with their customer counterparts. These platform teams are closely supported by divisional manufacturing, finance, quality, and advanced technology groups.

Lear's limited customer base, consisting of only a few dozen customers in all, allows Lear's sales teams to get very close to their customers. "Our teams don't call on purchasers; they're linked to customer operations at all levels," the marketer notes. "We try to put a system in place that creates continuous contact with customers." In fact, Lear often locates its sales offices in customers' plants. For example, the team that handles GM's light truck division works at GM's truck operation campus. "We can't just be there to give quotes and ask for orders," says the marketing executive. "We need to be involved with customers every step of the way—from vehicle concept through launch."

Such close customer involvement pays off handsomely. Last year, GM honored Lear as a Supplier of the Year. "[Lear's] performance and contributions have been critical in helping GM," says a senior GM purchasing executive. "They serve as a role model for other suppliers." GM also rewarded Lear with an innovative contract giving Lear complete responsibility for designing, engineering, purchasing, and delivery of interiors for two coming GM vehicles, a contract worth an average of $825 million in annual sales.

Lear's largest customers are worth billions of dollars in annual sales to the company. Maintaining profitable relationships with such large customers takes much more than a nice smile and a firm handshake. And certainly there's no place for the "smoke and mirrors" or "flim-flam" sometimes mistakenly associated with personal selling. Success in such a selling environment requires careful teamwork among well-trained, dedicated sales professionals who are bent on profitably taking care of their customers.[1]

In this chapter, we examine two more marketing communication and promotion tools— *personal selling* and *direct marketing*. Both involve direct connections with customers aimed toward building customer-unique value and lasting relationships.

Personal Selling

Robert Louis Stevenson once noted that "everyone lives by selling something." We are all familiar with the sales forces used by business organizations to sell products and services to customers around the world. But sales forces are also found in many other kinds of organizations. For example, colleges use recruiters to attract new students, and churches use membership committees to attract new members. Hospitals and museums use fund-raisers to contact donors and raise money. Even governments use sales forces. The U.S. Postal Service, for instance, uses a sales force to sell Express Mail and other services to corporate customers. In the first part of this chapter, we examine the role of personal selling in the organization, sales force management decisions, and the personal selling process.

The Nature of Personal Selling

Selling is one of the oldest professions in the world. The people who do the selling go by many names: *salespeople, sales representatives, account executives, sales consultants, sales engineers, agents, district managers, marketing representatives,* and *account development reps* to name just a few.

People hold many stereotypes of salespeople—including some unfavorable ones. "Salesman" may bring to mind the image of Arthur Miller's pitiable Willy Loman in *Death of a Salesman.* Or you might think of Meredith Willson's cigar-smoking, backslapping, joke-telling Harold Hill in *The Music Man.* Both examples depict salespeople as loners, traveling their territories, trying to foist their wares on unsuspecting or unwilling buyers.

However, modern salespeople are a far cry from these unfortunate stereotypes. Today, most salespeople are well-educated, well-trained professionals who work to build and maintain long-term customer relationships. They listen to their customers, assess customer needs, and organize the company's efforts to solve customer problems. Consider Boeing, the aerospace giant competing in the rough-and-tumble worldwide commercial aircraft market. It takes more than fast talk and a warm smile to sell expensive airplanes:

Selling high-tech aircraft at $70 million or more a copy is complex and challenging. A single big sale can easily run into billions of dollars. Boeing salespeople head up an extensive team of company specialists—sales and service technicians, financial analysts, planners, engineers—all dedicated to finding ways to satisfy airline customer needs. The salespeople begin by becoming experts on the airlines, much like Wall Street analysts would. They find out where each airline wants to grow, when it wants to replace planes, and details of its financial situation. The team runs Boeing and competing planes through

■ The term *salesperson* covers a wide range of positions, from the clerk selling in a retail store to the engineering salesperson who consults with client companies.

Salesperson

An individual acting for a company by performing one or more of the following activities: prospecting, communicating, servicing, and information gathering.

computer systems, simulating the airline's routes, cost per seat, and other factors to show that their planes are most efficient. Then the high-level negotiations begin. The selling process is nerve-wrackingly slow—it can take 2 or 3 years from the first sales presentation to the day the sale is announced. Sometimes top executives from both the airline and Boeing are brought in to close the deal. After getting the order, salespeople then must stay in almost constant touch to keep track of the account's equipment needs and to make certain the customer stays satisfied. Success depends on building solid, long-term relationships with customers, based on performance and trust. "When you buy an airplane, it is like getting married," says the head of Boeing's commercial airplane division. "It is a long-term relationship."[2]

The term **salesperson** covers a wide range of positions. At one extreme, a salesperson might be largely an *order taker,* such as the department store salesperson standing behind the counter. At the other extreme are *order getters*, whose positions demand the *creative selling* of products and services ranging from appliances, industrial equipment, and airplanes to insurance and information technology services. Here, we focus on the more creative types of selling and on the process of building and managing an effective sales force.

The Role of the Sales Force

Personal selling is the interpersonal arm of the promotion mix. Advertising consists of one-way, nonpersonal communication with target consumer groups. In contrast, personal selling involves two-way, personal communication between salespeople and individual customers—whether face-to-face, by telephone, through video or Web conferences, or by other means. Personal selling can be more effective than advertising in more complex selling situations. Salespeople can probe customers to learn more about their problems, then adjust the marketing offer to fit the special needs of each customer and negotiate terms of sale. They can build long-term personal relationships with key decision makers.

The role of personal selling varies from company to company. Some firms have no salespeople at all—for example, companies that sell only through mail-order catalogs or companies that sell through manufacturer's reps, sales agents, or brokers. In most firms, however, the sales force plays a major role. In companies that sell business products and services, such as IBM, Cisco Systems, and DuPont, the company's salespeople work directly with customers. In consumer product companies such as Procter & Gamble and Nike, which sell through intermediaries, final consumers rarely meet salespeople or even know about them. Still, the sales force plays an important behind-the-scenes role. It works with wholesalers and retailers to gain their support and to help them be more effective in selling the company's products.

The sales force serves as a critical link between a company and its customers. In many cases, salespeople serve both masters—the seller and the buyer. First, they *represent the company to customers*. They find and develop new customers and communicate information about the company's products and services. They sell products by approaching customers, presenting their products, answering objections, negotiating prices and terms, and closing sales. In addition, salespeople provide customer service and carry out market research and intelligence work.

At the same time, salespeople *represent customers to the company,* acting inside the firm as "champions" of customers' interests and managing the buyer–seller relationship. Salespeople relay customer concerns about company products and actions back inside to those who can handle them. They learn about customer needs and work with other marketing and nonmarketing people in the company to develop greater customer value. The old view was that salespeople should worry about sales and the company should worry about profit. However, the current view holds that salespeople should be concerned with more than just producing *sales*—they should work with others in the company to produce *customer satisfaction* and *company profit.*

Managing the Sales Force

We define **sales force management** as the analysis, planning, implementation, and control of sales force activities. It includes designing sales force strategy and structure and recruiting, selecting, training, compensating, supervising, and evaluating the firm's salespeople. These major sales force management decisions are shown in Figure 13.1 and are discussed in the following sections.

Designing Sales Force Strategy and Structure

Marketing managers face several sales force strategy and design questions. How should salespeople and their tasks be structured? How big should the sales force be? Should salespeople sell alone or work in teams with other people in the company? Should they sell in the field or by telephone? We address these issues below.

Sales Force Structure A company can divide up sales responsibilities along any of several lines. The decision is simple if the company sells only one product line to one industry with customers in many locations. In that case the company would use a *territorial sales force structure.* However, if the company sells many products to many types of customers, it might need either a *product sales force structure,* a *customer sales force structure,* or a combination of the two.

Territorial Sales Force Structure. In the **territorial sales force structure**, each salesperson is assigned to an exclusive geographic area and sells the company's full line of products or services to all customers in that territory. This organization clearly defines each salesperson's job and fixes accountability. It also increases the salesperson's desire to build local business relationships that, in turn, improve selling effectiveness. Finally, because each salesperson travels within a limited geographic area, travel expenses are relatively small.

A territorial sales organization is often supported by many levels of sales management positions. For example, Campbell Soup uses a territorial structure in which each salesperson is responsible for selling all Campbell Soup products. Starting at the bottom of the organization, *sales merchandisers* report to *sales representatives,* who report to *retail supervisors,* who report to *directors of retail sales operations,* who report to 1 of 22

Sales force management
The analysis, planning, implementation, and control of sales force activities. It includes setting and designing sales force strategy and structure; and recruiting, selecting, training, supervising, compensating, and evaluating the firm's salespeople.

Territorial sales force structure
A sales force organization that assigns each salesperson to an exclusive geographic territory in which that salesperson sells the company's full line.

FIGURE 13.1

Major Steps in Sales Force Management

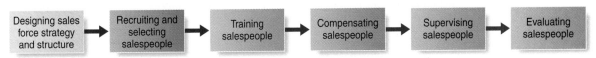

regional sales managers. Regional sales managers, in turn, report to 1 of 4 *general sales managers* (West, Central, South, and East), who report to a *vice president* and *general sales manager.*

Product sales force structure

A sales force organization under which salespeople specialize in selling only a portion of the company's products or lines.

Product Sales Force Structure. Salespeople must know their products—especially when the products are numerous and complex. This need, together with the growth of product management, has led many companies to adopt a **product sales force structure**, in which the sales force sells along product lines. For example, Kodak uses different sales forces for its film products than for its industrial products. The film products sales force deals with simple products that are distributed intensively, whereas the industrial products sales force deals with complex products that require technical understanding.

The product structure can lead to problems, however, if a single large customer buys many different company products. For example, Allegiance Healthcare Corporation, the large health care products and services company, has several product divisions, each with a separate sales force. Several Allegiance salespeople might end up calling on the same hospital on the same day. This means that they travel over the same routes and wait to see the same customer's purchasing agents. These extra costs must be compared with the benefits of better product knowledge and attention to individual products.

Customer sales force structure

A sales force organization under which salespeople specialize in selling only to certain customers or industries.

Customer Sales Force Structure. More and more companies are now using a **customer sales force structure**, in which they organize the sales force along customer or industry lines. Separate sales forces may be set up for different industries, for serving current customers versus finding new ones, and for major accounts versus regular accounts.

Organizing the sales force around customers can help a company to become more customer focused and build closer relationships with important customers. For example, IBM recently shifted from a product-based structure to a customer-based one. Before the shift, droves of salespeople representing different IBM software, hardware, and services divisions might call on a single large client, creating confusion and frustration. Such large customers wanted a "single face," one point of contact for all of IBM's vast array of products and services. After the restructuring, a single IBM "client executive" works with each large customer and manages a team of IBMers—product reps, systems engineers, consultants, and others—who work with the customer. The client executive becomes an expert in the customer's industry. Greg Buseman, a client executive in the distribution industry, who spends most of his time working with a major consumer packaged-goods customer, describes his role this way: "I am the owner of the business relationship with the client. If the client has a problem, I'm the one who pulls together software or hardware specialists or consultants. At the customer I work most closely with, we usually have 15 to 20 projects going at once, and I have to manage them."[3] Such an intense focus on customers is widely credited for IBM's dramatic turnaround in recent years.

Complex Sales Force Structures. When a company sells a wide variety of products to many types of customers over a broad geographic area, it often combines several types of sales force structures. Salespeople can be specialized by customer and territory, by product and territory, by product and customer, or by territory, product, and customer. No single structure is best for all companies and all situations. Each company should select a sales force structure that best serves the needs of its customers and fits its overall marketing strategy.

Sales Force Size Once the company has set its structure, it is ready to consider *sales force size.* Sales forces may range in size from only a few salespeople to many tens of thousands. Some sales forces are huge—for example, Microsoft employs 22,500 salespeople, PepsiCo 36,000, IBM 10,000, and Hartford Financial Services 111,000.[4] Salespeople constitute one of the company's most productive—and most expensive—assets. Therefore, increasing their number will increase both sales and costs.

Many companies use some form of *workload approach* to set sales force size. Using this approach, a company first groups accounts into different classes according to size,

Marketing at Work | 13.1

Point, Click, and Sell: Welcome to the Web-Based Sales Force

There are few rules at Fisher Scientific International's sales training sessions. The chemical company's salespeople are allowed to show up for new workshops in their pajamas. And no one flinches if they stroll in at midnight for their first class, take a dozen breaks to call clients, or invite the family cat to sleep in their laps while they take an exam. Sound unorthodox? It would be if Fisher's salespeople were trained in a regular classroom. But for the past few years, the company has been using the Internet to teach the majority of its salespeople in the privacy of their homes, cars, hotel rooms, or wherever else they bring their laptops.

To get updates on Fisher's pricing or refresh themselves on one of the company's highly technical products, all salespeople have to do is log on to the Web site and select from the lengthy index. Any time of the day or night, they can get information on a new product, take an exam, or post messages for product experts—all without ever entering a corporate classroom. Welcome to the world of the Web-based sales force.

In the past few years, sales organizations around the world have begun saving money and time by using a host of new Web approaches to train reps, hold sales meetings, and even conduct live sales presentations. "Web-based technologies are becoming really hot in sales because they save salespeople's time," says technology consultant Tim Sloane. Web-based technologies help companies save time and travel costs while keeping reps up to speed on their company's new products and sales strategies. Fisher Scientific's reps can dial up the Web site at their leisure, and whereas newer reps might spend hours online going through each session in order, more seasoned sellers might just log on for a quick refresher on a specific product before a sales call. "It allows them to manage their time better,

because they're only getting training when they need it, in the doses they need it in," says John Pavlik, director of the company's training department. If salespeople are spending less time on training, Pavlik says, they're able to spend more time on what they do best: selling.

Training is only one of the ways sales organizations are using the Internet. Many companies are using the Web to make sales presentations and service accounts. For example, computer and communications equipment maker NEC Corporation has adopted Web-based selling as an essential marketing tool.

After launching a new line of servers on September 11, 2001, NEC had to rethink its sales approach. Following the 9/11 terrorist attacks, the company began looking for ways to cut down on sales force travel. According to Dick Csaplar, marketing manager for the new server line, NEC's old sales approach—traveling to customer sites to pitch NEC products—became unworkable literally

overnight. Instead, NEC adopted a new Web-based sales approach. While the initial goal was to keep people off airplanes, however, Web selling has now grown into an intrinsic part of NEC's sales efforts. Web selling reduces travel time and costs. Whereas the average daily cost of salesperson travel is $663, an hour-long Web conference costs just $60. More importantly, Web selling lets sales reps meet with more prospective customers than ever before, creating a more efficient and effective sales organization. Csaplar estimates that he's doing 10 customer Web conferences a week, during which he and his sales team show prospects product features and benefits. Customers love it because they get a clear understanding of NEC's technology without having to host the NEC team on-site. And Csaplar was pleased to find that Web-based selling is an effective way to interact with customers and to build customer relationships. "By the time we're done with the Webcast, the customer understands the technology, the

Internet selling support: Sales organizations around the world are now using a host of new Web approaches to train reps, hold sales meetings, and even conducts live sales presentations.

(continued)

pricing, and the competition, and we understand the customer's business and needs," he says. Without Webcasts, "we'd be lost on how to communicate with the customer without spending a lot of money," says Csaplar. "People are very accepting of this [technology]," he concludes. "I don't see us ever going back to the heavy travel thing."

Other companies are using Web conferencing to find new prospects. Oracle Corporation, the $8 billion software and information technology services company, conducts online, live product seminars for prospective clients. Prospects can scan the high-tech company's Web site to see which seminars they might want to attend, and then log in at the appropriate time. The seminars, which usually consist of a live lecture describing the product's applications followed by a question-and-answer session, average about 125 prospective clients apiece. Once a seminar is completed, prospects are directed to another part of Oracle's Web site, from which they can order products. "It costs our clients nothing but time," says Oracle's manager of Internet marketing programs, "and we're reaching a much wider audience than we would if we were doing in-person seminars."

The Internet can also be a handy way to hold sales strategy meetings. Consider Cisco Systems, which provides networking solutions for the Internet. Sales meetings used to take an enormous bite out of Cisco's travel budget. Now the company saves about $1 million per month by conducting many of those sessions on the Web using PlaceWare Web conferencing software. Whenever Cisco introduces a new product, it holds a Web meeting to update salespeople, in groups of 100 or more, on the product's marketing and sales strategy.

Usually led by the product manager or a vice president of sales, the meetings typically begin with a 10-minute slide presentation that spells out the planned strategy. Then, salespeople spend the next 50 minutes or so asking questions via teleconference. The meeting's leader can direct attendees' browsers to competitors' Web sites or ask them to vote on certain issues by using the software's instant polling feature. "Our salespeople are actually meeting more online than they ever were face-to-face," says Mike Mitchell, Cisco's distance learning manager, adding that some salespeople who used to meet with other reps and managers only a few times a quarter are meeting online nearly every day. "That's very empowering for the sales force, because they're able to make suggestions at every step of the way about where we're going with our sales and marketing strategies."

Thus, Web-based technologies can produce big organizational benefits for sales forces. They help conserve salespeople's valuable time, save travel dollars, and give salespeople a new vehicle for selling and servicing accounts. But the technologies also have some drawbacks. For starters, they're not cheap. Setting up a Web-based system can cost up to several hundred thousand dollars. And such systems can intimidate low-tech salespeople or clients. "You must have a culture that is comfortable using computers," says one marketing communications manager. "As simple as it is, if your salespeople or clients aren't comfortable using the Web, you're wasting your money." Also, Web tools are susceptible to server crashes and other network difficulties, not a happy event when you're in the midst of an important sales meeting or presentation.

For these reasons, some high-tech experts recommend that sales executives use Web technologies for training, sales meetings, and preliminary client sales presentations, but resort to old-fashioned, face-to-face meetings when the time draws near to close the deal. "When push comes to shove, if you've got an account worth closing, you're still going to get on that plane and see the client in person," says sales consultant Sloane. "Your client is going to want to look you in the eye before buying anything from you, and that's still one thing you just can't do online."

Sources: Portions adapted from Melinda Ligos, "Point, Click, and Sell," *Sales & Marketing Management,* May 1999, pp. 51–55; and Tom Kontzer, "Web Conferencing Embraced," *Information Week,* May 26, 2003, pp. 68–70. Also see Ginger Conlon, "Ride the Wave," *Sales & Marketing Management,* December 2000, pp. 67–74; Cindy Waxer, "Better than Being There," *Selling Power,* November–December 2002, pp. 28–30; Julia Chang, "No Instructor Required," *Sales & Marketing Management,* May 2003, p. 26; and Nicole Ridgeway, "A Safer Place to Meet," *Forbes,* April 28, 2003, p. 97.

In many cases, the move to team selling mirrors similar changes in customers' buying organizations. According to a recent study by *Purchasing* magazine, nearly 70 percent of companies polled are using or are extremely interested in using multifunctional buying teams. Says the director of sales education at Dow Chemical, to sell effectively to such buying teams, "our sellers . . . have to captain selling teams. There are no more lone wolves."[10]

Some companies, such as IBM, Xerox, and Procter & Gamble, have used teams for a long time. P&G sales reps are organized into "customer business development (CBD) teams." Each CBD team is assigned to a major P&G customer. Teams consist of a customer business development manager, several account executives (each responsible for a specific category of P&G products), and specialists in marketing strategy, operations, information systems, logistics, and finance. This organization places the focus on serving the complete needs of each important customer.

Other companies have only recently reorganized to adopt the team concept. For example, Cutler-Hammer, which supplies circuit breakers, motor starters, and other electrical equipment to heavy industrial manufacturers such as Ford, recently developed "pods" of salespeople that focus on a specific geographical region, industry, or market. Each pod member contributes unique expertise and knowledge about a product or service that salespeople can leverage when selling to increasingly sophisticated buying teams.[11]

Team selling does have some pitfalls. For example, selling teams can confuse or overwhelm customers who are used to working with only one salesperson. Salespeople who are used to having customers all to themselves may have trouble learning to work with and trust others on a team. Finally, difficulties in evaluating individual contributions to the team selling effort can create some sticky compensation issues.

■ This Procter & Gamble "customer business development team" serves a major southeastern grocery retailer. It consists of a customer business development manager and five account executives (shown here), along with specialists from other functional areas.

Recruiting and Selecting Salespeople

At the heart of any successful sales force operation is the recruitment and selection of good salespeople. The performance difference between an average salesperson and a top salesperson can be substantial. In a typical sales force, the top 30 percent of the salespeople might bring in 60 percent of the sales. Thus, careful salesperson selection can greatly increase overall sales force performance. Beyond the differences in sales performance, poor selection results in costly turnover. When a salesperson quits, the costs of finding and training a new salesperson—plus the costs of lost sales—can be very high. Also, a sales force with many new people is less productive.

What sets great salespeople apart from all the rest? In an effort to profile top sales performers, Gallup Management Consulting Group, a division of the well-known Gallup polling organization, has interviewed as many as half a million salespeople. Its research suggests that the best salespeople possess four key talents: intrinsic motivation, disciplined work style, the ability to close a sale, and perhaps most important, the ability to build relationships with customers.[12]

Super salespeople are motivated from within. "Different things drive different people—pride, happiness, money, you name it," says one expert. "But all great salespeople have one thing in common: an unrelenting drive to excel." Some salespeople are driven by money, a hunger for recognition, or the satisfaction of competing and winning. Others are driven by the desire to provide service and to build relationships. The best salespeople possess some of each of these motivations. "A competitor with a strong sense of service will probably bring in a lot of business while doing a great job of taking care of customers," observes the managing director of the Gallup Management Consulting Group. "Who could ask for anything more?"

Whatever their motivations, salespeople must also have a disciplined work style. If salespeople aren't organized and focused, and if they don't work hard, they can't meet the ever-increasing demands customers are making these days. Great salespeople are tenacious about laying out detailed, organized plans, then following through in a timely, disciplined way. Says one sales trainer, "Some people say it's all technique or luck. But luck happens to the best salespeople when they get up early, work late, stay up till two in the morning

■ Great salespeople: The best salespeople possess intrinsic motivation, disciplined work style, the ability to close a sale, and perhaps most important, the ability to build relationships with customers.

working on a proposal, or keep making calls when everyone is leaving at the end of the day."

Other skills mean little if a salesperson can't close the sale. So what makes for a great closer? For one thing, it takes unyielding persistence. "Great closers are like great athletes," says one sales trainer. "They're not afraid to fail, and they don't give up until they close." Great closers also have a high level of self-confidence and believe that they are doing the right thing.

Perhaps most important in today's relationship-marketing environment, top salespeople are customer problem solvers and relationship builders. They have an instinctive understanding of their customers' needs. Talk to sales executives and they'll describe top performers in these terms: Empathetic. Patient. Caring. Responsive. Good listeners. Honest. Top performers can put themselves on the buyer's side of the desk and see the world through their customers' eyes. They don't want just to be liked, they want to add value for their customers.

When recruiting, companies should analyze the sales job itself and the characteristics of its most successful salespeople to identify the traits needed by a successful salesperson in their industry. Does the job require a lot of planning and paperwork? Does it call for much travel? Will the salesperson face a lot of rejections? Will the salesperson be working with high-level buyers? The successful salesperson should be suited to these duties.

After management has decided on needed traits, it must *recruit* salespeople. The human resources department looks for applicants by getting names from current salespeople, using employment agencies, placing classified ads, searching the Web, and contacting college students. Another source is to attract top salespeople from other companies. Proven salespeople need less training and can be immediately productive.

Recruiting will attract many applicants from whom the company must select the best. The selection procedure can vary from a single informal interview to lengthy testing and interviewing. Many companies give formal tests to sales applicants. Tests typically measure sales aptitude, analytical and organizational skills, personality traits, and other characteristics. Test results count heavily in companies such as IBM, Prudential, Procter & Gamble, and Gillette. Gillette claims that tests have reduced turnover by 42 percent and that test scores have correlated well with the later performance of new salespeople. But test scores provide only one piece of information in a set that includes personal characteristics, references, past employment history, and interviewer reactions.[13]

Training Salespeople

New salespeople may spend anywhere from a few weeks or months to a year or more in training. The average initial training period is 4 months. Then, most companies provide continuing sales training via seminars, sales meetings, and the Web throughout the salesperson's career. In all, U.S. companies spend more than $7 billion annually on training salespeople. Although training can be expensive, it can also yield dramatic returns on the training investment. For example, Nabisco did an extensive analysis of the return on investment of its 2-day Professional Selling Program, which teaches sales reps how to plan for and make professional presentations to their retail customers. Although it cost about $1,000 to put each sales rep through the program, the training resulted in additional sales of more than $122,000 per rep and yielded almost $21,000 of additional profit per rep.[14]

Training programs have several goals. Salespeople need to know and identify with the company, so most training programs begin by describing the company's history and objectives, its organization, its financial structure and facilities, and its chief products and markets. Salespeople also need to know the company's products, so sales trainees are shown how products are produced and how they work. They also need to know customers' and competitors' characteristics. So the training program teaches them about competitors' strategies and about different types of customers and their needs, buying motives, and buying habits. Because salespeople must know how to make effective presentations, they are trained in the principles of selling. Finally, salespeople need to understand field procedures and responsibilities. They learn how to divide time between active and potential accounts and how to use an expense account, prepare reports, and route communications effectively.

Today, many companies are adding Web-based training to their sales training programs. In fact, the industry for online training is expected to more than triple to $23.7 billion by 2006.[15] Such training may range from simple text-based product information to Internet-based sales exercises that build sales skills to sophisticated simulations that re-create the dynamics of real-life sales calls. Networking equipment and software maker Cisco Systems has learned that using the Internet to train salespeople offers many advantages:

> Keeping a large sales force up to speed on hundreds of complex, fast-changing products can be a daunting task. Under the old training process, newly hired Cisco salespeople traveled to a central location for several 5-day training sessions each year. "We used to fly people in and put them through a week of death-by-PowerPoint," says a Cisco training executive. This approach involved huge program-development and travel costs. Perhaps worse, it cost salespeople precious lost-opportunity time spent away from their customers. To address these issues, Cisco launched its Field E-Learning Connection—an internal learning portal through which Cisco's salespeople around the world can plan, track, develop, and measure their skills and knowledge. The site links salespeople to tens of thousands of Web-based learning aids. The new system offers a wide variety of convenient delivery formats. Learning involves the blending of

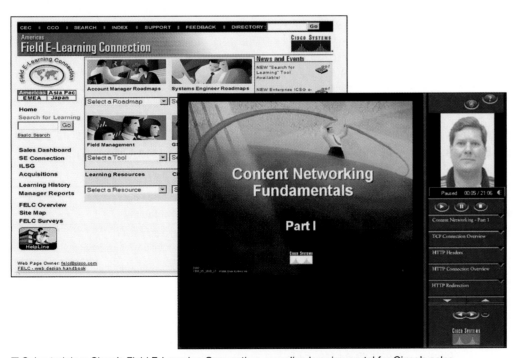

■ Sales training: Cisco's Field E-Learning Connection, an online learning portal for Cisco's sales force, blends audio and video, which can be turned into an MP3 file, viewed on-screen, downloaded to the computer, or even printed out in magazine form.

audio and video, live broadcasts of classes, and straight content. Content can be turned into an MP3 file, viewed on-screen, downloaded to the computer, even printed out in magazine form. Under the new system, Cisco can conduct a single training session that reaches up to 3,000 people at once, worldwide, by broadcasting it over the company's global intranet. Live events can then be archived as video-on-demand modules for viewers who missed the live broadcast. The system also provides electronic access to Cisco experts or "e-mentors," who can respond via e-mail or phone or meet learners in a virtual lab, connect to their screens, and walk them through exercises. The Field E-learning Connection has improved training by giving Cisco salespeople anywhere, anytime access to a vast system of training resources. At the same time, it has cut field training costs by 40 percent to 60 percent while boosting salesperson "face time" with customers by 40 percent.[16]

Compensating Salespeople

To attract salespeople, a company must have an appealing compensation plan. Compensation is made up of several elements—a fixed amount, a variable amount, expenses, and fringe benefits. The fixed amount, usually a salary, gives the salesperson some stable income. The variable amount, which might be commissions or bonuses based on sales performance, rewards the salesperson for greater effort. Expense allowances, which repay salespeople for job-related expenses, let salespeople undertake needed and desirable selling efforts. Fringe benefits, such as paid vacations, sickness or accident benefits, pensions, and life insurance, provide job security and satisfaction.

Management must decide what *mix* of these compensation elements makes the most sense for each sales job. Different combinations of fixed and variable compensation give rise to four basic types of compensation plans—straight salary, straight commission, salary plus bonus, and salary plus commission. A study of sales force compensation plans showed that 70 percent of all companies surveyed use a combination of base salary and incentives. The average plan consisted of about 60 percent salary and 40 percent incentive pay.[17]

The sales force compensation plan can both motivate salespeople and direct their activities. Compensation should direct the sales force toward activities that are consistent with overall marketing objectives. Table 13.1 illustrates how a company's compensation plan should reflect its overall marketing strategy. For example, if the strategy is to grow rapidly and gain market share, the compensation plan might include a larger com-

TABLE 13.1 The Relationship Between Overall Marketing Strategy and Sales Force Compensation

	Strategic Goal		
	To Gain Market Share Rapidly	To Solidify Market Leadership	To Maximize Profitability
Ideal salesperson	An independent self-starter	A competitive problem solver	A team player A relationship manager
Sales focus	Deal making Sustained high effort	Consultative selling	Account penetration
Compensation role	To capture accounts To reward high performance	To reward new and existing account sales	To manage the product mix To encourage team selling To reward account management

Source: Adapted from Sam T. Johnson, "Sales Compensation: In Search of a Better Solution," *Compensation & Benefits Review,* November–December 1993, pp. 53–60. Copyright © 1998 American Management Association, NY, www.amanet.org. All rights reserved, used with permission.

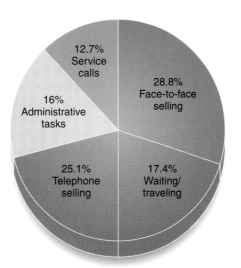

FIGURE 13.2

How Salespeople Spend Their Time

Source: Dartnell Corporation; *30th Sales Force Compensation Survey.* © 1999 Dartnell Corporation.

mission component coupled with a new-account bonus to encourage high sales performance and new-account development. In contrast, if the goal is to maximize current account profitability, the compensation plan might contain a larger base-salary component with additional incentives for current account sales or customer satisfaction. In fact, more and more companies are moving away from high commission plans that may drive salespeople to make short-term grabs for business. Notes one sales force expert, "The last thing you want is to have someone ruin a customer relationship because they're pushing too hard to close a deal." Instead, companies are designing compensation plans that reward salespeople for building customer relationships and growing the long-run value of each customer.[18]

Supervising Salespeople

New salespeople need more than a territory, compensation, and training—they need *supervision.* Through supervision, the company *directs* and *motivates* the sales force to do a better job.

Companies vary in how closely they supervise their salespeople. Many help their salespeople in identifying customer targets and setting call norms. Some may also specify how much time the sales forces should spend prospecting for new accounts and set other time management priorities. One tool is the *annual call plan* that shows which customers and prospects to call on in which months and which activities to carry out. Activities include taking part in trade shows, attending sales meetings, and carrying out marketing research. Another tool is *time-and-duty analysis.* In addition to time spent selling, the salesperson spends time traveling, waiting, eating, taking breaks, and doing administrative chores.

Figure 13.2 shows how salespeople spend their time. On average, actual face-to-face selling time accounts for less than 30 percent of total working time! If selling time could be raised from 30 percent to 40 percent, this would be a 33 percent increase in the time spent selling. Companies always are looking for ways to save time—using phones instead of traveling, simplifying record-keeping forms, finding better call and routing plans, and supplying more and better customer information. Consider the changes GE made to support its sales force[19]:

> When Jeff Immelt became General Electric's new chairman, one of his first actions was to survey the company's sales force. He was dismayed to find that members of the sales team were spending far more time on deskbound administrative chores than in face-to-face meetings with customers and

prospects. "He said we needed to turn that around," recalls Venki Rao, an IT leader in global sales and marketing at GE Power Systems, a division focused on energy systems and products. "[We need] to spend four days a week in front of the customer and one day for all the admin stuff." GE Power's salespeople spent much of their time at their desks because they had to go to many sources—some manual and some electronic, some internal and some external—for the information needed to sell multimillion-dollar turbines, turbine parts, and services to energy companies worldwide. To fix the problem, GE created a new sales portal, a kind of "one-stop shop" for just about everything they need. The sales portal connects the vast array of existing GE databases, providing everything from sales tracking and customer data to parts pricing and information on planned outages. GE also added external data, such as news feeds. "Before, you were randomly searching for things," says Bill Snook, a GE sales manager, "I'd go to a site, and if it didn't have the answer, I'd go to another site." Now, he says, "I have the sales portal as my home page, and I use it as the gateway to all the applications that I have." The sales portal has freed Snook and 2,500 other users around the globe from once time-consuming administrative tasks, greatly increasing their face time with customers.

Many firms have adopted *sales force automation systems,* computerized sales force operations for more efficient order-entry transactions, improved customer service, and better salesperson decision-making support. Salespeople use laptops, handheld computing devices, and Web technologies, coupled with customer-contact software and customer relationship management (CRM) software, to profile customers and prospects, analyze and forecast sales, manage account relationships, schedule sales calls, make presentations, enter orders, check inventories and order status, prepare sales and expense reports, process correspondence, and carry out many other activities. Sales force automation not only lowers sales force costs and improves productivity, it also improves the quality of sales management decisions. Here is an example of successful sales force automation[20]:

Owens-Corning has put its sales force online with FSA—its Field Sales Advantage system. FSA gives Owens-Corning salespeople a constant supply of information about their company and the people they're dealing with. Using laptop computers, each salesperson can access three types of programs. First, FSA gives them a set of *generic tools,* everything from word processing to fax and e-mail transmission to creating presentations online. Second, it provides *product information*—tech bulletins, customer specifications, pricing information, and other data that can help close a sale. Finally, it offers up a wealth of *customer information*—buying history, types of products ordered, and preferred payment terms. Before FSA, reps stored such information in loose-leaf books, calendars, and account cards. Now, FSA makes working directly with customers easier than ever. Salespeople can prime themselves on backgrounds of clients; call up prewritten sales letters; transmit orders and resolve customer-service issues on the spot during customer calls; and have samples, pamphlets, brochures, and other materials sent to clients with a few keystrokes. With FSA, "salespeople automatically become more

■ Owens-Corning's Field Sales Advantage system gives salespeople a constant supply of information about their company and the people with whom they're dealing.

empowered," says Charley Causey, regional general manager. "They become the real managers of their own business and their own territories."

Perhaps the fastest-growing sales force technology tool is the Internet. In a survey by Dartnell Corporation of 1,000 salespeople, 61 percent reported using the Internet regularly in their daily selling activities. The most common uses include gathering competitive information, monitoring customer Web sites, and researching industries and specific customers. As more and more companies provide their salespeople with Web access, experts expect continued growth in the use of the Internet by sales forces.[21]

Beyond directing salespeople, sales managers must also motivate them. Some salespeople will do their best without any special urging from management. To them, selling may be the most fascinating job in the world. But selling can also be frustrating. Salespeople often work alone and they must sometimes travel away from home. They may face aggressive competing salespeople and difficult customers. Therefore, salespeople often need special encouragement to do their best.

Management can boost sales force morale and performance through its organizational climate, sales quotas, and positive incentives. *Organizational climate* describes the feeling that salespeople have about their opportunities, value, and rewards for a good performance. Some companies treat salespeople as if they are not very important, and performance suffers accordingly. Other companies treat their salespeople as valued contributors and allow virtually unlimited opportunity for income and promotion. Not surprisingly, these companies enjoy higher sales force performance and less turnover.

Many companies motivate their salespeople by setting **sales quotas**—standards stating the amount they should sell and how sales should be divided among the company's products. Compensation is often related to how well salespeople meet their quotas. Companies also use various *positive incentives* to increase sales force effort. *Sales meetings* provide social occasions, breaks from routine, chances to meet and talk with "company brass," and opportunities to air feelings and to identify with a larger group. Companies also sponsor *sales contests* to spur the sales force to make a selling effort above what would normally be expected. Other incentives include honors, merchandise and cash awards, trips, and profit-sharing plans. In all, American companies spend some $27 billion a year on incentives to motivate and reward sales force performance.[22]

■ Sales force incentives: Many companies offer cash, trips, or merchandise as incentives. Marriott suggests that companies reward outstanding sales performers by letting them "spread their wings and reenergize" at fabulous Marriott resorts worldwide. "From comfortable lodging and fine dining to memorable golf outings and luxurious spa treatments, our incentives run deep."

Sales quotas
A standard that states the amount a salesperson should sell and how sales should be divided among the company's products.

Evaluating Salespeople

We have thus far described how management communicates what salespeople should be doing and how it motivates them to do it. This process requires good feedback. And good feedback means getting regular information about salespeople to evaluate their performance.

Management gets information about its salespeople in several ways. The most important source is *sales reports,* including weekly or monthly work plans and longer-term territory marketing plans. Salespeople also write up their completed activities on *call reports* and turn in *expense reports* for which they are partly or wholly repaid. Additional information comes from personal observation, customer surveys, and talks with other salespeople.

Using various sales force reports and other information, sales management evaluates members of the sales force. It evaluates salespeople on their ability to "plan their work and work their plan." Formal evaluation forces management to develop and communicate clear standards for judging performance. It also provides salespeople with constructive feedback and motivates them to perform well.

Linking the Concepts

Take a break and reexamine your thoughts about salespeople and sales management.

- As you did at the start of the chapter, close your eyes and envision a typical salesperson. Have your perceptions of salespeople changed after what you've just read? How? Be specific.
- Apply each of the steps in sales force management shown in Figure 13.1 to the chapter-opening Lear Corporation example.
- Find and talk with someone employed in professional sales. Ask about and report on how this salesperson's company designs its sales force and recruits, selects, trains, compensates, supervises, and evaluates its salespeople. Would you like to work as a salesperson for this company?

■■ The Personal Selling Process

Selling process

The steps that the salesperson follows when selling, which include prospecting and qualifying, preapproach, approach, presentation and demonstration, handling objections, closing, and follow-up.

We now turn from designing and managing a sales force to the actual personal selling process. The **selling process** consists of several steps that the salesperson must master. These steps focus on the goal of getting new customers and obtaining orders from them. However, most salespeople spend much of their time maintaining existing accounts and building long-term customer *relationships*. We discuss the relationship aspect of the personal selling process in a later section.

Steps in the Selling Process

As shown in Figure 13.3, the selling process consists of seven steps: prospecting and qualifying, preapproach, approach, presentation and demonstration, handling objections, closing, and follow-up.

Prospecting

The step in the selling process in which the salesperson identifies qualified potential customers.

Prospecting and Qualifying The first step in the selling process is **prospecting**—identifying qualified potential customers. Approaching the right potential customers is crucial to selling success. As one expert puts it: "If the sales force starts chasing anyone who is breathing and seems to have a budget, you risk accumulating a roster of expensive-to-serve, hard-to-satisfy customers who never respond to whatever value proposition you have." He continues, "The solution to this isn't rocket science. [You must] train salespeople to actively scout the right prospects. If necessary, create an incentive program to reward proper scouting."[23]

The salesperson must often approach many prospects to get just a few sales. Although the company supplies some leads, salespeople need skill in finding their own. They can ask current customers for referrals. They can cultivate referral sources, such as suppliers, dealers, noncompeting salespeople, and bankers. They can search for prospects in directo-

FIGURE 13.3
Major Steps in Effective Selling

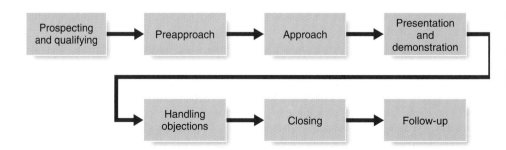

ries or on the Web and track down leads using the telephone and direct mail. Or they can drop in unannounced on various offices (a practice known as "cold calling").

Salespeople also need to know how to *qualify* leads—that is, how to identify the good ones and screen out the poor ones. Prospects can be qualified by looking at their financial ability, volume of business, special needs, location, and possibilities for growth.

Preapproach Before calling on a prospect, the salesperson should learn as much as possible about the organization (what it needs, who is involved in the buying) and its buyers (their characteristics and buying styles). This step is known as the **preapproach**. The salesperson can consult standard industry and online sources, acquaintances, and others to learn about the company. The salesperson should set *call objectives*, which may be to qualify the prospect, to gather information, or to make an immediate sale. Another task is to decide on the best approach, which might be a personal visit, a phone call, or a letter. The best timing should be considered carefully because many prospects are busiest at certain times. Finally, the salesperson should give thought to an overall sales strategy for the account.

Preapproach

The step in the selling process in which the salesperson learns as much as possible about a prospective customer before making a sales call.

Approach During the **approach** step, the salesperson should know how to meet and greet the buyer and get the relationship off to a good start. This step involves the salesperson's appearance, opening lines, and the follow-up remarks. The opening lines should be positive to build goodwill from the beginning of the relationship. This opening might be followed by some key questions to learn more about the customer's needs or by showing a display or sample to attract the buyer's attention and curiosity. As in all stages of the selling process, listening to the customer is crucial.

Approach

The step in the selling process in which the salesperson meets the customer for the first time.

Presentation and Demonstration During the **presentation** step of the selling process, the salesperson tells the product "story" to the buyer, presenting customer benefits and showing how the product solves the customer's problems. The problem-solver salesperson fits better with today's marketing concept than does a hard-sell salesperson or the glad-handing extrovert. Buyers today want solutions, not smiles; results, not razzle-dazzle. They want salespeople who listen to their concerns, understand their needs, and respond with the right products and services.

Presentation

The step in the selling process in which the salesperson tells the "product story" to the buyer, highlighting customer benefits.

This *need-satisfaction approach* calls for good listening and problem-solving skills. "I think of myself more as a . . . well, psychologist," notes one experienced salesperson. "I listen to customers. I listen to their wishes and needs and problems, and I try to figure out a solution. If you're not a good listener, you're not going to get the order." Another salesperson suggests, "It's no longer enough to have a good relationship with a client. You have to understand their problems. You have to feel their pain." One sales manager suggests that salespeople need to put themselves in their customers' shoes: "Make yourself a customer and see first-hand how it feels," he says.[24]

The qualities that buyers *dislike most* in salespeople include being pushy, late, deceitful, and unprepared or disorganized. The qualities they *value most* include empathy, good listening, honesty, dependability, thoroughness, and follow-through. Great salespeople know how to sell, but more importantly they know how to listen and to build strong customer relationships.

Today, advanced presentation technologies allow for full multimedia presentations to only one or a few people. Audio and video cassettes, CDs, online presentation technologies, and handheld and laptop computers with presentation software, have replaced the flip chart. Here's an example[25]:

> Until 6 months ago, Credant Technologies, a firm that sells security software programs for handhelds, used standard presentation equipment—laptops and LCD projectors—to showcase its products to potential clients. That's no longer the case. Each member of the company's sales team is now equipped with Presenter-to-Go, a credit card–sized device that slips into handheld PDAs or pocket PCs to make them compatible with projectors. The $200 device reads PowerPoint, Microsoft Word,

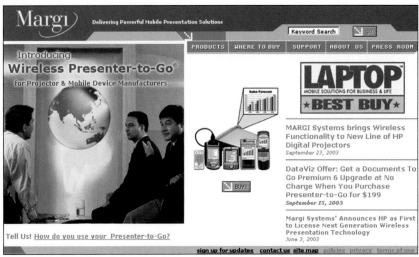

■ New presentation technologies: The old-fashioned flip chart has been replace by CDs, online presentation technologies, and hand-held and laptop computers. Each member of Credant Technologies' sales team is equipped with Presenter-to-Go, a credit card-sized device that slips into hand-held PDAs or pocket PCs to make them compatible with projectors.

and Excel files, as well as Web pages, allowing salespeople to create presentations on computers, then transfer them to a PDA. It also lets reps add notes to presentations instantaneously by transmitting handwriting on their pocket PC to the screen. And it includes a wireless remote control, so sales reps can move freely throughout the presentation room, unattached to their laptop or projector-advancing button. When Credant Regional Account Executive Tom Gore met recently with an important prospect, he wowed buying executives with a feature that enabled him to type some of their comments into his PDA. Within seconds, their comments appeared on screen. "It makes each presentation more personal and interactive," Gore says.

Handling objections

The step in the selling process in which the salesperson seeks out, clarifies, and overcomes customer objections to buying.

Handling Objections Customers almost always have objections during the presentation or when asked to place an order. The problem can be either logical or psychological, and objections are often unspoken. In **handling objections**, the salesperson should use a positive approach, seek out hidden objections, ask the buyer to clarify any objections, take objections as opportunities to provide more information, and turn the objections into reasons for buying. Every salesperson needs training in the skills of handling objections.

Closing

The step in the selling process in which the salesperson asks the customer for an order.

Closing After handling the prospect's objections, the salesperson now tries to close the sale. Some salespeople do not get around to **closing** or do not handle it well. They may lack confidence, feel guilty about asking for the order, or fail to recognize the right moment to close the sale. Salespeople should know how to recognize closing signals from the buyer, including physical actions, comments, and questions. For example, the customer might sit forward and nod approvingly or ask about prices and credit terms. Salespeople can use one of several closing techniques. They can ask for the order, review points of agreement, offer to help write up the order, ask whether the buyer wants this model or that one, or note that the buyer will lose out if the order is not placed now. The salesperson may offer the buyer special reasons to close, such as a lower price or an extra quantity at no charge.

Follow-up

The last step in the selling process in which the salesperson follows up after the sale to ensure customer satisfaction and repeat business.

Follow-up The last step in the selling process—**follow-up**—is necessary if the salesperson wants to ensure customer satisfaction and repeat business. Right after closing, the salesperson should complete any details on delivery time, purchase terms, and other matters. The salesperson then should schedule a follow-up call when the initial order is received, to make sure there is proper installation, instruction, and servicing. This visit would reveal any problems, assure the buyer of the salesperson's interest, and reduce any buyer concerns that might have arisen since the sale.

Personal Selling and Customer Relationship Management

The principles of personal selling as just described are *transaction oriented*—their aim is to help salespeople close a specific sale with a customer. But in many cases, the company is not seeking simply a sale: It has targeted a major customer that it would like to win and keep. The company would like to show that it has the capabilities to serve the customer over the long haul in a mutually profitable *relationship*. The sales force usually plays an important role in building and managing profitable customer relationships. "My company is selling something intangible," says one salesperson. "What we are really selling is 'Hey, when the time comes, we'll be there.' It all comes down to trust."[26]

Today's large customers favor suppliers who can sell and deliver a coordinated set of products and services to many locations and who can work closely with customer teams to improve products and processes. For these customers, the first sale is only the beginning of the relationship. Unfortunately, some companies ignore these new realities. They sell their products through separate sales forces, each working independently to close sales. Their technical people may not be willing to lend time to educate a customer. Their engineering, design, and manufacturing people may have the attitude that "it's our job to make good products and the salesperson's to sell them to customers." Other companies, however, recognize that winning and keeping accounts requires more than making good products and directing the sales force to close lots of sales. It requires a carefully coordinated whole-company effort to create value-laden, satisfying relationships with important customers.

■ Direct Marketing

Many of the marketing and promotion tools that we've examined in previous chapters were developed in the context of *mass marketing:* targeting broad markets with standardized messages and offers distributed through intermediaries. Today, however, with the trend toward more narrowly targeted or one-to-one marketing, many companies are adopting *direct marketing,* either as a primary marketing approach or as a supplement to other approaches. Increasingly, companies are using direct marketing to reach carefully targeted customers more efficiently and to build stronger, more personal, one-to-one relationships with them. In this section, we explore the exploding world of direct marketing.

Direct marketing consists of direct connections with carefully targeted individual consumers to both obtain an immediate response and cultivate lasting customer relationships. Direct marketers communicate directly with customers, often on a one-to-one, interactive basis. Using detailed databases, they tailor their marketing offers and communications to the needs of narrowly defined segments or even individual buyers. Beyond brand and image building, they usually seek a direct, immediate, and measurable consumer response. For example, Dell Computer interacts directly with customers, by telephone or through its Web site, to design built-to-order systems that meet customers' individual needs. Buyers order directly from Dell, and Dell quickly and efficiently delivers the new computers to their homes or offices.

Direct marketing
Direct communications with carefully targeted individual consumers to obtain an immediate response.

The New Direct-Marketing Model

Early direct marketers—catalog companies, direct mailers, and telemarketers—gathered customer names and sold goods mainly by mail and telephone. Today, however, fired by rapid advances in database technologies and new marketing media—especially the Internet—direct marketing has undergone a dramatic transformation.

In previous chapters, we've discussed direct marketing as direct distribution—as marketing channels that contain no intermediaries. We also include direct marketing as one element of the marketing communications mix—as an approach for communicating directly with consumers. In actuality, direct marketing is both these things.

Most companies still use direct marketing as a supplementary channel or medium for marketing their goods. Thus, Lexus markets mostly through mass-media advertising and its high-quality dealer network but also supplements these channels with direct marketing. Its direct marketing includes promotional CDs and other materials mailed directly to prospective buyers and a Web page (www.lexus.com) that provides consumers with information about various models, competitive comparisons, financing, and dealer locations. Similarly, office supply retailer Staples conducts most of its business through brick-and-mortar stores but also markets directly through its Web site. And most department stores sell the majority of their merchandise off their store shelves but also mail out catalogs.

However, for many companies today, direct marketing is more than just a supplementary channel or medium. For these companies, direct marketing—especially in its newest transformation, Internet marketing and e-commerce—constitutes a new and complete model for doing business. More than just another marketing channel or advertising medium, this new *direct model* is rapidly changing the way companies think about building relationships with customers.

Whereas most companies use direct marketing and the Internet as supplemental approaches, firms employing the direct model use it as the *only* approach. Some of these companies, such as Dell Computer, Amazon.com, and eBay, began as only direct marketers. Other companies—such as Cisco Systems, Charles Schwab, IBM, and many others—are rapidly transforming themselves into direct-marketing superstars. The company that perhaps best exemplifies this new direct-marketing model is Dell Computer (see Marketing at Work 13.2). Dell has built its entire approach to the marketplace around direct marketing. This direct model has proved highly successful, not just for Dell, but for the fast-growing number of other companies that employ it. Many strategists have hailed direct marketing as the new marketing model of the next millennium.

Benefits and Growth of Direct Marketing

Whether employed as a complete business model or as a supplement to a broader integrated marketing mix, direct marketing brings many benefits to both buyers and sellers. As a result, direct marketing is growing very rapidly.

For buyers, direct marketing is convenient, easy to use, and private. From the comfort of their homes or offices, they can browse mail catalogs or company Web sites at any time of the day or night. Direct marketing gives buyers ready access to a wealth of products and information, at home and around the globe. Finally, direct marketing is immediate and interactive—buyers can interact with sellers by phone or on the seller's Web site to create exactly the configuration of information, products, or services they desire, then order them on the spot.

For sellers, direct marketing is a powerful tool for building customer relationships. Using database marketing, today's marketers can target small groups or individual consumers, tailor offers to individual needs, and promote these offers through personalized communications. Direct marketing can also be timed to reach prospects at just the right moment. Because of its one-to-one, interactive nature, the Internet is an especially potent direct-marketing tool. Direct marketing also gives sellers access to buyers that they could not reach through other channels. For example, the Internet provides access to *global* markets that might otherwise be out of reach.

Finally, direct marketing can offer sellers a low-cost, efficient alternative for reaching their markets. For example, direct marketing has grown rapidly in B2B marketing, partly in response to the ever-increasing costs of marketing through the sales force. When personal sales calls cost $170 per contact, they should be made only when necessary and to high-potential customers and prospects. Lower cost-per-contact media—such as telemarketing, direct mail, and company Web sites—often prove more cost effective in reaching and selling to more prospects and customers.

As a result of these advantages to both buyers and sellers, direct marketing has become the fastest-growing form of marketing. Sales through traditional direct-marketing channels (telephone marketing, direct mail, catalogs, direct-response television, and others) have been growing rapidly. Last year direct sales to consumers and businesses in the United States reached more than $2 trillion, about 9 percent of the economy. Moreover, whereas total U.S. sales over the next 5 years will grow at an estimated 5 percent annually, direct-marketing sales will grow at an estimated 8 percent annually. According to the Direct Marketing Association, total U.S. spending on direct marketing exceeded $206 billion last year, or more than 55 percent of total U.S. advertising expenditures.[27]

Marketing at Work | *13.2*

Dell: Be Direct!

When 19-year-old Michael Dell began selling personal computers out of his college dorm room in 1984, competitors and industry insiders scoffed at the concept of mail-order computer marketing. PC buyers, they contended, needed the kind of advice and handholding that only full-service channels could provide. Yet young Michael Dell has proven the skeptics wrong—way wrong. In less than two decades, he has turned his dorm-room mail-order business into a burgeoning, $35 billion computer empire.

Dell is now the world's largest direct marketer of computer systems and the number-one PC maker worldwide. In the United States, Dell is number one in desktop PC sales, number one in laptops, and number-one in servers. Over the past 10 years, despite the recent tech slump, Dell has experienced a more than 12-fold increase in sales and a 14-fold increase in profits. During that period, Dell has delivered a dazzling 59 percent average annual return to shareholders. Dell's stock was the number-one performer of the 1990s, yielding an incredible 97 percent average annual return. Last year, while number-2 Hewlett Packard's PC sales fell 6 percent, Dell's grew 20 percent.

What's the secret to Dell's stunning success? Anyone at Dell can tell you without hesitation: It's the company's radically different business model—the *direct model*. "We have a tremendously clear business model," says Michael Dell, the 37-year-old founder. "There's no confusion about what the value proposition is, what the company offers, and why it's great for customers. That's a very simple thing, but it has tremendous power and appeal." An industry analyst agrees: "There's no better way to make, sell, and deliver PCs than the way Dell does it, and nobody executes that model better than Dell."

Dell's direct-marketing approach delivers greater customer value through an unbeatable combination of product customization, low prices, fast delivery, and award-winning customer service. A customer can talk by phone with a Dell representative or log onto www.dell.com on Monday morning; order a fully customized, state-of-the-art PC to suit his or her special needs; and have the machine delivered to his or her doorstep or desktop by Wednesday—all at a price that's 10 to 15 percent below competitors' prices for a comparably performing PC. Dell backs its products with high-quality service and support. As a result, Dell consistently ranks among the industry leaders in product reliability and service, and its customers are routinely among the industry's most satisfied.

Dell customers get exactly the machines they need. Michael Dell's initial idea was to serve individual buyers by letting them customize machines with the special features they wanted at low prices. However, this one-to-one approach also appeals strongly to corporate buyers, because Dell can so easily preconfigure each computer to precise requirements. Dell routinely preloads machines with a company's own software and even undertakes tedious tasks such as pasting inventory tags onto each machine so that computers can be delivered directly to a given employee's desk. As a result, more than 70 percent of Dell's sales now come from large corporate, government, and educational buyers.

Direct selling results in more efficient selling and lower costs, which translate into lower prices for customers. "Nobody, but nobody, makes [and markets] computer hardware more efficiently than Dell," says another analyst. "No unnecessary costs: This is an all-but-sacred mandate of the famous Dell direct business model." Because Dell builds machines to order, it carries barely any inventory—less than 5 days' worth

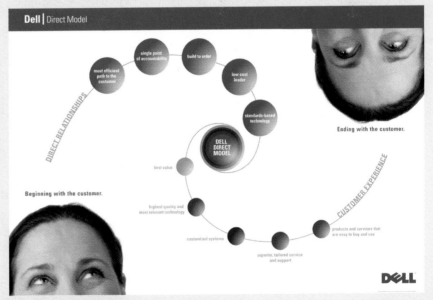

The Dell Direct Model: Dell's direct-marketing approach delivers greater customer value through an unbeatable combination of product customization, low prices, fast delivery, and award-winning customer service.

(continued)

by some accounts. Dealing one-to-one with customers helps the company react immediately to shifts in demand, so Dell doesn't get stuck with PCs no one wants. Finally, by selling directly, Dell has no dealers to pay. As a result, on average, Dell's costs are 12 percent lower than those of its leading PC competitor.

Dell knows that time is money, and the company is obsessed with "speed." For example, Dell has long been a model of just-in-time manufacturing and efficient supply chain management. Dell has also mastered the intricacies of today's lightning-fast electronic commerce. According to one account, Dell squeezes "time out of every step in the process—from the moment an order is taken to collecting the cash. [By selling direct, manufacturing to order, and] tapping credit cards and electronic payment, Dell converts the average sale to cash in less than 24 hours." By contrast, competitors selling through dealers might take 35 days or longer.

Such blazing speed results in more satisfied customers and still lower costs. For example, customers are often delighted to find their new computers arriving within as few as 36 hours of placing an order. And because Dell doesn't order parts until an order is booked, it can take advantage of ever-falling component costs. On average, its parts are 60 days newer than those in competing machines, and, hence, 60 days farther down the price curve. This gives Dell a 6 percent profit advantage from parts costs alone. It also gives Dell what one analysts calls a "negative cash

conversion cycle." Says the analyst, "Because it keeps only 5 days of inventories, manages receivables to 30 days, and pushes payables out to 59 days, the Dell model will generate cash even if the company were to report no profit whatsoever."

The Internet is a perfect extension of Dell's direct-marketing model. Customers who are already comfortable buying direct from Dell now have an even more powerful way to do so. Now, by simply clicking the "Buy a Dell" icon at Dell's Web site (www.dell.com), customers can design and price customized computer systems electronically. Then, with a click on the "purchase" button, they can submit an order, choosing from online payment options that include a credit card, company purchase order, or corporate lease. Dell dashes out a digital confirmation to customers within 5 minutes of receiving the order. After receiving confirmation, customers can check the status of the order online at any time. "The Internet," says Michael Dell, "is the ultimate direct model. . . . [Customers] like the immediacy, convenience, savings, and personal touches that the [Internet] experience provides. Not only are some sales done online, but people who call on the phone after having visited Dell.com are twice as likely to buy."

The direct-marketing pioneer now sells computers on some 80 country-specific Web sites, accounting for more than 50 percent of revenues. Buyers range from individuals purchasing home computers to large business users buying high-end $30,000 servers. "The

Internet is like a booster rocket on our sales and growth," proclaims Dell. "Our vision is to have *all* customers conduct *all* transactions on the Internet, globally."

As you might imagine, competitors are no longer scoffing at Michael Dell's vision of the future. In fact, competing and noncompeting companies alike are studying the Dell model closely. "Somehow Dell has been able to take flexibility and speed and build it into their DNA. It's almost like drinking water," says the CEO of another Fortune 500 company, who visited recently to absorb some of the Dell magic to apply to his own company. "I'm trying to drink as much water here as I can."

It's hard to argue with success, and Michael Dell has been very successful. By following his hunches, at the tender age of 37 he has built one of the world's hottest companies. In the process, he's become the world's richest man under 40, amassing a personal fortune of almost $17 billion.

Sources: Quotes, performance statistics, and other information from Kathryn Jones, "The Dell Way," *Business 2.0*, February 2003, pp. 60–66; Gary McWilliams, "Whirlwind on the Web," *Business Week*, April 7, 1997, pp. 132–136; "The InternetWeek Interview—Michael Dell," *InternetWeek*, April 13, 1999, p. 8; "America's 40 Richest Under 40," *Fortune*, September 16, 2002, p. 169; Andy Serwer, "Dell Does Domination," *Fortune*, January 21, 2002, pp. 71–75; Daniel Fisher, "The Best Little Factory in Texas," *Forbes*, June 10, 2002, p. 110; Mark Boslet, "PC Market Posts Fresh Growth as Dell Regains No. 1 Ranking," *Wall Street Journal*, April 18, 2003, p. B3; "Dell Computer Corporation," *Hoover's Company Profiles*, Austin, July 1, 2003, p. 13193; and www.dell.com/us/en/gen/corporate/access_company_direct_model.htm, September 2003.

Customer Databases and Direct Marketing

Customer database

An organized collection of comprehensive data about individual customers or prospects, including geographic, demographic, psychographic, and behavioral data.

Effective direct marketing begins with a good customer database. A **customer database** is an organized collection of comprehensive data about individual customers or prospects, including geographic, demographic, psychographic, and behavioral data. The database can be used to locate good potential customers, tailor products and services to the special needs of targeted consumers, and maintain long-term customer relationships. "If there's been any change in the past decade it's the knowledge we now can have about our customers," says one expert. "Strategically, the most essential tool is our customer database. A company is no better than what it knows."[28]

Many companies confuse a customer mailing list with a customer database. A customer mailing list is simply a set of names, addresses, and telephone numbers. A customer database contains much more information. In B2B marketing, the salesperson's customer profile might contain the products and services the customer has bought; past volumes and prices; key contacts (and their ages, birthdays, hobbies, and favorite foods); competitive suppliers; status of current contracts; estimated customer spending for the next few years; and assessments of competitive strengths and weaknesses in selling and servicing the account.

In consumer marketing, the customer database might contain a customer's demographics (age, income, family members, birthdays), psychographics (activities, interests, and opinions), buying behavior (past purchases, buying preferences), and other relevant information. Some of these databases are huge. For example, Ritz-Carlton's database holds more than 500,000 individual customer preferences. Pizza Hut's database lets it track the purchases of more than 50 million customers. Internet portal Yahoo! records every click made by every visitor, adding some 400 billion bytes of data per day to its database—the equivalent of 800,000 books. Ford's customer database contains information on more than 33 million customers, including warranty information, survey results, retail sales input, finance records, and more. And Wal-Mart's database contains more than 100 terabytes of data—that's 100 trillion bytes, equivalent to 16,000 bytes for every one of the world's 6 billion people.[29]

Armed with the information in their databases, these companies can identify small groups of customers to receive fine-tuned marketing offers and communications. Kraft Foods has amassed a list of more than 30 million users of its products who have responded to coupons or other Kraft promotions. Based on their interests, the company sends these customers tips on issues such as nutrition and exercise, as well as recipes and coupons for specific Kraft brands. FedEx uses its sophisticated database to create 100 highly targeted, customized direct-mail and telemarketing campaigns each year to its nearly 5 million customers shipping to 212 countries. By analyzing customers carefully and reaching the right customers at the right time with the right promotions, FedEx achieves response rates of 20 to 25 percent and earns an 8-to-1 return on its direct-marketing dollars.[30]

Companies use their databases in many ways. They can use a database to identify prospects and generate sales leads by advertising products or offers. Companies can use a database to deepen customer loyalty—they can build customers' interest and enthusiasm by remembering buyer preferences and sending appropriate information, gifts, or other materials. Or they can use the database to profile customers based on previous purchasing and to decide which customers should receive particular offers.

For example, Harrah's uses its sizable database to design different levels of service and rewards for its patrons. Through player cards and other means, Harrah's tracks individual customer activity in its casinos. It enters this data into a database containing millions of transactional data points about customers and their individual gambling preferences and spending. Harrah's then uses the database to tailor its messages and services to meet individual needs and to offer special rewards to loyal customers. As a result, the casino has the most devoted customers in the industry.[31]

Mars, a market leader in pet food as well as candy, maintains an exhaustive pet database. In Germany, the company has compiled the names of virtually every German family that owns a cat. It has obtained these names by contacting veterinarians, via its MyPetStop.com Web site, and by offering the public a free booklet titled "How to Take Care of Your Cat." People who request the booklet fill out a questionnaire, providing their cat's name, age, birthday, and other information. Mars then sends a free kitten starter kit to each registered cat owner, containing a cat food sample,

■ In Germany, Mars has compiled a database containing information on virtually every family that owns a pet. To build lasting relationships, it sends free kitten starter packs to cat owners in Germany who register online.

money-saving coupons on Mars brands, and other items. The result is a lasting relationship with the cat's owner.

Like many other marketing tools, database marketing requires a special investment. Companies must invest in computer hardware, database software, analytical programs, communication links, and skilled personnel. The database system must be user-friendly and available to various marketing groups, including those in product and brand management, new-product development, advertising and promotion, direct mail, telemarketing, Web marketing, field sales, order fulfillment, and customer service. A well-managed database should lead to sales gains that will more than cover its costs.

Forms of Direct Marketing

The major forms of direct marketing—as shown in Figure 13.4—include *personal selling, telephone marketing, direct-mail marketing, catalog marketing, direct-response television marketing, kiosk marketing,* and *online marketing.* We examined personal selling in depth earlier in this chapter and will look closely at online marketing in Chapter 14. Here, we examine the other direct-marketing forms.

Telephone marketing

Using the telephone to sell directly to customers.

Telephone Marketing **Telephone marketing**—using the telephone to sell directly to consumers and business customers—has become the major direct-marketing communication tool. Telephone marketing now accounts for more than 39 percent of all direct-marketing media expenditures and 36 percent of direct-marketing sales. We're all familiar with telephone marketing directed toward consumers, but B2B marketers also use telephone marketing extensively, accounting for 59 percent of all telephone marketing sales.[32]

Marketers use *outbound* telephone marketing to sell directly to consumers and businesses. *Inbound* toll-free 800 numbers are used to receive orders from television and print ads, direct mail, or catalogs. The use of 800 numbers has taken off in recent years as more and more companies have begun using them, and as current users have added new features such as toll-free fax numbers. Residential use has also grown. To accommodate this rapid growth, new toll-free area codes, such as 888, 877, and 866, have been added. After

FIGURE 13.4

Forms of Direct Marketing

the 800 area code was established in 1967, it took almost 30 years before its 8 million numbers were used up. In contrast, 888 area code numbers, established in 1996, were used up in only 2 years.[33]

Properly designed and targeted telemarketing provides many benefits, including purchasing convenience and increased product and service information. However, the recent explosion in unsolicited telephone marketing has annoyed many consumers, who object to the almost daily "junk phone calls" that pull them away from the dinner table or fill the answering machine. Lawmakers around the country are responding with legislation ranging from banning unsolicited telemarketing calls during certain hours to letting households sign up for "Do Not Call" lists. Consumers are responding enthusiastically. When the FTC opened registration for its "Do Not Call List" in mid-2003, nearly 10 million consumers registered more than 13 million phone numbers in just the first 3 days. The FTC expects that more than 60 million numbers will be added to the list. Most telemarketers also support some action against random and poorly targeted telemarketing. As a Direct Marketing Association executive notes, "We want to target people who want to be targeted."[34]

■ Marketers use Inbound toll-free 800 numbers to receive orders from television and print ads, direct mail, or catalogs. Here, the Carolina Cookie Company urges, "Don't wait another day. Call now to place an order or request a catalog."

Direct-Mail Marketing

Direct-mail marketing involves sending an offer, announcement, reminder, or other item to a person at a particular address. Using highly selective mailing lists, direct marketers send out millions of mail pieces each year—letters, ads, brochures, samples, video and audio tapes, CDs, and other "salespeople with wings." Direct mail accounts for nearly 23 percent of all direct-marketing media expenditures and more than 31 percent of direct-marketing sales. Together, telemarketing and direct-mail marketing account for some 62 percent of direct-marketing expenditures and 67 percent of direct-marketing sales.

Direct mail is well suited to direct, one-to-one communication. It permits high target-market selectivity, can be personalized, is flexible, and allows easy measurement of results. Although the cost per thousand people reached is higher than with mass media such as television or magazines, the people who are reached are much better prospects. Direct mail has proved successful in promoting all kinds of products, from books, magazine subscriptions, and insurance to gift items, clothing, gourmet foods, and industrial products. Direct mail is also used heavily by charities to raise billions of dollars each year.

The direct-mail industry constantly seeks new methods and approaches. For example, CDs are now among the fastest-growing direct-mail media. For instance, America Online has mailed out CDs by the hundreds of millions in one of the most successful direct mail campaigns in history. Now other marketers, especially those in technology or e-commerce, are using CDs in their direct mail offers. Used in conjunction with the Internet, CDs offer an affordable way to drive traffic to Web pages personalized for a specific market segment or a specific promotion. They can also be used to demonstrate computer-related products. For example, Sony sent out a CD that allowed PC users to try out its VAIO portable notebook on their own computers.

Direct-mail marketing
Direct marketing through single mailings that include letters, ads, samples, foldouts, and other "salespeople with wings" sent to prospects on mailing lists.

Until recently, all mail was paper based and handled by the U.S. Post Office or delivery services such as FedEx, UPS, DHL, or Airborne Express. Recently, however, three new forms of mail delivery have become popular:

■ *Fax mail:* Marketers now routinely send fax mail announcing special offers, sales, and other events to prospects and customers with fax machines. Fax mail messages can be sent and received almost instantaneously. However, some prospects and customers resent receiving unsolicited fax mail, which ties up their machines and consumes their paper.

■ *E-mail:* Many marketers now send sales announcements, offers, product information, and other messages to e-mail addresses—sometimes to a few individuals, sometimes to large groups. Today's e-mail messages have moved far beyond the drab text-only messages of old. The new breed of e-mail ad uses glitzy features such as animation, interactive links, streaming video, and personalized audio messages to reach out and grab attention. However, as people receive more and more e-mail, they resent the intrusion of unrequested messages. Smart marketers are using permission-based programs, sending e-mail ads only to those who want to receive them.

■ *Voice mail:* Some marketers have set up automated programs that exclusively target voice mailboxes and answering machines with prerecorded messages. These systems target homes between 10 A.M. and 4 P.M. and businesses between 7 P.M. and 9 P.M., when people are least likely to answer. If the automated dialer hears a live voice, it disconnects. Such systems thwart hang-ups by annoyed potential customers. However, they can also create substantial ill will.

Catalog marketing
Direct marketing through print, video, or electronic catalogs that are mailed to select customers, made available in stores, or presented online.

These new forms deliver direct mail at incredible speeds compared to the post office's "snail mail" pace. Yet, much like mail delivered through traditional channels, they may be resented as "junk mail" if sent to people who have no interest in them. For this reason, marketers must carefully identify appropriate targets so as not waste their money and recipients' time (see Marketing at Work 13.3).

Catalog Marketing Advances in technology, along with the move toward personalized, one-to-one marketing have resulted in exciting changes in **catalog marketing**. *Catalog Age* magazine used to define a *catalog* as "a printed, bound piece of at least eight pages, selling multiple products, and offering a direct ordering mechanism." Today, only a few years later, this definition is sadly out of date. With the stampede to the Internet, more and more catalogs are going electronic. Most print catalogers have added Web-based catalogs to their marketing mixes, and a variety of new Web-only catalogers have emerged. The Internet has not yet killed off printed catalogs—far from it. Web catalogs currently generate only about 13 percent of all catalog sales. Although the Internet has provided a new avenue for catalog sales, printed catalogs remain the primary medium. Most catalogers use the Internet as an added sales tool to augment their printed catalogs.[35]

Catalog marketing has grown explosively during the past 25 years. Annual catalog sales amounted to just under $126 billion last year and are expected to grow to more than $176

■ Catalog marketing has grown explosively during the past 25 years. Some 10,000 companies now produce 14,000 unique catalog titles in the United States.

Marketing at Work | 13.3

Misdirected Marketing: My Dead Dog May Already Be a Winner!

Poor database management and wrongly targeted direct marketing not only aggravates consumers, it costs companies millions of dollars each year and sometimes makes them look downright foolish. Take the following account, written by Lee Coppola, the bemused recipient of some of this misdirected mania:

Ever wonder what happens when a pet takes on a persona? Ashley could have told you, if he could have talked. Ashley was the family mutt, an SPCA special, part beagle and part spaniel. For years, most of them after he died, he also served as the family's representative in the local telephone book. He was picked for the role quite haphazardly one day when I tried to keep my number out of the book to avoid getting business calls at home. When I balked at the $60-a-year fee, the cheery telephone company representative suggested I list the number in one of my children's names.

I was munching on a sandwich at the time and Ashley followed me around the kitchen waiting for a crumb to fall. "Can I put the phone in any name?" I asked the rep as I sidestepped Ashley. "Certainly," she answered, and therein gave birth to 10 years of telephone calls and mail to a dog.

A remarkable new book about the Coppolas since the Civil War is about to make history—and you, Ashley Coppola, are in it," touted one letter asking Ashley to send $10 right away for "this one-time offer." Ashley received hundreds of pieces of mail, the bulk soliciting his money.

The most ironic pitches for cash were from the SPCA and the Buffalo Zoo, a kind of animal-helping-animal scenario. And we wondered how the chief executive of a local cemetery

might react if he knew he was asking a canine to buy a plot to give his family "peace of mind." Or a local lawn service's thoughts about asking a dog who daily messed the grass, "Is your lawn as attractive as it could be?" Then there was the letter offering Ashley "reliable electronic security to protect your home." One of the kids asked if that wasn't Ashley's job.

The kids soon got into the swing of having their dog receive mail and telephone calls. "He's sleeping under the dining room table," one would tell telemarketers. "He's out in the backyard taking a whiz," was the favorite reply of another. My wife would have nothing of that frivolity, preferring to simply reply, "He's deceased."

But that tack backfired on her one day when our youngest child took an almost pleading call from a survey-company employee looking for Ashley. "I'm Ashley," the 17-year-old politely replied, taking pity on the caller. He dutifully gave his age and answered a few questions before he realized he was late for an appointment and hurriedly cut short the conversation. "Can I call you again?" the surveyor asked. "OK," our son said as he hung up.

Sure enough, the surveyor called again the next day and asked for Ashley. But this time Mom answered and gave her standard reply. "Oh, my God," exclaimed the caller. "I'm so, so sorry." The surveyor's horrified grief puzzled my wife until our son explained how he had been a healthy teenage Ashley the day before.

Sometimes we worried about our dog's fate. You see, he broke several chain letters urging him to copy and send 20 others or risk some calamity. After all, Ashley was warned, didn't

one person die 9 days after throwing out the letter?

Did I mention credit cards? Ashley paid his bills on time, judging from the $5,000 lines-of-credit for which he "automatically" qualified. Made us wonder about the scrutiny of the nation's credit-card industry.

Of course, Ashley was no ordinary dog. He was an Italian dog. How else to explain the solicitation to Mr. Coppola Ashley that came all the way from Altamura, Italy, and sought donations to an orphanage? Then there was the offer to obtain his family's cherished crest, "fashioned hundreds of years ago in Italy," and purchase the Coppola family registry that listed him along with all the other Coppolas in America.

Is there some message to all this? Think of the saplings that were sacrificed to try to squeeze money from a canine. Or the time, energy, and money that were wasted each time a postage or bulk-mail stamp was affixed to an envelope being sent to a mutt. We did feel sheepish about the deception when the mail came from the self-employed trying to make a buck. We wondered if a local dentist really would have given Ashley a "complete initial consultation, exam, and bitewing X-rays for ONLY THREE DOLLARS." And what might have been the expression on the saleswoman's face if Ashley had shown up for his complimentary Mary Kay facial?

Ashley did appreciate, however, the coupon for dog food.

Source: Lee Coppola, "My Dead Dog May Already Be a Winner!" *Newsweek,* July 5, 1999, p. 11. Also, see Louella Miles, "Should DM Still Be Missing Its Mark?" *Marketing,* June 14, 2001, pp. 29–31; and Bob Levey, "How to Fight Back against Junk Mailers," *The Washington Post,* October 15, 2002, p. C11.

billion in 2008.[36] Some huge general-merchandise retailers—such as JCPenney and Spiegel—sell a full line of merchandise through catalogs. In recent years, these giants have been challenged by thousands of specialty catalogs that serve highly specialized market niches. According to one study, some 10,000 companies now produce 14,000 unique catalog titles in the United States.[37]

Consumers can buy just about anything from a catalog. Sharper Image sells $2,400 jet-propelled surfboards. The Banana Republic Travel and Safari Clothing Company features everything you would need to go hiking in the Sahara or the rain forest. And each year Lillian Vernon sends out 37 editions of its eight catalogs, with a total circulation of 162 million copies, to its 20-million-person database, selling more than 6,000 different items, ranging from shoes to decorative lawn birds and monogrammed oven mitts.[38] Specialty department stores, such as Neiman Marcus, Bloomingdale's, and Saks Fifth Avenue, use catalogs to cultivate upper-middle-class markets for high-priced, often exotic, merchandise. Several major corporations have also developed or acquired catalog divisions. For example, Avon now issues 10 women's fashion catalogs along with catalogs for children's and men's clothes. Walt Disney Company mails out over 6 million catalogs each year featuring videos, stuffed animals, and other Disney items.

Ninety-seven percent of all catalog companies now present merchandise and take orders over the Internet. Here's an example that illustrates this dramatic shift in catalog marketing:

> When novelty gifts marketer Archie McPhee launched its Web site in September 1995, response was underwhelming. But when the company added a shopping basket ordering feature in 1997, the site roared to life. According to Mark Pahlow, president of the catalog company, the site now has 35,000 unique visitors each month, generating 55 percent of the cataloger's total sales. The Web numbers are so positive that Archie McPhee has slashed circulation of its print catalog from 1 million to less than 300,000, and reduced the frequency from five issues a year to three. The Web site has saved the company more than 50 percent in the costs of producing, printing, and mailing its color catalog, which had been as high as $700,000 annually. The site can also offer much more merchandise. "A 48-page catalog would show fewer than 200 items, whereas the Web site offers more than 500," Pahlow notes. Another benefit is the site's real-time inventory feature. "The day a new product arrives, it is shown on the site. The moment we run out of an item, we pull it off. We are also able to show items we have small quantities of as Web-only specials." As an added benefit, the Web site also lets the cataloger build dynamic customer relationships using interactive features, such as its "world-famous Nerd Test" and a "Virtual Sarcastic Ball" which returns snide replies and put-downs to user questions. Customers can elect to join the "Cult of McPhee" e-mail list and receive free monthly e-mails announcing the direct marketer's upcoming events, contests, and specials. Cult members also get advance notice of our new products and qualify for special members-only deals.[39]

Along with the benefits, however, Web-based catalogs also present challenges. Whereas a print catalog is intrusive and creates its own attention, Web catalogs are passive and must be marketed. Attracting new customers is much more difficult for a Web catalog than for a print catalog. Thus, even catalogers who are sold on the Web are not likely to abandon their print catalogs. For example, Archie McPhee relies on its print catalogs to promote its site.

Direct-response television marketing

Direct marketing via television, including *direct-response television advertising* (infomercials) and *home shopping channels.*

Direct-Response Television Marketing **Direct-response television marketing** takes one of two major forms. The first is *direct-response advertising*. Direct marketers air television spots, often 60 or 120 seconds long, that persuasively describe a product and give customers a toll-free number for ordering. Television viewers often encounter 30-minute advertising programs, or *infomercials*, for a single product.

Some successful direct-response ads run for years and become classics. For example, Dial Media's ads for Ginsu knives ran for 7 years and sold almost 3 million sets of knives worth more than $40 million in sales; its Armourcote cookware ads generated more than twice that much. And over the past 40 years, infomercial czar Ron Popeil's company,

Ronco, has sold more than $1 billion worth of TV-marketed gadgets, including the original Veg-O-Matic, the Pocket Fisherman, Mr. Microphone, the Giant Food Dehydrator and Beef Jerky Machine, and the Showtime Rotisserie & BBQ.[40]

For years, infomercials have been associated with somewhat questionable pitches for juicers and other kitchen gadgets, get-rich-quick schemes, and nifty ways to stay in shape without working very hard at it. In recent years, however, a number of large companies—GTE, Johnson & Johnson, MCA Universal, Sears, Procter & Gamble, Revlon, IBM, Cadillac, Volvo, Land Rover, Anheuser-Busch, even the U.S. Navy—have begun using infomercials to sell their wares over the phone, refer customers to retailers, send out coupons and product information, or attract buyers to their Web sites (see Marketing at Work 13.4). Direct-response TV commercials are usually cheaper to make, and the media purchase is less costly. Moreover, results are easily measured. "Unlike branding campaigns, direct-response ads always include a 1-800 number or Web address, making it easier for marketers to gauge whether consumers are paying attention to their pitches," says an industry analyst.[41]

Home shopping channels, another form of direct-response television marketing, are television programs or entire channels dedicated to selling goods and services. Some home shopping channels, such as the Quality Value Channel (QVC), Home Shopping Network (HSN), and ValueVision, broadcast 24 hours a day. On QVC, the program's hosts offer bargain prices on products ranging from jewelry, lamps, collectible dolls, and clothing to power tools and consumer electronics—usually obtained by the home shopping channel at close-out prices. Viewers call a toll-free number to order goods from one of six QVC call centers.

With widespread distribution on cable and satellite television, the top three shopping networks combined now reach 248 million homes worldwide, selling more than $4 billion of goods each year. They are now combining direct-response television marketing with online and on-land selling. For example, QVC recently launched a feature called "61st Minute," in which QVC viewers are urged to go online immediately after a given product showcase. Once there, viewers find a Webcast continuation of the product pitch. Those who miss out on a deal on the tube or online can now visit one of six QVC outlet stores or the company's QVC's full-line store at the Mall of America.[42]

Kiosk Marketing Some companies place information and ordering machines—called *kiosks* (in contrast to vending machines, which dispense actual products)—in stores, airports, and other locations. Hallmark and American Greetings use kiosks to help customers create and purchase personalized greeting cards. Tower Records has listening kiosks that let customers listen to the music before purchasing. Kiosks in the do-it-yourself ceramics stores of California-based Color Me Mine Inc. contain clip-art images that customers can use to decorate the ceramics pieces they purchase in the store. At Car Max, the used-car superstore, customers use a kiosk with a touch-screen computer to get information about its vast inventory of as many as 1,000 cars and trucks. Customers can choose a handful and print out photos, prices, features, and locations on the store's lot. The use of such kiosks is expected to increase fivefold during the next 3 years and generate more than $6.5 billion in annual sales by 2006.[43]

Business marketers also use kiosks. For example, Dow Plastics places kiosks at trade shows to collect sales leads and to provide information on its 700 products. The kiosk system reads customer data from encoded registration badges and produces technical data sheets that can be printed at the kiosk or faxed or mailed to the customer. The system has resulted in a 400 percent increase in qualified sales leads.[44]

Like about everything else these days, kiosks are also going online, as many companies merge the powers of the real and virtual worlds. For example, in some Levi Strauss stores, you can plug your measurements into a Web kiosk and have custom-made jeans delivered to your home within 2 weeks. At the local Disney Store, kiosk guests can buy merchandise online, purchase theme-park passes, and learn more about Disney vacations and entertainment products. Gap has installed interactive kiosks, called Web lounges, in some of its stores that provide gift ideas or let customers match up outfits without trying them on in dressing rooms. Outdoor equipment retailer REI has at least four Web-enabled kiosks in each of its 63 stores that provide customers with product information and let them place orders online.[45]

Marketing at Work | 13.4

Infomercials: But Wait, There's More!

It's late at night and you can't get to sleep. So you grab the TV remote, surf channels, and chance upon a fast-talking announcer, breathlessly pitching some new must-have kitchen gadget. A grinning blonde co-announcer fawns over the gadget's every feature, and the studio audience roars its approval. After putting the gadget through its paces, the announcer asks, "How much would you expect to pay? Three hundred dollars? Two hundred? Well, think again! This amazing gadget can be yours for just four easy payments of $19.95 plus shipping and handling!" "Oooooh!" the audience screams. "But wait! There's more," declares the announcer. "If you act now, you will also receive an additional gadget, absolutely free. That's two for the price of one." With operators standing by, you don't have a minute to lose.

Sound familiar? We've all seen countless infomercials like this, hawking everything from kitchen gadgets, cleaning solutions, and exercise equipment to psychic advice and get-rich-quick schemes. Traditionally, such pitches have had a kind of fly-by-night feel about them. And in the cold light of day, such a purchase may not seem like such a good deal after all. You wait 6-to-8 weeks for delivery, learn that the device doesn't work nearly as well for you as it did for the smooth-talking announcer, and realize that the four easy payments (with an additional $9.95 S&H) added nearly $90 to your credit card bill. Such is the reputation of direct-response TV advertising. Yet, behind the hype is a powerful approach to marketing that is becoming more mainstream every day.

Ron Popeil pioneered direct-response product sales. Whether you realize it or not, you've probably been exposed to dozen's of Popeil's inventions over the years, and his direct-marketing model has become the standard for the infomercial industry. His company, Ronco, has brought us such classics as the Veg-O-Matic, the Electric Food Dehydrator, the Showtime Rotisserie Oven, the GLH Formula Hair

System, the Automatic 5-Minute Pasta and Sausage Maker, the Popeil Pocket Fisherman, the Inside the Egg Shell Electric Egg Scrambler, and the Dial-O-Matic Food Slicer.

Infomercials do work—two-thirds of Americans have seen the ads and one-third of viewers have bought goods they've "seen on TV." Since its beginning, Ronco has sold more than $1 billion worth of merchandise—that's mil-

Ronco and Ron Popeil, with his Veg-o-Matics, food dehydrators, and electric egg scramblers, paved the way for a host of mainstream marketers who now use direct-response ads.

lions of easy payments of just $14.95 each. The success of Ronco and its countless imitators hasn't gone unnoticed among the big hitters in corporate America. Direct-response television marketing is rapidly becoming a mainstay weapon in the marketing arsenals of even the most reputable companies.

Ronco's revenues aren't the only reason for the expansion of direct-response TV. It's also a matter of too many channels and too few shows. The explosion of cable and digital channels that reach a wide range of demographically targeted markets has created a glut of airtime, which can be snapped up at attractive rates. The channels offer both advertising slots for short-form direct response ads and off-primetime paid programming slots for long-form infomercials or shopping programs.

Changes in retailer reactions to direct-response TV products have also given infomercials a boost. Mass retailers are now embracing such direct-response staples as Orange Glo International's OxiClean. Some, such as drug-chain heavyweight Walgreens, devote entire front-of-store sections to such goods. "It used to take three to four years to get full retail distribution for direct-TV products," notes A.J. Kuhlbani, president of TeleBrands, which markets such products as Amber Vision sunglasses and the Roll-A-Hose. "Now, you see 'As Seen on TV' products in stores within a month of going on TV."

All this makes direct-response television advertising both attractive and cost-effective for an expanding range of companies and products, including the marketing heavyweights. Dell, Procter & Gamble, Volvo, Johnson & Johnson, Sears, Sharper Image, and many other mainstream marketers now use direct-response TV to peddle specific prod-

ucts and promotions, and to draw new customers into their other direct-to-consumer channels. Today's infomercials have evolved with the times—most now include highly professional pitches and Web sites to go along with the ever-present toll-free phone number.

Procter & Gamble, one of the nation's premier marketing companies, now routinely uses infomercials to sell products like the Swiffer WetJet and Dryel. A series of infomercials helped to propel the WetJet past rival Clorox's ReadyMop when other marketing efforts alone failed to do the trick. P&G launched its Swiffer Dusters product with a campaign that included direct-response ads and a tie-in to the DVD release of the Jennifer Lopez film *Maid in Manhattan*. Consumers contacting the 1-800 number got coupons for both the new Swiffer Duster and the DVD.

Beyond the usual domestic personal-care and home-care goods, interest in direct-response has now expanded to more serious products. For example, with the FDA's relaxation of regulations regarding direct-to-consumer advertising for prescription drugs, many pharmaceutical companies have jumped on the direct-response bandwagon. Pharmacia, which makes Celebrex, used infomercials to help introduce the drug to arthritis sufferers. It plans another infomercial-style marketing campaign to highlight how the drug improves the quality of life. Although consumers can't order the medicine directly from the company, they can request informative literature and receive coupons that defray the costs of required doctor visits or first pill purchases.

Since 1998, retailer Sharper Image has employed 2-minute infomercials to sell individual products, including vacuum cleaners, scooters, and air purifiers.

One Sharper Image VP boasts that the retailer's direct-response TV effort generates "a fairly good-size piece of our business! It pays for itself even without accounting for the advertising's impact on our stores. And we typically see sales in stores go up when we run the infomercials." The company buys time on a variety of major cable networks and runs the ads at all hours of the day and night.

Over the past several years, Sharper Image has increased its investment in direct-response television ads. By last year, infomercials accounted for about 32 percent of Sharper Image's total advertising budget. According to CEO Richard Thalheimer, the company "remains committed to our long-term strategy of growth through multiple sales channels, including . . . direct-response television." And with good reason. Consumer response to infomercials for the company's Ionic Breeze air purifier grew the company's month-to-month catalog sales by 49 percent.

So, direct-response TV ads are no longer just the province of Ron Popeil and his Veg-O-Matics, food dehydrators, and electric egg scramblers. While Popeil and his imitators paved the way, their success now has mainstream marketers dabbling in direct-response ads. What does the future hold for the direct-response industry? Wait, there's more!

Sources: Jack Neff, "Direct Response Getting Respect," *Advertising Age*, January 20, 2003, p. 4; Paul Miller, "Sharper Image Tunes in to Infomercials," *Catalog Age*, February 2001, p. 12; Bridget McCrea, "Removing the Blemishes," *Response*, March 2003, pp. 32–34; "Nearly Two-Thirds of Americans Are Exposed to Direct-Response TV," *Research Alert*, March 21, 2003, p. 9; Millie Takaki, "Now Available," *SHOOT*, April 25, 2003, p. 11; "Pharmaceutical Infomercial," *Back Stage*, April 18, 2003, p. 37; and Dean Tomasula, "Sharper Image Shares Soar on Ionic Breeze," July 18, 2003, accessed online at www.zephyr-media.com.

Linking the Concepts

Hold up a moment and think about the impact of direct marketing on your life.

- When was the last time you *bought* something via direct marketing? What did you buy, and why did you buy it direct? When was the last time that you *rejected* a direct-marketing offer? Why did you reject it? Based on these experiences, what advice would you give to direct marketers?
- For the next week, keep track of all the direct-marketing offers that come your way via direct mail and catalogs, telephone, and direct-response television. Then analyze the offers by type, source, and what you liked or disliked about each offer and the way it was delivered. Which offer best hit its target (you)? Which missed by the widest margin?

Integrated Direct Marketing

Too often, a company's individual direct-marketing efforts are not well integrated with one another or with other elements of its marketing and promotion mixes. For example, a firm's media advertising may be handled by the advertising department working with a traditional advertising agency. Meanwhile, its direct-mail and catalog business may be handled by direct-marketing specialists, while its Web site is developed and operated by an outside Internet firm. Even within a given direct-marketing campaign, too many companies use only a "one-shot" effort to reach and sell a prospect or a single vehicle in multiple stages to trigger purchases.

A more powerful approach is **integrated direct marketing**, which involves using carefully coordinated multiple-media, multiple-stage campaigns. Such campaigns can greatly improve response. Whereas a direct-mail piece alone might generate a 2 percent response, adding a Web site and toll-free phone number might raise the response rate by 50 percent. Then, a well-designed outbound telemarketing effort might lift response by an additional 500 percent. Suddenly, a 2 percent response has grown to 15 percent or more by adding interactive marketing channels to a regular mailing.

More elaborate integrated direct-marketing campaigns can be used. Consider the multimedia, multistage campaign shown in Figure 13.5. Here, the paid ad creates product awareness and stimulates phone, mail, or Web inquiries. The company immediately sends direct mail or e-mail responses to those who inquire. Within a few days, the company follows up with a phone call seeking an order. Some prospects will order by phone or the company's Web site; others might request a face-to-face sales call. In such a campaign, the marketer seeks to improve response rates and profits by adding media and stages that contribute more to additional sales than to additional costs.

Public Policy and Ethical Issues in Direct Marketing

Direct marketers and their customers usually enjoy mutually rewarding relationships. Occasionally, however, a darker side emerges. The aggressive and sometimes shady tactics of a few direct marketers can bother or harm consumers, giving the entire industry a black eye. Abuses range from simple excesses that irritate consumers to instances of unfair practices or even outright deception and fraud. The direct-marketing industry has also faced growing concerns about invasion-of-privacy issues.

Integrated direct marketing
Direct-marketing campaigns that use multiple vehicles and multiple stages to improve response rates and profits.

FIGURE 13.5
An Integrated Direct-Marketing Campaign

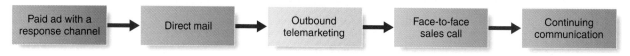

Irritation, Unfairness, Deception, and Fraud Direct-marketing excesses sometimes annoy or offend consumers. Most of us dislike direct-response TV commercials that are too loud, too long, and too insistent. Especially bothersome are dinnertime or late-night phone calls. Beyond irritating consumers, some direct marketers have been accused of taking unfair advantage of impulsive or less sophisticated buyers. TV shopping channels and program-long "infomercials" targeting television-addicted shoppers seem to be the worst culprits. They feature smooth-talking hosts, elaborately staged demonstrations, claims of drastic price reductions, "while they last" time limitations, and unequaled ease of purchase to inflame buyers who have low sales resistance.

Worse yet, so-called heat merchants design mailers and write copy intended to mislead buyers. Even well-known direct mailers have been accused of deceiving consumers. Sweepstakes promoter Publishers Clearing House recently paid $52 million to settle accusations that its high-pressure mailings confused or misled consumers, especially the elderly, into believing that they had won prizes or would win if they bought the company's magazines.[46]

Other direct marketers pretend to be conducting research surveys when they are actually asking leading questions to screen or persuade consumers. Fraudulent schemes, such as investment scams or phony collections for charity, have also multiplied in recent years. Crooked direct marketers can be hard to catch: Direct-marketing customers often respond quickly, do not interact personally with the seller, and usually expect to wait for delivery. By the time buyers realize that they have been bilked, the thieves are usually somewhere else plotting new schemes.

Invasion of Privacy Invasion of privacy is perhaps the toughest public policy issue now confronting the direct-marketing industry. These days, it seems that almost every time consumers enter a sweepstakes, apply for a credit card, take out a magazine subscription, or order products by mail, telephone, or the Internet, their names are entered into some company's already bulging database. Using sophisticated computer technologies, direct marketers can use these databases to "microtarget" their selling efforts.

Consumers often benefit from such database marketing—they receive more offers that are closely matched to their interests. However, many critics worry that marketers may know *too* much about consumers' lives and that they may use this knowledge to take unfair advantage of consumers. At some point, they claim, the extensive use of databases intrudes on consumer privacy.

For example, they ask, should AT&T be allowed to sell marketers the names of customers who frequently call the 800 numbers of catalog companies? Should a company such as American Express be allowed to make data on its millions of cardholders worldwide available to merchants who accept AmEx cards? Is it right for credit bureaus to compile and sell lists of people who have recently applied for credit cards—people who are considered prime direct-marketing targets because of their spending behavior? Or is it right for states to sell the names and addresses of driver's license holders, along with height, weight, and gender information, allowing apparel retailers to target tall or overweight people with special clothing offers?

In their drives to build databases, companies sometimes get carried away. For example, when first introduced, Intel's Pentium III chip contained an embedded serial number that allowed the company to trace users' equipment. When privacy advocates screamed, Intel disabled the feature. Similarly, Microsoft caused substantial privacy concerns when it introduced its Windows 95 software. It used a "Registration Wizard," which allowed users to register their new software online. However, when users went online to register, without their knowledge, Microsoft "read" the configurations of their PCs to learn about the major software products running on each customer's system. When users learned of this invasion, they protested loudly and Microsoft abandoned the practice.

These days, it's not only the large companies that can access such private information. The explosion of information technology has put these capabilities into the hands of almost any business. For example, one bar owner discovered the power of information technology after he acquired a simple, inexpensive device to check IDs.

About 10,000 people a week go to The Rack, a bar in Boston. . . . One by one, they hand over their driver's licenses to a doorman, who swipes them through a sleek black machine. If a license is valid and its holder is over 21, a red light blinks and the patron is waved through. But most of the customers are not aware that it also pulls up the name, address, birth date, and other personal details from a data strip on the back of the license. Even height, eye color, and sometimes Social Security number are registered. "You swipe the license, and all of a sudden someone's whole life as we know it pops up in front of you," said Paul Barclay, the bar's owner. "It's almost voyeuristic." Mr. Barclay bought the machine to keep out underage drinkers who use fake IDs. But he soon found that he could build a database of personal information, providing an intimate perspective on his clientele that can be useful in marketing. "It's not just an ID check," he said. "It's a tool." Now, for any given night or hour, he can break down his clientele by sex, age, ZIP code, or other characteristics. If he wanted to, he could find out how many blond women named Karen over 5 feet 2 inches came in over a weekend, or how many of his customers have the middle initial M. More practically, he can build mailing lists based on all that data—and keep track of who comes back.[47]

Such access to and use of information has caused much concern and debate among companies, consumers, and public policy makers. Consumer privacy has become a major regulatory issue.

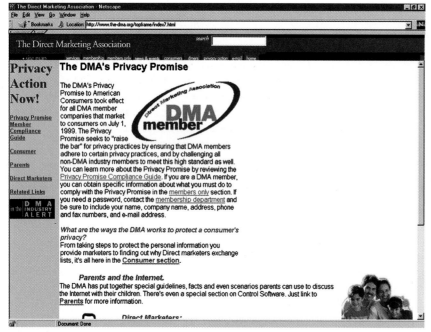

■ The DMA's "Privacy Promise to American Consumers" attempts to build customer confidence by requiring that all DMA members adhere to certain carefully developed consumer privacy rules.

The direct-marketing industry is addressing issues of ethics and public policy. For example, in an effort to build consumer confidence in shopping direct, the Direct Marketing Association (DMA)—the largest association for businesses practicing interactive and database marketing, with more than 4,600 member companies—launched a "Privacy Promise to American Consumers." The Privacy Promise requires that all DMA members adhere to a carefully developed set of consumer privacy rules. Members must agree to notify customers when any personal information is rented, sold, or exchanged with others. They must also honor consumer requests to "opt out" of information exchanges with other marketers or not to receive mail, telephone, or other solicitations again. Finally, they must abide by the DMA's Mail Preference Service (www. thedma.org/consumers/offmailinglist.html) and Telephone Preference Service (www. thedma.org/consumers/offtelephonelist.html), two national services to remove the names of consumers who wish not to receive mail or telephone offers at home.

Direct marketers know that, left untended, such problems will lead to increasingly negative consumer attitudes, lower response rates, and calls for more restrictive state and federal legislation. "Privacy and customer permission have become the cornerstones of customer trust, [and] trust has become the cornerstone to a continuing relationship," says one expert. Companies must "become the custodians of customer trust and protect the privacy of their customers."[48]

Most direct marketers want the same things that consumers want: honest and well-designed marketing offers targeted only toward consumers who will appreciate and respond to them. Direct marketing is just too expensive to waste on consumers who don't want it.

REST STOP:
Reviewing the Concepts

Hit the brakes, pull over, and revisit this chapter's key concepts. The chapter is the second of two chapters covering the final marketing mix element—promotion. The previous chapter dealt with advertising, sales promotion, and public relations. This one investigates personal selling and direct marketing.

Personal selling and direct marketing are both direct tools for communicating with and persuading current and prospective customers. Selling is the interpersonal arm of the communications mix. To be successful in personal selling, a company must first build and then manage an effective sales force. Firms must also be good at direct marketing, the process of forming one-to-one connections with customers. Today, many companies are turning to direct marketing in an effort to reach carefully targeted customers more efficiently and to build stronger, more personal, one-to-one relationships with them.

1. Discuss the role of a company's salespeople in creating value for customers and building customer relationships.

Most companies use salespeople, and many companies assign them an important role in the marketing mix. For companies selling business products, the firm's salespeople work directly with customers. Often, the sales force is the customer's only direct contact with the company and therefore may be viewed by customers as representing the company itself. In contrast, for consumer product companies that sell through intermediaries, consumers usually do not meet salespeople or even know about them. The sales force works behind the scenes, dealing with wholesalers and retailers to obtain their support and helping them become effective in selling the firm's products.

As an element of the promotion mix, the sales force is very effective in achieving certain marketing objectives and carrying out activities such as prospecting, communicating, selling and servicing, and information gathering. But with companies becoming more market oriented, a market-focused sales force also works to produce both *customer satisfaction* and *company profit*. To accomplish these goals, the sales force needs skills in marketing analysis and planning in addition to the traditional selling skills.

2. Identify and explain the six major sales force management steps.

High sales force costs necessitate an effective *sales management process* consisting of six steps: *designing sales force strategy and structure* and *recruiting and selecting, training, compensating, supervising,* and *evaluating* salespeople.

In designing a sales force, sales management must address issues such as what type of sales force structure will work best (territorial, product, customer, or complex structure); how large the sales force should be; who will be involved in the selling effort; and how its various sales and sales support people will work together (inside or outside sales forces and team selling).

To hold down the high costs of hiring the wrong people, salespeople must be *recruited* and *selected* carefully. In recruiting salespeople, a company may look to job duties and the characteristics of its most successful salespeople to suggest the traits it wants in its salespeople and then look for applicants through recommendations of current salespeople, employment agencies, classified ads, and the Internet and by contacting college students. In the selection process, the procedure can vary from a single informal interview to lengthy testing and interviewing. After the selection process is complete, *training* programs familiarize new salespeople not only with the art of selling but also with the company's history, its products and policies, and the characteristics of its market and competitors.

The sales force *compensation* system helps to reward, motivate, and direct salespeople. In compensating salespeople, companies try to have an appealing plan, usually close to the going rate for the type of sales job and needed skills. In addition to compensation, all salespeople need *supervision*, and many need continuous encouragement because they must make many decisions and face many frustrations. Periodically, the company must *evaluate* their performance to help them do a better job. In evaluating salespeople, the company relies on getting regular information gathered through sales reports, personal observations, customers' letters and complaints, customer surveys, and conversations with other salespeople.

3. Discuss the personal selling process, distinguishing between transaction-oriented marketing and relationship marketing.

The art of selling involves a seven-step *selling process*: *prospecting and qualifying, preapproach, approach, presentation and demonstration, handling objections, closing,* and *follow-up*. These steps help marketers close a specific sale and as such are *transaction oriented*. However, a seller's dealings with customers should be guided by the larger concept of *relationship marketing*. The company's sales force should help to orchestrate a whole-company effort to develop profitable long-term relationships with key customers based on superior customer value and satisfaction.

4. Define direct marketing and discuss its benefits to customers and companies.

Direct marketing consists of direct connections with carefully targeted individual consumers to both obtain an immediate response and cultivate lasting customer relationships. Using detailed databases, direct marketers tailor their offers and communications to the needs of narrowly defined segments or even individual buyers.

For buyers, direct marketing is convenient, easy to use, and private. It gives them ready access to a wealth of products and information, at home and around the globe. Direct marketing is also immediate and interactive, allowing buyers to create exactly the configuration of information, products, or services they desire, then order them on the spot. For sellers, direct marketing is a powerful tool for building customer relationships. Using database marketing, today's marketers can target small groups or individual consumers, tailor offers to individual needs, and promote these offers through personalized communications. It also offers them a low-cost, efficient alternative for reaching their markets. As a result of these advantages to both buyers and sellers, direct marketing has become the fastest-growing form of marketing.

5. Identify and discuss the major forms of direct marketing.

The main forms of direct marketing include *personal selling, telephone marketing, direct-mail marketing, catalog marketing, direct-response television marketing, kiosk marketing,* and *online marketing.* We discuss personal selling in the first part of this chapter and examined online marketing in detail in Chapter 3. *Telephone marketing* consists of using the telephone to sell directly to consumers. *Direct-mail marketing* consists of the company sending an offer, announcement, reminder, or other item to a person at a specific address. Recently, three new forms of mail delivery have become popular—*fax mail, e-mail,* and *voice mail.* Some marketers rely on *catalog marketing,* or selling through catalogs mailed to a select list of customers or made available in stores. *Direct-response television marketing* has two forms: *direct-response advertising* or *infomercials* and *home shopping channels. Kiosks* are information and ordering machines that direct marketers place in stores, airports, and other locations. *Online marketing,* discussed in Chapter 3, involves online channels and e-commerce, which electronically link consumers with sellers.

Navigating the Key Terms

Approach
Catalog marketing
Closing
Customer database
Customer sales force structure
Direct-mail marketing
Direct marketing
Direct-response television
  marketing

Follow-up
Handling objections
Inside sales force
Integrated direct marketing
Outside sales force (fields sales
  force)
Preapproach
Presentation
Product sales force structure

Prospecting
Sales force management
Sales quotas
Salesperson
Selling process
Team selling
Telephone marketing
Territorial sales force structure

Travel Log

Discussing the Issues

1. What is meant by "personal selling is the interpersonal arm of the promotion mix"? What advantages and disadvantages does the personal selling function have relative to advertising in convincing consumers to make a purchase?

2. Compare and contrast a territorial sales force structure, a product sales force structure, and a customer sales force structure. Under what circumstances might a company want to use each one?

3. In the selling process, the activities that occur before the potential client is contacted are of vital importance. Discuss the role of prospecting, qualifying, and the preapproach activities in making the actual sales presentations more successful.

4. Direct marketing is the fastest-growing form of marketing. What benefits do buyers and sellers receive from this marketing communications mix element that has led to its growth?

5. Study the direct marketing forms of telephone marketing, direct-mail marketing, catalog marketing, direct-response televi-sion marketing, and kiosk marketing presented in this chapter. Identify products or services that would be appropriate for each of these forms of direct marketing. What is it about the products or services you selected that make them appropriate for these forms?

Application Questions

1. In a small group, discuss entry-level sales positions appropriate for someone graduating from college with a marketing degree. Your discussion should include what a typical day would be like for this salesperson, and your group should identify the traits an individual should possess to be a successful salesperson in this industry. Write a newspaper advertisement recruiting an individual for this position.

2. Building on the sales position advertisement developed in the previous question, you are now asked to evaluate potential job applicants for the job. Each group member should bring a resumé to class with the individual's name removed. The group should then discuss what they will look for in a job candidate's resumé that will allow them to screen for the traits they discussed in the development of the advertisement. The group should then review the resumés and select the top two candidates they would invite to interview.

3. Select a product with which you are familiar and conduct a sales presentation/demonstration. Pair with another student and take turns role-playing the "salesperson" and the "prospect." The salesperson should tell the product story to the prospect, present customer benefits and show how the product solves the customer's problems. The prospect should raise objections to the sale so that the salesperson can practice handling objections. The selling role play should end with the salesperson attempting to close the sale. Several other students can observe the interaction and offer a critique of the salesperson.

Under the Hood: Focus on Technology

Many companies offer sales force automation products to assist salespeople in managing their clients. Visit the Web sites of these three sales force automation vendors (www.salesforce.com, www.avantgo.com/frontdoor/corpfrontdoor.html, and www.upshot.com) and read about their products. Next respond to the following questions.

1. What activities can sales force automation products help salespeople perform better?

2. What kinds of questions would you ask a sales force automation vendor if you were in charge of purchasing a system for your company?

3. What concerns might salespeople have to their company implementing a new sales force automation tool? What could be done to overcome these objections?

Focus on Ethics

Recruitment and selection are a big part of the sales management function. There are a variety of state and federal laws dictating what a sales manager can and cannot ask an applicant during the job interview. Generally, a sales manager should focus on questions that relate directly to knowing if the job candidate can or cannot perform the functions required of the job. Questions should not be asked that may lead to the potential for discrimination on the basis of age, disability, gender, national origin, race, or religion. Examples of inappropriate questions include: Are you married? How old are you?

Where were you born? Do you attend church regularly? Have you ever been arrested? Are you planning on having children? Have you ever filed for bankruptcy?

1. Why are laws in place that make it illegal to ask the types of questions listed above?

2. If you were asked one of these questions in an interview how would you handle it? What response options would you have?

3. What steps might a sales organization take to help reduce the possibility that inappropriate questions are asked during job interviews?

Videos

The Motorola video case that accompanies this chapter is located in Appendix 1 at the back of the book.

Student Materials

Need a tune-up? A study guide and OneKey access code are available to aid in your review of chapter material. Your instructor may choose to have these items shrink-wrapped with your text or you may purchase them separately at www.prenhall.com/marketing.

Office DEPOT
company information

Company Facts	Career Opportunities	International	Investor Relations	Women In Business	Media Relations	Real Estate	Community Relations

Home

COMPANY INFORMATION

4 EASY WAYS TO SHOP

**Shop Online
24 hours a day:**
www.officedepot.com
(AOL Keyword: office depot)

Call 24 Hours a day:
1-888-GO-DEPOT
(1-888-463-3768)

Fax 24 Hours a day:
1-800-685-5010

Locate a Store:
1-888-GO-DEPOT
(1-888-463-3768)

Office Depot, Inc. Founded in 1986, is one of the world's largest sellers of office products and an industry leader in every distribution channel, including stores, direct mail, contract delivery, the Internet and business-to-business electronic commerce.

Terms of Use	Security Statement	Privacy Policy	Contact Us

■ *After studying this chapter, you should be able to*

1. *Identify* the major forces shaping the new Digital Age **2.** *Explain* how companies have responded to the Internet and other powerful new technologies with e-business strategies, and how these strategies have resulted in benefits to both buyers and sellers **3.** *Describe* the four major e-commerce domains **4.** *Discuss* how companies go about conducting e-commerce to profitably deliver more value to customers **5.** *Give* an overview of the promise and challenges that e-commerce presents for the future

Marketing in the Digital Age

14

ROAD MAP | Previewing the Concepts

You've come a long way on your marketing journey. You've learned that the aim of marketing is to create value *for* customers in order to capture value *from* consumers in return. So far, you've learned the fundamentals of how good marketing companies win, keep, and grow customers by understanding customer needs, designing customer-driven marketing strategies, constructing value-delivering marketing programs, and building customer and marketing partner relationships. In the final two chapters, we'll extend these fundamentals to three special areas—marketing in the digital age, global marketing, and social responsibility and marketing ethics. Although we've visited these topics regularly in each previous chapter, because of their special importance, we will focus exclusively on them here at the end of your journey. In this chapter, we look into marketing in the new digital environment. Marketing strategy and practice have undergone dramatic changes during the past decade. Major technological advances, including the explosion of the Internet, have had a major impact on buyers and the marketers who serve them. To thrive in this new digital age—even to survive—marketers must rethink their strategies and adapt them to today's new environment.

As a tune-up, consider Office Depot. Each year, Office Depot sells billions of dollars worth of office supplies through its more than 1,000 superstores around the world. But why are we talking about a traditional "brick-and-mortar" retailer like Office Depot at the start our chapter on marketing in the digital age? Instead, shouldn't we be discussing Amazon.com? Or eBay? Roll on and see.

No one sells more office products to more customers in more countries," proclaims Office Depot, the giant office-supplies retailer. Office Depot's more than 1,000 office-supply superstores rack up annual sales of $11.4 billion in more than 20 countries. But you might be surprised to learn that most of Office Depot's recent growth has not come from its traditional "brick-and-mortar" channels. Instead, it's come from the Internet. Whereas Office Depot's store sales have flattened recently, its online sales have soared, more than doubling in just the past two years. The retailer's Web unit booked $2.1 billion in online revenues last year, accounting for 18.5 percent of total sales.

All of this makes Office Depot one of the best examples of the new breed of "*click*-and-mortar" companies that now dominate Internet marketing. Office Depot expanded to the Web in 1998, and adding "clicks" to its bricks-and-mortar foundation has strengthened not just growth and profits, it has strengthened customer relationships as well. Office Depot's click-and-mortar go-to-market strategy helps ensure that every customer experiences the company's promise: "What you need. What you need to know."

The combination of online and in-store selling gives Office Depot customers anywhere, anytime access to the retailer's wares, along with piles of helpful information. "Whether it's a self-employed entrepreneur shopping online at 3 A.M., a purchasing agent dealing with a trusted sales representative, or an administrative assistant hurriedly stopping by a store at lunchtime," says the company, Office Depot now offers a full range of contact points and delivery modes. Customers can search for and buy office supplies online, 24 hours a day. They can leaf through a paper catalog and phone in or fax an order. Or they can stop by the local Office Depot superstore to browse and buy. Then, they can either pick up purchased items or simply have them delivered to their doors and desktops. Returns are easy—just call for a pickup or return items to the store.

Selling on the Web lets Office Depot build deeper, more personalized relationships with customers large and small. "Contract customers"—the 80,000 or so larger businesses that have negotiated relationships with Office Depot—enjoy customized online ordering that includes company-specific product lists and pricing. For example, companies such as General Electric or Procter & Gamble can create lists of approved office products at discount prices, and then let company departments or even individuals do their own purchasing. This reduces ordering costs, cuts through the red tape, and speeds up the ordering process for customers. At the same time, it encourages companies to use Office Depot as a sole source for office supplies.

> Since the early 1990s, Bank of America executives have been letting employees order supplies from their desktop computers, but they were using an old-fashioned system that was expensive and difficult to operate. The bankers knew that there had to be a better way, but they couldn't figure it out on their own. That's when Monica Luechtefeld, Office Depot's chief of e-commerce, came calling. She explained how the office-supply retailer could easily plug its online store into Bank of America's internal network. Bank of America would be able to set it up to recognize who had clearance to buy an executive chair or a box of pencils. And Luechtefeld offered rebates for online purchases. It was a winning pitch. Today, Bank of America orders 85 percent of its supplies online through Office Depot and is saving millions of dollars a year.

But even the smallest companies and home-office workers can enjoy customized service at OfficeDepot.com. The Web site makes purchasing easier and more convenient. For example, the site keeps lists of prior purchases, making reorders a snap. OfficeDepot.com also delivers a ton of value-added information and services to small business customers. These include free weekly Webinars, online OSHA and tax forms, and a wide range of advice on how to run a small business. For example, at tax time in early April, Office Depot provided an online seminar entitled, "IRS: What the Small Business Needs to Know." Another popular feature at OfficeDepot.com is Web Café, a series of online seminars featuring nationally known experts discussing important small business topics.

Office Depot has also formed more than two dozen online partnerships to bring additional services to small business customers. Such services range from Internet postage (with Stamps.com) and Web hosting (with Microsoft) to sales intelligence data (TrueAdvantage.com), to online incorporation for new businesses (Business Filings). For example, says Luechtefeld, "Our partnership with Business Filings provides a way for our small business customers to work smarter not harder. It underscores our commitment to offering business customers the knowledge and support to help them to continue to grow and stay on top in today's competitive market."

Says Keith Butler, vice president of Office Depot online: "It's a natural extension of the Office Depot brand to add the service component. . . . It's a beautiful fit. Our strategy is to [make OfficeDepot.com] the destination area for small business."

Importantly, Office Depot's Web operations don't detract from store sales. Instead, Office Depot has created synergy between the "clicks" and the "bricks" by carefully connecting the online and stores sides of its business. Rather than stealing sales from stores, the OfficeDepot.com site actually builds store traffic by helping customers find a local store and check stock. Customers can check online, see that an item is available, and then visit the local store to see and buy it. In return, the local store promotes the Web site through in-store kiosks. If customers don't find what they need on the shelves, they can quickly order it via the Web from the kiosk.

So, when you think about it, it's not so surprising that we're talking about Office Depot to start this chapter on marketing in the digital age. Although "click-only" Web marketers such as Amazon.com, eBay, or PriceLine.com grab most of the online attention, integrated click-and-mortar companies such as Office Depot now capture a greater share of online sales than their Internet-only competitors. No click-only or brick-only seller can match the call, click, or visit convenience and support afforded by Office Depot's click-and-mortar model.

Office Depot is now the third largest e-tailer in the world—behind Amazon.com and Dell. More than half of Office Depot's major customers now use the online network to buy everything from printer cartridges, paper clips, and push pins to PDAs, computers, and solid cherry conference tables. What has made Office Depot so successful online? "Office Depot gets it," says an e-commerce consultant. "It uses the Web to build deeper relationships with customers." And deeper customer relationships mean more business. A former Office Depot executive summarizes the company's strategy this way: "There's value if you can build a sense of community among [customers] and yourself. You're doing more than just being a provider of supplies. You're a being a friend . . . and people buy from their friends."[1]

Recent technological advances, including the widespread use of the Internet, have created what some have called a New Economy. Although there has been widespread debate in recent years about the nature of—even the existence of—such a New Economy, few would disagree that the Internet and other powerful new connecting technologies are having a dramatic impact on marketers and buyers. Many standard marketing strategies and practices of the past—mass marketing, product standardization, media advertising, store retailing, and others—were well suited to the so-called Old Economy. These strategies and practices will continue to be important in the New Economy. However, marketers will also have to develop new strategies and practices better suited to today's new environment.

In this chapter, we first describe the key forces shaping the new digital age. Then we examine how marketing strategy and practice are changing to take advantage of today's new technologies.

■ Major Forces Shaping the Digital Age

Many forces are playing a major role in reshaping the world economy, including technology, globalization, environmentalism, and others. Here we discuss four specific forces that underlie the new digital age (see Figure 14.1): digitalization and connectivity, the explosion of the Internet, new types of intermediaries, and customization and customerization.

FIGURE 14.1

Forces Shaping the Digital Age

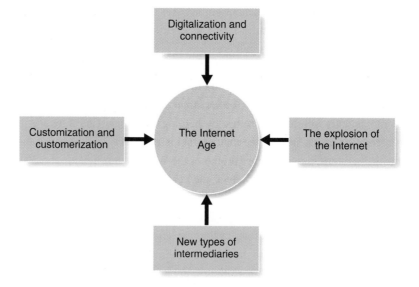

Digitalization and Connectivity

Many appliances and systems in the past—ranging from telephone systems, wristwatches, and musical recordings to industrial gauges and controls—operated on analog information. Analog information is continuously variable in response to physical stimuli. Today a growing number of appliances and systems operate on *digital information,* which comes as streams of zeros and ones, or *bits.* Text, data, sound, and images can be converted into *bit streams.* A laptop computer manipulates bits in its thousands of applications. Software consists of digital content for operating systems, games, information storage, and other applications.

For bits to flow from one appliance or location to another requires *connectivity,* a telecommunications network. Much of the world's business today is carried out over networks that connect people and companies. **Intranets** are networks that connect people within a company to each other and to the company network. **Extranets** connect a company with its suppliers, distributors, and other outside partners. And the **Internet**, a vast public web of computer networks, connects users of all types all around the world to each other and to an amazingly large "information repository." The Internet makes up one big "information highway" that can dispatch bits at incredible speeds from one location to another.

Internet Explosion

With the creation of the World Wide Web and Web browsers in 1990s, the Internet was transformed from a mere communication tool into a certifiably revolutionary technology. During the final decade of the twentieth century, the number of Internet users worldwide grew explosively. By early 2003, Internet penetration in the United States had reached 67 percent, with more than 160 million people now using the Internet. Each month, 2 million more Americans access the Internet for the first time.[2]

Although the dot-com crash in 2000 led to cutbacks in technology spending, research suggests that the growth of Internet access among the world's citizens will continue to explode. Not only are more people using the Web, they are increasingly moving faster when they get there. A recent study found that 31 percent of U.S. households with Internet access now go online through high-speed broadband connections.[3]

This explosive worldwide growth in Internet usage forms the heart of the so-called New Economy. The Internet has been *the* revolutionary technology of the new millennium, empowering consumers and businesses alike with blessings of connectivity. For nearly every New Economy innovation that has emerged during the past decade, the Internet has

Intranet

A network that connects people within a company to each other and to the company network.

Extranet

A network that connects a company with its suppliers and distributors.

Internet

A vast public web of computer networks that connects users of all types all around the world to each other and to an amazingly large "information repository."

played a starring—or at the very least a "best supporting"—role. The Internet enables consumers and companies to access and share huge amounts of information with just a few mouse clicks.

Recent studies have shown that consumers are accessing information on the Internet before making major life decisions. One in three consumers relies heavily on the Internet to gather information about choosing a school, buying a car, finding a job, dealing with a major illness, or making investment decisions. The average U.S. Internet user visits the Web 30 times a month at home and 66 times a month at work, spending more the 30 minutes per visit. As a result, to be competitive in today's new marketplace, companies must adopt Internet technology or risk being left behind.[4]

New Types of Intermediaries

New technologies have led thousands of entrepreneurs to launch Internet companies—the so-called dot-coms—in hopes of striking gold. The amazing success of early Internet-only companies, such as Amazon.com, Yahoo, eBay, Expedia, and dozens of others, struck terror in the hearts of many established manufacturers and retailers. For example, Barnes & Noble, which sold books only through retail stores, worried when Amazon grew quickly by selling books online. Toys "*R*" Us worried when eToys lured toy buyers to the Web. And even the largest travel agents began looking over their shoulders at Web travel merchants such as Expedia and Travelocity. Established store-based retailers of all kinds—from bookstores, music stores, and florists to travel agents, stockbrokers, and car dealers—began to doubt their futures as competitors sprung up selling their products and services via the Internet. They feared being *disintermediated* by the new e-tailers—being cut out by this new type of intermediary.

The formation of new types of intermediaries and new forms of channel relationships caused existing firms to reexamine how they served their markets. At first, the established *brick-and-mortar* firms—such as Staples, Barnes & Noble, and Merrill Lynch—dragged their feet hoping that the aggressive *click-only* firms would falter or disappear. Then they wised up and started their own online sales channels, becoming *click-and-mortar* competitors. Ironically, many click-and-mortar competitors have become stronger than the click-only competitors that pushed them reluctantly onto the Internet. In fact, although some click-only competitors are surviving and even prospering in today's marketplace, many once-formidable dot-coms—such as eToys, Pets.com, Garden.com, and Mothernature.com—have failed in the face of poor profitability and plunging stock values.

Customization and Customerization

The Old Economy revolved around *manufacturing companies* that focused mainly on standardizing their production, products, and business processes. They invested large sums in brand building to tout the advantages of their standardized market offerings. Through standardization and branding, manufacturers hoped to grow demand and take advantage of economies of scale. As a key to managing their assets, they set up command-and-control systems that would run their businesses like machines.

In contrast, the New Economy revolves around *information businesses*. Information has the advantages of being easy to differentiate, customize, personalize, and send at incredible speeds over networks. With rapid advances in Internet and other connecting technologies, companies have grown skilled in gathering information about individual customers and business partners (suppliers, distributors, retailers). In turn, they have become more adept at individualizing their products and services, messages, and media.

Dell Computer, for example, lets customers specify exactly what they want in their computers and delivers customer-designed units in only a few days. On its Reflect.com Web site, Procter & Gamble allows people to reflect their needs for, say, a shampoo by answering a set of questions. It then formulates a unique shampoo for each person.

Customization differs from *customerization*. Customization involves taking the initiative to customize the market offering. For example, a Levi's salesperson takes the person's

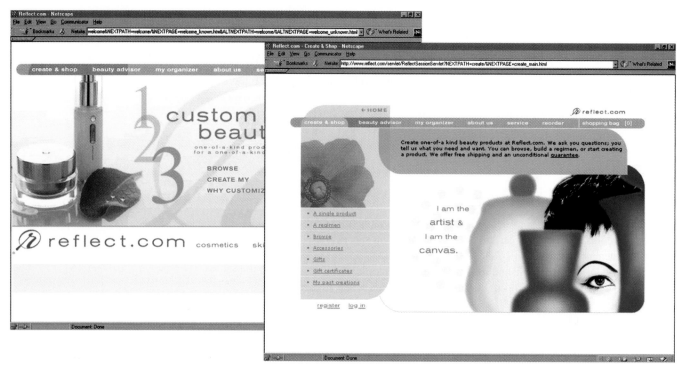

■ Customerization: At reflect.com, people formulate their own beauty products—it offers "one of a kind products for a one of a kind you." More than 650,000 people visit the site each month.

Customerization

Leaving it to individual customers to design the marketing offering—allowing customers to be *prosumers* rather than only consumers.

measurements and the company customizes the jeans at the factory. In **customerization**, the company leaves it to individual customers to design the offering. For example, jeans customers may take their own measurements and add specific features that they may want in their jeans, such as colorful patches.[5]

■ Marketing Strategy in the Digital Age

Conducting business in the new digital age will call for a new model for marketing strategy and practice. According to one strategist: "Sparked by new technologies, particularly the Internet, the corporation is undergoing a radical transformation that is nothing less than a new industrial revolution. . . . To survive and thrive in this century, managers will need to hard-wire a new set of rules into their brains. The twenty-first century corporation must adapt itself to management via the Web."[6] Suggests another, the Internet is "revolutionizing the way we think about . . . how to construct relationships with suppliers and customers, how to create value for them, and how to make money in the process; in other words, [it's] revolutionizing marketing."[7]

Some strategists envision a day when all buying and selling will involve direct electronic connections between companies and their customers. The new model has fundamentally changed customers' notions of convenience, speed, price, product information, and service. This new consumer thinking affects every business. Comparing the adoption of the Internet and other new marketing technologies to the early days of the airplane, Amazon.com CEO Jeff Bezos says, "It's the Kitty Hawk era of electronic commerce." Even those offering more cautious predictions agree that digital technologies will have a tremendous impact on future business strategies.

The fact is that today's marketing requires a mixture of Old Economy and New Economy thinking and action. Companies need to retain most of the skills and practices that have worked in the past. But they will also need to add major new competencies and practices if they hope to grow and prosper in the new environment. Marketing should play the lead role in shaping new company strategy.

E-business, E-commerce, and E-marketing in the Digital Age

E-business involves the use of electronic platforms—intranets, extranets, and the Internet—to conduct a company's business. The Internet and other technologies now help companies carry on their business faster, more accurately, and over a wider range of time and space.

Countless companies have set up Web sites to inform about and promote their products and services. Others use Web sites simply to build stronger customer relationships. For example, more than 70 percent of consumer packaged-goods manufacturers use their Web sites purely to inform and connect with consumers, rather than to sell products.

Most companies have also created intranets to help employees communicate with each other and to access information found in the company's computers. For example, some 14,000 employees regularly log on to P&G intranet, mNet, to receive training and to research marketing news from around the world.[8] Companies also set up extranets with their major suppliers and distributors to enable information exchange, orders, transactions, and payments. Companies such as Cisco, Microsoft, and Oracle run almost entirely as e-businesses, in which memos, invoices, engineering drawings, sales and marketing information—virtually everything—are exchanged over the Internet instead of on paper.[9]

E-commerce is more specific than e-business. E-business includes all electronics-based information exchanges within or between companies and customers. In contrast, e-commerce involves buying and selling processes supported by electronic means, primarily the Internet. *E-markets* are "market*spaces*," rather than physical market*places*. Sellers use e-markets to offer their products and services online. Buyers use them to search for information, identify what they want, and place orders using credit or other means of electronic payment.

E-commerce includes *e-marketing* and *e-purchasing* (*e-procurement*). **E-marketing** is the marketing side of e-commerce. It consists of company efforts to communicate about, promote, and sell products and services over the Internet. Thus, Amazon.com, Schwab.com, and Dell.com conduct e-marketing at their Web sites. The flip side of e-marketing is e-purchasing, the buying side of e-commerce. It consists of companies purchasing goods, services, and information from online suppliers.

In business-to-business buying, e-marketers and e-purchasers come together in huge e-commerce networks. For example, Global eXchange Services (GXS) operates one of the world's largest business-to-business e-commerce networks (www.gxs.com). Originally formed by General Electric and now independently owned, GXS consists of more than 100,000 trading partners in 58 countries—including giants such as General Electric, FedEx, DaimlerChrysler, JCPenney, Sara Lee, and Unilever. GXS completes some 1 billion transactions each year, accounting for $1 trillion worth of goods and services. GXS also operates the GE Global Supplier Network, one of the world's largest private marketplaces, serving a majority of GE's business units and their trading partners.[10]

E-commerce and the Internet bring many benefits to both buyers and sellers. Let's review some of these major benefits.

E-business

The use of electronic platforms—intranets, extranets, and the Internet—to conduct a company's business.

E-commerce

Buying and selling processes supported by electronic means, primarily the Internet.

E-marketing

The marketing side of e-commerce—company efforts to communicate about, promote, and sell products and services over the Internet.

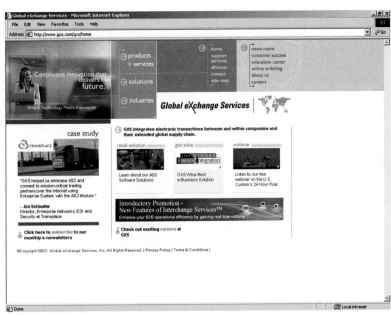

■ E-Commerce networks: Global eXchange Services (GXS) consists of more than 100,000 trading partners in 58 countries. GXS completes some 1 billion transactions each year, accounting for $1 trillion worth of goods and services.

Benefits to Buyers

Internet buying benefits both final buyers and business buyers in many ways. It can be *convenient:* Customers don't have to battle traffic, find parking spaces, and trek through stores and aisles to find and examine products. They can do comparative shopping by surfing Web sites. Web marketers never close their doors. Buying is *easy* and *private:* Customers encounter fewer buying hassles and don't have to face salespeople or open themselves up to persuasion and emotional pitches. Business buyers can learn about and buy products and services without waiting for and tying up time with salespeople.

In addition, the Internet often provides buyers with greater *product access and selection.* The world's the limit for the Web. Unrestrained by physical boundaries, cybersellers can offer an almost unlimited selection. Just compare the incredible selections offered by many Web merchants to the more meager assortments of their brick-and-mortar counterparts. For example, in books alone, Amazon.com offers a searchable selection of more than 3 million titles, 15 times more than in any physical bookstore. Web wine merchant www.wine.com carries more than 2,500 domestic and imported wines on its cybershelves, along with gourmet food items and an assortment of wine-related accessories.

Beyond a broader selection of sellers and products, e-commerce channels also give buyers access to a wealth of comparative *information,* information about companies, products, and competitors. Good sites often provide more information in more useful forms than even the most solicitous salesperson can. For example, Amazon.com offers top-10 product lists, extensive product descriptions, expert and user product reviews, and recommendations based on customers' previous purchases.

Finally, online buying is *interactive* and *immediate.* Buyers often can interact with the seller's site to create exactly the configuration of information, products, or services they desire, then order or download them on the spot. Moreover, the Internet gives consumers a greater measure of control. Like nothing else before it, the Internet has empowered consumers. These days, 27 percent of car buyers go online before showing up at a dealership, arming themselves with car and cost information. This is the new reality of consumer control.[11]

Benefits to Sellers

E-commerce also yields many benefits to sellers. First, the Internet is a powerful tool for *customer relationship building.* Because of its one-to-one, interactive nature, companies can interact online with customers to learn more about specific needs and wants. In turn, online customers can ask questions and volunteer feedback. Based on this ongoing interaction, companies can increase customer value and satisfaction through product and service refinements.

The Internet and other electronic channels can also *reduce costs* and *increase speed and efficiency.* By using the Internet to link directly to suppliers, factories, distributors, and customers, businesses such as Dell Computer and General Electric can cut costs and pass savings on to customers. E-marketers avoid the expense of maintaining a store and

■ Internet buying is easy and private: Final consumers can shop the world from home with few hassles; business buyers can learn about and obtain products and information without tying up time with salespeople.

the related costs of rent, insurance, and utilities. Because customers deal directly with sellers, e-marketing often results in lower costs and improved efficiencies for channel and logistics functions such as order processing, inventory handling, delivery, and trade promotion. Finally, communicating electronically often costs less than communicating on paper through the mail. For instance, a company can produce digital catalogs for much less than the cost of printing and mailing paper ones.

E-marketing can also offer greater *flexibility,* allowing the marketer to make ongoing adjustments to its offers and programs. For example, once a paper catalog is mailed to final consumer or business customers, the products, prices, and other catalog features are fixed until the next catalog is sent. However, an online catalog can be adjusted daily or even hourly, adapting product assortments, prices, and promotions to match changing market conditions.

Finally, the Internet is a truly *global* medium that allows buyers and sellers to click from one country to another in seconds. The GXS network provides business buyers with immediate access to suppliers in 58 countries, ranging from the United States and the United Kingdom to Hong Kong and the Philippines. A Web surfer from Paris or Istanbul can access an online L.L. Bean catalog as easily as someone living in Freeport, Maine, the direct retailer's hometown. Thus, even small e-marketers find that they have ready access to global markets.

◼▌E-Marketing Domains

The four major e-marketing domains are shown in Figure 14.2 and discussed below. They include B2C (business to consumer), B2B (business to business), C2C (consumer to consumer), and C2B (consumer to business).

B2C (Business to Consumer)

The popular press has paid the most attention to **B2C (business-to-consumer) e-commerce**—the online selling of goods and services to final consumers. Despite some gloomy predictions, online consumer buying continues to grow at a healthy rate. Last year, consumers worldwide spent more than $167 billion online. That number is expected to rise to $428 billion in 2004. The largest categories of consumer online spending include travel services, clothing, computer hardware and software, consumer electronics, books, music and video, health and beauty, home and garden, flowers and gifts, sports and fitness equipment, and toys.[12]

Online Consumers In its early days, the Internet was populated largely by pasty-faced computer nerds or young, techy, upscale male professionals. As the Web has matured, however, Internet demographics have changed significantly. Today, almost two-thirds of U.S. households surf the Internet. As more and more people find their way onto the Web, the cyberspace population is becoming more mainstream and diverse.

> Just a few years ago, the vast majority of Internet users fell predictably into the same group. They were overwhelmingly male, overwhelmingly young, overwhelmingly college educated, and overwhelmingly high-techy. How times have

B2C (business-to-consumer) e-commerce

The online selling of goods and services to final consumers.

	Targeted to consumers	Targeted to businesses
Initiated by business	B2C (business to consumer)	B2B (business to business)
Initiated by consumer	C2C (consumer to consumer)	C2B (consumer to business)

FIGURE 14.2

E-Marketing Domains

■ Online consumers: As more and more people find their way onto the Web, the online population is becoming more mainstream and diverse. The Web now offers marketers a palette of different kinds of consumers seeking different kinds of online experiences.

changed. Today, Internet users are found in all segments, even those with down-scale, late-adopting, technology-challenged families. This mixed portrait is a far cry from the old image of Net users as geeky white guys, technophiles who enjoyed hacking their way through chat rooms and bulletin boards. Since those early days, the Web community has exploded. For marketers, the Internet now presents a movable feast of different kinds of people seeking different types of online experiences. So, say farewell to the geeky white guys. The latest generation of connected Americans looks a lot more like the folks who cruise your local Wal-Mart.[13]

Thus, increasingly, the Internet provides e-marketers with access to a broad range of demographic segments. For example, one recent study found that consumers who have been buying online for more than six years have an average income exceeding $79,000. Thirty-four percent are women and 57 percent have college degrees. In contrast, consumers who've shopped online for less than one year have an average income of $52,000. About 57 percent are women and 39 percent have college degrees.[14] These days, just about everybody is logging on:

> Doral Main, a 51-year-old mother of two and office manager of a low-income property company in Oakland, CA, saves precious time by shopping the Internet for greeting cards and getaways. Her Net-newbie father, Charles, 73, goes online to buy supplies for his wood-carving hobby. Even niece Katrina, 11, finds excitement on the Web, picking gifts she wants from the Disney.com site. "It's addictive," Main says of the Internet. [Indeed,] the Web isn't mostly a hang-out for techno-nerds anymore.[15]

Growing Internet diversity continues to open new e-commerce targeting opportunities for marketers. For example, the Web now reaches consumers in all age groups. Children and teens are going online more than any other age group. Sixty-five percent of 10- to 14-year-olds and 75 percent of 14- to 17-year-olds now use the Internet.[16] Thus, these "net kids" and teen segments have attracted a host of e-marketers.

At the other end of the age spectrum, consumers aged 50 and older make up almost 20 percent of the online population. And more than 16 million Americans over the age of 65 are expected to be online by 2007. Whereas younger groups are more likely to use the Internet for entertainment and socializing, older Internet surfers go online for more serious matters. For example, 24 percent of people in this age group use the Internet for investment purposes, compared with only 3 percent of those 25 to 29. Thus, older Netizens make an attractive market for Web businesses, ranging from florists and automotive retailers to travel sites and financial services providers.[17]

Internet consumers differ from traditional offline consumers in their approaches to buying and in their responses to marketing. The exchange process via the Internet has become more customer initiated and customer controlled. People who use the Internet place greater value on information and tend to respond negatively to messages aimed only at selling. Traditional marketing targets a somewhat passive audience. In contrast, e-marketing targets people who actively select which Web sites they will visit and what marketing information they will receive about which products and under what conditions. Thus, the new world of e-commerce requires new marketing approaches.

B2C Web Sites Consumers can find a Web site for buying almost anything. The Internet is most useful for products and services when the shopper seeks greater ordering convenience or lower costs. The Internet also provides great value to buyers looking for information about differences in product features and value. However, consumers find the Internet less useful when buying products that must be touched or examined in advance. Still, even here there are exceptions. For example, who would have thought that people would order expensive computers from Dell or Gateway without seeing and trying them first?

People now go online to order a wide range of goods—clothing from Gap or L.L. Bean, books or electronics from Amazon.com, furniture from Ethan Allen, major appliances from Sears, flowers from Calyx & Corolla, or even home mortgages from Quicken Loans.

■ Calyx & Corolla, "The Flower Lover's Flower Company," sells fresh flowers directly to consumers. Customers can order bouquets or plants from a color catalog by phoning 1-800-877-0998 or place orders at the C&C Web site at www.calyxandcorolla.com. Orders go immediately to one of 25 growers in the C&C network, who pick and package the flowers and ship orders via FedEx. When the flowers arrive, they are fresher

 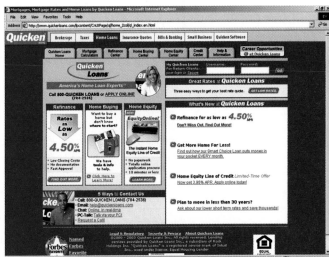

■ B2C Web sites: People now go online to order a wide range of goods and services—from fresh flowers to home mortgages.

and last about 10 days longer than flowers ordered from store-based retailers. Calyx and Corolla credits its success to a sophisticated information system and strong alliances with FedEx and the growers.

■ At Quicken Loans (www.quickenloans.com), prospective borrowers receive a high-tech, high-touch, one-stop mortgage shopping experience. At the site, customers can research a wide variety of home-financing and refinancing options, apply for a mortgage, and receive quick loan approval—all without leaving the comfort and security of their homes. The site provides useful interactive tools that help borrowers decide how much house they can afford, whether to rent or buy, whether to refinance a current mortgage, the economics of fixing up their current homes rather than moving, and much more. Customers can receive advice by phone or by chatting online with one of 1,700 mortgage experts and sign up for later e-mail rate updates. Quicken Loans originated more than $15 billion in mortgage loans in 2003.[18]

B2B (Business to Business)

B2B (business-to-business) e-commerce
Firms using B2B trading networks, auction sites, spot exchanges, online product catalogs, barter sites, and other online resources to reach new customers, serve current customers more effectively, and obtain buying efficiencies and better prices.

Open trading exchanges
Huge e-marketspaces in which B2B buyers and sellers find each other online, share information, and complete transactions efficiently.

Although the popular press has given the most attention to business-to-consumer (B2C) Web sites, consumer goods sales via the Web are dwarfed by **B2B (business-to-business) e-commerce**. In 2003, worldwide B2B e-commerce reached almost $4 trillion, compared with just $282 billion in 2000. One study estimates that by 2005, more than 500,000 enterprises will use e-commerce as buyers, sellers, or both. Another estimates that as much as one-third of all U.S. B2B spending will occur online by 2006.[19] These firms are using B2B trading networks, auction sites, spot exchanges, online product catalogs, barter sites, and other online resources to reach new customers, serve current customers more effectively, and obtain buying efficiencies and better prices.

Most major business-to-business marketers now offer product information, customer purchasing, and customer support services online. For example, corporate buyers can visit Sun Microsystems' Web site (www.sun.com), select detailed descriptions of Sun's products and solutions, request sales and service information, and interact with staff members. Some major companies conduct almost all of their business on the Web. Networking equipment and software maker Cisco Systems takes more than 80 percent of its orders over the Internet.

Some B2B e-commerce takes place in **open trading exchanges**—huge e-marketspaces in which buyers and sellers find each other online, share information, and complete transactions efficiently. Here is an example of an open B2B exchange:

> *Covisint* is the auto industry's public exchange. Created jointly by the Big Three auto makers—DaimlerChrysler, Ford, and General Motors—the site now connects a total of 11 auto makers with some 5,000 suppliers worldwide. Covisint handled more than $50 billion in auto-parts orders last year. Auto maker purchasing managers submit parts orders to Covisint's auction engineers, who in turn set up special auctions. "These auctions are for millions," says one auction engineer. "We're not messing around here with $10 at a time." In its biggest single auction ever, Covisint conducted a 4-day auction in which DaimlerChrysler purchased about $2.6 billion in auto parts. Compare that with eBay, the top consumer auction Web site, which recently reported gross merchandise sales of some $2.4 billion for the entire fourth quarter.[20]

The wisdom of experience.
The energy of youth.
Limitless potential.

covisint

Covisint, combining the heritage of the automotive industry and the promise of Internet technology to open a new window of possibility. Covisint is a global automotive business-to-business exchange developed by DaimlerChrysler, Ford Motor Company, General Motors, Nissan and Renault.

Here, connection increases organization. Collaboration transcends geography. Speed breeds efficiency. Knowledge is exchanged securely. This time, everyone gets to grow.

covisint.com

■ Trading networks: Covisint is the auto industry's public exchange. Created jointly by the Big Three auto makers, the site now connects 11 auto makers with some 5,000 suppliers worldwide. The exchange handled more than $50 billion in auto-parts orders last year.

Despite the use of such e-marketspaces, one Internet research firm estimates that 93 percent of all B2B e-commerce is conducted through private sites. Increasingly, online sellers are setting up their own **private trading networks**. Open trading exchanges such as Covisint facilitate transactions between a wide range of online buyers and sellers. In contrast, private trading exchanges link a particular seller with its own trading partners.

Private trading networks (PTNs)

B2B trading networks that link a particular seller with its own trading partners.

Rather than simply completing transactions, private exchanges give sellers greater control over product presentation and allow them to build deeper relationships with buyers and sellers by providing value-added services. As an example, take Trane Company, a maker of air-conditioning and heating systems:

> Since last autumn, Trane . . . has been red-hot with the business-to-business Internet crowd. Each of the horde of B2B [open trading] exchanges targeting the construction industry wants Trane to join. "Construction.com, MyPlant.com, MyFacility.com—we get up to five calls a week," says James A. Bierkamp, head of Trane's e-business unit. But after some consideration, Bierkamp did not see what any of those [third-party] e-marketplaces could offer that his company couldn't do itself. So in May, Trane rolled out its own private exchange, which allows its 5,000 dealers to browse, buy equipment, schedule deliveries, and process warranties. The site lets Trane operate with greater efficiency and trim processing costs—without losing control of the presentation of its brand name or running the risks of rubbing elbows with competitors in an open exchange. "Why let another party get between us and our customers?" asks Bierkamp.[21]

C2C (Consumer to Consumer)

Much **C2C (consumer-to-consumer) e-commerce** and communication occurs on the Web between interested parties over a wide range of products and subjects. In some cases, the Internet provides an excellent means by which consumers can buy or exchange goods or information directly with one another. For example, eBay, Amazon.com Auctions, and other auction sites offer popular marketspaces for displaying and selling almost anything, from art and antiques, coins and stamps, and jewelry to computers and consumer electronics. EBay's C2C online trading community of more than 42 million registered users worldwide transacted nearly $15 billion in trades last year. On any given day, the company's Web site lists more than 16 million items up for auction in more than 27,000 categories. EBay also maintains auction sites in several foreign countries, including Japan, the United Kingdom, and Germany.[22] Such C2C sites give people access to much larger audiences than the local flea market or newspaper classifieds (which, by the way, are now also going online).

C2C (consumer-to-consumer) e-commerce

Online exchanges of goods and information between final consumers.

In other cases, C2C involves interchanges of information through forums and Internet newsgroups that appeal to specific special-interest groups. Such activities may be organized for commercial or noncommercial purposes. *Forums* are discussion groups located on commercial online services such as AOL and CompuServe. A forum may take the form of a library, a "chat room" for real-time message exchanges, or even a classified ad directory. For example, AOL boasts some 14,000 chat rooms, which account for a third of its members' online time. It also provides "buddy lists," which alert members when friends are online, allowing them to exchange instant messages.

■ C2C e-commerce: Last year, EBay's C2C online trading community of more than 42 million registered users worldwide transacted nearly $15 billion in trades.

Newsgroups are the Internet version of forums. However, such groups are limited to people posting and reading messages on a specified topic, rather than managing libraries or conferencing. Internet users can participate in newsgroups without subscribing. There are tens of thousands of newsgroups dealing with every imaginable topic, from healthful eating and caring for your bonsai tree to collecting antique cars or exchanging views on the latest soap opera happenings.

C2C means that online visitors don't just consume product information—increasingly, they create it. They join Internet interest groups to share information, with the result that "word of Web" is joining "word of mouth" as an important buying influence. Word about good companies and products travels fast. Word about bad companies and products travels even faster. Many sites, including eComplaints.com, ConsumerReview.com, and BadDealings.com, have cropped up to provide consumers a forum in which to air complaints and share information about product and service experiences.

C2B (Consumer to Business)

C2B (consumer-to-business) e-commerce

Online exchanges in which consumers search out sellers, learn about their offers, and initiate purchases, sometimes even driving transaction terms.

The final e-commerce domain is **C2B (consumer-to-business) e-commerce**. Thanks to the Internet, today's consumers are finding it easier to communicate with companies. Most companies now invite prospects and customers to send in suggestions and questions via company Web sites. Beyond this, rather than waiting for an invitation, consumers can search out sellers on the Web, learn about their offers, initiate purchases, and give feedback. Using the Web, consumers can even drive transactions with businesses, rather than the other way around. For example, using Priceline.com, would-be buyers bid for airline tickets, hotel rooms, rental cars, and even home mortgages, leaving the sellers to decide whether to accept their offers.

Consumers can also use Web sites such as PlanetFeedback.com to ask questions, offer suggestions, lodge complaints, or deliver compliments to companies. The site provides letter templates for consumers to use based on their moods and reasons for contacting the company. The site then forwards the letters to the customer service manager at each company and helps to obtain a response. Last year, PlanetFeedback.com forwarded more than 330,000 consumer letters composed on their site. Not all of the letters were complaints. One-quarter of them offered compliments, while another one-fifth made suggestions for product or service improvements.[23]

■▌ Conducting E-Commerce

Companies of all types are now engaged in e-commerce. In this section, we first discuss different types of e-marketers shown in Figure 14.3. Then, we examine how companies go about conducting marketing online.

Click-Only Versus Click-and-Mortar E-Marketers

The Internet gave birth to a new species of e-marketers—the *click-only* dot-coms—which operate only online without any brick-and-mortar market presence. In addition, most traditional *brick-and-mortar* companies have now added e-marketing operations, transforming themselves into *click-and-mortar* competitors.

Click-only companies

The so-called dot-coms, which operate only online, without any brick-and-mortar market presence.

Click-Only Companies **Click-only companies** come in many shapes and sizes. They include *e-tailers,* dot-coms that sell products and services directly to final buyers via the Internet. Familiar e-tailers include Amazon.com, Expedia, and Wine.com. The click-only group also includes *search engines and portals* such as Google, Yahoo, and Excite, which began as search engines and later added services such as news, weather, stock reports, entertainment, and storefronts hoping to become the first port of entry to the Internet.

Internets service providers (ISPs) such as AOL, CompuServe, and Earthlink are click-only companies that provide Internet and e-mail connections for a fee. *Transaction sites,*

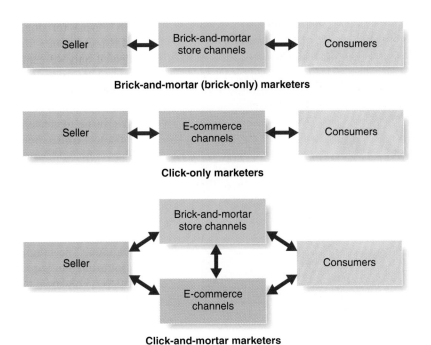

FIGURE 14.3

Types of e-Marketers

such as auction site eBay, take commissions for transactions conducted on their sites. Various *content sites,* such as *New York Times* on the Web (www.nytimes.com), ESPN.com, and Encyclopedia Britannica Online, provide financial, research, and other information. Finally, *enabler sites* provide the hardware and software that enable Internet communication and commerce.

The hype surrounding such click-only Web businesses reached astronomical levels during the "dot-com gold rush" of the late 1990s, when avid investors drove dot-com stock prices to dizzying heights. However, the investing frenzy collapsed in the year 2000, and many high-flying, overvalued dot-coms came crashing back to Earth. Even some of the strongest and most attractive e-tailers—eToys.com, Pets.com, Furniture.com, Mothernature.com, Garden.com, Living.com, and ValueAmerica.com—filed for bankruptcy. Survivors such as Amazon.com and Priceline.com saw their stock values plunge. Notes one analyst, "Once teeming with thousands of vibrant new ideas, the consumer Net [began] to look like the mall at midnight."[24]

Dot-coms failed for many reasons. Some rushed into the market without proper research or planning. Often, their primary goal was simply to launch an initial public offering (IPO) while the market was hot. Many relied too heavily on spin and hype instead of developing sound marketing strategies. Flush with investors' cash, the dot-coms spent lavishly offline on mass marketing in an effort to establish brand identities and attract customers to their sites. For example, during the fourth quarter of 1999, the average e-tailer spent an astounding 109 percent of sales on marketing and advertising.[25] The dot-coms tended to devote too much effort to acquiring new customers instead of building loyalty and purchase frequency among current customers. As one industry watcher concluded, many dot-coms failed because they "had dumb-as-dirt business models, not because the Internet lacks the power to enchant and delight customers in ways hitherto unimaginable."[26]

Pets.com, the now defunct online pet store, provides a good example of how many dot-coms failed to understand their marketplaces.

From the start, Pets.com tried to force its way to online success with unbeatable low prices and heavy marketing hype. In the end, however, neither worked. During its first year of operation, Pets.com lost $61.8 million on a meager $5.8 million in sales. During that time, it paid $13.4 million for the goods it sold for just $5.8 million. Thus, for every dollar that Pets.com paid suppliers

■ Like many other dot-coms, Pets.com never did figure out how to make money on the Web. Following the "dot-com meltdown," the once-bold e-tailer retired its popular Sock Puppet spokesdog and quietly closed its cyberdoors.

such as Purina for dog food and United Parcel Service for shipping, it collected only 43 cents from its customers. Moreover, by early spring of 1999, Pets.com had burned more than $21 million on marketing and advertising to create an identity and entice pet owners to its site. Its branding campaign centered on the wildly popular Sock Puppet character, a white dog with black patches. Sock Puppet even made an appearance in Macy's Thanksgiving Day Parade in New York as a 36-foot-high balloon. The singing mascot was also featured in Super Bowl ads that cost Pets.com more than $2 million. At first, investors bought into Pet.com's "landgrab" strategy—investing heavily to stake out an early share, and then finding ways later to make a profit. However, even though it attracted 570,000 customers, Pets.com never did figure out how to make money in a low-margin business with high shipping costs. Its stock price slid from a February 1999 high of $14 to a dismal 22 cents by the end of 2000. In early 2001, the once-bold e-tailer retired Sock Puppet and quietly closed its cyberdoors.[27]

At the same time, many click-only dot-coms are surviving and even prospering in today's marketspace. Of those that survived the crash, 50 percent were profitable by the end of last year. However, for many dot-coms, including Internet giants such as Amazon.com, the Web is still not a moneymaking proposition. Companies engaging in e-commerce need to describe to their investors how they will eventually make profits. They need to define a revenue and profit model. Table 14.1 shows that a dot-com's revenues may come from any of several sources.

Click-and-Mortar Companies   At first, many established companies moved quickly to open Web sites providing information about their companies and products. However, most resisted adding e-commerce to their sites. They worried that this would produce *channel conflict*—that selling their products or services online would be competing with their offline retailers and agents. For example, Hewlett-Packard feared that its retailers would drop HP's computers if the company sold the same computers directly online. Merrill Lynch hesitated to introduce online stock trading to compete with E*Trade, Charles Schwab, and other online brokerages, fearing that its own brokers would rebel. Even store-based bookseller Barnes & Noble delayed opening its online site to challenge Amazon.com.

These companies struggled with the question of how to conduct online sales without cannibalizing the sales of their own stores, resellers, or agents. However, they soon realized that the risks of losing business to online competitors were even greater than the risks of angering channel partners. If they didn't cannibalize these sales, online competitors soon would. Thus, most established brick-and-mortar companies are now prospering as **click-and-mortar companies**.

Most click-and-mortar marketers have found ways to resolve channel conflicts. For example, Gibson Guitars found that although its dealers were outraged when it tried to sell guitars directly to consumers, the dealers didn't object to direct sales of accessories such as guitar strings and parts. Liberty Mutual asks its online customers whether they

Click-and-mortar companies
Traditional brick-and-mortar companies that have added e-marketing to their operations.

TABLE 14.1   Sources of E-Commerce Revenue

Product and service sales income	Many e-commerce companies draw a good portion of their revenues from markups on goods and services they sell online.
Advertising income	Sales of online ad space can provide a major source of revenue. Google sells ad space adjacent to its search results, linked to key search words.
Sponsorship income	A dot-com can solicit sponsors for some of its content and collect sponsorship fees to help cover its costs.
Alliance income	Online companies can invite business partners to share costs in setting up a Web site and offer them free advertising on the site.
Membership and subscription income	Web marketers can charge subscription fees for use of their site. Many online newspapers (*Wall Street Journal* and *Financial Times*) require subscription fees for their online services. Auto-By-Tel receives income from selling subscriptions to auto dealers who want to receive hot car buyer leads.
Profile income	Web sites that have built databases containing the profiles of particular target groups may be able to sell these profiles if they get permission first. However, ethical and legal codes govern the use and sale of such customer information.
Transaction commissions and fees	Some dot-coms charge commission fees on transactions between other parties who exchange goods on their Web sites. For example, eBay puts buyers in touch with sellers and takes from a 1.25 percent to a 5 percent commission on each transaction.
Market research and information fees	Companies can charge for special market information or intelligence. For example, NewsLibrary charges a dollar or two to download copies of archived news stories. LifeQuote provides insurance buyers with price comparisons from approximately 50 different life insurance companies, then collects a commission of 50 percent of the first year's premium from the company chosen by the consumer.
Referral income	Companies can collect revenue by referring customers to others. Edmunds receives a "finder's fee" every time a customer fills out an Auto-By-Tel form at its Edmunds.com Web site, regardless of whether a deal is completed.

prefer to buy directly or through a financial adviser. It then refers interested customers and information about their needs to advisers, providing channel partners with a good source of new business. Avon worried that direct online sales might cannibalize the business of its Avon ladies, who had developed close relationships with their customers. Fortunately, Avon's research showed little overlap between existing customers and potential Web customers. Avon shared this finding with the reps and then moved into online marketing. As an added bonus for the reps, Avon also offered to help them set up their own Web sites.

Despite potential channel conflict issues, many click-and-mortar companies are now having more online success than their click-only competitors. In fact, in one study of the top 50 retail sites, ranked by the number of unique visitors, 56 percent were click-and-mortar retailers, whereas 44 percent were Internet-only retailers.[28]

What gives the click-and-mortar companies an advantage? Established companies such as Charles Schwab, Office Depot, and Gap have known and trusted brand names and greater financial resources. They have large customer bases, deeper industry knowledge and experience, and good relationships with key suppliers. By combining online marketing and established brick-and-mortar operations, they can offer customers more options. For example, consumers can choose the convenience and assortment of 24-hour-a-day online shopping, the more personal and hands-on experience of in-store shopping, or both. Customers can buy merchandise online, then easily return unwanted goods to a nearby store. For example, those wanting to do business with Charles Schwab can call a Schwab agent on the phone, go online to the company's Web site, or visit the local Schwab investment center. This lets Schwab issue a powerful invitation in its advertising: "Call, click, or visit Charles Schwab."

■ Click-and-mortar marketing: Those wanting to do business with Schwab can call a Schwab agent on the phone, go online to the company's Web site, or visit the local Schwab branch office. This lets Schwab issue a powerful invitation in its advertising: "Call, click, or visit Schwab Investments."

SPEED BUMP

Linking the Concepts

Pause here and cool your engine for a bit. Think about the relative advantages and disadvantages of *click-only*, *brick-and-mortar only*, and *click-and-mortar* retailers.

- Visit the Amazon.com Web site. Search for a specific book or DVD—perhaps one that's not too well known—and go through the buying process.
- Now visit www.bn.com and shop for the same book or video. Then visit a Barnes & Noble store and shop for the item there.
- What advantages does Amazon.com have over Barnes & Noble? What disadvantages? How does your local independent book store, with its store-only operations, fare against these two competitors?

Setting Up an E-Marketing Presence

Clearly all companies need to consider moving into e-marketing. Companies can conduct e-marketing in any of the four ways shown in Figure 14.4: creating a Web site, placing ads online, setting up or participating in Web communities, or using online e-mail or Webcasting.

Creating a Web Site For most companies, the first step in conducting e-marketing is to create a Web site. However, beyond simply creating a Web site, marketers must design an attractive site and find ways to get consumers to visit the site, stay around, and come back often.

Types of Web Sites. Web sites vary greatly in purpose and content. The most basic type is a **corporate Web site**. These sites are designed to build customer goodwill and to supplement other sales channels, rather than to sell the company's products directly. For example, you can't buy ice cream at benjerrys.com, but you can learn all about Ben & Jerry's company philosophy, products, and locations. Or you can send a free eCard to a friend, pick a great dessert recipe, subscribe to the Chunk Mail newsletter, or while away time in the Online Games area, playing Scooper Challenge or Virtual Checkers.

Corporate Web sites typically offer a rich variety of information and other features in an effort to answer customer questions, build closer customer relationships, and generate excitement about the company. They generally provide information about the company's history, its mission and philosophy, and the products and services that it offers. They might also tell about current events, company personnel, financial performance, and employment opportunities. Most corporate Web sites also provide entertainment features to attract and hold visitors. Finally, the site might also provide opportunities for customers to ask questions or make comments through e-mail before leaving the site.

Other companies create a **marketing Web site**. These sites engage consumers in an interaction that will move them closer to a direct purchase or other marketing outcome. Such sites might include a catalog, shopping tips, and promotional features such as coupons, sales events, or contests. For example, visitors to SonyStyle.com can search through dozens of categories of Sony products, review detailed features and specifications lists for specific items, read expert product reviews, and check out the latest hot deals. They can place an order for the desired Sony products online and pay by credit card, all with a few mouse clicks. Companies aggressively promote their marketing Web sites in offline print and broadcast advertising and through "banner-to-site" ads that pop up on other Web sites.

Corporate Web site
A Web site designed to build customer goodwill and to supplement other sales channels, rather than to sell the company's products directly.

Marketing Web site
A Web site that engages consumers in interactions that will move them closer to a direct purchase or other marketing outcome.

FIGURE 14.4

Setting Up for e-Marketing

Toyota operates a marketing Web site at www.toyota.com. Once a potential customer clicks in, the car maker wastes no time trying to turn the inquiry into a sale. The site offers plenty of useful information and a garage full of interactive selling features, such as detailed descriptions of current Toyota models and information on dealer locations and services, complete with maps and dealer Web links. Visitors who want to go further can use the Shop@Toyota feature to choose a Toyota, select equipment, and price it, then contact a dealer and even apply for credit. Or they fill out an online order form (supplying name, address, phone number, and e-mail address) for brochures and a free, interactive CD-ROM that shows off the features of Toyota models. The chances are good that before the CD-ROM arrives, a local dealer will call to invite the prospect in for a test drive. Toyota's Web site has now replaced its 800 number as the number one source of customer leads.

B2B marketers also make good use of marketing Web sites. For example, customers visiting GE Plastics' Web site can draw on more than 1,500 pages of information to get answers about the company's products anytime and from anywhere in the world. FedEx's Web site (www.fedex.com) allows customers to schedule their own shipments, request package pickup, and track their packages in transit.

Designing Attractive Web Sites. Creating a Web site is one thing; getting people to *visit* the site is another. The key is to create enough value and excitement to get consumers to come to the site, stick around, and come back again.

A recent survey of fervent online surfers shows that people's online expectations have skyrocketed over the past few years. Today's Web users are quick to abandon any Web site that doesn't measure up. "Whether people are online for work reasons or for personal reasons," says the chairman of the firm that ran the survey, "if a Web site doesn't meet their expectations, two-thirds say they don't return—now or ever. They'll visit you and leave and you'll never know. We call it the Internet death penalty."[29]

This means that companies must constantly update their sites to keep them current, fresh, and exciting. Doing so involves time and expense, but the expense is necessary if the e-marketer wishes to cut through the increasing online clutter. In addition, many online marketers spend heavily on good old-fashioned advertising and other offline marketing avenues to attract visitors to their sites. Says one analyst, "The reality today is you can't build a brand simply on the Internet. You have to go offline."[30]

For some types of products, attracting visitors is easy. Consumers buying new cars, computers, or financial services will be open to information and marketing initiatives from sellers. Marketers of lower-involvement products, however, may face a difficult challenge in attracting Web site visitors. As one veteran notes, "If you're shopping for a computer and you see a banner that says, 'We've ranked the top 12 computers to purchase,' you're going to click on the banner. [But] what kind of banner could encourage any consumer to visit dentalfloss.com?"[31]

For such low-interest products, the company can create a corporate Web site to answer customer questions, build goodwill and excitement, supplement selling efforts through other channels, and collect customer feedback. For example, although Kraft Food's LifeSavers Candystand Web site doesn't sell candy, it does generate a great deal of consumer excitement and sales support:

> The highly entertaining LifeSavers Candystand.com Web site, teeming with free video games, endless sweepstakes, and sampling offers, has cast a fresh face on a brand that kid consumers once perceived as a stodgy adult confection. Visitors to the site—mostly children and teenagers—are not just passing through. They're clicking the mouse for an average 27-minute stay playing Foul Shot Shootout, Stingin' Red Ants Run, Arctic 3D Racer, and dozens of other arcade-style games. All the while, they're soaking in a LifeSavers aura swirling with information about products. "Our philosophy is to create an exciting online experience that reflects the fun and quality associated with the LifeSavers brands," says the company's manager of new media. "For the production cost of about two television spots we have a marketing vehicle that lives 24 hours a day, 7 days a week, 365 days a year." While Candystand.com has not directly sold a single roll of candy, the buzz generated by the site makes it an ideal vehicle for offering consumers their first glimpse of a new product, usually with an offer to get free samples by mail. In addition, LifeSavers reps use the site as sales leverage to help seal distribution deals when they talk with retailers. And the site offers LifeSavers an efficient channel for gathering customer feedback. Its "What Do You Think?" feature has generated hundreds of thousands of responses since the site launched six years ago. "It's instant communication that we pass along directly to our brand people," says the manager. Comments collected from the Web site have resulted in improved packaging of one LifeSavers product and the resurrection of the abandoned flavor of another. Candystand is now the number-one consumer package-goods Web site, attracting 2.3 million unique visitors a month, more than twice the traffic of the number-two site.[32]

A key challenge is designing a Web site that is attractive on first view and interesting enough to encourage repeat visits. The early text-based Web sites have largely been replaced in recent years by graphically sophisticated Web sites that provide text, sound, and animation (for examples, see www.sonystyle.com, www.can.com or www.nike.com). To attract new visitors and to encourage revisits, suggests one expert, e-marketers should pay close attention to the seven *C*s of effective Web site design[33]:

- *Context:* the site's layout and design

- *Content:* the text, pictures, sound, and video that the Web site contains

- *Community:* the ways that the site enables user-to-user communication

- *Customization:* the site's ability to tailor itself to different users or to allow users to personalize the site

- *Communication:* the ways the site enables site-to-user, user-to-site, or two-way communication

- *Connection:* the degree to which the site is linked to other sites

- *Commerce:* the site's capabilities to enable commercial transactions

At the very least, a Web site should be easy to use and physically attractive. Beyond this, however, Web sites must also be interesting, useful, and challenging. Ultimately, it's the value of the site's *content* that will attract visitors, get them to stay longer, and bring them back for more. Effective Web sites contain deep and useful information, interactive tools that help buyers find and evaluate products of interest, links to other related sites, changing promotional offers, and entertaining features that lend relevant excitement.

For example, in addition to convenient online purchasing, Clinique.com offers in-depth information about cosmetics, a library of beauty tips, a computer for determining the buyer's skin type, advice from visiting experts, a bulletin board, a bridal guide, a directory of new products, and pricing information. Burpee.com provides aspiring gardeners with everything they need to make this year's garden the best ever. Besides selling seeds and plants by the thousands, the site offers an incredible wealth of information resources, including a Garden Wizard (to help new gardeners pick the best plants for specific sun and soil conditions), the Burpee Garden School (online classes about plants and plant care), an archive of relevant service articles, and a chance to subscribe to an e-mail newsletter containing timely tips and gardening secrets.

From time to time, a company needs to reassess its Web site's attractiveness and usefulness. One way is to invite the opinion of site-design experts. But a better way is to have users themselves evaluate what they like and dislike about the site. For example, Otis Elevator Company's Web site serves 20,000 registered customers, among them architects, general contractors, building managers, and others interested in elevators. The site, offered in 52 countries and 26 languages, provides a wealth of helpful information, from modernization, maintenance, and safety information to drawings of various Otis models. Otis uses two sources of information to gauge satisfaction with its complex site. First, in an effort to detect potential problems, it tracks hits, time spent on the site, frequently visited pages, and the sequence of pages the customer visits. Second, it conducts quarterly phone surveys with 200 customers each in half the countries in which Otis does business. Such customer satisfaction tracking has resulted in many site improvements. For example, Otis found that customers in other countries were having trouble linking to the page that would let them buy an elevator online. Now, the link is easier to find. Some customers were finding it hard to locate a local Otis office, so the company added an Office Locator feature.[34]

■ An effective Web site: The Burpee.com site is full of useful information, useful tools, and entertaining features that lend excitement. It provides aspiring gardeners with a wealth or resources, including the Burpee Garden School and a Garden Wizard to help them pick the best plants for specific conditions.

Placing Ads and Promotions Online   E-marketers can use **online advertising** to build their Internet brands or to attract visitors to their Web sites. Here, we discuss forms of online advertising and promotion and their future.

Forms of Online Advertising and Promotion.   Online ads pop up while Internet users are surfing online. Such ads include *banner ads* and *tickers* (banners that move across the screen). A Web user or America Online subscriber who is looking up airline schedules or fares might find a flashing banner on the screen exclaiming, "Rent a car from Alamo and get up to 2 days free!" To attract visitors to its own Web site, Toyota sponsors Web banner ads on other sites, ranging from ESPN SportZone (www.espn.com) to Parent Soup (www.parentsoup.com). Advertisers pay as much as $100,000 to post a banner ad atop ESPN.com's homepage for 24 hours.[35]

Other online ad formats include *skyscrapers* (tall, skinny ads at the side of a Web page) and *rectangles* (boxes that are much larger than a banner). *Interstitials* are online ads that pop up between changes on a Web site. Visitors to www.msnbc.com who visit the site's sports area might suddenly be viewing a separate window hawking wireless video cameras. Ads for Johnson & Johnson's Tylenol headache reliever pop up on brokers' Web sites whenever the stock market falls by 100 points or more.

Online advertising
Advertising that appears while consumers are surfing the Web, including banner and ticker ads, interstitials, skyscrapers, and other forms.

Content sponsorships are another form of Internet promotion. Many companies gain name exposure on the Internet by sponsoring special content on various Web sites, such as news or financial information. For example, Advil sponsors ESPN SportZone's Injury Report and General Mills sponsors an area on AOL called Quick Meals for Kids. The sponsor pays for showing the content and, in turn, receives recognition as the provider of the particular service on the Web site. Sponsorships are best placed in carefully targeted sites, where they can offer relevant information or service to the audience.

E-marketers can also go online with *microsites,* limited areas on the Web managed and paid for by an external company. For example, an insurance company might create a microsite on a car-buying site, offering insurance advice for car buyers and at the same time offering good insurance deals. Internet companies can also develop alliances and affiliate programs in which they work with other online companies to "advertise" each other. AOL has created many successful alliances with other companies and mentions their names on its site. Amazon.com has more than 350,000 affiliates who post Amazon.com banners on their Web sites.

Finally, online marketers use **viral marketing**, the Internet version of word-of-mouth marketing. Viral marketing involves creating an e-mail message or other marketing event that is so infectious that customers will want to pass it along to their friends. Because customers pass the message or promotion along to others, viral marketing can be very inexpensive. And when the information comes from a friend, the recipient is much more likely to open and read it. "The idea is to get your customers to do your marketing for you," notes a viral marketing expert. Consider these examples[36]:

> Seeking ways to get teenage girls to check out its Clean and Clear skin-care products, Johnson & Johnson created a pop-up microsite from which teens could "send a talking postcard to your friend." The site helped visitors design an e-greeting card, choosing decorations such as animated flowers or messages such as "Best Friends 4ever." Users were also offered a phone number to dictate a short voice message. Friends receiving the e-mail message heard the recording through their computer's speakers. As soon as they played the message, they were invited to click on a button called "Skin analyzer," linking them to Clean and Clear's main Web site.

Viral marketing
The Internet version of word-of-mouth marketing—e-mail messages or other marketing events that are so infectious that customers will want to pass them along to friends.

■ Gillette used viral marketing to introduce the three-bladed Venus razor for women, greatly expanding the audience reached by its "Reveal the Goddess in You" truck tour and beach-site promotions.

Gillette used viral marketing to introduce the three-bladed Venus razor for women. To reach college students, Gillette designed a truck that traveled around the Florida spring-break circuit, parking daily near a beach. Women were invited to come in and get some aromatherapy, learn about Venus, enter a "Celebrate the Goddess in You" sweepstakes, and make a digital greeting card with a picture of themselves enjoying the beach. The viral part came when they e-mailed the digital cards to friends. The e-mailed messages automatically included a chance for friends to enter the sweepstakes themselves. If e-mail recipients entered the contest, they saw a pitch for the Venus razor. Some 20 percent of the entries came from the viral-marketing cards, greatly expanding the audience reached by the beach-site promotions.

Viral marketing can also work well for B2B marketers. For example, to improve customer relationships, Hewlett-Packard recently sent tailored e-mail newsletters to customers who registered online. The newsletters contained information about optimizing the performance of HP products and services. Now that was good, but here's the best part: The newsletters also featured a button that let customers forward the newsletters to friends or colleagues. By clicking the button, customers entered a Web site where they could type in the friend's e-mail address and a comment, then hit Send. The system inserted the message above the newsletter and e-mailed the whole thing to the friend. New recipients were then asked if they'd like to receive future HP newsletters themselves. In this textbook case of viral marketing, Hewlett-Packard inexpensively met its goal of driving consumers to its Web site and ultimately increasing sales. "For those on our original e-mail list, the click-through rate was 10 to 15 percent," says an HP executive. "For those who received it from a friend or colleague, it was between 25 and 40 percent."[37]

The Future of Online Advertising. Online advertising serves a useful purpose, especially as a supplement to other marketing efforts. However, the Internet will not soon rival the major television and print media. Many marketers still question the value of Internet advertising as an effective tool. Costs are reasonable compared with those of other advertising media, but Web surfers can easily ignore such advertising and often do. As a result, Web advertising plays only a minor role in most promotion mixes. Last year, online advertising spending amounted to just $6.6 billion, 4 percent of the total spent offline.[38]

Still, online advertising is playing an increasingly important role in the marketing mixes of many advertisers. Recent studies by the Interactive Advertising Bureau suggest that online advertising should be as much as 10 to 15 percent of the overall media mix in low-involvement product categories such as packaged goods. Kimberly-Clark found that increasing the levels of online advertising boosted the impact of the ad campaign for its Kleenex SoftPack line[39]:

> Kimberly-Clark was spending 75 percent of its SoftPack budget on TV, 23 percent on print, and just 2 percent online. However, TV ads only reach about 42 percent of Kleenex's target audience. By boosting its online spending to more than 10 percent, Kimberly supplemented the light reach of TV and complemented its magazine advertising. The combination of print and online advertising helped raise brand awareness for SoftPack among its target audience from 34.7 percent to 42.7 percent; brand image from 35 percent to 41.8 percent; trial intent from 43.9 percent to 55.7 percent, and purchase intent from 24.2 to 34.0 percent. "It was surprising how impactful the lift on some of the brand [measures] were," says one Kimberly-Clark advertising executive.

Some Web sites, such as Google, have been very successful in creating effective online advertising processes and environments (see Marketing at Work 14.1). Companies themselves are also finding more effective forms and uses for Web advertising. They are taking advantage of new technologies to create bolder, higher-impact online ads. For example, the use of rich-media ads—ads that move across the screen or appear with full motion video and audio—is soaring. Delta Airlines recently showcased one such ad on

Marketing at Work | 14.1

"We Love You, Google Users"—and Advertisers, Too!

When you think back to the early dot-com boom, you probably think of brash, fast-growing start-ups led by offbeat, young entrepreneurs offering unique work environments to attract creative and talented employees. Google, the Web search services provider, is no different. Founded in September 1998 by Sergey Brin and Larry Page, then both 25 years old, Google got its start in a rented garage, complete with a washer, dryer, and hot tub.

Since then, it has grown from 3 employees to nearly 1,000. But Google still offers a relaxed and friendly environment to woo and keep the best employees. Working at the Googleplex (the company's headquarters) comes complete with setting your own hours, backrubs from a company masseuse, a self-playing ebony grand piano with Muppet-theme sheet music, and even baking bread from scratch if the mood strikes you.

Although this start-up story mirrors that of previous dot-coms, for Google there is one big difference. Whereas other dot-coms have struggled, Google is growing at a phenomenal rate: some 20 percent a *month*. More than 365 million unique visitors use Google's search engine each month to search 3 billion Web pages. They spend nearly 13 million hours a month searching on Google; second-place Yahoo! logs less than half that figure. Google users make more than 200 million queries each day—2000 per second during peak hours. Half of the queries originate from outside of the United States, where Google offers search services in 88 different languages. Even more amazing, most of these searches are answered within a quarter of a second.

Perhaps more surprising, unlike most other dot-coms, Google turns a profit. In fact, Google is three times more profitable than eBay was at the same stage in its development. What's behind this incredible success? Google's technology is an important part of the equation. Page and Brin started the company to promote their PageRank search technology, which has revolutionized Internet searching. The Google search engine returns results that are usually more reliable and more useful than those of other search engines.

Beyond this revolutionary technology, Google has triumphed because it has focused heavily on helping users search. Unlike Yahoo! and other competitors, Google opted not to offer e-mail, shopping, and other services. Its Web site promises "a laser-like focus on finding the right answer for each and every inquiry." In fact, the name of the company is a play on the word *googol,* a mathematical term for a 1 followed by 100 zeros. It's a very large number. Google chose the name to reflect its mission to organize and make accessible the immense amount of information available on the Web. By focusing only on Internet searching, Google positions itself as "the World's Best Search Engine—accurate and easy to use." Users rave about Google's simple, search-only home page, uncluttered with news reports or banner ads.

The best part is that Google's extraordinary services are free to users. But how, then, does Google make money? About half of Google's revenues come from contracts with corporate partners to provide search services for their own Internet and intranet sites. Today, more than 130 companies in 30 different countries rely on Google's WebSearch and SiteSearch technologies to power the search services on their Web sites.

These partners include companies such as Yahoo!, the *Washington Post,* Cisco, Red Hat, Palm, Nextel, Virgin, Netscape, Sony, and Cingular Wireless.

The other half of Google's revenues come from advertising sales. By attracting the largest online search audience in the world, Google has made itself a very attractive advertising medium. Here's how it works. Through constant data mining, Google determines which search terms are most popular. It then approaches companies who sell in those categories and offers them space for sponsored ad messages and links for a fee. Advertisers then bid on a search term. The highest bidder gets the highest position on the page. Then, when someone searches Google for a topic related to the sponsor's product or service, a tasteful ad box appears at the top or side of the Google results page, containing a short ad message and links to the sponsor's Web site.

Try it yourself. Go to the Google site (www.google.com), type in a search word or phrase, and see what advertiser messages and links appear. For example, if you search "Disneyland," you'll see ads and links at the top of the search list for online travel services Expedia and Orbitz. The ads promise "Save up to 70% on Disneyland Hotels with Expedia!" and "Incredible deals on Disneyland at Orbitz!" Search "barbeque grills" and you're greeted with "Shop Sears for brand name grills and all your barbeque needs" and a link to www.sears.com. Side sponsor boxes link you to a half-dozen other merchants, including GasGrillsDirect.com, grillstuff.com, woodstoves.com, and flaminggrills.com. A search of "outdoor gear" yields "Find the best selection at REI.com" with side boxes for five other

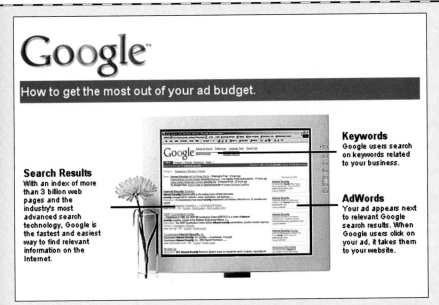

With world's largest online search audience, Google has become a very attractive advertising medium. It's highly targeted ads reach users when they are already searching for related information.

outfitters. Search "Rolling Stones" and you'll see ads and links for TicketsNow.com, stagefronttickets.com, ticketcity.com, and primetimetickets.com. You get the idea.

The advertising on Google is subtle, not like the pop-up ads that make Web-viewing on other sites like swatting flies. In fact, the ads are usually useful. Google "wants everything that appears on the page to be related to your search," says one reporter, "so a car company can't buy an ad to appear with your search for 'perfume.'" Sheryl Sandberg, one of Google's top advertising executives, loves it when people tell her that they didn't even realize that Google runs ads. "It means their advertising experience is not encroaching on their search experience," she says. "The goal is to make the ads as useful as the search results."

Whereas other forms of online advertising may produce questionable results

for advertisers, advertising on Google delivers. Google's highly targeted ads reach relevant users when they are already searching for information. Moreover, Google's matching process allows advertisers to tailor their ad messages or sites closely to users' search inquiries. As a result, "click-through" rates for the typical ad on Google are four to five times those of traditional banner ads.

Google works hard to make advertising on its site effective. Google's marketers assess each potential advertiser, pinpointing those they think will benefit from advertising on the site and those who won't. It proactively monitors ads to ensure their success. "People are looking for results," says a Google marketer. "When you spend money with us you can actually measure what the return is on investment by measuring the response on our site." Google even lets advertisers know when their ads

aren't working. One small business owner was shocked when he received an e-mail from Google suggesting that he pull his ads. "Google sent me an e-mail telling me what I was already thinking—that advertising with them was a waste of my money," he says.

This unique approach to selling advertising space has resulted in loyalty and satisfaction among the Google clients who do stay. Online advertisers, such as Acura, Expedia, Eddie Bauer, Ernst & Young, and REI, number more than 150,000 worldwide and regularly rank Google as their top online advertising choice. This, in turn, has fueled the company's financial success.

Almost from its first day, Google has been something of a cultural phenomenon. Within three months of starting up, it was picked as one of *PC Magazine's* top 100 Web sites. Google's success stems from its fervent passion to bring value to both the users who flock to its site and the advertisers wanting to reach them. In the company's lobby in Mountain View, California, a six-foot trophy case brims with awards, including a 2000 Webby (the Internet's equivalent of an Oscar), which cofounders Brin and Page accepted wearing hockey uniforms and rollerblades. Their shared acceptance speech was simply, "We love you, Google users." They might have added, "And you, too, Google advertisers."

Sources: Quotes and other information from Betsy Cummings, "Beating the Odds," *Sales and Marketing Management*, March 2002, pp. 24–28; Fred Vogelstein, "Looking for a Dot-Com Winner? Search No Further," *Fortune*, May 27, 2002, pp. 65–68; Leslie Walker, "In Trivial Pursuit of Shoppers," *The Washington Post*, April 6, 2003, p. H7; Keith Hammonds, "Growth Search," *Fast Company*, April 2003, pp. 74–81; David Kirkpatrick, "In the Hands of Geeks, Web Advertising Actually Works," *Fortune*, April 14, 2003, p. 388; and information gathered from www.google.com, September 2003.

several sports sites. The ad featured a baseball player, who appeared in the corner of the screen hitting a baseball. A pop-up appears on the screen with the sound and image of the ball breaking through a window. The ad ends with the message: "That ball's outta here. And so are you." It turns out to be an ad inviting fans to win a trip to see their favorite team play in another city. Such ads demand attention. "The creativity that's afforded right now [by rich media] is really astounding," says an online advertising executive. It makes advertising "a little more sexy, fun, and something to try."[40]

Web communities

Web sites where members can congregate online and exchange views on issues of common interest.

Creating or Participating in Web Communities   The popularity of forums and newsgroups has resulted in a rash of commercially sponsored Web sites called **Web communities**, which take advantage of the C2C properties of the Internet. Such sites allow members to congregate online and exchange views on issues of common interest. They are the cyberspace equivalent to a Starbucks coffeehouse, a place where everybody knows your e-mail address.

■ Web communities: iVillage.com, a Web community for women, provides an ideal environment for Web ads of companies such as Procter & Gamble, Kimberly Clark, Avon, Hallmark, and others.

For example, iVillage.com is a Web community in which women can exchange views and obtain information, support, and solutions on families, food, fitness, relationships, relaxation, home and garden, news and issues, or just about any other topic. The site draws 393 million page views per month, putting it in a league with magazines such as *Cosmopolitan, Glamour,* and *Vogue.* Another example is MyFamily.com, which aspires to be the largest and most active online community in the world for families. Its goal is to "connect families with their histories and one another." It provides free, private family Web sites on which family members can connect online to hold family discussions, share family news, create online family photo albums, maintain a calendar of family events, share family history information, jointly build family trees, and buy gifts for family members quickly and easily. "People talk about forming communities on the Internet," says co-founder Paul Allen. "Well, the oldest community is the family."[41]

Visitors to these Internet neighborhoods develop a strong sense of community. Such communities are attractive to advertisers because they draw consumers with common interests and well-defined demographics. Moreover, cyberhood consumers visit frequently and stay online longer, increasing the chance of meaningful exposure to the advertiser's message. For example, iVillage provides an ideal environment for the Web ads of companies such as Procter & Gamble, Kimberly-Clark, Avon, Clairol, Hallmark, and others who target women consumers. And MyFamily.com hosts The Shops@MyFamily, in which companies such as Disney, Kodak, Hallmark, Compaq, Hewlett-Packard, and Microsoft advertise and sell their family-oriented products.

Web communities can be either social or work related. One successful work-related community is @griculture Online. This site offers commodity prices, recent farm news, and chat rooms of all types. Rural surfers can visit the Electronic Coffee Shop and pick up the latest down-on-the-farm joke or join a hot discussion on controlling soybean cyst nematodes. @griculture Online has been highly successful, attracting as many as 5 million hits per month. As such, it provides an excellent advertising environment for such companies as John Deere, Chevy Truck, and Farm Bureau, all of which sponsor featured areas on the site.[42]

Using E-Mail   E-mail has exploded onto the scene as an important e-marketing tool. A recent study of ad, brand, and marketing managers found that nearly half of all the B2B and B2C companies surveyed use e-mail marketing to reach consumers. Another study found that almost 80 percent of consumers with Internet access see ads in e-mails at least once a day. Jupiter Media Metrix estimates that companies will be spending $7.3 billion annually on e-mail marketing by 2005, up from just $164 million in 1999.[43]

To compete effectively in this ever-more-cluttered e-mail environment, marketers are designing "enriched" e-mail messages—animated, interactive, and personalized messages full of streaming audio and video. Then, they are targeting these attention-grabbers more carefully to those who want them and will act on them.

As with other types of online marketing, companies must be careful that they don't cause resentment among Internet users who are already overloaded with "junk e-mail." The recent explosion of **spam**—unsolicited, unwanted commercial e-mail messages that clog up our e-mailboxes—has produced consumer frustration and anger (see Marketing at Work 14.2). E-mail marketers walk a fine line between adding value for consumers and being intrusive. Companies must beware of irritating consumers by sending unwanted e-mail to promote their products. Netiquette, the unwritten rules that guide Internet etiquette, suggests that marketers should ask customers for permission to e-mail marketing pitches. They should also tell recipients how to "opt in" or "opt out" of e-mail promotions at any time. This approach, known as permission-based marketing, has become a standard model for e-mail marketing.

Spam
Unsolicited, unwanted commercial e-mail messages.

◼◢ The Promise and Challenges of E-Commerce

E-commerce continues to offer both great promise and many challenges for the future. We now look at both the promises of e-commerce and the "darker side" of the Web.

The Continuing Promise of E-Commerce

Its most ardent apostles still envision a time when the Internet and e-commerce will replace magazines, newspapers, and even stores as sources for information and buying. For most, however, such "dot-com fever" has cooled, and a more realistic view has emerged. "It's time for Act II in the Internet revolution," suggests one analyst. "The first act belonged to dot-coms with big visions and small bank accounts. Now the [stage has been] taken by big companies that move their factories, warehouses, and customers onto the Web."[44]

To be sure, online marketing will become a successful business model for some companies, Internet firms such as Amazon.com, eBay, Expedia, and Earthlink and direct-marketing companies such as Dell Computer. Michael Dell's goal is one day "to have *all* customers conduct *all* transactions on the Internet, globally." However, for most companies, online marketing will remain just one important approach to the marketplace that works alongside other approaches in a fully integrated marketing mix.

Eventually, as companies become more adept at integrating e-commerce with their everyday strategy and tactics, the "e" will fall away from e-business or e-marketing. "The key question is not whether to deploy Internet technology—companies have no choice if they want to stay competitive—but how to deploy it," says business strategist Michael Porter. He continues: "We need to move away from the rhetoric about 'Internet industries,' 'e-business strategies,' and a 'new economy,' and see the Internet for what it is . . . a powerful set of tools that can be used, wisely or unwisely, in almost any industry and as part of almost any strategy."[45]

The Web's Darker Side

Along with its considerable promise, there is a "darker side" to Internet marketing. Here we examine two major sets of concerns: Internet profitability and legal and ethical issues.

Internet Profitability One major concern is profitability, especially for B2C dot-coms. Surprisingly few B2C Internet companies are profitable. Of the 456 Internet companies that went public since 1994, only 11 percent are still in business and profitable. Of

Marketing at Work | 14.2

E-Mail Marketing: The Hot New Marketing Medium or Pestering Millions for Profit?

E-mail is *the* hot new marketing medium. In ever-larger numbers, e-mail ads are popping onto our computer screens and filling up our e-mailboxes. And they're no longer just the quiet, plain-text messages of old. The new breed of in-your-face e-mail ad is designed to command your attention—loaded with glitzy features such as animation, interactive links, color photos, streaming video, and personalized audio messages.

But there's a dark side to the exploding use of e-mail marketing. The biggest problem? *Spam*—the deluge of unsolicited, unwanted commercial messages that now clutter up our e-mailboxes and our lives. Spam now accounts for an inbox-clogging 47 percent of the estimated 73 billion e-mails sent daily throughout the world, up from only 16 percent a year ago. If you're a typical e-mail user, the amount of spam you receive each day has nearly doubled, from 3.7 to 6.2 messages per day. America Online estimates that the amount of spam aimed at its customers has doubled in just the past six months and now approaches 70 percent of all messages received. AOL blocks some 2 billion spam messages sent to its subscribers each day.

Despite these dismal statistics, when used properly, e-mail can be the ultimate direct marketing medium. Blue-chip marketers such as Amazon.com, Schwab, Dell, L.L. Bean, Office Depot, and others use it regularly, and with great success. E-mail lets these marketers send highly-targeted, tightly personalized, relationship-building messages to consumers who actually *want* to receive them, at a cost of only a few cents per contact. E-mail ads really can command attention and get customers to act. ITM Strategies, a sales and marketing research firm, estimates that well-designed e-mail campaigns typically achieve 10 percent to 15 percent click-through rates. That's pretty good when compared with the 0.5 percent to 2 percent average response rates for traditional direct mail.

Consider Nintendo, a natural for e-mail based marketing:

Young computer-savvy gaming fans actually look forward to Nintendo's monthly e-mail newsletter for gaming tips and for announcements of exciting new games. When the company launched its Star Fox Adventure game in 2002, it created an intensive e-mail campaign in the weeks before and after the product launch. The campaign included a variety of messages targeting potential customers. "Each message has a different look and feel, and . . . that builds excitement for Nintendo," notes an executive working on the account. The response? More than a third of all recipients opened the e-mails. And they did more than just glance at the messages: click-through rates averaged more than 10 percent. Nearly two-thirds of those opening the message watched its 30-second streaming video in its entirety. Nintendo also gathered insightful customer data from the 20 percent of people who completed an embedded survey. Although the company feared that the barrage of messages might create "list fatigue" and irritate customers, the campaign received very few negative responses. The unsubscribe rate was under 1 percent.

However, while carefully designed e-mails may be effective, and may even be welcomed by selected consumers, critics argue that most commercial e-mail messages amount to little more than annoying "junk mail" to the rest of us. Too many bulk e-mailers blast out lowest-common-

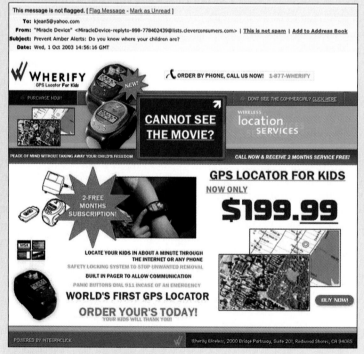

E-mail marketing: The new breed of in-your-face e-mail ads, loaded with glitzy features, commands attention and gets customers to act. But there's a dark side. Spam is ruining the rich potential of e-mail for companies that want to use it as a legitimate marketing tool.

denominator mailings to anyone with an e-mail address. There is no customization—no relationship building. Everyone gets the same hyperventilated messages. Moreover, too often, the spam comes from shady sources and pitches objectionable products—everything from Viagra and body enhancement products to pornography and questionable investments. And the messages are often sent from less-than-reputable marketers. Of the 11 million spam messages studied recently by the Federal Trade Commission, 44 percent came from phony addresses.

At least in part, it's e-mail economics that are to blame for our overflowing inboxes. Sending e-mail is so easy and so inexpensive that almost anyone can afford to do it, even at paltry response rates. For example, Data Resource Consulting, Inc. pumps out 720 million e-mails every year. That makes the company sound like a big-city direct marketing behemoth. But in reality, it's a home-based business run by a 41-year-old single mother, Laura Betterly, in Dunedin, Florida. Dubbed the Spam Queen by the *Wall Street Journal*, Betterly provides a good example of why spam is multiplying so quickly.

The sun was setting on . . . Betterly's six-bedroom house as she reviewed a pair of outgoing e-mail messages one last time. Satisfied, she moved her cursor to the "send" line icon and clicked. "It's that simple," [she] said triumphantly, swiping her palms. She had just dispatched e-mail messages to 500,000 strangers. Half saw the subject line: "Don't miss your chance to win a Lexus RX300." The other half saw: "Win a trip to NASCAR!" The company [Betterly] runs from her home sends out as many as 60 million such messages a month. [This e-mass mail captured only a 0.013 percent response rate—only 65 responses—generating $40 in revenue for her company.] But Betterly has discovered that she can make a profit [on] as few as 100 responses for every 10 million messages sent. She figures her income will be $200,000 this year.

The problem, of course, is that it's far easier for Betterly to hit the "send" button on an e-mail to a million strangers than it is for the beleaguered recipients to hit the delete key on all those messages. One analyst calculated that the recipient cost of Betterly's e-mails far exceeded the $40 in revenue that it produced for her.

Assume that the average time getting rid of the junk was two seconds, and that the average recipient values his time at the mean wage paid in the U.S., which is around $14 per hour, or $0.0039 per second. This implies a total cost, incurred by uninterested recipients, of 500,000 times two seconds times $.0039 per second, which gives $3,900. And such dollar calculations don't begin to account for the shear frustration of having to deal with all those many junk messages.

The impact of spam on consumers and businesses is alarming. According to one estimate, dealing with all the junk e-mail is costing U.S. organizations $13 billion a year. AOL and other Internet service providers are being inundated with complaints from subscribers. And spam is ruining the rich potential of e-mail for companies that want to use it as a legitimate marketing tool.

So, what's a marketer to do? Permission-based e-mail is one solution. Companies can send e-mails only to customers who "opt in"—those who grant permission in advance. They can let consumers specify what types of messages they'd like to receive. Financial services firms such as Charles Schwab use configurable e-mail systems that let customers choose what they want to get. Others, such as Yahoo or Amazon.com, include long lists of opt-in boxes for different categories of marketing material. Although such companies also send targeted promotions, they limit the volume of such e-mails. Moreover, every message gives customers an easy way to "opt out" of future messages.

Permission-based marketing ensures that e-mails are sent only to customers who want them. Still, marketers must

be careful not to abuse the privilege. There's a fine line between legitimate e-mail marketing and spam. Companies that cross the line will quickly learn that "opting out" is only a click away for disgruntled consumers.

If marketers themselves don't deal with the spam issues, others will. For example, more than two dozen states have banned spam in some fashion, and many consumer advocates are urging Congress or the Federal Trade Commission to enact aggressive "do not spam" laws. Anti-spam software makers and Internet service providers have also taken steps to help consumers to automatically remove spam. Solutions include elaborate spam filters, keyword recognition algorithms, communities of spam hunters, and spammer blacklists. Unfortunately, such solutions too often filter out the good e-mails with the bad.

Some companies attack such anti-spam regulations and actions as a violation of free-speech, or as bad for consumer choice and bad for business. But most legitimate e-mail marketers welcome such controls. Left unchecked, they reason, spam will make legitimate e-mail marketing less effective, or even impossible. "Long term, if the industry cannot deal with spam," says Joe Barrett, AOL's senior vice-president for network operations, "it's going to destroy e-mail."

Sources: Excerpts and other information from Saul Hansell, "Internet Is Losing Ground in Battle Against Spam," *New York Times*, April 22, 2003, p. A1; Matt Haig, "Building Brands Beyond the Internet," *Brand Strategy*, March 2002, p. 12; Mylene Mangalindan "Spam Queen: For Bulk E-Mailer, Pestering Millions Offers Path to Profit," *Wall Street Journal*, November 13, 2002, p. A1; "Dear Laura: You're Going to Have Mail," *Wall Street Journal*, November 26, 2002, p. A25; Mike France, "Needed Now: Laws to Can Spam," *Business Week*, October 7, 2002, p. 100; David Brosse, "Strategies for Successful Online Marketing," *Bank Marketing International*, November 2002, p. 9(2); Heidi Anderson, "Nintendo Case Study: Rules Are Made to Be Broken," *E-Mail Marketing Case Studies*, March 6, 2003, accessed online at http://www.clickz.com; Nikki Swartz, "Spam Costs Businesses $13 Billion Annually," *Information Management Journal*, March/April 2003, p. 9; Lorraine Woellert, "Slamming Spam," *Business Week*, May 12, 2003, p. 40; and David Kirkpatrick, "Taking Back the Net," *Fortune*, September 29, 2003, pp. 117–122.

those still in business and not acquired by another company, only 40 percent are profitable. One analysts calls this "the Web's pretty little secret."[46]

One problem is that, although expanding rapidly, online marketing still reaches only a limited marketspace. The Web audience is becoming more mainstream, but online users still tend to be somewhat more upscale and better educated than the general population. This makes the Internet ideal for marketing financial services, travel services, computer hardware and software, and certain other classes of products. However, it makes online marketing less effective for selling mainstream products. Moreover, in most product categories, users still do more window browsing and product research than actual buying.

Finally, the Internet offers millions of Web sites and a staggering volume of information. Thus, navigating the Internet can be frustrating, confusing, and time consuming for consumers. In this chaotic and cluttered environment, many Web ads and sites go unnoticed or unopened. Even when noticed, marketers will find it difficult to hold consumer attention. One study found that a site must capture Web surfers' attention within eight seconds or lose them to another site. That leaves very little time for marketers to promote and sell their goods.

Legal and Ethical Issues

From a broader societal viewpoint, Internet marketing practices have raised a number of ethical and legal questions. In previous sections, we've touched on some of the negatives associated with the Internet, such as unwanted e-mail and the annoyance of pop-up ads. Here we examine concerns about consumer online privacy and security and other legal and ethical issues.

Online Privacy and Security. *Online privacy* is perhaps the number one e-commerce concern. Most online marketers have become skilled at collecting and analyzing detailed consumer information. Marketers can easily track Web site visitors, and many consumers who participate in Web site activities provide extensive personal information. This may leave consumers open to information abuse if companies make unauthorized use of the information in marketing their products or exchanging databases with other companies. Many consumers and policy makers worry that marketers have stepped over the line and are violating consumers' right to privacy. A recent survey found that 69 percent of Americans agree that "consumers have lost all control over how personal information is collected and used by companies." Another study found that 7 of 10 consumers are concerned about online privacy.[47]

Many consumers also worry about *online security*. They fear that unscrupulous snoopers will eavesdrop on their online transactions or intercept their credit card numbers and make unauthorized purchases. In turn, companies doing business online fear that others will use the Internet to invade their computer systems for the purposes of commercial espionage or even sabotage. There appears to be an ongoing competition between the technology of Internet security systems and the sophistication of those seeking to break them.

In response to such online privacy and security concerns, the federal government has considered numerous legislative actions to regulate how Web operators obtain and use consumer information. Congress is considering an online privacy bill that would require online service providers and commercial Web sites to get customers' permission before they disclose important personal information. That would include financial, medical, ethnic, religious, and political information, along with Social Security data and sexual orientation. The bill would also direct the Federal Trade Commission to enact rules imposing similar requirements on both online and offline data collection. "I think this subject of privacy is a ticking time bomb, . . . because people do not want their personally identifiable medical and financial information spread all over every place," says one senator. "A doctor needs to know what ails you. But those ailments, your mortgage banker doesn't need to know that."[48]

Of special concern are the privacy rights of children. In 1998, the Federal Trade Commission surveyed 212 Web sites directed toward children. It found that 89 percent of the sites collected personal information from children. However, 46 percent of them did not include any disclosure of their collection and use of such information. As a result,

Congress passed the Children's Online Privacy Protection Act, which requires Web site operators targeting children to post privacy policies on their sites. They must also notify parents about the information they're gathering and obtain parental consent before collecting personal information from children under age 13.[49]

Many companies have responded to consumer privacy and security concerns with actions of their own. Companies such as Expedia and E-Loan have conducted voluntary audits of their privacy and security policies. Other companies have gone even further.

Royal Bank of Canada (RBC) relies on trust to build long-term customer relationships. The company's research suggests that 7 percent of a customer's buying decision relates to privacy issues. As a result, RBC has used progressive privacy practices to differentiate itself from competitors. During the past two years, the company has taken a number of internal actions to ensure that customers are protected (such as privacy risk self-assessments and internal audit reviews of privacy protection practices). It has also implemented a variety of programs to show customers that it strives to meet or exceed government-mandated privacy regulations. For example, RBC provides clients, at no cost, with a one-year subscripton to security and privacy software to help them feel more comfortable with their online experiences and to promote safe computing. It also provides clients with relevant information about its privacy and security practices on its public Web site.[50]

■ Online privacy and security: Royal Bank of Canada (RBC) has used a progressive privacy policy to differentiate itself from competitors. "At RBC Royal Bank, we're dedicated to protecting your privacy and securing your personal information."

Still others are taking a broad, industrywide approach. Founded in 1996, TRUSTe is a nonprofit, self-regulatory organization that works with a number of large corporate sponsors, including Microsoft, AT&T, and Intuit, to audit companies' privacy and security measures and help consumers navigate the Web safely. According to the company's Web site, "TRUSTe believes that an environment of mutual trust and openness will help make and keep the Internet a free, comfortable, and richly diverse community for everyone." To reassure consumers, the company lends it "trustmark" stamp of approval to Web sites that meet its privacy and security standards.[51]

Still, examples of companies aggressively protecting their customers' personal information are too few and far between. The costs of inaction could be great. Jupiter Media Metrix forecasts that in 2006 almost $25 billion in revenues will be lost as a result of consumers' privacy concerns. Moreover, they predict, online sales that year would be as much as 25 percent higher if consumers' concerns were adequately addressed.[52] Finally, if Web marketers don't act to curb privacy abuses, legislators most probably will.

Other Legal and Ethical Issues. Beyond issues of online privacy and security, Consumers are also concerned about *Internet fraud,* including identity theft, investment fraud, and financial scams. Last year alone, the federal Internet Fraud Complaint Center (IFCC) received nearly 50,000 complaints related to Internet fraud. Such fraud costs businesses and consumers more than $22 billion each year.[53] The IFCC reports that nearly 43 percent of reported incidents involve online auctions. Fraudulent activities are most often conducted through Web pages and e-mail, with 70 percent involving e-mail transactions.[54]

There are also concerns about *segmentation and discrimination* on the Internet. Some social critics and policy makers worry about the so-called *digital divide*—the gap between those who have access to the latest Internet and information technologies and those who don't. They are concerned that in this information age, not having equal access to information can be an economic and social handicap. They point out that 80 percent of American families with annual household incomes over $75,000 are online, compared with only 25 percent of the poorest U.S. families. Internationally, in most African countries, less than 1 percent of the population is online.[55] This leaves poorer people less informed about products, services, and prices. Some people consider the digital divide to be a national crisis; others see it as an overstated nonissue.

A final Internet marketing concern is that of *access by vulnerable or unauthorized groups*. For example, marketers of adult-oriented materials have found it difficult to restrict access by minors. In a more specific example, a while back, sellers using eBay.com found themselves the victims of a 14-year-old boy who'd bid on and purchased more than $3 million worth of high-priced antiques and rare artworks on the site. eBay has a strict policy against bidding by anyone under age 18 but works largely on the honor system. Unfortunately, this honor system did little to prevent the teenager from taking a cyberspace joyride.[56]

Despite these challenges, companies large and small are quickly integrating online marketing into their marketing strategies and mixes. As it continues to grow, online marketing will prove to be a powerful tool for building customer relationships, improving sales, communicating company and product information, and delivering products and services more efficiently and effectively.

REST STOP:
Reviewing the Concepts

In the first two chapters, you discovered the fundamentals of marketing and marketing strategy. In this chapter, you learned about some major changes in the marketing landscape that are having an impact on marketing practice. Recent technological advances have created a new digital age. To thrive in this new environment, marketers will have to add some Internet thinking to their strategies and tactics. This chapter introduces the forces shaping the new Internet environment and how marketers are adapting. In the next chapter, we'll take a look at other forces and factors affecting the complex and changing marketing environment.

1. Identify the major forces shaping the Digital Age.

Four major forces underlie the digital age: digitalization and connectivity, the explosion of the Internet, new types of intermediaries, and customization and customerization. Much of today's business operates on digital information, which flows through connected networks. Intranets, extranets, and the Internet now connect people and companies with each other and with important information. The Internet has grown explosively to become *the* revolutionary technology of the new millennium, empowering consumers and businesses alike with the blessings of connectivity.

The Internet and other new technologies have changed the ways that companies serve their markets. New Internet marketers and channel relationships have arisen to replace some types of traditional marketers. The new technologies are also helping marketers to tailor their offers effectively to targeted customers or even to help customers customerize their own marketing offers. Finally, the New Economy technologies are blurring the boundaries between industries, allowing companies to pursue opportunities that lie at the convergence of two or more industries.

2. Explain how companies have responded to the Internet and other powerful new technologies with e-business strategies, and how these strategies have resulted in benefits to both buyers and sellers.

Conducting business in the New Economy will call for a new model of marketing strategy and practice. Companies need to retain most of the skills and practices that have worked in the past. However, they must also add major new competencies and practices if they hope to grow and prosper in the New Economy. E-business is the use of electronic platforms to conduct a company's business. E-commerce involves buying and selling processes supported by electronic means, primarily the Internet. It includes e-marketing (the selling side of e-commerce) and e-purchasing (the buying side of e-commerce).

E-commerce benefits both buyers and sellers. For buyers, e-commerce makes buying convenient and private, provides greater product access and selection, and makes available a wealth of product and buying information. It is interactive and immediate and gives the consumer a greater measure of control over the buying process. For sellers, e-commerce is a powerful tool for building customer relationships. It also increases the sellers' speed and efficiency, helping to reduce selling costs.

E-commerce also offers great flexibility and better access to global markets.

3. Describe the four major e-commerce domains.

Companies can practice e-commerce in any or all of four domains. B2C (business-to-consumer) e-commerce is initiated by businesses and targets final consumers. Despite recent setbacks following the "dot-com gold rush" of the late 1990s, B2C e-commerce continues to grow at a healthy rate. Although online consumers are still somewhat higher in income and more technology oriented than traditional buyers, the cyberspace population is becoming much more mainstream and diverse. This growing diversity opens up new e-commerce targeting opportunities for marketers. Today, consumers can buy almost anything on the Web.

B2B (business-to-business) e-commerce dwarfs B2C e-commerce. Most businesses today operate Web sites or use B2B trading networks, auction sites, spot exchanges, online product catalogs, barter sites, or other online resources to reach new customers, serve current customers more effectively, and obtain buying efficiencies and better prices. Business buyers and sellers meet in huge marketspaces—or open trading networks—to share information and complete transactions efficiently. Or, they set up private trading networks that link them with their own trading partners.

Through C2C (consumer-to-consumer) e-commerce, consumers can buy or exchange goods and information directly from or with one another. Examples include online auction sites, forums, and Internet newsgroups. Finally, through C2B (consumer-to-business) e-commerce, consumers are now finding it easier to search out sellers on the Web, learn about their products and services, and initiate purchases. Using the Web, customers can even drive transactions with business, rather than the other way around.

4. Discuss how companies can go about conducting e-commerce to profitably deliver more value to customers.

Companies of all types are now engaged in e-commerce. The Internet gave birth to the *click-only* dot-coms, which operate only online. In addition, many traditional brick-and-mortar companies have now added e-marketing operations, transforming themselves into *click-and-mortar* competitors. Many click-and-mortar companies are now having more online success than their click-only competitors.

Companies can conduct e-marketing in any of four ways: creating a Web site, placing ads and promotions online, setting up or participating in Web communities, or using online e-mail or Webcasting. The first step typically is to set up a Web site. Corporate Web sites are designed to build customer goodwill and to supplement other sales channels, rather than to sell the company's products directly. Marketing Web sites engage consumers in an interaction that will move them closer to a direct purchase or other marketing outcome. Beyond simply setting up a site, companies must make their sites engaging, easy to use, and useful in order to attract visitors, hold them, and bring them back again.

E-marketers can use various forms of online advertising to build their Internet brands or to attract visitors to their Web sites. Beyond online advertising, other forms of online marketing include content sponsorships, microsites, and viral marketing, the Internet version of word-of-mouth marketing. Online marketers can also participate in Web communities, which take advantage of the C2C properties of the Web. Finally, e-mail marketing has become a hot new e-marketing tool for both B2C and B2B marketers.

5. Give an overview of the promise and challenges that e-commerce presents for the future.

E-commerce continues to offer great promise for the future. For most companies, online marketing will become an important part of a fully integrated marketing mix. For others, it will be the major means by which they serve the market. Eventually, the "e" will fall away from e-business or e-marketing as companies become more adept at integrating e-commerce with their everyday strategy and tactics. However, e-commerce also faces many challenges. One challenge is Web profitability—surprisingly few companies are using the Web profitably. The other challenge concerns legal and ethical issues—issues of online privacy and security, Internet fraud, and the Digital Divide. Despite these challenges, companies large and small are quickly integrating online marketing into their marketing strategies and mixes.

Navigating the Key Terms

B2B (business-to-business) e-commerce
B2C (business-to-consumer) e-commerce
C2B (consumer-to-business) e-commerce
C2C (consumer-to-consumer) e-commerce
Click-and-mortar companies

Click-only companies
Corporate Web site
Customerization
E-business
E-commerce
E-marketing
Extranet
Internet

Intranet
Marketing Web site
Online advertising
Open trading exchanges
Private trading exchanges
Spam
Viral marketing
Web communities

Travel Log

Discussing the Issues

1. Discuss the differences between intranets, extranets, and the Internet. What purpose does each serve for businesses?

2. How does e-commerce benefit both buyers and sellers? Can you think of any disadvantages for either buyers or sellers that are a result of e-commerce?

3. What channel conflict issues might a click-and-mortar company experience? How could the conflict be minimized? Use a specific company as an example.

4. How can the seven Cs encourage revisits to a company Web site? Are some of these factors more important than others? Why or why not?

5. Distinguish between the different forms of online advertising and promotion. What factors should a company consider in deciding between these different forms?

Application Questions

1. Getting consumers to spend time at a company's Web site and to come back again are critical goals in Web-site design.

What design options or features can a company use to get consumers to visit and explore their Web site? Identify a Web site that you feel does a good job at this and one that does not. What can the Web site doing the poor job learn from the one doing a good job?

2. Go to target.com. Browse the Web site and review the features and products offered. What would lead a consumer to purchase through this distribution outlet over going to their brick-and-mortar retail location? What fears might consumers purchasing online have that they would not be concerned with in a traditional retail store?

3. Customization involves the company taking the initiative to customize the market offering for consumers, while in customerization, the company leaves it up to individual customers to design the offering. What types of products do you think would lend themselves well to customerization and which do not? Could customerization be designed into an Internet-based Web ordering system for a consumer good? What obstacles would need to be overcome?

Under the Hood: Focus on Technology

Adware programs monitor the Web sites that a consumer visits and can be programmed to launch the Web sites of rival companies when a particular Web site is visited. Many consumers do not know they have these programs on their computers because they are typically bundled with other software that the consumer has downloaded. Recently, the moving company U-Haul lost a court decision to stop WhenU.com from displaying the Web sites of rival moving companies when consumers visited the U-Haul Web site. It is estimated that 30 million computers have WhenU.com's software installed.

1. How do you feel about pop-up advertising on the Internet? Do you find it useful or a burden?

2. Should adware programs be allowed to offer alternative purchase options to consumers? Do you think that this software gives more consumer choice or is it infringing on the rights of companies?

3. What form of online advertising do you find most and least objectionable? Do you feel that there might be a negative backlash against companies using more objectionable forms of online advertising?

Focus on Ethics

As noted in the chapter, concern over the security and privacy of sensitive personal information is a big issue for many consumers. Indeed it may lead some consumers to avoid online transactions. In an attempt to put consumers at ease with regard to how the company will and will not use their information, many have posted their privacy policies at their Web site. Visit Amazon.com and read their privacy policy (scroll to the bottom of the page and click on "privacy notice").

Be sure to read about the specific types of information they collect from you automatically, the information they capture with your consent, and the information they gather about you from third parties. After you have read their policies respond to the following questions.

1. What is your reaction to this privacy policy? Do you think it would give peace of mind to an individual concerned about others using their personal information?

2. As mentioned in the text, TRUSTe provides a seal of approval for those Web sites meeting its security and privacy standards. Go to the TRUSTe Web site (www.truste.org/consumers/users_how.html) and read about their four principles for online privacy. How does the Amazon.com privacy policy measure up on these four principles?

3. Do you feel that extra privacy measures should be taken to protect the privacy of individuals under the age of 18? What extra steps would you suggest?

Videos

The iwon.com video case that accompanies this chapter is located in Appendix 1 at the back of the book.

Student Materials

Need a tune-up? A study guide and OneKey access code are available to aid in your review of chapter material. Your instructor may choose to have these items shrink-wrapped with your text or you may purchase them separately at www.prenhall.com/marketing.

■ *After studying this chapter, you should be able to*

1. Discuss how the international trade system, economic, political–legal, and cultural environments affect a company's international marketing decisions   *2. Describe* three key approaches to entering international markets
3. Explain how companies adapt their marketing mixes for international markets   *4. Identify* the three major forms of international marketing organization

The Global Marketplace

15

ROAD MAP | Previewing the Concepts

We'll now look at global marketing. We've visited global topics throughout each previous chapter—it's difficult to find an area of marketing that doesn't contain at least some international issues. Here, however, we will examine the special considerations that companies face when they market their brands globally. As we move into the new millennium, advances in communication, transportation, and other technologies have made the world a much smaller place. Today, almost every firm, large or small, faces international marketing issues. In this chapter, we will examine six major decisions marketers make in going global.

Buckle up and let's get going! Our first stop is Coca-Cola—America's soft drink. Or *is* it just America's brand? Read on and see how finding the right balance between global standardization and local adaptation has made Coca-Cola the number-one brand worldwide.

What could be more American than Coca-Cola—right? The brand is as American as baseball and apple pie. Coke got its start in an Atlanta pharmacy in 1893, where it sold for five cents a glass. From there, the company's first president, savvy businessman Asa Candler, set out to convince America that Coca-Cola really was "the pause that refreshes." He printed coupons offering complimentary first tastes of Coca-Cola and outfitted pharmacists who distributed the brand with clocks, calendars, scales, and trays bearing the now-so-familiar red-and-white Coca-Cola logo. The beverage quickly became an all-American phenomenon; by 1895, the company had set up syrup plants in Chicago, Dallas, and Los Angeles.

But from the get-go, Coke was destined to be more than just America's soft drink. By 1900, Coca-Cola had already ventured beyond America's borders into numerous countries, including Cuba, Puerto Rico, and France. By the 1920s, Coca-Cola was slapping its logo on everything from dogsleds in Canada to the walls of bullfighting arenas in Spain. During World War II, Coca-Cola built bottling plants in Europe and Asia to supply American soldiers in the field.

As the years passed, Coca-Cola's persuasive and plentiful advertising cemented the brand at home as the all-American beverage. At the same time, strong marketing abroad fueled Coke's popularity throughout the world. In 1971, the company ran its legendary "I'd like to buy the world a Coke" television spot, in which a crowd of children sang the song from atop a hill in Italy. More recently, Coca-Cola's increased focus on emerging markets such as China, India, and

Indonesia—home to 2.4 billion people, half the world's population—has bolstered the brand's global success. Coca-Cola is now arguably the best-known and most admired brand in the world.

Coca-Cola's worldwide success results from a skillful balancing of global standardization and brand building with local adaptation. For years, the company has adhered to the mantra "Think globally, act locally." Coca-Cola spends lavishly on global Coke advertising—some $900 million a year—to create a consistent overall positioning for the brand across the 200 countries it serves. In addition, Coke's taste and packaging are largely standardized around the world—the bottle of Coke you'd drink in New York or Philadelphia looks and tastes much the same as one you might order in Paris, Hong Kong, Moscow, Sidney, or Abu Dhabi. As one ad agency executive asserts, "There are about two products that lend themselves to global marketing—and one of them is Coca-Cola."

Although Coke's taste and positioning are fairly consistent worldwide, in other ways Coca-Cola's marketing is relentlessly local. The company carefully adapts its mix of brands and flavors, promotions, price, and distribution to local customs and preferences in each market. For example, beyond its core Coca-Cola brand, the company makes nearly 300 different beverage brands, created especially for the taste buds of local consumers. It sells a pear-flavored drink in Turkey, a berry-flavored Fanta for Germany, a honey-flavored green tea in China, Sprite with a hint of mint in Canada, and a sports drink called Aquarius in Belgium and the Netherlands.

Consistent with this local focus, within the framework of its broader global positioning, Coca-Cola adapts specific ads to individual country markets. For example, a localized Chinese New Year television ad features a dragon in a holiday parade, adorned from head to tail with red Coke cans. The spot concludes, "For many centuries, the color red has been the color for good luck and prosperity. Who are we to argue with ancient wisdom?" Coke's now classic "Mean Joe" Greene TV ad from the United States—in which the weary football star reluctantly accepts a Coke from an admiring young fan and then tosses the awed kid his jersey in appreciation—was replicated in several different regions using the same format but substituting famous local athletes (ads in South America used Argentine soccer star Maradona; those in Asia used Thai soccer star, Niat).

More recently, Coke launched local ads to support its sponsorship of the 2002 World Cup. Based on careful research on local attitudes toward the event, ads were tailored to each country's experience with the competition. An Italian ad featured a bustling Roman marketplace. An emotional Turkish TV ad shows two kids stringing red and white light bulbs throughout Ankara, which light up the city in the team's colors. "There's even a special World Cup TV ad for the Netherlands—which scandalously failed to reach the tournament this time around," notes a global advertising analyst, "showing Dutch star Ruud Van Nistelroy quietly mowing his lawn while the drama unfolds in Japan and South Korea."

In India, Coca-Cola uses local promotions to aggressively cultivate a local image. It claimed official sponsorship for World Cup cricket, a favorite national sport, and used Indian cricket fans rather than actors to promote Coke products. Coca-Cola markets effectively in India to both retailers and imbibers. Observes one Coke watcher, "The company hosts massive gatherings of up to 15,000 retailers to showcase everything from the latest coolers and refrigerators, which Coke has for loan, to advertising displays. And its salespeople go house-to-house in their quest for new customers. In New Delhi alone, workers handed out more than 100,000 free bottles of Coke and Fanta last year."

Nothing better illustrates Coca-Cola's skill in balancing standardized global brand building with local adaptation than the explosive global growth of Sprite. Sprite's advertising uniformly targets the world's young people with the tag line "Image is nothing. Thirst is everything. Obey your thirst." The campaign taps into the rebellious side of teenagers and into their need to form individual identities. According to Sprite's director of brand marketing, "The meaning of [Sprite] and what we stand for is exactly the same globally. Teens tell us it's incredibly relevant in nearly every market we go into." However, as always, Coca-Cola tailors its message to local consumers. In China, for example, the campaign was given a softer edge: "You can't be irreverent in China, because it's not acceptable in that society. It's all about being relevant [to the specific audience]," notes the marketer. As a result of such smart targeting and powerful positioning, Sprite's worldwide sales surged 35 percent within three years of the start of the campaign, making it the world's number-four soft drink brand.

As a result of its international marketing prowess, Coca-Cola dominates the global soft drink market. More than 70 percent of the company's sales come from abroad. In the United States Coca-Cola captures an impressive 44 percent market share versus Pepsi's 32 percent. Overseas, however, it outsells Pepsi 2.5 to 1 and boasts four of the world's six leading soft drink brands: Coca-Cola, Diet Coke, Sprite, and Fanta.

Thus, Coca-Cola is truly an all-world brand. No matter where in the world you are, you'll find Coke "within an arm's length of desire." Yet, Coca-Cola also has a very personal meaning to consumers in different parts of the globe. Coca-Cola *is* as American as baseball and apple pie. But it's also as English as Big Ben and afternoon tea, as German as bratwurst and beer, as Japanese as sumo and sushi, and as Chinese as Ping-Pong and the Great Wall. Consumers in more than 200 countries think of Coke as *their* beverage. In Spain, Coke has been used as a mixer with wine; in Italy, Coke is served with meals in place of wine or cappuccino; in China, the beverage is served at special government occasions.

Says the company's Web site, "Our local strategy enables us to listen to all the voices around the world asking for beverages that span the entire spectrum of tastes and occasions. What people want in a beverage is a reflection of who they are, where they live, how they work and play, and how they relax and recharge. Whether you're a student in the United States enjoying a refreshing Coca-Cola, a woman in Italy taking a tea break, a child in Peru asking for a juice drink, or a couple in Korea buying bottled water after a run together, we're there for you. . . . It's a special thing to have billions of friends around the world, and we never forget it."[1]

In the past, U.S. companies paid little attention to international trade. If they could pick up some extra sales through exporting, that was fine. But the big market was at home, and it teemed with opportunities. The home market was also much safer. Managers did not need to learn other languages, deal with strange and changing currencies, face political and legal uncertainties, or adapt their products to different customer needs and expectations. Today, however, the situation is much different.

◼▮ Global Marketing in the Twenty-First Century

The world is shrinking rapidly with the advent of faster communication, transportation, and financial flows. Products developed in one country—Gucci purses, Sony electronics, McDonald's hamburgers, Japanese sushi, German BMWs—are finding enthusiastic acceptance in other countries. We would not be surprised to hear about a German businessman wearing an Italian suit meeting an English friend at a Japanese restaurant who later returns home to drink Russian vodka and watch *West Wing* on TV.

International trade is booming. Since 1969, the number of multinational corporations in the world's 14 richest countries has more than tripled, from 7,000 to 24,000. Imports of goods and services now account for 24 percent of gross domestic product (GDP) worldwide, twice the level of 40 years ago. International trade now accounts for a quarter of the United States' GDP, and between 1996 and 2006, U.S. exports are expected to increase 51 percent. World trade now accounts for 29 percent of the world GDP, a 10 percent increase from 1990.[2]

Many U.S. companies have long been successful at international marketing: Coca-Cola, McDonald's, IBM, Xerox, Gillette, Colgate, General Electric, Caterpillar, Ford,

■ Many American companies have made the world their market.

Kodak, 3M, Boeing, Motorola, and dozens of other American firms have made the world their market. And in the United States, names such as Sony, Toyota, Nestlé, Norelco, Nokia, BMW, Panasonic, and Prudential have become household words. Other products and services that appear to be American are in fact produced or owned by foreign companies: Bantam books, Baskin-Robbins ice cream, GE and RCA televisions, Carnation milk, Pillsbury food products, Universal Studios, and Motel 6, to name just a few. "Already two-thirds of all industry either operates globally or is in the process of doing so," notes one analyst. "Michelin, the oh-so-French tire manufacturer, now makes 35 percent of its money in the United States, while Johnson & Johnson does 43 percent of its business abroad. . . . The scope of every manager is the world."[3]

But today global competition is intensifying. Foreign firms are expanding aggressively into new international markets, and home markets are no longer as rich in opportunity. Few industries are now safe from foreign competition. Although some companies would like to stem the tide of foreign imports through protectionism, in the long run this would only raise the cost of living and protect inefficient domestic firms. The better way for companies to compete is to continuously improve their products at home and expand into foreign markets.

If companies delay taking steps toward internationalizing, they risk being shut out of growing markets in Western Europe, Eastern Europe, the Pacific Rim, and elsewhere. Firms that stay at home to play it safe not only might lose their chances to enter other markets but also risk losing their home markets. Domestic companies that never thought about foreign competitors suddenly find these competitors in their own backyards.

Ironically, although the need for companies to go abroad is greater today than in the past, so are the risks. Companies that go global confront several major problems. High debt, inflation, and unemployment in many countries have resulted in highly unstable governments and currencies, which limit trade and expose U.S. firms to many risks. Governments are placing more regulations on foreign firms, such as requiring joint ownership with domestic partners, mandating the hiring of nationals, and putting limits on the profits that can be taken from the country. Moreover, foreign governments often impose high tariffs or trade barriers in order to protect their own industries. Finally, corruption is an increasing problem—officials in several countries often award business not to the best bidder but to the highest briber.

Still, companies selling in global industries have no choice but to internationalize their operations. A *global industry* is one in which the competitive positions of firms in given local or national markets are affected by their global positions. A **global firm** is one that, by operating in more than one country, gains marketing, production, R&D, and financial advantages that are not available to purely domestic competitors.

The global company sees the world as one market. It minimizes the importance of national boundaries and develops "supranational" brands. It raises capital, obtains materials and components, and manufactures and markets its goods wherever it can do the best job. For example, Ford's "world truck" sports a cab made in Europe and a chassis built in North America. It is assembled in Brazil and imported to the United States for sale. Otis Elevator gets its elevators' door systems from France, small geared parts from Spain, electronics from Germany, and special motor drives from Japan. It uses the United States only for systems integration. Thus, global firms gain advantages by planning, operating, and coordinating their activities on a worldwide basis.

This does not mean that small and medium-size firms must operate in a dozen countries to succeed. These firms can practice global niching. But the world is becoming smaller, and every company operating in a global industry—whether large or small—must assess and establish its place in world markets.

The rapid move toward globalization means that all companies will have to answer some basic questions: What market position should we try to establish in our country, in our economic region, and globally? Who will our global competitors be, and what are their strategies and resources? Where should we produce or source our products? What strategic alliances should we form with other firms around the world?

As shown in Figure 15.1, a company faces six major decisions in international marketing. Each decision will be discussed in detail in this chapter.

◾▮ Looking at the Global Marketing Environment

Before deciding whether to operate internationally, a company must thoroughly understand the international marketing environment. That environment has changed a great deal in the past two decades, creating both new opportunities and new problems. The world economy has globalized. World trade and investment have grown rapidly, with many attractive markets opening up in Western and Eastern Europe, China and the Pacific Rim, Russia, and elsewhere. There has been a growth of global brands in automobiles, food, clothing, electronics, computers and software, and many other categories. The number of global companies has grown dramatically.

The International Trade System

The U.S. company looking abroad must start by understanding the international *trade system*. When selling to another country, the U.S. firm faces various trade restrictions. The most common is the **tariff**, which is a tax levied by a foreign government against certain imported products. The tariff may be designed either to raise revenue or to protect

Global firm
A firm that, by operating in more than one country, gains R&D, production, marketing, and financial advantages in its costs and reputation that are not available to purely domestic competitors.

Tariff
A tax levied by a government against certain imported products. Tariffs are designed to raise revenue or to protect domestic firms.

FIGURE 15.1
Major International Marketing Decisions

Quota

A limit on the amount of goods that an importing country will accept in certain product categories; it is designed to conserve on foreign exchange and to protect local industry and employment.

Embargo

A ban on the import of a certain product.

Exchange controls

Government limits on the amount of foreign exchange with other countries and on the exchange rate against other currencies.

Nontariff trade barriers

Nonmonetary barriers to foreign products, such as biases against a foreign company's bids or product standards that go against a foreign company's product features.

domestic firms. The exporter also may face a **quota**, which sets limits on the amount of goods the importing country will accept in certain product categories. The purpose of the quota is to conserve on foreign exchange and to protect local industry and employment. An **embargo**, or boycott, which totally bans some kinds of imports, is the strongest form of quota.

American firms may face **exchange controls** that limit the amount of foreign exchange and the exchange rate against other currencies. The company also may face **nontariff trade barriers**, such as biases against U.S. company bids or restrictive product standards or other rules that go against American product features:

> One of the cleverest ways the Japanese have found to keep foreign manufacturers out of their domestic market is to plead "uniqueness." Japanese skin is different, the government argues, so foreign cosmetics companies must test their products in Japan before selling there. The Japanese say their stomachs are small and have room for only the *mikan*, the local tangerine, so imports of U.S. oranges are limited. Now the Japanese have come up with what may be the flakiest argument yet: Their snow is different, so ski equipment should be too.[4]

At the same time, certain forces *help* trade between nations. Examples include the General Agreement on Tariffs and Trade and various regional free trade agreements.

The World Trade Organization and GATT The General Agreement on Tariffs and Trade (GATT) is a 56-year-old treaty designed to promote world trade by reducing tariffs and other international trade barriers. Since the treaty's inception in 1948, member nations (currently numbering 146) have met in eight rounds of GATT negotiations to reassess trade barriers and set new rules for international trade. The first seven rounds of negotiations reduced the average worldwide tariffs on manufactured goods from 45 percent to just 5 percent.[5]

The most recently completed GATT negotiations, dubbed the Uruguay Round, dragged on for seven long years before concluding in 1993. The benefits of the Uruguay Round will be felt for many years, as the accord promotes long-term global trade growth. It reduced the world's remaining merchandise tariffs by 30 percent, boosting global merchandise trade by as much as 10 percent, or $270 billion in current dollars, by 2002. The new agreement also extended GATT to cover trade in agriculture and a wide range of services, and it toughened international protection of copyrights, patents, trademarks, and other intellectual property.[6]

Beyond reducing trade barriers and setting international standards for trade, the Uruguay Round established the World Trade Organization (WTO) to enforce GATT rules. One of the WTO's first major tasks was to host negotiations on the General Agreement on Trade in Services, which deals with worldwide trade in banking, securities, and insurance services. In general, the WTO acts as an umbrella organization, overseeing GATT, the General Agreement on Trade in Services, and a similar agreement governing intellectual property. In addition, the WTO mediates global disputes and imposes trade sanctions, authorities that the previous GATT organization never possessed. A new round of GATT negotiations, the Doha round, began in Doha, Qatar, in late 2001 and is expected to conclude in January 2005.[7]

■ The WTO and GATT: The General Agreement on Tariffs and Trade (GATT) promotes world trade by reducing tariffs and other international trade barriers. The WTO, which oversees GATT, began a new round of negotiations in Doha, Qatar, in late 2001.

Regional Free Trade Zones Certain countries have formed *free trade zones* or **economic communities**—groups of nations organized to work toward common goals in the regulation of international trade. One such community is the *European Union*. Formed in 1957, the European Union (EU)—then called the Common Market—set out to create a single European market by reducing barriers to the free flow of products, services, finances, and labor among member countries and developing policies on trade with non-member nations. Today, the EU represents one of the world's single largest markets. Its

Economic community

A group of nations organized to work toward common goals in the regulation of international trade.

current 15 member countries contain more than 375 million consumers and account for 20 percent of the world's exports, and the EU is preparing to add 10 new eastern and southern European members in 2004. During the next decade, as more European nations gain admission, the EU could contain as many as 481 million people in 28 countries.[8]

European unification offers tremendous trade opportunities for U.S. and other non-European firms. However, it also poses threats. As a result of increased unification, European companies will grow bigger and more competitive. Perhaps an even greater concern, however, is that lower barriers *inside* Europe will create only thicker *outside* walls. Some observers envision a "Fortress Europe" that heaps favors on firms from EU countries but hinders outsiders by imposing obstacles such as stiffer import quotas, local content requirements, and other nontariff barriers.

Progress toward European unification has

■ Economic communities: The European Union represents one of the world's single largest markets. Its current 15 member countries contain more than 375 million consumers and account for 20 percent of the world's exports.

been slow—many doubt that complete unification will ever be achieved. However, on January 1, 1999, 11 of the 15 member nations took a significant step toward unification by adopting the euro as a common currency. In January 2001, Greece became the 12th member nation to adopt the euro. Currencies of the individual countries were phased out gradually until January 1, 2002, when the euro became the only currency. Adoption of the euro will decrease much of the currency risk associated with doing business in Europe, making member countries with previously weak currencies more attractive markets. In addition, by removing currency conversion hurdles, countries in the euro zone hope to increase cross-border trade and highlight differences in pricing and marketing from country to country.[9]

Even with the adoption of the euro as a standard currency, from a marketing viewpoint, creating an economic community will not create a homogeneous market. It is unlikely that the EU will ever go against 2,000 years of tradition and become the "United States of Europe." As one observer asks, "Can a community that speaks at least a dozen languages and has two dozen different cultures effectively come together and operate as a single unified entity?" Although economic and political boundaries may fall, social and cultural differences will remain, and companies marketing in Europe will face a daunting mass of local rules. Still, even if only partly successful, European unification will make a more efficient and competitive Europe a global force with which to reckon.[10]

In North America, the United States and Canada phased out trade barriers in 1989. In January 1994, the *North American Free Trade Agreement (NAFTA)* established a free trade zone among the United States, Mexico, and Canada. The agreement created a single market of 360 million people who produce and consume $6.7 trillion worth of goods and services. As it is implemented over a 15-year period, NAFTA will eliminate all trade barriers and investment restrictions among the three countries.

Thus far, the agreement has allowed trade between the countries to flourish. Each day the United States exchanges more than $1 billion in goods and services with Canada, its largest trading partner. And in 1998, Mexico passed Japan to become America's second largest trading partner. Since the agreement was signed in 1993, merchandise trade between Mexico and the United States has more than tripled, now totaling $232 billion. Given the apparent success of NAFTA, talks are now under way to investigate establishing a Free Trade Area of the Americas (FTAA). This mammoth free trade zone would include 34 countries stretching from the Bering Strait to Cape Horn, with a population of 800 million, a combined gross domestic product of more than $13 trillion, and more than $3.4 trillion in annual world trade.[11]

Other free trade areas have formed in Latin America and South America. For example, MERCOSUR now links six members, including full members Argentina, Brazil, Paraguay, and Uruguay and associate members Bolivia and Chile. With a population of more than 200 million and a combined economy of more than $1 trillion a year, these countries make up the largest trading bloc after NAFTA and the European Union. There is talk of a free trade agreement between the EU and MERCOSUR, and MERCOSUR's member countries are considering adopting a common currency, the merco.[12]

Although the recent trend toward free trade zones has caused great excitement and new market opportunities, this trend also raises some concerns. For example, in the United States, unions fear that NAFTA will lead to the further exodus of manufacturing jobs to Mexico, where wage rates are much lower. Environmentalists worry that companies that are unwilling to play by the strict rules of the U.S. Environmental Protection Agency will relocate in Mexico, where pollution regulation has been lax.

Each nation has unique features that must be understood. A nation's readiness for different products and services and its attractiveness as a market to foreign firms depend on its economic, political–legal, and cultural environments.

Economic Environment

The international marketer must study each country's economy. Two economic factors reflect the country's attractiveness as a market: the country's industrial structure and its income distribution.

The country's *industrial structure* shapes its product and service needs, income levels, and employment levels. The four types of industrial structures are as follows:

- *Subsistence economies:* In a subsistence economy, the vast majority of people engage in simple agriculture. They consume most of their output and barter the rest for simple goods and services. They offer few market opportunities.

- *Raw material exporting economies:* These economies are rich in one or more natural resources but poor in other ways. Much of their revenue comes from exporting these resources. Examples are Chile (tin and copper), Zaire (copper, cobalt, and coffee), and Saudi Arabia (oil). These countries are good markets for large equipment, tools and supplies, and trucks. If there are many foreign residents and a wealthy upper class, they are also a market for luxury goods.

- *Industrializing economies:* In an industrializing economy, manufacturing accounts for 10 to 20 percent of the country's economy. Examples include Egypt, the Philippines, India, and Brazil. As manufacturing increases, the country needs more imports of raw textile materials, steel, and heavy machinery, and fewer imports of finished textiles, paper products, and automobiles. Industrialization typically creates a new rich class and a small but growing middle class, both demanding new types of imported goods.

- *Industrial economies:* Industrial economies are major exporters of manufactured goods and investment funds. They trade goods among themselves and also export them to other types of economies for raw materials and semifinished goods. The varied manufacturing activities of these industrial nations and their large middle class make them rich markets for all sorts of goods.

The second economic factor is the country's *income distribution.* Countries with subsistence economies may consist mostly of households with very low family incomes. In contrast, industrialized nations may have low-, medium-, and high-income households.

Still other countries may have households with only either very low or very high incomes. However, in many cases, poorer countries may have small but wealthy segments of upper-income consumers. Also, even in low-income and developing economies, people may find ways to buy products that are important to them:

Philosophy professor Nina Gladziuk thinks carefully before shelling out her hard-earned zlotys for Poland's dazzling array of consumer goods. But spend she certainly does. Although she earns just $550 a month from two academic jobs, Gladziuk, 41, enjoys making purchases: They are changing her lifestyle after years of deprivation under communism. In the past year, she has furnished a new apartment in a popular neighborhood near Warsaw's Kabaty Forest, splurged on foreign-made beauty products, and spent a weekend in Paris before attending a seminar financed by her university. . . . Meet Central Europe's fast-rising consumer class. From white-collar workers like Gladziuk to factory workers in Budapest to hip young professionals in Prague, incomes are rising and confidence surging as a result of four years of economic growth. In the region's leading economies—the Czech Republic, Hungary, and Poland—the new class of buyers is growing not only in numbers but also in sophistication. . . . In Hungary, ad agency Young & Rubicam labels 11 percent of the country as "aspirers," with dreams of the good life and buying habits to match. Nearly one-third of all Czechs, Hungarians, and Poles—some 17 million people—are under 30 years old, eager to snap up everything from the latest fashions to compact disks.[13]

■ Developing economies: In Central Europe, companies are catering to the new class of buyers with dreams of the good life and buying habits to match who are eager to snap up everything from western consumer goods to high fashions and the latest cell phones.

Thus, international marketers face many challenges in understanding how the economic environment will affect decisions about which global markets to enter and how.

Political–Legal Environment

Nations differ greatly in their political–legal environments. At least four political–legal factors should be considered in deciding whether to do business in a given country: attitudes toward international buying, government bureaucracy, political stability, and monetary regulations.

In their *attitudes toward international buying,* some nations are quite receptive to foreign firms and others are quite hostile. For example, India has bothered foreign businesses with import quotas, currency restrictions, and limits on the percentage of the management team that can be nonnationals. As a result, many U.S. companies left India. In contrast, neighboring Asian countries such as Singapore, Thailand, Malaysia, and the Philippines court foreign investors and shower them with incentives and favorable operating conditions.[14]

A second factor is *government bureaucracy*—the extent to which the host government runs an efficient system for helping foreign companies: efficient customs handling, good market information, and other factors that aid in doing business. Americans are often shocked by how quickly barriers to trade disappear in some countries if a suitable payment (bribe) is made to some official.

Political stability is another issue. Governments change hands, sometimes violently. Even without a change, a government may decide to respond to new popular feelings. The foreign company's property may be taken, its currency holdings may be blocked, or import quotas or new duties may be set. International marketers may find it profitable to do business in an unstable country, but the unstable situation will affect how they handle business and financial matters.

Finally, companies must also consider a country's *monetary regulations*. Sellers want to take their profits in a currency of value to them. Ideally, the buyer can pay in the seller's currency or in other world currencies. Short of this, sellers might accept a blocked currency—one whose removal from the country is restricted by the buyer's government—if they can buy other goods in that country that they need themselves or can sell elsewhere for a needed currency. Besides currency limits, a changing exchange rate also creates high risks for the seller.

Most international trade involves cash transactions. Yet many nations have too little hard currency to pay for their purchases from other countries. They may want to pay with other items instead of cash, which has led to a growing practice called **countertrade**. Countertrade makes up an estimated 20 percent of all world trade.[15] It takes several forms: *Barter* involves the direct exchange of goods or services, as when Australian cattlemen swapped beef on the hoof for Indonesian goods, including beer, palm oil, and cement. Another form is *compensation* (or *buyback*), whereby the seller sells a plant, equipment, or technology to another country and agrees to take payment in the resulting products. Thus, Goodyear provided China with materials and training for a printing plant in exchange for finished labels. Another form is *counterpurchase*, in which the seller receives full payment in cash but agrees to spend some portion of the money in the other country within a stated time period. For example, Pepsi sells its cola syrup to Russia for rubles and agrees to buy Russian-made Stolichnaya vodka for sale in the United States.

Countertrade deals can be very complex. For example, a few years back, DaimlerChrysler agreed to sell 30 trucks to Romania in exchange for 150 Romanian jeeps, which it then sold to Ecuador for bananas, which were in turn sold to a German supermarket chain for German currency. Through this roundabout process, DaimlerChrysler finally obtained payment in German money.[16]

Countertrade
International trade involving the direct or indirect exchange of goods for other goods instead of cash.

Cultural Environment

Each country has its own folkways, norms, and taboos. When designing global marketing strategies, companies must understand how culture affects consumer reactions in each of its world markets. In turn, they must also understand how their strategies affect local cultures.

The Impact of Culture on Marketing Strategy The seller must examine the ways consumers in different countries think about and use certain products before planning a marketing program. There are often surprises. For example, the average French man uses almost twice as many cosmetics and beauty aids as his wife. The Germans and the French eat more packaged, branded spaghetti than do Italians. Italian children like to eat chocolate bars between slices of bread as a snack. Women in Tanzania will not give their children eggs for fear of making them bald or impotent.

Companies that ignore such differences can make some very expensive and embarrassing mistakes. Here's an example:

> McDonald's and Coca-Cola managed to offend the entire Muslim world by putting the Saudi Arabian flag on their packaging. The flag's design includes a passage from the Koran (the sacred text of Islam), and Muslims feel very strongly that their Holy Writ should never be wadded up and tossed in the garbage. Nike faced a similar situation in Arab countries when Muslims objected to a stylized "Air" logo on its shoes, which resembled "Allah" in Arabic script. Nike apologized for the mistake and pulled the shoes from distribution.[17]

Business norms and behavior also vary from country to country. American business executives need to be briefed on these factors before conducting business in another country. Here are some examples of different global business behavior[18]:

- South Americans like to sit or stand very close to each other when they talk business—in fact, almost nose-to-nose. The American business executive tends to keep backing away as the South American moves closer. Both may end up being offended.

- Fast and tough bargaining, which works well in other parts of the world, is often inappropriate in Japan and other Asian countries. Moreover, in face-to-face communications, Japanese business executives rarely say no. Thus, Americans tend to become impatient with having to spend time in polite conversation about the weather or other such topics before getting down to business. And they become frustrated when they don't know where they stand. However, when Americans come to the point quickly, Japanese business executives may find this behavior offensive.

- In France, wholesalers don't want to promote a product. They ask their retailers what they want and deliver it. If an American company builds its strategy around the French wholesaler's cooperation in promotions, it is likely to fail.

- When American executives exchange business cards, each usually gives the other's card a cursory glance and stuffs it in a pocket for later reference. In Japan, however, executives dutifully study each other's cards during a greeting, carefully noting company affiliation and rank. They show a business card the same respect they show a person. Also, they hand their card to the most important person first.

■ Overlooking cultural differences can result in embarrassing mistakes. When Nike learned that this stylized "Air" logo resembled "Allah" in Arabic script, it apologized and pulled the shoes from distribution.

By the same token, companies that understand cultural nuances can use them to advantage when positioning products internationally. Consider the following example:

> A television ad running these days in India shows a mother lapsing into a daydream: Her young daughter is in a beauty contest dressed as Snow White, dancing on a stage. Her flowing gown is an immaculate white. The garments of other contestants, who dance in the background, are a tad gray. Snow White, no surprise, wins the blue ribbon. The mother awakes to the laughter of her adoring family—and glances proudly at her Whirlpool White Magic washing machine. The TV spot is the product of 14 months of research by Whirlpool into the psyche of the Indian consumer. Among other things, [Whirlpool] learned that Indian homemakers prize hygiene and purity, which they associate with white. The trouble is, white garments often get discolored after frequent machine washing in local water. Besides appealing to this love of purity in its ads, Whirlpool custom-designed machines that are especially good with white fabrics. Whirlpool hasn't stopped there. It uses generous incentives to get thousands of Indian retailers to stock its goods. To reach every cranny of the vast nation, it uses local contractors conversant in India's 18 languages to collect payments in cash and deliver appliances by truck, bicycles, even oxcart. Since 1996, Whirlpool's sales in India have leapt 80 percent—and should hit $200 million this year. Whirlpool now is the leading brand in India's fast-growing market for fully automatic washing machines.[19]

Thus, understanding cultural traditions, preferences, and behaviors can help companies not only to avoid embarrassing mistakes but also to take advantage of cross-cultural opportunities.

■ Global cultural environment: By understanding cultural nuances, Whirlpool has become the leading brand in India's fast-growing market for automatic washing machines. It designed machines that keep whites whiter.

The Impact of Marketing Strategy on Cultures Whereas marketers worry about the impact of culture on their global marketing strategies, others may worry about the impact of marketing strategies on global cultures. For example, some critics argue that "globalization" really means "Americanization." They worry that the more people around the world are exposed to the American culture and lifestyle in the food they eat, the stores they shop, and television shows and movies they watch, the more they will lose their individual cultural identities. These critics contend that exposure to American values and products erodes other cultures and westernizes the world (see Marketing at Work 15.1).

■ Deciding Whether to Go International

Not all companies need to venture into international markets to survive. For example, most local businesses need to market well only in the local marketplace. Operating domestically is easier and safer. Managers need not learn another country's language and laws, deal with volatile currencies, face political and legal uncertainties, or redesign their products to suit different customer needs and expectations. However, companies that operate in global industries, where their strategic positions in specific markets are affected strongly by their overall global positions, must compete on a worldwide basis to succeed.

Any of several factors might draw a company into the international arena. Global competitors might attack the company's domestic market by offering better products or lower prices. The company might want to counterattack these competitors in their home markets to tie up their resources. Or the company might discover foreign markets that present higher profit opportunities than the domestic market does. The company's domestic market might be stagnant or shrinking, or the company might need an enlarged customer base in order to achieve economies of scale. The company might want to reduce its dependence on any one market so as to reduce its risk. Finally, the company's customers might be expanding abroad and require international servicing.

Before going abroad, the company must weigh several risks and answer many questions about its ability to operate globally. Can the company learn to understand the prefer-

Marketing at Work | 15.1

Globalization Versus Americanization: Does Globalization Wear Mickey Mouse Ears?

Many social critics argue that large American multinationals like McDonald's, Coca-Cola, Nike, Microsoft, Disney, and MTV aren't just "globalizing" their brands, they are "Americanizing" the world's cultures. "Today, globalization often wears Mickey Mouse ears, eats Big Macs, drinks Coke or Pepsi, and does its computing on an IBM PC, using Windows [software]," says Thomas Friedman, in his book *The Lexus and the Olive Tree.*

The critics worry that, in this new "McWorld," countries around the globe are losing their individual cultural identities. Teens in India watch MTV and ask their parents for more westernized clothes and other symbols of American pop culture and values. Grandmothers in small villas in northern Italy no longer spend each morning visiting local meat, bread, and produce markets to gather the ingredients for dinner. Instead, they now they shop at Wal-Mart

Supercenters. Women in Saudi Arabia see American films and question their societal roles. In China, most people never drank coffee before Starbucks entered the market. Now Chinese consumers rush to Starbucks stores "because it's a symbol of a new kind of lifestyle." Similarly, in China, where McDonald's operates 80 restaurants in Beijing alone, nearly half of all children identify the chain as a domestic brand.

An American reporter writing from Japan claimed:

> [It will] only be a matter of time before an Asian family [will] take cash from their corner U.S. bank, "drive off to Wal-Mart and fill the trunk of their Ford with the likes of Fritos and Snickers," then stop at the American-owned movie theater to see the latest Disney film before returning home to check their U.S. mutual fund accounts on America Online (on their IBM com-

puter with Microsoft software). Asians see this as no less than the U.S. "desire to bury Asian values," and they are not pleased.

Recently, such concerns have led to a backlash against American globalization. Well-known U.S. brands have become the targets of boycotts and protests in many international markets. As symbols of American capitalism, companies such as Coca-Cola, McDonald's, and KFC have been singled out by antiglobalization protestors in hot spots all around the world, especially when anti-American sentiment peaks. For example, almost immediately after U.S. armed forces unleashed their attack on Afghanistan following the September 11, 2001, terrorist attacks, McDonald's and KFC stores in Pakistan, India, and elsewhere around the world came under attack. In Karachi, Pakistan, thousands of protesters, chanting

Global marketing's impact on cultures: Concerns that "globalization" really means "Americanization" has sometimes led to a backlash against American globalization.

(continued)

"Death to America," mobbed the U.S. consulate. When police turned them back with barricades and tear gas, "they went for the next-best option: Colonel Sanders," said a reporter at the scene. "It didn't matter that the nearby KFC, one of 18 in Pakistan, was locally owned. The red, white, and blue KFC logo was justification enough." The protestors set fire to the store before police could turn them away.

Despite such images, defenders of globalization argue that concerns of "Americanization" are overblown. Most studies reveal that, although globalization may bridge cultural differences, it does not eliminate them. Instead, the cultural exchange goes both ways:

African consumers are more apt to be fans of Hindi musicals than MTV. And even American childhood has increasingly been shaped by Asian cultural imports. Most parents now know about the Power Rangers, Tamagotchi and Pokemon, Sega and Nintendo. For the moment, English remains cyberspace's dominant language, and having Web access often means that Third World youth have greater exposure to American popular culture. Yet these same technologies enable Balkan students studying in the United States to hear Webcast news and music from Serbia or Bosnia. Thanks to broadband communication, foreign media producers will distribute films and television programs directly to American consumers without having to pass by U.S. gatekeepers.

Thus, American companies have learned that to succeed abroad they must adapt to local cultural values and traditions rather than trying to force their own. McDonald's CEO Jack Greenberg notes that McDonald's is "a decentralized . . . network of locally owned stores that is very flexible and adapts very well to local conditions." This concept is echoed on the McDonald's Web site and throughout its corporate culture. The company encourages franchisees to introduce menu items that reflect local tastes, including the Maharaja Mac (made of mutton) in India, the Tatsuta Burger in Japan, the McPork Burger with Thai Basil in Thailand, and the McTempeh Burger (made from fermented soybeans) in Indonesia. In fact, McDonald's restaurants in Bombay and Delhi feature a menu that is more than 75 percent locally developed.

Similarly, Disneyland Paris flopped at first because it failed to take local cultural values and behaviors into account. According to Euro Disney Chief Executive Jay Rasulo, "When we first launched, there was the belief that it was enough to be Disney. Now we realize that our guests need to be welcomed on the basis of their own culture and travel habits." That realization, and the changes it spawned, has made Disneyland Paris the number one tourist attraction in Europe, even more popular than the Eiffel Tower. The park now attracts more than 13 million visitors each year. And Disney recently introduced a new movie-theme park to accompany the revitalized Paris attraction. The new park blends Disney entertainment and attractions with the history and culture of European film. A show celebrating the history of animation features Disney characters speaking six different languages. Rides are narrated by foreign-born stars, including Jeremy Irons, Isabella Rossellini, and Nastassja Kinski, speaking in their native tongues.

So, does globalization wear Mickey Mouse ears? American culture does seem to carry more weight these days than that of other countries—the United States is the world's largest exporter of culture. But globalization is a two-way street. As one expert concludes, "If globalization has Mickey Mouse ears, it is also wearing a French beret, [talking on a Nokia cell phone, driving a VW Beetle,] and listening to a Sony walkman."

Sources: Quotes and other information from Thomas L. Friedman, *The Lexus and the Olive Tree: Understanding Globalization* (New York: Anchor Books, 2000); Karl Moore and Alan Rugman, "Does Globalization Wear Mickey Mouse Ears?" *Across the Board*, January–February 2003, pp. 11–12; Walter LaFeber, *Michael Jordan and the New Global Capitalism* (New York: Norton, 1999), p. 23; Moises Naim, "McAtlas Shrugged," *Foreign Policy*, May–June 2001, pp. 26–37; Suh-Kyung Yoon, "Look Who's Going Native," *Far Eastern Economic Review*, February 1, 2001, pp. 68–69; Elisabeth Rosenthal, "Buicks, Starbucks and Fried Chicken. Still China?" *New York Times*, February 25, 2002, p. A4; Brian O'Keefe, "Global Brands," *Fortune*, November 26, 2001, pp. 102–110; Susan Postlewaite, "U.S. Marketers Try to Head Off Boycotts," *Advertising Age*, March 31, 2003, pp. 3, 90; Henry Jenkins, "Culture Goes Global," *Technology Review*, July–August 2001, p. 89; Paulo Prada and Bruce Orwall, "A Certain 'Je Ne Sais Quoi' at Disney's New Park—Movie-Themed Site Near Paris Is Multilingual, Serves Wine, and Better Sausage Variety," *Wall Street Journal*, March 12, 2002, p. B1; and "Euro Disney S. C. A.," *Hoover's Company Capsules*, Austin, July 2003, p. 90721.

ences and buyer behavior of consumers in other countries? Can it offer competitively attractive products? Will it be able to adapt to other countries' business cultures and deal effectively with foreign nationals? Do the company's managers have the necessary international experience? Has management considered the impact of regulations and the political environments of other countries?

Because of the risks and difficulties of entering international markets, most companies do not act until some situation or event thrusts them into the global arena. Someone—a domestic exporter, a foreign importer, a foreign government—may ask the company to sell abroad. Or the company may be saddled with overcapacity and need to find additional markets for its goods.

■ Deciding Which Markets to Enter

Before going abroad, the company should try to define its international *marketing objectives and policies.* It should decide what *volume* of foreign sales it wants. Most companies start small when they go abroad. Some plan to stay small, seeing international sales as a small part of their business. Other companies have bigger plans, seeing international business as equal to or even more important than their domestic business.

The company also needs to choose *how many* countries it wants to market in. Companies must be careful not to spread themselves too thin or to expand beyond their capabilities by operating in too many countries too soon. For example, although consumer products company Amway is now breaking into markets at a furious pace, it is doing so only after decades of gradually building up its overseas presence:

> Known for its neighbor-to-neighbor direct-selling networks, Amway expanded into Australia in 1971, a country far away but similar to the U.S. market. In the 1980s, Amway expanded into 10 more countries, and the pace increased rapidly from then on. By 1994, Amway was firmly established in 60 countries, including Hungary, Poland, and the Czech Republic. Following substantial success in Japan, China, and other Asian countries, the company entered India in 1998. Today, Amway sells its products in 80 countries and international proceeds contribute more than 70 percent of the company's overall revenues.[20]

Next, the company needs to decide on the *types* of countries to enter. A country's attractiveness depends on the product, geographical factors, income and population, political climate, and other factors. The seller may prefer certain country groups or parts of the world. In recent years, many major new markets have emerged, offering both substantial opportunities and daunting challenges.

After listing possible international markets, the company must screen and rank each one. Consider the following example:

> Many mass marketers dream of selling to China's more than 1.3 billion people. For example, Colgate is waging a pitched battle in China, seeking control of the world's largest toothpaste market. Yet, this country of infrequent brushers offers great potential. Only 20 percent of China's rural dwellers brush daily, so Colgate and its competitors are aggressively pursuing promotional and educational programs, from massive ad campaigns to visits to local schools to sponsoring oral care research. Through such efforts in this $350 million market, Colgate has expanded its market share from 7 percent in 1995 to 35 percent today, despite competing with a state-owned brand managed by Unilever and P&G's Crest.[21]

Colgate's decision to enter the Chinese market seems fairly simple and straightforward: China is a huge market without much established competition. Given the low rate of brushing, this already huge market can grow even larger. Yet we still can question whether market size *alone* is reason enough for selecting China. Colgate also must consider other factors: Will the Chinese government remain stable and supportive? Does China provide for the production and distribution technologies needed to produce and market Colgate's products profitably? Will Colgate be able to overcome cultural barriers and convince Chinese consumers to brush their teeth regularly? Can Colgate continue to compete effectively with dozens of local competitors? Colgate's

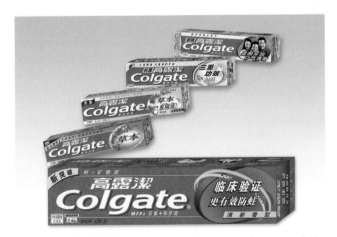

■ Colgate's decision to enter the huge Chinese market seems fairly straightforward. Using aggressive promotional and educational programs, Colgate has expanded its market share from 7 percent to 35 percent in less than a decade.

TABLE 15.1 Indicators of Market Potential

Demographic characteristies	Sociocultural factors
Education	Consumer lifestyles, beliefs, and values
Populaltion size and growth	Business norms and approaches
Population age composition	Social norms
Geographic characteristics	Languages
Climate	**Political and legal factors**
Country size	National priorities
Population density—urban, rural	Political stability
Transportation structure and market accessibility	Government attitudes toward global trade
Economic factors	Government bureaucracy
GDP size and growth	Monetary and trade regulations
Income distribution	
Industrial infrastructure	
Natural resources	
Financial and human resources	

current success in China suggests that it could answer yes to all of these questions. Still, the company's future in China is filled with uncertainties.

Possible global markets should be ranked on several factors, including market size, market growth, cost of doing business, competitive advantage, and risk level. The goal is to determine the potential of each market, using indicators such as those shown in Table 15.1. Then the marketer must decide which markets offer the greatest long-run return on investment.

■■ Deciding How to Enter the Market

Once a company has decided to sell in a foreign country, it must determine the best mode of entry. Its choices are *exporting, joint venturing,* and *direct investment.* Figure 15.2 shows three market entry strategies, along with the options each one offers. As the figure shows, each succeeding strategy involves more commitment and risk, but also more control and potential profits.

Exporting

Exporting
Entering a foreign market by selling goods produced in the company's home country, often with little modification.

The simplest way to enter a foreign market is through **exporting**. The company may passively export its surpluses from time to time, or it may make an active commitment to expand exports to a particular market. In either case, the company produces all its goods in its home country. It may or may not modify them for the export market. Exporting involves the least change in the company's product lines, organization, investments, or mission.

Companies typically start with *indirect exporting*, working through independent international marketing intermediaries. Indirect exporting involves less investment because the firm does not require an overseas sales force or set of contacts. It also involves less risk. International marketing intermediaries—domestic-based export merchants or agents, cooperative organizations, and export-management companies—bring know-how and services to the relationship, so the seller normally makes fewer mistakes.

FIGURE 15.2
Market-Entry Strategies

Exporting	Joint venturing	Direct investment
Indirect Direct	Licensing Contract manufacturing Management contracting Joint ownership	Assembly facilities Manufacturing facilities

Amount of commitment, risk, control, and profit potential

Sellers may eventually move into *direct exporting,* whereby they handle their own exports. The investment and risk are somewhat greater in this strategy, but so is the potential return. A company can conduct direct exporting in several ways: It can set up a domestic export department that carries out export activities. It can set up an overseas sales branch that handles sales, distribution, and perhaps promotion. The sales branch gives the seller more presence and program control in the foreign market and often serves as a display center and customer service center. The company can also send home-based salespeople abroad at certain times in order to find business. Finally, the company can do its exporting either through foreign-based distributors who buy and own the goods or through foreign-based agents who sell the goods on behalf of the company.

Joint Venturing

A second method of entering a foreign market is **joint venturing**—joining with foreign companies to produce or market products or services. Joint venturing differs from exporting in that the company joins with a host country partner to sell or market abroad. It differs from direct investment in that an association is formed with someone in the foreign country. There are four types of joint ventures: licensing, contract manufacturing, management contracting, and joint ownership.

Joint venturing
Entering foreign markets by joining with foreign companies to produce or market a product or service.

Licensing
A method of entering a foreign market in which the company enters into an agreement with a licensee in the foreign market, offering the right to use a manufacturing process, trademark, patent, trade secret, or other item of value for a fee or royalty.

Licensing **Licensing** is a simple way for a manufacturer to enter international marketing. The company enters into an agreement with a licensee in the foreign market. For a fee or royalty, the licensee buys the right to use the company's manufacturing process, trademark, patent, trade secret, or other item of value. The company thus gains entry into the market at little risk; the licensee gains production expertise or a well-known product or name without having to start from scratch.

Coca-Cola markets internationally by licensing bottlers around the world and supplying them with the syrup needed to produce the product. In Japan, Budweiser beer flows from Kirin breweries, Lady Borden ice cream is churned out at Meiji Milk Products dairies, and Marlboro cigarettes roll off production lines at Japan Tobacco, Inc. Online brokerage E*TRADE has set up E*TRADE-branded Web sites under licensing agreements in Canada, Australia/New Zealand, and France. And Tokyo Disneyland is owned and operated by Oriental L and Company under license from the Walt Disney

■ Licensing: Tokyo Disneyland is owned and operated by the Oriental Land Co., Ltd. (a Japanese development company), under license from the Walt Disney company.

Company. The 45-year license gives Disney licensing fees plus 10 percent of admissions and 5 percent of food and merchandise sales.[22]

Licensing has potential disadvantages, however. The firm has less control over the licensee than it would over its own production facilities. Furthermore, if the licensee is very successful, the firm has given up these profits, and if and when the contract ends, it may find it has created a competitor.

Contract manufacturing

A joint venture in which a company contracts with manufacturers in a foreign market to produce the product or provide its service.

Contract Manufacturing   Another option is **contract manufacturing**—the company contracts with manufacturers in the foreign market to produce its product or provide its service. Sears used this method in opening up department stores in Mexico and Spain, where it found qualified local manufacturers to produce many of the products it sells. The drawbacks of contract manufacturing are decreased control over the manufacturing process and loss of potential profits on manufacturing. The benefits are the chance to start faster, with less risk, and the later opportunity either to form a partnership with or to buy out the local manufacturer.

Management contracting

A joint venture in which the domestic firm supplies the management know-how to a foreign company that supplies the capital; the domestic firm exports management services rather than products.

Management Contracting   Under **management contracting**, the domestic firm supplies management know-how to a foreign company that supplies the capital. The domestic firm exports management services rather than products. Hilton uses this arrangement in managing hotels around the world.

Management contracting is a low-risk method of getting into a foreign market, and it yields income from the beginning. The arrangement is even more attractive if the contracting firm has an option to buy some share in the managed company later on. The arrangement is not sensible, however, if the company can put its scarce management talent to better uses or if it can make greater profits by undertaking the whole venture. Management contracting also prevents the company from setting up its own operations for a period of time.

Joint ownership

A joint venture in which a company joins investors in a foreign market to create a local business in which the company shares joint ownership and control.

Joint Ownership   **Joint ownership** ventures consist of one company joining forces with foreign investors to create a local business in which they share joint ownership and control. A company may buy an interest in a local firm, or the two parties may form a new business venture. Joint ownership may be needed for economic or political reasons. The firm may lack the financial, physical, or managerial resources to undertake the venture alone. Or a foreign government may require joint ownership as a condition for entry.

KFC entered Japan through a joint ownership venture with Japanese conglomerate Mitsubishi. KFC sought a good way to enter the large but difficult Japanese fast-food market. In turn, Mitsubishi, one of Japan's largest poultry producers, understood the Japanese culture and had money to invest. Together, they helped KFC succeed in the semiclosed Japanese market. Surprisingly, with Mitsubishi's guidance, KFC developed decidedly un-Japanese positioning for its Japanese restaurants:

> While its initial reception in Japan was great, KFC still had a number of obstacles to overcome. The Japanese were uncomfortable with the idea of fast food and franchising. They saw fast food as artificial, made by mechanical means, and unhealthy. KFC Japan knew that it had to build trust in the KFC brand and flew to Kentucky to do it. There it filmed the most authentic version of Colonel Sanders's beginnings possible. To show the philosophy of KFC—the southern hospitality, old American tradition, and authentic home cooking—the agency first created the quintessential southern mother. With "My Old Kentucky Home" by Stephen Foster playing in the background, the commercial showed Colonel Sanders's mother making and feeding her grandchildren KFC chicken made with 11 secret spices. It conjured up scenes of good home cookin' from the American South, positioning KFC as wholesome, aristocratic food. In the end, the Japanese people could not get

■ Joint ownership: KFC entered Japan through a joint ownership venture with Japanese conglomerate Mitsubishi.

enough of this special American chicken. The campaign was hugely successful, and in less than 8 years KFC expanded its presence from 400 locations to more than 1,000. Most Japanese now know "My Old Kentucky Home" by heart.[23]

Joint ownership has certain drawbacks. The partners may disagree over investment, marketing, or other policies. Whereas many U.S. firms like to reinvest earnings for growth, local firms often prefer to take out these earnings; and whereas U.S. firms emphasize the role of marketing, local investors may rely on selling.

Direct Investment

The biggest involvement in a foreign market comes through **direct investment**—the development of foreign-based assembly or manufacturing facilities. If a company has gained experience in exporting and if the foreign market is large enough, foreign production facilities offer many advantages. The firm may have lower costs in the form of cheaper labor or raw materials, foreign government investment incentives, and freight savings. The firm may improve its image in the host country because it creates jobs. Generally, a firm develops a deeper relationship with government, customers, local suppliers, and distributors, allowing it to adapt its products to the local market better. Finally, the firm keeps full control over the investment and therefore can develop manufacturing and marketing policies that serve its long-term international objectives.

The main disadvantage of direct investment is that the firm faces many risks, such as restricted or devalued currencies, falling markets, or government changes. In some cases, a firm has no choice but to accept these risks if it wants to operate in the host country.

■ Deciding on the Global Marketing Program

Companies that operate in one or more foreign markets must decide how much, if at all, to adapt their marketing mixes to local conditions. At one extreme are global companies that use a **standardized marketing mix**, selling largely the same products and using the same marketing approaches worldwide. At the other extreme is an **adapted marketing mix**. In this case, the producer adjusts the marketing mix elements to each target market, bearing more costs but hoping for a larger market share and return.

The question of whether to adapt or standardize the marketing mix has been much debated in recent years. The marketing concept holds that marketing programs will be

Direct investment
Entering a foreign market by developing foreign-based assembly or manufacturing facilities.

Standardized marketing mix
An international marketing strategy for using basically the same product, advertising, distribution channels, and other elements of the marketing mix in all the company's international markets.

Adapted marketing mix
An international marketing strategy for adjusting the marketing-mix elements to each international target market, bearing more costs but hoping for a larger market share and return.

more effective if tailored to the unique needs of each targeted customer group. If this concept applies within a country, it should apply even more in international markets. Consumers in different countries have widely varied cultural backgrounds, needs and wants, spending power, product preferences, and shopping patterns. Because these differences are hard to change, most marketers adapt their products, prices, channels, and promotions to fit consumer desires in each country.

However, global standardization is not an all-or-nothing proposition but rather a matter of degree. Companies should look for ways to standardize to help keep down costs and prices and to build greater global brand power. But they must not replace long-run marketing thinking with short-run financial thinking. Although standardization saves money, marketers must make certain that they offer what consumers in each country want.[24]

Many possibilities exist between the extremes of standardization and complete adaptation. For example, although Whirlpool ovens, refrigerators, clothes washers, and other major appliances share the same interiors worldwide, their outer styling and features are designed to meet the preferences of consumers in different countries. KFC restaurants look much the same worldwide, right down to images of Colonel Sanders. But the chain offers tempura crispy strips in Japan, fresh rice with sweet chili sauce in Thailand, potato-and-onion croquettes in Holland, and pastries alongside the chicken in France.

Similarly, McDonald's uses the same basic operating formula in its restaurants around the world but adapts its menu to local tastes. It uses chili sauce instead of ketchup on its hamburgers in Mexico. In Vienna, its restaurants include "McCafes," which offer coffee blended to local tastes, and in Korea, it sells roast pork on a bun with a garlicky soy sauce. In India, where cows are considered sacred, McDonald's serves chicken, fish, vegetable burgers, and the Maharaja Mac—two all-mutton patties, special sauce, lettuce, cheese, pickles, onions on a sesame-seed bun.[25]

■ Marketing mix adaptation: In India, McDonald's serves chicken, fish, and vegetable burgers, and the Maharaja Mac—two all-mutton patties, special sauce, lettuce, cheese, pickles, onions, on a sesame-seed bun.

Most international marketers suggest that companies should "think globally but act locally"—that they should seek a balance between standardization and adaptation. These marketers advocate a "glocal" strategy in which the firm standardizes certain core marketing elements and localizes others. The corporate level gives global strategic direction; local units focus on the individual consumer differences across global markets. L'Oreal, the highly successful international personal care products company, operates this way. It markets truly global brands but adapts them to meet the cultural nuances of each local market (see Marketing at Work 15.2). Simon Clift, head of marketing for global consumer goods giant Unilever, puts it this way: "We're trying to strike a balance between being mindlessly global and hopelessly local."

Product

Five strategies allow for adapting product and promotion to a global market (see Figure 15.3).[26] We first discuss the three product strategies and then turn to the two promotion strategies.

Straight product extension means marketing a product in a foreign market without any change. Top management tells its marketing people, "Take the product as is and find

Straight product extension

Marketing a product in a foreign market without any change.

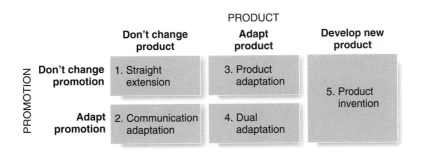

FIGURE 15.3

Five Global Product
and Promotion Strategies

customers for it." The first step, however, should be to find out whether foreign consumers use that product and what form they prefer.

Straight extension has been successful in some cases and disastrous in others. Kellogg cereals, Gillette razors, IBM computer services, Heineken beer, and Black & Decker tools are all sold successfully in about the same form around the world. But General Foods introduced its standard powdered Jell-O in the British market only to find that British consumers prefer a solid wafer or cake form. Likewise, Philips began to make a profit in Japan only after it reduced the size of its coffeemakers to fit into smaller Japanese kitchens and its shavers to fit smaller Japanese hands. Straight extension is tempting because it involves no additional product development costs, manufacturing changes, or new promotion. But it can be costly in the long run if products fail to satisfy foreign consumers.

Product adaptation involves changing the product to meet local conditions or wants. For example, Procter & Gamble's Vidal Sassoon shampoos contain a single fragrance worldwide, but the amount of scent varies by country: less in Japan, where subtle scents are preferred, and more in Europe. General Foods blends different coffees for the British (who drink their coffee with milk), the French (who drink their coffee black), and Latin Americans (who prefer a chicory taste). Gerber serves the Japanese baby food fare that might turn the stomachs of many Western consumers—local favorites include flounder and spinach stew, cod roe spaghetti, mugwort casserole, and sardines ground up in white radish sauce. Finnish cellular phone maker Nokia customized its 6100 series phone for every major market. Developers built in rudimentary voice recognition for Asia, where keyboards are a problem, and raised the ring volume so the phone could be heard on crowded Asian streets.

In some instances, products must also be adapted to local customs or spiritual beliefs. In Asia, the spiritual world often relates directly to sales. Hyatt Hotels' experience with the concept of *feng shui* is a good example:

> A practice widely followed in China, Hong Kong, and Singapore (and which has spread to Japan, Vietnam, and Korea), *feng shui* means "wind and water." Practitioners of *feng shui*, or geomancers, will recommend the most favorable conditions for any venture, particularly the placement of office buildings and the arrangement of desks, doors, and other items within. To have good *feng shui*, a building should face the water and be flanked by mountains. However, it should not block the view of the mountain spirits. The Hyatt Hotel in Singapore was designed without *feng shui* in mind, and as a result had to be redesigned to boost business. Originally the front desk was parallel to the doors and road, and this was thought to lead to wealth flowing out. Furthermore, the doors were facing northwest, which easily let undesirable spirits in. The geomancer recommended design alterations so that wealth could be retained and undesirable spirits kept out. Western businesses, from hotel chains, restaurants, and grocery retailers to Las Vegas casinos that serve many Asian visitors, are now incorporating *feng shui* principles into their facilities' designs.[27]

Product adaptation

Adapting a product to meet local conditions or wants in foreign markets.

Marketing at Work *15.2*

L'Oréal: Adapting Global Brands to Local Cultures

How does a French company with a British CEO successfully market a Japanese version of an American lipstick in Russia? Ask L'Oréal, the hugely successful international personal care products company. Headquartered in France, L'Oréal sells more than $14 billion worth of cosmetics, hair-care products, fragrances, and perfumes each year in 150 countries across the globe. That's 85 products sold every second, accounting for 13 percent of all cosmetics purchases made around the world. L'Oréal's broad portfolio of global brands includes, among others, Garnier, Maybelline, Redkin, Lancôme, Helena Rubinstein, Kiehl's, Biotherm, Softsheen-Carson, Vichy, and Ralph Lauren and Giorgio Armani Parfums. Impressively, L'Oréal has achieved 17 straight years of double-digit-profit international growth.

What's the secret to L'Oréal's amazing international success? The company markets its brands globally by understanding how they appeal to cultural nuances in specific local markets. Says one observer, "L'Oréal is French only when it wants to be. The rest of the time, it's happy being African, Asian, or anything else that sells." The giant cosmetics retailer buys local brands, tweaks them, and exports them globally, presenting a different face to each consumer around the world.

For example, in 1996, the company bought the stodgy American makeup producer, Maybelline. To reinvigorate and globalize the brand, it moved the unit's headquarters from Tennessee to New York City and added "New York" to the label. The resulting urban, street-smart, Big Apple image played well with the mid-price positioning of the workaday

makeup brand. The makeover earned Maybelline a 20 percent market share in its category in Western Europe. The young urban positioning also hit the mark in Asia. As one industry analyst recounts:

It's a sunny afternoon outside Parkson's department store in

Shanghai, and a marketing battle is raging for the attention of Chinese women. Tall, pouty models in beige skirts and sheer tops pass out flyers promoting Revlon's new spring colors. But their effort is drowned out by L'Oréal's eye-catching show for its Maybelline brand. To a pulsing

What's the secret to L'Oréal's amazing international success? The company markets its brands globally by understanding how they appeal to cultural nuances in specific local markets. It has become "the United Nations of Beauty."

Product invention

Creating new products or services for foreign markets.

Product invention consists of creating something new for a specific country market. This strategy can take two forms. It might mean reintroducing earlier product forms that happen to be well adapted to the needs of a given country. The National Cash Register Company reintroduced its crank-operated cash register at half the price of a modern cash register and sold large numbers in Asia, Latin America, and Spain. Or a company might

rhythm, two gangly models in shimmering lycra tops dance on a podium before a large backdrop depicting the New York City skyline. The music stops, and a makeup artist transforms a model's face while a Chinese saleswoman delivers the punch line. "This brand comes from America. It's very trendy," she shouts into her microphone. "If you want to be fashionable, just choose Maybelline." Few of the women in the crowd realize that the trendy "New York" Maybelline brand belongs to French cosmetics giant L'Oréal.

Although the Maybelline brand thrives on an infusion of American energy, L'Oréal does more than simply pitch a Western ideal. Instead, it recognizes different cultural perspectives on beauty throughout the world. In fact, the company often goes out of its way to challenge conventional preconceptions of beauty. For example, the cover of its annual report features a Japanese model with red hair and purple lipstick. Ads for Garnier hair dye posted in Moscow picture bleached blonde African and Asian models.

L'Oreal's CEO, Lindsay Owens-Jones, insists that the secret to good brand management is hitting the right audience with the right product. "Each brand is positioned on a very precise segment," he says. For L'Oréal, that means finding local brands, sprucing them up, positioning them for a specific target market, and exporting them to new customers all over the globe. To support that effort, the company spends $4 billion annually to tailor global marketing messages to local cultures around the world.

Take, for example, L'Oréal's recent acquisition and merger of the Soft Sheen and Carson brands. Originally marketed only in the United States, the Soft Sheen-Carson brand now generates more than 30 percent of its revenues abroad. In South Africa, where the brand has a 41 percent market share, L'Oréal has worked locally to encourage trials of its new products. In Senegal, the company's marketers are organizing a training session for hairdressers.

Beyond tailored messages and promotions, L'Oréal's products themselves must suit local needs across the very diverse range of people, cultures, and climates. Toward that end, as a proportion of revenues, L'Oréal spends 50 percent more than the industry average on product research and development and filed more than 490 patents last year alone. For example, research centers in Japan focus on the needs of Asian skin and hair types. The L'Oréal Institute for Ethnic Hair and Skin Research studies the needs of consumers of African descent. A climate-controlled wind tunnel in France provides insights into the impact of weather on cosmetics. R&D helps L'Oréal to formulate products for use in high-temperature, high-humidity environments such as India's. R&D also forms the basis for L'Oréal's fastest growing segment—so-called active cosmetics that are biomedically engineered by the company's scientists and dermatologists.

A seemingly conflicting array of words could be used to describe L'Oréal's brands: scientific and spiritual, mass-market and word-of-mouth, French sophistication and New York street smarts, conformity and uniqueness, luxury and affordability. How can a company stake a claim to all ends of the spectrum on so many different dimensions? For L'Oréal, being different things to different people means "conveying the allure of different cultures through its many products," says an industry analyst. Notes another observer:

In sharp contrast to other . . . Western brands such as Coca-Cola and McDonald's, which offer only a single cultural icon, L'Oréal can entice Asian consumers, for example, with a taste of French chic, New York attitude, or Italian elegance. You are anxious to buy into a part of the American dream—then Maybelline New York is there for the taking. [Want] 'Le latin way of life'—then Giorgio Armani is there for the taking.

L'Oréal products are found in chic shops, beauty salons, pharmacies, department stores, and even grocery stores. The company goes where the customer is and delivers what that customer wants—Vichy Laboratories in pharmacies, Giorgio Armani in upscale shops, mid-priced Maybelline at Wal-Mart. When CEO Owens-Jones recently addressed a UNESCO conference, nobody batted an eyelid when he described L'Oréal as "the United Nations of Beauty."

Sources: Quotes and other information from Gail Edmondson, "The Beauty of Global Branding," *Business Week*, June 28, 1999, pp.70–75; Richard Tomlinson, "L'Oréal's Global Makeover," *Fortune*, September 30, 2002, p. 141. See also "EuroFile Backgrounder: L'Oréal," September 11, 2001, accessed online at www.hemscott.co.uk; "Top Global Brands," *Global Cosmetic Industry*, February 2003, pp. 28–34; Jeremy Josephs, "O-J's Powers of Seduction Prove Hard to Resist," March 25, 2003, accessed online at www.jeremyjosephs.com; "History: Making Sure the Hair Creams Taste OK," accessed online at www.iwon.com, July 2003; and information accessed at www.loreal.com, September 2003.

create a new product to meet a need in a given country. For example, an enormous need exists for low-cost, high-protein foods in less-developed countries. Companies such as Quaker Oats, Swift, Monsanto, and Archer Daniels Midland are researching the nutrition needs of these countries, creating new foods, and developing advertising campaigns to gain product trial and acceptance.

As another example, Sony added the "U" model to its VAIO personal computer line to meet the unique needs of Japanese consumers, even though it wouldn't have much appeal in the United States and other world markets:

> The U may be the most "Japanese" product in the entire Sony VAIO line. The smallest laptop in the world, it is less than 7 inches wide, with a 6-inch diagonal screen, it makes an ordinary laptop look sumo sized. Sony noticed that rush-hour trains to Tokyo were simply too crowded to allow many commuters to use their laptops. "The only people in Tokyo who have the luxury of a lap are the first people on the train," says Mark Hanson, a Sony vice president. The point of the U, he explains, gripping its base with two hands and resting his thumbs on the keyboard, "is to give users the experience of what I'd call a standing computer." How would that translate into the U.S. market? The cultural differences are daunting. Far more Americans touch-type than do Japanese (a few Japanese characters convey a lot), and touch typists are likely to resist typing with their thumbs. And few Americans face a Tokyo-type rush-hour commute.[28]

Promotion

Companies can either adopt the same promotion strategy they used in the home market or change it for each local market. Consider advertising messages. Some global companies use a standardized advertising theme around the world. For example, to help communicate its global reach, IBM Global Services ran virtually identical "People Who Think. People Who Do. People Who Get It" ads in dozens of countries around the world. Of course, even in highly standardized promotion campaigns, some small changes might be required to adjust for language and minor cultural differences. For example, Guy Laroche uses virtually the same ads for its Drakkar Noir fragrances in Europe as in Arab countries. However, it subtly tones down the Arab versions to meet cultural differences in attitudes toward sensuality.

Colors also are changed sometimes to avoid taboos in other countries. Purple is associated with death in most of Latin America, white is a mourning color in Japan, and green is associated with jungle sickness in Malaysia. Even names must be changed. In Sweden, Helene Curtis changed the name of its Every Night Shampoo to Every Day because Swedes usually wash their hair in the morning. Kellogg also had to rename Bran Buds cereal in Sweden, where the name roughly translates as "burned farmer." (See Marketing at Work 15.3 for more on language blunders in international marketing.)

Communication adaptation
A global communication strategy of fully adapting advertising messages to local markets.

Other companies follow a strategy of **communication adaptation**, fully adapting their advertising messages to local markets. Kellogg ads in the United States promote the taste and nutrition of Kellogg's cereals versus competitors' brands. In France, where consumers drink little milk and eat little for breakfast, Kellogg's ads must convince consumers that cereals are a tasty and healthful breakfast. In India, where many consumers eat heavy, fried breakfasts, Kellogg's advertising convinces buyers to switch to a lighter, more nutritious breakfast diet.

Similarly, Coca-Cola sells its low-calorie beverage as Diet Coke in North America, the United Kingdom, and the Middle and Far East but as Light elsewhere. According to Diet

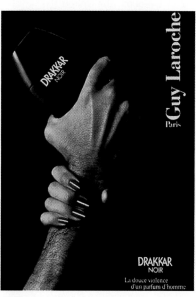

■ Some companies standardize their advertising around the world, adapting only to meet cultural differences. Guy Laroche uses similar ads in Europe (left) and Arab countries (right), but tones down the sensuality in the Arab version—the man is clothed and the woman barely touches him.

Coke's global brand manager, in Spanish-speaking countries Coke Light ads "position the soft drink as an object of desire, rather than as a way to feel good about yourself, as Diet Coke is positioned in the United States." This "desire positioning" plays off research showing that "Coca-Cola Light is seen in other parts of the world as a vibrant brand that exudes a sexy confidence."[29]

Media also need to be adapted internationally because media availability varies from country to country. TV advertising time is very limited in Europe, for instance, ranging from 4 hours a day in France to none in Scandinavian countries. Advertisers must buy time months in advance, and they have little control over airtimes. Magazines also vary in effectiveness. For example, magazines are a major medium in Italy and a minor one in Austria. Newspapers are national in the United Kingdom but are only local in Spain.[30]

Price

Companies also face many problems in setting their international prices. For example, how might Black & Decker price its power tools globally? It could set a uniform price all around the world, but this amount would be too high a price in poor countries and not high enough in rich ones. It could charge what consumers in each country would bear, but this strategy ignores differences in the actual costs from country to country. Finally, the company could use a standard markup of its costs everywhere, but this approach might price Black & Decker out of the market in some countries where costs are high.

Regardless of how companies go about pricing their products, their foreign prices probably will be higher than their domestic prices. A Gucci handbag may sell for $60 in Italy and $240 in the United States. Why? Gucci faces a *price escalation* problem. It must add the cost of transportation, tariffs, importer margin, wholesaler margin, and retailer margin to its factory price. Depending on these added costs, the product may have to sell for two to five times as much in another country to make the same profit. For example, a pair of Levi's jeans that sells for $30 in the United States typically fetches $63 in Tokyo and $88 in Paris. A computer that sells for $1,000 in New York may cost £1,000 in the United Kingdom. A DaimlerChrysler automobile priced at $20,000 in the United States might sell for more than $80,000 in South Korea.

Another problem involves setting a price for goods that a company ships to its foreign subsidiaries. If the company charges a foreign subsidiary too much, it may end up paying higher tariff duties even while paying lower income taxes in that country. If the company charges its subsidiary too little, it can be charged with *dumping*. Dumping occurs when a company either charges less than its costs or less than it charges in its home market. Thus, Harley-Davidson accused Honda and Kawasaki of dumping motorcycles on the U.S. market. The U.S. International Trade Commission agreed and responded with a special 5-year tariff on Japanese heavy motorcycles, starting at 45 percent in 1983 and gradually dropping to 10 percent by 1988. Various governments are always watching for dumping abuses, and they often force companies to set the price charged by other competitors for the same or similar products.[31]

Recent economic and technological forces have had an impact on global pricing. For example, in the European Union, the transition to the euro is reducing the amount of price differentiation. As consumers recognize price differentiation by country, companies are being forced to harmonize prices throughout the countries that have adopted the single currency. Companies and marketers that offer the most unique or necessary products or services will be least affected by such "price transparency."

For Marie-Claude Lang, a 72-year-old retired Belgian postal worker, the euro is the best thing since bottled water—or French country sausage. Always on the prowl for bargains, Ms. Lang is now stalking the wide aisles of an Auchan hypermarket in Roncq, France, a 15-minute drive from her Wervick home. . . . Ms. Lang has been coming to France every other week for years to stock up on bottled water,

Marketing at Work | 15.3

Watch Your Language!

Many global companies have had difficulty crossing the language barrier, with results ranging from mild embarrassment to outright failure. Seemingly innocuous brand names and advertising phrases can take on unintended or hidden meanings when translated into other languages. Careless translations can make a marketer look downright foolish to foreign consumers.

We've all run across examples when buying products from other countries. Here's one from a firm in Taiwan attempting to instruct children on how to install a ramp on a garage for toy cars: "Before you play with, fix waiting plate by yourself as per below diagram. But after you once fixed it, you can play with as is and no necessary to fix off again." Many U.S. firms are guilty of such atrocities when marketing abroad.

The classic language blunders involve standardized brand names that do not translate well. When Coca-Cola first marketed Coke in China in the 1920s, it developed a group of Chinese characters that, when pronounced, sounded like the product name. Unfortunately, the characters actually translated to mean "bite the wax tadpole." Now, the characters on Chinese Coke bottles translate as "happiness in the mouth."

Several U.S. car makers have had similar problems when their brand names crashed into the language barrier. Chevy's Nova translated into Spanish as *no va*—"it doesn't go." GM changed the name to Caribe and sales increased. Ford introduced its Fiera truck only to discover that the name means "ugly old woman" in Spanish. And Rolls-Royce avoided the name Silver Mist in German markets, where *mist* means "manure." Sunbeam, however, entered the German market with its Mist Stick hair curling iron. As should have been expected, the Germans had little use for a "manure wand." A similar fate awaited Colgate when it introduced a toothpaste in France called Cue, the name of a notorious porno magazine.

One well-intentioned firm sold its shampoo in Brazil under the name Evitol. It soon realized it was claiming to sell a "dandruff contraceptive." An American company reportedly had trouble marketing Pet milk in French-speaking areas. It seems that the word *pet* in French means, among other things, "to break wind." Hunt-Wesson introduced its Big John products in Quebec as Gros Jos before learning that it means "big breasts" in French. This gaffe had no apparent effect on sales. Interbrand of London, the firm that created household names such as Prozac and Acura, recently developed a brand-name "hall of shame" list, which contained these and other foreign brand names you're never likely to see inside the local A&P: Krapp toilet paper (Denmark), Crapsy Fruit cereal (France), Happy End toilet paper (Germany), Mukk yogurt (Italy), Zit lemonade (Germany), Poo curry powder (Argentina), and Pschitt lemonade (France).

Travelers often encounter well-intentioned advice from service firms that takes on meanings very different from those intended. The menu in one Swiss restaurant proudly stated, "Our wines leave you nothing to hope for." Signs in a Japanese hotel pronounced, "You are invited to take advantage of the chambermaid." At a laundry in Rome, it was, "Ladies, leave your clothes here and spend the afternoon having a good time." The brochure at a Tokyo car rental offered this sage advice: "When passenger of foot heave in sight, tootle the horn. Trumpet him melodiously at first, but if he still obstacles your passage, tootle him with vigor."

Advertising themes often lose—or gain—something in the translation. The Coors beer slogan "get loose with Coors" in Spanish came out as "get the runs with Coors." Coca-Cola's "Coke adds life" theme in Japanese translated into "Coke brings your ancestors back from the dead." The milk industry learned too late that its American advertising question "Got Milk?" translated in Mexico as a more provocative "Are you lactating?" In Chinese, the KFC slogan "finger-lickin' good" came out as "eat your fingers off." And Frank Perdue's classic line, "It takes a tough man to make a tender chicken," took on added meaning in Spanish: "It takes an aroused man to make a chicken affectionate." Even when the language is the same, word usage may differ from country to country. Thus, the British ad line for Electrolux vacuum cleaners—"Nothing sucks like an Electrolux"—would capture few customers in the United States.

Sources: See David A. Ricks, "Perspectives: Translation Blunders in International Business," *Journal of Language for International Business,* July 2, 1996, pp. 50–55; David W. Helin, "When Slogans Go Wrong," *American Demographics,* February 1992, p. 14; "But Will It Sell in Tulsa?" *Newsweek,* March 17, 1997, p. 8; "What You Didn't Learn in Marketing 101," *Sales & Marketing Management,* May 1997, p. 20; Ken Friedenreich, "The Lingua Too Franca," *World Trade,* April 1998, p. 98; Richard P. Carpenter, "What They Meant to Say Was . . . ," *Boston Globe,* August 2, 1998, p. M6; Thomas T. Sermon, "Cutting Corners in Language Risky Business," *Marketing News,* April 23, 2001, p. 9; and Lara L. Sowinski, "Ubersetzung, Traduzione, or Traduccion," *World Trade,* February 2002, pp. 48–49.

milk, and yogurt. But the launch of the euro . . . has opened her eyes to many more products that she now sees cost less across the border. Today she sees that "saucisse de campagne," is cheaper "by about five euro cents," a savings she didn't notice when she had to calculate the difference between Belgian and French francs. At Europe's borders, the euro is turning into the coupon clipper's delight. Sure, price-conscious Europeans have long crossed into foreign territory to find everything from cheaper television sets to bargain bottles of Coca-Cola. But the new transparency is making comparisons a whole lot easier.[32]

The Internet will also make global price differences more obvious. When firms sell their wares over the Internet, customers can see how much products sell for in different countries. They might even be able to order a given product directly from the company location or dealer offering the lowest price. This will force companies toward more standardized international pricing.

■ International pricing: Twelve European Union countries have adopted the euro as a common currency, creating "pricing transparency" and forcing companies to harmonize their prices throughout Europe.

Distribution Channels

The international company must take a **whole-channel view** of the problem of distributing products to final consumers. Figure 15.4 shows the three major links between the seller and the final buyer. The first link, the *seller's headquarters organization*, supervises the channels and is part of the channel itself. The second link, *channels between nations*, moves the products to the borders of the foreign nations. The third link, *channels within nations*, moves the products from their foreign entry point to the final consumers. Some U.S. manufacturers may think their job is done once the product leaves their hands, but they would do well to pay more attention to its handling within foreign countries.

Channels of distribution within countries vary greatly from nation to nation. First, there are the large differences in the *numbers and types of intermediaries* serving each foreign market. For example, a U.S. company marketing in China must operate through a frustrating maze of state-controlled wholesalers and retailers. Chinese distributors often carry competitors' products and frequently refuse to share even basic sales and marketing information with their suppliers. Hustling for sales is an alien concept to Chinese distributors, who are used to selling all they can obtain. Working with or getting around this system sometimes requires substantial time and investment.

When Coke first entered China, for example, customers bicycled up to bottling plants to get their soft drinks. Many shopkeepers still don't have enough electricity to run soft drink coolers. Now, Coca-Cola has set up direct-distribution channels, investing heavily in refrigerators and trucks, and upgrading wiring so that more retailers can install coolers. The company

Whole-channel view
Designing international channels that take into account all the necessary links in distributing the seller's products to final buyers, including the seller's headquarters organization, channels among nations, and channels within nations.

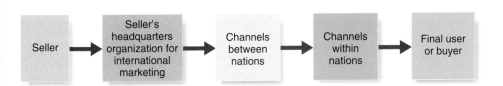

Seller → Seller's headquarters organization for international marketing → Channels between nations → Channels within nations → Final user or buyer

FIGURE 15.4
Whole-Channel Concept for International Marketing

■ A "neighborhood committee" member sells Coke in Shanghai.

has also built an army of more than 10,000 sales representatives that makes regular visits on resellers, often on foot or bicycle, to check on stocks and record sales. "Coke and its bottlers have been trying to map every supermarket, restaurant, barbershop, or market stall where a can of soda might be consumed," notes an industry observer. "Those data help Coke get closer to its customers, whether they are in large hypermarkets, Spartan noodle shops or schools."[33] Moreover, Coke is always on the lookout for innovative distribution approaches:

Stroll through any residential area in a Chinese city and sooner or later you'll encounter a senior citizen with a red armband eyeing strangers suspiciously. These are the pensioners who staff the neighborhood committees, which act as street-level watchdogs for the ruling Communist Party. In Shanghai, however, some of these socialist guardians have been signed up by the ultimate symbol of American capitalism, Coca-Cola. As part of its strategy to get the product to the customer, Coke approached 14 neighborhood committees . . . with a proposal. The head of Coke's Shanghai division outlines the deal: "We told them, 'You have some old people who aren't doing much. Why don't we stock our product in your office? Then you can sell it, earn some commission, and raise a bit of cash.'" Done. So . . . how are the party snoops adapting to the market? Not badly, reports the manager. "We use the neighborhood committees as a sales force," he says. Sales aren't spectacular, but because the committees supervise housing projects with up to 200 families, they have proved to be useful vehicles for building brand awareness.[34]

Another difference lies in the *size and character of retail units* abroad. Whereas large-scale retail chains dominate the U.S. scene, much retailing in other countries is done by many small, independent retailers. In India, millions of retailers operate tiny shops or sell in open markets. Their markups are high, but the actual price is lowered through haggling. Supermarkets could offer lower prices, but supermarkets are difficult to build and open because of many economic and cultural barriers. Incomes are low, and people prefer to shop daily for small amounts rather than weekly for large amounts. They also lack storage and refrigeration to keep food for several days. Packaging is not well developed because it would add too much to the cost. These factors have kept large-scale retailing from spreading rapidly in developing countries.

SPEED BUMP

Linking the Concepts

Slow down here and think again about McDonald's global marketing issues.

■ To what extent can McDonald's standardize for the Chinese market? What marketing strategy and program elements can be similar to those used in the United States and other parts of the Western world? Which ones must be adapted? Be specific.

■ To what extent can McDonald's standardize its products and programs for the Canadian market? What elements can be standardized and which must be adapted?

■ To what extent are McDonald's "globalization" efforts contributing to "Americanization" of countries and cultures around the world? What are the positives and negatives of such cultural developments?

◼◼▌ Deciding on the Global Marketing Organization

Companies manage their international marketing activities in at least three different ways: Most companies first organize an export department, then create an international division, and finally become a global organization.

A firm normally gets into international marketing by simply shipping out its goods. If its international sales expand, the company organizes an *export department* with a sales manager and a few assistants. As sales increase, the export department can expand to include various marketing services so that it can actively go after business. If the firm moves into joint ventures or direct investment, the export department will no longer be adequate.

Many companies get involved in several international markets and ventures. A company may export to one country, license to another, have a joint ownership venture in a third, and own a subsidiary in a fourth. Sooner or later it will create *international divisions* or subsidiaries to handle all its international activity.

International divisions are organized in a variety of ways. An international division's corporate staff consists of marketing, manufacturing, research, finance, planning, and personnel specialists. It plans for and provides services to various operating units, which can be organized in one of three ways. They can be *geographical organizations*, with country managers who are responsible for salespeople, sales branches, distributors, and licensees in their respective countries. Or the operating units can be *world product groups*, each responsible for worldwide sales of different product groups. Finally, operating units can be *international subsidiaries,* each responsible for its own sales and profits.

Many firms have passed beyond the international division stage and become truly *global organizations*. They stop thinking of themselves as national marketers who sell abroad and start thinking of themselves as global marketers. The top corporate management and staff plan worldwide manufacturing facilities, marketing policies, financial flows, and logistical systems. The global operating units report directly to the chief executive or executive committee of the organization, not to the head of an international division. Executives are trained in worldwide operations, not just domestic *or* international. The company recruits management from many countries, buys components and supplies where they cost the least, and invests where the expected returns are greatest.

Moving into the twenty-first century, major companies must become more global if they hope to compete. As foreign companies successfully invade their domestic markets, companies must move more aggressively into foreign markets. They will have to change from companies that treat their international operations as secondary to companies that view the entire world as a single borderless market.

REST STOP:
Reviewing the Concepts

It's time to stop and think back about the global marketing concepts you've covered in this chapter. In the past, U.S. companies paid little attention to international trade. If they could pick up some extra sales through exporting, that was fine. But the big market was at home, and it teemed with opportunities. Companies today can no longer afford to pay attention only to their domestic market, regardless of its size. Many industries are global industries, and firms that operate globally achieve lower costs and higher brand awareness. At the same time, *global marketing* is risky because of variable exchange rates, unstable governments, protectionist tar-

iffs and trade barriers, and several other factors. Given the potential gains and risks of international marketing, companies need a systematic way to make their global marketing decisions.

1. **Discuss how the international trade system, economic, political–legal, and cultural environments affect a company's international marketing decisions.**

A company must understand the *global marketing environment*, especially the international trade system. It must assess each foreign market's *economic*, *political–legal*, and *cultural characteristics.* The company must then decide whether it wants to go abroad and consider the potential risks and benefits. It must decide on the volume of international sales it wants, how many countries it wants to market in, and which specific markets it wants to enter. This decision calls for weighing the probable rate of return on investment against the level of risk.

2. Describe three key approaches to entering international markets.

The company must decide how to enter each chosen market—whether through *exporting, joint venturing,* or *direct investment.* Many companies start as exporters, move to joint ventures, and finally make a direct investment in foreign markets. In *exporting,* the company enters a foreign market by sending and selling products through international marketing intermediaries (indirect exporting) or the company's own department, branch, or sales representative or agents (direct exporting). When establishing a *joint venture,* a company enters foreign markets by joining with foreign companies to produce or market a product or service. In *licensing,* the company enters a foreign market by contracting with a licensee in the foreign market, offering the

right to use a manufacturing process, trademark, patent, trade secret, or other item of value for a fee or royalty.

3. Explain how companies adapt their marketing mixes for international markets.

Companies must also decide how much their products, promotion, price, and channels should be adapted for each foreign market. At one extreme, global companies use a *standardized marketing mix* worldwide. Others use an *adapted marketing mix,* in which they adjust the marketing mix to each target market, bearing more costs but hoping for a larger market share and return.

4. Identify the three major forms of international marketing organization.

The company must develop an effective organization for international marketing. Most firms start with an *export department* and graduate to an *international division.* A few become *global organizations,* with worldwide marketing planned and managed by the top officers of the company. Global organizations view the entire world as a single, borderless market.

Navigating the Key Terms

Adapted marketing mix	Exporting	Product adaptation
Communication adaptation	Global firm	Product invention
Contract manufacturing	Joint ownership	Quota
Countertrade	Joint venturing	Standardized marketing mix
Direct investment	Licensing	Straight product extension
Economic community	Management contracting	Tariff
Embargo	Nontariff trade barriers	Whole-channel view
Exchange controls		

Travel Log

Discussing the Issues

1. Discuss how tariffs, quotas, and nontariff trade barriers can restrict international trade. Why would a government choose to restrict the import of foreign products? How do regional free trade arrangements help to encourage trade between nations?

2. What are the advantages and disadvantages of the following types of joint ventures: licensing, contract manufacturing, management contracting, and joint ownership?

3. Identify a product that uses a standardized marketing mix and one that uses an adapted marketing mix. Evaluate the appropriateness of that strategy for those products.

4. Assume you are responsible for introducing the Ford Explorer into Pakistan. Explain what might be changed to the product and/or promotional strategy to make it fit into each of the five cells in Figure 15.3.

5. Explain the difference between organizing the international marketing function as an export department, international division, and a global organization. What drives the evolution from one organizational form to another?

Application Questions

1. Study the indicators of market potential listed in Table 15.1. Visit your school library and find either a print or online source of data for at least two indicators in each of the six major categories. Which of the information sources you identified seem the most reliable and which the least? What concerns would you have as a marketing manager making market potential evaluations using the least reliable data?

2. You have been asked by your boss to advise her on the best way to enter the Italian market with your company's new brand of sugar-free ice cream. What mode of entry would you recommend and why? What information would a company need to have before making this decision? For one of the entry modes you did not select, what would have to change for it to become the recommended choice?

3. Get into teams of three students. Assume that your team has been given responsibility for assessing the attractiveness of entering Mexico with your firm's line of laptop computers. Evaluate the opportunity of entering Mexico in terms of its economic, political–legal, and cultural environment for the laptop computer. Present your findings to the class.

Under the Hood: Focus on Technology

Everybody can use a little help now and then. But where can you go if you are a business owner who needs assistance expanding your operations internationally? Recognizing the need for American businesses to become more competitive in global markets, the U.S. Congress passed legislation to create the Centers for International Business Education and Research (CIBERs) in 1988. Currently, 30 universities from across the country are provided funding to develop programs, conduct research, provide language training, and make available other resources that will aid the international capabilities of businesses, teachers, and students. Visit the CIBER web site

(http://ciber.centers.purdue.edu/) and examine the type of information that is available to companies wishing to do business internationally. Then respond to these questions.

1. What resources are available to businesses and students to help understand international marketing concerns?

2. How might a small business owner interested in expanding their operations to Latin America utilize the CIBER resources?

3. What sorts of resources are available for business school faculty interested in advancing the international component of their curriculum?

Focus on Ethics

The global marketplace exposes marketing managers to a variety of customs and traditions as companies expand internationally. At times, business practices that may be disapproved of in one country (e.g., hiring from within one's family or offering gifts to secure business deals) may be common and accepted ways of doing business in other parts of the world. This can cause some concern among managers, who are unsure how to react to cultural differences. A "cultural relativism" approach would suggest that the customs of the local culture be adopted. At the other extreme, an "ethical imperialism" approach means that

an individual's home country rules are correct and should be applied universally.

1. Which approach should be taken, cultural relativism, ethical imperialism, or some middle position? Explain your choice.

2. Are there any guidelines that all companies should follow regardless of where the company operates (e.g., respect human dignity)?

3. How would you express your discomfort with business practices that are considered unethical in your culture, but are acceptable in the local culture in which you are operating?

Videos

The Starbucks video case that accompanies this chapter is located in Appendix 1 at the back of the book.

Student Materials

Need a tune-up? A study guide and OneKey access code are available to aid in your review of chapter material. Your instructor may choose to have these items shrink-wrapped with your text or you may purchase them separately at www.prenhall.com/marketing.

■ *After studying this chapter, you should be able to*

1. *Identify* the major social criticisms of marketing   **2.** *Define* consumerism and environmentalism, and explain how they affect marketing strategies   **3.** *Describe* the principles of socially responsible marketing   **4.** *Explain* the role of ethics in marketing

Marketing and Society: Social Responsibility and Marketing Ethics

16

ROAD MAP | Previewing the Concepts

You've almost completed your introductory marketing travels. In this final chapter, we'll focus on marketing as a social institution. First, we'll look at some common criticisms of marketing as it impacts individual consumers, other businesses, and society as a whole. Then, we'll examine consumerism, environmentalism, and other citizen and public actions to keep marketing in check. Finally, we'll see how companies themselves can benefit from proactively pursuing socially responsible and ethical practices. You'll see that social responsibility and ethical actions are more than just the right thing to do; they're also good for business.

Before traveling on, let's visit the concept of social responsibility in business. Over the past several years, Nike has been a lightning rod for social responsibility criticisms. Critics have accused Nike of putting profits ahead of the interests of consumers and the broader public, both at home and abroad. You've probably read headlines alleging foreign "sweatshops" abuses and possible exploitation of inner-city consumers. Are these criticisms justified? Read on.

I f you say "Nike" and "corporate social responsibility" in the same breath, most consumers will bring up the negatives. Many have read the headlines in recent years: "Nike Axes 'Sweatshop' after BBC Investigation," "Nike Accused of Exploiting Inner-City Youths with High-Priced Sneakers," or "Just Do It without Nike." However, while criticisms of Nike have grabbed the headlines, look a little deeper. You might be surprised to learn about all the socially responsible things that Nike does to make this world a better place.

Despite its success at selling shoes—or perhaps *because* of this success—Nike has been heavily criticized. As the headlines suggest, the company has been accused of everything from running sweatshops, using child labor, and exploiting low-income consumers to degrading the environment. The rights and wrongs concerning these issues are often hard to discern.

Consider the Nike "sweatshop" charges. Like many other companies these days, to be more cost and price competitive, Nike outsources production to contractors in low-wage countries, such as China, Vietnam, Thailand, Indonesia, the Philippines, and Pakistan. The problem is that, through the eyes of affluent Westerners, workplace conditions in many third-world factories are truly appalling. These factories have long hours, unsafe working conditions, child labor, and substandard pay for people desperate to have any job at all. As Nike has outsourced

more manufacturing to foreign subcontractors, reports of such abusive conditions have surfaced. The issue became very public in 1996, when a *New York Times* editorial accused Nike of running sweatshops and using child labor. Other critics quickly joined in, painting a picture of a greedy Nike, reaping profits at the expense of low-paid foreign laborers, many of them children, who were forced to work in the dismal conditions in suppliers' factories.

Nike responded that, years earlier, it had created a Code of Conduct, which demanded more socially responsible labor practices by its contractors. What's more, according to CEO Phil Knight, Nike was actually improving the working conditions in low-wage countries. "Nike has paid, on average, double the minimum wage as defined in countries where its products are produced under contract," he claimed. Besides, Nike argued, who are we to decide what rules are proper in other countries—to define who is a child, who has a right to work, and under what conditions? Some developing countries actually resent the paternalistic regulations of a multinational corporation. Still, Nike took the charges seriously and accepted some of the criticisms as legitimate. It commissioned Andrew Young, a civil rights leader and former UN ambassador, to visit Nike factories abroad. Although Young suggested there was room for improvement, he found none of the alleged extreme examples of abuse. Despite Nike's responses, the criticisms of its foreign manufacturing practices continued.

Nike has also received criticism at home. For example, it has been accused of inappropriately targeting its most expensive shoes to low-income families, making the shoes an expensive status symbol for poor urban street kids. Critics point to stories of youths gunned down in inner-city neighborhoods for a pair of $100 Nike sneakers. Nike isn't just selling utilitarian footwear, they claim. It's selling a hip athletic image created by a big-budget marketing campaign. The high price becomes the cost of membership in an artificial, "Just Do It" culture inhabited by the likes of Michael Jordan and LeBron James.

Although such criticisms have received most of the attention, a second look shows that Nike works hard at being a socially responsible global citizen. Click on the "Responsibility" tab at the company's Web site (www.nikebiz.com), and you'll learn that Nike pursues an active agenda of good works. "Our vision is to be an innovative and inspirational global citizen in a world where companies participate," says Nike. "As a company and as individuals, we ardently contribute to the communities where we live, work, and play throughout the world." Such words are cheap, but Nike backs this vision with actions.

Nike and the Nike Foundation contributed more than $29 million in cash and products last year to programs that encourage youth to participate in sports and that address challenges of globalization. The company's goal is to give 3 percent of annual pretax earnings to charities, nonprofit organizations, and community partners around the world. Here are just a few of the good things Nike is doing:

> The NikeGO program works closely with Boys & Girls Clubs of America to combat obesity, diabetes, and eating disorders among American youth resulting from poor diet, inactivity, and lack of safe facilities. The program funds kid-designed programs that increase club member activity—programs that get kids to "just Go!" The NikeGO Fund supports courts and facilities around the country. For example, it recently provided funds to refurbish every basketball court found in Portland's 10,000 acres of public parkland—new surfaces, rebuilt backboards, fresh nets, and all.

Nike's Jordan Fundamentals Grant Program awards grants to teachers or professionals who design innovative learning experiences for economically disadvantaged students in grades 6 to 12. Nike also supports Self Enhancement, Inc. (SEI), which works with schools and families to develop after-school programs in education, recreation, and the arts to help inner-city youth in Portland (Nike's home town) to realize their full potential.

Nike supports the Wings of America youth development program, which works with American Indian youth across the United States and Canada. The program uses running as a vehicle for leadership, self-esteem, wellness, and cultural pride among youths from 5 to 14 years of age.

Throughout the world, Nike works with governments, local communities, nongovernment organizations, and sports associations to actively promote kids' participation in sports through organized programs and better sports facilities. For example, Nike recently joined with its factory partners in China to donate a new, full-sized Nike Football Park located 15 minutes from Tiananmen Square. The facility is available to community soccer enthusiasts daily, free of charge. Nike also worked with the Shanghai Education Bureau to provide youth with safe places to play after school and on weekends.

Nike also donates money for education, community development, and small-business loans in the countries in which it operates. For example, Nike set up the Nike Village in Thailand, which combines progressive manufacturing with community development. This program encourages Nike contractors to set up satellite production facilities in rural areas to halt the migration into overcrowded Bangkok. The Nike Village hosts a community center, micro-loan programs, ecology and health education, and a women's advocacy group that provides business education and empowerment training.

Regarding its manufacturing practices, Nike has pledged to "make responsible sourcing a business reality that enhances workers' lives." For example, Nike's Code of Conduct is now available in 18 languages. It spells out Nike's position on child labor, forced labor, compensation, benefits, work hours, environment, safety, and health. Contractors must post the code where workers can read it and certify that they adhere to it. Today, Nike has 85 employees located in countries where Nike products are manufactured who visit suppliers' factories on a daily basis.

Nike is also committed to sustainable environmental practices. For example, it has developed environmentally responsible products such as PVC-free footware and a line of 100 percent organic cotton apparel. Nike's Reuse-A-Shoe program collects old shoes of any brand—some 2 millions pairs a year—then grinds them up and gives them new life as athletic surfaces or in other Nike products. Through its Air to Earth Program, Nike works with environmental organizations to educate students in grades 4 to 9 about conservation, reuse, and recycling.

Like most global companies, Nike isn't perfect when it comes to matters of social responsibility. "We made some mistakes," says CEO Knight. But the mistakes were not for a lack of trying to do what's right. Issues of social responsibility are seldom clear cut. Still, they are very, very important. In Knight's words:

> As a citizen of the world, Nike must Do the Right Thing. I know what makes for good performance when I see it on the running track. I know it when I read quarterly results from the finance department. I have to admit, though, I'm not sure how we measure good performance in corporate responsibility. I'm not convinced anybody [knows how]. Why not? Because there are no standards, no agreed-on definitions. . . . Until [we have such standards], we have to figure it out for ourselves. [No matter what the standards, however,] the performance of Nike and every other global company in the 21st century will be measured as much by our impact on quality of life as it is by revenue growth and profit margins.[1]

Responsible marketers discover what consumers want and respond with marketing offers that give satisfaction and value to buyers and profit to the producer. The *marketing concept* is a philosophy of customer satisfaction and mutual gain. Its practice leads the economy by an invisible hand to satisfy the many and changing needs of millions of consumers.

Not all marketers follow the marketing concept, however. In fact, some companies use questionable marketing practices, and some marketing actions that seem innocent in themselves strongly affect the larger society. Consider the sale of cigarettes. On the face of it, companies should be free to sell cigarettes and smokers should be free to buy them. But this transaction affects the public interest. First, the smokers are harming their health and may be shortening their own lives. Second, smoking places a financial burden on the smoker's family and on society at large. Third, other people around smokers may suffer discomfort and harm from second-hand smoke. Finally, marketing cigarettes to adults might also influence young people to begin smoking. Thus, the marketing of tobacco products has sparked substantial debate and negotiation in recent years.[2] This example shows that private transactions may involve larger questions of public policy.

This chapter examines the social effects of private marketing practices. We examine several questions: What are the most frequent social criticisms of marketing? What steps have private citizens taken to curb marketing ills? What steps have legislators and government agencies taken to curb marketing ills? What steps have enlightened companies taken to carry out socially responsible and ethical marketing? We examine how marketing affects and is affected by each of these issues.

■▌ Social Criticisms of Marketing

Marketing receives much criticism. Some of this criticism is justified; much is not. Social critics claim that certain marketing practices hurt individual consumers, society as a whole, and other business firms.

Marketing's Impact on Individual Consumers

Consumers have many concerns about how well the American marketing system serves their interests. Surveys usually show that consumers hold mixed or even slightly unfavorable attitudes toward marketing practices. Consumers, consumer advocates, government agencies, and other critics have accused marketing of harming consumers through high prices, deceptive practices, high-pressure selling, shoddy or unsafe products, planned obsolescence, and poor service to disadvantaged consumers.

High Prices   Many critics charge that the American marketing system causes prices to be higher than they would be under more "sensible" systems. They point to three factors—*high costs of distribution, high advertising and promotion costs,* and *excessive markups.*

High Costs of Distribution. A long-standing charge is that greedy intermediaries mark up prices beyond the value of their services. Critics charge that there are too many intermediaries, that intermediaries are inefficient and poorly run, or that they provide unnecessary or duplicate services. As a result, distribution costs too much, and consumers pay for these excessive costs in the form of higher prices.

How do resellers answer these charges? They argue that intermediaries do work that would otherwise have to be done by manufacturers or consumers. Markups reflect services that consumers themselves want—more convenience, larger stores and assortment, longer store hours, return privileges, and others. In fact, they argue, retail competition is so intense that margins are actually quite low. For example, after taxes, supermarket chains are typically left with barely 1 percent profit on their sales. If some resellers try to charge too much relative to the value they add, other resellers will step in with lower prices. Low-price stores such as Wal-Mart, Best Buy, and other discounters pressure their competitors to operate efficiently and keep their prices down.

High Advertising and Promotion Costs. Modern marketing is also accused of pushing up prices to finance heavy advertising and sales promotion. For example, a dozen tablets of a heavily promoted brand of aspirin sell for the same price as 100 tablets of less promoted brands. Differentiated products—cosmetics, detergents, toiletries—include promotion and packaging costs that can amount to 40 percent or more of the manufacturer's price to the retailer. Critics charge that much of the packaging and promotion adds only psychological value to the product rather than functional value. Retailers use additional promotion—advertising, displays, and sweepstakes—that adds several cents more to retail prices.

Marketers respond that consumers can usually buy functional versions of products at lower prices. However, they *want* and are willing to pay more for products that also provide psychological benefits—that make them feel wealthy, attractive, or special. Brand-name products may cost more, but branding gives buyers assurances of consistent quality. Heavy advertising adds to product costs but adds value by informing millions of potential buyers of the availability and merits of a brand. If consumers want to know what is available on the market, they must expect manufacturers to spend large sums of money on advertising. Also, heavy advertising and promotion may be necessary for a firm to match competitors' efforts—the business would lose "share of mind" if it did not match competitive spending. At the same time, companies are cost conscious about promotion and try to spend their money wisely.

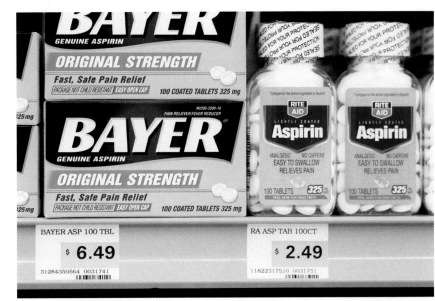

■ A heavily promoted brand of aspirin sells for much more than a virtually identical non-branded or store-branded product. Critics charge that promotion adds only psychological value to the product rather than functional value.

Excessive Markups. Critics also charge that some companies mark up goods excessively. They point to the drug industry, where a pill costing 5 cents to make may cost the consumer $2 to buy. They point to the pricing tactics of funeral homes that prey on the confused emotions of bereaved relatives and to the high charges for television repair and auto repair.

Marketers respond that most businesses try to deal fairly with consumers because they want repeat business. Most consumer abuses are unintentional. When shady marketers do take advantage of consumers, they should be reported to Better Business Bureaus and to state and federal agencies. Marketers also respond that consumers often don't understand the reasons for high markups. For example, pharmaceutical markups must cover the costs of purchasing, promoting, and distributing existing medicines plus the high research and development costs of formulating and testing new medicines.

Deceptive Practices Marketers are sometimes accused of deceptive practices that lead consumers to believe they will get more value than they actually do. Deceptive practices fall into three groups: deceptive pricing, promotion, and packaging. *Deceptive pricing* includes practices such as falsely advertising "factory" or "wholesale" prices or a large price reduction from a phony high retail list price. *Deceptive promotion* includes practices such as overstating the product's features or performance, luring the customer to the store for a bargain that is out of stock, or running rigged contests. *Deceptive packaging* includes exaggerating package contents through subtle design, not filling the package to the top, using misleading labeling, or describing size in misleading terms.

To be sure, questionable marketing practices do occur. For example, at one time or another, we've all gotten an envelope in the mail screaming something like "You have won $10,000,000!" or a pop-up Web screen promising free goods or discounted prices. In recent years, sweepstakes companies have come under the gun for their deceptive communication practices. Sweepstakes promoter Publishers Clearing House recently paid heavily to settle claims that its high-pressure tactics had misled consumers into believing that they had won prizes when they hadn't. The Wisconsin Attorney General asserted that "there are older consumers who send [sweepstakes companies] checks and money orders on a weekly basis

■ Questionable marketing practices: Sweepstakes promoter Publishers Clearing House recently paid heavily to settle claims that its high-pressure tactics had misled consumers into believing that they had won prizes when they hadn't.

with a note that says they were very upset that the prize patrol did not come."[3]

Deceptive practices have led to legislation and other consumer protection actions. For example, in 1938 Congress reacted to such blatant deceptions as Fleischmann's Yeast's claim to straighten crooked teeth by enacting the Wheeler–Lea Act giving the Federal Trade Commission (FTC) power to regulate "unfair or deceptive acts or practices." The FTC has published several guidelines listing deceptive practices. Despite new regulations, some critics argue that deceptive claims are still the norm. For example, a recent study found that almost two-thirds of unsolicited e-mails contain false or misleading claims.[4]

The toughest problem is defining what is "deceptive." For instance, Palm recently agreed to settle Federal Trade Commission accusations that ads for the company's handheld computers were deceptive. The ads claimed the Palm's devices provide built-in wireless access to the Internet. Now this was true, but only for some models. Many Palm models did not provide such access without separate wireless modems and additional software. What's more, the ads failed to tell buyers that one model providing wireless Internet and e-mail access requires that users pay monthly subscription fees to the company's Palm.Net Internet service. Thus, although the information in the ads was technically true, omissions left some consumers with the wrong impressions. The FTC ordered Palm to "disclose, clearly and conspicuously, when consumers have to buy add-ons in order to perform advertised functions."[5]

Marketers argue that most companies avoid deceptive practices because such practices harm their business in the long run. Profitable customer relationships are built upon a foundation of value and trust. If consumers do not get what they expect, they will switch to more reliable products. In addition, consumers usually protect themselves from deception. Most consumers recognize a marketer's selling intent and are careful when they buy, sometimes to the point of not believing completely true product claims.

However, one noted marketing thinker, Theodore Levitt, once claimed that some advertising puffery is bound to occur—and that it may even be desirable: "There is hardly a company that would not go down in ruin if it refused to provide fluff, because nobody will buy pure functionality. . . . Worse, it denies . . . people's honest needs and values. Without distortion, embellishment, and elaboration, life would be drab, dull, anguished, and at its existential worst."[6]

High-Pressure Selling Salespeople are sometimes accused of high-pressure selling that persuades people to buy goods they had no thought of buying. It is often said that insurance, real estate, and cars are *sold,* not *bought.* Salespeople are trained to deliver smooth, canned talks to entice purchase. They sell hard because sales contests promise big prizes to those who sell the most.

Marketers know that buyers often can be talked into buying unwanted or unneeded things. Laws require door-to-door and telephone salespeople to announce that they are selling a product. Buyers also have a "three-day cooling-off period" in which they can cancel a contract after rethinking it. In addition, consumers can complain to Better Business Bureaus or to state consumer protection agencies when they feel that undue selling pressure has been applied.

But in most cases, marketers have little to gain from high-pressure selling. Such tactics may work in one-time selling situations for short-term gain. However, most selling involves building long-term relationships with valued customers. High-pressure or deceptive selling can do serious damage to such relationships. For example, imagine a Procter & Gamble account manager trying to pressure a Wal-Mart buyer, or an IBM salesperson trying to browbeat a General Electric information technology manager. It simply wouldn't work.

Shoddy or Unsafe Products   Another criticism is that products lack the quality they should have. One complaint is that many products are not made well and services are not performed well. A second complaint is that many products deliver little benefit, or that they might even be harmful. For example, many critics have pointed out the dangers of today's fat-laden fast food. In fact, McDonald's recently faced a class-action lawsuit charging that its fare has contributed to a nationwide obesity epidemic:

> [Three years ago,] the parody newspaper *The Onion* ran a joke article under the headline "Hershey's Ordered to Pay Obese Americans $135 Billion." The hypothesized class-action lawsuit said that Hershey "knowingly and willfully" marketed to children "rich, fatty candy bars containing chocolate and other ingredients of negligible nutritional value," while "spiking" them with "peanuts, crisped rice, and caramel to increase consumer appeal." Some joke. Last summer New York City attorney Sam Hirsch filed a strikingly similar suit—against McDonald's—on behalf of a class of obese and overweight children. He alleged that the fast-food chain "negligently, recklessly, carelessly, and/or intentionally" markets to children food products that are "high in fat, salt, sugar, and cholesterol," while failing to warn of those ingredients' links to "obesity, diabetes, coronary heart disease, high blood pressure, strokes, elevated cholesterol intake, related cancers," and other conditions. . . . Rates of overweight among small children—to whom junk-food companies aggressively market their products—have doubled since 1980; rates among adolescents have tripled.[7]

Industry defenders decried the suit as frivolous. It is ridiculous, they claimed, to blame the fast-food industry for consumers "own nutritional ignorance, lack of willpower, genetic predispositions, failure to exercise, or whatever else may play a role in [their] obesity." A federal judge agreed and dismissed the suit, explaining that "it is not the place of the law to protect them from their own excess." However, the fast-food industry is listening. For example, McDonald's, Kraft, and Frito-Lay are now working to reduce the amount of artery-clogging trans fats in their foods.

A third complaint concerns product safety. Product safety has been a problem for several reasons, including manufacturer indifference, increased production complexity, poorly trained labor, and poor quality control. For years, Consumers Union—the nonprofit testing and information organization that publishes the *Consumer Reports* magazine and Web site—has reported various hazards in tested products: electrical dangers in appliances, carbon monoxide poisoning from room heaters, injury risks from lawn mowers, and faulty automobile design, among many others. The organization's testing and other activities have helped consumers make better buying decisions and encouraged businesses to eliminate product flaws (see Marketing at Work 16.1).

However, most manufacturers *want* to produce quality goods. The way a company deals with product quality and safety problems can damage or help its reputation. Companies selling poor-quality or unsafe products risk damaging conflicts with consumer groups and regulators. Moreover, unsafe products can result in product liability suits and large awards for damages. More fundamentally, consumers who are unhappy with a firm's products may avoid future purchases and talk other consumers into doing the same.

Consider what happened to Bridgestone/Firestone following its well-publicized recall of 6.5 million flawed Firestone tires. Product liability and safety concerns drove the company to the edge of bankruptcy:

> Profits have disappeared, and both customers and tire dealers alike are fleeing the Firestone make. Ford, the tire maker's biggest customer, recently

■ Product safety: Following its recall of 6.5 million flawed Firestone tires, product liability and safety concerns have driven Bridgestone/Firestone to the brink of bankruptcy.

announced plans to replace another 13 million Firestone tires that it believes are unsafe. "You have a serious risk of the Firestone brand imploding," warns an industry analyst. How bad will the financial hit get? Cutting ties with Ford will cost the company 4 percent of its $7.5 billion in revenues—about 40 percent of its sales to car companies. Mounting damages awards from rollover suits and legal bills could easily top the company's $463 million legal reserve. And if the National Highway Traffic & Safety Administration supports Ford's latest recall, Firestone could find itself liable for much of the $3 billion cost. For its part in the crisis, Ford is still recovering. The auto maker has lost more than $6.4 billion in the past 2 years.[8]

Thus, quality missteps can have severe consequences. Today's marketers know that customer-driven quality results in customer satisfaction, which in turn creates profitable customer relationships.

Planned Obsolescence Critics also have charged that some producers follow a program of planned obsolescence, causing their products to become obsolete before they actually should need replacement. For example, critics charge that some producers continually change consumer concepts of acceptable styles to encourage more and earlier buying. An obvious example is constantly changing clothing fashions.

Other producers are accused of holding back attractive functional features, then introducing them later to make older models obsolete. Critics claim that this occurs in the consumer electronics and computer industries. For example, Intel and Microsoft have been accused in recent years of holding back their next-generation computer chips and software until demand is exhausted for the current generation. Still other producers are accused of using materials and components that will break, wear, rust, or rot sooner than they should. One writer put it this way: "The marvels of modern technology include the development of a soda can which, when discarded, will last forever—and a . . . car, which, when properly cared for, will rust out in two or three years."[9]

Marketers respond that consumers *like* style changes; they get tired of the old goods and want a new look in fashion or a new design in cars. No one has to buy the new look, and if too few people like it, it will simply fail. For most technical products, customers *want* the latest innovations, even if older models still work. Companies that withhold new features run the risk that competitors will introduce the new feature first and steal the market. For example, consider personal computers. Some consumers grumble that the consumer electronics industry's constant push to produce "faster, smaller, cheaper" models means that they must continually buy new machines just to keep up. Others, however, can hardly wait for the latest model to arrive.

There was a time not so long ago when planned obsolescence was a troubling ghost in the machine. Four decades ago, consumer advocates described engineers at General Electric who intentionally shortened the life of light bulbs and automotive engineers who proposed limiting the life spans of cars. That was then. In today's topsy-turvy world of personal computers, obsolescence is not only planned, it is extolled by marketers as a principal virtue. Moreover, there has been hardly a peep from consumers, who dutifully line up to buy each new generation of faster, more powerful machines, eager to embrace the promise of simpler, happier, and more productive lives. Today's computer chips are no

Marketing at Work | *16.1*

When Consumer Reports *Talks, Buyers Listen*

For more than 65 years, *Consumer Reports* has given buyers the lowdown on everything from sports cars to luggage to lawn sprinklers. Published by Consumers Union, the nonprofit product-testing organization, the magazine's mission can be summed up by CU's motto: Test, Inform, Protect. With more than 4 million subscribers and several times that many borrowers, as dog-eared library copies will attest, *Consumer Reports* is one of the nation's most-read magazines. Its companion Consumer Reports Online site (www.consumerreports.org), established in 1997, is the Web's largest paid-subscriber site, with more than 1 million users.

Beyond being one of the most-read publications, *Consumer Reports* is also one of the most influential. In 1988, when its car testers rated Suzuki's topple-prone Samurai as "not acceptable"—meaning don't even take one as a gift—sales plunged 70 percent the following month. More recently, when it raved about Saucony's Jazz 3000 sneaker, sales doubled, leading to nationwide shortages.

Although some may view *Consumer Reports* as a deadly dull shopper's guide to major household appliances, it does a lot more than rate cars and refrigerators. It has looked at almost anything consumable—from mutual funds, home mortgages, and public health policies to retirement communities and prostate surgery.

When a recent Consumers Union study found that that less than one-third of consumers trust e-commerce Web sites, the organization launched Consumer WebWatch (www.consumer webwatch.org). The project's mission is "to investigate, inform, and improve the credibility of information published on the World Wide Web." The site gives ratings on everything from the disclosure of transaction fees and business partnerships to the publication of pri-

vacy policies and the labeling of pop-up ads. And when Consumers Union discovered that consumers wanted to voice their own complaints, it launched the Take Action Center on its Web site. The Center lets consumers offer their opinions directly to state and federal decision makers and to the media. It even offers help crafting the letters to better make the point.

In the 1930s, Consumers Union was one of the first organizations to urge a boycott of products imported from Nazi Germany, and it's been calling for nationalized health care since 1937. In the 1950s, it warned the nation that fallout from nuclear tests was contaminating milk supplies. In the 1960s and 1970s, it prodded car makers to install seat belts, then air bags.

Yet the magazine is rarely harsh or loud. Instead, it's usually understated, and it can even be funny. The very first issue in 1936 noted that Lifebuoy soap was itself so smelly that it simply overwhelmed your B.O. with L.O. And what reader didn't delight to find in a 1990 survey of soaps that the most expensive bar, Eau de Gucci at 31 cents per hand-washing, wound up dead last in a blind test.

Consumer Reports users clearly appreciate CU, its magazine, and its Web sites. It is unlikely that any other organization in the world could have raised $17 million toward a new building simply by asking users for donations. To avoid even the appearance of bias, CU has a strict no-ads, no-freebies policy. It buys all of its product samples on the open market and anonymously. CU's steadfast editorial independence has made *Consumer Reports* the bible of consumerism. "We're very single-minded about who we serve," says Rhoda Karpatkin, CU's recently retired president. "We serve the consumer."

A visit to CU's maze of labs confirms the thoroughness with which CU's testers carry out their mission. A chemist performs a cholesterol extraction test on a small white blob in a beaker: a ground-up piece of Turkey enchilada, you are told. Elsewhere you find the remains of a piston-driven machine called Fingers that added 1 + 1 on pocket calculators hundreds of thousands of times or until the calculators failed, whichever came first. You watch suitcases bang into one another inside a huge contraption—affectionately dubbed the "Mechanical

Consumers Union carries out its testing mission: Suitcases bang into one another inside the huge "Mechanical Gorilla," and a staffer coats the interior of self-cleaning ovens with a crusty concoction called "Monster Mash."

(continued)

Gorilla"—that looks like an 8-foot-wide clothes dryer.

Down the hall in the appliance department, a pair of "food soilers" will soon load 20 dishwashers with identical sets of dirty dishes. A sample dinner plate is marked off with scientific precision into eight wedge-shaped sections, each with something different caked to it—dried spaghetti, spinach, chipped beef, or something else equally difficult to clean. Next door, self-cleaning ovens are being tested, their interiors coated with a crusty substance—called "Monster Mash" by staffers—that suggests month-old chili sauce. The recipe includes tapioca, cheese, lard, grape jelly, tomato sauce, and cherry pie filling—mixed well and baked for one hour at 425 degrees. If an oven's self-cleaning cycle doesn't render the resulting residue into harmless-looking ash, 4 million readers will be so informed.

Some of the tests that CU runs are standard, but many are not. Several years ago, in a triumph of low-tech creativity, CU's engineers stretched paper towels across embroidery hoops, moistened the center of each with exactly 10 drops of water, then poured lead shot into the middle. The winner held 7 pounds of shot; the loser, less than 1. Who could argue with that? There is an obvious logic to such tests, and the results are plainly quantifiable.

From the start, Consumers Union has generated controversy. The second issue dismissed the Good Housekeeping Seal of Approval as nothing more than a fraudulent ploy by publisher William Randolph Hearst to reward loyal advertisers. Good Housekeeping responded by accusing CU of prolonging the Depression. To the business community, Consumer Reports was at first viewed as a clear threat to the American way of doing business. During its early years, more than 60 advertising-dependent publications, including the New York Times, Newsweek, and the New Yorker, refused to accept CU's subscription ads.

In 1939, in a move that would seem ludicrous today, Congress' new House UnAmerican Activities Committee (then known as the Dies Committee) branded CU a subversive organization. However, the controversy has more often helped than hurt subscriptions. And through the years, only 13 makers of panned products have filed suit against CU, challenging findings unfavorable to their products. To this day Consumers Union has never lost or settled a libel suit.

Sources: Portions adapted from Doug Stewart, "To Buy or Not to Buy, That Is the Question at Consumer Reports," Smithsonian, September 1993, pp. 34–43. Other quotes and information from Robin Finn, "Still Top Dog, Consumers' Pitt Bull to Retire," New York Times, October 5, 2000, p. B2; Barbara Quint, "Consumers Union Launches Consumer WebWatch," Information Today, June 2002, p. 48; Jim Guest, "What's Bugging You?" Consumer Reports: Publisher's Edition Including Supplemental Guides, May 2003, p. 7; and the Consumers Union Web site at www.consumersunion.org and the Consumer Reports Online site at www.consumerreports.org, September 2003.

longer designed to wear out; in fact, they will last for decades or longer. Even so, hapless consumers now rush back to the store ever more quickly, not to replace broken parts but to purchase new computers that will allow them to talk longer, see more vivid colors, or play cooler games.[10]

Thus, companies do not design their products to break down earlier, because they do not want to lose customers to other brands. Instead, they seek constant improvement to ensure that products will consistently meet or exceed customer expectations. Much of so-called planned obsolescence is the working of the competitive and technological forces in a free society—forces that lead to ever-improving goods and services.

Poor Service to Disadvantaged Consumers Finally, the American marketing system has been accused of serving disadvantaged consumers poorly. For example, critics claim that the urban poor often have to shop in smaller stores that carry inferior goods and charge higher prices. A Consumers Union study compared the food-shopping habits of low-income consumers and the prices they pay relative to middle-income consumers in the same city. The study found that the poor do pay more for inferior goods. The results suggested that the presence of large national chain stores in low-income neighborhoods made a big difference in keeping prices down. However, the study also found evidence of "redlining," a type of economic discrimination in which major chain retailers avoid placing stores in disadvantaged neighborhoods.[11]

Similar redlining charges have been leveled at the insurance, consumer lending, and banking industries. Home and auto insurers have been accused of assigning higher premiums to people with poor credit ratings. The insurers claim that individuals with bad credit tend to make more insurance claims, and that this justifies charging them higher premiums. However, critics and consumer advocates have accused the insurers of a new form of redlining. Says one writer, "This is a new excuse for denying coverage to the poor, elderly, and minorities." Not all of those affected by redlining are disadvantaged—some insurers have recently been accused of gouging residents of New York and Washington, D.C., in the wake of the September 11th terrorist attacks.[12]

Lenders and other businesses have also been accused of "Weblining," the Internet age version of redlining:

> As never before, the Internet lets companies identify (or "profile") high- and low-value customers, so firms can decide which product deals, prices, and services it will offer. For the most valued customers, this can mean better information and discounts. Low-value customers may pay the most for the least and sometimes get left behind. In lending, old-style redlining is unacceptable because it is based on geographic stereotypes, not concrete evidence that specific individuals are poor credit risks. Webliners may claim to have more evidence against the people they snub. But their classifications could also be based on irrelevant profiling data that marketing companies and others collect on the Web. How important to your mortgage status, say, is your taste in paperbacks, political discussion groups, or clothing? Yet all these far-flung threads are getting sewn into online profiles, where they are increasingly intertwined with data on your health, your education loans, and your credit history.[13]

Clearly, better marketing systems must be built to service disadvantaged consumers. Moreover, disadvantaged consumers clearly need consumer protection. The FTC has taken action against merchants who advertise false values, sell old merchandise as new, or charge too much for credit. The commission is also trying to make it harder for merchants to win court judgments against low-income people who were wheedled into buying something.

Linking the Concepts

SPEED BUMP

Hit the brakes for a moment and cool down. Few marketers *want* to abuse or anger consumers—it's simply not good business. Instead, as you know well by now, most marketers work to build long-term, profitable relationships with customers based on real value and caring. Yet, some marketing abuses do occur.

- Think back over the past three months or so and list the instances in which you've suffered a marketing abuse such as those just discussed. Analyze your list: What kinds of companies were involved? Were the abuses intentional? What did the situations have in common?

- Pick one of the instances you listed and describe it in detail. How might you go about righting this wrong? Write out an action plan, and then do something to remedy the abuse. If we all took such actions when wronged, there would be far fewer wrongs to right!

Marketing's Impact on Society as a Whole

The American marketing system has been accused of adding to several "evils" in American society at large. Advertising has been a special target—so much so that the American Association of Advertising Agencies launched a campaign to defend advertising against what it felt to be common but untrue criticisms.

False Wants and Too Much Materialism Critics have charged that the marketing system urges too much interest in material possessions. People are judged by what they *own* rather than by who they *are*. To be considered successful, people must own a large home, two cars, and the latest high-tech gadgets. This drive for wealth and possessions hit

■ The American Marketing Association runs ads to counter common advertising criticisms.

new highs in the 1980s, when phrases such as "greed is good" and "shop till you drop" seemed to characterize the times.

In the new millennium, many social scientists have noted a reaction against the opulence and waste of the previous decades and a return to more basic values and social commitment. However, our infatuation with material things continues.

It's hard to escape the notion that what Americans really value is stuff. Since 1987, we've had more shopping malls than high schools. We average 6 hours a week of shopping and only 40 minutes of playing with our children. Our rate of saving is 2 percent—only a quarter of what it was in the 1950s, when we earned less than half as much in real dollars. In each of the past 3 years, more U.S. citizens have declared personal bankruptcy than have graduated from college. All this acquisition isn't making us happier; the number of Americans calling themselves "very happy" peaked in 1957.[14]

Nearly two-thirds of adults agree that wearing "only the best designer clothing" conveys status. Even more feel this way about owning expensive jewelry. Big homes are back in vogue, which means Americans have more space to fulfill their acquisitive fantasies, from master bathrooms doubling as spas and gyms to fully wired home entertainment centers.[15]

The critics do not view this interest in material things as a natural state of mind but rather as a matter of false wants created by marketing. Businesses hire Madison Avenue (where the headquarters of many advertising agencies are located) to stimulate people's desires for goods, and Madison Avenue uses the mass media to create materialistic models of the good life. People work harder to earn the necessary money. Their purchases increase the output of American industry, and industry in turn uses Madison Avenue to stimulate more desire for the industrial output. Thus, marketing is seen as creating false wants that benefit industry more than they benefit consumers. Some critics even take their concerns to the streets.[16]

For the past four years, Bill Talen, also known as Reverend Billy, has taken to the streets, exhorting people to resist temptation—the temptation to shop. With the zeal of a street-corner preacher and the schmaltz of a street-corner Santa, Reverend Billy will tell anyone willing to listen that people are walking willingly into the hellfires of consumption. He believes that shoppers have almost no resistance to the media messages that encourage them, around the clock, to want things and buy them. He sees a population lost in consumption, the meaning of individual existence vanished in a fog of wanting, buying and owning too many things. To further his message, Billy started the Church of Stop Shopping. As Reverend Billy, he wears a televangelist's pompadour and a priest's collar, and is

■ Materialism: With the zeal of a street-corner preacher and the schmaltz of a street-corner Santa, Reverend Billy—founder of the Church of Stop Shopping—will tell anyone who will listen that people are walking willingly into the hellfires of consumption.

often accompanied by his gospel choir when he strides into stores he considers objectionable or shows up at protests like the annual post-Thanksgiving Buy Nothing Day event on Fifth Avenue in Manhattan. When the choir, which is made up of volunteers, erupts in song, it is hard to ignore: "Stop shopping! Stop shopping! We will never shop again!"

Other performers preach the same gospel, with their own twists. Ange Taggart, who lives in Nottingham, England, turns up in places like Troy, N.Y., to go into a store, buy a lot of things, and then return them. She recently filled a cart with Martha Stewart products at Kmart, then put them on the conveyor in a certain order, so that when she got her receipt, she said, the first letters on the itemized list spelled "Martha Stewart's hell." There is also Andrew Lynn, who created Whirl-Mart last year. He gets a group of people together, everyone with a shopping cart, and they stroll the aisles of Wal-Mart or Kmart, putting nothing in the carts. When store managers tell him to take his protest elsewhere, he tells them: "This isn't a protest. We're performing a consumption-awareness ritual."

These criticisms overstate the power of business to create needs, however. People have strong defenses against advertising and other marketing tools. Marketers are most effective when they appeal to existing wants rather than when they attempt to create new ones. Furthermore, people seek information when making important purchases and often do not rely on single sources. Even minor purchases that may be affected by advertising messages lead to repeat purchases only if the product performs as promised. Finally, the high failure rate of new products shows that companies are not able to control demand.

On a deeper level, our wants and values are influenced not only by marketers but also by family, peer groups, religion, ethnic background, and education. If Americans are highly materialistic, these values arose out of basic socialization processes that go much deeper than business and mass media could produce alone. Moreover, some social critics even see materialism as a positive and rewarding force:

. . . When we purchase an object, what we really buy is meaning. Commercialism is the water we swim in, the air we breathe, our sunlight and our shade. . . . Materialism is a vital source of meaning and happiness in the modern world. . . . We have not just asked to go this way, we have demanded. Now most of the world is lining up, pushing and shoving, eager to elbow into the mall. Getting and spending has become the most passionate, and often the most imaginative, endeavor of modern life. While this is dreary and depressing to some, as doubtless it should be, it is liberating and democratic to many more.[17]

Too Few Social Goods   Business has been accused of overselling private goods at the expense of public goods. As private goods increase, they require more public services that are usually not forthcoming. For example, an increase in automobile ownership (private good) requires more highways, traffic control, parking spaces, and police services (public goods). The overselling of private goods results in "social costs." For cars, the social costs include traffic congestion, air pollution, and deaths and injuries from car accidents.

A way must be found to restore a balance between private and public goods. One option is to make producers bear the full social costs of their operations. The government could require automobile manufacturers to build cars with even more safety features and better pollution control systems. Auto makers would then raise their prices to cover extra costs. If buyers found the price of some cars too high, however, the producers of these cars would disappear, and demand would move to those producers that could support the sum of the private and social costs.

A second option is to make consumers pay the social costs. A number of highway authorities around the world are starting to charge "congestion tolls" in an effort to reduce traffic congestion:

> Already, in Southern California, drivers are being charged premiums to travel in underused car pool lanes; Singapore, Norway, and France are managing traffic with varying tolls; peak surcharges are being studied for roads around New York, San Francisco, Los Angeles, and other cities. [Economists] point out that traffic jams are caused when drivers are not charged the costs they impose on others, such as delays. The solution: Make 'em pay.[18]

Interestingly, in San Diego, regular drivers can use the HOV (high-occupancy vehicle) lanes, but they must pay a price based on traffic usage at the time. The toll ranges from $.50 off-peak to $4.00 during rush hour. If the costs of driving rise high enough, consumers will travel at nonpeak times or find alternative transportation modes.

Cultural Pollution   Critics charge the marketing system with creating *cultural pollution*. Our senses are being constantly assaulted by advertising. Commercials interrupt serious programs; pages of ads obscure printed matter; billboards mar beautiful scenery. These interruptions continually pollute people's minds with messages of materialism, sex, power, or status. Although most people do not find advertising overly annoying (some even think it is the best part of television programming), some critics call for sweeping changes.

Marketers answer the charges of "commercial noise" with these arguments: First, they hope that their ads reach primarily the target audience. But because of mass-communication channels, some ads are bound to reach people who have no interest in the product and are therefore bored or annoyed. People who buy magazines addressed to their interests—such as

■ Cultural pollution: Our senses are sometimes assaulted by commercial messages.

Vogue or *Fortune*—rarely complain about the ads because the magazines advertise products of interest. Second, ads make much of television and radio free to users and keep down the costs of magazines and newspapers. Many people think commercials are a small price to pay for these benefits. Finally, today's consumers have alternatives. For example, they can zip and zap TV commercials or avoid them altogether on many cable or satellite channels. Thus, to hold consumer attention, advertisers are making their ads more entertaining and informative.

Too Much Political Power   Another criticism is that business wields too much political power. "Oil," "tobacco," "auto," and "pharmaceuticals" senators support an industry's interests against the public interest. Advertisers are accused of holding too much power over the mass media, limiting their freedom to report independently and objectively. One critic has asked, "How can [most magazines] afford to tell the truth about the scandalously low nutritional value of most packaged foods . . . when these magazines are being subsidized by such advertisers as General Foods, Kellogg's, Nabisco, and General Mills? . . . The answer is *they cannot and do not.*"[19]

American industries do promote and protect their own interests. They have a right to representation in Congress and the mass media, although their influence can become too great. Fortunately, many powerful business interests once thought to be untouchable have been tamed in the public interest. For example, Standard Oil was broken up in 1911, and the meat-packing industry was disciplined in the early 1900s after exposures by Upton Sinclair. Ralph Nader caused legislation that forced the automobile industry to build safer cars, and the Surgeon General's Report resulted in cigarette companies putting health warnings on their packages.

More recently, giants such as AT&T, R.J. Reynolds, Intel, and Microsoft have felt the impact of regulators seeking to balance the interests of big business against those of the public. Moreover, because the media receive advertising revenues from many different advertisers, it is easier to resist the influence of one or a few of them. Too much business power tends to result in counterforces that check and offset these powerful interests.

Marketing's Impact on Other Businesses

Critics also charge that a company's marketing practices can harm other companies and reduce competition. Three problems are involved: acquisitions of competitors, marketing practices that create barriers to entry, and unfair competitive marketing practices.

Critics claim that firms are harmed and competition reduced when companies expand by acquiring competitors rather than by developing their own new products. The large number of acquisitions and rapid pace of industry consolidation over the past several decades have caused concern that vigorous young competitors will be absorbed and that competition will be reduced. In virtually every major industry—retailing, entertainment, financial services, utilities, transportation, automobiles, telecommunications, health care—the number of major competitors is shrinking. Consider the glut of acquisitions in the food industry during just the past 2 years: "The consolidation frenzy led to Unilever's buying Bestfoods, Philip Morris's snatching Nabisco, General Mills' swallowing Pillsbury, Kellogg's taking over Keebler and PepsiCo's seizing of Quaker Oats."[20]

Acquisition is a complex subject. Acquisitions can sometimes be good for society. The acquiring company may gain economies of scale that lead to lower costs and lower prices. A well-managed company may take over a poorly managed company and improve its efficiency. An industry that was not very competitive might become more competitive after the acquisition. But acquisitions can also be harmful and, therefore, are closely regulated by the government.

Critics have also charged that marketing practices bar new companies from entering an industry. Large marketing companies can use patents and heavy promotion spending, and can tie up suppliers or dealers to keep out or drive out competitors. Those concerned with antitrust regulation recognize that some barriers are the natural result of the economic advantages of doing business on a large scale. Other barriers could be challenged by existing and new laws. For example, some critics have proposed a progressive tax on advertising spending to reduce the role of selling costs as a major barrier to entry.

Finally, some firms have in fact used unfair competitive marketing practices with the intention of hurting or destroying other firms. They may set their prices below costs, threaten to cut off business with suppliers, or discourage the buying of a competitor's products. Various laws work to prevent such predatory competition. It is difficult, however, to prove that the intent or action was really predatory. In recent years, Wal-Mart, American Airlines, Intel, and Microsoft have all been accused of various predatory practices. Take Microsoft, for example:

> Competitors and regulators have accused giant Microsoft of predatory "bundling" practices. That's the term used to describe Microsoft's practice of continually adding new features to Windows, the operating system installed on more than 90 percent of America's desktop computers. Because customers are essentially locked in to Windows, it's easy for the company to get them to use its other software—even if competitors make better products. That dampens competition, reduces choice, and could retard innovation. For example, in its zeal to become a leader not just in operating systems but on the Internet, the company bundled its Internet Explorer browser into its Windows software. This move sparked an antitrust suit by the government, much to the delight of Microsoft's rivals. After all, Web-browsing innovator Netscape has seen its market share plummet as it tries to sell what Microsoft now gives away for free.[21]

Although competitors and the government charge that Microsoft's actions are predatory, the question is whether this is unfair competition or the healthy competition of a more efficient company against the less efficient.

■■ Citizen and Public Actions to Regulate Marketing

Because some people view business as the cause of many economic and social ills, grass-roots movements have arisen from time to time to keep business in line. The two major movements have been *consumerism* and *environmentalism*.

Consumerism

American business firms have been the target of organized consumer movements on three occasions. The first consumer movement took place in the early 1900s. It was fueled by rising prices, Upton Sinclair's writings on conditions in the meat industry, and scandals in the drug industry. The second consumer movement, in the mid-1930s, was sparked by an upturn in consumer prices during the Great Depression and another drug scandal.

The third movement began in the 1960s. Consumers had become better educated, products had become more complex and potentially hazardous, and people were unhappy with American institutions. Ralph Nader appeared on the scene to force many issues, and other well-known writers accused big business of wasteful and unethical practices. President John F. Kennedy declared that consumers had the right to safety and to be informed, to choose, and to be heard. Congress investigated certain industries and proposed consumer-protection legislation. Since then, many consumer groups have been organized and several consumer laws have been passed. The consumer movement has spread internationally and has become very strong in Europe.

But what is the consumer movement? **Consumerism** is an organized movement of citizens and government agencies to improve the rights and power of buyers in relation to sellers. Traditional *sellers' rights* include:

Consumerism
An organized movement of citizens and government agencies to improve the rights and power of buyers in relation to sellers.

- The right to introduce any product in any size and style, provided it is not hazardous to personal health or safety; or, if it is, to include proper warnings and controls.

- The right to charge any price for the product, provided no discrimination exists among similar kinds of buyers.

- The right to spend any amount to promote the product, provided it is not defined as unfair competition.

- The right to use any product message, provided it is not misleading or dishonest in content or execution.

- The right to use any buying incentive schemes, provided they are not unfair or misleading.

Traditional *buyers' rights* include:

- The right not to buy a product that is offered for sale.

- The right to expect the product to be safe.

- The right to expect the product to perform as claimed.

Comparing these rights, many believe that the balance of power lies on the seller's side. True, the buyer can refuse to buy. But critics feel that the buyer has too little information, education, and protection to make wise decisions when facing sophisticated sellers. Consumer advocates call for the following additional consumer rights:

- The right to be well informed about important aspects of the product.

- The right to be protected against questionable products and marketing practices.

- The right to influence products and marketing practices in ways that will improve the "quality of life."

Each proposed right has led to more specific proposals by consumerists. The right to be informed includes the right to know the true interest on a loan (truth in lending), the true cost per unit of a brand (unit pricing), the ingredients in a product (ingredient labeling), the nutritional value of foods (nutritional labeling), product freshness (open dating), and the true benefits of a product (truth in advertising). Proposals related to consumer protection include strengthening consumer rights in cases of business fraud, requiring greater product safety, and giving more power to government agencies. Proposals relating to quality of life include controlling the ingredients that go into certain products and packaging, reducing the level of advertising "noise," and putting consumer representatives on company boards to protect consumer interests.

Consumers have not only the *right* but also the *responsibility* to protect themselves instead of leaving this function to someone else. Consumers who believe they got a bad deal have several remedies available, including contacting the company or the media; contacting federal, state, or local agencies; and going to small-claims courts.

■ Consumer desire for more information led to putting ingredients, nutrition, and dating information on product labels.

Environmentalism

Environmentalism

An organized movement of concerned citizens and government agencies to protect and improve people's living environment.

Whereas consumerists consider whether the marketing system is efficiently serving consumer wants, environmentalists are concerned with marketing's effects on the environment and with the costs of serving consumer needs and wants. **Environmentalism** is an organized movement of concerned citizens, businesses, and government agencies to protect and improve people's living environment.

Environmentalists are not against marketing and consumption; they simply want people and organizations to operate with more care for the environment. The marketing system's goal, they assert, should not be to maximize consumption, consumer choice, or consumer satisfaction, but rather to maximize life quality. And "life quality" means not only the quantity and quality of consumer goods and services, but also the quality of the environment. Environmentalists want environmental costs included in both producer and consumer decision making.

The first wave of modern environmentalism in the United States was driven by environmental groups and concerned consumers in the 1960s and 1970s. They were concerned about damage to the ecosystem caused by strip-mining, forest depletion, acid rain, loss of the atmosphere's ozone layer, toxic wastes, and litter. They also were concerned with the loss of recreational areas and with the increase in health problems caused by bad air, polluted water, and chemically treated food.

The second environmentalism wave was driven by the government, which passed laws and regulations during the 1970s and 1980s governing industrial practices that have an impact on the environment. This wave hit some industries hard. Steel companies and utilities had to invest billions of dollars in pollution control equipment and costlier fuels. The auto industry had to introduce expensive emission controls in cars. The packaging industry had to find ways to reduce litter. These industries and others have often resented and resisted environmental regulations, especially when they have been imposed too rapidly to allow companies to make proper adjustments. Many of these companies claim they have had to absorb large costs that have made them less competitive.

The first two environmentalism waves are now merging into a third and stronger wave in which companies are accepting responsibility for doing no harm to the environment. They are shifting from protest to prevention, and from regulation to responsibility. More and more companies are adopting policies of **environmental sustainability**—developing strategies that both sustain the environment and produce profits for the company (see Marketing at Work 16.2). According to one strategist, "The challenge is to develop a *sustainable global economy:* an economy that the planet is capable of supporting indefinitely. . . . [It's] an enormous challenge—and an enormous opportunity."[22]

Environmental sustainability

A management approach that involves developing strategies that both sustain the environment and produce profits for the company.

Figure 16.1 shows a grid that companies can use to gauge their progress toward environmental sustainability. At the most basic level, a company can practice *pollution prevention*. This involves more than pollution control—cleaning up waste after it has been created. Pollution prevention means eliminating or minimizing waste before it is created. Companies emphasizing prevention have responded with "green marketing" programs—developing ecologically safer products, recyclable and biodegradable packaging, better pollution controls, and more energy-efficient operations. They are finding that they can be both green *and* competitive. Consider how the Dutch flower industry has responded to its environmental problems:

> Intense cultivation of flowers in small areas was contaminating the soil and groundwater with pesticides, herbicides, and fertilizers. Facing increasingly strict regulation, . . . the Dutch understood that the only effective way to address the problem would be to develop a closed-loop system. In advanced Dutch greenhouses, flowers now grow in water and rock wool, not in soil. This lowers the risk of infestation, reducing the need for fertilizers and pesticides, which are delivered in water that circulates and is reused. The . . . closed-loop system also reduces variation in growing conditions, thus improving product quality. Handling costs have gone down because the flowers are cultivated on specially designed platforms. . . . The net result is not only dramatically lower

FIGURE 16.1

The Environmental Sustainability Grid

Source: Reprinted by permission of *Harvard Business Review*. From "Beyond Greening: Strategies for a Sustainable World," by Stuart L. Hart, January–February 1997, p. 74. Copyright © 1997 by the President and Fellows of Harvard College; all rights reserved.

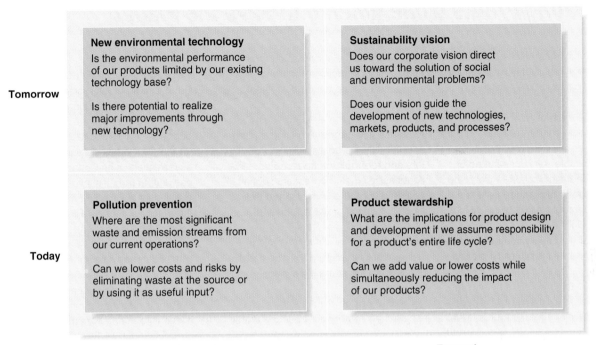

	Internal	**External**
Tomorrow	**New environmental technology** Is the environmental performance of our products limited by our existing technology base? Is there potential to realize major improvements through new technology?	**Sustainability vision** Does our corporate vision direct us toward the solution of social and environmental problems? Does our vision guide the development of new technologies, markets, products, and processes?
Today	**Pollution prevention** Where are the most significant waste and emission streams from our current operations? Can we lower costs and risks by eliminating waste at the source or by using it as useful input?	**Product stewardship** What are the implications for product design and development if we assume responsibility for a product's entire life cycle? Can we add value or lower costs while simultaneously reducing the impact of our products?

environmental impact but also lower costs, better product quality, and enhanced global competitiveness.[23]

At the next level, companies can practice *product stewardship*—minimizing not just pollution from production but all environmental impacts throughout the full product life cycle. Many companies are adopting *design for environment (DFE)* practices, which involve thinking ahead in the design stage to create products that are easier to recover, reuse, or recycle. DFE not only helps to sustain the environment, it can be highly profitable. An example is Xerox Corporation's Asset Recycle Management (ARM) program, which uses leased Xerox copiers as sources of high-quality, low-cost parts and components for new machines. Xerox takes back leased copiers, reconditions salvageable components, and reassembles them into new machines. Not only does this program provide lease customers with the latest product upgrades, it recycles old machines and saves the company money. Xerox estimates that ARM savings in raw materials, labor, and waste disposal in the first year alone ranged between $300 million and $400 million.

At the third level of environmental sustainability, companies look to the future and plan for *new environmental technologies.* Many organizations that have made good headway in pollution prevention and product stewardship are still limited by existing technologies. To develop fully sustainable strategies, they will need to develop new technologies. Monsanto is doing this by shifting its agricultural technology base from bulk chemicals to biotechnology. By controlling plant growth and pest resistance through bioengineering rather than through the application of pesticides or fertilizers, Monsanto hopes to fulfill its promise of environmentally sustainable agriculture. The Monsanto Pledge states the company's dedication to being capable stewards of the technologies it develops. The Pledge declares, "Monsanto is committed to providing high-quality products that benefit [both] our customers and the environment."[24]

Marketing at Work 16.2

Environmental Sustainability: Generating Profits while Helping to Save the Planet

Simply put, environmental sustainability is about generating profits while helping to save the planet. Sustainability is a crucial but difficult societal goal. John Browne, chairman of giant oil company BP, recently asked this question: "Is genuine progress still possible? Is development sustainable? Or is one strand of progress—industrialization—now doing such damage to the environment that the next generation won't have a world worth living in?"

Today, almost every company is taking at least some measures to protect and preserve the environment. Sony has reduced the amount of heavy metals—such as lead, mercury, and cadmium—in its electronic products. Nike produces PVC-free shoes, recycles old sneakers, and educates young people about conservation, reuse, and recycling. P&G's Tide still gets clothes clean, but the back of the box also mentions that the soap is biodegradable, comes in recycled-content packaging, and is safe for septic systems. Wal-Mart has opened "eco-friendly" stores in which the air-conditioning systems use non-ozone-depleting refrigerant, rainwater is collected from parking lots and rooftops for landscaping, skylights supplement fluorescent lighting adjusted by photo sensors, and the electronic signs are solar powered.

Some companies, however, are going even further. They are making sustainability central to their core missions. Here are some examples:

DuPont: Known during much of the 20th century as America's worst polluter, DuPont is now transforming itself from a down-and-dirty oil-and-chemicals business into a twenty-first century, eco-friendly life sciences firm. How? For starters, DuPont is polluting less and reducing waste, emissions, and energy usage. But it's doing much more—it is recreating itself as a collection of businesses that can operate forever without depleting natural resources. To do that, DuPont is spinning off businesses such as its Conoco oil and gas unit. In turn, it's investing in new businesses such as Pioneer Hi-Bred International. Pioneer Hi-Bred's seeds "produce not only food for people and livestock," notes an analyst, "but renewable materials for commercial uses—turning corn into stretch T-shirts, for example." DuPont is also introducing a bevy of new environmentally responsible products, such as Tyvek, a housing-insulation wrap that saves far more energy than is required to produce it. Other products include Super Solids, a paint that can be applied to cars

Environmental sustainability: BP sees the environmental sustainability challenge as an opportunity. It recently opened "the world's most environmentally friendly service station" near London, featuring solar panels, windmills, an array of other innovative green initiatives.

without discharging toxic solvents into the air; and Solae, a nutritional soy protein formulation that goes into more than 1000 food products. The company plans to almost double the percentage of its revenues from renewable sources by 2010, reaching 25 percent.

UPS: UPS is becoming greener by reducing its consumption of nonrenewable fossil fuels. UPS now operates some 1,800 alternative-fuel vehicles, 2,500 low-emissions vehicles, and a growing number of electric vehicles. In addition, in conjunction with DaimlerChrysler and the U.S. Environmental Protection Agency (EPA), UPS is testing fuel cells that run on hydrogen and other alternative fuels. The goal is to reduce greenhouse gas emissions and air pollution, and to improve the renewability of the resources that the company uses. As a side benefit, improving fuel efficiency and moving to alternative fuels reduces costs and shields UPS from fluctuations in foreign oil prices. It also reaffirms UPS's commitment to its consumers' well-being. UPS knows that every time one of its brown vehicles belches a malodorous cloud of black smoke into the air, its brand is tarnished. The company's recent ad campaign asks, "What can Brown do for you?" One of the answers, it seems: Brown can help you breathe a littler easier about the environment.

Dell: Like many companies, Dell understands that sustainability means more that just a clean factory. It also means proper handling of its products at the ends of their useful lives. Electronics are a fast-growing portion of America's trash, with 250 million computers destined to become obsolete by 2005. These computers contain both toxic metals and useful,

reusable materials, so Dell wants to keep them out of landfills. To accomplish this, the company set up Dell Recycling, an effort to reduce the environmental impact of old computers. Through this multipronged effort, Dell customers—big businesses and home buyers alike—can exchange, mail in, or drop off old computer equipment, or even have it picked up. Dell will accept any model of old computer, even competing brands. Then, if the old machine is still useful, Dell will refurbish it and donate it to one of several charities. If the old machine is obsolete or broken beyond repair, Dell will carefully disassemble it and either recycle or safely dispose of component materials. To promote Dell Recycling, the company recently organized a 15-city recycling tour that collected more than 1.5 million pounds of old computer equipment. In all, Dell estimates that it has recycled more than 2 million computers—keeping millions of pounds of electronics waste from going into the nation's landfills.

BP: BP sees the environmental sustainability challenge as an opportunity. "There are good commercial reasons to do right by the environment," says CEO John Browne. Under his leadership, BP has become active in public forums on global climate issues and has worked to reduce emissions in exploration and production. It has begun marketing cleaner fuels and invested significantly in exploring alternative energy sources, such as photovoltaic power and hydrogen. At the local level, BP recently opened "the world's most environmentally friendly service station" near London. The new BP Connect service station features an array of innovative green initiatives that show BP's commitment to envi-

ronmental responsibility. The station runs entirely on renewable energy and generates up to half of its own power, using solar panels installed on the roofs and three wind turbines. More than 60 percent of the water needed for the restrooms comes from rainwater collected on the shop roof, and water for hand washing is heated by solar panels. The site's vapor recovery systems collect and recycle even the fuel vapor released from customers' tanks as pump gas. BP has planted landscaping around the site with indigenous plant species. And, to promote biodiversity awareness, the company has undertaken several initiatives to attract local wildlife to the area, such as dragonflies and insect-feeding birds. The wildflower turf under the wind farm will even provide a habitat for bumblebees.

Some companies have responded to consumer environmental concerns by doing only what is required to avert new regulations or to keep environmentalists quiet. Enlightened companies, however, are taking action not because someone is forcing them to, or to reap short-run profits, but because it is the right thing to do—for both the company and for the planet's environmental future.

Sources: Marc Gunther, "Tree Huggers, Soy Lovers, and Profits," *Fortune*, June 23, 2003 pp. 98–104; Peter M. Senge, Goran Carstedt, and Patrick L. Porter, "Innovating Our Way to the Next Industrial Revolution," *MIT Sloan Management Review*, Winter 2001, pp. 24–38; "DuPont Discusses Sustainability," *Electronic Materials Update*, April 2003, p. 1; "Alternative Fuel Media Kit," accessed online at http://pressroom.ups.com/, August 2003; "Dell Recycling," accessed at www.dell.com, September 2003; "BP Launches World's Greenest Service Station," BP press release, April 25, 2002, accessed at www.bp.com/centres/press/media_resources/press_release/index.asp; and www.bp.com/centres/press/hornchurch/index.asp, September 2003.

Finally, companies can develop a *sustainability vision*, which serves as a guide to the future. It shows how the company's products and services, processes, and policies must evolve and what new technologies must be developed to get there. This vision of sustainability provides a framework for pollution control, product stewardship, and environmental technology.

Most companies today focus on the lower-left quadrant of the grid in Figure 16.1, investing most heavily in pollution prevention. Some forward-looking companies practice product stewardship and are developing new environmental technologies. Few companies have well-defined sustainability visions. Emphasizing only one or a few cells in the environmental sustainability grid in Figure 16.1 can be short-sighted. For example, investing only in the bottom half of the grid puts a company in a good position today but leaves it vulnerable in the future. In contrast, a heavy emphasis on the top half suggests that a company has good environmental vision but lacks the skills needed to implement it. Thus, companies should work at developing all four dimensions of environmental sustainability. Hewlett-Packard is doing just that:

> Hewlett-Packard has evolved through three distinct phases of environmental sustainability over the past two decades. In the 1980s, the environmental concerns were primarily pollution control and prevention, with a focus on reducing emissions from existing manufacturing processes. . . . In the 1990s, the focus shifted to . . . a product stewardship function, which focused on developing global processes for tracking and managing regulatory compliance issues, customer inquiry response systems, information management, public policy shaping, product take-back programs, green packaging, and integrating "design for the environment" and life cycle analysis into product development processes. Today, sustainability is about developing technologies that actually contribute a positive impact to environmental challenges. [However,] HP has recognized that pollution prevention and product stewardship have become baseline market expectations. To be an environmental leader in the twenty-first century, HP needs to integrate environmental sustainability into its fundamental business [vision and] strategy.[25]

Environmentalism creates some special challenges for global marketers. As international trade barriers come down and global markets expand, environmental issues are having an ever-greater impact on international trade. Countries in North America, Western Europe, and other developed regions are developing stringent environmental standards. In the United States, for example, more than two dozen major pieces of environmental legislation have been enacted since 1970, and recent events suggest that more regulation is on the way. A side accord to the North American Free Trade Agreement (NAFTA) set up a commission for resolving environmental matters. The European Union recently passed "end-of-life" regulations that require car makers to recycle or reuse at least 80 percent of their old automobiles by 2006. And the EU's Eco-Management and Audit Scheme provides guidelines for environmental self-regulation.[26]

However, environmental policies still vary widely from country to country, and uniform worldwide standards are not expected for many years. Although countries such as Denmark, Germany, Japan, and the United States have fully developed environmental policies and high public expectations, major countries such as China, India, Brazil, and Russia are in only the early stages of developing such policies. Moreover, environmental factors that motivate consumers in one country may have no impact on consumers in another. For example, PVC soft drink bottles cannot be used in Switzerland or Germany. However, they are preferred in France, which has an extensive recycling process for them. Thus, international companies are finding it difficult to develop standard environmental practices that work around the world. Instead, they are creating general policies and then translating these policies into tailored programs that meet local regulations and expectations.

Public Actions to Regulate Marketing

Citizen concerns about marketing practices will usually lead to public attention and legislative proposals. New bills will be debated—many will be defeated, others will be modified, and a few will become workable laws.

FIGURE 16.2

Major Marketing Decision Areas that may be Called into Question Under the Law

Many of the laws that affect marketing are listed in Chapter 3. The task is to translate these laws into the language that marketing executives understand as they make decisions about competitive relations, products, price, promotion, and channels of distribution. Figure 16.2 illustrates the major legal issues facing marketing management.

■■ Business Actions Toward Socially Responsible Marketing

At first, many companies opposed consumerism and environmentalism. They thought the criticisms were either unfair or unimportant. But by now, most companies have grown to accept the new consumer rights, at least in principle. They might oppose certain pieces of legislation as inappropriate ways to solve specific consumer problems, but they recognize the consumer's right to information and protection. Many of these companies have responded positively to consumerism and environmentalism in order to serve consumer needs better.

Enlightened Marketing

The philosophy of **enlightened marketing** holds that a company's marketing should support the best long-run performance of the marketing system. Enlightened marketing consists of five principles: *consumer-oriented marketing*, *innovative marketing*, *value marketing*, *sense-of-mission marketing*, and *societal marketing*.

Consumer-Oriented Marketing   **Consumer-oriented marketing** means that the company should view and organize its marketing activities from the consumer's point of view. It should work hard to sense, serve, and satisfy the needs of a defined group of customers. Every good marketing company that we've discussed in this textbook has had this in common: an all-consuming passion for delivering superior value to carefully chosen customers. Only by seeing the world through its customers' eyes can the company build lasting and profitable customer relationships. By creating value *for* consumers, the company can capture value *from* consumers in return.

Enlightened marketing
A marketing philosophy holding that a company's marketing should support the best long-run performance of the marketing system; its five principles include consumer-oriented marketing, innovative marketing, value marketing, sense-of-mission marketing, and societal marketing.

Consumer-oriented marketing
The philosophy of enlightened marketing that holds that the company should view and organize its marketing activities from the consumer's point of view.

Innovative marketing

A principle of enlightened marketing that requires that a company seek real product and marketing improvements.

Innovative Marketing The principle of **innovative marketing** requires that the company continuously seek real product and marketing improvements. The company that overlooks new and better ways to do things will eventually lose customers to another company that has found a better way. An excellent example of an innovative marketer is Colgate-Palmolive:

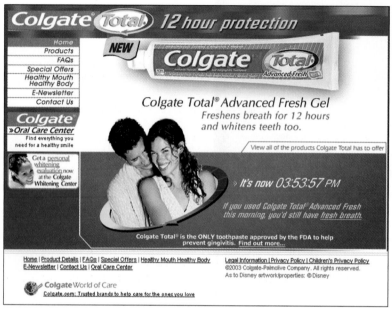

■ Innovative marketing: Colgate's Total toothpaste is perhaps the best example of Colgate's passion for innovation. This breakout brand provides a combination of benefits, including cavity prevention, tartar control, fresh breath, and long-lasting effects.

Colgate has become somewhat of a new-product machine in recent years. Worldwide, new products contribute 35 percent of Colgate's revenues, up from 26 percent 5 years earlier. In the United States, new products account for 58 percent of sales, up from 27 percent. During the past few years, Colgate has launched an abundance of innovative and highly successful new consumer products, including Colgate Total toothpaste. Total is perhaps the best example of the company's passion for continuous improvement. Marketing research showed shifts in consumer demographics and concerns—a growing population of aging, health-conscious, and better-educated consumers. For these consumers, Total became a breakout brand that provides a combination of benefits, including cavity prevention, tartar control, fresh breath, and long-lasting effects. The company also launched an innovative marketing program for the new product, which included advertising in health magazines targeting educated consumers who have high involvement in the health of their mouth and teeth. Consumers responded by making Colgate-Palmolive the toothpaste market leader for the first time since 1962. Colgate now captures a 35 percent market share versus Procter & Gamble's 25 percent, and its lead continues to grow.[27]

Value marketing

A principle of enlightened marketing that holds that a company should put most of its resources into value-building marketing investments.

Value Marketing According to the principle of **value marketing**, the company should put most of its resources into value-building marketing investments. Many things marketers do—one-shot sales promotions, minor packaging changes, advertising puffery—may raise sales in the short run but add less *value* than would actual improvements in the product's quality, features, or convenience. Enlightened marketing calls for building long-run consumer loyalty by continually improving the value consumers receive from the firm's marketing offer.

Sense-of-mission marketing

A principle of enlightened marketing that holds that a company should define its mission in broad social terms rather than narrow product terms.

Sense-of-Mission Marketing **Sense-of-mission marketing** means that the company should define its mission in broad *social* terms rather than narrow *product* terms. When a company defines a social mission, employees feel better about their work and have a clearer sense of direction. For example, defined in narrow product terms, the mission of Unilever's Ben & Jerry's unit might be "to sell ice cream and frozen yogurt." However, Ben & Jerry's states its mission more broadly as one of "linked prosperity," including product, economic, and social missions (see www.benjerrys.com/mission.html). Reshaping the basic task of selling consumer products into the larger mission of serving the interests of consumers, employees, and others in the company's various "communities" gives Ben & Jerry's a vital sense of purpose. Like Ben & Jerry's, many companies today are undertaking socially responsible actions and building concern for their communities into their underlying cultures (see Marketing at Work 16.3).

Marketing at Work | 16.3

Socially Responsible Marketing: Serving a Double Bottom Line of Values and Profits

Chances are, when you hear the term *socially responsible business*, a handful of companies—and their founders—leap to mind, companies such as Ben & Jerry's Homemade (Ben Cohen, Jerry Greenfield) and The Body Shop International (Anita Roddick). Such social revolutionaries pioneered the concept of "values-led business" or "caring capitalism." Their mission: Use business to make the world a better place.

Ben Cohen and Jerry Greenfield founded Ben & Jerry's Homemade in 1978 as a company that cared deeply about its social and environmental responsibilities. It bought only hormone-free milk and cream and used only organic fruits and nuts to make its ice cream, which it sold in environmentally friendly containers. It went to great lengths to buy from minority and disadvantaged suppliers. From its early Rainforest Crunch to its most recent One Sweet Whirled flavors and awareness campaigns, Ben & Jerry's has championed a host of social and environmental causes over the years. From the start, Ben & Jerry's donated a whopping 7.5 percent of pretax profits to support projects that exhibited "creative problem solving and hopefulness . . . relating to children and families, disadvantaged groups, and the environment." By the mid-1990s, Ben & Jerry's had become the nation's number two superpremium ice cream brand.

Anita Roddick opened The Body Shop in 1976 with a similar mission: "to dedicate our business to the pursuit of social and environmental change." The company manufactured and retailed natural-ingredient-based cosmetics in simple and appealing recyclable packaging. All products were formulated without any animal testing, and supplies were often sourced from developing countries. Roddick became a vocal advocate for putting "passion before profits," and The

Body Shop, which now operates nearly 1,850 stores in 47 countries, donates a percentage of profits each year to animal-rights groups, homeless shelters, Amnesty International, Save the Rain Forest, and other social causes.

Both companies set up shop in the late 1970s and grew fast and furiously through the 1980s and early 1990s. However, as competitors not shackled by their "principles before profits" missions invaded their markets, growth and profits flattened. In recent years, both Ben & Jerry's and The Body Shop have struggled. In 2000, after several years of less

than stellar financial returns, Ben & Jerry's was acquired by giant food producer Unilever. And Anita Roddick eventually handed over The Body Shop's reins to a more business-savvy turnaround team, taking the role of consultant.

What happened to the founders' lofty ideals of caring capitalism? Looking back, both companies may have focused on social issues at the expense of sound business management. Neither Ben Cohen nor Anita Roddick really wanted to be businesspeople. In fact, according to one analyst, Cohen and Roddick "saw businesspeople as tools

Societal marketing: Today's new activist entrepreneurs are not social activists with big hearts who hate capitalism, but well-trained business managers and company builders with a passion for a cause.

(continued)

of the military–industrial complex and profits as a dirty word." Cohen once commented, "There came a time [when I had to admit] 'I'm a businessman.' And I had a hard time mouthing those words." Likewise, Roddick admitted, "A lot of us would have slit our wrists if we ever thought we'd be part of corporate America or England. Big business was alien to me. . . . I was only ever interested in running a company that could break the rules of how business could be run. It wasn't about financial science or the science of retailing. It was about being a communications company."

Having a "double bottom line" of values and profits is no easy proposition. In the words of one especially harsh critic, "Ben and Jerry want to use ice cream to solve the world's problems. They call it running a values-led business; I call it a mess. Operating a business is tough enough. Once you add social goals to the demands of serving customers, making a profit, and returning value to shareholders, you tie yourself up in knots." For sure, it's often difficult to take good intentions to the bank.

The experiences of the 1980s revolutionaries taught the socially responsible business movement some hard lessons. The result is a new generation of activist entrepreneurs—not social activists with big hearts who hate capitalism, but well-trained business managers and company builders with a passion for a cause. According to a recent *Inc.* article, here are some of the lessons:

- *What you sell is important:* The product or service, not just the mission, must be socially responsible. Hence, Honest Tea Inc. markets barely sweetened iced tea and totally biodegradable tea bags; WorldWise Inc. offers garden, home, and pet products made from recycled or organic materials; Sustainable Harvest Inc. sells organic, shade-grown coffee with a guaranteed base price for growers; CitySoft Inc. does Web development using urban workers; Wild Planet Toys Inc. creates nonsexist, nonviolent toys; and Village Real Estate Services revitalizes communities and neighborhoods.
- *Be proud to be in business:* Unlike the 1980s revolutionaries, the new

young founders are businesspeople—and proud of it—and all appreciate solid business training. Honest Tea founder Seth Goldman won a business-plan competition as a student at the Yale School of Management and later started the company with one of his professors. Wild Planet CEO Daniel Grossman has an MBA from the Stanford Business School. Sustainable Harvest's David Griswold hires business school graduates because he believes that success "really depends on competing, using the rules of business. Good deeds alone don't work."

- *Make a solid commitment to change:* Cohen and Greenfield stumbled into making ice cream to make ends meet; Roddick owned a small hotel in England before opening her first store. By contrast the new social entrepreneurs' companies are a natural outgrowth of their long-held values. For example, Wild Planet's Grossman served for eight years in the U.S. Foreign Service. David Griswold cofounded and ran Aztec Harvest, a sales-and-marketing outfit for farmer-owned Mexican coffee cooperatives. And CitySoft CEO Nick Gleason was a community and labor organizer in Oakland, California, and ran his own urban-development consulting company, serving nonprofits, foundations, school districts, and governments.
- *Focus on two bottom lines:* Today's social entrepreneurs are just as dedicated to building a viable, profitable business as to shaping a mission. Worldwise's CEO Aaron Lamstein comments, "You can't be successful if you can't do both." Lamstein's strategy for getting Worldwise up and running, built around the concept of environmentally responsible products, illustrates such double-bottom-line thinking. "Our whole concept was that our products had to work as well as or better than others, look as good or finer, cost the same or less, and be better for the environment," says Lamstein. Honest Tea's Goldman agrees: "A commitment to socially responsible business cannot be used as an excuse to make poor business decisions. If we were to accept lower

margins, then we'd be doing the . . . socially responsible business movement a disservice, because we wouldn't be as competitive or as attractive to investors."

- *Forget the hype:* For these socially responsible companies, it's not about marketing and image. They go about doing their good deeds quietly. Village Real Estate Services concentrates primarily on marketing its services, not on publicizing the company's Village Fund, which funds the revitalization of urban neighborhoods. Honest Tea buys the peppermint leaves for its First Nation tea from I'tchik Herbal Tea, a small woman-owned company on the Crow Reservation in Montana. I'tchik gets royalties from the sales of the tea, as does a Native American organization called Pretty Shield Foundation, which includes foster care among its activities. However, "when we first brought out our peppermint tea, our label didn't mention that we were sharing the revenues with the Crow Nation," says Goldman. "We didn't want people to think that was a gimmick."

It remains to be seen how these new socially responsible companies will fare down the road. Many are less than five years old and post sales from $2 million to $10 million. Ben & Jerry's, by contrast, has sales of some $150 million (down from more than $350 million at its peak), and cash registers in Body Shop stores rang up nearly $1 billion in sales last year. Still, this much is clear: Social responsibility for the recent crop of company founders—at least at this early date—seems to be not about them nor even about their companies. It's about the mission.

Sources: Portions adapted from Thea Singer, "Can Business Still Save the World?" *Inc.*, April 30, 2001, pp. 58–71. Other information from Harriot Marsh, "Has the Body Shop Lost Its Direction for Good?" *Marketing*, May 10, 2001, p. 19; Mike Hoffman, "Ben Cohen: Ben & Jerry's Homemade, Established in 1978," *Inc.*, April 30, 2001, p. 68; Sarah Ellison, "Body Shop Hopes for New Image with an Omnilife Deal—Possible Takeover Could Spruce Up Brand That Has Lost Its Appeal over the Years," *Wall Street Journal*, June 8, 2001, p. B4; Sarah Ellison, "Body Shop's Two Founders to Step Aside; Sale Talks End," *Wall Street Journal*, February 13, 2002, p. A15; Renee Volpini, "Fight Global Warming with Ice Cream, Music and Activism," Ben & Jerry's press release, April 2, 2002, accessed online at http://lib.benjerry.com/pressrel/press040202osw.html; and "Anita Roddick," *Director*, June 2003, p. 60.

IMMEDIATE SATISFACTION

	Low	**High**
High	Salutary products	Desirable products
Low	Deficient products	Pleasing products

LONG-RUN CONSUMER BENEFIT

FIGURE 16.3

Societal Classification of Products

Societal Marketing Following the principle of **societal marketing**, an enlightened company makes marketing decisions by considering consumers' wants and interests, the company's requirements, and society's long-run interests. The company is aware that neglecting consumer and societal long-run interests is a disservice to consumers and society. Alert companies view societal problems as opportunities.

A societally oriented marketer wants to design products that are not only pleasing but are also beneficial. The difference is shown in Figure 16.3. Products can be classified according to their degree of immediate consumer satisfaction and long-run consumer benefit. **Deficient products**, such as bad-tasting and ineffective medicine, have neither immediate appeal nor long-run benefits. **Pleasing products** give high immediate satisfaction but may hurt consumers in the long run. An example is cigarettes. **Salutary products** have low appeal but may benefit consumers in the long run; for instance, seat belts and air bags. **Desirable products** give both high immediate satisfaction and high long-run benefits, such as a tasty *and* nutritious breakfast food.

Examples of desirable products abound. Philips Lightings Earth Light compact fluorescent light bulb provides good lighting at the same time that it gives long life and energy savings. Toyota's gas–electric hybrid Prius gives both a quiet ride and fuel efficiency. Maytag's front-loading Neptune washer provides superior cleaning along with water savings and energy efficiency. And Herman Miller's office chairs are not only attractive and functional but are also environmentally responsible:

Herman Miller, one of the world's largest office furniture makers, has received numerous awards for environmentally responsible products and business practices. More than a decade ago, the company formed a Design for the Environment team

Societal marketing

A principle of enlightened marketing that holds that a company should make marketing decisions by considering consumers' wants, the company's requirements, consumers' long-run interests, and society's long-run interests.

Deficient products

Products that have neither immediate appeal nor long-run benefits.

Pleasing products

Products that give high immediate satisfaction but may hurt consumers in the long run.

Salutary products

Products that have low appeal but may benefit consumers in the long run.

Desirable products

Products that give both high immediate satisfaction and high long-run benefits.

■ Herman Miller's Design for the Environment team is responsible for infusing the company's design process with its environmental values. For example, its new Mirra chair is made from 42 percent recycled materials and is 96 percent recyclable.

responsible for infusing the company's design process with its environmental values. The team carries out a "cradle-to-cradle" life cycle analyses on the company's products, including everything from how much of a product can be made from recycled materials to how much of the product itself can be recycled at the end of its useful life. For example, the team redesigned the company's chairs for the lowest possible ecological impact and high recyclability. Herman Miller's Aeron chair is constructed of 66 percent recycled materials (from pop bottles and recycled aluminum) and is 90 percent recyclable. The frames need no paint or other finish. No ozone-depleting materials are used. Chairs are shipped partially assembled, thus reducing the packaging and energy needed to ship them. Finally, materials schematics are imbedded in the bottoms of chair seats to help recycle chairs at the end of their lives. Herman Miller chairs are truly desirable products—they've won awards for design and function *and* for environmental responsibility. Most recently, Herman Miller introduced the Mirra chair, which is made from 42 percent recycled materials and is 96 percent recyclable.[28]

Companies should try to turn all of their products into desirable products. The challenge posed by pleasing products is that they sell very well but may end up hurting the consumer. The product opportunity, therefore, is to add long-run benefits without reducing the product's pleasing qualities. The challenge posed by salutary products is to add some pleasing qualities so that they will become more desirable in the consumers' minds.

SPEED BUMP

Linking the Concepts

Pause here, hold your place with your finger, and go way back and take another look at the Societal Marketing Concept section in Chapter 1.

- How does Figure 1.4 apply to the Enlightened Marketing section in this chapter?
- Use the five principles to assess the actions of a company that you believe exemplifies socially responsible marketing. (If you can't think of one, use Johnson & Johnson or one of the companies discussed in Marketing at Work 16.3.)
- Use the principles of enlightened marketing to assess the actions of a company that you believe falls short of socially responsible marketing.

Marketing Ethics

Conscientious marketers face many moral dilemmas. The best thing to do is often unclear. Because not all managers have fine moral sensitivity, companies need to develop *corporate marketing ethics policies*—broad guidelines that everyone in the organization must follow. These policies should cover distributor relations, advertising standards, customer service, pricing, product development, and general ethical standards.

The finest guidelines cannot resolve all the difficult ethical situations the marketer faces. Table 16.1 lists some difficult ethical situations marketers could face during their careers. If marketers choose immediate sales-producing actions in all these cases, their marketing behavior might well be described as immoral or even amoral. If they refuse to go along with *any* of the actions, they might be ineffective as marketing managers and unhappy because of the constant moral tension. Managers need a set of principles that will help them figure out the moral importance of each situation and decide how far they can go in good conscience.

But *what* principle should guide companies and marketing managers on issues of ethics and social responsibility? One philosophy is that such issues are decided by the free market and legal system. Under this principle, companies and their managers are not responsible for making moral judgments. Companies can in good conscience do whatever the system allows.

TABLE 16.1 Some Morally Difficult Situations in Marketing

1. You work for a cigarette company. Public policy debates over the past few years now leave no doubt in your mind that cigarette smoking and cancer are closely linked. What would you do?

2. Your R&D department has changed one of your products slightly. It is not really "new and improved," but you know that putting this statement on the package and in advertising will increase sales. What would you do?

3. You have been asked to add a stripped-down model to your line that could be advertised to pull customers into the store. The product won't be very good, but salespeople will be able to switch buyers up to higher-priced units. You are asked to give the green light for the stripped-down version. What would you do?

4. You are thinking of hiring a product manager who has just left a competitor's company. She would be more than happy to tell you all the competitor's plans for the coming year. What would you do?

5. One of your top dealers in an important territory recently has had family troubles, and his sales have slipped. It looks like it will take him a while to straighten out his family trouble. Meanwhile you are losing many sales. Legally, you can terminate the dealer's franchise and replace him. What would you do?

6. You have a chance to win a big account that will mean a lot to you and your company. The purchasing agent hints that a "gift" would influence the decision. Your assistant recommends sending a fine color television set to the buyer's home. What would you do?

7. You have heard that a competitor has a new product feature that will make a big difference in sales. The competitor will demonstrate the feature in a private dealer meeting at the annual trade show. You can easily send a spy to this meeting to learn about the new feature. What would you do?

8. You have to choose between three ad campaigns outlined by your agency. The first (a) is soft-sell, honest, straight-information campaign. The second (b) uses sex-loaded emotional appeals and exaggerates the product's benefits. The third (c) involves a noisy, somewhat irritating commercial that is sure to gain audience attention. Pretests show that the campaigns are effective in the following order: c, b, and a. What would you do?

9. You are interviewing a capable female applicant for a job as salesperson. She is better qualified than the men just interviewed. Nevertheless, you know that some of your important customers prefer dealing with men, and you will lose some sales if you hire her. What would you do?

A second philosophy puts responsibility not on the system but in the hands of individual companies and managers. This more enlightened philosophy suggests that a company should have a "social conscience." Companies and managers should apply high standards of ethics and morality when making corporate decisions, regardless of "what the system allows." History provides an endless list of examples of company actions that were legal but highly irresponsible. Consider the following example:

> Prior to the Pure Food and Drug Act, the advertising for a diet pill promised that a person taking this pill could eat virtually anything at any time and still lose weight. Too good to be true? Actually the claim was quite true; the product lived up to its billing with frightening efficiency. It seems that the primary active ingredient in this "diet supplement" was tapeworm larvae. These larvae would develop in the intestinal tract and, of course, be well fed; the pill taker would in time, quite literally, starve to death.[29]

Each company and marketing manager must work out a philosophy of socially responsible and ethical behavior. Under the societal marketing concept, each manager must look beyond what is legal and allowed and develop standards based on personal integrity, corporate conscience, and long-run consumer welfare. A clear and responsible philosophy will help the company deal with knotty issues such as the one faced recently by 3M:

> In late 1997, a powerful new research technique for scanning blood kept turning up the same odd result: Tiny amounts of a chemical 3M had made for nearly 40 years were showing up in blood drawn from people living all across the country. If the results held up, it meant that virtually all Americans may be carrying some minuscule amount of the chemical, called perfluorooctane sulfonate (PFOS), in their systems. Even though they had yet to come up with definitive answers—and they insisted that there was no evidence of danger to humans—the company reached a drastic decision. In mid-2000, although under no mandate to act, 3M decided to phase out products containing PFOS and related chemicals, including its popular Scotchgard fabric protector. This was no easy decision. Since there was as yet no replacement chemical, it meant a potential loss of $500 million in annual sales. 3M's voluntary actions drew praise from regulators. "3M deserves great credit for identifying the problem and coming forward," says an Environmental Protection Agency administrator. "It took guts," comments another government scientist. "The fact is that most companies . . . go into anger, denial, and the rest of that stuff. [We're used to seeing] decades-long arguments about whether a chemical is really toxic." For 3M, however, it wasn't all that difficult a decision—it was simply the right thing to do.[30]

As with environmentalism, the issue of ethics provides special challenges for international marketers. Business standards and practices vary a great deal from one country to the next. For example, whereas bribes and kickbacks are illegal for U.S. firms, they are standard business practice in many South American countries. One recent study found that companies from some nations were much more likely to use bribes when seeking contracts in emerging-market nations. The most flagrant bribe-paying firms were from Russia and China, with Taiwan and South Korea close behind. Other countries where corruption is common include India, Pakistan, and Bangladesh. The least corrupt were companies from Australia, Sweden, Switzerland, Austria, and Canada.[31] The question arises as to whether a company must lower its ethical standards to compete effectively in countries with lower standards. In one study, two researchers posed this question to chief executives of large international companies and got a unanimous response: No.[32]

For the sake of all of the company's stakeholders—customers, suppliers, employees, shareholders, and the public—it is important to make a commitment to a common set of shared standards worldwide. For example, John Hancock Mutual Life Insurance Company operates successfully in Southeast Asia, an area that by Western standards has widespread questionable business and government practices. Despite warnings from locals that Hancock would have to bend its rules to succeed, the company set out strict guidelines. "We told our people that we had the same ethical standards, same procedures, and same policies in these countries that we have in the United States, and we do," says Hancock Chairman Stephen Brown. "We just felt that things like payoffs were wrong—and if we had to do business that way, we'd rather not do business." Hancock employees feel good about the consistent levels of ethics. "There may be countries where you have to do that kind of thing," says Brown. "We haven't found that country yet, and if we do, we won't do business there."[33]

Many industrial and professional associations have suggested codes of ethics, and many companies are now adopting their own codes. For example, the American Marketing Association, an international association of marketing managers and scholars, developed the code of ethics shown in Table 16.2. Companies are also developing programs to teach managers about important ethics issues and help them find the proper responses. They hold ethics workshops and seminars and set up ethics committees. Furthermore, most major U.S. companies have appointed high-level ethics officers to champion ethics issues and to help resolve ethics problems and concerns facing employees.

PricewaterhouseCoopers (PwC) is a good example. In 1996 PwC established an ethics office and comprehensive ethics program, headed by a high-level chief ethics officer. The

TABLE 16.2 American Marketing Association Code of Ethics

Members of the American Marketing Association are committed to ethical, professional conduct. They have joined together in subscribing to this Code of Ethics embracing the following topics:

Responsibilities of the Marketer

Marketers must accept responsibility for the consequences of their activities and make every effort to ensure that their decisions, recommendations, and actions function to identify, serve, and satisfy all relevant publics: customers, organizations, and society.

Marketers' Professional Conduct Must Be Guided by

1. The basic rule of professional ethics: not knowingly to do harm.
2. The adherence to all applicable laws and regulations.
3. The accurate representation of their education, training, and experience.
4. The active support, practice, and promotion of this Code of Ethics.

Honesty and Fairness

Marketers shall uphold and advance the integrity, honor, and dignity of the marketing profession by:

1. Being honest in serving consumers, clients, employees, suppliers, distributors, and the public.
2. Not knowingly participating in conflict of interest without prior notice to all parties involved.
3. Establishing equitable fee schedules including the payment or receipt of usual, customary, and/or legal compensation for marketing exchanges.

Rights and Duties of Parties in the Marketing Exchange Process

Participants in the marketing exchange process should be able to expect that:

1. Products and services offered are safe and fit for their intended uses.
2. Communications about offered products and services are not deceptive.
3. All parties intend to discharge their obligations, financial and otherwise, in good faith.
4. Appropriate internal methods exist for equitable adjustment and/or redress of grievances concerning purchases.

It Is Understood That the Above Would Include, but are Not Limited to, the Following Responsibilities of the Marketer

In the area of product development and management,
- Disclosure of all substantial risks associated with product or service usage.
- Identification of any product component substitution that might materially change the product or impact on the buyer's purchase decision.
- Identification of extra cost-added features.

In the area of promotions,
- Avoidance of false and misleading advertising.
- Rejection of high-pressure manipulations, or misleading sales tactics.
- Avoidance of sales promotions that use deception or manipulation.

In the area of distribution,
- Not manipulating the availability of a product for purpose of exploitation.
- Not using coercion in the marketing channel.
- Not exerting undue influence over the reseller's choice to handle a product.

In the area of pricing,
- Not engaging in price fixing.
- Not practicing predatory pricing.
- Disclosing the full price associated with any purchase.

In the area of marketing research,
- Prohibiting selling or fundraising under the guise of conducting research.
- Maintaining research integrity by avoiding misrepresentation and omission of pertinent research data.
- Treating outside clients and suppliers fairly.

Organizational Relationships

Marketers should be aware of how their behavior may influence or impact on the behavior of others in organizational relationships. They should not demand, encourage, or apply coercion to obtain unethical behavior in their relationships with others, such as employees, suppliers, or customers.

1. Apply confidentiality and anonymity in professional relationships with regard to privileged information.
2. Meet their obligations and responsibilities in contracts and mutual agreements in a timely manner.
3. Avoid taking the work of others, in whole, or in part, and representing this work as their own or directly benefitting from it without compensation or consent of the originator or owner.
4. Avoid manipulations to take advantage of situations to maximize personal welfare in a way that unfairly deprives or damages the organization of others.

Any AMA member found to be in violation of any provision of this Code of Ethics may have his or her Association membership suspended or revoked.

■ Ethics programs: PricewaterhouseCoopers established a comprehensive ethics program, which begins with a code of conduct, called "The Way We Do Business," says PwC's CEO, "Ethics is in everything we say and do."

ethics program begins with a code of conduct, called "The Way We Do Business." PwC employees learn about the code of conduct and about how to handle thorny ethics issues in a comprehensive ethics training program, called "Navigating the Grey." The program also includes an ethics help line and continuous communications at all levels. "It is obviously not enough to distribute a document," says PwC's CEO, Samuel DiPiazza. "Ethics is in everything we say and do." Last year alone, the PwC training program involved 40,000 employees, and the help line received over 1,000 calls from people asking for guidance in working through difficult ethics dilemmas.[34]

Many companies have developed innovative ways to educate employees about ethics:

> Citicorp has developed an ethics board game, which teams of employees use to solve hypothetical quandaries. General Electric employees can tap into specially designed software on their personal computers to get answers to ethical questions. At Texas Instruments, employees are treated to a weekly column on ethics over an electronic news service. One popular feature: a kind of Dear Abby mailbag, answers provided by the company's ethics officer, . . . that deals with the troublesome issues employees face most often.[35]

Still, written codes and ethics programs do not ensure ethical behavior. Ethics and social responsibility require a total corporate commitment. They must be a component of the overall corporate culture. According to PwC's DiPiazza, "I see ethics as a mission-critical issue . . . deeply imbedded in who we are and what we do. It's just as important as our product development cycle or our distribution system. . . . It's about creating a culture based on integrity and respect, not a culture based on dealing with the crisis of the day. . . . We ask ourselves every day, 'Are we doing the right things?' "[36]

The future holds many challenges and opportunities for marketing managers as they move into the new millennium. Technological advances in every area, from telecommunications, information technology, and the Internet to health care and entertainment, provide abundant marketing opportunities. However, forces in the socioeconomic, cultural, and natural environments increase the limits under which marketing can be carried out. Companies that are able to create new customer value in a socially responsible way will have a world to conquer.

REST STOP:
Reviewing the Concepts

Well, here you are at the end of your introductory marketing travels! In this chapter, we've closed with many important concepts involving marketing's sweeping impact on individual consumers, other businesses, and society as a whole. You learned that responsible marketers discover what consumers want and respond with the right products, priced to give good value to buyers and profit to the producer. A marketing system should sense, serve, and satisfy consumer needs and improve the quality of consumers' lives. In working to meet consumer needs, marketers may take some actions that are not to everyone's liking or benefit. Marketing managers should be aware of the main *criticisms of marketing.*

1. Identify the major social criticisms of marketing.

Marketing's *impact on individual consumer welfare* has been criticized for its high prices, deceptive practices, high-pressure selling, shoddy or unsafe products, planned obsolescence, and poor service to disadvantaged consumers. Marketing's *impact on society* has been criticized for creating false wants and too much materialism, too few social goods, cultural pollution, and too much political power. Critics have also criticized marketing's *impact on other businesses* for harming competitors and reducing competition through acquisitions, practices that create barriers to entry, and unfair competitive marketing practices.

2. Define *consumerism* and *environmentalism,* and explain how they affect marketing strategies.

Concerns about the marketing system have led to *citizen action movements. Consumerism* is an organized social movement intended to strengthen the rights and power of consumers relative to sellers. Alert marketers view it as an opportunity to serve consumers better by providing more consumer information, education, and protection. *Environmentalism* is an organized social movement seeking to minimize the harm done to the environment and quality of life by marketing practices. The first wave of modern environmentalism was driven by environmental groups and concerned consumers, whereas the second wave was driven by government, which passed laws and regulations governing industrial practices that have an impact on the environment. Moving into the twenty-first century, the first two environmentalism waves are merging into a third and stronger wave in which companies are accepting responsibility for doing no environmental harm. Companies now are adopting policies of *environmental sustainability*—developing strategies that both sustain the environment and produce profits for the company.

3. Describe the principles of socially responsible marketing.

Many companies originally opposed these social movements and laws, but most of them now recognize a need for positive consumer information, education, and protection. Some companies have followed a policy of *enlightened marketing,* which holds that a company's marketing should support the best long-run performance of the marketing system. Enlightened marketing consists of five principles: *consumer-oriented marketing, innovative marketing, value marketing, sense-of-mission marketing,* and *societal marketing.*

4. Explain the role of ethics in marketing.

Increasingly, companies are responding to the need to provide company policies and guidelines to help their managers deal with questions of *marketing ethics.* Of course even the best guidelines cannot resolve all the difficult ethical decisions that individuals and firms must make. But there are some principles among which marketers can choose. One principle states that such issues should be decided by the free market and legal system. A second, and more enlightened principle, puts responsibility not in the system but in the hands of individual companies and managers. Each firm and marketing manager must work out a philosophy of socially responsible and ethical behavior. Under the societal marketing concept, managers must look beyond what is legal and allowable and develop standards based on personal integrity, corporate conscience, and long-term consumer welfare.

Because business standards and practices vary from country to country, the issue of ethics poses special challenges for international marketers. The growing consensus among today's marketers is that it is important to make a commitment to a common set of shared standards worldwide.

Navigating the Key Terms

Consumerism	Environmental sustainability	Salutary products
Consumer-oriented marketing	Environmentalism	Sense-of-mission marketing
Deficient products	Innovative marketing	Societal marketing
Desirable products	Pleasing products	Value marketing
Enlightened marketing		

Travel Log

Discussing the Issues

1. Discuss the claim that the high cost of distribution, high cost of advertising and promotion, and excessive markups lead to higher than necessary costs for American consumers. Do you agree or disagree with this position?

2. What is the difference between consumerism and environmentalism? How are they alike and different? Give an example of a cause that would be championed by each movement.

3. Distinguish between the five principles of enlightened marketing: consumer-oriented marketing, innovative marketing, value marketing, sense-of-mission marketing, and societal marketing.

4. Write a corporate marketing ethics policy for a company selling mortgage services online. How would such a policy influence ethical decision making among employees in this company?

5. Search through news reports to find a story about a company that is acting in a socially responsible manner. Would this information influence your buying decision if you were in the market to buy the type of product this firm sells? What impact do you think the socially responsible action reported in the news story has on the employees of the organization?

Application Questions

1. Get into small groups and consider the four issues regarding marketing's impact on society as a whole (materialism, few social goods, cultural pollution, and too much political power). Divide the group in half, with each half of the group supporting a different side of these issues. Debate each issue,

and after each debate take a poll of where your group stands on the issue.

2. One concern of environmentalists over the years has been the excessive packaging material some companies use to enclose and promote their product. At issue is that a larger package requires more resources for production (e.g., trees) and disposal (e.g., landfills). Visit a grocery store and identify a product whose packaging could be described as excessive. How does the packaging of this product compare with the packaging of rival products? What packaging modifications do you think an environmentalist would recommend?

3. Study Figure 16.1. Select two companies, one you feel is very environmentally considerate and one you feel is lacking in this area. Describe how you would rate each company in the areas of pollution prevention, product stewardship, new environmental technology, and sustainability vision. Do your initial attitudes regarding the environmental consciousness of each company still hold?

Under the Hood: Focus on Technology

A forest full of trees has been spared thanks to a new paperless wine list being used at Aureole restaurants in Las Vegas and New York. The wine selection boasts an awe-inspiring 4,000 different wine labels that would be impractical to print onto paper in the form of a manageable wine list. Instead of a paper wine list, customers are presented with a lightweight, wireless, computer tablet. Pages are turned and selections are made by the customer using either a stylus or their finger. Aside from the positive environmental impact, there are other marketing applications for the electronic wine list. For example, the tablet can be used to display brief wine reviews and narratives about the win-

ery, customers are allowed to bookmark favorite wine selections, and it has the ability to let customers request that wine selection information and special offers be e-mailed to them at home.

1. Consider other opportunities that electronic tablets have for replacing material that is traditionally printed on paper (e.g., textbooks, novels, etc.).

2. What sort of resistance do you think consumers may have to accessing printed material in an electronic format? How could such resistance be overcome?

3. What do you see as the environmental benefits to such a system?

Focus on Ethics

The text presents Figure 16.3 as a way to classify products in terms of their level of long-run benefit to consumers and the level of immediate satisfaction they provide. The goal of a societally oriented marketer is to design products that are both beneficial and pleasing—the "desirable products" cell in Figure 16.3.

1. Select products that are representative of each of the four cells in this classification scheme.

2. For products that fall into the deficient, salutary, and pleasing categories, consider what modifications could be made, if any, to move them to the desirable product classification.

3. Why do you think some companies continue to sell products that would be classified as deficient under this classification? What should society do, if anything, about such products?

Videos

The Honest Tea video case that accompanies this chapter is located in Appendix 1 at the back of the book.

Student Materials

Need a tune-up? A study guide and OneKey access code are available to aid in your review of chapter material. Your instructor may choose to have these items shrink-wrapped with your text or you may purchase them separately at www.prenhall.com/marketing.

Appendix 1   Video Cases

Managing Profitable Customer Relationships

Case in Point: Subaru

The auto-buying process generally is a simple one: You go to various car dealerships, compare prices and amenities, and buy a car. There is no way you could think of this as having a "relationship" with the automobile company. Yet Subaru of America, Inc., wants to have a relationship with you. What does *relationship* mean in this context? You get an excellent vehicle that "fits" you. Subaru gets—or wants—you to take four major actions: (1) It wants you to buy its auto—this sets everything in motion. (2) It wants you to recommend its car to other potential auto buyers. (3) It wants you to have your car serviced at its dealership. (4) It wants you to come back when you purchase your next car.

This seems clear enough, but consider this: Is this a *relationship* with a distant automaker, with a company that manufactures a heavy steel automobile as its product? When we think of a relationship, we normally think of a spouse or a loved one—of people. But an automaker? What's going on here?

The Product

Subaru designs and builds excellent products: Subaru vehicles. You know how sometimes a movie comes out that critics like but audiences hate, or vice versa? Subaru has the support of both critics and consumers. Experts and critics like Subaru—for example, they've voted Subaru's vehicles consistently onto *Car & Driver*'s 10 Best lists. Owners are also pleased—they consistently report high customer satisfaction with Subaru vehicles.

The Company

In the video, Subaru is described as relatively small, selling only 180,000 cars a year, far fewer than General Motors. To be fair, though, GM is huge. To put the numbers in perspective, consider that while Subaru enjoys only a 1.1 percent share of the automobile market, that still means more Subarus are sold in the United States than Acuras, Audis, Cadillacs, Infinitis, Lexuses, Lincolns, Mercedes, Oldsmobiles, Saabs, or Volvos. Think about how Subaru compares to these companies in terms of its marketing efforts, in getting to know its customers and trying to serve them as distinctive people.

The Customer

"Mr. Survey" (in the video) talks about using consumer insight data to try to understand the "mind of the customer." That includes the customer's *needs, wants,* and *demands*—all of that. The Subaru manager characterized the typical Subaru owner as intelligent and independent. Those are complimentary labels—don't we all want to be included in that segment?

The Subaru owner is also characterized as "quirky," which you can tell is still a positive label. The Subaru owner is said to "get it," as depicted in the ad where two people are appreciating their view of a deer in a natural setting when a bigger truck comes zooming by, making a lot of noise, scaring the deer away, wondering what the Subaru occupants were watching. The Subaru owners were trying to blend into nature and appreciate it, whereas the big, bad competitors' trucks are driven by people who are clueless and unsubtle. Or consider the ad in which the Subaru owners are admiring the Grand Canyon, compared to the guy, again zooming around in a big truck, who aims a camera at the vista, clicks, and drives off. The point is this: Non-Subaru people just *don't* get it.

Subaru sends its message consistently. For example, consistent with the environmental-appreciation theme, Subaru was one of a few sponsors of Canadian teams in Discovery Channel's *Eco-Challenge* (others included Schick and Advil), attracting many viewers (over two million adults ages 18 to 49 tuned in last April, even when a hockey game was broadcast in Canada at the same time!). As sponsors, Subaru sees its name on competitors' clothes, onsite signage, 60-second television advertising vignettes, and banner ads blanketing the Discovery Channel's Web site, www.exn.ca.

Customer Satisfaction

How do we know Subaru owners are happy? The customer satisfaction surveys tell us so.

With a 50 percent response rate, which is actually very high by marketing research industry standards, Subaru receives some 75,000 to 80,000 surveys to process each year. The company is moving toward even more contact points with its customers. For example, it mails a survey to every customer within 30 to 45 days of purchase to assess the customer's initial feelings about the newly purchased vehicle, to report on the nature of the transactions with the dealer, and to learn about any other element of the purchase. Subsequent to that initial contact, more surveys follow throughout the "lifetime" of the customer (that is, the duration of ownership of the car, on average 6 to 7 years) to assess longer-term satisfaction with the vehicle and the dealership regarding the vehicle's servicing. These days, some 500,000 surveys are mailed each year (contacts are also made via Web surveys).

What do surveys do? First, of course, they help Subaru collect information about its customers' perceptions regarding questions such as "How was your buying experience?" "How satisfied are you?" "What were the salespeople like?" "How was your service experience?" and "How does Subaru compare to other dealers you've visited?" If a problem is identified, Subaru executives want to make changes to keep customers happy, but they need information to diagnose the precise nature of the problem: Is it an issue with the vehicle, the dealer, the customer's lack of knowledge, or inappropriate expectations?

Consider other ways that the surveys function. For example, if you run a dealership and customers are being asked "How was our dealership?" you know that Subaru is going to be looking at your numbers and that you have to keep your customers happy. Hence, the act of surveying customers helps send a marketing message to Subaru's internal customers, its dealership managers, and its employees.

Similarly, as they get surveyed continually by Subaru, customers start forming additional expectations about the Subaru brand—that is, the survey becomes another form of communication from the company about the matters it cares about (Are those the same things the customer cares about?). The surveys become cues to customers forming expectations about the Subaru brand and experience. For example, if you get a survey that asks about the friendliness of the mechanics and the service write-up staff each time you use the dealership for an oil change or tune-up, you begin to develop expectations that the mechanics and service writers will be friendly. (Is that relevant to your car maintenance? Is it relevant to your loyalty?)

Customer Satisfaction Versus Loyalty

As marketers, we might think that customer satisfaction leads to loyalty. It is true that dissatisfied customer probably will not repurchase a Subaru. However, no guarantee exists that a satisfied customer will buy another Subaru.

Subaru wants its customers to be loyal, but of course most companies want that. The Subaru manager depicted in the video thinks it is easier to be loyal to something you buy frequently, such as a brand of beer, or a place you go to, such as a local coffee shop. (Do you agree? How does the purchase of a latté or a car differ? How do these differences translate into issues regarding repeat purchasing and loyalty?)

One goal, then, is to decrease the number of years between vehicle purchases. What can Subaru do to facilitate that goal? How might the surveys contribute to this initiative? The manager in the video thinks that the surveys signal that Subaru cares and that the surveys prompt the owners to think about their cars. If Subaru is confident that the vehicles are indeed of high quality, this prompting should result in good feelings that in turn might translate into including Subaru first when existing customers again want to buy a car.

Mr. George Dubinsky, the owner information manager at Subaru, says customer satisfaction is important but that loyalty is the real goal. For example, 10 to 15 years ago, Subaru dealers were getting great customer satisfaction scores but sales were starting to drop. Customers were "defecting" from using the dealership to have their cars serviced. The service end of the business is usually highly profitable, so this can be a big problem. Also, if you don't have your car serviced at a dealership, you might be less likely to think about the dealership when you buy again.

Consider the following numbers as a scenario: When a new vehicle is purchased, the dealer earns \$1,500 gross profit. Servicing can add up to be at least as profitable. Let's use conservative estimates and see. Say an owner makes two visits per year to have a car serviced. (We'll define that number as A.) Say each visit on average requires 1.5 hours of labor (at a going rate of, say, \$75 per hour). (We'll call the hours of labor B and the hourly wages C.) So far, we have three terms:

A = visits per year to have the car serviced (example: 2)

B = average hours of labor (1.5 hours)

C = labor hourly rate (\$75)

Now, say parts are about 70 percent of labor costs (call that D) and say that parts are marked up only 35 percent (call that E). Adding to our list of variables, we have:

D = ratio of parts to labor (example: 70 percent)

E = markup of parts (35 percent)

Let's plug these pieces into a formula to see how much we'd get *per car, per year* on *service* alone (call it S):

$$S = A\{(B \times C) + E[D(B \times C)]\}$$
$$= 2\{(1.5 \times \$75) + .35[.7(1.5 \times \$75)]\}$$
$$= \$280.12 \text{ per car, per year.}$$

Remember that these are conservative estimates. Thus, holding onto the customer for the five years between purchases almost doubles your gross profits. (How would the numbers change if you could get people to come to the dealer three times a year, rather than only twice?)

Where Does Subaru Go from Here?

Subaru's goals are to go from current sales of 180,000 vehicles per year to some 250,000 vehicles per year in three years. How is it going to achieve that growth?

Trying to stay true to the brand, Subaru's more recent marketing communications express what each of its car owners thinks and feels. For example, by replacing popular, longtime ad spokesperson Paul Hogan (of Crocodile Dundee fame) with Lance Armstrong (who conquered a devastating illness to return to world-class competition in bicycle racing) and by changing the advertisement tag line from "The beauty of all-wheel drive" to "Driven by what's inside," Subaru shifts its marketing focus from vehicle attributes to its drivers.

It's not just talk. The marketing messages are consistent with the company's product line extensions. Subaru is rolling out more performance-oriented vehicles, such as a 300-horsepower version of its WRX Impreza sports car, and a turbo-charged version of its

Forester crossover. In the other direction, Subaru's Baja combines the versatility of a pickup truck with the ride and handling of a passenger car. Subaru has incorporated a "switchback" system, which allows the reconfiguration of the rear seat to transport either more people or more cargo. It's kept the strut-type suspension in the front and a multilink in the rear, to allow the driver to handle twists and turns more easily, so the ride feels smoother, more like a passenger car than a typical rough-riding truck. Included in the base price of $25,000 are lots of extras, such as leather seating for four, a CD player, power windows, remote keyless entry, power driver's seat, a power moon roof, and more.

Subaru expects to pursue a "dual" strategy, bringing up the performance aspects of its vehicles, while maintaining the crossover theme of its car/truck positioning (which, after all, comprises some 70 percent of current volume). Given the identification of these niche markets, Subaru wants to maximize return by using a focused approach to advertising rather than a broader approach that would likely be less efficient.

Subaru's next challenges include going after younger customers, to grow a bigger loyal customer base. It also wishes to offer finance packages that are attractive enough to get people to turn over their cars more frequently than the current 6 to 7 years. Perhaps all these actions together will help Subaru achieve its ambitious growth goals.

Questions for Discussion

1. Do you think a brand or company can have a relationship with a customer?

2. What role does communication play in a relationship?

3. How does Subaru communicate with its customers? How do Subaru owners communicate to the company?

4. What does each party get from the relationship?

Video Case 2

Partnering to Build Customer Relationships

Case in Point: Dunkin' Donuts

Company Strengths

Lots of people love Dunkin' Donuts. The company has almost 5,000 stores worldwide. Those little stores with fast traffic flows brought in some $3 billion in sales this year. Dunkin' Donuts is a highly recognizable brand name. Its global presence, strong sales, and known brand name are qualities that many companies envy.

Dunkin' Donuts attracts customers in large part because of three key features of its offerings: quality, variety, and affordability.

First, the company prides itself on *quality*, which translates to freshness in the doughnut business. Dunkin' Donuts make doughnuts at least four times a day, and its coffee is considered stale and is tossed before it is 20 minutes old.

Second, Dunkin' Donuts offers *variety*—52 flavors of doughnuts. It's also offered some innovations over the years, like doughnut holes, new tastes in coffee (flavored coffees, decaf), and bagels. Dunkin' Donuts also offers convenience—good streetside locations for easy access.

Finally, Dunkin' Donuts is *affordable*. Just about any consumer can afford the Dunkin' Donuts doughnut experience. In addition, it appeals to just about everyone (the Mercedes and the pickup truck come together in an egalitarian Dunkin' Donuts parking lot).

What's on the Horizon?

Despite its strengths, Dunkin' Donuts now faces some serious challenges. Think about the main products that Dunkin' Donuts sells: the traditional combination of coffee and a doughnut. The coffee industry has become dominated by the coffeehouse experience, à la Starbucks, and the doughnut business has welcomed a strong newcomer in Krispy Kreme doughnuts.

So why should a consumer go to Dunkin' Donuts rather than to Starbucks or Krispy Kreme? Dunkin' Donuts offers coffee (which might or might not be as good as Starbucks coffee) and doughnuts (which might or might not be as good as Krispy Kreme doughnuts—and Krispy Kreme now enjoys a substantial "novelty" factor). Perhaps it's the doughnut *and* coffee combo where Dunkin' Donuts dominates. That is, Starbucks doesn't offer doughnuts, and Krispy Kreme coffee is just coffee. Perhaps Dunkin' Donuts can sell its combination as unique. Perhaps its traditional choices for convenient locations highlight that it's the one-stop coffee–doughnut shop.

Dunkin' Donuts might also leverage its value pricing. Although its doughnuts cost about the same as Krispy Kreme's, its coffee is certainly less expensive than Starbucks's.

Whichever strategy or tactic Dunkin' Donuts wants to pursue to fight off the competition, it has to be consistent with the company's corporate philosophies. Dunkin' Donuts likes to think of itself as a "fun" company. Think about its advertising: the sort of goofy-looking older fellow who says, "Time to make the doughnuts." This spokesman is usually shown rising from bed in his pajamas, emphasizing the strong work ethic of getting up early to go make a good, fresh product, just for you. The doughnut-maker helps personify the company. He gives the brand a real personality.

The company seems happy projecting an image that it's selling a straightforward product. It plays up the fact that the brand and the stores are "nothing fancy." This may signal something good (less expensive) or bad (not high quality) to customers. For example, would an advertising tag line of "We're not as fancy as Starbucks" signal something good (not as expensive) or something bad (not as high quality)? With competition nipping at both parts of its core business—doughnuts and coffee—Dunkin' Donuts ought to consider repositioning itself to a competitive advantage that is more sustainable. Alternatively, it could just retrench, saying "This is who we are" and hoping that customers see it as dominating on at least one attribute—for example, doughnut flavor or selection, coffee flavor or selection, price, or location. The company could hope that the Krispy Kreme movement is just a fad that will die down in a few years and that people will get tired of spending $3 to $4 for coffee at Starbucks when it's less than half that price that at Dunkin' Donuts.

What Next?

Dunkin' Donuts says it listens to its customers to get ideas about new doughnut flavors, which it then tries to create and test with other customers. How might customer feedback help Dunkin' Donuts now?

Business Partners

You've probably also noticed that Dunkin' Donuts stores have started branching with Baskin Robbins ice cream shops. (Let's see: 52 varieties of doughnuts, times 31 ice creams—that's 1,612 combinations!) More recently, retailers including 7-11 and Wal-Mart (anything Wal-Mart does, you should watch—just by its sheer size, it will be influential) are housing small Dunkin' Donuts shops within their own retail spaces. Dunkin' Donuts is "high profile" given its strong brand name, and coffee in particular is a high margin sale (retailers make tons of money on this alone).

International Presence

Dunkin' Donuts does have a worldwide presence, but there is no question that it's strongest in the United States. Right now, it's having difficulties with franchisers in Canada who blame sales declines on poor advertising and marketing support and with consumers in the United Kingdom who simply don't care that much for doughnuts. How might you adapt the basic coffee–doughnut experience to address different local tastes around the world?

Questions for Discussion

1. Would you say that Dunkin' Donuts is product-oriented or customer-oriented? Why?
2. What would you guess is Dunkin' Donuts' mission statement? What are its corporate goals?
3. How would you tackle the issues of Starbucks and Krispy Kreme invading Dunkin' Donuts' turf?

Video Case 3

The Marketing Environment

Case in Point: Nike

When you hit the age of 40, will everyone in the world know who you are? The founders of Nike have worked hard at building their brand for 40 years, and they have been extremely successful. They've built huge, worldwide brand awareness.

Nike is probably most familiar to the public for its athletic shoes. However, it also produces other athletic gear, such as clothing and equipment. It makes those products not just for "real" athletes but for all of us, or as Nike likes to say, "For the athlete in all of us." Nike doesn't challenge its customers to become pros—it challenges its customers to "Just do it."

Nike prides itself on innovation, and it uses celebrity athletes to endorse each new product line. The athletes help persuade shoppers that the shoes may help them perform better. An example is Michael Jordan's Nike Air shoes: The implication is that if you wear these light and bouncy shoes, perhaps you can play basketball as well as Jordan.

Nike employs the "opinion leader model." If you can convince those "market mavens" (as opinion leaders are also sometimes called) that you've got a good thing, they'll adopt it and become fiercely loyal, energetic supporters and vocal proponents. Later adopters fall in and buy, and sales can skyrocket, as Nike's have.

Nike considers premier competitive athletes to be their opinion leaders. The athletes lead by modeling. By simply wearing the shoes or other Nike gear, an athlete endorses the brand, sending a message that tells consumers that at least one top athlete thinks Nike is doing something right.

Nike perceives the athletes as more than just promotional material. It seeks feedback on its shoes to see what these excellent, knowledgeable, and presumably very picky athletes like and don't like. It uses the feedback to improve its product. For Nike, product is central, and promotional messages follow.

Of course, customers don't need to be professional athletes. If you like Nike's spokesperson, you'll think favorably about the Nike brand. In a sporting goods store or in a shoe store, the hope is that those positive attitudes make you gravitate toward the Nike shoe section, even if looking for a good shoe for another sport, such as tennis or walking.

The Company and the World

Americans love baseball. And football. And basketball. But the world's favorite game is soccer.

Nike, located in Oregon, had to switch gears a bit to appeal to the global consumer, who is far more likely to love soccer than American baseball. How did it proceed? Same ol' Nike story: Find top soccer players, find out what they look for in an excellent shoe, make such a shoe, and then get some of the athletes (and some entire teams) to wear the shoes and endorse them. If you shoe the players, the buying public will follow.

The Company Now

Why does Nike continue to sponsor sporting events? Its brand awareness is nearly 100 percent, and that's true throughout the world. Why spend the money?

First, the company is always looking to expand. It wants to grow new young customers into the product line to start their customer lifetime value with Nike. It wants to grow its share of dollars from each customer—that is, Nike would like all the sneakers in your closet to be Nikes.

In addition, positive publicity and continued advertising help to strengthen existing brand equity, building goodwill. A company never knows when it's going to need this. Nike was accused of poor labor practices when it was found to have paid very low wages to workers abroad. This hit Nike and its image hard. Nike recovered by fixing the problem and rebuilding the slightly tarnished brand image. In a sense, Nike has suffered from its own success. Most companies as big and omnipresent as Nike will sooner or later take a few hits from critics. If you continue to advertise and build goodwill in the marketplace, customers' attitudes may be inoculated against the hits, making it easier to fix problems before they overtake the brand.

Nike is tough. The company can take pressure. *Rolling Stone* magazine listed the Nike swoosh among the top American icons. Now that's cool.

Questions for Discussion

1. Do you own, or have you owned, a pair of Nike sneakers? What do you think about them? When you go shopping for new sports shoes, how does Nike fare in your shopping decisions?
2. What is your perception of Nike as a company?
3. With Nike's inclusive definition of an athlete, what would you say Nike's segmentation and targeting strategies are?

Video Case 4

Managing Marketing Information

Case in Point: Burke, Inc.

Marketing Research Has Come a Long Way

The Burke video opens with a description of marketing research as simple head counts, via telegrams (!) in the mid-1890s. Now, 115 years later, we still use head counts (as in the federal census) but also face-to-face interviews (as in mall intercepts), telephone interviews, mailed and faxed questionnaires, e-mail and Web surveys, focus groups, ethnographies, and much more. It's weird to hear the folks in the video talk about telephone penetration being low in the 1930s when now many of us have several phones (home, work, cell). The marketing research industry even has mini-surveys designed to be sent to cell-phone or pager users that they can answer via their keypads. Large marketing research suppliers collect data using all these multiple methods, and Burke is among the industry's leaders.

Marketing Research Process

The marketing research process includes four basic steps: (1) complete the problem audit, (2) identify the research objectives, (3) begin the field research, and (4) deliver the results. Talking about customers usually refers to the "end user" (the consumer), but a marketing research company first has to please its client—say, the clothing manufacturer trying to decide between two advertising campaigns, or the toothpaste manufacturer trying to decide whether the line extensions should address whiter teeth or fresher breath, or the bottling distributor trying to figure out whether to offer another flavor or a diet variety, or the retailer trying to decide how to occupy its shelf space with the array of choices that would be optimal to the consumer. These questions, and many more, can be answered with marketing intelligence, the product of marketing research.

Most marketing research companies' CEOs, such as Burke's Robert Tatum, worry about making their client companies happy. They believe that this goal is reached more readily if they work closely with their clients. Rather than thinking that the client gets in their way, they believe there is a great payoff in keeping the client informed and up-to-date regarding progress on a research project.

Getting the Client's Buy-In

In Burke's research process, it's important to get the client to agree to the basic research questions before proceeding, so that the client will have realistic expectations that will be addressed. Just like other consultants, marketing researchers spend much of their time helping define the precise nature of the problem before the project even begins. The client might think that its problem is one thing, whereas the outside researcher digs a little to find that the problem is probably something else. Had the research been designed to answer the client's initial hunches, the research would have been useless in the end—it would have answered the wrong question.

For example, consider this common scenario. Suppose that sales for a soft drink brand are stale or declining. The brand manager and his or her bosses think they need a sales promotion to stimulate short-term sales and a line extension (say, a new flavor) to stimulate longer-term sales. They conduct four focus groups on types of sales promotions and four on flavor tasting, costing at least $50,000 (not counting the engineering and chemistry time to create the new flavor formulations). Based on the results, they select a new flavor. They create, test, and launch advertising (some $1 million to $2 million for a national brand). Sales may be made, driven largely by the brand loyalty and curiosity of the consumers. If the sales drop had actually resulted from other causes (say, a concern to drink purer waters or vitaminized energy drinks, or a perception that this brand was no longer cool), all the expenditures (research, production, advertising) would be wasted—and the company still would have no diagnostic information about the ultimate source of their problems with consumers. In such a case, a few meetings in which the marketing researcher talked to the soft drink brand manager to explore different explanations and scenarios might well have led the research down the proper path.

It's also important to begin to educate the client to help shape realistic expectations. For example, the researchers in the video discuss drawing a sample of consumers and "doing the best we can" to create a sample that is representative so that the findings make sense for all the client's consumers or companies, not just for the several hundred in the sample.

Research Methods

Then the research begins. Usually a marketing researcher starts by poking around and seeing what is already known about the problem. Data that already exist are called "secondary data" and they may be "internal" (that is, the reports exist somewhere in the company) or "external" (for example, online or in industry trade magazines).

At some point, however, the researcher needs more than just background information to answer a particular question. For example, if a new product is being tested, no data will be available yet. However, relevant data about the category or brand might be available to help shape the research questions.

The marketing researchers at Burke meet with the client and design a research process. While they can do anything (e.g., mall, mail, Internet, etc.), they report that some 70 percent of their research is conducted via their phone centers. (This percentage might change, of course, if the "Do not call" legislation holds up.)

Multimedia Methodology

Burke talks about letting people respond in different ways. Doing so allows each person to interact with the company and to give his or her response easily and naturally (some people prefer phone to Web, some the reverse, on so on). In turn, this flexibility enhances response rates and even reduces the amount of time it takes to collect the data.

Web surveys, in particular, are the current favorite of the industry. The survey respondent clicks on buttons or moves cursors, and the computer automatically stores a number to a database, without the need for data entry staff (who are usually quite good but, of course, occasionally make mistakes). This immediacy also speeds up the research time, and the faster clients can get their answers, the faster they can take action in the marketplace, making or saving them even more dollars.

Some data collection is continuous, and some of that is even nearly secret. In one form of the big movement called "customer relationship management" (CRM), companies capture your online purchases via your clickstream data, the Web sites you visit, the banner ads you've been exposed to and clicked on, and other stealthy means.

You might be a member of a marketing research panel. In that case, Burke would also have information on your household demographics (number of people in the household, income, education levels, number of children and their ages, etc.). Other data might also be tied to your household identification number to provide an even richer understanding of your profile—for example, the scanner at your grocery enters your purchases into a database that indicates you prefer low-fat blueberry yogurt but that you also consume vast quantities of beer and M&Ms (Busted!).

These companies aren't just being nosey. All this information is used to try to serve you, the customer, better. The ad companies can tailor more appropriate ads for your viewing. The manufacturers can develop products and flavors according to your preferences. Retailers can provide coupons they think you'll value.

Delivering the Goods

Once the information is compiled and sorted and made sense of, the marketing research supplier, like Burke, makes the information available to the client who commissioned the work. This information is usually a big report, starting with an executive summary in which the basic findings are reported, with an eye toward answering the question that the client and Burke agreed was the focal business question.

If the client's expectations were clear and Burke's research is consistent with the expectations, Burke has done its job, regardless of whether or not the customers like or don't like the product or ad (or whatever the research was about). The client, in theory, should be happy.

Burke can encourage client satisfaction by reminding the client that the research was not done to answer a geeky marketing researcher's question but rather to address the client's business concern. For example, "Recall, here was the problem we agreed upon. Here's the information we gathered. Here's the decision it points to." Burke might even add "This is what we would recommend you do...."

In the video, Burke describes its "Digital Dashboard," which customizes the client's access to the data findings. Burke delivers the big report as a macro answer, but then the client can play with the data further to answer whatever questions it poses as a result of seeing the initial findings. For example, it can break the data out by segments (such as gender of consumer or size of business) to see where it is doing well or poorly.

Online Research

Perhaps the biggest question in the marketing research industry is how to use the Internet to gather information on customers. When Web surveys were first used, they were seen as "the answer." With time, of course, nothing is perfect, and the new method's warts began to show. For example, people have gotten truly annoyed with pop-up advertisers and spam e-mail, and the software that is being designed and disseminated now to prevent these pop-up ads will also effectively stop anything else from popping up, including marketing research surveys.

Burke has recently conducted meta-research (research about how to do research). It was worried about termination in a survey. This hasn't really been a problem to date—if people agree in a mall or on the phone to participate in a survey, they'll most likely finish it with the interviewer. However, online, no one can say "Oh wait, c'mon, just a few more minutes," so some people drop out. These people, in essence, agree to participate when they begin the survey. Yet they eventually lose interest and provide no more data.

A particular concern is whether the people who complete the entire survey online are somehow different from the people who drop out earlier (remember the previous claim that the researcher is trying to get a representative sample). So Burke created two online surveys. One was brief (10 questions taking an average of 5 minutes to complete), and the other was longer (20 questions, taking about 20 minutes to finish).

For the short form, 35 percent were completed. For the longer form, only 10 percent were completed. Hmm. Is this a problem? It is if it affects data quality.

Burke found some support for the hypothesis that only the most involved consumers stick with the longer surveys. For example, if the survey is about cars and I love cars, I'll answer every question asked. However, if the survey is about toothpaste, I might start your survey, but if it's boring, I'm going to drop out of the survey and go surf the Web. It looks like this hypothesis might be plausible, because in its research, Burke found that the attitudes of the people who terminated the survey later in the process were more positive than the attitudes of the people who quit the questionnaire earlier. (Presumably, it's not the survey itself that's making people happy!)

At the same time, in studies of customer satisfaction and dissatisfaction, Burke found that people who stuck with a survey were the ones who were the most angry and upset with the company (so they wanted every chance to answer questions negatively). In others words, those people who terminate later were actually more negative.

Therefore, it is essential to know exactly what the marketing and business problems are. Know that the data are imperfect but surely shed more light on the problem than having no information would. But be smart about using the information.

Questions for Discussion

1. Think about a brand of product you love (a soft drink, a fast food restaurant, your backpack, your bike, your jeans, etc.). Go online and try to find the market share of that brand compared to the others in its product category.

2. If this product is popular with you and your friends, is it because it's popular with a lot of young people? If so, go to www.census.gov, find the demographic projections about age, and see how long your brand might be sustained.

3. Often, products that are extremely popular turn out to be merely fads. People who are trend spotters are highly valued by industries when the trends they anticipate help form the industry's forecasts. Try it! Go online and find data to make a case for three growing trends. Then think about what categories and products are likely to enjoy growth and for how long. For example, if the trends you identify are an aging population, a tougher economy, and rising health care costs, you might develop a franchise plan for a low-cost, high-value living and care arrangement for the older population. What fashions are you likely to see on campus this coming year? What jobs are growing (therefore, what majors might you expect to grow)? What cars are hot right now?

Video Case 5

Consumer and Business Buyer Behavior

Case in Point: Sony Metreon

The Experience Economy

The United States began as a farming nation. The farming industry has been successful at helping to feed the world. The U.S. economy then moved on to manufacturing, which has been successful in producing goods very efficiently. More recently, we have been living in a service-oriented economy, emphasizing the purchase of many intangibles (such as hotel rooms and airline flights) in addition to tangible manufactured goods (such as cars and computers). Now we're undergoing another shift, toward what's being called an "experience" economy, in which the primary goal of what we purchase is an interesting experience (for example, theme parks or movies). No one has embraced the experiential nature of consumption better than Sony's entertainment center, Metreon.

What's going on? Is Sony trying to create a playground for adults, as well as for kids? Sony does refer to the Metreon center as its "Entertainment Destination." The company wants you to buy its electronics products, so the experiential center is partly a way to stimulate and motivate the consumer toward the goal of purchasing. The concept is an explicit acknowledgement that we take time to think about the buying process for some products, and we might want to try the product before committing to buying it. Sony figures "Why not?" So, consumers at Sony's retail store at Metreon are not only allowed but encouraged to touch and experience Sony's new products.

The Concept

Where better in the United States to create an electronics playground than in the heart of Silicon Valley: San Francisco? Here in "Geek City," younger children can climb through the interactive playhouse and older kids can interact with the arcade games or sit at the PlayStation bar to try the latest games. Even older kids (okay, 50-year-old quasi-adults—yes, your dad, yeek!) can try out Sony's new tech products, watch Imax films, see previews for Sony's—and its partners'—new movies and more.

Still, why would Sony do this? A 350,000-square-foot complex in San Francisco, California, is seriously expensive rental real estate. What does Sony get out of it?

If visitors to Sony's Metreon store can "See It, Buy It, Hear It, Experience It," as Sony puts it—all under one roof—they get a fun social occasion just by coming in. The store is likened to an arcade—that is, the store in and of itself is a fun time. The fact that you're quite explicitly gaining familiarity and exposure to Sony's latest product offerings, hopefully forming desires motivating you toward eventual purchasing them, contributes to Sony's ultimate financial goal of your buying the products you've played with and enjoyed.

Creating and Sustaining an Entertainment Destination

Relationships! In this experiential center, Sony encourages the consumer to "touch" whatever products they want to try. In providing these test market opportunities, Sony figures it's also "touching" the consumer. The company is making an impression, trying to reach the consumer on a deeper level than a TV or print ad could. Those media are informative, they can express product features, but they can't create the vivid interaction and trial of the store setting.

Marketers usually believe in a buying process that posits *awareness* before *trial,* and *satisfaction* with the product before *repeat purchasing.* Sony has a strong brand name, creating generally high awareness, and access to all of the hottest gadgets will ensure that awareness of any particular product will also be enhanced. The next stage is trial. When you're selling laundry detergent, you can put a small amount of your new soap in a little plastic envelope and co-package it with another product to encourage the consumer to try your new scent. When you're selling an electronic dog, though, how do you entice consumers to give it a trial? Electronics are not inexpensive toys, and most of us don't want to buy something that's fairly expensive when we're not sure we'll like it because we'd feel guilty about trying to return it (if we were even allowed to do so).

Thus, Metreon's interactivity is Sony's attempt to develop a deeper relationship with consumers. Sony believes that "making memories" is a way of forming a connection between the consumer and the brand or product.

Repeat purchasing is often confused with loyalty. Sometimes we buy the same brand because we don't care about the product enough to re-think the brand choice. Sometimes we buy the same brand for reasons other than a real liking for the brand. For example, we go to the same grocery store or gas station because it's conveniently located between school and home. These behaviors are characterized as repeat purchasing, and they translate into sales but don't indicate true loyalty. If a new, even more conveniently located grocer set up shop between your home and where you take classes, you'd start shopping there.

Loyalty is a notion that the product or brand has captured the heart of the consumer. Sony is aiming for this relationship by associating its name with fun.

Partners Getting into the Act

This video showed a number of other brands that offer consumers experiences at the Metreon Center. For example, the Discovery Channel Store and the Japanese animated film companies provide entertainment content delivered by the Sony technology. Jelly Belly, another example of a partner featured in the Metreon Center, is low-tech, but it also makes the experience fun for the store visitor. You can buy a bag of candies customized to exactly what you want (and nothing else) in terms of mixing and matching colors and flavors. The company fits with the Sony vision for the center because it's also fun.

Hands On

The environment Sony has created lets consumers get familiar with the latest in computers, technology, and games. While it might be the high-tech people who are particularly drawn into such a store, they are probably dragging friends into the store with them. Those friends might be a little less high-tech capable, but the center is set up to allow each visitor to interact with the new toys and games in his or her own time and at his or her own speed.

The Sony employees and taped demonstrations provide vivid depictions about how to use and operate the products. The virtual games allow learning by doing (dancing by matching foot motions to the lighted squares on the floor, the trackball Hyper-Bowling, snowmobiling simulations, and so on).

The video showed how Sony entertainment lets customers try out equipment in rooms in the Metreon store that look like real living rooms. When you go to a typical electronics store with the intent of trying and possibly buying audio equipment, you usually listen to speakers pound sound at you in a soundproof cubicle. Then you're left wondering, "Well, okay, it sounds great in here, but what's it going to sound like at my place?"

At Metreon, Sony overcomes such concerns by allowing customers to operate new Sony gadgets while simultaneously having fun playing and being entertained. Sony adds value beyond the point of merely displaying items and hoping consumers will reach for their wallets. The company has created products and an interactive playing environment in which to test the products, which makes the products come alive. Sony's betting that this type of store will translate into financial success.

What Else Is Going On?

We don't all live near Metreon, so Sony is trying to simulate some of the interactive experience of that store at a place near you—really near you: online.

Sony is exploring joint ventures with music downloads, helping consumers "try" and "listen" before they buy. The company also pays for inclusions in popular search engines and for banner and pop-up ads to entice you to its Web site to see pictures and price quotes for merchandise.

We'll probably see more of these types of brand–person interactions since Sony is on the forefront of marketing. Sony is seen worldwide as a premier marketing company, and whenever it tries and succeeds at something like the Metreon Center or its online efforts, other companies are sure to follow.

Questions for Discussion

1. Is your school near a city that has any experiential theme stores? Besides Sony's Metreon, others include NikeTown stores, ESPN Zones, American Girl (dolls), and others. If you can get to one of these retail outlets, check it out. What do you observe? What is the involvement level of the people at the store? What are the sales levels like? What are the employees like?

2. Do you think that a 13-year-old boy playing at Metreon's PlayStation bar will eventually buy the game he liked, or do you think he's taking advantage of Sony's hospitality to play and won't ever buy? Stated another way, do you think these stores really are instrumental in increasing Sony's sales, or do you think Sony is just kidding itself?

3. To what kinds of people do you think these stores appeal? Are there any particular demographics (social class, family background, gender, age), lifestyles (activities, interests, opinions), or personalities to whom these stores appeal?

4. What is the relationship between a store like Sony's Metreon and the types of people discussed in the model of "adoption of innovations"?

Video Case 6

*Building the Right Relationships
with the Right Customers*

Case in Point: Marriott

Marriott, the worldwide hospitality company, offers a diversity of hotels that serve a variety of customers: the family traveling on a budget, the business executive on an expense account, and everybody in between. The idea of segmentation wasn't always present in the hotel industry. Previously, a hotel company offered one kind of hotel at each of its locations, with a certain price per room, a certain level of service that customers expected, a certain level of amenities and on-site services, and so on. The property managers were much like franchise owners in that each property was supposed to be homogeneous, to maintain consistency, and to help toward brand building.

Segmentation

Then along came Marriott, pioneering segmentation in the hotel industry. It had established a strong, well-known brand name, and it wanted to leverage that brand equity to serve more customers.

A hotel company either appeals to a traveler, or it doesn't. So how can it grow? If it's too high priced for some travelers, it might lower price. However, that lowers profits, and higher-end customers might be somewhat annoyed by the riffraff who soon populate the hotel's properties.

Nothing is wrong with corporate goals of growth, but growth is difficult to achieve with a homogenous product. Therefore, Marriott divided its customers into segments, each of which had different customer needs.

Targeting

Marriott conducted some marketing research concept tests. Customers reacted favorably, so the company began rolling out additional kinds of hotels. "Courtyard by Marriott," with pricing and service levels scaled back from the big Marriott hotels, is targeted toward the price-sensitive frequent business traveler. Fairfield Inns are priced still more modestly to appeal to the traveler who is even more price sensitive.

However, the targeting isn't in pricing alone. For example, a family or a basic business traveler on a budget might be looking for convenient locations in addition to affordability. Hence, Marriott places Fairfield Inns along interstates and highways, figuring these targeted groups are likely traveling by car. Convenient locations become another attribute that adds value to a traveler's stay and enhances perception of the Marriott brand name.

Marriott also identified a substantial number of travelers who stay in Marriott hotels for more than a few nights. These extended-stay travelers have different needs. They might need meeting space to conduct business, a kitchenette to dine in occasionally, or a suitelike space so that they don't get sick of seeing the same four walls around their beds when they come "home" in the evening after yet another day on the road. For these travelers, Marriott offers several extended-stay and suite formats (Marriott Extended Stay, Townplace Suites, and Springhill Suites).

At the high end, Marriott offers even fuller service and higher prices with its Hotel Resorts & Suites and its Renaissance upscale business properties. Quite chic!

Positioning

Each hotel, whether "upscale" or intended for "value," has a distinct design and service level—each has its own personality. Yet all the hotels have in common the Marriott brand name and standards of excellence in operations. The common sharing of the Marriott brand name across the properties is intended to keep the brand name growing strong. The differences are intended to serve the unique segments appropriately.

Such differentiated positioning can be difficult to pull off. How do you express the concept that all these brands share the Marriott corporate name, yet each line is distinctive, serving a different customer group? Usually the encompassing brand name is played down a bit in advertisements. For example, in Courtyard by Marriott, the first part of the name is emphasized, but the Marriott association is made as well.

The hotel managers don't think the customers are confused, and they don't think the different hotel lines are cannibalizing each other (for example, that Fairfield Inns is taking business from Renaissance). Rather, each hotel line serves different customers, or sometimes the same customer but with changing needs (business travel vs. leisure travel, for example). Careful communications are also important so as to avoid confusion in the consumer's mind. You wouldn't want to set resort-level expectations and then deliver the perfectly acceptable but clearly simpler Fairfield standard of lodging and service.

To help stimulate travel, Marriott International has enlisted the help of some former coaches—including Mike Ditka, Jon Gruden, Lou Holtz, and Phil Jackson—in its advertising communications. The idea is that these personalities have "coached their teams out of slumps," so maybe they can also help business travelers "get back into the game," travel more frequently, and, of course, choose Marriott brand hotels. (The previous ad campaign had used *Survivor* host Jeff Probst and Robin Leach of *Lifestyles of the Rich and Famous* to target families.)

At the end of the spots promoting the Marriott Rewards loyalty program, viewers are getting travel advice from unexpected sources, such as David Copperfield suggesting the "magic" of a romantic weekend getaway. These ads have been successful: When the TV spots aired, www.Marriott.com saw spikes in Web site hits and bookings at reservation centers increased.

The Current Struggle

Some hotel managers, primarily those managing properties in California, are exploring surcharges to help cover increased energy costs. Marriott corporate was concerned with the possible negative impact of such fees on its brand image.

To see if its concern was legitimate, the company conducted 400 phone interviews with business travelers who had stayed recently at a Marriott or a Courtyard. These samples were further distinguished by whether or not the guest had stayed recently in a hotel in California—that is, had they experienced paying for the energy surcharge or not.

Marriott found support for its concern that the fees might have an impact on the long-term image of the brand. Further, this was definitely an issue where being "first mover" (the first company to do something in the marketplace) wasn't an advantage. The travelers who had stayed at a hotel chain (Marriott or another) in California and had been charged for energy were annoyed with that hotel chain. After experiencing the charge the first time, however, the next time they stayed at a hotel that charged such a fee, travelers began to think, "Oh, this must be how hotels are doing business now." Thus, the negative attitude toward the second hotel was nowhere near as intense as it was against the first hotel brand.

Well, the charges may be how hotels are doing business now, but Marriott didn't like it. Corporate headquarters was sufficiently concerned with the possibility of a tarnished brand name that it's now rolling back the fees. Of course, such fees might ultimately be incorporated into the pricing structure of hotel rooms, but a line item on your hotel bill for "State Energy Surcharge" gave customers the impression of being nickel-and-dimed, and Marriott wanted to retain the good faith of its customers by putting an end to the practice. Marriott will weather the energy surcharge issue. It's managed successfully through more delicate issues.

The main point to take away here is that there is no question that Marriott's *segmentation, targeting,* and *positioning* atrategies have played a major role in its expansion from one property 45 years ago to a presence today in 65 countries and $20 billion in annual sales.

Questions for Discussion

1. Why aren't most businesses satisfied going after one niche in a market?
2. If a company wants to go after the whole market, why can't it do that with one product offering?
3. Once a company segments its customer base into different segments, how should it go about deciding which group(s) to target?
4. Does positioning a product or service so that it's consistent with the defined target segment really matter? For example, why doesn't Marriott just say "We're Marriott" for all its lines of hotels?
5. Given the issues regarding segmentation, targeting, and positioning, would the surcharges, such as that discussed for energy or others (say, for early checkout) be more or less acceptable or appropriate for any particular Marriott hotel line(s)?

Video Case 7

*Product, Services, and
Branding Strategies*

Case in Point: Accenture

You've no doubt heard of the Arthur Andersen debacle (involving its doubtful Enron accounting practices and other problems) and the company's demise. Originally, the Andersen Consulting group was formed as a consulting arm of Arthur Andersen, the huge accounting firm. You might think that Andersen Consulting changed its name to Accenture because it didn't want to be associated with the Arthur Andersen accounting scandals, but that's not how it unfolded.

The Andersen Consulting group had been pulling away from the Arthur Andersen accounting firm for some years. A legal decision accelerated the split, necessitating a new name and identity for Andersen Consulting. After that, it was just timing and serendipity. The Arthur Andersen troubles surfaced only after Andersen Consulting became Accenture. Thus, while Andersen Consulting's name change was initiated for different reasons, the disassociation of Accenture from Arthur Andersen was a huge by-product of the change. Win–win!

Let's examine the name change. Andersen Consulting became Accenture on January 1, 2001. If the consultancy had been a soft drink, it would have said, "Same great taste, new packaging!" After all, it was still offering largely the same services: consulting with specialties in technology, systems integration, reengineering, and outsourcing. Yet it was disposing of the old brand name.

Usually a new name is the result of a company entering into a new market, or it is motivated by the merging of two companies. In this case, the legal system required the Andersen Consulting group to spin off and separate from Arthur Andersen, the accounting arm. Imagine that. At the time, the legal decision probably annoyed the consulting group. The top executives probably worried that giving up the Andersen Consulting name, which had served them so well, would result in a loss of short-term business. The name had a strong, positive brand equity, based on a strong, positive heritage and reputation in the business marketing world. Andersen Consulting managers knew the power of branding.

Yet given the subsequent developments with the accounting arm of the business, the name change was indeed a very fortunate move. Given that the Accenture brand name sounds so different from the Andersen Consulting brand name, few clients or potential clients would connect the two—and, hopefully, none of the negative practices, exposure, or baggage of Arthur Andersen would contaminate the newly named Accenture consulting group.

Choosing a Brand Name

Accenture wanted to be all that Andersen Consulting was and more. Andersen Consulting had a strong brand name in part because its work was good. However, just being good was not enough for you or me to have heard of it because it was good in B2B services, not consumer services. We heard of Andersen because it had done a thing rare in professional services circles: It had advertised.

Was all that money spent building the Andersen Consulting brand name wasted with the name change? No. In the advertisements announcing the name change, the company tried to show the transition. For example, one ad created for the transition by the Young & Rubicam advertising agency showed the name "Andersen Consulting" with the page looking torn to reveal what looked like the next page, which read "Reborn" and "Renamed." Such ads began to illustrate that what had been Andersen was gone and that now Accenture stood in its place. The emphasis was on the new, but Accenture wanted people to understand its relation to the former company so that it could transfer as much of the old, positive brand equity as possible.

When the legal decision came down that the company had to split away and cease and desist using the Andersen Consulting name, a scramble ensued to think up a new and good brand name. The company started in-house, obtaining some 2,500 name recommendations from employees (which, as the Accenture manager in the video argues, had the side benefit that it got employees thinking even more about forthcoming corporate changes).

Next, the company narrowed the list by deleting names it couldn't use (for example, those that were already trademarked or registered online) or shouldn't use (say, those that wouldn't translate well internationally). The partners selected from among the 29 final names and chose "Accenture." They believed that this name captured the brand essence of what they wanted their clients to think about when choosing Accenture for their consulting services. The "Acc" in the name connotes accomplishment or accessibility, and the name sounds like "adventure."

Thus, to choose a brand name, you first need a vision. Not just any name will do. In this case, Accenture wanted to use the name change as an opportunity to express its strategy to reposition itself in the marketplace. Beyond the name change, it wanted to tell the bigger story that it would be offering even more services for clients. Yes, it would continue to provide consulting and technology expertise, but it would also provide advice on alliances and venture capital.

Marketing

Once Accenture decided on the new name, it had many changes to make—from stationery to Web sites to nameplates to flags, and much more. The new services it was providing (for example, alliance expertise) were included in the tag lines. It worked to educate clients that it was adapting to their needs.

After spending some $175 million on the rebranding efforts, Accenture achieved almost the same level of brand awareness as its former Andersen Consulting name had (but with none of the negative baggage that the Arthur Andersen group would have brought).

The Company Now

This professional service consulting firm continues the excellent heritage of its predecessor, Andersen Consulting. Any time Accenture does anything, businesspeople take notice. For example, according to recent Accenture studies:

■ The Global 1000 is expected to grow its marketing expenditures from $825 billion to $1 trillion. Why? The spending is targeted predominantly at customer relationship management (CRM) investments. Firms want to find and target their most profitable customers, maximizing their share of wallet and improving their average lifetime revenue per customer.

■ This huge expenditure is in part attributable to the increasing difficulty of getting the attention of customers and having an impact on their attitudes. Accenture points to trends such as multiple media, resulting in the fragmenting of marketing audiences. These days, a consumer is confronted with some 3,000 marketing messages a day, compared with an estimated 650 just 20 years ago. At the same time, return on marketing investment is declining. For example, response rates to direct-mail solicitations for credit cards was a measly 3 percent in 1992 and has now dropped to 0.5 percent.

■ Further, while large CRM investments are required to achieve the aforementioned marketing goals, business execu-

tives are facing information technology (IT) investments with increased skepticism: "Don't we have big enough, fast enough computers already?" Accenture is getting together with some big IT players (such as Cisco, Hewlett-Packard, Intel, Microsoft, and Xerox) to form the Information Work Productivity Council, which will address this "prove it" attitude emanating from the boardroom.

■ If companies are paying more for equipment, they're also paying more to hire and hold onto good people. A global Accenture study showed that the number-one priority among business executives was to attract and retain skilled staff.

■ Finally, online is still all the buzz. Accenture identified two of the factors that explain most of the potential and promise of online exchange: (1) aggregation (the opportunity for one firm to do business with a large number of buyers and sellers) and (2) integration (the ability to communicate across organizations and link buyers' and sellers' processes).

Accenture has credibility—people believe their statements and estimates. Further, when Accenture says something like "Other firms in your industry are growing their marketing spending," it makes firms think "Well, then, we must do this also." Accenture makes things happen.

Questions for Discussion

1. What core service does Accenture offer? What supplemental services?

2. What are the tangibles and intangibles that a consulting firm delivers?

3. How does the client know it's getting its money's worth from the services that Accenture delivers?

4. What makes branding difficult for a professional service? Why is it critical to the firm's success?

Video Case 8

*New Product Development
and Product Life-Cycle Strategies*

Case in Point: eGO Vehicles

In the 1970s, McDonald's served its Big Mac sandwiches in polystyrene clamshell containers. Environmentalists protested that these materials were not biodegradable, and because of the volume of business that McDonald's does daily worldwide, great concern was expressed about contributing to mountainous landfills. McDonald's responded to this customer-based criticism by switching to paper containers.

Lots of companies find themselves in such jams. They go about their business, but then something internal or external sparks their conscience, such as customers, suppliers, or social critics censuring them for not being environmentally friendly. If they care (because, for example, lots of press or a large segment of dissatisfied customers is involved), the company might redesign its products to consume less energy, to produce less waste, and to fit in better with what is "natural."

Not so eGO Vehicles. From the very start, the goal of green marketing came before the product. What a concept!

The founders didn't start out to enter the bicycle, motorcycle, or moped markets and then claim "We are more environmentally friendly than the next guy." Their goal was to create an alternative form of transportation, one that was "green" yet practical. They wanted to design and market a vehicle that could be used for the endless errands we all run daily, out and about but near the house, errands for which you don't need a car for speed, storage capacity, or long distances.

The Product

The eGO Cycle—an electric bicycle—is priced at about $1,400. It can go about 20 to 25 miles on each electric charge at about 20 to 25 miles per hour (unless the driver is heavy or going up an incline). The cycle consumes no oil, no gas and generates no waste, not by-products, and no pollution.

These cycles are a little "distinctive" looking. (If you haven't seen one yet, take a look at www.egovehicles.com.) The designers sought such distinctiveness. They didn't want people to think "Oh, a motorcycle" (bad for the environment) or "Oh, a bike" (you have to pedal). It's a new and different concept, and its looks should—and do—reflect that.

The product is so novel in appearance that people stop owners and ask, "What is that?" "How does it work?" "Where did you get it?" "How much was it?" This reaction creates that most-valued of all marketing tools: customer buzz. Buzz, or "viral marketing" (as in "The enthusiasm is 'contagious' "), is valued because it's free (the company isn't spending advertising

dollars). It's also extremely effective. When you watch a TV ad, you think the advertiser is going to say "This is the best," but your reaction to a friend who's just bought a new computer will be "Oh, wow, this *is* the best!" Compare a company-sponsored message to one from a friend: Which is more vivid? Which strikes you as more compelling? Which seems most authentic?

Yet buzz is hard to generate. The eGO Vehicles people are trying to stimulate buzz by featuring the product at events such as football games. It shows the product to the people with the hope of making them want to know more.

The buzz is working because eGO Vehicles is selling hundreds of cycles each month to customers everywhere in the world. The word of mouth is strong and plentiful, and eGO Vehicles is smart: It's posting these word-of-mouth testimonials on its Web site. Given the product's novelty and its environmental friendliness, the company is also benefiting from great public relations and other favorable media coverage. The eGO Vehicle has garnered magazine coverage and high-quality TV airtime (on *Good Morning America, The Today Show,* CNN, and other channels). The eGO company says that even local word-of-mouth effects can be tracked—apparently, when someone buys an eGO Vehicle, a cluster of sales spikes in that local vicinity.

Introducing Products

The eGO Cycle is a little weird though, yes? How do you introduce this alternative means of transport to the market and help consumers find a place for it in their minds alongside bicycles or mopeds? Traditionally, introducing "new to the world" products requires huge advertising expenditures. The ads are basic education campaigns: Here's the product we sell, here's what it can do for you, here's why it's better than what you already have. Recent examples include DVD players and personal digital assistants (PDAs): The early ads had to explain why these inventions were better than what people had been using (e.g., VHS video or a DayBook calendar). However, eGO is saving on ad budget because its customers have become a massive de facto sales force. Current customers' in-market testimonials and potential customers seeing the vehicles essentially serve as free infomercials.

Yet it has been difficult for eGO Vehicles to get distributors to help it sell the transports. Traditional dealers don't want to devote floor space to non-bikes, and motorcycle dealerships don't want "bikes" on their lots. In this day and age, direct sales to customers might be successful. Customers can buy online at eGO Vehicles or its many partner sites.

Are you intrigued? Do you think you might buy one someday? Do you know of someone who might? Why? Is it the "cool vehicle" angle that would attract you as a customer? Or are you teased among your friends for being a tree-hugging environmentalist? How do you think eGO's word of mouth is functioning? Do you think it's just environmentally conscious people who are spreading the word of this alternative form of transportation? Could a person in that segment persuade a person who doesn't care as much about the environment to look at the vehicles and perhaps buy based on other attributes of the machines? How can eGO step into the buzz process and keep it going?

Questions for Discussion

1. How does one introduce new products to consumers in the marketplace? How do you, as a marketer, approach the problem if you have a new music CD to sell? A new flavor of Coca-Cola? A new car?

2. How do these strategies and tactics vary if you're introducing a so-called new-to-the-world product (like eGO Vehicles, or DVD players or Palm Pilots when they were new, etc.)?

3. What is eGO Vehicles' likely target segment(s)? What are your reasons for these suppositions?

4. Could eGO sell to motorcycle owners? Bicycle owners? Car owners? Walkers (e.g., New York City dwellers)? City dwellers (e.g., Los Angeles)? How would eGO appeal vary with the audience?

Video Case 9

Pricing

Case in Point: Nextel

Wireless phones demonstrate an interesting product growth curve—they've been around some 20 or more years, but growth at first was slow. Then, about 5 years ago, cell phone usage skyrocketed so that nearly half of U.S. consumers now subscribe (some 150 million users). Internationally, some countries exhibit even greater market penetration for cell phone usage (more than 75 percent in Finland and Italy).

Cell phones are part of our lives now because so many people have one. Business travelers have them, of course, but kids also have them to call mom after school.

The Product

What is it we buy when we get a cell phone? We buy a phone, of course, and a service provider—the communications network and the technology that carries the phone calls. The phones themselves are maturing as a product. It's difficult to tell a cell phone from a camera or from a personal digital assistant (PDA). The phone manufacturers are increasingly building in greater functionality, in part because there is so much competition.

Phone service plans are also becoming highly competitive. We want to know how much a plan will cost us, how many minutes (day, evening, weekend) we get, when "evening" starts, what the long-distance or roaming charges are, if any, and so on. Sometimes companies pride themselves on points of differentiation that the customers don't understand or don't care about. We might suffer "dropped calls," but do we really choose a carrier because of its reputation for better networks? Aren't all carriers using the same satellites? If we travel a lot by car and one phone plan doesn't pick up calls in the areas we travel through, do we really believe another phone plan will?

The Competition

The market is also maturing, though not yet slowing down. It is indeed a very competitive marketplace, with more than a hundred carriers in the United States alone.

Your own cell phone package is probably with one of the big six companies: AT&T Wireless, Cingular, Nextel, Sprint PCS, T-Mobile, or Verizon Wireless. However, all these providers aren't equally successful.

Even among the big six, the power is further concentrated. Nextel and T-Mobile control about 85 percent of the market in terms of subscribers. Still, it's the presence of all those competitors and the inherent customer choice that make the product category one that is responsive to customer needs.

Competitive Position

Nextel thinks it's different, but then who doesn't? It claims to offer products and services that competitors don't. Let's exam-

ine those so-called points of uniqueness. Further, let's look at how sustainable those differences are.

For example, Nextel points to its "nationwide direct connect," which allows customers to connect with each other regardless of a call's long-distance status. However, AT&T's Direct Rate plan also does this. Nextel might claim that it pioneered this feature, but honestly, do you care?

Nextel also says it's different from the competition in terms of a marketing strategy: It targets business customers because it knows that business customers tend to be high-value—though demanding—customers. However, if business customers are valuable, won't many of the other carriers eventually catch on and target them as well? And if AT&T or Sprint went after Nextel's business customers, would Nextel's customers remain loyal or would they jump ship? Even if Nextel is currently serving business customers better than the competition does, can Nextel sustain this difference? What is Nextel providing, especially for business customers, that they can't get elsewhere?

One unique service is an easy capacity for conference calling. Using Nextel Direct, a group of businesspeople can connect immediately and clearly. During this connection, Nextel is reaping profits because each person is connected via his or her plan minutes.

Also, if a company wants its sales force to be extremely responsive while on the road, it might institute the use of the walkie-talkie capabilities of the Nextel Direct plans. For the moment, if Nextel is the only game in town offering walkie-talkie features, a company's desire for a walkie-talkie capability drives it immediately to Nextel, with no consideration of a competitor (since, in its eyes, there would be none).

Still, AT&T, T-Mobile, and the other three players aren't going to stay put. Most of the differentiating features are easy to match. Nextel has to think about how it can stay one step ahead of these tough competitors. Should it drop price and start a price war? Could it do so, sustain its current reputation for innovativeness, and continue to create features that its core business customer would desire? Sustaining a competitive advantage is probably the most difficult challenge for any business.

Price Structure

If we accept for the moment that Nextel primarily seeks business customers, and business customers primarily seek Nextel, how does Nextel price its services to these customers? Behind the scenes, Nextel conducts a lot of sensitivity analyses to test customer reactions to price changes, as well as to new phone and service attributes, so it can make decisions about rolling out new options. Nextel prices its rate plans and then emphasizes that the fee includes many additional services. Is that how you like to purchase? Are those additional services really free, or are they cleverly bundled? If you're a business customer, perhaps someone else pays for your phone, so price is irrelevant to you.

Nextel customers like their "push to talk" service, which in turn yields high revenues per minute for Nextel. However, instead of passing "savings" (or part of the profits) on to customers, Nextel charges a premium for that service. It's raking in the bucks!

Nextel is also trying to add value with more services, including Internet access and the move toward GPS. Nextel believes that its customers know they're getting a lot for their money, so they're willing to pay more, and they'll still be satisfied that they're getting good value.

What's Next

Legislation passed recently supports "phone number portability" (PNP, which means wireless customers can keep their phone numbers even when they switch carriers). This has big implications for business customers, who don't want to print new business cards and stationery every time they switch phone carriers. Once this constraint is lifted, do you think business customers will stay with Nextel? That is, was it "loyalty" and "satisfaction" with Nextel's services that kept the business customer, or did the customer stay with Nextel because of a switching cost (a new number necessitating office supply changes, informing business associates, and so on)? One might certainly argue that Nextel and T-Mobile will be hurt more than the other carriers since they're the biggest right now (that is, we don't know whether some people have stayed with Nextel or T-Mobile because they're "loyal" or because they didn't want to lose their numbers).

Nextel is also hoping to expand its customer base, and so it's begun sponsoring NASCAR races. It turns out that about 12 percent of NASCAR fans have annual incomes between $75,00 and $100,000. In addition, sports marketing has traditionally been a means of enhancing awareness of brands, particularly among men, who in many instances might be the business customer decision makers.

That expansion and attempt for greater coverage and brand awareness can't hurt. They're all steps in the right direction. Nextel is really going to have to work hard to keep its marketplace advantages.

Questions for Discussion

1. Do most business customers pay for their own phones and phone service? Does this matter?
2. Have you switched cell phone carriers? Why did you switch? What might have kept you loyal? Are carriers a commodity, or might branding and product differentiation succeed in this industry?
3. Using the basic pricing principles presented in the chapter, how would you price a phone (with which bundle of features)? How would you price the calling plan service (with which bundle of features)?

Video Case 10

Distribution Channels and Logistics Management

Case in Point: Snapple

A consumer trend toward healthy foods, a production process break-through, and a corporate misstep: What do they all have in common? Snapple.

Consumer Trend toward Healthy Foods

Beverages are a huge industry. Sales are $70 billion a year, some 18 billion gallons, which translates to 66 gallons for each of us. Are you drinking your share? More? Less? That 66 gallons per year sounds like a lot, but it's only about 23 ounces a day. One can of soda is 12 ounces, so it's only about two cans a day.

Choices used to include only soft drinks, along with some flavored sugar mixes like Kool-Aid. Then came Snapple, a pioneer in addressing the trend toward health concerns, with its introduction of bottled iced tea that was "natural." Since the 1990s, Snapple has expanded its product line in efforts to satisfy consumers' desires for new varieties in taste. It now also offers other tea flavors and more exotic fruit blends. More recently, energy drinks have become popular, as has the purity promised by bottled waters.

Production Process Progress

If consumers were looking for healthier products to fit in their healthier lifestyles, for what drinks would they reach? Coke? Pepsi? Diet Coke and Diet Pepsi? What about something that had more than "empty" calories, such as fruit juice (but not too sugary)? Say you recognize tea as natural: How do you proceed to bottle it? If you insert preservatives in the bottling process, could you claim the drink was "natural"? If you do not use preservatives, the drink may be natural but not healthy.

How can Snapple position itself to consumers as "all natural"? It started 25 years ago by selling iced tea to New Yorkers. It then worked with suppliers, bottlers in this case, to find a production system whereby it could fill glass bottles with the beverage using a heated system that would kill microorganisms and do so without adding preservatives. Hence, Snapple contained no unnatural ingredients, just good-tasting, natural iced tea and fruit beverages.

Once the natural drink was bottled and capped, it could be distributed nationally, not just regionally in the Northeast, so marketing and advertising had to follow. When the drink rolled out nationally, the brand image was "offbeat," appealing to "unusual" consumers, with a "down to Earth," "fun" message.

People came to the drink like it was an oasis. Snapple devotees formed fan clubs, held Snapple conventions, and applauded themselves for being "cool" because they drank the "best stuff on Earth." That's quite a brand!

Corporate Missteps

It was a good deal 25 years ago, to pay $500 for the Snapple name. However, as the brand grew strong and the loyal customer base grew broader, the corporation floundered. It thought that sales could continue and grow with no marketing support. Sales sliding 8 percent might not seem like much, but that translates to a $100 million loss or market share plunge of 5 percent.

In 1994, Quaker Oats acquired the brand for $1.7 billion, apparently believing there was still life left in this tea. However, its actions belied those beliefs. It cut back on advertising at the same time that competitors started offering similar products of their own. Quaker explored changes that had nothing to do with the Snapple brand but rather simply reflected Quaker's own heritage (such as experimentation with bottle sizes, as Quaker had done successfully with Gatorade). It also cut the number of Snapple flavors from 50 to just over 30. Finally—yikes—it introduced a warehouse system, and this required preservatives. Uh oh. The end result? A big mistake, and Quaker took a big write-off.

Quaker thought that a new ad could stem the decline. That's expecting an awful lot from an ad.

Next, the Triarc Beverage Group, owner of R.C. Cola, bought Snapple. It sought to reinvent the beverage, to recapture its original brand personality. It hoped that it could successfully reconnect with the consumer. Previous sales had shown all kinds of promise and potential to help create a terrific brand.

Recovery Marketing

How do you reconnect with a consumer? One way is advertising, such as blatant product placements in popular television shows (then, *Seinfeld* and *Chicago Hope*). The company ran "goofy" ads in the personal columns in an attempt to retrace the offbeat nature of the drink's original customers.

More recently the company began an integrated advertising campaign. TV ads put dressed-up bottles in unexpected situations. For example, dressed-up Snapple bottles appeared to be running with the bulls in Spain or competing in a collegiate synchronized swim meet. Using other media, with a consistent message, fans of Snapple could log onto www.snapple.com to view the behind-the-scenes stories of these new TV commercials.

Snapple believes that if it can make a good first impression on a consumer who hasn't tried Snapple yet—for example, at a highly publicized and well-attended event—it can introduce the product to otherwise untapped customers. Sponsorships can be expensive, but Snapple believes that the money is a good investment in forming positive consumer impressions. For example, Snapple's YooHoo brand sponsored the "Big Stinking Summer Tour." The company converted a sanitation truck into a sampling vehicle (Gross!), and the truck followed the tour. In a similar move, Snapple became the "Official Iced Tea" for the New York Yankees.

Promotional products are also popular at Snapple. The video describes sandals ("flip flops") with a Snapple logo cutout on the soles, with the idea that as Snapple consumers walk along the beach, they'll leave imprints of the Snapple logo on the sand.

New products also contributed to the brand's regrowth. The company created smoothies, again to signal "fun." It targeted smaller packages to younger kids.

Finally, Snapple didn't ignore its marketing partners. Consumers who buy the drink are important, but the people who sell the drink (the retailers) are important, too. Snapple wanted their support, and it wanted to show the retailers it was back to stay.

Four years ago, sales started to turn around. Guess what? One year later, Snapple was sold again. Schweppes, the big beverage company, scooped up Snapple for a mere $1.4 billion! Schweppes is trying to keep the brand's quirky personality, even though $1.4 billion is a serious, not quirky, level of business.

The Company Now

Snapple is trying to extend its brand deeper into its consumers' lives. It targets primarily 18- to 24-year-olds. Last summer, it offered a promotion in which consumers could trade bottle caps they collected for backpacks, foosball tables, and other items. The cap collectors could shop on the Snapple Web site.

Snapple is also setting up retail stores and exploring categories of clothing, other foodstuffs, gaming consoles, and software. These are all thought to be products important to consumers' lives, and if developed consistent with the theme of "fun," they can all be adapted into the Snapple product line.

Questions for Discussion

1. How is a partner like a bottler important to Snapple, to the company?

2. How much do you, as the end consumer of the Snapple line of drinks, know about its suppliers and bottlers and other partners? How much do you need to know?

3. How central was the production process to the essence of the Snapple brand and the claims the company makes in its ads?

4. It is said that the Internet is the next best channel of distribution. For a product like a drink, which is not yet distributable electronically (wait for George Jetson!), can a company like Snapple use the Internet to its advantage? Why or why not? If so, how?

Video Case 11

Retailing and Wholesaling

Case in Point: Federated Direct Department Stores

The Retailing Environment

Today consumers can buy merchandise in many different venues: big department stores, little specialty boutiques, everyday-value discount stores, catalogs, and online shops. If you were the store manager for one of these shops, you would buy merchandise from different manufacturers in the hope that your customers would buy it from you. How can you know what your customers are going to want?

Federated Department Stores, which owns Macy's, Bloomingdale's, and other retail chains, is a merchandising group with an excellent reputation. It is so large that it produces ten of its own private label brands. Federated's brands include, among others, the popular INC, Alfani, Charter Club, and Style & Co. labels, which altogether account for 16 percent ($2 billion) of Macy's sales. Through its private labels, Federated's stores can provide excellent quality while keeping prices reasonable. Federated knows that even customers who are willing to spend quite a lot of money still want to feel like smart shoppers, getting good quality and value for their dollars. In fact, to stimulate sales, Federated and many of its competitors, have begun to push their post-holiday sales and promotions earlier in the fiscal year to "preholiday" schedules in the spirit of showing their customers they want to add value.

Beginning with the Bridal Business

Macy's bridal business might seem a peculiar place to have started, but consider the full scenario. Thinking about married life leads a couple to project their domestic needs. They don't need more jeans, so they don't need to visit The Gap. They need household goods, kitchen, bedding, and bathroom stuff, and they don't want junk but nice stuff. Above all, Macy's knew that you get a lot of gifts when you get married.

The Macy's buyers know that at this stage, early in the life cycle of a new family life, decision makers register at stores that are relatively new to them. If the couple is happy with the ease of their transactions—for example, putting together the items they want on their registry—and if they like the merchandise they receive, they'll have positive feelings toward that store. This will result in more frequent visits as the couple shops to satisfy their increased domestics needs. Further, even three years down the road, nearly all of those couples (96 percent!) are still shopping in the same stores that had provided their wedding registry service. That's remarkable. Thus, identifying a bridal registry opportunity is the store's best way to initiate a new customer relationship and to capture a long "customer lifetime value."

The Problem

Enticing young brides to the Macy's registry was a bit of a challenge. The brides-to-be didn't find the Macy's brand appealing. Macy's is associated with a big Thanksgiving Day parade—big deal—and it's basically where Mom shops. Since everybody knows that Mom's not cool, why would young women shop there?

That's a tricky mind-set for a marketer to overcome. Macy's has had a good brand image, but not with the brides-to-be segment. For Macy's to appeal to the hipper young women (in addition to their moms), it had to find out what the brides-to-be think is cooler. If they like places that range from Williams-Sonoma to Crate & Barrel to Target, Macy's needs to assess what those stores have that Macy's doesn't.

Another issue was that one of Macy's traditional strengths, excellent customer service, wasn't as valued by these couples. The young couples don't feel a need for advice. They come to the store more prepared than previous generations of couples. They've done some pre-purchasing homework, investigating brands and prices on the Web. Further, if they know what brands they want, sometimes they can find those brands cheaper at discount stores. Furthermore, if they don't need a salesperson following them around, they might as well register at Target rather than at Macy's.

Good marketing has to start with a good product—it's not just advertising. So in Macy's efforts to reposition its brand, or to "re-brand," it needed to stock cooler merchandise—that is, the product itself had to reflect the company's shifting strategy.

The in-store service had to change, also. Instead of having older women follow brides around the store while jotting down what to include in the registry, the young couples wandered around the store on their own, in "self-service" mode, with a registry electronic gun to scan items they wanted their families and friends to buy for them.

This also helped Macy's obtain a lot of information about each couple. Whether or not the bride and groom got the loot they'd registered for, Macy's now had a long list of items that they knew appealed to these customers. It knew which china patterns were more popular, and it could easily investigate (ask or experiment) whether this popularity was due to cool patterns or better prices. It knew which bedding was bought most often and with which towels and other bathroom goods, and this information gave Macy's ideas about what items to feature together and perhaps even bundle in pricing.

Macy's hope was that the new merchandise, still of excellent quality, along with the new high-tech registry service, would signal the new brand to younger couples. This new brand was to encompass luxury yet value, contemporary yet traditional, a new twist on the values that have long served Macy's and its customers so well.

The Company Now

When you walk through a store in the shoes of the customer, you think of many ways to make the shopping environment more inviting and user-friendly. For example, Macy's is exploring improvements to its fitting rooms, price-check scanners (prior to checkout), customer lounges, and more.

Some of Macy's private label fashion merchandise referred to earlier is so high-end that it is even being sold by non-Federated retailers in Australia, Bermuda, Canada, Peru, and Japan. Federated is taking quality in those private lines seriously. When it started selling luxurious high-thread-count sheets and top-of-the-line bedding that sells for some $3,000, it began to define a new "private brand luxury" category.

Federated is also sensitive to consumer trends. In a timely marketing twist, Macy's will be launching a collection of high-quality men's clothing called the Sopranos line, after the HBO hit. This line will include $40 silk ties, $50 shiny cotton sateen dress shirts in several solid colors, and $60 to $80 silk and wool knit shirts with patterned fronts and solid sleeves.

Federated is considered at the forefront of excellent marketing. Its best marketing executives are being hired by competitors. (Perhaps it needs to do a better job of internal marketing.)

Questions for Discussion

1. Is the proliferation of purchasing channels, such as the different kinds of stores, a good thing for the consumer? Why or why not?

2. If alternative channels are here to stay, how can a big department store like those under Federated's command make the best of it? What strengths can department stores play up as benefits to the consumer?

3. What other segments could Macy's go after that might grow into loyal customers, the way it found potential in young couples' future purchasing via its bridal business?

Video Case 12

Integrated Marketing Communications: Advertising, Sales Promotions, and Public Relations

Case in Point: AFLAC

AFLAC (American Family Life Assurance Company), the Columbus, Georgia insurer, was nearly unknown in the United States just 3 years ago. Now, nearly everyone knows the name. Thanks to that unflappable, curmudgeonly duck, 89 percent of us recognize the brand. The lighthearted advertising campaign took an unlikely insurance company from being virtually unknown to being one of the most recognizable brands in recent history.

Advertising Strategy

In the video, the AFLAC manager said she thought that maybe the company was taking a risk. After all, humor can backfire. What if people had seen the television commercials and thought, "How stupid!" or "A life insurance company should be more serious than that." The ads made fun of the company's name and also made it clear the company knew you didn't know who it was. This isn't the typical path to establishing brand equity.

How much of a risk was it really? The ad agency had done its homework. Its research indicated that no one had heard of the company (no surprise) and that the name AFLAC meant nothing to potential customers.

Even the creatives attested to being unable to remember the company's name. For goodness sake, this was AFLAC's client! The agency kept repeating the name over and over: AFLAC, AFLAC, AFLAC, eventually adding the goofy duck intonation. Thus was born the little avian mascot.

Repetition is the first rule in creating memory in advertising. It is a practice that connects a name to the associations or attributes of a product featured in an ad. The AFLAC name is now connected to the duck that quacks it, and to the insurance stories told by the human actors and narrators in the ad spots.

If you think only the serious customer thinking of buying insurance is listening, think again. A recent study showed that even "tweens" (kids ages 8 to 13) now know the name AFLAC. The other top-five TV ads recognized by this young segment include Geico, Pepsi, Old Navy, and M&Ms. Talk about great lifetime customer value potential—these young people aren't ready to buy supplemental insurance, but they'll have strong familiarity with the brand when they're ready to buy.

Who Is Buying?

AFLAC sells B2B as well as B2C, with more than $10 billion in annual sales. It has to offer better value and quality than competitors to get business customers to choose it for their company coverage.

AFLAC needs to have these strengths but also brand recognition to sell to consumers. Most of us make weekly grocery lists that include things like milk, bread, frozen burritos, or so on, but most of us aren't thinking, "Gee, I need to go buy some supplemental insurance." However, the TV commercial and that darned duck might prompt you to think about it. Maybe you do need some supplemental insurance. Maybe you can do better than your current policy. You're not buying because of the duck, exactly, but you sure know AFLAC's name because of it.

The sales force now has a tangible representative that opens the door in terms of name recognition. Other insurers have typically sought symbols that express the security that insurance represents—for example, the Traveler's "umbrella," All-State's "You're in good hands," Prudential's "rock" (strength, solidity), Merrill-Lynch's "bull" (strength, a good market economy), and Met-Life's "Snoopy" (hmm).

The salespeople need these symbols to help communicate what it is the insurance company can do for the buyers they're trying to persuade. Insurance is not a *search* good (like a pair of socks you know you'll like or not when you look at them because you can immediately assess their size, look, price, feel). Nor is it an *experience* good (like a dinner at a restaurant or a movie that you can't really judge until after you've consumed it). Instead, it's a *credence* purchase whose quality you can't be sure of even after you've bought it. Will the insurance cover you should you need it? The hope is that you never have to find out. So insurance companies use symbols to say "We're strong" and "We'll make you feel secure."

The video also alluded to how the duck campaign created fast growth, perhaps too fast to accommodate. The field organization has to coordinate sales and maintain helpful customer service staff to see sales through and to get policies started. In a sense, the salespeople might have been selling more than the company could handle while still providing quality service. A related phenomenon in many industries is that CEOs want more justification when their sales and marketing executives buy more expensive customer relationship or sales force management software packages. Yet it is true that a good computer system, like AFLAC's SmartApp, would help sales agents in the field. Using their laptops, the salespeople can transmit policy applications to headquarters electronically. The system may soon be paperless, which makes the field agents more efficient and saves the company dollars in the long run.

International Business

Is AFLAC a global company? Well, yes and no. It sells in countries other than the United States. In fact, most of its sales are from outside the United States. However, its international business is actually concentrated in Japan, where AFLAC brings in 70 percent of its operating earnings and has 80 percent of its $38 billion in assets.

Obviously, AFLAC is big in Japan, where it's the largest foreign insurer and the second most profitable company after IBM. Japan is a health-obsessed consumer market (think about the news reports showing everyone on a crowded train wearing cotton surgical masks to ward off colds), seemingly perfect for an insurance company.

This windfall of business came because, well, AFLAC got lucky. In 1974, Japan's Ministry of Finance handed AFLAC one of the rare licenses awarded to foreign firms. At the time, the big Japanese insurance companies didn't think there would be much of a market in such a niche business. Big mistake. AFLAC now insures 25 percent of Japan's citizens. AFLAC should do well in the future there as well, if you consider Japan's rapidly aging population.

Brands and Insurance

Branding is relatively new to the insurance industry. As insurance companies struggle to establish their own identities with business and consumer customers, some companies will stay conservative. Others, like AFLAC, think a little humor can never hurt. It may even help break through today's media clutter.

Questions for Discussion

1. What other industries, products, or brands have used humor to help position themselves in the marketplace? Do you think the strategies have worked? Where wouldn't humor work?

2. Now that AFLAC is a widely known brand name, do you think the company should drop the duck? What else might it feature?

3. What do you think the sales force's reaction was when it first saw the duck? Is it necessary for a sales force to buy into a campaign, or can it be shown later that a campaign is working?

Video Case 13

Integrated Marketing Communications: Personal Selling and Direct Marketing

Case in Point: Motorola

The video about Motorola opens by pointing out the obvious: It tells us that we're bombarded with tons of advertisements and other communications from companies every day. It's easy to get tired of this onslaught of media, to the point that we just about tune out. Companies and advertisers know this, too. Their usual answer, unfortunately, is to send even more "ad weight" (the term for spending even bigger advertising budgets) to expose you to even more messages, so that hopefully you'll see or hear at least one of them.

Integrated Marketing Communications

The frequency of advertisements is a huge issue. Another issue, though, is how to make sure that every communiqué that a company aims at customers sends a consistent image about the company and its products. That's the idea behind the new realm of marketing called "integrated marketing communications." If you run a TV and a radio spot, or a public announcement and a print ad, the essence of their messages must be the same in content and similar in execution so that the consumer starts putting two and two together. "Oh, this print ad in my magazine is advertising Motorola's new flip phone, like those posters I've seen on busses" or "Wow, the TV ad makes the phone look like fun, and there's a lot of information on the Web site about the phone's fun features."

A different form of the integrated marketing communications question is "How do you make your message consistent to customers all over the world?" On one hand, you might not think this is a big problem. For example, if you're a citizen of Taiwan, you'd see one set of ads and not the ones shown in, say, Canada, so why does it matter if the Taiwanese-targeted ads convey the same content as the Canadian-targeted ads? Well, it's the same company and product. And people travel. And people talk. And they e-mail one another. Thus, different messages might result in confused company and brand images.

Global Branding

Here comes the Moto, which is a cute name for Motorola's global branded cell phone. It's a name that will be easy to pronounce by anyone in the world, and a name that doesn't mean anything bad or weird anywhere in the world. It's also a name that carries some part of the Motorola name, a strong positive brand name that reminds consumers of the company's heritage.

The way Motorola's advertising agency, Ogilvy & Mather, talks about it, Motorola wants to express the same core idea about the product or brand, but it wants to do so in a way that makes sense to each local market. Reminiscent of the AFLAC story (in which the creatives at the ad agency simply kept repeating the name until the duck sound was born), the Taiwanese call their cells phones "moto."

Advertising Versus Building Brands

While Motorola has a reputation for high-quality products, the Moto name and product were intended to change the company's image to appeal to the younger, cooler crowd. Young adults comprise the target audience, and the mantra in sending ads to this group is to make the ads more irreverent and fast-paced. Further, Motorola's traditional strengths, those perceptions of quality, are taken as a given by consumers. So they're not choosing among phones by features but rather by whether the phone "fits" into their lives or considering "Is this phone me"? Motorola's marketing even challenged the company's own management to think of the phones not so much as engineered, functional devices but as fashion accessories to help consumers make statements about who they are.

Thus, the advertising agency was helping shift perceptions about the new "Moto" brand, rather than merely "advertising" it. It tried to try to address Motorola's business needs and desires to become more relevant and to be the first choice among young adult consumers.

Once the agency developed the positioning and message strategy, it had to reach its target, through whatever means. It considered using Superbowl ad slots but lots of other media are available. Motorola had to understand which media are important in its target market's life so that it could be confident about spending its ad dollars wisely, and it needed to integrate its messages so that they told a consistent story across varied media.

It wanted to build a brand that connects to its consumers, then to take the brand and make it work all over the world. The brand is defined globally, but the ad executions are tweaked in each local market.

It has succeeded. Motorola has consistently gained share at point-of-sale in recent years, and it's regained co-leadership with Nokia in the cell phone market in the United States.

The Current Global Market

China is everybody's biggest challenge. The potential is great, with China's population exceeding a billion people. China's cell phone market, for example, is bigger than that of the United States—in fact, it's now the world's largest, with 243 million subscribers.

Still, the Chinese government differs from many, and it's hard to do business in China the way it's done elsewhere. For cell phones, in particular, China currently relies mostly on suppliers. It is relabeling reconfigured Taiwanese handsets, and its engineers are designing cell phones into which they insert chips from the French company Sagem SA, the German company

Siemens AG, and others. The Chinese expect to have their own chip soon, and hence they have no need for these suppliers. Motorola has seen its own share of the cell phone market in China drop from 30 percent to 20 percent in just 2 years. Similar challenges exist for Motorola in Korea.

Other Issues at Motorola

High-technology products turn over quickly: Everyone wants the latest gadget with the most up-to-date features. That's understandable from the consumer's point of view, but if you're the high-tech company, how do you get rid of old inventory? About a year ago, Motorola started making some of its equipment (cell phones, radios) available on eBay. It's finding that eBay brings its selling prices with 35 percent higher average than its current channels for unloading these products. Selling on eBay is working so well that Motorola is looking into putting some of its B2B inventory online (for example, it sells some 11,000 pieces of equipment relevant to various kinds of testing, such as oscilloscopes, analyzers, and generators). Some companies are using eBay just for advertising: They put a high starting bid price on their merchandise, high enough that no one will bid on it, while they pay only $3.30 weekly to keep the item on the auction site. That's pretty inexpensive advertising.

While some things are going well for Motorola, others are a struggle. Motorola and IBM continue to vie for Steve Jobs's Apple business. At the moment, IBM's processors are a smidgen faster, and it's winning.

P.S.: Do you wonder where the name "Motorola" comes from? The founder, Paul Galvin, took a business trip to New York in 1929, where he heard that Long Island mechanics were installing car radios for $240. Galvin started making radios to install in cars and introduced the equipment just in time for the 1930 Radio Manufacturers' Association Convention in Atlantic City, New Jersey. Motorola's first big success was this creation—and domination—of the car radio market. The name originates in "Motor," from the car and "Rola," from Victrola—music. (Hey, we authors aren't that old. We've only seen them in pictures, too.)

Questions for Discussion

1. If you were to design an integrated marketing communications plan for the Moto in the United States, using billboards, the Internet, radio, and print, what features and benefits of the cell phone would you play up in each of these media? Why? What needs to be consistent across the media? What could differ?

2. Next, how would you modify your plans to promote the phone in China? In Finland (home of Nokia)? In Brazil (big youth market)?

3. Has Motorola "succeeded"? Do you consider it or its phones to be "cool"?

Video Case 14

Marketing in the Digital Age

Case in Point: iwon.com

Where do you go when you want to search the Web? Do you use Yahoo? Google? Why? How is that portal your special entrée into the World Wide Web?

The people at iwon.com think they've created the "portal with a difference." The core of what iwon.com provides is online information and entertainment, and there are many such content providers. To distinguish itself, iwon.com offers lotteries, a chance to win as you surf, just as you would surf from another site. What a great promotion. It's not a one-time gimmick but an integral part of iwon.com's brand definition.

Small Cost to the User

In exchange for this chance to win lots of cash, iwon.com wants your data: your demographics and psychographic profile. These data are sold to advertisers, who can then tailor ads for your particular tastes, or at least selectively post ads on your browser. The data are also sold, once you've given permission to iwon.com to do so, to retailers who are going to try their best to entice you to buy their stuff. In this Web-induced special era of permission-based marketing, some people have no problem offering their personal information and attitudes. Others resist, however, concerned about privacy and the potential for misuse of their data.

The Business Proposition

The ads, of course, are critical to iwon.com's business: No ad dollars, no prize money. Some 250 advertisers now help support iwon.com, with no end in sight—after all, every company wants information about you for its customer relationship management databases. Even the big-name players are involved: Amazon, Capital One, Dell, Kraft, Time, General Motors, Wal-Mart.

If the value to the company is information about you, what's the value to you, the user clicking onto iwon.com? The chance to win prizes, of course.

However, iwon.com also figures that it can shape your behavior. If you sign onto iwon.com to check the weather this morning, and you don't win, will you refuse to go back? Of course not. Look at the millions of people who buy lottery tickets every week. You don't expect to win every time. You're thinking about going to a movie some evening, and you go to iwon.com to check movie times. Did you win? Probably not. Does that deter you from making dinner reservations for the weekend at iwon.com? Nope.

Now they've got you: You've been trained by iwon.com to come to its site, get familiar with it, and keep coming back. After all, some day you might win cash, and now you've got a habit. When you want information, your fingers type iwon.com as if they have a mind of their own.

A Successful Strategy

The company has been greatly successful with its strategy. You've seen the huge names buying its advertising space. Since it's begun, iwon.com has doled out more than $50 million to almost 300,000 users. Your chances of winning seem better and better! The company can also boast to its potential advertisers that people come to its Web site and stay longer (They come to "play and stay"). Thus, an advertiser has a greater chance that you'll read its communication. Given the greater duration of your surf time, the advertiser even has a chance to reinforce that message with multiple exposures.

To be fair, iwon.com has not been successful just because its founders somehow found a magic business formula. It readily admits to being lucky, for example:

- Getting $100 million pumped in at the beginning from CBS
- Getting 100 investors to pop even more cash before Internet businesses started failing and funding evaporated
- Getting press conferences (partly given the CBS affiliation)
- Getting buzz, media, and word of mouth

If you have the entrepreneurial bug and try to start a business of your own someday, you'll appreciate what a huge advantage each of these elements has provided.

Questions for Discussion

1. Go to iwon.com. What do you think of the Web site? The information aspect? The entertainment aspect? Would you visit this site if there were no lottery?
2. How is this gimmick, offering a chance to win money, different from a retail store that offers "everyday low prices"? Is a Web site that offers money to attract visitors going to be perceived as the "cheap" site, or are the issues different because visiting every Web site is free?
3. What other promotions may be offered via the Web when companies want to be a stand-alone e-commerce company or when they want to extend their Internet business beyond their other business (retail, catalog, etc.)?
4. The video states that it was important that the founders had real world business experience before venturing into the dot-com world. What do you think?
5. The founders talk about running a tight ship, with relatively few employees. What do you think the impact of this efficiency is? Is this a good goal? What are the downsides?

Global Marketing

Case in Point: Starbucks

If you have a passion for something, you should go for it. Even if lots of people tell you you're crazy.

Starbucks: what a goofball concept. Let's recap. Forty-five years ago, coffee beans go up in price. At first, higher prices are passed along to the consumer, then coffee roasters start cutting back and using cheaper beans. The result: worse coffee at higher prices. This does not sound like a great value proposition for the consumer.

Coffee never went away, but consumption definitely declined. Then what? Ta da! Starbucks says, "Let's sell coffee! No, not the same old coffee—really good coffee. And yes, very expensive coffee. We'll even have a shop devoted to it. We'll convert the American lifestyle, make it more European."

It worked: 5,400 stores in 27 countries, fast growth (700 stores opening in the past 2 years), and revenues at almost $3 billion.

When a Brand Is More than the Product

The Starbucks vision is to serve people who care about coffee. More than that, though, it's to serve as a touchstone—to offer a coffeehouse where a consumer can make daily connections with other people. More than that, Starbucks wants to be seen as a socially responsible corporation that cares about community.

How do you keep that neighborhood coffee shop feeling as you grow to be nearly omnipresent? Starbucks knows that relationships are forged between its employees (its "partners") and its customers, so it treats them well, reasoning that a happy employee will help make a happy customer. Employees who like their jobs will come to work with a better attitude and will stay with the company longer. As a result, they'll know more about the products and be better able to serve customers. Customers are happier with the better service, and a positive, reinforcing cycle between the customer and the employee develops.

Taking the Company Global

This formula can work in any country. Whether people drink coffee or not (for example, Europeans do, but Asians don't drink much), people are always interested in other people. The interpersonal touch speaks to the fact that Starbucks grows through word of mouth, a really tricky "marketing" phenomenon. It's tricky because, although it's very powerful (for example, Starbucks doesn't have to spend money on a national advertising campaign), the company doesn't control it.

In the United States, word of mouth is sufficient enough that when the company announces its plans to open a shop in a particular location, people are primed and ready. Customers begin to patronize the store as soon as it opens.

How do you grow like this in other countries? In Europe, coffee consumption is big, and even the behavior of going to a coffee shop is familiar and appealing. The question is whether or not it will be as attractive to go to a—gasp— "U.S. export chain"?

In Asia, the issues are more fundamental. Coffee consumption isn't as prevalent, so Starbucks isn't just a choice among other options, as in Europe. Rather, Starbucks has to take on the challenge of pioneering the category and stimulating primary demand. That is, Starbucks first has to get the Asian consumer to think "I'd like to go get a coffee." When Starbucks is the only coffee shop in town, it'll clean up and get all the business.

Test Case: China

China is steeped in some 5,000 years of tea drinking, so the marketing savvy of Starbucks is really going to be put to the test if it is to achieve its goal of opening hundreds (!) of cafés in greater China in the next few years. It wants to tap into China's emerging middle class and help them develop a taste for coffee and going to coffee shops.

Starbucks's managers know their success is not just about the coffee per se, so they're trying to choose great locations for their stores—and doing it the old-fashioned way: observational marketing research techniques. They go to a potential store site, and with handheld counting devices, they click every time they see a target customer walk by.

In addition to cultural resistance, Starbucks might encounter other problems. Even for the so-called middle-class Chinese citizen, Starbucks is going to be seen as expensive. At the price of 22 renminbi ($2.65), even a medium latté costs a lot. The monthly disposable income of the average three-person household in China is $150. Starbucks has no immediate plans to cut prices. It would be seen as a luxury and that might have some appeal. However, compare that to Starbucks' positioning in the United States: Is it an item you have to save up for and can indulge in only occasionally?

In Japan, Starbucks is experimenting with offering alcohol, trying to revive the marketing buzz to counter the falling sales it's seen there. Yet in the end, this tactic might not be consistent with Starbucks. The alcohol might dilute the character of the store because it attracts a more boisterous crowd, which in turn spoils one of the chain's main benefits: the quiet and peaceful refuge the traditional Starbucks offers to the busy urban Japanese consumer.

The Social Environment

Coffee shops, and Starbucks in particular, have long served as the focal point for business people whose jobs are independent of an office, for example, consultants and writers: Have laptop, will travel to Starbucks. Even if you think five bucks is a lot for a cappuccino, it's still a smaller per diem than office rental in most cities.

In a weird twist, business analysts observed an upswing at Starbucks as the U.S. economy was in a downswing. Apparently, unemployed white-collar workers were going to the cafés as if they were job-search centers. They were going every day to get some coffee and network, which provided a routine similar to going to an office.

Other Happenings

- To answer the outcry of political activists, and to speak to their concern for community, Starbucks offers "fair trade coffee," which involves explicitly using fair business practices when selecting beans from farmers.

- Starbucks listens to its customers. Over the years, consumers have suggested extending the Starbucks product line to include sandwiches, gum, chocolate, wireless Internet access, iced and blended coffees and teas, and other items. Much of Starbucks's R&D originates not from the company but from these customer suggestions.

- Starbucks is entering the grocery store venue, disentangling the coffee offering from the coffee shop. It also has developed partnerships with United Airlines and Marriott Hotels.

- Starbucks has introduced its own "Frequent Java" card, with which your purchases accrue credits to apply to subsequent Starbucks purchases. It offers a prepaid card plan, which benefits the company by storing your purchase history.

Expect to see an ordering device soon where you're asked "Your usual?"

- Starbucks is sponsoring the Toronto International Film Festival because the demographics of these cinema viewers are consistent with their target market.

- In response to a segment of consumers demanding indulgence foods, Starbucks is selling more cream-based coffees.

Questions for Discussion

1. How do you apply the adage "Think globally, act locally" to brands?
2. In the video, the manager says, "A company owns a brand legally, but the consumer owns the brand in the market." What do you think that means? Do you agree?
3. Do you go to Starbucks or to a coffee shop like it? Do you go for the coffee or for the social buzz? How can a company market a product (the coffee)? How can it market an experience (the shop)?

Video Case 16

Marketing and Society: Social Responsibility and Marketing Ethics

Case in Point: Honest Tea

Honest Tea. Honesty.

Isn't that promising an awful lot from a drink company? These guys don't think so.

The Company Story

Reminiscent of the Snapple story, Honest Tea was the product of a desire to quench consumers' thirsts while at the same time doing so organically and authentically. Honest Teas are "natural," cleaner, less sweet, healthier.

The company's founder started by going to Whole Foods Market to see if it would be interested in carrying the home-brewed concoction. This first choice of a partner was brilliantly consistent with the Honest Tea image. Whole Foods is known for its organic foods and its sprouts-and-Birkenstocks consumers. Who better to appreciate a fine, natural, healthy tea?

The response was overwhelmingly positive: 15,000 bottles ordered at that first meeting, and even more during the next four years, making 11 varieties of Honest Tea available in more than 4,000 food and convenience stores nationwide. Honest Tea has started to turn a profit and it's started "giving back" to a number of communities.

Lots of people say they're going to "do good" but then take jobs with no redeeming social merit because they bring in large paychecks. In contrast, the guys at Honest Tea put their money where their mouths are.

Social Responsibility

Honest Tea is currently helping with economic and community development projects. Native Americans living within the boundaries of the Crow Nation reservation had high unemployment (67 percent), but with the portion of Honest Tea's sales that is returned to this group, it has begun to grow and cultivate the peppermint used in one of the company's teas. The peppermint is organic and the social mission is assisted—and both goals are important to the company.

With similarly high unemployment (70 percent) in Harlem, South Africa, farmers are cultivating the honeybush plants that grow there indigenously, and these plants are incorporated into the aptly named Harlem Honeybush Honest Tea. Again, the tea has organic ingredients and the company has assisted a community.

Instead of being just another foreign company that comes in and buys up a lot of crops, then moves on and forgets the people and providers as whatever fad fades, Honest Teas is continuing to forge and strengthen its relationships with these communities. As a South African businessman noted, the farmers are using their profits to buy computers and fax machines. Honest Tea is bringing them into the technological age. Tea leaves are doing that!

Are Honest Tea's teas vastly superior to other tea manufacturers' teas? Honest Tea probably would like you to believe that. In fact, we probably wouldn't know the difference in a blind taste test. However, consumers don't choose brands blindly. They buy in stores, and they make many positive (and negative) associations with the brands that face them as they reach toward shelves to address the line on their shopping list that says to "Pick up tea." If this tea and that tea pretty much taste like, well, tea, why not buy the one known to turn some of its profits into making the world a better place?

Honest Tea wants to succeed at quenching thirsts—physical thirsts for liquid, and humanity's thirst for helping one another. It's a player in the $7 billion food and beverage industry, but it wants to create "more than just a business." It wants to make a difference around the world.

Questions for Discussion

1. Just how far can marketing go? Can it be used to solve the world's problems? Reduce world hunger? Eliminate the AIDS crisis? Create peace instead of war? How would you envision it?
2. How could you integrate your wishes to do good with your life with the immediate demands of having a job to pay your bills?
3. How can companies "do better" at "doing good"?
4. Do you think companies like Honest Tea are naïve? Do you think people pay attention to attributes like "gives a percentage of profits to community development projects"? Or do people just want a good tasting tea for a reasonable price?

The Marketing Plan: An Introduction

As a marketer, you'll need a good marketing plan to provide direction and focus for your brand, product, or company. With a detailed plan, any business will be better prepared to launch a new product or build sales for existing products. Nonprofit organizations also use marketing plans to guide their fund-raising and outreach efforts. Even government agencies put together marketing plans for initiatives such as building public awareness of proper nutrition and stimulating area tourism.

The Purpose and Content of a Marketing Plan

Unlike a business plan, which offers a broad overview of the entire organization's mission, objectives, strategy, and resource allocation, a marketing plan has a more limited scope. It serves to document how the organization's strategic objectives will be achieved through specific marketing strategies and tactics, with the customer as the starting point. It is also linked to the plans of other departments within the organization. Suppose a marketing plan calls for selling 200,000 units annually. The production department must gear up to make that many units, the finance department must have funding available to cover the expenses, the human resources department must be ready to hire and train staff, and so on. Without the appropriate level of organizational support and resources, no marketing plan can succeed.

Although the exact length and layout will vary from company to company, a marketing plan usually contains the sections described in Table X on page Y. Smaller businesses may create shorter or less formal marketing plans, whereas corporations frequently require highly structured marketing plans. To guide implementation effectively, every part of the plan must be described in considerable detail. Sometimes a company will post its marketing plan on an internal Web site, which allows managers and employees in different locations to consult specific sections and collaborate on additions or changes.

The Role of Research

Marketing plans are not created in a vacuum. To develop successful strategies and action programs, marketers need up-to-date information about the environment, the competition, and the market segments to be served. Often, analysis of internal data is the starting point for assessing the current marketing situation, supplemented by marketing intelligence and research investigating the overall market, the competition, key issues, and threats and opportunities issues. As the plan is put into effect, marketers use advertising and other forms of research to measure progress toward objectives and identify areas for improvement if results fall short of projections. Finally, marketers use marketing research to learn more about their customers' requirements, expectations, perceptions, and satisfaction levels. This deeper understanding provides a foundation for building competitive advantage through well-informed segmenting, targeting, and positioning decisions. Thus, the marketing plan should outline what marketing research will be conducted and how the findings will be applied.

The Role of Relationships

The marketing plan shows how the company will establish and maintain profitable customer relationships. In the process, however, it also shapes a number of internal and external relationships. First, it affects how marketing personnel work with each other and with other departments to deliver value and satisfy customers. Second, it affects how the company works with suppliers, distributors, and strategic alliance partners to achieve the objectives listed in the plan. Third, it influences the company's dealings with other stakeholders, including government regulators, the media, and the community at large. All of these relationships are important to the organization's success, so they should be considered when a marketing plan is being developed.

From Marketing Plan to Marketing Action

Companies generally create yearly marketing plans, although some plans cover a longer period. Marketers start planning well in advance of the implementation date to allow time for marketing research, thorough analysis, management review, and coordination between departments. Then, after each action program begins, marketers monitor ongoing results, compare them with projections, analyze any differences, and take corrective steps as needed. Some marketers design contingency plans, as in the sample plan below, for implementation if certain conditions emerge. Because of inevitable and sometimes unpredictable environmental changes, marketers must be ready to update and adapt marketing plans at any time.

For effective implementation and control, the marketing plan should define how progress toward objectives will be measured. Managers typically use budgets, schedules, and performance standards for monitoring and evaluating results. With budgets, they can compare planned expenditures with actual expenditures for a given week, month, or other period. Schedules allow management to see when tasks were supposed to be completed—and when they were actually completed. Performance standards track the outcomes of marketing programs to see whether the company is moving forward toward its objectives. Some examples of performance standards are: market share, sales volume, product profitability, and customer satisfaction.

■■ Sample Marketing Plan for Sonic

This section takes you inside the sample marketing plan for Sonic, a hypothetical start-up company. The company's first product is the Sonic 1000, a multifunction personal digital assistant (PDA), also known as a handheld computer. Sonic will be competing with palmOne, Hewlett-Packard, and other well-established rivals in an increasingly crowded marketplace. The annotations explain more about what each section of the plan should contain—and why.

Executive Summary

Executive summary
This section summarizes the main goals, recommendations, and points as an overview for senior managers who must read and approve the marketing plan. Generally a table of contents follows this section, for management convenience.

Sonic is preparing to launch a new PDA product, the Sonic 1000, in a maturing market. Despite the dominance of PDA leader palmOne, we can compete because our offering combines exclusive features at a value-added price. We are targeting specific segments in the consumer and business markets, taking advantage of opportunities indicated by higher demand for easy-to-use, wireless-enabled PDAs with expanded communications functionality.

The primary marketing objectives of this plan are to achieve first-year U.S. market share of 3 percent and unit sales of 240,000. The primary financial objectives are to achieve first-year sales revenues of $60 million, keep first-year losses to less than $10 million, and break even early in the second year.

Current Marketing Situation

Current marketing situation
In this section, marketing managers discuss the overall market, identify the market segments they will target, and provide information about the company's current situation.

Sonic, founded 18 months ago by two entrepreneurs with experience in the PC market, is about to enter the PDA market dominated by palmOne. Now, however, overall PDA sales have slowed and profitability has suffered. The emergence of multifunction PDAs and advanced cell phones has increased competitive pressure. The estimated size of the market for multifunction PDAs and cell phones is $63.7 billion, with 50% growth expected within 4 years. To gain market share in this environment, Sonic must carefully target specific market segments.

Market Description Sonic's market consists of consumers and business users who need to conveniently store, communicate, and exchange information on the go. Specific segments being targeted during the first year include professionals, students, corporations, entrepreneurs, and medical users. Exhibit 1 shows how the Sonic 1000 addresses the needs of targeted consumer and business segments.

Market description
By describing the targeted segments in detail, marketers provide context for the marketing strategies and detailed action programs discussed later in the plan.

Benefits and product features
Exhibit 1 clarifies the benefits that product features will deliver to satisfy the needs of customers in each market segment.

PDA purchasers can choose between models based on two different operating systems, one created by Palm and one created by Microsoft. Sonic licenses the market-dominant Palm system because thousands of software applications and hardware peripherals are compatible with this system. Product proliferation and increased competition have resulted in lower prices and lower profit margins. Lower prices are helping sales of PDAs in the lower end of the consumer market, but at the expense of gross margins. Customers with first-generation PDAs are reentering the market by buying newer, high-end multifunction units.

Product review
The product review should summarize the main features for all of the company's products. The information may be organized by product line, by type of customer, by market, or (as here) by order of product introduction.

Product Review Our first product, the Sonic PDA 1000, offers the following standard features:

■ Voice recognition for hands-free commands and communication

■ Built-in cell phone functionality

■ Wireless Web access and e-mail capabilities

■ MP3 music downloading and player capabilities

■ Full organization and communication functions, including calendar, address book, memo pad, Internet browser, e-mail program, and text and instant messaging programs

Targeted Segment	Customer Need	Corresponding Feature/Benefit
Professionals (consumer market)	• Stay in touch while on the go	• Wireless e-mail to conveniently send and receive messages from anywhere; cell phone capability for voice communication from anywhere
	• Record information while on the go	• Voice recognition for no-hands recording
Students (consumer market)	• Perform many functions without carrying multiple gadgets	• Compatible with numerous applications and peripherals for convenient, cost-effective functionality
	• Express style and individuality	• Case wardrobe of different colors and patterns allows users to make a fashion statement
Corporate users (business market)	• Input and access critical data on the go	• Compatible with widely available software
	• Use for proprietary tasks	• Customizable to fit diverse corporate tasks and networks
Entrepreneurs (business market)	• Organize and access contacts, schedule details	• No-hands, wireless access to calendar and address book to easily check appointments and connect with contacts
Medical users (business market)	• Update, access, and exchange medical records	• No-hands, wireless recording and exchange of information to reduce paperwork and increase productivity

EXHIBIT 1

Needs and Corresponding
Features/Benefits of Sonic PDA

- Connectors to accommodate all palmOne-compatible peripherals

- Ability to run any palmOne-compatible application

- Large color display

- Keyboard for input

- Cradle for synchronizing data with PC

- Interchangeable case wardrobe of different colors and patterns

First-year sales revenues are projected to be $60 million, based on sales of 240,000 Sonic 1000 units at a wholesale price of $250 each. During the second year, we plan to introduce the Sonic 2000 as a higher-end product with the following standard features:

- Global positioning system for identifying locations, obtaining directions

- Built-in digital camera

- Translation capabilities to send English text as Spanish text (other languages to be offered as add-on options)

Competitive Review Increased entry of established computer and cell phone companies has pressured industry participants to continually add features and cut prices. Competition from specialized devices for text and e-mail messaging, such as Blackberry devices, is also a factor. Key competitors include:

Competitive review
The purpose of a competitive review is to identify key competitors, describe their market positions, and briefly discuss their strategies.

- *palmOne.* palmOne has had some financial struggles, in part because of the need to reduce prices for competitive reasons. Its acquisition of Handspring boosted its product development strength and expanded its product mix. As the best-known maker of PDAs, palmOne has achieved good distribution in nearly every channel and is gaining distribution among U.S. cell phone service carriers. At present, palmOne products lack some the voice recognition software that is standard in the Sonic 1000.

- *Hewlett-Packard.* HP is targeting business markets with its iPAQ Pocket PC devices, many with wireless capabilities to accommodate corporate users. For extra security, one model allows access by fingerprint match as well as by password. HP enjoys excellent distribution, and its products are priced from below $300 to more than $600.

Competitor	Model	Features	Price
PalmOne	Tungsten C	PDA functions, wireless capabilities, color screen, tiny keyboard, wireless capabilities	$499
palmOne	M130	PDA functions, color screen, expandable functionality	$199
Handspring	Treo 270	PDA and cell phone functions, color screen, tiny keyboard, speakerphone capabilities; no expansion slot	$499
Samsung	i500	PDA functions, cell phone functions, MP3 player, color screen, video capabilities	$599
Garmin	iQue 3600	PDA functions, global positioning system technology, voice recorder, expansion slot, MP3 player	$589
Dell	Axim X5	PDA functions, color screen, e-mail capable, voice recorder, speaker, expandable	$199
Sony	Clie PEG-NX73V	PDA functions, digital camera, tiny keyboard, games, presentation software, MP3 player, voice recorder	$499

EXHIBIT 2

Selected PDA Products and Pricing

- *Garmin.* Garmin's iQue 3600 was the first PDA with built-in global position system (GPS) capability. Priced at $589, its mapping software and verbal commands eliminate the need for an automotive device. Garmin's PDA uses the Palm operating system and has other unique functions, such as a digital voice recorder for brief memos.

- *Dell.* Dell's basic PDA model is priced starting at $199. However, this product is larger than competing palmOne products, and it lacks wireless functionality as a standard feature. New, slimmer models are expected at regular intervals from this low-cost competitor, which markets directly to customers.

- *Samsung.* This is one of several manufacturers that has married cell phone capabilities with multifunction PDA features. Its i500 uses the Palm operating system, provides speedy e-mail and MP3 downloads, plays video clips and offers PDA functions such as address book, calendar, and speed dial.

Despite this strong competition, Sonic can carve out a definite image and gain recognition among the targeted segments. Our licensing arrangement with Cellport Systems allows us to provide the exclusive feature of voice recognition for hands-off operation, a critical point of differentiation for competitive advantage. Exhibit 2 shows a selection of competitive PDA products and prices.

Distribution review

In this section, marketers list the most important channels, provide an overview of each channel arrangement, and mention any new developments or trends.

Distribution Review Sonic-branded products will be distributed through a network of select store and nonstore retailers in the top 50 U.S. markets. Among the most important channel partners being contacted are:

- *Office supply superstores.* Office Depot and Staples will both carry Sonic products in stores, in catalogs, and on Web sites.

- *Computer stores.* Gateway stores will carry Sonic products.

- *Electronic specialty stores.* Circuit City and Best Buy will carry Sonic PDAs.

- *Online retailers.* Amazon.com will carry Sonic PDAs and, for a promotional fee, will give Sonic prominent placement on its home page during the introduction.

Although distribution will initially be restricted to the United States, we plan to expand into Canada and beyond, according to demand. We will emphasize trade sales promotion in the first year.

Strengths, Weaknesses, Opportunities, and Threat Analysis

Sonic has several powerful strengths on which to build, but our major weakness is lack of brand awareness and image. The major opportunity is growing demand for multifunction

Strengths	Weaknesses
• Voice-recognition capabilities and multiple functions valued by customers	• Lack of brand awareness and image
• Value pricing	• Heavier than most competing models
• Compatibility with Palm add-ons	

Opportunities	Threats
• Increased demand for multiple communication methods	• Increasing competition
• Availability of diverse add-ons cycle	• Downward pricing pressure
• Availability of applications for consumer and business use	• Compressed product life

EXHIBIT 3

Sonic's Strengths, Weaknesses, Opportunities, and Threats

PDAs that deliver communication-specific benefits. We also face the threat of ever-higher competition and downward pressure on pricing. Exhibit 3 summarizes the main strengths, weaknesses, opportunities, and threats facing Sonic.

Strengths Sonic can build on three important strengths:

1. *Innovative product.*   The Sonic 1000 includes a voice-recognition system that simplifies usage and allows hands-free operation. It also offers features such as built-in cell phone functionality, wireless communication, and MP3 capabilities.

2. *Compatibility.*   Our PDA can work with the hundreds of Palm-compatible peripherals and applications currently available.

3. *Pricing.*   Our product is priced lower than competing multifunction models—all of which lack voice recognition—which gives us an edge with price-conscious customers.

Strengths
Strengths are internal capabilities that can help the company reach its objectives.

Weaknesses By waiting to enter the PDA market until the initial shakeout and consolidation of competitors has occurred, Sonic has learned from the successes and mistakes of others. Nonetheless, we have two main weaknesses:

1. *Lack of brand awareness.*   As a start-up, Sonic has not yet established a brand or image in the marketplace, whereas palmOne and other rivals have strong brand recognition. This is an area we will address with promotion.

2. *Heavier weight.*   To accommodate the multifunction features, the Sonic 100 is slightly heavier than most competing models. To counteract this, we will emphasize our multifunction features and value-added pricing, two important competitive strengths.

Weaknesses
Weaknesses are internal elements that may interfere with the company's ability to achieve its objectives.

Opportunities Sonic can take advantage of three major market opportunities:

1. *Increasing demand for multiple communication methods.*   The market for wireless Web-enabled PDAs with cell phone functionality is projected to grow faster than the market for nonwireless models. More prospects are seeing users with PDAs in work and educational settings, which is boosting primary demand. Also, customers who bought entry-level models are now trading up.

2. *Add-on peripherals.*   More peripherals, such as digital cameras and global positioning systems are available for PDAs that use the Palm operating system. Consumers and business users who are interested in any of these peripherals will see the Sonic 1000 as a value-priced device able to be conveniently and quickly expanded for multiple functions.

Opportunities
Opportunities are external elements that the company may be able to exploit to its advantage.

3. Diverse applications.   The wide range of Palm-compatible software applications available for home and business use allows the Sonic PDA to satisfy communication and information needs.

Threats   We face three main threats at the introduction of the Sonic 1000:

1. Increased competition.   More companies are entering the U.S. PDA market with models that offer some but not all of the features and benefits provided by Sonic's PDA. Therefore, Sonic's marketing communications must stress our clear differentiation and value-added pricing.

2. Downward pressure on pricing.   Increased competition and market-share strategies are pushing PDA prices down. Still, our objective of seeking a 10% profit on second-year sales of the original model is realistic, given the lower margins in the PDA market.

3. Compressed product life cycle.   PDAs seem to be reaching the maturity stage of their life cycle more quickly than earlier technology products. We have contingency plans to keep sales growing by adding new features, targeting additional segments, and adjusting prices.

Objectives and Issues

We have set aggressive but achievable objectives for the first and second years of market entry.

First-year Objectives   During the Sonic 1000's initial year on the market, we are aiming for a 3 percent share of the U.S. PDA market through unit sales volume of 240,000.

Second-year Objectives   Our second-year objectives are to achieve a 6 percent share based on sales of two models and to achieve break-even early in this period.

Issues   One major issue is our ability to establish a well-regarded brand name linked to a meaningful positioning. We will have to invest heavily in marketing to create a memorable and distinctive brand image projecting innovation, quality, and value. We also must measure awareness and response so we can adjust our marketing efforts if necessary.

Marketing Strategy

Sonic's marketing strategy is based on a positioning of product differentiation. Our primary consumer target is middle- to upper-income professionals who need one portable device to coordinate their busy schedules and communicate with family and colleagues. Our secondary consumer target is high school, college, and graduate students who need a multifunction device. This segment can be described demographically by age (16–30) and education status.

Our primary business target is mid- to large-sized corporations that want to help their managers and employees stay in touch and input or access critical data on the go. This segment consists of companies with more than $25 million in annual sales and more than 100 employees. A secondary business target is entrepreneurs and small-business owners. We are also targeting medical users who want to reduce paperwork and update or access patients' medical records.

Each of the four marketing-mix strategies conveys Sonic's differentiation to the target market segments identified above.

Positioning Using product differentiation, we are positioning the Sonic PDA as the most versatile, convenient, value-added model for personal and professional use. The marketing strategy will focus on the voice-recognition system as the main feature differentiating the Sonic 1000.

Product Strategy The Sonic 1000, including all the features described in the earlier Product Review section, will be sold with a one-year warranty. We will introduce a more compact, powerful high-end model (the Sonic 2000) during the following year, with GPS functionality and other features. Building the Sonic brand is an integral part of our product strategy. The brand and logo (Sonic's distinctive yellow thunderbolt) will be displayed on the product and its packaging, and reinforced by its prominence in the introductory marketing campaign.

Pricing Strategy The Sonic 1000 will be introduced at $250 wholesale/$350 estimated retail price per unit. We expect to lower the price of this first model when we expand the product line by launching the Sonic 2000, to be priced at $350 wholesale per unit. These prices reflect a strategy of (1) attracting desirable channel partners and (2) taking market share from palmOne.

Distribution Strategy Our channel strategy is to use selective distribution to have Sonic PDAs sold through well-known stores and online retailers. During the first year, we will add channel partners until we have coverage in all major U.S. markets and the product is included in the major electronics catalogs and Web sites. We will also investigate distribution through cell-phone outlets maintained by major carriers such as Cingular Wireless. In support of our channel partners, Sonic will provide demonstration products, detailed specification handouts, and full-color photos and displays featuring the product. We will also arrange special trade terms for retailers that place volume orders.

Marketing Communications Strategy By integrating all messages in all media, we will reinforce the brand name and the main points of product differentiation, especially our exclusive voice-recognition feature. Research about media consumption patterns will help our advertising agency choose appropriate media and timing to reach prospects before and during product introduction. Thereafter, advertising will appear on a pulsing basis to maintain brand awareness and communicate various differentiation messages. The agency will also coordinate public relations efforts to build the Sonic brand and support the differentiation message. To attract market attention and encourage purchasing, we will offer as a limited-time premium a leather carry-case. To attract, retain, and motivate channel partners for a push strategy, we will use trade sales promotions and personal selling to channel partners. Until the Sonic brand has been established, our communications will encourage purchases through channel partners rather than from our Web site.

Marketing Research Using research, we are identifying the specific features and benefits that our target market segments value. Feedback from market tests, surveys, and focus groups will help us develop the Sonic 2000. We are also measuring and analyzing customers' attitudes toward competing brands and products. Brand awareness research will help us determine the effectiveness and efficiency of our messages and media. Finally, we will use customer satisfaction studies to gauge market reaction.

Marketing Organization Sonic's chief marketing officer, Jane Melody, holds overall responsibility for marketing strategy and direction. Exhibit 4 shows the structure of the eight-person marketing organization. Sonic has hired Worldwide Marketing to handle national sales campaigns, trade and consumer sales promotions, and public relations efforts.

Positioning
A positioning built on meaningful differences, supported by appropriate strategy and implementation, can help the company build competitive advantage.

Marketing mix
These sections summarize the broad logic that will guide decisions made about the marketing mix in the period covered by the plan.

Marketing research
Management should explain in this section how marketing research will be used to support development, implementation, and evaluation of strategies and action programs.

Marketing organization
The marketing department may be organized by function, as in this sample, by geography, by product, or by customer (or some combination).

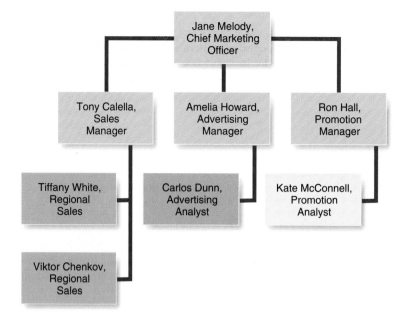

Action programs

Action programs should be coordinated with the resources and activities of other departments, including production, finance, purchasing, etc.

Action Programs

The Sonic 1000 will be introduced in February. Following are summaries of the action programs we will use during the first six months of next year to achieve our stated objectives.

January We will initiate a $200,000 trade sales promotion campaign to educate dealers and generate excitement for the product launch in February. We will exhibit at the major consumer electronics trade shows and provide samples to selected product reviewers, opinion leaders, and celebrities as part of our public relations strategy. Our training staff will work with sales personnel at major retail chains to explain the Sonic 1000's features, benefits, and competitive advantages.

February We will start an integrated print/radio/Internet campaign targeting professionals and consumers. The campaign will show how quickly Sonic PDA users can accomplish tasks using voice recognition. This multimedia campaign will be supported by point-of-sale signage as well as online-only specials.

March As the multimedia advertising campaign continues, we will add consumer sales promotion tactics such giving away leather carry-cases as a premium. We will also distribute new point-of-purchase displays to support our retailers.

April We will hold a trade sales contest offering prizes for the salesperson and retail organization that sells the most Sonic PDAs during the 4-week period.

May We plan to roll out a new national advertising campaign this month. The radio ads will feature celebrity voices using the voice-recognition system to operate their Sonic PDAs. The print ads will show these celebrities holding their Sonic PDAs.

June Our radio campaign will add a new voice-over tag line promoting the Sonic 1000 as a graduation gift. We will also exhibit at the semiannual electronics trade show and provide channel partners with new competitive comparison handouts as a sales aid. In addition, we will tally and analyze the results of customer satisfaction surveys for use in future promotions and to provide feedback for product and marketing activities.

Budgets

Total first-year sales revenue for the Sonic 1000 is projected at $60 million, with an average wholesale price of $250 per unit and variable cost per unit of $150 for unit sales volume of 240,000. We anticipate a first-year loss of up to $10 million on the Sonic 1000 model. Break-even calculations indicate that the Sonic 1000 will become profitable after the sales volume exceeds 267,500, early in the product's second year. Our break-even analysis of Sonic's first PDA product assumes per-unit wholesale revenue of $250 per unit, variable cost of $150 per unit, and estimated first-year fixed costs of $26,750,000. Based on these assumptions, the break-even calculation is:

$$\frac{26,750,000}{\$250 - \$150} = 267,500 \text{ units}$$

Budgets
Budgets serve two main purposes: to project profitability and to help managers plan for expenditures, scheduling, and operations related to each action program.

Controls

We are planning tight control measures to closely monitor quality and customer service satisfaction. This will enable us to react very quickly in correcting any problems that may occur. Other early warning signals that will be monitored for signs of deviation from the plan include monthly sales (by segment and channel) and monthly expenses.

Controls
Controls help management measure results after the plan is implemented and identify any problems or performance variations that need corrective action.

Marketing Plan Tools

Prentice Hall offers two valuable resources to assist you in developing a marketing plan:

- *The Marketing Plan: A Handbook* by Marian Burk Wood explains the process of creating a marketing plan, complete with checklists, real-world examples, and a listing of marketing-related Web sites.

- Marketing Plan Pro software is an award-winning package that includes sample marketing plans, step-by-step guides, help wizards, and customizable charts for documenting a marketing plan.

Sources: Background information and market data adapted from: Pui-Wing Tam, "Palm Unveils palmOne Name, after Breakup," *Wall Street Journal*, August 18, 2003, p. B4; Elaine C.Y. Chen, "Lean, Mean Multimedia Machine," *Laptop*, August 2003, p. 20; Michael V. Copeland, Om Malik, and Rafe Needleman, "The Next Big Thing," *Business 2.0*, July 2003, pp. 62–69; Steve Hamm, "Tech Comes Out Swinging," *Business Week*, June 23, 2003, pp. 62–66; "Dell Rides Wireless Wave," *eWeek*, July 7, 2003, http://www.eweek.com; Stephen H. Wildstrom, "Wi-Fi Handhelds? Not for the Footloose," *Business Week*, June 16, 2003, p. 24; Bob Brewin, "Palm to Buy Handspring to Bolster Hardware Unit," *Computerworld*, June 9, 2003, p. 12; "PDAs with Phones," *PC Magazine*, May 6, 2003, p. 108; "Handheld Market Declines in 2002," *Health Management Technology*, March 2003, p. 6; Bob Brewin, "Palm Slashes Pricing to Match the Competition," *Computerworld*, February 10, 2003, p. 36.

One aspect of marketing not discussed within the text is marketing arithmetic. The calculation of sales, costs, and certain ratios is important for many marketing decisions. This appendix describes three major areas of marketing arithmetic: the *operating statement, analytic ratios,* and *markups and markdowns.*

■■ Operating Statement

The operating statement and the balance sheet are the two main financial statements used by companies. The **balance sheet** shows the assets, liabilities, and net worth of a company at a given time. The **operating statement** (also called **profit-and-loss statement** or **income statement**) is the more important of the two for marketing information. It shows company sales, cost of goods sold, and expenses during a specified time period. By comparing the operating statement from one time period to the next, the firm can spot favorable or unfavorable trends and take appropriate action.

Table A3-1 shows the 2003 operating statement for Dale Parsons Men's Wear, a specialty store in the Midwest. This statement is for a retailer; the operating statement for a manufacturer would be somewhat different. Specifically, the section on purchases within the "cost of goods sold" area would be replaced by "cost of goods manufactured."

The outline of the operating statement follows a logical series of steps to arrive at the firm's $25,000 net profit figure:

Net sales	$300,000
Cost of goods sold	−175,000
Gross margin	$125,000
Expenses	−100,000
Net profit	$ 25,000

The first part details the amount that Parsons received for the goods sold during the year. The sales figures consist of three items: *gross sales, returns and allowances,* and *net sales.* **Gross sales** is the total amount charged to customers during the year for merchandise purchased in Parsons's store. As expected, some customers returned merchandise because of damage or a change of mind. If the customer gets a full refund or full credit on another purchase, we call this a *return.* Or the customer may decide to keep the item if Parsons will reduce the price. This is called an *allowance.* By subtracting returns and allowances from gross sales, we arrive at net sales—what Parsons earned in revenue from a year of selling merchandise:

Gross sales	$325,000
Returns and allowances	−25,000
Net sales	$300,000

The second major part of the operating statement calculates the amount of sales revenue Dale Parsons retains after paying the costs of the merchandise. We start with the inventory in the store at the beginning of the year. During the year, Parsons bought $165,000 worth of suits, slacks, shirts, ties, jeans, and other goods. Suppliers gave the store discounts totaling $15,000, so that net purchases were $150,000. Because the store is located away from regular shipping routes, Parsons had to pay an additional $10,000 to get the products delivered, giving the firm a net cost of $160,000. Adding the beginning inventory, the cost of goods available for sale amounted to $220,000. The $45,000 ending inventory of clothes in the store on December 31 is then subtracted to come up with the $175,000 **cost of goods sold.** Here again we have followed a logical series of steps to figure out the cost of goods sold:

Amount Parsons started with (beginning inventory)	$ 60,000
Net amount purchased	+150,000
Any added costs to obtain these purchases	+10,000
Total cost of goods Parsons had available for sale during year	$220,000
Amount Parsons had left over (ending inventory)	−45,000
Cost of goods actually sold	$175,000

The difference between what Parsons paid for the merchandise ($175,000) and what he sold it for ($300,000) is called the **gross margin** ($125,000).

In order to show the profit Parsons "cleared" at the end of the year, we must subtract from the gross margin the *expenses* incurred while doing business. *Selling expenses* included two sales employees, local newspaper and radio advertising, and the cost of delivering merchandise to customers after alterations. Selling expenses totaled $50,000 for the year. *Administrative expenses* included the salary for an office manager, office supplies such as stationery and business cards, and miscellaneous expenses including an administrative audit conducted by an outside consultant. Administrative expenses totaled $30,000 in 2003. Finally, the general expenses of rent, utilities, insurance, and depreciation came to $20,000. Total expenses were therefore $100,000 for the year. By subtracting expenses ($100,000) from the gross margin ($125,000), we arrive at the net profit of $25,000 for Parsons during 2003.

■■ Analytic Ratios

The operating statement provides the figures needed to compute some crucial ratios. Typically these ratios are called **operating ratios**—the ratio of selected operating statement items to net

TABLE A3-1   Operating Statement: Dale Parsons Men's Wear Year Ending December 31, 2003

Gross Sales			$325,000
Less: Sales returns and allowances			25,000
Net sales			$300,000
Cost of goods sold			
Beginning inventory, January 1, at cost		$ 60,000	
Gross purchases	$165,000		
Less: Purchase discounts	15,000		
Net Purchases	$150,000		
Plus: Freight-in	10,000		
Net cost of delivered purchases		$160,000	
Cost of goods available for sale		$220,000	
Less: Ending inventory, December 31, at cost		$ 45,000	
Cost of goods sold			$175,000
Gross margin			$125,000
Expenses			
Selling expenses			
Sales, salaries, and commissions	$ 40,000		
Advertising	5,000		
Delivery	5,000		
Total selling expenses		$ 50,000	
Administrative expenses			
Office salaries	$ 20,000		
Office supplies	5,000		
Miscellaneous (outside consultant)	5,000		
Total administrative expenses		$ 30,000	
General expenses			
Rent	$ 10,000		
Heat, light, telephone	5,000		
Miscellaneous (insurance, depreciation)	5,000		
Total general expenses		$ 20,000	
Total expenses			$100,000
Net profit			$ 25,000

sales. They let marketers compare the firm's performance in one year to that in previous years (or with industry standards and competitors in the same year). The most commonly used operating ratios are the *gross margin percentage,* the *net profit percentage,* the *operating expense percentage,* and the *returns and allowances percentage.*

Another useful ratio is the *stockturn rate* (also called *inventory turnover rate*). The stockturn rate is the number of times an inventory turns over or is sold during a specified time period (often one year). It may be computed on a cost, selling price, or units basis. Thus the formula can be:

$$\text{Stockturn rate} = \frac{\text{cost of goods sold}}{\text{average inventory at cost}}$$

or

Ratio		Formula	Computation from Table A3-1
Gross margin percentage	=	$\dfrac{\text{gross margin}}{\text{net sales}}$	$= \dfrac{\$125,000}{\$300,000} = 42\%$
Net profit percentage	=	$\dfrac{\text{net profit}}{\text{net sales}}$	$= \dfrac{\$ 25,000}{\$300,000} = 8\%$
Operating expense percentage	=	$\dfrac{\text{total expenses}}{\text{net sales}}$	$= \dfrac{\$100,000}{\$300,000} = 33\%$
Returns and allowances percentage	=	$\dfrac{\text{returns and allowances}}{\text{net sales}}$	$= \dfrac{\$ 25,000}{\$300,000} = 8\%$

$$\text{Stockturn rate} = \frac{\text{selling price of goods sold}}{\text{average selling price of inventory}}$$

or

$$\text{Stockturn rate} = \frac{\text{sales in units}}{\text{average inventory in units}}$$

We will use the first formula to calculate the stockturn rate for Dale Parsons Men's Wear:

$$\frac{\$175,000}{(\$60,000 = \$45,000)/2} = \frac{\$175,000}{\$52,500} = 3.3$$

That is, Parsons's inventory turned over 3.3 times in 2003. Normally, the higher the stockturn rate, the higher the management efficiency and company profitability.

Return on investment (ROI) is frequently used to measure managerial effectiveness. It uses figures from the firm's operating statement and balance sheet. A commonly used formula for computing ROI is:

$$\text{ROI} = \frac{\text{net profit}}{\text{sales}} \times \frac{\text{sales}}{\text{investment}}$$

You may have two questions about this formula: Why use a two-step process when ROI could be computed simply as net profit divided by investment? And what exactly is "investment"?

To answer these questions, let's look at how each component of the formula can affect the ROI. Suppose Dale Parsons Men's Wear has a total investment of $150,000. Then ROI can be computed as follows:

$$\text{ROI} = \frac{\$25,000(\text{net profit})}{\$300,000(\text{sales})} \times \frac{\$300,000(\text{sales})}{\$150,000(\text{investment})}$$
$$= 8.3\% \times 2 = 16.6\%$$

Now suppose that Parsons had worked to increase his share of market. He could have had the same ROI if his sales had doubled while dollar profit and investment stayed the same (accepting a lower profit ratio to get higher turnover and market share):

$$\text{ROI} = \frac{\$25,000(\text{net profit})}{\$600,000(\text{sales})} \times \frac{\$600,000(\text{sales})}{\$150,000(\text{investment})}$$
$$= 4.16\% \times 4 = 16.6\%$$

Parsons might have increased its ROI by increasing net profit through more cost cutting and more efficient marketing:

$$\text{ROI} = \frac{\$50,000(\text{net profit})}{\$300,000(\text{sales})} \times \frac{\$300,000(\text{sales})}{\$150,000(\text{investment})}$$
$$= 16.6\% \times 2 = 33.2\%$$

Another way to increase ROI is to find some way to get the same levels of sales and profits while decreasing investment (perhaps by cutting the size of Parsons's average inventory):

$$\text{ROI} = \frac{\$25,000(\text{net profit})}{\$300,000(\text{sales})} \times \frac{\$300,000(\text{sales})}{\$75,000(\text{investment})}$$
$$= 8.3\% \times 4 = 33.2\%$$

What is "investment" in the ROI formula? *Investment* is often defined as the total assets of the firm. But many analysts now use other measures of return to assess performance. These measures include *return on net assets (RONA)*, *return on stockholders' equity (ROE)*, or *return on assets managed (ROAM)*. Because investment is measured at a point in time, we usually compute ROI as the average investment between two time periods (say, January 1 and December 31 of the same year). We can also compute ROI as an "internal rate of return" by using discounted cash flow analysis (see any finance textbook for more on this technique). The objective in using any of these measures is to determine how well the company has been using its resources. As inflation, competitive pressures, and cost of capital increase, such measures become increasingly important indicators of marketing and company performance.

■ Markups and Markdowns

Retailers and wholesalers must understand the concepts of **markups** and **markdowns.** They must make a profit to stay in business, and the markup percentage affects profits. Markups and markdowns are expressed as percentages.

There are two different ways to compute markups—on *cost* or on *selling price*

$$\text{Markup percentage on cost} = \frac{\text{dollar markup}}{\text{cost}}$$

$$\text{Markup percentage on selling price} = \frac{\text{dollar markup}}{\text{selling price}}$$

Dale Parsons must decide which formula to use. If Parsons bought shirts for $15 and wanted to mark them up $10 to a price of $25, his markup percentage on cost would be $10/$15 = 67.7%. If Parsons based markup on selling price, the percentage would be $10/$25 = 40%. In figuring markup percentage, most retailers use the selling price rather than the cost.

Suppose Parsons knew his cost ($12) and desired markup on price (25%) for a man's tie, and wanted to compute the selling price. The formula is:

$$\text{Selling price} = \frac{\text{cost}}{1 - \text{markup}}$$

$$\text{Selling price} = \frac{\$12}{.75} = \$16$$

As a product moves through the channel of distribution, each channel member adds a markup before selling the product to the next member. This "markup chain" is shown for a suit purchased by a Parsons customer for $200:

		$ Amount	% of Selling Price
Manufacturer	Cost	$108	90%
	Markup	12	10
	Selling price	120	100
Wholeslaer	Cost	120	80
	Markup	30	20
	Selling price	150	100
Retailer	Cost	150	75
	Markup	50	25
	Selling price	200	100

The retailer whose markup is 25 percent does not necessarily enjoy more profit than a manufacturer whose markup is 10 percent. Profit also depends on how many items with that profit margin can be sold (stockturn rate) and on operating efficiency (expenses).

Sometimes a retailer wants to convert markups based on selling price to markups based on cost, and vice versa. The formulas are:

$$\text{Markup percentage on selling price} = \frac{\text{markup percentage on cost}}{100\% + \text{markup percentage on selling cost}}$$

$$\text{Markup percentage on cost} = \frac{\text{markup percentage on selling price}}{100\% - \text{markup percentage on selling price}}$$

Suppose Parsons found that his competitor was using a markup of 30 percent based on cost and wanted to know what this would be as a percentage of selling price. The calculation would be:

$$\frac{30\%}{100\% + 30\%} = \frac{30\%}{130\%} = 23\%$$

Because Parsons was using a 25 percent markup on the selling price for suits, he felt that his markup was suitable compared with that of the competitor.

Near the end of the summer Parsons still had an inventory of summer slacks in stock. Therefore, he decided to use a *markdown,* a reduction from the original selling price. Before the summer he had purchased 20 pairs at $10 each, and he had since sold 10 pairs at $20 each. He marked down the other pairs to $15 and sold 5 pairs. We compute his *markdown ratio* as follows:

$$\text{Markdown percentage} = \frac{\text{dollar markdown}}{\text{total net sales in dollars}}$$

The dollar markdown is $25 (5 pairs at $5 each) and total net sales are $275 (10 pairs at $20 + 5 pairs at $15). The ratio, then, is $25/$275 = 9%.

Larger retailers usually compute markdown ratios for each department rather than for individual items. The ratios provide a measure of relative marketing performance for each department and can be calculated and compared over time. Markdown ratios can also be used to compare the performance of different buyers and salespeople in a store's various departments.

■■ Key Terms

Balance sheet

Cost of goods sold

Gross margin

Gross sales

Markdown

Markup

Operating ratios

Operating statement (or profit-and-loss statement or income statement)

Return on investment (ROI)

Now that you have completed this course in marketing, you have a good idea of what the field entails. You may have decided you want to pursue a marketing career because it offers constant challenge, stimulating problems, the opportunity to work with people, and excellent advancement opportunities. But you still may not know which part of marketing best suits you—marketing is a very broad field offering a wide variety of career options. This appendix helps you discover what types of marketing jobs best match your special skills and interests, shows you how to conduct the kind of job search that will get you the position you want in the company of your choice, describes marketing career paths open to you, and suggests other information resources.

Marketing Careers Today

The field of marketing is booming in the twenty-first century, with nearly a third of all Americans now employed in marketing-related positions. Marketing salaries may vary by company, position, and region, and salary figures change constantly. In general, entry-level marketing salaries usually are only slightly below those for engineering and chemistry but equal or exceed starting salaries in economics, finance, accounting, general business, and the liberal arts. Moreover, if you succeed in an entry-level marketing position, it's likely that you will be promoted quickly to higher levels of responsibility and salary. In addition, because of the consumer and product knowledge you will gain in these jobs, marketing positions provide excellent training for the highest levels in an organization. A recent study by an executive recruiting firm found that more top executives come out of marketing than any other functional group.

Overall Marketing Facts and Trends

In conducting your job search, consider the following facts and trends that are changing the world of marketing.

Technology: Technology is changing the way marketers work. For example, price coding allows instantaneous retail inventorying. Software for marketing training, forecasting, and other functions is changing the ways we market. And the Internet is creating new jobs and new recruiting rules. Consider the explosive growth in new media marketing. Whereas advertising firms have traditionally recruited "generalists" in account management, "generalist" has now taken on a whole new meaning—advertising account executives must now have both broad and specialized knowledge.

Diversity: The number of women and minorities in marketing continues to rise. Traditionally, women were mainly in retailing. Now, women and minorities are rapidly moving into all industries. They also are rising rapidly into marketing management. For example, women now outnumber men by nearly two to one as advertising account executives. As marketing becomes more global, the need for diversity in marketing positions will continue to increase, opening new opportunities.

Global: Companies such as Coca-Cola, McDonald's, IBM, MTV, and Procter & Gamble have become multinational, with offices and manufacturing operations in hundreds of countries. Indeed, such companies often make more profit from sales outside the United States than from within. And it's not just the big companies that are involved in international marketing. Organizations of all sizes have moved into the global arena. Many new marketing opportunities and careers will be directly linked to the expanding global marketplace. The globalization of business also means that you will need more cultural, language, and people skills in the marketing world of the twenty-first century.

Nonprofit organizations: Increasingly, colleges, arts organizations, libraries, hospitals, and other nonprofit organizations are recognizing the need for effectively marketing their "products" and services to various publics. This awareness has led to new marketing positions—with these organizations hiring their own marketing directors and marketing vice presidents or using outside marketing specialists.

Looking for a Job in Today's Marketing World

To choose and find the right job, you will need to apply the marketing skills you've learned in this course, especially marketing analysis and planning. Follow these nine steps for marketing yourself: (1) Conduct a self-assessment and seek career counseling; (2) examine job descriptions; (3) develop job search objectives; (4) explore the job market and assess opportunities; (5) develop search strategies; (6) prepare résumés; (7) write cover letter and assemble supporting documents; (8) interview for jobs; and (9) follow up.

Conduct a Self-Assessment and Seek Career Counseling

If you're having difficulty deciding what kind of marketing position is the best fit for you, start out by doing some self-testing or get some career counseling. Self-assessments require that you honestly and thoroughly evaluate your interests, strengths, and weaknesses. What do you do well (your best and favorite skills) and not so well? What are your favorite interests? What are your career goals? What makes you stand out from other job seekers? The answers to such questions may suggest which marketing careers you should seek or avoid. For help in making an effective self-assessment, look at the following books in your local bookstore: Richard Bolles, *What Color Is Your Parachute?* (Berkeley, CA: Ten Speed Press, published annually); Susan Johnston, *The Career Adventure: Your Guide to Personal Assessment, Career Exploration, and Decision Making* (Prentice Hall, 2001); and Wilma R. Fellman, *Finding a Career That Works for You: A Step-by-Step Guide to Choosing a Career and Finding a Job* (Independent Publishers Group, 2000).

For help in finding a career counselor to guide you in making a career assessment, Richard Bolles's, *What Color Is Your Parachute?* contains a useful state-by-state sampling. (Some counselors can help you in your actual job search, too.) You can also consult the career counseling, testing, and placement services at your college or university.

Career Counseling on the Internet Today an increasing number of colleges, universities, and commercial career counselors offer career guidance on the Internet. In general, college and university sites are by far the best. But one useful commercial site you might look at is JobStar (jobstar.org/tools/career/index.cfm).

Examine Job Descriptions

After you have identified your skills, interests, and desires, you need to see which marketing positions are the best match for them. Two U.S. Labor Department publications in your local library, the *Occupation Outlook Handbook* and the *Dictionary of Occupational Titles,* describe the duties involved in various occupations, the specific training and education needed, the availability of jobs in each field, possibilities for advancement, and probable earnings.

Your initial career shopping list should be broad and flexible. Look for different ways to achieve your objectives. For example, if you want a career in marketing management, consider the public as well as the private sector, and regional as well as national firms. Be open initially to exploring many options, then focus on specific industries and jobs, listing your basic goals as a way to guide your choices. Your list might include "a job in a start-up company, near a big city, on the West Coast, doing new product planning, with a computer software firm."

Explore the Job Market and Assess Opportunities

At this stage, you need to look at the market and see what positions are actually available. You do not have to do this alone. Any of the following may assist you.

College Placement Centers Your college placement center is an excellent place to start. Besides posting specific job openings, placement centers have the current edition of the *College Placement Annual,* which lists job openings in hundreds of companies seeking college graduates for entry-level positions, as well as openings for people with experience or advanced degrees. More and more, schools are also going on the Internet. For example, the Web site of the career center of Emory University in Atlanta, Georgia, has a list of career links (www.emory.edu/CAREER/Students/Students_Main.htm).

In addition, find out everything you can about the companies that interest you by consulting business magazines, annual reports, business reference books, faculty, career counselors, and others. Try to analyze the industry's and the company's future growth and profit potential, advancement opportunities, salary levels, entry positions, travel time, and other factors of significance to you.

Job Fairs College placement offices often work with corporate recruiters to organize on-campus job fairs.

You might also use the Internet to check on upcoming career fairs in your region. For example, visit www.jobweb.com/employ/fairs/public_fairs.asp.

Networking and the Yellow Pages Networking, or asking for job leads from friends, family, people in your community, and career centers, is one of the best ways to find a marketing job. An estimated 33 percent of jobs are found through networking. The idea is to spread your net wide, contacting anybody and everybody.

The phone book's yellow pages are another effective way to job search. Check out employers in your field of interest in whatever region you want to work, then call and ask if they are hiring for the position of your choice.

Summer Jobs and Internships In some parts of the country one in seven students gets a job where he or she interned. On the Internet, many sites have separate internship areas. For examples, look at Wetfeet (www.wetfeet.internshipprograms.com), the Monster Board (www.monster.com), and Idealist (www.idealist.org). If you know a company for which you wish to work, go to that company's corporate Web site, enter the personnel area, and check for internships. If there are none listed, try e-mailing the personnel department, asking if internships are offered.

The Internet A constantly increasing number of sites on the Internet deal with job hunting. You can also use the Internet to make contacts with people who can help you gain information on companies and research companies that interest you. The Riley Guide offers a great introduction to what jobs are available (www.rileyguide.com). Other helpful sites are Employment Opportunities for People with Disabilities (www.dol.gov/odep/joblinks/joblinks.htm) and HireDiversity (www.hirediversity.com/), which contains information on opportunities for African Americans, Hispanic Americans, Asian Americans, and Native Americans.

Most companies have their own Web sites upon which they post job listings. This may be helpful if you have a specific and fairly limited number of companies that you are keeping your eye on for job opportunities. But if this is not the case, remember that to find out what interesting marketing jobs the companies themselves are posting, you may have to visit hundreds of corporate sites.

Develop Search Strategies

Once you've decided which companies you are interested in, you need to contact them. One of the best ways is through on-campus interviews. But not every company you are interested in will visit your school. In such instances, you can write (this includes e-mail) or phone the company directly or ask marketing professors or school alumni for contacts.

Prepare Résumés

A résumé is a concise yet comprehensive written summary of your qualifications, including your academic, personal, and professional achievements, that showcases why you are the best candidate for the job. Many organizations use résumés to decide which candidates to interview.

In preparing your résumé, remember that all information on it must be accurate and complete. Résumés typically begin with the applicant's full name, telephone and fax numbers, and traditional mail and e-mail addresses. A simple and direct statement of career objectives generally appears next, followed by work history and academic data (including awards and internships), and then by personal activities and experiences applicable to the job sought. The résumé usually ends with a list of references the employer may contact. If your work or internship experience is limited, nonexistent, or irrelevant, then it is a good idea to emphasize your academic and nonacademic achievements, showing skills related to those required for excellent job performance.

There are three types of résumés. *Chronological* résumés, which emphasize career growth, are organized in reverse chronological order, starting with your most recent job. They focus on job titles within organizations, describing the responsibilities required for each job. *Functional* résumés focus less on job titles and work history and more on assets and achievements. This format works best if your job history is scanty or discontinuous. *Mixed,* or *combined,* résumés take from each of the other two formats. First, the skills used for a specific job are listed, then the job title is stated. This format works best for applicants whose past jobs are in other fields or seemingly unrelated to the position.

Your local bookstore or library has many books that can assist you in developing your résumé. Popular guides are Tom Jackson, with Ellen Jackson, *The New Perfect Résumé* (Garden City, NY: Anchor Press/Doubleday, revised, 1996); Yana Parker, *The Damn Good Résumé Guide* (Berkeley, CA: Ten Speed Press, 2002); and Arthur Rosenberg and David Hizer, *The Résumé Handbook* (Adams Media Corporation, 2003). Computer software programs such as *WinWay Résumé,* provides hundreds of sample résumés and ready-to-use phrases while guiding you through the résumé preparation process.

Online Résumés Today more and more job seekers are posting their résumés on the Internet. Preparing an electronic résumé is somewhat different from preparing a traditional résumé. For example, you need to know the relevant rules about scanning (including that your computer will be unable to scan the attractive fonts you used in your original résumé) and keywords. Moreover, if you decide to post your résumé in a public area such as a Web site, then for security purposes you might not want to include your street or business address or the names of previous employers or references. (This information can be mailed later to employers after you have been contacted by them.) JobStar (www.jobstar.org/tools/resume/index.cfm) might assist you in writing your online résumé. In addition, placement centers usually assist you in developing a résumé. (Placement centers can also help with your cover letter and provide job interview workshops.)

After you have written your résumé, you need to post it. The following sites may be good locations to start: Monster.com (www.monster.com) and Yahoo! hotjobs (www.hotjobs.yahoo.com).

Résumé Tips

- Communicate your worth to potential employers in a concrete manner, citing examples whenever possible.

- Be concise and direct.

- Use active verbs to show you are a doer.

- Do not skimp on quality or use gimmicks. Spare no expense in presenting a professional résumé.

- Have someone critique your work. A single typo can eliminate you from being considered.

- Customize your résumé for specific employers. Emphasize your strengths as they pertain to your targeted job.

- Keep your résumé compact, usually one page.

- Format the text to be attractive, professional, and readable. Avoid too much "design" or gimmicky flourishes.

Write Cover Letter and Assemble Supporting Documents

Cover Letter You should include a cover letter informing the employer that a résumé is enclosed. But a cover letter does more than this. It also serves to summarize in one or two paragraphs the contents of the résumé and explains why you think you are the right person for the position. The goal is to persuade the employer to look at the more detailed résumé. A typical cover letter is organized as follows: (1) the name and position of the person you are contacting; (2) a statement identifying the position you are applying for, how you heard of the vacancy, and the reasons for your interest; (3) a summary of your qualifications for the job; (4) a description of what follow-ups you intend to make, such as phoning in two weeks to see if the résumé has been received; (5) an expression of gratitude for the opportunity of being a candidate for the job.

Letters of Recommendation and Other Supporting Documents Letters of recommendation are written references by professors, former and current employers, and others that testify to your character, skills, and abilities. A good reference letter tells why you would be an excellent candidate for the position. In choosing someone to write a letter of recommendation, be confident that the person will give you a good reference. In addition, do not assume the person knows everything about you or the position you are seeking. Rather, provide the person with your résumé and other relevant data. As a courtesy, allow the reference writer at least a month to complete the letter and enclose a stamped, addressed envelope with your materials.

In the packet containing your résumé, cover letter, and letters of recommendation, you may also want to attach other relevant documents that support your candidacy, such as academic transcripts, graphics, portfolios, and samples of writing.

Interview for Jobs

As the old saying goes, "The résumé gets you the interview; the interview gets you the job." The job interview offers you an opportunity to gather more information about the organization, while at the same time allowing the organization to gather more information about you. You'll want to present your best self. The interview process consists of three parts: before the interview, the interview itself, and after the interview. If you successfully pass through these stages, you will be called back for the follow-up interview.

Before the Interview In preparing for your interview, do the following:

1. Understand that interviewers have diverse styles, including the "chitchat," let's-get-to-know-each-other style; the interrogation style of question after question; and the tough-probing "why, why, why" style, among others. So be ready for anything.

2. With a friend, practice being interviewed and then ask for a critique. Or, videotape yourself in a practice interview so that you can critique your own performance. Your college placement service may also offer "mock" interviews to help you.

3. Prepare at least five good questions whose answers are not easily found in the company literature, such as "What is the future direction of the firm?" "How does the firm differentiate itself from competitors?" "Do you have a new-media division?"

4. Anticipate possible interview questions, such as "Why do you want to work for this company?" or "Why should we hire you?" Prepare solid answers before the interview. Have

a clear idea of why you are interested in joining the company and the industry to which it belongs.

5. Avoid back-to-back interviews—they can be exhausting and it is unpredictable how long they will last.

6. Dress conservatively and professionally. Be neat and clean.

7. Arrive 10 minutes early to collect your thoughts and review the major points you intend to cover. Check your name on the interview schedule, noting the name of the interviewer and the room number. Be courteous and polite to office staff.

8. Approach the interview enthusiastically. Let your personality shine through.

During the Interview During the interview, do the following:

1. Shake hands firmly in greeting the interviewer. Introduce yourself, using the same form of address the interviewer uses. Focus on creating a good initial impression.

2. Keep your poise. Relax, smile when appropriate, be upbeat throughout.

3. Maintain eye contact, good posture, and speak distinctly. Don't clasp your hands or fiddle with jewelry, hair, or clothing. Sit comfortably in your chair. Do not smoke, even if asked.

4. Carry extra copies of your résumé with you. Bring samples of your academic or professional work along.

5. Have your story down pat. Present your selling points. Answer questions directly. Avoid one-word or too-wordy answers.

6. Let the interviewer take the initiative but don't be passive. Find an opportunity to direct the conversation to things about yourself that you want the interviewer to hear.

7. To end on a high note, make your most important point or ask your most pertinent question during the last part of the interview.

8. Don't hesitate to "close." You might say, "I'm very interested in the position, and I have enjoyed this interview."

9. Obtain the interviewer's business card or address and phone number so that you can follow up later.

A tip for acing the interview: Before you open your mouth, find out *what it's like* to be a brand manager, sales representative, market researcher, advertising account executive, or other position for which you're interviewing.

After the Interview After the interview, do the following:

1. After leaving the interview, record the key points that arose. Be sure to note who is to follow up and when a decision can be expected.

2. Analyze the interview objectively, including the questions asked, the answers to them, your overall interview presentation, and the interviewer's responses to specific points.

3. Immediately send a thank-you letter, mentioning any additional items and your willingness to supply further information.

4. If you do not hear within the specified time, write or call the interviewer to determine your status.

Follow Up

If you are successful, you will be invited to visit the organization. The in-company interview will probably run from several hours to an entire day. The organization will examine your interest, maturity, enthusiasm, assertiveness, logic, and company and functional knowledge. You should ask questions about issues of importance to you. Find out about the working environment, job role, responsibilities, opportunity for advancement, current industrial issues, and the company's personality. The company wants to discover if you are the right person for the job, whereas you want to find out if it is the right job for you. The key is to determine if the right fit exists between you and the company.

■▌ *Marketing Jobs*

This section describes some of the key marketing positions.

Advertising

Advertising is one of today's hottest fields in marketing. In fact, *Money* magazine lists a position in advertising as among the 50 best jobs in America.

Job Descriptions Key advertising positions include copywriter, art director, production manager, account executive, and media planner/buyer. *Copywriters* write advertising copy and help find the concepts behind the written words and visual images of advertisements. *Art directors,* the other part of the creative team, help translate the copywriters' ideas into dramatic visuals called "layouts." Agency artists develop print layouts, package designs, television layouts (called "storyboards"), corporate logotypes, trademarks, and symbols. *Production managers* are responsible for physically creating ads, in-house or by contracting through outside production houses. *Account development executives* research and understand clients' markets and customers and help develop marketing and advertising strategies to impact them. *Account executives* serve as liaisons between clients and agencies. They coordinate the planning, creation, production, and implementation of an advertising campaign for the account. *Media planners* determine the best mix of television, radio, newspaper, magazine, and other media for the advertising campaign.

Skills Needed, Career Paths, and Typical Salaries
Work in advertising requires strong people skills in order to interact closely with an often difficult and demanding client base. In addition, advertising attracts people with high skills in planning, problem solving, creativity, communication, initiative, leadership, and presentation. Advertising involves working under high levels of stress and pressure created by unrelenting deadlines. Advertisers frequently have to work long hours to meet deadlines for a presentation. But work achievements are very apparent, with the results of creative strategies observed by thousands or even millions of people.

Because they are so sought after, positions in advertising sometimes require an MBA. But there are many jobs open for business, graphics arts, and liberal arts undergraduates. Advertising positions often serve as gateways to higher-level management. Moreover, with large advertising agencies opening offices all over the world, there is the possibility of eventually working on global campaigns.

Starting advertising salaries are relatively low compared to some other marketing jobs because of strong competition for entry-level advertising jobs. You may even want to consider working for free to break in. Compensation will increase quickly as you move into account executive or other management positions. For more facts and figures, see the Web pages of *Advertising Age,* a key ad industry publication (www. adage.com, click on the Job Bank button), and the American Association of Advertising Agencies (www.aaaa.org).

Brand and Product Management

Brand and product managers plan, direct, and control business and marketing efforts for their products. They are involved with research and development, packaging, manufacturing, sales and distribution, advertising, promotion, market research, and business analysis and forecasting.

Job Descriptions A company's brand management team consists of people in several positions. The *brand manager* guides the development of marketing strategies for a specific brand. The *assistant brand manager* is responsible for certain strategic components of the brand. The *product manager* oversees several brands within a product line or product group. The *product category manager* directs multiple product lines in the product category. The *market analyst* researches the market and provides important strategic information to the project managers. The *project director* is responsible for collecting market information on a marketing or product project. The *research director* oversees the planning, gathering, and analyzing of all organizational research.

Skills Needed, Career Paths, and Typical Salaries
Brand and product management requires high problem-solving, analytical, presentation, communication, and leadership skills, as well as the ability to work well in a team. Product management requires long hours and involves the high pressure of running large projects. In consumer goods companies, the newcomer—who usually needs an MBA—joins a brand team as an assistant and learns the ropes by doing numerical analyses and watching senior brand people. This person eventually heads the team and later moves on to manage a larger brand, then several brands. Many industrial goods companies also have product managers. Product management is one of the best training grounds for future corporate officers. Product management also

offers good opportunities to move into international marketing. Product managers command relatively high salaries. Because this job category encourages or requires a master's degree, starting pay tends to be higher than in other marketing categories such as advertising or retailing.

Sales, Sales Management

Sales and sales management opportunities exist in a wide range of profit and nonprofit organizations and in product and service organizations, including financial, insurance, consulting, and government organizations.

Job Descriptions

Key jobs include consumer sales, industrial sales, national account manager, service support, sales trainers, sales management, and teleseller. *Consumer* sales involves selling consumer products and services through retailers. *Industrial sales* includes selling products and services to other businesses. *National account managers (NAM)* oversee a few very large accounts. *Service support* personnel support salespeople during and after the sale of a product. *Sales trainers* train new hires and provide refresher training for all sales personnel. *Sales management* includes a sequence of positions ranging from district manager to vice president of sales. The *teleseller* (not to be confused with the home consumer telemarketer) offers service and support to field salespeople.

Salespeople enjoy active professional lives, working outside the office and interacting with others. They manage their own time and activities. Competition for top jobs can be intense. Every sales job is different, but some positions involve extensive travel, long workdays, and working under pressure, which can negatively impact personal life. You can also expect to be transferred more than once between company headquarters and regional offices.

Skills Needed, Career Paths, and Typical Salaries

Selling is a people profession in which you will work with people every day, all day long. Besides people skills, sales professionals need sales and communication skills. Most sales positions also require high problem-solving, analytical, presentation, and leadership ability as well as creativity and initiative. Teamwork skills are increasingly important.

Career paths lead from salesperson to district, regional, and higher levels of sales management and, in many cases, to the top management of the firm. Today, most entry-level sales management positions require a college degree. Increasingly, people seeking selling jobs are acquiring sales experience in an internship capacity or from a part-time job before graduating. Although there is a high turnover rate (one in four people leave their jobs in a year), sales positions are great springboards to leadership positions, with more CEOs starting in sales than in any other entry-level position. Possibly this explains why competition for top sales jobs is intense.

Starting base salaries in sales may be moderate, but compensation is often supplemented by significant commission, bonus, or other incentive plans. In addition, many sales jobs include a company car or car allowance. Successful salespeople are among most companies' highest paid employees.

Other Marketing Jobs

Retailing

Retailing provides an early opportunity to assume marketing responsibilities. Key jobs include store manager, regional manager, buyer, department manager, and salesperson. *Store managers* direct the management and operation of an individual store. *Regional managers* manage groups of stores across several states and report performance to headquarters. *Buyers* select and buy the merchandise that the store carries. The *department manager* acts as store manager of a department, such as clothing, but on the department level. The *salesperson* sells merchandise to retail customers. Retailing can involve relocation, but generally there is little travel, unless you are a buyer. Retailing requires high people and sales skills because retailers are constantly in contact with customers. Enthusiasm, willingness, and communication skills are very helpful for retailers, too.

Retailers work long hours, but their daily activities are often more structured than some types of marketing positions. Starting salaries in retailing tend to be low, but pay increases as you move into management or some retailing specialty job.

Marketing Research

Marketing researchers interact with managers to define problems and identify the information needed to resolve them. They design research projects, prepare questionnaires and samples, analyze data, prepare reports, and present their findings and recommendations to management. They must understand statistics, consumer behavior, psychology, and sociology. A master's degree helps. Career opportunities exist with manufacturers, retailers, some wholesalers, trade and industry associations, marketing research firms, advertising agencies, and governmental and private nonprofit agencies.

New-Product Planning

People interested in new-product planning can find opportunities in many types of organizations. They usually need a good background in marketing, marketing research, and sales forecasting; they need organizational skills to motivate and coordinate others; and they may need a technical background. Usually, these people work first in other marketing positions before joining the new-product department.

Marketing Logistics (Physical Distribution)

Marketing logistics, or physical distribution, is a large and dynamic field, with many career opportunities. Major transportation carriers, manufacturers, wholesalers, and retailers all employ logistics specialists. Increasingly, marketing teams include logistics specialists, and marketing managers' career paths include marketing logistics assignments. Coursework in quantitative methods, finance, accounting, and marketing will provide you with the necessary skills for entering the field.

Public Relations

Most organizations have a public relations staff to anticipate problems with various publics, handle complaints, deal with media, and build the corporate image. People interested in public relations should be able to speak and write clearly and persuasively, and they should have a background in journalism, communications, or the liberal arts. The challenges in this job are highly varied and very people oriented.

Nonprofit Services The key jobs in nonprofits include marketing director, director of development, event coordinator, publication specialist, and intern/volunteers. The *marketing director* is in charge of all marketing activities for the organization. The *director of development* organizes, manages, and directs the fund-raising campaigns that keep a nonprofit in existence. An *event coordinator* directs all aspects of fund-raising events, from initial planning through implementation. The *publication specialist* oversees publications designed to promote awareness of the organization. Although typically an unpaid position, the *intern/volunteer* performs various marketing functions, and this work can be an important step to gaining a full-time position. The nonprofit sector is typically not for someone who is money driven. Rather, most nonprofits look for people with a strong sense of community spirit and the desire to help others. So starting pay is usually lower than in other marketing fields. However, the bigger the nonprofit, the better your chance of rapidly increasing your income when moving into upper management.

■▌ *Other Resources*

Professional marketing associations and organizations are another source of information about careers. Marketers belong to many such societies. You may want to contact some of the following in your job search:

American Advertising Federation, 1101 Vermont Avenue, NW, Suite 500, Washington, DC 2005. (202) 898-0089 (www.aaf.org)

American Marketing Association, 250 South Wacker Drive, Suite 200, Chicago, IL 60606. (312) 648-0536 (www.marketingpower.com)

Council of Sales Promotion Agencies, 750 Summer Street, Stamford, CT 06901. (203) 325-3911

Market Research Association, 2189 Silas Deane Highway, Suite 5, Rocky Hill, CT 06067. (860) 257-4008 (www.mra-net.org)

National Council of Salesmen's Organization, 389 Fifth Avenue, Room 1010, New York, NY 10016. (718) 835-4591

National Management Association, 2210 Arbor Boulevard, Dayton, OH 45439. (513) 294-0421

National Retail Federation, 701 Pennsylvania Avenue NW, Suite 710, Washington, DC 20004. (202) 783-7971 (www.nrf.com)

Product Development and Management Association, 401 North Michigan Avenue, Chicago, IL 60611. (312) 527-6644 (www.pdma.org)

Public Relations Society of America, 33 Irving Place, Third Floor, New York, NY 10003. (212) 995-2230 (www.prsa.org)

Sales and Marketing Executives International, Statler Office Tower, Number 977, Cleveland, OH 44115. (216) 771-6650 (www.smei.org)

The Association of Women in Communications, 780 Ritchie Highway, Suite 28-S, Severna Park, MD 21146. (410) 544-7442

Women Executives in Public Relations, P.O. Box 609, Westport, CT 06881. (203) 226-4947 (www.wepr.org)

Glossary

adapted marketing mix   An international marketing strategy for adjusting the marketing-mix elements to each international target market, bearing more costs but hoping for a larger market share and return.

administered VMS   A vertical marketing system that coordinates successive stages of production and distribution, not through common ownership or contractual ties, but through the size and power of one of the parties.

adoption process   The mental process through which an individual passes from first hearing about an innovation to final adoption.

advertising   Any paid form of nonpersonal presentation and promotion of ideas, goods, or services by an identified sponsor.

advertising agency   A marketing services firm that assists companies in planning, preparing, implementing, and evaluating all or portions of their advertising programs.

advertising objective   A specific communication task to be accomplished with a specific target audience during a specific period of time.

affordable method   Setting the promotion budget at the level management thinks the company can afford.

age and life-cycle segmentation   Dividing a market into different age and life-cycle groups.

agent   A wholesaler who represents buyers or sellers on a relatively permanent basis, performs only a few functions, and does not take title to goods.

allowance   Promotional money paid by manufacturers to retailers in return for an agreement to feature the manufacturer's products in some way.

approach   The step in the selling process in which the salesperson meets the customer for the first time.

attitude   A person's consistently favorable or unfavorable evaluations, feelings, and tendencies toward an object or idea.

B2B (business-to-business) e-commerce   Firms using B2B trading networks, auction sites, spot exchanges, online product catalogs, barter sites, and other online resources to reach new customers, serve current customers more effectively, and obtain buying efficiencies and better prices.

B2C (business-to-consumer) e-commerce   The online selling of goods and services to final consumers.

baby boomers   The 78 million people born during the baby boom following World War II and lasting until the early 1960s.

behavioral segmentation   Dividing a market into groups based on consumer knowledge, attitude, use, or response to a product.

belief   A descriptive thought that a person holds about something.

benefit segmentation   Dividing the market into groups according to the different benefits that consumers seek from the product.

brand   A name, term, sign, symbol, or design, or a combination of these intended to identify the goods or services of one seller or group of sellers and to differentiate them from those of competitors.

brand equity   The positive differential effect that knowing the brand name has on customer response to the product or service.

brand extension   Using a successful brand name to launch a new or modified product in a new category.

breakeven pricing (target profit pricing)   Setting price to break even on the costs of making and marketing a product; or setting price to make a target profit.

broker   A wholesaler who does not take title to goods and whose function is to bring buyers and sellers together and assist in negotiation.

business analysis   A review of the sales, costs, and profit projections for a new product to find out whether these factors satisfy the company's objectives.

business buyer behavior   The buying behavior of the organizations that buy goods and services for use in the production of other products and services or for the purpose of reselling or renting them to others at a profit.

business portfolio   The collection of businesses and products that make up the company.

buying center   All the individuals and units that participate in the business buying-decision process.

by-product pricing   Setting a price for by-products in order to make the main product's price more competitive.

C2B (consumer-to-business) e-commerce   Online exchanges in which consumers search out sellers, learn about their offers, and initiate purchases, sometimes even driving transaction terms.

C2C (consumer-to-consumer) e-commerce   Online exchanges of goods and information between final consumers.

captive-product pricing   Setting a price for products that must be used along with a main product, such as blades for a razor and film for a camera.

catalog marketing   Direct marketing through print, video, or electronic catalogs that are mailed to select customers, made available in stores, or presented online.

category killer   Giant specialty store that carries a very deep assortment of a particular line and is staffed by knowledgeable employees.

causal research   Marketing research to test hypotheses about cause-and-effect relationships.

chain stores   Two or more outlets that are owned and controlled in common, have central buying and merchandising, and sell similar lines of merchandise.

channel conflict   Disagreement among marketing channel members on goals and roles—who should do what and for what rewards.

channel level   A layer of intermediaries that performs some work in bringing the product and its ownership closer to the final buyer.

click-and-mortar companies   Traditional brick-and-mortar companies that have added e-marketing to their operations.

click-only companies The so-called dotcoms, which operate only online, without any brick-and-mortar market presence.

closing The step in the selling process in which the salesperson asks the customer for an order.

co-branding The practice of using the established brand names of two different companies on the same product.

cognitive dissonance Buyer discomfort caused by postpurchase conflict.

commercialization Introducing a new product into the market.

communication adaptation A global communication strategy of fully adapting advertising messages to local markets.

competition-based pricing Setting prices based on the prices that competitors charge for similar products.

competitive advantage An advantage over competitors gained by offering consumers greater value, either through lower prices or by providing more benefits that justify higher prices.

concentrated (niche) marketing A market-coverage strategy in which a firm goes after a large share of one or a few segments, or niches.

concept testing Testing new-product concepts with a group of target consumers to find out if the concepts have strong consumer appeal.

consumer buyer behavior The buying behavior of final consumers—individuals and households who buy goods and services for personal consumption.

consumer market All the individuals and households who buy or acquire goods and services for personal consumption.

consumer product Product bought by final consumer for personal consumption.

consumerism An organized movement of citizens and government agencies to improve the rights and power of buyers in relation to sellers.

consumer-oriented marketing The philosophy of enlightened marketing that holds that the company should view and organize its marketing activities from the consumer's point of view.

contract manufacturing A joint venture in which a company contracts with manufacturers in a foreign market to produce the product or provide its service.

contractual VMS A vertical marketing system in which independent firms at different levels of production and distribution join together through contracts to obtain more economies or sales impact than they could achieve alone.

convenience product Consumer product that the customer usually buys frequently, immediately, and with a minimum of comparison and buying effort.

convenience store A small store, located near a residential area, that is open long hours 7 days a week and carries a limited line of high-turnover convenience goods.

conventional distribution channel A channel consisting of one or more independent producers, wholesalers, and retailers, each a separate business seeking to maximize its own profits even at the expense of profits for the system as a whole.

corporate VMS A vertical marketing system that combines successive stages of production and distribution under single ownership—channel leadership is established through common ownership.

corporate Web site A Web site designed to build customer goodwill and to supplement other sales channels, rather than to sell the company's products directly.

cost-plus pricing Adding a standard markup to the cost of the product.

countertrade International trade involving the direct or indirect exchange of goods for other goods instead of cash.

cultural environment Institutions and other forces that affect society's basic values, perceptions, preferences, and behaviors.

culture The set of basic values, perceptions, wants, and behaviors learned by a member of society from family and other important institutions.

customer database An organized collection of comprehensive data about individual customers or prospects, including geographic, demographic, psychographic, and behavioral data.

customer equity The total combined customer lifetime values of all of the company's customers.

customer lifetime value The value of the entire stream of purchases that the customer would make over a lifetime of patronage.

customer perceived value The difference between total customer value and total customer cost.

customer relationship management (CRM) Managing detailed information about individual customers and carefully managing customer "touch points" in order to maximize customer loyalty.

customer relationship management The overall process of building and maintaining profitable customer relationships by delivering superior customer value and satisfaction.

customer sales force structure A sales force organization under which salespeople specialize in selling only to certain customers or industries.

customer satisfaction The extent to which a product's perceived performance matches a buyer's expectations.

customerization Leaving it to individual customers to design the marketing offering—allowing customers to be prosumers rather than only consumers.

decline stage The product life-cycle stage in which a product's sales decline.

deficient products Products that have neither immediate appeal nor long-run benefits.

demand curve A curve that shows the number of units the market will buy in a given time period, at different prices that might be charged.

demands Human wants that are backed by buying power.

demarketing Marketing to reduce demand temporarily or permanently; the aim is not to destroy demand but only to reduce or shift it.

demographic segmentation Dividing the market into groups based on demographic variables such as age, sex, family size, family life cycle, income, occupation, education, religion, race, and nationality.

demography The study of human populations in terms of size, density, location, age, gender, race, occupation, and other statistics.

department store A retail organization that carries a wide variety of product lines—typically clothing, home furnishings, and household goods; each line is operated as a separate department managed by specialist buyers or merchandisers.

derived demand Business demand that ultimately comes from (derives from) the demand for consumer goods.

descriptive research Marketing research to better describe marketing problems, situations, or markets, such as the market potential for a product or the demographics and attitudes of consumers.

desirable products Products that give both high immediate satisfaction and high long-run benefits.

differentiated (segmented) marketing A market-coverage strategy in which a firm decides to target several market segments and designs separate offers for each.

direct investment Entering a foreign market by developing foreign-based assembly or manufacturing facilities.

direct marketing channel A marketing channel that has no intermediary levels.

direct marketing Direct communications with carefully targeted individual consumers to obtain an immediate response.

direct marketing Direct connections with carefully targeted individual consumers to both obtain an immediate response and cultivate lasting customer relationships—the use of telephone, mail, fax, email, the Internet, and other tools to communicate directly with specific customers.

direct-mail marketing Direct marketing through single mailings that include letters, ads, samples, foldouts, and other "salespeople with wings" sent to prospects on mailing lists.

direct-response television marketing Direct marketing via television, including direct-response television advertising or infomercials and home shopping channels.

discount A straight reduction in price on purchases during a stated period of time.

discount store A retail institution that sells standard merchandise at lower prices by accepting lower margins and selling at higher volume.

disintermediation The displacement of traditional resellers from a marketing channel by radical new types of intermediaries.

distribution center A large, highly automated warehouse designed to receive goods from various plants and suppliers, take orders, fill them efficiently, and deliver goods to customers as quickly as possible.

diversification A strategy for company growth through starting up or acquiring businesses outside the company's current products and markets.

downsizing Reducing the business portfolio by eliminating products or business units that are not profitable or that no longer fit the company's overall strategy.

dynamic pricing Charging different prices depending on individual customers and situations.

e-business The use of electronic platforms—intranets, extranets, and the Internet—to conduct a company's business.

e-commerce Buying and selling processes supported by electronic means, primarily the Internet.

economic community A group of nations organized to work toward common goals in the regulation of international trade.

economic environment Factors that affect consumer buying power and spending patterns.

e-marketing The marketing side of e-commerce—company efforts to communicate about, promote, and sell products and services over the Internet.

embargo A ban on the import of a certain product.

engel's laws Differences noted over a century ago by Ernst Engel in how people shift their spending across food, housing, transportation, health care, and other goods and services categories as family income rises.

enlightened marketing A marketing philosophy holding that a company's marketing should support the best long-run performance of the marketing system; its five principles include consumer-oriented marketing, innovative marketing, value marketing, sense-of-mission marketing, and societal marketing.

environmental management perspective A management perspective in which the firm takes aggressive actions to affect the publics and forces in its marketing environment rather than simply watching and reacting to them.

environmental sustainability A management approach that involves developing strategies that both sustain the environment and produce profits for the company.

environmentalism An organized movement of concerned citizens and government agencies to protect and improve people's living environment.

e-procurement Online purchasing.

exchange The act of obtaining a desired object from someone by offering something in return.

exchange controls Government limits on the amount of foreign exchange with other countries and on the exchange rate against other currencies.

exclusive distribution Giving a limited number of dealers the exclusive right to distribute the company's products in their territories.

experimental research The gathering of primary data by selecting matched groups of subjects, giving them different treatments, controlling related factors, and checking for differences in group responses.

exploratory research Marketing research to gather preliminary information that will help define problems and suggest hypotheses.

exporting Entering a foreign market by selling goods produced in the company's home country, often with little modification.

extranet A network that connects a company with its suppliers and distributors.

factory outlet Off-price retailing operation that is owned and operated by a manufacturer and that normally carries the manufacturer's surplus, discontinued, or irregular goods.

fad A fashion that enters quickly, is adopted with great zeal, peaks early, and declines very quickly.

fashion A currently accepted or popular style in a given field.

fixed costs Costs that do not vary with production or sales level.

focus group interviewing Personal interviewing that involves inviting 6 to 10 people to gather for a few hours with a trained interviewer to talk about a product, service, or organization. The interviewer "focuses" the group discussion on important issues.

follow-up The last step in the selling process, in which the salesperson follows up after the sale to ensure customer satisfaction and repeat business.

franchise   A contractual association between a manufacturer, wholesaler, or service organization (a franchiser) and independent businesspeople (franchisees) who buy the right to own and operate one or more units in the franchise system.

franchise organization   A contractual vertical marketing system in which a channel member, called a franchiser, links several stages in the production–distribution process.

gender segmentation   Dividing a market into different groups based on gender.

generation X   The 45 million people born between 1965 and 1976 in the "birth dearth" following the baby boom.

generation Y   The 72 million children of the baby boomers, born between 1977 and 1994.

geographic segmentation   Dividing a market into different geographical units such as nations, states, regions, counties, cities, or neighborhoods.

global firm   A firm that, by operating in more than one country, gains R&D, production, marketing, and financial advantages in its costs and reputation that are not available to purely domestic competitors.

group   Two or more people who interact to accomplish individual or mutual goals.

growth–share matrix   A portfolio-planning method that evaluates a company's strategic business units in terms of their market growth rate and relative market share. SBUs are classified as stars, cash cows, question marks, or dogs.

growth stage   The product life-cycle stage in which a product's sales start climbing quickly.

handling objections   The step in the selling process in which the salesperson seeks out, clarifies, and overcomes customer objections to buying.

horizontal marketing system   A channel arrangement in which two or more companies at one level join together to follow a new marketing opportunity.

idea generation   The systematic search for new-product ideas.

idea screening   Screening new-product ideas in order to spot good ideas and drop poor ones as soon as possible.

income segmentation   Dividing a market into different income groups.

independent off-price retailer   Off-price retailer that is either owned and run by entrepreneurs or is a division of a larger retail corporation.

indirect marketing channel   Channel containing one or more intermediary levels.

individual marketing   Tailoring products and marketing programs to the needs and preferences of individual customers—also labeled "markets-of-one marketing," "customized marketing," and "one-to-one marketing."

industrial product   Product bought by individuals and organizations for further processing or for use in conducting a business.

innovative marketing   A principle of enlightened marketing that requires that a company seek real product and marketing improvements.

inside sales force   Inside salespeople who conduct business from their offices via telephone or visits from prospective buyers.

integrated direct marketing   Direct-marketing campaigns that use multiple vehicles and multiple stages to improve response rates and profits.

integrated logistics management   The logistics concept that emphasizes teamwork, both inside the company and among all the marketing channel organizations, to maximize the performance of the entire distribution system.

integrated marketing communications (IMC)   The concept under which a company carefully integrates and coordinates its many communications channels to deliver a clear, consistent, and compelling message about the organization and its products.

intensive distribution   Stocking the product in as many outlets as possible.

interactive marketing   Marketing by a service firm that recognizes that perceived service quality depends heavily on the quality of buyer–seller interaction.

intermarket segmentation   Forming segments of consumers who have similar needs and buying behavior even though they are located in different countries.

intermodal transportation   Combining two or more modes of transportation.

internal databases   Electronic collections of information obtained from data sources within the company.

internal marketing   Marketing by a service firm to train and effectively motivate its customer-contact employees and all the supporting service people to work as a team to provide customer satisfaction.

internet   A vast public web of computer networks, which connects users of all types all around the world to each other and to an amazingly large information repository.

intranet   A network that connects people within a company to each other and to the company network.

introduction stage   The product life-cycle stage in which the new product is first distributed and made available for purchase.

joint ownership   A joint venture in which a company joins investors in a foreign market to create a local business in which the company shares joint ownership and control.

joint venturing   Entering foreign markets by joining with foreign companies to produce or market a product or service.

learning   Changes in an individual's behavior arising from experience.

licensing   A method of entering a foreign market in which the company enters into an agreement with a licensee in the foreign market, offering the right to use a manufacturing process, trademark, patent, trade secret, or other item of value for a fee or royalty.

lifestyle   A person's pattern of living as expressed in his or her activities, interests, and opinions.

line extension   Using a successful brand name to introduce additional items in a given product category under the same brand name, such as new flavors, forms, colors, added ingredients, or package sizes.

local marketing   Tailoring brands and promotions to the needs and wants of local customer groups—cities, neighborhoods, and even specific stores.

macroenvironment   The larger societal forces that affect the microenvironment—demographic, economic, natural, technological, political, and cultural forces.

management contracting   A joint venture in which the domestic firm supplies the management know-how to a foreign company that supplies the capital; the domestic firm exports management services rather than products.

manufacturers' sales branches and offices Wholesaling by sellers or buyers themselves rather than through independent wholesalers.

market The set of all actual and potential buyers of a product or service.

market development A strategy for company growth by identifying and developing new market segments for current company products.

market penetration A strategy for company growth by increasing sales of current products to current market segments without changing the product.

market-penetration pricing Setting a low price for a new product in order to attract a large number of buyers and a large market share.

market positioning Arranging for a product to occupy a clear, distinctive, and desirable place relative to competing products in the minds of target consumers.

market positioning Arranging for a product to occupy a clear, distinctive, and desirable place relative to competing products in the minds of target consumers.

market segment A group of consumers who respond in a similar way to a given set of marketing efforts.

market segmentation Dividing a market into distinct groups of buyers who have distinct needs, characteristics, or behavior and who might require separate products or marketing mixes.

market segmentation Dividing a market into distinct groups with distinct needs, characteristics, or behavior who might require separate products or marketing mixes.

market-skimming pricing Setting a high price for a new product to skim maximum revenues layer by layer from the segments willing to pay the high price; the company makes fewer but more profitable sales.

marketing A social and managerial process by which individuals and groups obtain what they need and want through creating and exchanging value with others.

marketing audit A comprehensive, systematic, independent, and periodic examination of a company's environment, objectives, strategies, and activities to determine problem areas and opportunities and to recommend a plan of action to improve the company's marketing performance.

marketing channel (distribution channel) A set of interdependent organizations involved in the process of making a product or service available for use or consumption by the consumer or business user.

marketing communications mix (promotion mix) The specific mix of advertising, personal selling, sales promotion, and public relations a company uses to pursue its advertising and marketing objectives.

marketing concept The marketing management philosophy that holds that achieving organizational goals depends on knowing the needs and wants of target markets and delivering the desired satisfactions better than competitors do.

marketing control The process of measuring and evaluating the results of marketing strategies and plans, and taking corrective action to ensure that objectives are achieved.

marketing environment The actors and forces outside marketing that affect marketing management's ability to build and maintain successful relationships with target customers.

marketing implementation The process that turns marketing strategies and plans into marketing actions in order to accomplish strategic marketing objectives.

marketing information system (MIS) People, equipment, and procedures to gather, sort, analyze, evaluate, and distribute needed, timely, and accurate information to marketing decision makers.

marketing intelligence The systematic collection and analysis of publicly available information about competitors and developments in the marketing environment.

marketing intermediaries Firms that help the company to promote, sell, and distribute its goods to final buyers; they include resellers, physical distribution firms, marketing service agencies, and financial intermediaries.

marketing logistics (physical distribution) The tasks involved in planning, implementing, and controlling the physical flow of materials, final goods, and related information from points of origin to points of consumption to meet customer requirements at a profit.

marketing management The art and science of choosing target markets and building profitable relationships with them.

marketing mix The set of controllable tactical marketing tools—product, price, place, and promotion—that the firm blends to produce the response it wants in the target market.

marketing offer Some combination of products, services, information, or experiences offered to a market to satisfy a need or want.

marketing plan A detailed plan for a product or brand that assesses the current marketing situation and outlines marketing objectives, a marketing strategy, action programs, budgets, and controls.

marketing research The systematic design, collection, analysis, and reporting of data relevant to a specific marketing situation facing an organization.

marketing strategy The marketing logic by which the company hopes to achieve strong and profitable customer relationships. It involves deciding which customers to serve (segmentation and targeting) and with what value proposition (differentiation and positioning).

marketing strategy development Designing an initial marketing strategy for a new product based on the product concept.

marketing Web site A Web site that engages consumers in interactions that will move them closer to a direct purchase or other marketing outcome.

maturity stage The stage in the product life cycle in which sales growth slows or levels off.

merchant wholesaler Independently owned business that takes title to the merchandise it handles.

microenvironment The actors close to the company that affect its ability to serve its customers—the company, suppliers, marketing intermediaries, customer markets, competitors, and publics.

micromarketing The practice of tailoring products and marketing programs to the needs and wants of specific individuals and local customer groups—includes local marketing and individual marketing.

mission statement A statement of the organization's purpose—what it wants to accomplish in the larger environment.

modified rebuy A business buying situation in which the buyer wants to modify product specifications, prices, terms, or suppliers.

motive (drive) A need that is sufficiently pressing to direct the person to seek satisfaction of the need.

multichannel distribution system A distribution system in which a single firm sets up two or more marketing channels to reach one or more customer segments.

natural environment   Natural resources that are needed as inputs by marketers or that are affected by marketing activities.

needs   States of felt deprivation.

new product   A good, service, or idea that is perceived by some potential customers as new.

new task   A business buying situation in which the buyer purchases a product or service for the first time.

new-product development   The development of original products, product improvements, product modifications, and new brands through the firm's own R&D efforts.

nontariff trade barriers   Nonmonetary barriers to foreign products, such as biases against a foreign company's bids, or product standards that go against a foreign company's product features.

objective-and-task method   Developing the promotion budget by (1) defining specific objectives; (2) determining the tasks that must be performed to achieve these objectives; and (3) estimating the costs of performing these tasks. The sum of these costs is the proposed

observational research   The gathering of primary data by observing relevant people, actions, and situations.

occasion segmentation   Dividing the market into groups according to occasions when buyers get the idea to buy, actually make their purchase, or use the purchased item.

off-price retailer   Retailer that buys at less-than-regular wholesale prices and sells at less than retail. Examples are factory outlets, independents, and warehouse clubs.

online advertising   Advertising that appears while consumers are surfing the Web, including banner and ticker ads, interstitials, skyscrapers, and other forms.

online databases   Computerized collections of information available from online commercial sources or via the Internet.

online (Internet) marketing research   Collecting primary data through Internet surveys and online focus groups.

open trading exchanges   Huge emarketspaces in which B2B buyers and sellers find each other online, share information, and complete transactions efficiently.

opinion leader   Person within a reference group who, because of special skills, knowledge, personality, or other characteristics, exerts influence on others.

optional-product pricing   The pricing of optional or accessory products along with a main product.

outside sales force (or field sales force)   Outside salespeople who travel to call on customers.

packaging   The activities of designing and producing the container or wrapper for a product.

partner relationship management   Working closely with partners in other company departments and outside the company to jointly bring greater value to customers.

percentage-of-sales method   Setting the promotion budget at a certain percentage of current or forecasted sales or as a percentage of the unit sales price.

perception   The process by which people select, organize, and interpret information to form a meaningful picture of the world.

personal selling   Personal presentation by the firm's sales force for the purpose of making sales and building customer relationships.

personality   The unique psychological characteristics that lead to relatively consistent and lasting responses to one's own environment.

pleasing products   Products that give high immediate satisfaction but may hurt consumers in the long run.

political environment   Laws, government agencies, and pressure groups that influence and limit various organizations and individuals in a given society.

portfolio analysis   A tool by which management identifies and evaluates the various businesses making up the company.

positioning statement   A statement that summarizes company or brand positioning—it takes this form: To (target segment and need) our (brand) is (concept) that (point-of-difference).

preapproach   The step in the selling process in which the salesperson learns as much as possible about a prospective customer before making a sales call.

presentation   The step in the selling process in which the salesperson tells the "product story" to the buyer, highlighting customer benefits.

price   The amount of money charged for a product or service, or the sum of the values that consumers exchange for the benefits of having or using the product or service.

price elasticity   A measure of the sensitivity of demand to changes in price.

primary data   Information collected for the specific purpose at hand.

private (or store) brand   A brand created and owned by a reseller of a product or service.

private trading networks (PTNs)   B2B trading networks that link a particular seller with its own trading partners.

product   Anything that can be offered to a market for attention, acquisition, use, or consumption that might satisfy a want or need.

product adaptation   Adapting a product to meet local conditions or wants in foreign markets.

product bundle pricing   Combining several products and offering the bundle at a reduced price.

product concept   A detailed version of the new-product idea stated in meaningful consumer terms.

product concept   The idea that consumers will favor products that offer the most quality, performance, and features and that the organization should therefore devote its energy to making continuous product improvements.

product development   A strategy for company growth by offering modified or new products to current market segments.

product development   Developing the product concept into a physical product in order to ensure that the product idea can be turned into a workable product.

product invention   Creating new products or services for foreign markets.

product life cycle   The course of a product's sales and profits over its lifetime. It involves five distinct stages: product development, introduction, growth, maturity, and decline.

product line pricing   Setting the price steps between various products in a product line based on cost differences between the products, customer evaluations of different features, and competitors' prices.

product line   A group of products that are closely related because they function in a similar manner, are sold to the same customer groups, are marketed through the same types of outlets, or fall within given price ranges.

product mix (or product assortment)   The set of all product lines and items that a particular seller offers for sale.

product position   The way the product is defined by consumers on important attributes—the place the product occupies in consumers' minds relative to competing products.

product quality   The ability of a product to perform its functions; it includes the product's overall durability, reliability, precision, ease of operation and repair, and other valued attributes.

product sales force structure   A sales force organization under which salespeople specialize in selling only a portion of the company's products or lines.

product/market expansion grid   A portfolio-planning tool for identifying company growth opportunities through market penetration, market development, product development, or diversification.

production concept   The idea that consumers will favor products that are available and highly affordable.

promotional pricing   Temporarily pricing products below the list price, and sometimes even below cost, to increase short-run sales.

prospecting   The step in the selling process in which the salesperson identifies qualified potential customers.

psychographic segmentation   Dividing a market into different groups based on social class, lifestyle, or personality characteristics.

psychological pricing   A pricing approach that considers the psychology of prices and not simply the economics; the price is used to say something about the product.

public   Any group that has an actual or potential interest in or impact on an organization's ability to achieve its objectives.

public relations   Building good relations with the company's various publics by obtaining favorable publicity, building up a good "corporate image," and handling or heading off unfavorable rumors, stories, and events. Major PR tools include press relations, product publicity, corporate communications, lobbying, and public service.

pull strategy   A promotion strategy that calls for spending a lot on advertising and consumer promotion to build up consumer demand. If the strategy is successful, consumers will ask their retailers for the product, the retailers will ask the wholesalers,

push strategy   A promotion strategy that calls for using the sales force and trade promotion to push the product through channels. The producer promotes the product to wholesalers, the wholesalers promote to retailers, and the retailers promote to consumers.

quota   A limit on the amount of goods that an importing country will accept in certain product categories; it is designed to conserve on foreign exchange and to protect local industry and employment.

reference prices   Prices that buyers carry in their minds and refer to when they look at a given product.

retailer   Business whose sales come primarily from retailing.

retailing   All activities involved in selling goods or services directly to final consumers for their personal, nonbusiness use.

sales force management   The analysis, planning, implementation, and control of sales force activities. It includes setting and designing sales force strategy; and recruiting, selecting, training, supervising, compensating, and evaluating the firm's salespeople.

sales promotion   Short-term incentives to encourage the purchase or sale of a product or service.

sales quota   A standard that states the amount a salesperson should sell and how sales should be divided among the company's products.

salesperson   An individual acting for a company by performing one or more of the following activities: prospecting, communicating, servicing, and information gathering.

salutary products   Products that have low appeal but may benefit consumers in the long run.

sample   A segment of the population selected for marketing research to represent the population as a whole.

secondary data   Information that already exists somewhere, having been collected for another purpose.

segmented pricing   Selling a product or service at two or more prices, where the difference in prices is not based on differences in costs.

selective distribution   The use of more than one, but fewer than all, of the intermediaries who are willing to carry the company's products.

selling concept   The idea that that consumers will not buy enough of the firm's products unless it undertakes a large-scale selling and promotion effort.

selling process   The steps that the salesperson follows when selling, which include prospecting and qualifying, preapproach, approach, presentation and demonstration, handling objections, closing, and follow-up.

sense-of-mission marketing   A principle of enlightened marketing that holds that a company should define its mission in broad social terms rather than narrow product terms.

sequential product development   A new-product development approach in which one company department works to complete its stage of the process before passing the new product along to the next department and stage.

service   Any activity or benefit that one party can offer to another that is essentially intangible and does not result in the ownership of anything.

service inseparability   A major characteristic of services—they are produced and consumed at the same time and cannot be separated from their providers, whether the providers are people or machines.

service intangibility   A major characteristic of services—they cannot be seen, tasted, felt, heard, or smelled before they are bought.

service perishability   A major characteristic of services—they cannot be stored for later sale or use.

service-profit chain   The chain that links service firm profits with employee and customer satisfaction.

service variability   A major characteristic of services—their quality may vary greatly, depending on who provides them and when, where, and how.

share of customer   The portion of the customer's purchasing in its product categories that a company gets.

shopping center   A group of retail businesses planned, developed, owned, and managed as a unit.

shopping product   Consumer good that the customer, in the process of selection and purchase, characteristically compares on bases such as suitability, quality, price, and style.

simultaneous (or team-based) product development   An approach to developing new products in which various company departments work closely together, overlapping the steps in the product-development process to save time and increase effectiveness.

single-source data systems   Electronic monitoring systems that link consumers' exposure to television advertising and promotion (measured using television meters) with what they buy in stores (measured using store checkout scanners).

social class   Relatively permanent and ordered divisions in a society whose members share similar values, interests, and behaviors.

social marketing   The design, implementation, and control of programs seeking to increase the acceptability of a social idea, cause, or practice among a target group.

societal marketing concept   A principle of enlightened marketing that holds that a company should make good marketing decisions by considering consumers' wants, the company's requirements, consumers' long-run interests, and society's long-run interests.

societal marketing   A principle of enlightened marketing that holds that a company should make marketing decisions by considering consumers' wants, the company's requirements, consumers' long-run interests, and society's long-run interests.

spam   Unsolicited, unwanted commercial e-mail messages.

specialty product   Consumer product with unique characteristics or brand identification for which a significant group of buyers is willing to make a special purchase effort.

specialty store   A retail store that carries a narrow product line with a deep assortment within that line.

standardized marketing mix   An international marketing strategy for using basically the same product, advertising, distribution channels, and other elements of the marketing mix in all the company's international markets.

straight product extension   Marketing a product in a foreign market without any change.

straight rebuy   A business buying situation in which the buyer routinely reorders something without any modifications.

strategic planning   The process of developing and maintaining a strategic fit between the organization's goals and capabilities and its changing marketing opportunities. It involves defining a clear company mission, setting supporting objectives, designing a sound business portfolio, and coordinating functional strategies.

style   A basic and distinctive mode of expression.

subculture   A group of people with shared value systems based on common life experiences and situations.

supermarket   Large, low-cost, low-margin, high-volume, self-service store that carries a wide variety of food, laundry, and household products.

superstore   A store much larger than a regular supermarket that carries a large assortment of routinely purchased food and nonfood items and offers services such as dry cleaning, post offices, photo finishing, check cashing, bill paying, lunch counters, car care, and pet care.

supply chain management   Managing upstream and downstream value-added flows of materials, final goods, and related information among suppliers, the company, resellers, and final consumers.

survey research   The gathering of primary data by asking people questions about their knowledge, attitudes, preferences, and buying behavior.

systems selling   Buying a packaged solution to a problem from a single seller, thus avoiding all the separate decisions involved in a complex buying situation.

target costing   Pricing that starts with an ideal selling price, then targets costs that will ensure that the price is met.

target market   A set of buyers sharing common needs or characteristics that the company decides to serve.

target marketing   The process of evaluating each market segment's attractiveness and selecting one or more segments to enter.

target marketing   The process of evaluating each market segment's attractiveness and selecting one or more segments to enter.

tariff   A tax levied by a government against certain imported products. Tariffs are designed to raise revenue or to protect domestic firms.

team selling   Using teams of people from sales, marketing, engineering, finance, technical support, and even upper management to service large, complex accounts.

technological environment   Forces that create new technologies, creating new product and market opportunities.

telephone marketing   Using the telephone to sell directly to customers.

territorial sales force structure   A sales force organization that assigns each salesperson to an exclusive geographic territory in which that salesperson sells the company's full line.

test marketing   The stage of new-product development in which the product and marketing program are tested in more realistic market settings.

third-party logistics (3PL) provider   An independent logistics provider that performs any or all of the functions required to get their client's product to market.

total costs   The sum of the fixed and variable costs for any given level of production.

transaction   A trade of values between two parties.

undifferentiated (mass) marketing   A market-coverage strategy in which a firm decides to ignore market segment differences and go after the whole market with one offer.

unsought product   Consumer product that the consumer either does not know about or knows about but does not normally think of buying.

value analysis   An approach to cost reduction in which components are studied carefully to determine if they can be redesigned, standardized, or made by less costly methods of production.

value chain The series of departments that carry out value-creating activities to design, produce, market, deliver, and support a firm's products.

value delivery network A network made up of the company, suppliers, distributors, and ultimately customers who "partner" with each other to improve the performance of the entire system.

value marketing A principle of enlightened marketing that holds that a company should put most of its resources into value-building marketing investments.

value pricing Offering just the right combination of quality and good service at a fair price.

value proposition The full positioning of a brand—the full mix of benefits on which it is positioned.

value-based pricing Setting price based on buyers' perceptions of value rather than on the seller's cost.

value-delivery network The network made up of the company, suppliers, distributors, and ultimately customers who "partner" with each other to improve the performance of the entire system.

variable costs Costs that vary directly with the level of production.

vertical marketing system (VMS) A distribution channel structure in which producers, wholesalers, and retailers act as a unified system. One channel member owns the others, has contracts with them, or has so much power that they all cooperate.

viral marketing The Internet version of word-of-mouth marketing—e-mail messages or other marketing events that are so infectious that customers will want to pass them along to friends.

wants The form human needs take as shaped by culture and individual personality.

warehouse club Off-price retailer that sells a limited selection of brand-name grocery items, appliances, clothing, and a hodgepodge of other goods at deep discounts to members who pay annual membership fees.

web communities Web sites where members can congregate online and exchange views on issues of common interest.

wheel-of-retailing concept A concept of retailing that states that new types of retailers usually begin as low-margin, low-price, low-status operations but later evolve into higher-priced, higher-service operations, eventually becoming like the conventional retailers they replaced.

whole-channel view Designing international channels that take into account all the necessary links in distributing the seller's products to final buyers, including the seller's headquarters organization, channels among nations, and channels within nations.

wholesaler A firm engaged primarily in wholesaling activity.

wholesaling All activities involved in selling goods and services to those buying for resale or business use.

zone pricing A geographical pricing strategy in which the company sets up two or more zones. All customers within a zone pay the same total price; the more distant the zone, the higher the price.

Notes

Chapter 1

1. See Stewart Alsop, "I'm Betting on Amazon," *Fortune,* April 30, 2001, p. 48; Kathleen Doler, "Interview: Jeff Bezos, Founder and CEO of Amazon.com Inc.," *Upside,* September 1998, pp. 76–80; Susan Stellin, Geoffrey Colvin, "Shaking Hands on the Web," *Fortune,* May 14, 2001, p. 54; Fred Vogelstein, "Amazon's Second Act," September 2, 2002, pp. 186–188; Jonathon Krim and Dina ElBoghdady, "Amazon Posts Profit for 2nd Time; Firm May Prove to Be a Rare E-Commerce Site with Staying Power," *The Washington Post,* January 24, 2003; Nick Wingfield, "Amazon Narrows Loss as Revenue Increases by 28%," *Wall Street Journal,* April 25, 2003, p. B8; Fred VogelStein, "Mighty Amazon," *Fortune,* May 26, 2003, pp. 60–74; and annual reports and other information accessed at www.amazon.com, August 2003.

2. The American Marketing Association offers this definition: "*Marketing* is the process of planning and executing the conception, pricing, promotion, and distributing of ideas, goods, and services to create exchanges that satisfy individual and organizational objectives." See www.marketingpower.com/live/content.php?Item_ID=4620, July 2003.

3. For an interesting discussion of creating customer value and extracting value in return, see Natalie Mizik and Robert Jacobson, "Trading Off Between Value Creation and Value Appropriation: The Financial Implications of Shifts in Strategic Emphasis," *Journal of Marketing,* January 2003, pp. 63–76.

4. Jack Neff, "Humble Try," *Advertising Age,* February 18, 2002, pp. 3, 12; and Mark Ritson, "The Best Research Comes from Living the Life of Your Customer," *Marketing,* July 18, 2002, p. 16.

5. See Theodore Levitt's classic article, "Marketing Myopia," *Harvard Business Review,* July-August 1960, pp. 45–56. For more recent discussions, see Colin Grant, "Theodore Levitt's Marketing Myopia," *Journal of Business Ethics,* February 1999, pp. 397–406; Jeffrey M. O'Brien, "Drums in the Jungle," *MC Technology Marketing Intelligence,* March 1999, pp. 22–30; Hershell Sarbin, "Overcoming Marketing Myopia," *Folio,* May 2000, pp. 55–56; and James R. Stock, "Marketing Myopia Revisited: Lessons for Logistics," *International Journal of Physical Distribution Logistics Management,* vol. 2, issue 1/2, 2002, pp. 12–21.

6. Erika Rasmusson, "Marketing More than a Product," *Sales Marketing Management,* February 2000, p. 99. Also see B. Joseph Pine II and James Gilmore, "Welcome to the Experience Economy," *Harvard Business Review,* July–August 1998, p. 99; Stephen E. DeLong, "The Experience Economy," *Upside,* November 2001, p. 28; and Pat Esgate, "Pine and Gilmore Stage a Fourth Think About Experience," *Strategy Leadership,* vol. 30, issue 3, 2002, pp. 47–48.

7. For more discussion on demand states, see Philip Kotler, *Marketing Management: Analysis, Planning, Implementation, and Control,* 11th ed. (Upper Saddle River, NJ: Prentice Hall, 2003), p. 6.

8. Ralph Waldo Emerson offered this advice: "If a manmakes a better mousetrap the world will beat a path to his door." Several companies, however, have built better mousetraps yet failed. One was a laser mousetrap costing $1,500. Contrary to popular assumptions, people do not automatically learn about new products, believe product claims, or willingly pay higher prices.

9. See James Bandler, "Kodak Advances in Marketing Share of Digital Cameras," *Wall Street Journal,* December 21, 2001, p. B2; and Bandler, "Leading the News: Kodak Posts Disappointing Net, Plans New Layoffs," January 23, 2003, p. A3.

10. See John Goodman and Steve Newman, "Understand Customer Behavior and Complaints," *Quality Progress,* January 2003, pp. 51–55.

11. Kotler, *Marketing Management: Analysis, Planning, Implementation, and Control,* 11th ed., p. 19. Also see Kotler, *Marketing Insights from A to Z* (Hoboken, NJ: Wiley, 2003), pp. 32–34.

12. See Gary Hamel and C. K. Prahalad, "Seeing the Future First," *Fortune*, September 5, 1994, pp. 64–70; Philip Kotler, *Kotler on Marketing* (New York: Free Press, 1999), pp. 20–24; and Anthony W. Ulwick, "Turn Customer Input Into Innovation," *Harvard Business Review,* January 2002, pp. 91–97.

13. See Sonia Reyes, "Fighting the Fat Backlash," *Brandweek,* May 5, 2003, pp. 24–30; and Nat Ives, "Fast-Food Chains Are Adding Premium Salads to Their Menus After Success of Rival," *New York Times,* May 5, 2003, p. C10.

14. See "Leaders of the Most Admired," *Fortune,* January 29, 1990, pp. 40–54; Thomas A. Stewart, "America's Most Admired Companies," *Fortune,* March 2, 1998, pp. 70–82; and www.jnj.com/our_company/credo_heading.htm, September 2003.

15. Neil A. Martin, "A New Ground War," *Barron's,* April 21, 2003, pp. 21–26.

16. For more on customer satisfaction, see Regina Fazio Marcuna, "Mapping the World of Customer Satisfaction, *Harvard Business Review,* May–June 2000, p. 30; David M. Szymanski, "Customer Satisfaction: A Meta-Analysis of the Empirical Evidence," *Academy of Marketing Science Journal,* Winter 2001, pp. 16–35; Vikas Mittal and Wagner Kamakura, "Satisfaction, Repurchase Intent, and Repurchase Behavior: Investigating the Moderating Effect of Customer Characteristics," *Journal of Marketing Research,* February 2001, pp. 131–142; and Robert C. Blattberg, Gary Getz, Jacquelyn S. Thomas, *Customer Equity* (Boston, MA: Harvard Business School Press, 2001), pp. 75; and Marc R. Okrant, "How to Convert '3's and '4's into '5's," *Marketing News,* October 14, 2002, pp. 14, 17.

17. For more on this measure and for recent customer satisfaction scores, see Eugene W. Anderson and Claes Fornell, "Foundations of the American Customer Satisfaction Index," *Total Quality Management,* September 2000, pp. S869–S882; and Fornell, "The Science of Satisfaction," *Harvard Business Review*, March 2001, pp. 120–121. Cited facts accessed online at the ACSI Web site at www.theacsi.org, September 2003.

18. Leonard L. Berry and A. Parasuraman, *Marketing Services: Competing Through Quality* (New York: Free Press, 1991), pp. 136–142. Also see Richard Cross and Janet Smith, *Customer Bonding: Pathways to Lasting Customer Loyalty* (Lincolnwood, IL: NTC Business Books, 1995); and Michelle L. Roehm, Ellen Bolman Pullins, and Harpeer A. Roehm, "Building Loyalty-Building Programs for Packaged Goods Brands," *Journal of Marketing Research,* May 2002, 202–213.

19. See Mary M. Long and Leon G. Schiffman, "Consumption Values and Relationships: Segmenting the Market for Frequency Programs," *The Journal of Consumer Marketing,* 2000, pp. 214+; and Patrick LePointe, "Loyalty Marketing's Newest Challenges," *Marketing News,* October 14, 2002, pp. 16–17. Examples based on information accessed online at www.hog.com and www.swatch.com, September 2003.

20. See Rick Brooks, "Unequal Treatment: Alienating Customers Isn't Always a Bad Idea, Many Firms Discover," *Wall Street Journal,*

January 7, 1999, p. A1; Erika Rasmusson, "Wanted: Profitable Customers," *Sales Marketing Management*, May 1999, pp. 28–34; Peter Cockburn, "CRM for Profit," *Telecommunications,* December 2000, pp. 89–93; Chris Serres, "Banks Get Customers' Numbers," *Raleigh News Observer,* March 19, 2002, pp. A1, A4; and "Customer Profitability," *Chief Executive,* April 2003, pp. 1–4.

21. See Erika Rasmusson, "Complaints Can Build Relationships," *Sales Marketing Management*, September 1999, p. 89; "King Customer," *Selling Power,* October 2000, pp. 124–125; Renee Houston Zemansky and Jeff Weiner, "Just Hang On to What You Got," *Selling Power,* March 2002, pp. 60–64; and Marc R. Okrant, "How to Convert '3's and '4's into '5's," *Marketing News,* October 14, 2002, pp. 14, 17.

22. Kotler, *Kotler on Marketing,* p. 20.

23. Thor Valdmanis, "Alliances Gain Favor over Risky Mergers," *USA Today*, February 4, 1999, p. 3B. Also see Gabor Gari, "Leveraging the Rewards of Strategic Alliances," *Journal of Business Strategy*, April 1999, pp. 40–43; Rosabeth Moss Kanter, "Why Collaborate?" *Executive Excellence*, April 1999, p. 8; Matthew Schifrin, "Partner or Perish," *Forbes*, May 21, 2001, pp. 26–28; and Kim T. Gordan, "Strong Partnerships Build Marketing Muscle," *CRN,* February 10, 2003, p. 14A.

24. See Thomas O. Jones and W. Earl Sasser Jr. "Why Satisfied Customers Defect," *Harvard Business Review*, November–December 1995, pp. 88–99, Thomas A. Stewart, "A Satisfied Customer Isn't Enough," *Fortune,* July 21, 1997, pp. 112–113; and Philip Kotler, *Marketing Insights from A to Z* (Hoboken, NJ: Wiley, 2003), pp. 36–40.

25. Information accessed online at www.stew-leonards'com, August 2002.

26. See Libby Estell, "This Call Center Accelerates Sales," *Sales Marketing Management*, February 1999, p. 72; Mark McMaster, "A Lifetime of Sales," *Sales Marketing Management,* September 2001, p. 55; and Lauren Keller Johnson, "The Real Value of Customer Loyalty," *MIT Sloan Management Review,* Winter 2002, pp. 14–17.

27. Erin Stout, "Keep Them Coming Back for More," *Sales and Marketing Management,* February 2002, pp. 51–52.

28. See Roland T. Rust, Valerie A. Zeithaml, and Katherine A. Lemon, *Driving Customer Equity* (New York Free Press 2000); Rust, Lemon, and Zeithaml, "Where Should the Next Marketing Dollar Go?" *Marketing Management,* September–October 2001, pp. 24–28; Robert C. Blattberg, Gary Getz, Jacquelyn S. Thomas, *Customer Equity* (Boston, MA: Harvard Business School Press, 2001); and John E. Hogan, Katherine N. Lemon, and Roland T. Rust, "Customer Equity Management: Charting New Directions for the Future of Marketing," *Journal of Service Research,* August 2002, pp. 4–12.

29. This example is adapted from Rust, Lemon, and Zeithaml, "Where Should the Next Marketing Dollar Go?" *Marketing Management,* p. 25. For in-depth discussions of how to measure customer equity, see Blattberg, Getz, and Thomas, *Customer Equity.*

30. Ravi Dhar and Rashi Glazer, "Hedging Customers," *Harvard Business Review,* May 2003, pp. 86–92.

31. Werner Reinartz and V. Kumar, "The Mismanagement of Customer Loyalty," *Harvard Business Review,* July 2002, pp. 86–94. For more on customer equity management, see Kotler, *Marketing Insights from A to Z,* pp. 38–40; Blattberg, Getz, and Thomas, *Customer Equity,* chapters 3–6; Sunil Gupta and Donald R. Lehman, "Customers as Assets," *Journal of Interactive Marketing,* Winter 2003, pp. 9–24; and Reinartz and Kumar, "The Impact of Customer Relationship Characteristics on Profitable Lifetime Duration," *Journal of Marketing,* January 2003, pp. 77–79.

32. Michael J. Weiss, "Online America," *American Demographics,* March 2001, pp. 53–60; Taylor, Humphrey, "Internet Penetration at 66% of Adults (137 Million) Nationwide," *The Harris Poll,* April 17, 2002; "Internet Penetration Rate Slows," *Silicon Valley/San Jose Business*

Journal, February 5, 2003, accessed online at www.eastbay.bizjournals.com/sanjose; and "Population Explosion!" *CyberAtlas,* March 14, 2003, accessed online at www.cyberatlas.com.

33. Robert D. Hof, "Survive and Prosper," *Business Week,* May 14, 2001, p. EB60; and Timothy Mullaney, "E-biz Surprise," *Business Week,* May 12, 2003, pp. 60–68.

34. Steve Hamm, "E-Biz: Down but Hardly Out," *Business Week,* March 26, 2001, pp. 126–130; "B2B E-Commerce Headed for Trillions," March 6, 2002, accessed online at www.cyberatlas.internet.com; and Mullaney, "E-biz Surprise," pp. 60–68.

35. See Ben Jerry's full mission statement online at www.benjerry.com.

36. Example adapted from Alison Stein Wellner, "Oh Come All Ye Faithful," *American Demographics,* June 2001, pp. 52–55. Other information from www.marblechurch.org, August 2003.

37. For other examples, and for a good review of nonprofit marketing, see Philip Kotler and Alan R. Andreasen, *Strategic Marketing for Nonprofit Organizations*, 6th ed. (Upper Saddle River, NJ: Prentice Hall, 2003); Philip Kotler and Karen Fox, *Strategic Marketing for Educational Institutions* (Upper Saddle River, NJ: Prentice Hall, 1995); Norman Shawchuck, Philip Kotler, Bruce Wren, and Gustave Rath, *Marketing for Congregations: Choosing to Serve People More Effectively* (Nashville, TN: Abingdon Press, 1993); and Philip Kotler, John Bowen, and James Makens, *Marketing for Hospitality and Tourism,* 3d ed. (Upper Saddle River, NJ: Prentice Hall, 2003).

38. Trevor Jensen, "USPS Brings a New Campaign," *Adweek,* February 25, 2002, p. xxx; Trevor Jensen, p. 2. For more on social marketing, see Philip Kotler, Ned Roberto, and Nancy R. Lee, *Social Marketing: Improving the Quality of Life*, 2nd ed. (Upper Saddle River, NJ: Prentice Hall, 2002).

Chapter 2

1. "The Walt Disney Company," *Hoover Company Profiles,* Austin, May 1, 2003; Robert C. Ford, Cherrill P. Heaton, and Stephen W. Brown, "Delivering Excellent Service: Lessons from the Best Firms," *California Management Review*, Fall 2001, pp. 39–56; "Who Owns What?" *Columbia Journal Review*, posted February 19, 2002 at www.cjr.org; Laura M. Holson, "Surviving at Disney, Eisner Faces Difficult Year," *New York Times,* March 17, 2003; and information accessed online at www.Disney.go.com/corporate, August 2003.

2. For a more detailed discussion of corporate- and business-level strategic planning as they apply to marketing, see Philip Kotler, *Marketing Management*, 11th ed. (Upper Saddle River, NJ: Prentice Hall, 2003), chapter 4.

3. Digby Anderson, "Is This the Perfect Mission Statement?" *Across the Board*, May–June 2001, p. 16.

4. Found at www.celestialseasonings.com/whowear/corporatehistory/mission.html, June 2003. For more on mission statements, see Barbara Bartkus, Myron Glassman, and R. Bruce McAfee, "Mission Statements: Are They Smoke and Mirrors?" *Business Horizons*, November–December 2000, pp. 23–28; George S. Day, "Define Your Business," *Executive Excellence*, February 2001, p. 12; and Forest R. David and Fred R. David, "It's Time to Redraft Your Mission Statement," *The Journal of Business Strategy,* January–February 2003, pp. 11–14.

5. For more on strategic planning, see John A. Byrne, "Strategic Planning," *Business Week,* August 26, 1996, pp. 46–51; Pete Bogda, "Fifteen Years Later, the Return of Strategy," *Brandweek,* February 1997, p. 18; Ian Wilson, "Strategic Planning for the Millennium: Resolving the Dilemma," *Long Range Planning*, August 1998, pp. 507–513; Tom Devane, "Ten Cardinal Sins of Strategic Planning," *Executive Excellence,* October 2000, p. 15; Dave Lefkowith, "Effective Strategic Planning," *Management Quarterly*, Spring 2001, pp. 7–11; and Stan Abraham, "The Association of Strategic Planning: Strategy Is

Still Management's Core Challenge," *Strategy Leadership,* 2002, pp. 38–42.

6. H. Igor Ansoff, "Strategies for Diversification," *Harvard Business Review*, September–October 1957, pp. 113–124. Also see Philip Kotler, *Kotler on Marketing* (New York: Free Press, 1999), pp. 46–48; and Kevin Lane Keller, *Strategic Brand Management,* 2nd ed. (Upper Saddle River, NJ: Prentice Hall, 2003), pp. 576–578.

7. Michael Krauss, "Starbucks Adds Value by Taking on Wireless," *Marketing News,* February 2003, p. 9; and "How the Starbucks Card Stimulated New Markets," *Credit Card Management,* February 2003, p. 44.

8. Leslie Brokaw, "The Secrets of Great Planning," *Inc.,* October 1992, p. 152; and Kotler, *Marketing Management,* chapter 3.

9. Bradford McKee, "Think Ahead, Set Goals, and Get Out of the Office," *Nation's Business,* May 1993, p. 10. For more on small business strategic planning see Nancy Upton, Elisabeth J. Teal, and Joe T. Felan, "Strategic and Business Planning Practices of Fast Growth Family Firms," *Journal of Small Business Management,* January 2001, pp. 60–72; Jennifer Keeney, "How to Prepare for the Dawn of a New Economy," *FSB: Fortune Small Business,* April 2002, pp. 10–13; and Paulette Thomas, "Entrepreneurs' Biggest Problems—And How They Solve Them—Among the Ingredients for Success: Flexibility, Realism, and Passion," *Wall Street Journal,* March 17, 2003, p. R1.

10. Michael E. Porter, *Competitive Advantage: Creating and Sustaining Superior Performance* (New York: Free Press, 1985); and Michel E. Porter, "What Is Strategy?" *Harvard Business Review,* November–December 1996, pp. 61–78. Also see Jim Webb and Chas Gile, "Reversing the Value Chain," *Journal of Business Strategy,* March–April 2001, pp. 13–17.

11. Kotler, *Kotler on Marketing,* pp. 20–22. Also see Philip Kotler, *Marketing Insights from A to Z* (Hoboken, NJ: Wiley, 2003), pp. 102–107.

12. David Stires, "Fallen Arches," *Fortune,* April 29, 2002, pp. 74–76; and Sherri Day, "After Years at the Top, McDonald's Strives to Regain Ground," *New York Times,* March 3, 2003, p. A1.

13. Myron Magnet, "The New Golden Rule of Business," *Fortune*, February 21, 1994, pp. 60–63. For more on supply-chain management and strategic alliances, also see Hau Lee, "Survey: Chain Reaction," *The Economist,* February 2002, pp. S13–S15; James P. Morgan and Robert M. Monczka, "Why Supply Chains Must Be Managed," *Purchasing,* April 17, 2003, pp. 42–45; and Philip Kotler, *Marketing Management,* 11th ed. (Upper Saddle River, NJ: Prentice Hall, 2003), pp. 70–71.

14. Accessed online at Ad Age Dataplace, www.adage.com/dataplace, June 2003.

15. The four *Ps* classification was first suggested by E. Jerome McCarthy, *Basic Marketing: A Managerial Approach* (Homewood, IL: Irwin, 1960). For the 4Cs, other proposed classifications, and more discussion, see Robert Lauterborn, "New Marketing Litany: 4P's Passé; C-Words Take Over," *Advertising Age,* October 1, 1990, p. 26; Don E. Schultz, "Marketers: Bid Farewell to Strategy Based on Old 4Ps," *Marketing News,* February 12, 2001, p. 7, John Farrell, "Highlighting the 4Rs of Marketing," *Incentive,* April 2002, p. 101; and Elliott Ettenberg, "Goodbye 4Ps, Hello 4Rs," *Marketing Magazine,* April 14, 2003, p. 8.

16. For a good discussion of gaining advantage through implementation effectiveness versus strategic differentiation, see Michael E. Porter, "What Is Strategy," *Harvard Business Review,* November–December 1996, pp. 61–78. Also see Charles H. Noble and Michael P. Mokwa, "Implementing Marketing Strategies: Developing and Testing a Managerial Theory," *Journal of Marketing,* October 1999, pp. 57–73; and Thomas W. Porter and Stephen C. Harper, "Tactical Implementation," *Business Horizons,* January–February 2003, pp. 53–60.

17. Brian Dumaine, "Why Great Companies Last," *Business Week*, January 16, 1995, p. 129. See James C. Collins and Jerry I. Porras, *Built to Last: Successful Habits of Visionary Companies* (New York: Harper-Business, 1995); Rob Goffee and Gareth Jones, *The Character of a Corporation: How Your Company's Culture Can Make or Break Your Business* (New York: HarperBusiness, 1998); Thomas A. Atchison, "What Is Corporate Culture?" *Trustee,* April 2002, p. 11; and Jeff Rosenthal and Mary Ann Masarech, "High-Performance Cultures: How Values Can Drive Vision," *Journal of Organizational Excellence,* Spring 2003, pp. 3–18.

18. For more on brand and product management, see Kevin Lane Keller, *Strategic Brand Management,* 2nd ed. (Upper Saddle River, NJ: Prentice Hall, 2003).

19. See Roland T. Rust, Valerie A. Zeithaml, and Katherine N. Lemon, *Driving Customer Equity: How Lifetime Customer Value Is Reshaping Corporate Strategy* (New York: Free Press, 2000); and Rust, Lemon, and Zeithaml, "Where Should the Next Marketing Dollar Go?" *Marketing Management,* September–October 2001, pp. 24–28; Robert C. Blattberg, Gary Getz, and Jacquelyn S. Thomas, *Customer Equity* (Boston, MA: Harvard Business School Press, 2001); and John E. Hogan, Katherine N. Lemon, and Roland T. Rust, "Customer Equity Management: Charting New Directions for the Future of Marketing," *Journal of Service Research,* August 2002, pp. 4–12.

20. For details, see Kotler, *Marketing Management,* pp. 695–699. Also see Neil A. Morgan, Bruce H. Clark, and Rich Gooner, "Marketing Productivity, Marketing Audits, and Systems for Marketing Performance Assessment: Integrating Multiple Perspectives," *Journal of Marketing,* May 2002, pp. 363–375.

Chapter 3

1. Quotes from Theresa Howard, "Nostalgia Helps Beetle Score," *USA Today*, February 23, 2003, accessed online at www.usatoday.com; James R. Rosenfield, "Millennial Fever," *American Demographics,* December 1997, pp. 47–51; Keith Naughton and Bill Vlasic, "The Nostalgia Boom: Why the Old Is New Again," *Business Week,* March 23, 1998, pp. 58–64, Marc Peyser, "Everything Old Is . . . Even Older," *Newsweek,* May 6, 2002, p. 14; and "A Top-Popping Good Time," *The Washington Post,* April 24, 2003, p. G18. Also see James R. Rosenfield, "Millennial Fever Revisited," *Direct Marketing*, June 2000, pp. 43–47; Jeff Green, "Heavy Traffic on Memory Lane," *Business Week,* January 15, 2001, p. 40; Sholnn Freeman and Beth Demain Reigber, "The VW Bus Is Back," *Wall Street Journal,* June 12, 2002, p. D1; and "Flashback to '80s Brings in Cute, Cuddly Cash Cows," *DSN Retailing Today,* February 10, 2003, p. 16.

2. See Sarah Lorge, "The Coke Advantage," *Sales Marketing Management,* December 1998, p. 17; "The Fight for the Fountain Pushes Forward," *Beverage World,* January 15, 2001, pp. 48–49; and "Coca-Cola Inks New Deal with Jack in the Box Chain," *Nation's Restaurant News,* January 13, 2003, p. 52.

3. World POPClock, U.S. Census Bureau, accessed online at www.census.gov, August 2003. This Web site provides continuously updated projections of the U.S. and world populations.

4. Information accessed online at www.questconnect.org/global_citizen.htm, August 2003.

5. Sally D. Goll, "Marketing: China's (Only) Children Get the Royal Treatment," *Wall Street Journal*, February 8, 1995, pp. B1, B3; James L. Watson, "China's Big Mac Attack," *Foreign Affairs,* May–June 2000, pp. 120–134; and Mark Dunn, "Feeding China's Little Emperors: Food, Children, and Social Change," *The China Business Review*, September–October 2000, p. 32.

6. U.S. Census Bureau projections and POPClock Projection, U.S. Census Bureau, accessed online at www.census.gov, March 2003; and

Alison Stein Wellner, "The Next 25 Years," American Demographics, April 2003, pp. 23–27.

7. Alison Stein Wellner, "The Wealth Effect," *American Demographics*, January 2003, p. 35; and Rebecca Gardyn, "Whitewashed," *American Demographics*, February 2003, pp. 13–15.

8. Diana McKeon Charkalis, "Boomers Remodel Empty Nests Their Way," *USA Today*, March 21, 2003, accessed online at www.usatoday.com.

9. Michael Weiss, "Chasing Youth," *American Demographics,* October 2002, pp. 35–41.

10. See Joan Raymond, "The Joy of Empty Nesting," *American Demographics,* May 2000, pp. 49–54; David Rakoff, "The Be Generation," *Adweek*, March 5, 2001, pp. SR18–SR22; Gene Koretz, "Bless the Baby Boomers," *Business Week,* June 10, 2002, p. 30; and Greg Schneider, "Rebels with Disposable Income; Aging baby Boomers Line Up to Buy High-End Versions of Youthful Indulgences," *The Washington Post,* April 27, 2003, p. F01.

11. See Jean Chatzky, "Gen Xers Aren't Slackers after All," *Time,* April 8, 2002, p. 87; Alison Wellner, "The Power of the Purse," *American Demographics*, August 2002, pp. S3–S10; and Marybeth Matzek, "GenXers Take a Piece of the Pie," *The Cincinnati Enquirer,* March 3, 2003, accessed online at www.enquirer.com.

12. Example adapted from information found in Jura Koncius, "Chicago: In a Gritty Northside . . . ," *The Washington Post*, February 20, 2003, p. H1; and "The Core CB Shopper," *The Washington Post,* February 20, 2003, p. 115.

13. See Ken Gronback, "Marketing to Generation Y," *DSN Retailing Today,* July 24, 2000, p. 14; and Joanna Krotz, "Tough Customers: How to reach Gen Y," accessed online at www.bcentral.com, March 21, 2003.

14. Tobi Elkin, "Gen Y Quizzed about On-Demand," *Advertising Age,* February 14, 2003, p. 37. Also see Pamela Paul, "Getting Inside Gen Y," *American Demographics,* September 2001, pp. 43–49; and Rebecca Gardyn, "Born to be Wired," *American Demographics,* April 2003, pp. 14–15.

15. See Gronback, "Marketing to Generation Y," p. 14; "Study Compares Gen Y to Boomers," *Home Textiles Today,* September 11, 2000, p. 14; and Rebecca Gardyn, "Granddaughters of Feminism," *American Demographics*, April 2001, pp. 43–47.

16. See J. Walker Smith and Ann Clurman, *Rocking the Ages* (New York: HarperBusiness, 1998); Mercedes M. Cardona, "Hilfiger's New Apparel Lines Getting Individual Efforts," *Advertising Age,* February 8, 1999, p. 24; and Alison Stein Wellner, "Generational Divide," *American Demographics,* October 2000, pp. 53–58.

17. Alison Stein Wellner, "The American Family in the 21st Century," *American Demographics,* August 2001, p. 20.

18. Information on household composition accessed online at www.census.gov/population/projections/nation/hh-fam/table5n.txt, August 2003.

19. U.S. Census Bureau, "Women and Men in the United States," accessed online at www.census.gov/prod/2003pubs/p20-544.pdf, March 2003.

20. For these and other examples, see Kelly Shermach, "Niche Malls: Innovation for an Industry in Decline," *Marketing News,* February 26, 1996, p. 1; Sue Shellenbarger, "'Child-Care Cams': Are They Good News for Working Parents?" *Wall Street Journal,* August 19, 1998, p. B1; and Michelle Conlin, "Mommy Is Really Home from Work," *Business Week*, November 25, 2002, pp. 101–104.

21. U.S. Census Bureau, "Geographical Mobility: Population Characteristics," May 2001, accessed online at www.census.gov/prod/2001pubs/p20-538.pdf.

22. See Alison Stein Wellner, "Size Doesn't Matter," *American Demographics,* May 2001, pp. 23–24; Roderick J. Harrison, "The New White Flight," *American Demographics,* June 2002, pp. 20–24; and U.S. Census Bureau, "Geographical Mobility: Population Characteristics," pp. 4–5.

23. Lauri J. Flynn, "Not Just a Copy Shop Any Longer, Kinko's Pushes Its Computer Services," *New York Times,* July 6, 1998, p. D1. Also see Carol Leonetti Dannhauser, "Who's in the Home Office," *American Demographics,* June 1999, pp. 50–56; David Bouchier, "Working from Home, I Think," *New York Times,* January 20, 2002, PLI.13; John Fetto, "You *Can* Take It with You," *American Demographics*, February 2002, pp. 10–11; and Patrick Thibodeau, "Telecommuters Weather Storm," *Computerworld,* February 24, 2003, pp. 1, 16.

24. U.S. Census Bureau, "Women and Men in the United States," p. 3; and Peter Francese, "Top Trends for 2003," *American Demographics,* January 2003, pp. 48–51.

25. See Rebecca Piirto Heath, "The New Working Class," *American Demographics,* January 1998, pp. 51–55; *Digest of Education Statistics 1997,* National Center for Education Statistics, January 1998, at http://nces01.ed.gov/pubs/digest97; and U.S. Bureau of Labor Statistics, "Labor Force, Employment, and Earnings," p. 416, accessed at http://landview.census.gov/prod/2001pubs/statab/sec13.pdf, August 2003.

26. Karen Raugust, "Advertising Age's Multicultural Guide," *Advertising Age,* November 4, 2002, pp. M1–M3; Peter Francese, "Top Trends for 2003," *American Demographics,* January 2003, pp. 48–51; Alison Stein Wellner, "The Next 25 Years," American Demographics, April 2003, pp. 23–27; and U.S. Census Bureau reports accessed online at www.census.gov, August 2003.

27. Adapted from an example in Laurel Wentz, "Bank of America Goes Multicultural," *Advertising Age,* April 15, 2002, p. 3. Also see Shawn Tully, "Bank of the Americas," Fortune, April 14, 2003, pp. 145–148.

28. The Ford, Miller, and Avis examples are adapted from Dianne Solis, "Mainstream Marketing Increasing Gay Themes in Ads," *The Raleigh News and Observer,* August 8, 2003, pp. 2D, 6D. For other examples, see Laura Koss-Feder, "Out and About," *Marketing News,* May 25, 1998, pp. 1, 20; Jennifer Gilbert, "Ad Spending Booming for Gay-Oriented Sites," *Advertising Age,* December 6, 1999, p. 58; John Fetto, "In Broad Daylight," *American Demographics,* February 2001, pp. 16, 20; Robert Sharoff, "Diversity in the Mainstream," *Marketing News*, May 21, 2001, pp. 1, 13; David Goetzl, "Showtime, MTV Gamble on Gay Net," *Advertising Age,* January 14, 2002, p. 4; Kristi Nelson, "Canada's Gay TV Network Gets Ready for U.S.," *Electronic Media,* Chicago, May 6, 2002; and Sandra Yin, "Coming Out in Print," *American Demographics,* February 2003, pp. 18–21.

29. For these and other examples, see "Marketing to Americans with Disabilities," *Packaged Facts,* New York, 1997; Dan Frost, "The Fun Factor: Marketing Recreation to the Disabled," *American Demographics*, February 1998, pp. 53–58; Michelle Wirth Fellman, "Selling IT Goods to Disabled End-Users," *Marketing News,* March 15, 1999, pp. 1, 17; Alison Stein Wellner, "The Internet's Nest Niche," *American Demographics,* September 2000, pp. 18–19; Alan Hughes, "Taking the 'Dis' Out of Disability," *Black Enterprise,* March 2002, p. 102; and information accessed online at Volkswagen's Web site (www.vw.com), August 2002.

30. Alison Stein Wellner, "The Next 25 Years," *American Demographics,* April 2003, pp. 23–27.

31. James W. Hughes, "Understanding the Squeezed Consumer," *American Demographics,* July 1991, pp. 43–50. For more on consumer spending trends, see Cheryl Russell, "The New Consumer Paradigm," *American Demographics*, April 1999, pp. 50–58.

32. For an excellent summary, see Michael J. Weiss, "Inconspicuous Spending," *American Demographics,* April 2002, pp. 31–39.

33. See Alison Stein Wellner, "The Money in the Middle," *American Demographics,* April 2000, pp. 56–64; and Wellner, "The Wealth Effect," *American Demographics*, January 2003, p. 35.

34. Debra Goldman, "Paradox of Pleasure," *American Demographics*, May 1999, pp. 50–53. Also see Kate Fitzgerald, "Luxury Marketing," *Advertising Age*, August 14, 2000, pp. S1, S6.

35. David Leonhardt, "Two-Tier Marketing," *Business Week*, March 17, 1997, pp. 82–90. Also see "Market Looks: The U.S. Affluent Market," a research report by Packaged Facts, January 1, 2002; and Rebecca Gardyn, "Love Richly," *American Demographics*, April 2003, pp. 16–18.

36. For more discussion, see the "Environmentalism" section in Chapter 16. Also see Stuart L. Hart, "Beyond Greening: Strategies for a Sustainable World," *Harvard Business Review*, January–February 1997, pp. 67–76; "Earth in the Balance," *American Demographics*, January 2001, p. 24; Subhabrata Bobby Banerjee, "Corporate Environmentalism: The Construct and Its Measurement," *Journal of Business Research*, March 2002, pp. 177–191; Marc Gunther, "Tree Huggers, Soy Lovers, and Profits," *Fortune*, June 23, 2003, pp. 98–104; and information accessed online at www.3m.com and www.mcdonalds.com, August 2003.

37. See "U.S. RD Spending up 3.4%," *Research Technology Management*, March–April 2003, p. 8.

38. A.J. Vogl, "Does It Pay to Be Good?" *Across the Board*, January/February 2003, pp. 16–23.

39. For more on online privacy, see William M. Savino, "Protecting Online Privacy," *Marketing Management*, September–October 2002, pp. 49–51; Deborah L. Vence, "Marketers Expect to See Federal Law on Online Privacy Soon," *Marketing News*, June 24, 2002, p. 4; and Eric Goldman, "The Internet Privacy Fallacy," *Computer and Internet Lawyer*, January 2003, p. 20.

40. See Kevin T. Higgins, "Marketing with a Conscience," *Marketing Management*, July–August 2002, pp. 12–15; Sonoo Singh, "Success Is All in a Good Cause," *Marketing Week*, April 10, 2003, pp. 28–19; Linda I. Nowak and T.K. Clarke, "Cause-Related Marketing: Keys to Successful Relationships with Corporate Sponsors," *Journal of Nonprofit Public Sector Marketing*, 2003, pp. 137–149; and "Cause-Related Marketing Comes of Age in 2003," accessed online at www.porternovelli.com, April 2003.

41. For more on Yankelovich Monitor, see http://secure.yankelovich.com/solutions/monitor/y-monitor.asp.

42. Portions of this example are adapted from information in Eileen Daspin, "The End of Nesting," *Wall Street Journal*, May 16, 2003, p. W1. Also see "The Cocoon Cracks Open," *Brandweek*, April 28, 2003, pp. 32–36.

43. See Jesse Wong and Erik Guyot, "Asian Flag Maker Says Old Glory Means New Cash," *Wall Street Journal*, October 15, 2001, p. A19; and Paula Szuchman, "Stars, Stripes . . . and Lines," *Wall Street Journal*, May 23, 2003, p. W1.

44. For these and other examples, see Patricia Callahan and Amy Merrick, "Greeting-Card Firms Hasten to Serve Nation's New Mood—Sales Surge Shifts Focus to Patriotism, but Taste Remains Paramount Concern," *Wall Street Journal*, October 4, 2001; William Grimes, "On Menus Everywhere, A Big Slice of Patriotism," *New York Times*, October 24, 2001, p. F1; "What's Hot: Patriotism," *Dsn Retailing Today*, January 7, 2002, p. 23; Eleena de Lisser, "Shoes, Diapers Salute the Flag," *Wall Street Journal*, February 5, 2002, p. B1; and Karen Springen, "Glory Days," *Newsweek*, February 11, 2002, p. 10.

45. Steve Jarvis, "Red, White, and Blues," *Marketing News*, May 27, 2002, pp. 1, 9; and Alison Stein Wellner, "The Perils of Patriotism," *American Demographics*, September 2002, pp. 49–51.

46. See Debbie Howell, "Health Food, Like Bell Bottoms, Puts Mojo Back in Mass," *DSN Retailing Today*, April 16, 2001, pp. 21–22; Victoria Furness, "McDonald's Organic Bid to Lure Customers," *Marketing Week*, January 9, 2003, p. 5; and *Lisa Van Der Pool*, "Soy-Milk Sales Boom Leads to First TV ads," *Adweek*, March 3, 2003, p. 14.

47. Myra Stark, "Celestial Season," *Brandweek*, November 16, 1998, pp. 25–26. Also see Pamela Paul, "Convictions and Contradictions," *American Demographics*, June 2002, p. 17; Paul, "Religious Identity and Mobility," *American Demographics*, March 2003, pp. 20–21; and J. Walker Smith, "Marketing That's Good for the Soul," *Marketing Management*, January–February 2003, p. 52.

48. See Philip Kotler, *Kotler on Marketing* (New York: Free Press, 1999), p. 3; and Kotler, *Marketing Insights from A to Z* (Hoboken, NJ: Wiley, 2003), pp. 23–24.

49. See Carl P. Zeithaml and Valerie A. Zeithaml, "Environmental Management: Revising the Marketing Perspective," *Journal of Marketing*, Spring 1984, pp. 46–53.

50. Howard E. Butz, Jr. and Leonard D. Goodstein, "Measuring Customer Value: Gaining the Strategic Advantage," *Organizational Dynamics*, Winter 1996, pp. 66–67.

Chapter 4

1. See "Coke 'Family' Sales Fly as New Coke Stumbles," *Advertising Age*, January 17, 1986, p. 1; Jack Honomichl, "Missing Ingredients in 'New' Coke's Research," *Advertising Age*, July 22, 1985, p. 1; Rick Wise, "Why Things Go Better with Coke," *The Journal of Business Strategy*, January–February 1999, pp. 15–19; Catherine Fredman, "Smart People, Stupid Choices," *Chief Executive*, August/September 2002, pp. 64–68; "Special Issue: Top-10 U.S. Carbonated Soft Drink Companies and Brands for 2002," *Beverage Digest*, February 24, 2003, accessed at www.beverage-digest.com/pdf/top-10_2003.pdf; and "The Real Story of New Coke" accessed online at www.coca-cola.com, August 2003.

2. Christina Le Beau, "Mountains to Mine," *American Demographics*, August 2000, pp. 40–44. Also see David Shenk, *Data Smog: Surviving the Information Glut* (San Francisco: HarperSanFrancisco, 1997); Diane Trommer, "Information Overload—Study Finds Intranet Users Overwhelmed with Data," *Electronic Buyers' News*, April 20, 1998, p. 98; and Julie Schlosser, "Looking for Intelligence in Ice Cream," *Fortune*, March 17, 2003, pp. 114–120.

3. Alice LaPlante, "Still Drowning!" *Computer World*, March 10, 1997, pp. 69–70; and Jennifer Jones, "Looking Inside," *InfoWorld*, January 7, 2002, pp. 22–26.

4. See Philip Kotler, *Marketing Insights from A to Z* (Hoboken, NJ: Wiley, 2003), pp. 80–82.

5. See Geoffrey Brewer, "The Customer Stops Here," *Sales Marketing Management*, March 1998, pp. 31–36; Andy Patrizio, "Home-Grown CRM," *Insurance Technology*, February 2001, pp. 49–50; and "USAA," *Hoover Company Capsules*, Austin, May 15, 2003.

6. James Curtis, "Behind Enemy Lines," *Marketing*, May 24, 2001, pp. 28–29.

7. Robert O'Harrow Jr., "Oracle Admits to Probe; Company Paid for Dirt on Microsoft," *The Washington Post*, June 29, 2000, p. E1; and Andy Serwer, "PG's Covert Operation," *Fortune*, September 17, 2001, pp. 42–44.

8. Adapted from information in Ellen Neuborne, "Know Thy Enemy," *Sales Marketing Management*, January 2003, pp. 29–33.

9. James Curtis, "Behind Enemy Lines," pp. 28–29.

10. For more on research firms that supply marketing information, see Jack Honomichl, "Honomichl 50," special section, *Marketing News*, June 10, 2002, pp. H1–H43.

11. Example adapted from Douglas McGray, "Babes in RD Toyland," *Fast Company*, December 2002, p. 46.

12. Alison Stein Wellner, "Watch Me Now," *American Demographics*, October 2002, pp. S1–S4.

13. For more on ethnographic research, see Lawrence Osborne, "Consuming Rituals of the Suburban Tribe," *New York Times*, January 13, 2002,

p. 6.29; Gerry Khermouch, "Consumers in the Mist," *Business Week,* February 26, 2001, p. 92; Tim Henderson, "Shopping Guinea Pigs," *Stores,* December 2002, p. 8; and Ju Long, Kerem Tomak, and Andrew B. Whinston, "Calling All Customers," *Marketing News,* January 20, 2003, pp. 18–22.

14. Example adapted from Alison Stein Wellner, "The New Science of Focus Groups," *American Demographics,* March 2003, pp. 29–33.

15. See "Cybersurveys Come of Age," *Marketing Research,* Spring 2003, pp. 32–37.

16. Adapted from examples in Gary H. Anthes, "Smile, You're on Candid Computer," *Computerworld,* December 3, 2001, p. 50; Brandon Mercer, "Can Computers Read Your Mind?" *Techlive,* May 29, 2002, accessed at www.techtv.com/news/computing/story/0,24195,3386341,00.html; and "Creating Computers that Know How You Feel: Blue Eyes," accessed at www.almaden.ibm.com/cs/BlueEyes/index.html, July 2003.

17. Kate Maddox, "CRM to Outpace Other IT Spending," *B to B,* March 11, 2002, pp. 2, 33.

18. See Marc L. Songini, "FedEx Expects CRM System to Deliver," *Computerworld,* November 6, 2000, p. 10. The Marks Spencer example is adapted from "SAS Outfits Marks Spencer with Customer Intelligence," accessed at www.sas.com/success/marksandspencer.html, August 2003.

19. Darrell K. Rigby, "Avoid the Four Perils of CRM," *Harvard Business Review,* February 2002, pp. 101–109.

20. Michael Krauss, "At Many Firms, Technology Obscures CRM," *Marketing News,* March 18, 2002, p. 5.

21. Robert McLuhan, "How to Reap the Benefits of CRM," *Marketing,* May 24, 2001, p. 35; Sellar, "Dust Off That Data," p. 72; and Stewart Deck, "Data Mining," *Computerworld,* March 29, 1999, p. 76. Also see Eric Almquist, Carla Heaton, and Nick Hall, "Making CRM Make Money," *Marketing Management,* May–June 2002, pp. 16–21; "Six Changes in CRM," *Selling Power,* source book, 2003, pp. 26–30.

22. Ravi Kalakota and Marcia Robinson, *E-Business: Roadmap for Success* (Reading, MA: Addison-Wesley, 1999); and "Maximizing Relationships," *Chain Store Age,* August 2001, pp. 21A–23A.

23. "Business Bulletin: Studying the Competition," *Wall Street Journal,* March 19, 1995, pp. A1, A5.

24. Alison Stein Wellner, "Research on a Shoestring," *American Demographics,* April 2001, pp. 38–39. Also see "Bissell, Inc.," *Hoover Company Profiles,* Austin, May 15, 2003.

25. For some good advice on conducting market research in a small business, see "Marketing Research . . . Basics 101," accessed at www.onlinewbc.gov/docs/market/mkt_res_basics.html, June 2003; and "Researching Your Market," U.S. Small Business Administration, accessed at www.sba.gov/library/pubs/mt-8.doc, August 2003.

26. Jack Honomichl, "Honomichl Global 25," special section, *Marketing News,* August 19, 2002, pp. H3–H27; and the AC Nielsen Worldwide, accessed online at www.acnielsen.com/markets/, August 2003.

27. Many of the examples in this section, along with others, are found in Subhash C. Jain, *International Marketing Management,* 3d ed. (Boston: PWS-Kent, 1990), pp. 334–339. Ken Gofton, "Going Global with Research," *Marketing,* April 15, 1999, p. 35; Naresh K. Malhotra, *Marketing Research,* 3rd ed. (Upper Saddle River, NJ: Prentice Hall, 1999), chapter 23; Tim R.V. Davis and Robert B. Young, "International Marketing Research," *Business Horizons,* March–April 2002, pp. 31–38; and Warren J. Keegan, *Global Marketing Management,* 7th ed. (Upper Saddle River, NJ: Prentice Hall, 2002), chapter 6.

28. Jain, *International Marketing Management,* p. 338. Also see Alvin C. Burns and Ronald F. Bush, *Marketing Research,* 3d ed. (Upper Saddle River, NJ: Prentice Hall, 2000), pp. 317–318.

29. Steve Jarvis, "Status Quo = Progress," *Marketing News,* April 29, 2002, pp. 37–38.

30. See "DoubleClick Settles Online-Privacy Suits, Plans to Ensure Protections, Pay Legal Fees," *Wall Street Journal,* April 1, 2002, p. B8; and Yochi J. Dreazen, "The Best Way to Guard Your Privacy," *Wall Street Journal,* November 18, 2002, p. R4.

31. See Craig Frazier, "What Are Americans Afraid Of?" *American Demographics,* July 2001, pp. 43–49; Steve Jarvis, "CMOR Finds Survey Refusal Rate Still Rising," *Marketing News,* February 4, 2002, p. 4; and Peter Tuckel and Harry O'Neill, "The Vanishing Respondent in Telephone Surveys," *Journal of Advertising Research,* September–October 2002, pp. 26–48.

32. "ICC/ESOMAR International Code of Marketing and Social Research Practice," accessed at www.iccwbo.org/home/menu_advert_marketing.asp, June 2003.

33. Catherine Siskos, "In the Service of Guarding Secrets," *Kiplinger's Personal Finance,* February 2003, p. 26. Also see John Schwartz, "Chief Privacy Officers Forge Evolving Corporate Roles," *New York Times,* February 12, 2001, p. C1; J. Michael Pemberton, "Chief Privacy Officer: Your Next Career?" *Information Management Journal,* May–June 2002, pp. 57–58; and Edward Hurley, "Companies Creating More Chief Privacy Officer Jobs," January 15, 2003, accessed at http://searchsecurity.techtarget.com/originalContent/0,289142,sid14_g ci874297,00.html.

34. Schwartz, "Chief Privacy Officers Forge Evolving Corporate Roles," p. C1.

35. Cynthia Crossen, "Studies Galore Support Products and Positions, but Are They Reliable?" *Wall Street Journal,* November 14, 1991, pp. A1, A9. Also see Allan J. Kimmel, "Deception in Marketing Research and Practice: An Introduction," *Psychology and Marketing,* July 2001, pp. 657–661.

Chapter 5

1. Quotes and other information from Greg Schneider, "Rebels with Disposable Income; Aging Baby Boomers Line Up to Buy High-End Versions of Youthful Indulgences," *The Washington Post,* April 27, 2003, p. F1; Richard A. Melcher, "Tune-Up Time for Harley," *Business Week,* April 8, 1997, pp. 90–94; Ian P. Murphy, "Aided by Research, Harley Goes Whole Hog," *Marketing News,* December 2, 1996, pp. 16, 17; Ted Bolton, "Tattooed Call Letters: The Ultimate Test of Brand Loyalty," accessed online at www.boltonresearch.com, April 2003; "Harley-Davidson, Inc.," *Hoover Company Profiles,* Austin, May 15, 2003; and the Harley-Davidson Web site at www.Harley-Davidson.com, August 2003.

2. World POPClock, U.S. Census Bureau, www.census.gov, July 2003. This Web site provides continuously updated projections of the U.S. and world populations.

3. Brad Weiners, "Getting Inside—Way Inside—Your Customer's Head," *Business 2.0,* April 2003, pp. 54–55.

4. Statistics from Joan Raymond, "¿Tienen Numeros?" *American Demographics,* March 2002, pp. 22–25; U.S. Census Bureau reports accessed online at www.census.gov, March 2003; Eduardo Porter, "Buying Power of Hispanics Is Set to Soar," *Wall Street Journal,* April 18, 2003, p. B1; and Allison Stein Wellner, "The Next 25 Years," *American Demographics,* April 2003, pp. 24–27.

5. See Roberta Bernstein, "Food for Thought," *American Demographics,* May 2000, pp. 39–42; Jack Neff, "Suavitel Generates Waft of Success," *Advertising Age,* February 21, 2000, p. S4; Catherine P. Taylor, "BarbieLatina Says 'Hola' to Net," *Advertising Age,* October 1, 2001, p. 54; Laurel Wentz, "Doors Opening Wide," *Advertising Age,* May 6, 2002, p. 24; and Rebecca Garden and John Fetto, "Race, Ethnicity, and

the Way We Shop," *American Demographics*, February, 2003, pp. 30–33.

6. Calmetta Y. Coleman, "Attention Shoppers: Target Makes a Play for Minority Group Sears Has Cultivated," *Wall Street Journal*, April 12, 1999, p. A1; Robert Sharoff, "Diversity in the Mainstream," *Marketing News*, May 21, 2001, pp. 1, 13+; and Cecile B. Corral, "Sear Habla Espanol, ¿y Usted?" *Home Textiles Today*, February 3, 2003.

7. "The U.S. African American Market," Packaged Facts, January 2002; Garden and Fetto, "Race, Ethnicity, and the Way We Shop," p. 31; and U.S. Census Bureau reports accessed online at www.census.gov, August 2003.

8. See Steve Jarvis, "Ethnic Sites Draw New Ad Wave," *Marketing News*, August 5, 2002; pp. 4, 6; information accessed at www.BlackPlanet.com, July 2003; and a list of the most popular African American Web sites at www.freemaninstitute.com/AfAmSites.htm, August 2003.

9. Drawn from U.S. Census Bureau reports accessed online at www.census.gov, July 2003; Garden and Fetto, "Race, Ethnicity, and the Way We Shop," p. 31; and Wellner, "The Next 25 Years," p. 26.

10. Information for this example from Louise Lee, "Speaking the Customer's Language—Literally," *Business Week*, September 25, 2000, p. 178; and Hassan Fattah, "Asia Rising," *American Demographics*, July–August 2002, pp. 38–43.

11. See Peter Francese, "Older and Wealthier," *American Demographics*, November 2002, pp. 40–41; and Wellner, "The Next 25 Years," pp. 24–27.

12. See D. Allen Kerr, "Where There's Gray, There's Green," *Marketing News*, May 25, 1998, p. 2; "Fewer Seniors in the 1990s but Their Ranks Are Set to Explode," *Business Week*, May 28, 2001, p. 30; Laura Petrecca, "Savvy, Aging Boomers Buy into Pharma Mantra," *Advertising Age*, July 8, 2002, pp. S8–S9; and Peter Francese, "Consumers Today," *American Demographics*, April 2003, pp. 28–29.

13. For more on social class, see Leon G. Schiffman and Leslie L. Kanuk, *Consumer Behavior*; Terrell G. Williams, "Social Class Influences on Purchase Evaluation Criteria," *Journal of Consumer Marketing*, vol. 19, no. 2/3, 2002, pp. 248–276; and Michael R. Solomon, *Consumer Behavior*, 5th ed. (Upper Saddle River, NJ: Prentice Hall, 2002), chapter 13.

14. See Edward Keller and Jonathan Berry, *The Influentials* (New York: Free Press, 2003); "The Chattering Class," *Fast Company*, January 2003, p. 48; and information found at www.amazon.com, July 2003.

15. Daniel Eisenberg and Laura Bradford, "It's an Ad, Ad, Ad, Ad World," *Time*, September 2, 2002, pp. 38–41.

16. Example adapted from Michael Witte, "Buzz-z-z Marketing," *Business Week*, July 30, 2001, pp. 50–56. For other examples, see Alf Nucifora, "Keeping Up with the Buzz on Buzz Marketing," December 2, 2002, accessed online at www.bizjournals.com.

17. See Darla Dernovsek, "Marketing to Women," *Credit Union Magazine*, October 2000, pp. 90–96; Sharon Goldman Edry, "No Longer Just Fun and Games," *American Demographics*, May 2001, pp. 36–38; Hillary Chura, "Marketing Messages for Women Fall Short," *Advertising Age*, September 23, 2002, pp. 4, 14–15; and Jennifer Pendleton, "Ford at 100: Targeting the Female Market," *Advertising Age*, March 31, 2003, F38–F40.

18. Adapted from information in Bruce Upbin, "Merchant Princes," *Forbes*, January 20, 2003, pp. 52–56.

19. Example drawn from Karl Greenberg, "The Kids Stay in the Future," *Brandweek*, March 31, 2003.

20. Tobi Elkin, "Sony Marketing Aims at Lifestyle Segments," *Advertising Age*, March 18, 2002, pp. 3, 72; and Kenneth Hein, "When Is Enough Enough?" *Brandweek*, December 2, 2002, pp. 26–28.

21. See Rebecca Piirto, "Measuring Minds in the 1990s," *American Demographics*, December 1990, pp. 35–39; Rebecca Piirto, "VALS the Sec-

ond Time," *American Demographics*, July 1991, p. 6; and www.sric-bi.com/VALS/projects.shtml, July 2003. For good discussions of other lifestyle topics, see Solomon, *Consumer Behavior*, chapter 6.

22. Accessed at www.forrester.com/Technographics/0,6438,,FF.html, July 2003.

23. Jennifer Aaker, "Dimensions of Measuring Brand Personality," *Journal of Marketing Research*, August 1997, pp. 347–356. Also see Aaker, "The Malleable Self: The Role of Self Expression in Persuasion," *Journal of Marketing Research*, May 1999, pp. 45–57; and Swee Hoon Ang, "Personality Influences on Consumption: Insights from the Asian Economic Crisis," *Journal of International Consumer Marketing*, 2001, pp. 5–20.

24. Charles Pappas, "Ad Nauseam," *Advertising Age*, July 10, 2000, pp. 16–18.

25. Bob Garfield, "'Subliminal' Seduction and Other Urban Myths," *Advertising Age*, September 18, 2000, pp. 4, 105.

26. Jill Venter, "Milk Mustache Campaign Is a Hit with Teens," *St. Louis Post-Dispatch*, April 1, 1998, p. E1; Gay Verne, "Milk, the Magazine," *American Demographics*, February 2000, pp. 32–33; Rebecca Flass, "California Processors Vote to Continue 'Got Milk,'" *Adweek*, March 26, 2001, p. 5; Kate Fitzgerald, "Milk Tailors Effort to Teens," *Advertising Age*, February 18, 2002, p. 16; Rebecca Flass, "'Got Milk?' Takes a Serious Look Inside the Body," *Adweek*, January 27, 2003, p. 5; Katie Koppenhoefer, "MilkPEP Ads Make Big Impact with Hispanics," press release, International Dairy Foods Association, March 3, 2003, accessed at www.idfa.org/news/gotmilk/2003/milkpepads.cfm; and information from www.whymilk.com, August 2003.

27. See Leon Festinger, *A Theory of Cognitive Dissonance* (Stanford, CA: Stanford University Press, 1957); Schiffman and Kanuk, *Consumer Behavior*, pp. 219–220; Jeff Stone, "A Radical New Look at Cognitive Dissonance," *American Journal of Psychology*, Summer 1998, pp. 319–326; Thomas R. Schultz, Elene Leveille, and Mark R. Lepper, "Free Choice and Cognitive Dissonance Revisited: Choosing 'Lesser Evils' Versus 'Greater Goods,'" *Personality and Social Psychology Bulletin*, January 1999, pp. 40–48; Jillian C. Sweeney, Douglas Hausknecht, and Geoffrey N. Soutar, "Cognitive Dissonance after Purchase: A Multidimensional Scale," *Psychology Marketing*, May 2000, pp. 369–385; and Patti Williams and Jennifer L. Aaker, "Can Mixed Emotions Peacefully Coexist?" March 2002, pp. 636–649.

28. The following discussion draws from Everett M. Rogers, *Diffusion of Innovations*, 4th ed. (New York: Free Press, 1995). Also see Peter J. Danaher, Bruce G. S. Hardie, and William P. Putsis, "Marketing-Mix Variables and the Diffusion of Successive Generations of a Technological Innovation," *Journal of Marketing Research*, November 2001, pp. 501–514; Eric Waarts, Yvonne M. van Everdingen, and Jos van Hillegersberg, "The Dynamics of Factors Affecting the Adoption of Innovations," *Journal of Product Innovation Management*, November 2002, pp. 412–423; and Jae H. Pae and Donald R. Lehmann, "Multigeneration Innovation Diffusion," *Academy of Marketing Science Journal*, Winter 2003, pp. 36–45.

29. See Kate Macarthur, "Teflon Togs Get $40 Million Ad Push," *Advertising Age*, April 8, 2002, p. 3; and "Neat Pants for Sloppy People," *Consumer Reports: Publisher's Edition Including Supplemental Guides*, May 2003, p. 10.

30. Sarah Lorge, "Purchasing Power," *Sales Marketing Management*, June 1998, pp. 43–46.

31. Patrick J. Robinson, Charles W. Faris, and Yoram Wind, *Industrial Buying Behavior and Creative Marketing* (Boston: Allyn Bacon, 1967). Also see Erin Anderson, Weyien Chu, and Barton Weitz, "Industrial Purchasing: An Empirical Exploration of the Buyclass

Framework," *Journal of Marketing*, July 1987, pp. 71–86; Michael D. Hutt and Thomas W. Speh, *Business Marketing Management*, 7th ed. (Upper Saddle River, NJ: Prentice Hall, 2001), pp. 56–66; and Junyean Moon and Surinder Tikoo, "Buying Decision Approaches of Organizational Buyers and Users," *Journal of Business Research*, April 2002, pp. 293–299.

32. See "BJ's Knows . . . Our System Is Their Solution," *Insights*, March 2002, p. 1; and information accessed online at www.chemstation.com, August 2003.

33. Thomas V. Bonoma, "Major Sales: Who Really Does the Buying," *Harvard Business Review*, May–June 1982, p. 114. Also see Ajay Kohli, "Determinants of Influence in Organizational Buying: A Contingency Approach," *Journal of Marketing*, July 1989, pp. 50–65; and Jeffrey E. Lewin, "The Effects of Downsizing on Organizational Buying Behavior: An Empirical Investigation," *Academy of Marketing Science*, Spring 2001, pp. 151–164.

34. Robinson, Faris, and Wind, *Industrial Buying Behavior*, p. 14.

35. Unless otherwise noted, quotes and spending information in this section are from Michael A. Verespej, "E-Procurement Explosion," *Industry Week,* March 2002, pp. 24–28; "E-Procurement Still Less Popular than Paper Orders," *Supply Management,* March 13, 2003, p. 10; and Jennifer Baljko, "Online Purchasing Activity on the Rise—But OEM Cost-Cutting Initiatives Are Limiting Process Changes," *EBN*, April 21, 2003, p. 6.

36. See Verespej, "E-Procurement Explosion," pp. 25–28; "E-Procurement: Certain Value in Changing Times," *Fortune,* April 30, 2001, pp. S2–S3; and Susan Avery, "Microsoft Moves Entire PC Buy Online, Saves 6%," *Purchasing* January 16, 2003, pp. 14–18.

Chapter 6

1. See Erin White and Sarah Ellison, "Unilever Ads Offer Tribute to Dirt," *Wall Street Journal,* June 2, 2003, p. B3; and information accessed online at www.pg.com and www.tide.com, July 2003.

2. These and other examples found in Nelson D. Schwartz, "Still Perking After All These Years," *Fortune*, May 24, 1999, pp. 203–210; and www.usaopoly.com, July 2003.

3. See Bruce Hager, "Podunk Is Beckoning," *Business Week*, December 2, 1991, p. 76; David Greisling, "The Boonies Are Booming," *Business Week*, October 9, 1995, pp. 104–110; Mike Duff, "Home Depot Drops Villager's Hardware for New Concept," *DSN Retailing Today*, April 22, 2002, pp. 5, 28; "Home Depot Lite," *Chain Store Age*, January 2002, p. 39; and Mike Troy, "Neighborhood Market Caps Year with Round of New Market Entries," *DSN Retailing Today*, January 27, 2003, pp. 3, 22.

4. Rob Turner, "Toothpaste for Women?" *Fortune,* March 3, 2003, p. 182; and information accessed online at www.olay.com, August 2003.

5. For these and other examples, see Patricia Sellers, "Gap's New Guy Upstairs," *Fortune,* April 24, 2003, pp. 110–116; Karen M. Kroll, "Plasma Video Screens Prove Customer Hit in Eddie Bauer," *Stores,* February 2001, pp. 74–75; and information accessed at www.crestkids.com and www.crest-re.com, July 2003.

6. See Hillary Chura, "Marketing Messages for Women Fall Short," *Advertising Age*, September 23, 2002, pp. 1, 14–15; Alice Z. Cuneo, "Advertisers Target Women, but Market Remains Elusive," *Advertising Age,* November 10, 1997, pp. 1, 24; and Bruce Upbin, "Merchant Princes," *Forbes*, January 20, 2003, pp. 52–56.

7. Michael McCarthy, "Marketers, NFL Focus on Game's Audience of 40 Million Women," *USA Today*, January 25, 2001, p. 1; Sam Walker, "Super Bowl XXXVI: The NFL Tackles Mom," *Wall Street Journal,* February 1, 2002, p. W1; and Isabel C. Gonzalez, "All-Star Fashion," *Time*, May 19, 2003, p. 83.

8. Michelle Orecklin, "What Women Watch," *Time,* May 13, 2002, pp. 65–66; and information accessed online at www.iVillage.com and www.oxygen.com, July 2003.

9. Information accessed at www.neimanmarcus.com/store/sitelets/incircle/index.jhtml, August 2003.

10. Brian Bremner, "Looking Downscale without Looking Down," *Business Week*, October 8, 1990, pp. 62–67; "Greyhound Lines, Inc.," *Hoover's Company Profiles,* Austin, May 15, 2003; Dan Hogsett, "Family Dollar Drives 1Q Profits," *Home Textiles Today*, January 14, 2002, p. 16; Debbie Howell, "Humbled Dollar General Rebounds with Verve," *DSN Retailing Today,* April 8, 2002, p. 7; and "Family Dollar Stores, Inc.," *Hoover's Company Profiles,* Austin, May 15, 2003.

11. Tracie Rozhon, "Setting Its Sights High, Levi's Aims Low with New Jeans," *New York Times*, October 31, 2002; and Sally Beatty, "Levi's Strives to Keep a Hip Image," *Wall Street Journal*, January 23, 2003, p. B12.

12. "Lifestyle Marketing," *Progressive Grocer*, August 1997, pp. 107–110; and Philip Kotler, *Marketing Management: Analysis, Planning, Implementation, and Control,* 11th ed. (Upper Saddle River, NJ: Prentice Hall, 2003), pp. 291–292.

13. "Scooter Wars," *Cycle World*, February 1998, p. 26; Laurie Freeman and Cleveland Horton, "Spree: Honda's Scooters Ride the Cutting Edge," *Advertising Age*, September 5, 1985, pp. 3, 35; Jonathon Welsh, "Transport: The Summer of the Scooter: Boomers Get a New Retro Toy," *Wall Street Journal*, April 13, 2001, p. W1; and Honda's Web site at www.hondamotorcycle.com/scooter, August 2003.

14. Information from www.kodak.com, August 2003.

15. See Jennifer Ordonez, "Cash Cows: Hamburger Joints Call Them 'Heavy Users,' " *Wall Street Journal*, January 12, 2000, p. A1; and Brian Wonsink and Sea Bum Park, "Methods and Measures that Profile Heavy Users," *Journal of Advertising Research*, July–August 2000, pp. 61–72.

16. Kendra Parker, "How Do You Like Your Beef?" *American Demographics*, January 2000, pp. 35–37.

17. Information about the PRIZM segmentation system accessed at http://cluster2.claritas.com/YAWYL/aboutprism.wjsp, July 2003. To look up specific ZIP codes, see http://cluster2.claritas.com/YAWYL/Default.wjsp?System=WL.

18. Daniel S. Levine, "Justice Served," *Sales Marketing Management*, May 1995, pp. 53–61.

19. For more on segmenting business markets, see James C. Anderson and James A. Narus, *Business Market Management* (Upper Saddle River, NJ: Prentice Hall, 1999), pp. 44–47; Andy Dexter, "Egotists, Idealists, and Corporate Animals—Segmenting Business Markets," *International Journal of Marketing Research,* First Quarter 2002, pp. 31–51; and Turan Senguder, "An Evaluation of Consumer and Business Segmentation Approaches," *Journal of the Academy of Business,* March 2003, pp. 618–624.

20. See Warren J. Keegan, *Global Marketing Management* (Upper Saddle River, NJ, 2002), p. 194; Arundhati Parmar, "Global Youth United," *Marketing News*, October 28, 2002, pp. 1, 49; the MTV Worldwide Web site, www.mtv.com/mtvinternational; and "MTV: Music Television: The Facts," accessed online at www.viacom.com/prodbyunit1.tin?ixBusUnit=19, July 2003.

21. See Michael Porter, *Competitive Advantage* (New York: Free Press, 1985), pp. 4–8, 234–236. For more recent discussions, see Leyland Pitt, "Total E-clipse: Five New Forces for Strategy in the Digital Age," *Journal of General Management,* Summer 2001, pp. 1–15; Stanley Slater and Eric Olson, "A Fresh Look at Industry and Market Analysis," *Business Horizons,* January–February 2002, pp. 15–22; and Kotler, *Marketing Management*, pp. 242–243.

22. Nina Munk, "Why Women Find Lauder Mesmerizing," *Fortune,* May 25, 1998, pp. 97–106; Christine Bittar, "New Faces, Same Name," *Brandweek,* March 11, 2002, pp. 28–34; and information accessed at www.elcompanies.com, August 2003.

23. Peter Burrows, "How to Milk an Apple," *Business Week,* February 3, 2003, p. 44.

24. Gerry Khermouch, "Call It the Pepsi Blue Generation," *Business Week,* February 3, 2003, p. 96.

25. Paul Davidson, "Entrepreneurs Reap Riches from Net Niches," *USA Today,* April 20, 1998, p. B3; and information accessed online at www.ostrichesonline.com, July 2003.

26. See Philip Kotler, *Kotler on Marketing* (New York: Free Press, 1999), pp. 149–150; and Faith Keenan, "A Mass Market of One," *Business Week,* December 2, 2002, pp. 68–72.

27. See Jerry Wind and Arvid Rangaswamy, "Customerization: The Next Revolution in Mass Customization," *Journal of Interactive Marketing,* Winter 2001, pp. 13–32; and Yoram Wind and Vijay Mahajan, "Convergence Marketing," *Journal of Interactive Marketing,* Spring 2002, pp. 64–69.

28. Sony A. Grier, "The Federal Trade Commission's Report on the Marketing of Violent Entertainment to Youths: Developing Policy-Tuned Research," *Journal of Public Policy and Marketing,* Spring 2001, pp. 123–132; and Greg Winter, "Tobacco Company Reneged on Youth Ads, Judge Rules," *New York Times,* June 7, 2002, p. A18. Also see Deborah L. Vence, "Marketing to Minors Still under Careful Watch," *Marketing News,* March 31, 2003, pp. 5–6.

29. See "PowerMaster," *Fortune,* January 13, 1992, p. 82; Herbert Rotfeld, "The FTC and Marketing Abuse," *Marketing News,* March 17, 1997, p. 4; and George G. Brenkert, "Marketing to Inner-City Blacks: Power-Master and Moral Responsibility," *Business Ethics Quarterly,* January 1998, pp. 1–18.

30. Joseph Turow, "Breaking Up America: The Dark Side of Target Marketing," *American Demographics,* November 1997, pp. 51–54; and Bette Ann Stead and Jackie Gilbert, "Ethical Issues in Electronic Commerce," *Journal of Business Ethics,* November 2001, pp. 75–85.

31. Adapted from a positioning map prepared by students Brian May, Josh Payne, Meredith Schakel, and Bryana Sterns, University of North Carolina, April 2003. SUV sales data furnished by WardAuto.com, June 2003. Price data from www.edmunds.com, June 2003.

32. See Kotler, *Kotler on Marketing,* pp. 59–63.

33. See Bobby J. Calder and Steven J. Reagan, "Brand Design," in Dawn Iacobucci, ed. *Kellogg on Marketing* (New York: Wiley, 2001) p. 61.

34. The Palm Pilot and Mountain Dew examples are from Alice M. Tybout and Brian Sternthal, "Brand Positioning," in Iacobucci, *Kellogg on Marketing,* p. 54.

Chapter 7

1. Excerpt adapted from Penelope Green, "Spiritual Cosmetics. No Kidding," *New York Times,* January 10, 1999, p. 1. Also see Elizabeth Wellington, "The Success of Smell," *The News Observer,* June 11, 2001, p. E1; Mary Tannen, "Cult Cosmetics," *New York Times Magazine,* Spring 2001, p. 96; Sandra Yin, "The Nose Knows," *American Demographics,* February 2002, pp. 14–15; and "Pots of Promise—The Beauty Business," *The Economist,* May 24, 2003, pp. 69–71.

2. Excerpt adapted from Toys R Us ad featured in *Playbill,* December 2002, with additional information from www.wirednewyork.com/toys_rus.htm, August 2003.

3. For more on experience marketing, see B. Joseph Pine and James H. Gilmore, *The Experience Economy* (New York: Free Press, 1999); Jane E. Zarem, "Experience Marketing," *Folio: The Magazine for Magazine Management,* Fall 2000, pp. 28–32; Scott Mac Stravic, "Make Impressions Last: Focus on Value," *Marketing News,* October 23, 2000, pp. 44–45; and Stephen E. DeLong, "The Experience Economy," *Upside,* November 2001, p. 28.

4. See Kate Fitzgerald, "Buick Rides the Tiger," *Advertising Age,* April 15, 2002, p. 41; and "He Sold Fame; We Bought It," *Los Angeles Times,* May 20, 2003, p. B14.

5. Check out the tourism Web pages of these states at www.TravelTex.com, www.michigan.org, and www.iloveny.state.ny.us.

6. See Philip Kotler, Irving J. Rein, and Donald Haider, *Marketing Places: Attracting Investment, Industry, and Tourism to Cities, States, and Nations* (New York: Free Press, 1993), pp. 202, 273. Additional information accessed at www.ireland.travel.ie and www.ida.ie, August 2003.

7. Accessed online at www.social-marketing.org/aboutus.html, August 2003.

8. See Alan R. Andreasen, Rob Gould, and Karen Gutierrez, "Social Marketing Has a New Champion," *Marketing News,* February 7, 2000, p. 38. Also see Philip Kotler, Ned Roberto, and Nacy Lee, *Social Marketing: Improving the Quality of Life,* 2nd ed. (Thousand Oaks, CA: Sage Publications, 2002); and www.social-marketing.org, August 2003.

9. Quotes and definitions from Philip Kotler, *Kotler on Marketing* (New York: Free Press, 1999), p. 17; and www.asq.org, August 2003.

10. See Roland T. Rust, Anthony J. Zahorik, and Timothy L. Keiningham, "Return on Quality (ROQ): Making Service Quality Financially Accountable," *Journal of Marketing,* April 1995, pp. 58–70; and Roland T. Rust, Christine Moorman, and Peter R. Dickson, "Getting Return on Quality: Revenue Expansion, Cost Reduction, or Both?" *Journal of Marketing,* October 2002, pp. 7–24.

11. Quote from Mike Musgrove, "Think Discontinued: Apple Retires Its Original iMac Line," *The Washington Post,* March 19, 2003, p. E2. Also see "Hot R.I.P.: The Floppy Disk," *Rolling Stone,* August 20, 1998, p. 86; Robert Dwek, "Apple Pushes Design to Core of Marketing," *Marketing Week,* January 24, 2002, p. 20; "John Markoff, "Apple Computer Beats Earnings Estimates in Second Quarter," *New York Times,* April 18, 2002, p. C7; and Chee Pearlman, "Designer of iMac Winds Designer of the Year Award," *New York Times,* June 5, 2003, p. 3.

12. Adapted from information found in Mark Schwanhausser, "Thinking Outside the Wallet," *The News Observer,* May 12, 2002, p. 12E; and "Discover on the Go," *Credit Card Management,* May 2002, p. 9. Additional information from "Best Products of 2002," *USAToday Online,* December 6, 2003, accessed at www.usatoday.com/money/2002-12-03-products.htm; and "Discover 2GO Card," accessed at www.discover2go.com, July 2003.

13. See Kate Fitzgerald, "Packaging Is the Capper," *Advertising Age,* May 5, 2003, p. 22.

14. Adapted from examples found in Julie Dunn, "Pouring Paint, Minus a Mess," *New York Times,* October 27, 2002, p. 3.2; "Look Ma, No Drip," *Business Week,* December 16, 2002, p. 74; and Seth Godin, "In Praise of the Purple Cow," *Fast Company,* February 2003, pp. 74–85.

15. Robert M. McMath, "Chock Full of (Pea)nuts," *American Demographics,* April 1997, p. 60. For more on packaging, see Robert L. Underwood, "The Communicative Power of Product Packaging: Creating Brand Identity via Lived and Mediate Experience," *Journal of Marketing Theory and Proactice,* Winter 2003, p. 62.

16. Bro Uttal, "Companies That Serve You Best," *Fortune,* December 7, 1987, p. 116; and American Customer Satisfaction Index ratings accessed at www.theasci.org, July 2003.

17. See "On Mother's Day, Advice Goes a Long Way," *PR Newswire,* Ziff Communications, May 2, 1995; Mike Campbell, "Floral Web Site Ends Online Stress," *Bank Marketing,* April 1999, p. 8; David L. Margulius, "Smarter Call Centers: At Your Service?" *New York Times,*

March 14, 2002, p. G1, and information found at www.1800flowers.com, July 2003.

18. Information accessed online at www.marriott.com, August 2003.

19. Information about PG's product lines accessed at www.pg.com and www.crest.com, August 2003. For more on product line strategy, see Robert Bordley, "Determining the Appropriate Depth and Breadth of a Firm's Product Portfolio," *Journal of Marketing Research,* February 2003, pp. 39–53.

20. See "McAtlas Shrugged," *Foreign Policy,* May–June 2001, pp. 26–37; and Philip Kotler, *Marketing Management,* 11th ed. (Upper Saddle River, NJ: Prentice Hall, 2003), p. 423.

21. Douglas Holt, "What Becomes an Icon Most?" *Harvard Business Review,* March 2003, pp. 43–49.

22. David C. Bello and Morris B. Holbrook, "Does an Absence of Brand Equity Generalize Across Product Classes?" *Journal of Business Research,* October 1995, p. 125; and Scott Davis, *Brand Asset Management: Driving Profitable Growth through Your Brands* (San Francisco: Jossey-Bass, 2000). Also see Kevin Lane Keller, *Building, Measuring, and Managing Brand Equity,* 2nd ed. (Upper Saddle River, NJ: Prentice Hall, 2003), chapter 2.

23. "Brands in an Age of Anti-Americanism," *Business Week,* August 4, 2003, pp. 69–78.

24. See Roland T. Rust, Valerie A. Zeithaml, and Katherine A. Lemon, *Driving Customer Equity* (New York Free Press, 2000); Rust, Lemon, and Zeithaml, "Where Should the Next Marketing Dollar Go?" *Marketing Management,* September–October 2001, pp. 24–28; Robert C. Blattberg, Gary Getz, and Jacquelyn S. Thomas, *Customer Equity* (Boston: Harvard Business School Press, 2001); and John E. Hogan, Katherine N. Lemon, and Roland T. Rust, "Customer Equity Management: Charting New Directions for the Future of Marketing," *Journal of Service Research,* August 2002, pp. 4–12.

25. See Davis, *Brand Asset Management*; and Kotler, *Marketing Management,* pp. 419–420.

26. Marc Gobe, *Emotional Branding* (New York: Allworth Press, 2001).

27. See Paul N. Bloom, Gregory T. Gundlach, and Joseph P. Cannon, "Slotting Allowances and Fees: School of Thought and the Views of Practicing Managers," *Journal of Marketing,* April 2000, pp. 92–108; Julie Forster, "The Hidden Cost of Shelf Space," *Business Week,* April 15, 2002, p. 103; William Wilkie, "Marketing Research and Public Policy: The Case of Slotting Fees," *Journal of Public Policy and Marketing,* Fall 2002, pp. 175–189; and Gene Epstein, "Envelope, Please," *Barron's,* November 4, 2002, p. 37.

28. Warren Thayer, "Loblaws Exec Predicts: Private Labels to Surge," *Frozen Food Age,* May 1996, p. 1; "President's Choice Continues Brisk Pace," *Frozen Food Age,* March 1998, pp. 17–18; David Dunne and Chakravarthi Narasimhan, "The New Appeal of Private Labels," *Harvard Business Review,* May–June 1999, pp. 41–52; "New Private Label Alternatives Bring Changes to Supercenters, Clubs," *Dsn Retailing Today,* February 5, 2001, p. 66; and "The President's Choice Story," accessed at www.presidentschoice.ca/products/pc_story.aspx, July 2003.

29. See "The Private Label Connection," *Beverage Industry,* February 2003, p. 48; and Shelley Branch, "Going Private (Label)," *Wall Street Journal,* June 12, 2003, p. B1.

30. See Doug Desjardins, "Popularized Entertainment Icons Continue to Dominate Licensing," *Dsn Retailing Today,* July 9, 2001, p. 4; Patricia Winters Lauro, "Licensing Deals Are Putting Big Brand Name into New Categories at the Supermarket," *New York Times,* June 18, 2002, p. C14; Derek Manson, "Spidy Cents," *Money,* July 2002, p. 40; Tobi Elkin, "Mopping Up the Licensing Buck," *Advertising Age,* March 24, 2003, p. S4; and David D. Kirkpatrick, "A New Sign on Harry's Forehead: For Sale," *New York Times,* June 16, 2003, p. 1.

31. See Terry Lefton, "Warner Brothers' Not Very Looney Path to Licensing Gold," *Brandweek,* February 14, 1994, pp. 36–37; Robert Scally, "Warner Builds Brand Presence, Strengthens 'Tunes' Franchise," *Discount Store News,* April 6, 1998, p. 33; "Looney Tunes Launched on East Coast," *Dairy Foods,* April 2001, p. 9; "Looney Tunes Entering 696 Publix Super Markets," *Dairy Foods,* April 2002, p. 11; and Tobi Elkin, "Struggling Toy Industry Looks to Licensing," *Advertising Age,* February 17, 2003, pp. 4, 36.

32. See Laura Petrecca, "'Corporate Brands' Put Licensing in the Spotlight," *Advertising Age,* June 14, 1999, p. 1; and Bob Vavra, "The Game of the Name," *Supermarket Business,* March 15, 2001, pp. 45–46.

33. Phil Carpenter, "Some Cobranding Caveats to Obey," *Marketing News,* November 7, 1994, p. 4; Gabrielle Solomon, "Co-Branding Alliances: Arranged Marriages Made by Marketers," *Fortune,* October 12, 1998, p. 188; "Kmart Licensing Will Continue," *New York Times,* March 21, 2002, p. C5; and Michael Barbaro, "Indictment Tests Shoppers' Loyalty," *The Washington Post,* June 5, 2003, p. E1.

34. For more on the use of line and brand extensions and consumer attitudes toward them, see Deborah Roedder John, Barbara Loken, and Christopher Joiner, "The Negative Impact of Extensions: Can Flagship Brands Be Eroded?" *Journal of Marketing,* January 1998, pp. 19–32; Zeynep Gurrhan-Canli and Durairaj Maheswaran, "The Effects of Extensions on Brand Name Dilution and Enhancement," *Journal of Marketing,* November 1998, pp. 464–473; Vanitha Swaminathan, Richard J. Fox, and Srinivas K. Reddy, "The Impact of Brand Extension Introduction on Choice," *Journal of Marketing,* October 2001, pp. 1–15; Kalpesh Kaushik Desai and Kevin Lane Keller, "The Effect of Ingredient Branding Strategies on Host Brand Extendibility," *Journal of Marketing,* January 2002, pp. 73–93; and Subramanian Balachander and Sanjoy Ghose, "Reciprocal Spillover Effects: A Strategic Benefit of Brand Extensions," *Journal of Marketing,* January 2003, pp. 4–13.

35. "Top 200 Megabrands," accessed at www.adage.com, June 2003.

36. See Kevin Lane Keller, "The Brand Report Card," *Harvard Business Review,* January 2000, pp. 147–157; and Keller, *Strategic Brand Management,* pp. 766–767.

37. Steve Jarvis, "Refocus, Rebuild, Reeducate, Refine, Rebrand," *Marketing News,* March 26, 2001, pp. 1, 11; and "Top 10 Wireless Phone Brands," *Advertising Age,* June 24, 2002, p. S-18.

38. See Ronald Henkoff, "Service Is Everybody's Business," *Fortune,* June 27, 1994, pp. 48–60; Valerie Zeithaml and Mary Jo Bitner, *Services Marketing,* 3rd ed. (New York: McGraw-Hill, 2002), pp. 8–9; and Margaret Popper, "Services: Slowed but Still Strong," *Business Week,* December 12, 2002, accessed online at www.businessweek.com.

39. Adapted from information in Leonard Berry and Neeli Bendapudi, "Clueing in Customers," *Harvard Business Review,* February 2003, pp. 100–106.

40. See James L. Heskett, Thomas O. Jones, Gary W. Loveman, W. Earl Sasser Jr., and Leonard A. Schlesinger, "Putting the Service-Profit Chain to Work," *Harvard Business Review,* March–April, 1994, pp. 164–174; James L. Heskett, W. Earl Sasser Jr., and Leonard A. Schlesinger, *The Service Profit Chain: How Leading Companies Link Profit and Growth to Loyalty, Satisfaction, and Value* (New York: Free Press, 1997); and Heskett, Sasser, and Schlesinger, *The Value Profit Chain: Treat Employees Like Customers and Customers Like Employees* (New York: Free Press, 2003).

41. See Louise Lee, "Schwab vs. Wall Street," *Business Week,* June 3, 2002, pp. 65–71.

42. For discussions of service quality, see A. Parasuraman, Valerie A. Zeithaml, and Leonard L. Berry, "A Conceptual Model of Service Quality and Its Implications for Future Research," *Journal of Marketing,* Fall 1985, pp. 41–50; Zeithaml, Berry, and Parasuraman, "The Behavioral

Consequences of Service Quality," *Journal of Marketing,* April 1996, pp. 31–46; Thomas J. Page Jr., "Difference Scores Versus Direct Effects in Service Quality Measurement," *Journal of Service Research,* February 2002, pp. 184–192; Richard A. Spreng; James J. Jiang, Gary Klein, and Christopher L. Carr, "Measuring Information System Service Quality: SERVQUAL from the Other Side," *MIS Quarterly,* June 2002, pp. 145–166; and Y. H. Hung, M. L. Huang, and K. S. Chen, "Service Quality Evaluation by Service Quality Performance Matrix," *Total Quality Management Business Excellence,* January 2003, pp. 79–89.

43. See James L. Heskett, W. Earl Sasser Jr., and Christopher W. L. Hart, *Service Breakthroughs* (New York: Free Press, 1990).

44. See Paula Mergenbagen, "Product Liability: Who Sues?" *American Demographics*, June 1995, p. 48; "A Primer on Product Liability Laws," *Purchasing,* May 6, 1999, pp. 32–34; Pamela L. Moore, "The Litigation Machine," *Business Week,* January 29, 2001, pp. 115–123; and "Jury Awards in Product Liability Cases Increasing in Recent Years," *Chemical Market Reporter,* February 12, 2001, p. 5.

45. See James A. Bruen, "Product Liability: The Role of the Product Steward," *Risk Management,* February 2002, p. 34.

46. See Philip Cateora, *International Marketing,* 8th ed. (Homewood, IL: Irwin, 1993), p. 270; David Fairlamb, "One Currency—But 15 Economies," *Business Week,* December 31, 2001, p. 59; and www. walkabouttravelgear.com, July 2003.

47. Information accessed online at www.deutsche-bank.com, August 2003.

48. Information accessed online at www.interpublic.com and www. mccann.com, July 2003.

49. See Mike Troy, "The Super Growth Leaders—Wal-Mart: Global Dominance Puts Half Trillion in Sight," *DSN Retailing Today,* December 10, 2001, p. 17; "Wal-Mart International Operations," accessed at www.walmartstores.com, August 2003; and "Top 200 Global Retailers," *Stores,* January 2003, accessed at www.stores.org.

Chapter 8

1. Quotes, extracts, and other information from Jay Greene, "Microsoft: How It Became Stronger Than Ever," *Business Week,* June 4, 2001, pp. 74–85; Brent Schlender, "Microsoft: The Beast Is Back," *Fortune,* June 11, 2001, pp. 74–86; Greene, "On to the Living Room," *Business Week,* January 21, 2002, pp. 68–72; Greene, "Bill Has Designs on Your Wrist," *Business Week,* January 20, 2003, pp. 68–69; "Microsoft Hotmail," Cade Metz, *PC Magazine,* May 7, 2002, accessed online at www.pcmag.com; Greene, "Ballmer's Microsoft," *Business Week,* June 17, 2002, pp. 66–76; Brent Schlender, "All You Need Is Love, $50 Billion, and Killer Software Code-Named Longhorn," *Fortune,* July 8, 2002, pp. 56–68; "The Forbes 400," accessed at www.forbes. com/richlist, July 2003; "Connected Services from Microsoft," accessed at www.microsoft.com/net/services, July 2003; and Aaron Ricadela, "Microsoft in Every Pot," *InformationWeek,* March 31, 2003, pp. 45–48.

2. For these and other examples, see Cliff Edwards, "Where Have All the Edsels Gone?" *Greensboro News Record,* May 24, 1999, p. B6; Simon Romero, "Once Proudly Carried, and Now Mere Carrion," *New York Times,* November 22, 2001, p. G5; and Kelly Carroll, "Satellite Telephony: Not for the Consumer," *Telephony,* March 4, 2002, p. 17.

3. See Eric Berggren, "Introducing New Products Can Be Hazardous to Your Company: Use the Right New-Solutions Delivery Tools," *The Academy of Management Executive,* August 2001, p. 92; Bruce Tait, "The Failure of Marketing 'Science,'" *Brandweek,* April 8, 2002, pp. 20–22; Alison Stein Wellner, "The New Science of Focus Groups," *American Demographics,* March 2003, p. 30; and Kevin J. Clancy and Peter C. Krieg, "Surviving Innovation," *Marketing Management,* March/April 2003, pp. 14–20.

4. Quotes from Gary Slack, "Innovations and Idiocities," *Beverage World,* November 15, 1998, p. 122; and Edwards, "Where Have All the Edsels Gone?" p. B6. Other information and examples from Robert M. McMath and Thom Forbes, *What Were They Thinking? Money-Saving, Time-Saving, Face-Saving Marketing Lessons You Can Learn from Products That Flopped* (New York: Times Business, 1999), various pages; Melissa Master, "Spectacular Failures," *Across the Board,* March–April 2001, p. 24; and information from www.new productworks.com/product_poll/hm_index.html, August 2003.

5. Gary Hamel, "Innovation's New Math," *Fortune,* July 9, 2001, pp. 130–131.

6. See Tim Stevens, "Idea Dollars," *Industry Week,* February 16, 1998, pp. 47–49; Michael Arndt, "3M: A Lab for Growth," *Business Week,* January 21, 2002, pp. 50–51; and "Innovation at 3M," accessed at www.3m.com/about3m/innovation/index.jhtml, July 2003.

7. Paul Lukas, "Marketing: The Color of Money and Ketchup," *Fortune,* September 18, 2000, p. 38; ". . . And Adds a Ketchup Mystery Bottle for Kids," *Packaging Digest,* April 2002, p. 4; Sonia Reyes, "Shopping List: Quick, Classic, and Cool for Kids," *Brandweek,* June 17, 2002, pp. S52–S54; and "Heinz EZ Squirt Shoots for the Stars with Its Latest Creation; Stellar Blue Has Landed on Store Shelves," Heinz press release, April 7, 2003, accessed at www.heinz.com/jsp/news_f.jsp.

8. Pam Weisz, "Avon's Skin-So-Soft Bugs Out," *Brandweek,* June 6, 1994, p. 4; and information accessed online at www.avon.com, August 2003.

9. Stefan Thomke and Eric von Hippel, "Customers as Innovators: A New Way to Create Value," *Harvard Business Review,* April 2002, pp. 74–81; and Faith Keenan, "A Mass Market of One," *Business Week,* December 2, 2002, pp. 68–72.

10. Anthony W. Ulwick, "Turn Customer Input into Innovation," *Harvard Business Review,* January 2002, pp. 91–97.

11. Philip Kotler, *Kotler on Marketing* (New York, NY: The Free Press, 1999), pp. 43–44. For more on developing new-product ideas, see Darrell Rigby and Chris Zook, "Open-Market Innovation," *Harvard Business Review,* October 2002, pp. 80–89; and Jacob Goldenberg, Roni Horowitz, Amnon Levav, and David Mazursky, "Finding Your Innovation Sweetspot," *Harvard Business Review,* March 2003, pp. 120–129.

12. Brian O'Reilly, "New Ideas, New Products," *Fortune,* March 3, 1997, pp. 61–64. Also see Michael Schrage, "Getting beyond the Innovation Fetish," *Fortune,* November 13, 2000, pp. 225–232.

13. See Stuart F. Brown, "A Wild Vision for Fuel-Cell Vehicles," *Fortune,* April 1, 2002, p. 72; "The Fuel Cell on Its Way to the Customer," accessed at www.daimlerchrysler.com/specials/fuelcell2002/necar5_e. htm; July 2003; and Katherine Mieszkowski, "Fill 'er Up with Hydrogen," *Fast Company,* March 2003, p 34.

14. See Raymond R. Burke, "Virtual Reality Shopping: Breakthrough in Marketing Research," *Harvard Business Review,* March–April 1996, pp. 120–131; Mike Hoffman, "Virtual Shopping," *Inc,* July 1998, p. 88; Christopher Ryan, "Virtual Reality in Marketing," *Direct Marketing,* April 2001, pp. 57–62; and Patrick Waurzyniak, "Going Virtual," *Manufacturing Engineering,* May 2002, pp. 77–88.

15. Adrienne Ward Fawcett, "Oreo Cones Make Top Grade in Poll," *Advertising Age,* June 14, 1993, p. 30; Becky Ebenkamp, "The New Gold Standards," *Brandweek,* April 19, 1999, p. 34; Ebencamp, "It's Like Cheers and Jeers, Only for Brands," *Brandweek,* March 19, 2001; and Ebenkamp, "The Focus Group Has Spoken," *Brandweek,* April 23, 2001, p. 24.

16. "Hershey Research Sees Net Gain," *Marketing News,* November 25, 2002, p. 17.

17. Examples adapted from those found in Faye Rice, "Secrets of Product Testing," *Fortune,* November 28, 1994, pp. 172–174; Linda Grant, "Gillette Knows Shaving—and How to Turn Out Hot New Products,"

Fortune, October 14, 1996, pp. 207–210; Emily Nelson, "Focus Groupies: PG Keeps Cincinnati Busy with All Its Studies—While Her Sons Test Old Spice, Linda Geil Gets Swabbed," *Wall Street Journal,* January 24, 2002, p. A1; and "Real Hot Stuff," *Marketing Magazine,* April 28, 2003, p. 31.

18. Judann Pollack, "Baked Lays," *Advertising Age,* June 24, 1996, p. S2; Jack Neff and Suzanne Bidlake, "PG, Unilever Aim to Take Consumers to the Cleaners," *Advertising Age,* February 12, 2001, pp. 1, 2; and Dean Takahashi, "Nokia's N-Gage Shakes Up the Gaming Market," *Electronic Business,* April 1, 2003, p. 28.

19. The McDonald's, Nabisco, and other examples can be found in Robert McMath, "To Test or Not to Test," *Advertising Age,* June 1998, p. 64; and Bret Thron, "Lessons Learned: Menu Miscues," *Nation's Restaurant News,* May 20, 2002, pp. 102–104. Also see Jerry W. Thomas, "Skipping Research a Major Error," *Marketing News,* March 4, 2002, p. 50.

20. Jack Neff, "Is Testing the Answer?" *Advertising Age,* July 9, 2001, p. 13; and Dale Buss, "PG's Rise," *Potentials,* January 2003, pp. 26–30.

21. Emily Nelson, "Colgate's Net Rose 10% in Period, New Products Helped Boost Sales," *Wall Street Journal,* February 2, 2001, p. B6.

22. For a good review of research on new-product development, see Rajesh Sethi, "New Product Quality and Product Development Teams," *Journal of Marketing,* April 2000, pp. 1–14; Shikhar Sarin and Vijay Mahajan, "The Effect of Reward Structures on the Performance of Cross-Functional Product Development Teams," *Journal of Marketing,* April 2001, pp. 35–54; Joseph M. Bonner, Robert W. Ruekert, and Orville C. Walker Jr., "Upper Management Control of New Product Development Projects and Project Performance," *Journal of Product Innovation Management,* May 2002, pp. 233–245; Avan R. Jassawalla and Hemant C. Sashittal, "Building Collaborative New Product Processes," *S.A.M. Advanced Management Journal,* Winter 2003, pp. 27–36; and Sandra Valle and Lucia Avella, "Cross-Functionality and Leadership of the New Product Development Teams," *European Journal of Innovation Management,* 2003, pp. 32–47.

23. Laurie Freeman, "Study: Leading Brands Aren't Always Enduring," *Advertising Age,* February 28, 2000, p. 26.

24. See David Stipp, "The Theory of Fads," *Fortune,* October 14, 1996, pp. 49–52; "Fads vs. Trends," *The Futurist,* March–April 2000, p. 67; Irma Zandl, "How to Separate Trends from Fads," *Brandweek,* October 23, 2000, pp. 30–33; "Scooter Fad Fades, as Warehouses Fill and Profits Fall," *Wall Street Journal,* June 14, 2001, p. B4; and Katya Kazakina, "Toy Story: Yo-Yos Make a Big Splash," *Wall Street Journal,* April 11, 2003, p. W-10.

25. For interesting discussions of how brand performance is affected by the product life-cycle stage at which the brand enters the market, see Venkatesh Shankar, Gregory S. Carpenter, and Lekshman Krishnamurthi, "The Advantages of Entry in the Growth Stage of the Product Life Cycle: An Empirical Analysis," *Journal of Marketing Research,* May 1999, pp. 269–276; William Boulding and Markus Christen, "First-Mover Disadvantage," *Harvard Business Review,* October 2001, pp. 20–21; and William T. Robinson and Sungwook Min, "Is the First to Market the First to Fail? Empirical Evidence for Industrial Goods Businesses," *Journal of Marketing Research,* February 2002, p. 120; and William T. Robinson and Jeongwen Chaing, "Product Development Strategies for Established Market Pioneers, Early Followers, and Late Entrants," *Strategic Management Journal,* September 2002, pp. 855–866.

26. Mark McMaster, "Putting a New Spin on Old Products," *Sales Marketing Management,* April 2001, p. 20; Emily Nelson, "Is Wet TP All Dried Up?" *Wall Street Journal,* April 25, 2002, p. B1; and www.cottenelle.com/moist/rollwipes.asp, August 2003.

27. Example from Stephanie Thompson, "Sprucing Up Spam for New Generation," *Advertising Age,* October 28, 2002, p. 6. Additional information from see "The Lighter Side of Spam," December 9, 2002, accessed at www.msn.com/id/2074884/; and information from www.spam.com, August 2003.

28. Michael Hartnett, "Cracker Jack: Chris Neugent," *Advertising Age,* June 26, 2000, p. S22.

29. For a more comprehensive discussion of marketing strategies over the course of the product life cycle, see Philip Kotler, *Marketing Management,* 11th ed. (Upper Saddle River, NJ: Prentice Hall, 2003), chapter 10.

Chapter 9

1. Thomas T. Nagle and Reed K. Holden, *The Strategy and Tactics of Pricing,* 3d ed. (Upper Saddle River, NJ: Prentice Hall, 2002), chapter 1.

2. Excerpts from "Business: It Was My Idea," *The Economist,* August 15, 1998, p. 54; Karl Taro Greenfeld, "Be Your Own Barcode," *Time,* July 10, 2000, pp. 96–97; Ben Rosier, "The Price Is Right," *Marketing,* February 22, 2001, p. 26; and www.priceline.com, July 2003. See also Julia Angwin, "Priceline Founder Closes Online Bidding Site for Gas and Groceries," *Wall Street Journal,* October 6, 2000, p. B1; "Priceline.com's Online 'Reach' Up 810% vs. a Year Ago," June 7, 2002, accessed online at www.priceline.com; "Priceline, Incorporated," *Hoover's Company Profiles,* Austin, June 15, 2003; and "Priceline.com Reports 1st Quarter 2003 Financial Results; Hotel Service Sets All-Time Records," May 1, 2003, accessed online at www.priceline.com.

3. Dean Foust, "Raising Prices Won't Fly," *Business Week,* June 3, 2002, p. 34; and Stephanie N. Mehta, "How to Thrive When Prices Fall," *Fortune,* May 12, 2003, pp. 131–134.

4. Philip Kotler, *Marketing Management,* 11th ed. (Upper Saddle River, NJ: Prentice Hall, 2003), p. 470.

5. See Michael Vizard, Ed Scannell, and Dan Neel, "Suppliers Toy with Dynamic Pricing," *InfoWorld,* May 14, 2001, p. 28; and Faith Keenan, "The Price Is Really Right," *Business Week,* March 31, 2003, pp. 60–68.

6. For an excellent discussion of factors affecting pricing decisions, see Nagle and Holden, *The Strategy and Tactics of Pricing,* chapter 1.

7. See Robert Berner, "Why PG's Smile Is So Bright," *Business Week,* August 12, 2002, pp. 58–60; and Jack Neff, "Power Brushes a Hit at Every Level," *Advertising Age,* May 26, 2003, p. 10.

8. Joshua Rosenbaum, "Guitar Maker Looks for a New Key," *Wall Street Journal,* February 11, 1998, p. B1; and information accessed online at www.gibson.com, July 2003.

9. See Nagle and Holden, *The Strategy and Tactics of Pricing,* chapter 4.

10. See Mike Troy, "Kmart: 2. Drop EDLP—Continue Promoting the Value Message," *DSN Retailing Today,* March 11, 2002, p. 33; and Laura Heller, "Simple Messages Reinforce EDLP," *DSN Retailing Today,* June 10, 2002, p. 129; and Christine Tierney, "Kmart's Toughest Sell," *Business Week,* May 15, 2003, accessed online at www.businessweek.com.

11. Erin Stout, "Keep Them Coming Back for More," *Sales Marketing Management,* February 2002, pp. 51–52. Also see Beth Cox, "'Value Pricing' Key to Boosting Profits," *Internet News,* February 26, 2003, accessed online at www.internetnews.com.

12. For other examples of value-added pricing, see Stephanie N. Mehta, "How to Thrive When Prices Fall," *Fortune,* May 12, 2003, pp. 131–134; and Alison Smith, "The Flip Side of Price," *Selling Power,* May 2003, pp. 28–30.

13. For a comprehensive discussion of pricing strategies, see Nagle and Holden, *The Strategy and Dynamics of Pricing.* Also see Robert J.

Dolan and Hermann Simon, *Power Pricing: How Managing Price Transforms the Bottom Line* (New York: The Free Press, 1997).

14. Kotler, *Marketing Management*, p. 474; Kara Swisher, "Electronics 2001: The Essential Guide," *Wall Street Journal*, January 5, 2001; Cliff Edwards, "HDTV: High-Anxiety Television," *Business Week,* June 10, 2002, pp. 142–146; and Eric Taub, "HDTV's Acceptance Picks Up Pace as Prices Drop and Networks Sign On," *New York Times*, March 31, 2003, p. C1.

15. Seanna Browder, "Nintendo: At the Top of Its Game," *Business Week,* June 9, 1997, pp. 72–73; "Console Competition Lowers Opening Price Points," *DSN Retailing Today*, March 25, 2002, p. 18; and Ken Belson, "Sony Profits Climb 96% in Quarter," *New York Times*, January 30, 2003, p. W1.

16. E.M. Phillips, "Capitalizing on Your Wood By-Products," *FDM*, March 2002, pp. 48–51; and information accessed online at www.woodworkingsite.com, July 2003.

17. Susan Krafft, "Love, Love Me Doo," *American Demographics*, June 1994, pp. 15–16; Damon Darlin, "Zoo Doo," *Forbes,* May 22, 1995, p. 92; information from www.zoodoo.com, September 2003; and "Time Again for Zoo's Annual Spring Fecal Fest!" Woodland Park Zoo Press Release, February 28, 2003, accessed online at www.zoo.org.

18. See Nagle and Holden, *The Strategy and Tactics of Pricing*, pp. 244–247; and Stefan Stremersch and Gerard J. Tellis, "Strategic Bundling of Products and Prices: A New Synthesis for Marketing," *Journal of Marketing Research,* January 2002, pp. 55–72.

19. Example adapted from Charles Fishman, "Which Price Is Right?" *Fast Company,* March 2003, pp. 92–96. For more on yield management, see Susan Greco, "Are Your Prices Right?" *Inc.,* January 1997, pp. 88–89; Robert G. Cross, *Revenue Management: Hard-Core Tactics for Market Domination* (New York: Broadway Books, 1998); Steven M. Shugan, "Strategic Service Pricing and Yield Management," *Journal of Marketing,* January 1999, pp. 44–56; Sheryl E. Kimes, "Perceived Fairness of Yield Management," *Cornell Hotel and Restaurant Administration Quarterly,* February 2002, p. 21; and Anthony Ingold, Una McMahon-Beattie, and Ian Yeoman, *Yield Management* (New York, NY: Continuum Publishing, 2002).

20. Example adapted from Greco, "Are Your Prices Right?" p. 88.

21. For more reading on reference prices and psychological pricing, see Robert M. Schindler and Patrick N. Kirby, "Patterns of Right-Most Digits Used in Advertised Prices: Implications for Nine-Ending Effects," *Journal of Consumer Research,* September 1997, pp. 192–201; Dhruv Grewal, Kent B. Monroe, Chris Janiszewski, and Donald R. Lichtenstein, "A Range Theory of Price Perception," *Journal of Consumer Research,* March 1999, pp. 353–368; Tridib Mazumdar and Purushottam Papatla, "An Investigation of Reference Price Segments," *Journal of Marketing Research,* May 2000, pp. 246–258; Indrajit Sinha and Michael Smith, "Consumers' Perceptions of Promotional Framing of Price," *Psychology Marketing,* March 2000, pp. 257–271; Tulin Erdem, Glenn Mayhew, and Baohong Sun, "Understanding Reference-Price Shoppers: A Within- and Across-Category Analysis," *Journal of Marketing Research,* November 2001, pp. 445–457; and Nagle and Holden, *The Strategy and Tactics of Pricing,* pp. 83–90.

22. Tim Ambler, "Kicking Price Promotion Habit Is Like Getting Off Heroin—Hard," *Marketing,* May 27, 1999, p. 24. Also see Robert Gray, "Driving Sales at Any Price?" *Marketing,* April 11, 2002, p. 24; and Lauren Kellere Johnson, "Dueling Pricing Strategies," *MIT Sloan Management Review,* Spring 2003, pp. 10–11.

23. Adapted from Andrew Park and Peter Burrows, "Dell, the Conqueror," *Business Week*, September 24, 2001, pp. 92–102. See also Andy Serwer, "Dell Does Domination," *Fortune,* January 21, 2002, pp. 70–75; Gary McWilliams, "Dell Computer's Kevin Rollins Becomes a Driv-

ing Force," *Wall Street Journal*, April 4, 2002, p. B6; and Terril Yue Jones, "Dell Launches First Line of Printers; The Move Reflects the PC Maker's Ambition to Compete with HP in the Computer Systems Market," *The Los Angeles Times*, March 25, 2003, p. C3.

24. Philip R. Cateora, *International Marketing*, 7th ed. (Homewood, IL: Irwin, 1990), p. 540. Also see S. Tamer Cavusgil, "Pricing for Global Markets," *Columbia Journal of World Business,* Winter 1996, pp. 66–78; Barbara Stottinger, "Strategic Export Pricing: A Long and Winding Road," *Journal of International Marketing,* 2001, pp. 40–63; and Warren J. Keegan, *Global Marketing Management* (Upper Saddle River, NJ: Prentice Hall, 2002), chapter 12.

25. See John Greenwald, "Cereal Showdown," *Time,* April 29, 1996, p. 60; "Cereal Thriller," *The Economist,* June 15, 1996, p. 59; Terril Yue Jones, "Outside the Box," *Forbes,* June 14, 1999, pp. 52–53; "Kellogg Concedes Top Spot to General Mills," *New York Times,* February 22, 2001, p. C4; and "Kellogg Company," *Hoover's Company Profiles*, Austin, June 15, 2003.

26. Jeff Ansell, "Luvs," *Advertising Age,* June 30, 1997, p. S16; Jack Neff, "Kimberly-Clark Looses 'Bounty Killer,' " *Advertising Age*, April 2, 2001, p. 34; and information accessed at www.scottbrand.com/products/towels, July 2003.

27. For an excellent discussion of these issues, see Dhruv Grewel and Larry D. Compeau, "Pricing and Public Policy: A Research Agenda and Overview of Special Issue," *Journal of Marketing and Public Policy,* Spring 1999, pp. 3–10.

28. Ralph Blumenthal, "Ex-Executive of Christie's Tells of Collusion Scheme," *New York Times,* November 15, 2001, pg. D1; Paul Hofheinz, "EU Accuses Auction Houses of Running Price-Fixing Cartel," *Wall Street Journal*, April 22, 2002, p. B6; and Brooks Barnes, "*Sotheby's, Christie's to Settle Claims by Overseas Customers,*" *Wall Street Journal,* March 12, 2003, p. B.2.

29. David Barboza, "Archer Daniels Executive Said to Tell of Price-Fixing Talks with Cargill Counterpart," *New York Times,* June 17, 1999, p. 6; Stephen Labaton, "The World Gets Tough on Fixing Prices," *New York Times,* June 3, 2001, p. 3.1; Scott Kilman, "Court Reinstates Suit Alleging Archer Rigged Sweetener Market," *Wall Street Journal*, June 19, 2002, p. D2; Jennifer Ordonez, "*The Record Industry Owes You $20—For Music Buyers, a Deadline Is Approaching to File Claims in a Big CD Price-Fixing Case,*" *Wall Street Journal,* February 5, 2003, p. D1; and "Vitamin Firms Are Guilty of Price Fixing," *Wall Street Journal,* June 16, 2003, p. B3.

30. Excerpts from Dan Carney, "Predatory Pricing: Cleared for Takeoff," *Business Week,* May 14, 2001, p. 50. For more information on predatory pricing, see James Helgeson and Eric Gorger, "The Price Weapon: Developments in U.S. Predatory Pricing Law," *Journal of Business to Business Marketing*, 2003, pp. 3–22.

31. See "Nike's Pricing Practices Under Investigation in Florida," *New York Times,* February 19, 2003, p. C4.

32. Grewel and Compeau, "Pricing and Public Policy," p. 8.

33. FTC Guides Against Deceptive Pricing," accessed at www.ftc.gov/bcp/guides/decptprc.htm, July 2003.

34. For more on public policy and pricing, see Louis W. Stern and Thomas L. Eovaldi, *Legal Aspects of Marketing Strategy* (Upper Saddle River, NJ: Prentice Hall, 1984), chapter 5; Robert J. Posch, *The Complete Guide to Marketing and the Law* (Upper Saddle River, NJ: Prentice Hall, 1988), chapter 28; Joseph P. Guiltinan and Gregory Gunlach, "Aggressive and Predatory Pricing: A Framework for Analysis," *Journal of Marketing,* July 1996, pp. 87–102; Bruce Upbin, "Vindication," *Forbes,* November 17, 1997, pp. 52–56; Grewel and Compeau, "Pricing and Public Policy," pp. 3–10; and Nagle and Holden, *The Strategy and Tactics of Pricing,* chapter 14.

Chapter 10

1. Quotes and other information from Donald V. Fites, "Make Your Dealers Your Partners," *Harvard Business Review,* March–April 1996, pp. 84–95; Sandra Ward, "The Cat Comes Back," *Barron's,* February 25, 2002, pp. 21–24; DeAnn Weimer, "A New Cat on the Hot Seat," *Business Week,* March 1998, pp. 56–62; "The 2003 Fortune 500," *Fortune,* April 14, 2003, pp. F28–F31; "Caterpillar, Inc.," *Hoover's Company Profiles,* Austin, June 15, 2003; and information accessed online at www.caterpillar.com, July 2003.

2. For definitions and a complete discussion of distribution channel topics, see Anne T. Coughlin, Erin Anderson, Louis W. Stern, and Adel El-Ansary, *Marketing Channels,* 6th ed. (Upper Saddle River, NJ: Prentice Hall, 2001), pp. 2–3.

3. For these and other examples, see Drew Villard, "Franchisees Fight with Parents Over Internet Sales," *Sacramento Business Journal,* February 16, 2001, pp. 34+; Chuck Moozakis, "Herman Miller Builds Three-Pronged Strategy—Furniture Company Tailors Web Efforts to Size of Customer," *Internetweek,* June 11, 2001, pp. PG61–PG62; Laura Heller, "Tupperware Takes Its Party to the Aisles of SuperTarget," *DSN Retailing Today,* August 6, 2001, pp. 2, 42; David Rocks, "Herman Miller," *Business Week,* October 29, 2001, p. EB23; Kate Macarthur, "McD's Boss Blasts Chain 'Naysayers,' " *Advertising Age,* March 18, 2002, p. 1; and Lisa W. Foderaro, "Tupperware Parties for the Cosmo Set," *New York Times,* February 1, 2003, p. B1.

4. William Keenan Jr., "Sales and Marketing—(Pet) Food for Thought," *Industry Week,* March 5, 2001, p. 23; "PG Plans Overhaul of Iams Brand," *Marketing Week,* May 30, 2002, p. 6; and Sarah Ellison and Robin Sidel, "Procter Gamble May Buy Wella," *Wall Street Journal,* March 18, 2003, p. B7.

5. Coughlin, Anderson, Stern, and El-Ansary, *Marketing Channels*, 6th ed., p. 160; and information accessed at www.giantfoods.com and www.luxottica.com/english/profilo_aziendale/index_keyfacts.html, July 2003.

6. "Business Floating on Air," *The Economist,* May 19, 2001, pp. 56–57; Richard Heller, "Galician Beauty," *Forbes,* May 28, 2001, p. 98; Carlta Vitzthum, "Just-in-Time Fashion—Spanish Retailer Zara Makes Low-Cost Lines in Weeks by Running Its Own Show," *Wall Street Journal,* May 18, 2001, p. B1; Miguel Helft, "Fashion Fast Forward," *Business 2.0,* May 2002, p. 60; and John Tagliabue, "A Rival to Gap That Operates Like Dell," *New York Times,* May 30, 2003, p. W-1.

7. See Ilan Alon, "The Use of Franchising by U.S.-Based Retailers," *Journal of Small Business Management,* April 2001, pp. 111–122; James H. Amos Jr., "Franchising, More than Any Act of Government, Will Strengthen the Global Economy," *Franchising World,* May–June 2001, p. 8; Anne Field, "Your Ticket to a New Career," *Business Week,* May 12, 2003, pp. 100–101; and "Answers to the 21 Most Commonly Asked Questions About Franchising," accessed online at the International Franchise Association Web site: www.franchise.org, August 2003.

8. Amanda Miller, Peter Rose, and Michael Voeller, "General Mills, Inc.," Krause Fund Research, Fall 2002, accessed at www.biz.uiowa.edu/krause/General_Mills_F02.pdf; and information accessed at www.nestle.com/html/brands/breakfast.asp.

9. See Subhash C. Jain, *International Marketing Management,* 3rd ed. (Boston: PWS-Kent Publishing, 1990), pp. 489–491; and Warren J. Keegan, *Global Marketing Management* (Upper Saddle River, NJ: Prentice Hall, 2002), pp. 403–404.

10. See Aruna Chandra and John K. Ryans Jr., "Why India Now?" *Marketing Management,* March–April 2002, pp. 43–45; Dana James, "Dark Clouds Should Part for International Marketers," *Marketing News,* January 7, 2002, pp. 9, 13; and Russell Flannery, "Red Tape," *Forbes,* March 3, 2003, pp. 97–100.

11. For more on channel relationships, see James A. Narus and James C. Anderson, "Rethinking Distribution," *Harvard Business Review,* July–August 1996, pp. 112–120; James C. Anderson and James A. Narus, *Business Market Management* (Upper Saddle River, NJ: Prentice Hall, 1999), pp. 276–288; Jonathon D. Hibbard, Nirmalya Kumar, and Louis W. Stern, "Examining the Impact of Destructive Acts in Marketing Channel Relationships," *Journal of Marketing Research,* February 2001, pp. 45–61; and Stavros P. Kalafatis, "Buyer–Seller Relationships Among Channels of Distribution," *Industrial Marketing Management,* April 2002, pp. 215–228.

12. Mitch Betts, "GE Appliance Park Still an IT Innovator," *Computerworld,* January 29, 2001, pp. 20–21; and "What Is GE CustomerNet?" accessed online at www.geappliances.com/buildwithge/index_cnet.htm, August 2003.

13. See Heather Harreld and Paul Krill, "Channel Management," *InfoWorld,* October 8, 2001, pp. 46–52; Mitch Wagner, "PRM Software Delivers Tighter Channel Ties," *BtoB,* October 14, 2002, p. 17; and Barbara Darrow, "Comergent 6.3 Extends PRM Suite Capabilities," *CRN,* March 17, 2003, p. 40.

14. For a full discussion of laws affecting marketing channels, see Coughlin, Anderson, Stern, and El-Ansary, *Marketing Channels,* chapter 12.

15. James R. Stock, "The Seven Deadly Sins of Reverse Logistics," *Material Handling Management,* March 2001, pp. MHS5–MHS11; and Martin Piszczalksi, "Logistics: A Difference Between Winning and Losing," *Automotive Manufacturing Production,* May 2001, pp. 16–18; and "The Logistics Industry," accessed online at www.menlolog.com/shtml/about_us/logistics_industry.shtml, June 2003.

16. Shlomo Maital, "The Last Frontier of Cost Reduction," *Across the Board,* February 1994, pp. 51–52; and "Wal-Mart to Expand Supercenters to California," *Business Journal,* May 15, 2002, accessed online at http://sanjose.bizjournals.com; and information accessed online at www.walmart.com, August 2003.

17. John Huey, "Wal-Mart: Will It Take Over the World?" *Fortune,* January 30, 1989, pp. 52–64; Mike Troy, "Wal-Mart: Behind the Scenes Efficiency Keeps Growth Curve on Course," *Dsn Retailing Today,* June 4, 2001, pp. 80, 91; Gail Braccidiferro, "One Town's Rejection Is Another's 'Let's Do Business,' " *New York Times,* June 15, 2003, p. 2; and "Wal-Mart Centers Benefit from Quick Start," accessed online at www.dtae.org/quickstart/News7/walmart.html, July 2003.

18. J. William Gurley, "Why Dell's War Isn't Dumb," *Fortune,* July 9, 2001, pp. 134–136; Bob Evans, "Real-Time Business: More Than a Fad," *Information Week,* March 10, 2003, p. 74.

19. See Jack Neff, "A Chip Over Your Shoulder?" *Advertising Age,* April 22, 2002, p. 4; Kimberly Hill, "Prada Uses Smart Tags to Personalize Shopping," April 24, 2002, accessed online at www.crmdaily.com; "Business: The Best Thing Since the Bar-Code: The IT Revolution," *The Economist,* February 8, 2003, p. 57–58; "Gillette, Michelin Begin RFID Pilots," *Frontline Solutions,* March 2003, p. 8; "RFID Benefits Apparent," *Chain Store Age,* March 2003, p. 63; Faith Keenan, "If Supermarket Shelves Could Talk," *Business Week,* March 31, 2003, pp. 66–67; and information accessed online at www.autoidcenter.org, August 2003.

20. For statistics on freight shipments, see *United States 1997 Economic Census: Transportation,* U.S. Department of Transportation, issued December 1999, accessed online at www.bts.gov.Statistics; and information found at www.bts.gov/publications/pocket_guide_to_transportation/2003/html/table_19.html, July 2003.

21. See Amy Rogers, "Supply Chain Players Toss a Few Barbs as Competition Heats Up," *Crn,* April 22, 2002, pp. 29–30; Emily Kay, "Coordinating Supply Chain Data," *Frontline Solutions,* May 2003, pp. 21–24; and William C. Copacino, "Supply Chain Software Still Has Much to Offer," *Logistics Management,* May 2003, p. 76.

22. Reed Stith, "Customer-Driven Supply Chain," *Frontline Solutions,* May 2002, p. 40.

23. Robert E. Lieb, "3PLs Eye Further Supply Chain Integration," *Purchasing,* March 20, 2003, pp. S4–S8; Mike Verespej, "Logistics' New Look? Now It's Service," *Frontline Solutions,* June 2002, pp. 24–33; and "3PL Providers Work to Close the Gap," *Logistics Management,* February 2003, p. E64.

24. Verespej, "Logistics' New Look? Now It's Service," p. 24.

Chapter 11

1. Quotes and other information from Bill Saporito, "Is Wal-Mart Unstoppable?" *Fortune,* May 6, 1991, pp. 50-59; Carol J. Loomis, "Sam Would Be Proud," *Fortune,* April 17, 2001, pp. 131–144; Stephanie Thompson, "Wal-Mart Tops List for New Food Lines," *Advertising Age,* April 29, 2002, pp. 4, 61; Cait Murphy, "Introduction: Wal-Mart Rules," *Fortune,* April 15, 2002, pp. 94–98; *Wal-Mart Annual Report 2003,* accessed online at www.walmartstores.com; Jerry Useem, "One Nation Under Wal-Mart," *Fortune,* March 3, 2003, pp. 65–78; Gerald Chichester, "No. 1 Wal-Mart," *Fortune,* March 31, 2003, p. 26; and Jerry Useem, "Fortune 500: The Stories," *Fortune,* April 14, 2003, pp. 81–90.

2. See Bob Tedeschi, "The History of Online Grocery Shopping: First as Web Farce, Now a Lucrative Field for Older Companies," *New York Times,* May 6, 2002, p. C7; and Katy McLaughlin, "Back from the Dead: Buying Groceries Online," *Wall Street Journal,* February 25, 2003, p. D-1.

3. See "2003 SOI Highlights," National Association of Convenience Stores, accessed online at www.cstorecentral.com, September 2003.

4. Richard Turcsik and Jenny Summerour, "David vs. Goliath," *Progressive Grocer,* March 2001, p. 7; Laura Heller, "Wal-Mart Out-prices Atlanta Competition," *Dsn Retailing,* June 18, 2001, pp. 1, 42; Mike Duff, "Supercenters Take Lead in Food Retailing," *Dsn Retailing Today,* May 6, 2002. pp. F8–F9; and Patricia Callahan and Ann Zimmerman, "Price War in Aisle 3—Wal-Mart Tops Grocery List with Supercenter Format," *Wall Street Journal,* May 27, 2003, p. B-1.

5. See Ray A. Smith, "Outlet Centers Go Upmarket with Amenities," *Wall Street Journal,* June 6, 2001, p. B12; *Mervyn Rothstein,* "At a Shoppers' Mecca, Now, Retail for Locals," *New York Times,* April 10, 2002, p. C6; and Sally Beatty, "Paying Less for Prada," *Wall Street Journal,* April 29, 2003, p. D.1.

6. Wendy Zellner, "Warehouse Clubs: When the Going Gets Tough . . . ," *Business Week,* July 16, 2001, p. 60; "Warehouse Clubs Lead Growth," *Chain Store Age,* May 2002, p. 160; and Doug Desjardins, "Costco Home Poised to Revolutionize High-End Furniture," *DSN Retailing Today,* January 6, 2003, pp. 5, 50.

7. See David Stires, "Fallen Arches," *Fortune,* April 29, 2002, pp. 74–76; information accessed online at www.subway.com, September 2003; and information accessed online at www.mcdonalds.com/corporate, September 2003.

8. Quotes and information from Shelly Branch, "How Target Got Hot," *Fortune,* May 24, 1999, pp. 169–174; "Target Works Its Market Magic," *Dsn Retailing Today,* April 2, 2001, pp. 43, 64; Constance L. Hayes, "Can Target Survive in Wal-Mart's Cross Hairs?" *New York Times,* June 9, 2002, p. 3.1; and Julie Schlosser, "Is Retail Back in Fashion?" *Fortune,* April 14, 2003, pp. 374–376.

9. Myron Magnet, "Let's Go for Growth," *Fortune,* March 7, 1994, pp. 60–72. Also see Dierdre Donahue, "Bookstores: A Haven for the Intellect," *USA Today,* July 10, 1997, pp. D1, D2; and Christina Nifong, "Beyond Browsing," *Raleigh News Observer,* May 25, 1999, p. E1.

10. "Mall of America Starts 10th Year Celebration," *Home Textiles Today,* June 24, 2002, p. 42; and "The History of Mall of America," accessed online at www.mallofamerica.com, September 2003.

11. Andrea Bermudez, "Bijan Dresses the Wealthy for Success," *Apparel News.Net,* December 1-7, 2000, accessed online at www.apparelnews.net/Archieve/120100/News/newsfeat.htm; and Mimi Avins, "FASHION; More Is More; Over-the-Top Isn't High Enough for Bijan, Whose Boutique Embraces Excess," *The Los Angeles Times,* January 5, 2003, p. E.1.

12. John Fetto, "Mall Rats," *American Demographics,* March 2002, p. 10; Robert Berner and Gerry Khermouch, "Retail Reckoning," *Business Week,* December 10, 2001, pp. 71–77; Matt Valley, "The Remalling of America," *National Real Estate Investor,* May 2002, pp. 18–24; Brian Libby, "Shopping Around for Second Lives," *New York Times,* June 15, 2003, p. 32.

13. Dean Starkman, "The Mall, Without the Haul—'Lifestyle Centers' Slip Quietly into Upscale Areas, Mixing Cachet and 'Curb Appeal,'" *Wall Street Journal,* July 25, 2001, p. B1.

14. Amy Barrett, "A Retailing Pacesetter Pulls Up Lame," *Business Week,* July 12, 1993, pp. 122–123.

15. See Malcolm P. McNair and Eleanor G. May, "The Next Revolution of the Retailing Wheel," *Harvard Business Review,* September–October 1978, pp. 81–91; Stephen Brown, "The Wheel of Retailing: Past and Future," *Journal of Retailing,* Summer 1990, pp. 143–147; Stephen Brown, "Variations on a Marketing Enigma: The Wheel of Retailing Theory," *Journal of Marketing Management,* 7, no. 2, 1991, pp. 131–155; Jennifer Negley, "Retrenching, Reinventing and Remaining Relevant," *Discount Store News,* April 5, 1999, p. 11; and Don E. Schultz, "Another Turn of the Wheel," *Marketing Management,* March–April 2002, pp. 8–9.

16. Charles Haddad, "Office Depot's E-Diva," *Business Week,* August 6, 2001, pp. EB22–EB24; Meryl Davids Landau, "*Sweet Revenge,*" *Chief Executive,* May 2002, pp. 58–62; and "Consumer Products Brief—Office Depot Inc.: Fourth-Period Net Soared 56%; Forecast for 2003 Is Cautious," *Wall Street Journal,* February 14, 2003, p. A10.

17. Excerpt adapted from Alice Z. Cuneo, "What's in Store?" *Advertising Age,* February 25, 2002, pp. 1, 30–31. Also see Robert Berner, "Dark Days in White Goods for Sears," *Business Week,* March 10, 2003, pp. 78–79.

18. See "The Fortune 500," *Fortune,* April 14, 2003, p. F1.

19. Regina Fazio Maruca, "Retailing: Confronting the Challenges That Face Bricks-and-Mortar Stores," *Harvard Business Review,* July–August 1999, pp. 159–168. Also see Marshall L. Fisher, Ananth Raman, and Anna Sheen McClelland, "Rocket Science Retailing Is Almost Here: Are You Ready?" *Harvard Business Review,* July–August 2000, pp. 115–124.

20. James Cox, "Red-Letter Day as East Meets West in the Aisles," *USA Today,* September 11, 1996, p. B1; and "Wal-Mart International Operations," July 2003, accessed online at www.walmartstores.com.

21. Carla Rapoport, "Retailers Go Global," *Fortune,* February 20, 1995, pp. 102–108; "Global Retailing in the Connected Economy," *Chain Store Age,* December 1999, pp. 69–82; Tim Craig, "Global Retailing's Defining Moments Are Getting Lost in the Mix," *Dsn Retailing Today,* April 21, 2003, p. 7; and "World's 100 Largest Retailers," accessed at www.chainstoreage.com, July 2003.

22. Adapted from Tim Craig, "Carrefour: At the Intersection of Global," *Dsn Retailing Today,* September 18, 2000, p. 16. Additional information from Richard Tomlinson, "Who's Afraid of Wal-Mart?" *Fortune,* June 26, 2000, pp. 186–196; "Carrefour SA," *Euroweek,* April 25, 2003, p. 1; and www.carrefour.com, September 2003.

23. Nifong, "Beyond Browsing," p. E1. Also see Fred Brock, "Catering to the Elderly Can Pay Off," *New York Times,* February 2002, p. 3.11.

24. Kathleen Cholewka, "Standing Out Online: The Five Best e-Marketing Campaigns," *Sales Marketing Management,* January 2001, pp. 51–58. Other information from www.playstation.com, September 2003.

25. Information from "About the Company" and "Supply Management Online," accessed online at www.mckesson.com, August 2003.
26. Facts accessed at www.supervalu.com, July 2003; and from "Super-Valu Inc.," *Hoover's Company Capsules,* Austin, June 15, 2003.

Chapter 12

1. Quotes and other information from Lisa Bertagnoli, "Duck Campaign Is Firm's Extra Insurance," *Marketing News,* August 27, 2001, pp. 5–6; "AFLAC's Duck Is Endearing to Customers, Bottom Line," *Best's Review,* November 2000, p. 100; Meg Green, "Duck Preens Feathers for Dental Pitch," *Best's Review,* July 2001, p. 38; Bethany McLean, "Duck and Coverage," *Fortune,* August 13, 2001, pp. 142–143; Stuart Elliott, "Why a Duck? Because It Sells Insurance," *New York Times,* June 24, 2002, p. C11; Lori Chordas, "The Mighty Duck," *Best's Review,* May 2003, pp. 82–87; and "AFLAC Tames Its Duck for Japanese Market," *The Los Angeles Times,* May 13, 2003, p. C7.
2. The first four of these definitions are adapted from Peter D. Bennett, *Dictionary of Marketing Terms* (Chicago: American Marketing Association, 1995).
3. Don E. Schultz, "New Media, Old Problem: Keep Marcom Integrated," *Marketing News,* March 29, 1999, p. 11. Also see Michael McLaren, "Key to Tech Marketing Is Integrated Message," *B to B,* February 10, 2003, p. 16; and Claire Atkinson, "Integration Still a Pipe Dream for Many," *Advertising Age,* March 10, 2003, pp. 1, 47.
4. See Don E. Schultz, Stanley I. Tannenbaum, and Robert F. Lauterborn, *Integrated Marketing Communications* (Chicago, IL: NTC, 1992), chapters 3 and 4. Also see James R. Ogdan, *Developing a Creative and Innovative Integrated Marketing Communications Plan* (Upper Saddle River, NJ: Prentice Hall, 1998); Don E. Schultz and Philip J. Kitchen, *Communication Globally: An Integrated Marketing Approach* (New York: McGraw Hill, 2000); and Anders Gronstedt, *The Customer Century: Lessons from World Class Companies in Integrated Communications* (New York: Routledge, 2000).
5. P. Griffith Lindell, "You Need Integrated Attitude to Develop IMC," *Marketing News,* May 26, 1997, p. 6. For more discussion of integrated marketing communications, see Stephen J. Gould, "The State of IMC Research and Applications," *Journal of Advertising Research,* September–October 2000, pp. 22–23; Don E. Schultz, "Marcom Model Reverses Traditional Pattern," *Marketing News,* April 1, 2002, p. 8; and Schultz, "Rethink How Sales, Marketing Work Together," *Marketing News,* March 17, 2003, p. 10.
6. Bill Carter, "After Super Bowl, 'Survivor' Is the Season's Top Hit on TV," *New York Times,* January 30, 2001, p. C8; Howard Fendrich, "Super Bowl Ratings Are Best Since '98," January 26, 2003, accessed online at http://newslink.nandomedia.com/; and "Oscar's Fallout and Future," *The Los Angeles Times,* March 25, 2003, p. E1.
7. Michele Marchetti, "What a Sales Call Costs," *Sales Marketing Management,* September 2000, p. 80.
8. Information on U.S. and international advertising spending accessed at the Ad Age Dataplace, www.adage.com, August 2003; Mercedes M. Cardona, "Ad Industry Looks Ahead with Cautious Optimism," *Advertising Age,* December 16, 2003, p. 4; and the International Advertising Association Web page at www.iaaglobal.org, September 2003.
9. For more on advertising budgets, see George E. Belch and Michael A. Belch, *Advertising and Promotion: An Integrated Marketing Communications Perspective,* 6th ed. (New York: McGraw Hill, 2004), pp. 211–232.
10. David Allen, "Excessive Use of the Mirror," *Management Accounting,* June 1966, p. 12. Also see Laura Petrecca, "4A's Will Study Financial Return on Ad Spending," *Advertising Age,* April 7, 1997, pp. 3, 52; and Dana W. Hayman and Don E. Schultz, "How Much Should You Spend on Advertising," *Advertising Age,* April 26, 1999, p. 32.
11. Information from Gary Levin, " 'Meddling' in Creative More Welcome," *Advertising Age,* April 9, 1990, pp. S4, S8; Eleftheria Parpis, "TBWA: Absolut," *Adweek,* November 9, 1998, p. 172; Sarah Theodore, "Absolut Secrets," *Beverage Industry,* July 2000, p. 50; Hillary Chura, "Absolut Vanilla Part of Plan to Boost Flat Market Share," *Advertising Age,* December 16, 2002, p. 8; and the QA section at www.absolut.com, September 2003.
12. "Swimming the Channels," *American Demographics,* June 1998, p. 37; and information accessed online at www.magazine.org, July 2003.
13. Charles Pappas, "Ad Nauseam," *Advertising Age,* July 10, 2000, pp. 16–18; and Mark Ritson, "Marketers Need to Find a Way to Control the Contagion of Clutter," *Marketing,* March 6, 2003, p. 16.
14. Wayne Friedman, "TV Networks' New Reality," *Advertising Age,* September 24, 2001, pp. 1, 70; Steve McClellan, "How High Is Too High?" *Broadcasting Cable,* January 20, 2003, pp. 50–53; Andrew Green, "Clutter Crisis Countdown," *Advertising Age,* April 21, 2003, p. 22; and Wayne Friedman, "PG Takes $2.4 Million Super Bowl Spot," *Advertising Age,* July 1, 2003, accessed at www.adage.com, July 2003.
15. Edward A. Robinson, "Frogs, Bears, and Orgasms: Think Zany if You Want to Reach Today's Consumers," *Fortune,* June 9, 1997, pp. 153–156. Also see Chuck Ross, "NBC Blasts Beyond the 15-Minute Barrier," *Advertising Age,* August 7, 2000, p. 3; and Tobi Elkin, "Courting Craftier Consumers," July 1, 2002, p. 28.
16. Wayne Friedman, "PVR Users Skip Most Ads: Study," *Advertising Age,* July 1, 2002, pp. 4, 46; and Jeff Goodby, "The Next Golden Age," *Advertising Age,* February 10, 2003, p. 23.
17. Tobi Elkin, "Porsche, Acura Latest to Try Out TiVo Showcases," *Advertising Age,* February 24, 2003; Elkin, "Getting Viewers to Opt In, Not Tune Out," *Advertising Age,* November 4, 2002, p. 10; and Jon Healey, "California; TiVo to Sell Statistics on Ads Skipped," *Los Angeles Times,* June 2, 2003, p. C2.
18. *Newsweek* and *Business Week* cost and circulation data accessed online at http://mediakit.businessweek.com and www.newsweekmediakit.com, August 2003.
19. See Ariane Herrera, "AAAA Survey Finds Three Percent Drop in Cost to Produce 30-Second TV Commercials," news release, American Association of Advertising Agencies, December 13, 2001, accessed online at www.aaaa.org.
20. Information on advertising agency income and billings from "World's Top 25 Ad Organization," *Advertising Age,* April 21, 2003, p. S-4; and the Advertising Age Data Center, accessed at www.adage.com/datacenter, September 2003.
21. See Belch and Belch, *Advertising and Promotion,* pp. 666–668.
22. *2002 Trade Promotion Spending Merchandising Industry Study* (Wilton, CT: Cannondale Associates, 2002), p. 13; and *Trade Promotion Spending Merchandising 2003 Industry Study* (Wilton, CT: Cannondale Associates, 2003), p. 7.
23. Kenneth Hein, "Coke Puts New Twist on Plain Vanilla Sampler, Summer Tours," *Brandweek,* July 1, 2002, p. 35; and Larry Burns, "Sampling Success," *Global Cosmetic Industry,* January 2003, pp. 32–36.
24. Debra Aho Williamson, "PG's Reformulated Pert Plus Builds Consumer Relationships," *Advertising Age,* June 28, 1999, p. 52.
25. See "Do Coupons Make Cents?" *Incentive,* May 2003, p. 19; and Catherine Arnold, "No Coup Online," *Marketing News,* May 26, 2003, p. 3.
26. See "Electronic Coupon Clipping," *USA Today,* May 11, 1999, p. 1B; Cara Beardi, "Catalina Expands in Cyberworld," *Advertising Age,* January 22, 2001, p. 19; Roger O. Crockett, "Penny-Pinchers' Paradise," *Business Week,* January 22, 2001, p. EB12; and Lucia Moses, "Coupons Make Move Online," *Editor Publisher,* February 24, 2003, p. 10.

27. See Kate Bertrand, "Premiums Prime the Market," *Advertising Age's Business Marketing,* May 1998, p. S6; and Paul Nolan, "Promotions Come Alive with the Sound of Music," *Potentials,* April 1999, p. 10. For other examples, see Elinor Dumont, "Today's Version of the Toaster," *Bank Marketing,* September 2001, pp. 12–14; and Kenneth Hein, "Frito-Lay Supplies Pieces to the Star Wars Puzzle," *Brandweek,* March 25, 2002, p. 10.

28. See William F. Kendy, "The Great Giveaway," *Selling Power,* September 2002, pp. 98–105; and information found at the Promotional Products Association International Web site, www.ppai.org, July 2003.

29. See Richard Szathmary, "Trade Shows," *Sales Marketing Management,* May 1992, pp. 83–84; Srinath Gopalakrishna, Gary L. Lilien, Jerome D. Williams, and Ian Sequeira, "Do Trade Shows Pay Off?" *Journal of Marketing,* July 1995, pp. 75–83; Peter Jenkins, "Making the Most of Trade Shows," *Nation's Business,* June 1999, p. 8; and Ben Chapman, "The Trade Show Must Go On," *Sales Marketing Management,* June 2001, p. 22.

30. Adapted from Scott Cutlip, Allen Center, and Glen Broom, *Effective Public Relations,* 8th ed. (Upper Saddle River, NJ: Prentice Hall, 1999), chapter 1.

31. Diane Brady, "Wizard of Marketing," *Business Week,* July 24, 2000, pp. 84–87. Also see Dick Lynch, "The Magic of 'Harry Potter,' " *Advertising Age,* December 10, 2001, p. 26; Stephen Brown, "*Marketing for Muggles: The Harry Potter Way to Higher Profits,*" *Business Horizons,* January–February 2002, pp. 6–14; and "Harry Potter and the Publishing Goldmine," www.Economist.com, June 23, 2003.

32. See Kathleen Sampey, "Crest Whitestrips to Get $90M Push," *Brandweek,* June 4, 2001, p. 27; and Sampey, "Breaking the Rules of PR/Fashion Results in White-Hot Campaign," *PR News,* February 25, 2002.

33. See Al Ries and Laura Ries, *The Fall of Advertising and the Rise of PR* (New York: HarperBusiness, 2002). For counterpoints, see O. Burtch Drake, " 'Fall' of Advertising? I Differ," *Advertising Age,* January 13, 2003, p. 23.

34. Al Ries and Laura Ries, "First Do Some Publicity," *Advertising Age,* February 8, 1999, p. 42. Also see Ries and Ries, *The Fall of Advertising and the Rise of PR.* For counterpoints, see Drake, " 'Fall' of Advertising? I Differ," p. 23.

35. Portions adapted from Kate Fitzgerald, "Marketing on the Move," *Advertising Age,* March 18, 2002, p. 59. Also see Jack Neff, "Ries' Thesis: Ads Don't Build Brands, PR Does," *Advertising Age,* July 15, 2002, pp. 14–15; Scott Hume, Janice Matsumoto, Allison Perlik, and Margaret Sheridan, "Krispy Kreme's Movable Feast," *Restaurants Institutions,* June 1, 2002, p. 26; Kate Fitzgerald, "Branding Face to Face," *Advertising Age,* October 21, 2002, pp. 46–47; and Margaret Sheridan, "RI Choice in Chains," *Restaurants Institutions,* March 1, 2003, p. 62.

36. See Mark Gleason, "Edelman Sees Niche in Web Public Relations," *Advertising Age,* January 20, 1997, p. 30; Michael Krauss, "Good PR Critical to Growth on the Net," *Marketing News,* January 18, 1999, p. 8; Steve Jarvis, "How the Internet Is Changing Fundamentals of Publicity," *Marketing News,* July 17, 2000, p. 6; and G. A. Markin, "Why Doesn't the Press Call?"

Chapter 13

1. Quotes from "Lear Corporation Honored by General Motors as a 2002 Supplier of the Year," Lear press release, April 14, 2003, accessed at www.lear.com; and Andy Cohen, "Top of the Charts: Lear Corporation," *Sales Marketing Management,* July 1998, p. 40. Also see Fara Warner, "Lear Won't Take a Back Seat," *Fast Company,* June 2001, pp. 178–185; "America's 25 Best Sales Forces," *Sales Marketing Management,* accessed online at www.salesandmarketing.com, July 2002; "Automotive Brief: Lear Corp.: Auto-Parts Firm Posts Profit; New GM Accord Is Unveiled; "Lear Corporation," *Hoover's Company Profiles,* Austin, July 1, 2003, p. 17213; and "About Lear," accessed online at www.lear.com, September 2003.

2. Quote from Laurence Zuckerman, "Selling Airplanes with a Smile," *New York Times,* February 17, 2002, p. 3.2. Also see Bill Kelley, "How to Sell Airplanes, Boeing-Style," *Sales Marketing Management,* December 9, 1985, pp. 32–34; Andy Cohen, "Boeing," *Sales Marketing Management,* October 1997, p. 68; Stanley Holmes, "Rumble over Tokyo," *Business Week,* April 2, 2001, pp. 80–81; and J. Lynn Lunsford, "Boeing Beats Out Airbus to Sell Virgin Blue $3 Billion in Jets," *Wall Street Journal,* January 16, 2003, p. B6.

3. Geoffrey Brewer, "Love the Ones You're With," *Sales Marketing Management,* February 1997, pp. 38–45; *Edward F. Moltzen* and *Jennifer Hagendorf,* "IBM Unleashes E-Business Army," *Computer Reseller News,* January 24, 2000, pp. 3, 8; and Erin Stout, "Blue Skies Ahead?" *Sales Marketing Management,* March 2003, pp. 25–29.

4. "America's 500 Largest Sales Forces," *Selling Power,* October 2002, pp. 55–58.

5. Michele Marchetti, "What a Sales Call Costs," *Sales Marketing Management,* September 2000, p. 80.

6. See Martin Everett, "Selling by Telephone," *Sales Marketing Management,* December 1993, pp. 75–79. Also see Terry Arnold, "Telemarketing Strategy," *Target Marketing,* January 2002, pp. 47–48.

7. Geoffrey Brewer, "Lou Gerstner Has His Hands Full," *Sales Marketing Management,* May 8, 1998, pp. 36–41; and Michelle Cioci, "Marketing to Small Businesses," *Sales Marketing Management,* December 2000, pp. 94–100.

8. See "A Phone Is Better than a Face," *Sales Marketing Management,* October 1987, p. 29. Also see Michele Marchetti, "Look Who's Calling," *Sales Marketing Management,* May 1998, pp. 43–46; and "Climax Portable Machine Tools Case Study," accessed online at www.selltis.com/case_climax.html, August 2003.

9. Karen J. Bannan, "Call Center's Role Evolves with CRM," *B to B,* May 5, 2003, p. 14. Also see Julia Chang, "Dialing for Dollars," *Sales Marketing Management,* July 2003, p. 28.

10. Rick Mullin, "From Lone Wolves to Team Players," *Chemical Week,* January 14, 1998, pp. 33–34; and James P. Morgan, "Cross-Functional Buying: Why Teams Are Hot," *Purchasing,* April 5, 2001, pp. 27–32.

11. Robert Hiebeler, Thomas B. Kelly, and Charles Ketteman, *Best Practices: Building Your Business with Customer-Focused Solutions* (New York: Arthur Andersen/Simon Schuster, 1998), pp. 122–124. For more on team selling, also see Mark A. Moon and Susan Forquer Gupta, "Examining the Formation of Selling Centers: A Conceptual Framework," *Journal of Personal Selling and Sales Management,* Spring 1997, pp. 31–41; and Christian Homburg, John P. Workman Jr., and Ove Jensen, "A Configurational Perspective on Key Account Management," *Journal of Marketing,* April 2002, pp. 38–60; and Thomas N. Ingram, Raymond W. LaForge, Ramon A. Avila, Charles H. Schwepker Jr., and Michael R. Williams, *Sales Management: Analysis and Decision Making,* 5th ed. (Mason, OH: South-Western, 2004), pp. 66–67.

12. Quotes and other information in this section from Geoffrey Brewer, "Mind Reading: What Drives Top Salespeople to Greatness?" *Sales Marketing Management,* May 1994, pp. 82–88; Larry Blaine, "Sales Fundamentals," *American Salesman,* May 2002, p. 14–17; Erika Rasmusson, "The 10 Traits of Top Salespeople," *Sales Marketing Management,* August 1999, pp. 34–37; Andy Cohen, "The Traits of Great Sales Forces," *Sales Marketing Management,* October 2000, pp. 67–72; and Julia Chang, "Born to Sell?" *Sales Marketing Management,* July 2003, pp. 34–38.

13. See "To Test or Not to Test," *Sales Marketing Management*, May 1994, p. 86; Elena Harris, "Reduce Recruiting Risks," *Sales Marketing Management*, May 2000, p. 18; Erin Stout, "Recruiting and Hiring for Less," *Sales Marketing Management*, May 2002, p. 61; and Ingram, LaForge, Avila, Schwepker, and Williams, *Sales Management: Analysis and Decision Making*, pp. 136–139.

14. Robert Klein, "Nabisco Sales Soar after Sales Training," *Marketing News*, January 6, 1997, p. 23. Also see Malcolm Fleschner, "Training: How to Find the Best Training Solutions for Your Sales Team," *Selling Power*, June 2001, pp. 93–97; and Christine Galea, "2002 Sales Training Survey," *Sales Marketing Management*, July 2002, pp. 34–37.

15. Julia Chang, "No Instructor Required," *Sales Marketing Management*, May 2003, p. 26.

16. See "SMM's Best of Sales and Marketing: Best Trained Sales Force—Cisco Systems," *Sales Marketing Magazine*, September 2001, pp. 28–29; and "E-Learning: Field Training—How Cisco Spends Less Time in the Classroom and More Time with Customers," accessed at http://business.cisco.com/prod/tree.taf%3Fpublic_view=truekbns=1asset_id=86360.html, August 2003.

17. See Christen P. Heide, "All Levels of Sales Reps Post Impressive Earnings," press release, www.dartnell.com, May 5, 1997; *Dartnell's 30th Sales Force Compensation Survey*, Dartnell Corporation, August 1999; and Christine Galea, "2003 Salary Survey," *Sales Marketing Management*, May 2003, pp. 32–41.

18. Geoffrey Brewer, "Brain Power," *Sales Marketing Management*, May 1997, pp. 39–48; Don Peppers and Martha Rogers, "The Price of Customer Service," *Sales Marketing Management*, April 1999, pp. 20–21; Michelle Marchetti, "Pay Changes Are on the Way," *Sales Marketing Management*, August 2000, p. 101; Erin Stout, "Is Your Pay Plan on Target?" *Sales Marketing Management*, January 2002, p. 18; Peter Gundy, "Sales Compensation Programs: Built to Last," *Compensation Benefits and Review*, September/October 2002, pp. 21–28; and Ellen Neuborne, "A Compensation Plan Check-Up," *Sales Marketing Management*, May 2003, pp. 38–42.

19. See Gary H. Anthes, "Portal Powers GE Sales," *Computerworld*, June 2, 2003, pp. 31–32.

20. David Prater, "The Third Time's the Charm," *Sales Marketing Management*, September 2000, pp. 101–104. For more on sales force automation (SFA), see Chris Pullig, James G. Maxham III, and Joseph F. Hair Jr., "Salesforce Automation Systems: An Exploratory Examination of Organizational Factors Associated with Effective Implementation and Sales-Force Productivity," *Journal of Business Research*, May 2002, pp. 401–415; Cheri Speier and Viswanath Venkatesh, "The Hidden Minefields in the Adoption of Sales Force Automation Technologies," *Journal of Marketing*, July 2002, pp. 98–111; and Steve Levy, "A Call to Integrate CI, Customer Relationship Management, and Sales Force Automation," *Competitive Intelligence Magazine*, March–April 2003, pp. 36–39.

21. Melinda Ligos, "Point, Click, and Sell," *Sales Marketing Management*, May 1999, pp. 51–56; Tim Wilson, "Salespeople Leverage the Net," *InternetWeek*, June 4, 2001, pp. PG11, PG13; Amy J. Morgan and Scott A. Inks, "Technology and the Sales Force: Increasing Acceptance of Sales Force Automation," *Industrial Marketing Management*, July 2001, pp. 463–472; Eilene Zimmerman, "Casting the Net Wide," *Sales Marketing Management*, April 2002, pp. 50–56; and Paul N. Romani, "The Internet and Personal Selling," *The American Salesman*, March 2003, pp. 3–10.

22. Christine Neuberger, "Incentives to Perform," *Selling Power Sourcebook*, 2002, pp. 12–16.

23. Bob Donath, "Delivering Value Starts with Proper Prospecting," *Marketing News*, November 10, 1997, p. 5. Also see "Skills Workshop: Prospecting," *Selling Power*, October 2000, pp. 54–56; Steve Atlas, "Prospecting at Large Companies," *Selling Power*, January–February 2002, pp. 30–32; and Andy Cohen, "The Art of the Cold Call," *Sales Marketing Management*, February 2003, p. 12.

24. Quotes from David Stamps, "Training for a New Sales Game," *Training*, July 1997, pp. 46–52; Erin Stout, "Throwing the Right Pitch," *Sales Marketing Management*, April 2001, pp. 61–63; and Andy Cohen, "Customers Know Best," *Sales Marketing Management*, January 2003, p. 10.

25. Adapted from Betsy Cummings, "On the Cutting Edge," *Sales Marketing Management*, June 3, 2003, pp. 39–43.

26. Renee Houston Zemanski, "Well Connected," *Selling Power*, March 2003, pp. 32–34.

27. For these and other direct-marketing statistics in this section, see "Economic Impact: U.S. Direct and Interactive Marketing Today," along with a wealth of other information, accessed at www.the-dma.org/research, August 2003.

28. Alicia Orr Suman, "Ideas You Can Take to the Bank! 10 Big Things All Direct Marketers Should Be Doing Now," *Target Marketing*, February 2003, pp. 31–33.

29. Carol Krol, "Pizza Hut's Database Makes Its Couponing More Efficient," *Advertising Age*, November 30, 1998, p. 27; Dana Blakenhorn, "Marketers Hone Targeting," *Advertising Age*, June 18, 2001, p. T16; Thomas H. Davenport, "How Do They Know Their Customers So Well?" *MIT Sloan Management Review*, Winter 2001, pp. 63–73; and "The Customer Is Job 1 at Ford," accessed at www.sas.com/success/ford.html, August 2003.

30. For these and other examples, see Jonathan Berry, "A Potent New Tool for Selling: Database Marketing," *Business Week*, September 4, 1994, pp. 56–62; Weld F. Royal, "Do Databases Really Work?" *Sales Marketing Management*, October 1995, pp. 66–74; Daniel Hill, "Love My Brand," *Brandweek*, January 19, 1998, pp. 26–29; "FedEx Taps into Data Warehousing," *Advertising Age's Business Marketing*, January 1999, p. 25; and Harriet Marsh, "Dig Deeper into the Database Goldmine," *Marketing*, January 11, 2001, pp. 29–30.

31. Gary Loveman, "Diamonds in the Data Mine," *Harvard Business Review*, May 2003, pp. 109–113.

32. Statistics on direct media expenditures and sales throughout this section are from "Economic Impact: U.S. Direct and Interactive Marketing Today," accessed at www.the-dma.org/research, August 2003.

33. Matthew L. Wald, "Third Area Code Is Added in the Land of the Toll-Free," *New York Times*, April 4, 1998, p. 10; and "ATT Offers Toll-Free Number Availability Tool Online," *Direct Marketing*, May 2001, p. 24.

34. See Don Oldenberg, "Millions Answer Yes to No-Call," *The Washington Post*, July 8, 2003, p. C9; and " 'Do Not Call' List Registers Millions," *Wall Street Journal*, July 1, 2003, p. A4.

35. Facts about the catalog industry in this section are from "The DMA State of the Catalog Industry Report," accessed at www.the-dma.org, August 2003.

36. "Live from ACC: Catalog Sales Growth Outpaces Employment Growth," *Catalog Age*, June 2 2003, accessed online at http://catalogagemag.com/ar/marketing_live_acc_catalog/.

37. "Catalog Study Now Available," *Business Forms, Labels, and Systems*, June 20, 2001, p. 24; Richard S. Hodgson, "It's Still the Catalog Age," *Catalog Age*, June 2001, p. 156; and "JCPenney 100th Anniversary: Rewriting the Book on Catalog Sales," *Chain Store Age*, June 2002, p. 68.

38. Lillian Vernon 2002 Annual Report, accessed online at www.lillianvernon.com/pdf/LV-AR_2002_final.pdf; and "Lillian Vernon Corporation," *Hoover's Company Capsules*, Austin, July 1, 2003.

39. Example adapted in part from Moira Pascale, "Archie's Online Boom," *Catalog Age*, August 1999, p. 10. Other information accessed online at www.mcphee.com, August 2003.

40. Ron Donoho, "One-Man Show," *Sales Marketing Management,* June 2001, pp. 36–42.

41. Suzanne Vranica, "Blue Chips Using Ads with 1-800 Numbers," *Wall Street Journal,* November 30, 2001, p. B8.

42. See Steve Sullivan, "Shopping Channels: Less Hard Sell," *Broadcasting Cable,* November 27, 2000, pp. 86–90; Bob Tedeschi, "Television Shopping Channels May Become the Big Winners in the Competition for Online Sales," *New York Times,* April 16, 2001, p. C4; and "QVC, Inc.," *Hoover's Company Capsules,* Austin, July 1, 2003.

43. "Lining Up for Interactive Kiosks," *Nation's Business,* February 1998, p. 46; Warren S. Hersch, "Kiosks Poised to Be a Huge Growth Market," *Computer Reseller News,* May 18, 1998, p. 163; Catherine Yang, "No Web Site Is an Island," *Business Week,* March 22, 1999, p. EB38; "Kiosk: Disney Store," *Chain Store Age,* December 2000, p. 14A; Larry Beck, "The Kiosk's Ship Has Come In," *Dsn Retailing Today,* February 19, 2001, p. 14; and Shayn Ferriolo, "The Key to Kiosks," *Catalog Age,* June 2003, pp. 103–108.

44. "Interactive: Ad Age Names Finalists," *Advertising Age,* February 27, 1995, pp. 12–14.

45. Yang, "No Web Site Is an Island," p. EB38; and Matthew Haeberle, "REI Overhauls Its E-Commerce," *Chain Store Age,* January 2003, p. 64.

46. "Sweepstakes Groups Settles with States," *New York Times,* June 27, 2001, p. A14; and "*PCH Reaches $34 Million Sweepstakes Settlement with 26 States,*" *Direct Marketing,* September 2001, p. 6.

47. Jennifer Lee, "Welcome to the Database Lounge," *New York Times,* March 21, 2002, p. G1.

48. Debbie A. Connon, "The Ethics of Database Marketing," *Information Management Journal,* May-June 2002, pp. 42–44.

Chapter 14

1. Ranja Gulati and Jason Garino, "Get the Right Mix of Bricks and Clicks," *Harvard Business Review,* May–June 2000, pp. 107–108; Eric Berkman, "Clicklayer" *CIO,* February 1, 2001, p. 92; "Office Depot Helps Small Business Owners Get Ready for Tax Season with a Special 'Web Cafe' Online Seminar Session," *Business Wire,* March 31, 2003, p. 5775; "Office Depot, Inc.," *Hoover's Online,* Austin, August 15, 2003, p. 14308; and information accessed at www.officedepot.com, September 2003.

2. See "U.S. Internet Population Continues to Grow," February 6, 2002, accessed at http://cyberatlas.internet.com; "Internet Users Will Top 1 Billion in 2005," press release, Computer Industry Almanac Inc., March 12, 2002, accessed online at www.c-i-a.com; "Internet Penetration Rate Slows," *Silicon Valley/San Jose Business Journal,* February 5, 2003, accessed online at http://eastbay.bizjournals.com/sanjose; and "Population Explosion!" *CyberAtlas,* June 23, 2003, accessed at http://cyberatlas.internet.com.

3. Timothy J. Mullaney, "At Last, the Web Hits 100 MPH," *Business Week,* June 23, 2003, pp. 80-81; and Pamela Paul, "Hurry Up and Wait," *American Demographics,* June 2003, pp. 20-24.

4. Robyn Greenspan, "The Web as a Way of Life," accessed online at http://cyberatlas.internet.com, May 21, 2002; and "June 2003 Internet Usage Stats," accessed at http://cyberatlas.internet.com, September, 2003.

5. See Jerry Wind and Arvid Rangaswamy, "Customerization: The Next Revolution in Mass Customization," *Journal of Interactive Marketing,* Winter 2001, pp. 114–132; Yoram Wind and Vijay Mahajan, "Convergence Marketing," *Journal of Interactive Marketing,* Spring 2002, pp. 64–79. For other examples, including B2B examples, see Stefan Thomke and Eric Von Hippel, "Customers as Innovators," *Harvard Business Review,* April 2002, pp. 74–81. For a thoughtful discussion of customizing communication on the Internet, see Asim Ansari and Carl

F. Mena, "E-Customization," *Journal of Marketing Research* May 2003, pp. 131-145.

6. John A. Byrne, "Management by the Web," *Business Week,* August 28, 2000, pp. 84–96.

7. Alan Mitchell, "Internet Zoo Spawns New Business Models," *Marketing Week,* January 21, 1999, pp. 24–25. Also see Philip Kotler, *Marketing Moves: A New Approach to Profits, Growth, and Renewal* (Boston: Harvard Business School Press, 2002).

8. Paola Hjelt, "Flying on the Web in a Turbulent Economy," *Business Week,* April 30, 2001, pp. 142–148; and Lisa Sanders, "E-Packaging the Goods," *Advertising Age,* May 13, 2002, p. 28.

9. Jack Neff, "Using Tech Tools to Speed Marketing," *Advertising Age,* October 28, 2002, p. 14.

10. Information accessed online at www.gxs.com/gxs/aboutus, September 2003.

11. See Greenspan, "The Web as a Way of Life," and Mike Molesworth and Jukka-Petten Suortti, "Buying Cars Online: The Adoption of the Web for High-Involvement Purchases," *Journal of Consumer Behavior,* December 2002, pp. 155–169.

12. See Timothy Mullaney, "The E-Biz Surprise," *Business Week,* May 12, 2003, pp. 60–68; and Ken Kenjale and Arnie Phatak, "B2B Exchanges: How to Move Forward from Here," *World Trade,* June 2003, p. 26.

13. Adapted from Michael J. Weiss, "Online America," *American Demographics,* March 2001, pp. 53–60. Also see "A Nation Online: How Americans Are Expanding Their Use of the Internet," Department of Commerce, February 2002; Robyn Greenspan, "The Web as a Way of Life," May 21, 2002, accessed online at http://cyberatlas.internet.com; and Rebecca Gardyn, "Target Practice," *American Demographics,* October 2002, pp. 18–19.

14. See Michael Totty, "E-Commerce (A Special Report): Selling Strategies—Demographics: The Masses Have Arrived—And E-Commerce Will Never Be the Same," *Wall Street Journal,* January 27, 2003, p. R8.

15. Roger O. Crockett, "A Web That Looks Like the World," *Business Week,* March 22, 1999, p. EB46–EB47. Also see Robyn Greenspan, "Internet Not for Everyone," April 16, 2003, accessed at http://cyberatlas.internet.com.

16. See "A Nation Online: How Americans Are Expanding Their Use of the Internet," Department of Commerce, February 2002; Michael Pastore, "Internet Key to Communication Among Youth," January 25, 2002, accessed online at http://cyberatlas.internet.com; and John Fetto, "Teen Chatter," *American Demographics,* April 2002, p. 14.

17. See Joanne Cleaver, "Surfing for Seniors," *Marketing News,* July 19, 1999, pp. 1, 7; Sara Teasdale Montgomery, "Senior Surfers Grab Web Attention," *Advertising Age,* July 10, 2000, p. S4; Hassan Fattah, "Hollywood, the Internet, Kids," *American Demographics,* May 2001, pp. 51–56; Michael Pastore, "Online Seniors Enthusiastic About Internet Use," September 10, 2001, accessed online at http://cyberatlas.internet.com; and Robyn Greenspan, "Surfing with Seniors and Boomers," *CyberAtlas,* January 23, 2003, accessed at http://cyberatlas.internet.com.

18. Information accessed online at http://quickenloans.com, October 2003.

19. See Steve Hamm, "E-Biz: Down but Hardly Out," *Business Week,* March 26, 2001, pp. 126–130; "B2B E-Commerce Headed for Trillions," March 6, 2002, accessed at http://cyberatlas.internet.com; Kenjale and Phatak, "B2B Exchanges," p. 26; and Timothy Mullaney, "The E-Biz Surprise," *Business Week,* May 12, 2003, pp. 60–68.

20. See Peter Loftis, "E-Commerce: Business to Business—Exchanges: Making It Work," *Wall Street Journal,* February 2002, p. R16; Robert Simons, "Can E-Sourcing Win Auto Supplier's Hearts?" *Frontline Solutions,* May 2003, p. 43; and information accessed at www.covisint.com, September 2003. Also see George S. Day, Adam J. Fein, and Gregg Ruppersberger, "Shakeouts in Digital Markets: Lessons from

B2B Exchanges," *California Management Review,* Winter 2003, p. 131.

21. Darnell Little, "Let's Keep This Exchange to Ourselves," *Business Week,* December 4, 2000, p. 48. Also see Eric Young, "Web Marketplaces That Really Work," *Fortune/CNET Tech Review,* Winter 2002, pp. 78–86.

22. Facts from eBay annual reports and other information accessed at www.ebay.com, September 2003; and Robert Hof, "eBay Rules," *Business Week,* Spring 2003, p. 172. Also see Adam Lashinsky, "Meg and the Machine," *Fortune,* September 1, 2003, pp. 68-78.

23. Gary M. Stern, "You Got a Complaint?" *Link-Up,* September–October 2001, p. 28; Bob Tedeschi, "In the Current Internet Wilderness, Some Consumer Community Sites Are Hanging On, and Even Making Money," *New York Times,* January 7, 2002, p. C6; Susan Stellin, "Unhappy Math in Car Rentals," *New York Times,* February 23, 2003, p. 5.4; and information from www.planetfeedback.com/consumer, September 2003.

24. Heather Green, "How to Reach John Q. Public," *Business Week,* March 26, 2001, pp. 132–134. Also see Ellen Florian, "Dot-Com Deathwatch: Dead and (Mostly) Gone," *Fortune,* December 24, 2001, pp. 46–47.

25. Bradley Johnson, "Out-of-Sight Spending Collides with Reality," *Advertising Age,* August 7, 2000, pp. S4–S8.

26. Gary Hamel, "Is This All You Can Build with the Net? Think Bigger," *Fortune,* April 30, 2001, pp. 134–138.

27. See Ann Weintraub, "For Online Pet Stores, It's Dog-Eat-Dog," *Business Week,* March 6, 2000, pp. 78–80; "Death of a Spokespup," *Adweek,* December 11, 2000, pp. 44–46; Jacques R. Chevron, "Name Least of Pet.com's Woes," *Advertising Age,* January 22, 2001, p. 24; Norm Alster, "Initial Offerings Take a Turn to the Traditional," *New York Times,* May 19, 2002, p. 3.4; and "Marketing Hits and Misses," *Sales Marketing Management,* August 2002, p. 16.

28. "E-Commerce Trudges through Current Slowdown," accessed at www.cyberatlas.internet.com, May 22, 2001. Also see Eyal Biyalogorsky and Prasad Naik, "Click and Mortar: The Effect of On-line Activities on Off-line Sales," *Marketing Letters,* February 2003, pp. 1–21.

29. Sharon Gaudin, "The Site of No Return," *DataMation,* accessed at www.internet.com, May 28, 2002.

30. Laurie Freeman, "Why Internet Brands Take Offline Avenues," *Marketing News,* July 1999, p. 4; and Paul C. Judge, "The Name's the Thing," *Business Week,* November 15, 1999, pp. 35–39.

31. John Deighton, "The Future of Interactive Marketing," *Harvard Business Review,* November–December 1996, p. 154.

32. Don Peppers and Martha Rogers, "Opening the Door to Consumers," *Sales Marketing Management,* October 1998, pp. 22–29; Mike Beirne, "Marketers of the Next Generation: Silvio Bonvini," *Brandweek,* November 8, 1999, p. 64; Jack Neff, "PG vs. Martha," *Advertising Age,* April 8, 2002, p. 24; Hassan Fattah and Pamela Paul, "Gaming Gets Serious," *American Demographics,* May 2002, pp. 38–43; and information from www.candystand.com, June 2002.

33. Jeffrey F. Rayport and Bernard J. Jaworski, *e-Commerce* (New York: McGraw-Hill, 2001), p. 116. Also see Goutam Chakraborty, "What Do Customers Consider Important in B2B Websites?" *Journal of Advertising,* March 2003, p. 50; and David Sparrow, "Get 'Em to Bite," *Catalog Age,* April 1, 2003, pp. 35–36.

34. Lisa Bertagnoli, "Getting Satisfaction," *Marketing News,* May 7, 2001, p. 11.

35. Tobi Elkin, "Size Matters; So Does Price," *Advertising Age,* January 13, 2003, p. 46.

36. For these and other examples, see William M. Bulkeley, "E-Commerce (A Special Report): Cover Story—Pass It On: Advertisers Discover They Have a Friend in 'Viral' Marketing," *Wall Street Journal,* January 14, 2002, p. R6.

37. Eilene Zimmerman, "Catch the Bug," *Sales and Marketing Management,* February 2001, pp. 78–82. Also see Ellen Neuborne, "Viral Marketing Alert," *Business Week,* March 19, 2001, p. EB8.

38. Heather Green, "Online Ads Take Off—Again," *Business Week,* May 5, 2003, p. 75.

39. Tobi Elkin, "Net Advantages," *Advertising Age,* February 10, 2003, p. 29.

40. Debra Aho Williamson, "Web Giants Cash in on Rich Media," *Advertising Age,* November 18, 2002, p. S-12. Also see, Tobi Elkin, "Marketing beyond the Pop-Up," *Advertising Age,* March 10, 2003, pp. 40, 42.

41. Information from the iVillage Top-Line Metrics section of www.ivillage.com, September 2003; and Dennis Callaghan, "Brands to Watch: Paul Allen: MyFamily.com," *MC Technology Marketing Intelligence,* February 2000, pp. 44–46; and information from www.MyFamily.com, September 2003.

42. See Thane Peterson, "E-I-E-I-E-Farming," *Business Week,* May 1, 2000, p. 202; "Survival of the Fittest," *Agri Marketing,* March 2002, pp. 18–24; and www.agriculture.com, September 2003.

43. Arlene Weintraub, "When E-Mail Ads Aren't Spam," *Business Week,* October 16, 2000, pp. 112–113; Rebecca Gardyn, "Target Practice," *American Demographics,* October 2002, pp. 18–20; and "DoubleClick Marketing Spending Index," accessed online at www.DoubleClick.com, March 2003.

44. Elizabeth Corcoran, "The E Gang," *Fortune,* July 24, 2000, p. 145.

45. Michael Porter, "Strategy and the Internet," *Harvard Business Review,* March 2001, pp. 614–678.

46. Timothy J. Mullaney, "Break Out the Black Ink," *Business Week,* May 13, 2002, pp. 74–76; and Timothy Mullaney, "The Web Is Finally Catching Profits," *Business Week,* February 17, 2003, p. 66.

47. See Peter Han and Angus Maclaurin, "Do Consumers Really Care About Online Privacy?" *Marketing Management,* January–February 2002, pp. 35–38; *Eric Goldman,* "The Internet Privacy Fallacy," *Computer and Internet Lawyer,* January 2003, p. 20; and Nancy Wong, "Getting Pragmatic about Privacy," *American Demographics,* June 2003, pp. 14–15.

48. See Adam Clymer, "Senator Prevents Action on Online Privacy Bill," *New York Times,* May 17, 2002, p. A16; Donna Doyle, "Privacy Legislation Updates," *Target Marketing,* July 2002, p. 19; and Deborah L. Vence, "Moving Forward," *Marketing News,* December 9, 2002, p. 15.

49. See Jennifer DiSabatino, "FTC OKs Self-Regulation to Protect Children's Privacy," *Computerworld,* February 12, 2001, p. 32; and Laurie Flynn, "New Efforts Are Being Made to Keep Online Merchants from Collecting Personal Information from Children," *New York Times,* May 12, 2003, p. C4.

50. Bob Tedeschi, "Everybody Talks About Online Privacy, but Few Do Anything about It," *New York Times,* June 3, 2002, p. C6; and Ivan Schneideer, "RBC Promotes Company-Wide High Standards," *Bamk Systems Technology,* December 2002, p. 14; and information accessed online at www.truste.com, August 2003.

51. Information on TRUSTe accessed at www.truste.com, September 2003.

52. See "Seventy Percent of US Consumers Worry About Online Privacy, but Few Take Protective Action, Reports Jupiter Media Metrix," Jupiter Media Metrix press release, June 3, 2002, accessed online at www.jmm.com.

53. Ira Sager, "The Underground Web," *Business Week,* September 2, 2002, pp. 67–74.

54. "VeriSign Signs Pact with eBay to Fight Fraud on Auction Site," *Wall Street Journal,* May 8, 2002, p. A9; and the Internet Fraud Complaint Center Annual Report, accessed online at www.ifccfbi.gov, March 2003.

55. Mark Warschauer, "Demystifying the Digital Divide," *Scientific American,* August 2003, p. 42.

56. "14-Year-Old Bids over $3M for Items in eBay Auctions," *USA Today,* April 30, 1999, p. 10B.

Chapter 15

1. Mark L. Clifford and Nicole Harris, "Coke Pours into Asia," *Business Week,* October 28, 1996, pp. 72–77; Mark Gleason, "Sprite Is Riding Global Ad Effort to No. 4 Status," *Advertising Age,* November 18, 1996, p. 30; Hillary Chura and Richard Linnett, "Coca-Cola Readies Global Assault," *Advertising Age,* April 2, 2001, pp. 1, 34; Daniel Rogers, "Coke's Local World Cup Tactics," *Marketing,* May 30, 2002, p. 15; Ken Hein, "Soft Drinks," *Mediaweek,* April 21, 2003, p. SR29; "Sprite Shows Off Hint of Mint Up North," *Packaging Digest,* May 2003, p. 4; and "Our Company," accessed online at www.coca-cola.com, September 2003.

2. John Alden, "What in the World Drives UPS?" *International Business,* April 1998, pp. 6–7; Karen Pennar, "Two Steps Forward, One Step Back," *Business Week,* August 31, 1998, p. 116; Michelle Wirth Fellman, "A New World for Marketers," *Marketing News,* May 10, 1999, p. 13; Alan Greenspan, "International Trade: Globalization vs. Protectionism," *Vital Speeches of the Day,* April 15, 2001, pp. 386–388, and *International Trade Statistics 2002,* WTO, p. 1, accessed online at www.wto.org/english/res_e/statis_e/its2002_e/its02_toc_e.htm, August 2003.

3. Gail Edmondson, "See the World, Erase Its Borders," *Business Week,* August 28, 2000, pp. 113–114.

4. "The Unique Japanese," *Fortune,* November 24, 1986, p. 8; and James D. Southwick, "Addressing Market Access Barriers in Japan Through the WTO," *Law and Policy in International Business,* Spring 2000, pp. 923–976. For more on nontariff and other barriers, see Warren J. Keegan and Mark C. Green, *Principles of Global Marketing* (Upper Saddle River, NJ: Prentice Hall, 2000), chapter 8; and Simon P. Anderson and Nicholas Schmidt, "Nontariff Barriers and Trade Liberalization," *Economic Inquiry,* January 2003, pp. 80–98.

5. "What Is the WTO?" accessed at www.wto.org/english/thewto_e/whatis_e.htm, September 2003.

6. See Douglas Harbrecht and Owen Ullmann, "Finally GATT May Fly," *Business Week,* December 29, 1993, pp. 36–37; Ping Deng, "Impact of GATT Uruguay Round on Various Industries," *American Business Review,* June 1998, pp. 22–29; Helene Cooper, "U.S. Seeks a New Rounds of WTO Talks," *Wall Street Journal,* July 18, 2001, p. A12; Michael Finger, Julio J. Nogues, "The Unbalanced Uruguay Outcome: The New Areas in Future WTO Negotiations," *The World Economy,* March 2002, pp. 321–340; and *WTO Annual Report 2003,* accessed online at www.wto.org/english/res_e/anrep_e/anrep03_e.pdf, September 2003.

7. "Leaders: Deadlocked in Doha; World Trade," *The Economist,* March 29, 2003, p. 13.

8. Jeffrey Lewis, "The European Union," *AFP Exchange,* March/April 2003, pp. 46–50; and "The European Union at a Glance," accessed online at http://europa.eu.int, September 2003.

9. Allyson L. Stewart-Allen, "Changeover to Euro Has Hidden Expenses," *Marketing News,* July 30, 2001, p. 6; "Finance and Economics: Up for Adoption: Central Europe and the Euro," *The Economist,* June 1, 2002, pp. 69–70; and "Finance and Economics: The Euro, Trade and Growth; Economic Focus," *The Economist,* July 12, 2003, p. 74.

10. For more on the European Union, see "Around Europe in 40 Years," *The Economist,* May 31, 1997, p. S4; "European Union to Begin Expansion," *New York Times,* March 30, 1998, p. A5; Joan Warner, "Mix Us Culturally? It's Impossible," *Business Week,* April 27, 1998,

p. 108; Paul J. Deveney, "World Watch," *Wall Street Journal,* May 20, 1999, p. A12; and Stephen J. Dannhauser, "Can Europe Become a Global Superpower? Europe Must Have Unification," *Vital Speeches of the Day,* April 1, 2003, pp. 382–385.

11. Charles J. Whalen, "NAFTA's Scorecard: So Far, So Good," *Business Week,* July 9, 2001, pp. 54–56; Geri Smith, "Betting on Free Trade: Will the Americas Be One Big Market?" *Business Week,* April 23, 2001, pp. 60–62; Ernesto Zedillo, "Commentary: Free Trade Is the Best Diplomacy," *Forbes,* July 23, 2001, p. 49; Fay Hansen, "World Trade Update," *Business Finance,* March 2002, pp. 9–11; Daniel T. Griswold, "NAFTA at 10," *World Trade,* March 2003, p. 10; and Kenneth G. Weigel, "The FTAA," *World Trade,* July 2003, p. 44.

12. Larry Rohter, "Latin America and Europe to Talk Trade," *New York Times,* June 26, 1999, p. 2; Bernard Malamud and Wayne A. Label, "The Merco: A Common Currency for Mercosur and Latin America," *American Business Review,* June 2002, pp. 132–139; and Terry Wade, "Latin Trade Bloc Flexes Its Muscle—New Leaders in Argentina, Brazil Give Mercosur Clout; Another Challenge for U.S." *Wall Street Journal,* June 16, 2003, p. A.13.

13. David Woodruff, "Ready to Shop Until They Drop," *Business Week,* June 22, 1998, pp. 104–108. Also see "Card-Carrying Consumers," *Country Monitor,* July 15, 2002, p. 5; William Drozdiak, "What's New about Europe? The Economy," *The Washington Post,* February 9, 2003, p. B3; and Lara L. Sowinsky, "Follow the Money," *World Trade,* July 2003, p. 20.

14. Virginia Postrel, "The Wealth of Nations Depends on How Open They Are to International Trade," *New York Times,* May 17, 2001, p. C2.

15. Dan West, "Countertrade," *Business Credit,* April 2001, pp. 64–67. Also see Dan West, "Countertrade," *Business Credit,* April 2002, pp. 48–51.

16. For this and other examples, see Louis Kraar, "How to Sell to Cashless Buyers," *Fortune,* November 7, 1988, pp. 147–154; Nathaniel Gilbert, "The Case for Countertrade," *Across the Board,* May 1992, pp. 43–45; Darren McDermott and S. Karen Witcher, "Bartering Gains Currency," *Wall Street Journal,* April 6, 1998, p. A10; Anne Millen Porter, "Global Economic Meltdown Boosts Barter Business," *Purchasing,* February 11, 1999, pp. 21–25; S. Jayasankaran, "Fire-Fighting," *Far Eastern Economic Review,* May 31, 2001, p. 52; and Dalia Marin and Monika Schnitzer, "The Economic Institution of International Barter," *Economic Journal,* April 2002, pp. 293–316.

17. Rebecca Piirto Heath, "Think Globally," *Marketing Tools,* October 1996, pp. 49–54; and "The Power of Writing," *National Geographic,* August 1999, pp. 128–129.

18. For other examples, see *Dun Bradstreet's Guide to Doing Business Around the World* (Upper Saddle River, NJ: Prentice Hall, 2000); Betsy Cummings, "Selling Around the World," *Sales Marketing Management,* May 2001, p. 70; James K. Sebenius, "The Hidden Challenge of Cross-Border Negotiations," *Harvard Business Review,* March 2002, pp. 76–85; and Philip Kotler, *Marketing Management,* 11th ed. (Upper Saddle River, NJ: Prentice Hall, 2003), chapter 7.

19. Pete Engardio, Manjeet Kripalani, and Alysha Webb, "Smart Globalization," *Business Week,* August 27, 2001, pp. 132–136.

20. Charles A. Coulombe, "Global Expansion: The Unstoppable Crusade," *Success,* September 1994, pp. 18–20; "Amway Hopes to Set Up Sales Network in India," *Wall Street Journal,* February 17, 1998, p. B8; Gerald S. Couzens, "Dick Devos," *Success,* November 1998, pp. 52–57; information accessed online at www.amway.com/OurStory/o-hist.asp, August 2003; and information accessed online at www.amway.com/infocenter/i-mediFact.asp, September 2003.

21. See "Crest, Colgate Bare Teeth in Competition for China," *Advertising Age International,* November 1996, p. I3; and Jack Neff, "Submerged," *Advertising Age,* March 4, 2002, p. 14.

22. Robert Neff, "In Japan, They're Goofy about Disney," *Business Week*, March 12, 1990, p. 64; "In Brief: E*Trade Licensing Deal Gives It an Israeli Link," *American Banker*, May 11, 1998; John Engen, "Going Going Global," *USBanker*, February 2000, pp. 22S–25S; "Cowboys and Samuri: The Japanizing of Universal," *Wall Street Journal*, March 22, 2001, p. B1; Chester Dawson, "Will Toyko Embrace Another Mouse?" *Business Week*, September 10, 2001; Bruce Orwall, "Eisner Contends Disney Is Primed for Turnaround," *Wall Street Journal*, August 9, 2002, p. B1; and "Walt Disney Parks Resorts," *Hoover's Company Capsules*, Austin, July 1, 2003, p. 104368.

23. See Cynthia Kemper, "KFC Tradition Sold Japan on Chicken," *Denver Post*, June 7, 1998, p. J4; and Milford Prewitt, "Chains Look for Links Overseas," *Nation's Restaurant News*, February 18, 2002, pp. 1, 6.

24. Laurel Wentz, "Far-Flung Units Connected," *Advertising Age*, April 7, 2003, p. S2.

25. See "In India, Beef-Free Mickie D," *Business Week*, April 7, 1995, p. 52; Jeff Walters, "Have Brand Will Travel," *Brandweek*, October 6, 1997, pp. 22–26; David Barboza, "From Abroad, McDonald's Finds Value in Local Control," *New York Times*, February 12, 1999, p. 1; Nanette Byrnes, "Brands in a Bind," *Business Week*, August 28, 2000, pp. 234–238; *Suh-Kyung Yoon*, "Look Who's Going Native," *Far Eastern Economic Review*, February 1, 2001, pp. 68–69; and O'Keefe, "Global Brands," p. 104.

26. For more, see Warren J. Keegan, *Global Marketing Management*, 7th ed. (Upper Saddle River, NJ: Prentice Hall, 2002), pp. 346–351.

27. Bernd H. Schmitt and Yigang Pan, "In Asia, the Supernatural Means Sales," *New York Times*, February 19, 1995, 3, 11; Sally Taylor, "Tackling the Curse of Bad Feng Shui," *Publishers Weekly*, April 27, 1998, p. 24; Michael Schrage, "Sorry About the Profits, Boss. My Feng Shui Is Off," *Fortune*, November 27, 2000, p. 306; Barry Janoff, "East Meets West," *Progressive Grocer*, January 2001, pp. 47–49; and Branden Phillips, "A Swath of Enterprise Where Feng Shui Fits," *New York Times*, May 6, 2003, p. G9.

28. Adapted from Douglas McGray, "Translating Sony into English," *Fast Company*, January 2003, p. 38.

29. Kate MacArthur, "Coca-Cola Light Employs Local Edge," *Advertising Age*, August 21, 2000, pp. 18–19.

30. See Alicia Clegg, "One Ad One World?" *Marketing Week*, June 20, 2002, pp. 51–52; and George E. Belch and Machael A. Belch, *Advertising and Promotion: An Integrated Marketing Communications Perspective*, 6th ed. (New York: McGraw Hill, 2004), pp. 666–668.

31. See Michael Oneal, "Harley-Davidson: Ready to Hit the Road Again," *Business Week*, July 21, 1986, p. 70; "EU Proposes Dumping Change," *East European Markets*, February 14, 1997, pp. 2–3. For more on dumping, see Dobrin R. Kolev and Thomas J. Pruse, "Dumping and Double Crossing: The (In)effectiveness of Cost-Based Trade Policy Under Incomplete Information," *International Economic Review*, August 2002, pp. 895–918; and William Baldwin, "Please Dump on Me," *Forbes*, April 14, 2003.

32. Sarah Ellison, "Revealing Price Discrepancies, the Euro Aids Bargain-Hunters," *Wall Street Journal*, January 30, 2002, p. A15.

33. See Patrick Powers, "Distribution in China: The End of the Beginning," *China Business Review*, July–August, 2001, pp. 8–12; Drake Weisert, "Coca-Cola in China: Quenching the Thirst of a Billion," *The China Business Review*, July–August 2001, pp. 52–55; and Gabriel Kahn, "Coke Works Harder at being the Real Thing in Hinterland," *Wall Street Journal*, November 26, 2002, p. B1.

34. Richard Tomlinson, "The China Card," *Fortune*, May 25, 1998, p. 82; and Paul Mooney, "Deals on Wheels," *Far East Economic Review*, May 20, 1999

Chapter 16

1. Quotes and other information for this Nike story from Rebecca De Winter, "The Anti-Sweatshop Movement," *Ethics International Affairs*, October 2001, pp. 99–117; Richard Locke, "The Promise and Perils of Globalization: The Case of Nike," *Management: Inventing and Delivering Its Future*, 2003; and www.nike.com/nikebiz/nikebiz.jhtml?page=24, September 2003.

2. See Greg Winter, "Tobacco Producers Are Willing to Talk with Justice Department," *New York Times*, June 22, 2001, p. C1; Gordan Fairclough, "*Study Slams Philip Morris Ads Telling Teens Not to Smoke—How a Market Researcher Who Dedicated Years to Cigarette Sales Came to Create Antismoking Ads*," Wall Street Journal, May 29, 2002, p. B1; and Christina Cheddar Berk, "Cigarette Makers Spending on Ads, Promotions Rises," *Wall Street Journal*, June 18, 2003, p. B5.

3. James Heckman, "Don't Shoot the Messenger: More and More Often, Marketing Is the Regulators' Target," *Marketing News*, May 24, 1999, pp. 1, 9; "Sweepstakes Group Settles with States," *The New York Times*, June 27, 2001, p. A.14; "Business Brief—Publishers Clearing House: Payment of $34 Million Set to Settle with 26 States," *Wall Street Journal*, June 27, 2001, p. B8; "PCH Reaches $34 Million Sweepstakes Settlement with 26 States," *Direct Marketing*, September 2001, p. 6; and "'You're a Guaranteed Winner': Composing 'You' in a Consumer Culture," Helen Rothschild Ewald and Roberta Vann, *The Journal of Business Communication*, April 2003, pp. 98–128.

4. Mylene Mangalindan, "Subject: Spam Messages Often Are Misleading," *Wall Street Journal*, April 30, 2003, p. D2.

5. Palm Settles Deceptive Ad Charges," *New York Times*, March 7, 2002, p. 6.

6. Theodore Levitt, "The Morality (?) of Advertising," *Harvard Business Review*, July–August 1970, pp. 84–92. For counterpoints, see Heckman, "Don't Shoot the Messenger," pp. 1, 9.

7. Roger Parloff, "Is Fat the Next Tobacco?" *Fortune*, February 3, 2003, pp. 51–54; and "'Big Food' Get the Obesity Message," *New York Times*, July 10, 2003, p. A22.

8. David Welch, "Firestone: Is This Brand Beyond Repair?" *Business Week*, June 11, 2001, p. 48. Also see Ken Belson and Micheline Maynard, "Big Recall Behind It, Tire Maker Regains Its Footing," *New York Times*, August 10, 2002, p. 1; and Keith Naughton, "Bill Ford's Rainy Days," *Newsweek*, June 16, 2003, p. 38.

9. Cliff Edwards, "Where Have All the Edsels Gone?" *Greensboro News Record*, May 24, 1999, p. B6. For a thought-provoking short case involving planned obsolescence, see James A. Heely and Roy L. Nersesian, "The Case of Planned Obsolescence," *Management Accounting*, February 1994, p. 67. Also see Joel Dryfuss, "Planned Obsolescence Is Alive and Well," *Fortune*, February 15, 1999, p. 192; Atsuo Utaka, "Planned Obsolescence and Marketing Strategy," *Managerial and Decision Economics*, December 2000, pp. 339–344.

10. Adapted from John Markoff, "Is Planned Obsolescence Obsolete?" *New York Times*, February 17, 2002, p. 4.6.

11. See Judith Bell and Bonnie Maria Burlin, "In Urban Areas: Many More Still Pay More for Food," *Journal of Public Policy and Marketing*, Fall 1993, pp. 268–270; Kathryn Graddy and Diana C. Robertson, "Fairness of Pricing Decisions," *Business Ethics Quarterly*, April 1999, pp. 225–243; Gordon Matthews, "Does Everyone Have the Right to Credit?" *USBanker*, April 2001, pp. 44-48.

12. See Brian Grow and Pallavi Gogoi, "A New Way to Squeeze the Weak?" *Business Week*, January 28, 2002, p. 92; and Mark A. Hofmann, "Redlining Becomes Less of an Issue for Agents, Brokers," *Business Insurance*, May 5, 2003, p. 14C.

13. Marcia Stepanek, "Weblining," *Business Week,* April 3, 2000, pp. EB26–EB43. Also see Karin Helperin, "Wells Fargo Online Service Accused of Redlining," *Bank Systems Technology,* September 2000, p. 19.

14. John De Graaf, "The Overspent American/Luxury Fever," *The Amicus Journal*, Summer 1999, pp. 41–43. Also see, James E. Burroughs and Aric Rindfleisch, "Materialism and Well-Being: A Conflicting Values Perspective," *Journal of Consumer Research,* December 2002, pp. 348–362; and Tim Kasser, *The High Price of Materialism* (Cambridge, MA: MIT Press, 2002).

15. Carolyn Setlow, "Profiting from America's New Materialism," *Discount Store News,* April 17, 2000, p. 16. For interesting discussions on materialism and consumption, see Mark Rotella, Sarah F. Gould, Lynn Andriani, and Michael Scharf, "The High Price of Materialism," *Publishers Weekly,* July 1, 2002, p. 67; and LinChiat Chang and Robert M. Arkin, "Materialism as an Attempt to Cope with Uncertainty," *Psychology Marketing,* May 2002, pp. 389–406.

16. Adapted from Constance L. Hays, "Preaching to Save Shoppers from 'Evil' of Consumerism," *New York Times,* January 1, 2003, p. C1.

17. James Twitchell, "Two Cheers for Materialism," *The Wilson Quarterly,* Spring 1999, pp. 16–26. Also see Twitchell, *Lead Us into Temptation: The Triumph of American Materialism* (New York: Columbia University Press, 1999); and Twitchell, *Living It Up: Our Love Affair with Luxury* (New York: Columbia University Press, 2002).

18. Kim Clark, "Real-World-O-Nomics: How to Make Traffic Jams a Thing of the Past," *Fortune,* March 31, 1997, p. 34. Also see Lee Hultgreen and Kim Kawada, "San Diego's Interstate 15 High-Occupancy/Toll Lane Facility Using Value Pricing," *ITE Journal,* June 1999, pp. 22–27; "Variably Priced Express Lanes Gaining Interest Nationwide," *ENR,* March 17, 2003, p. 17; and "HOT Idea in Traffic Management," *The Washington Post,* June 15, 2003, p. B8.

19. From an advertisement for *Fact* magazine, which does not carry advertisements.

20. Greg Winter, "Hershey Is Put on the Auction Block," *New York Times,* July 26, 2002, p. 5.

21. Adapted from information found in Steve Hamm, "Microsoft's Future," *Business Week,* January 19, 1998, pp. 58–68; and Dan Carney and Mike France, "The Microsoft Case: Tying It All Together," *Business Week,* December 3, 2001, pp. 68–69. Also see James G. Helgeson and Eric G. Gorger, "The Price Weapon: Developments in U.S. Predatory Pricing Law," *Journal of Business to Business Marketing,* 2003, p. 3.

22. Stuart L. Hart, "Beyond Greening: Strategies for a Sustainable World," *Harvard Business Review,* January–February 1997, pp. 66–76. Also see Trevor Price and Doug Probert, "The Need for Environmentally-Sustainable Developments," *International Need for Environmentally-Sustainable Developments,* 2002, pp. 1–22; and "Four Different Versions of the Environmental Future," *Futurist,* January–February 2003, pp. 12–14.

23. Michael E. Porter and Claas van der Linde, "Green *and* Competitive: Ending the Stalemate," *Harvard Business Review,* September–October 1995, pp. 120–134.

24. Hart, "Beyond Greening," p. 73; Carl Pope, "Billboards of the Garden Wall," *Sierra,* January/February 1999, pp. 12–13; Hendrik A. Verfaille, "A New Pledge for a New Company," *Executive Speeches,* February–March 2001, pp. 10–13; and www.monsanto.com/monsanto/layout/our_pledge/default.asp, September 2003.

25. Lynelle Preston, "Sustainability at Hewlett-Packard: From Theory to Practice," *California Management Review,* Spring 2001, pp. 26–36.

26. See Lars K. Hallstrom, "Industry Versus Ecology: Environment in the New Europe," *Futures,* February 1999, pp. 25–38; Joe McKinney, "NAFTA: Four Years Down the Road," *Baylor Business Review*, Spring 1999, pp. 22–23; Andreas Diekmann and Axel Franzen, "The Wealth of Nations and Environmental Concern," *Environment and Behavior*, July 1999, pp. 540–549; "EMAS-Newsletter: The Eco-Management and Audit Scheme," June 2002, accessed online at http://europa.eu.int/comm/environment/emas; Michelle Conlin and Paul Raeburn, "Industrial Evolution," *Business Week,* April 8, 2002, pp. 70–72; and N. Kanari, J.L. Pineau, and S. Shallari, "End-of-Life Vehicle Recycling in the European Union," *Journal of Minerals, Metals Materials,* August 2003, pp. 15–19.

27. Michelle Wirth Fellman, "New Product Marketer of 1997," *Marketing News,* March 30, 1998, pp. E2, E12; Mercedes M. Cardona, "Colgate Boosts Budget to Further 5-Year Plan," *Advertising Age,* May 15, 2000, p. 6; Emily Nelson, "Colgate's Net Rose 10 percent in Period, New Products Helped Boost Sales," *Wall Street Journal,* February 2, 2001, p. B6; and Christina Cheddar Berk, "Colgate Posts Rise of 10% in Profit for Second Period," *Wall Street Journal,* July 23, 2003, p. A8.

28. Jacquelyn A. Ottman, "Green Marketing: Wake Up to the Truth about Green Consuming," *In Business,* May–June 2002, p. 31; Marc Gunther, "Son of Aeron," *Fortune,* May 12, 2003, p. 134; and information accessed online at www.HermanMiller.com, October 2003.

29. Dan R. Dalton and Richard A. Cosier, "The Four Faces of Social Responsibility," *Business Horizons,* May–June 1982, pp. 19–27.

30. Joseph Webber, "3M's Big Cleanup," *Business Week,* June 5, 2000, pp. 96–98. Also see Kara Sissell, "3M Defends Timing of Scotchgard Phaseout," *Chemical Week,* April 11, 2001, p. 33; Peck Hwee Sim, "Ausimont Targets Former Scotchgard Markets," *Chemical Week,* August 7, 2002, p. 32; and Jennifer Lee, "E.P.A. Orders Companies to Examine Effect of Chemicals," *New York Times,* April 15, 2003, p. F2.

31. Barbara Crossette, "Russia and China Top Business Bribers," *New York Times,* May 17, 2002, p. A10; and Jakob Svensson, "Who Must Pay Bribes and How Much? Evidence from a Cross Section of Firms," *The Quarterly Journal of Economics*, February 2003, p. 207.

32. John F. Magee and P. Ranganath Nayak, "Leaders' Perspectives on Business Ethics," *Prizm,* Arthur D. Little, Inc., Cambridge, MA, first quarter, 1994, pp. 65–77. Also see Turgut Guvenli and Rajib Sanyal, "Ethical Concerns in International Business: Are Some Issues More Important Than Others?" *Business and Society Review,* Summer 2002, pp. 195–206.

33. Guvenli and Sanyal, "Ethical Concerns in International Business," pp. 71–72. Also see Thomas Donaldson, "Values in Tension: Ethics away from Home," *Harvard Business Review,* September–October 1996, pp. 48–62; Patrick E. Murphy, "Character and Virtue Ethics in International Marketing: An Agenda for Managers, Researchers, and Educators," *Journal of Business Ethics,* January 1999, pp. 107–124; and Gopalkrishnan, "International Exchanges as the Basis for Conceptualizing Ethics in International Business," *Journal of Business Ethics,* February 2001, pp. 3–25.

34. See Samuel A. DiPiazza, "Ethics in Action," *Executive Excellence,* January 2002, pp. 15–16; and Samuel A. DiPiazza, Jr, "It's All Down to Personal Values," accessed online at www.pwcglobal.com, August 2003.

35. Kenneth Labich, "The New Crisis in Business Management," *Fortune,* April 20, 1992, pp. 167–176.

36. DiPiazza, "Ethics in Action," p. 15.

Credits

Ranch. **270** Courtesy of Daimler/Chrysler Corporation **274** Courtesy of Gillette **275** Courtesy of Nokia **278** Courtesy of 3M **282** Courtesy of WD-40. All rights reserved. **283** Courtesy of Stock Boston **284** SPAM and all SPAM derived terms are registered trademarks of Hormel Foods, LCC and are used with permission from Hormel Foods. **285** Courtesy of CrackerJack

Chapter 9

290 Courtesy of Priceline.com. All rights reserved. **295** Used with permission of PriceSCAN.com, Inc. All rights reserved. **296** Courtesy of Four Seasons Hotels **299** Used with permission of Robin Hood Multifoods Corporation. **300** Used with permission of Gibson Guitar. All rights reserved. **303** Courtesy of Steinway & Sons **305** Reprinted courtesy of Caterpillar Inc. **307** Courtesy of Gramophone. All rights reserved. **309** Courtesy of CityPass. **311** Courtesy of Continental Airlines and MapQuest. All rights reserved. **312** Courtesy of D. Young-Wolff/PhotoEdit **313** Courtesy of Wide World Photos **313** Courtesy of Wide World Photos **313** Courtesy of Photo Edit **313** Courtesy of Getty Images Inc. **315** Courtesy of Big KMart **318** Courtesy of McDonalds **319** Courtesy of Joy perfume **321** Courtesy of Kimberly Clark **322** Reprinted with permission of AARP **325** Courtesy of Getty Images Inc.

Chapter 10

330 Reprinted courtesy of Caterpillar Inc. **334** Courtesy of Palm, Inc. Photographer: Amanda Marsalis. **335** © 1995-2001 FedEx. All rights reserved. **339** Courtesy of Churchill & Klehr Photography **340** (Right) Jan Staller, TimePix; (Left) AP/Wide World Photos **341** Used with permission of Cereal Partners UK **344** Reprinted with permission of Expedia, Inc. Courtesy of Deutsch Inc. Photo © Roy Lipstein **347** Courtesy of GEICO and The Martin Agency. Photography: John Henley **348** Courtesy of Medicrome—The Stock Shop, Inc. **349** Courtesy of Stock Boston **350** Courtesy of GE Consumer Products **351** Copyright 1994-2000 Hewlett-Packard Company. Reproduced with permission. **356** Courtesy of Gillette **357** Courtesy of Roadway Express **358** Copyright Oracle. All rights reserved. **359** Reprinted with permission of Ryder Systems, Inc. © 2003 Ryder Systems, Inc. All rights reserved.

Chapter 11

364 Courtesy of Brian Coates Photography. © 1999 Brian Coates. **369** Used with permission of Safeway **370** Davis Barber **373** Used with permission of Doctor's Associates Inc and Subway **374** Courtesy of Whole Foods **376** Courtesy of the Target Corporation **377** Courtesy of Getty Images Inc. **379** Courtesy of Mall of America **381** Used with permission of Staples **381** Used with permission of Travelocity **384** Courtesy Wide World Photos **385** Courtesy of Sony Entertainment America. All rights reserved. **387** Courtesy of W.W. Grainger, Inc. **391** Courtesy of McKesson, Inc.

Chapter 12

396 Courtesy of AFLAC. All rights reserved. **400** Used with permission of Discovery Communications, Inc. Photographer: Neil Gabriel, Jay Silverman productions. All rights reserved. **401** Courtesy of The Saturn Corporation **403** Courtesy of The Procter & Gamble Company. Used by permission. **403** Courtesy of PhotoEdit **406** Courtesy of Michael Newman **409** Courtesy of General Mills, Inc. All rights reserved. **411** (Both) Under permission by V&S Vin & Spirit AB. Absolut country of Sweden Vodka and logo, Absolut, Absolut bottle design, and Absolut calligraphy are trademarks owned by V&S Vin & Spirit AB **413** Reprinted with permission of Callard & Bowser-Suchard, Inc. **414** Used with permission of TiVo Inc. All rights reserved. **416** © Houghton Mifflin Company and Mullen. All rights reserved. **419** AP/Wide World Photo; Corbis/Bettmann; Medialink WirePix Worldwide Photographic Solutions; Spencer Grant/PhotoEdit **422** Used with permission of Gillette. All rights reserved. **424** Used with permission of Lladro USA **426** Courtesy of Catalina Marketing **427** Courtesy of Getty Images Inc. **428** Used with permission of Empire State Development **429** Courtesy of John Storey Photography **430** Courtesy of Crest **432** Courtesy of BMW of North American, LLC

Chapter 13

438 Courtesy of Lear Corporation **442** © Bonn Sequenz/Imapress/The Image Works; Gabe Palmer/Corbis/Stock Market **445** Stone/Getty Images Inc. **446** © Paul Barton/CORBIS **447** Courtesy of Corbis/Bettmann **449** Courtesy of AP/Wide World Photos **450** AP/Wide World Photos **451** Courtesy of Cisco Systems, Inc. All rights reserved. **454** Rob Nelson/Black Star **455** Courtesy of Marriott International, Inc. All Rights Reserved. **458** Used with permission of Margi Systems. All rights reserved. **461** Used with permission of Dell Inc. All rights reserved. **463** Used with permission of MyPetStop.com and Mars Incorporated. All rights reserved. **465** Used with permission of the Carolina Cookie Company. All rights reserved. **466** Courtesy of photographer: Amanda B. Kamen **470** Courtesy of Ronco/Ron Popeil **474** Used with permission of the Direct Marketing Association. All rights reserved.

Chapter 14

478 Used with permission of Office Depot. All rights reserved. **484** The Procter & Gamble Company. Used by permission. **485** Used with permission of Global Exchange Services. All rights reserved. **486** Francisco Cruz/SuperStock, Inc. **488** David Yound-Wolff/PhotoEdit; Michael Newman/PhotoEdit; SuperStock, Inc.; SuperStock, Inc. **489** (Left) Courtesy of Calyx & Corolla. All rights reserved; (Right) Courtesy of Quicken Loans. All rights reserved. **490** Courtesy of Covisint. All rights reserved. **491** These materials have been reproduced with the permission of eBay Inc. Copyright © EBAY INC. All rights reserved. **494** Courtesy Getty Images Inc. **495** Courtesy of FMR Corp. **495** Courtesy of Charles Schwab & Company, Inc. All rights reserved. **499** Used with permission of W. Atlee Burpee & Co. All rights reserved. **500** Courtesy of The Gillette Co. **503** Used with permission of Google Inc. All rights reserved. **504** Courtesy of iVillage. **506** Courtesy of Wherify Wireless, Inc. All rights reserved. **509** Used with permission of RBC Royal Bank. All rights reserved.

Chapter 15

514 Courtesy of Arthur Meyerson **518** Courtesy of Arthur Meyerson **518** Jeffrey Aaronson/Network Aspen; Pablo Bartholomew/Getty Images, Inc.—Liaison; Eugene Hoshiko/AP Wide World Photos **520** Courtesy of Corbis/Bettmann; © AFP/CORBIS **521** Courtesy of the European Commission Audiovisual Librar **523** Courtesy of Regina Maria Anzeenberger **525** Cary Sol Wolinsky **526** Courtesy of Whirlpool of India, LTD. All rights reserved. **527** Courtesy of AP/Wide World Photos **529** Courtesy of Colgate-Palmolive. All rights reserved. **531** Courtesy of Walt Disney Attractions Japan, LTD © Disney. Tokyo Disneyland Park **533** Donald Dietz/Stock Boston **534** Douglas E. Curran/Agence France-Presse **536** Courtesy of L'Oreal **538** (Both) © Prestige & Collections **541** Courtesy of the Audiovisual Library, European Commission **542** © Fritz Hoffmann/Fritz Hoffmann

Chapter 16

546 Used with permission of Nike. All rights reserved. **551** © Rachel Epstein/PhotoEdit **552** Courtesy AP/Wide World Photos **554** Courtesy of AP/Wide World Photos **555** Courtesy of Enrico Ferorelli **558** (Both) Courtesy of the American Association of Advertising Agencies **559** Courtesy of Charles Eshelman Photography **560** Lester Lefkowitz/CORBIS **563** Courtesy of Campbell Soup Company **566** Courtesy of BP p.l.c. **570** Courtesy of Colgate-Palmolive. All rights reserved. **571** Courtesy of Worldwise; Used with permission Village Real Estate Services; Courtesy of Wild Planet Toys, Inc.; Used with permission of Honest Tea; These materials have been reproduced with the permission of Ben & Jerry's Homemade Holdings Inc. Copyright © Ben & Jerry's Homemade Inc. All rights reserved. **573** Used with permission of Herman Miller, Inc. All rights reserved. **578** Reprinted with permission of PricewaterhouseCoopers LLP. Copyright 2003 PWC. All rights reserved.

Indexes

Company, Brand, and Organization

Subject Index